THE CRICKETERS' WHO'S WHO 2002

Introduction by
STEVE JAMES

Edited by
CHRIS MARSHALL

Statistics by
RICHARD LOCKWOOD

Portraits photographed or researched by
BILL SMITH

Queen Anne Press

QUEEN ANNE PRESS
a division of Lennard Associates Limited
Mackerye End, Harpenden, Herts AL5 5DR

Published in association with
The Cricketers' Who's Who Limited

First published in Great Britain 2002

© The Cricketers' Who's Who Limited

British Library Cataloguing in Publication is available

ISBN 1 85291 643 5

Typeset in Times and Univers Condensed
Editor (for Queen Anne Press): Kirsty Ennever
Quiz compiled by Chris Marshall
Cover design by Paul Cooper

Printed and bound by
Butler and Tanner Limited, Frome and London

ACKNOWLEDGEMENTS

Cover photographs by Allsport UK
'Leading performers in the County Championship 2001'
Front (l to r): Richard Dawson, David Fulton, Warren Hegg and Neil Burns
Back: Richard Montgomerie and Martin Bicknell

The publishers would also like to thank the county clubs, the players
and their families for their assistance in helping to assemble
the information and photographs in this book.

Extra information has also been gathered from the pages of
The Cricketer, *The Times*, *The Sunday Times* and *The Sunday Telegraph*

Thanks also to the following for providing additional photographs:
Allsport UK, BBC, Martin Bennett, Neville Chadwick, Bowles Associates,
Channel 4, Ilford Recorder, Victor Isaacs, Hugh John, Graham Morris,
Scarborough Evening News, SkySports, Somerset County Times,
Roger Wootton and York Evening Press

CONTENTS

INTRODUCTION

Whither county cricket now? That is, and has been for some time, a burning question. It is certainly a much-maligned trade, which regularly bears the brunt of criticism for failings at international level.

I have been fortunate enough to be part of this game for almost 16 years, and am not about to bite the hand which has fed me so heartily and generously over that period of time. A lucrative benefit in the past year is testament to the enormous debt I owe to it. However, I do feel that the years of experience place me in a position in which to make some pertinent and hopefully constructive comments.

We inhabit a sporting world, which is constantly evolving, changing beyond recognition, but ultimately improving. In Wales, where I am now happily ensconced and settled, a similar problem is arising as to the future of Welsh club rugby. Age-old traditions and institutions are being threatened. And it is not edifying. In fact it is all becoming rather acrimonious because the natural inclination is to resist change. We find ourselves in a similar dilemma as regards domestic cricket in this country.

There has been change – much of it, in fact: two divisions in both four-day and one-day competitions, an increase in the amount of floodlit cricket and central contracts for the elite. Still, all does not seem well, there being a lingering feeling that more is to come. By March of this year we should know how much more, when plans for 2003 and beyond are revealed.

The county system has glaring deficiencies. Nobody can dispute that. Anyone setting up such a system today would surely never set about it using the geographical spread of counties which has evolved down the ages. The Midlands is heavily over-populated for instance.

In my opinion there are too many professional cricketers in this country earning a decent living; and too many of those are in a comfort zone with no real ambition to represent their country, which should always be the ultimate aim. Too many are more interested in the pampered lifestyle, fretting about such trivial peripherals as securing a sponsored car rather than putting in extra work in the nets or in the gym. For some, things come too easy.

That is not to say that the majority are not dedicated, ambitious and committed professionals whose values and intentions are honourable and well meaning. They play as hard as the system permits, enjoy themselves too and are a credit to their profession. But at times the system lets them down. It does not prepare them sufficiently for the step up to the higher level, for the voracious glare and unforgiving intensity of Test cricket.

Our county cricket can lack intensity, purely because of its quantity. But it is not soft, as has often been purported by many uninformed critics. The two-division split has increased the intensity and excitement. At Glamorgan every County Championship game we have played in the last two years, bar a soporific draw against Surrey at the end of last year, has been fervidly competitive and meaningful. But still fatigue plays too big a part in a season – the need for quantity of matches to satisfy memberships and justify budgets overrules the delicate balance required to initiate the play, rest and practice cycle.

I do not personally agree with the three up, three down formula – three out of nine is far too high a proportion in my view. But this was passed for a specific reason, because the counties – some more than others – were pusillanimous about their very existence and future. That is an understandable fear, but a compromise must be reached whereby we reach an optimum number of games for a season. My personal preference would be for 12 four-day games and I would jettison one of the one-day cups. How we reach this Utopia I am not yet sure, but I am convinced that the answer lies in striking a balance between ensuring we produce England cricketers capable of beating the best in the world – which must surely be the overriding purpose – and at the same time recognising that county cricket must strive to sustain itself and exist as an entertainment in its own right.

In Australia – I know that we should not keep trying to mimic them but they are streets ahead at present, and to learn from the best is not plagiarism – everything is geared towards the national team. Wage structures are such that the highest earners are the national players, which is how it should be. That is why I am becoming increasingly concerned by some of the inflated wages being offered and paid to some run-of-the-mill county cricketers – good cricketers, no question – but not our nation's finest.

This, in turn, is causing problems for the rest of the counties because, as happens, other county cricketers soon learn about the magnitude of these wages and go knocking on their chief executive's door requesting a raise. I am not sure that such exaggerated demands can be sustained.

The central contracts system – I agree with its principle and its results are there for all to see – has almost inadvertently exacerbated this problem. To the counties the most valuable players are now those just below England standard because they are likely to be available for the whole season.

I applaud the new national academy – after all it was the brainchild of my former opening partner Hugh Morris, so I could hardly take issue! – for I fear that 'A' tours were not serving their purpose. There were exceptions, and last winter's successful sortie into the Busta Cup may well have been one of them, but in general the reluctance of our authorities to play 'A' Tests at home meant that the standard of opposition encountered abroad was variable to say the least. As a result some cricketers returned home with inflated opinions of themselves, and the selectors received distorted pictures of their capacity to step up to the higher level.

I know from the harsh reality of my brief flirtation with Test cricket that there is a considerable gulf between playing at county and Test level. I was preparing one day to play Leicestershire at a damp and deserted Sophia Gardens, only to receive a summons to face South Africa the next day, in front of a capacity crowd, at Lord's. The contrast could not have been sharper and the baptism more chastening. I think it was too much to ask of anyone, however talented, of whatever temperament, and of whatever mental fortitude.

I recognise a need for there to be some intermediate level between county and Test cricket. Regional cricket has been mooted, but I fear that it would go the same way as divisional rugby did in the 1980s – lacking both a spectator base and a specific allure for the players; rather play some representative matches against the tourists – either regional sides or an 'A' team – with all the selectors in attendance, pressurising the players in a very different environment to the comfortable existence with their county side.

Tourist matches for counties merit differing levels of gravity, but one factor remains constant – they are not as important as County Championship fixtures, certainly not in cricketing terms. If a player has a slight niggle he might be risked in the latter but certainly not in the former, despite the calibre of the opposition and the lure of a big crowd. However, the marketing men may not concur.

Another bugbear of mine at present is the increasing hiring of 'overseas' players with tenuous claims to be domestically qualified. They cannot play for England but are taking the salaries and places of homebred cricketers who could go on to represent their country. One cannot blame the players because the money is attractive and the opportunity to play county cricket is rarely sniffed at, even by the most vociferous of foreign critics.

The counties will point to the fact that they are only operating within the regulations and there can be no disputing that, but surely we should all be looking at the bigger picture and recognising that short-term gain could mean long-term pain. Hopefully the introduction of the counties' academy system will rectify this.

Maybe there should be an immediate limit on the number of such players per team – I would say one at the most. But this is not to say that I am against overseas players. Far from it. Bona fide high-profile overseas players are highly beneficial for the game in my view; you only have to look at the impact which the likes of Viv Richards, Waqar Younis, Jacques Kallis and Matthew Elliott have had at Glamorgan – brilliant cricketers whose contributions have extended way beyond the boundary rope and dressing-room, exciting the Welsh nation with their charisma, skill and personalities. Jimmy Maher may not have possessed the same profile before he arrived but his contribution was also telling and we all knew who he was by the time he left! With the advent of central contracts I would not be averse to the idea of having two overseas players per side.

But still our county game excites, attracts and enthrals in differing measures. Crowds may not be as large at the grounds as we might like (although maybe not as paltry as some would lead us to believe) but many, many people also follow the scorecards through various forms of media – and from all around the world too. It may cop a lot of flak but it is also the object of much envy from abroad and I for one am proud to be a part of it.

I must conclude by congratulating Yorkshire for their Championship success last year and Nasser Hussain and his England side for their continuing upward trend. They may have just lost 1-0 in the Tests out in India but for me that series – and the subsequent One-Day Internationals – epitomised the resilience, character, determination and no little skill which Hussain and coach Duncan Fletcher have brought to the table.

Continued good luck to them and to all who pour their heart and soul into county cricket again this year.

Steve James
January 2002

(Steve James is a regular contributor to The Sunday Telegraph*)*

THE PLAYERS

THE FIRST 39 YEARS
A quiz to celebrate the 40th year of the Gillette Cup/NatWest Trophy/C&G Trophy

Throughout the book there are 100 quiz questions based on the oldest one-day knockout competition – from the first Gillette Cup contested in 1963.

The answers can be found on page 815.

Editor's Notes

The cricketers listed in this volume include all those who played 1st XI cricket for a first-class county at least once last season, in any form of cricket, and all those registered (at the time of going to press at the end of February) to play for the 18 first-class counties in 2002, even those who have yet to make a first-team appearance. All statistics are complete to the end of the last English season (the Stop press sections for individual players cover subsequent highlights). Figures about 1000 runs, 50 wickets and 50 dismissals in a season refer to matches in England only. All first-class figures include figures for Test matches which are also extracted and listed separately. One-Day 100s and One-Day five wickets in an innings are for the English domestic competitions and all One-Day Internationals, home and abroad. Career records include 'rebel' tours to South Africa. In the interests of space 2001 statistics are not given for those whose appearances in first-class cricket or One-Day competitions were only for teams other than the county to which they are now contracted i.e. universities, Board XIs, minor counties etc (excluding international cricketers on tours to England). These appearances are, however, reflected in their career statistics and reference is made in the Extras section to the team for which they played.

The following abbreviations apply: * means not out; All First – all first-class matches; 1-day Int – One-Day Internationals; 1-day Lge – Norwich Union League (including former Sunday leagues); C&G – C&G Trophy (incl NatWest); B&H – Benson and Hedges Cup (including the Super Cup). The figures for batting and bowling averages refer to the full first-class English list for 2001, followed in brackets by the 2000 figures. Inclusion in the batting averages depends on a minimum of six completed innings, a bowler has to have taken at least 10 wickets. Strike rate refers to a bowler's record of balls bowled per wicket taken. The Stop press page (p.744) includes some late-breaking signings and there are also details (p.743) of non-registered players who made guest appearances for counties last season in non-competitive matches.

Each year in *The Cricketers' Who's Who*, in addition to those cricketers who are playing during the current season, we also include the biographical and career details of those who played in the previous season but retired at the end of it. The purpose of this is to have, on the record, the full and final cricketing achievements of every player when his career has ended.

A book of this complexity and detail has to be prepared several months in advance of the cricket season, and occasionally there are recent changes in a player's circumstances or the structure of the game which cannot be included in time. Many examples of facts, statistics and even opinions which can quickly become outdated in the period between the actual compilation of the book and its publication, months later, will spring to the reader's mind, and I ask him or her to make the necessary commonsense allowance and adjustments.

Chris Marshall, March 2002

ABDUR RAZZAQ   Middlesex

Name: Abdur Razzaq
Role: Right-hand bat, right-arm
fast-medium bowler
Born: 2 December 1979, Lahore
Height: 5ft 11in
County debut: No first-team appearance
Test debut: 1999-2000
Tests: 14
One-Day Internationals: 84
1st-Class 50s: 11
1st-Class 100s: 4
1st-Class 5 w. in innings: 6
1st-Class 10 w. in match: 2
1st-Class catches: 14
One-Day 5 w. in innings: 2
Place in batting averages: 174th av. 22.16
Place in bowling averages: 94th av. 35.90
Strike rate: 63.30 (career 46.79)

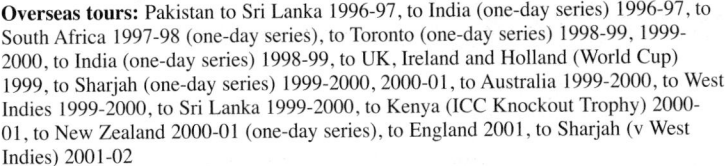

Education: Furqan Model Secondary School, Lahore
Overseas tours: Pakistan to Sri Lanka 1996-97, to India (one-day series) 1996-97, to South Africa 1997-98 (one-day series), to Toronto (one-day series) 1998-99, 1999-2000, to India (one-day series) 1998-99, to UK, Ireland and Holland (World Cup) 1999, to Sharjah (one-day series) 1999-2000, 2000-01, to Australia 1999-2000, to West Indies 1999-2000, to Sri Lanka 1999-2000, to Kenya (ICC Knockout Trophy) 2000-01, to New Zealand 2000-01 (one-day series), to England 2001, to Sharjah (v West Indies) 2001-02
Overseas teams played for: Khan Research Labs; Lahore Cricket Association
Extras: Took 7-51 on first-class debut, for Lahore City v Karachi Whites 1996-97. Took Test hat-trick (Kaluwitharana, Herath, Pushpakumara) v Sri Lanka at Galle in June 2000, becoming the youngest player – and the second Pakistan bowler, after Wasim Akram (twice) – to take a hat-trick in Tests. FICA Young Player of the Year 2001
Best batting: 117 KRL v Customs, Faisalabad 1997-98
Best bowling: 7-51 Lahore City v Karachi Whites, Thatta 1996-97   ·
Stop press: Man of the Match for his century (134) and match figures of 4-71 in first Test v Bangladesh at Dhaka 2001-02. Returned his best one-day figures of 6-35 v Bangladesh at Dhaka 2001-02

2001 Season

	M	Inns	NO	Runs	HS	Avge	100s	50s	Ct	St	O	M	Runs	Wkts	Avge	Best	5wI	10wM
Test	2	4	0	98	53	24.50	-	1	2	-	53	9	162	5	32.40	3-61	-	-
All First	5	7	1	133	53	22.16	-	1	2	-	105.3	19	359	10	35.90	3-61	-	-
1-day Int	6	6	0	125	75	20.83	-	1	2	-	46.3	3	187	5	37.40	2-41	-	
C & G																		
B & H																		
1-day Lge																		

Career Performances

	M	Inns	NO	Runs	HS	Avge	100s	50s	Ct	St	Balls	Runs	Wkts	Avge	Best	5wI	10wM
Test	14	22	1	480	100 *	22.85	1	3	6	-	2315	1026	26	39.46	4-56	-	-
All First	46	67	8	1700	117	28.81	4	11	14	-	6738	4543	144	31.54	7-51	6	2
1-day Int	84	71	14	1418	75 *	24.87	-	9	9	-	3930	2848	116	24.55	5-31	2	
C & G																	
B & H																	
1-day Lge																	

ADAMS, C. J.   Sussex

Name: <u>Christopher</u> John Adams
Role: Right-hand bat, right-arm medium
bowler, slip fielder, county captain
Born: 6 May 1970, Whitwell, Derbyshire
Height: 6ft **Weight:** 13st 7lbs
Nickname: Grizzly, Grizwold
County debut: 1988 (Derbyshire),
1998 (Sussex)
County cap: 1992 (Derbyshire),
1998 (Sussex)
Test debut: 1999-2000
Tests: 5
One-Day Internationals: 5
1000 runs in a season: 5
1st-Class 50s: 65
1st-Class 100s: 28
1st-Class 200s: 2
1st-Class catches: 279
One-Day 100s: 16
One-Day 5 w. in innings: 1
Place in batting averages: 27th av. 51.71 (2000 40th av. 39.69)
Place in bowling averages: 1st av. 11.10

Strike rate: 24.20 (career 75.68)
Parents: John and Eluned (Lyn)
Wife and date of marriage: Samantha Claire, 26 September 1992
Children: Georgia Louise, 4 October 1993; Sophie Victoria, 13 October 1998
Family links with cricket: Brother David played 2nd XI cricket for Derbyshire and Gloucestershire. Father played for Yorkshire Schools and uncle played for Essex 2nd XI
Education: Tapton House School; Chesterfield Boys Grammar School; Repton School
Qualifications: 6 O-levels, NCA coaching awards, Executive Development Certificate in Coaching and Management Skills
Off-season: 'Barbados and Hong Kong with Blade. Coaching football, rugby and cricket at Christ's Hospital School. Enjoying the family'
Overseas tours: Repton School to Barbados 1987; England NCA North to Northern Ireland 1987; England XI to New Zealand (Cricket Max) 1997; England to South Africa and Zimbabwe 1999-2000; Sussex to Grenada 2001; Blade to Barbados 2001
Overseas teams played for: Takapuna, New Zealand 1987-88; Te Puke, New Zealand 1989-90; Primrose, Cape Town, South Africa 1991-92; Canberra Comets, Australia 1998-99; University of NSW, Australia 2000-01
Career highlights to date: 'Has to be Test debut for England'
Cricketers particularly admired: Mike Atherton, Ian Botham
Young players to look out for: Ian Bell, Mike Yardy
Other sports played: Football ('mad on it'), golf
Other sports followed: Football (Arsenal FC)
Injuries: Out for one month with a broken thumb
Relaxations: 'My kids'
Extras: Beat Richard Hutton's 25-year-old record for most runs scored in a season at Repton. Represented English Schools U15 and U19, MCC Schools U19 and, in 1989, England YC. Took two catches as 12th man for England v India at Old Trafford in 1990. Set county records for the highest score in the Sunday League (141*) v Kent at Chesterfield 1992 and for the fastest century by a Derbyshire batsman (57 mins). Whittingdale Young Player Award 1992. His 239 v Hampshire at Southampton 1996 is the highest score by a Derbyshire No. 3. Released by Derbyshire at the end of the 1997 season and joined Sussex for 1998 as captain. Scored 135 and 105 v Essex at Chelmsford 1998, becoming the third player to score centuries in each innings of a match for two counties; he had also done so for Derbyshire. Sussex Player of the Year 1998 and 1999. Set individual one-day record score for Sussex of 163 (off 107 balls) v Middlesex in the National League at Arundel 1999; the innings included nine sixes, a Sussex Sunday/National League record. CGU Player of the Month July/August 1999. Top run-scorer in the 1999 National League competition with 798 runs at 79.80. Passed 5000 career runs in Sunday/National League v Northamptonshire Steelers at Eastbourne 2000. Sussex 1st XI Fielder of the Season 2000. C&G Man of the Match award for his 89* v Cornwall at Truro 2001. Topped first-class bowling averages in 2001 (10 wickets av. 11.10). BBC South Cricketer of the Year 2001
Opinions on cricket: 'Four-day cricket: more pressure, more interest, better cricket – less money. What is going on?'

17

Best batting: 239 Derbyshire v Hampshire, Southampton 1996
Best bowling: 4-28 Sussex v Durham, Riverside 2001

2001 Season

	M	Inns	NO	Runs	HS	Avge	100s	50s	Ct	St	O	M	Runs	Wkts	Avge	Best	5wI	10wM
Test																		
All First	15	23	2	1086	192	51.71	3	7	28	-	40.2	6	111	10	11.10	4-28	-	-
1-day Int																		
C & G	2	2	1	103	89*	103.00	-	1	-	-	3	0	15	0	-		-	-
B & H	1	1	0	37	37	37.00	-	-	-	-	7	0	27	0	-		-	-
1-day Lge	12	11	2	322	100*	35.77	1	1	3	-	27	0	147	4	36.75	2-49	-	

Career Performances

	M	Inns	NO	Runs	HS	Avge	100s	50s	Ct	St	Balls	Runs	Wkts	Avge	Best	5wI	10wM
Test	5	8	0	104	31	13.00	-	-	6	-	120	59	1	59.00	1-42	-	-
All First	231	376	29	12936	239	37.27	30	65	279	-	3103	1830	41	44.63	4-28	-	-
1-day Int	5	4	0	71	42	17.75	-	-	3	-							
C & G	25	24	6	1111	129*	61.72	4	7	9	-	114	91	1	91.00	1-15	-	
B & H	42	39	5	1355	138	39.85	3	9	17	-	186	147	1	147.00	1-41	-	
1-day Lge	175	167	27	5447	163	38.90	9	35	92	-	872	799	27	29.59	5-16	1	

ADADAMS, J. H. K.   Hampshire

ADAMS, J. H. K.   Hampshire

Name: James Henry Kenneth Adams
Role: Left-hand bat, left-arm medium bowler
Born: 23 September 1980, Winchester
Height: 6ft 1in **Weight:** 13st 7lbs
Nickname: Jimmy, Bison, Baron
County debut: No first-team appearance
Parents: Jenny and Mike
Marital status: Single
Family links with cricket: 'Dad played a bit for Kent Schoolboys. Brothers Ben and Tom played/play for Hampshire age groups'
Education: Hursley Keble Memorial; Twyford School; Sherborne School; Loughborough University
Qualifications: 9 GCSEs, 3 A-levels, Level 1 coaching
Career outside cricket: 'Student/tax dodger'
Off-season: 'Uni'

Overseas tours: England U19 to Sri Lanka (U19 World Cup) 1999-2000; West of England to West Indies 1995; Sherborne School to Pakistan
Overseas teams played for: Woodville, Adelaide 1999-2000; Melville, Perth 2000-01
Career highlights to date: 'England U19 and 2nd XI Championship'
Cricket moments to forget: 'Kidderminster, June 2000'
Cricketers particularly admired: 'Lara, Smith, Thorpe...'
Young players to look out for: J. Francis, J. Tomlinson, C. Denison 'and others from Hants Academy'
Other sports played: Hockey (Dorset age group when 14), football, bass fishing
Other sports followed: Football (Aston Villa); 'fair interest in most sports'
Injuries: Out for one month with partial tear of posterior cruciate ('still giving me gyp')
Relaxations: Music, PlayStation, 'kick about with mates'
Extras: Played in U15 World Cup 1996. Hampshire Young Player of the Year 1998. Called up as an injury replacement for England U19 tour to Sri Lanka for U19 World Cup 1999-2000. Represented England U19 v Sri Lanka U19 in 'Test' series 2000. Part of Hampshire's 2nd XI Championship winning side 2001
Opinions on cricket: 'I'll wait until I've played some first-class before I stick my neck out, though two divisions seems to have worked well.'

ADSHEAD, S. J.   Leicestershire

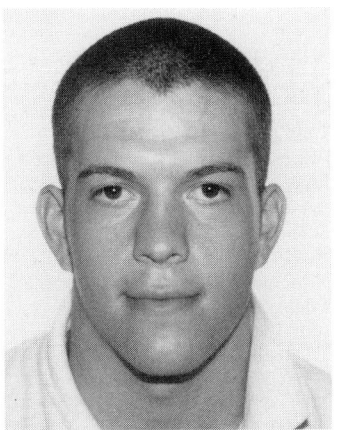

Name: <u>Stephen</u> John Adshead
Role: Right-hand bat, wicket-keeper
Born: 29 January 1980, Worcester
Height: 5ft 8in **Weight:** 12st 7lbs
Nickname: Adzo, Shed, Monkey Boy
County debut: 2000
1st-Class stumpings: 1
Parents: David and Julie
Marital status: Single
Family links with cricket: 'Dad and brother play local club cricket'
Education: Beoley First; Ridgeway Middle; Bridley Moor HS, Redditch
Qualifications: 10 GCSEs, 2 A-levels, ECB Level 2 coaching
Off-season: Playing and coaching in New Zealand
Overseas tours: Leicestershire to Potchefstroom, South Africa 2001
Overseas teams played for: Fish Hoek, Cape Town 1998-99; Witwatersrand

Technical, Johannesburg 1999-2000; Central Hawkes Bay, New Zealand 2000-01
Career highlights to date: 'Winning AON Trophy 2000; Man of Match in final'
(*Top-scored for Leicestershire 2nd XI with 58*)
Cricket moments to forget: 'All good so far'
Cricketers particularly admired: Alec Stewart, Steve Waugh, Trevor Ward
Young players to look out for: David Brignall
Other sports followed: Football (Nottingham Forest)
Relaxations: Fishing, scuba diving
Extras: Averaged 90 for Worcestershire U19 in county U19 competition in 1998, in which Worcestershire reached the semi-finals. Played a few games for Worcestershire 2nd XI. Played for Herefordshire in Minor Counties and NatWest 1999. Played for Leicestershire Board XI in the second round of the C&G 2002, which was played in September 2001
Opinions on cricket: 'Well, I enjoy it!'

2001 Season (did not make any first-class or one-day appearances)

Career Performances

	M	Inns	NO	Runs	HS	Avge	100s	50s	Ct	St	Balls	Runs	Wkts	Avge	Best	5wI	10wM
Test																	
All First	1	1	0	0	0	0.00	-	-	-	1							
1-day Int																	
C & G	3	3	0	70	29	23.33	-	-	3	2							
B & H																	
1-day Lge																	

AFZAAL, U. Nottinghamshire

Name: Usman Afzaal
Role: Left-hand bat, slow left-arm bowler
Born: 9 June 1977, Rawalpindi, Pakistan
Height: 6ft **Weight:** 12st 7lbs
Nickname: Saeed, Gulfraz, Usy Bhai, Trevor
County debut: 1995
County cap: 2000
Test debut: 2001
Tests: 3
1000 runs in a season: 2
1st-Class 50s: 29
1st-Class 100s: 7
1st-Class catches: 47

Place in batting averages: 78th av. 37.44
(2000 24th av. 44.26)
Place in bowling averages: 145th av. 57.90
Strike rate: 95.00 (career 95.09)
Parents: Firdous and Shafi Mahmood
Marital status: Single
Family links with cricket: Older brother
Kamran played for NAYC and for
Nottinghamshire U15-U19 ('top player');
younger brother Aqib played for Notts and
England U15; 'Uncle Mac and Uncle Raja
great players'
Education: Blue Bell Hill School; Manvers
Pierrepont School; South Notts College
Qualifications: Coaching certificates
Career outside cricket: Printing company
Off-season: '*Inshallah*, going to India and
New Zealand'

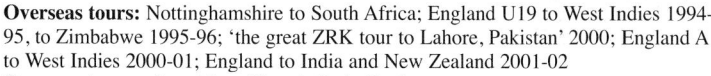

Overseas tours: Nottinghamshire to South Africa; England U19 to West Indies 1994-95, to Zimbabwe 1995-96; 'the great ZRK tour to Lahore, Pakistan' 2000; England A to West Indies 2000-01; England to India and New Zealand 2001-02
Overseas teams played for: Victoria Park, Perth
Career highlights to date: 'Playing for England in the Ashes'
Cricket moments to forget: 'Every time I get out'
Cricketers particularly admired: David Gower, Saeed Anwar, Ian Botham, Clive Rice, Uncle Raja and Uncle Mac
Young players to look out for: Bilal Shafayat, Aqib Afzaal, Nadeem Malik
Other sports played: Indoor football, 'want to start playing squash'
Other sports followed: Football ('a bit of Man U')
Relaxations: 'Praying; spending time with friends and family; listening to Indian music'
Extras: Played for England U15 against South Africa and, in 1994, for England U17 against India. Broke the U16 bowling record in the Texaco Trophy. Won Denis Compton Award 1996. Made Test debut in first Test v Australia at Edgbaston 2001. Took wicket (Adam Gilchrist) with third ball in Test cricket v Australia at The Oval 2001
Opinions on cricket: 'Fantastic game. Love it more every day. Give it 100 per cent and enjoy it.'
Best batting: 151* Nottinghamshire v Worcestershire, Trent Bridge 2000
Best bowling: 4-101 Nottinghamshire v Gloucestershire, Trent Bridge 1998

2001 Season

	M	Inns	NO	Runs	HS	Avge	100s	50s	Ct	St	O	M	Runs	Wkts	Avge	Best	5wI	10wM
Test	3	6	1	83	54	16.60	-	1	-	-	9	0	49	1	49.00	1-49	-	-
All First	15	28	1	1011	138	37.44	1	8	9	-	158.2	29	579	10	57.90	3-88	-	-
1-day Int																		
C & G	2	1	0	49	49	49.00	-	-	-	-								
B & H	7	7	2	199	56 *	39.80	-	2	1	-	20	0	110	5	22.00	3-51	-	
1-day Lge	12	12	3	449	94 *	49.88	-	4	2	-	25	1	128	3	42.66	2-13	-	

Career Performances

	M	Inns	NO	Runs	HS	Avge	100s	50s	Ct	St	Balls	Runs	Wkts	Avge	Best	5wI	10wM
Test	3	6	1	83	54	16.60	-	1	-	-	54	49	1	49.00	1-49	-	-
All First	101	176	15	4891	151 *	30.37	7	29	47	-	5896	3153	62	50.85	4-101	-	-
1-day Int																	
C & G	6	4	1	119	49	39.66	-	-	1	-	66	57	0	-		-	-
B & H	13	13	3	381	78	38.10	-	4	2	-	132	114	5	22.80	3-51	-	
1-day Lge	40	34	8	971	95 *	37.34	-	8	13	-	452	400	15	26.66	2-13	-	

ALDRED, P.   Derbyshire

Name: Paul Aldred
Role: Right-hand bat, right-arm medium bowler
Born: 4 February 1969, Chellaston, Derby
Height: 5ft 10in   **Weight:** 12st
Nickname: Jack, Aldo, Mr Ed, Dred
County debut: 1995
County cap: 1999
50 wickets in a season: 1
1st-Class 50s: 1
1st-Class 5 w. in innings: 5
1st-Class 10 w. in match: 1
1st-Class catches: 32
Place in batting averages: 259th av. 10.00 (2000 259th av. 11.46)
Place in bowling averages: 143rd av. 57.07 (2000 116th av. 36.70)
Strike rate: 87.46 (career 64.55)
Parents: Harry (deceased) and Lynette
Marital status: Single
Family links with cricket: Father played local cricket
Education: Chellaston and Curbar Primary School; Lady Manners, Bakewell

Qualifications: 'None of interest'
Career outside cricket: Builder
Overseas teams played for: Bentley CC, Melbourne 1994-95
Cricketers particularly admired: Ian Botham, Viv Richards
Young players to look out for: Ian Blackwell
Other sports played: Golf; hockey for Derbyshire U16, U19, U21 and senior squad
Other sports followed: Golf, rugby, horse racing
Relaxations: 'Most sports; golf, fishing, rugby, horse racing'
Extras: Played against New Zealand with NCA in 1994. Played for Derbyshire U21 hockey team at the age of 15. His 1999 season included a spell of 27 wickets in three matches
Opinions on cricket: 'Two divisions seems to have improved the standard. You have more to play for at the end of the season; in past years that may not have been the case. Channel 4's coverage of the Test series has made younger people get interested in the game. It makes it easier to understand. They have people presenting the coverage who know about the game.'
Best batting: 83 Derbyshire v Hampshire, Chesterfield 1997
Best bowling: 7-101 Derbyshire v Lancashire, Derby 1999

2001 Season

	M	Inns	NO	Runs	HS	Avge	100s	50s	Ct	St	O	M	Runs	Wkts	Avge	Best	5wl	10wM
Test																		
All First	8	13	1	120	35	10.00	-	-	5	-	189.3	30	742	13	57.07	3-102	-	-
1-day Int																		
C & G																		
B & H	2	2	0	7	7	3.50	-	-	1	-	19	0	100	2	50.00	2-55	-	
1-day Lge	9	5	1	63	37	15.75	-	-	3	-	58	4	298	14	21.28	3-17	-	

Career Performances

	M	Inns	NO	Runs	HS	Avge	100s	50s	Ct	St	Balls	Runs	Wkts	Avge	Best	5wl	10wM
Test																	
All First	58	78	11	766	83	11.43	-	1	32	-	8199	4351	127	34.25	7-101	5	1
1-day Int																	
C & G	5	3	1	21	17	10.50	-	-	1	-	236	151	7	21.57	4-30	-	
B & H	13	5	1	45	24 *	11.25	-	-	2	-	627	471	18	26.16	3-12	-	
1-day Lge	64	35	11	294	39 *	12.25	-	-	11	-	2406	2097	68	30.83	4-41	-	

ALI, K.   Worcestershire

Name: Kabir Ali
Role: Right-hand bat, right-arm medium-fast
bowler
Born: 24 November 1980, Birmingham
Height: 6ft **Weight:** 12st 7lbs
Nickname: Kabby, Taxi
County debut: 1999
1st-Class 50s: 2
1st-Class 5 w. in innings: 1
1st-Class catches: 5
Place in batting averages: (2000 202nd
av. 17.75)
Place in bowling averages: 4th av. 18.07
(2000 132nd av. 40.55)
Strike rate: 36.14 (career 52.43)
Parents: Shabir Ali and M. Begum
Marital status: Single
Family links with cricket: Father played

club cricket in Birmingham. Cousin Kadeer Ali also plays for Worcestershire
Education: Moseley School; Wolverhampton University
Qualifications: GNVQ (Advanced) Leisure and Tourism
Career outside cricket: Student
Off-season: Playing in Perth, Australia
Overseas tours: Warwickshire Youth U19 to South Africa 1998
Career highlights to date: 'Opening the bowling with Glenn [McGrath]'
Cricketers particularly admired: Ian Botham, Wasim Akram
Young players to look out for: Aatif Ali, Kadeer Ali, Moeen Munir
Other sports played: Football, badminton, snooker
Other sports followed: Badminton, football
Relaxations: 'Playing snooker, spending time with family and friends'
Extras: Warwickshire Youth Young Player of the Year award. Won Gold Award on
B&H debut for his 4-29 v Glamorgan 2000. Represented England U19 v Sri Lanka
U19 in one-day and 'Test' series 2000. NBC Denis Compton Award for the most
promising young Worcestershire player 2000. Played for Worcestershire Board XI and
Worcestershire in the C&G 2001. Recorded maiden first-class five-wicket return
(5-22) v Gloucestershire at Worcester 2001. Junior Royals Player of the Year 2001
Opinions on cricket: 'Should play more day/night cricket.'
Best batting: 50* Worcestershire v Nottinghamshire, Worcester 2000
                50* Worcestershire v Durham UCCE, Worcester 2001
Best bowling: 5-22 Worcestershire v Gloucestershire, Worcester 2001

2001 Season

	M	Inns	NO	Runs	HS	Avge	100s	50s	Ct	St	O	M	Runs	Wkts	Avge	Best	5wI	10wM
Test																		
All First	4	5	1	138	50 *	34.50	-	1	-	-	84.2	18	253	14	18.07	5-22	1	-
1-day Int																		
C & G	4	2	0	7	5	3.50	-	-	1	-	24	5	88	6	14.66	3-35	-	
B & H																		
1-day Lge	7	2	0	10	6	5.00	-	-	-	-	45.5	6	210	13	16.15	4-22	-	

Career Performances

	M	Inns	NO	Runs	HS	Avge	100s	50s	Ct	St	Balls	Runs	Wkts	Avge	Best	5wI	10wM
Test																	
All First	15	21	4	362	50 *	21.29	-	2	5	-	1940	1122	37	30.32	5-22	1	-
1-day Int																	
C & G	6	3	0	14	7	4.66	-	-	2	-	264	185	10	18.50	3-35	-	
B & H	3	0	0	0	0	-	-	-	-	-	94	94	4	23.50	4-29	-	
1-day Lge	18	9	4	24	7	4.80	-	-	4	-	656	528	26	20.30	4-22	-	

ALI, K. Worcestershire

Name: Kadeer Ali
Role: Right-hand bat
Born: 7 March 1983, Birmingham
Height: 6ft 2in **Weight:** 10st 7lbs
Nickname: Kaddy
County debut: 2000
1st-Class catches: 3
Place in batting averages: 268th av. 8.12
(2000 308th av. 1.85)
Parents: Munir Ali and Maqsood Begum
Marital status: Single
Family links with cricket: Father a cricket coach and club cricketer. Cousin Kabir Ali also plays for Worcestershire
Education: Handsworth Grammar; Moseley Sixth Form College
Qualifications: 5 GCSEs
Career outside cricket: Studying
Off-season: England U19 tour to Australia and New Zealand
Overseas tours: England U19 to India 2000-01, to Australia and (U19 World Cup) New Zealand 2001-02
Cricketers particularly admired: Sachin Tendulkar, Vikram Solanki

Young players to look out for: Kabir Ali, Depesh Patel
Other sports played: Football
Other sports followed: Football (Liverpool FC)
Relaxations: Listening to music, going out with friends
Extras: Young Player awards at Warwickshire CCC. Played for the Worcestershire Board XI in the NatWest Trophy in 1999. Represented England U19 v Sri Lanka U19 in 'Test' series 2000 and v West Indies U19 in one-day series (3/3) and 'Test' series (3/3) 2001, scoring century (155) in the second 'Test' at Trent Bridge
Opinions on cricket: 'Need to play longer version of game more than limited over game.'
Best batting: 38 Worcestershire v Middlesex, Worcester 2001

2001 Season

	M	Inns	NO	Runs	HS	Avge	100s	50s	Ct	St	O	M	Runs	Wkts	Avge	Best	5wI	10wM
Test																		
All First	5	8	0	65	38	8.12	-	-	2	-	17	5	57	0	-	-	-	-
1-day Int																		
C & G																			
B & H																			
1-day Lge																			

Career Performances

	M	Inns	NO	Runs	HS	Avge	100s	50s	Ct	St	Balls	Runs	Wkts	Avge	Best	5wI	10wM
Test																	
All First	9	15	0	78	38	5.20	-	-	3	-	102	57	0	-	-	-	-
1-day Int																	
C & G	1	1	0	24	24	24.00	-	-	-	-							
B & H																	
1-day Lge	1	1	0	20	20	20.00	-	-	-	-							

ALLEYNE, D.   Middlesex

Name: David Alleyne
Role: Right-hand bat, wicket-keeper
Born: 17 April 1976, York
Height: 5ft 11in **Weight:** 13st
Nickname: Bones, Gears
County debut: 1999 (one-day), 2001 (first-class)
1st-Class catches: 4
Parents: Jo and Darcy
Marital status: Engaged to Dawn

Family links with cricket: Father played for local club Northampton Exiles
Education: Raglan; Enfield Grammar; Hertford Regional College, Ware; City and Islington College
Qualifications: 6 GCSEs, City and Guilds, Diploma in Leisure Studies, senior coaching award
Off-season: Playing for Karori CC in New Zealand
Overseas tours: Middlesex to Johannesburg 2000
Overseas teams played for: Stratford, Inglewood, New Zealand 1997-98; Sturt, Adelaide 1999-2000; Midland-Guildford, Perth 2000-01; Karori CC, Wellington, New Zealand 2001-02
Cricketers particularly admired: Desmond Haynes, Carl Hooper, Jack Russell, Keith Piper
Young players to look out for: Ed Joyce, Ben Hutton, Andrew Strauss, Owais Shah, Nick Compton
Other sports played: Football
Other sports followed: Football (Liverpool FC)
Relaxations: Music, sleeping, 'very interested in the workings of the female mind, i.e. Dawn's'
Extras: Represented Middlesex U11 to U17. Represented Middlesex Cricket Board. Played football for Middlesex U15 and U16 and for Enfield Borough U16. Middlesex 2nd XI Player of the Year 1999 and 2000
Opinions on cricket: 'Pitch quality needs to improve massively, then you will see our game improve.'
Best batting: 44 Middlesex v Gloucestershire, Lord's 2001

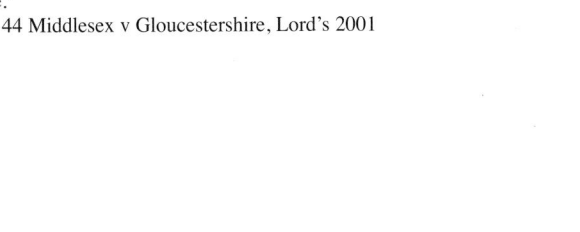

1. Who are the only two batsmen to have scored a double hundred in the Gillette/NatWest/C&G?

2001 Season

	M	Inns	NO	Runs	HS	Avge	100s	50s	Ct	St	O	M	Runs	Wkts	Avge	Best	5wI	10wM
Test																		
All First	2	4	0	55	44	13.75	-	-	4	-								
1-day Int																		
C & G																		
B & H																		
1-day Lge	1	1	0	8	8	8.00	-	-	2	-								

Career Performances

	M	Inns	NO	Runs	HS	Avge	100s	50s	Ct	St	Balls	Runs	Wkts	Avge	Best	5wI	10wM
Test																	
All First	2	4	0	55	44	13.75	-	-	4	-							
1-day Int																	
C & G	2	2	0	8	7	4.00	-	-	2	-							
B & H																	
1-day Lge	13	13	0	200	58	15.38	-	1	14	6							

ALLEYNE, M. W. — Gloucestershire

Name: <u>Mark</u> Wayne Alleyne
Role: Right-hand bat, right-arm medium
bowler, occasional wicket-keeper,
county captain
Born: 23 May 1968, Tottenham
Height: 5ft 10in **Weight:** 14st
Nickname: Boo-Boo
County debut: 1986
County cap: 1990
Benefit: 1999
One-Day Internationals: 10
1000 runs in a season: 6
50 wickets in a season: 1
1st-Class 50s: 67
1st-Class 100s: 20
1st-Class 200s: 1
1st-Class 5 w. in innings: 8
1st-Class catches: 247
1st-Class stumpings: 3
One-Day 100s: 4
One-Day 5 w. in innings: 3
Place in batting averages: 114th av. 31.21 (2000 212th av. 17.08)

Place in bowling averages: 42nd av. 26.31 (2000 72nd av. 27.36)
Strike rate: 54.82 (career 63.14)
Parents: Euclid (deceased) and Hyacinth
Wife and date of marriage: Louise Maria, 9 October 1998
Family links with cricket: Brother played for Gloucestershire 2nd XI and Middlesex YC. Father played club cricket in Barbados and England
Education: Harrison College, Barbados; Cardinal Pole School, East London
Qualifications: 6 O-levels, NCA Senior Coaching Award, volleyball coaching certificate
Career outside cricket: 'Business and lifestyle management'
Off-season: 'Recharging and working on a part-time basis at Gloucestershire CCC with our chief executive and marketing department'
Overseas tours: England YC to Sri Lanka 1986-87, to Australia 1987-88; England XI to New Zealand (Cricket Max) 1997; England A to Bangladesh and New Zealand 1999-2000 (captain), to West Indies 2000-01 (captain); England to Australia 1998-99 (CUB Series), to South Africa and Zimbabwe 1999-2000 (one-day series), to Kenya (ICC Knockout Trophy) 2000-01, to Pakistan and Sri Lanka 2000-01 (one-day series)
Career highlights to date: '1) England debut in Brisbane 2) England Man of the Match in East London, South Africa 3) Each one of our five consecutive trophies'
Cricket moments to forget: 'Missing promotion in the Championship and being relegated in the Norwich Union League in the same week [2001]'
Cricketers particularly admired: Gordon Greenidge, Viv Richards, Jack Russell, Steve Waugh
Players to look out for: 'Lads at Gloucestershire have got a lot to offer the game. Bodes well for the future'
Other sports played: Basketball, football 'and various ball games interpreted by John Bracewell'
Other sports followed: 'Still follow Tottenham religiously but support our local football and rugby teams'
Relaxations: 'Sport crazy but also an avid gardener. Keen historian'
Extras: In 1986 became (at 18 years 54 days) the youngest player to score a century for Gloucestershire, with his 116* v Sussex at Bristol. In 1990 also became the youngest to score a double hundred for the county. Graduate of Haringey Cricket College. Cricket Select Sunday League Player of the Year 1992. In 1992 struck then highest Sunday League score for Gloucestershire (134*). Scored 112 in the B&H Super Cup final v Yorkshire at Lord's 1999, winning the Man of the Match award. Leading all-rounder in the single-division four-day era of the County Championship with 6409 runs (av. 32.53) and 216 wickets (av. 31.18) 1993-99. Man of the Match in One-Day International v South Africa at East London February 2000 (53, 3-55 and a catch to dismiss Jonty Rhodes). Captain of Gloucestershire's one-day double-winning side (NatWest and B&H Super Cup) 1999 and of treble-winning side (NatWest, B&H and Norwich Union National League) 2000. Played 393 consecutive competitive games, a Gloucestershire record, between 28 July 1990 and 24 June 2000. One of *Wisden*'s Five Cricketers of the Year 2001. B&H Gold Award for his 79* (following

2-36) v Glamorgan at Bristol 2001. Honorary fellowship from University of
Gloucestershire, October 2001. Gloucestershire captain since 1997
Opinions on cricket: 'It appears that a lot more thought goes into each game now,
and the introduction of the divisional format can claim responsibility for this. It
certainly has focused teams more, and if we can just reduce the amount of cricket, I
think we will have a very good product.'
Best batting: 256 Gloucestershire v Northamptonshire, Northampton 1990
Best bowling: 6-49 Gloucestershire v Middlesex, Lord's 2000

2001 Season

	M	Inns	NO	Runs	HS	Avge	100s	50s	Ct	St	O	M	Runs	Wkts	Avge	Best	5wI	10wM
Test																		
All First	16	26	3	718	136	31.21	2	2	12	1	374.4	87	1079	41	26.31	5-50	1	-
1-day Int																		
C & G	2	2	0	29	22	14.50	-	-	1	-	18	1	80	3	26.66	2-37	-	
B & H	7	7	1	203	79 *	33.83	-	1	3	-	64.3	3	267	10	26.70	3-51	-	
1-day Lge	15	15	2	211	68	16.23	-	1	8	-	105	5	395	10	39.50	2-17	-	

Career Performances

	M	Inns	NO	Runs	HS	Avge	100s	50s	Ct	St	Balls	Runs	Wkts	Avge	Best	5wI	10wM
Test																	
All First	300	491	45	13957	256	31.29	21	67	247	3	23806	12012	377	31.86	6-49	8	-
1-day Int	10	8	1	151	53	21.57	-	1	3	-	366	280	10	28.00	3-27	-	
C & G	40	33	5	606	73	21.64	-	1	15	-	1653	1042	41	25.41	5-30	1	
B & H	65	56	11	1193	112	26.51	1	3	33	-	2746	1961	62	31.62	5-27	1	
1-day Lge	235	215	45	4820	134 *	28.35	3	20	96	-	7907	6414	207	30.98	5-28	1	

AMBROSE, T. R.   Sussex

Name: <u>Timothy</u> Raymond Ambrose
Role: Right-hand bat, wicket-keeper
Born: 1 December 1982, Newcastle, New South Wales
Height: 5ft 7in
Nickname: Shambrose
County debut: 2001
1st-Class 50s: 1
1st-Class catches: 3
Parents: Raymond and Sally
Marital status: Single
Family links with cricket: 'Cousin played Sydney first grade; father is captain of
local grade D4 team'

Education: Tighes Hill, Newcastle; Merewether Selective High, NSW
Qualifications: Third year of greenkeeping apprenticeship
Career outside cricket: Greenkeeping
Off-season: 'Playing cricket in Newcastle, where I live, and working'
Overseas tours: Sussex to Grenada 2001
Overseas teams played for: Wallsend, NSW 2000; Nelson Bay, NSW 2001; Newcastle, NSW 2002
Career highlights to date: 'Making my debut in the match that secured Sussex promotion. Winning Man of the Match in my second one-dayer'
Cricketers particularly admired: Steve Waugh, Adam Gilchrist, Ian Healy
Young players to look out for: Mike Yardy, Matt Prior, Dominic Clapp, Carl Hopkinson

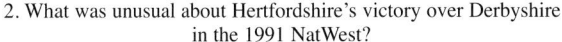

Other sports played: Football, squash, golf, rugby league, rugby union, AFL, 'I'll have a go at anything'
Other sports followed: Rugby league (Newcastle Knights), Australian Rules (Sydney Swans), football (Tottenham Hotspur)
Relaxations: Guitar, music, surfing
Extras: Captained Newcastle U16 1999 Bradman Cup winning side. 'Scored 138 in first ever game.' Played for New South Wales U17. Won NSW Junior Cricketer of the Year three years running. Played for Eastbourne in the Sussex League in 2000. Scored 87 and took two catches and a stumping in his second one-day match, in the Norwich Union League v Lancashire at Hove 2001. Scored 52 on first-class debut v Warwickshire at Edgbaston 2001. Is not considered an overseas player
Opinions on cricket: 'Haven't been around long enough to have any, except it's the best game in the world.'
Best batting: 52 Sussex v Warwickshire, Edgbaston 2001

---

2. What was unusual about Hertfordshire's victory over Derbyshire
in the 1991 NatWest?

2001 Season

	M	Inns	NO	Runs	HS	Avge	100s	50s	Ct	St	O	M	Runs	Wkts	Avge	Best	5wI	10wM
Test																		
All First	2	3	0	92	52	30.66	-	1	3	-								
1-day Int																		
C & G																		
B & H																		
1-day Lge	4	4	0	164	87	41.00	-	1	3	3								

Career Performances

	M	Inns	NO	Runs	HS	Avge	100s	50s	Ct	St	Balls	Runs	Wkts	Avge	Best	5wI	10wM
Test																	
All First	2	3	0	92	52	30.66	-	1	3	-							
1-day Int																	
C & G																	
B & H																	
1-day Lge	4	4	0	164	87	41.00	-	1	3	3							

AMIN, R. M. Surrey

Name: <u>Rupesh</u> Mahesh Amin
Role: Right-hand bat, slow left-arm bowler
Born: 20 August 1977, Clapham, London
Height: 5ft 11in **Weight:** 10st 7lbs
Nickname: Idi, Plug
County debut: 1997
1st-Class catches: 6
Strike rate: 122.40 (career 100.20)
Parents: Mahesh and Aruna
Marital status: Single
Family links with cricket: Father played club cricket
Education: Stanford Middle School; Riddlesdown High School; John Ruskin Sixth Form; Croydon College
Qualifications: 8 GCSEs, 3 A-levels, ECB Level 1 cricket coaching
Overseas tours: Bishen Bedi Academy to Sharjah 1999
Overseas teams played for: Manly-Warringah District CC, Sydney 1997-98; University of New South Wales 1999-2000
Cricketers particularly admired: Saqlain Mushtaq, Sachin Tendulkar

Young players to look out for: Tim Murtagh, Michael Carberry
Other sports played: Snooker ('socially'), five-a-side football
Other sports followed: Football (Liverpool), snooker (Ronnie O'Sullivan), boxing (Prince Naseem Hamed)
Relaxations: Going to cinema, eating good food, going out and seeing places
Extras: Played for Croydon District U15 side that won Hobbs Trophy against London Schools. Attended Bishen Bedi Academy in Delhi for coaching purposes 1998-99. Released by Surrey at the end of the 2001 season
Best batting: 12 Surrey v Leicestershire, The Oval 1998
Best bowling: 4-87 Surrey v Somerset, The Oval 1999

2001 Season

	M	Inns	NO	Runs	HS	Avge	100s	50s	Ct	St	O	M	Runs	Wkts	Avge	Best	5wI	10wM
Test																		
All First	3	4	1	1	1	0.33	-	-	2	-	102	28	272	5	54.40	3-80	-	-
1-day Int																		
C & G																		
B & H																		
1-day Lge	1	0	0	0	0	-	-	-	-	-	3	0	21	0	-		-	-

Career Performances

	M	Inns	NO	Runs	HS	Avge	100s	50s	Ct	St	Balls	Runs	Wkts	Avge	Best	5wI	10wM
Test																	
All First	14	18	8	35	12	3.50	-	-	6	-	2505	1053	25	42.12	4-87	-	-
1-day Int																	
C & G																	
B & H																	
1-day Lge	3	0	0	0	0	-	-	-	1	-	66	64	2	32.00	2-43	-	

3. Which current county cricketer who represented his country in the 1996 World Cup was run out for 99 v Worcestershire in the 1997 NatWest?

Name: <u>James</u> Michael Anderson
Role: Left-hand bat, right-arm medium-fast bowler
Born: 30 July 1982, Burnley
Height: 6ft 2in **Weight:** 12st 5lbs
Nickname: Jimmy
County debut: 2001 (one-day)
Parents: Michael and Catherine
Marital status: Single
Family links with cricket: Father and uncle played for Burnley
Education: St Mary's RC Primary School; St Theodore's RC High School; St Theodore's RC Sixth Form Centre (all Burnley)
Qualifications: 10 GCSEs, 1 A-level, 1 GNVQ (Advanced)
Career highlights to date: 'Taking a hat-trick for Lancashire 2nd XI last season. Making 1st XI debut in Norwich Union League game at end of last season [2001]'
Cricketers particularly admired: Michael Atherton, Darren Gough, Courtney Walsh, Shaun Pollock
Young players to look out for: David Brown, Jonathan Clare (both Burnley CC)
Other sports played: Golf, football, 'most active sports'
Other sports followed: Football (Burnley FC), golf
Relaxations: Television, music, all sports
Extras: Played for Lancashire Board XI in the NatWest 2000. Represented England U19 v West Indies U19 in 'Test' series (3/3) 2001, taking 5-45 in the West Indies U19 second innings in the first 'Test' at Leicester
Opinions on cricket: 'Too much cricket is played both at amateur and professional levels in England. The emphasis seems to be on quantity rather than quality.'

2001 Season

	M	Inns	NO	Runs	HS	Avge	100s	50s	Ct	St	O	M	Runs	Wkts	Avge	Best	5wI	10wM
Test																		
All First																		
1-day Int																		
C & G																		
B & H																		
1-day Lge	1	0	0	0	0	-	-	-	-	-	4	0	33	1	33.00	1-33	-

Career Performances

	M	Inns	NO	Runs	HS	Avge	100s	50s	Ct	St	Balls	Runs	Wkts	Avge	Best	5wl	10wM
Test																	
All First																	
1-day Int																	
C & G	2	1	1	5	5*	-	-	-	-	-	120	98	3	32.66	2-64	-	
B & H																	
1-day Lge	1	0	0	0	0	-	-	-	-	-	24	33	1	33.00	1-33	-	

ANDERSON, R. S. G.   Northamptonshire

Name: Ricaldo (<u>Ricky</u>) Sherman Glenroy Anderson
Role: Right-hand bat, right-arm medium-fast bowler
Born: 22 September 1976, Hammersmith, London
Height: 5ft 10in **Weight:** 11st 11lbs
County debut: 1999 (Essex)
50 wickets in a season: 1
1st-Class 50s: 1
1st-Class 5 w. in innings: 8
1st-Class 10 w. in match: 1
1st-Class catches: 7
Place in batting averages: 232nd av. 14.00
Place in bowling averages: 11th av. 19.97 (2000 94th av. 30.37)
Strike rate: 39.62 (career 46.46)
Parents: Heather and Junior
Marital status: Single
Education: Lyon Park School; Alperton High School; Barnet College; NWL College; London Cricket College
Qualifications: 6 GCSEs, BTEC National in Engineering
Overseas tours: Middlesex U16 to Jersey; BWIA to Trinidad and Tobago 1998, 1999, 2000
Overseas teams played for: Coronation CC, South Africa 1996-97
Cricketers particularly admired: Malcolm Marshall, Stuart Law, Carl Hooper
Young players to look out for: James Foster
Other sports followed: Football (Liverpool)
Injuries: Out for last eight Championship matches with a shin injury
Relaxations: Music

Extras: Took 50 first-class wickets in his first season 1999. Left Essex in the 2001-02 off-season and has joined Northamptonshire for 2002
Best batting: 67* Essex v Sussex, Chelmsford 2000
Best bowling: 6-34 Essex v Northamptonshire, Ilford 2000

2001 Season

	M	Inns	NO	Runs	HS	Avge	100s	50s	Ct	St	O	M	Runs	Wkts	Avge	Best	5wl	10wM
Test																		
All First	8	11	0	154	45	14.00	-	-	2	-	231.1	54	699	35	19.97	5-21	3	-
1-day Int																		
C & G																		
B & H	1	0	0	0	0	-	-	-	1	-	10	1	63	1	63.00	1-63	-	
1-day Lge	5	5	0	35	22	7.00	-	-	-	-	33.4	1	159	2	79.50	1-5	-	

Career Performances

	M	Inns	NO	Runs	HS	Avge	100s	50s	Ct	St	Balls	Runs	Wkts	Avge	Best	5wl	10wM
Test																	
All First	32	39	5	471	67*	13.85	-	1	7	-	5065	2701	109	24.77	6-34	8	1
1-day Int																	
C & G																	
B & H	4	0	0	0	0	-	-	-	1	-	198	172	3	57.33	1-33	-	
1-day Lge	15	12	1	62	22	5.63	-	-	-	-	606	509	7	72.71	3-32	-	

ATHERTON, M. A.   Lancashire

Name: <u>Michael</u> Andrew Atherton
Role: Right-hand bat, leg-break bowler
Born: 23 March 1968, Manchester
Height: 6ft **Weight:** 13st 5lbs
Nickname: Athers, Dread
County debut: 1987
County cap: 1989
Benefit: 1997 (£307,000)
Test debut: 1989
Tests: 115
One-Day Internationals: 54
1000 runs in a season: 7
1st-Class 50s: 104
1st-Class 100s: 52
1st-Class 200s: 2
1st-Class 5 w. in innings: 3

1st-Class catches: 268
One-Day 100s: 12
Place in batting averages: 104th av. 32.45
(2000 46th av. 38.14)
Strike rate: (career 83.15)
Parents: Alan and Wendy
Marital status: Single
Family links with cricket: Father played
club cricket
Education: Briscoe Lane County Primary;
Manchester GS; Downing College,
Cambridge
Qualifications: 10 O-levels, 3 A-levels,
BA (Hons) (Cantab)
Overseas tours: England YC to Sri Lanka
1986-87, to Australia 1987-88; England A to
Zimbabwe 1989-90; England to Australia
1990-91, to India and Sri Lanka 1992-93, to

West Indies 1993-94, to Australia 1994-95, to South Africa 1995-96, to India and
Pakistan (World Cup) 1995-96, to Zimbabwe and New Zealand 1996-97, to West
Indies 1997-98, to Australia 1998-99, to South Africa 1999-2000, to Pakistan and
Sri Lanka 2000-01
Cricketers particularly admired: Allan Border
Other sports followed: Golf, squash, football
Injuries: Recurring back injury
Relaxations: 'Decent novels (Heller, Kundera, etc.), good movies, food and wine,
travelling, most sports, music'
Extras: First captained England U19 aged 16. In 1987 was first player to score 1000
runs in his debut season since Paul Parker in 1976. Shared in a Lancashire record
partnership for the third wicket (364) with Neil Fairbrother at The Oval 1990. Became
youngest Lancastrian to score a Test century (151 v NZ at Trent Bridge in 1990);
second Lancastrian to score a Test century at Old Trafford (138 v India in 1990). One
of *Wisden*'s Five Cricketers of the Year 1991. Appointed England captain in 1993.
Cornhill England Player of the Year 1993-94. Voted England's Player of the Series
against the West Indies in 1995. Hit 185 not out in the second Test against South
Africa in Johannesburg in 1995-96 series; the innings lasted 645 minutes and was the
fourth longest by an Englishman in Test matches. Carried bat for 94* in first innings of
third Test v New Zealand at Christchurch 1996-97, going on to score 118 in the second
innings. Passed Peter May's long-standing record of most Tests as England captain
(41), against Australia during the Ashes campaign in 1997. Relinquished England
captaincy after 1997-98 Test series v West Indies. Was England's Man of the Series v
South Africa 1998. Run of 62 consecutive Test matches ended when he pulled out of
the Test v Sri Lanka at The Oval 1998. Selected for England's 1999 World Cup squad
but forced to withdraw ahead of Coca-Cola Cup tournament in Sharjah in April 1999

because of back injury. Scored 136 in the second Test v Zimbabwe 2000, thus equalling Denis Compton's record of five Test centuries at Trent Bridge. Shared in Lancashire Sunday/National League record first-wicket partnership (192), with Saurav Ganguly v Somerset Sabres at Taunton 2000. Made 100th Test appearance in third Test v West Indies on his home ground of Old Trafford 2000. Won Man of the Match award for his 83 and 108 v West Indies in the fifth Test at The Oval 2000 – in England's first innings he shared in a new record first-wicket stand for England v West Indies at The Oval (159) with Marcus Trescothick; in England's second innings he was last man out, having scored 108 out of 217. Passed 7000 runs in Test cricket in the first Test v Pakistan at Lahore 2000-01. Scored a 430-ball 125 and a 33-ball 26 in England's victory in the third Test v Pakistan at Karachi 2000-01, winning the Man of the Match award and moving into fifth place above Wally Hammond in the list of England Test run-scorers. England central contract 2001. Captained England in second and third Tests v Australia 2001 in the absence of the injured Nasser Hussain; in the second Test he passed Colin Cowdrey's career total of 7624 runs to become England's fourth highest run-scorer in Tests. Retired at the end of the 2001 season and received an ECB Special Award at the PCA awards dinner at the Royal Albert Hall. Has joined Channel 4 as a broadcaster

Best batting: 268* Lancashire v Glamorgan, Blackpool 1999
Best bowling: 6-78 Lancashire v Nottinghamshire, Trent Bridge 1990

2001 Season

	M	Inns	NO	Runs	HS	Avge	100s	50s	Ct	St	O	M	Runs	Wkts	Avge	Best	5wl	10wM
Test	7	13	0	319	57	24.53	-	3	13	-								
All First	11	21	1	649	160	32.45	1	3	17	-								
1-day Int																		
C & G	3	3	0	40	18	13.33	-	-	5	-								
B & H	5	5	1	147	77*	36.75	-	2	2	-								
1-day Lge	4	4	0	107	62	26.75	-	1	6	-								

Career Performances

	M	Inns	NO	Runs	HS	Avge	100s	50s	Ct	St	Balls	Runs	Wkts	Avge	Best	5wl	10wM
Test	115	212	7	7728	185*	37.69	16	46	83	-	408	302	2	151.00	1-20	-	-
All First	336	584	47	21929	268*	40.83	54	107	268	-	8981	4733	108	43.82	6-78	3	-
1-day Int	54	54	3	1791	127	35.11	2	12	15	-							
C & G	35	35	3	1171	115	36.59	2	9	15	-	188	154	6	25.66	2-15	-	
B & H	72	70	7	2259	121*	35.85	3	15	36	-	252	228	7	32.57	4-42	-	
1-day Lge	107	104	8	3508	111	36.54	5	20	37	-	216	248	7	35.42	3-33	-	

AUSTIN, I. D.   Lancashire

Name: <u>Ian</u> David Austin
Role: Left-hand bat, right-arm medium
bowler
Born: 30 May 1966, Haslingden, Lancs
Height: 5ft 10in **Weight:** 14st 7lbs
Nickname: Oscar, Bully
County debut: 1986
County cap: 1990
Benefit: 2000
One-Day Internationals: 9
1st-Class 50s: 20
1st-Class 100s: 2
1st-Class 5 w. in innings: 6
1st-Class 10 w. in match: 1
1st-Class catches: 35
One-Day 5 w. in innings: 1
Strike rate: (career 65.88)
Parents: Jack and Ursula
Wife and date of marriage: Alexandra, 27 February 1993
Children: Victoria, 28 January 1995; Matthew, 26 January 1998
Family links with cricket: Father opened batting for Haslingden CC
Education: Haslingden High School
Qualifications: 4 O-levels, NCA coaching certificate
Overseas tours: NAYC to Bermuda 1985; Lancashire to Jamaica 1986-87, 1987-88, to Zimbabwe 1988-89, to Tasmania and Western Australia 1989-90, 1990-91; England XI to New Zealand (Cricket Max) 1997; England to Bangladesh (Wills International Cup) 1998, to Sharjah (Coca-Cola Cup) 1998-99
Overseas teams played for: Maroochydore, Queensland 1987-88, 1991-92; Randwick, Sydney 1990-91
Cricketers particularly admired: Ian Botham, Hartley Alleyne
Young players to look out for: Andrew Flintoff
Other sports followed: Football (Burnley), golf
Relaxations: Golf, and listening to music
Extras: Set amateur Lancashire League record for highest individual score (147*). Set Lancashire CCC season record for most wickets in the Sunday League (29) in 1991. Won the Walter Lawrence Trophy in 1991 for the fastest first-class century of the season, 64 balls off authentic bowling v Yorkshire at Scarborough, batting at No. 10. Man of the Match in the 1996 B&H final and Lancashire's 1996 NatWest semi-final v Yorkshire. Lancashire Player of the Year for 1997. Man of the Match in the 1998 NatWest final. One of *Wisden's* Five Cricketers of the Year 1999. Represented England in the 1999 World Cup. Retired at the end of the 2001 season

Best batting: 115* Lancashire v Derbyshire, Blackpool 1992
Best bowling: 6-43 Lancashire v Sri Lanka A, Old Trafford 1999

2001 Season

	M	Inns	NO	Runs	HS	Avge	100s	50s	Ct	St	O	M	Runs	Wkts	Avge	Best	5wI	10wM
Test																		
All First																			
1-day Int																			
C & G																			
B & H	5	3	0	16	14	5.33	-	-	-	-	46	8	158	4	39.50	2-18	-	
1-day Lge	1	0	0	0	0	-	-	-	-	-	6.5	1	32	1	32.00	1-32	-	

Career Performances

	M	Inns	NO	Runs	HS	Avge	100s	50s	Ct	St	Balls	Runs	Wkts	Avge	Best	5wI	10wM
Test																	
All First	124	173	37	3778	115 *	27.77	2	20	35	-	17261	8042	262	30.69	6-43	6	1
1-day Int	9	6	1	34	11 *	6.80	-	-	-	-	475	360	6	60.00	2-25	-	
C & G	33	23	10	361	97	27.76	-	2	4	-	2133	1203	44	27.34	3-14	-	
B & H	69	44	12	684	80	21.37	-	2	11	-	3928	2434	84	28.97	4-8	-	
1-day Lge	194	117	47	1177	48	16.81	-	-	34	-	8087	5789	217	26.67	5-56	1	

AVERIS, J. M. M. Gloucestershire

Name: <u>James</u> Maxwell Michael Averis
Role: Right-hand bat, right-arm
fast-medium bowler
Born: 28 May 1974, Bristol
Height: 5ft 11in **Weight:** 13st
Nickname: Fish, Avo
County debut: 1994 (one-day),
1997 (first-class)
County cap: 2001
1st-Class 5 w. in innings: 2
1st-Class catches: 6
One-Day 5 w. in innings: 3
Place in batting averages: 284th av. 2.18
(2000 273rd av. 10.00)
Place in bowling averages: 105th av. 37.69
Strike rate: 64.48 (career 77.90)
Parents: Mike and Carol
Marital status: Single
Family links with cricket: 'Father and grandfather played and have lots of advice'

Education: Bristol Cathedral School; Portsmouth University; St Cross College, Oxford University
Qualifications: 10 GCSEs, 3 A-levels, BSc (Hons) Geographical Science, Diploma in Social Studies (Oxon), FPC I and II
Career outside cricket: 'Financial advisor? (this winter)'
Off-season: 'Taking more financial planning exams; seeing friends I don't see during the season and sorting my house out'
Overseas tours: Bristol Schools to Australia 1990-91; Gloucestershire to Zimbabwe 1997, to South Africa 1999, to Cape Town 2000; Bristol RFC to South Africa 1996; Oxford University RFC to Japan and Australia 1997
Overseas teams played for: Union CC, Port Elizabeth, South Africa; Kraifontaine, Boland, South Africa 2001
Cricket moments to forget: 'This year's [2001] B&H final v Surrey'
Cricketers particularly admired: Jack Russell, Ian Harvey, Malcolm Marshall, Ian Botham
Young players to look out for: Chris Taylor, Dominic Jago
Other sports played: Rugby (Bristol RFC – first-team debut 1994; Oxford University – Blue 1996)
Other sports followed: Football (Liverpool FC), rugby (Bristol RFC)
Relaxations: 'Reading, music and gossip mags'
Extras: Double Oxford Blue in 1996-97. Captain of South West U21 rugby in 1995. Played in every one-day game in Gloucestershire's treble-winning season 2000. Gloucestershire Player of the Year 2001. Awarded Gloucestershire cap 2001
Opinions on cricket: 'More time between matches would allow for quality practice time, which would probably bring the standard up. More international cricket played outside Test grounds would take the game to the public.'
Best batting: 42 Oxford University v Durham, The Parks 1997
  42 Oxford University v Sussex, The Parks 1997
Best bowling: 5-55 Gloucestershire v Middlesex, Lord's 2001

---

4. Off which unfortunate bowler did Lancashire's David Hughes strike 24 from an over to set up victory over Gloucestershire in the gathering gloom at Old Trafford in the Gillette Cup semi-finals of 1971?

2001 Season

	M	Inns	NO	Runs	HS	Avge	100s	50s	Ct	St	O	M	Runs	Wkts	Avge	Best	5wI	10wM
Test																		
All First	15	19	3	35	7 *	2.18	-	-	3	-	462.1	102	1621	43	37.69	5-55	1	-
1-day Int																		
C & G	2	2	2	12	12 *	-	-	-	-	-	16	1	63	6	10.50	4-42	-	
B & H	8	3	0	23	19	7.66	-	-	2	-	66	6	322	11	29.27	2-16	-	
1-day Lge	15	8	3	51	17 *	10.20	-	-	3	-	121.3	8	546	27	20.22	5-40	2	

Career Performances

	M	Inns	NO	Runs	HS	Avge	100s	50s	Ct	St	Balls	Runs	Wkts	Avge	Best	5wI	10wM
Test																	
All First	34	48	11	417	42	11.27	-	-	6	-	5921	3579	76	47.09	5-55	2	-
1-day Int																	
C & G	8	4	3	26	12 *	26.00	-	-	1	-	410	310	15	20.66	4-36	-	
B & H	15	3	0	23	19	7.66	-	-	3	-	706	555	25	22.20	4-8	-	
1-day Lge	44	26	11	124	23 *	8.26	-	-	5	-	1973	1478	69	21.42	5-20	3	

AYMES, A. N.   Hampshire

Name: <u>Adrian</u> Nigel Aymes
Role: Right-hand bat, wicket-keeper
Born: 4 June 1964, Southampton
Height: 6ft **Weight:** 13st
Nickname: Adi
County debut: 1987
County cap: 1991
Benefit: 2000
50 dismissals in a season: 5
1st-Class 50s: 38
1st-Class 100s: 8
1st-Class catches: 500
1st-Class stumpings: 43
Place in batting averages: 67th av. 40.85
(2000 148th av. 23.41)
Strike rate: 36.00 (career 41.00)
Parents: Michael and Barbara
Wife and date of marriage: Marie,
14 November 1992
Children: Lucie, 9 November 1994
Family links with cricket: 'Brother Gary bowled at me in the drive; he's 6ft 7in
(good practice for Curtly and Courtney!!)'

Education: Shirley Middle; Bellemoor Secondary; Hill College
Qualifications: 4 O-levels, 1 A-level, NCA coaching award
Career outside cricket: Building sites, selling
Off-season: 'Promoting "Get-Zet-Go" (the future)'
Overseas tours: Hampshire CCC to Isle of Wight 1992, to Portugal 1993, to Guernsey 1994, to Anguilla 1997, to South Africa
Career highlights to date: '1991 NatWest win; 1992 B&H win'
Cricket moments to forget: 'All the semi-final losses'
Cricketers particularly admired: Jack Russell, 'all Hursley Park players'
Young players to look out for: Nicky Peng, 'all Hampshire's youngsters'
Other sports played: Football (Gosport Borough, Lymington, Bristol City trials)
Other sports followed: Non-sport martial arts, football (Arsenal, Southampton)
Relaxations: Spending time with friends and family; 'letting my neighbour "Old Stu" teach me about wine and food'
Extras: Equalled county record of six catches in an innings and ten in a match. Hampshire Exiles Young Player of the Year 1990. Was quickest wicket-keeper to 100 dismissals and 1000 runs in the Sunday League. Took 500th first-class catch (Usman Afzaal off Shaun Udal) v Nottinghamshire at Trent Bridge 2001. Hampshire Players' Fielder of the Season Award 2001
Opinions on cricket: 'Still a great game.'
Best batting: 133 Hampshire v Leicestershire, Leicester 1998
Best bowling: 2-101 Hampshire v Nottinghamshire, Trent Bridge 2001

2001 Season

	M	Inns	NO	Runs	HS	Avge	100s	50s	Ct	St	O	M	Runs	Wkts	Avge	Best	5wI	10wM
Test																		
All First	16	19	5	572	112 *	40.85	1	4	43	2	12	0	107	2	53.50	2-101	-	-
1-day Int																		
C & G																		
B & H	4	3	1	34	17 *	17.00	-	-	4	2								
1-day Lge	1	1	1	9	9 *	-	-	-	-	-								

Career Performances

	M	Inns	NO	Runs	HS	Avge	100s	50s	Ct	St	Balls	Runs	Wkts	Avge	Best	5wI	10wM
Test																	
All First	210	307	77	7286	133	31.67	8	38	500	43	246	438	6	73.00	2-101	-	-
1-day Int																	
C & G	25	11	4	277	73 *	39.57	-	2	38	4							
B & H	43	28	8	404	63	20.20	-	1	41	11							
1-day Lge	151	110	43	1511	60 *	22.55	-	3	134	38							

BAILEY, R. J.   Derbyshire

Name: Robert (Rob) John Bailey
Role: Right-hand bat, off-spin bowler
Born: 28 October 1963, Biddulph,
Stoke-on-Trent
Height: 6ft 3in **Weight:** 14st 7lbs
Nickname: Setter
County debut: 1982 (Northants),
2000 (Derbys)
County cap: 1985 (Northants),
2000 (Derbys)
Benefit: 1993 (Northants)
Test debut: 1988
Tests: 4
One-Day Internationals: 4
1000 runs in a season: 13
1st-Class 50s: 111
1st-Class 100s: 43
1st-Class 200s: 4
1st-Class 5 w. in innings: 2
1st-Class catches: 272
One-Day 100s: 9
One-Day 5 w. in innings: 1

Place in batting averages: 184th av. 21.45 (2000 17th av. 48.53)
Strike rate: 65.57 (career 80.27)
Parents: Marie, father deceased
Wife and date of marriage: Rachel, 11 April 1987
Children: Harry John, 7 March 1991; Alexandra Joy, 13 November 1993
Family links with cricket: Brother plays for Betley-North Staffs with Dominic Cork's two brothers
Education: Biddulph High School
Qualifications: 6 CSEs, 1 O-level, NCA advanced cricket coach
Career outside cricket: Seller of promotional ceramics
Overseas tours: England to Sharjah 1984-85, 1986-87, to West Indies 1989-90; Northants to Durban 1991-92, to Cape Town 1992-93, to Zimbabwe 1994-95; Singapore Sixes October 1994
Overseas teams played for: Rhodes University, South Africa 1982-83; Uitenhage, Melbourne 1983-84, 1984-85; Fitzroy, Melbourne 1985-86; Gosnells, Perth 1987-88
Cricket moments to forget: 'Getting run out by my runner – Steve Stubbings, 2000 – just after tearing my calf. (I knew G. Fowler would be laughing in the TV box)'
Other sports played: Was Staffordshire badminton champion U12-U16

Other sports followed: Football (Stoke City, Northampton Town, Rushden & Diamonds), rugby (Northampton Saints)
Relaxations: Walking, and drinking at the local village pub
Extras: Played for Staffordshire. Played for Young England v Young Australia 1983. Selected for cancelled England tour of India 1988-89. In 1990 became youngest Northamptonshire player to score 10,000 first-class runs. Won three consecutive NatWest Man of the Match Awards 1995. Northamptonshire captain 1996-97. In 1999 v Gloucestershire, passed 20,000 first-class runs for Northamptonshire, becoming only the sixth player to do so. Left Northamptonshire at end of 1999 season and joined Derbyshire for 2000. Scored hundred (118) on first-class debut for Derbyshire, v Leics at Derby 2000. Scored 112* v West Indians at Derby 2000; this was the first century by a Derbyshire batsman in matches between the county and the West Indians. Derbyshire Supporters' Club Player of the Year 2000
Best batting: 224* Northamptonshire v Glamorgan, Swansea 1986
Best bowling: 5-54 Northamptonshire v Nottinghamshire, Northampton 1993

2001 Season

	M	Inns	NO	Runs	HS	Avge	100s	50s	Ct	St	O	M	Runs	Wkts	Avge	Best	5wI	10wM
Test																		
All First	14	25	1	515	136 *	21.45	1	2	8	-	76.3	17	245	7	35.00	2-17	-	-
1-day Int																		
C & G	1	1	0	34	34	34.00	-	-	-	-	0.2	0	4	0	-		-	-
B & H	4	4	0	148	62	37.00	-	2	-	-								
1-day Lge	14	14	2	402	94	33.50	-	3	4	-	46	0	227	4	56.75	2-28	-	

Career Performances

	M	Inns	NO	Runs	HS	Avge	100s	50s	Ct	St	Balls	Runs	Wkts	Avge	Best	5wI	10wM
Test	4	8	0	119	43	14.87	-	-	-	-							
All First	374	628	89	21844	224 *	40.52	47	111	272	-	9713	5144	121	42.51	5-54	2	-
1-day Int	4	4	2	137	43 *	68.50	-	-	1	-	36	25	0	-		-	-
C & G	49	49	13	1629	145	45.25	1	10	18	-	656	411	16	25.68	3-47	-	
B & H	78	73	12	2837	134	46.50	4	22	21	-	450	305	8	38.12	5-45	1	
1-day Lge	254	239	36	7031	125 *	34.63	4	45	67	-	1744	1632	43	37.95	3-23	-	

---

5. Which two counties were required to replay their third-round tie in the NatWest 2000 after one of them fielded a player who was deemed to be ineligible?

BAILEY, T. M. B.   Northamptonshire

Name: <u>Tobin</u> Michael Barnaby Bailey
Role: Right-hand bat, wicket-keeper
Born: 28 August 1976, Kettering
Height: 5ft 11in **Weight:** 13st 8lbs
Nickname: Bill, Mad Dog, Scruff
County debut: 1996
1st-Class 50s: 1
1st-Class catches: 22
1st-Class stumpings: 2
Place in batting averages: 218th av. 16.14
Parents: Terry and Penny
Marital status: Single
Family links with cricket: 'Step-dad
watches a lot'
Education: Bedford School; Loughborough
University
Qualifications: 3 A-levels, BA (Hons)
Politics, Level II coaching award
Career outside cricket: Coaching
Off-season: Playing cricket in Perth

Overseas tours: Bedford to South Africa 1994, to Bermuda; Northamptonshire to
Grenada 2000, 2001
Cricketers particularly admired: Jack Russell, Mike Atherton, Alan Knott
Young players to look out for: Mark Powell
Other sports played: Hockey and tennis (both for Beds at youth level), golf ('badly')
Other sports followed: Rugby (Bedford RFC), football (Leicester City FC)
Relaxations: Watching videos, playing golf and eating out
Extras: Bedfordshire Young Player of the Year and Northants County League Young
Player of the Year in 1995. Holmwoods Schools Cricketer of the Year. Played for
England Schools U19 and was a reserve for the England U19 tour to Zimbabwe
1995-96. Won the BUSA Championship with Loughborough University in 1996 and
captained the university to BUSA Championship shared win with Durham University
in 1998 (final washed out by rain). Represented British Universities 1997 and 1998.
Northamptonshire Young Player of the Year 2000. NBC Denis Compton Award for the
most promising young Northamptonshire player 2000. 'Took part in AON Risk game
in 2000 that started with 12 players'. PCA representative for Northamptonshire
Opinions on cricket: 'Three up/three down is too many. I would prefer
two up/two down.'
Best batting: 96* Northamptonshire v Worcestershire, Worcester 2000

2001 Season

	M	Inns	NO	Runs	HS	Avge	100s	50s	Ct	St	O	M	Runs	Wkts	Avge	Best	5wI	10wM
Test																		
All First	5	7	0	113	41	16.14	-	-	3	-								
1-day Int																		
C & G	1	1	0	4	4	4.00	-	-	-	-								
B & H																		
1-day Lge	6	4	0	49	22	12.25	-	-	2	1								

Career Performances

	M	Inns	NO	Runs	HS	Avge	100s	50s	Ct	St	Balls	Runs	Wkts	Avge	Best	5wI	10wM
Test																	
All First	18	22	3	394	96 *	20.73	-	1	22	2							
1-day Int																	
C & G	1	1	0	4	4	4.00	-	-	-	-							
B & H	10	8	1	97	52	13.85	-	1	5	7							
1-day Lge	13	5	0	59	22	11.80	-	-	11	2							

BAKER, T. M.   Northamptonshire

Name: <u>Thomas</u> Michael Baker
Role: Right-hand bat, right-arm
fast-medium bowler
Born: 6 July 1981, Dewsbury, West
Yorkshire
Height: 6ft 5in **Weight:** 12st 8lbs
Nickname: Tosh
County debut: 2001 (one-day, Yorkshire)
Parents: Mike and Carol
Marital status: Single
Family links with cricket: 'Grandad played
in local league. Brother James plays at Spen
Victoria in the Bradford League'
Education: Gomersal First School; Gomersal
Middle School; Whitcliffe Mount School;
Huddersfield Technical College
Qualifications: NCA Level 1 coaching,
BTEC Sports Science, GNVQ Leisure
and Tourism

Career outside cricket: Sports scientist
Off-season: 'Relaxing, keeping fit, playing golf'
Overseas tours: Yorkshire to Cape Town 2000

Overseas teams played for: Edgemead CC, Cape Town 2000-01
Career highlights to date: 'Making one-day debut on TV. Playing day/night game at Newlands, Cape Town, and hitting a straight six'
Cricket moments to forget: 'None so far (touch wood)!'
Cricketers particularly admired: Allan Donald, Steve Waugh, Jacques Kallis
Young players to look out for: David Paynter, Joe Sayers, Chris Taylor
Other sports played: Golf, football, 'any really'
Other sports followed: Football (Leeds United)
Injuries: Out for ten days after back spasm on tour to Cape Town; for three weeks with a groin strain
Relaxations: 'Following Leeds United, socialising'
Extras: Yorkshire CCC Most Promising U17 Cricketer. Took wicket (Steve Stubbings) with first legitimate ball of his career (the first delivery was a wide) v Derbyshire in the B&H at Headingley 2001. Released by Yorkshire at the end of the 2001 season and has joined Northamptonshire for 2002
Opinions on cricket: 'A day/night league would be a good idea. Too many one-day competitions.'

2001 Season

	M	Inns	NO	Runs	HS	Avge	100s	50s	Ct	St	O	M	Runs	Wkts	Avge	Best	5wI	10wM
Test																		
All First																		
1-day Int																		
C & G																		
B & H	3	1	0	3	3	3.00	-	-	2	-	16	1	67	3	22.33	2-13	-	
1-day Lge	1	0	0	0	0	-	-	-	1	-	5	1	22	1	22.00	1-22	-	

Career Performances

	M	Inns	NO	Runs	HS	Avge	100s	50s	Ct	St	Balls	Runs	Wkts	Avge	Best	5wI	10wM
Test																	
All First																	
1-day Int																	
C & G																	
B & H	3	1	0	3	3	3.00	-	-	2	-	96	67	3	22.33	2-13	-	
1-day Lge	1	0	0	0	0	-	-	-	1	-	30	22	1	22.00	1-22	-	

6. Which current first-class umpire kept wicket for Middlesex
in their victory in the 1977 Gillette Cup final?

BALL, M. C. J.   Gloucestershire

Name: <u>Martyn</u> Charles John Ball
Role: Right-hand bat, off-spin bowler,
slip fielder
Born: 26 April 1970, Bristol
Height: 5ft 9in **Weight:** 12st 10lbs
Nickname: Benny, Barfo
County debut: 1988
County cap: 1996
1st-Class 50s: 12
1st-Class 5 w. in innings: 10
1st-Class 10 w. in match: 1
1st-Class catches: 187
One-Day 5 w. in innings: 1
Place in batting averages: 131st av. 29.15
(2000 176th av. 20.33)
Place in bowling averages: 35th av. 25.76
(2000 137th av. 43.86)

Strike rate: 61.52 (career 79.20)
Parents: Kenneth Charles and Pamela Wendy
Wife and date of marriage: Mona, 28 September 1991
Children: Kristina, 9 May 1990; Alexandra, 2 August 1993; Harrison, 5 June 1997
Education: Stanshawes Court; King Edmund Secondary School, Yate; Bath College
of Further Education
Qualifications: 6 O-levels, 2 A-levels, advanced cricket coach
Career outside cricket: Sports marketing
Overseas tours: Gloucestershire to Namibia 1991, to Kenya 1992, to Sri Lanka 1993,
to Zimbabwe 1996, 1997, to South Africa 1999; MCC to New Zealand 1998-99
(*see **Stop press***)
Overseas teams played for: North Melbourne, Australia 1988-89; Old Hararians,
Zimbabwe 1990-91
Cricketers particularly admired: Ian Botham, Vic Marks, John Emburey,
Jack Russell
Young players to look out for: Stephen Pope, Alastair Bressington
Other sports played: Rugby, football (both to County Schoolboys level), 'enjoy golf
and skiing'
Other sports followed: 'All sport – massive Man City fan'
Relaxations: 'Spending some quality time at home with family'
Extras: Represented county schools. Played for Young England against Young New
Zealand in 1989. Produced best match bowling figures for the Britannic County
Championship 1993 season – 14-169 against Somerset. Granted a benefit for 2002.
PCA representative for Gloucestershire

Opinions on cricket: 'The divisional aspect has already shown signs of improvement to our national team. A form of the game has to be pushed that is quicker, more thrilling, more exciting and over in a couple of hours if we are to fill stadiums and attract big sponsors.'
Best batting: 71 Gloucestershire v Nottinghamshire, Bristol 1993
Best bowling: 8-46 Gloucestershire v Somerset, Taunton 1993
Stop press: Called up for England Test tour of India 2001-02 after withdrawal of Robert Croft

2001 Season

	M	Inns	NO	Runs	HS	Avge	100s	50s	Ct	St	O	M	Runs	Wkts	Avge	Best	5wl	10wM
Test																		
All First	12	16	3	379	68	29.15	-	3	19	-	348.4	94	876	34	25.76	6-23	2	-
1-day Int																		
C & G	2	2	1	32	18	32.00	-	-	2	-	15.2	0	60	3	20.00	2-26	-	
B & H	5	5	3	48	27	24.00	-	-	4	-	41	1	166	8	20.75	2-19	-	
1-day Lge	14	12	5	132	38	18.85	-	-	11	-	111	2	518	21	24.66	3-15	-	

Career Performances

	M	Inns	NO	Runs	HS	Avge	100s	50s	Ct	St	Balls	Runs	Wkts	Avge	Best	5wl	10wM
Test																	
All First	154	237	42	3779	71	19.37	-	12	187	-	23049	10767	291	37.00	8-46	10	1
1-day Int																	
C & G	25	17	5	161	31	13.41	-	-	16	-	1176	776	26	29.84	3-39	-	
B & H	35	24	5	211	28	11.10	-	-	17	-	1812	1221	36	33.91	4-23	-	
1-day Lge	135	98	35	827	38	13.12	-	-	51	-	4882	4003	116	34.50	5-42	1	

BANES, M. J.   Kent

Name: Matthew (<u>Matt</u>) John Banes
Role: Right-hand bat, right-arm medium bowler
Born: 10 December 1979, Pembury
Height: 5ft 9in **Weight:** 12st 7lbs
Nickname: Bano
County debut: 1999
1st-Class 50s: 2
1st-Class catches: 2
Strike rate: 92.00 (career 92.00)
Parents: Chris and Jane Ann
Marital status: Single
Education: Holmewood House Prep School; Tonbridge School; Durham University
Qualifications: 10 GCSEs, 4 A-levels

Off-season: Durham University; 'Yellowhammers tour to Cape Town, 26 December 2001'

Overseas tours: Tonbridge School to Australia 1996-97; Durham University CC to Cape Town 2000; Yellowhammers to Cape Town 2001-02

Career highlights to date: 'A fifty [53] on debut for Kent v New Zealanders on TV'

Cricketers particularly admired: Mike Atherton, Steve Waugh

Young players to look out for: Rob Ferley, Charlie van der Gucht

Other sports played: Hockey (Durham University 1st XI)

Other sports followed: Football (Arsenal)

Injuries: Osteoma on shin; broken finger

Relaxations: Reading, films, 'Klute'

Extras: Set record for most centuries (11 in three years) for Tonbridge School 1st XI. Played in Old Tonbridgians side that won *The Cricketer* Cup 1999. Scored 53 on first-class debut v New Zealanders at Canterbury 1999. Represented British Universities 2000 and 2001. Played for Durham University CCE 2001 (captain). Played for Kent Board XI in the second round of the C&G 2002, which was played in September 2001

Opinions on cricket: 'Two divisions seems to be the way forward – more competitive.'

Best batting: 53 Kent v New Zealanders, Canterbury 1999

Best bowling: 3-65 DUCCE v Lancashire, Durham 2001

2001 Season (did not make any first-class or one-day appearances)

Career Performances

	M	Inns	NO	Runs	HS	Avge	100s	50s	Ct	St	Balls	Runs	Wkts	Avge	Best	5wI	10wM
Test																	
All First	7	11	1	171	53	17.10	-	2	2	-	276	162	3	54.00	3-65	-	-
1-day Int																	
C & G	1	1	0	82	82	82.00	-	1	-	-							
B & H																		
1-day Lge																		

BARNETT, K. J. Gloucestershire

Name: <u>Kim</u> John Barnett
Role: Right-hand bat, leg-break bowler
Born: 17 July 1960, Stoke-on-Trent
Height: 6ft **Weight:** 13st
Nickname: The Vicar
County debut: 1979 (Derbyshire),
1999 (Gloucestershire)
County cap: 1982 (Derbyshire),
1999 (Gloucestershire)
Benefit: 1993 (Derbyshire, £37,056)
Test debut: 1988

Tests: 4
One-Day Internationals: 1
1000 runs in a season: 16
1st-Class 50s: 152
1st-Class 100s: 54
1st-Class 200s: 4
1st-Class 5 w. in innings: 3
1st-Class catches: 283
One-Day 100s: 14
One-Day 5 w. in innings: 2
Place in batting averages: 52nd av. 44.73 (2000 20th av. 45.71)
Strike rate: (career 75.53)
Parents: Derek and Doreen
Wife and date of marriage: Janet, 8 August 1995
Children: Michael Nicholas, 24 April 1990; Christina Natalie, 11 June 1996;
Gregory John, 26 September 2000
Family links with cricket: 'Father local sportsman, mainly football'
Education: Ipstones C of E; Leek High School, Staffs
Qualifications: 7 O-levels, advanced mathematics
Career outside cricket: Bank clerk
Off-season: Training
Overseas tours: English Schools to India 1977-78; England YC to Australia 1978-79;
England B to Sri Lanka 1985-86 (vice-captain); unofficial English XI to South Africa
1989-90
Overseas teams played for: Boland, South Africa 1980-81, 1982-83
Career highlights to date: 'Six finals in succession'
Cricket moments to forget: 'Losing the first and last'
Cricketers particularly admired: Gordon Greenidge
Young players to look out for: Chris Taylor, Mark Hardinges
Other sports played: Football (Stafford Rangers, Leek Town)

Other sports followed: Football (Stoke City)
Relaxations: Horse racing, golf
Extras: Played for Northamptonshire 2nd XI when aged 15; also played for
Staffordshire and Warwickshire 2nd XI. Appointed Derbyshire captain 1983, becoming
youngest captain of a first-class county; relinquished captaincy at end of 1995 season.
One of *Wisden*'s Five Cricketers of the Year 1989. Banned from Test cricket after
joining tour to South Africa; suspension remitted in 1992. Leading century-maker and
run-scorer in all competitions in the history of Derbyshire cricket. Left Derbyshire in
1998-99 off-season and joined Gloucestershire for 1999. Appeared in six successive
domestic one-day finals – 1998 NatWest with Derbyshire; 1999 B&H Super Cup and
NatWest, 2000 B&H and NatWest and 2001 B&H, all with Gloucestershire; also holds
distinction of having played in the first (1981) and last (2000) NatWest finals. Is
second highest run-scorer in B&H Cup history behind Graham Gooch (who scored
5176 runs). Scored 101 v Northamptonshire in the Norwich Union League at
Northampton 2001, passing Graham Gooch's domestic one-day league run record
(8573) with his hundredth run
Best batting: 239* Derbyshire v Leicestershire, Leicester 1988
Best bowling: 6-28 Derbyshire v Glamorgan, Chesterfield 1991

2001 Season

	M	Inns	NO	Runs	HS	Avge	100s	50s	Ct	St	O	M	Runs	Wkts	Avge	Best	5wI	10wM
Test																		
All First	14	25	2	1029	114	44.73	1	7	10	-	16	4	35	0	-		-	-	-
1-day Int																		
C & G	2	2	0	40	32	20.00	-	-	-	-	4	0	25	0	-		-	-
B & H	8	8	0	225	85	28.12	-	1	-	-	10	0	50	0	-		-	-
1-day Lge	15	15	0	473	101	31.53	2	1	3	-	30.2	2	130	6	21.66	4-12	-

Career Performances

	M	Inns	NO	Runs	HS	Avge	100s	50s	Ct	St	Balls	Runs	Wkts	Avge	Best	5wI	10wM
Test	4	7	0	207	80	29.57	-	2	1	-	36	32	0	-		-	-	-
All First	471	769	73	27952	239 *	40.16	58	152	283	-	14085	7034	186	37.81	6-28	3	-
1-day Int	1	1	0	84	84	84.00	-	1	-	-							
C & G	57	55	3	2032	113 *	39.07	2	14	22	-	790	548	25	21.92	6-24	2
B & H	103	94	6	3165	115	35.96	4	21	35	-	690	479	16	29.93	3-52	-
1-day Lge	320	308	43	8920	131 *	33.66	8	47	103	-	1941	1676	62	27.03	4-12	-

BASSANO, C. W. G.   Derbyshire

Name: <u>Christopher</u> Warwick Godfrey
Bassano
Role: Right-hand bat, leg-spin bowler
Born: 11 September 1975, East London,
South Africa
Height: 6ft 2in   **Weight:** 13st 7lbs
Nickname: Bass, Bassy
County debut: 2001
1st-Class 50s: 2
1st-Class 100s: 2
1st-Class catches: 5
Place in batting averages: 57th av. 43.58
Parents: Brian and Allison
Marital status: Single
Family links with cricket: 'Father played
throughout his life, was a radio commentator,
provincial manager, and held development
positions in South Africa; also wrote books
on cricket etc.'

Education: Grey School, Port Elizabeth; Launceston Church Grammar School,
Tasmania; University of Tasmania, Hobart
Qualifications: Bachelor of Applied Science (Horticulture)
Career outside cricket: Trout fishing guide
Off-season: 'Fishing and playing cricket in Tasmania as well as spending some time
with the family'
Career highlights to date: 'Being selected to play representative cricket or to play at
a higher level is always a highlight'
Cricket moments to forget: 'Losing'
Cricketers particularly admired: Graeme Pollock, Steve Waugh
Young players to look out for: Tom Lungley, Nathan 'Roach' Dumelow,
Shane Watson (Tasmania)
Other sports played: Hockey
Other sports followed: Rugby union
Injuries: Out for one week with a groin strain
Relaxations: Fly fishing
Extras: Captained Eastern Province U13 1987-88. Played for Tasmania U16, U17,
U19 (captain), U23 (captain) and 2nd XI. Has played for the 2nd XIs of Sussex, Essex,
Kent and Gloucestershire. Became the first player to score a century in each innings of
his Championship debut, 186* and 106 v Gloucestershire at Derby 2001; his first
innings lasted 8¼ hours and also produced the highest score by a Derbyshire
batsman on Championship debut. Is diabetic. His ancestry includes a set of brothers

from Venice who were musicians at the court of Henry VIII. Is not considered an overseas player

Opinions on cricket: 'As long as each player leaves the game in a better state than when he arrived, we will all be better for it.'

Best batting: 186* Derbyshire v Gloucestershire, Derby 2001

2001 Season

	M	Inns	NO	Runs	HS	Avge	100s	50s	Ct	St	O	M	Runs	Wkts	Avge	Best	5wl	10wM
Test																		
All First	8	14	2	523	186 *	43.58	2	2	5	-	2	0	11	0	-		-	-	-
1-day Int																		
C & G																		
B & H	1	1	0	9	9	9.00	-	-	1	-								
1-day Lge	8	8	1	180	45	25.71	-	-	2	-								

Career Performances

	M	Inns	NO	Runs	HS	Avge	100s	50s	Ct	St	Balls	Runs	Wkts	Avge	Best	5wl	10wM
Test																	
All First	8	14	2	523	186 *	43.58	2	2	5	-	12	11	0	-		-	-	-
1-day Int																	
C & G																		
B & H	1	1	0	9	9	9.00	-	-	1	-							
1-day Lge	8	8	1	180	45	25.71	-	-	2	-							

7. How many overs per side did the first Gillette Cup competition comprise in 1963?

BATTY, G. J.   Worcestershire

Name: <u>Gareth</u> Jon Batty
Role: Right-hand bat, off-spin bowler
Born: 13 October 1977, Yorkshire
Height: 5ft 11in   **Weight:** 12st 4lbs
Nickname: Ging, Bats
County debut: 1997 (Yorkshire),
1998 (one-day, Surrey),
1999 (first-class, Surrey)
1st-Class catches: 2
Strike rate: (career 48.00)
Parents: David and Rosemary
Marital status: Single
Family links with cricket: 'Dad is Yorkshire
Academy coach and U17 manager; brother
played for Yorkshire and Somerset'

Education: Cullingworth First; Parkside
Middle; Bingley Grammar
Qualifications: 9 GCSEs, BTEC Art and
Design, coaching certificate
Career outside cricket: 'Property tycoon and a bit of wheeling and dealing'
Off-season: 'Getting very fit and working hard on my game in the nets in England'
Overseas tours: England U15 to South Africa 1993; England U19 to Zimbabwe
1995-96, to Pakistan 1996-97
Overseas teams played for: Marist Newman, Australia
Career highlights to date: 'Every time I'm on the winning team'
Cricket moments to forget: 'Every time I lose'
Cricketers particularly admired: Alec Stewart, Adam Hollioake, Mark Butcher,
Saqlain Mushtaq, Ian Salisbury, Graham Thorpe, Ali Brown
Young players to look out for: 'Everyone who played in the 2nd XI Trophy for
Surrey last year'
Other sports played: Rugby union, golf
Other sports followed: Rugby (Leeds)
Injuries: Calf injury
Relaxations: Going to the gym
Extras: National U15 bowling award. *Daily Telegraph* Young Player of the Year 1993.
Made first-class debut for Yorkshire v Lancashire 1997 in non-Championship match.
Joined Surrey for 1998. Played for Weybridge side that won Surrey Championship
1999; scored 201* for Weybridge v Spencer 1999. Scored a 61-ball 54 and took 2-20 v
Gloucestershire at Bristol in the Norwich Union League 2001. Surrey Supporters' Club
Most Improved Player Award and Young Player of the Year Award 2001. Surrey CCC
Young Player of the Year Award 2001. ECB 2nd XI Player of the Year 2001. Released
by Surrey at the end of the 2001 season and has joined Worcestershire for 2002

Opinions on cricket: 'Let's keep the kids interested, whatever it takes.'
Best batting: 25* Surrey v Sri Lanka A, The Oval 1999
Best bowling: 2-45 Surrey v Sri Lanka A, The Oval 1999

2001 Season

	M	Inns	NO	Runs	HS	Avge	100s	50s	Ct	St	O	M	Runs	Wkts	Avge	Best	5wI	10wM
Test																		
All First	1	2	0	44	25	22.00	-	-	2	-								
1-day Int																		
C & G																		
B & H																		
1-day Lge	12	11	2	317	83 *	35.22	-	3	2	-	54.3	4	256	11	23.27	4-36	-	

Career Performances

	M	Inns	NO	Runs	HS	Avge	100s	50s	Ct	St	Balls	Runs	Wkts	Avge	Best	5wI	10wM
Test																	
All First	3	6	1	98	25 *	19.60	-	-	2	-	192	128	4	32.00	2-45	-	-
1-day Int																	
C & G	1	1	0	7	7	7.00	-	-	2	-	56	42	2	21.00	2-42	-	
B & H																	
1-day Lge	22	21	5	450	83 *	28.12	-	3	6	-	717	591	15	39.40	4-36	-	

BATTY, J. N. Surrey

Name: Jonathan (<u>Jon</u>) Neil Batty
Role: Right-hand bat, wicket-keeper
Born: 18 April 1974, Chesterfield
Height: 5ft 10in **Weight:** 11st 6lbs
Nickname: JB
County debut: 1997
County cap: 2001
50 dismissals in a season: 1
1st-Class 50s: 6
1st-Class 100s: 1
1st-Class catches: 161
1st-Class stumpings: 25
Place in batting averages: 220th av. 15.93
(2000 182nd av. 19.71)
Strike rate: (career 78.00)
Parents: Roger and Jill
Marital status: Single
Family links with cricket: Father played to a
high standard of club cricket

Education: Blyth CofE; Oakley Parochial; Wheatley Park; Repton; Durham University (St Chad's); Keble College, Oxford
Qualifications: 10 GCSEs, 4 A-levels, BSc (Hons) in Natural Sciences, Diploma in Social Studies (Oxon)
Off-season: 'Working on my game'
Overseas tours: Repton School to Holland 1991; MCC to Bangladesh 1996; Surrey to South Africa 1997, 2001
Overseas teams played for: Mount Lawley CC, Perth 1997-2001
Career highlights to date: 'Winning two County Championships'
Cricket moments to forget: 'None!'
Cricketers particularly admired: David Gower, Alec Stewart, Jack Russell
Other sports played: Golf, squash
Other sports followed: Football (Nottingham Forest)
Relaxations: Reading, listening to music, movies
Extras: Oxford Blue 1996. Has also played for Oxfordshire and represented Minor Counties. Awarded Surrey cap in 2001
Best batting: 100* Surrey v Somerset, The Oval 2000
Best bowling: 1-21 Surrey v Lancashire, Old Trafford 2000

2001 Season

	M	Inns	NO	Runs	HS	Avge	100s	50s	Ct	St	O	M	Runs	Wkts	Avge	Best	5wI	10wM
Test																		
All First	10	16	1	239	59	15.93	-	1	26	2								
1-day Int																		
C & G	1	0	0	0	0	-	-	-	1	-								
B & H	2	1	0	3	3	3.00	-	-	-	-								
1-day Lge	14	10	2	83	21 *	10.37	-	-	18	2								

Career Performances

	M	Inns	NO	Runs	HS	Avge	100s	50s	Ct	St	Balls	Runs	Wkts	Avge	Best	5wI	10wM
Test																	
All First	69	90	15	1641	100 *	21.88	1	6	161	25	78	61	1	61.00	1-21	-	-
1-day Int																	
C & G	2	1	0	1	1	1.00	-	-	1	-							
B & H	12	9	3	86	26 *	14.33	-	-	9	-							
1-day Lge	50	36	9	355	40	13.14	-	-	46	9							

BELL, I. R. — Warwickshire

Name: Ian Ronald Bell
Role: Right-hand bat, right-arm medium bowler
Born: 11 April 1982, Coventry
Height: 5ft 10in **Weight:** 11st
Nickname: Belly
County debut: 1999
County cap: 2001
1st-Class 50s: 4
1st-Class 100s: 3
1st-Class catches: 13
Place in batting averages: 9th av. 64.30
Strike rate: 102.00 (career 102.00)
Parents: Terry and Barbara
Marital status: Single
Family links with cricket: Brother has played for England U18 and is a member of the Warwickshire Academy
Education: Bilton Middle; Princethorpe College, Rugby
Off-season: Attending ECB Academy in Australia
Overseas tours: Warwickshire U19 to Cape Town 1998-99; England U19 to New Zealand 1998-99, to Malaysia and (U19 World Cup) Sri Lanka 1999-2000, to India 2000-01 (captain); England A to West Indies 2000-01; ECB National Academy to Australia 2001-02
Career highlights to date: 'Selection for ECB Academy and as replacement for England A tour to West Indies. Captaining England U19. Receiving my county cap and scoring my first County Championship century'
Cricket moments to forget: 'Being bowled for a duck when making county debut'
Cricketers particularly admired: Michael Atherton, Steve Waugh, Alec Stewart, Nick Knight
Young players to look out for: Keith Bell
Other sports played: Football (was at Coventry City School of Excellence), rugby, golf
Other sports followed: Football (Aston Villa), rugby union (Northampton Saints)
Relaxations: Golf, listening to music
Extras: Played for England U14, U15, U16, U17. Scored first international century (115) v New Zealand U19 in Alexandra 1998-99. Player of the Series for England U19 v New Zealand U19 in 'Test' series 1998-99. Scored 190 v Northants 2nd XI and 140 v Glos 2nd XI 1999. Represented England U19 in one-day and 'Test' series v Australia U19 1999. NBC Denis Compton Award for the most promising young Warwickshire player 1999, 2000. Gray-Nicolls Trophy for Best Young Schools Cricketer 2000.

Scored 109 for England U19 v India U19 in the first 'Test' at Mumbai 2000-01 and was England U19 leading run-scorer in 'Test' series (332 av. 55.33) and one-day series (169 av. 56.33). On his return from India, he was drafted into the England A squad in West Indies as injury cover in the batting department and made his England A debut v Leeward Islands at Anguilla. Captained England U19 in one-day and 'Test' series (bar second 'Test') v Sri Lanka U19 2000. Represented England U19 in one-day series (3/3, captain) and 'Test' series (1/3, captain) v West Indies U19 2001. Scored maiden first-class century (130) v Oxford University CCE at The Parks 2001, becoming (at 19 years 56 days) the youngest player to score a first-class century for Warwickshire. Scored maiden Championship century (103) v Nottinghamshire at Edgbaston 2001, becoming (at 19 years 115 days) the youngest Warwickshire batsman to score a Championship 100. Awarded Warwickshire cap 2001

Best batting: 135 Warwickshire v Derbyshire, Derby 2001
Best bowling: 1-24 Warwickshire v Nottinghamshire, Edgbaston 2001
Stop press: Scored century (104) in ECB National Academy's innings victory over Commonwealth Bank [Australian] Cricket Academy in Adelaide 2001-02

2001 Season

	M	Inns	NO	Runs	HS	Avge	100s	50s	Ct	St	O	M	Runs	Wkts	Avge	Best	5wl	10wM
Test																		
All First	11	16	3	836	135	64.30	3	4	11	-	17	4	40	1	40.00	1-24	-	-
1-day Int																		
C & G																		
B & H																		
1-day Lge	1	1	0	48	48	48.00	-	-	-	-								

Career Performances

	M	Inns	NO	Runs	HS	Avge	100s	50s	Ct	St	Balls	Runs	Wkts	Avge	Best	5wl	10wM
Test																	
All First	13	19	3	886	135	55.37	3	4	13	-	102	40	1	40.00	1-24	-	-
1-day Int																	
C & G	1	1	0	10	10	10.00	-	-	-	-	3	2	0	-		-	-
B & H																	
1-day Lge	1	1	0	48	48	48.00	-	-	-	-							

8. Which England Test batsman skippered Kent in the 1983 NatWest final against Somerset, a county he would later also captain?

BENHAM, C. C.   Hampshire

Name: Christopher (<u>Chris</u>) Charles Benham
Role: Right-hand bat, right-arm off-spin bowler
Born: 24 March 1983, Frimley, Surrey
Height: 6ft 1in **Weight:** 13st
Nickname: Benny, Beano
County debut: No first-team appearance
Parents: Frank and Sandie
Marital status: Single
Family links with cricket: 'Both older brothers, Nick and Andy, played local club cricket'
Education: Westsfield Junior School; Yateley Comprehensive School; Yateley Sixth Form College; Loughborough University
Qualifications: 10 GCSEs, 3 A-levels
Career outside cricket: Studying Sports Science and Physical Education degree at Loughborough University
Off-season: At Loughborough University; training with Loughborough ECB Academy squad
Overseas tours: West of England U15 to West Indies 1998
Career highlights to date: 'Being part of Hampshire 2nd XI squad that won the 2nd XI Championship in 2001'
Cricketers particularly admired: Ian Botham, Alec Stewart, Steve Waugh, Jacques Kallis
Young players to look out for: James Tomlinson, David Wheeler 'and other young Hampshire Academy players'
Other sports played: Football (school, district and county sides; trials with Swindon and Crystal Palace), tennis, golf
Other sports followed: Football (Arsenal, 'who will soon be dominating the European football scene'), tennis (Anna Kournikova), 'enjoy watching most sports'
Relaxations: 'Playing "Championship Manager" on my PC, which I'm addicted to; listening to music; having a good night out'
Extras: Played for ESCA U15 v Scotland. Represented England U16 v Denmark. Played for Hampshire Board XI in the C&G 2001
Opinions on cricket: 'Feel that the technology available in modern sport should be taken advantage of in cricket to prevent controversial decisions.'

2001 Season (did not make any first-class or one-day appearances)

Career Performances

	M	Inns	NO	Runs	HS	Avge	100s	50s	Ct	St	Balls	Runs	Wkts	Avge	Best	5wI	10wM
Test																	
All First																	
1-day Int																	
C & G	1	1	0	0	0	0.00	-	-	-	-							
B & H																	
1-day Lge																	

BETTS, M. M. Warwickshire

Name: <u>Melvyn</u> Morris Betts
Role: Right-hand bat, right-arm medium-fast bowler
Born: 26 March 1975, Sacriston
Height: 5ft 11in **Weight:** 11st 4lbs
Nickname: Village
County debut: 1993 (Durham), 2001 (Warwickshire)
County cap: 1998 (Durham), 2001 (Warwickshire)
1st-Class 50s: 2
1st-Class 5 w. in innings: 12
1st-Class 10 w. in match: 2
1st-Class catches: 30
Place in batting averages: 251st av. 11.50 (2000 240th av. 13.71)
Place in bowling averages: 43rd av. 26.45 (2000 16th av. 18.90)
Strike rate: 50.00 (career 48.98)
Parents: Melvyn and Shirley
Wife and date of marriage: Angela, 3 October 1998
Children: Chloe
Family links with cricket: Father and uncle played for Sacriston
Education: Fyndoune Comprehensive
Qualifications: 9 GCSEs, plus qualifications in engineering and sports and recreational studies
Off-season: 'Spending time with my daughter'
Overseas tours: England U19 to Sri Lanka 1993-94; England A to Zimbabwe and South Africa 1998-99; Durham CCC to South Africa 1996

Career highlights to date: '9-64 v Northamptonshire'
Cricketers particularly admired: David Boon
Young players to look out for: Mark Wagh, Ian Bell, Nicky Peng
Other sports played: Golf
Other sports followed: Football (Newcastle United FC)
Relaxations: 'Local pub with friends outside cricket'
Extras: Played for England U19 in home series against India in 1994. Left Durham at the end of the 2000 season and joined Warwickshire for 2001. B&H Gold Award for his 4-22 v Somerset at Taunton 2001. Took 5-22 on his Championship debut for Warwickshire against his old county, Durham, at Edgbaston 2001. Awarded Warwickshire cap 2001
Opinions on cricket: 'Less cricket – more time for training and developing own game.'
Best batting: 57* Durham v Sussex, Hove 1996
Best bowling: 9-64 Durham v Northamptonshire, Northampton 1997

2001 Season

	M	Inns	NO	Runs	HS	Avge	100s	50s	Ct	St	O	M	Runs	Wkts	Avge	Best	5wI	10wM
Test																		
All First	12	11	3	92	19	11.50	-	-	9	-	308.2	72	979	37	26.45	5-22	2	-
1-day Int																		
C & G	1	0	0	0	0	-	-	-	-	-	7	1	39	0	-		-	-
B & H	3	0	0	0	0	-	-	-	-	-	28.4	3	135	6	22.50	4-22	-	
1-day Lge																		

Career Performances

	M	Inns	NO	Runs	HS	Avge	100s	50s	Ct	St	Balls	Runs	Wkts	Avge	Best	5wI	10wM
Test																	
All First	80	116	26	1049	57 *	11.65	-	2	30	-	12833	7227	262	27.58	9-64	12	2
1-day Int																	
C & G	9	7	1	40	14	6.66	-	-	2	-	552	427	15	28.46	4-34	-	
B & H	15	9	4	51	20 *	10.20	-	-	1	-	683	512	19	26.94	4-22	-	
1-day Lge	49	34	16	195	21	10.83	-	-	9	-	2089	1722	53	32.49	4-39	-	

9. Three players named Smith played in the final
of the 1993 NatWest. Name them.

BEVAN, M. G. Leicestershire

Name: <u>Michael</u> Gwyl Bevan
Role: Left-hand bat, slow left-arm wrist-spin
bowler
Born: 8 May 1970, Canberra, Australia
County debut: 1995 (Yorkshire),
1998 (Sussex)
County cap: 1995 (Yorkshire),
1998 (Sussex)
Test debut: 1994-95
Tests: 18
One-Day Internationals: 164
1000 runs in a season: 3
1st-Class 50s: 62
1st-Class 100s: 45
1st-Class 200s: 2
1st-Class 5 w. in innings: 1
1st-Class 10 w. in match: 1
1st-Class catches: 101
One-Day 100s: 8
One-Day 5 w. in innings: 1
Strike rate: (career 73.65)
Wife: Tracy
Education: Australian Cricket Academy
Off-season: Playing for New South Wales and Australia
Overseas tours: Australia to Sharjah 1994, to Pakistan 1994-95, to India and Pakistan
(World Cup) 1995-96, to Sri Lanka 1996-97, to India 1996-97, to South Africa 1996-
97, to England 1997, to New Zealand 1997-98, to India and Sharjah 1997-98,
to Pakistan and Bangladesh 1998-99 (one-day series), to West Indies 1998-99 (one-day
series), to UK, Ireland and Holland (World Cup) 1999, to Sri Lanka 1999-2000 (one-
day series), to Zimbabwe 1999-2000 (one-day series), to New Zealand 1999-2000
(one-day series), to South Africa 1999-2000 (one-day series), to Kenya (ICC Knockout
Trophy) 2000-01, to India 2000-01 (one-day series), to England 2001 (one-day series)
Overseas teams played for: South Australia 1989-90; New South Wales 1990-91 –
Extras: Struck century for South Australia v Western Australia on first-class debut
1989-90. In 1990-91 he became the first player to score a century in five successive
Sheffield Shield matches. Made 82 on his Test debut against Pakistan in Karachi,
1994-95. Played for Rawtenstall in the Lancashire League in 1993 and 1994. Played
for Yorkshire 1995-96 (vice-captain for the 1996 season). Joined Sussex for 1998 and
was appointed vice-captain. Averaged 106.00 in the 1998-99 Australian first-class
season. Was in Australia's 1999 World Cup winning side and did not play county
cricket that season. Won Man of the Match award for his 185 from 132 balls for a

World XI v an Asia XI in Dhaka 2000; chasing 321 for victory, the World XI lost by just one run, Bevan just failing to hit a six from the final ball. Returned to Sussex as overseas player and vice-captain in 2000. Scored 150-plus (166 and 174) in each innings v Nottinghamshire at Hove 2000; in his next Championship match, v Middlesex at Southgate, he became the first batsman to pass 1000 first-class runs in the 2000 season during his second innings 173*, his fourth score of 150-plus in five Championship innings. Scored 106 for Australia in the inaugural indoor One-Day International v South Africa at Melbourne 2000. Topped English first-class batting averages in 2000 with 1124 runs at 74.93. Top run-scorer in the 2000 National League competition with 706 runs at 117.66. Sussex Player of the Year 2000. Left Sussex at the end of the 2000 season. Scored 135* in New South Wales's victory over Western Australia in the 2000-01 Mercantile Mutual Cup final at Perth, winning the Man of the Match award. New South Wales Player of the Year 2000-01. Australian Cricket Board central contract 2001-02. Has joined Leicestershire as overseas player for 2002
Best batting: 203* New South Wales v Western Australia, Sydney 1993-94
Best bowling: 6-82 Australia v West Indies, Adelaide 1996-97
Stop press: Equalled career-best 203* v Western Australia 2001-02, in the process becoming the highest first-class run-scorer in New South Wales cricket history by overtaking Alan Kippax's total of 8005 runs. Man of the Match for his 93-ball century (102*) in Australia's victory over New Zealand in the VB Series One-Day International at Melbourne 2001-02; Australia were at one point 82-6 chasing 246. Selected for the Australian one-day squad for the series in South Africa 2001-02

2001 Season

	M	Inns	NO	Runs	HS	Avge	100s	50s	Ct	St	O	M	Runs	Wkts	Avge	Best	5wI	10wM
Test																		
All First	1	2	0	67	34	33.50	-	-	-	-	5	0	28	0	-		-	-	-
1-day Int	5	4	2	102	56 *	51.00	-	1	3	-	3.2	0	16	1	16.00	1-4	-
C & G																		
B & H																		
1-day Lge																		

Career Performances

	M	Inns	NO	Runs	HS	Avge	100s	50s	Ct	St	Balls	Runs	Wkts	Avge	Best	5wI	10wM
Test	18	30	3	785	91	29.07	-	6	8	-	1285	703	29	24.24	6-82	1	1
All First	189	316	56	14420	203 *	55.46	49	64	105	-	8168	4952	112	44.21	6-82	1	1
1-day Int	164	145	51	5387	108 *	57.30	5	36	54	-	1978	1659	36	46.08	3-36	-
C & G	11	10	2	456	91 *	57.00	-	5	2	-	223	174	4	43.50	2-47	-
B & H	16	15	7	1055	157 *	131.87	1	11	1	-	198	185	1	185.00	1-25	-
1-day Lge	52	50	15	2141	103 *	61.17	2	19	22	-	680	608	36	16.88	5-29	1

BICHEL, A. J.   Worcestershire

Name: Andrew (<u>Andy</u>) John Bichel
Role: Right-hand bat, right-arm fast-medium bowler
Born: 27 August 1970, Laidley, Queensland
Height: 5ft 11in **Weight:** 13st 9lbs
Nickname: Bic, Andre
County debut: 2001
Test debut: 1996-97
Tests: 5
One-Day Internationals: 17
50 wickets in a season: 1
1st-Class 50s: 8
1st-Class 100s: 1
1st-Class 5 w. in innings: 20
1st-Class 10 w. in match: 3
1st-Class catches: 42
One-Day 100s: 1
One-Day 5 w. in innings: 1

Place in batting averages: 147th av. 26.12
Place in bowling averages: 46th av. 27.33
Strike rate: 50.53 (career 48.69)
Parents: Trevor and Shirley
Wife: Dionn
Children: Keegan
Family links with cricket: 'Uncle Don played for Queensland. Cricket is a huge part of our family in Southeast Queensland'
Education: Laidley North SS; Laidley High; Ipswich TAFE College
Qualifications: Carpenter and joiner
Career outside cricket: Project management
Off-season: Playing for Queensland
Overseas tours: Queensland Academy to South Africa 1994; Australian Academy to South Africa 1996; Australia A to Scotland and Ireland 1998; Australia to South Africa 1996-97, to England 1997, to New Zealand (one-day series) 1997-98, to Kuala Lumpur (Commonwealth Games) 1998, to West Indies 1998-99, to South Africa 2001-02
Overseas teams played for: Queensland 1992-93 –
Career highlights to date: 'Queensland winning the Sheffield Shield for the first time in 1994-95. Being selected for Australia in 1997. Playing my first Test for Australia on Australia Day at the Adelaide Oval against West Indies'
Cricket moments to forget: 'Any game that is close that you lose – always makes it hard to forget. But in sport you have to learn from your mistakes'

Cricketers particularly admired: Allan Border, Sachin Tendulkar, Glenn McGrath, Dennis Lillee
Young players to look out for: Simon Katich
Other sports played: Rugby league (first grade TRL); tennis (first grade LTA)
Other sports followed: Rugby league (Brisbane Broncos), AFL (Brisbane Lions)
Relaxations: 'Fishing in my boat on Moreton Bay; going to the beach; golf'
Extras: Sheffield Shield Player of the Year 1996-97. Was due to play for Hampshire as their overseas player in 1998 but was selected for Australia A tour of Scotland and Ireland. Queensland Player of the Year in the 1998-99 Australian season. Took 60 first-class wickets at 20.11 in the 1999-2000 Australian season, including 6-47 for Queensland in Victoria's first innings in the Pura Milk Cup final. Recorded maiden Test five-wicket return (5-60) v West Indies at Melbourne 2000-01. Joined Worcestershire as overseas player for 2001. Won the Dick Lygon Award 2001 as Worcestershire's Player of the Year; was also the Worcestershire Supporters' Association Player of the Year 2001 and the winner of the inaugural Don Kenyon Award for the season's best first-class match-winning performance (113 runs and seven wickets v Glamorgan). Has same birthday as the late Sir Donald Bradman
Opinions on cricket: 'Test and international cricket will always be OK if we keep working and developing the game in schools around the world. Pura Cup and county cricket need to play more day/night cricket because people today like plenty of action, and day/night cricket provides this excitement for everyone that likes cricket.'
Best batting: 110 Queensland v Victoria, Brisbane 1997-98
Best bowling: 6-44 Worcestershire v Gloucestershire, Bristol 2001
Stop press: Selected for Australia tour to South Africa 2001-02

2001 Season

	M	Inns	NO	Runs	HS	Avge	100s	50s	Ct	St	O	M	Runs	Wkts	Avge	Best	5wI	10wM
Test																		
All First	16	24	0	627	78	26.12	-	3	5	-	555.5	137	1804	66	27.33	6-44	4	1
1-day Int																		
C & G	3	2	0	30	27	15.00	-	-	-	-	25	2	102	8	12.75	3-9	-	
B & H	5	5	0	177	100	35.40	1	-	4	-	50	10	189	9	21.00	3-38	-	
1-day Lge	15	12	1	148	36 *	13.45	-	-	7	-	115.4	22	428	27	15.85	5-21	1	

Career Performances

	M	Inns	NO	Runs	HS	Avge	100s	50s	Ct	St	Balls	Runs	Wkts	Avge	Best	5wI	10wM
Test	5	7	0	58	18	8.28	-	-	2	-	780	421	9	46.77	5-60	1	-
All First	83	111	8	2089	110	20.28	1	8	42	-	17238	8560	354	24.18	6-44	20	3
1-day Int	17	11	4	99	27*	14.14	-	-	2	-	890	701	21	33.38	3-17	-	
C & G	3	2	0	30	27	15.00	-	-	-	-	150	102	8	12.75	3-9	-	
B & H	5	5	0	177	100	35.40	1	-	4	-	300	189	9	21.00	3-38	-	
1-day Lge	15	12	1	148	36 *	13.45	-	-	7	-	694	428	27	15.85	5-21	1	

BICKNELL, D. J. Nottinghamshire

Name: <u>Darren</u> John Bicknell
Role: Left-hand opening bat, occasional slow
left-arm bowler
Born: 24 June 1967, Guildford
Height: 6ft 4½in **Weight:** 14st
Nickname: Denzil, Bickers
County debut: 1987 (Surrey), 2000 (Notts)
County cap: 1990 (Surrey), 2000 (Notts)
Benefit: 1999 (Surrey)
1000 runs in a season: 7
1st-Class 50s: 65
1st-Class 100s: 35
1st-Class 200s: 2
1st-Class catches: 89
One-Day 100s: 10
Place in batting averages: 83rd av. 36.20
(2000 63rd av. 34.32)

Strike rate: (career 53.82)
Parents: Vic and Valerie
Wife and date of marriage: Rebecca, 21 September 1992
Children: Lauren Elizabeth, 21 September 1993; Sam, 9 November 1995; Emily,
16 December 1997
Family links with cricket: Brother Martin plays at Surrey
Education: Robert Haining County Secondary; Guildford County College
of Technology
Qualifications: 8 O-levels, 2 A-levels, senior coaching award
Off-season: 'Working, decorating and playing golf'
Overseas tours: Surrey to Sharjah 1988, 1989, to Dubai 1990, to Perth 1995;
Nottinghamshire to Johannesburg 2000, 2001; England A to Zimbabwe and Kenya
1989-90, to Pakistan 1990-91, to Bermuda and West Indies 1991-92
Overseas teams played for: Coburg, Melbourne 1986-87
Career highlights to date: 'Representing England A and winning the Championship
at Surrey'
Cricket moments to forget: 'Getting out to my brother twice – although both times it
was to his slower ball; perhaps he should consider a change of career?'
Cricketers particularly admired: Mark Taylor, Steve Waugh, Alec Stewart,
Mike Atherton
Young players to look out for: Ian Bell, Kevin Pietersen
Other sports played: Golf (12 handicap) 'and any other sport that I get time to play'
Other sports followed: Football (West Ham United, 'and a passing interest in
Nottingham Forest FC')

Relaxations: Family, computer

Extras: Shared Surrey record third-wicket stand of 413 with David Ward v Kent at Canterbury in 1990 – both made career bests. Surrey Batsman of the Year four times. Left Surrey and joined Notts for 2000. Became first English cricketer to take part in more than one partnership of 400-plus when he scored 180* in a first-wicket stand of 406* with Guy Welton (200*) v Warwickshire at Edgbaston 2000; the stand broke several records, including that for the highest Nottinghamshire partnership for any wicket, formerly 398 by Arthur Shrewsbury and William Gunn v Sussex at Trent Bridge 1890, and that for the highest unbeaten first-wicket partnership in Championship history. B&H Gold Awards for his 89 v Lancashire at Trent Bridge and 117* in the quarter-final v Warwickshire at Trent Bridge 2001. Scored 120-ball 115 v Northamptonshire at Trent Bridge in the Norwich Union League 2001, in the process passing 4000 career runs in the one-day league. Was acting captain of Nottinghamshire in 2001 during the absence through injury of Jason Gallian

Opinions on cricket: 'Pitches are getting better, but our practice facilities are diabolical.'

Best batting: 235* Surrey v Nottinghamshire, Trent Bridge 1994

Best bowling: 3-7 Surrey v Sussex, Guildford 1996

2001 Season

	M	Inns	NO	Runs	HS	Avge	100s	50s	Ct	St	O	M	Runs	Wkts	Avge	Best	5wI	10wM
Test																		
All First	16	29	0	1050	167	36.20	3	3	8	-								
1-day Int																		
C & G	2	2	1	81	48 *	81.00	-	-	-	-								
B & H	7	7	1	361	117 *	60.16	1	2	3	-								
1-day Lge	16	15	0	592	115	39.46	1	6	7	-								

Career Performances

	M	Inns	NO	Runs	HS	Avge	100s	50s	Ct	St	Balls	Runs	Wkts	Avge	Best	5wI	10wM
Test																	
All First	243	426	38	15108	235 *	38.93	37	65	89	-	1238	789	23	34.30	3-7	-	-
1-day Int																	
C & G	23	23	5	860	135 *	47.77	1	5	1	-							
B & H	44	43	5	1677	119	44.13	3	12	16	-							
1-day Lge	135	130	16	4190	125	36.75	6	29	34	-	42	45	2	22.50	1-11	-	

BICKNELL, M. P. Surrey

Name: <u>Martin</u> Paul Bicknell
Role: Right-hand bat, right-arm fast-medium bowler
Born: 14 January 1969, Guildford
Height: 6ft 4in **Weight:** 15st
Nickname: Bickers
County debut: 1986
County cap: 1989
Benefit: 1997
Test debut: 1993
Tests: 2
One-Day Internationals: 7
50 wickets in a season: 10
1st-Class 50s: 22
1st-Class 100s: 1
1st-Class 5 w. in innings: 35
1st-Class 10 w. in match: 4
1st-Class catches: 83
One-Day 5 w. in innings: 2

Place in batting averages: 42nd av. 46.75 (2000 84th av. 31.25)
Place in bowling averages: 17th av. 21.36 (2000 13th av. 17.53)
Strike rate: 45.15 (career 51.65)
Parents: Vic and Val
Wife and date of marriage: Loraine, 29 September 1995
Children: Eleanor, 31 March 1995; Charlotte, 22 July 1996
Family links with cricket: 'Brother plays, but with no luck'
Education: Robert Haining County Secondary
Qualifications: 2 O-levels, NCA coach
Career outside cricket: 'Running "Martin Bicknell Golf"'
Overseas tours: England YC to Sri Lanka 1986-87, to Australia 1987-88; England A to Zimbabwe and Kenya 1989-90, to Bermuda and West Indies 1991-92, to South Africa 1993-94; England to Australia 1990-91
Career highlights to date: '*Wisden* Cricketer of the Year 2001'
Cricket moments to forget: 'It's all been an experience!!'
Cricketers particularly admired: 'All honest county trundlers'
Young players to look out for: Tim Murtagh, Gareth Batty
Other sports played: Golf
Other sports followed: Football (Leeds United), golf
Injuries: Out for four days with Achilles problems
Relaxations: 'Playing golf, reading; spending time with my children'
Extras: His figures of 9 for 45 v Cambridge University at Fenner's in 1988 were the

best for the county for 30 years. One of four players on stand-by as reserves for England's World Cup squad 1991-92. Took 7-30 in National League v Glamorgan at The Oval 1999, the best Sunday/National League return by a Surrey bowler. Took 800th first-class wicket (Darren Lehmann) v Yorkshire at The Oval 2000. His 16-119 (including 9-47 in the second innings) v Leicestershire at his home ground of Guildford in 2000 equalled the Surrey record for wickets taken in a match and is the second best match return in Surrey history behind Tony Lock's 16-83 v Kent at Blackheath in 1956. One of *Wisden*'s Five Cricketers of the Year 2001. Took 7-60 v Northamptonshire at his home ground of Guildford 2001. Scored maiden first-class century (110*) v Kent at Canterbury 2001 out of a total of 193-8, having scored 78 in the first innings and taken 4-47 in Kent's only innings. Scored 748 runs (av. 46.75) and took 72 wickets (av. 21.36) in the County Championship 2001. Surrey Supporters' Player of the Year 1993, 1997, 1999, 2000, 2001. Surrey Players' Player of the Year 1997, 1998, 1999, 2000, 2001. Surrey CCC Bowler of the Season Award 2001
Opinions on cricket: 'Could all the people with a negative effect on the game please find something else to do?'
Best batting: 110* Surrey v Kent, Canterbury 2001
Best bowling: 9-45 Surrey v Cambridge University, The Oval 1988

2001 Season

	M	Inns	NO	Runs	HS	Avge	100s	50s	Ct	St	O	M	Runs	Wkts	Avge	Best	5wI	10wM
Test																		
All First	15	22	6	748	110 *	46.75	1	4	5	-	541.5	132	1538	72	21.36	7-60	3	1
1-day Int																		
C & G	2	1	0	16	16	16.00	-	-	-	-	20	3	62	5	12.40	3-34	-	
B & H	7	4	0	50	24	12.50	-	-	3	-	57	8	196	6	32.66	2-29	-	
1-day Lge	11	8	2	70	23 *	11.66	-	-	2	-	84	8	310	13	23.84	3-20	-	

Career Performances

	M	Inns	NO	Runs	HS	Avge	100s	50s	Ct	St	Balls	Runs	Wkts	Avge	Best	5wI	10wM
Test	2	4	0	26	14	6.50	-	-	-	-	522	263	4	65.75	3-99	-	-
All First	243	293	71	5092	110 *	22.93	1	22	83	-	46387	21681	898	24.14	9-45	35	4
1-day Int	7	6	2	96	31 *	24.00	-	-	2	-	413	347	13	26.69	3-55	-	
C & G	39	19	8	213	66 *	19.36	-	1	16	-	2415	1348	55	24.50	4-35	-	
B & H	63	33	12	364	43	17.33	-	-	13	-	3545	2287	90	25.41	4-38	-	
1-day Lge	178	89	42	684	57 *	14.55	-	1	38	-	7633	5318	215	24.73	7-30	2	

BISHOP, J. E. Essex

Name: <u>Justin</u> Edward Bishop
Role: Left-hand lower middle order bat, left-arm fast-medium opening bowler
Born: 4 January 1982, Bury St Edmunds
Height: 6ft **Weight:** 13st 2lbs
Nickname: Bish, Bash, Basher, Sweaty, Tractor Boy
County debut: 1999
1st-Class 5 w. in innings: 1
Place in batting averages: 271st av. 7.40
Place in bowling averages: 107th av. 38.12
Strike rate: 56.00 (career 59.33)
Parents: Keith and Anne
Marital status: 'Very single'
Family links with cricket: 'Dad plays for Bury St Edmunds and used to play for Suffolk; Mum does teas; Grandad played for Nowton'

Education: Ickworth Park Primary School, Bury St Edmunds; Horringer Court Middle School; County Upper School, Bury St Edmunds; Durham University
Qualifications: GCSEs, 1 A-level (PE), GNVQ (Advanced) Science, Level 1 coaching award
Career outside cricket: Student
Off-season: 'Working and playing hard at uni'
Overseas tours: England U19 to Malaysia and (U19 World Cup) Sri Lanka 1999-2000, to India 2000-01
Career highlights to date: 'Taking first first-class five wickets, against Leicestershire in August 2001'
Cricketers particularly admired: Mark Ilott ('ability to swing ball back into right-handers')
Young players to look out for: Mark Nunn, Brian Wilson, Peter Hambling, Mark Pettini
Other sports played: Football (Suffolk and West Suffolk Schools, Bury Town Youth)
Other sports followed: Football (Ipswich Town FC 'on their European tour 2001')
Relaxations: 'Watching "the Tractor Boys" win and "Naaridge" lose'
Extras: Played for England U15 1997. Represented England U17 at the ECC Colts Festival in Northern Ireland 1999. Took 7-42 for England U19 in Sri Lanka U19 first innings in third 'Test' at Worcester, August 2000. Took 5-64 in India U19's first innings in the third U19 'Test' at Hyderabad 2000-01. Represented England U19 v West Indies U19 in one-day series (2/3) and 'Test' series (2/3) 2001, taking 7-41, the best England U19 figures in a 'One-Day International', in second 'ODI' at

Chelmsford. Recorded maiden first-class five-wicket return (5-148) v Leicestershire at Chelmsford 2001

Best batting: 18 Essex v Somerset, Chelmsford 2001
Best bowling: 5-148 Essex v Leicestershire, Chelmsford 2001

2001 Season

	M	Inns	NO	Runs	HS	Avge	100s	50s	Ct	St	O	M	Runs	Wkts	Avge	Best	5wI	10wM
Test																		
All First	8	12	2	74	18	7.40	-	-	-	-	224	39	915	24	38.12	5-148	1	-
1-day Int																		
C & G	2	2	0	3	3	1.50	-	-	-	-	14.1	1	61	2	30.50	2-34	-	
B & H																		
1-day Lge	11	7	2	28	14	5.60	-	-	3	-	79	2	411	15	27.40	3-33	-	

Career Performances

	M	Inns	NO	Runs	HS	Avge	100s	50s	Ct	St	Balls	Runs	Wkts	Avge	Best	5wI	10wM
Test																	
All First	10	13	2	91	18	8.27	-	-	-	-	1602	1095	27	40.55	5-148	1	-
1-day Int																	
C & G	3	3	0	3	3	1.00	-	-	-	-	127	78	3	26.00	2-34	-	
B & H																	
1-day Lge	14	10	4	46	16 *	7.66	-	-	3	-	516	464	16	29.00	3-33	-	

10. Who scored a century before lunch for Hampshire on his NatWest debut, v Norfolk in 1996?

BLACKWELL, I. D.   Somerset

Name: <u>Ian</u> David Blackwell
Role: Left-hand bat, slow left-arm bowler
Born: 10 June 1978, Chesterfield
Height: 6ft 2in **Weight:** 16st 7lbs
Nickname: Blacko, Blackie, Albert, Pip, Yuf
County debut: 1997 (Derbyshire),
2000 (Somerset)
County cap: 2001 (Somerset)
1st-Class 50s: 9
1st-Class 100s: 5
1st-Class 5 w. in innings: 2
1st-Class catches: 23
Place in batting averages: 31st av. 49.35
(2000 115th av. 27.71)
Place in bowling averages: 128th av. 44.80
(2000 138th av. 43.91)
Strike rate: 87.50 (career 98.16)
Parents: John and Marilyn
Marital status: Engaged to Clare
Children: 'None; just a big, fat, lazy cat – Max'
Family links with cricket: Father played for Derbyshire Over 50s and is also involved at Chesterfield CC
Education: Old Hall Primary School; Manor Community School (GCSEs); Brookfield Community School (A-levels)
Qualifications: 9 GCSEs, 1 A-level, NCA senior coaching award
Career outside cricket: Work in the club office
Off-season: 'I have the pleasure of working in the club office. Big shoes to fill, however, as I follow in the footsteps of legend Michael Burns. Also selected for England to Hong Kong Sixes'
Overseas tours: Somerset to Cape Town 2000, 2001; England VI to Hong Kong 2001
Overseas teams played for: Delacombe Park CC, Melbourne, Australia 1997, 1999
Career highlights to date: 'By far the C&G final win v Leicestershire at Lord's 2001. Also getting Steve Waugh out on my debut for Derbyshire 1997; he was my first first-class wicket'
Cricket moments to forget: 'Scoring 0 and 5 against Lancashire in the Championship 1998; in the same game Graham Lloyd hit me for 28 in an over – the Kellogg's factory was in danger!!!'
Cricketers particularly admired: Phillip DeFreitas, Ian Botham, Brian Lara, Glenn McGrath, Jamie Cox, Marcus Trescothick
Players to look out for: Matt Wood, Arul Suppiah, Ian Bell
Other sports played: 'Golf mainly – partner Bully in matchplay – but can turn to most sports'

Other sports followed: Golf, football (Chesterfield FC)
Injuries: Missed four weeks at start of season with a bad back
Relaxations: Golf ('but it's not that relaxing!!'); 'use my laptop quite a lot'
Extras: Played for Derbyshire from the age of eight through to the 1st XI. Set record for number of balls lost (7) in a score of 213 not out off 156 balls at Bolsover, which included 21 fours and 15 sixes and equalled the Bassetlaw League 1A record. Left Derbyshire at end of 1999 season and joined Somerset for 2000. B&H Gold Award for his 64 v Worcestershire at Worcester 2001. Scored two centuries (103 and 122) in a match v Northamptonshire at Northampton 2001; in the process of scoring his 103 he equalled with Keith Dutch the record seventh-wicket partnership for Somerset in matches against Northamptonshire. Scored 102 v Glamorgan at Taunton 2001, in the process sharing with Peter Bowler in a record fifth-wicket stand for Somerset in matches v Glamorgan (163). Awarded Somerset cap 2001
Opinions on cricket: 'Having two divisions has increased interest towards the end of the season, but three up/three down is a little excessive. I know there are reasons for it, but two up/two down would be more appropriate.'
Best batting: 122 Somerset v Northamptonshire, Northampton 2001
Best bowling: 5-115 Derbyshire v Surrey, The Oval 1998

2001 Season

	M	Inns	NO	Runs	HS	Avge	100s	50s	Ct	St	O	M	Runs	Wkts	Avge	Best	5wI	10wM
Test																		
All First	11	17	0	839	122	49.35	4	3	5	-	291.4	72	896	20	44.80	5-122	1	-
1-day Int																		
C & G	5	4	0	95	50	23.75	-	1	3	-	11	0	69	1	69.00	1-25	-	
B & H	6	4	0	116	64	29.00	-	1	2	-	22	0	111	1	111.00	1-41	-	
1-day Lge	15	14	1	433	86	33.30	-	4	2	-	71.5	4	328	12	27.33	3-15	-	

Career Performances

	M	Inns	NO	Runs	HS	Avge	100s	50s	Ct	St	Balls	Runs	Wkts	Avge	Best	5wI	10wM
Test																	
All First	54	79	4	2073	122	27.64	5	9	23	-	6970	3252	71	45.80	5-115	2	-
1-day Int																	
C & G	10	9	1	135	50	16.87	-	1	3	-	282	218	6	36.33	2-34	-	
B & H	14	10	1	206	64	22.88	-	1	5	-	186	178	1	178.00	1-41	-	
1-day Lge	52	48	5	1157	97	26.90	-	8	15	-	1555	1185	42	28.21	4-36	-	

BLAIN, J. A. R.   Northamptonshire

Name: <u>John</u> Angus Rae Blain
Role: Right-hand bat, right-arm fast-medium
bowler
Born: 4 January 1979, Edinburgh
Height: 6ft 2in **Weight:** 13st 7lbs
Nickname: Blainey, Haggis, Hag
County debut: 1997
One-Day Internationals: 5
1st-Class 5 w. in innings: 1
1st-Class catches: 3
One-Day 5 w. in innings: 1
Strike rate: 54.00 (career 68.10)
Place in bowling averages: 112th av. 39.58
Parents: John and Elma
Marital status: Single
Education: Eastfield Primary School;
Penicuik HS; Jewel and Esk Valley College

Qualifications: 8 GCSEs, 1 A-level,
HNC Leisure and Recreation, Level 1 coaching award
Career outside cricket: 'Maybe some coaching but no other career'
Overseas tours: Northants CCC to Zimbabwe 1997; Scotland U19 to Holland
(International Youth Tournament) 1994-95, to Bermuda (International Youth
Tournament) 1997, to South Africa (U19 World Cup) 1997-98 (captain);
Scotland to Denmark (European Championships) 1996, to Malaysia (ICC Trophy)
1997, to Malaysia (Commonwealth Games) 1998, to Sharjah 1999, to Canada (ICC
Trophy) 2001
Overseas teams played for: New Plymouth Old Boys, New Zealand 1998-99;
Taranaki Cricket Association, New Zealand 1998-99
Cricketers particularly admired: Devon Malcolm, Steve Waugh
Young players to look out for: Mark Powell
Other sports played: Football (schoolboy forms with Hibernian FC and Falkirk FC,
making youth and reserve team appearances), golf
Other sports followed: Football (Hibernian FC)
Relaxations: 'Listening to music, going out for a drink, going back to Scotland to
spend time with family; watching football, going to the gym and sleeping!'
Extras: Was youngest ever player to play for Scotland national side, at 17 years and
114 days. Played for Scotland in the B&H and NatWest competitions. Made his first-
class debut for Scotland against Ireland in 1996. Took 5 for 24 on Sunday League
debut for Northants against Derbyshire 1997. Represented Scotland in the 1999 World
Cup, taking 10 wickets and finishing top of the strike rate chart for the tournament.
Recorded maiden first-class five-wicket return (6-42) v Kent at Canterbury 2001

Opinions on cricket: 'The two divisional set-up has been a very beneficial move, creating more competitiveness. Young players expect too much too early once a little success has been gained. There is no substitute for hard work. Second XI cricket should be played at first-class venues more often, where possible. Too many times facilities and wickets are substandard. I prepare myself professionally to play and expect to have professional standards. It sometimes makes the step to first class a little harder.'

Best batting: 34 Northamptonshire v Surrey, Northampton 2001
Best bowling: 6-42 Northamptonshire v Kent, Canterbury 2001

2001 Season

	M	Inns	NO	Runs	HS	Avge	100s	50s	Ct	St	O	M	Runs	Wkts	Avge	Best	5wI	10wM
Test																		
All First	5	9	4	66	34	13.20	-	-	-	-	153	16	673	17	39.58	6-42	1	-
1-day Int																		
C & G																		
B & H	2	1	0	11	11	11.00	-	-	-	-	18	0	110	2	55.00	1-41	-	
1-day Lge	3	2	2	3	3 *	-	-	-	2	-	18	0	122	3	40.66	3-45	-	

Career Performances

	M	Inns	NO	Runs	HS	Avge	100s	50s	Ct	St	Balls	Runs	Wkts	Avge	Best	5wI	10wM
Test																	
All First	9	11	5	97	34	16.16	-	-	3	-	1362	955	20	47.75	6-42	1	-
1-day Int	5	5	1	15	9	3.75	-	-	1	-	223	210	10	21.00	4-37	-	
C & G	1	0	0	0	0	-	-	-	1	-	66	56	2	28.00	2-56	-	
B & H	5	3	1	25	11	12.50	-	-	-	-	198	250	5	50.00	2-82	-	
1-day Lge	6	2	2	3	3 *	-	-	-	3	-	252	232	10	23.20	5-24	1	

11. Which England batsman won the Man of the Match award
on his competition debut in the 1988 NatWest final?

BLAKEY, R. J.   Yorkshire

Name: <u>Richard</u> John Blakey
Role: Right-hand bat, wicket-keeper
Born: 15 January 1967, Huddersfield
Height: 5ft 10in **Weight:** 11st 4lbs
Nickname: Dick
County debut: 1985
County cap: 1987
Benefit: 1998
Test debut: 1992-93
Tests: 2
One-Day Internationals: 3
1000 runs in a season: 4
50 dismissals in a season: 6
1st-Class 50s: 78
1st-Class 100s: 9
1st-Class 200s: 2
1st-Class catches: 717
1st-Class stumpings: 55
One-Day 100s: 3

Place in batting averages: 142nd av. 27.00 (2000 225th av. 15.52)
Strike rate: (career 63.00)
Parents: Brian and Pauline
Wife and date of marriage: Michelle, 28 September 1991
Children: Harrison Brad, 22 September 1993
Family links with cricket: Father played local cricket
Education: Woodhouse Primary; Rastrick Grammar School
Qualifications: 4 O-levels, Senior NCA Coach
Career outside cricket: Started own leisure company
Overseas tours: England YC to West Indies 1984-85; Yorkshire to Barbados 1986-87, to Cape Town 1990-91; England A to Zimbabwe and Kenya 1989-90, to Pakistan 1990-91; England to India and Sri Lanka 1992-93
Overseas teams played for: Waverley, Sydney 1985-87; Mt Waverley, Sydney 1987-88; Bionics, Zimbabwe 1989-90
Cricketers particularly admired: Martyn Moxon, Dermot Reeve, Ian Botham, Alan Knott
Other sports followed: All
Relaxations: All sports, particularly golf and squash, eating out, drawing, photography
Extras: Established himself in Huddersfield League. Made record 2nd XI score – 273* v Northamptonshire 1986. Yorkshire's Young Player of the Year 1989. Was awarded a citation by the International Committee for Fair Play in 1995, the only cricketer among the 25 winners worldwide

Best batting: 221 England A v Zimbabwe, Bulawayo 1989-90
Best bowling: 1-68 Yorkshire v Nottinghamshire, Sheffield 1986

2001 Season

	M	Inns	NO	Runs	HS	Avge	100s	50s	Ct	St	O	M	Runs	Wkts	Avge	Best	5wl	10wM
Test																		
All First	15	21	6	405	78 *	27.00	-	3	49	5								
1-day Int																		
C & G	3	2	1	2	2 *	2.00	-	-	7	1								
B & H	7	5	4	85	35 *	85.00	-	-	9	1								
1-day Lge	16	16	8	280	52	35.00	-	1	20	4								

Career Performances

	M	Inns	NO	Runs	HS	Avge	100s	50s	Ct	St	Balls	Runs	Wkts	Avge	Best	5wl	10wM
Test	2	4	0	7	6	1.75	-	-	2	-							
All First	319	506	78	13165	221	30.75	11	78	717	55	63	68	1	68.00	1-68	-	-
1-day Int	3	2	0	25	25	12.50	-	-	2	1							
C & G	38	30	11	461	75	24.26	-	2	43	3							
B & H	68	58	17	1238	80 *	30.19	-	6	68	4							
1-day Lge	215	191	46	5046	130 *	34.80	3	26	207	39							

BLEWETT, G. S.   Nottinghamshire

Name: Gregory (Greg) Scott Blewett
Role: Right-hand bat, right-arm
medium bowler
Born: 28 October 1971, Adelaide
Height: 6ft **Weight:** 11st
Nickname: Blewy
County debut: 1999 (Yorkshire),
2001 (Nottinghamshire)
County cap: 1999 (Yorkshire),
2001 (Nottinghamshire)
Test debut: 1994-95
Tests: 46
One-Day Internationals: 32
1000 runs in a season: 1
1st-Class 50s: 67
1st-Class 100s: 30
1st-Class 200s: 5
1st-Class 5 w. in innings: 1

1st-Class catches: 152
Place in batting averages: 37th av. 47.85
Strike rate: 113.00 (career 83.13)
Parents: Bob and Shirley
Wife and date of marriage: Jodie, 26 June 1998
Family links with cricket: Father played for South Australia
Education: Angaston Primary School, Adelaide; Prince Alfred College, Adelaide
Overseas tours: Australian Institute of Sport to Sri Lanka 1990-91; Australia U19
to England 1991; Australia to West Indies 1994-95, to South Africa 1996-97,
to England 1997, to India 1997-98, to West Indies 1998-99, to Sri Lanka 1999-2000,
to Zimbabwe 1999-2000, to New Zealand 1999-2000
Overseas teams played for: Kensington, Adelaide; South Australia 1991-92 –
Cricketers particularly admired: Greg Chappell, Gordon Greenidge, Viv Richards
Other sports played: Golf
Other sports followed: Australian Football League (Adelaide Crows)
Relaxations: Golf, films, socialising
Extras: Scored centuries (102* and 115) in his first two Test matches, v England at
Adelaide and Perth in 1994-95. Scored 214 at Johannesburg 1996-97, sharing in record
fifth-wicket partnership for Australia in Tests v South Africa, 385 with Steve Waugh.
Was due to play for Middlesex in 1997 but was selected for Ashes tour. Was the only
Australian to make 1000 Test runs in 1997 calendar year. Holds the unenviable record
of being the first Australian to be out for 99 twice in Test cricket. In 1998-99, made
1175 first-class runs (av. 146.86 and including five 100s and a 200) before Christmas
in the Australian season, breaking David Hookes' record of 1163 set in 1982-83 and
becoming only the sixth Australian to score four consecutive first-class 100s. Averaged
118.70 in full Australian first-class season 1998-99. Joined Yorkshire as overseas
player for 1999 season; released by Yorkshire at end of 1999 season. Made match-
saving 260* in 10 hours 29 minutes after South Australia had been forced to follow on
v Queensland at Brisbane in the Pura Cup 2000-01. Leading run-scorer in the Pura
Cup 2000-01 with 1162 runs (av. 68.35). Australian Cricket Board central contract
2001-02. Joined Nottinghamshire as overseas player for 2001. Scored 133 v Durham at
Trent Bridge 2001, becoming only the second player to score a century on
Championship debut for Notts and the seventh to score one on first-class debut for the
county. B&H Gold Award for his 84 v Yorkshire at Headingley 2001. Awarded
Nottinghamshire cap 2001; released by Nottinghamshire at the end of the 2001 season
Best batting: 268 South Australia v Victoria, Melbourne 1993-94
Best bowling: 5-29 Australian XI v West Indies, Hobart 1996-97

2001 Season

	M	Inns	NO	Runs	HS	Avge	100s	50s	Ct	St	O	M	Runs	Wkts	Avge	Best	5wI	10wM
Test																		
All First	16	30	3	1292	137 *	47.85	5	5	24	-	113	24	374	6	62.33	2-20	-	-
1-day Int																		
C & G	2	2	1	28	25	28.00	-	-	1	-	15	2	42	0	-		-	-
B & H	7	7	1	264	84	44.00	-	2	3	-	15	0	83	4	20.75	3-41	-
1-day Lge	16	16	0	501	89	31.31	-	3	6	-	41	1	272	3	90.66	1-30	-

Career Performances

	M	Inns	NO	Runs	HS	Avge	100s	50s	Ct	St	Balls	Runs	Wkts	Avge	Best	5wI	10wM
Test	46	79	4	2552	214	34.02	4	15	45	-	1436	720	14	51.42	2-9	-	-
All First	179	319	22	13608	268	45.81	35	67	152	-	9228	4802	111	43.26	5-29	1	-
1-day Int	32	30	3	551	57 *	20.40	-	2	7	-	749	647	14	46.21	2-6	-
C & G	5	5	1	111	77	27.75	-	1	2	-	190	99	7	14.14	4-18	-
B & H	10	10	1	348	84	38.66	-	3	3	-	108	106	4	26.50	3-41	-
1-day Lge	27	27	0	679	89	25.14	-	3	12	-	397	388	7	55.42	1-14	-

BLOOMFIELD, T. F.   Middlesex

Name: Timothy (<u>Tim</u>) Francis Bloomfield
Role: Right-hand bat, right-arm
fast-medium bowler
Born: 31 May 1973, Ashford, Middlesex
Height: 6ft 2in **Weight:** 14st
Nickname: Bloomers, Boof, Frank
County debut: 1997
County cap: 2001
50 wickets in a season: 1
1st-Class 5 w. in innings: 6
1st-Class catches: 6
Place in batting averages: 272nd av. 7.08
(2000 307th av. 2.66)
Place in bowling averages: 87th av. 34.18
(2000 114th av. 36.26)
Strike rate: 57.56 (career 52.02)
Parents: Richard and Pauline
Marital status: Engaged to Emma
Education: Staines Preparatory School; Halliford Independent School
Qualifications: 8 GCSEs, NCA coaching award
Off-season: Training; MCC tour to Kenya

Overseas tours: Berkshire U25 to Barbados 1996; Middlesex to South Africa 2000; MCC to Sri Lanka 2001, to Kenya 2002
Career highlights to date: 'Getting capped by Middlesex at Lord's'
Cricketers particularly admired: Ian Botham, Viv Richards, Angus Fraser
Young players to look out for: Alan Coleman, Nick Compton
Other sports played: Football, golf, tennis, snooker
Other sports followed: Football (Liverpool)
Injuries: Out for three weeks with a side strain
Relaxations: Sport, music, 'nice cold Stella in "the Bells"'
Extras: Has also played for Sussex 2nd XI and Berkshire. Took 4-17 v Somerset at Southgate in the NatWest 2000, winning the Man of the Match award. Awarded Middlesex cap 2001
Opinions on cricket: 'I think the two division system has been a success. Central contracts have worked well. In 2001 the standard of cricket balls was poor!! They were too soft and fell apart very easily. This made for some very, very dull cricket from 80-100 overs in the Championship. Maybe we could have new balls at 80-85 overs.'
Best batting: 28 Middlesex v Sussex, Hove 2001
Best bowling: 5-36 Middlesex v Glamorgan, Cardiff 1999

2001 Season

	M	Inns	NO	Runs	HS	Avge	100s	50s	Ct	St	O	M	Runs	Wkts	Avge	Best	5wl	10wM
Test																		
All First	16	16	4	85	28	7.08	-	-	2	-	479.4	79	1709	50	34.18	5-58	2	-
1-day Int																		
C & G																		
B & H	3	2	2	7	7*	-	-	-	-	-	26	2	105	2	52.50	1-33	-	
1-day Lge	10	4	1	6	2	2.00	-	-	2	-	81	11	295	5	59.00	2-16	-	

Career Performances

	M	Inns	NO	Runs	HS	Avge	100s	50s	Ct	St	Balls	Runs	Wkts	Avge	Best	5wl	10wM
Test																	
All First	49	54	22	222	28	6.93	-	-	6	-	7335	4468	141	31.68	5-36	6	-
1-day Int																	
C & G	5	2	1	7	7*	7.00	-	-	-	-	216	140	6	23.33	4-17	-	
B & H	5	2	2	7	7*	-	-	-	-	-	240	195	2	97.50	1-33	-	
1-day Lge	32	10	4	37	15	6.16	-	-	6	-	1350	973	26	37.42	2-8	-	

BOPARA, R. S. Essex

Name: Ravinder (<u>Rav</u>) Singh Bopara
Role: Right-hand bat, right-arm fast bowler
Born: 4 May 1985, Newham, London
Height: 5ft 8in **Weight:** 11st 8lbs
Nickname: Puppy
County debut: No first-team appearance
Parents: Charanjit Singh Bopara and Baldish
Kaur Bopara
Marital status: Single
Education: Central Park School; Brampton
Manor School; Barking Abbey Sports College
Qualifications: 7 GCSEs, ECB Level 1
coaching
Career outside cricket: Student
Off-season: Studying

Career highlights to date: '102* against
Hertfordshire for Essex 2nd XI on debut
2001. 153* against Yorkshire Academy for
England U17 on debut 2001'
Cricket moments to forget: 'I went out to bat once and didn't realise I didn't have a
box on until I got hit there'
Cricketers particularly admired: Sachin Tendulkar, Jacques Kallis
Young players to look out for: Tim Bresnan
Other sports played: Football
Other sports followed: Football (Arsenal)
Relaxations: 'I enjoy DJ-ing in my spare time and listening to music (hip-hop,
R 'n' B, garage)'
Extras: Played for Development of Excellence XI (South) v West Indies U19 at
Arundel 2001. Played for Essex Board XI in the first round of the C&G 2002, which
was played in August 2001
Opinions on cricket: 'It is getting more and more competitive and aggressive, which I
see as a strong point. Also, to succeed in cricket you not only need talent but you also
have to be physically fit, as this can affect one's game and selection.'

Career Performances

	M	Inns	NO	Runs	HS	Avge	100s	50s	Ct	St	Balls	Runs	Wkts	Avge	Best	5wl	10wM
Test																	
All First																	
1-day Int																	
C & G	1	1	0	1	1	1.00	-	-	-	-							
B & H																	
1-day Lge																	

BOSWELL, S. A. J.   Leicestershire

Name: <u>Scott</u> Antony John Boswell
Role: Right-hand bat, right-arm fast-medium
bowler
Born: 11 September 1974, Fulford, York
Height: 6ft 4in **Weight:** 14st 2lbs
Nickname: Bossy, Joey, Grandad
County debut: 1995 (one-day, Northants),
1996 (first-class, Northants), 1999
(Leicestershire)
1st-Class 5 w. in innings: 1
1st-Class catches: 6
Strike rate: 45.50 (career 63.52)
Parents: Tony and Judy
Marital status: Single
Education: Ebor Prep School; Pocklington
School; Wolverhampton University
('Wolly Poly')
Qualifications: 9 GCSEs, 3 A-levels

Overseas tours: Northamptonshire to Zimbabwe 1998
Overseas teams played for: Hutt Valley, New Zealand 1994-95; Koeburg CC,
South Africa 1997-98
Cricketers particularly admired: Richard Hadlee ('for his dedication')
Young players to look out for: Graeme Swann
Other sports played: Rugby ('toured Zimbabwe in '92 with school')
Other sports followed: Football (York City), rugby (York)
Relaxations: Watching TV, socialising and spending time with friends
Extras: Attended Dennis Lillee's Pace Foundation in India 1996. Released by
Northamptonshire at the end of the 1998 season and joined Leicestershire for 1999.
Made Championship debut for Leics against his former county at Northampton 1999.

Took 4-44 in the C&G semi-final v Lancashire at Leicester 2001. Released by Leicestershire at the end of the 2001 season
Best batting: 35 Northamptonshire v Leicestershire, Northampton 1997
Best bowling: 5-94 Northamptonshire v Worcestershire, Northampton 1997

2001 Season

	M	Inns	NO	Runs	HS	Avge	100s	50s	Ct	St	O	M	Runs	Wkts	Avge	Best	5wI	10wM
Test																		
All First	2	3	1	20	16 *	10.00	-	-	2	-	45.3	7	161	6	26.83	3-74	-	-
1-day Int																		
C & G	5	2	1	2	2	2.00	-	-	1	-	33	4	147	6	24.50	4-44	-	
B & H	4	2	1	0	0 *	0.00	-	-	-	-	19.2	3	72	2	36.00	1-17	-	
1-day Lge	13	7	4	27	23 *	9.00	-	-	3	-	89.3	9	398	12	33.16	3-32	-	

Career Performances

	M	Inns	NO	Runs	HS	Avge	100s	50s	Ct	St	Balls	Runs	Wkts	Avge	Best	5wI	10wM
Test																	
All First	22	30	10	249	35	12.45	-	-	6	-	2668	1665	42	39.64	5-94	1	-
1-day Int																	
C & G	5	2	1	2	2	2.00	-	-	1	-	198	147	6	24.50	4-44	-	
B & H	14	8	2	24	14	4.00	-	-	1	-	652	557	8	69.62	3-39	-	
1-day Lge	23	10	6	34	23 *	8.50	-	-	3	-	915	668	23	29.04	3-32	-	

12. Which pair of cricketing brothers stand in first and second places in the list of Gillette/NatWest/C&G century-makers?

BOULTON, N. R.   Worcestershire

Name: <u>Nicholas</u> Ross Boulton
Role: Left-hand bat, right-arm slow-medium
bowler
Born: 22 March 1979, Johannesburg,
South Africa
Height: 6ft 1in **Weight:** 12st 6lbs
Nickname: Boults
County debut: 1997 (Somerset),
2001 (Worcestershire)
1st-Class catches: 1
Parents: Michael and Pauline
Marital status: Single
Education: Ridge School, Johannesburg;
King's School, Taunton
Overseas tours: King's School 1st XI
to Australia 1995, to South Africa 1997
Overseas teams played for: Wanderers CC,
Johannesburg 1996-98
Other sports followed: Hockey, rugby, golf, fly fishing, football (Liverpool FC)
Relaxations: Fly fishing, reading, going back to South Africa
Extras: Awarded Holmwoods Schoolboy Cricketer of the Year. Played ESCA U19 and
Transvaal U14. Formerly with Somerset. Released by Worcestershire at the end of the
2001 season
Best batting: 47 Worcestershire v Durham UCCE, Worcester 2001

13. In which year was the Duckworth/Lewis system first applied in a
Gillette/NatWest/C&G final?

2001 Season

	M	Inns	NO	Runs	HS	Avge	100s	50s	Ct	St	O	M	Runs	Wkts	Avge	Best	5wl	10wM
Test																		
All First	4	5	0	75	47	15.00	-	-	1	-	17	4	48	0	-	-	-	-
1-day Int																		
C & G	1	1	0	39	39	39.00	-	-	-	-								
B & H	3	3	2	32	22 *	32.00	-	-	-	-								
1-day Lge	3	3	0	22	20	7.33	-	-	-	-								

Career Performances

	M	Inns	NO	Runs	HS	Avge	100s	50s	Ct	St	Balls	Runs	Wkts	Avge	Best	5wl	10wM
Test																	
All First	5	7	0	90	47	12.85	-	-	1	-	102	48	0	-	-	-	-
1-day Int																	
C & G	1	1	0	39	39	39.00	-	-	-	-							
B & H	3	3	2	32	22 *	32.00	-	-	-	-							
1-day Lge	3	3	0	22	20	7.33	-	-	-	-							

BOWLER, P. D. Somerset

Name: Peter Duncan Bowler
Role: Right-hand opening bat, occasional off-spin bowler, occasional wicket-keeper
Born: 30 July 1963, Plymouth
Height: 6ft 2in **Weight:** 13st 10lbs
Nickname: Tom
County debut: 1986 (Leicestershire), 1988 (Derbyshire), 1995 (Somerset)
County cap: 1989 (Derbyshire), 1995 (Somerset)
Benefit: 2000 (Somerset)
1000 runs in a season: 9
1st-Class 50s: 86
1st-Class 100s: 39
1st-Class 200s: 3
1st-Class catches: 188
1st-Class stumpings: 1
One-Day 100s: 6
Place in batting averages: 62nd av. 41.35 (2000 6th av. 62.14)
Strike rate: (career 97.69)
Parents: Peter and Etta
Wife and date of marriage: Joanne, 10 October 1992

Children: Peter Robert, 21 September 1993; Rebekah, 25 August 1995
Education: Scots College, Sydney, Australia; Daramalan College, Canberra, Australia; Nottingham Trent University
Qualifications: Australian Year 12 certificate, LLB
Cricketers particularly admired: Gus Valence, Rob Jeffery, Bill Carracher, Phil Russell
Other sports followed: Rugby union
Relaxations: Family and reading
Extras: First Leicestershire player to score a first-class century on debut (100* v Hampshire 1986). Moved to Derbyshire at the end of the 1987 season and scored a hundred (155*) on debut v Cambridge University in 1988, becoming the first player to score hundreds on debut for two counties. His 241* v Hampshire at Portsmouth 1992 is the highest score by a Derbyshire No. 1. First batsman to 2000 runs in 1992, finishing equal leading run-scorer (2044) with Mike Roseberry of Middlesex. Derbyshire Player of the Year 1992. Joined Somerset for 1995. Took over the Somerset captaincy mid-season 1997 after Andy Hayhurst was released. Relinquished captaincy after 1998 season. Passed 5000 runs in Sunday/National League, v Durham 1999. Has set up a sports management agency with Nottinghamshire's John Morris. Top-scoring English batsman in first-class cricket in his benefit season (2000) with 1305 runs (av. 62.14). Scored 164 v Glamorgan at Taunton 2001, in the process sharing with Ian Blackwell in a record fifth-wicket stand for Somerset in matches v Glamorgan (163)
Best batting: 241* Derbyshire v Hampshire, Portsmouth 1992
Best bowling: 3-25 Somerset v Northamptonshire, Taunton 1998

2001 Season

	M	Inns	NO	Runs	HS	Avge	100s	50s	Ct	St	O	M	Runs	Wkts	Avge	Best	5wl	10wM
Test																		
All First	14	22	2	827	164	41.35	2	4	14	-	2	0	9	0	-	-	-	-
1-day Int																		
C & G	5	5	0	113	43	22.60	-	-	-	-								
B & H	5	5	0	143	62	28.60	-	2	5	-								
1-day Lge	11	11	0	560	104	50.90	1	5	4	-								

Career Performances

	M	Inns	NO	Runs	HS	Avge	100s	50s	Ct	St	Balls	Runs	Wkts	Avge	Best	5wl	10wM
Test																	
All First	279	475	50	17290	241 *	40.68	42	86	188	1	3224	2018	33	61.15	3-25	-	-
1-day Int																	
C & G	31	31	0	821	111	26.48	1	3	12	-	36	26	0	-	-	-	-
B & H	55	54	1	1592	109	30.03	2	13	26	1	309	182	5	36.40	1-15	-	
1-day Lge	207	200	19	6127	138 *	33.85	3	50	75	1	308	323	8	40.37	3-31	-	

BRANDY, D. G. — Leicestershire

Name: <u>Damian</u> Gareth Brandy
Role: Right-hand bat, right-arm medium bowler
Born: 14 September 1981, Highgate, London
Height: 6ft 1in **Weight:** 15st 7lbs
Nickname: Damo
County debut: No first-team appearance
Parents: Judy May and Aubrey Winston
Marital status: Single
Family links with cricket: 'Dad was a good cricketer and played for a club in Chingford'
Education: Henry Maynard; St John's, Epping; Harlow College
Qualifications: 10 GCSEs, 3 A-levels, Level 1 ACB coaching award
Off-season: 'Working for GlaxoSmithKlein'
Overseas teams played for: Bankstown, Sydney 2000-01
Career highlights to date: 'Scoring century in first 2nd XI game for Leicestershire, v Durham 2001'
Cricket moments to forget: 'Shouldering arms in two consecutive games against the same team and the same bowler and being bowled first ball each time'
Cricketers particularly admired: Steve Waugh, Curtly Ambrose
Young players to look out for: Andrew McGarry, Jarrad Burke (Australia U19)
Other sports played: Golf (18 handicap), football (captain of school 1st XI)
Other sports followed: Football (Arsenal)
Relaxations: Playing golf, socialising
Extras: Played for Essex from U11 to 2nd XI
Opinions on cricket: 'Standard of pitches should be improved. Cricketers in England settle into comfort zone too easily and need to be pushed.'

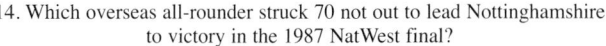

14. Which overseas all-rounder struck 70 not out to lead Nottinghamshire to victory in the 1987 NatWest final?

BRESNAN, T.   Yorkshire

Name: Timothy Bresnan
Role: Right-hand bat, right-arm medium-fast
bowler
Born: 28 February 1985, Pontefract
Height: 6ft **Weight:** 12st 2lbs
Nickname: Brez
County debut: 2001 (one-day)
Parents: Ray and Julie
Marital status: Single
Family links with cricket: 'Dad played local
league cricket'
Education: Three Lane Ends Primary
School; Castleford High School; Pontefract
New College
Qualifications: 8 GCSEs
Off-season: England U19 tour to Australia
and New Zealand
Overseas tours: Yorkshire U16 to Cape

Town 2001; England U17 to Australia 2000-01; England U19 to Australia and
(U19 World Cup) New Zealand 2001-02
Career highlights to date: 'Afridi caught by Wood off first ball of opening spell
v Leicester in Norwich Union League [2001]'
Cricket moments to forget: 'Eight ducks in a row in 2000 season, for various teams'
Cricketers particularly admired: Ian Botham
Young players to look out for: Joseph Sayers, Chris Gilbert, David Stiff
Other sports played: Golf, football
Other sports followed: Football (Leeds United)
Relaxations: Golf, PlayStation
Extras: Bunbury Festival Best All-rounder and Most Outstanding Player. Made one-
day debut v Kent at Headingley 2001 aged 16 years 102 days, making him the
youngest player to represent Yorkshire since Paul Jarvis in 1981
Opinions on cricket: 'Local league cricket should be publicised better, drawing better
crowds and should all play 50 overs with circles and fielding restrictions.'

2001 Season

	M	Inns	NO	Runs	HS	Avge	100s	50s	Ct	St	O	M	Runs	Wkts	Avge	Best	5wI	10wM
Test																		
All First																		
1-day Int																		
C & G																		
B & H																		
1-day Lge	4	3	2	12	7	12.00	-	-	2	-	23	3	86	4	21.50	2-27	-	

Career Performances

	M	Inns	NO	Runs	HS	Avge	100s	50s	Ct	St	Balls	Runs	Wkts	Avge	Best	5wI	10wM
Test																	
All First																	
1-day Int																	
C & G																	
B & H																	
1-day Lge	4	3	2	12	7	12.00	-	-	2	-	138	86	4	21.50	2-27	-	

BRESSINGTON, A. N.   Gloucestershire

Name: <u>Alastair</u> Nigel Bressington
Role: Left-hand bat, right-arm fast-medium bowler; all-rounder
Born: 28 November 1979, Bristol
Height: 6ft 1in **Weight:** 14st
Nickname: Magic, Bressy
County debut: 2000
1st-Class catches: 3
Place in bowling averages: 96th av. 36.09
Strike rate: 65.81 (career 52.75)
Parents: Adrian and Marjorie
Marital status: Single
Family links with cricket: Brother Nathan plays for county 2nd XI
Education: Croft School, Painswick; Marling Grammar School, Stroud; UWIC
Qualifications: 12 GCSEs, 4 A-levels
Career outside cricket: Student
Off-season: University
Cricketers particularly admired: Jack Russell, Ian Botham
Other sports played: Rugby (Gloucestershire Colts; Gloucester RFC U21; Newbury – National Division 3)

Other sports followed: Rugby (Bristol RFC), football (Liverpool FC)
Relaxations: Music, reading
Extras: Played for Gloucestershire Board XI in the NatWest 1999 and 2000. Took wicket with third ball in first-class cricket and took five wickets in debut match, including that of Matthew Maynard. Played for Cardiff University CCE 2001 (captain)
Best batting: 17* Gloucestershire v Hampshire, Cheltenham 2001
Best bowling: 4-36 Gloucestershire v Glamorgan, Bristol 2000

2001 Season

	M	Inns	NO	Runs	HS	Avge	100s	50s	Ct	St	O	M	Runs	Wkts	Avge	Best	5wI	10wM
Test																		
All First	5	5	2	40	17 *	13.33	-	-	2	-	120.4	31	397	11	36.09	3-42	-	-
1-day Int																		
C & G																		
B & H																		
1-day Lge	3	2	0	20	15	10.00	-	-	2	-	23	3	96	1	96.00	1-31	-	

Career Performances

	M	Inns	NO	Runs	HS	Avge	100s	50s	Ct	St	Balls	Runs	Wkts	Avge	Best	5wI	10wM
Test																	
All First	6	6	3	42	17 *	14.00	-	-	3	-	844	446	16	27.87	4-36	-	-
1-day Int																	
C & G	3	2	0	98	54	49.00	-	1	2	-	150	86	5	17.20	3-21	-	
B & H																	
1-day Lge	3	2	0	20	15	10.00	-	-	2	-	138	96	1	96.00	1-31	-	

BRIDGE, G. D. Durham

Name: <u>Graeme</u> David Bridge
Role: Right-hand bat, left-arm spin bowler
Born: 4 September 1980, Sunderland
Height: 5ft 8in **Weight:** 12st 7lbs
Nickname: Bridgy
County debut: 1999
1st-Class 5 w. in innings: 1
1st-Class catches: 6
Place in batting averages: 252nd av. 11.36
Place in bowling averages: 24th av. 22.94
Strike rate: 57.33 (career 68.21)
Parents: Anne and John
Marital status: Single

Family links with cricket: 'Dad played village cricket badly'
Education: Ryhope Junior School; Southmoor School
Qualifications: 4 GCSEs
Career outside cricket: 'Wrestling'
Off-season: 'A bit of this and that'
Overseas tours: England U19 to New Zealand 1998-99, to Malaysia and (U19 World Cup) Sri Lanka 1999-2000
Career highlights to date: 'Getting promoted'
Cricket moments to forget: 'Twisting my ankle on TV'
Cricketers particularly admired: Martin Love, David Boon
Young players to look out for: Nicky Peng, Ian Pattison, Steve Symington
Other sports followed: Football (Sunderland AFC)
Relaxations: Socialising

Extras: Represented England U19 in the one-day series v Australia U19 1999. Played for Durham Board XI in the NatWest 1999. C&G Man of the Match award on county one-day debut for his 3-44 v Gloucestershire at Bristol 2001. Recorded maiden first-class five-wicket return (6-84) v Hampshire at Riverside 2001; also posted successive career bests with the bat in the same game, scoring 31 and 39*
Opinions on cricket: 'Too many games.'
Best batting: 39* Durham v Hampshire, Riverside 2001
Best bowling: 6-84 Durham v Hampshire, Riverside 2001

15. Who scored a 111-ball 135 not out v Surrey to put Lancashire in the semi-finals of the 2000 NatWest?

2001 Season

	M	Inns	NO	Runs	HS	Avge	100s	50s	Ct	St	O	M	Runs	Wkts	Avge	Best	5wI	10wM
Test																		
All First	7	13	2	125	39 *	11.36	-	-	5	-	172	48	413	18	22.94	6-84	1	-
1-day Int																		
C & G	2	2	0	6	6	3.00	-	-	-	-	19	0	89	4	22.25	3-44	-	
B & H																		
1-day Lge	7	5	3	20	14 *	10.00	-	-	3	-	51	1	218	6	36.33	2-42	-	

Career Performances

	M	Inns	NO	Runs	HS	Avge	100s	50s	Ct	St	Balls	Runs	Wkts	Avge	Best	5wI	10wM
Test																	
All First	8	15	2	136	39 *	10.46	-	-	6	-	1296	523	19	27.52	6-84	1	-
1-day Int																	
C & G	5	4	1	30	15	10.00	-	-	1	-	276	212	5	42.40	3-44	-	
B & H																	
1-day Lge	7	5	3	20	14 *	10.00	-	-	3	-	306	218	6	36.33	2-42	-	

BRIGNULL, D. S. Leicestershire

Name: David (<u>Dave</u>) Stephen Brignull
Role: Right-hand bat, right-arm medium-fast bowler
Born: 27 November 1981, Forest Gate, London
Height: 6ft 4in **Weight:** 14st 8lbs
Nickname: Briggers
County debut: No first-team appearance
Parents: Sharon Penfold and Stephen Brignull
Marital status: Single
Education: Avenue Junior School; Lancaster Boys School; Wyggeston and Queen Elizabeth I College
Qualifications: 11 GCSEs, 3 A-levels
Career outside cricket: Barman
Overseas tours: Leicestershire U19 to South Africa 2000-01
Overseas teams played for: Lafarge CC, Lichtenburg, South Africa 2000-01
Career highlights to date: 'Debut for England U17 and winning ECC Colts Festival'
Cricket moments to forget: 'First game for Leicestershire 2nd XI – got out first ball against Lancashire'

Cricketers particularly admired: Robin Smith, Darren Gough
Young players to look out for: Tom New
Other sports played: Rugby (Wigston RFC), volleyball (for college team that came fourth in nationals)
Other sports followed: Rugby (Leicester Tigers), football (West Ham)
Injuries: Could not throw properly last season because of instability of shoulder
Relaxations: Listening to music; darts, snooker
Extras: Represented England U17 at the ECC Colts Festival in Northern Ireland 1999. Leicestershire Youth Bowler of the Year and U19 Player of the Season 2001. Hat-trick against Derbyshire U19. Played for Leicestershire Board XI in the NatWest 1999 and the C&G 2001

2001 Season (did not make any first-class or one-day appearances)

Career Performances

	M	Inns	NO	Runs	HS	Avge	100s	50s	Ct	St	Balls	Runs	Wkts	Avge	Best	5wl	10wM
Test																	
All First																	
1-day Int																	
C & G	2	2	1	15	9 *	15.00	-	-	1	-	112	85	4	21.25	2-35	-	
B & H																	
1-day Lge																	

16. Which player holds the record for the highest individual score in a Gillette/NatWest/C&G final?

BRINKLEY, J. E. Durham

Name: <u>James</u> Edward Brinkley
Role: Right-hand bat, right-arm medium-fast bowler
Born: 13 March 1974, Helensburgh, Scotland
Height: 6ft 3in **Weight:** 15st 11lbs
Nickname: JB, Sweat Monster
County debut: 1993-94 (Worcestershire), 1998 (one-day, Essex), 2001 (Durham)
One-Day Internationals: 5
1st-Class 50s: 1
1st-Class 5 w. in innings: 4
1st-Class catches: 9
Place in batting averages: 257th av. 10.09
Place in bowling averages: 18th av. 21.38
Strike rate: 43.00 (career 55.35)
Parents: Tom and Sharon
Wife and date of marriage: Kim, 11 October 1997
Children: Emma, 2001
Family links with cricket: 'Brother plays club cricket in Worcester and Dad played for the Navy'
Education: Marist College, Canberra; Trinity College, Perth; Manchester Metropolitan University
Qualifications: Fitness instructor, cricket and rugby coach, studying for BSc Sports Science
Career outside cricket: PE teacher at The Grange and RGS Worcester
Overseas tours: Worcestershire to Zimbabwe 1993-94, to Barbados 1996; Scotland to Malaysia (Commonwealth Games) 1998, to Sharjah 1999, to Zimbabwe 2000, to Canada (ICC Trophy) 2001
Overseas teams played for: Scarborough, Perth 1990-93; Western Australia U19 1993; Matabeleland, Zimbabwe 1994-95
Cricketers particularly admired: Glenn McGrath, Darren Gough, 'Dod, Badger and Asim'
Young players to look out for: Thomas Williams ('shame he is Welsh!')
Other sports played: Rugby union, golf
Other sports followed: Rugby union (Worcester RFC)
Relaxations: Good movies, sports science (psychology), 'getting my 2000m rowing time lower'
Extras: Took a hat-trick in both the 2nd XI Championship and the Bain Clarkson Trophy, against Surrey and Somerset respectively. Made first-class debut on Worcestershire tour of Zimbabwe 1993-94. Took 6-98 (the top six) for Worcestershire

v Surrey at The Oval 1994 on County Championship debut, the best Championship debut figures for Worcestershire in the 20th century. Coached Zimbabwe U19 in South African provincial Coca-Cola Cup 1994. Joined Essex for part of 1998 season and was released at end of season. Represented Scotland in the 1999 World Cup. Has also represented Scotland in first-class and NatWest cricket. Played for Herefordshire's ECB 38-County Cup winning side 2000. Scottish born but brought up in Australia, where he attended the same school as Simon Katich. Joined Durham for 2001. Took 6-32 on Championship debut for Durham v Gloucestershire at Riverside 2001, becoming, as far as can be ascertained, the first bowler to take six wickets in an innings on Championship debut for two counties. Took 6-14 from ten overs v Derbyshire at Riverside 2001. Scored 65 v Hants at Riverside 2001, in the process sharing with Danny Law in a record seventh-wicket partnership for Durham (127)
Opinions on cricket: 'Great game!'
Best batting: 65 Durham v Hampshire, Riverside 2001
Best bowling: 6-14 Durham v Derbyshire, Riverside 2001

2001 Season

	M	Inns	NO	Runs	HS	Avge	100s	50s	Ct	St	O	M	Runs	Wkts	Avge	Best	5wI	10wM
Test																		
All First	10	13	2	111	65	10.09	-	1	4	-	222.1	61	663	31	21.38	6-14	2	-
1-day Int																		
C & G	1	0	0	0	0	-	-	-	-	-	5	0	14	0	-	-	-	-
B & H	6	1	0	2	2	2.00	-	-	-	-	50.4	6	190	9	21.11	2-17	-	
1-day Lge	9	3	2	2	1 *	2.00	-	-	3	-	56.3	5	234	8	29.25	2-19	-	

Career Performances

	M	Inns	NO	Runs	HS	Avge	100s	50s	Ct	St	Balls	Runs	Wkts	Avge	Best	5wI	10wM
Test																	
All First	29	35	7	300	65	10.71	-	1	12	-	4539	2116	82	25.80	6-14	4	-
1-day Int	5	5	0	52	23	10.40	-	-	1	-	168	117	2	58.50	1-29	-	
C & G	3	2	0	1	1	0.50	-	-	2	-	132	51	3	17.00	2-13	-	
B & H	17	7	3	47	30 *	11.75	-	-	-	-	822	583	20	29.15	2-17	-	
1-day Lge	14	6	3	9	7	3.00	-	-	3	-	513	375	11	34.09	2-19	-	

BROPHY, G. L.   Northamptonshire

Name: <u>Gerard</u> Louis Brophy
Role: Right-hand bat, wicket-keeper
Born: 26 November 1975, Welkom,
South Africa
Height: 5ft 11in   **Weight:** 12st
Nickname: Scuba
County debut: No first-team appearance
1st-Class 50s: 5
1st-Class 100s: 1
1st-Class catches: 73
1st-Class stumpings: 5
Parents: Gerard and Trish
Marital status: Single
Education: Christian Brothers College,
Boksburg; Wits Technikon
Qualifications: Level 2 coach
Off-season: 'Sales rep, N. Ireland'
Overseas tours: South Africa U17 to

England 1993; South African Academy to Zimbabwe 1999-2000
Overseas teams played for: Gauteng (Wanderers); Free State; Bloemfontein
Career highlights to date: 'Captaincy of Free State. First dismissal with
Allan Donald'
Cricket moments to forget: 'Totally messed up a live interview after a match'
Cricketers particularly admired: Ray Jennings, Ian Healy, Allan Donald,
Hansie Cronje
Young players to look out for: Jacques Rudolph
Other sports played: Golf, rugby
Other sports followed: Golf (Ernie Els), South African rugby
Injuries: Out for three weeks after operation to left knee; also broken finger
Relaxations: Fishing, travelling, stock market, scuba diving
Extras: Captained South Africa U17. Parents live in Brisbane, Australia. Is not
considered an overseas player
Best batting: 185 South African Academy v President's XI, Harare 1999-2000

2001 Season (did not make any first-class or one-day appearances)

Career Performances

	M	Inns	NO	Runs	HS	Avge	100s	50s	Ct	St	Balls	Runs	Wkts	Avge	Best	5wI	10wM
Test																	
All First	23	38	3	1030	185	29.42	1	5	73	5							
1-day Int																	
C & G																	
B & H																	
1-day Lge																	

BROWN, A. D. Surrey

Name: Alistair Duncan Brown
Role: Right-hand bat, off-spin bowler, occasional wicket-keeper
Born: 11 February 1970, Beckenham
Height: 5ft 10in **Weight:** 12st 8lbs
Nickname: Lordy
County debut: 1992
County cap: 1994
One-Day Internationals: 12
1000 runs in a season: 5
1st-Class 50s: 37
1st-Class 100s: 25
1st-Class 200s: 2
1st-Class catches: 162
1st-Class stumpings: 1
One-Day 100s: 13
One-Day 200s: 1
Place in batting averages: 112th av. 31.50
(2000 12th av. 51.94)
Strike rate: (career 798.00)
Parents: Robert and Ann
Wife and date of marriage: Sarah, 10 October 1998
Children: Max Charles, 9 March 2001
Family links with cricket: Father played for Surrey Young Amateurs in the 1950s
Education: Cumnor House School; Caterham School; 'David Ward's card school for the technically gifted'
Qualifications: 5 O-levels, NCA Senior Coach
Off-season: 'Looking after my son Max for three days a week and working on my benefit year in 2002'

Overseas tours: England VI to Singapore 1993, 1994, 1995, to Hong Kong 1997; England to Sharjah (Champions Trophy) 1997-98, to Bangladesh (Wills International Cup) 1998-99
Overseas teams played for: North Perth, Western Australia 1989-90
Cricketers particularly admired: Ian Botham, Viv Richards
Young players to look out for: Jimmy Ormond
Other sports played: Golf, football, snooker, 'winner of the Lanzarote Open Pool Championship 1990'
Other sports followed: Football (West Ham United), rugby league (London Broncos)
Injuries: Out for one week with a broken thumb
Extras: Scored three of the eight fastest centuries of the 1992 season (71, 78 & 79 balls). Awarded Man of the Match for 118 against India in the third One-Day International 1996. Recorded the highest-ever score in the Sunday League with 203 off 119 balls against Hampshire at Guildford in 1997 and received an individual award at the PCA Dinner for that achievement. Scored 72-ball 100 v Northamptonshire to become joint winner (with Carl Hooper) of the EDS Walter Lawrence Trophy for the fastest first-class 100 of the 1998 season. Scored 31-ball 50 v South Africa in the Texaco Trophy match at Headingley 1998, the fastest 50 in the history of the Texaco Trophy. B&H Gold Award for his 108* in the quarter-final v Sussex at Hove 2001. Granted a benefit for 2002. Surrey CCC Batsman of the Season Award 2001
Opinions on cricket: 'Two divisions has improved the standard of first-class cricket – there aren't too many dead games any more. Floodlit cricket is still a must, and perhaps we could get the white ball to do a bit more and then go softer earlier!'
Best batting: 295* Surrey v Leicestershire, Oakham School 2000
Best bowling: 1-56 Surrey v Lancashire, Old Trafford 2000

2001 Season

	M	Inns	NO	Runs	HS	Avge	100s	50s	Ct	St	O	M	Runs	Wkts	Avge	Best	5wI	10wM
Test																		
All First	13	20	0	630	122	31.50	3	2	3	-	23	1	97	0	-	-	-	-
1-day Int	3	3	0	21	12	7.00	-	-	-	-								
C & G	2	1	0	3	3	3.00	-	-	-	-								
B & H	7	6	1	219	108 *	43.80	1	-	2	-								
1-day Lge	13	13	1	565	130	47.08	3	1	7	-	8	0	54	1	54.00	1-40	-	

Career Performances

	M	Inns	NO	Runs	HS	Avge	100s	50s	Ct	St	Balls	Runs	Wkts	Avge	Best	5wI	10wM
Test																	
All First	154	241	24	9356	295 *	43.11	27	37	162	1	798	425	1	425.00	1-56	-	-
1-day Int	15	15	0	348	118	23.20	1	1	4	-							
C & G	27	23	2	552	72	26.28	-	3	8	-	6	9	0	-	-	-	-
B & H	49	48	7	1501	117 *	36.60	2	6	14	-							
1-day Lge	164	159	5	4926	203	31.98	12	17	52	-	269	252	8	31.50	3-39	-	

BROWN, D. R. Warwickshire

Name: Douglas (<u>Dougie</u>) Robert Brown
Role: Right-hand bat, right-arm
fast-medium bowler
Born: 29 October 1969, Stirling, Scotland
Height: 6ft 2in **Weight:** 14st 7lbs
Nickname: Hoots
County debut: 1992
County cap: 1995
One-Day Internationals: 9
50 wickets in a season: 2
1st-Class 50s: 28
1st-Class 100s: 2
1st-Class 200s: 1
1st-Class 5 w. in innings: 13
1st-Class 10 w. in match: 4
1st-Class catches: 84
One-Day 5 w. in innings: 1
Place in batting averages: 73rd av. 39.17

(2000 45th av. 38.87)
Place in bowling averages: 63rd av. 30.57 (2000 124th av. 38.20)
Strike rate: 67.45 (career 51.37)
Parents: Alastair and Janette
Wife and date of marriage: Brenda, 2 October 1993
Children: Lauren, 14 September 1998
Family links with cricket: 'Both grandads played a bit'
Education: St John's Primary, Alloa; Alloa Academy; West London Institute of Higher
Education (Borough Road College)
Qualifications: 9 O-Grades, 5 Higher Grades, BEd (Hons) Physical Education,
ECB Level III coach
Career outside cricket: PE teacher
Overseas tours: Scotland XI to Pakistan 1988-89; England VI to Hong Kong 1997;
England A to Kenya and Sri Lanka 1997-98; England to Sharjah (Champions Trophy)
1997-98, to West Indies 1997-98 (one-day series), to Bangladesh (Wills International
Cup) 1998
Overseas teams played for: Primrose, Cape Town 1992-93; Vredenburg Saldhana,
Cape Town 1993-94; Eastern Suburbs, Wellington 1995-96; Wellington, New Zealand
1995-96
Career highlights to date: 'Playing in a Lord's final for the first time, in 1995
v Northants'
Cricketers particularly admired: Dermot Reeve, 'and as I play more, the likes of
Angus Fraser, Devon Malcolm and Phillip DeFreitas, who keep running in each day'

Young players to look out for: Ian Bell 'who looks the genuine article'
Other sports played: Golf
Other sports followed: Football (Alloa Athletic), 'most sports'
Relaxations: Sport, music
Extras: Played football at Hampden Park for Scotland U18. Played first-class and B&H cricket for Scotland in 1989, and played again for Scotland against Ireland in 1992. His maiden first-class century v Northants on 15 April 1999 is the earliest Championship 100 in an English season. Scored maiden double century v Sussex at Hove 2000 (203; the highest score recorded by a Warwickshire No. 7), during which he shared in a record Warwickshire partnership for 8th wicket (289 with Ashley Giles). His 4-20 v Derbyshire at Derby 2001 included a spell of 3-6 from nine overs; also took 6-60 in second innings. PCA representative for Warwickshire
Opinions on cricket: 'If pitches are to continue improving as they are, please give the bowlers a ball that will do something, so that they can practise their skills too. Also, balls used in one-day games should be rock hard, so that boundaries can be hit at the end of an innings too. At the moment, balls are like tennis balls at the end of a game.'
Best batting: 203 Warwickshire v Sussex, Hove 2000
Best bowling: 8-89 First-Class Counties v Pakistan A, Chelmsford 1997
Stop press: Called into the England squad to the Hong Kong Sixes 2001 to replace Richard Johnson, who was drafted into the England Test tour party to India

2001 Season

	M	Inns	NO	Runs	HS	Avge	100s	50s	Ct	St	O	M	Runs	Wkts	Avge	Best	5wI	10wM
Test																		
All First	16	20	3	666	104	39.17	1	6	16	-	472.1	123	1284	42	30.57	6-60	1	1
1-day Int																		
C & G	4	4	1	154	70	51.33	-	2	-	-	37	5	154	4	38.50	2-41	-	
B & H	6	6	1	57	18	11.40	-	-	1	-	57	4	263	13	20.23	3-36	-	
1-day Lge	15	11	1	320	73	32.00	-	4	7	-	116.4	16	529	29	18.24	4-56	-	

Career Performances

	M	Inns	NO	Runs	HS	Avge	100s	50s	Ct	St	Balls	Runs	Wkts	Avge	Best	5wI	10wM
Test																	
All First	130	194	25	4811	203	28.46	3	28	84	-	17931	9336	349	26.75	8-89	13	4
1-day Int	9	8	4	99	21	24.75	-	-	1	-	324	305	7	43.57	2-28	-	
C & G	22	21	3	429	70	23.83	-	4	2	-	1048	698	20	34.90	2-18	-	
B & H	34	26	3	609	62	26.47	-	4	9	-	1637	1143	37	30.89	5-31	1	
1-day Lge	118	98	14	1756	78 *	20.90	-	9	34	-	4138	3089	133	23.22	4-42	-	

BROWN, J. F.   Northamptonshire

Name: <u>Jason</u> Fred Brown
Role: Right-hand bat, off-spin bowler
Born: 10 October 1974,
Newcastle-under-Lyme
Height: 6ft **Weight:** 13st
Nickname: Cheese, Fish, Brownie
County debut: 1996
County cap: 2000
50 wickets in a season: 1
1st-Class 5 w. in innings: 9
1st-Class 10 w. in match: 3
1st-Class catches: 9
Place in batting averages: 270th av. 8.00
(2000 304th av. 3.33)
Place in bowling averages: 134th av. 50.25
(2000 24th av. 20.62)
Strike rate: 101.53 (career 64.14)
Parents: Peter and Cynthia
Wife and date of marriage: Sam, 26 September 1998
Education: St Joseph's RC School, Stoke-on-Trent; St Margaret Ward RC School,
Stoke-on-Trent
Qualifications: 9 GCSEs, Level 1 coaching qualification
Overseas tours: Kidsgrove League U18 to Australia 1990; Northants CCC to
Zimbabwe 1998, to Grenada 2000; England A to West Indies 2000-01; England
to Sri Lanka 2000-01
Overseas teams played for: North East Valley, Dunedin, New Zealand 1996-97
Cricketers particularly admired: John Emburey, Carl Hooper
Young players to look out for: Mark Powell, Tim Roberts, James Foster
Other sports played: Golf
Other sports followed: Football (Port Vale)
Relaxations: 'Reading, listening to music, walking my dog Spike'
Extras: Represented Staffordshire at all junior levels and in Minor Counties. Once took
10 for 16 in a Kidsgrove League game against Haslington U18 playing for Sandyford
U18. Played for Staffordshire in the 1995 NatWest competition. Took 100th first-class
wicket in 23rd match, v Sussex at Northampton 2000, going on to take his 50th wicket
of the season in the same game, only his seventh of the summer. Drafted into England
Test squad for tour to Sri Lanka 2000-01
Best batting: 35* Northamptonshire v Leicestershire, Northampton 2001
Best bowling: 7-78 Northamptonshire v Sussex, Northampton 2000

2001 Season

	M	Inns	NO	Runs	HS	Avge	100s	50s	Ct	St	O	M	Runs	Wkts	Avge	Best	5wI	10wM
Test																		
All First	11	12	5	56	35 *	8.00	-	-	2	-	473.5	102	1407	28	50.25	5-107	1	-
1-day Int																		
C & G	2	1	1	2	2 *	-	-	-	-	-	20	4	79	2	39.50	1-33	-	
B & H	3	2	2	10	5 *	-	-	-	-	-	26	1	125	0	-	-	-	
1-day Lge	15	7	3	12	5	3.00	-	-	3	-	108.4	3	461	13	35.46	3-25	-	

Career Performances

	M	Inns	NO	Runs	HS	Avge	100s	50s	Ct	St	Balls	Runs	Wkts	Avge	Best	5wI	10wM
Test																	
All First	40	50	22	139	35 *	4.96	-	-	9	-	9879	4433	154	28.78	7-78	9	3
1-day Int																	
C & G	6	3	3	3	2 *	-	-	-	-	-	372	288	7	41.14	3-35	-	
B & H	3	2	2	10	5 *	-	-	-	-	-	156	125	0	-	-	-	
1-day Lge	28	12	5	22	5	3.14	-	-	7	-	1261	865	30	28.83	4-26	-	

BROWN, M. J. Middlesex

Name: <u>Michael</u> James Brown
Role: Right-hand bat, part-time wicket-keeper
Born: 9 February 1980, Burnley
Height: 6ft **Weight:** 11st 7lbs
Nickname: Weasel, Browny
County debut: 1999
1st-Class 50s: 2
1st-Class catches: 4
Place in batting averages: 157th av. 24.62
Parents: Peter and Valerie
Marital status: Single
Family links with cricket: Father played for Burnley CC (Lancashire League) and some games for Lancashire 2nd XI in 1970s. Also played for Southgate CC 1976-78, winning National Club Knockout in 1977. Brother David plays for Lancashire U17 and U19
Education: Rosehill Junior School, Burnley; Queen Elizabeth's Grammar School, Blackburn; Durham University
Qualifications: 10 GCSEs, 4 A-levels
Career outside cricket: Business

Off-season: 'Durham University – third year of Economics and Politics degree'
Overseas teams played for: Western Province CC, Cape Town 1998-99
Career highlights to date: 'Watching James Foster slogsweep Mushtaq Ahmed to point, British Universities v Pakistan, May 2001; team bowled out for 74 by Wasim and Waqar – fantastic experience'
Cricket moments to forget: 'Whenever I leave straight balls'
Cricketers particularly admired: Dale Benkenstein, Mike Atherton, Glenn McGrath, James Foster
Young players to look out for: David Brown, Ian Bell, Will Jefferson
Other sports played: Football ('town team')
Other sports followed: Football (Burnley FC)
Relaxations: 'Sleeping, "Kluting", and security for James Foster'
Extras: Opened batting for Burnley CC in Lancashire League 1995-98. Lancashire League Under-25 Batsman of the Season 1997, 1998. Represented Lancashire Schools at U11, U13, U15 and U17 level 1989-97. Represented Lancashire U19 Federation 1997-98. Played for Lancashire 2nd XI 1997-98. Represented ECB U19 A v Pakistan U19 in two one-day games 1998. Played for Durham University CCE and British Universities 2001, scoring two fifties (55 and 60*) for DUCCE v Worcestershire at Worcester. 'Was at non-striker's end as five wickets fell in one over, Middlesex 2nd XI v Glamorgan 2nd XI, July 2001'
Opinions on cricket: 'Too many passport grabbers.'
Best batting: 60* Durham UCCE v Worcestershire, Worcester 2001

2001 Season

	M	Inns	NO	Runs	HS	Avge	100s	50s	Ct	St	O	M	Runs	Wkts	Avge	Best	5wI	10wM
Test																		
All First	5	9	1	197	60*	24.62	-	2	2	-								
1-day Int																		
C & G																		
B & H																		
1-day Lge																		

Career Performances

	M	Inns	NO	Runs	HS	Avge	100s	50s	Ct	St	Balls	Runs	Wkts	Avge	Best	5wI	10wM
Test																	
All First	7	12	3	245	60*	27.22	-	2	4	-							
1-day Int																	
C & G																	
B & H																	
1-day Lge																	

BROWN, S. J. E.   Durham

Name: <u>Simon</u> John Emmerson Brown
Role: Right-hand bat, left-arm medium-fast
bowler, gully fielder
Born: 29 June 1969, Cleadon Village,
Sunderland
Height: 6ft 3in **Weight:** 13st
Nickname: Chubby
County debut: 1987 (Northamptonshire),
1992 (Durham)
County cap: 1998 (Durham)
Benefit: 2001 (Durham)
Test debut: 1996
Tests: 1
50 wickets in a season: 7
1st-Class 50s: 2
1st-Class 5 w. in innings: 36
1st-Class 10 w. in match: 2
1st-Class catches: 42
One-Day 5 w. in innings: 2

Place in batting averages: (2000 278th av. 9.11)
Place in bowling averages: 29th av. 23.78 (2000 32nd av. 21.57)
Strike rate: 49.28 (career 52.23)
Parents: Ernest and Doreen
Marital status: Single
Education: Cleadon Village Junior School; Boldon Comprehensive, Tyne & Wear;
South Tyneside Marine and Technical College
Qualifications: 6 O-levels, qualified electrician
Career outside cricket: Electrician
Overseas tours: England YC to Sri Lanka 1986-87, to Australia (U19 World Cup)
1987-88; MCC to Bahrain 1994-95
Overseas teams played for: Marist, Christchurch, New Zealand
Cricketers particularly admired: John Lever, Ian Botham, Dennis Lillee
Young players to look out for: Steve Harmison
Other sports played: Golf
Relaxations: Playing golf
Extras: Offered basketball scholarship in America. Durham Supporters' Player of the
Year 1992. Durham Player of the Year 1994. Took his 500th first-class wicket (Steve
Stubbings caught by Martin Speight) v Derbyshire at Darlington 2000
Best batting: 69 Durham v Leicestershire, Durham University 1994
Best bowling: 7-51 Durham v Lancashire, Riverside 2000

2001 Season

	M	Inns	NO	Runs	HS	Avge	100s	50s	Ct	St	O	M	Runs	Wkts	Avge	Best	5wI	10wM
Test																		
All First	4	5	2	64	29	21.33	-	-	1	-	115	29	333	14	23.78	6-70	1	-
1-day Int																		
C & G	1	0	0	0	0	-	-	-	-	-	8	1	22	0	-		-	-
B & H																		
1-day Lge																		

Career Performances

	M	Inns	NO	Runs	HS	Avge	100s	50s	Ct	St	Balls	Runs	Wkts	Avge	Best	5wI	10wM
Test	1	2	1	11	10 *	11.00	-	-	1	-	198	138	2	69.00	1-60	-	-
All First	158	221	72	1796	69	12.05	-	2	42	-	28623	15735	548	28.71	7-51	36	2
1-day Int																	
C & G	12	7	3	20	8	5.00	-	-	1	-	748	503	19	26.47	5-22	1	
B & H	22	9	5	41	12	10.25	-	-	5	-	1199	726	30	24.20	6-30	1	
1-day Lge	77	36	12	156	18	6.50	-	-	17	-	3297	2746	81	33.90	4-20	-	

BRUNNSCHWEILER, I.   Hampshire

Name: Iain Brunnschweiler
Role: Right-hand bat, wicket-keeper
Born: 10 December 1979, Southampton
Height: 6ft   **Weight:** 12st 7lbs
Nickname: Bruno, Brown, Brunchy
County debut: 2000
1st-Class catches: 9
Parents: Arthur and Joan
Marital status: Single
Family links with cricket: 'They mostly dislike it!'
Education: Highfield C of E; King Edward VI School, Southampton
Qualifications: 9 GCSEs, 3 A-levels, ECB Level 1 cricket coaching award, UEFA Part B football coaching award
Career outside cricket: Journalism for local paper (*Southern Daily Echo*)
Off-season: 'Playing grade cricket for Perth CC in Western Australia and taking part in Paul Terry's "Academy"'
Overseas tours: England U17 to Bermuda 1997; King Edward VI School to South Africa 1998; Hampshire CCC to Cape Town 2001

Overseas teams played for: Belmont DCC, Newcastle, NSW 1998-99; Nullamara, Perth 2000-01

Career highlights to date: 'Hitting the winning runs for Hampshire against Australia in 2001'

Cricket moments to forget: 'Losing the U17 Texaco Trophy final against Northants in 1997 (and getting a golden duck)'

Cricketers particularly admired: Robin Smith, Adi Aymes, Jack Russell, Ian Healy

Young players to look out for: John Francis, Chris Benham, James Tomlinson, Neil Mullally

Other sports played: Football (Southampton Youth), hockey, rugby

Other sports followed: Football (Southampton FC)

Relaxations: 'Music; going out with my friends and enjoying good food and liquid'

Extras: 'Longest surname in English county cricket?'

Opinions on cricket: 'The two-divisional structure has been a great success, and in the long run I'm sure the national side will reap the rewards. Also, the national academy is another step in the right direction.'

Best batting: 19 Hampshire v New Zealand A, Portsmouth 2000

2001 Season

	M	Inns	NO	Runs	HS	Avge	100s	50s	Ct	St	O	M	Runs	Wkts	Avge	Best	5wI	10wM
Test																		
All First	1	2	1	11	10 *	11.00	-	-	5	-								
1-day Int																		
C & G																		
B & H																		
1-day Lge																		

Career Performances

	M	Inns	NO	Runs	HS	Avge	100s	50s	Ct	St	Balls	Runs	Wkts	Avge	Best	5wI	10wM
Test																	
All First	2	4	1	33	19	11.00	-	-	9	-							
1-day Int																	
C & G																	
B & H																	
1-day Lge																	

BULBECK, M. P. L.   Somerset

Name: <u>Matthew</u> Paul Leonard Bulbeck
Role: Left-hand bat, left-arm
fast-medium bowler
Born: 8 November 1979, Taunton
Height: 6ft 4in **Weight:** 14st 7lbs
Nickname: Bully
County debut: 1998
50 wickets in a season: 1
1st-Class 50s: 1
1st-Class 5 w. in innings: 3
1st-Class 10 w. in match: 1
1st-Class catches: 6
One-Day 5 w. in innings: 1
Strike rate: 165.00 (career 46.42)
Parents: Paul and Carolyn
Marital status: Single
Family links with cricket: Father plays for
local club; sister plays for same club
Education: Bishops Hall Primary School; Castle School; Taunton School; Richard
Huish College
Qualifications: 8 GCSEs
Overseas tours: West of England U15 to West Indies; Somerset U16 to South Africa;
England U19 to New Zealand 1998-99
Cricketers particularly admired: Wasim Akram, Andy Caddick, Graham Rose
Young players to look out for: Ian Blackwell
Other sports played: Football (goalkeeper), golf (12 handicap)
Other sports followed: Football (Manchester United), rugby union (Bath RFC)
Injuries: Recovering from back operation
Relaxations: 'PlayStation with Blackie; occasional drink with friends'
Extras: Went to Madras Pace Foundation and was coached by Dennis Lillee and Jeff
Thomson in September 1997. Represented England U19 in one-day and 'Test' series
v Australia U19 1999. NBC Denis Compton Award 1999. Played for Somerset Board
XI in the second round of the C&G 2002, which was played in September 2001
Opinions on cricket: 'Every National League game should be played under
floodlights. It brings in bigger crowds and gets the younger people in to watch and
gets them interested in cricket.'
Best batting: 76* Somerset v Durham, Riverside 1999
Best bowling: 5-45 Somerset v Northamptonshire, Northampton 1999

2001 Season

	M	Inns	NO	Runs	HS	Avge	100s	50s	Ct	St	O	M	Runs	Wkts	Avge	Best	5wI	10wM
Test																		
All First	5	7	2	50	18	10.00	-	-	3	-	110	6	501	4	125.25	2-46	-	-
1-day Int																		
C & G	1	0	0	0	0	-	-	-	-	-	9.1	3	18	5	3.60	5-18	1	
B & H																		
1-day Lge	1	0	0	0	0	-	-	-	-	-	2	0	22	0	-	-	-	

Career Performances

	M	Inns	NO	Runs	HS	Avge	100s	50s	Ct	St	Balls	Runs	Wkts	Avge	Best	5wI	10wM
Test																	
All First	31	35	17	462	76 *	25.66	-	1	6	-	4364	2675	94	28.45	5-45	3	1
1-day Int																	
C & G	1	0	0	0	0	-	-	-	-	-	55	18	5	3.60	5-18	1	
B & H	1	1	1	1	1 *	-	-	-	-	-	42	27	0	-	-	-	
1-day Lge	9	3	0	7	5	2.33	-	-	2	-	276	240	5	48.00	4-40	-	

BURNS, M.   Somerset

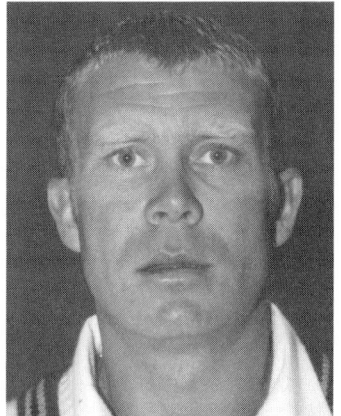

Name: Michael Burns
Role: Right-hand bat, right-arm medium
bowler, occasional wicket-keeper
Born: 6 February 1969, Barrow-in-Furness
Height: 6ft **Weight:** 14st
Nickname: George, Ashley, Butch, Onslow
County debut: 1991 (Warwickshire),
1997 (Somerset)
County cap: 1999 (Somerset)
1st-Class 50s: 28
1st-Class 100s: 4
1st-Class 200s: 1
1st-Class 5 w. in innings: 1
1st-Class catches: 92
1st-Class stumpings: 7
One-Day 100s: 2
Place in batting averages: 85th av. 35.59
(2000 36th av. 40.78)
Place in bowling averages: 130th av. 44.91 (2000 73rd av. 27.64)
Strike rate: 69.41 (career 71.23)
Parents: Robert and Linda, stepfather Stan
Wife and date of marriage: Carolyn, 9 October 1994

Children: Elizabeth, 12 January 1997; Adam, 3 August 2000

Family links with cricket: 'Grandfather was a great back-garden bowler'

Education: Walney Comprehensive; Barrow College of Further Education

Qualifications: 'Few CSEs, couple of GCEs', qualified fitter at VSEL in Barrow, coaching award

Career outside cricket: 'Would like to get involved in sports marketing'

Overseas teams played for: Gill College, South Africa 1991-92; Motueka, Nelson, New Zealand 1992-93; Alex Sports Club, Harare 1993-94; Lindisfarne, Tasmania 1999-2000

Career highlights to date: '2001 Cheltenham & Gloucester final'

Cricket moments to forget: 'Losing the 1999 NatWest final to Gloucestershire'

Cricketers particularly admired: Marcus Trescothick

Young players to look out for: Adam Burns ('if he's no good at golf')

Other sports played/followed: Rugby league ('had trials for Barrow RLFC and Carlisle RLFC') and golf

Injuries: Out for one Norwich Union match with chickenpox

Relaxations: TV, family, cinema, Indian food

Extras: Had a trial with Glamorgan. Went to La Manga with Lancashire junior side 1984. Played for Cumberland 1989-90. Player of the Tournament at Benson and Hedges Thailand International Cricket Sixes in 1989. Left Warwickshire and joined Somerset for the 1997 season. Scored club record of 217 for Lindisfarne in 1999-2000 season. Scored 160 v Oxford Universities at Taunton on 7 April 2000, setting new record for the earliest ever 100 in a first-class cricket season in this country. His 221 v Yorkshire at Bath in 2001 set a new record for the highest score by a Somerset player at Bath (overtaking Mark Lathwell) and for the highest score by a Somerset player against Yorkshire (overtaking Viv Richards). C&G Man of the Match award for his 83-ball 71 in the quarter-final v Kent at Canterbury 2001. Recorded maiden first-class five-wicket return (6-54) v Leicestershire at Taunton 2001

Opinions on cricket: 'Two up/two down in both forms of the game. Prize money needs to be reviewed. Nothing for third in first division and prize money for second in the second is hardly fair.'

Best batting: 221 Somerset v Yorkshire, Bath 2001

Best bowling: 6-54 Somerset v Leicestershire, Taunton 2001

2001 Season

	M	Inns	NO	Runs	HS	Avge	100s	50s	Ct	St	O	M	Runs	Wkts	Avge	Best	5wI	10wM
Test																		
All First	17	28	1	961	221	35.59	1	7	13	-	138.5	23	539	12	44.91	6-54	1	-
1-day Int																		
C & G	5	5	0	134	71	26.80	-	1	2	-	14	1	48	2	24.00	2-30	-	
B & H	6	5	1	63	24 *	15.75	-	-	-	-	7.4	0	50	0	-	-	-	
1-day Lge	14	13	4	331	101 *	36.77	1	1	3	-	15	0	70	1	70.00	1-32	-	

Career Performances

	M	Inns	NO	Runs	HS	Avge	100s	50s	Ct	St	Balls	Runs	Wkts	Avge	Best	5wI	10wM
Test																	
All First	95	147	6	4251	221	30.14	5	28	92	7	2707	1630	38	42.89	6-54	1	-
1-day Int																	
C & G	18	18	3	440	84 *	29.33	-	3	7	-	186	150	4	37.50	2-30	-	
B & H	26	23	2	607	95	28.90	-	5	7	2	206	189	8	23.62	3-18	-	
1-day Lge	108	100	11	2044	115 *	22.96	2	10	49	9	885	813	28	29.03	4-39	-	

BURNS, N. D. — Leicestershire

Name: Neil David Burns
Role: Left-hand bat, wicket-keeper
Born: 19 September 1965, Chelmsford
Height: 5ft 10in **Weight:** 12st
Nickname: Burnsie, Ern, George
County debut: 1986 (Essex),
1987 (Somerset), 2000 (Leicestershire)
County cap: 1987 (Somerset),
2001 (Leicestershire)
50 dismissals in a season: 4
1st-Class 50s: 35
1st-Class 100s: 6
1st-Class catches: 417
1st-Class stumpings: 36
Place in batting averages: 64th av. 41.04
(2000 129th av. 26.17)
Parents: Roy and Marie
Family links with cricket: Father played
club cricket for Finchley CC; brother Ian captained Essex U19
Education: Mildmay Junior; Moulsham High School
Qualifications: 6 O-levels, advanced cricket coach
Career outside cricket: Neil Burns Company Ltd (NBC), specialising in sports
marketing and PR

Overseas tours: England YC to West Indies 1984-85; Essex to Barbados 1985-86; Christians in Sport to India 1989-90
Overseas teams played for: Northerns/Goodwood, Cape Town 1984-87, 1992; Western Province B 1985-86
Cricketers particularly admired: Alan Knott, Bob Taylor, Rod Marsh, Graham Gooch, Allan Border, Graeme Pollock, David Gower
Other sports followed: Most sports but particularly soccer (West Ham)
Relaxations: Watching/playing sport, reading newspapers, relaxing at home
Extras: Former schoolboy footballer with Tottenham Hotspur and Orient. Once took a hat-trick of stumpings off Nasser Hussain's leg-breaks for Essex U11 v Berkshire U11. Made eight stumpings in match v Kent 2nd XI at Dartford in 1984. Joined Somerset in 1987 after spending four years at Essex. Scored maiden first-class century (100*) v former county at Chelmsford 1987. Equalled Steve Rhodes's one-day record of four stumpings in an innings, v Kent in Sunday League at Taunton 1991. Stumped Mike Roseberry off a wide bowled by Ken MacLeay at Lord's in 1992. Retired in 1994. Has also played for Bucks and been their director of cricket. Joined Leicestershire for 2000. Took five catches against his former club Somerset in their first innings at Leicester 2000. Took a Leicestershire record seven catches in an innings against his former club Somerset at Leicester 2001; also took six in an innings v Yorkshire at Leicester 2001. Scored a 96-ball 90* v Northamptonshire at Leicester in the Norwich Union League 2001, in the process sharing in a Leicestershire competition-record eighth-wicket partnership (116) with Phillip DeFreitas. Scored century (111) then took six first innings catches v Glamorgan at Leicester 2001. Scored 834 runs (av. 41.70) and made 67 dismissals in the Championship 2001, and was the leading first-class wicket-keeper overall in 2001 with 68 dismissals. Leicestershire Player of the Year 2001. Awarded Leicestershire cap 2001
Best batting: 166 Somerset v Gloucestershire, Taunton 1990

---

17. When Kent met Lancashire in the 1974 Gillette Cup final,
each side had a wicket-keeper who had played Test cricket.
Name the wicket-keepers.

2001 Season

	M	Inns	NO	Runs	HS	Avge	100s	50s	Ct	St	O	M	Runs	Wkts	Avge	Best	5wl	10wM
Test																		
All First	17	28	7	862	111	41.04	1	6	65	3								
1-day Int																		
C & G	5	2	0	22	16	11.00	-	-	7	-								
B & H	5	5	2	96	46	32.00	-	-	5	1								
1-day Lge	16	12	3	376	90 *	41.77	-	3	14	4								

Career Performances

	M	Inns	NO	Runs	HS	Avge	100s	50s	Ct	St	Balls	Runs	Wkts	Avge	Best	5wl	10wM
Test																		
All First	189	283	63	6656	166	30.25	6	35	417	36	3	8	0	-	-	-	-
1-day Int																		
C & G	27	20	3	253	51	14.88	-	1	34	7							
B & H	41	34	11	551	51	23.95	-	1	37	9							
1-day Lge	135	104	26	1537	90 *	19.70	-	6	145	23							

BUTCHER, G. P. *Surrey*

Name: <u>Gary</u> Paul Butcher
Role: Right-hand middle-order bat, right-arm medium bowler
Born: 11 March 1975, Clapham, London
Height: 5ft 9in **Weight:** 12st
Nickname: Butch, Uncle Bib, Robert, 'the Iron and Steel Business'
County debut: 1994 (Glamorgan), 1999 (Surrey)
1st-Class 50s: 12
1st-Class 100s: 1
1st-Class 5 w. in innings: 2
1st-Class catches: 19
Place in batting averages: 153rd av. 25.00
Strike rate: 104.00 (career 58.11)
Parents: Alan and Elaine
Marital status: Girlfriend Roz
Family links with cricket: Brother Mark plays for Surrey and England. Father Alan played for Surrey, England, and captained Glamorgan. Uncle Ian played for Gloucestershire and Leicestershire. Uncle Martin played for Surrey

Education: Cumnor House Prep School, South Croydon; Riddlesdown Comprehensive; Heath Clark College
Qualifications: 5 GCSEs, BTEC 1st Diploma in Leisure Studies, badminton coaching award, cricket coaching award
Career outside cricket: 'Varies from off-season to off-season'
Overseas tours: England U18 to Denmark 1993; England U19 to Sri Lanka 1993-94; Glamorgan to Zimbabwe 1995, to Pretoria 1996, to Jersey 1998
Overseas teams played for: Northern Natal, South Africa 1995-96; Hawkesbury Hawks, Sydney 1996-97
Cricketers particularly admired: Brian Lara, Malcolm Marshall, Viv Richards, Curtly Ambrose, Michael Holding, Steve Waugh, David Gower
Young players to look out for: Carl Greenidge
Other sports played: Football
Other sports followed: Football (Liverpool FC)
Relaxations: Music, playing bass guitar, spending time with friends
Extras: Took wicket (N. A. Folland) with first ball on Sunday League debut, for Glamorgan v Somerset at Swansea 1994. Won Glamorgan's Most Improved Player Award 1996. Nominated for Young Player of the Year award 1996. Released by Glamorgan at end of 1998 season and joined Surrey for 1999. Played in three Championship-winning sides in four years (Glamorgan 1997; Surrey 1999, 2000). Took four wickets (Aldred, Munton, Dean, Wharton) in four balls v Derbyshire at The Oval 2000, the first Championship four-in-four since Pat Pocock achieved the feat for Surrey v Sussex at Eastbourne 1972. Man of the Match for his 115-ball 131 in Surrey 2nd XI's victory over Somerset 2nd XI in the 2nd XI Trophy final at Taunton 2001. Released by Surrey at the end of the 2001 season
Best batting: 101* Glamorgan v Oxford University, The Parks 1997
Best bowling: 7-77 Glamorgan v Gloucestershire, Bristol 1996

18. Who captained Middlesex to victory in the 1980 Gillette Cup final, winning the Man of the Match award in the process?

2001 Season

	M	Inns	NO	Runs	HS	Avge	100s	50s	Ct	St	O	M	Runs	Wkts	Avge	Best	5wI	10wM
Test																		
All First	4	8	1	175	56	25.00	-	1	1	-	34.4	5	138	2	69.00	1-8	-	-
1-day Int																		
C & G																		
B & H	1	1	1	1	1 *	-	-	-	-	-	7	0	42	0	-		-	-
1-day Lge	7	6	1	61	17	12.20	-	-	-	-	16	0	94	2	47.00	1-23	-	

Career Performances

	M	Inns	NO	Runs	HS	Avge	100s	50s	Ct	St	Balls	Runs	Wkts	Avge	Best	5wI	10wM
Test																	
All First	53	78	12	1841	101 *	27.89	1	12	19	-	3661	2390	63	37.93	7-77	2	-
1-day Int																	
C & G	4	3	1	77	48	38.50	-	-	-	-	120	122	4	30.50	2-33	-	
B & H	14	11	4	59	17	8.42	-	-	1	-	241	214	4	53.50	2-21	-	
1-day Lge	49	40	8	548	47	17.12	-	-	5	-	815	936	18	52.00	4-32	-	

BUTCHER, M. A.   Surrey

Name: <u>Mark</u> Alan Butcher
Role: Left-hand bat, right-arm medium bowler
Born: 23 August 1972, Croydon
Height: 5ft 11in **Weight:** 13st
Nickname: Butch, Baz
County debut: 1991
County cap: 1996
Test debut: 1997
Tests: 32
1000 runs in a season: 6
1st-Class 50s: 58
1st-Class 100s: 17
1st-Class 200s: 2
1st-Class 5 w. in innings: 1
1st-Class catches: 160
Place in batting averages: 19th av. 56.52
(2000 30th av. 42.42)
Strike rate: 44.25 (career 60.99)
Parents: Alan and Elaine
Wife and date of marriage: Judy, 4 October 1997
Children: Alita, 1999

Family links with cricket: Father Alan played for Glamorgan, Surrey and England and is now coach with Surrey; brother Gary played for Glamorgan and Surrey; uncle Ian played for Gloucestershire and Leicestershire; uncle Martin played for Surrey

Education: Cumnor House School; Trinity School; Archbishop Tenison's, Croydon

Qualifications: 5 O-levels, senior coaching award

Career outside cricket: Singer, guitar player

Off-season: Touring India and New Zealand with England

Overseas tours: England YC to New Zealand 1990-91; Surrey to Dubai 1990 and 1993, to Perth 1995; England A to Australia 1996-97; England to West Indies 1997-98, to Australia 1998-99, to South Africa 1999-2000, to India and New Zealand 2001-02

Overseas teams played for: South Melbourne, Australia 1993-94; North Perth 1994-95

Cricketers particularly admired: Ian Botham, David Gower, Viv Richards, Larry Gomes, Graham Thorpe, Alec Stewart, Michael Holding

Other sports followed: Football (Crystal Palace)

Relaxations: Music, playing the guitar, novels, wine

Extras: Played his first game for Surrey in 1991 against his father's Glamorgan in the Refuge Assurance League at The Oval, the first-ever match of any sort between first-class counties in which a father and son have been in opposition. Carried his bat for 109* in second innings v Somerset at Taunton 1998. Made his maiden Test century (116) v South Africa at Headingley in 1998, earning the Man of the Match award. Captained Surrey during Adam Hollioake's absence on World Cup duty 1999. His 259 v Leicestershire 1999 was the highest score by a left-hander at Grace Road and the fourth highest individual score recorded there overall. Captained England in third Test v New Zealand at Old Trafford 1999, deputising for Nasser Hussain who missed the match through injury. B&H Gold Award for his 84 in the semi-final v Nottinghamshire at The Oval 2001. His 4-42 in the first Test v Australia at Edgbaston 2001 included four wickets in 14 balls. Scored 145* v Glamorgan 2001, becoming the first Surrey batsman to carry his bat at The Oval since Grahame Clinton did so in 1984. Man of the Match in the fourth Test v Australia at Headingley 2001 for his match-winning 173*, having also scored 47 in the first innings; England's Man of the Series v Australia 2001 with 456 runs (more than any other batsman on either side) at an average of 50.66. Slazenger Sheer Instinct Award 2001 for the cricketer who has impressed the most in the recent season

Best batting: 259 Surrey v Leicestershire, Leicester 1999

Best bowling: 5-86 Surrey v Lancashire, Old Trafford 2000

Stop press: Scored 92 v India in second Test at Ahmedabad 2001-02, batting for four hours and 13 minutes despite being under the weather with a stomach bug

2001 Season

	M	Inns	NO	Runs	HS	Avge	100s	50s	Ct	St	O	M	Runs	Wkts	Avge	Best	5wI	10wM
Test	5	10	1	456	173*	50.66	1	1	4	-	14	4	63	4	15.75	4-42	-	-
All First	15	25	2	1300	230	56.52	3	6	15	-	59	9	225	8	28.12	4-42	-	-
1-day Int																		
C & G	2	2	1	91	73*	91.00	-	1	-	-	4	0	20	0	-		-	-
B & H	4	4	0	132	84	33.00	-	1	-	-								
1-day Lge	8	8	1	147	55	21.00	-	2	-	-								

Career Performances

	M	Inns	NO	Runs	HS	Avge	100s	50s	Ct	St	Balls	Runs	Wkts	Avge	Best	5wI	10wM
Test	32	61	2	1709	173*	28.96	3	5	25	-	416	232	7	33.14	4-42	-	-
All First	167	288	23	10292	259	38.83	19	58	160	-	6831	3705	112	33.08	5-86	1	-
1-day Int																	
C & G	19	19	5	659	91	47.07	-	6	9	-	306	216	5	43.20	2-57	-	
B & H	31	27	6	564	84	26.85	-	2	8	-	480	396	7	56.57	3-37	-	
1-day Lge	91	78	14	1406	85*	21.96	-	5	27	-	1717	1571	37	42.45	3-23	-	

BYAS, D. Lancashire

Name: David Byas
Role: Left-hand bat, right-arm medium bowler
Born: 26 August 1963, Middledale, Kilham
Height: 6ft 4in **Weight:** 14st 7lbs
Nickname: Bingo, Gadgett
County debut: 1986
County cap: 1991
Benefit: 2000
1000 runs in a season: 5
1st-Class 50s: 79
1st-Class 100s: 27
1st-Class 200s: 1
1st-Class catches: 351
One-Day 100s: 5
Place in batting averages: 49th av. 44.89 (2000 137th av. 24.83)
Strike rate: (career 93.16)
Parents: Richard and Anne
Wife and date of marriage: Rachael Elizabeth, 26 October 1990
Children: Olivia Rachael, 16 December 1991; Georgia Elizabeth, 30 December 1993; Benjamin, 1997

Family links with cricket: Father played local leagues
Education: Kilham Primary School; Lisvane School, Scarborough;
Scarborough College
Qualifications: 1 O-level (Engineering)
Career outside cricket: Partner in family farming business
Off-season: Farming
Overseas teams played for: Papatoetoe, Auckland 1990-91
Career highlights to date: 'Leading Yorkshire to County Championship in 2001.
Receiving county cap'
Cricket moments to forget: 'Losing B&H final 1999'
Cricketers particularly admired: David Gower, Viv Richards, Ian Botham
Young players to look out for: Matthew Wood, Richard Dawson, Steve Kirby
Other sports played: Hockey (international and county player)
Other sports followed: Most other sports
Relaxations: 'Spending time with the family, and gardening'
Extras: Set Yorkshire League record for runs in a season (1350). Became youngest
captain (aged 21) of Scarborough CC in 1985. Runner-up in the Sunday League
averages 1994, breaking John Hampshire's 1976 Sunday League Yorkshire record with
702 runs. Played hockey for Young England (U21) in the European Cup in Portugal.
Passed 5000 runs in the Sunday/National League v Somerset at Scarborough 2000;
passed Geoffrey Boycott's Yorkshire one-day league run record (5051) v Somerset at
Headingley in the Norwich Union League 2001. Captain of Yorkshire 1996-2001.
Scored a century (104) and took the final catch in the victory over Glamorgan at his
home ground of Scarborough that brought the 2001 County Championship to
Yorkshire. Retired at the end of the 2001 season but later accepted an invitation to play
for Lancashire in 2002
Best batting: 213 Yorkshire v Worcestershire, Scarborough 1995
Best bowling: 3-55 Yorkshire v Derbyshire, Chesterfield 1990

19. Which No. 11 batsman propelled Essex into the 1997 NatWest final
with his only scoring shot of that year's competition, v Glamorgan?

2001 Season

	M	Inns	NO	Runs	HS	Avge	100s	50s	Ct	St	O	M	Runs	Wkts	Avge	Best	5wI	10wM
Test																		
All First	16	24	5	853	110 *	44.89	4	2	38	-								
1-day Int																		
C & G	3	3	0	44	17	14.66	-	-	1	-								
B & H	7	7	1	115	55	19.16	-	1	3	-								
1-day Lge	16	16	0	347	81	21.68	-	2	11	-								

Career Performances

	M	Inns	NO	Runs	HS	Avge	100s	50s	Ct	St	Balls	Runs	Wkts	Avge	Best	5wI	10wM
Test																	
All First	268	449	42	14398	213	35.37	28	79	351	-	1118	727	12	60.58	3-55	-	-
1-day Int																	
C & G	34	32	3	912	73 *	31.44	-	8	23	-	18	23	1	23.00	1-23	-	
B & H	58	55	5	1427	116 *	28.54	2	7	17	-	283	155	5	31.00	2-38	-	
1-day Lge	217	211	27	5352	111 *	29.08	3	28	88	-	529	463	19	24.36	3-19	-	

CADDICK, A. R. Somerset

Name: <u>Andrew</u> Richard Caddick
Role: Right-hand bat, right-arm fast-medium bowler
Born: 21 November 1968, Christchurch, New Zealand
Height: 6ft 5in **Weight:** 14st 13lbs
Nickname: Des, Shack
County debut: 1991
County cap: 1992
Benefit: 1999
Test debut: 1993
Tests: 50
One-Day Internationals: 35
50 wickets in a season: 7
100 wickets in a season: 1
1st-Class 50s: 5
1st-Class 5 w. in innings: 53
1st-Class 10 w. in match: 14
1st-Class catches: 61
One-Day 5 w. in innings: 3
Place in batting averages: 253rd av. 11.09 (2000 266th av. 10.84)
Place in bowling averages: 58th av. 29.27 (2000 6th av. 15.41)

Strike rate: 44.85 (career 49.48)
Parents: Christopher and Audrey
Wife and date of marriage: Sarah, 27 January 1995
Children: Ashton Faye, 24 August 1998; Fraser Michael, 12 October 2001
Education: Papanui High School, Christchurch, New Zealand
Qualifications: Qualified plasterer and tiler
Career outside cricket: Plasterer and tiler
Off-season: Touring with England
Overseas tours: New Zealand YC to Australia (U19 World Cup) 1987-88, to England 1988; England A to Australia 1992-93; England to West Indies 1993-94, to Zimbabwe and New Zealand 1996-97, to West Indies 1997-98, to South Africa and Zimbabwe 1999-2000, to Kenya (ICC Knockout Trophy) 2000-01, to Pakistan and Sri Lanka 2000-01, to India (one-day series) and New Zealand 2001-02 (*see Stop press*)
Career highlights to date: 'Bowling West Indies out at Lord's [2000] and thus getting my name up on the board'
Cricketers particularly admired: Dennis Lillee, Richard Hadlee, Robin Smith, Jimmy Cook
Players to look out for: Matthew Hoggard, Owais Shah, Aftab Habib
Other sports followed: 'Mostly all'
Relaxations: Golf
Extras: Rapid Cricketline 2nd XI Championship Player of the Year 1991. Whyte and Mackay Bowler of the Year 1997. Took 105 first-class wickets in 1998 season. Leading wicket-taker in the single-division four-day era of the County Championship with 422 wickets (av. 22.48) 1993-99. England's Man of the Series v New Zealand 1999, taking 20 wickets at an average of 20.60. Returned 7-46 in South Africa's first innings of the third Test at Durban, December 1999; shared Man of the Match award with Gary Kirsten. Cornhill England Player of the Year 1999-2000. Played for a World XI v an Asia XI in Dhaka 2000. Took 5-16 from 13 overs as West Indies were bowled out for 54 in their second innings in the second Test at Lord's 2000. Took 5-14 in fourth Test v West Indies at Headingley 2000, becoming in the process the fifth England bowler to take four wickets in an over in a Test match and recording the cheapest five-wicket Test return by an England bowler since Ian Botham's 5-11 v Australia at Edgbaston in 1981. Shared the new ball with Darren Gough in each Test of the West Indies series 2000, the first time the same pair had opened the bowling for England throughout a series since Fred Trueman and Brian Statham did so v South Africa in 1960. One of *Wisden*'s Five Cricketers of the Year 2001. England central contract 2001. Man of the Match in first Test v Pakistan at Lord's 2001 for his match figures of 8-106. Took 18 wickets (including three five-wicket returns) in his two County Championship matches in 2001. Scored a 40-ball 49* v Australia at Edgbaston 2001, in the process sharing with Alec Stewart in the first century stand for the last wicket (103) since 1903-04 for England in Tests v Australia
Opinions on cricket: 'I do approve of the two divisional system now in place, but I do believe that only two teams should be relegated or promoted each year.'
Best batting: 92 Somerset v Worcestershire, Worcester 1995

Best bowling: 9-32 Somerset v Lancashire, Taunton 1993
Stop press: Withdrew from England Test tour to India 2001-02; replaced by Richard Johnson

2001 Season

	M	Inns	NO	Runs	HS	Avge	100s	50s	Ct	St	O	M	Runs	Wkts	Avge	Best	5wI	10wM
Test	7	12	2	107	49 *	10.70	-	-	1	-	262.4	36	1057	29	36.44	5-101	1	-
All First	9	15	4	122	49 *	11.09	-	-	1	-	351.2	53	1376	47	29.27	5-81	4	1
1-day Int	4	4	1	60	36	20.00	-	-	-	-	38	4	161	5	32.20	2-37	-	
C & G	4	1	1	0	0 *	-	-	-	-	-	40	4	152	4	38.00	2-35	-	
B & H	3	1	1	2	2 *	-	-	-	-	-	27	4	130	3	43.33	2-42	-	
1-day Lge	1	0	0	0	0	-	-	-	-	-	9	2	21	1	21.00	1-21	-	

Career Performances

	M	Inns	NO	Runs	HS	Avge	100s	50s	Ct	St	Balls	Runs	Wkts	Avge	Best	5wI	10wM
Test	50	77	9	739	49 *	10.86	-	-	17	-	10728	5392	181	29.79	7-46	10	-
All First	181	242	46	2937	92	14.98	-	5	61	-	38799	19468	784	24.83	9-32	53	14
1-day Int	35	22	9	145	36	11.15	-	-	8	-	1932	1216	45	27.02	4-19	-	
C & G	27	13	5	29	8	3.62	-	-	5	-	1640	887	45	19.71	6-30	2	
B & H	27	17	10	130	38	18.57	-	-	4	-	1479	1021	34	30.02	5-51	1	
1-day Lge	93	36	11	277	39	11.08	-	-	14	-	4031	2903	114	25.46	4-18	-	

CAIRNS, C. L.   Nottinghamshire

Name: Christopher (<u>Chris</u>) Lance Cairns
Role: Right-hand bat, right-arm
fast-medium bowler
Born: 13 June 1970, Picton, New Zealand
Height: 6ft 2in   **Weight:** 14st
County debut: 1988
County cap: 1993
Test debut: 1989-90
Tests: 49
One-Day Internationals: 137
1000 runs in a season: 1
50 wickets in a season: 3
1st-Class 50s: 60
1st-Class 100s: 11
1st-Class 5 w. in innings: 26
1st-Class 10 w. in match: 6
1st-Class catches: 70
One-day 100s: 5

One-Day 5 w. in innings: 3
Strike rate: (career 52.82)
Parents: Lance and Sue
Family links with cricket: Father played for New Zealand, uncle played first-class cricket in New Zealand
Education: Christchurch Boys' High School, New Zealand
Qualifications: 5th and 6th form certificates
Off-season: Playing for New Zealand
Overseas tours: New Zealand YC to Australia (U19 World Cup) 1987-88; New Zealand to Australia 1989-90, 1993-94, to India 1995-96, to India and Pakistan (World Cup) 1995-96, to Pakistan 1996-97, to Zimbabwe 1997-98, to Australia 1997-98, to Sri Lanka 1997-98, to UK, Ireland and Holland (World Cup) 1999, to England 1999, to India 1999-2000, to Zimbabwe 2000-01, to Australia 2001-02
Overseas teams played for: Northern Districts 1988-89; Canterbury 1990-91 –
Cricketers particularly admired: Mick Newell, Richard Hadlee, Dennis Lillee
Other sports followed: Most sports
Extras: Represented New Zealand in the 1991-92 World Cup. Hit the fastest first-class hundred of the 1995 season (65 balls v Cambridge University). In the 1999 World Cup, struck a ball from Shane Warne out of the ground at Cardiff and into the River Taff. New Zealand's Man of the Series on tour of England 1999; performances included 5-31 followed by a 94-ball 80 in final Test at The Oval. Took 7-27 v West Indies at Hamilton 1999-2000, returning 10-100 in the match to make himself and his father Lance the only father and son to have taken ten wickets in a Test match; topped New Zealand series bowling averages with 17 wickets at 9.94 and averaged 51.50 with the bat. Topped New Zealand batting averages in Test series v Australia 1999-2000 (341 runs av. 56.83). National Bank Player of the Year 1999-2000 in New Zealand and won the Redpath Cup for batting and the Winsor Cup for bowling (only the second player, after John Reid in 1954-55, to win the batting and bowling trophies in one year). Canterbury of New Zealand Sportsperson of the Year 2000. One of *Wisden*'s Five Cricketers of the Year 2000. Played for a World XI v an Asia XI in Dhaka 2000. Man of the Match award for his 102* in the ICC Knockout Trophy final v India in Kenya 2000-01. Has rejoined Nottinghamshire as overseas player for 2002
Opinions on cricket: 'Great game.'
Best batting: 126 New Zealand v India, Hamilton 1998-99
Best bowling: 8-47 Nottinghamshire v Sussex, Arundel 1995
Stop press: Had first innings figures of 5-146 and scored 61 and 43 in the first Test v Australia at Brisbane 2001-02, his first international match after a year out with a knee injury. Had second innings figures of 7-53 (including 5-7 in 38 balls) v Bangladesh in first Test at Hamilton, December 2001. Captained New Zealand to victory over Australia at Sydney in a VB one-day series match 2001-02 in the absence of the injured Stephen Fleming. Scored a 99-ball 102* in New Zealand's win over South Africa at Brisbane in the VB one-day series 2001-02. Took his 150th One-Day International wicket (Nasser Hussain) v England at Auckland 2001-02 in his 150th One-Day International

Career Performances

	M	Inns	NO	Runs	HS	Avge	100s	50s	Ct	St	Balls	Runs	Wkts	Avge	Best	5wI	10wM
Test	49	82	3	2553	126	32.31	4	19	14	-	9381	4995	171	29.21	7-27	10	1
All First	183	285	32	8883	126	35.11	11	60	70	-	29897	15625	566	27.60	8-47	26	6
1-day Int	137	124	12	3217	115	28.72	3	16	44	-	5612	4419	131	33.73	5-42	1	
C & G	7	7	1	306	77	51.00	-	3	2	-	482	279	14	19.92	4-18	-	
B & H	12	8	0	112	46	14.00	-	-	3	-	617	454	16	28.37	4-47	-	
1-day Lge	60	50	10	1655	126*	41.37	2	9	17	-	2363	1858	86	21.60	6-52	2	

CARBERRY, M. A.   Surrey

Name: Michael Alexander Carberry
Role: Left-hand bat, right-arm off-spin
bowler
Born: 29 September 1980, Croydon
Height: 6ft **Weight:** 12st 7lbs
Nickname: Carbs
County debut: 2001
1st-Class 50s: 1
1st-Class catches: 6
Place in batting averages: 116th av. 31.10
Parents: Maria and Neville
Marital status: Single
Family links with cricket: 'My dad played
club cricket'
Education: Winterbourne Junior School;
St John Rigby RC College
Qualifications: 10 GCSEs
Off-season: 'Resting'
Overseas tours: Surrey U17 to South Africa 1997; England U19 to New Zealand
1998-99, to Malaysia and (U19 World Cup) Sri Lanka 1999-2000
Overseas teams played for: Portland CC, Melbourne
Career highlights to date: 'Getting chance to play first-class cricket'
Cricketers particularly admired: Brian Lara, Steve Waugh, Mark Butcher,
Graham Thorpe
Young players to look out for: Tim Murtagh, Carl Greenidge, Scott Newman
Other sports played: Basketball, football
Other sports followed: Football (Tottenham Hotspur)
Relaxations: 'Nightclubbing, weights, DJ-ing'
Extras: Second schoolboy to score a century for Croydon U13 since Ali Brown.
Scored century (126*) for ECB U18 v Pakistan U19 at Abergavenny 1998. Scored his

first Surrey 2nd XI century v Lancashire. Represented England U19 in one-day and 'Test' series v Australia U19 1999, scoring 50 in the third 'Test' at Chester-le-Street. Played for Surrey Board XI in 1999 NatWest. NBC Denis Compton Award for the most promising young Surrey player 1999, 2000. Represented England U19 v Sri Lanka U19 in one-day series 2000

Best batting: 84 Surrey v Glamorgan, Cardiff 2001

2001 Season

	M	Inns	NO	Runs	HS	Avge	100s	50s	Ct	St	O	M	Runs	Wkts	Avge	Best	5wI	10wM
Test																		
All First	6	10	0	311	84	31.10	-	1	6	-								
1-day Int																		
C & G																		
B & H																		
1-day Lge	5	5	0	33	20	6.60	-	-	1	-								

Career Performances

	M	Inns	NO	Runs	HS	Avge	100s	50s	Ct	St	Balls	Runs	Wkts	Avge	Best	5wI	10wM
Test																	
All First	6	10	0	311	84	31.10	-	1	6	-							
1-day Int																	
C & G	2	2	0	23	19	11.50	-	-	-	-							
B & H																	
1-day Lge	5	5	0	33	20	6.60	-	-	1	-							

20. Which Northamptonshire player (now at Derbyshire) won three successive Man of the Match awards in the 1995 NatWest?

CARPENTER, J. R.   Sussex

Name: <u>James</u> Robert Carpenter
Role: Left-hand bat, slow left-arm bowler
Born: 20 October 1975, Birkenhead
Height: 6ft 1in **Weight:** 13st
Nickname: Carps
County debut: 1997
1st-Class 50s: 2
1st-Class catches: 5
Strike rate: (career 129.00)
Parents: John and Jo
Marital status: Single
Family links with cricket: Father played
Minor Counties cricket for Cheshire
Education: Gayton Primary School;
Birkenhead School

Qualifications: 9 GCSEs, 4 A-levels
Off-season: Working and training
Overseas tours: Sussex to Grenada 2001
Overseas teams played for: Randwick CC, Sydney, Australia 1996-99
Cricketers particularly admired: Ian Botham, Allan Border, Steve Waugh
Young players to look out for: Brett Lee, Jamie Keggin (Bootle CC), Adam Warren
Other sports played: Played county schools rugby for Cheshire and schoolboy
football with Liverpool FC. Also had schoolboy forms with Everton and trials with
Bolton Wanderers and played for Runcorn FC in Vauxhall Conference
Relaxations: Golf and 'lying on Coogee beach, Sydney, in the off-season'
Extras: Captained MCC Young Professionals at Lord's. *Daily Telegraph* Bowling
Award. Awarded the Wetherall Trophy by the Cricket Society for the year's
outstanding schoolboy cricketer. Leading catcher in AXA League for 1998 season
Best batting: 65 Sussex v Nottinghamshire, Trent Bridge 1998
Best bowling: 1-50 Sussex v Nottinghamshire, Hove 1997

2001 Season

	M	Inns	NO	Runs	HS	Avge	100s	50s	Ct	St	O	M	Runs	Wkts	Avge	Best	5wI	10wM
Test																		
All First																		
1-day Int																		
C & G	1	1	0	14	14	14.00	-	-	-	-								
B & H																		
1-day Lge	5	3	0	28	18	9.33	-	-	1	-								

Career Performances

	M	Inns	NO	Runs	HS	Avge	100s	50s	Ct	St	Balls	Runs	Wkts	Avge	Best	5wl	10wM
Test																	
All First	13	24	0	383	65	15.95	-	2	5	-	129	81	1	81.00	1-50	-	-
1-day Int																	
C & G	2	2	0	69	55	34.50	-	1	-	-							
B & H	8	7	2	154	53 *	30.80	-	1	3	-							
1-day Lge	41	32	8	496	64 *	20.66	-	3	23	-	6	15	0	-		-	-

CARTER, N. M.   Warwickshire

Name: <u>Neil</u> Miller Carter
Role: Left-hand 'cultured' bat, left-arm
fast-medium swing bowler
Born: 29 January 1975, Cape Town
Height: 6ft 2in **Weight:** 14st 4lbs
Nickname: Carts
County debut: 2001
1st-Class 5 w. in innings: 3
1st-Class catches: 4
Strike rate: 51.42 (career 51.87)
Place in bowling averages: 77th av. 32.57
Parents: John and Heather
Marital status: Single
Education: Somerset House Preparatory
School; Hottentots Holland High School;
Cape Technicon
Qualifications: Diploma in Financial
Information Systems, Certified Novell
Engineer, Level 2 coaching
Off-season: Playing for Boland

Overseas tours: SA Country Schools U15 to England 1992
Overseas teams played for: Boland 1998 –
Career highlights to date: 'Winning Standard Bank Cup for Boland 1999-2000'
Cricket moments to forget: 'Any performance under par'
Cricketers particularly admired: Jacques Kallis
Young players to look out for: Ian Bell, Justin Ontong
Other sports played: Golf, swimming, chess ('grandmaster')
Other sports followed: Rugby union (Western Stormers, Springboks), football
(Sheffield Wednesday)
Injuries: Out for five weeks with injury to lower back
Relaxations: 'Trying to find F.M.C.; surfing the Net; film making'

Extras: Made his first-class debut for Boland during the 1999-2000 season. Recorded maiden first-class five-wicket return (6-63) in the Supersport Series v Griqualand West in Kimberley 2000-01. Won Man of the Match award in first one-day match for Warwickshire (4-21 and a 43-ball 40), in C&G Trophy v Essex at Edgbaston 2001. Recorded maiden Championship five-wicket return (5-78) v Worcestershire at Edgbaston 2001. Is not considered an overseas player
Opinions on cricket: 'Too many games with too many players "enjoying the ride".'
Best batting: 37 Boland v Eastern Province, Port Elizabeth 1999-2000
Best bowling: 6-63 Boland v Griqualand West, Kimberley 2000-01

2001 Season

	M	Inns	NO	Runs	HS	Avge	100s	50s	Ct	St	O	M	Runs	Wkts	Avge	Best	5wI	10wM
Test																		
All First	6	4	1	10	5	3.33	-	-	2	-	120	12	456	14	32.57	5-78	1	-
1-day Int																		
C & G	3	1	0	40	40	40.00	-	-	-	-	26.3	5	97	7	13.85	4-21	-	
B & H																		
1-day Lge	4	2	0	13	13	6.50	-	-	-	-	29	2	119	7	17.00	3-28	-	

Career Performances

	M	Inns	NO	Runs	HS	Avge	100s	50s	Ct	St	Balls	Runs	Wkts	Avge	Best	5wI	10wM
Test																	
All First	15	19	3	144	37	9.00	-	-	4	-	2542	1406	49	28.69	6-63	3	-
1-day Int																	
C & G	3	1	0	40	40	40.00	-	-	-	-	159	97	7	13.85	4-21	-	
B & H																	
1-day Lge	4	2	0	13	13	6.50	-	-	-	-	174	119	7	17.00	3-28	-	

CASSAR, M. E.   Northamptonshire

Name: <u>Matthew</u> Edward Cassar
Role: Right-hand bat, right-arm medium-fast bowler, occasional wicket-keeper
Born: 16 October 1972, Sydney, Australia
Height: 6ft **Weight:** 14st
Nickname: Cass, Chach
County debut: 1994 (Derbyshire), 2001 (Northants)
1st-Class 50s: 9
1st-Class 100s: 1
1st-Class 5 w. in innings: 2
1st-Class catches: 16
One-Day 100s: 4
Place in batting averages: (2000 191st av. 18.94)

Place in bowling averages: (2000 46th av. 23.40)
Strike rate: (career 51.22)
Parents: Edward and Joan
Marital status: Separated
Education: Punchbowl Primary School, Sydney; Sir Joseph Banks High School, Sydney; Manchester Metropolitan University
Qualifications: School certificate and senior coaching award
Off-season: 'Doing Sports Science degree and rehab'
Overseas tours: Northamptonshire to Grenada 2001
Overseas teams played for: Petersham-Marrickville, Sydney 1988-95, 1999-2001

Career highlights to date: 'Getting Steve Waugh out caught behind first ball during a grade game in Sydney 2000'
Cricket moments to forget: 'My first season at Northamptonshire, when I hardly played because of a groin injury'
Cricketers particularly admired: Dennis Lillee, Viv Richards, Steve Waugh, Rod Marsh, Ian Botham
Young players to look out for: Ian Blackwell, Trevor Smith, Lian Wharton, Rob Weston, 'Phillip DeFreitas', Kevin Dean
Other sports played: Golf, squash, tennis, football
Other sports followed: Football (Derby County)
Injuries: Out for virtually the whole season with a groin injury
Relaxations: Cinema, music, TV, golf
Extras: Played for New South Wales Colts. Took three wickets in final over of National League match at Southampton 2000, preventing Hampshire scoring the nine runs required for victory. Left Derbyshire at the end of the 2000 season and joined Northamptonshire for 2001
Opinions on cricket: 'To improve the standard of pitches, groundsmen should be employed by the ECB and not the counties. I like the new two-divisional structure, as I think it does produce more competitive cricket. One overseas player per team is the right balance, because whilst playing with and against the best players in the world is of great benefit, I would hate to see cricket go the same way as football has in this country.'
Best batting: 121 Derbyshire v Sussex, Horsham 1998
Best bowling: 6-76 Derbyshire v Yorkshire, Derby 2000

2001 Season

	M	Inns	NO	Runs	HS	Avge	100s	50s	Ct	St	O	M	Runs	Wkts	Avge	Best	5wI	10wM
Test																		
All First	1	2	0	9	9	4.50	-	-	2	-								
1-day Int																		
C & G																		
B & H																		
1-day Lge	4	4	0	99	58	24.75	-	1	2	-	6.3	0	52	0	-		-	-

Career Performances

	M	Inns	NO	Runs	HS	Avge	100s	50s	Ct	St	Balls	Runs	Wkts	Avge	Best	5wI	10wM
Test																	
All First	56	89	11	1812	121	23.23	1	9	16	-	3842	2287	75	30.49	6-76	2	-
1-day Int																	
C & G	6	6	1	175	90 *	35.00	-	2	-	-	78	63	1	63.00	1-31	-	
B & H	5	4	0	69	43	17.25	-	-	1	-	126	82	2	41.00	2-8	-	
1-day Lge	46	45	4	1264	134	30.82	4	5	15	-	935	833	30	27.76	4-29	-	

CATTERALL, D. N. Worcestershire

Name: <u>Duncan</u> Neil Catterall
Role: Right-hand bat, right-arm
medium-fast bowler
Born: 19 September 1978, Preston
Height: 5ft 11in **Weight:** 12st 2lbs
Nickname: Cats
County debut: 1998
1st-Class 50s: 2
1st-Class catches: 1
Strike rate: (career 46.00)
Parents: David and Christine
Marital status: Single
Family links with cricket: Brother plays and
father played for Leyland DAF in the
Northern League
Education: Horncliffe School, Blackburn;
Queen Elizabeth's Grammar School,
Blackburn; Loughborough University
Qualifications: 11 GCSEs and 4 A-levels
Overseas tours: Queen Elizabeth's Grammar School to Australia, December 1996
Overseas teams played for: Manly CC, Sydney 1999-2000
Cricketers particularly admired: Steve Waugh

Young players to look out for: Kabir Ali
Other sports followed: Football (Preston North End)
Relaxations: Music, socialising
Extras: Represented England Schools U19 in 1998
Best batting: 60 Worcestershire v Essex, Chelmsford 1999
                    60 Worcestershire v Middlesex, Worcester 1999
Best bowling: 4-50 Worcestershire v West Indians, Worcester 2000

2001 Season

	M	Inns	NO	Runs	HS	Avge	100s	50s	Ct	St	O	M	Runs	Wkts	Avge	Best	5wl	10wM
Test																		
All First																		
1-day Int																		
C & G																		
B & H																		
1-day Lge	1	1	0	0	0	0.00	-	-	1	-	4	0	31	0	-		-	-

Career Performances

	M	Inns	NO	Runs	HS	Avge	100s	50s	Ct	St	Balls	Runs	Wkts	Avge	Best	5wl	10wM
Test																	
All First	4	5	0	157	60	31.40	-	2	1	-	506	308	11	28.00	4-50	-	-
1-day Int																	
C & G	1	1	0	1	1	1.00	-	-	-	-	57	40	1	40.00	1-40	-	
B & H																	
1-day Lge	11	6	2	27	11 *	6.75	-	-	3	-	336	267	3	89.00	2-35	-	

---

21. Which county won the Gillette Cup on most occasions,
including a hat-trick of victories 1970-72?

CAWDRON, M. J.   Northamptonshire

Name: Michael (<u>Mike</u>) John Cawdron
Role: Left-hand bat, right-arm
medium-fast bowler
Born: 7 October 1974, Luton
Height: 6ft 3in **Weight:** 13st 7lbs
Nickname: Muscles
County debut: 1995 (one-day,
Gloucestershire),
1999 (first-class, Gloucestershire)
1st-Class 5 w. in innings: 5
1st-Class 10 w. in match: 1
1st-Class catches: 3
Place in batting averages: 247th av. 11.71
(2000 224th av. 15.62)
Place in bowling averages: 120th av. 41.50
(2000 30th av. 21.36)
Strike rate: 84.00 (career 53.16)
Parents: William and Mandy
Marital status: 'Very single'
Family links with cricket: Father and brother played local village cricket
Education: Cheltenham College
Qualifications: 10 GCSEs, 3 A-levels, NCA coaching award
Off-season: 'House hunting in Northampton'
Overseas tours: West of England U14 to Holland; Cheltenham College to Zimbabwe
1992; Gloucestershire YC to Sri Lanka 1993-94; Gloucestershire Gypsies to
Zimbabwe 1994-95, to Cape Town 1997; Christians in Sport to Zimbabwe 1998,
to South Africa 2000; Gloucestershire to Kimberley and Cape Town 2001
Career highlights to date: 'Playing in 1999 NatWest final v Somerset'
Cricketers particularly admired: Jack Russell, Jeremy Snape, Kim Barnett ('they are
all very tough players who make the most of their talents')
Young players to look out for: David Sales
Other sports followed: Rugby, hockey, rackets, clay-pigeon shooting, golf
Relaxations: Cinema, videos, eating and going out with friends
Extras: Winner of the *Daily Telegraph* Regional Bowling Award 1993. Captain of
MCC Schools and ESCA U19 1993. 'Made 50 off 32 balls on Sunday League debut
against Essex at my old school' (Cheltenham College). Scored 42 and took 5-35 on
first-class debut, v Hampshire at Bristol 1999; went on to take two more five-wicket
hauls in his next two Championship games. Released by Gloucestershire at the end of
the 2001 season and has joined Northamptonshire for 2002
Best batting: 42 Gloucestershire v Hampshire, Bristol 1999
Best bowling: 6-25 First-Class Counties XI v New Zealand A, Milton Keynes 2000

2001 Season

	M	Inns	NO	Runs	HS	Avge	100s	50s	Ct	St	O	M	Runs	Wkts	Avge	Best	5wI	10wM
Test																		
All First	6	9	2	82	29	11.71	-	-	1	-	168	50	498	12	41.50	4-79	-	-
1-day Int																		
C & G	2	2	1	4	3	4.00	-	-	-	-	17	2	67	4	16.75	2-24	-	
B & H	5	2	1	9	9 *	9.00	-	-	-	-	43.5	3	224	4	56.00	2-26	-	
1-day Lge	5	4	2	36	29 *	18.00	-	-	-	-	39.2	6	168	5	33.60	2-43	-	

Career Performances

	M	Inns	NO	Runs	HS	Avge	100s	50s	Ct	St	Balls	Runs	Wkts	Avge	Best	5wI	10wM
Test																	
All First	18	26	4	333	42	15.13	-	-	3	-	2818	1298	53	24.49	6-25	5	1
1-day Int																	
C & G	9	6	3	26	17	8.66	-	-	1	-	420	307	12	25.58	4-34	-	
B & H	12	4	3	16	9 *	16.00	-	-	-	-	528	437	17	25.70	4-28	-	
1-day Lge	32	22	7	251	50	16.73	-	1	4	-	1154	929	25	37.16	4-17	-	

CHAPPLE, G. Lancashire

Name: Glen Chapple
Role: Right-hand bat, right-arm medium-fast bowler
Born: 23 January 1974, Skipton, Yorkshire
Height: 6ft 2in **Weight:** 12st 7lbs
Nickname: Chappy, Boris, Boomor, Cheeky
County debut: 1992
County cap: 1994
50 wickets in a season: 3
1st-Class 50s: 8
1st-Class 100s: 2
1st-Class 5 w. in innings: 15
1st-Class catches: 40
One-Day 5 w. in innings: 4
Place in batting averages: 118th av. 31.06 (2000 251st av. 12.11)
Place in bowling averages: 21st av. 22.15 (2000 49th av. 23.97)
Strike rate: 42.94 (career 54.76)
Parents: Eileen and Michael
Marital status: Single
Family links with cricket: Father played in Lancashire League for Nelson and was a professional for Darwen and Earby

Education: West Craven High School; Nelson and Colne College
Qualifications: 8 GCSEs, 2 A-levels
Overseas tours: England U18 to Canada 1991; England YC to New Zealand 1990-91, to Pakistan 1991-92, to India 1992-93; England A to India 1994-95, to Australia 1996-97
Cricketers particularly admired: Dennis Lillee, Robin Smith
Other sports followed: Football (Liverpool), golf
Relaxations: 'Watching films, cinema, music, socialising'
Extras: Set record for fastest century in first-class cricket (21 minutes; against declaration bowling) v Glamorgan at Old Trafford 1993. Man of the Match in the 1996 NatWest final against Essex for his 6 for 18. Shared in a record eighth-wicket partnership for Lancashire in matches against Northamptonshire (136*) with Warren Hegg at Northampton 2001, scoring 72*; also scored 31 in the first innings and took nine wickets in the match. Scored 155 v Somerset at Old Trafford 2001, equalling Wasim Akram's record, set in 1998 v Nottinghamshire, for the highest score by a Lancashire No. 8
Best batting: 155 Lancashire v Somerset, Old Trafford 2001
Best bowling: 6-42 Lancashire v Durham, Riverside 2000

2001 Season

	M	Inns	NO	Runs	HS	Avge	100s	50s	Ct	St	O	M	Runs	Wkts	Avge	Best	5wI	10wM
Test																		
All First	13	19	3	497	155	31.06	1	2	3	-	379.2	87	1174	53	22.15	6-46	4	-
1-day Int																		
C & G	3	3	0	36	23	12.00	-	-	-	-	23	1	111	2	55.50	1-22	-	
B & H	3	3	1	14	8	7.00	-	-	-	-	29	2	124	3	41.33	2-38	-	
1-day Lge	13	11	0	204	56	18.54	-	2	2	-	93.1	5	403	17	23.70	3-19	-	

Career Performances

	M	Inns	NO	Runs	HS	Avge	100s	50s	Ct	St	Balls	Runs	Wkts	Avge	Best	5wI	10wM
Test																	
All First	130	176	47	2785	155	21.58	2	8	40	-	21029	10725	384	27.92	6-42	15	-
1-day Int																	
C & G	21	12	1	62	23	5.63	-	-	6	-	1104	807	27	29.88	6-18	2	
B & H	29	14	7	56	11	8.00	-	-	5	-	1462	1115	33	33.78	5-7	1	
1-day Lge	104	46	14	445	56	13.90	-	2	20	-	4123	3206	115	27.87	6-25	1	

CHERRY, D. D.   Glamorgan

Name: <u>Daniel</u> David Cherry
Role: Left-hand bat, right-arm
medium bowler
Born: 7 February 1980, Newport, Gwent
Height: 5ft 9in **Weight:** 13st
Nickname: Rhino, Banners
County debut: 1998
Parents: David and Elizabeth
Marital status: Single
Family links with cricket: Father is a
qualified coach and played club cricket
Education: Feltonfleet Prep School,
Cobham, Surrey; Tonbridge School, Kent;
University of Wales, Swansea
Qualifications: 10 GCSEs, 3 A-levels,
degree in History
Off-season: 'Play some rugby. Do
coaching award'
Overseas tours: Tonbridge School to Australia 1996-97
Career highlights to date: 'First-class debut'
Cricket moments to forget: 'Bagging a pair on 2nd XI Championship debut'
Cricketers particularly admired: Michael Atherton, Graham Thorpe,
Steve James
Young players to look out for: Mark Wallace, Simon Jones, Ian Thomas,
David Harrison
Other sports played: Rugby, rackets (Public Schools doubles champion)
Other sports followed: Rugby (Wales), football (Everton)
Relaxations: Reading crime books, 'drinking plenty of pots'
Extras: Played for ECB U19 XI v Pakistan U19 1998
Opinions on cricket: 'Second XI cricket should be played on 1st XI-standard
grounds.'
Best batting: 11 Glamorgan v Derbyshire, Cardiff 1998

2001 Season (did not make any first-class or one-day appearances)

Career Performances

	M	Inns	NO	Runs	HS	Avge	100s	50s	Ct	St	Balls	Runs	Wkts	Avge	Best	5wI	10wM
Test																	
All First	1	1	0	11	11	11.00	-	-	-	-							
1-day Int																	
C & G																	
B & H																	
1-day Lge																	

CHILTON, M. J. Lancashire

Name: <u>Mark</u> James Chilton
Role: Right-hand bat, right-arm medium bowler
Born: 2 October 1976, Sheffield
Height: 6ft 2in **Weight:** 12st 10lbs
Nickname: Dip, Chill
County debut: 1997
1st-Class 50s: 8
1st-Class 100s: 3
1st-Class catches: 41
One-Day 5 w. in innings: 1
Place in batting averages: 124th av. 29.73
(2000 160th av. 22.00)
Strike rate: (career 159.00)
Parents: Jim and Sue
Marital status: Single
Family links with cricket: Father played local cricket
Education: Brooklands Primary School; Manchester Grammar School; Durham University
Qualifications: 10 GCSEs, 3 A-levels, BA (Hons) Business Economics, senior coaching award
Overseas tours: Manchester Grammar School to Barbados 1993-94, to South Africa 1995-96; Durham University to Zimbabwe 1997-98
Overseas teams played for: East Torrens, Adelaide 2000-01
Career highlights to date: 'Championship centuries'
Cricketers particularly admired: Michael Atherton
Young players to look out for: Kyle Hogg
Other sports played: Football, golf

Other sports followed: Football (Manchester United)

Relaxations: Music, playing guitar

Extras: Represented England U14, U15, U17. Awarded England U15 Batsman of the Year in 1992. Played for North of England v New Zealand U19 in 1996. Played for British Universities in 1997 Benson and Hedges Cup, winning the Gold Award against Sussex. Awarded 2nd XI cap 1998. His maiden first-class century (106*) v Cambridge University at Fenner's on 9 April 1999 was then the earliest ever 100 in a first-class cricket season in this country (superseded by Michael Burns's century v Oxford Universities on 7 April 2000)

Opinions on cricket: 'Things have changed for the better since the divisional changes. Games have remained competitive throughout the season.'

Best batting: 106* Lancashire v Cambridge University, Fenner's 1999

Best bowling: 1-1 Lancashire v Sri Lanka A, Old Trafford 1999

2001 Season

	M	Inns	NO	Runs	HS	Avge	100s	50s	Ct	St	O	M	Runs	Wkts	Avge	Best	5wI	10wM
Test																		
All First	14	24	1	684	104	29.73	1	4	10	-	5	0	18	0	-		-	-
1-day Int																		
C & G																		
B & H	3	3	1	54	42*	27.00	-	-	1	-	0.1	0	2	0	-		-	-
1-day Lge	9	8	1	84	34	12.00	-	-	2	-								

Career Performances

	M	Inns	NO	Runs	HS	Avge	100s	50s	Ct	St	Balls	Runs	Wkts	Avge	Best	5wI	10wM
Test																	
All First	46	75	5	1964	106*	28.05	3	8	41	-	318	171	2	85.50	1-1	-	-
1-day Int																	
C & G	3	3	0	112	50	37.33	-	1	2	-	42	42	2	21.00	1-20	-	
B & H	14	14	2	351	56	29.25	-	2	5	-	370	318	14	22.71	5-26	1	
1-day Lge	29	27	2	371	44	14.84	-	-	4	-	180	182	7	26.00	3-41	-	

22. Which current Hampshire spinner won the Man of the Match
award for his 3-35 for the Hampshire Board XI
v Glamorgan in the 1999 NatWest?

CLAPP, D. A.   Sussex

Name: <u>Dominic</u> Adrian Clapp
Role: Right-hand bat, right-arm medium
bowler
Born: 25 May 1980, Southport, Merseyside
Height: 6ft 0½ **Weight:** 13st 7lbs
Nickname: Hans, Poppa, Gruber, Rhino,
Link, Cornelius
County debut: No first-team appearance
Parents: Adrian and Sarah
Marital status: Single
Family links with cricket: Brother plays for
his local club side, Broadwater
Education: Sompting Abbotts Prep School;
Lancing College; Worthing Sixth Form
College
Qualifications: 6 GCSEs, 1 A-level, Level 1
and 2 cricket coach
Career outside cricket: Coaching/journalism

Off-season: Coaching and working at Lancing Leisure Centre
Overseas tours: Sussex U14 to Jersey 1994; Lancing College to Australia 1996;
Sussex U19 to Barbados 1997; Sussex Martlets to Australia 2000; Sussex
to Grenada 2001
Overseas teams played for: St Bernhards CC, Melbourne
Career highlights to date: 'Being awarded my first Sussex contract'
Cricketers particularly admired: Murray Goodwin, Steve Waugh, Jacques Kallis,
Damien Martyn, Mike Atherton, Tony Cottey, Ray Beiber, John Kaye
Young players to look out for: Matt Prior, Ian Bell, Nicky Peng, Ian Hunter,
Lawrence Prittipaul, Jimmy Adams
Other sports played: Tennis (Sussex U10, U11, U12), golf, two-touch football
Other sports followed: Football (Tottenham Hotspur), rugby, golf, tennis, athletics,
boxing
Relaxations: 'Reading newspapers, magazines, books; spending time with my friends;
playing cards'
Extras: Sussex U14 Player of the Year 1994. Set record for highest score in Sussex
Youth cricket, 189 v Middlesex 1998. Played two Development of Excellence games
v Australia U19 1999. Sussex Young Cricketer of the Year 1999. Played for Sussex
Board XI in the NatWest 2000
Opinions on cricket: '1. 2nd XI cricket should mirror the first-class game. 2. All
pitches should be prepared for what you would expect for a Test match. 3. All
groundsmen should be employed by the ECB so home captains do not influence the
kind of pitch being prepared.'

2001 Season (did not make any first-class or one-day appearances)

Career Performances

	M	Inns	NO	Runs	HS	Avge	100s	50s	Ct	St	Balls	Runs	Wkts	Avge	Best	5wl	10wM
Test																	
All First																		
1-day Int																		
C & G	2	2	0	14	10	7.00	-	-	-	-	36	46	3	15.33	3-46	-	
B & H																		
1-day Lge																		

CLARKE, A. J. Essex

Name: Andrew (<u>Andy</u>) John Clarke
Role: Left-hand bat, right-arm fast-medium
bowler
Born: 9 November 1975, Harold Wood,
Essex
Height: 6ft 2in **Weight:** 12st 8lbs
Nickname: Vicram, Nobby, Ken
County debut: 2001 (one-day)
Parents: Mary and John (both deceased)
Marital status: Single
Family links with cricket: 'Dad played club
cricket'
Education: Hutton All Saints, Hutton,
Brentwood; St Martins School, Hutton;
Brentwood College of Higher Education
Qualifications: 7 GCSEs, 1 AS-level,
2 A-levels, Level 2 coaching
Career outside cricket: 'Property'
Off-season: Coaching at the Essex Indoor Cricket School
Overseas tours: MCC to Amsterdam 1998
Career highlights to date: '7-19 v Basildon away'
Cricketers particularly admired: 'My dad'
Young players to look out for: Simon Thurston, Steve Cotton, Andy Bliss, Richard
Lewis, Simon Lambett, Daniel Shepheard
Other sports played: Football, squash
Other sports followed: Football (West Ham)
Injuries: Out for two weeks with a hamstring injury
Relaxations: 'Listening to music; time with family and friends'

Extras: MCC Young Cricketers cap and Player of the Year 1998. Played for Essex Board XI and Essex in the C&G 2001
Opinions on cricket: 'Starts should be later.'

2001 Season

	M	Inns	NO	Runs	HS	Avge	100s	50s	Ct	St	O	M	Runs	Wkts	Avge	Best	5wI	10wM
Test																		
All First																		
1-day Int																		
C & G	2	2	0	9	9	4.50	-	-	-	-	16	2	38	1	38.00	1-19	-	
B & H																		
1-day Lge	10	5	1	10	5	2.50	-	-	1	-	54	3	284	7	40.57	2-39	-	

Career Performances

	M	Inns	NO	Runs	HS	Avge	100s	50s	Ct	St	Balls	Runs	Wkts	Avge	Best	5wI	10wM
Test																	
All First																	
1-day Int																	
C & G	2	2	0	9	9	4.50	-	-	-	-	96	38	1	38.00	1-19	-	
B & H																	
1-day Lge	10	5	1	10	5	2.50	-	-	1	-	324	284	7	40.57	2-39	-	

CLARKE, R. Surrey

Name: Rikki Clarke
Role: Right-hand bat, right-arm fast-medium bowler
Born: 29 September 1981, Orsett, Essex
Height: 6ft 4in
Nickname: Clarkey, Rocka, Goofy
County debut: 2001 (one-day)
Parents: Janet and Bob
Marital status: Girlfriend Becky
Family links with cricket: 'Dad played a bit when he was younger'
Education: Godalming Middle School; Broadwater; Godalming College
Qualifications: 5 GCSEs, GNVQ Leisure and Tourism
Off-season: 'Fitness training and netting and spending time with the family'

Overseas tours: Surrey Cricket Board to Barbados; MCC Young Cricketers to South Africa
Career highlights to date: 'Being selected for England U17 squad. Winning the 2nd XI Trophy 2001 with Surrey'
Cricketers particularly admired: Ian Botham, Glenn McGrath
Young players to look out for: Mark Wright, Tim Murtagh, Alex Gidman, Nicky Peng, Phil Sampson
Other sports played: Football, 'all sports really'
Other sports followed: Football (Tottenham Hotspur)
Relaxations: 'Cinema and pub'
Extras: Represented England U17 at the ECC Colts Festival in Northern Ireland 1999. Played for Surrey Board XI in the second round of the C&G 2002, which was played in September 2001
Opinions on cricket: 'Second XI Trophy games to be played in coloured kits to attract crowds.'

2001 Season

	M	Inns	NO	Runs	HS	Avge	100s	50s	Ct	St	O	M	Runs	Wkts	Avge	Best	5wI	10wM
Test																		
All First																		
1-day Int																		
C & G	1	1	0	2	2	2.00	-	-	-	-	4	0	14	1	14.00	1-14	-	
B & H																		
1-day Lge	2	2	0	7	7	3.50	-	-	1	-								

Career Performances

	M	Inns	NO	Runs	HS	Avge	100s	50s	Ct	St	Balls	Runs	Wkts	Avge	Best	5wI	10wM
Test																		
All First																		
1-day Int																		
C & G	1	1	0	2	2	2.00	-	-	-	-	24	14	1	14.00	1-14	-	
B & H																		
1-day Lge	2	2	0	7	7	3.50	-	-	1	-							

CLINTON, R. S. Essex

Name: <u>Richard</u> Selvey Clinton
Role: Left-hand opening bat, right-arm
medium bowler
Born: 1 September 1981, Sidcup, Kent
Height: 6ft 3in **Weight:** 13st 9lbs
Nickname: Bill, Clint, Norman
County debut: 2001
1st-Class 50s: 1
1st-Class catches: 2
Place in batting averages: 191st av. 20.21
Strike rate: 27.00 (career 27.00)
Parents: Grahame and Catherine
Marital status: Single
Family links with cricket: 'Grandfather and
uncles successful club cricketers. Father
played professionally for Kent and Surrey'
Education: Harenc Prep School;
Colfes School

Qualifications: 9 GCSEs, 3 A-levels
Career outside cricket: Student
Off-season: Playing cricket in Australia
Overseas teams played for: Kensington CC, Adelaide; Valleys CC, Brisbane
Career highlights to date: 'Making first-class debut'
Cricket moments to forget: 'Fielding in a Sunday League game against Glamorgan
with half-and-half spikes after five days of rain, therefore being unable to stand up or
stop running'
Cricketers particularly admired: Graham Thorpe, Mark Butcher, Ricky Ponting
Young players to look out for: Justin Bishop, James Hockley
Other sports played: Football, rugby
Other sports followed: Football (Chelsea FC)
Injuries: Out for two weeks with a broken thumb
Relaxations: Doing crosswords; playing sport in general; listening to dance music
Extras: Scored 36 and 58* on first-class debut v Surrey at Ilford 2001; scored 56 the
following day on Norwich Union League debut v Durham at the same ground
Opinions on cricket: 'Should be more use of floodlights to allow Championship
games to start and finish later, thereby allowing the supporters to watch the game
after work.'
Best batting: 58* Essex v Surrey, Ilford 2001
Best bowling: 2-30 Essex v Australians, Chelmsford 2001

2001 Season

	M	Inns	NO	Runs	HS	Avge	100s	50s	Ct	St	O	M	Runs	Wkts	Avge	Best	5wI	10wM
Test																		
All First	8	15	1	283	58 *	20.21	-	1	2	-	9	1	30	2	15.00	2-30	-	-
1-day Int																		
C & G	1	1	0	13	13	13.00	-	-	-	-								
B & H																		
1-day Lge	9	6	2	125	56	31.25	-	1	-	-	3	0	25	0	-		-	-

Career Performances

	M	Inns	NO	Runs	HS	Avge	100s	50s	Ct	St	Balls	Runs	Wkts	Avge	Best	5wI	10wM
Test																	
All First	8	15	1	283	58 *	20.21	-	1	2	-	54	30	2	15.00	2-30	-	-
1-day Int																	
C & G	1	1	0	13	13	13.00	-	-	-	-							
B & H																	
1-day Lge	9	6	2	125	56	31.25	-	1	-	-	18	25	0	-		-	-

CLOUGH, G. D. Nottinghamshire

Name: <u>Gareth</u> David Clough
Role: Right-hand bat, right-arm medium bowler
Born: 23 May 1978, Leeds
Height: 6ft **Weight:** 12st
Nickname: Banga, Cloughie
County debut: 1998 (Yorkshire), 2001 (Nottinghamshire)
1st-Class catches: 2
Place in batting averages: 282nd av. 3.66
Strike rate: 100.00 (career 102.00)
Parents: David and Gillian
Marital status: Single
Family links with cricket: Brother-in-law plays local league cricket in Leeds
Education: Pudsey Greenside Primary School; Pudsey Grangefield
Qualifications: 9 GCSEs, 3 A-levels, Level 1 cricket coach
Off-season: Melbourne – playing for Deepdene Bears
Overseas tours: Yorkshire to Durban and Cape Town 1999; Nottinghamshire to Johannesburg 2001

Overseas teams played for: Somerset West, Cape Town 1996-97; Deepdene Bears, Melbourne 1999-2000, 2001-02
Career highlights to date: 'Making my first-class debut – Yorkshire v Glamorgan 1998, Sophia Gardens'
Cricket moments to forget: 'B&H semi-final v Surrey at The Oval 2001'
Cricketers particularly admired: Ian Botham, Steve Waugh
Young players to look out for: Bilal Shafayat, Samit Patel
Other sports played: Golf, football (Royal FC), tennis, snooker, nine-ball pool
Other sports followed: Football (Everton FC), rugby league (Leeds Rhinos)
Injuries: Out for three weeks with groin trouble
Relaxations: Socialising with friends, watching films
Extras: Formerly with Yorkshire. Played for Nottinghamshire 2nd XI in 2000, topping the bowling averages with 37 wickets at 19.05 and scoring 400 runs
Opinions on cricket: 'I don't think it is a coincidence that the upturn in England's fortunes has coincided with the introduction of a two-divisional structure in the domestic game. This has made the game more competitive throughout the season and floodlit games have made cricket more of a spectator sport – which are both big positives.'
Best batting: 33 Yorkshire v Glamorgan, Cardiff 1998
Best bowling: 3-69 Nottinghamshire v Gloucestershire, Trent Bridge 2001

2001 Season

	M	Inns	NO	Runs	HS	Avge	100s	50s	Ct	St	O	M	Runs	Wkts	Avge	Best	5wI	10wM
Test																		
All First	4	6	0	22	8	3.66	-	-	1	-	100	14	353	6	58.83	3-69	-	-
1-day Int																		
C & G																		
B & H	7	1	0	0	0	0.00	-	-	1	-	60.2	2	308	7	44.00	2-36	-	
1-day Lge	13	8	2	73	24	12.16	-	-	2	-	86.1	1	429	13	33.00	2-33	-	

Career Performances

	M	Inns	NO	Runs	HS	Avge	100s	50s	Ct	St	Balls	Runs	Wkts	Avge	Best	5wI	10wM
Test																	
All First	5	8	0	56	33	7.00	-	-	2	-	612	364	6	60.66	3-69	-	-
1-day Int																	
C & G																	
B & H	7	1	0	0	0	0.00	-	-	1	-	362	308	7	44.00	2-36	-	
1-day Lge	13	8	2	73	24	12.16	-	-	2	-	517	429	13	33.00	2-33	-	

COLEMAN, A. J.   Middlesex

Name: <u>Alan</u> James Coleman
Role: Right-hand bat, right-arm
medium-fast bowler
Born: 13 December 1983, Ashford
Height: 6ft 2in **Weight:** 12st 4lbs
Nickname: Coley
County debut: 2001 (one-day)
Parents: Pamela and Philip
Marital status: Single
Family links with cricket: Father played
club cricket. Brother Chris is wicket-keeper
for Loughborough University CCE
Education: Bedfont Primary School;
Longford Community School
Qualifications: 11 GCSEs, 3 AS-levels,
ECB Level 1 coach, community sports leader
Career outside cricket: Student
Off-season: Studying for A-levels at school
Overseas tours: England U17 to Australia 2000-01
Career highlights to date: 'Making Norwich Union League debut v Sussex in 2001'
Cricketers particularly admired: Owais Shah
Young players to look out for: Tim Bresnan, Bilal Shafayat, Gary Scott
Other sports played: Football, squash
Other sports followed: Football (Brentford FC)
Relaxations: 'Watching Brentford; listening to music'

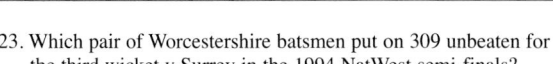

23. Which pair of Worcestershire batsmen put on 309 unbeaten for
the third wicket v Surrey in the 1994 NatWest semi-finals?

2001 Season

	M	Inns	NO	Runs	HS	Avge	100s	50s	Ct	St	O	M	Runs	Wkts	Avge	Best	5wI	10wM
Test																		
All First																		
1-day Int																		
C & G																		
B & H																		
1-day Lge	3	2	2	15	11 *	-	-	-	1	-	13.1	1	61	0	-		-	-

Career Performances

	M	Inns	NO	Runs	HS	Avge	100s	50s	Ct	St	Balls	Runs	Wkts	Avge	Best	5wI	10wM
Test																	
All First																	
1-day Int																	
C & G																	
B & H																	
1-day Lge	3	2	2	15	11 *	-	-	-	1	-	79	61	0	-		-	-

COLLINGWOOD, P. D.   Durham

Name: <u>Paul</u> David Collingwood
Role: Right-hand bat, right-arm
medium bowler
Born: 26 May 1976, Shotley Bridge,
Tyneside
Height: 5ft 11in **Weight:** 11st 8lbs
Nickname: Colly
County debut: 1995 (one-day),
1996 (first-class)
County cap: 1998
One-Day Internationals: 4
1000 runs in a season: 1
1st-Class 50s: 22
1st-Class 100s: 7
1st-Class catches: 87
Place in batting averages: 24th av. 52.76
(2000 134th av. 25.22)
Place in bowling averages: (2000 129th
av. 39.50)
Strike rate: 110.00 (career 91.05)
Parents: David and Janet
Marital status: Single

Family links with cricket: Father and brother play in the Tyneside Senior League for Shotley Bridge CC

Education: Benfieldside Junior School; Blackfyne Comprehensive School; Derwentside College

Qualifications: 9 GCSEs and 2 A-levels

Career outside cricket: 'Whatever job I can find'

Off-season: Hong Kong Sixes and England one-day squads to Zimbabwe, India and New Zealand

Overseas tours: Durham Cricket Academy to Sri Lanka 1996 (captain); England VI to Hong Kong 2001; England to Zimbabwe (one-day series) 2001-02, to India and New Zealand 2001-02 (one-day series)

Overseas teams played for: Bulleen CC, Melbourne 1995-96, 1996-97 ('won flag on both occasions'); Cornwall CC, Auckland 1997-98; Alberton CC, Johannesburg 1998-99; Richmond CC, Melbourne 2000-01

Cricketers particularly admired: Steve Waugh, Simon Katich, Jacques Kallis

Players to look out for: Simon Katich

Other sports played: Golf

Other sports followed: Football ('The Red and Whites' – Sunderland)

Extras: Took wicket (David Capel) with first ball on first-class debut against Northants, then scored 91 in Durham's first innings. Durham Player of the Year 2000. Awarded the Ron Brierley Scholarship 2000 through the ECB in conjunction with the Victorian Cricket Association, Australia; joint winner of the Jack Ryder Medal, awarded by the umpires, for his performances in Victorian Premier Cricket 2000-01. B&H Gold Awards for his 89 v Derbyshire at Derby and 95* v Leicestershire at Riverside 2001. Made One-Day International debut v Pakistan at Edgbaston in the NatWest Series 2001. Scored 103 v Worcestershire at Riverside 2001, in the process passing 1000 runs in a season for the first time

Best batting: 153 Durham v Warwickshire, Edgbaston 2001

Best bowling: 3-7 Durham v Glamorgan, Cardiff 1999

Stop press: Man of the Match (77 and 1-31) in fourth ODI v Zimbabwe at Bulawayo 2001-02; followed up with 56* (50 from 43 balls) in fifth ODI at Bulawayo. Man of the Match in One-Day International v India at Cuttack 2001-02 for his all-round performance, including 71*. Took 4-38 in One-Day International v New Zealand at Napier 2001-02, winning the Man of the Match award

2001 Season

	M	Inns	NO	Runs	HS	Avge	100s	50s	Ct	St	O	M	Runs	Wkts	Avge	Best	5wI	10wM
Test																		
All First	13	24	3	1108	153	52.76	3	6	10	-	165	50	465	9	51.66	2-2	-	-
1-day Int	4	4	0	20	9	5.00	-	-	-	-	7.1	0	49	0	-	-	-	
C & G	3	3	1	157	60	78.50	-	2	-	-	18	1	118	1	118.00	1-31	-	
B & H	6	6	2	284	95 *	71.00	-	2	6	-	43.4	3	189	5	37.80	2-39	-	
1-day Lge	11	11	0	294	84	26.72	-	1	6	-	67.5	1	293	11	26.63	3-21	-	

Career Performances

	M	Inns	NO	Runs	HS	Avge	100s	50s	Ct	St	Balls	Runs	Wkts	Avge	Best	5wI	10wM
Test																	
All First	84	145	10	4094	153	30.32	7	22	87	-	4644	2143	51	42.01	3-7	-	-
1-day Int	4	4	0	20	9	5.00	-	-	-	-	43	49	0	-	-	-	
C & G	11	10	1	262	60	29.11	-	2	1	-	246	196	4	49.00	2-7	-	
B & H	24	23	5	643	95 *	35.72	-	2	11	-	791	601	18	33.38	4-31	-	
1-day Lge	78	75	6	1911	86	27.69	-	14	41	-	1558	1234	40	30.85	3-20	-	

COMPTON, N. R. D.   Middlesex

Name: Nicholas (<u>Nick</u>) Richard Denis Compton
Role: Right-hand bat, right-arm off-spin bowler
Born: 26 June 1983, Durban, South Africa
Height: 6ft 1in **Weight:** 12st 8lbs
Nickname: Compo
County debut: 2001 (one-day)
Parents: Richard and Glynis
Marital status: Single
Family links with cricket: Grandfather Denis Compton played for Middlesex and England
Education: Clifton, Durban; Hilton College/DHS, South Africa; Harrow School
Qualifications: 3 A-levels
Career outside cricket: Student
Off-season: University; winter tours
Overseas tours: England U19 to Australia and (U19 World Cup) New Zealand 2001-02
Overseas teams played for: University of Western Australia, Perth 2001
Career highlights to date: 'A fifty at age 15 to win a game against a President's XI which included a number of West Indians'

Cricket moments to forget: 'Dropping three catches against Australia 2002'
Cricketers particularly admired: Jacques Kallis, Damien Martyn
Young players to look out for: Shaun Marsh (Australian), Hasim Amla and Jon Kent (South African), Kyle Hogg, Paul McMahon
Other sports played: Golf (six handicap), represented Natal at junior level at tennis, hockey, football and rugby
Other sports followed: Football (Arsenal), rugby union (Natal Sharks)
Relaxations: Music, films and friends
Extras: Played for Natal U13 and U15. Represented Harrow v Eton in 1999 (match abandoned), 2000, and 2001 (captain). Natal Academy award 1997. Middlesex U17 Batsman of the Season 1999. Middlesex U19 Player of the Season 2000. NBC Denis Compton Award for the most promising young Middlesex player 2001
Opinions on cricket: 'Far too individual. Players driven by money and bonuses rather than their so-called passion for the game.'

2001 Season

	M	Inns	NO	Runs	HS	Avge	100s	50s	Ct	St	O	M	Runs	Wkts	Avge	Best	5wI	10wM
Test																		
All First																		
1-day Int																		
C & G																		
B & H																		
1-day Lge	1	1	0	6	6	6.00	-	-	-	-								

Career Performances

	M	Inns	NO	Runs	HS	Avge	100s	50s	Ct	St	Balls	Runs	Wkts	Avge	Best	5wI	10wM
Test																	
All First																	
1-day Int																	
C & G																	
B & H																	
1-day Lge	1	1	0	6	6	6.00	-	-	-	-							

COOK, J. W. Northamptonshire

Name: <u>Jeffrey</u> William Cook
Role: Left-hand bat, right-arm
medium bowler
Born: 2 February 1972, Sydney
Height: 6ft 4in **Weight:** 14st
Nickname: Cookie
County debut: 2000
1st-Class 50s: 5
1st-Class 100s: 2
1st-Class catches: 9
One-Day 100s: 1
Place in batting averages: 148th av. 26.06
(2000 83rd av. 31.37)
Strike rate: 282.00 (career 288.00)
Parents: Roma and Les
Wife and date of marriage: Fiona,
10 October 1998
Children: Alexander, 21 April 2000

Family links with cricket: Mother represented New South Wales
Education: Rockdale Public School, Rockdale, NSW; James Cook High School,
Kogarah, NSW
Qualifications: NCA Level 2 coaching award, ACB Level 1 coaching award
Off-season: Playing in Sydney
Overseas tours: Northamptonshire to Grenada 2000, 2001
Overseas teams played for: St George DCC, Sydney 1987-93;
Easts CC, Sydney 1999 –
Career highlights to date: 'First [first-class] century (137) v Glos in my second
game. Winning second division of Championship in 2000 with Northants. Fielding for
England v Pakistan at Lord's 2001'
Cricket moments to forget: 'First ever pair – v Yorkshire at Headingley 2001'
Cricketers particularly admired: David Gower, Mark Taylor, Mark Waugh,
Steve Waugh
Young players to look out for: Tobin Bailey
Other sports played: Football, tennis
Other sports followed: Football (Liverpool), rugby league (Parramatta)
Relaxations: 'Time with family'
Extras: Represented NSW at U17, U19 and Colts levels. Represented New South
Wales and Australia at indoor cricket. Played for Northants Board XI in 1999 NatWest,
scoring 130 v Wiltshire at Northampton and winning the Man of the Match award.
Shared in record second-wicket stand for Northants in matches v Surrey (168) with
Mike Hussey at Northampton 2001

Opinions on cricket: 'More day/night matches.'
Best batting: 137 Northamptonshire v Gloucestershire, Cheltenham 2000
Best bowling: 1-17 Northamptonshire v Somerset, Northampton 2001

2001 Season

	M	Inns	NO	Runs	HS	Avge	100s	50s	Ct	St	O	M	Runs	Wkts	Avge	Best	5wI	10wM
Test																		
All First	9	16	1	391	88	26.06	-	4	5	-	47	16	124	1	124.00	1-17	-	-
1-day Int																		
C & G																		
B & H	5	5	0	160	86	32.00	-	1	1	-	8	0	43	0	-		-	-
1-day Lge	8	8	0	129	55	16.12	-	1	5	-	18	2	81	3	27.00	2-44	-	

Career Performances

	M	Inns	NO	Runs	HS	Avge	100s	50s	Ct	St	Balls	Runs	Wkts	Avge	Best	5wI	10wM
Test																	
All First	20	33	2	893	137	28.80	2	5	9	-	288	131	1	131.00	1-17	-	-
1-day Int																	
C & G	4	4	0	235	130	58.75	1	-	-	-	48	50	0	-		-	-
B & H	5	5	0	160	86	32.00	-	1	1	-	48	43	0	-		-	-
1-day Lge	22	22	0	315	55	14.31	-	1	10	-	108	81	3	27.00	2-44	-	

COOK, S. J.   Middlesex

Name: <u>Simon</u> James Cook
Role: Right-hand bat, right-arm
fast bowler
Born: 15 January 1977, Oxford
Height: 6ft 4in **Weight:** 13st
Nickname: Donk, Cookie
County debut: 1997 (one-day),
1999 (first-class)
1st-Class 50s: 2
1st-Class catches: 8
Place in batting averages: 129th av. 29.50
(2000 234th av. 14.50)
Place in bowling averages: 89th av. 34.80
(2000 95th av. 30.45)
Strike rate: 65.45 (career 65.36)
Parents: Phil and Sue
Marital status: Single

Education: Botley Primary School; Matthew Arnold School
Qualifications: GCSEs, NVQ Business Administration II
Career outside cricket: Sales and marketing within the computer industry
Off-season: Coaching for Middlesex
Overseas tours: Middlesex to South Africa 2000
Overseas teams played for: Rockingham, Western Australia
Cricketers particularly admired: Angus Fraser, Allan Donald, Mark Waugh
Young players to look out for: Jamie Dalrymple, Nick Hatch
Other sports followed: Football (Liverpool), 'any other ball sport'
Relaxations: 'Sleeping, playing any sport, watching television and videos'
Extras: Scored career best 93* v Nottinghamshire at Lord's 2001, helping Middlesex to avoid the follow-on, then took a wicket with the first ball of his opening spell
Best batting: 93* Middlesex v Nottinghamshire, Lord's 2001
Best bowling: 4-13 Middlesex v Essex, Lord's 2000

2001 Season

	M	Inns	NO	Runs	HS	Avge	100s	50s	Ct	St	O	M	Runs	Wkts	Avge	Best	5wI	10wM
Test																		
All First	10	11	3	236	93 *	29.50	-	1	3	-	218.1	47	696	20	34.80	3-10	-	-
1-day Int																		
C & G																		
B & H	5	3	0	12	11	4.00	-	-	1	-	41	2	199	5	39.80	2-63	-	
1-day Lge	11	9	2	111	50	15.85	-	1	1	-	72.3	4	366	8	45.75	2-33	-	

Career Performances

	M	Inns	NO	Runs	HS	Avge	100s	50s	Ct	St	Balls	Runs	Wkts	Avge	Best	5wI	10wM
Test																	
All First	27	37	6	618	93 *	19.93	-	2	8	-	3791	1985	58	34.22	4-13	-	-
1-day Int																	
C & G	3	3	1	14	7	7.00	-	-	-	-	120	79	2	39.50	1-29	-	
B & H	6	4	0	18	11	4.50	-	-	1	-	300	270	5	54.00	2-63	-	
1-day Lge	40	30	5	318	50	12.72	-	1	7	-	1684	1257	46	27.32	3-16	-	

CORK, D. G.   Derbyshire

Name: <u>Dominic</u> Gerald Cork
Role: Right-hand bat, right-arm fast-medium bowler, county captain
Born: 7 August 1971, Newcastle-under-Lyme, Staffordshire
Height: 6ft 3in **Weight:** 14st 10lbs
Nickname: Corky
County debut: 1990
County cap: 1993

Benefit: 2001
Test debut: 1995
Tests: 31
One-Day Internationals: 25
50 wickets in a season: 5
1st-Class 50s: 34
1st-Class 100s: 4
1st-Class 200s: 1
1st-Class 5 w. in innings: 20
1st-Class 10 w. in match: 2
1st-Class catches: 133
One-Day 5 w. in innings: 4
Place in batting averages: 161st av. 23.81
(2000 31st av. 41.69)
Place in bowling averages: 137th av. 51.50
(2000 29th av. 21.09)
Strike rate: 103.41 (career 54.78)
Parents: Gerald and Mary
Wife and date of marriage: Donna-Marie, 28 August 2000
Children: Ashleigh, 28 April 1990; Gregory Theodore Gerald, 29 September 1994
Family links with cricket: 'Father and brothers played for Betley CC in local North
Staffs & South Cheshire League with myself'
Education: The Convent, Newcastle, Staffs; St Joseph's College, Trent Vale,
Stoke-on-Trent
Qualifications: 3 O-levels, Level 2 coach
Off-season: 'Holidays, relaxing, watching my children play sport; hopefully
representing my country'
Overseas tours: England YC to Australia 1989-90; England A to Bermuda and West
Indies 1991-92, to Australia 1992-93, to South Africa 1993-94, to India 1994-95;
England to South Africa 1995-96, to India and Pakistan (World Cup) 1995-96,
to New Zealand 1996-97, to Australia 1998-99, to Pakistan and Sri Lanka 2000-01
Overseas teams played for: East Shirley, Christchurch, New Zealand 1990-91
Career highlights to date: 'Making my debut for England'
Cricket moments to forget: 'Losing any game'
Cricketers particularly admired: Ian Botham, Malcolm Marshall, Imran Khan
Young players to look out for: Luke Sutton
Other sports played: Football, skiing
Other sports followed: Football (Stoke City)
Injuries: Hamstring tear; recovering from spinal stress fracture
Extras: Played Minor Counties cricket for Staffordshire in 1989 and 1990. In 1990 he
took a wicket in his first over in first-class cricket, v New Zealanders at Derby, and
scored a century as nightwatchman for England U19 v Pakistan at Taunton. Took 8-53
before lunch on his 20th birthday, v Essex at Derby 1991. Selected for England A in
1991 – his first full season of first-class cricket. Won the Professional Cricketers'
Association (PCA) Young Player of the Year award 1991. Achieved first-class hat-trick

against Kent 1994. Took 7-43 on Test debut against West Indies at Lord's 1995, the best innings figures by an England debutant. Achieved hat-trick against the West Indies at Old Trafford in the fourth Test 1995 – the first by an Englishman in Test cricket for 38 years. Voted Player of the Year by the PCA for 1995. Finished at the top of the Whyte and Mackay ratings for bowling in 1995. Cornhill England Player of the Year 1995-96. One of *Wisden*'s Five Cricketers of the Year 1996. Man of the Match in the second Test v West Indies at Lord's 2000; on his recall to the Test side he recorded match figures of 7-52 followed by a match-winning 33* in England's second innings. Scored maiden first-class 200 (200*, the highest score by a Derbyshire No. 8) v Durham at Derby 2000, setting in the process a new record seventh-wicket partnership for Derbyshire (258) with Mathew Dowman; then took wicket with first ball of Durham's second innings. C&G Man of the Match award for his 50 followed by 4-35 v Glamorgan at Cardiff 2001. Derbyshire captain since 1998. England central contract 2001

Opinions on cricket: 'Too many games. Too little quality. The game should be run by England and counties by owners.'

Best batting: 200* Derbyshire v Durham, Derby 2000
Best bowling: 9-43 Derbyshire v Northamptonshire, Derby 1995

2001 Season

	M	Inns	NO	Runs	HS	Avge	100s	50s	Ct	St	O	M	Runs	Wkts	Avge	Best	5wI	10wM
Test	3	5	0	57	25	11.40	-	-	1	-	95.3	20	284	6	47.33	3-41	-	-
All First	7	11	0	262	128	23.81	1	-	6	-	206.5	44	618	12	51.50	4-122	-	-
1-day Int	5	4	0	42	18	10.50	-	-	-	-	41.5	0	215	6	35.83	2-32	-	
C & G	1	1	0	50	50	50.00	-	1	1	-	10	0	35	4	8.75	4-35	-	
B & H	4	4	0	45	21	11.25	-	-	-	-	35	6	141	6	23.50	2-23	-	
1-day Lge	2	2	1	87	83 *	87.00	-	1	3	-	18	2	60	3	20.00	3-38	-	

Career Performances

	M	Inns	NO	Runs	HS	Avge	100s	50s	Ct	St	Balls	Runs	Wkts	Avge	Best	5wI	10wM
Test	34	53	8	781	59	17.35	-	2	17	-	7195	3647	124	29.41	7-43	5	-
All First	195	289	41	6225	200 *	25.10	5	34	133	-	33307	16360	608	26.90	9-43	20	2
1-day Int	30	19	2	174	31 *	10.23	-	-	6	-	1691	1286	41	31.36	3-27	-	
C & G	20	18	4	543	93	38.78	-	6	8	-	1257	761	42	18.11	5-18	2	
B & H	30	23	6	431	92 *	25.35	-	2	15	-	1696	1111	35	31.74	5-49	1	
1-day Lge	98	82	9	1365	83 *	18.69	-	6	44	-	4186	3230	114	28.33	6-21	1	

COSKER, D. A.   Glamorgan

Name: <u>Dean</u> Andrew Cosker
Role: Right-hand bat, slow left-arm bowler
Born: 7 January 1978, Weymouth, Dorset
Height: 5ft 10½in **Weight:** 12st 5lbs
Nickname: Lurks
County debut: 1996
County cap: 2000
1st-Class 5 w. in innings: 2
1st-Class catches: 55
Place in batting averages: 221st av. 15.90
(2000 287th av. 8.00)
Place in bowling averages: 121st av. 42.12
(2000 105th av. 32.55)
Strike rate: 77.06 (career 76.57)
Parents: Des and Carol
Marital status: Girlfriend Katie
Education: Ravenswood Prep School, Devon;
Millfield School; 'The University of Higher
Education, Hawker Close'

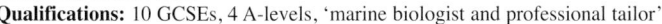

Qualifications: 10 GCSEs, 4 A-levels, 'marine biologist and professional tailor'
Career outside cricket: 'Weatherman'
Off-season: Pre-season tour to Cape Town with Glamorgan
Overseas tours: West of England U15 to West Indies 1993-94; Millfield School to Sri
Lanka 1994-95; England U17 to Holland 1995; England U19 to Pakistan 1996-97;
England A to Kenya and Sri Lanka 1997-98, to Zimbabwe and South Africa 1998-99;
Glamorgan CCC to Cape Town and Jersey
Overseas teams played for: Gordon CC, Sydney 1996-97; Crusaders, Durban
2000-01
Career highlights to date: 'Receiving my county cap in 2000. Winning the
Championship in 1997. Having the pleasure of sitting next to Darren Thomas in the
Glamorgan changing room for five years!!'
Cricket moments to forget: 'Losing the NatWest semi v Essex in 1997. Not being
able to play in the Lord's [B&H] final 2000, and watching it as well'
Cricketers particularly admired: Matthew Maynard, Steve Watkin, Hugh Morris,
Steve Barwick
Young players to look out for: Tim Ambrose, Mark Wallace, Simon 'Horse' Jones
Other sports followed: Soccer (Tottenham Hotspur FC)
Relaxations: 'Alan Partridge (comic), yoga, t'ai chi, Ammanford and my car'
Extras: *Daily Telegraph* Regional Bowling Award. England U15 and U17. Played for
U19 TCCB Development of Excellence XI against South Africa U19 in 1995. Played
for England U19 against Zimbabwe U19 in 1997. Leading wicket-taker on England A

tour of Zimbabwe and South Africa 1998-99. Third youngest Glamorgan player to receive county cap
Opinions on cricket: 'If at any time throughout your cricketing career you stop enjoying, smiling, loving playing with the players around you, or lose respect for any of them, you might as well hang up your boots and join the dole queue!!'
Best batting: 49 Glamorgan v Sussex, Cardiff 1999
Best bowling: 6-140 Glamorgan v Lancashire, Colwyn Bay 1998

2001 Season

	M	Inns	NO	Runs	HS	Avge	100s	50s	Ct	St	O	M	Runs	Wkts	Avge	Best	5wI	10wM
Test																		
All First	11	15	4	175	35	15.90	-	-	10	-	423.5	84	1390	33	42.12	4-48	-	-
1-day Int																		
C & G	2	0	0	0	0	-	-	-	1	-	18	1	88	1	88.00	1-37	-	
B & H	2	1	0	0	0	0.00	-	-	-	-	19	3	79	2	39.50	1-35	-	
1-day Lge	12	4	1	22	14 *	7.33	-	-	6	-	85	5	391	14	27.92	3-40	-	

Career Performances

	M	Inns	NO	Runs	HS	Avge	100s	50s	Ct	St	Balls	Runs	Wkts	Avge	Best	5wI	10wM
Test																	
All First	83	96	27	752	49	10.89	-	-	55	-	15544	7191	203	35.42	6-140	2	-
1-day Int																	
C & G	7	4	3	16	5	16.00	-	-	1	-	368	240	8	30.00	3-26	-	
B & H	7	5	2	2	1 *	0.66	-	-	1	-	288	207	6	34.50	2-26	-	
1-day Lge	53	27	9	172	27 *	9.55	-	-	16	-	2274	1863	59	31.57	3-18	-	

COTTEY, P. A.   Sussex

Name: Phillip Anthony (<u>Tony</u>) Cottey
Role: Right-hand bat
Born: 2 June 1966, Swansea
Height: 5ft 5in **Weight:** 10st 10lbs
Nickname: Cotts, Rudy, Baba
County debut: 1986 (Glamorgan), 1999 (Sussex)
County cap: 1992 (Glamorgan), 1999 (Sussex)
1000 runs in a season: 7
1st-Class 50s: 65
1st-Class 100s: 23
1st-Class 200s: 1
1st-Class catches: 162
Place in batting averages: (2000 74th av. 32.17)
Strike rate: (career 84.87)

Parents: Bernard John and Ruth
Wife and date of marriage: Gail, 5 October 1992
Children: Lowri Rhiannon, 16 October 1993; Seren Nia, 6 August 1997
Family links with cricket: Father played club cricket for Swansea CC
Education: Crwys Primary; Bishopston Comprehensive School, Swansea
Qualifications: 9 O-levels, advanced coach (Level 3)
Career outside cricket: 'Undecided'
Off-season: 'Setting up a possible business venture'
Overseas tours: Glamorgan to La Manga, Barbados, Trinidad, Zimbabwe and Cape Town 1987-96, to Jersey 1998
Overseas teams played for: Penrith, Sydney 1986-88; Benoni, Johannesburg 1990-93; Eastern Transvaal 1991-92
Career highlights to date: 'Winning Championship with Glamorgan 1997. Winning Sunday League with Glamorgan 1993. Winning second division of one-day league with Sussex 1999'
Cricket moments to forget: 'Any of the four semi-final losses at Glamorgan and the semi-final loss at Gloucestershire 1999 in Super Cup with Sussex'
Cricketers particularly admired: Ian Botham, Matthew Maynard, Sachin Tendulkar, Mark Robinson
Young players to look out for: Tim Ambrose
Other sports played: Golf, road running, soccer
Other sports followed: Rugby (Dunvant RFC), football (Swansea City AFC)
Injuries: Out for the whole of the 2001 season with 'tennis elbow' (torn tendon)
Relaxations: 'Night out with friends; time with family; golf'
Extras: Left school at 16 to play for Swansea City AFC for three years as a professional. Three Welsh Youth caps (one as captain). Glamorgan Player of the Year in 1994. Ran the New York Marathon in 1995 and the Athens Marathon in 1996. Left Glamorgan at the end of the 1998 season and joined Sussex. Sussex Clubman of the Year 1999
Opinions on cricket: 'Two-divisional cricket is great – just worry that an elitist band is going to be created, resulting in some counties going out of business.'
Best batting: 203 Glamorgan v Leicestershire, Swansea 1996
Best bowling: 4-49 Glamorgan v Leicestershire, Swansea 1996

	M	Inns	NO	Runs	HS	Avge	100s	50s	Ct	St	O	M	Runs	Wkts	Avge	Best	5wI	10wM
Test																		
All First	2	3	1	70	46	35.00	-	-	1	-								
1-day Int																		
C & G																		
B & H																		
1-day Lge	1	1	0	0	0	0.00	-	-	1	-								

Career Performances

	M	Inns	NO	Runs	HS	Avge	100s	50s	Ct	St	Balls	Runs	Wkts	Avge	Best	5wI	10wM
Test																	
All First	238	384	51	12209	203	36.66	24	65	162	-	1358	862	16	53.87	4-49	-	-
1-day Int																	
C & G	29	28	7	567	68	27.00	-	4	8	-	150	96	3	32.00	1-9	-	
B & H	39	37	6	638	96	20.58	-	3	15	-	78	53	1	53.00	1-49	-	
1-day Lge	161	137	27	2790	92 *	25.36	-	16	55	-	509	523	15	34.86	4-56	-	

COUSINS, D. M.   Northamptonshire

Name: Darren Mark Cousins
Role: Right-hand bat, right-arm
fast-medium bowler
Born: 24 September 1971, Cambridge
Height: 6ft 1in **Weight:** 14st
Nickname: Cuz, Mad Dog, Gimp, Hooks, T
County debut: 1993 (Essex), 1999 (one-day,
Surrey), 2000 (Northants)
County cap: 2000 (Northants)
50 wickets in a season: 1
1st-Class 5 w. in innings: 4
1st-Class catches: 8
Place in batting averages: 241st av. 12.42
(2000 244th av. 13.12)
Place in bowling averages: 78th av. 32.66
(2000 21st av. 19.67)
Strike rate: 55.61 (career 54.20)
Parents: Dennis Charles and Deanna
Maureen (deceased)
Marital status: Single – 'living with girlfriend Anna and her two boys; if she has her
own way we'll be married by the time this goes to print'
Family links with cricket: Father opened the bowling for and was capped by
Cambridgeshire

Education: Milton Primary School; Impington Village College
Qualifications: 7 GCSEs, basic and senior coaching awards
Off-season: 'Hopefully touring India with MCC, then maybe going overseas after Christmas to make sure I'm fully fit for next season. Depends on my feet'
Overseas tours: Northamptonshire to Grenada 1999-2000, 2000-01
Overseas teams played for: Gold Coast Dolphins, Queensland 1994-95; Maritzburg Old Boys, Pietermaritzburg, South Africa 1995-96; Shell Harbour, NSW 1996-97; Bellville, Cape Town 1999-2000; Greenpoint, Cape Town 2000-01
Career highlights to date: 'Winning the second division championship in 2000. Receiving my cap and Player of the Year award'
Cricket moments to forget: 'All the times I realise that an injury is going to put me out of action for a long time'
People particularly admired: 'Alan Butcher, the man who got me back into first-class cricket. Anna, my calming influence when things go pear-shaped!'
Young players to look out for: Monty Panesar, Richard Logan, John Blain
Other sports played: Football (represented Cambridgeshire at all youth levels), swimming (represented Cambridgeshire)
Other sports followed: Football (Liverpool, Cambridge United), rugby union ('I hope to watch Northampton more')
Injuries: Out for second half of season with bilateral navicular stress fractures
Relaxations: 'X-rated'
Extras: Represented Cambridgeshire at every level at cricket. Played for a Bull Development Squad against Australia in 1991, taking four wickets in each innings. Played 2nd XI cricket for Northants and Worcs. Set record both for number of wickets in any single Colts festival (21) and for number of wickets taken in the Hilda Overy Festival overall (74). Spent seven years at Essex, undergoing four back and two knee operations. Awarded 2nd XI cap and Essex Young Player of the Year 1994. Essex Cricket Society 2nd XI Player of the Year 1994. Leading Essex wicket-taker in Sunday League and top of the bowling averages in 1994. Released by Essex at end of 1998 season after only full season on the staff. Played as a pro for Cambridge St Giles and Cambridgeshire 1999. Played three National League matches for Surrey 1999; offered one-year contract at end of 1999 but chose to join Northants for 2000. His 4-62 v Essex at Chelmsford 2001 was his third four-wicket return in as many Championship matches against his old county. Took all seven wickets to fall (7-120) in Lancashire's second innings at Northampton 2001. Took 100th Championship wicket for Northants (Peter Bowler lbw) v Somerset at Northampton 2001 in only his 23rd Championship match for the county
Opinions on cricket: 'It seems to be a batsman's game. The balls this year were terrible and pitches were flat as farts.'
Best batting: 29* Northamptonshire v Glamorgan, Northampton 2000
Best bowling: 8-102 Northamptonshire v Yorkshire, Headingley 2001

2001 Season

	M	Inns	NO	Runs	HS	Avge	100s	50s	Ct	St	O	M	Runs	Wkts	Avge	Best	5wI	10wM
Test																		
All First	8	10	3	87	27	12.42	-	-	-	-	333.4	54	1176	36	32.66	8-102	2	-
1-day Int																		
C & G	1	0	0	0	0	-	-	-	1	-	10	0	39	1	39.00	1-39	-	
B & H	4	2	0	9	6	4.50	-	-	3	-	40	4	171	9	19.00	4-23	-	
1-day Lge	5	2	1	8	5 *	8.00	-	-	1	-	43	2	226	4	56.50	3-34	-	

Career Performances

	M	Inns	NO	Runs	HS	Avge	100s	50s	Ct	St	Balls	Runs	Wkts	Avge	Best	5wI	10wM
Test																	
All First	39	58	15	456	29 *	10.60	-	-	8	-	7046	3632	130	27.93	8-102	4	-
1-day Int																	
C & G	8	4	2	23	12	11.50	-	-	2	-	389	312	8	39.00	3-39	-	
B & H	12	5	1	41	12 *	10.25	-	-	4	-	587	415	16	25.93	4-23	-	
1-day Lge	57	25	10	69	18	4.60	-	-	7	-	2469	1874	75	24.98	3-18	-	

COVERDALE, P. S.   Northamptonshire

Name: <u>Paul</u> Stephen Coverdale
Role: Right-hand bat, right-arm medium bowler
Born: 24 July 1983, Harrogate
Height: 5ft 10in **Weight:** 11st
Nickname: Covers, Drill Sergeant, Flaps, Sec Jr.
County debut: No first-team appearance
Parents: Stephen and Jane
Marital status: Single
Family links with cricket: Father played for Yorkshire CCC and Cambridge University and is now Chief Executive of Northamptonshire
Education: Spratton Hall School; Wellingborough School; 'Loughborough University in 2002'
Qualifications: 9 GCSEs, 3 A-levels
Career outside cricket: Further education
Off-season: 'Am taking a gap year from education and will spend the winter playing cricket in Australia'
Overseas tours: Northamptonshire U19 to South Africa 2000

Cricketers particularly admired: Allan Lamb, Steve Waugh, Michael Atherton, Jacques Kallis
Young players to look out for: Mark Powell, David Paynter, Monty Panesar, Andrew Daniels
Other sports played: Rugby, golf ('or at least attempt to!')
Other sports followed: Rugby (Northampton Saints), football
Injuries: Out for three weeks with 'slight shin problem'
Relaxations: Socialising and going out with friends; listening to music; watching and playing sports
Extras: Progressed through county age groups, captaining at U14, U15, U17 and U19. Played for Northamptonshire Board XI in the C&G 2001 and in the first round of the C&G 2002, which was played in August 2001. Represented East England Schools U18. Joined the Northants Academy in 2000
Opinions on cricket: 'English cricket is beginning to show signs of improvement, resulting from the changes introduced by the ECB. I feel, therefore, that people ought to recognise these improvements and not return to the same old "doomed English cricket" attitude at the first sign of failure. It should be remembered that Team England is not yet the finished article.'

2001 Season (did not make any first-class or one-day appearances)

Career Performances

	M	Inns	NO	Runs	HS	Avge	100s	50s	Ct	St	Balls	Runs	Wkts	Avge	Best	5wl	10wM
Test																	
All First																	
1-day Int																	
C & G	2	2	0	21	19	10.50	-	-	2	-	96	48	1	48.00	1-21	-	
B & H																	
1-day Lge																	

24. Which current county chairman bowled his 12 overs at a cost of only three runs v Suffolk in the 1985 NatWest?

COWAN, A. P. Essex

Name: <u>Ashley</u> Preston Cowan
Role: Right-hand bat, right-arm fast-medium bowler, 'benefit-only wicket-keeper'
Born: 7 May 1975, Hitchin, Hertfordshire
Height: 6ft 5in **Weight:** 15st
Nickname: Dic Dic, Wallace, Vic
County debut: 1995
County cap: 1997
50 wickets in a season: 1
1st-Class 50s: 7
1st-Class 5 w. in innings: 7
1st-Class catches: 42
One-Day 5 w. in innings: 2
Place in batting averages: 214th av. 17.14 (2000 204th av. 17.50)
Place in bowling averages: 132nd av. 46.12 (2000 56th av. 25.00)
Strike rate: 84.12 (career 60.71)
Parents: Jeff and Pam
Wife and date of marriage: Cath, 14 October 2001
Family links with cricket: 'Father played village cricket. Mother made the teas'
Education: Kingshott Pre-Prep; Framlingham College; 'Essex County Cricket Club'
Qualifications: 8 GCSEs, 3 A-levels
Career outside cricket: Business
Off-season: 'Working for an IT company in London'
Overseas tours: England to West Indies 1997-98
Overseas teams played for: Zingari CC, Durban 1995-97
Career highlights to date: 'Getting England blazer. Winning finals at Lord's'
Cricket moments to forget: 'Any time I get smashed around the park. Losing [NatWest] final at Lord's 1996'
Cricketers particularly admired: Ian Botham, Allan Donald, Curtly Ambrose, Glenn McGrath
Young players to look out for: Mark Pettini, Justin Bishop
Other sports played: Rugby, hockey (Chelmsford), golf (single-figure handicap), squash
Other sports followed: Rugby (Saracens), golf, football ('anybody who plays Man U')
Injuries: Out for two weeks with damaged knee ligaments
Relaxations: Sports, sleeping, reading
Extras: Played rugby and hockey for East of England U18. Was the youngest person

to play for Cambridgeshire. Became first Essex player to take a first-class hat-trick at Castle Park, Colchester, v Gloucestershire in 1996. Took three wickets in four balls in the final over of National League match at Southend 2000 to prevent Glamorgan scoring the six runs needed for victory; the over also contained a run-out

Opinions on cricket: 'More day/night cricket. Change balls back to those used in 2000 season. Keep pitches as good as 2001 season.'

Best batting: 94 Essex v Leicestershire, Leicester 1998

Best bowling: 6-47 Essex v Glamorgan, Cardiff 1999

2001 Season

	M	Inns	NO	Runs	HS	Avge	100s	50s	Ct	St	O	M	Runs	Wkts	Avge	Best	5wl	10wM
Test																		
All First	15	24	3	360	68	17.14	-	2	8	-	462.4	104	1522	33	46.12	3-64	-	-
1-day Int																		
C & G	2	2	0	16	14	8.00	-	-	1	-	19.4	4	66	3	22.00	2-26	-	
B & H	3	3	2	69	45	69.00	-	-	-	-	25.1	1	127	2	63.50	1-37	-	
1-day Lge	16	15	0	204	31	13.60	-	-	4	-	129.1	10	568	22	25.81	5-14	1	

Career Performances

	M	Inns	NO	Runs	HS	Avge	100s	50s	Ct	St	Balls	Runs	Wkts	Avge	Best	5wl	10wM
Test																	
All First	90	134	26	1873	94	17.34	-	7	42	-	14511	7934	239	33.19	6-47	7	-
1-day Int																	
C & G	14	10	4	59	17 *	9.83	-	-	5	-	803	528	19	27.78	3-29	-	
B & H	19	13	8	168	45	33.60	-	-	1	-	1024	745	20	37.25	5-28	1	
1-day Lge	79	62	14	589	40 *	12.27	-	-	32	-	3428	2590	95	27.26	5-14	1	

25. Who was the first woman to adjudicate on the
Man of the Match award in a NatWest tie?

COX, J. Somerset

Name: Jamie Cox
Role: Right-hand bat, off-spin bowler,
county captain
Born: 15 October 1969, Burnie, Tasmania
Height: 6ft **Weight:** 12st 7lbs
Nickname: Buzz, Skippy
County debut: 1999
County cap: 1999
1000 runs in a season: 2
1st-Class 50s: 60
1st-Class 100s: 38
1st-Class 200s: 3
1st-Class catches: 81
One-Day 100s: 3
Place in batting averages: 18th av. 57.45
(2000 42nd av. 39.32)
Strike rate: (career 129.75)

Parents: David and Kaye
Marital status: Engaged to Helen
Children: Lachlan William Joseph, December 2001
Family links with cricket: Father played State colts and is life member of local club
Education: Wynyard Primary; Wynyard High; Deakin University (current)
Qualifications: School Certificate, Diploma of Management; currently studying for
Bachelor of Business degree
Off-season: Playing for Tasmania
Overseas tours: Australia U19 to West Indies 1988; Australia A to Zimbabwe 1989,
to Malaysia (Super 8s) 1997; Australia XI to Zimbabwe 1991-92; Tasmania
to Zimbabwe 1995-96
Overseas teams played for: Tasmania 1987-88 –
Cricketers particularly admired: Ian Botham, Geoff Marsh, David Boon,
Steve Waugh
Other sports played: Golf
Other sports followed: Australian Rules football (Western Bulldogs)
Relaxations: Music, home design
Extras: Scored 1349 runs in the 1996-97 Australian season, with five 100s, including
two in one match v New South Wales. Players' Player of the Year 1996-97. Tasmanian
Cricket Player of the Year 1996-97. Scored an unbeaten 115 in the first innings of the
1997-98 Sheffield Shield final v Western Australia, becoming the first player to carry
his bat in a Shield final. Joined Somerset in 1999 as overseas player and captain.
Became the first Somerset player to score a 200 (216) and a 100 (129*) in a match, v
Hampshire at Southampton 1999; scored 153 at the same ground in 2000 to make it

three successive scores of 100 or more there. Scored 94 for Australia A v West Indies at Hobart 2000-01. Scored 1070 runs (av. 66.88) in the Pura Cup 2000-01, passing during the season David Boon's record of 9096 career first-class runs for Tasmania to become the state's leading run-scorer. *Wisden Australia* Pura Cup Cricketer of the Year 2000-01; also Pura Cup Player of the Series 2000-01 (voted on by the umpires). Took over captaincy of Tasmania in 1999-2000 in succession to David Boon; handed over to Ricky Ponting for the 2001-02 season

Opinions on cricket: 'In good shape. Must be careful not to overprotect centrally contracted players. Points for a draw to be reduced or removed. Unlimited time to get full bowling points; 120 overs for batting points.'

Best batting: 245 Tasmania v New South Wales, Hobart 1999-2000
Best bowling: 3-46 Somerset v Middlesex, Taunton 1999
Stop press: Played in his 140th first-class match for Tasmania against Western Australia at Hobart in January 2002, in the process overtaking David Boon's record of 139 matches to become Tasmania's most-capped first-class player

2001 Season

	M	Inns	NO	Runs	HS	Avge	100s	50s	Ct	St	O	M	Runs	Wkts	Avge	Best	5wI	10wM
Test																		
All First	15	25	3	1264	186	57.45	1	9	6	-								
1-day Int																		
C & G	4	4	1	167	63 *	55.66	-	1	2	-								
B & H	4	4	0	191	72	47.75	-	2	1	-								
1-day Lge	12	12	1	331	76 *	30.09	-	2	4	-								

Career Performances

	M	Inns	NO	Runs	HS	Avge	100s	50s	Ct	St	Balls	Runs	Wkts	Avge	Best	5wI	10wM
Test																	
All First	185	326	23	13910	245	45.90	41	60	81	-	519	323	4	80.75	3-46	-	-
1-day Int																	
C & G	11	11	1	430	114	43.00	1	2	2	-							
B & H	7	7	0	269	72	38.42	-	3	1	-							
1-day Lge	42	42	1	1409	110	34.36	2	8	20	-	96	82	3	27.33	3-28	-	

CRAVEN, V. J.   Yorkshire

Name: <u>Victor</u> John Craven
Role: Left-hand middle/top order bat, right-arm medium bowler
Born: 31 July 1980, Harrogate
Height: 6ft **Weight:** 13st 8lbs
Nickname: Cow, Magoo
County debut: 2000
1st-Class 50s: 2
1st-Class catches: 8
Place in batting averages: (2000 135th av. 25.10)
Parents: Vic and Sue
Marital status: Single
Family links with cricket: 'Father played local cricket and introduced me to the game'
Education: Beckwithshaw County Primary; Harrogate Grammar School
Qualifications: 10 GCSEs, GNVQ (Advanced) Business, Level 2 cricket coaching
Career outside cricket: Gym instructor
Off-season: 'Training, working on technical parts of the game'
Overseas tours: Yorkshire to South Africa
Overseas teams played for: Tatura CC, Victoria 1998-99; Deepdene Bears, Melbourne 2000-01
Career highlights to date: 'Playing against West Indies and scoring 53 [for Yorkshire in 2000]'
Cricket moments to forget: 'All bad drops and misfields'
Cricketers particularly admired: Michael Atherton, Graham Thorpe
Young players to look out for: John Sadler, Michael Lumb
Other sports played: Soccer, golf, snooker
Other sports followed: Football (Leeds United), rugby league (Leeds Rhinos)
Injuries: Out for a week with a dislocated finger
Relaxations: 'Cinema, gym, socialising with pals'
Extras: Has Yorkshire 2nd XI cap
Best batting: 58 Yorkshire v Derbyshire, Derby 2000

2001 Season

	M	Inns	NO	Runs	HS	Avge	100s	50s	Ct	St	O	M	Runs	Wkts	Avge	Best	5wl	10wM
Test																		
All First	2	4	1	33	23 *	11.00	-	-	2	-	13	1	69	0	-		-	-	-
1-day Int																		
C & G	1	1	0	26	26	26.00	-	-	-	-								
B & H																		
1-day Lge	3	3	0	66	55	22.00	-	1	-	-								

Career Performances

	M	Inns	NO	Runs	HS	Avge	100s	50s	Ct	St	Balls	Runs	Wkts	Avge	Best	5wl	10wM
Test																	
All First	10	15	2	284	58	21.84	-	2	8	-	126	84	0	-		-	-	-
1-day Int																	
C & G	1	1	0	26	26	26.00	-	-	-	-							
B & H	1	1	0	1	1	1.00	-	-	1	-							
1-day Lge	8	8	0	143	55	17.87	-	1	5	-							

CRAWLEY, J. P.   Lancashire

Name: <u>John</u> Paul Crawley
Role: Right-hand bat, occasional wicket-keeper
Born: 21 September 1971, Maldon, Essex
Height: 6ft 2in **Weight:** 13st 2lbs
Nickname: Creeps, Jonty, JC
County debut: 1990
County cap: 1994
Test debut: 1994
Tests: 29
One-Day Internationals: 13
1000 runs in a season: 7
1st-Class 50s: 90
1st-Class 100s: 35
1st-Class 200s: 5
1st-Class catches: 162
One-Day 100s: 3
Place in batting averages: 69th av. 40.81
(2000 22nd av. 45.28)
Strike rate: (career 132.00)
Parents: Frank and Jean
Family links with cricket: Father played in Manchester Association; brother Mark

played for Lancashire and Nottinghamshire; brother Peter plays for Warrington CC and has played for Scottish Universities and Cambridge University; uncle was excellent fast bowler; godfather umpires in Manchester Association

Education: Manchester Grammar School; Trinity College, Cambridge

Qualifications: 10 O-levels, 2 AO-Levels, 3 A-levels, 2 S-levels, BA in History

Overseas tours: England YC to Australia 1989-90, to New Zealand 1990-91 (captain); England A to South Africa 1993-94, to West Indies 2000-01; England to Australia 1994-95, to South Africa 1995-96, to Zimbabwe and New Zealand 1996-97, to West Indies 1997-98, to Australia 1998-99

Overseas teams played for: Midland-Guildford, Perth 1990

Cricketers particularly admired: Michael Atherton, Neil Fairbrother, Graham Gooch, Alec Stewart, David Gower, Allan Donald, Ian Salisbury

Other sports followed: Football (Manchester United), golf

Relaxations: 'Playing or trying to play the guitar'

Extras: Played for England YC in three home series – v New Zealand 1989, Pakistan 1990 and Australia (as captain) 1991. First to score 1000 runs in U19 'Tests'. Scored 286 for England A against Eastern Province at Port Elizabeth in 1994, the highest score by an Englishman on an England or England A tour for almost 30 years. Finished top of the first-class batting averages on England's tour to South Africa in 1995-96 with 336 runs at 67.20. Lancashire vice-captain for the 1998 season. Scored century in each innings (124 and 136) v Glamorgan at Colwyn Bay 1998. Topped first-class batting averages for 1998 season. Lancashire Player of the Year 1998. Lancashire captain 1999-2001

Best batting: 286 England A v Eastern Province, Port Elizabeth 1993-94

Best bowling: 1-90 Lancashire v Sussex, Hove 1992

2001 Season

	M	Inns	NO	Runs	HS	Avge	100s	50s	Ct	St	O	M	Runs	Wkts	Avge	Best	5wl	10wM
Test																		
All First	14	24	2	898	280	40.81	2	5	4	-	1	0	2	0	-	-	-	-
1-day Int																		
C & G	3	3	0	67	33	22.33	-	-	-	-								
B & H	5	4	0	100	52	25.00	-	1	1	-								
1-day Lge	13	13	3	357	84 *	35.70	-	3	9	-								

Career Performances

	M	Inns	NO	Runs	HS	Avge	100s	50s	Ct	St	Balls	Runs	Wkts	Avge	Best	5wl	10wM
Test	29	47	5	1329	156 *	31.64	3	7	26	-							
All First	237	387	36	16530	286	47.09	40	90	162	-	132	201	1	201.00	1-90	-	-
1-day Int	13	12	1	235	73	21.36	-	2	1	1							
C & G	26	25	3	814	113 *	37.00	1	5	9	-	6	4	0	-	-	-	
B & H	49	47	1	1522	114	33.08	1	9	15	-							
1-day Lge	111	108	9	2766	100	27.93	1	18	32	3							

CREESE, M. L.   Middlesex

Name: <u>Matthew</u> Leonard Creese
Role: Left-hand bat, left-arm spin bowler
Born: 13 February 1982, Enfield
Height: 6ft 2in **Weight:** 14st
Nickname: Creesey, 'and many others
around that theme'
County debut: 1999
Strike rate: (career 153.00)
Parents: John and Christine
Marital status: Single
Family links with cricket: Father played
club cricket for Calthorpe CC
Education: Millbrook JMI; Goffs GM
School; Durham University
Qualifications: 10 GCSEs, 4 A-levels,
Level 1 cricket coach, YMCA qualified
fitness instructor

Career outside cricket: Student
Off-season: At university
Overseas tours: Middlesex to Portugal 1998, 1999; Durham University to Vienna
(Indoor Championships) 2001
Career highlights to date: 'Second-team and first-class debuts. Learning to pick
Rob Ferley's wrong 'un in corridor cricket'
Cricket moments to forget: 'Getting a golden duck padding up against Glamorgan on
2nd XI debut'
Cricketers particularly admired: Phil Tufnell, Ian Botham, Steve Waugh,
Paul Weekes
Young players to look out for: James Foster, Michael Brown, Will Jefferson,
Nick Compton, Alex Loudon
Other sports played: Rugby, football (Durham University 2nd XI), golf, 'anything I
find time for'
Other sports followed: Rugby (Saracens), football (Arsenal)
Relaxations: '"Swan and Three"; playing bass guitar; socialising; losing money to
various people while playing three-card brag and shoot-the-pot when rain stops play'
Extras: Middlesex Seaxe Young Player of the Year 1997. Played for England U15.
Played for ECB U19 XI v Australia U19 1999 and v Sri Lanka U19 2000. Played
for Middlesex Board XI in the first round of the C&G 2002, which was played in
August 2001
Opinions on cricket: 'University centres of excellence are a step in the right direction
to stop players "drifting" in terms of their skill development while at university, as
they are able to play a high standard of cricket all year round.'

Best batting: 4 Middlesex v Cambridge University, Fenner's 1999
Best bowling: 1-37 Middlesex v Cambridge University, Fenner's 1999

2001 Season (did not make any first-class or one-day appearances)

Career Performances

	M	Inns	NO	Runs	HS	Avge	100s	50s	Ct	St	Balls	Runs	Wkts	Avge	Best	5wI	10wM
Test																	
All First	1	1	0	4	4	4.00	-	-	-	-	153	98	1	98.00	1-37	-	-
1-day Int																	
C & G	1	1	0	34	34	34.00	-	-	-	-	60	35	2	17.50	2-35	-	
B & H																	
1-day Lge																	

CROFT, R. D. B.   Glamorgan

Name: <u>Robert</u> Damien Bale Croft
Role: Right-hand bat, off-spin bowler, county vice-captain
Born: 25 May 1970, Morriston, Swansea
Height: 5ft 11in **Weight:** 13st 7lbs
Nickname: Crofty
County debut: 1989
County cap: 1992
Benefit: 2000
Test debut: 1996
Tests: 21
One-Day Internationals: 50
50 wickets in a season: 5
1st-Class 50s: 32
1st-Class 100s: 2
1st-Class 5 w. in innings: 30
1st-Class 10 w. in match: 5
1st-Class catches: 126
One-Day 5 w. in innings: 1
One-Day 100s: 1
Place in batting averages: 141st av. 27.15 (2000 162nd av. 21.69)
Place in bowling averages: 109th av. 38.62 (2000 113th av. 35.80)
Strike rate: 82.12 (career 79.28)
Parents: Malcolm and Susan
Wife: Marie
Children: Callum James Bale Croft

Family links with cricket: Father and grandfather played league cricket
Education: Hendy CP School; St John Lloyd Catholic School, Llanelli; Neath Tertiary College; West Glamorgan Institute of Higher Education
Qualifications: 6 O-levels, OND Business Studies, HND Business Studies, NCA senior coaching certificate
Career outside cricket: 'Don't know. Media perhaps'
Off-season: Training for the new season
Overseas tours: England A to Bermuda and West Indies 1991-92, to South Africa 1993-94; England to Zimbabwe and New Zealand 1996-97, to West Indies 1997-98, to Australia 1998-99, to Sharjah (Coca-Cola Cup) 1998-99, to Sri Lanka 2000-01 (*see **Stop press***)
Career highlights to date: 'Playing for England and winning the Championship with Glamorgan in 1997'
Cricket moments to forget: 'None. This career is too short to forget any of it'
Cricketers particularly admired: Ian Botham, Viv Richards, Shane Warne
Young players to look out for: 'Everyone at Glamorgan'
Other sports played: 'Give anything a go'
Other sports followed: Football (Liverpool FC), rugby (Llanelli and Wales)
Interests/relaxations: 'Everything'
Extras: Captained England South to victory in International Youth Tournament 1989 and was voted Player of the Tournament. Glamorgan Young Player of the Year 1992. Scored Test-best 37* at Old Trafford 1998, resisting for 190 minutes to deny South Africa victory. Represented England in the 1999 World Cup. Made his 16th England Test appearance v West Indies at Edgbaston 2000, passing Jeff Jones's total of 15 Tests to become the most capped Welshman. Had match figures of 10-191 from 90.3 overs v Northamptonshire at Cardiff 2001. Scored maiden one-day century (114*; hundred from 105 balls) v Middlesex at Cardiff in the Norwich Union League 2001. Honorary fellow of West Glamorgan Institute of Higher Education. Appointed Glamorgan vice-captain for 2002
Opinions on cricket: 'Too many people sticking their noses in when they haven't got a clue what they are talking about.'
Best batting: 143 Glamorgan v Somerset, Taunton 1995
Best bowling: 8-66 Glamorgan v Warwickshire, Swansea 1992
Stop press: Selected for England Test party to India and New Zealand 2001-02 but withdrew from tour to India and was replaced by Martyn Ball; subsequently omitted from revised party to New Zealand

2001 Season

	M	Inns	NO	Runs	HS	Avge	100s	50s	Ct	St	O	M	Runs	Wkts	Avge	Best	5wI	10wM
Test	1	2	0	3	3	1.50	-	-	-	-	3	0	10	1	10.00	1-8	-	-
All First	10	15	2	353	93	27.15	-	3	6	-	328.3	86	927	24	38.62	5-95	2	1
1-day Int	2	1	0	20	20	20.00	-	-	1	-	14	2	67	1	67.00	1-21	-	
C & G	2	2	0	21	21	10.50	-	-	-	-	20	2	99	3	33.00	3-56	-	
B & H	5	4	1	47	28 *	15.66	-	-	1	-	49	1	242	4	60.50	2-53	-	
1-day Lge	15	15	1	570	114 *	40.71	1	5	3	-	102.2	5	363	16	22.68	4-33	-	

Career Performances

	M	Inns	NO	Runs	HS	Avge	100s	50s	Ct	St	Balls	Runs	Wkts	Avge	Best	5wI	10wM
Test	21	34	8	421	37 *	16.19	-	-	10	-	4619	1825	49	37.24	5-95	1	-
All First	249	362	72	7180	143	24.75	2	32	126	-	53597	24402	676	36.09	8-66	30	5
1-day Int	50	36	12	344	32	14.33	-	-	11	-	2466	1743	45	38.73	3-51	-	
C & G	32	26	6	426	64	21.30	-	3	5	-	1924	1167	39	29.92	4-47	-	
B & H	38	33	8	722	77	28.88	-	5	9	-	2021	1335	41	32.56	4-30	-	
1-day Lge	152	125	28	2286	114 *	23.56	1	10	41	-	6340	4592	147	31.23	6-20	1	

CROWE, C. D. Leicestershire

Name: <u>Carl</u> Daniel Crowe
Role: Right-hand bat, right-arm off-spinner
Born: 25 November 1975, Leicester
Height: 6ft **Weight:** 12st 7lbs
Nickname: 'Crowey!'
County debut: 1995
1st-Class catches: 14
Place in batting averages: 269th av. 8.11
(2000 211th av. 17.16)
Place in bowling averages: (2000 93rd
av. 30.20)
Strike rate: 78.11 (career 67.21)
Parents: Jeannette and Eddie (deceased)
Wife and date of marriage: Helen,
14 October 2000
Family links with cricket: Brother Craig on
Leicestershire staff 2001
Education: Lutterworth High School;
Lutterworth Grammar School
Qualifications: 11 GCSEs, 2 A-levels, NCA Senior Coach
Career outside cricket: 'Business world'
Off-season: 'Training before Christmas; Cape Town after Christmas; doing
business degree'

Overseas tours: Leicestershire U19 to South Africa 1993-94; Leicestershire to Holland 1996, 1998, to Barbados 1998, to Sri Lanka 1999, to Anguilla 2000, to South Africa 2001

Overseas teams played for: Old Mentonians, Melbourne 1997-99

Career highlights to date: 'Championship medal'

Cricket moments to forget: 'Playing and missing in nets to Wardy last June'

Cricketers particularly admired: The Waughs

Other sports played: 'Try all sports.' 'Had a hole in one'

Other sports followed: 'Support Leicester at everything and follow Spurs'

Injuries: Out for one month with injury to spinning finger

Relaxations: 'P52; reading true crime and military operations'

Extras: Played for Leicestershire U12-U19 and Midlands Schools U14-U19. One of the Cricketers of the Festival at Cambridge U19 Festival 1994. Won Leics 2nd XI batting award 1998. Played in Leicestershire's victory in the AON Trophy final 2000. PCA representative for Leicestershire

Opinions on cricket: 'Day/night games are the way forward.'

Best batting: 44* Leicestershire v Northamptonshire, Northampton 1999

Best bowling: 4-47 Leicestershire v Surrey, The Oval 2001

2001 Season

	M	Inns	NO	Runs	HS	Avge	100s	50s	Ct	St	O	M	Runs	Wkts	Avge	Best	5wI	10wM
Test																		
All First	7	10	1	73	42	8.11	-	-	4	-	117.1	30	326	9	36.22	4-47	-	-
1-day Int																		
C & G																		
B & H																		
1-day Lge	2	1	0	5	5	5.00	-	-	2	-	7.3	0	30	4	7.50	4-30	-	

Career Performances

	M	Inns	NO	Runs	HS	Avge	100s	50s	Ct	St	Balls	Runs	Wkts	Avge	Best	5wI	10wM
Test																	
All First	26	33	6	409	44 *	15.14	-	-	14	-	2756	1332	41	32.48	4-47	-	-
1-day Int																	
C & G																	
B & H																	
1-day Lge	5	3	2	14	5 *	14.00	-	-	2	-	51	40	4	10.00	4-30	-	

CULLINAN, D. J. Kent

Name: <u>Daryll</u> John Cullinan
Role: Right-hand bat, off-spin bowler
Born: 4 March 1967, Kimberley,
South Africa
Height: 5ft 10in
County debut: 1995 (Derbyshire),
2001 (Kent)
Test debut: 1992-93
Tests: 70
One-Day Internationals: 138
1st-Class 50s: 67
1st-Class 100s: 35
1st-Class 200s: 2
1st-Class 300s: 1
1st-Class catches: 208
One-Day 100s: 5
Strike rate: 84.00 (career 90.28)
Marital status: Married with one son

Family links with cricket: Elder brother Ralph (R. E. Cullinan) played for Border and
Orange Free State B from 1984-85 to 1990-91
Education: Queens College, Queenstown, South Africa; Stellenbosch University
Overseas tours: South Africa to Sri Lanka 1993-94, to Australia 1993-94, to England
1994, to New Zealand 1994-95, to Zimbabwe 1995-96, to India and Pakistan (World
Cup) 1995-96, to India 1996-97, to Pakistan 1997-98, to Australia 1997-98, to England
1998, to New Zealand 1998-99, to UK, Ireland and Holland (World Cup) 1999, to
Zimbabwe 1999-2000, to India 1999-2000, to Sri Lanka 2000-01, to Australia (Super
Challenge one-day series) 2000-01, to West Indies 2000-01
Overseas teams played for: Border 1983-84 – 1984-85, 1994-95 – 1995-96; Western
Province 1985-86 – 1990-91; Transvaal/Gauteng 1991-92 – 1993-94, 1996-97 –
Other sports played: Rugby union (as schoolboy)
Extras: Represented South African Schools in 1983 and (as captain) 1984. In 1983-84
became the youngest player to score a first-class century in South Africa. One of South
Africa's six Players of the Year 1989 and one of five Players of the Year 1996 and
1999. In 1993-94 set the record for the highest first-class score in South African
cricket, 337* for Transvaal v Northern Transvaal at Johannesburg. Was Derbyshire's
overseas player in 1995, becoming the first player to score a Championship century
(134) on debut for the county. Set record individual Test score for South Africa, 275* v
New Zealand at Eden Park 1999 (since equalled by Gary Kirsten). Man of the Series v
England 1999-2000 (386 runs av. 55.14). His 112 v Sri Lanka at Cape Town in
January 2001 was his fourth successive Test 100 at that ground. Scored 459 runs (av.
51.00 and including two centuries) in Test series in West Indies 2000-01. Joined Kent

as overseas player for 2001 but his season was cut short by a knee injury; replaced by Andrew Symonds

Best batting: 337* Transvaal v Northern Transvaal, Johannesburg 1993-94
Best bowling: 2-27 Border v Natal B, East London 1983-84

2001 Season

	M	Inns	NO	Runs	HS	Avge	100s	50s	Ct	St	O	M	Runs	Wkts	Avge	Best	5wI	10wM
Test																		
All First	3	3	0	122	63	40.66	-	2	-	-	14	6	29	1	29.00	1-24	-	-
1-day Int																		
C & G																			
B & H	5	4	0	48	20	12.00	-	-	-	-								
1-day Lge	2	2	0	100	70	50.00	-	1	1	-								

Career Performances

	M	Inns	NO	Runs	HS	Avge	100s	50s	Ct	St	Balls	Runs	Wkts	Avge	Best	5wI	10wM
Test	70	115	12	4555	275 *	44.22	14	20	67	-	120	71	2	35.50	1-10	-	-
All First	219	373	53	14110	337 *	44.09	38	67	208	-	632	329	7	47.00	2-27	-	-
1-day Int	138	133	16	3860	124	32.99	3	23	62	-	190	130	5	26.00	2-30	-	
C & G	3	3	2	148	119 *	148.00	1	-	2	-							
B & H	8	7	2	154	101 *	30.80	1	-	1	-							
1-day Lge	14	13	3	465	76 *	46.50	-	4	5	-							

26. Which non-first-class side put Durham out of the 1999 NatWest?

CUNLIFFE, R. J.   Leicestershire

Name: <u>Robert</u> John Cunliffe
Role: Right-hand bat, cover fielder
Born: 8 November 1973, Oxford
Height: 5ft 10in   **Weight:** 12st 8lbs
Nickname: 'Forrest Gump for some reason'
County debut: 1993 (one-day, Gloucs),
1994 (first-class, Gloucs)
1st-Class 50s: 10
1st-Class 100s: 3
1st-Class catches: 52
One-Day 100s: 3
Place in batting averages: 192nd av. 20.14
(2000 219th av. 16.35)
Parents: Barry and Janet
Family links with cricket: 'Dad played in
his younger days for his wife's village team
and was groundsman for nine years at
Banbury Twenty CC'
Education: Grimsbury Primary; Banbury School; Banbury Technical College
Qualifications: Carpentry course, coaching award
Career outside cricket: Coaching
Overseas tours: England U19 to India 1992-93
Overseas teams played for: Richmond City CC, Melbourne 1995-97
Cricketers particularly admired: Robin Smith
Other sports played: Football
Relaxations: Walking the dog, watching TV
Extras: Played in England U19 home series against West Indies in 1993. B&H Gold
Award for his 143-ball 137 v Surrey at The Oval 1996; scored 116* in following round
v Ireland, sharing in a Gloucestershire record B&H partnership (221) with A. J. Wright
(123). Left Gloucestershire during the 2001-02 off-season and has joined
Leicestershire for 2002
Best batting: 190* Gloucestershire v Oxford University, Bristol 1995

2001 Season

	M	Inns	NO	Runs	HS	Avge	100s	50s	Ct	St	O	M	Runs	Wkts	Avge	Best	5wI	10wM
Test																		
All First	5	8	1	141	48	20.14	-	-	5	-								
1-day Int																		
C & G																		
B & H	6	6	0	100	75	16.66	-	1	1	-								
1-day Lge	6	6	1	118	32	23.60	-	-	4	-								

Career Performances

	M	Inns	NO	Runs	HS	Avge	100s	50s	Ct	St	Balls	Runs	Wkts	Avge	Best	5wI	10wM
Test																	
All First	62	103	6	2421	190 *	24.95	3	10	52	-							
1-day Int																	
C & G	12	10	0	234	69	23.40	-	1	2	-							
B & H	26	25	3	910	137 *	41.36	3	5	11	-							
1-day Lge	39	37	5	709	66	22.15	-	5	9	-							

DAGNALL, C. E.   Leicestershire

Name: <u>Charles</u> Edward Dagnall
Role: Right-hand bat, right-arm medium 'dobber'
Born: 10 July 1976, Bury, Lancashire
Height: 6ft 3in **Weight:** 14st 'on a good day'
Nickname: Daggers, Dog Face, Fitzpatrick, Palms, Perrers
County debut: 1999 (Warwickshire)
1st-Class 5 w. in innings: 1
Place in bowling averages: 26th av. 23.25
Strike rate: 41.50 (career 42.91)
Parents: Mike and Jackie
Marital status: Single – 'don't do relationships'
Family links with cricket: 'Dad ran town team'
Education: Bolton School; Bridgewater School, Worsley; UMIST
Qualifications: 9 GCSEs, 4 A-levels, BSc (Hons) Chemistry
Career outside cricket: Singer (Frisco Crabbe and the Atlantic Frantics); shopping channel presenter (Shop! 'The Home Shopping Channel')
Off-season: 'Growing my hair'
Overseas tours: Warwickshire to Bloemfontein 2000, to Cape Town 2001
Overseas teams played for: Newtown and Chilwell, Geelong, Australia 1994-95; St Josephs, Geelong 1998-99
Career highlights to date: 'Winning B&H Gold Award v Worcestershire in 2001'
Cricket moments to forget: 'The dropped catch in Paarl would have to be up there'
Cricketers particularly admired: Gower, Holding, Perryman, Hart
Young players to look out for: Ian Bell, Alan Richardson, Jamie Spires ('no, really')
Other sports played: Golf, football

177

Other sports followed: Football (Burnley FC, 'soft spot for Forest and Villa; hate Stoke')

Injuries: Out for one match with a stiff neck

Relaxations: 'Educating the masses about music; meeting new people; talking'

Extras: Played for Cumberland. Man of the Match, Board XI final 1999 (Warwickshire v Essex). Topped 2nd XI batting averages 1998 and was second in bowling averages. Awarded 2nd XI cap 1999. Took a wicket with his fourth ball in first-class cricket v Oxford University at The Parks 1999. B&H Gold Award for his 21* batting at No. 11 (following 2-18) v Worcestershire at Worcester 2001. Recorded maiden first-class five-wicket return (6-50) v Derbyshire at Derby 2001. Left Warwickshire at the end of the 2001 season and has joined Leicestershire for 2002

Opinions on cricket: 'Too many complaints to make. However, the loan system, which at the moment is useless, could be a huge success. Ask me for details.'

Best batting: 6* Warwickshire v Essex, Chelmsford 2000

Best bowling: 6-50 Warwickshire v Derbyshire, Derby 2001

2001 Season

	M	Inns	NO	Runs	HS	Avge	100s	50s	Ct	St	O	M	Runs	Wkts	Avge	Best	5wl	10wM
Test																		
All First	3	1	0	1	1	1.00	-	-	-	-	83	16	279	12	23.25	6-50	1	-
1-day Int																		
C & G																		
B & H	3	1	1	21	21*	-	-	-	1	-	29	2	125	4	31.25	2-18	-	
1-day Lge	12	2	1	5	3*	5.00	-	-	-	-	88.5	13	301	13	23.15	2-18	-	

Career Performances

	M	Inns	NO	Runs	HS	Avge	100s	50s	Ct	St	Balls	Runs	Wkts	Avge	Best	5wl	10wM
Test																	
All First	6	4	2	12	6*	6.00	-	-	-	-	987	548	23	23.82	6-50	1	-
1-day Int																	
C & G	1	1	0	4	4	4.00	-	-	-	-	54	37	1	37.00	1-37	-	
B & H	3	1	1	21	21*	-	-	-	1	-	174	125	4	31.25	2-18	-	
1-day Lge	17	3	1	6	3*	3.00	-	-	1	-	785	443	25	17.72	4-34	-	

27. Which wicket-keeper holds the Gillette/NatWest/C&G record for most dismissals in an innings?

DAKIN, J. M.   Essex

Name: <u>Jonathan</u> Michael Dakin
Role: Left-hand bat, right-arm
fast-medium bowler, 'benefit wicket-keeper'
Born: 28 February 1973, Hitchin, Herts
Height: 6ft 6in   **Weight:** 16st
Nickname: JD, Babe Ruth
County debut: 1993 (Leicestershire)
County cap: 2000 (Leicestershire)
1st-Class 50s: 10
1st-Class 100s: 5
1st-Class catches: 16
One-Day 100s: 2
One-Day 5 w. in innings: 1
Place in batting averages: 200th av. 19.18
(2000 32nd av. 41.63)
Place in bowling averages: 44th av. 26.68
(2000 140th av. 45.78)
Strike rate: 45.93 (career 73.56)
Parents: Fred John and Gloria May
Marital status: Single
Family links with cricket: Brother plays for club side Ivanhoe
Education: King Edward VII School, Johannesburg, South Africa
Qualifications: Matriculation
Career outside cricket: Furniture removal man
Off-season: Playing in Tasmania for North Hobart
Overseas tours: Rutland Tourists to Jersey 1992; Leicestershire CCC to South Africa
1996, 1997, to Barbados, to Sri Lanka, to Anguilla
Overseas teams played for: Wanderers, South Africa 1986-92; Alberts, South Africa
1993; Kaponga CC, New Zealand 1995-96; North Hobart, Tasmania 2001-02
Career highlights to date: 'Winning two Championships'
Cricket moments to forget: 'Losing two Lord's finals'
Cricketers particularly admired: Daz 'fast and nasty' Maddy, Tim Mason,
Aftab Habib, Ian Blackwell, 'Mr T' Malcolm
Young players to look out for: Tom New
Other sports followed: Rugby union (Leicester Tigers)
Injuries: Out for about eight weeks with a 'torn oblique'
Relaxations: Eating out
Extras: Won three Bain Hogg trophies in four years. Scored 193 against Middlesex in
the Bain Hogg in 1996. Won the Gold Award against Durham in the 1996 B&H. C&G
Man of the Match award for his 179 v Wales at Swansea 2001; it was the fourth
highest individual score in Gillette/NatWest/C&G history and the highest in the

50-over format of the competition. Left Leicestershire at the end of the 2001 season and has joined Essex for 2002

Opinions on cricket: 'Sunday League should be 40 overs with two white balls.'
Best batting: 190 Leicestershire v Northamptonshire, Northampton 1997
Best bowling: 4-27 Leicestershire v Worcestershire, Worcester 1999

2001 Season

	M	Inns	NO	Runs	HS	Avge	100s	50s	Ct	St	O	M	Runs	Wkts	Avge	Best	5wI	10wM
Test																		
All First	7	11	0	211	69	19.18	-	1	1	-	122.3	23	427	16	26.68	4-53	-	-
1-day Int																		
C & G	3	3	0	207	179	69.00	1	-	1	-	16	0	65	4	16.25	2-23		
B & H	5	5	2	88	39	29.33	-	-	1	-	32.1	1	145	3	48.33	1-19	-	
1-day Lge	12	10	1	262	65	29.11	-	1	1	-	60.3	3	237	7	33.85	3-14	-	

Career Performances

	M	Inns	NO	Runs	HS	Avge	100s	50s	Ct	St	Balls	Runs	Wkts	Avge	Best	5wI	10wM
Test																	
All First	49	71	6	1957	190	30.10	5	10	16	-	5444	2750	74	37.16	4-27	-	-
1-day Int																	
C & G	10	10	0	275	179	27.50	1	-	1	-	324	224	7	32.00	2-23	-	
B & H	21	17	5	402	108 *	33.50	1	-	6	-	664	539	16	33.68	3-68	-	
1-day Lge	102	89	12	1324	68 *	17.19	-	2	19	-	2727	2328	85	27.38	5-30	1	

DALE, A.   Glamorgan

Name: Adrian Dale
Role: Right-hand bat, right-arm medium bowler
Born: 24 October 1968, Johannesburg, South Africa
Height: 5ft 11in **Weight:** 11st 11lbs
Nickname: Arthur
County debut: 1989
County cap: 1992
1000 runs in a season: 4
1st-Class 50s: 53
1st-Class 100s: 18
1st-Class 200s: 2
1st-Class 5 w. in innings: 4
1st-Class catches: 85
One-Day 100s: 2
One-Day 5 w. in innings: 2
Place in batting averages: 28th av. 51.30 (2000 60th av. 34.87)

Place in bowling averages: (2000 78th av. 28.04)
Strike rate: 100.28 (career 69.04)
Parents: John and Maureen
Wife and date of marriage: Ruth, 9 January 1999
Children: Jessica, 12 January 2001
Family links with cricket: Father played occasionally for Glamorgan 2nd XI
Education: Chepstow Primary School; Chepstow Comprehensive; Swansea University
Qualifications: 9 O-levels, 3 A-levels, BA (Hons) Economics
Career outside cricket: Estate agency. Glamorgan marketing department

Overseas tours: Welsh Schools U16 to Australia 1986-87; Combined Universities to Barbados 1988-89; Glamorgan to Trinidad 1989-90, to Zimbabwe 1990-91, to Trinidad 1991-92, to Cape Town 1992-93, 1999; England A to South Africa 1993-94
Overseas teams played for: Bionics, Zimbabwe 1990-91; Cornwall, New Zealand 1991-93, 1995-97
Career highlights to date: '1997 County Championship win'
Cricketers particularly admired: Ian Botham, Michael Holding, Mike Gatting
Young players to look out for: Christopher Tremlett
Other sports followed: Football (Arsenal), rugby union (Wales)
Relaxations: Travelling, eating out
Extras: Played in successful Combined Universities sides of 1989 and 1990. Only batsman to score two half-centuries against the West Indies tourists in the same match in 1991. Took a wicket with his first delivery at Lord's. Recorded Glamorgan's then best one-day bowling figures, 6-22, against Durham 1993. Shared in Glamorgan's highest ever partnership, 425*, with Viv Richards against Middlesex 1993. Scored two centuries in Championship match v Gloucestershire at Cardiff 1999. Glamorgan CCC Player of the Year 2000, 2001. Vice-captain of Glamorgan in 2001. Glamorgan Supporters' Player of the Year 2001. Granted a benefit for 2002. PCA representative for Glamorgan
Opinions on cricket: 'The two divisions system is working well, although there should be less prize money for teams winning the second division and more for those doing well in the first division.'
Best batting: 214* Glamorgan v Middlesex, Cardiff 1993
Best bowling: 6-18 Glamorgan v Warwickshire, Cardiff 1993

2001 Season

	M	Inns	NO	Runs	HS	Avge	100s	50s	Ct	St	O	M	Runs	Wkts	Avge	Best	5wI	10wM
Test																		
All First	15	23	3	1026	204	51.30	3	4	9	-	117	25	410	7	58.57	3-34	-	-
1-day Int																		
C & G	2	2	0	12	12	6.00	-	-	-	-	13	1	43	3	14.33	3-15	-	-
B & H	5	5	1	133	98 *	33.25	-	1	1	-	35.3	3	180	0	-	-	-	-
1-day Lge	16	9	1	221	52 *	27.62	-	1	3	-	59.2	1	254	12	21.16	3-22	-	

Career Performances

	M	Inns	NO	Runs	HS	Avge	100s	50s	Ct	St	Balls	Runs	Wkts	Avge	Best	5wI	10wM
Test																	
All First	213	349	30	10829	214 *	33.94	20	53	85	-	14361	7614	208	36.60	6-18	4	-
1-day Int																	
C & G	34	31	3	805	110	28.75	1	3	6	-	1340	946	29	32.62	3-15	-	
B & H	44	43	7	1073	100	29.80	1	3	12	-	1726	1247	43	29.00	5-41	1	
1-day Lge	176	152	20	3727	82	28.23	-	21	39	-	5369	4597	144	31.92	6-22	1	

DALEY, J. A.   Durham

Name: <u>James</u> Arthur Daley
Role: Right-hand bat
Born: 24 September 1973, Sunderland
Height: 5ft 11in **Weight:** 12st
Nickname: Bebs, Jonty
County debut: 1992
County cap: 1999
1st-Class 50s: 19
1st-Class 100s: 4
1st-Class catches: 43
One-Day 100s: 1
Place in batting averages: 134th av. 28.53
(2000 233rd av. 14.52)
Strike rate: (career 126.00)
Parents: William and Christine
Marital status: Single
Family links with cricket: Brother played
representative cricket for Durham
Education: Hetton Comprehensive
Qualifications: 5 GCSEs
Career outside cricket: Travel agent
Overseas tours: Durham to Zimbabwe 1991-92; England U19 to India 1992-93;
England XI to Holland 1993

Cricketers particularly admired: David Graveney, Wayne Larkins, Jimmy Adams
Other sports followed: Most sports
Relaxations: Socialising, listening to all types of music
Extras: Scored three centuries in 1991 for MCC Young Cricketers at Lord's. Northern Electric Foundation for Sport award winner 1992
Best batting: 159* Durham v Hampshire, Portsmouth 1994
Best bowling: 1-12 Durham v Cambridge University, Fenner's 1998

2001 Season

	M	Inns	NO	Runs	HS	Avge	100s	50s	Ct	St	O	M	Runs	Wkts	Avge	Best	5wI	10wM
Test																		
All First	9	16	1	428	128*	28.53	1	1	1	-								
1-day Int																		
C & G																		
B & H	5	5	1	192	92	48.00	-	2	-	-								
1-day Lge	5	5	1	124	35	31.00	-	-	-	-								

Career Performances

	M	Inns	NO	Runs	HS	Avge	100s	50s	Ct	St	Balls	Runs	Wkts	Avge	Best	5wI	10wM
Test																	
All First	91	158	12	4142	159*	28.36	4	19	43	-	126	81	1	81.00	1-12	-	-
1-day Int																	
C & G																	
B & H	16	15	1	298	92	21.28	-	2	-	-	12	19	0	-		-	-
1-day Lge	51	47	9	1260	105	33.15	1	7	11	-	1	4	0	-		-	-

28. Which county won the first ever Gillette Cup in 1963?

DALRYMPLE, J. W. M. — Middlesex

Name: James (Jamie) William
Murray Dalrymple
Role: Right-hand bat, off-spin bowler
Born: 21 January 1981, Nairobi, Kenya
Height: 6ft **Weight:** 13st 7lbs
Nickname: JD, Nipple
County debut: 2000 (one-day),
2001 (first-class)
1st-Class 50s: 1
1st-Class catches: 8
Place in batting averages: 172nd av. 22.55
Place in bowling averages: 144th av. 57.80
Strike rate: 122.10 (career 122.10)
Parents: Douglas and Patricia
Marital status: Single
Family links with cricket: 'Dad played lots
of club cricket'
Education: Ashfold School, Dorton; Radley
College, Abingdon; St Peter's College, Oxford University
Qualifications: 10 GCSEs, 5 A-levels
Off-season: At university
Overseas tours: Middlesex to South Africa 2000
Career highlights to date: 'Four-day debut. Being part of a [Norwich Union League]
win with 16 required off the last over'
Cricket moments to forget: 'Any duck. Dropping any catches'
Cricketers particularly admired: 'Many – Gower, Hooper, the Waughs,
Ian Botham …'
Young players to look out for: Ed Joyce, Chad Keegan, John Francis, Joe Sayers
Other sports played: Rugby (college), hockey (university)
Other sports followed: Football (Tottenham), rugby (Northampton RUFC)
Relaxations: Reading, music
Extras: Represented England U19 v Sri Lanka U19 in one-day and 'Test' series
2000. Played for Oxford University CCE 2001, making first-class debut against his
county club, Middlesex, at The Parks. Represented British Universities 2001. Oxford
Blue 2001
Opinions on cricket: 'There are too many games played on poor pitches throughout
the levels of the game. The facilities are the biggest difference between England and
Australia – oh, and the weather. We need more facilities such as the new ground at
West End. I think there is a need for more positivity – i.e. not "we are bad" but "how
can we improve?"'
Best batting: 70 Oxford UCCE v Warwickshire, The Parks 2001
Best bowling: 4-86 Oxford University v Cambridge University, Fenner's 2001

2001 Season

	M	Inns	NO	Runs	HS	Avge	100s	50s	Ct	St	O	M	Runs	Wkts	Avge	Best	5wl	10wM
Test																		
All First	5	10	1	203	70	22.55	-	1	8	-	203.3	47	578	10	57.80	4-86	-	-
1-day Int																		
C & G																		
B & H																		
1-day Lge	9	8	3	114	38 *	22.80	-	-	2	-	37.3	3	157	7	22.42	4-14	-	

Career Performances

	M	Inns	NO	Runs	HS	Avge	100s	50s	Ct	St	Balls	Runs	Wkts	Avge	Best	5wl	10wM
Test																	
All First	5	10	1	203	70	22.55	-	1	8	-	1221	578	10	57.80	4-86	-	-
1-day Int																	
C & G																	
B & H																	
1-day Lge	10	8	3	114	38 *	22.80	-	-	2	-	267	194	8	24.25	4-14	-	

DAVIES, A. P.　　　　　　　Glamorgan

Name: <u>Andrew</u> Philip Davies
Role: Left-hand bat, right-arm
medium-fast bowler
Born: 7 November 1976, Neath
Height: 5ft 11in **Weight:** 12st
Nickname: Diver
County debut: 1995
1st-Class catches: 3
One-Day 5 w. in innings: 1
Place in batting averages: 230th av. 14.16
Strike rate: 57.33 (career 65.24)
Parents: Phil and Anne
Marital status: Engaged to Nerys James
Family links with cricket: Father and
brother play in local league
Education: Coedffranc; Dwr-y-Felin
Comprehensive School; Christ College,
Brecon

Qualifications: 6 GCSEs, A-levels, Level 2 coach
Career outside cricket: 'Policeman and possible sales rep'

Off-season: 'Moving into new house. Planning wedding. Working for Lansing Linde, Severnside'

Overseas tours: Wales MC to Barbados; Glamorgan to Pretoria, to Cape Town

Overseas teams played for: Marist CC, Whangarei, New Zealand 1995-96

Career highlights to date: 'Winning division two of the one-day league last year [2001]. Beating Surrey at The Oval in division one of the Championship last year [2001]'

Cricket moments to forget: 'Dropping a catch on Sky in the B&H against Gloucestershire'

Cricketers particularly admired: Steve Watkin

Young players to look out for: Mark Wallace

Other sports played: 'Used to play football (trials for Birmingham City)'

Other sports followed: Football (Swansea City)

Relaxations: Listening to music

Extras: Rugby trials for Wales U17. Welsh U19 Player of the Year 1995. Wales Player of the Year 1996. 2nd XI cap 1998. 2nd XI Player of the Year 1998, 1999. 1st XI Player of the Month August-September 1998. Recorded maiden one-day five-wicket return (5-39; five of the top six) v Essex at Cardiff in the Norwich Union League 2001. Glamorgan's leading wicket-taker (21) in the Norwich Union League 2001

Opinions on cricket: 'All teams to have floodlights installed with the possibility of starting Championship cricket a little later with the prospect of getting more people to watch after work has finished.'

Best batting: 40 Glamorgan v Essex, Cardiff 2001

Best bowling: 3-76 Glamorgan v Surrey, The Oval 2001

2001 Season

	M	Inns	NO	Runs	HS	Avge	100s	50s	Ct	St	O	M	Runs	Wkts	Avge	Best	5wI	10wM
Test																		
All First	4	7	1	85	40	14.16	-	-	2	-	86	16	341	9	37.88	3-76	-	-
1-day Int																		
C & G																		
B & H	4	1	1	3	3 *	-	-	-	-	-	37.3	1	189	2	94.50	1-38	-	
1-day Lge	10	3	2	35	24	35.00	-	-	3	-	68.5	5	301	21	14.33	5-39	1	

Career Performances

	M	Inns	NO	Runs	HS	Avge	100s	50s	Ct	St	Balls	Runs	Wkts	Avge	Best	5wI	10wM
Test																	
All First	13	16	3	164	40	12.61	-	-	3	-	1631	944	25	37.76	3-76	-	-
1-day Int																	
C & G																	
B & H	4	1	1	3	3 *	-	-	-	-	-	225	189	2	94.50	1-38	-	
1-day Lge	20	10	5	62	24	12.40	-	-	4	-	783	582	33	17.63	5-39	1	

DAVIES, M. A.   Durham

Name: <u>Mark</u> Anthony Davies
Role: Right-hand bat, right-arm medium-fast bowler
Born: 4 October 1980, Stockton-on-Tees
Height: 6ft 3in **Weight:** 13st 6lbs
Nickname: Davo
County debut: 1998 (one-day)
Parents: Howard and Mandy
Marital status: Single
Family links with cricket: Grandfather keen fan of Durham
Education: Billingham C of E School; Northfield School, Billingham
Qualifications: 5 GCSEs, NVQ Level 3 Sport and Recreation
Overseas teams played for: North Kalgoorlie CC, Western Australia
Cricketers particularly admired: Andrew Caddick, Glenn McGrath
Young players to look out for: Nicky Peng, Ian Bell
Other sports played: Football, golf, boxing
Other sports followed: Football (Middlesbrough)
Injuries: Collapsed lung
Relaxations: Socialising, golf
Extras: Represented England U19 in one-day series v Sri Lanka U19 2000. Played for Durham Board XI in the NatWest 2000 and for Durham Board XI and Durham in the C&G 2001. Attended Durham Academy

29. Which current broadcaster captained Hampshire to victory
in the 1991 NatWest final in the absence of another,
Mark Nicholas, through injury?

2001 Season

	M	Inns	NO	Runs	HS	Avge	100s	50s	Ct	St	O	M	Runs	Wkts	Avge	Best	5wI	10wM
Test																		
All First																		
1-day Int																		
C & G	3	3	1	6	6	3.00	-	-	-	-	28	3	100	3	33.33	1-30	-	
B & H																		
1-day Lge	5	3	0	14	10	4.66	-	-	-	-	34	5	134	7	19.14	4-13	-	

Career Performances

	M	Inns	NO	Runs	HS	Avge	100s	50s	Ct	St	Balls	Runs	Wkts	Avge	Best	5wI	10wM
Test																	
All First																	
1-day Int																	
C & G	6	4	1	6	6	2.00	-	-	-	-	276	165	5	33.00	1-11	-	
B & H																	
1-day Lge	7	4	0	14	10	3.50	-	-	1	-	288	193	12	16.08	4-13	-	

DAVIES, M. K. Essex

Name: <u>Michael</u> Kenton Davies
Role: Right-hand bat, slow left-arm bowler
Born: 17 July 1976, Ashby-de-la-Zouch
Height: 6ft **Weight:** 12st
Nickname: Dicky
County debut: 1997 (Northamptonshire),
2001 (Essex)
1st-Class 5 w. in innings: 5
1st-Class catches: 8
Place in batting averages: (2000 274th
av. 9.87)
Strike rate: 76.00 (career 67.27)
Parents: Lyndon and Ann
Marital status: Single
Education: Fairfield Primary School,
Loughborough; Loughborough Grammar
School; Loughborough University
Qualifications: 8 GCSEs, 4 A-levels,
BSc PE, Sports Science and Recreation Management
Overseas tours: England A to Bangladesh and New Zealand 1999-2000
Overseas teams played for: Techs CC, Cape Town 1999
Cricketers particularly admired: Nick Cook, Steve Waugh

Young players to look out for: Mark Powell, Monty Panesar
Other sports played: Golf
Other sports followed: 'Wales at anything, especially rugby'
Relaxations: Music, cinema, socialising
Extras: Leicestershire U19 Player of the Year. Represented British Universities; was a member of BUSA's cricket squad in the 1997 Benson and Hedges Cup. NBC Denis Compton Award 1999. Released by Northants at the end of the 2000 season and joined Essex for 2001. Released by Essex at the end of the 2001 season
Best batting: 32* Northamptonshire v Durham, Northampton 1999
Best bowling: 6-49 Northamptonshire v Hampshire, Northampton 1999

2001 Season

	M	Inns	NO	Runs	HS	Avge	100s	50s	Ct	St	O	M	Runs	Wkts	Avge	Best	5wI	10wM
Test																		
All First	2	4	1	22	10 *	7.33	-	-	-	-	38	4	141	3	47.00	3-121	-	-
1-day Int																		
C & G																		
B & H																		
1-day Lge																		

Career Performances

	M	Inns	NO	Runs	HS	Avge	100s	50s	Ct	St	Balls	Runs	Wkts	Avge	Best	5wI	10wM
Test																	
All First	33	48	14	338	32 *	9.94	-	-	8	-	6458	2566	96	26.72	6-49	5	-
1-day Int																	
C & G																	
B & H	6	3	2	4	2 *	4.00	-	-	-	-	272	238	5	47.60	3-11	-	
1-day Lge	2	2	1	4	4	4.00	-	-	-	-	72	57	3	19.00	2-29	-	

30. Which Pakistan Test player took 6-32 for
Warwickshire v Hampshire in the quarter-finals of the 1965 Gillette Cup?

DAVIS, M. J. G. Sussex

Name: <u>Mark</u> Jeffrey Gronow Davis
Role: Right-hand bat, right-arm
off-spin bowler
Born: 10 October 1971, Port Elizabeth,
South Africa
Height: 6ft 2in **Weight:** 12st 8lbs
Nickname: Doxy, Davo, Sparky
County debut: 2001
1st-Class 50s: 5
1st-Class 5 w. in innings: 4
1st-Class 10w. in match: 1
1st-Class catches: 50
Place in batting averages: 158th av. 24.38
Place in bowling averages: 114th av. 39.83
Strike rate: 87.37 (career 79.45)
Parents: Jeremy and Marilyn
Wife and date of marriage: Candice,
8 April 2000
Family links with cricket: Father supported Sussex
Education: Woodridge Preparatory School; Grey High School; University of Pretoria
Qualifications: BA Psychology and English
Off-season: Coaching spin bowling at Port Elizabeth Academy, South Africa
Overseas tours: South Africa U24 to Sri Lanka 1995; Northern Transvaal to
Zimbabwe 1992-93, to Kenya 1994-95, 1995-96
Overseas teams played for: Northern Transvaal/Northerns 1991-92 – 2000-01
Cricketers particularly admired: Malcolm Marshall, Tim May, Roy Pienaar,
Shane Warne
Players to look out for: Herschelle Gibbs
Other sports played: Golf, tennis
Other sports followed: Rugby ('support the Springboks'), football (Middlesbrough)
Relaxations: 'Golf, music, going out with friends, watching good movies'
Extras: Made first-class debut for Northern Transvaal B 1990-91. Captain of Northern
Transvaal/Northerns 1997-2000, during which time the province won the first two
trophies in its history. Represented South Africa A v Zimbabwe 1995. Member of
MCC; played for MCC against Sri Lanka A at Shenley in 1999 and against New
Zealand A at The Parks in 2000. Is not considered an overseas player
Opinions on cricket: 'Still the best game in the world.'
Best batting: 71 Northerns v Free State, Bloemfontein 1995-96
Best bowling: 8-37 Northerns B v North West, Potchefstroom 1994-95

2001 Season

	M	Inns	NO	Runs	HS	Avge	100s	50s	Ct	St	O	M	Runs	Wkts	Avge	Best	5wI	10wM
Test																		
All First	15	22	4	439	52	24.38	-	1	5	-	349.3	82	956	24	39.83	6-116	1	-
1-day Int																		
C & G	2	2	2	41	30 *	-	-	-	-	-	20	3	59	3	19.66	2-37	-	
B & H	4	2	2	2	2 *	-	-	-	1	-	39.2	0	145	2	72.50	1-28	-	
1-day Lge	14	8	1	87	27	12.42	-	-	1	-	105.1	6	523	12	43.58	4-24	-	

Career Performances

	M	Inns	NO	Runs	HS	Avge	100s	50s	Ct	St	Balls	Runs	Wkts	Avge	Best	5wI	10wM
Test																	
All First	85	133	21	1953	71	17.43	-	5	50	-	13110	5687	165	34.46	8-37	4	1
1-day Int																	
C & G	2	2	2	41	30 *	-	-	-	-	-	120	59	3	19.66	2-37	-	
B & H	4	2	2	2	2 *	-	-	-	1	-	236	145	2	72.50	1-28	-	
1-day Lge	14	8	1	87	27	12.42	-	-	1	-	631	523	12	43.58	4-24	-	

DAVIS, R. P. Leicestershire

Name: Richard Peter Davis
Role: Right-hand bat, slow left-arm bowler
Born: 18 March 1966, Westbrook, Margate
Height: 6ft 4in **Weight:** 14st 4lbs
Nickname: Dicky
County debut: 1986 (Kent),
1994 (Warwickshire), 1996 (Gloucestershire),
1998 (one-day, Sussex), 2001 (Leicestershire)
County cap: 1990 (Kent),
1994 (Warwickshire)
50 wickets in a season: 2
1st-Class 50s: 5
1st-Class 5 w. in innings: 17
1st-Class 10 w. in match: 2
1st-Class catches: 157
One-Day 5 w. in innings: 1
Strike rate: 36.00 (career 74.22)
Parents: Brian and Sylvia
Wife and date of marriage: Samantha Jane, 3 March 1990
Family links with cricket: Father played club cricket and is a coach;
father-in-law, Colin Tomlin, helped with England's fitness training for tours 1990-93;
brother-in-law, Raj Sharma, played for Derbyshire

Education: King Ethelbert's School, Birchington; Thanet Technical College
Qualifications: CSEs, NCA Coaching Certificate
Overseas tours: Kent Schools to Canada 1983; Kent to Zimbabwe 1992-93; Warwickshire to Zimbabwe 1993-94, to Cape Town 1994-95
Other sports followed: Football (Derby County), rugby, squash, golf, badminton
Relaxations: 'Eating out with my wife, Sam; television and reading'
Extras: Moved to Warwickshire at the end of the 1993 season after nine years with Kent. Released by Warwickshire at the end of the 1995 season and joined Gloucestershire for the 1996 season. Retired from first-class cricket at the end of the 1997 season to become cricket development officer for Greater London. Joined Sussex for 1998 as a one-day player. Released by Sussex at the end of the 1998 season. Player/coach of Berkshire 2001, for whom he played in the C&G 2001 and in the first round of the C&G 2002, which was played in August 2001. Is also an assistant coach with the England women's team. Joined Leicestershire on special registration during the 2001 season, scoring a 50 (51, batting at No. 10) and recording a five-wicket innings return (6-73) v Northamptonshire at Northampton in his first first-class match since 1997. Released by Leicestershire at the end of the 2001 season
Best batting: 67 Kent v Hampshire, Southampton 1989
Best bowling: 7-64 Kent v Durham, Gateshead Fell 1992

2001 Season

	M	Inns	NO	Runs	HS	Avge	100s	50s	Ct	St	O	M	Runs	Wkts	Avge	Best	5wl	10wM
Test																		
All First	1	2	0	51	51	25.50	-	1	2	-	42	7	161	7	23.00	6-73	1	-
1-day Int																		
C & G	3	2	0	57	56	28.50	-	1	2	-	27	5	99	4	24.75	2-27	-	
B & H																		
1-day Lge																		

Career Performances

	M	Inns	NO	Runs	HS	Avge	100s	50s	Ct	St	Balls	Runs	Wkts	Avge	Best	5wl	10wM
Test																	
All First	170	210	46	2503	67	15.26	-	5	157	-	31250	14704	421	34.92	7-64	17	2
1-day Int																	
C & G	17	9	2	104	56	14.85	-	1	12	-	963	535	19	28.15	3-19	-	
B & H	29	12	5	81	18 *	11.57	-	-	12	-	1508	1063	20	53.15	2-26	-	
1-day Lge	97	49	19	265	40 *	8.83	-	-	31	-	3584	2841	101	28.12	5-52	1	

DAWSON, R. K. J. Yorkshire

Name: <u>Richard</u> Kevin James Dawson
Role: Right-hand bat, right-arm
off-spin bowler
Born: 4 August 1980, Doncaster
Height: 6ft 4in **Weight:** 11st 4lbs
Nickname: Billy Dog
County debut: 2001
1st-Class 5 w. in innings: 2
1st-Class catches: 6
Place in batting averages: 264th av. 9.50
Place in bowling averages: 84th av. 33.80
Strike rate: 63.16 (career 67.70)
Parents: Kevin and Pat
Marital status: Single
Family links with cricket: Brother Gareth
plays for Doncaster Town CC
Education: Hill House Preparatory School;
Batley Grammar School; Exeter University

Qualifications: 10 GCSEs, 4 A-levels, degree in Exercise and Sports Science
Off-season: Touring with England
Overseas tours: England U18 to Bermuda 1997; England U19 to New Zealand
1998-99; England to India and New Zealand 2001-02
Cricketers particularly admired: Steve Waugh, Graeme Swann
Young players to look out for: Graeme Bridge, Ian Bell
Other sports played: Football
Other sports followed: Football (Doncaster Rovers FC)
Relaxations: Sleeping, listening to music
Extras: Sir John Hobbs Jubilee Memorial Prize 1995. Captained England U15. Played
for Devon 1999 and 2000. Represented England U19 in one-day and 'Test' series v
Australia U19 in 1999. Has Yorkshire 2nd XI cap. Captained British Universities 2000.
Recorded maiden first-class five-wicket return (6-98) v Surrey at Headingley 2001
Best batting: 37 Yorkshire v Leicestershire, Headingley 2001
Best bowling: 6-82 Yorkshire v Glamorgan, Scarborough 2001
Stop press: Made Test debut in first Test v India at Mohali 2001-02, taking 4-134 in
India's first innings

2001 Season

	M	Inns	NO	Runs	HS	Avge	100s	50s	Ct	St	O	M	Runs	Wkts	Avge	Best	5wI	10wM
Test																		
All First	9	11	1	95	37	9.50	-	-	6	-	315.5	69	1014	30	33.80	6-82	2	-
1-day Int																		
C & G	2	0	0	0	0	-	-	-	-	-	17	0	71	1	71.00	1-32	-	
B & H																		
1-day Lge	10	7	1	25	10 *	4.16	-	-	4	-	57	4	266	9	29.55	3-28	-	

Career Performances

	M	Inns	NO	Runs	HS	Avge	100s	50s	Ct	St	Balls	Runs	Wkts	Avge	Best	5wI	10wM
Test																	
All First	10	12	1	96	37	8.72	-	-	6	-	2099	1129	31	36.41	6-82	2	-
1-day Int																	
C & G	5	3	0	14	7	4.66	-	-	1	-	233	159	5	31.80	2-32	-	
B & H																	
1-day Lge	10	7	1	25	10 *	4.16	-	-	4	-	342	266	9	29.55	3-28	-	

DEAN, K. J.   Derbyshire

Name: <u>Kevin</u> James Dean
Role: Left-hand bat, left-arm
medium bowler ('still swing it, though')
Born: 16 October 1975, Derby
Height: 6ft 5in **Weight:** 14st
Nickname: Deany, Red Face, The Wall,
George
County debut: 1996
County cap: 1998
50 wickets in a season: 1
1st-Class 5 w. in innings: 11
1st-Class 10 w. in match: 2
1st-Class catches: 7
One-Day 5 w. in innings: 1
Place in batting averages: 248th av. 11.70
(2000 302nd av. 4.08)
Place in bowling averages: 37th av. 26.11
(2000 14th av. 17.84)
Strike rate: 44.26 (career 40.61)
Parents: Ken and Dorothy
Marital status: Single
Education: Waterhouses Primary School; Leek High School; Leek College of
Further Education

Qualifications: 8 GCSEs, 3 A-levels, 1 AS-level
Career outside cricket: Working for Ladbrokes
Off-season: 'Working for Ladbrokes at Derby County and Uttoxeter Racecourse. Writing for cricnet.com'
Overseas teams played for: Sturt CC, Adelaide 1996-97
Career highlights to date: 'Can't split – 1) Hitting the winning runs against Australia for Derbys in 1997; 2) Getting either hat-trick'
Cricket moments to forget: 'Losing in the NatWest final [1998]'
Cricketers particularly admired: Dominic Cork, Wasim Akram, Michael Holding
Young players to look out for: Ed Joyce, Tom Lungley
Other sports played: Football (Blue Circle), golf, tennis, squash
Other sports followed: Football (Derby County), horse racing
Relaxations: 'Going horse racing. Talking with Sutts and trying to keep it vaguely interesting. Trying to stay one step ahead of the practical jokers, Aldred, Wells, Krikken. Playing golf and trying to get my handicap down so less people think I am a bandit'
Extras: A member of the Staffordshire U16 Texaco winning team. Achieved first-class hat-trick against Kent at Derby 1998. Took second first-class hat-trick (Habib, Kumble, Ormond) v Leicestershire at Leicester 2000. PCA representative for Derbyshire
Opinions on cricket: 'As many one-day games as possible should be played under floodlights, as so far they have proved to be a great success. Children should also be admitted free in Championship cricket. The away team should decide whether they want to bat or bowl; this would eradicate pitch doctoring.'
Best batting: 27* Derbyshire v South Africans, Derby 1998
Best bowling: 8-52 Derbyshire v Kent, Canterbury 2000

2001 Season

	M	Inns	NO	Runs	HS	Avge	100s	50s	Ct	St	O	M	Runs	Wkts	Avge	Best	5wI	10wM
Test																		
All First	8	12	2	117	23	11.70	-	-	2	-	250.5	58	888	34	26.11	6-73	2	1
1-day Int																		
C & G																		
B & H																		
1-day Lge	6	2	0	9	7	4.50	-	-	-	-	40.3	4	232	4	58.00	2-25	-	

Career Performances

	M	Inns	NO	Runs	HS	Avge	100s	50s	Ct	St	Balls	Runs	Wkts	Avge	Best	5wI	10wM
Test																	
All First	56	70	25	447	27 *	9.93	-	-	7	-	8447	4725	208	22.71	8-52	11	2
1-day Int																	
C & G	11	3	2	8	8	8.00	-	-	4	-	630	421	20	21.05	3-13	-	
B & H	6	2	1	20	14 *	20.00	-	-	-	-	240	211	5	42.20	2-62	-	
1-day Lge	56	24	15	112	16 *	12.44	-	-	9	-	2348	1850	60	30.83	5-32	1	

DEFREITAS, P. A. J.   Leicestershire

Name: <u>Phillip</u> Anthony Jason DeFreitas
Role: Right-hand bat, right-arm
fast-medium bowler
Born: 18 February 1966, Scotts Head,
Dominica
Height: 6ft **Weight:** 13st 7lbs
Nickname: Daffy, Lunchy
County debut: 1985 (Leics),
1989 (Lancs), 1994 (Derbys)
County cap: 1986 (Leics),
1989 (Lancs), 1994 (Derbys)
Test debut: 1986-87
Tests: 44
One-Day Internationals: 103
50 wickets in a season: 12
1st-Class 50s: 48
1st-Class 100s: 8
1st-Class 5 w. in innings: 55
1st-Class 10 w. in match: 5
1st-Class catches: 110
One-Day 5 w. in innings: 6

Place in batting averages: 194th av. 19.69 (2000 23rd av. 45.13)
Place in bowling averages: 47th av. 27.47 (2000 108th av. 33.48)
Strike rate: 53.47 (career 57.30)
Parents: Sybil and Martin
Wife and date of marriage: Nicola, 10 December 1990
Children: Alexandra Elizabeth Jane, 5 August 1991
Family links with cricket: Father played in Windward Islands. All six brothers play
Education: Willesden High School
Qualifications: 2 O-levels
Overseas tours: England YC to West Indies 1984-85; England to Australia 1986-87,
to Pakistan, Australia and New Zealand 1987-88, to India (Nehru Cup) and West
Indies 1989-90, to Australia 1990-91, to New Zealand 1991-92, to India and Sri Lanka
1992-93, to Australia 1994-95, to South Africa 1995-96, to India and Pakistan
(World Cup) 1995-96; England XI to New Zealand (Cricket Max) 1997
Overseas teams played for: Port Adelaide, South Australia 1985; Mosman, Sydney
1988; Boland, South Africa 1993-94, 1995-96
Cricketers particularly admired: Ian Botham, Graham Gooch, Geoff Boycott,
Mike Gatting
Other sports followed: Football (Manchester City) and rugby league (Warrington)
Relaxations: 'Golf, gardening, visiting stately homes, spending spare time with wife
and daughter Alexandra'

Extras: Left Leicestershire and joined Lancashire at end of 1988 season. Man of the Match in 1990 NatWest Trophy final. One of *Wisden*'s Five Cricketers of the Year 1992. Man of the Tournament in the Hong Kong Sixes 1993. Left Lancashire at the end of the 1993 season and joined Derbyshire. Player of the Series against New Zealand 1994. Captained Derbyshire for part of 1997 season after the departure of Dean Jones. Is the only playing English cricketer to have appeared in two World Cup finals. Took 1000th first-class wicket (Usman Afzaal caught by Karl Krikken) v Notts at Trent Bridge 1999. Left Derbyshire at end of 1999 season and rejoined Leicestershire for 2000. Scored 97 and 123* v Lancashire at Leicester 2000 (also bowled 47 overs in Lancashire's only innings). Shared in a Leicestershire record eighth-wicket partnership for the one-day league (116) with Neil Burns v Northamptonshire at Leicester in the Norwich Union League 2001
Best batting: 123* Leicestershire v Lancashire, Leicester 2000
Best bowling: 7-21 Lancashire v Middlesex, Lord's 1989

2001 Season

	M	Inns	NO	Runs	HS	Avge	100s	50s	Ct	St	O	M	Runs	Wkts	Avge	Best	5wI	10wM
Test																		
All First	9	14	1	256	97	19.69	-	2	-	-	303	66	934	34	27.47	6-65	1	-
1-day Int																		
C & G	5	2	0	49	35	24.50	-	-	1	-	41	3	159	5	31.80	2-17	-	
B & H																		
1-day Lge	10	7	1	68	33 *	11.33	-	-	1	-	74.3	7	324	6	54.00	2-29	-	

Career Performances

	M	Inns	NO	Runs	HS	Avge	100s	50s	Ct	St	Balls	Runs	Wkts	Avge	Best	5wI	10wM
Test	44	68	5	934	88	14.82	-	4	14	-	9838	4700	140	33.57	7-70	4	-
All First	323	458	43	9433	123 *	22.73	8	48	110	-	62692	30302	1094	27.69	7-21	55	5
1-day Int	103	66	23	690	67	16.04	-	1	26	-	5712	3775	115	32.82	4-35	-	
C & G	43	27	4	427	69	18.56	-	1	7	-	2613	1370	57	24.03	5-13	4	
B & H	63	43	9	736	75 *	21.64	-	3	16	-	3427	1960	87	22.52	5-16	1	
1-day Lge	198	150	24	2351	72 *	18.65	-	6	37	-	8121	5916	208	28.44	5-26	1	

31. Which pair of brothers played for Sussex in their
1986 NatWest final victory?

DIVENUTO, M. J. — Derbyshire

Name: <u>Michael</u> James DiVenuto
Role: Left-hand bat, right-arm medium/leg-break bowler, county vice-captain
Born: 12 December 1973, Hobart, Tasmania
Height: 5ft 11in **Weight:** 12st 12lbs
Nickname: Diva
County debut: 1999 (Sussex), 2000 (Derbyshire)
County cap: 1999 (Sussex), 2000 (Derbyshire)
One-Day Internationals: 9
1000 runs in a season: 2
1st-Class 50s: 57
1st-Class 100s: 17
1st-Class catches: 117
One-Day 100s: 2
Place in batting averages: 48th av. 45.08 (2000 70th av. 32.95)
Strike rate: 180.00 (career 143.40)
Parents: Enrico and Elizabeth
Marital status: Single
Family links with cricket: 'Dad and older brother Peter both played grade cricket in Tasmania.' Brother Peter also plays for Italy
Education: St Peter's School, Hobart; St Virgil's College, Hobart
Qualifications: HSC (5 x Level III subjects), Level 3 cricket coach
Career outside cricket: Part-time sports journalist with Southern Cross TV, Hobart
Off-season: Playing first-class cricket for Tasmania
Overseas tours: Australian Cricket Academy to India and Sri Lanka 1993, to South Africa 1996; Australia A to Malaysia (Super 8s) 1997 (captain), to Scotland and Ireland 1998 (captain), to Los Angeles 1999; Australia to South Africa 1996-97 (one-day series), to Hong Kong (Super 6s) 1997, to Malaysia (Super 8s) 1998; Tasmania to Zimbabwe 1995-96
Overseas teams played for: North Hobart CC, Tasmania; Kingborough, Tasmania; Tasmania 1991-92 –
Career highlights to date: 'Playing for Australia. Man of the Match award v South Africa at Johannesburg 1997. Dismissing Jamie Cox at Taunton in 1999, my first wicket in first-class cricket'
Cricket moments to forget: 'Being dismissed by Jamie Cox at Taunton in 1999, *his* first wicket in first-class cricket'
Cricketers particularly admired: David Boon, Dean Jones, Kepler Wessels, Mark and Steve Waugh

198

Young players to look out for: Shane Watson ('young Tasmanian all-rounder')
Other sports played: Australian Rules (Tasmanian U15, U16 and Sandy Bay FC)
Other sports followed: Australian Rules football (Geelong Cats)
Injuries: Out for two weeks with a sprained ankle; for two weeks with a strained groin
Relaxations: Golf, sleeping and eating
Extras: Scored career-best 189 v Western Australia in 1997-98 Sheffield Shield final, contributing more than 50 per cent of Tasmania's total in their second innings. Joined Sussex as overseas player for 1999. Joined Derbyshire as overseas player for 2000. Scored 173* v Derbyshire Board XI at Derby in NatWest 2000, a record for Derbyshire in one-day cricket. B&H Gold Award for his 108 v Leicestershire at Leicester 2001. Took five slip catches in an innings v Durham at Riverside 2001, later scoring 111 in victory chase
Opinions on cricket: 'We should have PLOs for one-day pitches. Some of the wickets we play on are a disgrace. Old, used slow wickets that turn square won't help the problems England are facing in the limited overs game at international level.'
Best batting: 189 Tasmania v Western Australia, Perth 1997-98
Best bowling: 1-0 Tasmania v Queensland, Brisbane 1999-2000

2001 Season

	M	Inns	NO	Runs	HS	Avge	100s	50s	Ct	St	O	M	Runs	Wkts	Avge	Best	5wI	10wM
Test																		
All First	14	25	1	1082	165	45.08	4	5	15	-	30	2	124	1	124.00	1-16	-	-
1-day Int																		
C & G	1	1	0	18	18	18.00	-	-	3	-								
B & H	5	5	0	209	108	41.80	1	-	3	-								
1-day Lge	12	12	0	342	71	28.50	-	2	2	-	5	0	30	0	-		-	-

Career Performances

	M	Inns	NO	Runs	HS	Avge	100s	50s	Ct	St	Balls	Runs	Wkts	Avge	Best	5wI	10wM
Test																	
All First	134	231	11	8755	189	39.79	17	57	117	-	717	401	5	80.20	1-0	-	-
1-day Int	9	9	0	241	89	26.77	-	2	1	-							
C & G	5	5	1	348	173 *	87.00	1	2	4	-							
B & H	12	11	1	432	108	43.20	1	2	4	-							
1-day Lge	42	42	4	1310	94 *	34.47	-	9	13	-	30	30	0	-		-	-

DOWMAN, M. P.   Derbyshire

Name: <u>Mathew</u> Peter Dowman
Role: Left-hand bat, right-arm
medium bowler
Born: 10 May 1974, Grantham, Lincs
Height: 5ft 10in   **Weight:** 12st
Nickname: Doomer
County debut: 1993 (one-day,
Nottinghamshire), 1994 (first-class,
Nottinghamshire), 2000 (Derbyshire)
County cap: 1998 (Nottinghamshire),
2000 (Derbyshire)
1000 runs in a season: 1
1st-Class 50s: 17
1st-Class 100s: 9
1st-Class catches: 50
Place in batting averages: 171st av. 22.68
(2000 78th av. 32.03)
Strike rate: (career 89.04)
Parents: Clive and Jackie

Wife and date of marriage: Joanne, 6 October 2001
Family links with cricket: 'Dad and three brothers all used to play for Grantham
Town; two brothers represented Lincolnshire Schools and Lincolnshire U19'
Education: Earlsfield County Primary; St Hugh's Comprehensive; Grantham College
Qualifications: 3 GCSEs, national sports award, senior coach
Off-season: 'Getting married; studying at home; working for DCCC; training for
new season'
Overseas tours: Lincolnshire U16 to Zimbabwe 1988-89; England U19 to India
1992-93; Nottinghamshire to Cape Town 1992-93, to Johannesburg 1996-97, 1997-98,
1998-99; Derbyshire to Portugal 2000
Overseas teams played for: South Barwon, Geelong, Melbourne 1995-96; East
Shirley, Christchurch, New Zealand 1997-98 ('didn't complete season')
Career highlights to date: 'Probably 145* v Pakistan on my birthday this year
[2001], plus any first-class hundred scored'
Cricket moments to forget: 'Dropping a catch and breaking my nose for Notts v
Derbys. Most of 2001 season'
Cricketers particularly admired: Robin Smith, Mike Gatting, Malcolm Marshall,
Jimmy Adams
Young players to look out for: Nathan Dumelow
Other sports played: Golf (nine handicap), squash
Other sports followed: Ice hockey (Nottingham Panthers, New York Rangers), 'most
football', golf

Injuries: Out for three weeks with a groin injury
Relaxations: 'TV, generally relaxing at home; golf, films, music'
Extras: Played in winning Midlands team at ESCA Festival 1989. Set record for most runs in a season for Lincolnshire Schools and record for most runs in Lincolnshire Schools career. Played for England U19 in home series against West Indies in 1993, scoring 267 in second 'Test'. Winner of the 1997 Uncapped Whyte and Mackay Batting Award. Released by Nottinghamshire at end of 1999 season and joined Derbyshire for 2000. Scored 140 v Durham at Derby 2000, in the process sharing with Dominic Cork in a new record seventh-wicket partnership for Derbyshire (258). B&H Gold Award for his 76* against his old county, Nottinghamshire, at Derby 2001
Opinions on cricket: 'One way or another the third umpire issue needs to be resolved. There is too much talk about their role rather than the cricket being played. There is a role for them in the game, but the people at the top don't seem to know what that is or how much power to give them.'
Best batting: 149 Nottinghamshire v Leicestershire, Leicester 1997
Best bowling: 3-10 Nottinghamshire v Pakistan A, Trent Bridge 1997

2001 Season

	M	Inns	NO	Runs	HS	Avge	100s	50s	Ct	St	O	M	Runs	Wkts	Avge	Best	5wI	10wM
Test																		
All First	14	26	1	567	145 *	22.68	1	1	4	-	10	3	53	0	-		-	-	-
1-day Int																		
C & G	1	1	0	25	25	25.00	-	-	-	-								
B & H	5	5	1	193	76 *	48.25	-	1	-	-								
1-day Lge	15	15	0	309	64	20.60	-	1	4	-	4	0	38	0	-		-	-

Career Performances

	M	Inns	NO	Runs	HS	Avge	100s	50s	Ct	St	Balls	Runs	Wkts	Avge	Best	5wI	10wM
Test																	
All First	93	164	11	4350	149	28.43	9	17	50	-	2226	1171	25	46.84	3-10	-	-
1-day Int																	
C & G	9	8	0	170	47	21.25	-	-	3	-	222	134	4	33.50	2-49	-
B & H	24	19	4	600	92	40.00	-	4	5	-	398	299	14	21.35	3-21	-
1-day Lge	90	90	4	1593	74 *	18.52	-	6	21	-	1013	971	21	46.23	2-16	-

32. Who became the first captain to lead his county to all four domestic titles when his side won the NatWest Trophy in 1985?

DRAKES, V. C.   Warwickshire

Name: <u>Vasbert</u> Conniel Drakes
Role: Right-hand bat, right-arm fast bowler
Born: 5 August 1969, St Michael's, Barbados
Height: 6ft 2in **Weight:** 12st
County debut: 1996 (Sussex),
1999 (Nottinghamshire), 2001
(Warwickshire)
County cap: 1996 (Sussex),
1999 (Nottinghamshire), 2001
(Warwickshire)
One-Day Internationals: 5
50 wickets in a season: 1
1st-Class 50s: 16
1st-Class 100s: 4
1st-Class 5 w. innings: 23
1st-Class 10 w. in match: 3
1st-Class catches: 40
One-Day 5 w. in innings: 2

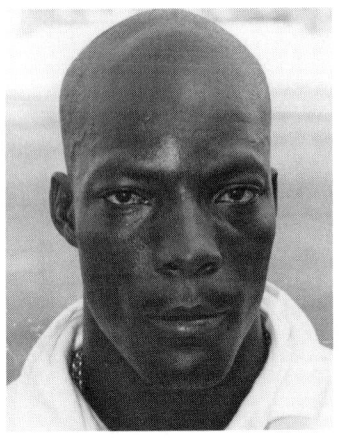

Place in batting averages: 188th av. 20.90
Place in bowling averages: 101st av. 36.59
Strike rate: 72.19 (career 48.90)
Parents: Leon and Caroline
Family links with cricket: 'Sir Francis Drake is the famous bowler in the family – the only bowler to receive a knighthood. Introduced cricket to Barbados on an away day'
Education: St Lucy Secondary and College School, Barbados
Qualifications: NCA coach
Career outside cricket: Electrician
Overseas tours: Barbados U19 to UK 1987; Barbados U21 to UK 1990; Barbados to South Africa 1992; West Indies to England 1995
Overseas teams played for: Barbados 1991-92 – 1997-98; Border, South Africa 1996-97 –
Cricketers particularly admired: Desmond Haynes, Malcolm Marshall, 'and all successful fast bowlers throughout the world'
Other sports followed: Tennis, golf, basketball, football (Arsenal) and volleyball
Relaxations: Listening to music
Extras: Played for West Indies in One-Day International series against Australia in 1994-95. Once took 9-2 for Lamhey CC. Was Sussex overseas player in 1996 and 1997. Took 56 wickets for Border 1998-99, two short of the South African record shared by Peter Pollock and Sylvester Clarke. Joined Nottinghamshire as overseas player for 1999 on one-year contract. Took nine wickets on Championship debut for the county, v Worcestershire at Trent Bridge 1999. Took four wickets in four balls for

Nottinghamshire in the final over of their National League victory v Derbyshire at Trent Bridge 1999; Derbyshire started the over needing ten runs with five wickets in hand. Awarded Nottinghamshire cap 1999; released by Nottinghamshire at the end of the 1999 season. Took 60 first-class wickets (av. 16.31) for Border in the SuperSport Series 1999-2000 to set a new competition record. One of South Africa's five Players of the Year 2000. Joined Warwickshire as overseas player for 2001. Awarded Warwickshire cap 2001, becoming the first overseas player to be capped by three counties. Released by Warwickshire at the end of the 2001 season

Best batting: 180* Barbados v Leeward Islands, Anguilla 1994-95
Best bowling: 8-59 Border v KwaZulu-Natal, Durban 1996-97

2001 Season

	M	Inns	NO	Runs	HS	Avge	100s	50s	Ct	St	O	M	Runs	Wkts	Avge	Best	5wI	10wM
Test																		
All First	14	13	3	209	50	20.90	-	1	1	-	505.2	107	1537	42	36.59	5-37	1	-
1-day Int																		
C & G	4	1	0	7	7	7.00	-	-	1	-	38.3	5	145	3	48.33	2-31	-	
B & H	6	4	1	13	9	4.33	-	-	-	-	56.2	14	164	7	23.42	3-35	-	
1-day Lge	8	4	2	64	43	32.00	-	-	1	-	70.4	11	279	9	31.00	3-35	-	

Career Performances

	M	Inns	NO	Runs	HS	Avge	100s	50s	Ct	St	Balls	Runs	Wkts	Avge	Best	5wI	10wM
Test																	
All First	131	205	24	4026	180*	22.24	4	16	40	-	24843	12848	508	25.29	8-59	23	3
1-day Int	5	2	0	25	16	12.50	-	-	1	-	239	204	3	68.00	1-36	-	
C & G	12	6	1	118	35	23.60	-	-	1	-	732	442	21	21.04	4-62	-	
B & H	14	10	2	143	58	17.87	-	1	-	-	734	453	18	25.16	5-19	1	
1-day Lge	46	36	8	458	43	16.35	-	-	7	-	2062	1652	57	28.98	5-31	1	

33. Whose brilliant catch dismissed Asif Iqbal in the 1971 Gillette Cup final as he seemed on the verge of winning the match for Kent?

DRIVER, R. C.   Lancashire

Name: <u>Ryan</u> Craig Driver
Role: Left-hand bat, right-arm
medium bowler
Born: 30 April 1979, Truro
Height: 6ft 4in **Weight:** 15st
Nickname: Screw
County debut: 1998 (Worcestershire),
2001 (Lancashire)
1st-Class 50s: 1
1st-Class catches: 8
Place in batting averages: 249th av. 11.62
(2000 149th av. 23.25)
Strike rate: (career 46.00)
Parents: Les and Jan
Marital status: Engaged
Family links with cricket: Grandfather and
uncle played club cricket. Father was captain
of Truro CC for six years and still plays in
Cornwall League. Mother and fianceé keen supporters
Education: St Gluvias CP and Trewirgie School, Redruth; Redruth Technology
College; Durham University
Qualifications: 9 GCSEs, 3 A-levels, 2.2 degree in Sport in Community, Level 3
coaching award
Off-season: 'Training and catching up with people'
Overseas tours: ESCA West U14 to West Indies 1993-94; Cornwall Colts to South
Africa 1996, 1997; Lancashire to South Africa 2001
Career highlights to date: 'Man of the Match award, Worcestershire v
Gloucestershire in NatWest Trophy 2000'
Cricket moments to forget: 'Ducking a yorker from Ian Hunter in 2nd XI game at
Old Trafford and having stumps spread everywhere'
Cricketers particularly admired: Steve Waugh
Young players to look out for: Kadeer Ali, Adam Barber
Other sports played: Football ('apparently')
Other sports followed: Football (Derby County)
Relaxations: Music, 'getting beaten at squash by Tim Roberts'
Extras: CSCA Batting Award 1993-96. Played for Cornwall CCC from 1995. West
Region *Daily Telegraph* Batsman of the Year 1995. Opening bat for Truro CC
(Cornwall champions in 1996 and 1997). Played for ESCA U19 and MCC Schools in
1997. England Schoolboy Cricketer of the Year 1997. 2nd XI Player of the Month
August/September 1998. Durham University 1st XI 1998-2000; played in Durham
University's BUSA Championship winning side 1999. Won NatWest Man of the

Match award for his 61* v Gloucestershire 2000 (the game was later declared void and replayed but award stood). British Universities 1999-2000. Durham University Sportsman of the Year 2000. Released by Worcestershire at the end of the 2000 season and joined Lancashire for 2001

Opinions on cricket: 'Introduction of two divisions has added an edge to county cricket in both four-day and one-day competitions.'

Best batting: 64 Worcestershire v Sussex, Worcester 2000

Best bowling: 1-13 Worcestershire v Northamptonshire, Worcester 2000

2001 Season

	M	Inns	NO	Runs	HS	Avge	100s	50s	Ct	St	O	M	Runs	Wkts	Avge	Best	5wI	10wM
Test																		
All First	5	8	0	93	35	11.62	-	-	5	-	4	0	33	0	-		-	-
1-day Int																		
C & G																		
B & H																		
1-day Lge	2	2	0	9	9	4.50	-	-	-	-	3	0	23	0	-		-	-

Career Performances

	M	Inns	NO	Runs	HS	Avge	100s	50s	Ct	St	Balls	Runs	Wkts	Avge	Best	5wI	10wM
Test																	
All First	20	35	4	573	64	18.48	-	1	8	-	92	77	2	38.50	1-13	-	-
1-day Int																	
C & G	3	3	1	61	61 *	30.50	-	1	-	-							
B & H																	
1-day Lge	11	11	0	140	52	12.72	-	1	1	-	54	65	1	65.00	1-17	-	

> 34. Which Somerset player won the Man of the Match award
> for his 61 not out in his county's victory over Warwickshire in
> the semi-finals of the 2001 C&G?

DUMELOW, N. R. C.   Derbyshire

Name: <u>Nathan</u> Robert Charles Dumelow
Role: Right-hand bat, right-arm
off-spin bowler
Born: 30 April 1981, Derby
Height: 5ft 10in   **Weight:** 12st 2lbs
Nickname: Pig
County debut: 2001
1st-Class 50s: 2
1st-Class catches: 2
Place in batting averages: 182nd av. 21.71
Place in bowling averages: 138th av. 51.64
Strike rate: 79.64 (career 79.64)
Parents: Kate and Robert
Marital status: Single
Family links with cricket: 'Dad plays for
Derbyshire Over 50s'
Education: Foremark Hall; Denstone College
Qualifications: 7 GCSEs

Career outside cricket: Farmer
Off-season: Playing in Tasmania
Overseas tours: Derbyshire U16 to Barbados; Derbyshire U17 to South Africa
Overseas teams played for: Schoeman Park CC, Bloemfontein 2000-01
Career highlights to date: 'Taking four wickets against Pakistan'
Cricket moments to forget: 'Day/night game against Worcestershire'
Cricketers particularly admired: Viv Richards
Young players to look out for: Lian Wharton, Chris Bassano, Tom Lungley
Other sports played: Golf, snooker
Other sports followed: Football (Derby County FC)
Relaxations: Fishing, shooting
Extras: Won all Derbyshire age-group awards. Played for Derbyshire Board XI in the
NatWest 1999 and 2000. Took 4-81 on first-class debut v Pakistanis at Derby 2001,
including the wickets of Yousuf Youhana, Inzamam-ul-Haq and Abdur Razzaq.
Scored 50* on Championship debut v Hampshire at Derby 2001; his first
Championship wicket (Will Kendall, caught at the wicket) was also Karl Krikken's
500th first-class dismissal
Opinions on cricket: 'More young players should play.'
Best batting: 61 Derbyshire v Middlesex, Southgate 2001
Best bowling: 4-81 Derbyshire v Pakistanis, Derby 2001

2001 Season

	M	Inns	NO	Runs	HS	Avge	100s	50s	Ct	St	O	M	Runs	Wkts	Avge	Best	5wI	10wM
Test																		
All First	9	15	1	304	61	21.71	-	2	2	-	185.5	34	723	14	51.64	4-81	-	-
1-day Int																		
C & G	1	1	0	0	0	0.00	-	-	-	-	7	0	27	0	-		-	-
B & H	1	1	0	18	18	18.00	-	-	-	-	10	0	46	1	46.00	1-46	-	
1-day Lge	10	9	2	145	33	20.71	-	-	1	-	65	3	345	11	31.36	3-32	-	

Career Performances

	M	Inns	NO	Runs	HS	Avge	100s	50s	Ct	St	Balls	Runs	Wkts	Avge	Best	5wI	10wM
Test																	
All First	9	15	1	304	61	21.71	-	2	2	-	1115	723	14	51.64	4-81	-	-
1-day Int																	
C & G	3	3	0	56	32	18.66	-	-	-	-	132	90	2	45.00	2-21	-	
B & H	1	1	0	18	18	18.00	-	-	-	-	60	46	1	46.00	1-46	-	
1-day Lge	10	9	2	145	33	20.71	-	-	1	-	390	345	11	31.36	3-32	-	

DUTCH, K. P.   Somerset

Name: <u>Keith</u> Philip Dutch
Role: Right-hand bat, off-spin bowler
Born: 21 March 1973, Harrow, Middlesex
Height: 5ft 9in **Weight:** 11st 4lbs
Nickname: Dutchy, Oik
County debut: 1993 (Middlesex),
2001 (Somerset)
County cap: 2001 (Somerset)
1st-Class 50s: 6
1st-Class 100s: 1
1st-Class 5 w. in innings: 1
1st-Class catches: 41
One-Day 5 w. in innings: 2
Place in batting averages: 130th av. 29.44
(2000 151st av. 22.85)
Place in bowling averages: 98th av. 36.22
(2000 31st av. 21.52)
Strike rate: 62.19 (career 63.84)
Parents: Alan and Ann
Wife and date of marriage: Emma, 11 November 2000
Children: Lauren Beth Amy, 15 January 1999
Family links with cricket: Father coached

Education: Nower Hill High School, Pinner; Weald College, Harrow
Qualifications: 5 GCSEs, 1 AS-level, staff tutor coach
Off-season: Coaching
Overseas tours: MCC to Central and East Africa 1997, to Canada 2000-01
Overseas teams played for: Worcester United, South Africa 1992-93; Geelong City, Australia, 1994; Rygersdal CC, Cape Town 1997-98
Career highlights to date: 'Man of the Match award in C&G semi-final and winning C&G final 2001'
Cricketers particularly admired: Mark Ramprakash, John Emburey
Young players to look out for: Owais Shah, David Nash, Stephen Peters, Ed Joyce
Other sports followed: Football (Arsenal FC)
Relaxations: Music, TV and shopping for clothes
Extras: Middlesex 2nd XI Player of the Year 1995. In 1996 scored over 1,000 2nd XI Championship runs and took 63 wickets, setting in the process a record for the highest-ever batting total (261 v Somerset) and best bowling figures (15 for 157 v Leicestershire) by a Middlesex player in the history of the 2nd XI Championship. 2nd XI Championship Player of the Year in 1993, 1996 and 1999. Took five catches in Cambridge University's first innings at Fenner's 2000. Scored 91 and took 6-62 (both then career bests) in a single day v Essex at Chelmsford 2000. Released by Middlesex at the end of the 2000 season and joined Somerset for 2001. Scored maiden first-class century (118) v Essex at Taunton 2001. Scored 84 v Northamptonshire at Northampton 2001, in the process equalling with Ian Blackwell the Somerset record seventh-wicket partnership in matches against Northamptonshire. C&G Man of the Match award for his 54-ball 61 in the semi-final v Warwickshire at Taunton 2001. Awarded Somerset cap 2001
Opinions on cricket: 'Going in right direction. Could benefit from a few less counties. Two divisions seems to be strengthening the game.'
Best batting: 118 Somerset v Essex, Taunton 2001
Best bowling: 6-62 Middlesex v Essex, Chelmsford 2000

2001 Season

	M	Inns	NO	Runs	HS	Avge	100s	50s	Ct	St	O	M	Runs	Wkts	Avge	Best	5wI	10wM
Test																		
All First	16	22	4	530	118	29.44	1	3	19	-	367	64	1268	35	36.22	4-32	-	-
1-day Int																		
C & G	5	3	1	68	61*	34.00	-	1	6	-	31	1	141	5	28.20	2-28	-	
B & H	6	6	1	96	55	19.20	-	1	-	-	37	3	134	5	26.80	2-22	-	
1-day Lge	15	13	3	159	28	15.90	-	-	8	-	96	2	452	16	28.25	6-40	1	

	M	Inns	NO	Runs	HS	Avge	100s	50s	Ct	St	Balls	Runs	Wkts	Avge	Best	5wI	10wM
Test																	
All First	43	57	6	1027	118	20.13	1	6	41	-	4661	2459	73	33.68	6-62	1	-
1-day Int																	
C & G	14	11	5	228	61 *	38.00	-	1	11	-	648	443	13	34.07	2-28	-	
B & H	12	12	2	144	55	14.40	-	1	2	-	408	286	12	23.83	4-42	-	
1-day Lge	77	66	17	854	58	17.42	-	2	23	-	2599	2033	84	24.20	6-40	2	

EALHAM, M. A.   Kent

Name: <u>Mark</u> Alan Ealham
Role: Right-hand bat, right-arm
medium bowler; all-rounder
Born: 27 August 1969, Ashford, Kent
Height: 5ft 10in **Weight:** 14st 4lbs
Nickname: Ealy, Skater, Boarder, Ealberg
County debut: 1989
County cap: 1992
Test debut: 1996
Tests: 8
One-Day Internationals: 64
1000 runs in a season: 1
1st-Class 50s: 42
1st-Class 100s: 6
1st-Class 5 w. in innings: 16
1st-Class 10 w. in match: 1
1st-Class catches: 64
One-Day 100s: 1
One-Day 5 w. in innings: 4
Place in batting averages: 168th av. 23.00 (2000 155th av. 22.53)
Place in bowling averages: 25th av. 22.96 (2000 86th av. 29.29)
Strike rate: 54.44 (career 59.39)
Parents: Alan and Sue
Wife and date of marriage: Kirsty, 24 February 1996
Family links with cricket: Father played for Kent
Education: Chartham; Stour Valley Secondary School
Qualifications: 9 CSEs
Career outside cricket: Plumber
Overseas tours: England A to Australia 1996-97, to Kenya and Sri Lanka 1997-98;
England VI to Hong Kong 1997, 2001; England to Sharjah (Champions Trophy) 1997-
98, to Bangladesh (Wills International Cup) 1998, to Australia 1998-99 (CUB Series),

to Sharjah (Coca-Cola Cup) 1998-99, to South Africa and Zimbabwe 1999-2000
(one-day series), to Kenya (ICC Knockout Trophy) 2000-01, to Pakistan and Sri Lanka
2000-01 (one-day series)
Overseas teams played for: South Perth, Australia 1992-93; University, Perth
1993-94
Cricketers particularly admired: Ian Botham, Viv Richards, Robin Smith,
Steve Waugh, Paul Blackmore and Albert 'for his F and G'
Young players to look out for: Pete Trego, James Hockley
Other sports followed: Football (Manchester United) and most other sports
Relaxations: Playing golf and snooker, watching films
Extras: Set record for fastest Sunday League century (44 balls), v Derbyshire at
Maidstone 1995. Represented England in the 1999 World Cup. Returned a new
England best One-Day International bowling analysis with his 5-15 v Zimbabwe at
Kimberley in January 2000; all five were lbw. Vice-captain of Kent 2001. His 5-13 v
Essex at Southend 2001 included spells of 2-6 and 3-5 either side of lunch
Opinions on cricket: 'In the one-day competitions where fixtures are "drawn", give
the visiting side the choice of the toss to ensure the best possible surfaces are prepared.
Two-divisional cricket is a success, but only two teams from each division to go up
and down.'
Best batting: 153* Kent v Northamptonshire, Canterbury 2001
Best bowling: 8-36 Kent v Warwickshire, Edgbaston 1996

2001 Season

	M	Inns	NO	Runs	HS	Avge	100s	50s	Ct	St	O	M	Runs	Wkts	Avge	Best	5wI	10wM
Test																		
All First	12	15	2	299	153*	23.00	1	-	8	-	226.5	68	574	25	22.96	6-64	2	-
1-day Int	3	2	0	4	4	2.00	-	-	1	-	25.3	0	127	1	127.00	1-32	-	
C & G	3	2	1	42	27*	42.00	-	-	-	-	27	4	74	5	14.80	2-22	-	
B & H	5	4	0	49	19	12.25	-	-	3	-	35	1	123	4	30.75	2-42	-	
1-day Lge	10	10	4	177	34	29.50	-	-	3	-	85	10	359	16	22.43	3-19	-	

Career Performances

	M	Inns	NO	Runs	HS	Avge	100s	50s	Ct	St	Balls	Runs	Wkts	Avge	Best	5wI	10wM
Test	8	13	3	210	53*	21.00	-	2	4	-	1060	488	17	28.70	4-21	-	-
All First	161	255	40	6636	153*	30.86	6	42	64	-	21324	10166	359	28.31	8-36	16	1
1-day Int	64	45	4	716	45	17.46	-	-	9	-	3222	2193	67	32.73	5-15	2	
C & G	24	22	7	444	58*	29.60	-	2	6	-	1307	658	31	21.22	4-10	-	
B & H	46	42	9	908	75	27.51	-	7	17	-	2290	1481	69	21.46	4-17	-	
1-day Lge	151	126	35	2334	112	25.64	1	9	39	-	5999	4448	147	30.25	6-53	2	

EDWARDS, A. D.   Derbyshire

Name: <u>Alexander</u> David Edwards
Role: Right-hand bat, right-arm
fast-medium bowler
Born: 2 August 1975, Cuckfield, Sussex
Height: 6ft **Weight:** 12st 9lbs
Nickname: Al, Steads, Elvis
County debut: 1994 (one-day, Sussex),
1995 (first-class, Sussex), 2001 (Derbyshire)
1st-Class 5 w. in innings: 1
1st-Class catches: 11
Strike rate: (career 65.38)
Parents: Richard John and Angela Janet
Marital status: Single
Family links with cricket: 'Parents drove
me everywhere to play or practise cricket and
have been absolutely wonderful'
Education: Felbridge Primary; Imberhorne
Comprehensive; Loughborough University
Qualifications: 10 GCSEs, 4 A-levels

Overseas tours: Sussex U18 to India 1990-91; England U18 to South Africa 1992-93,
to Denmark 1993
Cricketers particularly admired: Dennis Lillee, Michael Holding, Viv Richards,
Stan Berry and Pat Cale 'for their tremendous support, belief and encouragement'
Other sports followed: Football (Liverpool FC)
Relaxations: Snooker, swimming, training, listening to a variety of music, watching
sport on television
Extras: Lord's Taverners U15 Young Cricketer of the Year 1991 and a *Cricketer*
magazine Young Cricketer of the Month in the same year. Played for England U19
against India U19 in 1994. Released by Sussex at the end of the 1999 season and
joined Middlesex for 2000. Released by Middlesex at the end of the 2000 season.
Emergency registration by Derbyshire during the 2001 season; released by Derbyshire
at the end of the 2001 season
Best batting: 23 Derbyshire v Hampshire, West End 2001
Best bowling: 5-34 Sussex v Pakistan A, Hove 1997

2001 Season

	M	Inns	NO	Runs	HS	Avge	100s	50s	Ct	St	O	M	Runs	Wkts	Avge	Best	5wI	10wM
Test																		
All First	1	2	1	27	23	27.00	-	-	-	-	13	3	40	0	-		-	-	-
1-day Int																		
C & G																		
B & H																		
1-day Lge	7	3	1	18	17	9.00	-	-	1	-	45	1	242	3	80.66	1-25	-

Career Performances

	M	Inns	NO	Runs	HS	Avge	100s	50s	Ct	St	Balls	Runs	Wkts	Avge	Best	5wI	10wM
Test																	
All First	16	25	3	183	23	8.31	-	-	11	-	1700	1109	26	42.65	5-34	1	-
1-day Int																	
C & G																	
B & H	10	9	2	101	43	14.42	-	-	5	-	585	511	8	63.87	2-51	-
1-day Lge	27	15	2	85	20	6.53	-	-	5	-	911	737	18	40.94	3-34	-

ELSTUB, C. J.   Yorkshire

Name: <u>Christopher</u> John Elstub
Role: Right-hand bat, right-arm
medium-fast bowler
Born: 3 February 1981, Dewsbury
Height: 5ft 11in **Weight:** 12st
Nickname: Shrub, Elly
County debut: 2000
1st-Class catches: 1
Strike rate: 51.00 (career 52.30)
Parents: Richard and Susan
Marital status: Single
Family links with cricket: Father played
club cricket and for Yorkshire 2nd XI
Education: Gomersal Middle School;
Whitcliffe Mount School; Leeds Metropolitan
University
Qualifications: 9 GCSEs, 1 A-level, GNVQ
(Advanced) Leisure and Tourism, NCA
coaching award Levels 1 and 2
Career outside cricket: Teacher
Cricketers particularly admired: Darren Gough, Darren Lehmann, Courtney Walsh
Young players to look out for: Michael Lumb, Joe Sayers
Other sports played: Hockey (Bradford)

Other sports followed: Football (Emley FC and Manchester United)
Relaxations: Sleeping, listening to music, socialising with friends
Extras: Played for Bradford/Leeds University CCE and British Universities 2001
Opinions on cricket: 'There are too many games played in the season, which leads to injuries. More NUL matches should be played under floodlights.'
Best batting: 6* British Universities v Pakistanis, Trent Bridge 2001
Best bowling: 3-37 Yorkshire v West Indians, Headingley 2000

2001 Season

	M	Inns	NO	Runs	HS	Avge	100s	50s	Ct	St	O	M	Runs	Wkts	Avge	Best	5wl	10wM
Test																		
All First	1	2	1	6	6 *	6.00	-	-	-	-	17	4	65	2	32.50	2-65	-	-
1-day Int																		
C & G																		
B & H																		
1-day Lge	6	2	2	0	0 *	-	-	-	-	-	41	5	161	10	16.10	4-25	-	

Career Performances

	M	Inns	NO	Runs	HS	Avge	100s	50s	Ct	St	Balls	Runs	Wkts	Avge	Best	5wl	10wM
Test																	
All First	5	6	4	12	6 *	6.00	-	-	1	-	523	240	10	24.00	3-37	-	-
1-day Int																	
C & G																	
B & H																	
1-day Lge	8	2	2	0	0 *	-	-	-	-	-	320	228	10	22.80	4-25	-	

---

35. When Hampshire beat Surrey in the 1991 NatWest final,
both overseas players were Pakistan Test fast bowlers. Who were they?

EVANS, A. W.   Glamorgan

Name: <u>Alun</u> Wyn Evans
Role: Right-hand bat, right-arm
medium bowler, occasional wicket-keeper
Born: 20 August 1975, Glanamman, Dyfed
Height: 5ft 8in **Weight:** 12st 6lbs
Nickname: Troll
County debut: 1996
1st-Class 50s: 6
1st-Class 100s: 1
1st-Class catches: 24
One-Day 100s: 1
Place in batting averages: (2000 190th
av. 19.00)
Parents: Gareth and Lynfa
Marital status: Girlfriend Heidi
Family links with cricket: 'Brother played
for Glamorgan 2nd XI, Ammanford, British
Police, South Wales Cricket Association. Dad
played for Ammanford'

Education: Glanamman Primary; Fishguard Primary; Fishguard Secondary School;
Neath Tertiary College
Qualifications: 11 GCSEs, BTEC National Diploma in Sports Science, Senior Cricket
Coaching Award
Overseas tours: Welsh Schools U17 to Sydney, Australia 1992-93
Overseas teams played for: Marist CC, Whangarei, New Zealand 1995, 1996, 1997;
Gordon, Sydney 1999-2000
Career highlights to date: 'Hitting Wasim Akram for six against Pakistan at
Pontypridd'
Cricket moments to forget: 'The beginning of the 2001 season'
Cricketers particularly admired: 'After the 2001 season, it would have to be
Matthew Hayden'
Young players to look out for: Ian Bell
Other sports played: Football (Wimbledon FC U13-U15), rugby (Fishguard RFC)
Other sports followed: Golf, football (Tottenham Hotspur FC)
Injuries: Out for three weeks after brain scan and lumbar puncture
Relaxations: Classical music, reading autobiographies
Extras: Welsh Schools Player of the Year 1994. MCC Young Cricketer 1995.
Balconiers 2nd XI Player of the Year 1996. ASW Young Player of the Year
Opinions on cricket: 'Standard of pitches in second-team cricket was absolutely
dreadful last season – therefore gives limited opportunity for players to perform to
reach first-team standard.'
Best batting: 125 Glamorgan v Cambridge University, Fenner's 1998

2001 Season

	M	Inns	NO	Runs	HS	Avge	100s	50s	Ct	St	O	M	Runs	Wkts	Avge	Best	5wI	10wM
Test																		
All First	2	3	0	54	41	18.00	-	-	1	-	1	0	2	0	-	-	-	-
1-day Int																		
C & G																		
B & H	1	1	0	0	0	0.00	-	-	-	-								
1-day Lge	1	1	0	4	4	4.00	-	-	1	-								

Career Performances

	M	Inns	NO	Runs	HS	Avge	100s	50s	Ct	St	Balls	Runs	Wkts	Avge	Best	5wI	10wM
Test																		
All First	38	63	7	1503	125	26.83	1	6	24	-	12	5	0	-	-	-	-
1-day Int																		
C & G	3	3	0	93	52	31.00	-	1	-	-								
B & H	3	3	0	24	14	8.00	-	-	-	-								
1-day Lge	36	31	5	545	108	20.96	1	2	13	-								

FAIRBROTHER, N. H. Lancashire

Name: Neil Harvey Fairbrother
Role: Left-hand bat, left-arm medium bowler
Born: 9 September 1963, Warrington
Height: 5ft 8in **Weight:** 11st 4lbs
Nickname: Harvey
County debut: 1982
County cap: 1985
Benefit: 1995
Test debut: 1987
Tests: 10
One-Day Internationals: 75
1000 runs in a season: 10
1st-Class 50s: 104
1st-Class 100s: 42
1st-Class 200s: 3
1st-Class 300s: 1
1st-Class catches: 280
One-Day 100s: 7
Place in batting averages: 10th av. 62.60 (2000 19th av. 45.72)
Strike rate: 36.00 (career 108.42)
Parents: Les and Barbara
Wife and date of marriage: Audrey, 23 September 1988

Children: Rachael Elizabeth, 4 April 1991; Sam, 3 April 1994
Family links with cricket: Father and two uncles played local league cricket
Education: St Margaret's Church of England School, Oxford; Lymm Grammar School
Qualifications: 5 O-levels
Overseas tours: England A to Pakistan 1990-91; England to Sharjah 1986-87, to India and Pakistan (World Cup) 1987-88, to Australia and New Zealand 1987-88, to New Zealand 1991-92, to India 1992-93, to Australia 1994-95, to South Africa 1995-96, to India and Pakistan (World Cup) 1995-96, to Bangladesh (Wills International Cup) 1998-99, to Australia 1998-99 (CUB Series), to Sharjah (Coca-Cola Cup) 1998-99
Cricketers particularly admired: Clive Lloyd, Allan Border, David Gower
Other sports followed: Football, rugby union, rugby league
Relaxations: Music and playing sport
Extras: 'I was named after the Australian cricketer Neil Harvey, who was my mum's favourite cricketer.' Played for England YC v Australia 1983. His 366 v Surrey in 1990 was the third (now fourth) highest score ever made in the County Championship, the second highest first-class score by a Lancashire batsman and the highest individual score recorded at The Oval; during the innings he shared in a Lancashire record partnership for the third wicket (364) with Michael Atherton. Appointed Lancashire captain for 1992 but resigned in 1993. Has appeared in ten domestic one-day finals, a record he shares with Derek Underwood. Represented England in the 1999 World Cup. Passed 20,000 career first-class runs v Northamptonshire at Old Trafford 2001
Best batting: 366 Lancashire v Surrey, The Oval 1990
Best bowling: 2-91 Lancashire v Nottinghamshire, Old Trafford 1987

2001 Season

	M	Inns	NO	Runs	HS	Avge	100s	50s	Ct	St	O	M	Runs	Wkts	Avge	Best	5wI	10wM
Test																		
All First	12	19	4	939	179 *	62.60	4	1	16	-	6	1	20	1	20.00	1-18	-	-
1-day Int																		
C & G	4	4	2	94	73	47.00	-	1	1	-								
B & H	2	2	0	54	32	27.00	-	-	-	-								
1-day Lge	12	11	3	390	101	48.75	1	2	4	-								

Career Performances

	M	Inns	NO	Runs	HS	Avge	100s	50s	Ct	St	Balls	Runs	Wkts	Avge	Best	5wI	10wM
Test	10	15	1	219	83	15.64	-	1	4	-	12	9	0	-	-	-	-
All First	354	561	79	20206	366	41.92	46	104	280	-	759	473	7	67.57	2-91	-	-
1-day Int	75	71	18	2092	113	39.47	1	16	33	-	6	9	0	-	-	-	
C & G	49	46	10	1670	93 *	46.38	-	13	23	-	48	44	1	44.00	1-28	-	
B & H	84	80	23	2849	116 *	49.98	1	23	36	-	54	67	1	67.00	1-17	-	
1-day Lge	249	231	59	6961	116 *	40.47	5	48	74	-	48	48	1	48.00	1-33	-	

FELLOWS, G. M. Yorkshire

Name: <u>Gary</u> Matthew Fellows
Role: Right-hand bat, right-arm
medium bowler
Born: 30 July 1978, Halifax
Height: 5ft 9in **Weight:** 11st
Nickname: Mousey, Mick
County debut: 1998
1st-Class 50s: 4
1st-Class catches: 13
Place in batting averages: 135th av. 28.43
(2000 164th av. 21.31)
Place in bowling averages: 81st av. 33.16
Strike rate: 78.00 (career 83.45)
Parents: Eric and Tina
Marital status: Single
Family links with cricket: Dad and two
brothers play league cricket
Education: Whitehill Primary School,
Illingworth, Halifax; North Halifax Grammar School, Illingworth, Halifax
Qualifications: 10 GCSEs, 1 A-level, coaching award
Overseas teams played for: Bulawayo Athletic Club, Zimbabwe 1996-97
Cricketers particularly admired: Craig White, Mark Waugh
Other sports played: Football (on Bradford City books for one season)
Other sports followed: Football (Halifax Town)
Relaxations: Most sports 'and a laugh with the lads after the game'. Golf
Extras: Set record for most catches by a fielder in a season (11) for Yorkshire Schools
U15 1993. Awarded Yorkshire 2nd XI cap 1998. C&G Man of the Match award for his
89-ball 80* v Surrey at Headingley 2001
Best batting: 63 Yorkshire v Somerset, Bath 2001
Best bowling: 3-23 Yorkshire v Essex, Chelmsford 2001

2001 Season

	M	Inns	NO	Runs	HS	Avge	100s	50s	Ct	St	O	M	Runs	Wkts	Avge	Best	5wI	10wM
Test																		
All First	12	17	1	455	63	28.43	-	3	4	-	156	43	398	12	33.16	3-23	-	-
1-day Int																		
C & G	3	3	1	97	80*	48.50	-	1	1	-	9	0	35	0	-		-	-
B & H	7	6	1	69	38	13.80	-	-	1	-	22	0	97	3	32.33	2-15	-	
1-day Lge	14	14	1	261	67	20.07	-	1	3	-	36	1	185	6	30.83	3-34	-	

Career Performances

	M	Inns	NO	Runs	HS	Avge	100s	50s	Ct	St	Balls	Runs	Wkts	Avge	Best	5wI	10wM
Test																	
All First	32	48	6	957	63	22.78	-	4	13	-	1836	865	22	39.31	3-23	-	-
1-day Int																	
C & G	7	6	1	144	80 *	28.80	-	1	1	-	72	55	0	-		-	-
B & H	14	12	3	185	38	20.55	-	-	1	-	150	109	3	36.33	2-15	-	
1-day Lge	44	37	3	641	67	18.85	-	3	12	-	363	318	8	39.75	3-34	-	

FERLEY, R. S. Kent

Name: <u>Robert</u> Steven Ferley
Role: Right-hand bat, left-arm spin bowler
Born: 4 February 1982, Norwich
Height: 5ft 8in **Weight:** 12st 4lbs
Nickname: Deadly, Bob Turkey
County debut: No first-team appearance
1st-Class catches: 1
Strike rate: 85.71 (career 85.71)
Parents: Pam and Tim (divorced)
Marital status: Single
Education: North Wootton CP; King Edward
VII High School; Sutton Valence School
(A-levels); Grey College, Durham University
Qualifications: 10 GCSEs, 3 A-levels
Career outside cricket: Student
Overseas tours: England U19 to India
2000-01
Cricketers particularly admired:
Steve Waugh, Mike Atherton, Derek Underwood
Young players to look out for: Paddy Bush, Ian Bell, Mark Wallace, Rob Joseph
Other sports played: Rugby, hockey, tennis, football
Other sports followed: Football (Liverpool)
Relaxations: Socialising with friends, sleeping, running, snooker
Extras: Represented England U17 at the ECC Colts Festival in Northern Ireland 1999.
Took 4-32 (including 3-2 in nine balls) on his 19th birthday to help England U19 to
victory over India U19 in the second 'One-Day International' at Vijayawada 2000-01.
Played for Durham University CCE and British Universities 2001. Represented
England U19 v West Indies U19 in one-day series (3/3) 2001. Played for Kent Board
XI in the second round of the C&G 2002, which was played in September 2001
Opinions on cricket: 'I love the game. I want to be involved as long as possible.'
Best batting: 17* DUCCE v Worcestershire, Worcester 2001
Best bowling: 3-52 DUCCE v Lancashire, Durham 2001

2001 Season (did not make any first-class or one-day appearances)

Career Performances

	M	Inns	NO	Runs	HS	Avge	100s	50s	Ct	St	Balls	Runs	Wkts	Avge	Best	5wI	10wM
Test																	
All First	4	5	1	41	17 *	10.25	-	-	1	-	600	337	7	48.14	3-52	-	-
1-day Int																	
C & G	1	1	0	6	6	6.00	-	-	-	-	30	13	1	13.00	1-13	-	
B & H																	
1-day Lge																	

FISHER, I. D.   Gloucestershire

Name: Ian Douglas Fisher
Role: Left-hand bat, left-arm spin bowler
Born: 31 March 1976, Bradford
Height: 5ft 11in **Weight:** 13st 6lbs
Nickname: Fish, Flash, Fishy
County debut: 1995-96 (Yorkshire)
1st-Class 50s: 2
1st-Class 5 w. in innings: 2
1st-Class catches: 1
Place in batting averages: (2000 153rd
av. 22.62)
Place in bowling averages: (2000 117th
av. 36.75)
Strike rate: 78.00 (career 68.81)
Parents: Geoff and Linda
Marital status: Single
Family links with cricket: Father played
club cricket
Education: Denholme First School; Parkside Middle School; Beckfoot
Grammar School
Qualifications: 9 GCSEs, NCA coaching award, Sports Leader's Award, Lifesaver
(bronze), YMCA Gym Instructor
Off-season: 'Training, resting, moving'
Overseas tours: Yorkshire to Zimbabwe 1996, to South Africa 1998, 1999, 2001,
to Perth 2000; MCC to Sri Lanka 2001
Overseas teams played for: Somerset West, Cape Town 1994-95; Petone Riverside,
Wellington, New Zealand 1997-98
Career highlights to date: 'Winning the Championship with Yorkshire [2001]'
Cricket moments to forget: 'None so far'

Cricketers particularly admired: Darren Lehmann, Shane Warne
Young players to look out for: Tim Bresnan
Other sports played: Football (Westbrook)
Other sports followed: Football (Leeds United)
Relaxations: Music, movies, catching up with friends, shopping, eating out
Extras: Played England U17 and Yorkshire Schools U15, U16 and Yorkshire U19.
Awarded Yorkshire 2nd XI cap. Bowled the last first-class ball delivered at the
Northlands Road ground, Southampton, September 2000. Released by Yorkshire at the
end of the 2001 season and has joined Gloucestershire for 2002
Best batting: 68* Yorkshire v Somerset, Taunton 2000
Best bowling: 5-35 Yorkshire v Mashonaland, Harare 1995-96

2001 Season

	M	Inns	NO	Runs	HS	Avge	100s	50s	Ct	St	O	M	Runs	Wkts	Avge	Best	5wI	10wM
Test																		
All First	1	1	1	28	28 *	-	-	-	-	-	13	3	32	1	32.00	1-32	-	-
1-day Int																		
C & G																		
B & H																		
1-day Lge	2	1	0	0	0	0.00	-	-	-	-	15	0	86	1	86.00	1-53	-	

Career Performances

	M	Inns	NO	Runs	HS	Avge	100s	50s	Ct	St	Balls	Runs	Wkts	Avge	Best	5wI	10wM
Test																	
All First	24	32	9	545	68 *	23.69	-	2	1	-	2959	1384	43	32.18	5-35	2	-
1-day Int																	
C & G	3	1	0	5	5	5.00	-	-	2	-	150	87	3	29.00	1-21	-	
B & H	1	0	0	0	0	-	-	-	1	-	48	26	1	26.00	1-26	-	
1-day Lge	24	11	3	63	20	7.87	-	-	3	-	843	595	25	23.80	3-20	-	

FLEMING, M. V. Kent

Name: <u>Matthew</u> Valentine Fleming
Role: Right-hand bat, right-arm
medium bowler, county club captain and one-day captain
Born: 12 December 1964, Macclesfield
Height: 5ft 11ins **Weight:** 13st
Nickname: Jazzer
County debut: 1988
County cap: 1990
Benefit: 2001
One-Day Internationals: 11

1st-Class 50s: 42
1st-Class 100s: 10
1st-Class 5 w. in innings: 2
1st-Class catches: 83
One-Day 100s: 4
One-Day 5 w. in innings: 3
Place in batting averages: 177th av. 21.83
(2000 100th av. 29.43)
Place in bowling averages: 118th av. 41.36
(2000 68th av. 26.89)
Strike rate: 82.54 (career 76.34)
Parents: Valentine and Elizabeth
Wife and date of marriage: Caroline,
23 September 1989
Children: Hannah, 9 October 1992; Victoria,
16 June 1994; Mathilda, 13 February 1997
Family links with cricket: Great-grandfather
C.F.H. Leslie played four Tests for England

on 1882-83 tour of Australia; once hit an all-run seven at Lord's. Father played for
Eton 2nd XI; mother opened the bowling for Heathfield School
Education: St Aubyns School, Rottingdean; Eton College
Qualifications: 8 O-levels, 3 A-levels, granted short-service commission in Royal
Green Jackets 1985
Career outside cricket: 'Sadly I am going to have to decide very soon!'
Overseas tours: England VI to Hong Kong 1997; England to Sharjah (Champions
Trophy) 1997-98, to West Indies 1997-98 (one-day series), to Bangladesh (Wills
International Cup) 1998
Overseas teams played for: Avendale, Cape Town 1983-84
Other sports played: 'Most sports; none with distinction'
Other sports followed: Football (Arsenal), rugby union (London Wasps)
Relaxations: 'Field sports, bonfiring, my family'
Extras: Is great-nephew of James Bond author Ian Fleming. First two scoring shots in
Championship cricket were sixes. Chairman of the Professional Cricketers'
Association. Out twice before lunch batting at number three for Kent against West
Indies in 1995. Took 4-13 and scored a 20-ball 63* (reaching 50 from 16 balls) in a
reduced (ten-over) AXA League match v Yorkshire at Canterbury in 1996. Player of
the Tournament in the 1997 Hong Kong Sixes. Director of *The Cricketer* magazine.
Shared in a new NatWest record sixth-wicket stand of 226 with Nigel Llong v
Cheshire at Bowdon 1999, scoring 117* in the process; the second 50 of his 100 came
off 13 balls. Ran out four opposition batsmen, including three in four balls, with direct
hits on the stumps v Surrey at Canterbury in the Norwich Union League 2001. Top-
scored with 58 and took 5-40 v Gloucestershire at Bristol and scored 125 and took
3-28 v Northamptonshire at Canterbury in the Norwich Union League 2001. Kent
Player of the Year (Cowdrey Award) 2001. Captain of Kent 1999-2001; appointed club
captain and one-day captain for 2002 (*see entry on David Fulton*)

Best batting: 138 Kent v Essex, Canterbury 1997
138 Kent v Worcestershire, Worcester 1999
Best bowling: 5-51 Kent v Nottinghamshire, Trent Bridge 1997

2001 Season

	M	Inns	NO	Runs	HS	Avge	100s	50s	Ct	St	O	M	Runs	Wkts	Avge	Best	5wI	10wM
Test																		
All First	17	23	5	393	59	21.83	-	1	6	-	302.4	59	910	22	41.36	4-53	-	-
1-day Int																		
C & G	1	1	0	40	40	40.00	-	-	-	-	10	0	58	0	-		-	-
B & H	5	4	0	69	24	17.25	-	-	1	-	32	3	110	6	18.33	3-25	-	
1-day Lge	13	13	3	345	125	34.50	1	1	3	-	83	4	354	13	27.23	5-40	1	

Career Performances

	M	Inns	NO	Runs	HS	Avge	100s	50s	Ct	St	Balls	Runs	Wkts	Avge	Best	5wI	10wM
Test																	
All First	214	340	42	8995	138	30.18	10	42	83	-	21681	10123	284	35.64	5-51	2	-
1-day Int	11	10	1	139	33	15.44	-	-	1	-	523	434	17	25.52	4-45	-
C & G	25	23	2	507	117 *	24.14	1	1	11	-	1011	642	23	27.91	3-28	-
B & H	54	49	3	1136	105 *	24.69	1	5	17	-	2506	1757	72	24.40	5-27	2
1-day Lge	198	174	24	3677	125	24.51	2	15	44	-	7129	6031	236	25.55	5-40	1

FLEMING, S. P. Middlesex

Name: <u>Stephen</u> Paul Fleming
Role: Left-hand bat, occasional right-arm
slow-medium bowler
Born: 1 April 1973, Christchurch,
New Zealand
Height: 6ft 3in
County debut: 2001
County cap: 2001
Test debut: 1993-94
Tests: 60
One-Day Internationals: 156
1000 runs in a season: 1
1st-Class 50s: 53
1st-Class 100s: 16
1st-Class catches: 179
One-Day 100s: 3
Place in batting averages: 26th av. 51.95

Education: Cashmere High School; Christchurch College of Education
Overseas tours: New Zealand to England 1994, to South Africa 1994-95, to India 1995-96, to West Indies 1995-96, to Pakistan 1996-97, to Zimbabwe 1997-98 (captain), to Australia 1997-98 (captain), to Sri Lanka 1997-98 (captain), to UK, Ireland and Holland (World Cup) 1999 (captain), to England 1999 (captain), to India 1999-2000 (captain), to Zimbabwe 2000-01 (captain), to Kenya (ICC Knockout Trophy) 2000-01 (captain), to South Africa 2000-01 (captain), to Australia 2001-02 (captain)
Overseas teams played for: Canterbury 1991-92 –
Extras: Captain of New Zealand since 1996-97. Scored career best 174* at Colombo 1997-98, in the process sharing with Craig McMillan in a record fourth-wicket partnership for New Zealand in Tests against Sri Lanka (240). Led his country to series victory in England in 1999, which included New Zealand's first wins at Lord's and The Oval. Topped New Zealand Test batting averages (52.20) on tour of India 1999-2000. Averaged 66.50 in two-match Test series v West Indies 1999-2000. Led New Zealand to victory in the ICC Knockout Trophy in Kenya 2000-01. Scored 60 v Pakistan at Dunedin 2000-01, in the process sharing with Nathan Astle in a record partnership for any wicket for New Zealand in One-Day Internationals (193). Joined Middlesex as overseas player for 2001; released by Middlesex at the end of the 2001 season
Best batting: 174* New Zealand v Sri Lanka, Colombo 1997-98

2001 Season

	M	Inns	NO	Runs	HS	Avge	100s	50s	Ct	St	O	M	Runs	Wkts	Avge	Best	5wI	10wM
Test																		
All First	14	23	2	1091	151	51.95	4	6	22	-	2	0	19	0	-		-	-	-
1-day Int																		
C & G																		
B & H	5	4	0	121	73	30.25	-	1	3	-								
1-day Lge	10	9	0	107	28	11.88	-	-	2	-								

Career Performances

	M	Inns	NO	Runs	HS	Avge	100s	50s	Ct	St	Balls	Runs	Wkts	Avge	Best	5wI	10wM
Test	60	105	8	3615	174 *	37.26	2	29	91	-							
All First	137	227	22	8536	174 *	41.63	16	53	179	-	102	129	0	-		-	-	-
1-day Int	156	150	14	4165	116 *	30.62	3	26	69	-	29	28	1	28.00	1-8	-	
C & G																	
B & H	5	4	0	121	73	30.25	-	1	3	-							
1-day Lge	10	9	0	107	28	11.88	-	-	2	-							

FLINTOFF, A. Lancashire

Name: Andrew Flintoff
Role: Right-hand bat, right-arm
fast-medium bowler, county vice-captain
Born: 6 December 1977, Preston
Height: 6ft 4in
County debut: 1995
County cap: 1998
Test debut: 1998
Tests: 9
One-Day Internationals: 23
1st-Class 50s: 20
1st-Class 100s: 7
1st-Class 5 w. in innings: 1
1st-Class catches: 100
One-Day 100s: 2
Place in batting averages: 115th av. 31.18
(2000 59th av. 35.05)
Place in bowling averages: 110th av. 38.73
(2000 20th av. 19.33)
Strike rate: 77.52 (career 74.73)
Parents: Colin and Susan
Family links with cricket: Brother Chris and father both play local league cricket
Education: Greenlands County Primary; Ribbleton Hall High School
Qualifications: 9 GCSEs
Off-season: ECB National Academy in Australia, Hong Kong Sixes, touring with
England
Overseas tours: England Schools U15 to South Africa 1993; England U19 to West
Indies 1994-95, to Zimbabwe 1995-96, to Pakistan 1996-97 (captain); England A
to Kenya and Sri Lanka 1997-98, to Zimbabwe and South Africa 1998-99; England
to Sharjah (Coca-Cola Cup) 1998-99, to South Africa and Zimbabwe 1999-2000,
to Kenya (ICC Knockout Trophy) 2000-01, to Pakistan and (one-day series) Sri Lanka
2000-01, to Zimbabwe (one-day series) 2001-02, to India and New Zealand 2001-02
(one-day series); ECB National Academy to Australia 2001-02; England VI to Hong
Kong 2001 (*see Stop press*)
Cricketers particularly admired: Jason Gallian, John Crawley, Stephen Titchard,
Warren Hegg
Other sports followed: Football (Preston North End and Liverpool FC)
Relaxations: Listening to music and sleeping
Extras: Won a *Daily Telegraph* regional award for batting. Represented England U14
to U19. Captained England U19 in the series against Zimbabwe U19 in 1997. Scored
61 off 24 balls in Championship match v Surrey at Old Trafford in June 1998,
including 34 from one over by Alex Tudor. Became the 50th recipient of the Cricket

Writers' Club Young Player of the Year award in September 1998. Professional Cricketers' Association's Young Player of the Year 1998. Topped England A batting averages for tour to Zimbabwe and South Africa 1998-99 with 542 runs at an average of 77.42. Struck 50 (including four sixes) on One-Day International debut, v Pakistan, Sharjah 1998-99. Scored 143 off 66 balls, including nine sixes, in National League v Essex at Chelmsford 1999. His 160 v Yorkshire at Old Trafford 1999 included 111 runs before lunch, the first century before lunch by a Lancashire batsman in a Roses match. Won the EDS Walter Lawrence Trophy 1999 (for the fastest first-class century of the season) for his hundred off 61 balls (before lunch) for Lancashire v Gloucestershire at Bristol. Represented England in the 1999 World Cup. Forced to return home early from England tour of South Africa and Zimbabwe 1999-2000 after breaking a foot in the fourth Test at Cape Town. NatWest Man of the Match award for his 111-ball 135* in the quarter-final v Surrey at The Oval 2000. Lancashire Player of the Year 2000. Struck 84 from 60 balls to win Man of the Match award in England's victory in the first One-Day International v Pakistan at Karachi 2000-01; returned home early from Pakistan because his long-standing back problem prevented him from bowling; later recalled as cover for the injured Michael Vaughan and for one-day series in Sri Lanka. C&G Man of the Match awards for his 2-19 and 65* v Sussex at Old Trafford and his 2-46 and 72* in the quarter-final v Durham at Blackpool 2001. Appointed vice-captain of Lancashire for 2002

Best batting: 160 Lancashire v Yorkshire, Old Trafford 1999

Best bowling: 5-24 Lancashire v Hampshire, Southampton 1999

Stop press: Called up from the ECB National Academy tour in Australia into the England Test squad in India 2001-02, recording Test best bowling figures (4-50) in the third Test at Bangalore to win the Man of the Match award; retained in Test squad for tour to New Zealand. Scored 36-ball 50 (52) in One-Day International v India at Delhi 2001-02, then scored 40 and took 3-38 in England's series-equalling victory at Mumbai (Bombay). Man of the Match for his 4-17 in One-Day International v New Zealand at Auckland 2001-02

2001 Season

	M	Inns	NO	Runs	HS	Avge	100s	50s	Ct	St	O	M	Runs	Wkts	Avge	Best	5wl	10wM
Test																		
All First	14	23	1	686	120	31.18	1	2	17	-	245.3	48	736	19	38.73	3-36	-	-
1-day Int																		
C & G	4	4	2	182	72 *	91.00	-	2	3	-	33	2	126	4	31.50	2-19	-	
B & H	4	3	0	24	15	8.00	-	-	2	-	18	1	52	5	10.40	3-12	-	
1-day Lge	13	13	0	269	78	20.69	-	1	2	-	60.5	4	271	12	22.58	3-16	-	

Career Performances

	M	Inns	NO	Runs	HS	Avge	100s	50s	Ct	St	Balls	Runs	Wkts	Avge	Best	5wI	10wM
Test	9	14	0	233	42	16.64	-	-	4	-	827	385	7	55.00	2-31	-	-
All First	80	124	10	3941	160	34.57	7	20	100	-	5306	2412	71	33.97	5-24	1	-
1-day Int	23	18	1	342	84	20.11	-	2	4	-	266	248	7	35.42	2-3	-	
C & G	17	15	4	567	135 *	51.54	1	3	10	-	485	294	8	36.75	2-19	-	
B & H	20	17	1	345	92	21.56	-	2	9	-	570	305	14	21.78	3-12	-	
1-day Lge	54	53	2	1282	143	25.13	1	6	14	-	1235	900	43	20.93	4-24	-	

FLOWER, A. Essex

Name: Andrew (<u>Andy</u>) Flower
Role: Left-hand bat, wicket-keeper,
occasional right-arm medium/off-spin bowler
Born: 28 April 1968, Cape Town,
South Africa
Nickname: Petals
County debut: No first-team appearance
Test debut: 1992-93
Tests: 52
One-Day Internationals: 172
1st-Class 50s: 42
1st-Class 100s: 21
1st-Class 200s: 2
1st-Class catches: 237
1st-Class stumpings: 18
One-Day 100s: 2
Strike rate: (career 115.50)
Family links with cricket: Younger brother
Grant also plays for Zimbabwe
Education: North Park School, Harare; Vainona High School
Overseas tours: Zimbabwe to Australia and New Zealand (World Cup) 1991-92,
to India 1992-93, to Pakistan 1993-94, to Australia (one-day series) 1994-95, to New
Zealand 1995-96, to India and Pakistan (World Cup) 1995-96, to Sri Lanka and
Pakistan 1996-97, to Sri Lanka and New Zealand 1997-98, to Pakistan 1998-99,
to UK, Ireland and Holland (World Cup) 1999, to South Africa 1999-2000, to Sri
Lanka 1999-2000, to West Indies 1999-2000, to England 2000, to India and New
Zealand 2000-01, to Australia (one-day series) 2000-01, to Bangladesh, Sri Lanka and
India 2001-02
Overseas teams played for: Mashonaland 1993-94 –
Other sports played: Tennis, squash; rugby, hockey (at school)
Extras: Captained Zimbabwe Schools. Made first-class debut for ZCU President's XI

v Young West Indies at Harare 1986. Has represented Zimbabwe since 1988-89. Has played club cricket in the Birmingham League, the Central Lancashire League and in Holland. Scored century (115*) on One-Day International debut v Sri Lanka at New Plymouth in the 1992 World Cup, batting right through the Zimbabwe innings. Appeared in Zimbabwe's inaugural Test, v India at Harare 1992-93, scoring 59. Captain of Zimbabwe 1993-94 – 1995-96 and 1999-2000. Scored 156 v Pakistan at Harare 1994-95 in Zimbabwe's first Test win, in the process sharing with Grant Flower (201*) in a fourth-wicket stand of 269, the highest partnership between brothers in Test cricket and at the time the highest partnership for Zimbabwe for any wicket in Tests. Coached Oxford University 1997. Scored 100* v Pakistan at Bulawayo 1997-98, in the process sharing with Murray Goodwin in a new record partnership for Zimbabwe for any wicket in Tests (277*). Scored maiden Test double century (232*) v India at Nagpur 2000-01 to help save the match after Zimbabwe had followed on; was Man of the Series, having scored 183*, 70 and 55 in his other three innings for a series average of 270.00. Scored 73 v Bangladesh at Bulawayo 2000-01, in the process equalling Everton Weekes's world record, set 1947-49, of seven consecutive Test half-centuries. FICA International Player of the Year 2001. Scored 142 and 199* v South Africa in the first Test at Harare 2001, becoming the first wicket-keeper to score a century in each innings of a Test match and the first Zimbabwe player to reach 4000 Test runs; his performance took him to the top of the PricewaterhouseCoopers ratings for Test batsmen, making him the first wicket-keeper/batsman to achieve the feat

Best batting: 232* Zimbabwe v India, Nagpur 2000-01

Best bowling: 1-1 Mashonaland v Mashonaland CD, Harare South 1993-94

Stop press: Equalled Zimbabwe's highest individual score in One-Day Internationals with his 142* (century from 97 balls) v England in the third One-Day International at Harare 2001-02, in the process of scoring which he shared with Heath Streak in a new world record seventh-wicket partnership for ODIs (130)

2001 Season (did not make any first-class or one-day appearances)

Career Performances

	M	Inns	NO	Runs	HS	Avge	100s	50s	Ct	St	Balls	Runs	Wkts	Avge	Best	5wI	10wM
Test	52	92	16	3908	232*	51.42	9	24	136	7	1	0	0	-	-	-	-
All First	116	191	38	8048	232*	52.60	23	42	237	18	462	189	4	47.25	1-1	-	-
1-day Int	172	169	12	5268	120*	33.55	2	44	124	30	30	23	0	-	-	-	-
C & G																	
B & H																		
1-day Lge																		

FOSTER, J. S.   Essex

Name: <u>James</u> Savin Foster
Role: Right-hand bat, wicket-keeper
Born: 15 April 1980, Whipps Cross, London
Height: 6ft **Weight:** 12st
Nickname: Fozzy, Chief
County debut: 2000
County cap: 2001
1st-Class 50s: 6
1st-Class 100s: 1
1st-Class catches: 46
1st-Class stumpings: 9
Place in batting averages: 143rd av. 26.56
Parents: Martin and Diana
Marital status: Single
Family links with cricket: 'Dad played for
Essex Amateurs'
Education: Forest School; Durham
University

Qualifications: 10 GCSEs, 3 A-levels, hockey and cricket Level 1 coaching awards
Off-season: Touring Zimbabwe, India and New Zealand with England; also studying
at Durham University
Overseas tours: BUSA to South Africa 1999; Durham University to South Africa
1999, to Vienna (European Indoor Championships) 1999; England A to West Indies
2000-01; England to Zimbabwe (one-day series) 2001-02, to India and New Zealand
2001-02
Career highlights to date: 'Being picked to play for England. Playing for Essex
against Australia'
Cricketers particularly admired: Nasser Hussain, Stuart Law, Robert Rollins,
Ian Healy, Jack Russell, Alec Stewart, Adam Gilchrist
Young players to look out for: John Chambers, Adnan Akram, Arfan Akram,
Tony Palladino
Other sports played: Hockey (Essex U21), tennis (played for GB U14 v Sweden
U14; national training squad)
Other sports followed: Football (Wimbledon FC)
Relaxations: Socialising, 'Klute and Rixy's'
Extras: Essex U17 Player of the Year 1997. Represented ECB U19 v Pakistan U19
1998. Represented England U19 v Australia U19 in 'Test' series 1999. Represented
BUSA v South Africa Universities 1999, v New Zealand A and Zimbabweans 2000
and v Pakistan 2001. Awarded 2nd XI cap at end of 2000 season. Voted Essex Cricket
Society 2nd XI Player of the Year 2000. Scored 52 on debut v Glamorgan at Southend
2000. Scored 53 on England A debut v Guyana in Grenada 2000-01. Scored maiden

first-class century (103) for Durham University CCE v Worcestershire at Worcester 2001. Awarded Essex cap 2001

Opinions on cricket: 'Less first-class cricket should be played, and county cricket regulations should comply with those of Test/international cricket. Lunch and tea should be longer.'

Best batting: 103 DUCCE v Worcestershire, Worcester 2001

Stop press: Made One-Day International debut in first ODI v Zimbabwe at Harare 2001-02; made Test debut in first Test v India at Mohali 2001-02. Scored 40 in second Test v India at Ahmedabad 2001-02, in the process sharing with Craig White in a record seventh-wicket partnership for England in Tests in India (105)

2001 Season

	M	Inns	NO	Runs	HS	Avge	100s	50s	Ct	St	O	M	Runs	Wkts	Avge	Best	5wI	10wM
Test																		
All First	16	25	0	664	103	26.56	1	4	31	8	2	0	6	0	-		-	-	-
1-day Int																		
C & G	1	1	0	33	33	33.00	-	-	2	-								
B & H																		
1-day Lge	14	13	5	207	56 *	25.87	-	1	17	1								

Career Performances

	M	Inns	NO	Runs	HS	Avge	100s	50s	Ct	St	Balls	Runs	Wkts	Avge	Best	5wI	10wM
Test																		
All First	23	34	3	911	103	29.38	1	6	46	9	12	6	0	-		-	-	-
1-day Int																		
C & G	1	1	0	33	33	33.00	-	-	2	-								
B & H																		
1-day Lge	20	19	8	288	56 *	26.18	-	1	23	2								

36. Why were Holland not permitted to stage home games when they first entered the Gillette/NatWest/C&G?

FRANCIS, J. D.   Hampshire

Name: <u>John</u> Daniel Francis
Role: Left-hand bat, slow left-arm bowler
Born: 13 November 1980, Bromley, Kent
Height: 5ft 11in **Weight:** 13st
Nickname: Long John, Franky, Junior
County debut: 2001
1st-Class 50s: 1
1st-Class catches: 1
Strike rate: 36.00 (career 36.00)
Parents: Linda and Daniel
Marital status: Single
Family links with cricket: Brother Simon
played for Hampshire 1997-2001; will play
for Somerset 2002. Father played club
cricket. Grandfather played for the services
Education: Yardley Court, Tonbridge; King
Edward VI, Southampton; Durham and
Loughborough Universities
Qualifications: 10 GCSEs, 3 A-levels, ECB Level 1 coaching award
Off-season: Studying at Loughborough University
Overseas tours: Twyford School to Barbados 1993; West of England U15 to West
Indies 1995; King Edward VI, Southampton to South Africa 1998; Durham University
to South Africa 2000
Career highlights to date: 'Receiving Sir John Hobbs Silver Jubilee Memorial Prize
for National U15 Player of the Year'
Cricket moments to forget: 'Losing semi-final against Pakistan' (*In the U15 World
Cup 1996*)
Cricketers particularly admired: Graham Thorpe, Neil Johnson, Simon Francis,
Greg Johnson
Young players to look out for: Simon Francis
Other sports played: Hockey (England U18), golf, squash
Relaxations: Drawing and painting, socialising
Extras: Hampshire Young Sportsman of the Year 1995. Leading run-scorer in U15
World Cup 1996. Played for Loughborough University CCE in 2001, scoring a century
(107) v Leicestershire at Leicester. Scored match-winning 81-ball 78* in his second
Norwich Union League match, v Worcestershire at Worcester 2001
Best batting: 72* Hampshire v Nottinghamshire, Trent Bridge 2001
Best bowling: 1-34 Hampshire v Nottinghamshire, Trent Bridge 2001

2001 Season

	M	Inns	NO	Runs	HS	Avge	100s	50s	Ct	St	O	M	Runs	Wkts	Avge	Best	5wI	10wM
Test																		
All First	2	4	2	131	72 *	65.50	-	1	1	-	6	0	34	1	34.00	1-34	-	-
1-day Int																		
C & G																			
B & H																			
1-day Lge	6	6	3	189	78 *	63.00	-	2	1	-								

Career Performances

	M	Inns	NO	Runs	HS	Avge	100s	50s	Ct	St	Balls	Runs	Wkts	Avge	Best	5wI	10wM
Test																	
All First	2	4	2	131	72 *	65.50	-	1	1	-	36	34	1	34.00	1-34	-	-
1-day Int																	
C & G																		
B & H																		
1-day Lge	6	6	3	189	78 *	63.00	-	2	1	-							

FRANCIS, S. R. G.   Somerset

Name: <u>Simon</u> Richard George Francis
Role: Right-hand bat, right-arm
fast-medium bowler
Born: 15 August 1978, Bromley, Kent
Height: 6ft 2in **Weight:** 15st
Nickname: Franky, Hulk
County debut: 1997 (Hampshire)
1st-Class catches: 1
Place in batting averages: (2000 269th
av. 10.66)
Place in bowling averages: (2000 130th
av. 40.13)
Strike rate: (career 84.08)
Parents: Daniel and Linda
Marital status: Single
Family links with cricket: Brother John
plays for Hampshire. Father played club
cricket. Grandfather played for the Navy
Education: Yardley Court, Tonbridge/Twyford, Winchester; King Edward VI,
Southampton; Durham University
Qualifications: 9 GCSEs, 1 AS-Level, 3 A-levels, BA (Hons) Sport in the
Community, Level 1 coaching in cricket and hockey

Career outside cricket: Coaching
Off-season: 'Training in Taunton. Playing lots of golf!!'
Overseas tours: England U17 to Holland (International Youth Tournament) 1995;
England U19 to Pakistan 1996-97; Durham University to Zimbabwe 1997-98;
Hampshire to Boland 2001
Overseas teams played for: 'Maties'-Stellenbosch University, South Africa 2000;
Melville CC, Perth 2001
Cricketers particularly admired: Malcolm Marshall, Richard Hadlee, Allan Donald,
Graham Dilley
Young players to look out for: John Francis, Scott Charlton
Other sports played: Golf (second in PCA Players' Team Competition 2000)
Injuries: Stress fracture of spine
Relaxations: Golf, films
Extras: *Daily Telegraph* West Region Bowling Award U15. Played hockey for
England U18 1995. Played in Durham University's BUSA Championship-winning
side 1999. Put on 90 for the tenth wicket with Dimitri Mascarenhas v Surrey at The
Oval 2000, the pair falling just two runs short of pulling off a remarkable
Championship victory. Released by Hampshire at the end of the 2001 season and has
joined Somerset for 2002
Opinions on cricket: 'More day/night games – more entertaining; bigger crowds.'
Best batting: 30* Hampshire v Surrey, The Oval 2000
Best bowling: 4-95 Hampshire v Surrey, The Oval 2000

2001 Season (did not make any first-class or one-day appearances)

Career Performances

	M	Inns	NO	Runs	HS	Avge	100s	50s	Ct	St	Balls	Runs	Wkts	Avge	Best	5wI	10wM
Test																	
All First	16	22	10	91	30 *	7.58	-	-	1	-	2102	1232	25	49.28	4-95	-	-
1-day Int																	
C & G	1	0	0	0	0	-	-	-	-	-	36	10	0	-		-	-
B & H																	
1-day Lge	10	5	3	18	8 *	9.00	-	-	2	-	348	242	6	40.33	2-28	-	

FRANKS, P. J. Nottinghamshire

Name: <u>Paul</u> John Franks
Role: Left-hand bat, right-arm fast-medium bowler
Born: 3 February 1979, Sutton-in-Ashfield
Height: 6ft 1½in **Weight:** 13st 10lbs
Nickname: Pike, Franno, The General
County debut: 1996

County cap: 1999
One-Day Internationals: 1
50 wickets in a season: 2
1st-Class 50s: 8
1st-Class 5 w. in innings: 8
1st-Class catches: 30
One-Day 5 w. in innings: 2
Place in batting averages: (2000 126th av. 26.29)
Place in bowling averages: 80th av. 33.00 (2000 92nd av. 29.69)
Strike rate: 68.84 (career 54.79)
Parents: Pat and John
Marital status: Single
Family links with cricket: 'Dad was a local league legend'
Education: Walter D'Ayncourt Primary School; Minster School, Southwell; West Notts College
Qualifications: 7 GCSEs, GNVQ (Advanced) Leisure Management, coaching Level 1
Career outside cricket: 'Applied for a job as bar manager at "Spearmint Rhino"'
Off-season: 'Taking it generally steady the same as last season'
Overseas tours: England U19 to Pakistan 1996-97, to South Africa (including U19 World Cup) 1997-98; England A to Zimbabwe and South Africa 1998-99, to Bangladesh and New Zealand 1999-2000, to West Indies 2000-01; Notts CCC to South Africa 1998, 1999
Career highlights to date: 'England [one-day] debut v West Indies on home ground in 2000'
Cricket moments to forget: 'Any time I get my poles removed or go the distance'
Cricketers particularly admired: Glenn McGrath, Mike Atherton, Allan Donald, Phil 'bowls like me' DeFreitas
Young players to look out for: Kyle Hogg, Nadeem Malik, Bilal Shafayat, Matt Prior, Richard Hodgkinson
Other sports played: Golf, pre-match soccer ('midfield dynamo')
Other sports followed: Football (Mansfield Town 'the future of football')
Injuries: Out for four months with patellar tendonitis
Relaxations: 'Taking it generally steady'
Extras: Became youngest ever Notts player (and third-youngest player ever, aged 18 years 163 days) to take a hat-trick, v Warwickshire in July 1997. Won U19 World Cup winner's medal in Johannesburg 1998. Attended Dennis Lillee coaching school, Chennai (Madras), March 1997, February 1998 and March 1999. NBC Denis Compton Award 1999. Cricket Writers' Young Player of the Year 2000. Scored 85 v Middlesex at Lord's 2001, in the process sharing in a record seventh-wicket stand for Notts in matches against Middlesex (199) with Kevin Pietersen

Opinions on cricket: 'Pitches are now much better. However, whoever had the idea to use very soft cricket balls was a complete fool. Next year we might as well use tennis balls.'
Best batting: 85 Nottinghamshire v Middlesex, Lord's 2001
Best bowling: 7-56 Nottinghamshire v Middlesex, Lord's 2000

2001 Season

	M	Inns	NO	Runs	HS	Avge	100s	50s	Ct	St	O	M	Runs	Wkts	Avge	Best	5wI	10wM
Test																		
All First	5	8	4	217	85	54.25	-	1	2	-	149.1	33	429	13	33.00	4-65	-	-
1-day Int																		
C & G																			
B & H	6	0	0	0	0	-	-	-	-	-		58	6	275	4	68.75	2-39	-
1-day Lge	3	3	3	9	4 *	-	-	-	-	-		24	1	119	3	39.66	2-26	-

Career Performances

	M	Inns	NO	Runs	HS	Avge	100s	50s	Ct	St	Balls	Runs	Wkts	Avge	Best	5wI	10wM
Test																	
All First	71	105	19	1862	85	21.65	-	8	30	-	12767	6434	233	27.61	7-56	8	-
1-day Int	1	1	0	4	4	4.00	-	-	1	-	54	48	0	-	-	-	-
C & G	9	7	3	110	26 *	27.50	-	-	3	-	480	329	15	21.93	3-7	-
B & H	10	4	2	32	14	16.00	-	-	-	-	492	362	8	45.25	2-14	-
1-day Lge	50	38	16	373	40	16.95	-	-	6	-	2238	1713	70	24.47	6-27	2

FRASER, A. R. C. Middlesex

Name: Angus Robert Charles Fraser
Role: Right-hand lower-order bat, right-arm medium-fast bowler, county captain
Born: 8 August 1965, Billinge, Wigan
Height: 6ft 6in **Weight:** 16st
Nickname: Gus, Lard, Wiggy, Recall
County debut: 1984
County cap: 1988
Benefit: 1997
Test debut: 1989
Tests: 46
One-Day Internationals: 42
50 wickets in a season: 7
1st-Class 50s: 2
1st-Class 5 w. in innings: 33
1st-Class 10 w. in match: 4
1st-Class catches: 54

One-Day 5 w. in innings: 1
Place in batting averages: 242nd av. 12.41
(2000 236th av. 14.18)
Place in bowling averages: 104th av. 37.62
(2000 44th av. 23.14)
Strike rate: 88.06 (career 63.53)
Parents: Don and Irene
Wife and date of marriage: Denise,
March 1996
Children: Alexander Charles Mitchell, May
1993; Bethan Louise, July 1995
Family links with cricket: 'Mum and Dad
keen followers. Brother Alastair played for
Middlesex, Essex, then Middlesex again'
Education: Weald Junior and Middle School;
Gayton High School, Harrow; Orange Hill
Senior High School, Edgware
Qualifications: 7 O-levels, qualified
cricket coach

Career outside cricket: 'I would love to still be involved in and around the game
when I retire, whether it be coaching, commentating or writing. I also enjoy working
for Hardy's in the wine trade'
Off-season: 'Commentating for *Test Match Special* in Zimbabwe, India and
New Zealand. Working for Middlesex CCC. Working for Sky TV. Getting fit for
next season'
Overseas tours: Thames Valley Gentlemen to Barbados 1985; Middlesex to La
Manga 1985, 1986, to Portugal 1991-93, to Malta 2001; England to India (Nehru Cup)
1989-90, to West Indies 1989-90, to Australia 1990-91, to West Indies 1993-94, to
Australia 1994-95, to South Africa 1995-96, to West Indies 1997-98, to Australia
1998-99, to Sharjah (Coca-Cola Cup) 1998-99
Overseas teams played for: Plimmerton, Wellington 1985-86, 1987-88; Western
Suburbs, Sydney 1988-89, 1994-95
Career highlights to date: 'Difficult to pull out one. Fortunately there have been a
few highlights. Obviously playing and winning games/series for England and winning
trophies for Middlesex stand out'
Cricket moments to forget: 'Remember the bad days as they make the good ones feel
that much better. I have no regrets'
Cricketers particularly admired: Graham Gooch, Curtly Ambrose, Courtney Walsh,
Allan Border, Mike Atherton
Young players to look out for: Chris Tremlett, Ian Bell, 'the Middlesex top six'
Other sports played: 'Golf with a sombrero on'
Other sports followed: 'Follow Liverpool FC keenly. Enjoy watching rugby
internationals at my local rugby club, Harrow'
Injuries: Out for two games 'with torn lat under armpit'; for one game with bruised
ribs; for one game with sore Achilles and hip

Relaxations: Spending time with family, golf, Liverpool FC, drinking good red wine
Extras: Middlesex Player of the Year 1988 and 1989. Took a hat-trick in the Benson and Hedges Cup in 1989. Took his 100th Test wicket (Brian Lara) against West Indies in 1995. Finished 2nd in the Whyte and Mackay bowling ratings for 1995. One of *Wisden*'s Five Cricketers of the Year 1996. His 8-53 v West Indies at Trinidad in 1998 is the best return by an English bowler in the West Indies. Peter Smith Award 1998. Winner of the Kumala Cape Wines 'Century of Bottles' award for the best individual performance against the 1998 South Africans. Awarded MBE in New Year honours list 1999. Represented England in 1999 World Cup. Captain of Middlesex since 2001
Opinions on cricket: 'The greed of players will lead to their premature exclusion from the game. Higher salaries don't make you a better player. Reward success, not potential. You have to work hard for success.'
Best batting: 92 Middlesex v Surrey, The Oval 1990
Best bowling: 8-53 England v West Indies, Port of Spain 1997-98

2001 Season

	M	Inns	NO	Runs	HS	Avge	100s	50s	Ct	St	O	M	Runs	Wkts	Avge	Best	5wI	10wM
Test																		
All First	13	12	0	149	41	12.41	-	-	4	-	469.4	140	1204	32	37.62	3-46	-	-
1-day Int																		
C & G	1	0	0	0	0	-	-	-	-	-	10	0	63	1	63.00	1-63	-	
B & H	5	3	2	11	8	11.00	-	-	-	-	45	6	152	8	19.00	3-30	-	
1-day Lge	7	3	1	29	17	14.50	-	-	1	-	61	12	159	15	10.60	3-13	-	

Career Performances

	M	Inns	NO	Runs	HS	Avge	100s	50s	Ct	St	Balls	Runs	Wkts	Avge	Best	5wI	10wM
Test	46	67	15	388	32	7.46	-	-	9	-	10876	4836	177	27.32	8-53	13	2
All First	288	342	82	2898	92	11.14	-	2	54	-	55843	24087	879	27.40	8-53	35	5
1-day Int	42	20	9	141	38 *	12.81	-	-	5	-	2392	1412	47	30.04	4-22	-	
C & G	36	13	10	80	19	26.66	-	-	6	-	2301	1180	50	23.60	4-34	-	
B & H	50	27	14	128	30 *	9.84	-	-	10	-	2925	1716	63	27.23	4-49	-	
1-day Lge	188	77	35	489	33	11.64	-	-	30	-	8418	5397	213	25.33	5-32	1	

FROST, T.   Warwickshire

Name: Tony Frost
Role: Right-hand bat, wicket-keeper
Born: 17 November 1975, Stoke-on-Trent
Height: 5ft 10in **Weight:** 10st 6lbs
County debut: 1997
County cap: 1999
1st-Class 50s: 3

1st-Class 100s: 1
1st-Class catches: 76
1st-Class stumpings: 5
Parents: Ivan and Christine
Marital status: Single
Family links with cricket: Father played for Staffordshire
Education: James Brinkley High School; Stoke-on-Trent College
Qualifications: 5 GCSEs
Overseas tours: Kidsgrove U18 to Australia 1990-91
Cricketers particularly admired: Ashley Giles 'could be described as a legend', 'Pop' Welch and George Burns 'in the JT bracket'
Other sports followed: Football, golf
Relaxations: Listening to music, watching films, reading aircraft magazines

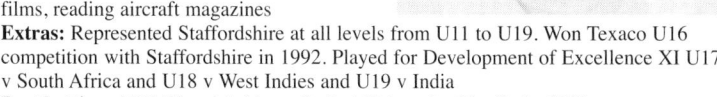

Extras: Represented Staffordshire at all levels from U11 to U19. Won Texaco U16 competition with Staffordshire in 1992. Played for Development of Excellence XI U17 v South Africa and U18 v West Indies and U19 v India
Best batting: 111* Warwickshire v Oxford University, The Parks 1998

2001 Season

	M	Inns	NO	Runs	HS	Avge	100s	50s	Ct	St	O	M	Runs	Wkts	Avge	Best	5wI	10wM
Test																		
All First	1	2	1	17	17	17.00	-	-	5	2								
1-day Int																		
C & G																		
B & H																		
1-day Lge	1	0	0	0	0	-	-	-	-	-	-							

Career Performances

	M	Inns	NO	Runs	HS	Avge	100s	50s	Ct	St	Balls	Runs	Wkts	Avge	Best	5wI	10wM
Test																	
All First	31	45	6	912	111 *	23.38	1	3	76	5	6	6	0	-	-	-	-
1-day Int																	
C & G	2	2	0	5	5	2.50	-	-	4	1							
B & H	3	2	1	11	10 *	11.00	-	-	3	-							
1-day Lge	23	9	3	88	22 *	14.66	-	-	15	3							

FULTON, D. P. Kent

Name: David (<u>Dave</u>) Paul Fulton
Role: Right-hand top-order bat, left-arm spin bowler, occasional wicket-keeper, county captain in Championship
Born: 15 November 1971, Lewisham
Height: 6ft 2in **Weight:** 12st 7lbs
Nickname: Tav, Rave
County debut: 1992
County cap: 1998
1000 runs in a season: 1
1st-Class 50s: 30
1st-Class 100s: 14
1st-Class 200s: 2
1st-Class catches: 185
Place in batting averages: 5th av. 75.68 (2000 159th av. 22.26)
Strike rate: (career 175.00)
Parents: John and Ann
Marital status: Single
Children: 'Millie' ('Staffordshire bull terrier; 13 February 2000')
Family links with cricket: Father played for village
Education: Otford County Primary; The Judd School, Tonbridge; University of Kent at Canterbury
Qualifications: 10 GCSEs, 3 A-levels, BA (Hons) Politics and International Relations, advanced cricket coach, rugby coach, gym instructor qualification
Career outside cricket: Journalist
Off-season: 'Standby for England Test tour. Journalist for *Kent Messenger* group. Writing my first novel'
Overseas tours: Kent SCA U17 to Singapore and New Zealand 1987-88; Kent to France 1998, to Port Elizabeth 2001
Overseas teams played for: Avendale CC, Cape Town 1993-94; Victoria CC, Cape Town 1994-95; University of WA, Perth 1995-96; Petersham-Marrickville CC, Sydney 1998-99, 1999-2000
Career highlights to date: 'Will Kendall caught and bowled Fulton (first and only first-class victim). PCA Player of the Year 2001'
Cricket moments to forget: 'Already forgotten'
Cricketers particularly admired: Gordon Greenidge, Graham Gooch, Courtney Walsh, Steve Waugh
Young players to look out for: James Tredwell, Rob Joseph
Other sports played: Chess (England junior), table tennis ('top 10 in UK as a junior'; played for South England juniors); rugby, football, tennis, golf, squash

Other sports followed: Football (Nottingham Forest), rugby (Harlequins)
Relaxations: 'Walking the dog, music, chilling (getting old)'
Extras: Was the last person to catch Viv Richards in a first-class match, in 1993.
Opened the batting and the bowling against South Africa in their first county game
1994. Helped Dean Headley's hat-trick against Derbyshire 1996 by catching Kim
Barnett and Chris Adams. Set record for the longest innings ever played by a Kent
batsman in scoring his 207 against Yorkshire at Maidstone in 1998. Wrote 'Dr Love'
column for *For Me* magazine in Australia. Has best catching strike rate in Kent
fielding history. Scored double century (208*) and century (104*) v Somerset at
Canterbury 2001, also taking seven catches in the match; followed up with 197 v
Northamptonshire at Northampton in next Championship innings. Scored 196 v
Northamptonshire at Canterbury 2001, in the process equalling Arthur Fagg's 1938
season tally of nine centuries for Kent, one behind Frank Woolley's Kent record of ten,
set in 1928 and 1934. First batsman to 1000 first-class runs in 2001 and the season's
leading English batsman in terms of runs scored (second overall) and average (fifth
overall) with 1892 runs (av. 75.68). Kent Batsman of the Year (Denness Award) 2001.
PCA Player of the Year 2001. Appointed captain of Kent in County Championship for
2002 (*see entry on Matthew Fleming*). PCA representative for Kent
Opinions on cricket: 'Have to be progressive. Would love to see a few mergers of
clubs and changes of format. Let's shake it up and do it better.'
Best batting: 208* Kent v Somerset, Canterbury 2001
Best bowling: 1-37 Kent v Oxford University, Canterbury 1996

2001 Season

	M	Inns	NO	Runs	HS	Avge	100s	50s	Ct	St	O	M	Runs	Wkts	Avge	Best	5wI	10wM
Test																		
All First	18	27	2	1892	208 *	75.68	9	3	27	-	1	0	2	0	-		-	-	-
1-day Int																		
C & G	3	3	0	104	63	34.66	-	1	7	-								
B & H																			
1-day Lge	14	14	0	334	82	23.85	-	1	10	-								

Career Performances

	M	Inns	NO	Runs	HS	Avge	100s	50s	Ct	St	Balls	Runs	Wkts	Avge	Best	5wI	10wM
Test																	
All First	125	217	14	7185	208 *	35.39	16	30	185	-	175	112	1	112.00	1-37	-	-
1-day Int																	
C & G	11	11	0	192	63	17.45	-	1	8	-	6	9	0	-		-	-
B & H	2	2	0	42	25	21.00	-	-	3	-							
1-day Lge	33	33	0	538	82	16.30	-	2	18	-							

GAIT, A. I. Derbyshire

Name: <u>Andrew</u> Ian Gait
Role: Right-hand opening bat
Born: 19 December 1978, Bulawayo, Zimbabwe
Height: 6ft 1in **Weight:** 13st 7lbs
Nickname: Bob
County debut: No first-team appearance
1st-Class 50s: 5
1st-Class 100s: 2
1st-Class catches: 19
Parents: Roger and Hazel
Marital status: Single
Education: Warner Beach Primary School, KwaZulu-Natal, South Africa; Kearsney College, KwaZulu-Natal; 'busy studying through University of South Africa'
Qualifications: Level 2 coaching, studying Bachelor of Commerce

Off-season: Back in South Africa visiting family; possibly travelling
Overseas tours: South African National Academy to Kenya and Zimbabwe 1998
Overseas teams played for: South Africa U19; Free State 1998-2001
Career highlights to date: 'Chasing 400-plus in fourth innings and winning v Natal; scored 101'
Cricket moments to forget: 'Losing to Natal in a Standard Bank game in the 2000-01 season' (*Free State lost by 12 runs under the Duckworth/Lewis method, four wickets falling in a single over bowled by Jonathan Bastow*)
Cricketers particularly admired: Allan Donald, Steve Waugh, Jacques Kallis
Young players to look out for: Kevin Pietersen, Jacques Rudolph, Dewald Pretorius
Other sports played: Squash
Other sports followed: Rugby (Natal Sharks)
Relaxations: Gym, running; beach, outdoors; music
Extras: Represented South Africa U19 in U19 World Cup 1997-98. Set Free State record for highest individual score in one-day cricket (138*). Scored 101 in the highest successful fourth-innings run chase by a South African province – 443 by Free State v KwaZulu-Natal at Durban 1999-2000
Opinions on cricket: 'The game is constantly developing, and as a player one needs to adapt and maintain a positive frame of mind in order to stay ahead of the pack!'
Best batting: 112 Free State v Border, Bloemfontein 2000-01

2001 Season (did not make any first-class or one-day appearances)

Career Performances

	M	Inns	NO	Runs	HS	Avge	100s	50s	Ct	St	Balls	Runs	Wkts	Avge	Best	5wI	10wM
Test																	
All First	19	35	0	937	112	26.77	2	5	19	-							
1-day Int																	
C & G																	
B & H																	
1-day Lge																	

GALLIAN, J. E. R. Nottinghamshire

Name: Jason Edward Riche Gallian
Role: Right-hand bat, right-arm
medium bowler, county captain
Born: 25 June 1971, Manly, NSW, Australia
Height: 6ft **Weight:** 14st
Nickname: Gal
County debut: 1990 (Lancashire),
1998 (Nottinghamshire)
County cap: 1994 (Lancashire),
1998 (Nottinghamshire)
Test debut: 1995
Tests: 3
1000 runs in a season: 2
1st-Class 50s: 36
1st-Class 100s: 17
1st-Class 300s: 1
1st-Class 5 w. in innings: 1
1st-Class catches: 112
One-Day 100s: 7
One-Day 5 w. in innings: 1
Place in batting averages: (2000 62nd av. 34.60)
Strike rate: (career 71.40)
Parents: Ray and Marilyn
Wife and date of marriage: Charlotte, 2 October 1999
Children: Tom, 12 April 2001
Family links with cricket: Father played for Stockport
Education: The Pittwater House Schools, Australia; Oxford University
Qualifications: Higher School Certificate, Diploma in Social Studies
(Keble College, Oxford)

Off-season: 'Rehabbing knee injury; finding a job; giving my sister away at her wedding in Australia'
Overseas tours: Australia U20 to West Indies 1989-90; England A to India 1994-95, to Pakistan 1995-96, to Australia 1996-97; England to South Africa 1995-96; Nottinghamshire to Johannesburg 2000, to South Africa 2001
Overseas teams played for: NSW and Australia U19 1988-89; NSW Colts and NSW 2nd XI 1990-91; Manly 1993-94
Career highlights to date: 'Playing Test cricket'
Cricket moments to forget: 'Breaking a finger in my first Test match'
Cricketers particularly admired: Desmond Haynes, Mike Gatting
Young players to look out for: Bilal Shafayat
Other sports followed: Rugby league and union, football
Injuries: Out for six months with a knee injury
Relaxations: Listening to music, playing golf
Extras: Captained Australia YC v England YC 1989-90. Represented Australia U20 and U21 1991-92. Took wicket of D. A. Hagan of Oxford University with his first ball in first-class cricket 1990. Played for Oxford University in 1992 and for Combined Universities in the B&H Cup. Captained Oxford University 1993. Recorded highest individual score in history of Old Trafford with his 312 v Derbyshire in 1996. Left Lancashire during the 1997-98 off-season and joined Nottinghamshire for 1998, being appointed captain after resignation of Paul Johnson
Opinions on cricket: 'Two divisions is very good. Four-day cricket needs to be more intense.'
Best batting: 312 Lancashire v Derbyshire, Old Trafford 1996
Best bowling: 6-115 Lancashire v Surrey, Southport 1996

2001 Season

	M	Inns	NO	Runs	HS	Avge	100s	50s	Ct	St	O	M	Runs	Wkts	Avge	Best	5wI	10wM
Test																		
All First	1	1	1	23	23 *	-	-	-	-	-								
1-day Int																		
C & G																		
B & H																		
1-day Lge	1	1	0	1	1	1.00	-	-	-	-								

Career Performances

	M	Inns	NO	Runs	HS	Avge	100s	50s	Ct	St	Balls	Runs	Wkts	Avge	Best	5wI	10wM
Test	3	6	0	74	28	12.33	-	-	1	-	84	62	0	-	-	-	-
All First	141	245	23	8124	312	36.59	18	36	112	-	6712	3825	94	40.69	6-115	1	-
1-day Int																	
C & G	14	14	1	442	101 *	34.00	1	3	8	-	162	122	1	122.00	1-11	-	
B & H	34	33	2	995	134	32.09	2	6	6	-	725	621	17	36.52	5-15	1	
1-day Lge	90	88	9	2656	130	33.62	4	14	32	-	844	825	28	29.46	2-10	-	

GANNON, B. W.   Gloucestershire

Name: <u>Benjamin</u> Ward Gannon
Role: Right-hand bat, right-arm
medium bowler
Born: 5 September 1975, Oxford
Height: 6ft 3in **Weight:** 13st 7lbs
Nickname: Louis, Ganja
County debut: 1999
1st-Class 5 w. in innings: 3
1st-Class catches: 7
Place in batting averages: (2000 249th
av. 12.33)
Place in bowling averages: (2000 60th
av. 25.24)
Strike rate: 72.75 (career 47.85)
Parents: Martin and Jane
Marital status: Single
Education: Dragon School, Oxford;
Abingdon School; Cheltenham and
Gloucester College of Higher Education

Qualifications: 3 A-levels, BSc (Hons) Sports Science and Physical Geography,
coaching awards in football, rugby and cricket, fitness qualifications
Career outside cricket: 'The demands of professional cricket make another career
difficult'
Off-season: 'Furthering education/experience for life after cricket. Getting fit for 2002
season. Spending some time in South Africa in preparation for new season'
Overseas tours: Gloucestershire to Zimbabwe 1997, to South Africa 2000, 2001;
Forest Nomads to Zimbabwe 1998
Overseas teams played for: Waverley, Sydney 1993-94; Union CC, Port Elizabeth
2000; Easterns CC, Cape Town 2001
Career highlights to date: 'Making debut against Glamorgan'
Cricketers particularly admired: Courtney Walsh, Curtly Ambrose, Glenn McGrath,
'Syd' Lawrence
Young players to look out for: Steve Harmison, Simon Jones
Other sports played: 'I'll have a go at most sports'
Other sports followed: Boxing, rugby, tennis, athletics, climbing
Injuries: Achilles tendon strain
Relaxations: Listening to music, keeping fit, travelling, photography
Extras: NBC Denis Compton Award 1999
Opinions on cricket: 'Opinions often fall on deaf ears anyway, so take the view that the
individual should be given the responsibility and trust to make his/her own destiny.'
Best batting: 28 Gloucestershire v Essex, Colchester 2000
Best bowling: 6-80 Gloucestershire v Glamorgan, Cardiff 1999

2001 Season

	M	Inns	NO	Runs	HS	Avge	100s	50s	Ct	St	O	M	Runs	Wkts	Avge	Best	5wI	10wM
Test																		
All First	5	6	4	12	10 *	6.00	-	-	-	-	97	12	380	8	47.50	3-47	-	-
1-day Int																		
C & G																			
B & H																			
1-day Lge																			

Career Performances

	M	Inns	NO	Runs	HS	Avge	100s	50s	Ct	St	Balls	Runs	Wkts	Avge	Best	5wI	10wM
Test																	
All First	24	28	12	156	28	9.75	-	-	7	-	3350	2104	70	30.05	6-80	3	-
1-day Int																	
C & G																		
B & H																		
1-day Lge																		

GAZZARD, C. M.   Somerset

Name: <u>Carl</u> Matthew Gazzard
Role: Right-hand bat, wicket-keeper
Born: 15 April 1982, Penzance
Height: 6ft **Weight:** 13st
Nickname: Gazza, Slinger, Hoggard
County debut: No first-team appearance
Parents: Paul and Alison
Marital status: Single
Family links with cricket: Father and brother both played for Cornwall Schools; mother's a keen follower
Education: St Mary's Roman Catholic School, Penzance; Mounts Bay Comprehensive; Richard Huish College, Taunton
Qualifications: 10 GCSEs, 2 A-levels, Level 1 and 2 coaching
Off-season: 'Training – trying to get fit for next year and coaching'
Overseas tours: Cornwall Schools U13 to Johannesburg; West of England U15 to West Indies; Somerset Academy to Durban 1999
Overseas teams played for: Subiaco-Floreat, Perth 2000-01

Career highlights to date: 'England U19 v Sri Lanka U19 2000 – 3-0 victory in ODIs and 1st "Test" victory'

Cricket moments to forget: 'Dislocating my shoulder in Perth – kept me out for 2001 season'

Cricketers particularly admired: Ian Allen, Shakil Ahmed, Ian Healy, Alec Stewart, Marcus Trescothick

Young players to look out for: Matthew Wood, Peter Trego

Other sports played: Football (played through the age groups for Cornwall)

Other sports followed: Football (West Ham United)

Injuries: Out for 2001 season with dislocated shoulder

Relaxations: Any sport, watching TV, socialising

Extras: Played for England U13, U14, U15, U19. Won the Graham Kersey Award for Best Wicket-keeper at Bunbury Festival. Played for Cornwall in Minor Counties aged 16 and in the NatWest Trophy 1999

Opinions on cricket: 'The game is becoming quicker and harder to force your way into, but with the right attitude and self-belief we can add to the quality and entertainment already provided. Second XI playing regulations should be the same as in first-class matches.'

2001 Season (did not make any first-class or one-day appearances)

Career Performances

	M	Inns	NO	Runs	HS	Avge	100s	50s	Ct	St	Balls	Runs	Wkts	Avge	Best	5wI	10wM
Test																	
All First																	
1-day Int																	
C & G	1	1	0	16	16	16.00	-	-	2	-							
B & H																	
1-day Lge																	

37. Which Nottinghamshire pace bowler took 5-22 and the Man of the Match award as Gloucestershire were shot out for 82 in the semi-finals of the 1987 NatWest?

GIDDINS, E. S. H. Surrey

Name: Edward (<u>Ed</u>) Simon Hunter Giddins
Role: Right-hand bat, right-arm
medium-fast bowler
Born: 20 July 1971, Eastbourne
Height: 6ft 4in **Weight:** 13st 10lbs
Nickname: The Chief
County debut: 1991 (Sussex), 1998
(Warwickshire), 2001 (Surrey)
County cap: 1994 (Sussex), 1998
(Warwickshire)
Test debut: 1999
Tests: 4
50 wickets in a season: 4
1st-Class 5 w. in innings: 22
1st-Class 10 w. in match: 2
1st-Class catches: 21
One-Day 5 w. in innings: 1
Place in batting averages: 276th av. 6.00

(2000 305th av. 3.12)
Place in bowling averages: 102nd av. 36.73 (2000 77th av. 28.03)
Strike rate: 70.56 (career 52.79)
Parents: Simon and Pauline
Marital status: Single
Family links with cricket: 'A keen interest'
Education: St Bede's School, Eastbourne; Eastbourne College
Qualifications: O-levels, A-levels, national coaching certificate
Overseas tours: England A to Pakistan 1995-96; Rumsey Tours to Barbados 2000
Overseas teams played for: Mosman, Sydney 1994-95
Cricketers particularly admired: Graham Gooch, Eddie Hemmings, Ian Gould
Other sports played: 'Love golf'
Other sports followed: Football (Fulham FC)
Relaxations: Travel
Extras: Joined Warwickshire for the 1998 season. Recorded maiden Test five-wicket return (5-15; 7-42 in match) in the first Test v Zimbabwe, Lord's 2000, winning the Man of the Match award. Left Warwickshire during the 2000-01 off-season and joined Surrey for 2001. C&G Man of the Match award for his 2-21 v Surrey Board XI at Guildford 2001
Opinions on cricket: 'Sunday League cricket should not be 40 overs; it should be 10 overs a side but on a "best of three" basis – i.e. first to secure two wins gets the four points.'
Best batting: 34 Sussex v Essex, Hove 1995
Best bowling: 6-47 Sussex v Yorkshire, Eastbourne 1996

2001 Season

	M	Inns	NO	Runs	HS	Avge	100s	50s	Ct	St	O	M	Runs	Wkts	Avge	Best	5wI	10wM
Test																		
All First	12	14	8	36	9 *	6.00	-	-	2	-	352.5	83	1102	30	36.73	5-48	1	-
1-day Int																		
C & G	2	1	1	0	0 *	-	-	-	1	-	20	3	62	2	31.00	2-21	-	
B & H	7	3	1	2	2	1.00	-	-	2	-	54	2	224	8	28.00	3-31	-	
1-day Lge	15	6	1	4	3	0.80	-	-	5	-	109.5	14	519	15	34.60	3-31	-	

Career Performances

	M	Inns	NO	Runs	HS	Avge	100s	50s	Ct	St	Balls	Runs	Wkts	Avge	Best	5wI	10wM
Test	4	7	3	10	7	2.50	-	-	-	-	444	240	12	20.00	5-15	1	-
All First	137	164	69	501	34	5.27	-	-	21	-	23390	12490	443	28.19	6-47	22	2
1-day Int																	
C & G	19	7	4	27	13	9.00	-	-	4	-	1163	692	21	32.95	3-24	-	
B & H	29	10	6	8	4 *	2.00	-	-	7	-	1520	958	38	25.21	5-21	1	
1-day Lge	110	43	16	41	9 *	1.51	-	-	18	-	4649	3677	118	31.16	4-23	-	

GIDMAN, A. P. R. Gloucestershire

Name: Alexander (<u>Alex</u>) Peter
Richard Gidman
Role: Right-hand bat, right-arm fast-medium
bowler; all-rounder
Born: 22 June 1981, High Wycombe
Height: 6ft 2in **Weight:** 13st 8lbs
Nickname: A.P.R., Gidders, Giddo
County debut: 2001 (one-day)
Parents: Alistair and Jane
Marital status: Single
Family links with cricket: 'All male family
members love it. Younger brother plays
GCCC Youth'
Education: Dean Close; Wycliffe College
Qualifications: 7 GCSEs, 1 A-level, GNVQ
in Leisure and Tourism
Off-season: Brendon Bracewell's Cricket
Academy, New Zealand
Overseas tours: MCC Young Cricketers to Cape Town 1999
Overseas teams played for: Albion, New Zealand
Career highlights to date: 'Debut for Gloucestershire'
Cricket moments to forget: 'Surrey 2nd XI scoring 400 v MCC Young Cricketers in
one-day game'

Cricketers particularly admired: Steve Waugh, Brett Lee
Young players to look out for: Will Gidman, Mark Wright
Other sports played: Rugby (Gloucester U17 trials), football (Stroud district)
Other sports followed: Rugby (Gloucester RFC), football (Wolverhampton Wanderers)
Relaxations: Golf, drinking coffee
Extras: Played for Gloucestershire Board XI in the C&G 2001 and in the first and second rounds of the C&G 2002, which were played in August and September 2001
Opinions on cricket: 'Encourage people to be positive rather than negative towards the game.'

2001 Season

	M	Inns	NO	Runs	HS	Avge	100s	50s	Ct	St	O	M	Runs	Wkts	Avge	Best	5wI	10wM
Test																		
All First																		
1-day Int																		
C & G	3	3	0	50	23	16.66	-	-	1	-	21.3	0	106	1	106.00	1-43	-	
B & H																		
1-day Lge	1	1	0	7	7	7.00	-	-	-	-								

Career Performances

	M	Inns	NO	Runs	HS	Avge	100s	50s	Ct	St	Balls	Runs	Wkts	Avge	Best	5wI	10wM
Test																	
All First																	
1-day Int																	
C & G	3	3	0	50	23	16.66	-	-	1	-	129	106	1	106.00	1-43	-	
B & H																	
1-day Lge	1	1	0	7	7	7.00	-	-	-	-							

GILES, A. F.   Warwickshire

Name: <u>Ashley</u> Fraser Giles
Role: Right-hand bat, slow left-arm bowler
Born: 19 March 1973, Chertsey
Height: 6ft 4in **Weight:** 15st 7lbs
Nickname: Splash, Skinny
County debut: 1993
County cap: 1996
Test debut: 1998
Tests: 8
One-Day Internationals: 9
50 wickets in a season: 2

1st-Class 50s: 13
1st-Class 100s: 3
1st-Class 5 w. in innings: 15
1st-Class 10 w. in match: 2
1st-Class catches: 47
One-Day 100s: 1
One-Day 5 w. in innings: 2
Place in batting averages: (2000 39th av. 40.36)
Place in bowling averages: 93rd av. 35.75 (2000 42nd av. 23.07)
Strike rate: 77.41 (career 67.27)
Parents: Michael and Paula
Wife and date of marriage: Stine, 9 October 1999
Children: Anders Fraser, 29 May 2000; Matilde, February 2002
Family links with cricket: 'Dad played and brother Andrew still plays club cricket at Ripley, Surrey'
Education: Kingfield Primary School, Old Woking; George Abbott County Secondary, Burpham, Guildford
Qualifications: 9 GCSEs, 2 A-levels, coaching certificate
Career outside cricket: 'Baby sitting'
Off-season: Touring with England to India and New Zealand
Overseas tours: Surrey U19 to Barbados 1990-91; Warwickshire to Cape Town 1996, 1997, to Bloemfontein 1998; England A to Australia 1996-97, to Kenya and Sri Lanka 1997-98; England to Sharjah (Champions Trophy) 1997-98, to Bangladesh (Wills International Cup) 1998, to Australia 1998-99 (CUB Series), to South Africa and Zimbabwe 1999-2000 (one-day series), to Kenya (ICC Knockout Trophy) 2000-01, to Pakistan and Sri Lanka 2000-01, to India and New Zealand 2001-02
Overseas teams played for: Vredenburg/Saldanha, Cape Town 1992-95; Avendale CC, Cape Town 1995-96
Cricketers particularly admired: Dermot Reeve, Tim Munton, Dougie Brown, Ian Botham
Young players to look out for: Ian Bell
Other sports played: Golf (14 handicap), football ('Klinsmann')
Other sports followed: Football (QPR)
Injuries: Out for much of 2001 season with an Achilles tendon injury
Relaxations: 'Cinema, music, spending lots of time with my family'
Extras: Surrey Young Cricketer of the Year 1991. Shared in record Warwickshire partnership for tenth wicket, 141 with Tim Munton v Worcestershire at Worcester 1996. NBC Denis Compton Award for Warwickshire in 1996. Warwickshire Player of the Year in 1996 and 2000. Warwickshire Most Improved Player 1996. Cricket Society Young Allrounder of the year 1996. Scored hundred (123*) and took five wickets in an innings (5-28) in same match (v Oxford University at The Parks) in 1999, the first

time this feat had been performed by a Warwickshire player since Tom Cartwright achieved it v Lancashire at Edgbaston in 1961. Shared in record Warwickshire partnership for eighth wicket (289 with Dougie Brown v Sussex at Hove 2000), in the process scoring 128*, the best by a Warwickshire No. 8. Took 23 wickets (12-135 and 11-196) in two games v Northamptonshire 2000. Followed first innings score of 98 with five wickets in an innings (6-58) v Sussex at Edgbaston 2000. Recorded maiden five-wicket return in Tests (5-75) in the second Test v Pakistan at Faisalabad 2000-01; finished the series with 17 wickets, the highest total by an England bowler in a series in Pakistan. Returned figures of 4-11 from 9.1 overs as Sri Lanka were bowled out for 81 in their second innings of the third Test at Colombo 2000-01. England central contract 2001

Opinions on cricket: 'Two divisions pulling the game in the right direction. Central contracts are the future of our game.'

Best batting: 128* Warwickshire v Sussex, Hove 2000

Best bowling: 8-90 Warwickshire v Northamptonshire, Northampton 2000

Stop press: Returned innings figures of 5-67 from 43.3 overs v India at Ahmedabad 2001-02 on his return to Test cricket after an Achilles tendon operation in July. Man of the Match for his 5-57 (including spell of 5-10 in 19 balls) in One-Day International v India at Delhi 2001-02

2001 Season

	M	Inns	NO	Runs	HS	Avge	100s	50s	Ct	St	O	M	Runs	Wkts	Avge	Best	5wI	10wM
Test	1	2	0	7	7	3.50	-	-	-	-	25	0	108	1	108.00	1-108	-	-
All First	4	7	2	72	40*	14.40	-	-	4	-	154.5	41	429	12	35.75	5-46	1	-
1-day Int																		
C & G	3	1	1	19	19*	-	-	-	1	-	29	1	119	2	59.50	2-23	-	
B & H																		
1-day Lge	5	5	3	27	23	13.50	-	-	1	-	45	1	228	8	28.50	2-41	-	

Career Performances

	M	Inns	NO	Runs	HS	Avge	100s	50s	Ct	St	Balls	Runs	Wkts	Avge	Best	5wI	10wM
Test	8	13	4	95	37*	10.55	-	-	5	-	2185	933	26	35.88	5-75	1	-
All First	108	146	32	3162	128*	27.73	3	13	48	-	22134	8657	329	26.31	8-90	15	2
1-day Int	9	6	2	38	11	9.50	-	-	1	-	426	336	8	42.00	2-37	-	
C & G	20	14	4	373	107	37.30	1	2	3	-	1067	703	31	22.67	5-21	1	
B & H	19	14	3	188	37	17.09	-	-	9	-	712	554	22	25.18	3-22	-	
1-day Lge	81	53	11	766	57	18.23	-	1	26	-	2993	2171	107	20.28	5-36	1	

38. Which left-arm seamer took 3-26 for Surrey v Warwickshire in the 1982 NatWest final, winning the Man of the Match award?

GOLDING, J. M.   Kent

Name: <u>James</u> Matthew Golding
Role: Right-hand bat, right-arm
fast-medium bowler; all-rounder
Born: 19 July 1977, Canterbury
Height: 6ft 4in **Weight:** 16st 7lbs
Nickname: Goldy, Jingo
County debut: 1999
1st-Class catches: 2
Place in batting averages: 227th av. 15.00
Strike rate: 94.50 (career 100.12)
Parents: Marilyn and Adrian
Marital status: Single
Education: St Anne's, Canterbury; Kent
College, Canterbury; University College,
Worcester
Qualifications: 9 GCSEs, 3 A-levels,
BSc (Hons) Geography with Sports Science,
Level II cricket coach, Level I hockey coach
Off-season: 'In Perth, Western Australia; training with Neil 'Noddy' Holder and
Matt Nicholson'
Overseas tours: Kent to Port Elizabeth 2001
Overseas teams played for: Kensington District CC, Adelaide 1995-96; Balcatta CC,
Perth 2000-01
Career highlights to date: 'Kent winning Norwich Union League 2001'
Cricket moments to forget: 'Being struck into the top tier of the Frank Woolley
Stand at Canterbury'
Cricketers particularly admired: Ian Botham, David Gower, Jacques Kallis,
Allan Donald, Graeme Hick
Young players to look out for: Robin Jackson, Ian Gascoigne, Andy Alford,
Rupert Swetman
Other sports played: 'All ball sports, particularly hockey, golf and tennis'
Other sports followed: 'Keep an eye on most, apart from horse racing'
Injuries: Out for final two months of season after having 'os trigonum' removed from
left ankle
Relaxations: Socialising, other sports, gym
Extras: Man of the Match playing for Kent Cricket Board v Hampshire in NatWest
third round 1999. Made first-class debut for Kent v New Zealanders 1999 while still
an amateur; his first wicket was New Zealand captain Stephen Fleming
Opinions on cricket: 'More day/nighters – encourages younger audience.'
Best batting: 30 Kent v Glamorgan, Maidstone 2001
Best bowling: 3-23 Kent v Somerset, Taunton 2001

2001 Season

	M	Inns	NO	Runs	HS	Avge	100s	50s	Ct	St	O	M	Runs	Wkts	Avge	Best	5wI	10wM
Test																		
All First	5	8	2	90	30	15.00	-	-	2	-	94.3	17	330	6	55.00	3-23	-	-
1-day Int																		
C & G	1	0	0	0	0	-	-	-	-	-	3	0	19	0	-		-	-
B & H	5	4	2	76	33 *	38.00	-	-	-	-	25.1	0	139	7	19.85	3-25	-	
1-day Lge	5	5	2	42	15	14.00	-	-	-	-	34	2	139	4	34.75	2-18	-	

Career Performances

	M	Inns	NO	Runs	HS	Avge	100s	50s	Ct	St	Balls	Runs	Wkts	Avge	Best	5wI	10wM
Test																	
All First	7	11	4	111	30	15.85	-	-	2	-	801	442	8	55.25	3-23	-	-
1-day Int																	
C & G	4	2	0	52	47	26.00	-	-	2	-	168	160	0	-		-	-
B & H	7	5	2	83	33 *	27.66	-	-	2	-	235	208	11	18.90	3-20	-	
1-day Lge	8	7	2	42	15	8.40	-	-	-	-	282	177	5	35.40	2-18	-	

GOODE, C. M. Northamptonshire

Name: <u>Chris</u> Martin Goode
Role: Right-hand middle/lower-order bat, right-arm fast bowler
Born: 12 October 1984, Kettering
Height: 6ft 2in **Weight:** 12st
Nickname: Goodey
County debut: No first-team appearance
Parents: Martin and Carla
Marital status: Single
Family links with cricket: 'Dad played local cricket – got me started'
Education: Finedon Mulso C of E School; Huxlow; Tresham College
Qualifications: 9 GCSEs
Career outside cricket: Full-time education
Off-season: 'Resting (first half); getting fitter (second half)'
Overseas tours: Northamptonshire U17-U19 to South Africa 1999-2000; Northampton Town FC U14 to Italy 1998-99
Career highlights to date: 'Second-team appearance v Yorkshire'
Cricketers particularly admired: Allan Donald
Young players to look out for: Tim Bresnan
Other sports played: Football ('played for Northampton Town U10-U16')

Other sports followed: Football (Rushden & Diamonds)
Injuries: Out for second half of season with back problem
Relaxations: Music
Extras: Represented England U15 in Costcutter U15 World Challenge 2000, taking 4-22 v India
Opinions on cricket: 'Enjoy it!'

GOODWIN, M. W. Sussex

Name: Murray William Goodwin
Role: Right-hand bat, right-arm medium/leg-spin bowler
Born: 11 December 1972, Harare, Zimbabwe
Height: 5ft 9in **Weight:** 11st 2lbs
Nickname: Muzza, Fuzz, Goodie
County debut: 2001
County cap: 2001
Test debut: 1997-98
Tests: 19
One-Day Internationals: 71
1000 runs in a season: 1
1st-Class 50s: 25
1st-Class 100s: 14
1st-Class 200s: 1
1st-Class catches: 51
One-Day 100s: 3
Place in batting averages: 12th av. 61.25
(2000 5th av. 65.10)
Strike rate: (career 93.28)
Parents: Penny and George
Wife and date of marriage: Tarsha, 13 December 1997
Family links with cricket: 'Dad is a coach. Eldest brother played for Zimbabwe'
Education: St Johns, Harare, Zimbabwe; Newtonmoore Senior High, Bunbury, Western Australia
Qualifications: Level II coach
Career outside cricket: Coaching, commentating; business
Off-season: Playing for Western Australia
Overseas tours: Australian Cricket Academy to South Africa 1992, to Sri Lanka and India 1993; Zimbabwe to Sri Lanka and New Zealand 1997-98, to Bangladesh (Wills International Cup) 1998-99, to Pakistan 1998-99, to UK, Ireland and Holland (World Cup) 1999, to South Africa 1999-2000, to West Indies 1999-2000, to England 2000
Overseas teams played for: Excelsior, Holland 1997; Mashonaland 1997-98 – 1998-99; Western Australia 1994-95 – 1996-97, 2000-01 –

Career highlights to date: 'Playing international cricket'
Cricket moments to forget: 'Test against Sri Lanka – we felt the umpiring to be very dubious' (*In the second Test v Zimbabwe 1997-98 at Colombo, chasing 326 to win, Sri Lanka won by five wickets having been 137 for five*)
Cricketers particularly admired: Allan Border, Steve Waugh, Curtly Ambrose, Sachin Tendulkar
Young players to look out for: Shaun Marsh
Other sports played: Hockey (WA Country), golf, tennis
Other sports followed: 'All'
Relaxations: 'Socialising with friends'
Extras: Emigrated to Australia aged 13. Attended Australian Cricket Academy. Made first-class debut for Western Australia v England, Perth 1994-95, scoring 91 and 77. Has played league cricket in England. Scored century (111) in only his second One-Day International, v Sri Lanka at Colombo 1997-98, winning Man of the Match award. Scored 166* v Pakistan at Bulawayo 1997-98, in the process sharing with Andy Flower in the highest partnership for Zimbabwe for any wicket in Tests (277*). Scored 148* for Zimbabwe v England in second Test at Trent Bridge 2000, winning Man of the Match award. Scored 112* v West Indies in NatWest Triangular Series at Riverside 2000, winning Man of the Match award. Retired from international cricket in 2000. Scored 167 for Western Australia v New South Wales at Perth in the Mercantile Mutual Cup 2000-01, setting a new record for the highest individual score in Australian domestic one-day cricket. Joined Sussex as overseas player for 2001. B&H Gold Award for his 108 v Middlesex at Hove 2001. Scored maiden first-class double century (203*) v Nottinghamshire at Trent Bridge 2001, having already scored a century (115) in the first innings; in the process of scoring his 203* he shared with Richard Montgomerie in a record partnership for any wicket for Sussex in matches against Notts (372*). Scored 87 v Essex at Hove in the Norwich Union League 2001, in the process sharing with Richard Montgomerie in a Sussex record opening partnership in the one-day league (176). Joint Sussex Player of the Year (with Richard Montgomerie) 2001. Awarded Sussex cap 2001
Opinions on cricket: 'Play long hours and lots of practice for little financial gain.'
Best batting: 203* Sussex v Nottinghamshire, Trent Bridge 2001
Best bowling: 2-23 Zimbabweans v Lahore City, Lahore 1998-99

2001 Season

	M	Inns	NO	Runs	HS	Avge	100s	50s	Ct	St	O	M	Runs	Wkts	Avge	Best	5wI	10wM
Test																		
All First	17	32	5	1654	203 *	61.25	7	5	8	-	13	13	40	0	-	-	-	-
1-day Int																		
C & G	2	2	0	105	66	52.50	-	1	-	-								
B & H	4	4	0	222	108	55.50	1	1	1	-								
1-day Lge	15	15	3	484	87	40.33	-	6	4	-								

Career Performances

	M	Inns	NO	Runs	HS	Avge	100s	50s	Ct	St	Balls	Runs	Wkts	Avge	Best	5wI	10wM
Test	19	37	4	1414	166 *	42.84	3	8	10	-	118	69	0	-	-	-	-
All First	72	128	13	5282	203 *	45.93	15	25	51	-	653	337	7	48.14	2-23	-	-
1-day Int	71	70	3	1818	112 *	27.13	2	8	20	-	248	210	4	52.50	1-12	-	
C & G	3	3	0	109	66	36.33	-	1	-	-	30	28	1	28.00	1-28	-	
B & H	4	4	0	222	108	55.50	1	1	1	-							
1-day Lge	15	15	3	484	87	40.33	-	6	4	-							

GOUGH, D. Yorkshire

Name: Darren Gough
Role: Right-hand bat, right-arm fast bowler
Born: 18 September 1970, Barnsley
Height: 5ft 11in **Weight:** 13st 9lbs
Nickname: Rhino, Dazzler
County debut: 1989
County cap: 1993
Benefit: 2001
Test debut: 1994
Tests: 56
One-Day Internationals: 95
50 wickets in a season: 4
1st-Class 50s: 12
1st-Class 100s: 1
1st-Class 5 w. in innings: 27
1st-Class 10 w. in match: 3
1st-Class catches: 41
One-Day 5 w. in innings: 6
Place in batting averages: 176th av. 21.90 (2000 245th av. 13.10)
Place in bowling averages: 66th av. 31.07 (2000 18th av. 18.98)
Strike rate: 49.48 (career 49.86)
Parents: Trevor and Christine
Wife and date of marriage: Anna Marie, 16 October 1993
Children: Liam James, 24 November 1994; Brennan Kyle, 9 December 1997
Education: St Helens Junior; Priory Comprehensive; Airedale and Wharfdale College (part-time)
Qualifications: 2 O-levels, 5 CSEs, BTEC Leisure, NCA coaching award
Off-season: 'Being a dad for first time in seven years and playing one-day cricket for England'
Overseas tours: England YC to Australia 1989-90; Yorkshire to Barbados 1989-90, to South Africa 1991-92 and 1992-93; England A to South Africa 1993-94; England to

Australia 1994-95, to South Africa 1995-96, to India and Pakistan (World Cup) 1995-96, to Zimbabwe and New Zealand 1996-97, to Australia 1998-99, to Sharjah (Coca-Cola Cup) 1998-99, to South Africa and Zimbabwe 1999-2000, to Kenya (ICC Knockout Trophy) 2000-01, to Pakistan and Sri Lanka 2000-01, to India and New Zealand 2001-02 (one-day series)

Overseas teams played for: East Shirley, Christchurch, New Zealand 1991-92
Cricketers particularly admired: Shane Warne, Steve Waugh, Ian Botham, Michael Atherton, Malcolm Marshall
Young players to look out for: Michael Lumb
Other sports played: Golf, football
Other sports followed: Football (Barnsley and Tottenham Hotspur)
Relaxations: Golf, cinema, 'spending time with family'
Extras: Scored 65 in his first Test innings, v New Zealand at Old Trafford 1994, batting at No. 9. Yorkshire Sports Personality of the Year 1994. Cornhill England Player of the Year 1994-95. Took a hat-trick against Kent at Headingley in 1995. Whyte and Mackay Bowler of the Year in 1996. England Player of the Series in the Texaco one-day rubber v South Africa 1998. Took 100th Test wicket (Jonty Rhodes) v South Africa at Headingley 1998. Took Test hat-trick (Healy, MacGill, Miller) v Australia at Sydney in January 1999, the first Ashes hat-trick by an England bowler since J. Hearne's at Leeds in 1899. Was third English cricketer to reach 100 One-Day International wickets. *Sheffield Star* Sports Personality of the Year. Cornhill England Player of the Year (for the second time) 1998-99. One of *Wisden*'s Five Cricketers of the Year 1999. Represented England in the 1999 World Cup. Won Freeserve Fast Ball award 2000 (for the fastest recorded ball bowled in a televised match) for a delivery timed at 93.1 mph at Lord's on 20 May during the first Test v Zimbabwe. Shared the new ball with Andrew Caddick in each Test of the West Indies series 2000, the first time the same pair had opened the bowling for England throughout a series since Fred Trueman and Brian Statham did so v South Africa in 1960. Took 25 Test wickets v West Indies 2000 and was named England's Man of the Series. Man of the Series v Sri Lanka 2000-01 (14 wickets av. 19.57). England central contract 2001. *GQ* Sportsman of the Year 2001. Vodafone England Cricketer of the Year 2000-01. Took 200th Test wicket (Rashid Latif) v Pakistan at Lord's 2001 in his 50th Test, in the same match passing John Snow's total of 202 wickets to move into seventh place in the list of England Test wicket-takers; his 5-61 in Pakistan's first innings was also his first Test five-wicket return at Lord's. Took 146th ODI wicket (Shahid Afridi) v Pakistan at Headingley 2001, passing Ian Botham's England record of 145 ODI wickets. Made himself unavailable for Test tour of India 2001-02
Opinions on cricket: 'Does it matter what a player has to say? Nobody takes notice. They'll only do what's best financially for themselves.'
Best batting: 121 Yorkshire v Warwickshire, Headingley 1996
Best bowling: 7-28 Yorkshire v Lancashire, Headingley 1995
Stop press: Became first England bowler to take 150 One-Day International wickets, v India at Cuttack 2001-02

2001 Season

	M	Inns	NO	Runs	HS	Avge	100s	50s	Ct	St	O	M	Runs	Wkts	Avge	Best	5wI	10wM
Test	7	12	4	110	39 *	13.75	-	-	-	-	233.4	37	937	31	30.22	5-61	2	-
All First	9	15	5	219	96	21.90	-	1	-	-	321.4	55	1212	39	31.07	5-61	2	-
1-day Int	6	5	1	49	40 *	12.25	-	-	2	-	54	5	244	9	27.11	2-31	-	
C & G	2	1	1	6	6 *	-	-	-	-	-	20	2	88	0	-	-	-	
B & H	4	1	0	13	13	13.00	-	-	-	-	39	2	149	3	49.66	1-18	-	
1-day Lge	2	2	1	29	16 *	29.00	-	-	-	-	16	3	53	4	13.25	3-15	-	

Career Performances

	M	Inns	NO	Runs	HS	Avge	100s	50s	Ct	St	Balls	Runs	Wkts	Avge	Best	5wI	10wM
Test	56	83	18	806	65	12.40	-	2	12	-	11503	6288	228	27.57	6-42	9	-
All First	192	260	50	3379	121	16.09	1	12	41	-	35158	18627	705	26.42	7-28	27	3
1-day Int	95	62	24	415	45	10.92	-	-	14	-	5249	3665	147	24.93	5-44	2	
C & G	26	14	1	234	46	18.00	-	-	3	-	1643	939	54	17.38	7-27	2	
B & H	39	19	6	177	48 *	13.61	-	-	11	-	2042	1245	45	27.66	4-17	-	
1-day Lge	106	70	20	673	72 *	13.46	-	1	19	-	4563	3291	135	24.37	5-13	2	

GOUGH, M. A.　　　　　　　　　　　Durham

Name: <u>Michael</u> Andrew Gough
Role: Right-hand bat, off-spin bowler,
specialist gully fielder
Born: 18 December 1979, Hartlepool
Height: 6ft 5in **Weight:** 14st
Nickname: Goughy
County debut: 1998
1st-Class 50s: 8
1st-Class 100s: 1
1st-Class 5 w. in innings: 1
1st-Class catches: 43
Place in batting averages: 196th av. 19.56
(2000 231st av. 14.66)
Place in bowling averages: 71st av. 32.07
Strike rate: 67.50 (career 82.72)
Parents: Michael and Jean
Marital status: Single
Family links with cricket: 'Dad played
Minor Counties cricket for Durham. Cousin Paul played for Durham U19. Uncle John
was a good opening bat'
Education: Sacred Heart RC Primary School, Hartlepool; English Martyrs School and
Sixth Form College, Hartlepool

Qualifications: 10 GCSEs, cricket coaching award

Overseas tours: Durham U21 to Sri Lanka November 1996; Durham to Sri Lanka 2001; England U17 to Bermuda (International Youth Tournament) June 1997; England U19 to South Africa (including U19 World Cup) 1997-98, to New Zealand 1998-99 (captain); England A to Bangladesh and New Zealand 1999-2000

Cricketers particularly admired: Mike Atherton, Steve Waugh, Jacques Kallis, Shane Warne, Simon Katich, Saqlain Mushtaq, Ronnie Irani

Young players to look out for: Gary Pratt, Nicky Peng, James Foster, Ian Hunter, Chris Lawson (Hartlepool CC)

Other sports played: Football (had trials with Arsenal, Sheffield United and Hartlepool, and attended Middlesbrough FC School of Excellence)

Other sports followed: Football (Hartlepool United season-ticket holder – 'for my sins!!!')

Relaxations: 'Music, TV, sport, socialising, spending time with girlfriend Nicola, cinema, eating out, spending time with friends, football'

Extras: Captained North of England and England U15. Part of winning England U17 team at the International Youth Tournament in Bermuda 1997. Durham CCC Young Player of the Year 1997. Scored 62 on first-class debut, against Essex 1998. Became youngest player to score a first-class century for Durham, 123 against Cambridge University at Fenner's 1998, aged 18 years and 151 days. Captained England U19 v Australia U19 in one-day and 'Test' series 1999. 'Hit Shane Warne for a four!' Recorded maiden first-class five-wicket return (5-66) v Middlesex at Riverside 2001

Opinions on cricket: 'Far too much cricket played, therefore players lose hunger and desire. Extend tea break by ten minutes. Should play more day/night cricket – great to play in, great spectacle for spectators, great attraction for kids, therefore more involvement in game. More fast bowlers on central contracts for monitoring progress and injury prevention.'

Best batting: 123 Durham v Cambridge University, Fenner's 1998

Best bowling: 5-66 Durham v Middlesex, Riverside 2001

2001 Season

	M	Inns	NO	Runs	HS	Avge	100s	50s	Ct	St	O	M	Runs	Wkts	Avge	Best	5wI	10wM
Test																		
All First	13	23	0	450	79	19.56	-	1	8	-	157.3	34	449	14	32.07	5-66	1	-
1-day Int																		
C & G	3	2	0	53	27	26.50	-	-	2	-	11	0	64	0	-	-	-	-
B & H	6	6	0	136	58	22.66	-	1	2	-	33.1	0	152	6	25.33	3-36	-	
1-day Lge	8	6	2	115	35	28.75	-	-	1	-	53	3	247	7	35.28	2-27	-	

Career Performances

	M	Inns	NO	Runs	HS	Avge	100s	50s	Ct	St	Balls	Runs	Wkts	Avge	Best	5wI	10wM
Test																	
All First	46	80	1	1752	123	22.17	1	8	43	-	2068	1109	25	44.36	5-66	1	-
1-day Int																	
C & G	4	3	0	63	27	21.00	-	-	2	-	66	64	0	-	-	-	-
B & H	6	6	0	136	58	22.66	-	1	2	-	199	152	6	25.33	3-36	-	
1-day Lge	16	13	3	223	36	22.30	-	-	3	-	390	322	7	46.00	2-27	-	

GRANT, J. B. Essex

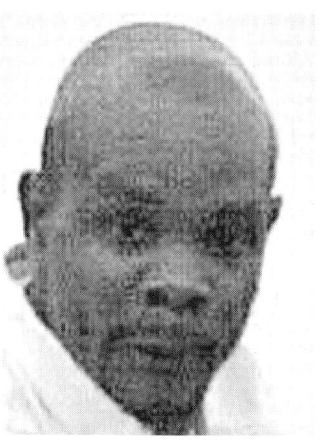

Name: Joseph (<u>Joe</u>) Benjamin Grant
Role: Right-hand bat, right-arm
fast-medium bowler
Born: 17 December 1967, White House,
St James, Jamaica
County debut: 2001
Strike rate: 38.00 (career 66.90)
Overseas teams played for: Jamaica
1990-91 – 1995-96
Extras: Opened the bowling for Jamaica with
Courtney Walsh. Has played in the Yorkshire
leagues. Played for Cambridgeshire in the
Minor Counties Championship in 2001,
taking 21 wickets (av. 12.38) in three
matches. Is not considered an overseas player
Best batting: 36* Jamaica v Guyana, Albion
1994-95
Best bowling: 3-43 Jamaica v Trinidad and
Tobago, Kingston 1994-95

2001 Season

	M	Inns	NO	Runs	HS	Avge	100s	50s	Ct	St	O	M	Runs	Wkts	Avge	Best	5wI	10wM
Test																		
All First	1	1	1	1	1*	-	-	-	-	-	19	0	101	3	33.66	3-81	-	-
1-day Int																		
C & G																		
B & H																		
1-day Lge																		

Career Performances

	M	Inns	NO	Runs	HS	Avge	100s	50s	Ct	St	Balls	Runs	Wkts	Avge	Best	5wI	10wM
Test																	
All First	15	19	9	90	36 *	9.00	-	-	6	-	1539	980	23	42.60	3-43	-	-
1-day Int																	
C & G																	
B & H																	
1-day Lge																	

GRAY, A. K. D.   Yorkshire

Name: Andrew (<u>Andy</u>) Kenneth
Donovan Gray
Role: Right-hand bat, right-arm
off-spin bowler
Born: 19 May 1974, Armadale,
Western Australia
Nickname: Graysie
County debut: 2001
1st-Class catches: 2
Place in bowling averages: 53rd av. 28.10
Strike rate: 55.20 (career 55.20)
Overseas teams played for: Willetton,
Western Australia
Extras: Played for Wilberfoss in division one
of the York Senior League. Played for
Scarborough CC for part of 2001. Played for
Worcestershire 2nd XI v Yorkshire 2nd XI at
Scarborough 2001 before joining Yorkshire.
Is not considered an overseas player
Best batting: 3 Yorkshire v Surrey, The Oval 2001
Best bowling: 4-128 Yorkshire v Surrey, The Oval 2001

2001 Season

	M	Inns	NO	Runs	HS	Avge	100s	50s	Ct	St	O	M	Runs	Wkts	Avge	Best	5wI	10wM
Test																		
All First	3	4	0	4	3	1.00	-	-	2	-	92	23	281	10	28.10	4-128	-	-
1-day Int																		
C & G																		
B & H																		
1-day Lge	2	2	1	21	19 *	21.00	-	-	1	-	9.1	0	49	1	49.00	1-45	-	

Career Performances

	M	Inns	NO	Runs	HS	Avge	100s	50s	Ct	St	Balls	Runs	Wkts	Avge	Best	5wI	10wM
Test																	
All First	3	4	0	4	3	1.00	-	-	2	-	552	281	10	28.10	4-128	-	-
1-day Int																	
C & G																	
B & H																	
1-day Lge	2	2	1	21	19 *	21.00	-	-	1	-	55	49	1	49.00	1-45	-	

GRAYSON, A. P. Essex

Name: Adrian <u>Paul</u> Grayson
Role: Right-hand opening bat, slow left-arm bowler, county vice-captain
Born: 31 March 1971, Ripon
Height: 6ft 1in **Weight:** 12st
Nickname: Larry
County debut: 1990 (Yorkshire), 1996 (Essex)
County cap: 1996 (Essex)
One-Day Internationals: 1
1000 runs in a season: 4
1st-Class 50s: 37
1st-Class 100s: 14
1st-Class 5 w. in innings: 1
1st-Class catches: 109
Place in batting averages: 33rd av. 49.03 (2000 114th av. 27.82)
Place in bowling averages: (2000 139th av. 44.30)
Strike rate: 108.00 (career 94.15)
Parents: Adrian and Carol
Wife and date of marriage: Alison, 30 September 1994
Children: Oliver, 30 January 1997; Beth, 3 February 1999
Family links with cricket: 'Father is a staff coach; brother Simon plays when free from football commitments'
Education: Bedale; Bedale Comprehensive School
Qualifications: 8 CSEs, BTEC in Leisure Studies, advanced cricket coach
Career outside cricket: Working for Ridley's Brewery
Off-season: England one-day tour to Zimbabwe
Overseas tours: England YC to Australia 1989-90; England to Kenya (ICC Knockout Trophy) 2000-01, to Pakistan 2000-01 (one-day series), to Zimbabwe (one-day series)

2001-02; Yorkshire to Barbados 1989-90, to Cape Town 1991, 1992, 1993, to Leeward Islands 1994

Overseas teams played for: Petone, Wellington 1991-92, 1995-96

Cricketers particularly admired: Graham Gooch, Martyn Moxon, Darren Gough

Young players to look out for: James Foster, Oliver Grayson

Other sports played: Golf (16 handicap), football (Essex CCC charity side; was offered apprentice forms with Middlesbrough FC at 16 but signed for Yorkshire)

Other sports followed: Football (Leeds United)

Relaxations: 'Spending time with my wife and children; playing golf; watching football'

Extras: Played for England YC v New Zealand 1989 and Pakistan 1990. Brother plays professional football. Yorkshire Player of the Year 1994. Released by Yorkshire at end of 1995 and joined Essex for 1996. Essex Player of the Year 1997. Drafted into England one-day squad for ICC Knockout Trophy in Kenya 2000-01 as cover for the injured Ashley Giles (making One-Day International debut v South Africa), and for one-day element of tour to Pakistan. B&H Gold Award for his 2-24 (following 22) v Middlesex at Chelmsford 2001. Recorded maiden first-class five-wicket return (5-20) v Yorkshire at Scarborough 2001. Scored two centuries (173 and 149) in match v Northamptonshire at Northampton 2001. Essex Player of the Year 2001. Appointed vice-captain of Essex for 2002. PCA representative for Essex

Opinions on cricket: 'Two divisions are an excellent idea and is working well. Central contracts have worked and should be applauded. County staffs should be reduced, but there should be an increase in wages for retained players.'

Best batting: 189 Essex v Glamorgan, Chelmsford 2001

Best bowling: 5-20 Essex v Yorkshire, Scarborough 2001

2001 Season

	M	Inns	NO	Runs	HS	Avge	100s	50s	Ct	St	O	M	Runs	Wkts	Avge	Best	5wI	10wM
Test																		
All First	16	29	3	1275	189	49.03	6	1	7	-	162	24	602	9	66.88	5-20	1	-
1-day Int																		
C & G	2	2	0	37	36	18.50	-	-	-	-	20	1	55	4	13.75	2-27	-	
B & H	3	3	0	55	23	18.33	-	-	-	-	28	3	100	3	33.33	2-24	-	
1-day Lge	16	15	1	320	52	22.85	-	1	6	-	116	3	501	18	27.83	3-23	-	

Career Performances

	M	Inns	NO	Runs	HS	Avge	100s	50s	Ct	St	Balls	Runs	Wkts	Avge	Best	5wI	10wM
Test																	
All First	158	261	23	7593	189	31.90	14	37	109	-	11205	5242	119	44.05	5-20	1	-
1-day Int	1	1	0	0	0	0.00	-	-	-	-	30	20	0	-	-	-	-
C & G	24	20	1	446	82 *	23.47	-	3	7	-	989	737	25	29.48	3-24	-	
B & H	31	26	6	408	49 *	20.40	-	-	7	-	1185	833	28	29.75	3-30	-	
1-day Lge	142	118	17	1921	69 *	19.01	-	6	39	-	4790	4120	130	31.69	4-25	-	

GREENIDGE, C. G.　　　Northamptonshire

Name: <u>Carl</u> Gary Greenidge
Role: Right-hand bat, right-arm
fast bowler
Born: 20 April 1978, Basingstoke
Height: 5ft 10in **Weight:** 12st 7lbs
Nickname: Carlos, Carlito, G
County debut: 1998 (one-day, Surrey),
1999 (first-class, Surrey)
1st-Class 5 w. in innings: 1
1st-Class catches: 3
Strike rate: (career 55.83)
Parents: Gordon and Anita
Marital status: Single
Family links with cricket: Father Gordon
played for Hampshire and West Indies, as did
cousin (on mother's side) Andy Roberts
Education: St Paul's, Barbados; St
Michael's, Barbados; Heathcote School,
Chingford; City of Westminster College

Qualifications: GNVQ Leisure and Tourism, NCA senior coaching award
Cricketers particularly admired: Malcolm Marshall, Dennis Lillee, Carl Hooper,
Mark Waugh, Graham Thorpe, Ricaldo Anderson, Muazam Ali, Gareth Batty,
Rupesh Amin, 'and many more'
Other sports followed: Football (Arsenal), basketball (LA Lakers)
Relaxations: 'Music, kung fu movies, PlayStation, and my bed'
Extras: Spent a year on Lord's groundstaff. Took eight wickets on his Championship
debut for Surrey, v Yorkshire at The Oval 1999. Released by Surrey at the end of the
2001 season and has joined Northamptonshire for 2002
Best batting: 14 Surrey v Sri Lanka A, The Oval 1999
Best bowling: 5-60 Surrey v Yorkshire, The Oval 1999

2001 Season

	M	Inns	NO	Runs	HS	Avge	100s	50s	Ct	St	O	M	Runs	Wkts	Avge	Best	5wI	10wM
Test																		
All First																		
1-day Int																		
C & G																		
B & H																		
1-day Lge	4	3	1	1	1	0.50	-	-	3	-	20	2	112	5	22.40	2-17	-	

Career Performances

	M	Inns	NO	Runs	HS	Avge	100s	50s	Ct	St	Balls	Runs	Wkts	Avge	Best	5wI	10wM
Test																	
All First	5	5	0	29	14	5.80	-	-	3	-	670	337	12	28.08	5-60	1	-
1-day Int																	
C & G	2	0	0	0	0	-	-	-	-	-	-	84	87	0	-		-	-
B & H	1	0	0	0	0	-	-	-	-	-	-	24	22	0	-		-	-
1-day Lge	13	5	3	6	3 *	3.00	-	-	7	-	434	403	9	44.77	2-17	-

GRIFFITHS, P. Leicestershire

Name: Paul Griffiths
Role: Right-hand bat, right-arm medium-fast bowler
Born: 14 September 1975, Wolverhampton
Height: 6ft 7in **Weight:** 14st
Nickname: Kinder, Egg, Express, Longshanks, Gimp, Useless
County debut: 2000
Strike rate: 60.00 (career 82.00)
Parents: Tony and Val
Marital status: Single
Family links with cricket: 'Dad played club cricket. Brother plays for Wolverhampton CC and has played for Staffordshire'
Education: St Nicholas School, Codsall, Wolverhampton; Codsall High School; Cheltenham and Gloucester College of Higher Education
Qualifications: 3 A-levels, BSc (Hons) Physical Geography and Sports and Exercise Science
Cricketers particularly admired: Michael Holding, Allan Donald, Ian Botham, Curtly Ambrose
Young players to look out for: Steve Adshead, Ashley Wright, 'my brother Simon'
Other sports played: Golf (Staffordshire Boys' Champion 1991)
Other sports followed: Football (Wolverhampton Wanderers)
Relaxations: Socialising, cinema, gambling
Extras: Took wicket (Adrian Griffith) with his third ball in first-class cricket, v West Indians at Leicester 2000. Released by Leicestershire at the end of the 2001 season
Opinions on cricket: 'Second XI cricket should be played on first-class grounds. More day/night games to bring in the crowds.'
Best batting: 4* Leicestershire v Pakistanis, Leicester 2001
Best bowling: 2-51 Leicestershire v Pakistanis, Leicester 2001

2001 Season

	M	Inns	NO	Runs	HS	Avge	100s	50s	Ct	St	O	M	Runs	Wkts	Avge	Best	5wI	10wM
Test																		
All First	1	2	1	5	4 *	5.00	-	-	-	-	20	7	51	2	25.50	2-51	-	-
1-day Int																		
C & G																		
B & H																		
1-day Lge																		

Career Performances

	M	Inns	NO	Runs	HS	Avge	100s	50s	Ct	St	Balls	Runs	Wkts	Avge	Best	5wI	10wM
Test																	
All First	2	2	1	5	4 *	5.00	-	-	-	-	246	116	3	38.66	2-51	-	-
1-day Int																	
C & G																	
B & H																	
1-day Lge																	

GROVE, J. O. Leicestershire

Name: <u>Jamie</u> Oliver Grove
Role: Right-hand bat, right-arm
fast-medium bowler
Born: 3 July 1979, Bury St Edmunds
Height: 6ft 2in **Weight:** 12st 6lbs
Nickname: Groover, Grover
County debut: 1998 (Essex),
2000 (Somerset)
1st-Class 5 w. in innings: 1
1st-Class catches: 2
Place in bowling averages: (2000 112th
av. 34.90)
Strike rate: 88.33 (career 62.82)
Parents: Chris and Pat
Marital status: Single
Family links with cricket: 'Dad played
Minor Counties and brother plays local
cricket. Mum is a keen fan!'
Education: Whepstead Primary School; St James Middle School, Bury St Edmunds;
County Upper School, Bury St Edmunds; Saxon Training College
Qualifications: 9 GCSEs, Modern Apprenticeship in Precision Engineering
Career outside cricket: Engineer

Off-season: Training and working
Overseas tours: England U19 to South Africa (including U19 World Cup) 1997-98
Career highlights to date: 'Taking five wickets on debut for Somerset'
Cricket moments to forget: 'Anything that involved me being hit out of the park'
Cricketers particularly admired: Ian Botham
Young players to look out for: Sam Waterson, Taylor Waterson, Matthew Wood (Somerset), Pete Trego
Other sports played: 'All sports'
Other sports followed: Football (West Ham United)
Injuries: 'Repetitive strain disorder from carrying drinks tray!'
Relaxations: 'Listening to music, chillin' with mates'
Extras: Played for England at U15, U17 and U19 level. Was part of the successful England U19 World Cup winning squad in South Africa in 1997-98. Released by Essex at the end of the 1999 season and joined Somerset for 2000. Recorded maiden first-class five-wicket return (5-90) v Leicestershire at Leicester 2000 on debut for Somerset. Member of Somerset's 2nd XI Trophy runners-up side 2001. Member of Somerset's C&G Trophy winning squad 2001. Released by Somerset at the end of the 2001 season and has joined Leicestershire for 2002
Opinions on cricket: 'Take every day as it comes.'
Best batting: 33 Essex v Surrey, Chelmsford 1998
Best bowling: 5-90 Somerset v Leicestershire, Leicester 2000

2001 Season

	M	Inns	NO	Runs	HS	Avge	100s	50s	Ct	St	O	M	Runs	Wkts	Avge	Best	5wI	10wM
Test																		
All First	4	5	2	30	19 *	10.00	-	-	2	-	88.2	8	489	6	81.50	2-46	-	-
1-day Int																		
C & G	1	0	0	0	0	-	-	-	-	-	10	1	36	4	9.00	4-36	-	
B & H																		
1-day Lge	12	3	1	9	6	4.50	-	-	3	-	80	2	438	9	48.66	3-24	-	

Career Performances

	M	Inns	NO	Runs	HS	Avge	100s	50s	Ct	St	Balls	Runs	Wkts	Avge	Best	5wI	10wM
Test																	
All First	22	27	9	191	33	10.61	-	-	2	-	2576	1873	41	45.68	5-90	1	-
1-day Int																	
C & G	1	0	0	0	0	-	-	-	-	-	60	36	4	9.00	4-36	-	
B & H																	
1-day Lge	12	3	1	9	6	4.50	-	-	3	-	480	438	9	48.66	3-24	-	

GUNTER, N. E. L.   Derbyshire

Name: <u>Neil</u> Edward Lloyd Gunter
Role: Left-hand bat, right-arm
medium-fast bowler
Born: 12 May 1981, Basingstoke
Height: 6ft
Nickname: Gunts, Green Beret, Rodney
County debut: No first-team appearance
Parents: Tim and Caroline
Marital status: Single
Family links with cricket: 'Dad played for
The Mote, Maidstone'
Education: Woolton Hill Primary School;
The Clere School; Newbury College
Qualifications: GCSEs and A-levels
Off-season: 'Work, coaching, in the gym or
going to Durban'
Career highlights to date: 'Signing for
Derbyshire and Berkshire debut'
Cricket moments to forget: 'Finishing below Matt Thomas in club averages'
Cricketers particularly admired: Shaun Pollock, Merv Hughes
Young players to look out for: Matt Thomas, James and Richard Morris
Other sports played: Golf, snooker
Other sports followed: 'Passing interest in most sports'
Relaxations: 'Yoga, going to gigs, cinema, reading up on polar explorers; Super
Extreme Highball'
Extras: Berkshire Young Player of the Year 2000. Played for Berkshire in the C&G
2001. MCC Groundstaff 2001
Opinions on cricket: 'There are a lot more good players than are credited for.
Improvements concerning the game should be done with the paying public more
in mind.'

2001 Season (did not make any first-class or one-day appearances)

Career Performances

	M	Inns	NO	Runs	HS	Avge	100s	50s	Ct	St	Balls	Runs	Wkts	Avge	Best	5wI	10wM
Test																	
All First																	
1-day Int																	
C & G	1	1	0	5	5	5.00	-	-	-	-	24	25	0	-		-	-
B & H																	
1-day Lge																	

GUY, S. M.   Yorkshire

Name: <u>Simon</u> Mark Guy
Role: Right-hand bat, wicket-keeper
Born: 17 November 1978, Rotherham
Height: 5ft 7in **Weight:** 10st 7lbs
Nickname: Roland Rat, Fez
County debut: 2000
1st-Class catches: 21
1st-Class stumpings: 2
Place in batting averages: (2000 184th
av. 19.42)
Parents: Darrell and Denise
Wife and date of marriage: Suzanne,
13 October 2001
Family links with cricket: 'Father played for
Notts and Worcs 2nd XI and for Rotherham
Town CC. Brothers play local cricket for
Treeton CC'
Education: Listerdale Junior School;
Wickersley Comprehensive School

Qualifications: GNVQ in Leisure and Recreation, qualified cricket coach, 'two years
at the Yorkshire Cricket School under Ralph Middlebrook'
Career outside cricket: 'Coaching or sports management'
Overseas tours: Yorkshire to South Africa 1999
Overseas teams played for: Orange Cyrus, NSW 1999-2000
Career highlights to date: 'Playing the last ever County Championship game at
Southampton and winning off the last ball with 13 Yorkshire and past Yorkshire men
on the pitch at the same time'
Cricket moments to forget: 'On my debut against the Zimbabweans, smashing a door
after getting out – but I still say it was an accident'
Cricketers particularly admired: Darren Lehmann
Young players to look out for: Joe Sayers
Other sports played: 'All sports', rugby (played for South Yorkshire and Yorkshire)
Other sports followed: Rugby (Rotherham RUFC), 'Treeton Welfare CC, where all
my family play'
Relaxations: 'Playing all sports, socialising with friends, watching cartoons, and
eating a lot'
Extras: Set fifth-wicket partnership record in Yorkshire League (199 unbroken).
Topped Yorkshire 2nd XI batting averages 1998 (106.00). Awarded 2nd XI cap 2000.
Took off pads to bowl on his Championship debut v Somerset at Taunton 2000. Took
five catches in an innings for first time for Yorkshire 1st XI 2000
Best batting: 42 Yorkshire v Somerset, Taunton 2000

2001 Season

	M	Inns	NO	Runs	HS	Avge	100s	50s	Ct	St	O	M	Runs	Wkts	Avge	Best	5wI	10wM
Test																		
All First	1	2	1	12	12 *	12.00	-	-	-	-								
1-day Int																		
C & G																		
B & H																		
1-day Lge																		

Career Performances

	M	Inns	NO	Runs	HS	Avge	100s	50s	Ct	St	Balls	Runs	Wkts	Avge	Best	5wI	10wM
Test																	
All First	7	11	3	148	42	18.50	-	-	21	2	24	8	0	-	-	-	-
1-day Int																	
C & G																		
B & H																		
1-day Lge																		

HABIB, A.   Essex

Name: Aftab Habib
Role: Right-hand bat, right-arm
net bowler
Born: 7 February 1972, Reading
Height: 5ft 10in **Weight:** 11st 7lbs
Nickname: Afie, Tabby, Scabby, Habiby,
Alvin, Inzy
County debut: 1992 (Middlesex),
1995 (Leicestershire)
County cap: 1998 (Leicestershire)
Test debut: 1999
Tests: 2
1000 runs in a season: 2
1st-Class 50s: 26
1st-Class 100s: 14
1st-Class 200s: 1
1st-Class catches: 47
One-Day 100s: 1
Place in batting averages: 65th av. 41.00 (2000 18th av. 47.18)
Parents: Tahira (deceased) and Hussain
Marital status: Single
Family links with cricket: Cousin of Zahid Sadiq (ex-Surrey and Derbyshire)

Education: Alfred Sutton Primary School; Millfield Junior School; Taunton School
Qualifications: 7 GCSEs, NCA coaching certificate
Career outside cricket: 'I would like to teach'
Off-season: 'At home this year, relaxing'
Overseas tours: Berkshire CCC to South Africa 1996; England YC to Australia 1989-90; England U19 to New Zealand 1990-91; England A to Bangladesh and New Zealand 1999-2000, to West Indies 2000-01
Overseas teams played for: Globe Wakatu, Nelson, New Zealand 1992-93, 1996-97; Riccarton CC, Christchurch, New Zealand 1997-98
Career highlights to date: 'Playing for England in 1999'
Cricket moments to forget: 'We lost two one-day competitions in 2001 – one final [C&G] and the Sunday League'
Cricketers particularly admired: Phil Simmons, Steve Waugh, Sachin Tendulkar, Matthew Maynard
Young players to look out for: Owais Shah, Paul Franks, Nicky Peng
Other sports played: 'Enjoy most sports'
Other sports followed: Football ('follow Reading FC and enjoy watching Liverpool'), rugby (Leicester Tigers)
Relaxations: 'Music, cinema, reading books, relaxing with girlfriend, playing golf'
Extras: Played for England U15-U19. Played football for Reading Schools. Middlesex 2nd XI Seaxe Player of the Year 1992. Released by Middlesex at end of 1994 season. Played for Berkshire and had trials with Essex and Somerset. Leicestershire 2nd XI Player of the Year in 1995. With James Whitaker, set then record partnership for Leicestershire for fifth wicket (320), v Worcestershire at Leicester in 1996. Championship medal with Leicestershire in 1996 and 1998. Gold Award winner in the Benson and Hedges Cup with 111 against Durham in 1997. Scored 101* for England A v New Zealand A to help save the first 'Test' at Lincoln 1999-2000. Forced to return home early from England A tour of West Indies 2000-01 with a shoulder injury. Left Leicestershire during the 2001-02 off-season and has joined Essex for 2002
Opinions on cricket: 'Better wickets needed. Too many low-scoring games, both one-dayers and four-dayers. More day/night games. Start on Fridays.'
Best batting: 215 Leicestershire v Worcestershire, Leicester 1996

2001 Season

	M	Inns	NO	Runs	HS	Avge	100s	50s	Ct	St	O	M	Runs	Wkts	Avge	Best	5wI	10wM
Test																		
All First	13	21	2	779	153	41.00	3	3	8	-								
1-day Int																		
C & G	5	3	1	56	22 *	28.00	-	-	1	-	1	0	6	0	-		-	-
B & H	4	4	0	16	10	4.00	-	-	1	-								
1-day Lge	12	9	3	183	44	30.50	-	-	5	-								

Career Performances

	M	Inns	NO	Runs	HS	Avge	100s	50s	Ct	St	Balls	Runs	Wkts	Avge	Best	5wI	10wM
Test	2	3	0	26	19	8.66	-	-	-	-							
All First	103	150	23	5686	215	44.77	15	26	47	-	48	52	0	-	-	-	-
1-day Int																	
C & G	15	12	1	257	67	23.36	-	2	5	-	10	11	2	5.50	2-5	-	
B & H	21	17	2	397	111	26.46	1	2	10	-							
1-day Lge	72	64	16	1347	99 *	28.06	-	5	23	-	1	4	0	-	-	-	

HAMBLIN, J. R. C.   Hampshire

Name: <u>James</u> Rupert Christopher Hamblin
Role: Right-hand bat, right-arm
fast-medium bowler
Born: 16 August 1978, Pembury, Kent
Height: 6ft **Weight:** 14st
Nickname: Hambo
County debut: 2001
Strike rate: 108.00 (career 108.00)
Parents: Bryan and Amanda
Marital status: Single
Family links with cricket: 'Father (C.B.
Hamblin) played for Oxford University
1971-73 and scored a first-class hundred'
Education: Vinehall Preparatory School;
Charterhouse School; University of the West
of England, Bristol
Qualifications: 9 GCSEs, 2 A-levels,
BA (Hons) Social Science
Off-season: 'Rackets tour in October; three months in Perth, January-March'
Overseas tours: British Universities to South Africa 1999; Hampshire to
Cape Town 2000
Overseas teams played for: Harare Sports Club, Zimbabwe 1996-97; Old
Edwardians, Johannesburg 2000-01
Career highlights to date: 'Hampshire v Sussex 2001 – 61 and 3-23'
Cricket moments to forget: 'Missing out on the Hampshire v Australians game 2001'
Cricketers particularly admired: Jim Williams, James Kirtley
Young players to look out for: John Francis, James Pyemont, Mark Hardinges
Other sports played: Rackets, golf, 'any sport really'
Other sports followed: 'All sports'
Relaxations: Playing golf and snooker
Extras: 2nd XI Player of the Month for August/September 1999 and for

August/September 2001. Played in Charterhouse Friars' *Cricketer* Cup winning side 2000. Took 3-23 and scored a 42-ball 60 (50 from 28 balls) v Sussex at Hove in the Norwich Union League 2001

Opinions on cricket: 'Great to see clubs and countries having the confidence to play younger cricketers.'

Best batting: 5 Hampshire v Warwickshire, Edgbaston 2001
Best bowling: 1-88 Hampshire v Warwickshire, Edgbaston 2001

2001 Season

	M	Inns	NO	Runs	HS	Avge	100s	50s	Ct	St	O	M	Runs	Wkts	Avge	Best	5wI	10wM
Test																		
All First	1	1	0	5	5	5.00	-	-	-	-	18	1	88	1	88.00	1-88	-	-
1-day Int																		
C & G																			
B & H																			
1-day Lge	14	8	2	129	61	21.50	-	1	5	-	86	3	431	17	25.35	4-29	-	

Career Performances

	M	Inns	NO	Runs	HS	Avge	100s	50s	Ct	St	Balls	Runs	Wkts	Avge	Best	5wI	10wM
Test																	
All First	1	1	0	5	5	5.00	-	-	-	-	108	88	1	88.00	1-88	-	-
1-day Int																	
C & G																		
B & H																		
1-day Lge	14	8	2	129	61	21.50	-	1	5	-	516	431	17	25.35	4-29	-	

HAMILTON, G. M.   Yorkshire

Name: <u>Gavin</u> Mark Hamilton
Role: Left-hand bat, right-arm medium-fast bowler
Born: 16 September 1974, Broxburn
Height: 6ft 3in **Weight:** 13st
Nickname: Hammy, Jock, Dits, 'anything Scottish'
County debut: 1994
County cap: 1998
Test debut: 1999-2000
Tests: 1
One-Day Internationals: 5
50 wickets in a season: 1
1st-Class 50s: 14
1st-Class 100s: 1
1st-Class 5 w. in innings: 9

1st-Class 10 w. in match: 2
1st-Class catches: 27
One-Day 5 w. in innings: 2
Place in batting averages: 238th av. 12.66
(2000 106th av. 28.71)
Place in bowling averages: 36th av. 25.84
(2000 33rd av. 21.65)
Strike rate: 48.76 (career 48.95)
Parents: Gavin and Wendy
Marital status: Single
Family links with cricket: Father 'long-term
fast bowler at club level' (Sidcup, Kent; West
Lothian, Scotland). Brother opening bat for
Sidcup CC and has opened batting for
Scotland

Education: Dulverton Primary School, New
Eltham; Hurstmere School, Sidcup
Qualifications: 10 GCSEs and two
coaching awards
Overseas tours: England to South Africa and Zimbabwe 1999-2000; Yorkshire
pre-season tours to South Africa, Zimbabwe and West Indies
Overseas teams played for: Welling, Municipals, and Stellenbosch University –
all South Africa; Spotswood, Melbourne
Cricketers particularly admired: Craig White, Mark Robinson, Chris Adams
Young players to look out for: Matthew Wood, Vikram Solanki, Gary Fellows
Other sports played: Golf ('a lot of it'), football (Arsenal YTS)
Other sports followed: Football (Falkirk FC)
Relaxations: Listening to music and reading the paper
Extras: Took 10 wickets and scored 149 runs v Glamorgan at Cardiff in 1998, the
second best all-round contribution in Yorkshire history. First-class All-rounder of the
Year 1998; Yorkshire Players' Player of the Year 1998; Yorkshire Supporters' Player of
the Year 1998. Scored 76 for Scotland v Pakistan at Chester-le-Street in the 1999
World Cup, the first 50 scored by a Scotland player in World Cup cricket. Scored 217
runs (av. 54.25) in the 1999 World Cup, more than any England batsman. Finished in
top 15 of first-class batting and bowling averages 1999. Scored 57* and took 5-34 v
Sussex Sharks in the National League at Scarborough 2000. PCA representative for
Yorkshire
Best batting: 125 Yorkshire v Hampshire, Headingley 2000
Best bowling: 7-50 Yorkshire v Surrey, Headingley 1998

2001 Season

	M	Inns	NO	Runs	HS	Avge	100s	50s	Ct	St	O	M	Runs	Wkts	Avge	Best	5wI	10wM
Test																		
All First	8	9	0	114	34	12.66	-	-	1	-	211.2	43	672	26	25.84	5-27	1	-
1-day Int																		
C & G	2	2	1	59	30 *	59.00	-	-	-	-	7	0	47	2	23.50	1-11	-	
B & H	3	3	0	72	31	24.00	-	-	-	-	20.4	5	103	5	20.60	3-56	-	
1-day Lge	10	10	1	171	57	19.00	-	1	3	-	47	3	221	9	24.55	3-14	-	

Career Performances

	M	Inns	NO	Runs	HS	Avge	100s	50s	Ct	St	Balls	Runs	Wkts	Avge	Best	5wI	10wM
Test	1	2	0	0	0	0.00	-	-	-	-	90	63	0	-	-	-	-
All First	78	103	20	2230	125	26.86	1	14	27	-	11652	6002	238	25.21	7-50	9	2
1-day Int	5	5	1	217	76	54.25	-	2	1	-	214	149	3	49.66	2-36	-	
C & G	11	9	3	148	39	24.66	-	-	3	-	504	340	19	17.89	3-27	-	
B & H	19	11	4	178	31	25.42	-	-	1	-	772	516	22	23.45	4-33	-	
1-day Lge	71	50	12	712	57 *	18.73	-	2	11	-	2435	2033	81	25.09	5-16	2	

HANCOCK, T. H. C.　　　　Gloucestershire

Name: Timothy (Tim) Harold
Coulter Hancock
Role: Right-hand bat, right-arm medium
bowler, county vice-captain
Born: 20 April 1972, Reading
Height: 5ft 11in **Weight:** 12st 7lbs
Nickname: Herbie
County debut: 1991
County cap: 1998
1000 runs in a season: 1
1st-Class 50s: 40
1st-Class 100s: 5
1st-Class 200s: 1
1st-Class catches: 95
One-Day 100s: 1
One-Day 5 w. in innings: 1
Place in batting averages: 187th av. 20.90
(2000 186th av. 19.38)
Strike rate: 168.00 (career 65.38)
Parents: John and Jennifer
Wife and date of marriage: Rachael, 26 September 1998
Children: George, 30 January 2000; Annabel Rachael, 28 August 2001

Family links with cricket: 'Dad and brother very keen players'
Education: St Piran's, Maidenhead; St Edward's, Oxford; Henley College
Qualifications: 8 GCSEs, senior coaching award
Overseas tours: Gloucestershire to Kenya 1991, to Sri Lanka 1992-93, to Zimbabwe (two visits)
Overseas teams played for: CBC Old Boys, Bloemfontein 1991-92; Wynnum Manley, Brisbane 1992-93; Harlequins, Durban 1994-95
Career highlights to date: 'Winning at Lord's four times and doing the treble in one-day competitions in 2000'
Cricket moments to forget: 'Breaking my hand in fielding practice days before the 2001 B&H final'
Cricketers particularly admired: Viv Richards, Gordon Greenidge, Ian Botham
Young players to look out for: 'Nicky Peng of Durham has plenty of talent'
Other sports played: Hockey, golf
Other sports followed: 'I like to play and watch rugby, but don't do either enough'
Injuries: Out for four weeks with a broken hand
Relaxations: 'Family life and a round of golf'
Extras: Played hockey for Oxfordshire U19. Vice-captain of Gloucestershire since 2000. Scored maiden one-day century (110) to win Man of the Match award in the NatWest quarter-final v Northamptonshire at Bristol 2000
Opinions on cricket: 'I feel the way the game is marketed needs to change. Certainly the game should be spun a bit more positively. Having said that, pitches are generally terrible, very slow and dead – and this year especially so with the balls being so soft.'
Best batting: 220* Gloucestershire v Nottinghamshire, Trent Bridge 1998
Best bowling: 3-5 Gloucestershire v Essex, Colchester 1998

2001 Season

	M	Inns	NO	Runs	HS	Avge	100s	50s	Ct	St	O	M	Runs	Wkts	Avge	Best	5wI	10wM
Test																		
All First	6	11	0	230	55	20.90	-	1	7	-	28	5	100	1	100.00	1-67	-	-
1-day Int																		
C & G	1	1	0	29	29	29.00	-	-	-	-								
B & H	4	4	0	104	42	26.00	-	-	1	-	3	0	21	0	-		-	-
1-day Lge	11	11	0	223	67	20.27	-	1	1	-	2	0	13	0	-		-	-

Career Performances

	M	Inns	NO	Runs	HS	Avge	100s	50s	Ct	St	Balls	Runs	Wkts	Avge	Best	5wI	10wM
Test																	
All First	150	262	16	6737	220 *	27.38	6	40	95	-	2877	1658	44	37.68	3-5	-	-
1-day Int																	
C & G	17	16	0	659	110	41.18	1	5	6	-	233	178	13	13.69	6-58	1	
B & H	40	37	3	843	71 *	24.79	-	3	8	-	337	264	10	26.40	3-13	-	
1-day Lge	123	113	2	2031	73	18.29	-	8	44	-	696	654	22	29.72	3-18	-	

HARDINGES, M. A. Gloucestershire

Name: <u>Mark</u> Andrew Hardinges
Role: Right-hand bat, right-arm medium-fast bowler
Born: 5 February 1978, Gloucester
Height: 6ft 1in **Weight:** 13st 7lbs
Nickname: Dinges
County debut: 1999
1st-Class catches: 2
Strike rate: 79.00 (career 91.20)
Parents: David and Jean
Marital status: Single
Family links with cricket: Brother and father played club cricket
Education: Hillstone School; Malvern College; Bath University
Qualifications: 10 GCSEs, 3 A-levels, BSc (Hons) Economics and Politics
Off-season: 'Perth for winter training'
Overseas tours: Malvern College to South Africa 1996; Gloucestershire to South Africa 1999, 2000
Overseas teams played for: Newtown and Chilwell, Geelong, Australia 1997
Career highlights to date: 'Norwich Union debut v Notts 2001 – scored 65 and set domestic one-day seventh-wicket partnership record (165) with J. Snape. Also Lord's final v Surrey'
Cricket moments to forget: 'Glos v Somerset [Norwich Union 2001] – bowled three overs for 30 and was run out for 0 on Sky TV'
Cricketers particularly admired: Kim Barnett, Steve Waugh, Mark Alleyne
Young players to look out for: Steven Pope, J. Pearson, Neil Stovold, David Nash, Gavin Franklin
Other sports played: Golf, tennis (Gloucester U14), football (university first team)
Other sports followed: Football (Tottenham)
Injuries: Out for last two weeks of the season with a broken toe and a patellar tendon operation
Relaxations: Golf
Extras: Represented British Universities in 2000. Scored 65 v Nottinghamshire at Trent Bridge on Norwich Union League debut 2001, in the process sharing in a record seventh-wicket partnership for domestic one-day competitions (164) with Jeremy Snape
Opinions on cricket: 'Pre-match preparation is having too much emphasis on it. Warm-up should start at 10.00. Practise your skills!'
Best batting: 22 Gloucestershire v Nottinghamshire, Trent Bridge 2001
Best bowling: 2-16 Gloucestershire v Essex, Bristol 2000

2001 Season

	M	Inns	NO	Runs	HS	Avge	100s	50s	Ct	St	O	M	Runs	Wkts	Avge	Best	5wI	10wM
Test																		
All First	4	3	0	56	22	18.66	-	-	2	-	79	15	295	6	49.16	2-36	-	-
1-day Int																		
C & G	1	1	0	0	0	0.00	-	-	1	-	3	0	11	1	11.00	1-11	-	
B & H	1	1	0	12	12	12.00	-	-	-	-	7	0	31	1	31.00	1-31	-	
1-day Lge	8	8	2	114	65	19.00	-	1	1	-	32	1	169	3	56.33	1-30	-	

Career Performances

	M	Inns	NO	Runs	HS	Avge	100s	50s	Ct	St	Balls	Runs	Wkts	Avge	Best	5wI	10wM
Test																	
All First	7	7	0	60	22	8.57	-	-	2	-	912	454	10	45.40	2-16	-	-
1-day Int																	
C & G	1	1	0	0	0	0.00	-	-	1	-	18	11	1	11.00	1-11	-	
B & H	1	1	0	12	12	12.00	-	-	-	-	42	31	1	31.00	1-31	-	
1-day Lge	8	8	2	114	65	19.00	-	1	1	-	192	169	3	56.33	1-30	-	

HARMISON, S. J.   Durham

Name: <u>Stephen</u> James Harmison
Role: Right-hand bat, right-arm fast bowler
Born: 23 October 1978, Ashington, Northumberland
Height: 6ft 4in **Weight:** 13st
Nickname: Harmy
County debut: 1996
County cap: 1999
50 wickets in a season: 2
1st-Class 5 w. in innings: 4
1st-Class catches: 9
Place in batting averages: 263rd av. 9.70 (2000 280th av. 8.66)
Place in bowling averages: 95th av. 36.05 (2000 102nd av. 31.61)
Strike rate: 71.97 (career 61.23)
Parents: Margaret and James
Wife and date of marriage: Hayley, 8 October 1999
Children: Emily Alice, 1 June 1999
Family links with cricket: Brothers Ben and James and father play in the local league
Education: Ashington High School

Off-season: Australia with England Academy
Overseas tours: England U19 to Pakistan 1996-97; England A to Zimbabwe and South Africa 1998-99; ECB National Academy to Australia 2001-02
Career highlights to date: 'Durham being promoted to first division of the Norwich Union League, September 2001'
Sportsmen particularly admired: Alan Shearer, David Boon, Courtney Walsh
Young players to look out for: Nicky Peng, Ian Bell
Other sports played: Football, golf
Other sports followed: Football (Newcastle United)
Injuries: Calf injury; heart problems
Relaxations: Spending time with family
Extras: Represented Northumberland U17. Played football for Ashington in the Northern League. Was selected for England A tour of Bangladesh and New Zealand 1999-2000 but was forced to withdraw with a knee injury. Included in the England party for the two Tests v Zimbabwe and for the first Test v West Indies 2000 before developing shin problems. Was selected for England A tour of West Indies 2000-01 but was forced to withdraw with a shin problem
Best batting: 36 Durham v Kent, Canterbury 1998
              36 Durham v Worcestershire, Worcester 1998
Best bowling: 6-111 Durham v Sussex, Riverside 2001
Stop press: Returned match figures of 7-120 (4-78 and 3-42) in ECB National Academy's innings victory over Commonwealth Bank [Australian] Cricket Academy in Adelaide 2001-02. Placed on stand-by for England Test tour to New Zealand 2001-02

2001 Season

	M	Inns	NO	Runs	HS	Avge	100s	50s	Ct	St	O	M	Runs	Wkts	Avge	Best	5wI	10wM
Test																		
All First	12	14	4	97	27	9.70	-	-	-	-	419.5	86	1262	35	36.05	6-111	2	-
1-day Int																		
C & G	1	1	0	2	2	2.00	-	-	-	-	10	1	46	0	-	-	-	-
B & H	1	0	0	0	0	-	-	-	-	-	10	1	50	1	50.00	1-50	-	
1-day Lge	7	3	1	18	11 *	9.00	-	-	1	-	45	3	248	8	31.00	4-43	-	

Career Performances

	M	Inns	NO	Runs	HS	Avge	100s	50s	Ct	St	Balls	Runs	Wkts	Avge	Best	5wI	10wM
Test																	
All First	58	81	22	540	36	9.15	-	-	9	-	11206	5753	183	31.43	6-111	4	-
1-day Int																	
C & G	3	3	1	4	2 *	2.00	-	-	1	-	132	122	2	61.00	1-34	-	
B & H	8	4	2	17	8 *	8.50	-	-	-	-	348	281	9	31.22	2-34	-	
1-day Lge	21	9	5	24	11 *	6.00	-	-	3	-	905	786	19	41.36	4-43	-	

HARRIS, A. J.   Nottinghamshire

Name: <u>Andrew</u> James Harris
Role: Right-hand bat, right-arm
fast-medium bowler
Born: 26 June 1973, Ashton-under-Lyne,
Lancashire
Height: 6ft   **Weight:** 11st 9lbs
Nickname: AJ, Honest
County debut: 1994 (Derbyshire),
2000 (Nottinghamshire)
County cap: 1996 (Derbyshire),
2000 (Nottinghamshire)
1st-Class 5 w. in innings: 9
1st-Class 10 w. in match: 1
1st-Class catches: 20
One Day 5 w. in innings: 1
Place in batting averages: 275th av. 6.07
(2000 228th av. 15.30)
Place in bowling averages: 111th av. 39.17
(2000 96th av. 30.86)
Strike rate: 70.85 (career 56.55)
Parents: Norman (deceased) and Joyce
Wife and date of marriage: Kate, 7 October 2000
Education: Tintwistle Primary School; Hadfield Comprehensive School;
Glossopdale Community College
Qualifications: 6 GCSEs, 1 A-level
Career outside cricket: Studying book-keeping and accountancy
Off-season: As above
Overseas tours: England A to Australia 1996-97
Overseas teams played for: Ginninderra, West Belconnen, Australia 1992-93;
Victoria University of Wellington CC, New Zealand 1997-98
Career highlights to date: 'Helping Nottinghamshire achieve first-division status in
the National League 2000'
Cricket moments to forget: 'Having forgotten my shirt I had to walk out to field in
the last Norwich Union game of the 2001 season (which happened to be on TV)
wearing the diminutive Guy Welton's shirt'
Cricketers particularly admired: Merv Hughes, Allan Donald
Young players to look out for: Ed Joyce, David Lucas
Other sports played: Golf, snooker, 'as well as being player/manager of the Derby
Rejects, winners of the JJB Soccerdome six-a-side Monday night premier division'
Other sports followed: 'Rossendale (brother), and Man City as they push for a place
in Europe during season 2002-03 in the Premiership'

Injuries: Out for six weeks after tearing a tendon in right shoulder during pre-season
Relaxations: 'Good food, good wine and the odd game of golf'
Extras: Left Derbyshire at end of the 1999 season and joined Notts for 2000
Best batting: 39 Nottinghamshire v Worcestershire, Trent Bridge 2000
Best bowling: 6-40 Derbyshire v Middlesex, Derby 1996

2001 Season

	M	Inns	NO	Runs	HS	Avge	100s	50s	Ct	St	O	M	Runs	Wkts	Avge	Best	5wI	10wM
Test																		
All First	9	15	2	79	20 *	6.07	-	-	-	-	330.4	84	1097	28	39.17	6-98	1	-
1-day Int																		
C & G	2	1	0	0	0	0.00	-	-	-	-	16	3	68	0	-		-	-
B & H	1	1	0	0	0	0.00	-	-	-	-	10	0	63	1	63.00	1-63	-	
1-day Lge	9	3	0	9	8	3.00	-	-	3	-	72	4	397	17	23.35	4-24	-	

Career Performances

	M	Inns	NO	Runs	HS	Avge	100s	50s	Ct	St	Balls	Runs	Wkts	Avge	Best	5wI	10wM
Test																	
All First	66	94	24	624	39	8.91	-	-	20	-	11821	6990	209	33.44	6-40	9	1
1-day Int																	
C & G	9	5	3	21	11 *	10.50	-	-	1	-	493	343	9	38.11	3-10	-	
B & H	13	5	1	12	5	3.00	-	-	4	-	672	537	18	29.83	3-41	-	
1-day Lge	64	22	10	75	10 *	6.25	-	-	16	-	2736	2359	86	27.43	5-35	1	

HARRISON, D. S.   Glamorgan

Name: <u>David</u> Stuart Harrison
Role: Right-hand bat, right-arm medium-fast bowler; all-rounder
Born: 31 July 1981, Newport
Height: 6ft 4in **Weight:** 13st 9lbs
Nickname: Harry, Hazza
County debut: 1999
Strike rate: (career 192.00)
Parents: Stuart and Susan
Marital status: 'Very single!!'
Family links with cricket: 'Dad played for Glamorgan in early 1970s; brother Adam played for England U15 in U15 World Cup 2000 and won BBC Sports Young Cricketer of the Year Award and Sir John Hobbs Memorial Award 2001'
Education: Greenlawn Junior School, Pontypool; West Monmouth Comprehensive, Pontypool; Pontypool College
Qualifications: 8 GCSEs, 2 A-levels, BTEC National Diploma in Sports Science, Levels 1 and 2 coaching awards

Career outside cricket: 'Coaching, feeding certain animals (!!), modelling'

Off-season: 'Hopefully visiting a friend in Durban for a few months. Visiting Dennis Lillee's MRF Pace Foundation, Chennai (Madras) Jan-Feb'

Overseas tours: Gwent U15 to Cape Town 1996; Wales to Jersey 1996, 1997; England U19 to Malaysia and (U19 World Cup) Sri Lanka 1999-2000

Career highlights to date: 'Making my Glamorgan debut April 1999 – fifth youngest ever to play for Glamorgan in County Championship! England U19 debut 1999. U19 World Cup 2000'

Cricket moments to forget: 'My dad hooking me for a boundary in a charity game, then walking down the pitch and saying, "Son, you're not quick enough!!"'

Cricketers particularly admired: Steve James, Rob Bailey, Glenn McGrath, Matthew Maynard

Young players to look out for: Adam Harrison ('little bro'), Mark Wallace, Ian Bell, Nicky Peng

Other sports played: Squash ('played for Wales U11, U12, U13'), rugby union ('played for Wales Schools until I was 14'; represented Pontypool Schools XV in Welsh Cup final), 'handy golfer', five-a-side football (Super Dragon Rovers)

Other sports followed: Football (Manchester United, Cardiff City, 'the Super Dragon Rovers!')

Relaxations: 'Sleeping, playing golf, walking my dog (Jake), Sky Digital, shopping'

Extras: Represented Wales from 12 to 16. Played for Glamorgan U17 and U19 ('playing two years young'). Represented England at U17, U18 and U19 levels. Missed U19 tour to New Zealand 1998-99 and home series v Australia U19 1999 through injury. Represented England U19 v Sri Lanka U19 in 'Test' series 2000

Opinions on cricket: 'A lot of people would give anything to become a professional cricketer. I am happy to be a cricketer and I enjoy every minute of it (most of the time)!'

Best batting: 27 Glamorgan v Gloucestershire, Bristol 2000

Best bowling: 1-15 Glamorgan v Oxford University, The Parks 1999

---

39. Which current county player top-scored with 73
for Ireland v Warwickshire in the 1998 NatWest?

2001 Season (did not make any first-class or one-day appearances)

Career Performances

	M	Inns	NO	Runs	HS	Avge	100s	50s	Ct	St	Balls	Runs	Wkts	Avge	Best	5wI	10wM
Test																	
All First	3	4	0	56	27	14.00	-	-	-	-	192	109	1	109.00	1-15	-	-
1-day Int																	
C & G																	
B & H																	
1-day Lge	3	3	1	11	5 *	5.50	-	-	1	-	84	96	0	-		-	-

HARVEY, I. J.   Gloucestershire

Name: <u>Ian</u> Joseph Harvey
Role: Right-hand bat, right-arm
fast-medium bowler
Born: 10 April 1972, Wonthaggi, Victoria,
Australia
Height: 5ft 9in **Weight:** 12st 8lbs
Nickname: Freak
County debut: 1999
County cap: 1999
One-Day Internationals: 35
1st-Class 50s: 24
1st-Class 100s: 7
1st-Class 5 w. in innings: 10
1st-Class 10 w. in match: 1
1st-Class catches: 71
One-Day 5 w. in innings: 5
Place in batting averages: 68th av. 40.84
(2000 89th av. 30.38)

Place in bowling averages: 7th av. 18.85 (2000 9th av. 16.45)
Strike rate: 42.24 (career 56.99)
Overseas tours: Australian Academy to New Zealand 1994-95; Australia to Sharjah
(Coca-Cola Cup) 1997-98, to New Zealand 1999-2000 (one-day series), to Kenya
(ICC Knockout Trophy) 2000-01, to India 2000-01 (one-day series), to England 2001
(one-day series)
Overseas teams played for: Dandenong, Victoria; Fitzroy-Doncaster, Victoria;
Victoria 1993-94 –
Extras: The nickname 'Freak' is a reference to his brilliant fielding and was
reportedly coined by Shane Warne. Took a wicket (Jonty Rhodes) with his second ball
in One-Day International cricket in 1997-98. Top scorer (57) for Victoria in their

Mercantile Mutual Cup final victory over New South Wales 1998-99. Joined Gloucestershire in 1999 as overseas player. Won NatWest Man of the Match award v Durham Cricket Board XI at Riverside 1999. Top wicket-taker in the 1999 National League competition with 30 wickets at 15.80. Had match figures of 10-32 from 25 overs (and scored 60 in Gloucestershire's only innings) v Sussex at Hove 2000. Australian Cricket Board central contract 2001-02. B&H Gold Awards for his 5-32 v Warwickshire at Edgbaston and 92 (followed by 2-35) v Worcestershire at Bristol 2001. Won the Walter Lawrence Trophy for the season's fastest first-class hundred with his 61-ball century (ending up with 104 from 65) v Derbyshire at Bristol 2001; also took 5-89 in Derbyshire's second innings

Best batting: 136 Victoria v South Australia, Melbourne 1995-96
Best bowling: 7-44 Victoria v South Australia, Melbourne 1996-97
Stop press: Selected for the Australian one-day squad for the series in South Africa 2001-02

2001 Season

	M	Inns	NO	Runs	HS	Avge	100s	50s	Ct	St	O	M	Runs	Wkts	Avge	Best	5wI	10wM
Test																		
All First	10	15	2	531	130 *	40.84	2	1	8	-	288.4	92	773	41	18.85	5-33	2	-
1-day Int	5	2	1	19	19 *	19.00	-	-	1	-	38.1	4	153	7	21.85	2-18	-	
C & G	2	2	0	32	23	16.00	-	-	-	-	15.2	2	62	3	20.66	2-40	-	
B & H	7	7	0	173	92	24.71	-	1	3	-	62.5	7	248	16	15.50	5-32	1	
1-day Lge	9	9	0	226	67	25.11	-	1	1	-	64.1	7	261	10	26.10	4-42	-	

Career Performances

	M	Inns	NO	Runs	HS	Avge	100s	50s	Ct	St	Balls	Runs	Wkts	Avge	Best	5wI	10wM
Test																	
All First	92	154	11	4371	136	30.56	7	24	71	-	14249	6806	250	27.22	7-44	10	1
1-day Int	35	25	8	363	47 *	21.35	-	-	10	-	1660	1260	38	33.15	4-28	-	
C & G	12	11	0	190	47	17.27	-	-	6	-	627	371	25	14.84	4-29	-	
B & H	13	11	0	344	92	31.27	-	2	3	-	697	448	32	14.00	5-32	2	
1-day Lge	37	37	2	922	67	26.34	-	4	6	-	1705	1107	74	14.95	5-19	3	

40. Which Test fast bowler, now a bowling coach, took 5-29 for Worcestershire v Middlesex in the 1988 NatWest final?

HATCH, N. G.   Durham

Name: <u>Nicholas</u> Guy Hatch
Role: Right-hand bat, right-arm
medium-fast bowler
Born: 21 April 1979, Darlington
Height: 6ft 7in **Weight:** 14st 10lbs
Nickname: Tony
County debut: 2001
1st-Class catches: 1
Place in batting averages: 219th av. 16.12
Place in bowling averages: 83rd av. 33.34
Strike rate: 57.38 (career 57.38)
Parents: Mike and Paula
Marital status: Single
Family links with cricket: Father played
club cricket with Darlington CC for over 20
years. Brother plays club cricket in London
Education: Raventhorpe Prep School;
Barnard Castle School; Hull University
Qualifications: 11 GCSEs, 5 A-levels, BA History and Politics
Off-season: Playing club cricket in Perth, Western Australia
Overseas teams played for: Claremont-Nedlands CC, Perth 2000-01, 2001-02
Career highlights to date: 'First-class debut'
Cricketers particularly admired: Courtney Walsh, Steve Waugh, Curtly Ambrose
Young players to look out for: Nicky Peng, Gordon Muchall
Other sports played: Rugby union (played for North of England U19)
Other sports followed: All sports
Relaxations: Reading, socialising with friends
Extras: Represented British Universities v New Zealand A in one-day match 2000
Opinions on cricket: 'Too much cricket. Should be less, and cricket played both at
club and county level more competitive.'
Best batting: 24 Durham v Sussex, Riverside 2001
Best bowling: 3-42 Durham v Hampshire, West End 2001

2001 Season

	M	Inns	NO	Runs	HS	Avge	100s	50s	Ct	St	O	M	Runs	Wkts	Avge	Best	5wI	10wM
Test																		
All First	9	16	8	129	24	16.12	-	-	1	-	248.4	43	867	26	33.34	3-42	-	-
1-day Int																		
C & G	1	0	0	0	0	-	-	-	-	-	10	0	51	2	25.50	2-51	-	
B & H																		
1-day Lge	5	2	1	13	8 *	13.00	-	-	-	-	33	3	144	7	20.57	3-26	-	

Career Performances

	M	Inns	NO	Runs	HS	Avge	100s	50s	Ct	St	Balls	Runs	Wkts	Avge	Best	5wI	10wM
Test																	
All First	9	16	8	129	24	16.12	-	-	1	-	1492	867	26	33.34	3-42	-	-
1-day Int																	
C & G	1	0	0	0	0	-	-	-	-	-	60	51	2	25.50	2-51	-	
B & H																		
1-day Lge	5	2	1	13	8 *	13.00	-	-	-	-	198	144	7	20.57	3-26	-	

HAVELL, P. M. R. Sussex

Name: <u>Paul</u> Matthew Roger Havell
Role: Left-hand bat, right-arm
fast-medium bowler
Born: 4 July 1980, Melbourne, Australia
Height: 6ft 3in **Weight:** 12st
Nickname: Trigger
County debut: 2001
Parents: Roger and Caroline
Marital status: Single
Family links with cricket: Brother Mark
played for Sussex U19
Education: Great Walstead School; Warden
Park School; Haywards Heath College
Qualifications: 9 GCSEs, 1 A-level, Level 2
coaching award
Off-season: 'Off to Australia (Jan 10-March
10) to train and get some sun!'
Overseas tours: Sussex U19 to Barbados
1997-98; Sussex to Grenada 2000-01
Overseas teams played for: East Doncaster CC, Australia 1998-99; Carlton CC,
Melbourne 2000-01
Career highlights to date: 'Getting 12 wickets in the 2nd XI game against Kent at
Canterbury'
Cricketers particularly admired: James Kirtley 'and all Sussex players!'
Young players to look out for: Paul Havell
Other sports played: Golf, football, ice hockey
Other sports followed: Football (Brighton & Hove Albion)
Extras: Sussex Young Cricketer of the Year 1995

2001 Season

	M	Inns	NO	Runs	HS	Avge	100s	50s	Ct	St	O	M	Runs	Wkts	Avge	Best	5wl	10wM
Test																		
All First	1	0	0	0	0	-	-	-	-	-	7	3	16	0	-	-	-	-
1-day Int																		
C & G																			
B & H																			
1-day Lge	1	0	0	0	0	-	-	-	-	-	4	0	20	0	-	-	-	

Career Performances

	M	Inns	NO	Runs	HS	Avge	100s	50s	Ct	St	Balls	Runs	Wkts	Avge	Best	5wl	10wM
Test																	
All First	1	0	0	0	0	-	-	-	-	-	42	16	0	-	-	-	-
1-day Int																	
C & G																	
B & H																	
1-day Lge	1	0	0	0	0	-	-	-	-	-	24	20	0	-	-	-	

HAYNES, J. J. Lancashire

Name: Jamie Jonathan Haynes
Role: Right-hand bat, wicket-keeper
Born: 5 July 1974, Bristol
Height: 5ft 10in **Weight:** 12st 8lbs
Nickname: JJ
County debut: 1996
1st-Class 50s: 2
1st-Class catches: 28
1st-Class stumpings: 2
Place in batting averages: 216th av. 16.62
Parents: Steve Haynes and Moiya Ford
Marital status: Single
Family links with cricket: Father and uncle both played for Gloucestershire CCC
Education: Garran Primary, Canberra, Australia; St Edmunds College, Canberra; University of Canberra ('nearly completed BA Sports Media')

Qualifications: Year 12 Certificate, coaching certificate
Off-season: Training as part of 12-month contract at Lancashire; 'holiday in Oz'
Overseas tours: Lancashire CCC to Cape Town 1999
Overseas teams played for: Weston Creek CC, Canberra; Queanbeyan CC, Canberra; Tuggeranong Valley CC, Canberra 1995-96; South Canberra CC 1996-97

Career highlights to date: 'Making first-class debut'
Cricket moments to forget: 'Losing four front teeth while keeping wicket'
Cricketers particularly admired: Ian Healy, Jack Russell, Alan Knott, Steve Waugh, Mike Atherton
Young players to look out for: Kyle Hogg
Other sports played: Australian Rules football (Queanbeyan Tigers)
Other sports followed: Football (Manchester United, 'a soft spot for Burnley FC as well'), Australian Rules (Carlton)
Relaxations: 'Eating fine food, drinking fine wine, cooking, going to the movies, golf'
Extras: Top scorer with 80 as nightwatchman in Lancashire's first innings v Sri Lanka A at Old Trafford 1999
Opinions on cricket: 'Wickets in second-class cricket need to be comparable to first-class tracks.'
Best batting: 80 Lancashire v Sri Lanka A, Old Trafford 1999

2001 Season

	M	Inns	NO	Runs	HS	Avge	100s	50s	Ct	St	O	M	Runs	Wkts	Avge	Best	5wl	10wM
Test																		
All First	5	8	0	133	57	16.62	-	1	7	-								
1-day Int																		
C & G	1	1	1	59	59 *	-	-	1	1	-								
B & H	1	1	0	29	29	29.00	-	-	2	-								
1-day Lge	4	2	0	11	11	5.50	-	-	2	1								

Career Performances

	M	Inns	NO	Runs	HS	Avge	100s	50s	Ct	St	Balls	Runs	Wkts	Avge	Best	5wl	10wM
Test																	
All First	11	17	3	348	80	24.85	-	2	28	2							
1-day Int																	
C & G	1	1	1	59	59 *	-	-	1	1	-							
B & H	1	1	0	29	29	29.00	-	-	2	-							
1-day Lge	7	3	0	23	12	7.66	-	-	5	2							

41. Which two counties share the title of most frequent winners of the NatWest, each having won the trophy three times?

HEGG, W. K.　　　　　　Lancashire

Name: <u>Warren</u> Kevin Hegg
Role: Right-hand bat, wicket-keeper,
county captain
Born: 23 February 1968, Manchester
Height: 5ft 9in **Weight:** 12st 10lbs
Nickname: Chucky
County debut: 1986
County cap: 1989
Benefit: 1999 (£178,000)
Test debut: 1998-99
Tests: 2
50 dismissals in a season: 6
1st-Class 50s: 49
1st-Class 100s: 7
1st-Class catches: 698
1st-Class stumpings: 79
Place in batting averages: 34th av. 48.87

(2000 55th av. 35.50)
Parents: Kevin (deceased) and Glenda
Wife and date of marriage: Joanne, 29 October 1994
Children: Chloe Louise, 13 November 1998
Family links with cricket: Brother Martin plays in local leagues
Education: Unsworth High School; Stand College, Whitefield
Qualifications: 5 O-levels, 7 CSEs, qualified coach
Off-season: Touring India and New Zealand with England
Overseas tours: NCA North U19 to Bermuda 1985; England YC to Sri Lanka 1986-87,
to Australia (U19 World Cup) 1987-88; England A to Pakistan and Sri Lanka 1990-91,
to Australia 1996-97; England to Australia 1998-99, to India and New Zealand 2001-02
Overseas teams played for: Sheffield, Tasmania 1988-90, 1992-93
Cricketers particularly admired: Ian Botham, Alan Knott, Bob Taylor,
Gehan Mendis, Ian Healy
Young players to look out for: Peter Devaney, Jamie Haynes ('for his fine glovework'),
Gordon Howarth ('right-arm fast bowler at Whitefield')
Other sports played: Football (Old Standians)
Other sports followed: Rugby league (Salford City Reds), football
(Manchester United)
Relaxations: 'Golf, golf, golf'
Extras: Became youngest player for 30 years to score a century for Lancashire with
his 130 v Northamptonshire at Northampton in 1987 aged 19 in his fourth first-class
game. Took 11 catches in match v Derbyshire at Chesterfield in 1989, equalling world
first-class record. Wombwell Cricket Lovers' Society joint Wicket-keeper of the Year

1993. Vice-captain of Lancashire in 1999 and 2001. Scored 107* v Northamptonshire at Northampton 2001, in the process sharing in a record eighth-wicket partnership for Lancashire in matches against Northants (136*) with Glen Chapple. Lancashire Player of the Year 2001. Appointed Lancashire captain for 2002, the first wicket-keeper to hold the post in an official capacity

Opinions on cricket: 'Prize money should not be given for runners-up in division two – the reward of promotion is enough! – enabling monies to be awarded to third place in division one.'

Best batting: 134 Lancashire v Leicestershire, Old Trafford 1996

2001 Season

	M	Inns	NO	Runs	HS	Avge	100s	50s	Ct	St	O	M	Runs	Wkts	Avge	Best	5wI	10wM
Test																		
All First	13	20	4	782	133	48.87	2	5	35	3								
1-day Int																		
C & G	4	1	0	60	60	60.00	-	1	1	-								
B & H	4	3	0	60	31	20.00	-	-	3	-								
1-day Lge	10	9	2	105	29	15.00	-	-	11	6								

Career Performances

	M	Inns	NO	Runs	HS	Avge	100s	50s	Ct	St	Balls	Runs	Wkts	Avge	Best	5wI	10wM
Test	2	4	0	30	15	7.50	-	-	8	-							
All First	288	421	81	9524	134	28.01	7	49	698	79	6	7	0	-		-	-	-
1-day Int																	
C & G	42	22	1	411	60	19.57	-	1	49	6							
B & H	72	38	14	622	81	25.91	-	2	96	6							
1-day Lge	211	128	50	1578	52	20.23	-	1	214	38							

42. Which current first-class umpire won the Man of the Match award in the 1969 Gillette Cup final?

HEMP, D. L. — Glamorgan

Name: <u>David</u> Lloyd Hemp
Role: Left-hand bat, right-arm
medium bowler
Born: 15 November 1970,
Hamilton, Bermuda
Height: 6ft 1in **Weight:** 13st
Nickname: Hempy, Jonesy
County debut: 1991 (Glamorgan),
1997 (Warwickshire)
County cap: 1994 (Glamorgan),
1997 (Warwickshire)
1000 runs in a season: 3
1st-Class 50s: 44
1st-Class 100s: 17
1st-Class catches: 107
One-Day 100s: 4
Place in batting averages: 32nd av. 49.35
(2000 47th av. 37.90)
Strike rate: (career 60.70)

Parents: Clive and Elisabeth
Wife and date of marriage: Angie, 16 March 1996
Children: Cameron, January 2002
Family links with cricket: Brother Tim captains Swansea CC
Education: Parklands Junior; Olchfa Comprehensive School; Millfield School;
West Glamorgan Institute of Higher Education; Birmingham University
Qualifications: 5 O-levels, 2 A-levels, Level III coaching award
Off-season: 'Hoping to complete MBA degree at Birmingham University. Working on
my game, training (fitness). Getting used to being a father'
Overseas tours: Welsh Cricket Association U18 to Barbados 1986; Welsh Schools
U19 to Australia 1987-88; Glamorgan to Trinidad 1990; South Wales Cricket
Association to New Zealand and Australia 1991-92; England A to India 1994-95
Overseas teams played for: Crusaders, Durban 1992-98
Career highlights to date: 'Career best 186 not out v Worcestershire 2001'
Cricketers particularly admired: David Gower, Viv Richards
Young players to look out for: Ian Bell
Other sports followed: Football (Swansea City, West Ham United)
Relaxations: Golf, listening to music, reading
Extras: Scored 258* for Wales v MCC 1991. In 1989 scored 104* and 101* for Welsh
Schools U19 v Scottish Schools U19 and 120 and 102* v Irish Schools U19. Left
Glamorgan at the end of the 1996 season and joined Warwickshire. Scored two 100s
(138 and 114*) for Warwicks v Hants at Southampton 1997; Matthew Hayden scored a

200 and a 100 for Hants in the same match. Vice-captain of Warwickshire in 2001. Left Warwickshire in the 2001-02 off-season and has rejoined Glamorgan for 2002

Opinions on cricket: 'Reduce amount of cricket played, which would allow for more quality practice in between games. Bowlers would remain fairly fresh all season. Batters should become more disciplined because of less innings, which would hopefully raise standard and competitiveness of cricket played. Away captain should have choice of whether to bat or bowl. Cricketers are only as good as the surface they play on. Improve the wickets, which will improve the standard of players. Pitch inspectors less tolerant; more points deducted for poor surfaces. Keep two divisions with three up/three down as majority of games will remain competitive up till end of season.'

Best batting: 186* Warwickshire v Worcestershire, Edgbaston 2001
Best bowling: 3-23 Glamorgan v South Africa A, Cardiff 1996

2001 Season

	M	Inns	NO	Runs	HS	Avge	100s	50s	Ct	St	O	M	Runs	Wkts	Avge	Best	5wI	10wM
Test																		
All First	17	25	5	987	186 *	49.35	4	2	12	-	14	1	37	0	-		-	-	-
1-day Int																		
C & G	2	2	0	11	11	5.50	-	-	-	-								
B & H																		
1-day Lge	12	8	1	121	43 *	17.28	-	-	2	-								

Career Performances

	M	Inns	NO	Runs	HS	Avge	100s	50s	Ct	St	Balls	Runs	Wkts	Avge	Best	5wI	10wM
Test																	
All First	161	268	24	8465	186 *	34.69	17	44	107	-	1032	778	17	45.76	3-23	-	-
1-day Int																	
C & G	21	20	2	753	112	41.83	3	3	5	-	48	43	1	43.00	1-40	-	
B & H	22	20	0	546	121	27.30	1	4	2	-	49	32	4	8.00	4-32	-	
1-day Lge	110	94	11	1664	83 *	20.04	-	7	45	-	74	86	3	28.66	2-43	-	

---

43. Which player, selected at the last minute, scored 158 for Sussex
as they successfully chased 328 for victory v Derbyshire
in the quarter-finals of the 1997 NatWest?

HEWISON, C. J.   Nottinghamshire

Name: Christopher (<u>Chris</u>) Jon Hewison
Role: Right-hand bat, right-arm
medium bowler
Born: 6 October 1979, Gateshead
Height: 6ft 1in **Weight:** 13st
Nickname: Spuggy, Hewey, Mutly, Houston
County debut: 2000
1st-Class catches: 5
Parents: Neil and Kay
Marital status: Single
Family links with cricket: 'Dad played for
Durham (when Minor County) 1974-75 and
was a professional in local leagues'
Education: Marley Hill Primary; Whickham
Comprehensive; Whickham Comprehensive
Sixth Form
Qualifications: 9 GCSEs, 2 A-levels
Overseas tours: Durham U21 to Sri Lanka

1997; England U18 to Bermuda (International Youth Tournament) 1997
Overseas teams played for: Hallam Kallora Park 1998-99, 2000-01
Cricketers particularly admired: Viv Richards, Robin Smith, Curtly Ambrose
Young players to look out for: Paul Armstrong, Ian Hunter, Imran Shah
Other sports played: Football, tennis, snooker
Other sports followed: Football (Newcastle United FC), rugby league (Wigan)
Relaxations: 'Watching or playing any sports; snooker against my dad; socialising
with my mates'
Extras: *Daily Telegraph* U14 Cricketer of the Year. North East Junior Cricketer of the
Year. Colin Milburn Trophy. Formerly with Durham. Played for Durham Board XI in
the NatWest 1999. Top run-scorer for Nottinghamshire 2nd XI 2000. Released by
Nottinghamshire at the end of the 2001 season
Opinions on cricket: 'Still too much cricket, especially one-dayers, but the two
divisions proved to be a good idea, as the end of last season showed.'
Best batting: 24 Nottinghamshire v Glamorgan, Trent Bridge 2000

	M	Inns	NO	Runs	HS	Avge	100s	50s	Ct	St	O	M	Runs	Wkts	Avge	Best	5wl	10wM
Test																		
All First																		
1-day Int																		
C & G																			
B & H																			
1-day Lge	1	1	0	20	20	20.00	-	-	1	-								

Career Performances

	M	Inns	NO	Runs	HS	Avge	100s	50s	Ct	St	Balls	Runs	Wkts	Avge	Best	5wl	10wM
Test																	
All First	1	2	0	30	24	15.00	-	-	5	-							
1-day Int																	
C & G	2	2	0	19	19	9.50	-	-	1	-							
B & H																		
1-day Lge	1	1	0	20	20	20.00	-	-	1	-							

HEWITT, J. P.   Kent

Name: James Peter Hewitt
Role: Left-hand bat, right-arm medium-fast bowler
Born: 26 February 1976, Southwark, London
Height: 6ft 3in   **Weight:** 14st 7lbs
Nickname: Hewie, Shoes, Dog
County debut: 1995 (one-day, Middlesex), 1996 (first-class, Middlesex)
County cap: 1998 (Middlesex)
50 wickets in a season: 1
1st-Class 50s: 3
1st-Class 5 w. in innings: 5
1st-Class catches: 23
Place in bowling averages: 108th av. 38.60
Strike rate: 49.80 (career 48.99)
Parents: Gill Underhay and Terry Hewitt
Marital status: Engaged to Joanne
Family links with cricket: Father and grandfather played club cricket and had trials with Surrey
Education: Buckingham School, Hampton; Teddington School, Middlesex; Richmond College
Qualifications: GCSEs; City and Guilds Parts I, II and III in Recreation and Leisure; GNVQ Leisure and Tourism; coaching awards I, II and advanced staff coach

Career outside cricket: Coaching
Off-season: Getting fit for the new cricket season and going to Perth
Overseas teams played for: University, Perth 1997-98; Shenton Park 2000-02
Career highlights to date: 'Beating Australians at Lord's for Middlesex [2001]'
Cricket moments to forget: 'Ask Kevin Pietersen! It only took two overs (was going well until then). Then getting a call from Dusty Miller' (*Pietersen was severe on Hewitt during his innings of 165* for Nottinghamshire v Middlesex at Lord's 2001*)
Cricketers particularly admired: Richard Hadlee, David Gower, Sachin Tendulkar, Curtly Ambrose
Young players to look out for: Ed Joyce, Andrew Strauss, Matthew Todd, Scott Newman
Other sports played: Athletics ('represented South of England at cross-country'), football ('played for Chelsea Youth'); 'I will play any sports'
Other sports followed: 'All sports', football (Chelsea)
Injuries: Out for one and a half months with a side strain; 'went in the brain August/September'
Relaxations: Watching TV
Extras: First Middlesex bowler since 1902 to take a wicket (R. I. Dawson of Gloucestershire) with first ball in first-class cricket. Released by Middlesex at the end of the 2001 season and has joined Kent for 2002
Opinions on cricket: 'Too much cricket played. Second team pitches are terrible. Tea should be half an hour!'
Best batting: 75 Middlesex v Essex, Chelmsford 1997
Best bowling: 6-14 Middlesex v Glamorgan, Cardiff 1997

2001 Season

	M	Inns	NO	Runs	HS	Avge	100s	50s	Ct	St	O	M	Runs	Wkts	Avge	Best	5wI	10wM
Test																		
All First	4	5	1	22	10 *	5.50	-	-	1	-	83	8	386	10	38.60	3-72	-	-
1-day Int																		
C & G	1	0	0	0	0	-	-	-	-	-	9	0	75	1	75.00	1-75	-	
B & H																		
1-day Lge	4	4	2	24	11 *	12.00	-	-	1	-	22	2	108	3	36.00	1-16	-	

Career Performances

	M	Inns	NO	Runs	HS	Avge	100s	50s	Ct	St	Balls	Runs	Wkts	Avge	Best	5wI	10wM
Test																	
All First	60	81	12	1216	75	17.62	-	3	23	-	8329	4856	170	28.56	6-14	5	-
1-day Int																	
C & G	6	3	2	23	14 *	23.00	-	-	2	-	288	249	4	62.25	1-26	-	
B & H	9	5	0	30	14	6.00	-	-	2	-	444	384	6	64.00	2-49	-	
1-day Lge	58	34	13	268	32 *	12.76	-	-	19	-	2055	1526	55	27.74	4-24	-	

HEWSON, D. R. Derbyshire

Name: Dominic (<u>Dom</u>) Robert Hewson
Role: Right-hand bat, right-arm
medium bowler
Born: 3 October 1974, Cheltenham
Height: 5ft 9in **Weight:** 13st
Nickname: Chopper
County debut: 1996 (Gloucestershire)
1st-Class 50s: 13
1st-Class 100s: 2
1st-Class catches: 23
Place in batting averages: 87th av. 35.47
(2000 156th av. 22.40)
Strike rate: (career 72.00)
Parents: Robert and Julie
Wife and date of marriage: Amy,
14 October 2000
Education: Cheltenham College; University
of West of England

Qualifications: 10 GCSEs, 3 A-levels, City and Guilds in Tree Surgery
Career outside cricket: Tree surgeon
Off-season: Working/training
Overseas teams played for: Constantia, Cape Town 1995-96; Central, Hawkes Bay,
New Zealand 1998-99
Career highlights to date: 'Playing at Gloucestershire CCC during their successes of
1999 and 2000'
Cricketers particularly admired: Courtney Walsh
Other sports followed: Rugby (Gloucester RFC)
Relaxations: Seeing friends, fishing, and watching sport
Extras: Made debut for Gloucestershire 2nd XI in July 1993. Scored maiden first-
class century (100*) v Derbyshire at Derby 2001. Left Gloucestershire in the 2001-02
off-season and has joined Derbyshire for 2002
Best batting: 168 Gloucestershire v Derbyshire, Bristol 2001
Best bowling: 1-7 Gloucestershire v Kent, Bristol 1998

2001 Season

	M	Inns	NO	Runs	HS	Avge	100s	50s	Ct	St	O	M	Runs	Wkts	Avge	Best	5wI	10wM
Test																		
All First	14	25	2	816	168	35.47	2	4	6	-	3	1	7	0	-	-	-	-
1-day Int																		
C & G	1	1	0	35	35	35.00	-	-	-	-								
B & H	1	1	0	11	11	11.00	-	-	-	-								
1-day Lge	8	8	0	120	52	15.00	-	1	4	-								

Career Performances

	M	Inns	NO	Runs	HS	Avge	100s	50s	Ct	St	Balls	Runs	Wkts	Avge	Best	5wI	10wM
Test																	
All First	51	94	7	2172	168	24.96	2	13	23	-	72	44	1	44.00	1-7	-	-
1-day Int																	
C & G	5	5	0	141	45	28.20	-	-	1	-							
B & H	5	4	1	62	30 *	20.66	-	-	1	-							
1-day Lge	20	16	0	234	52	14.62	-	1	5	-							

HICK, G. A.   Worcestershire

Name: <u>Graeme</u> Ashley Hick
Role: Right-hand bat, off-spin bowler, county captain
Born: 23 May 1966, Harare, Zimbabwe
Height: 6ft 3in **Weight:** 14st 7lbs
Nickname: Hicky, Ash
County debut: 1984
County cap: 1986
Benefit: 1999
Test debut: 1991
Tests: 65
One-Day Internationals: 120
1000 runs in a season: 16
1st-Class 50s: 127
1st-Class 100s: 104
1st-Class 200s: 11
1st-Class 300s: 1
1st-Class 400s: 1
1st-Class 5 w. in innings: 5
1st-Class 10 w. in match: 1
1st-Class catches: 523
One-Day 100s: 29

One-Day 5 w. in innings: 1
Place in batting averages: 20th av. 56.36 (2000 57th av. 35.13)
Strike rate: 90.57 (career 89.02)
Parents: John and Eve
Wife and date of marriage: Jackie, 5 October 1991
Children: Lauren Amy, 12 September 1992
Family links with cricket: Father has served on Zimbabwe Cricket Union Board of Control since 1984 and played representative cricket in Zimbabwe
Education: Banket Primary; Prince Edward Boys' High School, Zimbabwe
Qualifications: 4 O-levels, NCA coaching award
Overseas tours: Zimbabwe to England (World Cup) 1983, to Sri Lanka 1983-84, to England 1985; England to New Zealand and Australia (World Cup) 1991-92, to India and Sri Lanka 1992-93, to West Indies 1993-94, to Australia 1994-95, to South Africa 1995-96, to India and Pakistan (World Cup) 1995-96, to Sharjah 1997-98, to West Indies 1997-98 (one-day series), to Bangladesh (Wills International Cup) 1998-99, to Australia 1998-99, to Sharjah (Coca-Cola Cup) 1998-99, to South Africa and Zimbabwe 1999-2000 (one-day series), to Kenya (ICC Knockout Trophy) 2000-01, to Pakistan and Sri Lanka 2000-01
Overseas teams played for: Old Hararians, Zimbabwe 1982-90; Northern Districts, New Zealand 1987-89; Queensland, Australia 1990-91; Auckland 1997-98
Cricketers particularly admired: Steve Waugh
Other sports followed: Football (Liverpool FC), golf, tennis, squash, hockey
Relaxations: 'Leaning against Steve Rhodes at first slip'
Extras: Made first century aged six for school team. Youngest player participating in 1983 Prudential World Cup (aged 17); youngest player to represent Zimbabwe. Scored 1234 runs in Birmingham League and played for Worcestershire 2nd XI in 1984 – hitting six successive centuries. In 1986, at age 20, he became the youngest player to score 2000 runs in an English season. One of *Wisden*'s Five Cricketers of the Year 1987. In 1988 he made 405* v Somerset at Taunton, the highest individual score in England since 1895, and scored 1000 first-class runs by end of May, hitting a record 410 runs in April. In 1990 became youngest batsman ever to make 50 first-class centuries and scored 645 runs without being dismissed – a record for English cricket. Also in 1990 became the fastest to 10,000 runs in county cricket (179 innings). Qualified as an English player in 1991. Scored first Test century v India in Bombay 1992-93 and was England's leading batsman, bowler and fielder. Published *Hick 'n' Dilley Circus* and *A Champion's Diary*. Also played hockey for Zimbabwe. Finished third in the Whyte and Mackay batting ratings in 1995 and top of the first-class batting averages in 1997. Scored hundredth first-class 100 v Sussex at Worcester in 1998 with his second 100 of the match; at the age of 32, he became the second youngest player after Wally Hammond to score one hundred 100s; received an Individual Performance Award from the PCA in recognition of his achievement. Represented England in the 1999 World Cup. Scored two centuries in a match for the fourth time, v Essex at Chelmsford 1999; the second 100, his 108th, put him level with Zaheer Abbas at 15th in the all-time century-scoring list. Won One-Day International Man of the Match awards v Zimbabwe, the country of his birth, for his match-winning 87* at Bulawayo

and his 80 and 5-33 at Harare, February 2000. Scored 101 in England's only innings in his first Test v Zimbabwe at Lord's 2000; it was his first Test century at Lord's. Scored 40 in match-winning 91-run partnership with Graham Thorpe in third Test at Karachi 2000-01. C&G Man of the Match award for his 113-ball 155 v Hertfordshire at Hertford 2001. Scored 200* v Durham at Riverside 2001, in the process equalling Sir Donald Bradman's career figure of 117 hundreds and achieving the feat of having recorded centuries against each of the other 17 counties, both home and away. Passed Allan Lamb's career total of 32,502 runs during the 2001 season, becoming the highest scoring African-born cricketer. Captain of Worcestershire since 2000

Opinions on cricket: 'The wickets need to improve drastically.'
Best batting: 405* Worcestershire v Somerset, Taunton 1988
Best bowling: 5-18 Worcestershire v Leicestershire, Worcester 1995

2001 Season

	M	Inns	NO	Runs	HS	Avge	100s	50s	Ct	St	O	M	Runs	Wkts	Avge	Best	5wI	10wM
Test																		
All First	17	28	3	1409	201	56.36	6	3	20	-	105.4	30	287	7	41.00	3-33	-	-
1-day Int																		
C & G	3	3	1	258	155	129.00	2	-	1	-	1	0	16	0	-		-	-
B & H	5	5	0	50	19	10.00	-	-	4	-	20	2	66	6	11.00	3-23	-	
1-day Lge	15	14	1	406	87	31.23	-	4	8	-	27.4	1	145	7	20.71	3-41	-	

Career Performances

	M	Inns	NO	Runs	HS	Avge	100s	50s	Ct	St	Balls	Runs	Wkts	Avge	Best	5wI	10wM
Test	65	114	6	3383	178	31.32	6	18	90	-	3057	1306	23	56.78	4-126	-	-
All First	422	695	65	33793	405 *	53.63	117	127	523	-	20565	10126	231	43.83	5-18	5	1
1-day Int	120	118	15	3846	126 *	37.33	5	27	64	-	1236	1026	30	34.20	5-33	1	
C & G	43	43	7	1950	172 *	54.16	6	9	23	-	1247	791	23	34.39	4-54	-	
B & H	70	68	13	2822	127 *	51.30	7	19	45	-	852	628	18	34.88	3-23	-	
1-day Lge	215	205	34	7589	130	44.38	11	55	72	-	2816	2440	87	28.04	4-21	-	

HOCKLEY, J. B.   Kent

Name: James Bernard Hockley
Role: Right-hand bat, right-arm off-spin bowler
Born: 16 April 1979, Beckenham
Height: 6ft 2in **Weight:** 12st 7lbs
Nickname: Hockers, Ice
County debut: 1998
1st-Class 50s: 1
1st-Class catches: 8
Place in batting averages: 233rd av. 13.83

Strike rate: 138.00 (career 122.00)
Parents: Bernard and Joan
Wife and date of marriage: Wendy,
28 September 2001
Education: Churchfields Primary School,
Beckenham; Kelsey Park Secondary School,
Beckenham
Qualifications: 7 GCSEs, NCA coaching
award Level 1
Career outside cricket: Coaching
Off-season: 'Possibility of going to Perth for
two months to improve my batting technique'
Overseas tours: Kent to Jamaica 1999;
pre-season tour to South Africa 2001
Overseas teams played for: North City,
Wellington 1999-2000
Career highlights to date: 'Winning the
Norwich Union League trophy with Kent
in 2001'

Cricket moments to forget: 'Playing at Lord's for the first time – out for a duck and
dropped a catch!'
Cricketers particularly admired: Ian Botham, Aravinda De Silva, Carl Hooper
Young players to look out for: Ben Trott, Rob Key, Geraint Jones
Other sports played: Football, golf, snooker
Other sports followed: Football (Arsenal)
Relaxations: 'Spending time with my wife; listening to music; beating Martin
Saggers at golf'
Extras: AKCL Player of the Year Award in 1995. Equalled Trevor Ward's Kent U15
batting record with a total of 1,000 runs in the season. Kent Schools Player of the Year
in 1996. Scored a 102-ball 90 in title-clinching Norwich Union League victory v
Warwickshire at Edgbaston 2001
Opinions on cricket: 'Two divisional system seems to be a success; lots of
competitive cricket to make better, tougher players. In my opinion we should make
better use of the technology available so that umpires can correctly make decisions
that could either make or break a game.'
Best batting: 74 Kent v Zimbabweans, Canterbury 2000
Best bowling: 1-21 Kent v Glamorgan, Maidstone 2001

2001 Season

	M	Inns	NO	Runs	HS	Avge	100s	50s	Ct	St	O	M	Runs	Wkts	Avge	Best	5wI	10wM
Test																		
All First	7	13	1	166	29	13.83	-	-	6	-	46	7	176	2	88.00	1-21	-	-
1-day Int																		
C & G	3	3	1	67	48 *	33.50	-	-	-	-								
B & H	5	4	0	92	55	23.00	-	1	-	-								
1-day Lge	14	14	1	403	90	31.00	-	3	6	-								

Career Performances

	M	Inns	NO	Runs	HS	Avge	100s	50s	Ct	St	Balls	Runs	Wkts	Avge	Best	5wI	10wM
Test																	
All First	14	21	1	341	74	17.05	-	1	8	-	366	233	3	77.66	1-21	-	-
1-day Int																	
C & G	4	4	1	75	48 *	25.00	-	-	-	-							
B & H	6	5	0	106	55	21.20	-	1	-	-							
1-day Lge	25	24	3	666	90	31.71	-	4	11	-							

HOGG, K. W.   Lancashire

Name: <u>Kyle</u> William Hogg
Role: Left-hand bat, right-arm
fast-medium opening bowler
Born: 2 July 1983, Birmingham
Height: 6ft 4in **Weight:** 12st
Nickname: Hoggy
County debut: 2001
Strike rate: 18.00 (career 18.00)
Parents: Sharon and William
Marital status: Single
Family links with cricket: 'Dad played for
Lancs and Warwickshire; grandad Sonny
Ramadhin played for Lancs and West Indies'
Education: St Anne's, Oldham; Saddleworth
High School
Qualifications: GCSEs
Off-season: U19 World Cup
Overseas tours: England U19 to India
2000-01, to Australia and (U19 World Cup) New Zealand 2001-02
Career highlights to date: 'First-class and one-day debuts'
Cricketers particularly admired: Andrew Flintoff
Young players to look out for: Gordon Muchall, Nicky Peng

Other sports played: Football
Other sports followed: Football (Man Utd)
Relaxations: Going out, shopping
Extras: Represented England U19 v West Indies U19 in one-day series (2/3) and
'Test' series (2/3) 2001, taking 5-88 (including three wickets in four balls) in the first
innings of the second 'Test' at Trent Bridge and 4-31 in the first innings of the third
'Test' at Riverside
Opinions on cricket: 'Haven't played enough to comment.'
Best batting: 19 Lancashire v DUCCE, Durham 2001
Best bowling: 3-17 Lancashire v DUCCE, Durham 2001

2001 Season

	M	Inns	NO	Runs	HS	Avge	100s	50s	Ct	St	O	M	Runs	Wkts	Avge	Best	5wl	10wM
Test																		
All First	1	1	0	19	19	19.00	-	-	-	-	9	3	17	3	5.66	3-17	-	-
1-day Int																		
C & G																		
B & H																		
1-day Lge	2	0	0	0	0	-	-	-	1	-	9	1	36	1	36.00	1-14	-	

Career Performances

	M	Inns	NO	Runs	HS	Avge	100s	50s	Ct	St	Balls	Runs	Wkts	Avge	Best	5wl	10wM
Test																	
All First	1	1	0	19	19	19.00	-	-	-	-	54	17	3	5.66	3-17	-	-
1-day Int																	
C & G																	
B & H																	
1-day Lge	2	0	0	0	0	-	-	-	1	-	54	36	1	36.00	1-14	-	

44. Which pair of Essex quick bowlers took 5-8 and 5-22
as Middlesex were dismissed for 41 at Westcliff in the Gillette Cup 1972?

HOGGARD, M. J. Yorkshire

Name: <u>Matthew</u> James Hoggard
Role: Right-hand bat, right-arm
fast-medium bowler
Born: 31 December 1976, Leeds
Height: 6ft 2in **Weight:** 14st
Nickname: Oggie
County debut: 1996
County cap: 2000
Test debut: 2000
Tests: 2
50 wickets in a season: 1
1st-Class 5 w. in innings: 8
1st-Class catches: 11
One-Day 5 w. in innings: 2
Place in batting averages: 285th av. 1.83
(2000 293rd av. 7.35)
Place in bowling averages: 23rd av. 22.90
(2000 65th av. 26.46)
Strike rate: 45.00 (career 48.20)

Parents: Margaret and John
Marital status: Living with girlfriend Sarah
Family links with cricket: 'Dad is a cricket badger'
Education: Lowtown Junior and Infants; Pudsey Grangefield
Qualifications: GCSEs and A-levels
Off-season: England tours to Zimbabwe, India and New Zealand
Overseas tours: Yorkshire CCC to South Africa; England U19 to Zimbabwe 1995-96;
England to Kenya (ICC Knockout Trophy) 2000-01, to Pakistan and Sri Lanka
2000-01, to Zimbabwe (one-day series) 2001-02, to India and New Zealand 2001-02
Overseas teams played for: Pirates, Johannesburg 1995-97; Free State 1998-2000
Career highlights to date: 'Taking my first Test wicket (Younis Khan)'
Cricketers particularly admired: Allan Donald, Courtney Walsh
Young players to look out for: Joe Sayers, Michael Lumb, Tim Bresnan
Other sports played: Rugby
Other sports followed: Rugby league (Leeds Rhinos)
Injuries: Out for four weeks with a bulging disk in the back; for seven weeks with a
stress fracture of the left foot
Relaxations: Dog walking
Extras: Was top wicket-taker in the 2000 National League competition with 37
wickets at 12.37, in the process superseding Howard Cooper's Yorkshire one-day
league season record of 29 wickets set in 1975. PCA Young Player of the Year 2000.
Drafted into England one-day squad for Kenya and Pakistan 2000-01 as replacement

for the injured Alan Mullally; was already selected for winter Test squads. Returned match figures of 8-30 (4-13 and 4-17) from 22.3 overs v Pakistan Board XI at Lahore and took 17 wickets in total in his two matches in Pakistan. England central contract 2001. Was called up by England halfway through Yorkshire v Kent Championship match at Headingley 2001 and replaced by Steve Kirby

Opinions on cricket: 'The two league system has worked well with vital games being played at the end of the season, but I think we need zonal teams to make the sides stronger – e.g. Yorkshire, Lancashire, Durham could play Surrey, Essex, Middlesex.'

Best batting: 21* Free State v Gauteng, Johannesburg 1999-2000

Best bowling: 6-51 Yorkshire v Essex, Scarborough 2001

Stop press: Made One-Day International debut in first ODI v Zimbabwe at Harare 2001-02. Man of the Match (3-37) in second ODI v Zimbabwe at Harare 2001-02. Recorded maiden ODI five-wicket return (5-49) in third ODI v Zimbabwe at Harare 2001-02. Recorded Test best bowling figures (4-80) v India in the third Test at Bangalore 2001-02

2001 Season

	M	Inns	NO	Runs	HS	Avge	100s	50s	Ct	St	O	M	Runs	Wkts	Avge	Best	5wI	10wM
Test	1	2	1	0	0 *	0.00	-	-	-	-	48	8	172	6	28.66	3-79	-	-
All First	8	8	2	11	4	1.83	-	-	-	-	240	58	733	32	22.90	6-51	2	-
1-day Int																		
C & G																			
B & H	1	0	0	0	0	-	-	-	-	-	10	0	54	2	27.00	2-54	-	
1-day Lge	11	2	1	7	5 *	7.00	-	-	2	-	74.3	11	329	9	36.55	2-14	-	

Career Performances

	M	Inns	NO	Runs	HS	Avge	100s	50s	Ct	St	Balls	Runs	Wkts	Avge	Best	5wI	10wM
Test	2	3	2	12	12 *	12.00	-	-	1	-	366	221	6	36.83	3-79	-	-
All First	53	63	19	269	21 *	6.11	-	-	11	-	9495	4460	197	22.63	6-51	8	-
1-day Int																	
C & G	1	0	0	0	0	-	-	-	-	-	30	6	0	-		-	-
B & H	8	1	1	2	2 *	-	-	-	-	-	361	230	10	23.00	4-39	-	
1-day Lge	31	13	7	15	5 *	2.50	-	-	3	-	1368	937	52	18.01	5-28	2	

---

45. Who skippered Lancashire to their 1990 NatWest final victory, thereby adding a NatWest winner's medal to his four Gillette winner's medals?

HOLLIOAKE, A. J.   Surrey

Name: <u>Adam</u> John Hollioake
Role: Right-hand bat, right-arm
medium bowler, county captain
Born: 5 September 1971,
Melbourne, Australia
Height: 5ft 11in **Weight:** 13st 10lbs
Nickname: Smokey
County debut: 1992 (one-day),
1993 (first-class)
County cap: 1995
Test debut: 1997
Tests: 4
One-Day Internationals: 35
1000 runs in a season: 2
1st-Class 50s: 45
1st-Class 100s: 13
1st-Class 5 w. in innings: 1
1st-Class catches: 130
One-Day 100s: 1
One-Day 5 w. in innings: 4
Place in batting averages: 70th av. 39.89 (2000 96th av. 29.95)
Strike rate: 108.00 (career 74.10)
Parents: John and Daria
Marital status: Single
Family links with cricket: Brother plays
Education: St Joseph's College, Sydney; St Patrick's College, Ballarat, Australia;
St George's College, Weybridge; Surrey Tutorial College, Guildford
Qualifications: 'Some GCSEs and A-levels'
Overseas tours: School trip to Zimbabwe; Surrey YC to Australia; England YC to
New Zealand 1990-91; England A to Australia 1996-97 (captain); England VI to Hong
Kong 1997 (captain); England to Sharjah (Champions Trophy) 1997-98 (captain), to
West Indies 1997-98 (captain in one-day series), to Bangladesh (Wills International
Cup) 1998-99 (captain), to Australia 1998-99 (CUB Series), to Sharjah (Coca-Cola
Cup) 1998-99
Overseas teams played for: Fremantle, Western Australia 1990-91; North Shore,
Sydney 1992-93; Geelong, Victoria; North Perth, Western Australia 1995-97
Cricketers particularly admired: 'Every cricketer who gives their best and takes up
the challenge to compete'
Young players to look out for: Tim Murtagh, Nicky Peng, Michael Carberry
Other sports played: 'Boxing – grappling'
Other sports followed: 'No holds barred fighting'

Extras: Played rugby for London Counties, Middlesex and South of England as well as having a trial for England U18. Scored a century (123) on first-class debut against Derbyshire 1993. Surrey Young Player of the Year 1993. Scored fastest ever one-day 50 – in 15 balls v Yorkshire in the Sunday League at Scarborough 1994. Surrey Supporters' Player of the Year and Surrey Players' Player of the Year 1996. His 39 wickets in the Sunday League in 1996 is a season record for the domestic one-day league. Man of the Match in the first One-Day International against Australia at Headingley in 1997. He and brother Ben became the first brothers to make their England Test debut together this century in the fifth Test against Australia at Trent Bridge 1997. Captained England in the Texaco Trophy one-day series v South Africa 1998. Represented England in the 1999 World Cup. Coached Hong Kong in the Asian Cricket Council Trophy in Sharjah 2000. Surrey captain since 1997

Opinions on cricket: 'We are lucky to have such a good game to play, and it is an honour for me to have the opportunity to compete every day.'

Best batting: 182 Surrey v Middlesex, Lord's 1997

Best bowling: 5-62 Surrey v Glamorgan, Swansea 1998

2001 Season

	M	Inns	NO	Runs	HS	Avge	100s	50s	Ct	St	O	M	Runs	Wkts	Avge	Best	5wI	10wM
Test																		
All First	13	20	1	758	97	39.89	-	7	15	-	54	11	165	3	55.00	1-19	-	-
1-day Int																		
C & G	2	1	0	12	12	12.00	-	-	1	-	10.2	1	63	2	31.50	2-34	-	
B & H	7	5	0	71	39	14.20	-	-	1	-	33	1	157	9	17.44	4-36	-	
1-day Lge	15	15	2	399	70	30.69	-	3	6	-	56.4	3	278	15	18.53	4-19	-	

Career Performances

	M	Inns	NO	Runs	HS	Avge	100s	50s	Ct	St	Balls	Runs	Wkts	Avge	Best	5wI	10wM
Test	4	6	0	65	45	10.83	-	-	4	-	144	67	2	33.50	2-31	-	-
All First	139	212	17	7538	182	38.65	13	45	130	-	7633	4159	103	40.37	5-62	1	-
1-day Int	35	30	6	606	83 *	25.25	-	3	13	-	1208	1019	32	31.84	4-23	-	
C & G	24	18	3	480	88	32.00	-	3	10	-	778	618	23	26.86	4-53	-	
B & H	40	31	3	720	85	25.71	-	4	12	-	1346	1171	42	27.88	4-34	-	
1-day Lge	127	116	16	2701	111	27.01	1	12	32	-	4032	3748	177	21.17	5-29	4	

HOLLIOAKE, B. C.   Surrey

Name: Benjamin (<u>Ben</u>) Caine Hollioake
Role: Right-hand bat, right-arm fast-medium
bowler, 'new generation of gully fielder'
Born: 11 November 1977,
Melbourne, Australia
Height: 6ft 1in **Weight:** 13st 7lbs
Nickname: Pely, Oaksy
County debut: 1996
County cap: 1999
Test debut: 1997
Tests: 2
One-Day Internationals: 13
1st-Class 50s: 14
1st-Class 100s: 3
1st-Class 5 w. in innings: 1
1st-Class catches: 67
One-Day 5 w. in innings: 1
Place in batting averages: 120th av. 30.84
(2000 264th av. 10.92)
Place in bowling averages: (2000 118th av. 37.00)
Strike rate: 88.88 (career 57.88)
Parents: John and Daria
Marital status: Single
Family links with cricket: 'Dad played for Victoria. Uncle Rex "the Recca"
Hollioake was fast as hell. Brother managed to captain England'
Education: Edgarley Hall; Millfield School; Wesley College, Perth, Western Australia;
'Joey Benjamin's house'
Qualifications: 'A couple of GCSEs and NCA coaching award'
Career outside cricket: 'Hollysmoke Developments'
Off-season: Touring with England. Hong Kong Sixes. 'Working on my fitness and
batting with Carly and bowling with Mr Dilley via email'
Overseas tours: Millfield to Zimbabwe 1992; West of England to West Indies 1992;
England U19 to Pakistan 1996-97; England A to Kenya and Sri Lanka 1997-98;
England VI to Hong Kong 1997, 2001; England to Sharjah (Champions Trophy)
1997-98, to West Indies 1997-98 (one-day series), to Australia 1998-99, to Zimbabwe
(one-day series) 2001-02, to India and New Zealand 2001-02 (one-day series)
Overseas teams played for: Melville, Perth 1992-95; North Perth 1996-97;
South Perth 1999-2000
Career highlights to date: 'Every Surrey trophy I've won and every time I pull an
England shirt on!'
Cricket moments to forget: 'Getting beaten five balls in a row by Chris Schofield,

then getting stumped off the sixth in NatWest quarter-finals 2000 on TV when we were already in trouble!'

Cricketers particularly admired: 'Mr Dilley, Messrs Younis and Akram, Messrs M. and S. Waugh'

Young players to look out for: Michael Carberry, Carl Greenidge

Other sports played: Golf, body surfing, touch ('bloody hard') rugby

Other sports followed: AFL (West Coast Eagles), football ('Chelsea, Man U, Leeds, Arsenal, Barcelona, Real Madrid, England, Brazil, Argentina, France and Perth Glory')

Injuries: Out for two weeks with a pulled hamstring

Relaxations: 'Walking Horace, my lab; spending time with Janaya doing various things'

Extras: Played England U14 and U15. Played Western Australia U17 and U19. Became the youngest player to take five wickets in a Sunday League game when he took 5-10 v Derbyshire at The Oval in 1996. His first two appearances at Lord's both resulted in him winning Man of the Match awards – his 63 off 48 balls in the third One-Day International against Australia in 1997 (his England one-day debut) and his 98 off 113 balls for Surrey against Kent in the Benson and Hedges Cup final in 1997. Became the youngest player (aged 19 and after only 11 first-class games) to make his Test debut for England since Brian Close in 1949 and he and brother Adam became the first brothers to make their Test debuts together for England this century. Was voted the Young Cricketer of the Year by both the Cricket Writers' Club and the PCA in 1997. B&H Gold Award for his 3-29 v Hampshire at West End 2001. Scored 73 off 76 balls in Surrey's B&H final win over Gloucestershire in 2001, becoming the first player to win two B&H final Gold Awards. Scored maiden Championship century (118) v Yorkshire at The Oval 2001. Surrey CCC Fielder of the Year Award and Most Improved Player Award 2001

Opinions on cricket: 'Two up/two down system should be put in place for the Sunday League with top two teams playing division one and division two finals.'

Best batting: 163 England A v Sri Lanka A, Moratuwa 1997-98

Best bowling: 5-51 Surrey v Glamorgan, The Oval 1999

2001 Season

	M	Inns	NO	Runs	HS	Avge	100s	50s	Ct	St	O	M	Runs	Wkts	Avge	Best	5wI	10wM
Test																		
All First	12	19	0	586	118	30.84	1	4	18	-	133.2	21	530	9	58.88	2-39	-	-
1-day Int	6	6	1	118	53	23.60	-	1	2	-	31	0	179	0	-		-	-
C & G	2	1	0	0	0	0.00	-	-	-	-	3	0	22	0	-		-	-
B & H	6	5	2	195	73	65.00	-	2	1	-	31.2	1	145	7	20.71	3-13	-	
1-day Lge	12	11	3	368	70 *	46.00	-	3	2	-	81	8	384	21	18.28	3-10	-	

Career Performances

	M	Inns	NO	Runs	HS	Avge	100s	50s	Ct	St	Balls	Runs	Wkts	Avge	Best	5wI	10wM
Test	2	4	0	44	28	11.00	-	-	2	-	252	199	4	49.75	2-105	-	-
All First	75	114	6	2794	163	25.87	3	14	67	-	7293	4214	126	33.44	5-51	1	-
1-day Int	13	12	1	240	63	21.81	-	2	3	-	336	301	2	150.50	2-43	-	
C & G	14	9	0	95	33	10.55	-	-	6	-	492	398	8	49.75	2-28	-	
B & H	26	23	3	751	98	37.55	-	6	7	-	996	876	29	30.20	3-13	-	
1-day Lge	65	56	6	1121	70 *	22.42	-	4	19	-	2338	1913	84	22.77	5-10	1	

HOLLOWAY, P. C. L. Somerset

Name: <u>Piran</u> Christopher Laity Holloway
Role: Left-hand bat, off-spin bowler,
wicket-keeper
Born: 1 October 1970, Helston, Cornwall
Height: 5ft 8in **Weight:** 11st 5lbs
Nickname: Oggy, Leg, Piras
County debut: 1988 (Warwickshire),
1994 (Somerset)
County cap: 1997 (Somerset)
1st-Class 50s: 28
1st-Class 100s: 9
1st-Class catches: 82
1st-Class stumpings: 1
One-Day 100s: 2
Place in batting averages: 137th av. 28.35
(2000 180th av. 19.84)
Parents: Chris and Mary
Family links with cricket: 'Mum and Dad
are keen'
Education: Nansloe CP School, Helston; Millfield School; Taunton School;
Loughborough University
Qualifications: 7 O-levels, 2 A-levels, BSc (Hons) Sports Science
Career outside cricket: Coaching
Overseas tours: Millfield School to Barbados 1986; England YC to Australia 1989-
90; Warwickshire CCC to Cape Town 1992 and 1993; Somerset CCC to Holland 1994
Overseas teams played for: North Perth, 1993-94; Nedlands, Perth 1994-96;
Claremont-Nedlands, Perth 1996-98
Cricketers particularly admired: Ian Botham, David Gower
Young players to look out for: Matt Bulbeck, Steve Harmison
Other sports followed: Squash, football, rugby, tennis, surfing
Relaxations: Music, surfing, travel

Extras: Won the Jack Hobbs Trophy in 1990. Played Young England for three years. Was fourth in the county averages in 1991 (av. 65.75). Somerset Young Player of the Year 1995. Scored the most runs in A-grade cricket in Perth in 1997-98 season in which Claremont-Nedlands won the Bank West Cup. Took part in Somerset record opening stand in matches v Glamorgan (240) with Marcus Trescothick at Cardiff 2001
Best batting: 168 Somerset v Middlesex, Uxbridge 1996

2001 Season

	M	Inns	NO	Runs	HS	Avge	100s	50s	Ct	St	O	M	Runs	Wkts	Avge	Best	5wI	10wM
Test																		
All First	12	21	1	567	85	28.35	-	4	3	-	4	0	19	0	-		-	-	-
1-day Int																		
C & G	1	1	0	12	12	12.00	-	-	-	-								
B & H	1	1	0	14	14	14.00	-	-	-	-								
1-day Lge	6	5	0	19	11	3.80	-	-	-	-								

Career Performances

	M	Inns	NO	Runs	HS	Avge	100s	50s	Ct	St	Balls	Runs	Wkts	Avge	Best	5wI	10wM
Test																	
All First	119	200	28	5358	168	31.15	9	28	82	1	76	69	0	-		-	-	-
1-day Int																	
C & G	16	15	3	549	90	45.75	-	4	8	1							
B & H	11	11	1	233	78	23.30	-	2	8	-							
1-day Lge	94	84	16	1742	117	25.61	2	10	36	7							

46. Which former England spinner was Man of the Match for his
4-13 for Berkshire v Durham in the 2000 NatWest?

Name: <u>Carl</u> Daniel Hopkinson
Role: Right-hand bat, right-arm medium-fast
bowler; 'batter that bowls'
Born: 14 September 1981, Brighton
Height: 5ft 11in
Nickname: Hoppo
County debut: 2001 (one-day)
Parents: Jane and Jerry
Marital status: Single
Family links with cricket: 'Dad played in
the local team, which got me interested, and
coached me from a young age'
Education: Barcombe; Chailey;
Brighton College
Qualifications: 7 GCSEs, 3 A-levels, Level 1
coaching

Off-season: 'Training in England; coaching;
maybe go to Australia after Christmas'
Overseas tours: Tours to India 1997-98, to South Africa 1999
Overseas teams played for: Rockingham-Mandurah, Western Australia 2000-01
Career highlights to date: 'Playing in my first day/night game on TV; also my debut'
Cricket moments to forget: 'Playing on my debut and taking guard before the
incoming batsman was announced; in other words, they didn't know who I was!'
Cricketers particularly admired: Dennis Lillee, Ian Botham, Viv Richards,
Graham Thorpe
Young players to look out for: Krishna Singh
Other sports played: Rugby ('won Rosslyn Park National Sevens'), squash, football
Other sports followed: Football (Leeds United and Brighton & Hove Albion)
Relaxations: 'Going out in Brighton with my mates, cinema etc.'
Extras: South of England and England squads until U17. Sussex Young Player of the
Year 2000. 2nd XI Fielder of the Year 2001. Played for Sussex Board XI in the C&G
2001 and in the second round of the C&G 2002, which was played in September 2001.
Took wicket (John Wood) with his third ball on county debut, in the Norwich Union
League v Lancashire at Hove 2001. Took four catches and achieved a run out v
Glamorgan at Hove in the Norwich Union League 2001
Opinions on cricket: 'I like the idea of the new academies that are being set up.
Having come through an academy, they seem like a superb opportunity for the players
involved. Apart from that, I think I need to play a little more cricket to further my
opinions.'

2001 Season

	M	Inns	NO	Runs	HS	Avge	100s	50s	Ct	St	O	M	Runs	Wkts	Avge	Best	5wI	10wM
Test																		
All First																		
1-day Int																		
C & G	2	2	0	58	43	29.00	-	-	1	-	15	0	88	0	-		-	-
B & H																		
1-day Lge	2	1	1	10	10 *	-	-	-	5	-	2	0	2	1	2.00	1-2	-

Career Performances

	M	Inns	NO	Runs	HS	Avge	100s	50s	Ct	St	Balls	Runs	Wkts	Avge	Best	5wI	10wM
Test																	
All First																	
1-day Int																	
C & G	2	2	0	58	43	29.00	-	-	1	-	90	88	0	-		-	-
B & H																	
1-day Lge	2	1	1	10	10 *	-	-	-	5	-	12	2	1	2.00	1-2	-

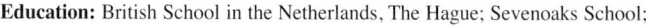

HOUSE, W. J. Sussex

Name: William (<u>Will</u>) John House
Role: Left-hand top-order bat, right-arm medium bowler
Born: 16 March 1976, Sheffield
Height: 5ft 10in **Weight:** 13st
Nickname: Housey, Curry, Etna
County debut: 1997 (Kent), 2000 (Sussex)
1st-Class 50s: 8
1st-Class 100s: 2
1st-Class catches: 21
One-Day 5 w. in innings: 1
Place in batting averages: (2000 248th av. 12.44)
Strike rate: (career 365.75)
Parents: Bill and Anna
Marital status: Girlfriend Felicity
Family links with cricket: 'Dad played in the Yorkshire League and now plays with both my brothers for "the Chart"'
Education: British School in the Netherlands, The Hague; Sevenoaks School; University of Cambridge (Gonville and Caius College)
Qualifications: 11 GCSEs, International Baccalaureate, BA (Hons) History, NCA coaching award

Career outside cricket: 'Working for Long Reach International (www.longreachint.com) – new company providing expertise to the managers of the commercial and risk management activities of sport'

Overseas tours: MCC to Australia 1999, to Bangladesh 2000; Sussex to Grenada 2001

Overseas teams played for: Royal Hague CC 1985-89; University CC, Adelaide 1994-95

Career highlights to date: 'First first-class hundred'

Cricket moments to forget: 'Getting out for two on my Championship debut for Kent in 1997 and it then starting to rain just as I was walking off – terrible feeling'

Cricketers particularly admired: David Gower, Ian Botham

Young players to look out for: Tim Ambrose, Matt Prior

Other sports played: Rugby (Cambridge University U21 XV 1996-97), football (Cambridge Blue 1998)

Other sports followed: Rugby, football (Sheffield Wednesday), golf

Injuries: Out for two weeks 'and a limp for the rest of the season' with a pulled muscle in the back of the knee

Relaxations: Music, history

Extras: Cricket Society's leading all-rounder in schools cricket in 1993. Kent CCC's Most Improved Player 1996. Cambridge University's Player of the Year 1996 and 1998. Benson and Hedges Gold Awards for British Universities v Surrey 1997 (93 runs) and v Gloucestershire 1998 (5-34). Left Kent at end of 1999 season and joined Sussex for 2000

Opinions on cricket: 'Two divisions has helped ensure intense cricket right through to the end of the season. There seems little doubt now that a gulf in standard will open up sooner rather than later between the two divisions and will inevitably result in division one attracting greater interest and revenue.'

Best batting: 136 Cambridge University v Derbyshire, Fenner's 1996

Best bowling: 1-34 Cambridge University v Oxford University, Lord's 1998
1-34 Sussex v Glamorgan, Colwyn Bay 2000

2001 Season

	M	Inns	NO	Runs	HS	Avge	100s	50s	Ct	St	O	M	Runs	Wkts	Avge	Best	5wI	10wM
Test																		
All First	3	4	0	80	46	20.00	-	-	1	-								
1-day Int																		
C & G	1	1	0	18	18	18.00	-	-	-	-	4	0	24	0	-		-	-
B & H	4	4	0	71	35	17.75	-	-	1	-								
1-day Lge	15	13	3	240	39	24.00	-	-	4	-	22	0	112	2	56.00	2-50	-	

Career Performances

	M	Inns	NO	Runs	HS	Avge	100s	50s	Ct	St	Balls	Runs	Wkts	Avge	Best	5wI	10wM
Test																	
All First	37	57	8	1443	136	29.44	2	8	21	-	1463	964	4	241.00	1-34	-	-
1-day Int																	
C & G	4	3	0	38	18	12.66	-	-	3	-	48	47	0	-		-	-
B & H	19	19	0	405	93	21.31	-	2	4	-	185	190	10	19.00	5-58	1	
1-day Lge	50	43	8	820	80 *	23.42	-	1	8	-	524	425	13	32.69	3-34	-	

HUGGINS, T. B. Northamptonshire

Name: Thomas (<u>Tom</u>) Benjamin Huggins
Role: Right-hand bat, right-arm
medium bowler
Born: 8 March 1983, Peterborough
Height: 6ft 3in **Weight:** 14st
County debut: No first-team appearance
Parents: John and Elizabeth
Marital status: Single
Education: Kimbolton Prep School;
Kimbolton School
Qualifications: 9 GCSEs, 3 A-levels, Level 2
coaching award
Off-season: Training
Overseas tours: Huntingdon Cricket 2000 to
Zimbabwe 1999
Career highlights to date: 'Setting three
records for Kimbolton 1st XI in 2001 – most
runs in a season (1069); most centuries in a
season (five); highest individual score (150*)'
Cricket moments to forget: 'Getting bowled for nought in an ECB U18 trial match'
Cricketers particularly admired: Graham Thorpe
Other sports played: Football, hockey
Other sports followed: Football (Liverpool FC)
Relaxations: Listening to music; playing snooker; cars; going out with friends
Extras: Huntingdonshire Youth Player of the Year 1997, 1998, 2000. Recorded highest
individual score in Huntingdonshire Youth cricket (185* v Norfolk U19 2000). Played
for Cambridgeshire in the second round of the C&G 2002, which was played in
September 2001
Opinions on cricket: 'Generally standards are improving due to better and more
innovative coaching techniques and facilities.'

2001 Season (did not make any first-class or one-day appearances)

Career Performances

	M	Inns	NO	Runs	HS	Avge	100s	50s	Ct	St	Balls	Runs	Wkts	Avge	Best	5wI	10wM
Test																	
All First																	
1-day Int																	
C & G	1	1	0	2	2	2.00	-	-	-	-							
B & H																	
1-day Lge																	

HUGHES, J. Glamorgan

Name: Jonathan Hughes
Role: Right-hand bat, right-arm medium bowler
Born: 30 June 1981, Pontypridd
Height: 5ft 11in
Nickname: Jonny, Tuck Box, Hughesy
County debut: 2001
Parents: Steve and Anne
Marital status: Single
Family links with cricket: 'Dad and brothers Matthew (16) and Gareth (22) play for Hopkinstown'
Education: Trehoplyn; Coed y Lan Comprehensive, Pontypridd
Qualifications: MCC coaching badges
Off-season: 'Not a lot – chill out, do a bit of work for my father (plumbing)'
Overseas tours: Hopkinstown to Barbados 1998
Overseas teams played for: Easts-Redlands, Brisbane 2000, 2001
Career highlights to date: 'Debut v Surrey for Glamorgan in County Championship'
Cricketers particularly admired: Matthew Maynard, Ian Botham
Young players to look out for: Mark Wallace
Other sports played: Football (Hopkinstown)
Other sports followed: Rugby (Pontypridd), football (Everton)
Injuries: Out for two weeks with a back strain
Relaxations: Going to the pub
Extras: Captained Welsh Schools. Was on Lord's groundstaff 1998-99. Glamorgan 2nd XI Player of the Year 2001. Glamorgan Young Player of the Year 2001

Opinions on cricket: 'Just get on with it.'
Best batting: 49 Glamorgan v Surrey, Cardiff 2001

2001 Season

	M	Inns	NO	Runs	HS	Avge	100s	50s	Ct	St	O	M	Runs	Wkts	Avge	Best	5wI	10wM
Test																		
All First	1	2	0	87	49	43.50	-	-	-	-								
1-day Int																		
C & G																		
B & H																		
1-day Lge																		

Career Performances

	M	Inns	NO	Runs	HS	Avge	100s	50s	Ct	St	Balls	Runs	Wkts	Avge	Best	5wI	10wM
Test																		
All First	1	2	0	87	49	43.50	-	-	-	-							
1-day Int																		
C & G																		
B & H																		
1-day Lge																		

HUNT, T. A.   Middlesex

Name: <u>Thomas</u> Aaron Hunt
Role: Left-hand bat, right-arm
medium-fast bowler
Born: 19 January 1982, Melbourne, Australia
Height: 6ft 3in **Weight:** 13st 4lbs
Nickname: Hopalong, Peg-leg
County debut: No first-team appearance
(*see Extras*)
Parents: Jennifer Hunt and Tim Woodbridge
Marital status: Single
Education: Brackenbury, Hammersmith;
Acton High; St Clement Danes
Qualifications: 9 GCSEs, 1 A-level, Level 1
coaching award
Off-season: 'Getting fit'
Cricket moments to forget: '1st XI debut at
Lord's'
Cricketers particularly admired:
Curtly Ambrose, Waqar Younis

Young players to look out for: Ian Bell, Andrew Strauss, Tim Bloomfield

Other sports played: 'Keen skier, also played school and Sunday league football'
Other sports followed: Football (Man Utd)
Injuries: Injury to left knee
Relaxations: 'Music; spending time with girlfriend'
Extras: Has not appeared in a domestic competition but played for Middlesex v Australians in a one-day fixture at Lord's 2001

HUNTER, I. D. Durham

Name: <u>Ian</u> David Hunter
Role: Right-hand bat, right-arm fast-medium bowler
Born: 11 September 1979, Durham City
Height: 6ft 2in **Weight:** 11st 9lbs
Nickname: Sticks, Hunts
County debut: 1999 (one-day), 2000 (first-class)
1st-Class 50s: 1
1st-Class catches: 4
Place in batting averages: 210th av. 18.09
Place in bowling averages: 123rd av. 43.75
Strike rate: 68.06 (career 68.45)
Parents: Ken and Linda
Marital status: Single
Family links with cricket: Brother plays for local village side
Education: Sacriston Junior School; Fyndoune Community College, Sacriston; New College, Durham
Qualifications: 9 GCSEs, 1 A-level (PE), BTEC National Diploma in Sports Science, Level I and II cricket coaching awards
Off-season: 'Relaxing/socialising; preparing for next season'
Overseas tours: Durham U21 to Sri Lanka 1996
Career highlights to date: 'Scoring 63 on first-class debut' (*v Leicestershire at Riverside 2000 as nightwatchman*)
Cricketers particularly admired: Allan Donald, Steve Waugh
Young players to look out for: 'Simon Brown', Gordon Muchall, Gary Pratt
Other sports played: Football, golf
Other sports followed: Football (Newcastle United FC)
Relaxations: Socialising with friends; keeping fit, golf, football
Extras: Set a new Durham best analysis for the 2nd XI Championship with his 11-155 v Lancashire 2nd XI 1999. Represented England U19 in 'Test' series v Australia U19 1999. Played for Durham Board XI in the second round of the C&G 2002, which was played in September 2001

Opinions on cricket: 'Standards of pitches have improved considerably "especially at Riverside". Two divisions has improved the standard and competitiveness of cricket but two up/two down would be more appropriate. The ECB Academy is a step in the right direction.'

Best batting: 63 Durham v Leicestershire, Riverside 2000
Best bowling: 4-55 Durham v Warwickshire, Edgbaston 2001

2001 Season

	M	Inns	NO	Runs	HS	Avge	100s	50s	Ct	St	O	M	Runs	Wkts	Avge	Best	5wI	10wM
Test																		
All First	8	14	3	199	37	18.09	-	-	4	-	181.3	27	700	16	43.75	4-55	-	-
1-day Int																		
C & G	1	1	0	13	13	13.00	-	-	-	-	9	1	29	1	29.00	1-29	-	
B & H	4	2	1	1	1 *	1.00	-	-	2	-	36	4	164	5	32.80	4-48	-	
1-day Lge	6	4	1	47	21	15.66	-	-	1	-	38	5	186	8	23.25	3-47	-	

Career Performances

	M	Inns	NO	Runs	HS	Avge	100s	50s	Ct	St	Balls	Runs	Wkts	Avge	Best	5wI	10wM
Test																	
All First	11	18	3	282	63	18.80	-	1	4	-	1506	928	22	42.18	4-55	-	-
1-day Int																	
C & G	2	2	0	14	13	7.00	-	-	-	-	78	47	1	47.00	1-29	-	
B & H	4	2	1	1	1 *	1.00	-	-	2	-	216	164	5	32.80	4-48	-	
1-day Lge	24	13	4	84	21	9.33	-	-	3	-	984	748	29	25.79	4-29	-	

47. The twin brother of a current county cricketer captained
the Somerset Board XI in the 2001 C&G. Name him.

HUSSAIN, N. Essex

Name: Nasser Hussain
Role: Right-hand bat, leg-break bowler,
county club captain
Born: 28 March 1968, Madras, India
Height: 6ft **Weight:** 12st 7lbs
Nickname: Nashwan
County debut: 1987
County cap: 1989
Benefit: 1999 (£271,500)
Test debut: 1989-90
Tests: 63
One-Day Internationals: 50
1000 runs in a season: 5
1st-Class 50s: 86
1st-Class 100s: 43
1st-Class 200s: 1
1st-Class catches: 314
One-Day 100s: 5

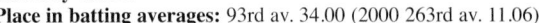

Place in batting averages: 93rd av. 34.00 (2000 263rd av. 11.06)
Strike rate: (career 156.00)
Parents: Joe and Shireen
Wife and date of marriage: Karen, 24 September 1993
Children: Jacob, 8 June 2001
Family links with cricket: Father played zonal cricket in India. Played for Madras in Ranji Trophy 1966-67. Brother Mel played for Hampshire. Brother Abbas played for Essex 2nd XI
Education: Forest School, Snaresbrook; Durham University
Qualifications: 10 O-levels, 3 A-levels, BSc (Hons) in Natural Sciences, NCA cricket coaching award
Off-season: Touring Zimbabwe, India and New Zealand with England
Overseas tours: England YC to Sri Lanka 1986-87, to Australia (U19 World Cup) 1987-88; England A to Pakistan and Sri Lanka 1990-91, to Bermuda and West Indies 1991-92, to Pakistan 1995-96 (captain); England to India (Nehru Cup) 1989-90, to West Indies 1989-90, to West Indies 1993-94, to Zimbabwe and New Zealand 1996-97, to West Indies 1997-98, to Australia 1998-99, to South Africa and Zimbabwe 1999-2000 (captain), to Kenya (ICC Knockout Trophy) 2000-01 (captain), to Pakistan and Sri Lanka 2000-01 (captain), to Zimbabwe (one-day series) 2001-02 (captain), to India and New Zealand 2001-02 (captain)
Overseas teams played for: Madras 1986-87; Petersham, Sydney 1992-93; Adelaide University 1990; Stellenbosch University, South Africa 1994-95; Primrose, Cape Town
Cricketers particularly admired: Mark Waugh, Graham Gooch, Sachin Tendulkar

Other sports played: Golf (10 handicap), football
Other sports followed: Football (Leeds United)
Injuries: Suffered a fractured right thumb in Lord's Test v Pakistan and a fractured little finger of left hand in Edgbaston Test v Australia
Relaxations: Listening to music. Listening to Mark Ilott. Watching television
Extras: Played for England Schools U15 for two years (one as captain). Became youngest player to play for Essex Schools U11 at the age of eight and U15 at the age of 12. Took hat-trick for Essex U11 v Berkshire U11 – all stumped by Neil Burns, now of Leics – and at 15 was considered the best young leg-break bowler in the country. Cricket Writers' Club Young Cricketer of the Year 1989. Set records for third (347* v Lancashire at Ilford 1992), fourth (314 v Surrey at The Oval 1991) and fifth (316 v Leicestershire at Leicester 1991) wicket partnerships for Essex (with Mark Waugh, Salim Malik and Mike Garnham respectively). Essex Player of the Year 1993. Appointed Essex vice-captain 1996. Finished 2nd in the Whyte and Mackay batting ratings in 1995. Appointed England vice-captain in 1996-97. Shared in record fourth-wicket partnership for England in Tests v Australia (288) with Graham Thorpe at Edgbaston 1997. Appointed Essex captain for 1999. Represented England in the 1999 World Cup. Appointed England captain after 1999 World Cup. Topped England batting averages in the 1999-2000 Test series v South Africa with 370 runs at 61.66; during the series he became the first player to bat for 1000 minutes in Test cricket without being out. Handed over Essex team captaincy to Ronnie Irani at the start of the 2000 season but remains Essex club captain. In 2000 led England to victory in the NatWest triangular one-day series, to a Test series win over Zimbabwe, and to a first Test series win over West Indies for 31 years; followed up with series wins in Pakistan and Sri Lanka in the winter of 2000-01, which made England only the second touring side to win two Test rubbers on the sub-continent in the same season. England central contract 2001. npower Contribution to Cricket Award 2001
Best batting: 207 England v Australia, Edgbaston 1997
Best bowling: 1-38 Essex v Worcestershire, Kidderminster 1992
Stop press: Awarded OBE in New Year honours list 2001-02

48. What was unusual about the result of the 1981 NatWest final?

2001 Season

	M	Inns	NO	Runs	HS	Avge	100s	50s	Ct	St	O	M	Runs	Wkts	Avge	Best	5wI	10wM
Test	4	7	1	241	64	40.16	-	3	-	-								
All First	6	10	1	306	64	34.00	-	3	-	-	1	0	1	0	-	-	-	-
1-day Int																		
C & G	1	1	0	10	10	10.00	-	-	1	-								
B & H	3	3	0	162	63	54.00	-	2	2	-								
1-day Lge	2	2	0	28	21	14.00	-	-	-	-								

Career Performances

	M	Inns	NO	Runs	HS	Avge	100s	50s	Ct	St	Balls	Runs	Wkts	Avge	Best	5wI	10wM
Test	63	113	12	3535	207	35.00	9	17	42	-	30	15	0	-	-	-	-
All First	286	463	47	17349	207	41.70	44	86	314	-	312	323	2	161.50	1-38	-	-
1-day Int	50	50	8	1206	95	28.71	-	9	29	-							
C & G	28	26	3	913	108	39.69	2	4	19	-							
B & H	53	48	8	1888	118	47.20	2	17	23	-							
1-day Lge	145	134	18	3692	114	31.82	1	25	63	-							

HUSSEY, M. E. K.　　　Northamptonshire

Name: Michael (<u>Mike</u>) Edward Killeen Hussey
Role: Left-hand bat, right-arm medium bowler, county captain
Born: 27 May 1975, Perth, Western Australia
Height: 6ft **Weight:** 12st 7lbs
Nickname: Huss
County debut: 2001
County cap: 2001
1000 runs in a season: 1
1st-Class 50s: 32
1st-Class 100s: 15
1st-Class 200s: 2
1st-Class 300s: 1
1st-Class catches: 70
One-Day 100s: 1
Place in batting averages: 4th av. 79.03
Strike rate: 54.00 (career 87.20)
Parents: Helen and Ted
Marital status: Engaged to Amy
Family links with cricket: Brother Dave was in the Western Australia state squad
Education: Whitfords Catholic; Prendiville; Curtin

Career outside cricket: Teacher
Overseas tours: Australia U19 to India 1994; Australian Cricket Academy to Pakistan 1995; Australia A to Scotland and Ireland 1998
Overseas teams played for: Wanneroo, Western Australia; Western Australia 1994-95 –
Cricketers particularly admired: Steve Waugh, Mark Taylor, Sachin Tendulkar, Dennis Lillee
Young players to look out for: Shaun Marsh
Other sports played: Golf, squash, tennis
Other sports followed: Australian Rules (West Coast Eagles), football (Man Utd)
Relaxations: Movies, beach
Extras: Attended the Australian Academy in 1995. Finished third in the Sheffield Shield Player of the Year award in his first full season 1995-96. Played league cricket in Scotland for Ferguslie CC in 1998. Sir Donald Bradman Young Cricketer of the Year 1998. Excalibur Award (Western Australia) 1998-2000. Scored maiden Mercantile Cup century (100*) v Victoria at Melbourne 1999-2000, sharing in a competition record sixth-wicket partnership of 173 with Brad Hogg. Carried his bat for 172* v South Australia in the Pura Milk Cup 1999-2000. Joined Northamptonshire as overseas player for 2001. B&H Gold Awards for his 93 v Warwickshire at Northampton and 114* v Glamorgan at Cardiff (his maiden century for Northants) 2001. Shared in record second-wicket stand for Northants in matches v Surrey (168) with Jeff Cook at Northampton 2001. Scored maiden first-class double century (232) v Leicestershire at Northampton 2001. Scored maiden first-class triple century (329*) v Essex at Northampton 2001, in the process overtaking Mal Loye's record for the highest individual score by a Northants player (322*); followed up with a 33-ball 70* in the second innings and was on the field for the entire match. Scored 208 v Somerset at Taunton 2001, in the process sharing with Russell Warren in a record third-wicket partnership for Northants in matches against Somerset (287). Leading run-scorer in English first-class cricket 2001 with 2055 runs (all in the Championship) at 79.03, at the same time becoming the first Northants batsman to score 2000 Championship runs in a season since Allan Lamb did so in 1981. Northamptonshire Player of the Year 2001. Awarded Northamptonshire cap 2001. Appointed Northamptonshire captain for 2002
Best batting: 329* Northamptonshire v Essex, Northampton 2001
Best bowling: 2-21 Western Australia v Queensland, Perth 1998-99

2001 Season

	M	Inns	NO	Runs	HS	Avge	100s	50s	Ct	St	O	M	Runs	Wkts	Avge	Best	5wI	10wM
Test																		
All First	16	30	4	2055	329 *	79.03	5	9	19	-	18	2	78	2	39.00	1-14	-	-
1-day Int																		
C & G	2	2	0	67	59	33.50	-	1	1	-	5	0	30	1	30.00	1-20	-	
B & H	5	5	1	253	114 *	63.25	1	1	3	-	3	0	15	1	15.00	1-15	-	
1-day Lge	15	15	1	510	96 *	36.42	-	4	4	-								

Career Performances

	M	Inns	NO	Runs	HS	Avge	100s	50s	Ct	St	Balls	Runs	Wkts	Avge	Best	5wI	10wM
Test																	
All First	88	161	12	7437	329 *	49.91	18	32	70	-	436	248	5	49.60	2-21	-	-
1-day Int																	
C & G	2	2	0	67	59	33.50	-	1	1	-	30	30	1	30.00	1-20	-	
B & H	5	5	1	253	114 *	63.25	1	1	3	-	18	15	1	15.00	1-15	-	
1-day Lge	15	15	1	510	96 *	36.42	-	4	4	-							

HUTCHISON, P. M. Sussex

Name: <u>Paul</u> Michael Hutchison
Role: Left-hand bat, left-arm swing bowler
Born: 9 June 1977, Leeds
Height: 6ft 4in **Weight:** 12st 4lbs
Nickname: Hutch
County debut: 1995-96 (Yorkshire)
County cap: 1998 (Yorkshire)
50 wickets in a season: 1
1st-Class 5 w. in innings: 7
1st-Class 10 w. in match: 1
1st-Class catches: 9
Place in batting averages: (2000 310th av. 0.50)
Place in bowling averages: (2000 64th av. 26.25)
Strike rate: 51.42 (career 42.58)
Parents: David Hutchison and Rita Laycock (deceased)
Marital status: Engaged to Emma
Family links with cricket: Brother Richard plays at Pudsey St Lawrence in the Bradford League
Education: Pudsey Greenside; Pudsey Crawshaw High; 'the Yorks changing room!!'

Qualifications: 8 GCSEs, GNVQ Leisure and Tourism, qualified cricket coach, basic IT ('thanks to PCA')

Career outside cricket: 'Not just yet, thanks!'

Off-season: 'At home fitness training until the New Year, then out to Oz to work on my game. Joining the county on pre-season ready for the new season'

Overseas tours: England U19 to Zimbabwe 1995-96; England A to Kenya and Sri Lanka 1997-98, to Zimbabwe and South Africa 1998-99; Yorkshire CCC to Zimbabwe and Botswana 1996, to South Africa 1998, 1999, 2001

Career highlights to date: 'My Championship debut at Portsmouth – 7-50. My Yorkshire cap. My two England A tours'

Cricket moments to forget: 'Dropping Mark Alleyne in the Super Cup final at Lord's [1999]. Continually being overlooked at Yorks last season!'

Cricketers particularly admired: Matt Maynard, Neil Fairbrother, Courtney Walsh, Craig White, Darren Gough, Graham Dilley, Malcolm Marshall

Young players to look out for: Michael Lumb, Ian Bell, Vik Solanki, John Sadler

Other sports played: Golf, football

Other sports followed: 'Most sports; anything on Sky Sports; any team from my area (Leeds/Bradford)'

Relaxations: Golf, cinema, socialising with friends

Extras: Represented England at U17, U18 and U19 levels. Played for Pudsey St Lawrence in the Bradford League. Had a place at the Yorkshire Academy. Took 7-38 on first first-class appearance of 1997, against Pakistan A. Took 7-50 against Hampshire at Portsmouth 1997, the best Championship debut figures for Yorkshire since Wilfred Rhodes took 7-24 v Somerset in 1898. Voted Wombwell Cricket Lovers' Young Player of the Year for 1997. Was PCA representative for Yorkshire CCC. Released by Yorkshire at the end of the 2001 season and has joined Sussex for 2002

Opinions on cricket: 'Great game to be involved with. Two divisions is a success. Would probably change it to two up/two down as gaining promotion to the top flight from third place is too easy. Floodlit matches are also a success as they get the crowds in. TV coverage is also improving, which then lends itself to better marketing for the players.'

Best batting: 30 Yorkshire v Essex, Scarborough 1998

Best bowling: 7-31 Yorkshire v Sussex, Hove 1998

2001 Season

	M	Inns	NO	Runs	HS	Avge	100s	50s	Ct	St	O	M	Runs	Wkts	Avge	Best	5wI	10wM
Test																		
All First	3	3	3	22	11 *	-	-	-	-	-	60	11	224	7	32.00	2-33	-	-
1-day Int																		
C & G																		
B & H																		
1-day Lge	3	0	0	0	0	-	-	-	1	-	23	2	102	7	14.57	3-26	-	

Career Performances

	M	Inns	NO	Runs	HS	Avge	100s	50s	Ct	St	Balls	Runs	Wkts	Avge	Best	5wI	10wM
Test																	
All First	44	45	25	200	30	10.00	-	-	9	-	6600	3562	155	22.98	7-31	7	1
1-day Int																	
C & G	3	1	1	4	4 *	-	-	-	-	-	132	62	5	12.40	3-18	-	
B & H	6	2	2	6	4 *	-	-	-	-	-	191	112	10	11.20	3-14	-	
1-day Lge	23	8	5	8	2 *	2.66	-	-	3	-	920	670	28	23.92	4-34	-	

HUTTON, B. L.   Middlesex

Name: Benjamin (<u>Ben</u>) Leonard Hutton
Role: Left-hand bat, right-arm
medium bowler
Born: 29 January 1977,
Johannesburg, South Africa
Height: 6ft 2in **Weight:** 12st
Nickname: Gibbo
County debut: 1999
1st-Class 50s: 5
1st-Class 100s: 3
1st-Class catches: 33
One-Day 5 w. in innings: 1
Place in batting averages: 72nd av. 39.30
(2000 235th av. 14.46)
Strike rate: 144.00 (career 102.88)
Parents: Richard and Charmaine
Marital status: Single
Family links with cricket: Len Hutton
(grandfather) Yorkshire and England; Richard Hutton (father) Yorkshire and England
Education: Holmewood House Prep School; Radley College; Durham University
Qualifications: 10 GCSEs, 3 A-levels, BA (Hons) Social Sciences, NCA
coaching award

Off-season: Playing grade cricket in Perth
Overseas tours: Durham University to Zimbabwe 1997-98; Middlesex to Portugal 1997, 1998, 1999, to South Africa 2000, to Malta 2001
Overseas teams played for: Wanderers CC, Johannesburg 1996-97; Pirates CC, Johannesburg 1997; Gosnells, Perth 2000-01, 2001-02
Career highlights to date: 'First Championship century [139 v Derbyshire at Southgate 2001]. Scoring 73 against the Australians 2001'
Cricket moments to forget: 'Middlesex losing 16 wickets in a day against Gloucestershire [Lord's 2001] and at the same time breaking my hand, ruling me out for the remainder of the season. The defeat severely dented our promotion hopes'
Cricketers particularly admired: Len Hutton, Richard Hutton, Justin Langer, Mark Ramprakash, Michael Atherton
Young players to look out for: Alan Coleman, Ian Bell, Nicky Peng
Other sports played: Golf (12 handicap)
Other sports followed: Football, rugby
Injuries: Out for six weeks with a broken hand
Relaxations: Reading, music
Extras: BUSA Halifax medal 1997. Opened for Middlesex v Essex at Southend 1999 with Andrew Strauss, his former opening partner at Radley. Played in Durham University's BUSA Championship winning side 1999. His maiden first-class century, 133 v Oxford University CCE at The Parks, was the first first-class century of the 2001 season. Scored maiden Championship century (139) v Derbyshire at Southgate 2001. Recorded maiden one-day five-wicket return (5-45) v Derbyshire at Southgate in the Norwich Union League 2001
Opinions on cricket: 'The two divisional system is working. However, two up/two down would suffice and mean that sides would have to go all out for victory, instead of being content with taking full bonus and a drawn result (as the improvement in four-day wickets this season has often made it hard to take 20 wickets). Why not award bonus points for winning on first innings; that may lead to more intense cricket that would mirror the Test arena. By contrast, the very poor nature of wickets for Sunday League cricket has meant low-scoring, unexciting matches that are failing to capture the attention of audiences and don't prepare players for ODIs.'
Best batting: 139 Middlesex v Derbyshire, Southgate 2001
Best bowling: 2-9 Middlesex v Glamorgan, Southgate 2000

2001 Season

	M	Inns	NO	Runs	HS	Avge	100s	50s	Ct	St	O	M	Runs	Wkts	Avge	Best	5wI	10wM
Test																		
All First	14	22	2	786	139	39.30	3	2	20	-	24	4	91	1	91.00	1-24	-	-
1-day Int																		
C & G	1	1	0	14	14	14.00	-	-	1	-	6	1	42	2	21.00	2-42	-	
B & H	5	4	0	66	52	16.50	-	1	3	-	7	0	51	1	51.00	1-15	-	
1-day Lge	8	8	0	187	77	23.37	-	1	3	-	44	2	188	8	23.50	5-45	1	

Career Performances

	M	Inns	NO	Runs	HS	Avge	100s	50s	Ct	St	Balls	Runs	Wkts	Avge	Best	5wI	10wM
Test																	
All First	33	53	4	1315	139	26.83	3	5	33	-	926	576	9	64.00	2-9	-	-
1-day Int																	
C & G	1	1	0	14	14	14.00	-	-	1	-	36	42	2	21.00	2-42	-	
B & H	9	6	0	70	52	11.66	-	1	4	-	169	152	5	30.40	2-43	-	
1-day Lge	23	18	2	359	77	22.43	-	1	11	-	450	384	14	27.42	5-45	1	

HYAM, B. J.   Essex

Name: <u>Barry</u> James Hyam
Role: Right-hand bat, wicket-keeper
Born: 9 September 1975, Romford
Height: 5ft 11in **Weight:** 12st
Nickname: Bazza
County debut: 1993
County cap: 1999
50 dismissals in a season: 1
1st-Class 50s: 3
1st-Class catches: 168
1st-Class stumpings: 11
Place in batting averages: 185th av. 21.42
(2000 268th av. 10.66)
Parents: Peter and Gloria
Wife and date of marriage: Villene,
30 September 2000
Family links with cricket: 'Mum and Dad
are keen fans; brother Matthew is captain of
Harold Wood CC; brother Richard plays for Harold Wood'
Education: Marshalls Park; Havering Sixth Form College; Westminster College;
Capel Manor College
Qualifications: 9 GCSEs, 1 A-level, NCA coaching award

Career outside cricket: Artist
Off-season: 'I am currently training to be a garden designer at Capel Manor College'
Overseas tours: MCC to Bangladesh 1999-2000
Career highlights to date: 'Receiving my county cap'
Cricket moments to forget: 'I can't remember!'
Cricketers particularly admired: Jack Russell, Nasser Hussain
Young players to look out for: Justin Bishop, Tim Phillips
Other sports played: Golf, football
Other sports followed: Football (West Ham United)
Injuries: Out for one week with a spasm in the lower back
Relaxations: Drawing
Extras: Made first-class debut on his 18th birthday. Joint leading wicket-keeper (along with Steve Rhodes) in first-class cricket in the 2000 season with 55 dismissals
Opinions on cricket: 'The idea of reducing 2nd XI matches during the season was not successful, because there were not enough grass net facilities available to practise. Artificial nets are not good enough preparation for games because surfaces are so different.'
Best batting: 63 Essex v Glamorgan, Chelmsford 2001

2001 Season

	M	Inns	NO	Runs	HS	Avge	100s	50s	Ct	St	O	M	Runs	Wkts	Avge	Best	5wl	10wM
Test																		
All First	6	9	2	150	63	21.42	-	1	20	1								
1-day Int																		
C & G	1	1	1	36	36 *	-	-	-	-	1								
B & H	3	2	0	7	7	3.50	-	-	1	1								
1-day Lge	3	3	1	40	30 *	20.00	-	-	1	-								

Career Performances

	M	Inns	NO	Runs	HS	Avge	100s	50s	Ct	St	Balls	Runs	Wkts	Avge	Best	5wl	10wM
Test																	
All First	60	95	11	1381	63	16.44	-	3	168	11	12	8	0	-	-	-	-
1-day Int																	
C & G	4	3	1	41	36 *	20.50	-	-	2	1							
B & H	6	5	0	49	24	9.80	-	-	2	1							
1-day Lge	33	23	5	217	37	12.05	-	-	27	4							

ILLINGWORTH, R. K.   Derbyshire

Name: <u>Richard</u> Keith Illingworth
Role: Right-hand bat, slow left-arm bowler
Born: 23 August 1963, Bradford
Height: 6ft **Weight:** 13st 7lbs
Nickname: Lucy, Harry
County debut: 1982 (Worcestershire), 2001 (Derbyshire)
County cap: 1986 (Worcestershire)
Benefit: 1997 (Worcestershire, £271,275)
Test debut: 1991
Tests: 9
One-Day Internationals: 25
50 wickets in a season: 5
1st-Class 50s: 21
1st-Class 100s: 4
1st-Class 5 w. in innings: 27
1st-Class 10 w. in match: 6
1st-Class catches: 161
One-Day 5 w. in innings: 2
Place in batting averages: 211th av. 17.85 (2000 227th av. 15.40)
Place in bowling averages: 67th av. 31.60 (2000 119th av. 37.15)
Strike rate: 76.00 (career 79.25)
Parents: Keith and Margaret
Wife and date of marriage: Anne, 20 September 1985
Children: Miles, 28 August 1987; Thomas, 20 April 1989
Family links with cricket: Father played Bradford League cricket
Education: Wrose Brow Middle; Salts Grammar School ('same school as the late Jim Laker')
Qualifications: 6 O-levels, Level 3 coaching award
Overseas tours: England A to Zimbabwe and Kenya 1989-90, to Pakistan and Sri Lanka 1990-91; England to New Zealand and Australia (World Cup) 1991-92, to South Africa 1995-96, to India and Pakistan (World Cup) 1995-96
Overseas teams played for: Natal 1988-89
Cricketers particularly admired: Ian Botham, Wasim Akram
Other sports played: Golf
Other sports followed: Football (Leeds United), rugby league (Bradford Bulls), rugby union (Worcester)
Relaxations: 'Playing golf and watching Miles and Thomas in their sporting activities'
Extras: Took 11 for 108 on South African first-class debut for Natal B v Boland 1988. In 1991, v West Indies, became 11th person in history to take a wicket (Phil Simmons)

with first ball in Test cricket. Took a hat-trick in Sunday League v Sussex in 1993, the first Worcestershire player to take hat-trick in one-day cricket. Won 1993 Dick Lygon award for contribution to Worcestershire CCC. Has made three centuries as a nightwatchman. Released by Worcestershire at the end of the 2000 season and joined Derbyshire for 2001. Took 4-37 from 20 overs on Derbyshire debut, v Middlesex at Derby 2001. Retired at the end of the 2001 season

Opinions on cricket: 'I've been very fortunate to play this game for 20 years and enjoyed most of it. I hope everyone gets the same enjoyment as myself.'
Best batting: 120* Worcestershire v Warwickshire, Worcester 1987
Best bowling: 7-50 Worcestershire v Oxford University, The Parks 1985

2001 Season

	M	Inns	NO	Runs	HS	Avge	100s	50s	Ct	St	O	M	Runs	Wkts	Avge	Best	5wI	10wM
Test																		
All First	5	8	1	125	61*	17.85	-	1	-	-	126.4	39	316	10	31.60	4-37	-	-
1-day Int																		
C & G																		
B & H	5	4	1	15	10*	5.00	-	-	2	-	43	2	174	4	43.50	2-40	-	
1-day Lge	6	3	3	45	21*	-	-	-	2	-	47.1	0	209	9	23.22	3-52	-	

Career Performances

	M	Inns	NO	Runs	HS	Avge	100s	50s	Ct	St	Balls	Runs	Wkts	Avge	Best	5wI	10wM
Test	9	14	7	128	28	18.28	-	-	5	-	1485	615	19	32.36	4-96	-	-
All First	376	435	122	7027	120*	22.45	4	21	161	-	65868	26213	831	31.54	7-50	27	6
1-day Int	25	11	5	68	14	11.33	-	-	8	-	1501	1059	30	35.30	3-33	-	
C & G	37	20	9	187	29*	17.00	-	-	11	-	2179	1157	32	36.15	4-20	-	
B & H	66	33	17	275	36*	17.18	-	-	15	-	3232	1883	59	31.91	4-27	-	
1-day Lge	233	111	52	780	31	13.22	-	-	54	-	8938	6413	273	23.49	5-24	2	

49. In the 1973 Gillette Cup final Sussex had an opening batsman called Greenidge and a pace bowler called Marshall. What were their first names?

ILOTT, M. C.   Essex

Name: <u>Mark</u> Christopher Ilott
Role: Left-hand bat, left-arm
medium-fast swing bowler
Born: 27 August 1970, Watford
Height: 6ft 1in **Weight:** 13st 8lbs
Nickname: Ramble, Chook
County debut: 1988
County cap: 1993
Test debut: 1993
Tests: 5
50 wickets in a season: 5
1st-Class 50s: 4
1st-Class 5 w. in innings: 27
1st-Class 10 w. in match: 3
1st-Class catches: 50
One-Day 5 w. in innings: 1
Place in batting averages: 215th av. 16.90

(2000 243rd av. 13.22)
Place in bowling averages: 85th av. 34.11 (2000 75th av. 27.84)
Strike rate: 63.77 (career 55.42)
Parents: John and Glenys
Wife and date of marriage: Sandra, 14 October 1994
Children: James Christopher Mark, 6 October 1996; Madeleine-Rose, 3 March 1999
Family links with cricket: 'Father now umpires at Minor Counties level. Brother
skippers Langleybury in the Hertfordshire League Premier Division'
Education: Kingsway Junior; Francis Combe Secondary Modern
Qualifications: 8 O-levels, 2 A-levels, first two coaching awards, diploma in Fitness
and Nutrition
Career outside cricket: 'Hospitality business and website publisher – markilott.com
for rivals.net'
Off-season: 'I have a benefit year, so I'll not be "working" on that, but I will be
trying to get my committee to organise events on my behalf. And getting extremely fit
for 2002'
Overseas tours: England A to Sri Lanka 1990-91, to Australia 1992-93, to South
Africa 1993-94, to India 1994-95; England to South Africa 1995-96
Overseas teams played for: East Torrens District, Adelaide 1989-91
Career highlights to date: 'England games – all five of them. B&H victory 1998;
NatWest victory 1997; Essex cap 1993'
Cricket moments to forget: 'The various times I have limped off with injury, or last
season when Keith Newell despatched all over Chelmsford for 40 in two overs'
Cricketers particularly admired: Malcolm Marshall, Graham Gooch, John Lever,
Nasser Hussain

Young players to look out for: James Foster, Justin Bishop
Other sports played: Snooker (Rolls-Royce E side in the Watford League),
badminton
Other sports followed: Football (Liverpool and Watford)
Injuries: Out for two weeks with a hamstring injury; for five weeks with a broken
finger; for three weeks with tendonitis of the shoulder
Relaxations: Guitar playing and cutting grass ('no one's in particular')
Extras: Took his 450th wicket for Essex (Nick Knight) v Warwickshire at Chelmsford
1999. Granted a benefit for 2002
Opinions on cricket: 'I love it and want to keep on loving it for the next six years
at least!'
Best batting: 60 England A v Warwickshire, Edgbaston 1995
Best bowling: 9-19 Essex v Northamptonshire, Luton 1995

2001 Season

	M	Inns	NO	Runs	HS	Avge	100s	50s	Ct	St	O	M	Runs	Wkts	Avge	Best	5wI	10wM
Test																		
All First	10	12	1	186	34	16.90	-	-	6	-	287	65	921	27	34.11	5-85	1	-
1-day Int																		
C & G																			
B & H																			
1-day Lge	4	3	2	5	3 *	5.00	-	-	1	-	28	0	189	3	63.00	3-20	-	

Career Performances

	M	Inns	NO	Runs	HS	Avge	100s	50s	Ct	St	Balls	Runs	Wkts	Avge	Best	5wI	10wM
Test	5	6	2	28	15	7.00	-	-	-	-	1042	542	12	45.16	3-48	-	-
All First	186	240	49	2785	60	14.58	-	4	50	-	34196	16898	617	27.38	9-19	27	3
1-day Int																	
C & G	23	13	6	125	54 *	17.85	-	1	6	-	1440	876	25	35.04	3-20	-	
B & H	36	14	4	107	26 *	10.70	-	-	4	-	1944	1205	56	21.51	5-21	1	
1-day Lge	122	75	27	522	56 *	10.87	-	1	20	-	5126	3892	147	26.47	4-15	-	

INNES, K. J.   Northamptonshire

Name: <u>Kevin</u> John Innes
Role: Right-hand bat, right-arm
medium bowler
Born: 24 September 1975, Wellingborough
Height: 5ft 10in **Weight:** 11st 5lbs
Nickname: KJ, Squirrel, Ernie
County debut: 1994
1st-Class 50s: 1
1st-Class catches: 10
Place in batting averages: 229th av. 14.33
Strike rate: 55.88 (career 52.42)
Parents: Peter and Jane
Wife and date of marriage: Caroline, 2001
Education: Boothville Middle School;
Weston Favell Upper School, Northampton
Qualifications: 6 GCSEs, 4 O-levels, NCA
coaching awards Levels 1 and 2

Overseas tours: England U18 to South
Africa 1992-93, to Denmark 1993; England U19 to Sri Lanka 1993-94
Overseas teams played for: Karori, New Zealand 1995-97
Cricketers particularly admired: Glenn McGrath, Steve Waugh
Young players to look out for: Mark Powell
Other sports played: Golf, snooker, fishing
Relaxations: 'Spending time with my wife; sleeping and eating out; music, reading
books/magazines'
Extras: Played for England U19 in home series against India U19 in 1994. Won the
MCC Lord's Taverners Award U13 and U15. Became youngest player to play for
Northants 2nd XI, aged 14 years 9 months. 2nd XI Championship Player of the Year
1998. Left Northamptonshire during the 2001-02 off-season
Opinions on cricket: 'There are too many games/fixtures throughout the season,
and players are therefore not able to get in as much quality practice. Play should also
start at 10.30 all through the year, enabling the teams to have an hour for lunch and
also for tea.'
Best batting: 63 Northamptonshire v Lancashire, Northampton 1996
Best bowling: 4-61 Northamptonshire v Lancashire, Northampton 1996

2001 Season

	M	Inns	NO	Runs	HS	Avge	100s	50s	Ct	St	O	M	Runs	Wkts	Avge	Best	5wI	10wM
Test																		
All First	4	7	1	86	40	14.33	-	-	1	-	83.5	15	331	9	36.77	4-76	-	-
1-day Int																		
C & G																			
B & H	5	3	1	56	37	28.00	-	-	-	-	47.1	3	215	4	53.75	1-35	-	
1-day Lge	8	6	2	61	19	15.25	-	-	2	-	53.2	5	294	9	32.66	3-60	-	

Career Performances

	M	Inns	NO	Runs	HS	Avge	100s	50s	Ct	St	Balls	Runs	Wkts	Avge	Best	5wI	10wM
Test																	
All First	21	32	6	522	63	20.07	-	1	10	-	1992	1117	38	29.39	4-61	-	-
1-day Int																	
C & G	5	3	2	33	25	33.00	-	-	2	-	123	114	5	22.80	3-26	-	
B & H	9	5	1	76	37	19.00	-	-	-	-	427	372	6	62.00	1-25	-	
1-day Lge	42	28	10	380	55	21.11	-	1	12	-	1328	1216	42	28.95	4-36	-	

IRANI, R. C. Essex

Name: Ronald (<u>Ronnie</u>) Charles Irani
Role: Right-hand bat, right-arm
medium bowler, county team captain
Born: 26 October 1971, Leigh, Lancashire
Height: 6ft 4in **Weight:** 14st 4lbs
Nickname: Reggie
County debut: 1990 (Lancashire),
1994 (Essex)
County cap: 1994 (Essex)
Test debut: 1996
Tests: 3
One-Day Internationals: 10
1000 runs in a season: 5
50 wickets in a season: 1
1st-Class 50s: 49
1st-Class 100s: 15
1st-Class 5 w. in innings: 8
1st-Class catches: 64
One-Day 100s: 3
One-Day 5 w. in innings: 1
Place in batting averages: 132nd av. 28.85 (2000 11th av. 54.36)
Place in bowling averages: 72nd av. 32.50 (2000 50th av. 24.00)

Strike rate: 66.53 (career 61.21)

Parents: Jimmy and Anne

Wife's name: Lorraine

Children: Simone

Family links with cricket: 'Father played league cricket for over 30 years. Mum did teas for years as well'

Education: Church Road Primary School; Smithills Comprehensive School

Qualifications: 9 GCSEs

Off-season: 'Spending time at home with wife, family and Eric the Dobermann!'

Overseas tours: England YC to Australia 1989-90; England A to Pakistan 1995-96, to Bangladesh and New Zealand 1999-2000; England to Zimbabwe and New Zealand 1996-97

Overseas teams played for: Technicol Natal, Durban 1992-93; Eden-Roskill, Auckland 1993-94

Career highlights to date: 'Playing for England. Winning one-day trophies with Essex'

Cricketers particularly admired: Graham Gooch, Javed Miandad, Viv Richards, Wasim Akram

Young players to look out for: Will Jefferson, Justin Bishop

Other sports played: Golf, pool

Other sports followed: Football (Manchester United), Muay Thai boxing

Relaxations: Fly fishing

Extras: Played for England YC in home series v Australian YC 1991, scoring a century and three 50s in six innings and being named Bull Man of the Series. Appointed vice-captain of Essex in 1999. Achieved double of 1000 first-class runs and 50 first-class wickets in 1999. Took over team captaincy of Essex at the start of the 2000 season, Nasser Hussain remaining as club captain. His career best innings of 168* v Glamorgan at Cardiff 2000 lasted nine hours and 20 minutes, during which time he received 479 balls. His 5-43 v Northamptonshire at Chelmsford 2001 included a spell of 4-5 from 10 overs. Scored a 55-ball century (ending up 108*) v Glamorgan at Chelmsford in the Norwich Union League 2001. Recorded a five-wicket innings return (5-58) and scored a century (119) for Essex v Surrey at Ilford 2001, following up with a wicket with the first ball of his opening spell in Surrey's second innings. C&G Man of the Match award for his 55 and 3-37 v Berkshire at Reading 2001. Has website: www.ronnieirani.com

Opinions on cricket: 'Would like to see more money in the game all round; not just wages but facilities, stadiums etc.'

Best batting: 168* Essex v Glamorgan, Cardiff 2000

Best bowling: 6-79 Essex v Lancashire, Colchester 2001

2001 Season

	M	Inns	NO	Runs	HS	Avge	100s	50s	Ct	St	O	M	Runs	Wkts	Avge	Best	5wI	10wM
Test																		
All First	17	29	2	779	119	28.85	1	6	4	-	354.5	96	1040	32	32.50	6-79	3	-
1-day Int																		
C & G	2	2	0	103	55	51.50	-	1	2	-	17	1	70	3	23.33	3-37	-	
B & H	3	3	0	79	33	26.33	-	-	3	-	24	1	104	6	17.33	3-48	-	
1-day Lge	16	15	3	402	108 *	33.50	1	1	5	-	115.5	13	527	16	32.93	3-51	-	

Career Performances

	M	Inns	NO	Runs	HS	Avge	100s	50s	Ct	St	Balls	Runs	Wkts	Avge	Best	5wl	10wM
Test	3	5	0	86	41	17.20	-	-	2	-	192	112	3	37.33	1-22	-	-
All First	161	266	32	8461	168 *	36.15	15	49	64	-	18422	9171	301	30.46	6-79	8	-
1-day Int	10	10	2	78	45 *	9.75	-	-	2	-	329	246	4	61.50	1-23	-	
C & G	21	19	2	712	124	41.88	1	6	7	-	1244	820	30	27.33	4-41	-	
B & H	29	23	2	777	82 *	37.00	-	4	6	-	1368	1029	38	27.07	4-30	-	
1-day Lge	129	122	18	2788	108 *	26.80	2	14	30	-	4626	3507	144	24.35	5-33	1	

JAMES, S. P.   Glamorgan

Name: Stephen Peter James
Role: Right-hand opening bat, county captain
Born: 7 September 1967, Lydney
Height: 6ft **Weight:** 13st
Nickname: Sid, Jamo
County debut: 1985
County cap: 1992
Benefit: 2001
Test debut: 1998
Tests: 2
1000 runs in a season: 8
1st-Class 50s: 55
1st-Class 100s: 38
1st-Class 200s: 4
1st-Class 300s: 1
1st-Class catches: 165
One-Day 100s: 7
Place in batting averages: 39th av. 47.33
(2000 35th av. 41.15)
Parents: Peter and Margaret
Wife and date of marriage: Jane Louise, 26 September 1997
Children: Bethan Amy, 28 August 1998 ('during Test match!')

Family links with cricket: Father played for Gloucestershire 2nd XI. Distant relative of Dominic Ostler

Education: Monmouth School; University College, Swansea; Cambridge University

Qualifications: BA (Hons) Wales – Classics; BA (Hons) Cantab – Land Economy

Off-season: 'Finishing off benefit. Rugby writing for *Sunday Telegraph*'

Overseas tours: Welsh Schools to Barbados 1984; Monmouth Schools to Sri Lanka 1985; Combined Universities to Barbados 1989; Glamorgan to Trinidad 1989-90, to Zimbabwe 1990-91, to Cape Town 1993-94, to Pretoria 1995-96; England A to Kenya and Sri Lanka 1997-98 (vice-captain)

Overseas teams played for: Bionics, Zimbabwe 1990-92; Universals Sports Club, Zimbabwe 1992-96

Career highlights to date: 'Winning the Sunday League in 1993; winning the Championship in 1997'

Cricket moments to forget: 'Pair in a day, Luton 1992'

Cricketers particularly admired: Michael Atherton, Graham Burgess

Young players to look out for: Jonathan Hughes, Ian Thomas, Mark Wallace, Simon Jones

Other sports played/followed: Rugby union (Cardiff RFC and Lydney RFC; 'played for Lydney, Gloucestershire and Cambridge University and was on bench for Varsity Match'), football (West Ham United)

Injuries: Out for three weeks after pre-season cartilage operations; for five weeks with a broken hand

Relaxations: Reading, *Telegraph* crosswords, videos, weight-training

Extras: Scored maiden century in only second first-class game. In 1995 broke Matthew Maynard's club record for number of one-day runs in a season with 1263; in same season, also broke Hugh Morris's club record for number of Sunday League runs in a season with 815. First player to reach 1000 runs in 1997 and was voted the Cricketer of the Year by both the Wombwell Cricket Lovers' Society and the PCA. Appointed vice-captain of Glamorgan in 1999. Set record for highest post-war score by a Glamorgan batsman, with 259* v Notts at Colwyn Bay 1999 (his fifth successive century v Notts and still the highest score by a Glamorgan No. 1), beating Matthew Maynard's 243 in 1991. Set record (batting at No. 2) for highest individual score ever by a Glamorgan batsman, with 309* v Sussex at Colwyn Bay in 2000, setting in the process a new record first-wicket partnership for Glamorgan of 374 with Matthew Elliott (177); during his innings he also became the first Glamorgan batsman to record five scores of 200-plus. Carried his bat for 61* v Leicestershire at Leicester 2001. Captain of Glamorgan since 2001

Opinions on cricket: 'Four-day wickets have been excellent this year; one-day not so good.'

Best batting: 309* Glamorgan v Sussex, Colwyn Bay 2000

2001 Season

	M	Inns	NO	Runs	HS	Avge	100s	50s	Ct	St		O	M	Runs	Wkts	Avge	Best	5wI	10wM
Test																			
All First	9	15	3	568	156	47.33	1	4	5	-									
1-day Int																			
C & G	2	2	0	46	46	23.00	-	-	1	-									
B & H	4	4	1	112	49	37.33	-	-	-	-									
1-day Lge	9	8	1	210	93	30.00	-	2	2	-									

Career Performances

	M	Inns	NO	Runs	HS	Avge	100s	50s	Ct	St		Balls	Runs	Wkts	Avge	Best	5wI	10wM
Test	2	4	0	71	36	17.75	-	-	-	-								
All First	230	400	32	14765	309 *	40.12	43	55	165	-		2	3	0	-	-	-	-
1-day Int																		
C & G	29	28	3	1097	123	43.88	3	6	9	-								
B & H	43	43	4	1324	135	33.94	2	9	12	-								
1-day Lge	140	135	17	3987	107	33.78	2	29	33	-								

JEFFERSON, W. I.   Essex

Name: William (Will) Ingleby Jefferson
Role: Right-hand bat, right-arm
medium bowler
Born: 25 October 1979, Derby ('but native
of Norfolk')
Height: 6ft 10in **Weight:** 15st 2lbs
Nickname: Jeffo
County debut: 2000
1st-Class 50s: 1
1st-Class catches: 3
Parents: Richard and Pauline
Marital status: Single
Family links with cricket: Grandfather
Jefferson played for the Army and Combined
Services in the 1920s. Father, R. I. Jefferson,
played for Cambridge University 1961 and
Surrey 1961-66
Education: Beeston Hall School, Norfolk;
Oundle School, Northants; Durham University (reading Sport in the Community)
Qualifications: 9 GCSEs, 3 A-levels, Levels 1 and 2 cricket coaching awards
Career outside cricket: Student
Off-season: 'Third and final year at Durham University'

Overseas tours: Oundle School to South Africa 1995
Overseas teams played for: Young People's Club, Paarl, South Africa 1998-99
Career highlights to date: 'Being hit on the head by Wasim Akram'
Cricket moments to forget: 'Losing to Loughborough in the final of the BUSA Championships in 2000 off the last ball of the match'
Cricketers particularly admired: Mark Waugh, Shaun Pollock, Jacques Kallis, Steve Waugh, Nasser Hussain
Young players to look out for: Jamie Dalrymple, Michael Brown, John Francis, Justin Ontong (South African), Andrew and Simon Hollingsworth
Other sports played: Golf (12 handicap), tennis, squash, swimming
Other sports followed: Rugby union
Injuries: Out from 7 May to end of season after back operation on prolapsed disc
Relaxations: 'Listening to music, watching sport on television, catching up with family and friends'
Extras: Aged 15, received a letter handwritten by Sir Colin Cowdrey congratulating him on scoring 83 and 106* in his two games in the Sun Life of Canada U15 Club Championships. Holmwoods School Cricketer of the Year 1998. Represented British Universities 2000 and 2001. Played for Durham University CCE 2001
Opinions on cricket: 'Levels of fitness have to keep improving if English cricket is going to compete with the Australians and South Africans. We must use new technologies in any ways we can to help assist improvements, especially in coaching. Still far too much cricket when set against the miles that have to be travelled.'
Best batting: 69 Essex v Leicestershire, Leicester 2001

2001 Season

	M	Inns	NO	Runs	HS	Avge	100s	50s	Ct	St	O	M	Runs	Wkts	Avge	Best	5wl	10wM
Test																		
All First	3	5	0	160	69	32.00	-	1	2	-								
1-day Int																		
C & G																		
B & H																		
1-day Lge	1	1	0	2	2	2.00	-	-	-	-								

Career Performances

	M	Inns	NO	Runs	HS	Avge	100s	50s	Ct	St	Balls	Runs	Wkts	Avge	Best	5wl	10wM
Test																		
All First	5	8	0	206	69	25.75	-	1	3	-								
1-day Int																		
C & G																		
B & H																		
1-day Lge	4	4	0	119	65	29.75	-	2	1	-								

JOHNSON, N. C.   Hampshire

Name: <u>Neil</u> Clarkson Johnson
Role: Left-hand bat, right-arm
fast-medium bowler
Born: 24 January 1970, Harare, Zimbabwe
Nickname: Johnno
County debut: 1997 (Leicestershire),
2001 (Hampshire)
County cap: 1997 (Leicestershire),
2001 (Hampshire)
Test debut: 1998-99
Tests: 13
One-Day Internationals: 48
1000 runs in a season: 1
1st-Class 50s: 40
1st-Class 100s: 8
1st-Class 5 w. in innings: 2
1st-Class catches: 157
One-Day 100s: 6
Place in batting averages: 53rd av. 44.70 (2000 68th av. 33.25)
Place in bowling averages: 113th av. 39.60 (2000 125th av. 38.46)
Strike rate: 65.95 (career 62.64)
Education: Kingswood College, Grahamstown, South Africa; University of
Port Elizabeth
Overseas tours: South Africa A to Zimbabwe 1994-95; Zimbabwe to Pakistan
1998-99, to South Africa 1999-2000, to West Indies 1999-2000, to England 2000
Overseas teams played for: Eastern Province B 1989-90 – 1991-92; Natal 1992-93 –
1997-98; Matabeleland 1998-99; Western Province 2000-01 –
Extras: Moved from Zimbabwe to South Africa at the age of ten. Represented Eastern
Province Schools, opening the bowling with Brett Schultz. Represented South African
Schools 1988. Has played league cricket in England. Leicestershire's overseas player
in 1997. Scored maiden Test century (107, after going in on hat-trick ball) in his
second Test, for Zimbabwe v Pakistan at Peshawar 1998-99. Scored 59 and took 4-42
v Kenya, scored 76 and took 3-27 v South Africa and scored 132* v Australia in the
1999 World Cup, winning Man of the Match award on each occasion. Scored 95* in
the NatWest Triangular Series international v West Indies at Bristol 2000, winning the
Man of the Match award. Retired from international cricket after the NatWest
Triangular Series v England and West Indies in 2000. Played for a World XI v an Asia
XI in Dhaka 2000. Joined Hampshire as overseas player for 2001. Man of the Match
for his 88 and 29-ball 37 in Hampshire's victory over the Australians in the Vodafone
Challenge match at West End 2001. Awarded Hampshire cap 2001
Best batting: 150 Leicestershire v Lancashire, Leicester 1997
Best bowling: 5-79 Natal v Boland, Stellenbosch 1993-94

2001 Season

	M	Inns	NO	Runs	HS	Avge	100s	50s	Ct	St	O	M	Runs	Wkts	Avge	Best	5wI	10wM
Test																		
All First	17	27	3	1073	105 *	44.70	2	8	28	-	252.5	42	911	23	39.60	4-20	-	-
1-day Int																		
C & G	1	1	1	113	113 *	-	1	-	-	-	3	0	27	0	-		-	-
B & H	4	4	1	77	40	25.66	-	-	1	-	24	0	120	3	40.00	3-41	-	
1-day Lge	15	15	1	481	105 *	34.35	1	2	15	-	66	1	362	10	36.20	2-13	-	

Career Performances

	M	Inns	NO	Runs	HS	Avge	100s	50s	Ct	St	Balls	Runs	Wkts	Avge	Best	5wI	10wM
Test	13	23	1	532	107	24.18	-	4	12	-	1186	594	15	39.60	4-77	-	-
All First	125	193	23	5744	150	33.78	8	40	157	-	12341	6299	197	31.97	5-79	2	-
1-day Int	48	48	2	1679	132 *	36.50	4	6	19	-	1503	1220	35	34.85	4-42	-	
C & G	3	3	1	132	113 *	66.00	1	-	1	-	36	46	0	-		-	-
B & H	12	12	2	207	58	20.70	-	2	2	-	462	427	11	38.81	3-41	-	
1-day Lge	26	26	2	781	105 *	32.54	1	4	21	-	680	687	24	28.62	3-37	-	

JOHNSON, P.　　　　　Nottinghamshire

Name: Paul Johnson
Role: Right-hand bat, right-arm
'occasional' bowler
Born: 24 April 1965, Newark
Height: 'Below average' **Weight:** 'Above
average'
Nickname: Johno, Midge
County debut: 1982
County cap: 1986
Benefit: 1995
1000 runs in a season: 8
1st-Class 50s: 114
1st-Class 100s: 40
1st-Class catches: 229
1st-Class stumpings: 1
One-Day 100s: 13
Place in batting averages: 117th av. 31.09
(2000 170th av. 20.76)
Strike rate: (career 107.66)
Parents: Donald Edward and Joyce
Wife and date of marriage: Jackie, 24 December 1993
Children: Ruth, 28 September 1994; Eve, 9 September 1996

Family links with cricket: Father played local cricket and is a qualified coach
Education: Grove Comprehensive School, Newark
Qualifications: 9 CSEs, Level 3 coach
Career outside cricket: Coaching
Off-season: Coaching. Christians in Sport to India, Nepal and Bangladesh ('trouble permitting!')
Overseas tours: England A to Bermuda and West Indies 1991-92; Christians in Sport to Zimbabwe 1997, 1998, to India, Nepal and Bangladesh 2001-02
Overseas teams played for: RAU Johannesburg 1985-86; Hutt District, Wellington, New Zealand 1988-89
Career highlights to date: 'Winning all four domestic honours'
Cricket moments to forget: 'Losing never gets easier!'
Cricketers particularly admired: Clive Rice, Mike Gatting, Michael Atherton
Young players to look out for: Gary Pratt, Samit Patel
Other sports played: '"Royal Oak" pool team, golf, squash, indoor powerboat racing'
Other sports followed: Ice hockey (Nottingham Panthers), football (Nottingham Forest)
Relaxations: Listening to music, crosswords and reading autobiographies
Extras: Played for English Schools in 1980-81 and England YC 1982 and 1983. Youngest player to join the Nottinghamshire staff. Made 235 for Nottinghamshire 2nd XI, July 1982, aged 17. Scored 125 v Gloucestershire at Bristol 1983, in the process becoming (at 18 years 128 days) the youngest player to score a first-class century for Nottinghamshire. Won Man of the Match award in his first NatWest game (101* v Staffordshire) in 1985, but missed the final owing to appendicitis. Sunday morning soccer referee in Nottingham. Took over the Nottinghamshire captaincy from Tim Robinson at the start of the 1996 season. Relinquished captaincy during 1998 season. Against Surrey at Trent Bridge 2001, passed Derek Randall's record of 7062 runs to become Notts highest run-scorer in the domestic one-day league
Opinions on cricket: 'Too many people have too many opinions who have not played too many matches.'
Best batting: 187 Nottinghamshire v Lancashire, Old Trafford 1993
Best bowling: 1-9 Nottinghamshire v Cambridge University, Trent Bridge 1984

2001 Season

	M	Inns	NO	Runs	HS	Avge	100s	50s	Ct	St	O	M	Runs	Wkts	Avge	Best	5wI	10wM
Test																		
All First	13	24	2	684	149	31.09	2	2	7	-	1	1	0	0	-	-	-	-
1-day Int																		
C & G	2	1	0	10	10	10.00	-	-	-	-								
B & H	7	6	2	162	71*	40.50	-	1	-	-								
1-day Lge	15	14	1	384	88*	29.53	-	3	5	-	0.4	0	2	1	2.00	1-2	-	

Career Performances

	M	Inns	NO	Runs	HS	Avge	100s	50s	Ct	St	Balls	Runs	Wkts	Avge	Best	5wl	10wM
Test																	
All First	357	599	57	19872	187	36.66	40	114	229	1	646	605	6	100.83	1-9	-	-
1-day Int																	
C & G	38	37	2	1058	146	30.22	3	3	12	-	18	20	0	-		-	-
B & H	69	64	13	1677	104 *	32.88	2	11	15	-							
1-day Lge	257	243	29	7074	167 *	33.05	8	42	80	-	5	3	1	3.00	1-2	-	

JOHNSON, R. L. Somerset

Name: Richard Leonard Johnson
Role: Right-hand bat, right-arm
fast-medium bowler
Born: 29 December 1974, Chertsey
Height: 6ft 2in **Weight:** 14st 3lbs
Nickname: Jono, Lenny, The Greek
County debut: 1992 (Middlesex),
2001 (Somerset)
County cap: 1995 (Middlesex),
2001 (Somerset)
50 wickets in a season: 4
1st-Class 50s: 5
1st-Class 5 w. in innings: 12
1st-Class 10 w. in match: 2
1st-Class catches: 45
One-Day 5 w. in innings: 1
Place in batting averages: 111th av. 31.58
(2000 171st av. 20.70)
Place in bowling averages: 28th av. 23.77 (2000 83rd av. 28.58)
Strike rate: 44.83 (career 50.90)
Parents: Roger and Mary Anne
Marital status: Single
Family links with cricket: Father and grandfather played club cricket
Education: Sunbury Manor School; Spelthorne College
Qualifications: 9 GCSEs, A-level in Physical Education, NCA senior coaching award
Off-season: 'Hong Kong Sixes; staying fit and relaxing' (*see Stop press*)
Overseas tours: England U18 to South Africa 1992-93; England U19 to Sri Lanka
1993-94; England A to India 1994-95; MCC to Bangladesh 1999-2000, to Canada
2000-01
Cricketers particularly admired: Ian Botham, Richard Hadlee and Angus Fraser 'for
his quality bowling and his dedication to moaning'

Young players to look out for: Matthew Wood, Ed Joyce
Other sports followed: Football (Tottenham), rugby (London Irish)
Relaxations: 'Waiting for Nashy's phone call to tell me who's to blame for him getting out this time! And having a quiet couple with my mates'
Extras: Represented Middlesex at all levels from U11. Took 10 for 45 v Derbyshire in July 1994, becoming first person to take ten wickets in an innings since Ian Thomson (Sussex) in 1964; also most economical ten-wicket haul since Hedley Verity's 10 for 10 in 1932. Had to pull out of England's 1995-96 tour to South Africa due to a persistent back injury. Left Middlesex at the end of the 2000 season and joined Somerset for 2001. Took five-wickets in an innings in his first two Championship matches for Somerset – 5-107 v Lancashire and 5-106 v Glamorgan. Included in England squad for third, fourth and fifth Tests v Australia 2001. Awarded Somerset cap 2001
Opinions on cricket: 'Two divisions has improved the competitiveness of the Championship – always something to play for, but still too much cricket.'
Best batting: 69 Middlesex v Essex, Chelmsford 2000
Best bowling: 10-45 Middlesex v Derbyshire, Derby 1994
Stop press: Called up for England Test tour of India 2001-02 after withdrawal of Andrew Caddick; replaced by Dougie Brown in the England squad to the Hong Kong Sixes

2001 Season

	M	Inns	NO	Runs	HS	Avge	100s	50s	Ct	St	O	M	Runs	Wkts	Avge	Best	5wI	10wM
Test																		
All First	13	15	3	379	68	31.58	-	2	3	-	463.2	89	1474	62	23.77	5-40	5	-
1-day Int																		
C & G	4	1	0	0	0	0.00	-	-	1	-	36	1	181	9	20.11	3-42	-	
B & H	4	2	0	35	24	17.50	-	-	-	-	35	5	126	4	31.50	2-26	-	
1-day Lge	7	5	1	69	24 *	17.25	-	-	-	-	57	4	290	8	36.25	3-51	-	

Career Performances

	M	Inns	NO	Runs	HS	Avge	100s	50s	Ct	St	Balls	Runs	Wkts	Avge	Best	5wI	10wM
Test																	
All First	105	145	17	2127	69	16.61	-	5	45	-	17155	9186	337	27.25	10-45	12	2
1-day Int																	
C & G	21	13	3	176	45 *	17.60	-	-	3	-	1092	787	31	25.38	5-50	1	
B & H	19	14	0	154	26	11.00	-	-	2	-	1026	764	22	34.72	3-33	-	
1-day Lge	88	60	16	504	29	11.45	-	-	9	-	3608	3077	92	33.44	4-45	-	

JONES, G. O.   Kent

Name: <u>Geraint</u> Owen Jones
Role: Right-hand bat, wicket-keeper
Born: 14 July 1976, Kundiawa,
Papua New Guinea
Height: 5ft 10in **Weight:** 11st
Nickname: Jonesy, Oink
County debut: 2001
1st-Class catches: 1
Parents: Emrys
Marital status: Single
Family links with cricket: 'Father was
the star off-spinner for Blaenau Ffestiniog
School side'
Education: Wilsonton Primary School,
Toowoomba, Queensland, Australia;
Harristown State High School, Toowoomba;
MacGregor State HS, Brisbane
Qualifications: NVQ Level 3 Pharmacy
Technician

Off-season: 'Brisbane, Australia. Seeing family, travelling and preparing for
2002 season'
Overseas tours: Beenleigh-Logan U19 to New Zealand 1995
Overseas teams played for: Beenleigh-Logan, Brisbane 1995-98
Career highlights to date: 'NUL debut v Surrey at The Oval. Didn't know much
about Saqlain's first ball, but did all right from then on'
Cricket moments to forget: 'Kent 2nd XI v Nottinghamshire 2nd XI 2001 – out lbw
in first innings leaving one down legside which swung back and hit my right pad dead
in front of all three stumps'
Cricketers particularly admired: Ian Healy, Steve Waugh, Jack Russell
Young players to look out for: Robert Key, James Hockley, Ben Phillips, Rob Ferley
Other sports played: Rugby
Other sports followed: Rugby (Crickhowell RFC)
Relaxations: 'Golf, video sessions with Rob Ferley'
Extras: Scored a 39-ball 39 on Norwich Union League debut v Surrey at The Oval
2001, having arrived at the crease with his side on 59 for 5
Opinions on cricket: 'Second XI competition needs to mirror first-class, not in terms
of games played but promotion and relegation, otherwise season just drifts along if
you don't play any first-team cricket. More floodlit cricket required – gets the crowds
in and enjoying the sport.'
Best batting: 5 Kent v Somerset, Taunton 2001

2001 Season

	M	Inns	NO	Runs	HS	Avge	100s	50s	Ct	St	O	M	Runs	Wkts	Avge	Best	5wI	10wM
Test																		
All First	1	1	0	5	5	5.00	-	-	1	-	1	0	4	0	-	-	-	-
1-day Int																		
C & G	1	0	0	0	0	-	-	-	1	-								
B & H																		
1-day Lge	4	4	0	59	39	14.75	-	-	-	-								

Career Performances

	M	Inns	NO	Runs	HS	Avge	100s	50s	Ct	St	Balls	Runs	Wkts	Avge	Best	5wI	10wM
Test																	
All First	1	1	0	5	5	5.00	-	-	1	-	6	4	0	-	-	-	-
1-day Int																	
C & G	1	0	0	0	0	-	-	-	1	-							
B & H																	
1-day Lge	4	4	0	59	39	14.75	-	-	-	-							

JONES, I.   Somerset

Name: Ian Jones
Role: Right-hand bat, right-arm fast bowler
Born: 11 March 1977, London
Height: 6ft 4in **Weight:** 17st
Nickname: Bubba, Jonah
County debut: 1999
Strike rate: (career 79.33)
Parents: Dianne and Ronnie
Marital status: Single
Family links with cricket: Brother plays in Durham League for Kimblesworth CC
Education: Fyndoune Community College, Sacriston, Durham
Qualifications: 9 GCSEs, City and Guilds Diploma in Engineering, Level 1 coaching award
Overseas tours: Durham Academy to Sri Lanka 1996
Cricketers particularly admired: Glenn McGrath, Andrew Caddick, Allan Donald
Young players to look out for: Matt Bulbeck, Ian Blackwell, Ian Hunter
Other sports played: Football, shooting

Other sports followed: Football (Sunderland AFC)

Relaxations: 'Shooting, walking, listening to music, odd pint with Bully'

Extras: First player to sign on at Durham Cricket Academy. Played for Somerset Board XI in the C&G 2001. Took 3-14 v Surrey at The Oval in the Norwich Union League 2001 after being called up from the stands to replace Richard Johnson, who was unwell. Released by Somerset at the end of the 2001 season

Opinions on cricket: 'More competition since two divisions have been brought in. Should be more day/night matches. Televised games should be spread evenly between counties instead of certain clubs being on all of the time.'

Best batting: 35 Somerset v Durham, Riverside 1999

Best bowling: 3-81 Somerset v New Zealanders, Taunton 1999

2001 Season

	M	Inns	NO	Runs	HS	Avge	100s	50s	Ct	St	O	M	Runs	Wkts	Avge	Best	5wI	10wM
Test																		
All First																		
1-day Int																		
C & G	1	1	0	6	6	6.00	-	-	1	-	10	1	33	2	16.50	2-33	-	
B & H																		
1-day Lge	1	0	0	0	0	-	-	-	-	-	2	0	14	3	4.66	3-14	-	

Career Performances

	M	Inns	NO	Runs	HS	Avge	100s	50s	Ct	St	Balls	Runs	Wkts	Avge	Best	5wI	10wM
Test																	
All First	3	4	1	78	35	26.00	-	-	-	-	476	341	6	56.83	3-81	-	-
1-day Int																	
C & G	1	1	0	6	6	6.00	-	-	1	-	60	33	2	16.50	2-33	-	
B & H																	
1-day Lge	2	1	1	5	5 *	-	-	-	-	-	55	67	4	16.75	3-14	-	

JONES, P. S.   Somerset

Name: Philip Steffan Jones

Role: Right-hand bat, right-arm fast-medium bowler

Born: 9 February 1974, Llanelli

Height: 6ft 1in **Weight:** 14st

Nickname: Myfanwy, Elvis, Delilah, Jona

County debut: 1997

50 wickets in a season: 1

1st-Class 50s: 1

1st-Class 100s: 1

1st-Class 5 w. in innings: 3

1st-Class catches: 14
One-Day 5 w. in innings: 1
Place in batting averages: 217th av. 16.36
(2000 271st av. 10.16)
Place in bowling averages: 86th av. 34.15
(2000 104th av. 32.35)
Strike rate: 56.94 (career 61.29)
Parents: Lyndon and Ann
Marital status: Single
Family links with cricket: Father played
cricket for Glamorgan 2nd XI and
Wales Schools; also played first-class rugby
Education: Llangennech Primary School;
Ysgol Gyfun y Strade, Llanelli;
Loughborough University; Homerton
College, Cambridge University
Qualifications: BSc Sports Science,
PGCE in Physical Education
Career outside cricket: Teaching

Overseas tours: Wales Minor Counties to Barbados 1996; Somerset CCC to South
Africa 1999, 2000
Cricketers particularly admired: 'Everyone who gives 100 per cent and does not
blame others!'
Young players to look out for: Joe Tucker, Luke Sutton
Other sports played: Rugby union (Welsh Schools, Youth, U20, U21; Loughborough
University, Cambridge University; Swansea, Bristol, Exeter and Moseley)
Other sports followed: Rugby union (New Zealand All Blacks), athletics
Relaxations: 'Training in my own gym, dining out with my very supportive
girlfriend Alex'
Extras: Schoolboy international from U13 to U19. Represented Wales Minor
Counties. Took nine wickets in the Varsity match at Lord's in 1997. Man of the Match
(5-23) in Sunday League game against Warwickshire 1998. Played first-class cricket
and first-class rugby for two years ('last dual player, I think')
Opinions on cricket: 'Good to see young so-called "unknowns" like "Banger" given
the chance. Playing at the highest level is 60-70 per cent confidence, and if you
believe in yourself, then other people's opinions mean nothing. As long as you can
look at yourself in the mirror and say "I'm giving my all and I believe in myself and
what I'm doing", then anything is possible. Too many players blame others, play at 50
per cent effort and play for external benefits (i.e. money). These players let
themselves, their team-mates and the club down.'
Best batting: 105 Somerset v New Zealanders, Taunton 1999
Best bowling: 6-67 Cambridge University v Oxford University, Lord's 1997

2001 Season

	M	Inns	NO	Runs	HS	Avge	100s	50s	Ct	St	O	M	Runs	Wkts	Avge	Best	5wI	10wM
Test																		
All First	16	16	5	180	29 *	16.36	-	-	3	-	560	100	2015	59	34.15	5-115	1	-
1-day Int																		
C & G	5	1	1	14	14 *	-	-	-	-	-	45.1	3	222	7	31.71	3-40	-	
B & H	5	3	2	9	4 *	9.00	-	-	-	-	42	6	155	7	22.14	3-38	-	
1-day Lge	14	7	5	41	17 *	20.50	-	-	2	-	111.4	8	560	22	25.45	4-40	-	

Career Performances

	M	Inns	NO	Runs	HS	Avge	100s	50s	Ct	St	Balls	Runs	Wkts	Avge	Best	5wI	10wM
Test																	
All First	54	64	18	756	105	16.43	1	1	14	-	9010	5138	147	34.95	6-67	3	-
1-day Int																	
C & G	13	4	3	47	26 *	47.00	-	-	2	-	643	547	16	34.18	4-25	-	
B & H	13	7	4	35	12	11.66	-	-	2	-	589	403	13	31.00	3-38	-	
1-day Lge	59	30	16	130	27	9.28	-	-	11	-	2598	2207	94	23.47	5-23	1	

JONES, S. P.   Glamorgan

Name: <u>Simon</u> Philip Jones
Role: Left-hand bat, right-arm fast bowler
Born: 25 December 1978, Swansea
Height: 6ft 3in **Weight:** 14st
Nickname: Racehorse, Horsey, Ray, Raymond
County debut: 1998
1st-Class 5 w. in innings: 1
1st-Class catches: 3
Place in batting averages: 266th av. 8.30
Place in bowling averages: 139th av. 52.17 (2000 120th av. 37.40)
Strike rate: 70.00 (career 67.50)
Parents: Jeff and Irene
Marital status: Single
Family links with cricket: Father played for Glamorgan and England (15 Tests)
Education: Halfway CP School; Coedcae Comprehensive School; Millfield School
Qualifications: 12 GCSEs, 1 A-level, basic and senior coaching awards
Career outside cricket: 'Fitness instructor etc.'
Off-season: Selected for England National Academy tour of Australia

Overseas tours: Dyfed Schools to Zimbabwe 1994; Glamorgan to South Africa 1998; ECB National Academy to Australia 2001-02
Career highlights to date: 'Being selected for England Academy'
Cricketers particularly admired: Allan Donald, Steve Watkin
Young players to look out for: Mark Wallace, Ian Thomas, Jonathan Hughes, Matthew Wood (Yorkshire), Andrew Davies
Other sports followed: Football (Manchester United)
Relaxations: 'Having a few pots with friends'
Opinions on cricket: 'Too many games. Not enough rest in between games. It's a batter's game. Tea time is too short.'
Best batting: 46 Glamorgan v Yorkshire, Scarborough 2001
Best bowling: 5-31 Glamorgan v Sussex, Cardiff 1999

2001 Season

	M	Inns	NO	Runs	HS	Avge	100s	50s	Ct	St	O	M	Runs	Wkts	Avge	Best	5wI	10wM
Test																		
All First	8	11	1	83	46	8.30	-	-	-	-	198.2	29	887	17	52.17	3-36	-	-
1-day Int																		
C & G																		
B & H																		
1-day Lge																		

Career Performances

	M	Inns	NO	Runs	HS	Avge	100s	50s	Ct	St	Balls	Runs	Wkts	Avge	Best	5wI	10wM
Test																	
All First	26	30	7	175	46	7.60	-	-	3	-	3578	2382	53	44.94	5-31	1	-
1-day Int																	
C & G	1	0	0	0	0	-	-	-	-	-	30	30	0	-		-	-
B & H	1	0	0	0	0	-	-	-	-	-	30	47	0	-		-	-
1-day Lge	1	1	1	12	12 *	-	-	-	-	-	42	39	1	39.00	1-39	-	

50. Of the Gloucestershire side that won the 1973 Gillette Cup final, one member is now chairman of the England selectors, another is chief executive of the MCC and a third is one of the modern game's most respected Test umpires. Name the three players.

JOYCE, E. C.   Middlesex

Name: <u>Edmund</u> Christopher Joyce
Role: Left-hand bat, right-arm medium
bowler, occasional wicket-keeper
Born: 22 September 1978, Dublin
Height: 5ft 10in **Weight:** 12st 2lbs
Nickname: Joycie, Spud
County debut: 1999
1st-Class 50s: 1
1st-Class 100s: 2
1st-Class catches: 14
Place in batting averages: (2000 113th
av. 27.85)
Parents: Maureen and Jim
Marital status: Single
Family links with cricket: Both brothers
have played for Ireland and both sisters have
played for Ireland ladies.
Education: St Patrick's, Bray;Presentation
College, Bray, County Wicklow; Trinity College, Dublin
Qualifications: Irish Leaving Certificate; BA (Hons) Economics and Geography
Overseas tours: Ireland U19 to Bermuda (International Youth Tournament) 1997,
to South Africa (U19 World Cup) 1997-98; Ireland to Canada (ICC Trophy) 2001
Overseas teams played for: Coburg CC, Melbourne 1996-97; University CC, Perth
2001-02
Career highlights to date: 'Making 100 at Lord's in 2001'
Cricket moments to forget: 'Being bowled first ball by Allan Donald, The
commentator said it was the worst shot he had ever seen!'
Cricketers particularly admired: Larry Gomes, Brian Lara
Young players to look out for: Brett Jones (University of Western Australia)
Other sports played: Golf
Other sports followed: Rugby (Leinster), football (Manchester United)
Relaxations: Cinema, eating out, listening to music
Extras: Leinster U19 to Oxford Festival. Was only player to score a century at the
International Youth Tournament, Bermuda 1997. Has represented Ireland senior side
since 1997, including appearances in the Triple Crown tournament. NBC Denis
Compton Award for the most promising young Middlesex player 2000. Scored maiden
first-class century (104) v Warwickshire at Lord's 2001, becoming the first born and
bred Irishman to record a 100 in the County Championship. Is not considered an
overseas player.
Opinions on cricket: 'Very happy with it.'
Best batting: 108* Middlesex v Worcestershire, Worcester 2001

2001 Season

	M	Inns	NO	Runs	HS	Avge	100s	50s	Ct	St	O	M	Runs	Wkts	Avge	Best	5wI	10wM
Test																		
All First	3	6	1	234	108 *	46.80	2	-	5	-								
1-day Int																		
C & G																		
B & H																		
1-day Lge	6	5	0	63	38	12.60	-	-	3	-								

Career Performances

	M	Inns	NO	Runs	HS	Avge	100s	50s	Ct	St	Balls	Runs	Wkts	Avge	Best	5wI	10wM
Test																		
All First	12	19	2	520	108 *	30.58	2	1	14	-	114	102	0	-	-	-	-
1-day Int																		
C & G	5	5	2	196	73	65.33	-	1	1	-								
B & H	3	3	0	76	42	25.33	-	-	1	-								
1-day Lge	12	11	3	193	40 *	24.12	-	-	4	-								

KEEDY, G.   Lancashire

Name: Gary Keedy
Role: Left-hand bat, slow left-arm bowler
Born: 27 November 1974, Wakefield
Height: 5ft 11in **Weight:** 12st 4lbs
Nickname: Keeds
County debut: 1994 (Yorkshire),
1995 (Lancashire)
County cap: 2000 (Lancashire)
1st-Class 5 w. in innings: 6
1st-Class 10 w. in match: 2
1st-Class catches: 21
One-Day 5 w. in innings: 1
Place in batting averages: 250th av. 11.57
(2000 253rd av. 12.00)
Place in bowling averages: 117th av. 41.07
(2000 70th av. 27.16)
Strike rate: 82.96 (career 79.21)
Parents: Roy and Pat
Marital status: Engaged
Family links with cricket: Twin brother plays for Castleford in the Yorkshire League
Education: Green Lane; Garforth Comprehensive; 'the School of Life'
Qualifications: 8 GCSEs, Level 2 coaching award

Off-season: 12-month contract – full-time training
Overseas tours: England U18 to South Africa 1992-93, to Denmark 1994; England U19 to Sri Lanka 1993-94; Lancashire to Portugal 1995, to Jamaica 1996, to South Africa 1997
Overseas teams played for: Frankston, Melbourne 1995-96
Career highlights to date: 'Probably bowling Yorkshire out at Headingley. My involvement with Lancashire in general; receiving my county cap was a proud moment'
Cricketers particularly admired: Shane Warne, Graham Gooch
Young players to look out for: Kyle Hogg, James Anderson
Other sports played: Football, snooker
Other sports followed: Football (Leeds United), rugby league (Leeds Rhinos)
Relaxations: PlayStation
Extras: Player of the Series for England U19 v West Indies U19 in 1993. Graduate of the Yorkshire Cricket Academy. Played for England U19 in the home series against India U19 in 1994. His match return of 10-155 v Durham at Old Trafford 2000 included second innings figures of 6-56 from 50 overs
Opinions on cricket: 'Do we need overseas players? Let's find out who's the best team without them!'
Best batting: 34 Lancashire v Surrey, Old Trafford 2000
Best bowling: 6-56 Lancashire v Durham, Old Trafford 2000

2001 Season

	M	Inns	NO	Runs	HS	Avge	100s	50s	Ct	St	O	M	Runs	Wkts	Avge	Best	5wI	10wM
Test																		
All First	13	15	8	81	20 *	11.57	-	-	6	-	387.1	76	1150	28	41.07	5-73	2	-
1-day Int																		
C & G																			
B & H																			
1-day Lge	1	1	0	2	2	2.00	-	-	-	-	4	0	37	1	37.00	1-37	-	

Career Performances

	M	Inns	NO	Runs	HS	Avge	100s	50s	Ct	St	Balls	Runs	Wkts	Avge	Best	5wI	10wM
Test																	
All First	78	89	49	444	34	11.10	-	-	21	-	15685	7132	198	36.02	6-56	6	2
1-day Int																	
C & G	1	0	0	0	0	-	-	-	-	-	60	40	1	40.00	1-40	-	
B & H																	
1-day Lge	12	3	1	3	2	1.50	-	-	1	-	400	361	11	32.81	5-30	1	

KEEGAN, C. B.   Middlesex

Name: <u>Chad</u> Blake Keegan
Role: Right-hand bat, right-arm
fast-medium bowler
Born: 30 July 1979, Sandton, South Africa
Height: 6ft 1in **Weight:** 12st
Nickname: Wick
County debut: 2001
1st-Class catches: 1
One-Day 5 w. in innings: 1
Place in batting averages: 278th av. 5.62
Place in bowling averages: 79th av. 32.66
Strike rate: 56.66 (career 56.66)
Parents: Sharon and Blake
Marital status: Single
Education: Northlands Senior Primary,
Durban, South Africa; Durban High School
Qualifications: YMCA fitness instructor
Off-season: 'Travelling'

Overseas tours: MCC to Argentina and Chile 2001
Overseas teams played for: Durban High School Old Boys 1994-97; Crusaders, Durban 1998-99
Career highlights to date: 'Beating Australia at Lord's and getting Steve Waugh's wicket [2001]'
Cricket moments to forget: 'Getting hit for eight off the first ball of an innings by Atherton'
Cricketers particularly admired: Malcolm Marshall, Neil Johnson
Young players to look out for: Thos ('Mare Man') Hunt
Other sports played: 'Any extreme sports, golf'
Other sports followed: Football (Liverpool)
Injuries: Sprained ankle; stressed rotator cuff
Relaxations: 'Making and listening to music (guitar); sketching'
Extras: Represented KwaZulu-Natal U13, KwaZulu-Natal Schools, KwaZulu-Natal U19, KwaZulu-Natal Academy. MCC Young Cricketer. Recorded maiden one-day five-wicket return (5-17) v Hampshire at Southgate in the Norwich Union League 2001. Is not considered an overseas player
Opinions on cricket: 'More floodlit games.'
Best batting: 30* Middlesex v Warwickshire, Edgbaston 2001
Best bowling: 4-54 Middlesex v Hampshire, West End 2001

2001 Season

	M	Inns	NO	Runs	HS	Avge	100s	50s	Ct	St	O	M	Runs	Wkts	Avge	Best	5wI	10wM
Test																		
All First	7	10	2	45	30 *	5.62	-	-	1	-	170	38	588	18	32.66	4-54	-	-
1-day Int																		
C & G																		
B & H	5	3	1	4	3	2.00	-	-	1	-	42	2	201	6	33.50	3-39	-	
1-day Lge	14	11	3	72	16	9.00	-	-	2	-	106.5	7	461	26	17.73	5-17	1	

Career Performances

	M	Inns	NO	Runs	HS	Avge	100s	50s	Ct	St	Balls	Runs	Wkts	Avge	Best	5wI	10wM
Test																	
All First	7	10	2	45	30 *	5.62	-	-	1	-	1020	588	18	32.66	4-54	-	-
1-day Int																	
C & G																	
B & H	5	3	1	4	3	2.00	-	-	1	-	252	201	6	33.50	3-39	-	
1-day Lge	14	11	3	72	16	9.00	-	-	2	-	641	461	26	17.73	5-17	1	

KENDALL, W. S.   Hampshire

Name: William (<u>Will</u>) Salwey Kendall
Role: Right-hand bat, right-arm medium
bowler, occasional wicket-keeper, county
vice-captain
Born: 18 December 1973, Wimbledon
Height: 5ft 10in **Weight:** 12st 7lbs
Nickname: Villy, Lemon, Baldy, Wiggy
County debut: 1996
County cap: 1999
1000 runs in a season: 3
1st-Class 50s: 27
1st-Class 100s: 8
1st-Class 200s: 1
1st-Class catches: 93
Place in batting averages: 165th av. 23.62
(2000 34th av. 41.28)
Strike rate: (career 78.50)
Parents: Tom and Sue
Marital status: Single
Family links with cricket: Father played club cricket with East Horsley, Hampshire
Hogs and MCC. Older brother James played for Durham University. Younger brother,
Ed, took new ball for Nottingham University

Education: Bradfield College, Berkshire; Keble College, Oxford University
Qualifications: 10 GCSEs, 3 A-levels, 1 AS-level, BA (Hons) Modern History
Career outside cricket: 'Dabbling in a little journalism'
Off-season: 'Mainly at home until January, then spending February in South Africa and March on tour with MCC in Kenya'
Overseas tours: Bradfield College to Barbados 1991; Troubadours to Argentina 1997; Hampshire CCC to Anguilla 1997, to Cape Town 2001; MCC to Kenya 2001-02
Overseas teams played for: Frankston Peninsular CC, Melbourne 1997-98
Career highlights to date: 'Being part of the Hampshire side that beat the Aussies in 2001 – an unforgettable three days. Receiving my county cap on the same day I made my career best score v Sussex 1999'
Cricket moments to forget: 'About half of my batting efforts last year'
Cricketers particularly admired: Robin Smith, Graham Thorpe, Mark Ramprakash, Shane Warne, 'and anyone playing over 36'
Young players to look out for: Derek Kenway, Charlie van der Gucht, Lawrence Prittipaul, James Adams
Other sports played: Hockey (Oxford Blue), football (Independent Schools 1992, Old Bradfieldians, Corinthian Casuals; offered terms by Reading), squash, golf
Other sports followed: 'All sports'
Relaxations: Playing or watching sport, socialising with friends, relaxing at home; 'hacking up golf courses, travelling and quiet days with girlfriend, Emily'
Extras: Surrey Young Cricketer of the Year 1992. Awarded Gray-Nicolls Trophy for Schoolboy Cricketer of the Year in memory of Len Newbery 1992. Made first-class debut for Oxford University in 1994. Hampshire Exiles Player of the Year for 1996. Vice-captain of Hampshire since 2001
Opinions on cricket: 'We clearly need to up the standard, but regional cricket is not the answer. Why not restrict full-time county staffs to 17-18, abandon registration and allow all players outside of this core to be free agents? Counties could receive less central funding and be allowed to sink or swim – the cream will soon rise. And bring back an "A" side for summer and winter matches. They should truly be England's 2nd XI.'
Best batting: 201 Hampshire v Sussex, Southampton 1999
Best bowling: 3-37 Oxford University v Derbyshire, The Parks 1995

2001 Season

	M	Inns	NO	Runs	HS	Avge	100s	50s	Ct	St	O	M	Runs	Wkts	Avge	Best	5wI	10wM
Test																		
All First	17	30	3	638	94	23.62	-	3	11	-	16	2	36	0	-	-	-	-
1-day Int																		
C & G	1	1	0	15	15	15.00	-	-	-	-								
B & H	4	3	0	65	33	21.66	-	-	1	-								
1-day Lge	11	9	0	108	47	12.00	-	-	8	-								

Career Performances

	M	Inns	NO	Runs	HS	Avge	100s	50s	Ct	St	Balls	Runs	Wkts	Avge	Best	5wI	10wM
Test																	
All First	106	172	22	5488	201	36.58	9	27	93	-	785	453	10	45.30	3-37	-	-
1-day Int																	
C & G	9	8	2	127	39	21.16	-	-	3	-							
B & H	16	15	1	224	33	16.00	-	-	2	-							
1-day Lge	64	57	8	1070	85 *	21.83	-	4	33	-	12	22	0	-		-	-

KENWAY, D. A. Hampshire

Name: <u>Derek</u> Anthony Kenway
Role: Right-hand bat, wicket-keeper
Born: 12 June 1978, Fareham
Height: 6ft **Weight:** 14st 7lbs
Nickname: Kenners, Big Dog
County debut: 1997
County cap: 2001
1000 runs in a season: 1
1st-Class 50s: 15
1st-Class 100s: 4
1st-Class catches: 44
1st-Class stumpings: 1
Place in batting averages: 92nd av. 34.51
(2000 125th av. 26.34)
Strike rate: 48.00 (career 40.00)
Parents: Keith and Geraldine
Marital status: Engaged
Family links with cricket: Brother plays
local club cricket
Education: Botley Primary School; St George's, Southampton; Barton Peveril College
Qualifications: 6 GCSEs, NCA coaching award
Off-season: England Academy in Australia
Overseas tours: West of England U15 to West Indies 1993; ECB National Academy
to Australia 2001-02
Overseas teams played for: Beaumaris CC, Melbourne 1997-98
Career highlights to date: 'Being picked for the Academy'
Cricket moments to forget: 'Leaving a straight one on my debut'
Cricketers particularly admired: Steve Waugh
Young players to look out for: Chris Tremlett
Other sports played: Football, 'all pub games (local teams)'
Other sports followed: Football (Southampton FC)

Injuries: Out for two weeks with a broken toe
Relaxations: 'Music, TV, sleeping'
Extras: *Daily Telegraph* Batting Award (West) 1994. Southern League Young Player of the Year 1996. NBC Denis Compton Award 1999. Hampshire Cricket Society Player of the Year 2001. Awarded Hampshire cap 2001
Best batting: 166 Hampshire v Nottinghamshire, West End 2001
Best bowling: 1-5 Hampshire v Warwickshire, Southampton 1997
Stop press: Scored half-century (60) in ECB National Academy's innings victory over Commonwealth Bank [Australian] Cricket Academy in Adelaide 2001-02

2001 Season

	M	Inns	NO	Runs	HS	Avge	100s	50s	Ct	St	O	M	Runs	Wkts	Avge	Best	5wI	10wM
Test																		
All First	16	30	3	932	166	34.51	2	4	16	-	8	0	66	1	66.00	1-66	-	-
1-day Int																		
C & G	1	1	0	26	26	26.00	-	-	-	1								
B & H	4	3	0	57	30	19.00	-	-	-	-								
1-day Lge	14	14	2	404	93 *	33.66	-	3	14	-								

Career Performances

	M	Inns	NO	Runs	HS	Avge	100s	50s	Ct	St	Balls	Runs	Wkts	Avge	Best	5wI	10wM
Test																	
All First	54	95	11	2812	166	33.47	4	15	44	1	120	142	3	47.33	1-5	-	-
1-day Int																	
C & G	3	3	0	126	53	42.00	-	1	1	1							
B & H	9	8	0	152	47	19.00	-	-	5	1							
1-day Lge	45	41	2	1080	93 *	27.69	-	8	26	4							

---

51. Which Essex opening bat scored 110 to take the Man of the Match award in his county's one run win over Nottinghamshire in the 1985 NatWest final?

KERR, J. I. D. Derbyshire

Name: <u>Jason</u> Ian Douglas Kerr
Role: Right-hand bat, right-arm
fast-medium bowler, (wicket-keeper
'if required')
Born: 7 April 1974, Bolton
Height: 6ft 3in **Weight:** 12st 6lbs
Nickname: Junior B
County debut: 1993 (Somerset)
1st-Class 50s: 5
1st-Class 5 w. in innings: 2
1st-Class catches: 16
Place in batting averages: 160th av. 23.85
Strike rate: 124.44 (career 63.62)
Parents: Len and Janet
Marital status: Single
Education: Withins High School; Bolton
Met College
Qualifications: 5 GCSEs, BTEC National
Diploma in Business Studies, cricket coach

Off-season: 'In the gym, walking round town and visiting Pain et Vin with
R. J. Dewar!'
Overseas tours: England U19 to India 1992-93; Lancashire U19 to Isle of Man
Overseas teams played for: Gordon Districts CC, Sydney, Australia 1994-95;
Taita CC, Wellington, New Zealand 1996-97; Subiaco-Floreat, Perth
Cricketers particularly admired: A.R. Caddick ('bowling machine')
Other sports followed: Football (Bolton 'The Great' Wanderers)
Extras: His 7-23 v Leics at Taunton 1999 included a spell of 5-6 from 3.1 overs.
Completed hat-trick (Lara, McLean, Collymore) v West Indians at Taunton 2000 in his
first game of the 2000 season; Collymore was also his 100th first-class wicket. Left
Somerset in the 2001-02 off-season and has joined Derbyshire for 2002
Opinions on cricket: 'There's enough of those out there!'
Best batting: 80 Somerset v West Indians, Taunton 1995
Best bowling: 7-23 Somerset v Leicestershire, Taunton 1999

2001 Season

	M	Inns	NO	Runs	HS	Avge	100s	50s	Ct	St	O	M	Runs	Wkts	Avge	Best	5wl	10wM
Test																		
All First	8	12	5	167	36	23.85	-	-	1	-	186.4	36	645	9	71.66	3-51	-	-
1-day Int																		
C & G	1	1	0	11	11	11.00	-	-	-	-	8	0	49	1	49.00	1-49	-	
B & H	6	4	1	29	11	9.66	-	-	-	-	49.5	3	197	11	17.90	3-14	-	
1-day Lge	12	8	3	53	16	10.60	-	-	1	-	85	3	493	12	41.08	2-33	-	

Career Performances

	M	Inns	NO	Runs	HS	Avge	100s	50s	Ct	St	Balls	Runs	Wkts	Avge	Best	5wl	10wM
Test																	
All First	58	83	16	1394	80	20.80	-	5	16	-	7190	4558	113	40.33	7-23	2	-
1-day Int																	
C & G	10	8	2	43	21	7.16	-	-	2	-	390	346	9	38.44	3-32	-	
B & H	12	7	1	60	17	10.00	-	-	-	-	533	370	18	20.55	3-14	-	
1-day Lge	73	47	14	439	56	13.30	-	1	11	-	2725	2501	82	30.50	4-28	-	

KEY, R. W. T.   Kent

Name: <u>Robert</u> William Trevor Key
Role: Right-hand bat, off-spin bowler
Born: 12 May 1979, Dulwich
Height: 6ft 1in **Weight:** 12st 7lbs
Nickname: Keysy
County debut: 1998
County cap: 2001
1000 runs in a season: 1
1st-Class 50s: 18
1st-Class 100s: 7
1st-Class catches: 44
Place in batting averages: 46th av. 45.75
(2000 167th av. 20.85)
Parents: Trevor and Lynn
Marital status: Single
Family links with cricket: Mother played for Kent Ladies. Father played club cricket in Derby. Sister Elizabeth played for her junior school side
Education: Worsley Bridge Primary School; Langley Park Boys' School
Qualifications: 10 GCSEs, NCA coaching award, GNVQ Business Studies
Career outside cricket: 'Work in the futures market'

Off-season: Selected for National Academy tour of Australia
Overseas tours: Kent U13 to Holland; England U17 to Bermuda 1997; England U19 to South Africa (including U19 World Cup) 1997-98; England A to Zimbabwe and South Africa 1998-99; ECB National Academy to Australia 2001-02
Overseas teams played for: Green Point CC, Cape Town 1996-97
Career highlights to date: 'Winning the Sunday League with Kent [2001] and the U19 World Cup [1997-98]'
Cricket moments to forget: 'Any time I have lost to Min at cards'
Cricketers particularly admired: Min Patel, Neil Taylor, Alan Wells, Mark Ealham 'for his enthusiasm'
Young players to look out for: Duncan 'Pies' Spencer, Jason Billimoria
Other sports played: Hockey, football, snooker
Other sports followed: Football (Chelsea), basketball (Chicago Bulls)
Relaxations: 'Listening to Jim Sly talk about Dave Fulton'
Extras: Played for England U17 and England U19 Development XI. Also played for South England U14 and U19. County tennis player. Played for England U19 against Zimbabwe in 1997 and captained the England U17 side to victory in the International Youth Tournament in Bermuda in July. Played for the victorious England side in the U19 World Cup in South Africa. Shared England U19 Man of the Series award with Graeme Swann v Pakistan U19 1998. Scored century (119) v Pakistanis at Canterbury 2001 on his 22nd birthday. Scored century (132) v Lancashire at Old Trafford 2001, in the process passing 1000 runs in a season for the first time. Scored a 33-ball 50 in title-clinching Norwich Union League victory v Warwickshire at Edgbaston 2001. Awarded Kent cap 2001
Opinions on cricket: 'If Duncan Fletcher ever wishes to step down as England coach, the selectors should have a look at Jim Sly from Otford.'
Best batting: 132 Kent v Lancashire, Old Trafford 2001
Stop press: Scored century (177) in ECB National Academy's innings victory over Commonwealth Bank [Australian] Cricket Academy in Adelaide 2001-02

2001 Season

	M	Inns	NO	Runs	HS	Avge	100s	50s	Ct	St	O	M	Runs	Wkts	Avge	Best	5wI	10wM
Test																		
All First	18	28	0	1281	132	45.75	4	7	7	-	1	0	5	0	-	-	-	-
1-day Int																		
C & G	3	3	1	88	58	44.00	-	1	-	-								
B & H	5	4	0	97	45	24.25	-	-	1	-								
1-day Lge	10	9	1	201	59	25.12	-	2	2	-								

Career Performances

	M	Inns	NO	Runs	HS	Avge	100s	50s	Ct	St	Balls	Runs	Wkts	Avge	Best	5wl	10wM
Test																	
All First	70	118	3	3365	132	29.26	7	18	44	-	70	40	0	-	-	-	-
1-day Int																	
C & G	7	7	1	245	67	40.83	-	3	1	-
B & H	6	5	0	101	45	20.20	-	-	1	-
1-day Lge	36	32	4	797	76 *	28.46	-	7	3	-

KHAN, A. Kent

Name: Amjad Khan
Role: Right-hand bat, right-arm fast bowler
Born: 14 October 1980, Copenhagen, Denmark
Height: 6ft **Weight:** 11st 7lbs
County debut: 2001
Strike rate: 50.00 (career 50.00)
Parents: Aslam and Raisa
Marital status: Single
Education: Skolen på Duevej, Denmark; Falkonĕrgårdens Gymnasium
Overseas tours: Denmark U19 to Canada 1996, to Bermuda 1997, to South Africa and Wales 1998, to Ireland 1999; Denmark to Holland 1998, to Zimbabwe 1999, to Canada (ICC Trophy) 2001

Overseas teams played for: Kjøbenhavns Boldklub, Denmark
Cricketers particularly admired: Wasim Akram, Sachin Tendulkar, Allan Donald
Other sports followed: Football (Denmark)
Relaxations: Working out, listening to music, sleeping
Extras: The youngest Danish international ever, at age of 17. Played for Denmark in the NatWest Trophy 1999 and 2000
Best bowling: 1-46 Kent v Pakistanis, Canterbury 2001

2001 Season

	M	Inns	NO	Runs	HS	Avge	100s	50s	Ct	St	O	M	Runs	Wkts	Avge	Best	5wl	10wM
Test																		
All First	1	0	0	0	0	-	-	-	-	-	8.2	2	46	1	46.00	1-46	-	-
1-day Int																		
C & G																		
B & H	2	1	1	0	0*	-	-	-	-	-	6	0	35	1	35.00	1-23	-	
1-day Lge																		

Career Performances

	M	Inns	NO	Runs	HS	Avge	100s	50s	Ct	St	Balls	Runs	Wkts	Avge	Best	5wl	10wM
Test																	
All First	1	0	0	0	0	-	-	-	-	-	50	46	1	46.00	1-46	-	-
1-day Int																	
C & G	2	2	0	2	2	1.00	-	-	-	-	105	93	3	31.00	2-38	-	
B & H	2	1	1	0	0*	-	-	-	-	-	36	35	1	35.00	1-23	-	
1-day Lge																	

KHAN, R. M.   Derbyshire

Name: <u>Rawait</u> Mahmood Khan
Role: Right-hand bat
Born: 5 March 1982, Birmingham
Height: 5ft 9in **Weight:** 9st 7lbs
Nickname: Ray
County debut: 2001
Parents: Hashim Khan and Barish Begum
Marital status: Single
Family links with cricket: Father played for Warwickshire 2nd XI. Brother Zubair was also with Derbyshire
Education: Parkhill School; Moseley School; Solihull College
Cricketers particularly admired: Steve Waugh
Other sports played: Football, badminton
Relaxations: 'Socialising with friends'
Extras: Played for Derbyshire Board XI in the NatWest 2000
Best batting: 13 Derbyshire v Gloucestershire, Bristol 2001

2001 Season

	M	Inns	NO	Runs	HS	Avge	100s	50s	Ct	St	O	M	Runs	Wkts	Avge	Best	5wl	10wM
Test																		
All First	1	2	0	18	13	9.00	-	-	-	-								
1-day Int																		
C & G																		
B & H																		
1-day Lge																		

Career Performances

	M	Inns	NO	Runs	HS	Avge	100s	50s	Ct	St	Balls	Runs	Wkts	Avge	Best	5wl	10wM
Test																	
All First	1	2	0	18	13	9.00	-	-	-	-							
1-day Int																	
C & G	1	1	0	29	29	29.00	-	-	-	-							
B & H																	
1-day Lge																	

KHAN, W. G.   Derbyshire

Name: <u>Wasim</u> Gulzar Khan
Role: Left-hand bat, leg-break bowler
Born: 26 February 1971, Birmingham
Height: 6ft 1in **Weight:** 11st 11lbs
Nickname: Mowgli, Jai ('son of Tarzan')
County debut: 1992 (one-day, Warwicks),
1995 (first-class, Warwicks), 1998 (Sussex),
2001 (Derbyshire)
1st-Class 50s: 17
1st-Class 100s: 5
1st-Class catches: 36
Place in batting averages: (2000 144th
av. 23.83)
Parents: Gulzar Ahmed (deceased) and
Zarina Begum
Marital status: Single
Education: Somerville; Small Heath
Comprehensive; Josiah Mason Sixth Form
College (all Birmingham)
Qualifications: 6 O-levels, 1 A-level, coaching qualifications
Career outside cricket: Personal fitness training
Overseas tours: Warwickshire to Cape Town 1993, 1995

Overseas teams played for: Western Suburbs, Sydney 1990-91; North Perth 1991-93; Albion, Melbourne 1993-95; Petone Riverside, Wellington, New Zealand 1996-97
Cricketers particularly admired: Dermot Reeve, Saeed Anwar, Graham Thorpe, Michael DiVenuto
Other sports played: Squash, football
Other sports followed: Football (Birmingham City FC)
Relaxations: Reading, listening to music
Extras: Most Promising Young Cricketer 1990. Scored four centuries in a row for Warwickshire U19. Scored 171* v Northants in second trial game for Warwickshire 2nd XI. England Schools U19. Won Oxford/Cambridge U19 Festival 1989, 1990. Left Warwickshire at the end of the 1997 season to join Sussex. Released by Sussex at the end of the 2000 season and joined Derbyshire for 2001. Retired at the end of the 2001 season
Best batting: 181 Warwickshire v Hampshire, Southampton 1995

2001 Season

	M	Inns	NO	Runs	HS	Avge	100s	50s	Ct	St	O	M	Runs	Wkts	Avge	Best	5wI	10wM
Test																		
All First	1	1	0	1	1	1.00	-	-	-	-								
1-day Int																		
C & G	1	1	0	1	1	1.00	-	-	-	-								
B & H	3	3	1	38	18	19.00	-	-	-	-	7	0	46	0	-	-	-	-
1-day Lge	4	4	1	58	30 *	19.33	-	-	2	-	2	1	7	1	7.00	1-7	-	

Career Performances

	M	Inns	NO	Runs	HS	Avge	100s	50s	Ct	St	Balls	Runs	Wkts	Avge	Best	5wI	10wM
Test																	
All First	58	102	8	2835	181	30.15	5	17	36	-	132	62	0	-	-	-	-
1-day Int																	
C & G	2	2	0	3	2	1.50	-	-	1	-							
B & H	5	5	2	71	33	23.66	-	-	1	-	42	46	0	-	-	-	-
1-day Lge	21	19	1	201	33	11.16	-	-	5	-	12	7	1	7.00	1-7	-	

KILLEEN, N.   Durham

Name: Neil Killeen
Role: Right-hand bat, right-arm medium-fast bowler
Born: 17 October 1975, Shotley Bridge
Height: 6ft 1in **Weight:** 15st
Nickname: Killer, Bully, Quinny, Squeaky, Bull
County debut: 1995
County cap: 1999

50 wickets in a season: 1
1st-Class 5 w. in innings: 6
1st-Class catches: 12
One-Day 5 w. in innings: 2
Place in batting averages: (2000 270th av. 10.28)
Place in bowling averages: 13th av. 20.18 (2000 103rd av. 31.68)
Strike rate: 48.54 (career 55.58)
Parents: Glen and Thora
Wife and date of marriage: Clare Louise, 5 February 2000
Children: Jonathan David
Family links with cricket: 'Dad best armchair player in the game'
Education: Anfield Plain; Greencroft Comprehensive School; Derwentside College, University of Teesside
Qualifications: 8 GCSEs, 2 A-levels, first year Sports Science, Level III coaching award, Level I staff coach
Career outside cricket: Cricket coaching
Off-season: 'Working in own business, Neil Killeen Cricket Coaching, and also running cricket supporters tours with Beyond the Boundary Cricket Tours'
Overseas tours: Durham CCC to Zimbabwe 1992; England U19 to West Indies 1994-95; MCC to Bangladesh 1999-2000
Career highlights to date: 'My county cap and first-class debut'
Cricket moments to forget: 'Injury causing me to miss most of 2001 season'
Cricketers particularly admired: Ian Botham, Curtly Ambrose, Courtney Walsh, David Boon
Young players to look out for: Nicky Peng
Other sports played: Athletics (English Schools javelin)
Other sports followed: Football (Sunderland AFC), cricket (Anfield Plain CC)
Injuries: Out for all but one month of the 2001 season with a torn ligament in the left ankle
Relaxations: 'Good food, good wine; golf; spending time with wife and family'
Extras: Was first Durham bowler to take five wickets in a Sunday League game (5-26 against Northamptonshire in 1995). Took three wickets in final over of National League game at Derby 2000, preventing Derbyshire scoring the six runs required for victory. B&H Gold Award for his 4-18 v Lancashire at Liverpool 2001. PCA representative for Durham
Best batting: 48 Durham v Somerset, Chester-le-Street 1995
Best bowling: 7-85 Durham v Leicestershire, Leicester 1999

2001 Season

	M	Inns	NO	Runs	HS	Avge	100s	50s	Ct	St	O	M	Runs	Wkts	Avge	Best	5wI	10wM
Test																		
All First	4	3	0	6	5	2.00	-	-	-	-	89	29	222	11	20.18	3-14	-	-
1-day Int																		
C & G																		
B & H	5	1	0	0	0	0.00	-	-	3	-	45.3	3	144	10	14.40	4-18	-	
1-day Lge	2	0	0	0	0	-	-	-	-	-	17	0	73	1	73.00	1-37	-	

Career Performances

	M	Inns	NO	Runs	HS	Avge	100s	50s	Ct	St	Balls	Runs	Wkts	Avge	Best	5wI	10wM
Test																	
All First	45	64	12	629	48	12.09	-	-	12	-	7726	3838	139	27.61	7-85	6	-
1-day Int																	
C & G	6	4	1	4	2	1.33	-	-	1	-	348	217	8	27.12	2-15	-	
B & H	27	14	4	60	24 *	6.00	-	-	7	-	1422	957	31	30.87	4-18	-	
1-day Lge	70	42	14	279	32	9.96	-	-	12	-	3061	2395	93	25.75	6-31	2	

KING, R.   Northamptonshire

Name: Richard King
Role: Right-hand bat, left-arm medium-fast bowler
Born: 3 January 1984, Hitchin
Height: 6ft **Weight:** 13st
Nickname: Kingie
County debut: No first-team appearance
Parents: Roger and Rosemary
Marital status: Single
Education: Fernwood School; Bedford Modern School
Qualifications: 10 GCSEs, 4 A/S-Levels, 'ongoing 3 A-levels', Level 1 ECB coach
Off-season: 'At school. Developing at NCCC'
Overseas tours: Bedford Modern to Barbados 1999
Career highlights to date: 'Breaking school record with 200* (from 140 balls) in 2001, then scoring 185* a week later'
Cricketers particularly admired: Ian Botham, Viv Richards, Shane Warne
Young players to look out for: Ian Bell, Gareth Andrews (Somerset)
Other sports played: Rugby (school 1st XV, Midlands)

Other sports followed: Rugby (Saracens)
Relaxations: Spending time with friends
Extras: MCC Lord's Taverners Player of the Year U13. Played for Northamptonshire Board XI in the first round of the C&G 2002, which was played in August 2001
Opinions on cricket: 'Fitness is key. Self-analysis is important for improvement. Technology is improving the game, but soon it will become disruptive and the game may slide downhill.'

2001 Season (did not make any first-class or one-day appearances)

Career Performances

	M	Inns	NO	Runs	HS	Avge	100s	50s	Ct	St	Balls	Runs	Wkts	Avge	Best	5wI	10wM
Test																	
All First																	
1-day Int																	
C & G	1	1	0	2	2	2.00	-	-	1	-	36	27	0	-		-	-
B & H																	
1-day Lge																	

KIRBY, S. P. Yorkshire

Name: <u>Steven</u> Paul Kirby
Role: Right-hand bat, right-arm fast bowler
Born: 4 October 1977, Bury
Height: 6ft 3in **Weight:** 12st 10lbs
Nickname: Tango
County debut: 2001
1st-Class 5 w. in innnings: 3
1st-Class 10 w. in match: 1
1st-Class catches: 4
Place in batting averages: 274th av. 6.12
Place in bowling averages: 16th av. 20.85
Strike rate: 35.81 (career 35.81)
Parents: Paul and Allison
Marital status: Engaged
Education: St Joseph's Primary, Heywood, Lancs; Elton High School, Walshaw, Bury, Lancs; Bury College
Qualifications: 10 GCSEs, BTEC/GNVQ

Advanced Leisure and Tourism, Level 1 coaching award
Career outside cricket: Sports management
Off-season: ECB National Academy to Australia

Overseas tours: Yorkshire to Grenada 2001; ECB National Academy to Australia 2001-02
Overseas teams played for: Taranaki, Egmont Plains, New Zealand 1997-98
Career highlights to date: 'Being selected to go to Australia with the Academy'
Cricketers particularly admired: Michael Atherton, Curtly Ambrose, Malcolm Marshall, Glenn McGrath, Darren Gough
Young players to look out for: Tim Bresnan, John Sadler, Ian Bell
Other sports played: Basketball, table tennis, tennis, squash, golf
Other sports followed: Football (Manchester United), rugby (Leicester Tigers), golf (Tiger Woods)
Relaxations: 'Spending time with my girlfriend and family and friends; socialising; golf and playing any other sports; big *Star Trek* fan'
Extras: Formerly with Leicestershire. Took 14 wickets (41-18-47-14) in one day for Egmont Plains v Hawera in a New Zealand club match 1997-98. Took 7-50 in Kent's second innings at Headingley 2001, the best bowling figures by a Yorkshire player on first-class debut (Paul Hutchison's similar figures were on his Championship debut only); Kirby had replaced Matthew Hoggard (called up for England) halfway through the match. Took 12-72 against Leicestershire, his former club, at Headingley 2001. Awarded Yorkshire 2nd XI cap 2001
Opinions on cricket: '1. We play too much cricket, which reduces a) intensity; b) recovery; c) preparation. 2. Pitches are too inconsistent – a) bad techniques; b) lack of fast bowlers. 3. Need to have better practice facilities.'
Best batting: 15* Yorkshire v Lancashire, Headingley 2001
Best bowling: 7-50 Yorkshire v Kent, Headingley 2001
Stop press: Returned first innings figures of 4-100 in ECB National Academy's victory over Commonwealth Bank [Australian] Cricket Academy in Adelaide 2001-02

2001 Season

	M	Inns	NO	Runs	HS	Avge	100s	50s	Ct	St	O	M	Runs	Wkts	Avge	Best	5wl	10wM
Test																		
All First	10	10	2	49	15*	6.12	-	-	4	-	280.3	60	980	47	20.85	7-50	3	1
1-day Int																		
C & G	1	1	0	0	0	0.00	-	-	-	-	10	1	53	1	53.00	1-53	-	
B & H																		
1-day Lge	4	1	1	4	4*	-	-	-	-	1	-	27	1	158	6	26.33	3-35	-

Career Performances

	M	Inns	NO	Runs	HS	Avge	100s	50s	Ct	St	Balls	Runs	Wkts	Avge	Best	5wl	10wM
Test																	
All First	10	10	2	49	15*	6.12	-	-	4	-	1683	980	47	20.85	7-50	3	1
1-day Int																	
C & G	1	1	0	0	0	0.00	-	-	-	-	60	53	1	53.00	1-53	-	
B & H																	
1-day Lge	4	1	1	4	4*	-	-	-	-	1	-	162	158	6	26.33	3-35	-

KIRTLEY, R. J.   Sussex

Name: Robert <u>James</u> Kirtley
Role: Right-hand bat, right-arm
fast-medium bowler, county vice-captain
Born: 10 January 1975, Eastbourne
Height: 6ft **Weight:** 12st
Nickname: Ambi, Hurtler, Springer
County debut: 1995
County cap: 1998
50 wickets in a season: 4
1st-Class 50s: 2
1st-Class 5 w. in innings: 20
1st-Class 10 w. in match: 3
1st-Class catches: 29
One-Day 5 w. in innings: 1
Place in batting averages: 254th av. 10.88
(2000 285th av. 8.11)
Place in bowling averages: 27th av. 23.32
(2000 54th av. 24.74)
Strike rate: 45.32 (career 48.21)
Parents: Bob and Pip
Marital status: Girlfriend Jenny
Family links with cricket: Brother plays league cricket
Education: St Andrews School, Eastbourne; Clifton College, Bristol
Qualifications: 9 GCSEs, 2 A-levels, NCA coaching first level
Career outside cricket: 'Teaching?'
Off-season: Touring Zimbabwe with England one-day team
Overseas tours: Sussex YC to Barbados 1993, to Sri Lanka 1995; Sussex to Grenada 2001; England A to Bangladesh and New Zealand 1999-2000; England to Zimbabwe (one-day series) 2001-02
Overseas teams played for: Mashonaland, Zimbabwe 1996-97; Namibian Cricket Board/Wanderers, Windhoek, Namibia 1998-99
Career highlights to date: 'Winning the second division Championship with Sussex [2001]. Being selected for the England one-day squad. Hopefully more to come'
Cricket moments to forget: 'The three times I've bagged a pair'
Cricketers particularly admired: Curtly Ambrose, Jim Andrew, Darren Gough
Other sports followed: Hockey, golf, football (Brighton & Hove Albion)
Relaxations: 'Inviting friends round for a braii (barbeque) and enjoying a cold beer with them'
Extras: Played in the Mashonaland side which defeated England on their 1996-97 tour of Zimbabwe, taking seven wickets in the match. Winner of an NBC Denis Compton Award for promising cricketers. Vice-captain of Sussex since 2001. Took hat-trick

(A. Morris, Z. Morris, Aymes) in the B&H v Hampshire at West End 2001. Took 100th one-day league wicket (Joe Scuderi) v Lancashire at Old Trafford in the Norwich Union League 2001. Took 6-35 v Gloucestershire at Hove in the Championship 2001, in the process passing 100 wickets in all county cricket for the season. Leading wicket-taker in English first-class cricket 2001 with 75 wickets (av. 23.32)

Best batting: 59 Sussex v Durham, Eastbourne 1998
Best bowling: 7-21 Sussex v Hampshire, Southampton 1999
Stop press: Made One-Day International debut in first ODI v Zimbabwe at Harare 2001-02

2001 Season

	M	Inns	NO	Runs	HS	Avge	100s	50s	Ct	St	O	M	Runs	Wkts	Avge	Best	5wl	10wM
Test																		
All First	16	24	6	196	51 *	10.88	-	1	8	-	566.3	135	1749	75	23.32	6-34	5	2
1-day Int																		
C & G	1	1	0	0	0	0.00	-	-	-	-	4	0	37	0	-		-	-
B & H	4	1	0	8	8	8.00	-	-	3	-	37	5	146	9	16.22	3-29	-	
1-day Lge	15	7	3	48	11	12.00	-	-	3	-	116	9	493	18	27.38	2-8	-	

Career Performances

	M	Inns	NO	Runs	HS	Avge	100s	50s	Ct	St	Balls	Runs	Wkts	Avge	Best	5wl	10wM
Test																	
All First	93	131	38	970	59	10.43	-	2	29	-	16876	8837	350	25.24	7-21	20	3
1-day Int																	
C & G	8	3	1	13	7 *	6.50	-	-	1	-	462	344	15	22.93	5-39	1	
B & H	11	5	2	25	10 *	8.33	-	-	3	-	611	426	20	21.30	3-29	-	
1-day Lge	75	34	19	175	17 *	11.66	-	-	21	-	3093	2419	107	22.60	4-21	-	

KNIGHT, N. V.   Warwickshire

Name: Nicholas Verity Knight
Role: Left-hand bat, right-arm medium-fast bowler, close fielder
Born: 28 November 1969, Watford
Height: 6ft 1in **Weight:** 13st
Nickname: Stitch, Fungus
County debut: 1991 (Essex), 1995 (Warwickshire)
County cap: 1994 (Essex), 1995 (Warwickshire)
Test debut: 1995
Tests: 17
One-Day Internationals: 60
1000 runs in a season: 2
1st-Class 50s: 48

1st-Class 100s: 23
1st-Class 200s: 1
1st-Class catches: 232
One-Day 100s: 15
Place in batting averages: 54th av. 44.64
(2000 41st av. 39.53)
Strike rate: (career 159.00)
Parents: John and Rosemary
Wife and date of marriage: Trudie,
3 October 1998
Family links with cricket: Father played for
Cambridgeshire. Brother Andy plays club
cricket in local Cambridge leagues
Education: St John's School, Cambridge;
Felsted Prep; Felsted School; Loughborough
University
Qualifications: 9 O-levels, 3 A-levels,
BSc (Hons) Sociology, coaching qualification
Off-season: Touring with England

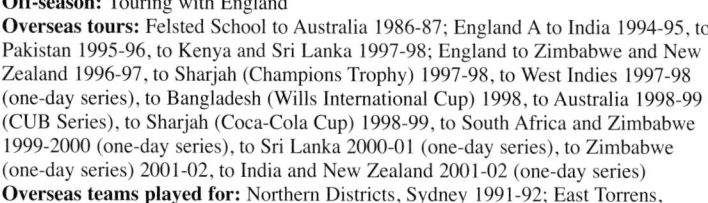

Overseas tours: Felsted School to Australia 1986-87; England A to India 1994-95, to Pakistan 1995-96, to Kenya and Sri Lanka 1997-98; England to Zimbabwe and New Zealand 1996-97, to Sharjah (Champions Trophy) 1997-98, to West Indies 1997-98 (one-day series), to Bangladesh (Wills International Cup) 1998, to Australia 1998-99 (CUB Series), to Sharjah (Coca-Cola Cup) 1998-99, to South Africa and Zimbabwe 1999-2000 (one-day series), to Sri Lanka 2000-01 (one-day series), to Zimbabwe (one-day series) 2001-02, to India and New Zealand 2001-02 (one-day series)
Overseas teams played for: Northern Districts, Sydney 1991-92; East Torrens, Adelaide 1992-94
Cricketers particularly admired: David Gower, Graham Gooch
Other sports played: Rugby, hockey
Relaxations: Eating good food, painting
Extras: Captained English Schools 1987 and 1988, England YC v New Zealand 1989 and Combined Universities 1991. Played hockey for Essex and Young England. Played rugby for Eastern Counties. Won *Daily Telegraph* award 1988; voted Gray-Nicolls Cricketer of the Year 1988, Cricket Society Cricketer of the Year 1989, Essex Young Player of the Year 1991 and Essex U19 Player of the Year. Left Essex at the end of the 1994 season to join Warwickshire. Scored successive centuries (113 and 125*) in the Texaco Trophy against Pakistan in 1996. Man of the Match after striking 96 off 117 balls in first Test v Zimbabwe at Bulawayo 1996-97 as England chased 205 for victory; he was run out off the last ball of the match while attempting the winning run and the match was drawn with the scores level (the first such Test result). Won successive one-day Man of the Match awards v West Indies 1997-98. Warwickshire vice-captain 1999. Member of England's 1999 World Cup squad. With Anurag Singh, shared in record NatWest first-wicket stand for Warwickshire (185), v Hampshire at Edgbaston 2000. Forced to withdraw from England one-day squads to Kenya and

Pakistan 2000-01 with knee problem. B&H Gold Award for his 107* v Glamorgan at Edgbaston 2001 (his second century in two days)
Best batting: 233 Warwickshire v Glamorgan, Edgbaston 2000
Best bowling: 1-61 Essex v Middlesex, Uxbridge 1994
Stop press: Man of the Match (80*) in fifth ODI v Zimbabwe at Bulawayo 2001-02 and Man of the Series (302 runs av. 100.67). Scored 105 in England's One-Day International victory over India at Delhi 2001-02

2001 Season

	M	Inns	NO	Runs	HS	Avge	100s	50s	Ct	St	O	M	Runs	Wkts	Avge	Best	5wI	10wM
Test	1	2	0	15	15	7.50	-	-	2	-								
All First	13	19	2	759	140	44.64	2	3	18	-								
1-day Int	6	6	1	213	84	42.60	-	2	2	-								
C & G	4	4	0	111	45	27.75	-	-	1	-								
B & H	6	6	1	340	107 *	68.00	3	-	-	-								
1-day Lge	12	10	2	301	84 *	37.62	-	2	4	-								

Career Performances

	M	Inns	NO	Runs	HS	Avge	100s	50s	Ct	St	Balls	Runs	Wkts	Avge	Best	5wI	10wM
Test	17	30	0	719	113	23.96	1	4	26	-							
All First	166	274	27	10024	233	40.58	24	48	232	-	159	191	1	191.00	1-61	-	-
1-day Int	60	60	6	2144	125 *	39.70	3	14	22	-							
C & G	25	25	2	975	151	42.39	4	3	9	-							
B & H	41	37	4	1226	107 *	37.15	4	4	10	-	6	4	0	-	-	-	-
1-day Lge	124	112	16	3136	134	32.66	4	14	52	-	84	85	2	42.50	1-14	-	

KOENIG, S. G.   Middlesex

Name: Sven Gaetan Koenig
Role: Left-hand bat
Born: 9 December 1973, Durban, South Africa
Height: 5ft 9in **Weight:** 12st 2lbs
Nickname: Blackie
County debut: No first-team appearance
1st-Class 50s: 25
1st-Class 100s: 7
1st-Class catches: 46
Strike rate: (career 122.00)
Parents: Gaetan and Barbara
Marital status: Girlfriend
Education: Highbury; Hilton College; University of Cape Town
Qualifications: Law degree, Economics degree, Level 2 coach

Career outside cricket: Business
Overseas tours: Western Province to Australia 1995; South Africa A to England 1996; Transvaal to Australia 1997
Overseas teams played for: Western Province 1993-96; Transvaal/Gauteng 1997-2000
Career highlights to date: 'Opening the batting with Desmond Haynes for three seasons at Western Province'
Cricket moments to forget: 'First-ball duck – lbw Malcolm Marshall – on Currie Cup debut, Western Province v Natal'
Cricketers particularly admired: Desmond Haynes, Steve Waugh, Gary Kirsten
Young players to look out for: Eddie Cowan (Sydney University)
Other sports played: Golf, surfing
Other sports followed: Rugby (Springboks), football (Newcastle United)
Interests/relaxations: Surfing, business
Extras: Leading run-scorer in South African domestic first-class cricket 2000-01 with 789 runs (av. 60.69). South African Young Player of the Year 1994. Gauteng Player of the Year 2000-01. Is not considered an overseas player
Opinions on cricket: 'Australia leading the way forward in bringing crowds to Test cricket. First-class cricket worldwide needs to follow their example by playing attacking cricket.'
Best batting: 155 Gauteng v Griqualand West, Kimberley 2000-01
Best bowling: 1-0 Gauteng/Northerns v Sri Lanka A, Johannesburg 1999-2000

2001 Season (did not make any first-class or one-day appearances)

Career Performances

	M	Inns	NO	Runs	HS	Avge	100s	50s	Ct	St	Balls	Runs	Wkts	Avge	Best	5wI	10wM
Test																	
All First	75	131	5	4642	155	36.84	7	25	46	-	122	67	1	67.00	1-0	-	-
1-day Int																	
C & G																	
B & H																	
1-day Lge																	

KRIKKEN, K. M. Derbyshire

Name: <u>Karl</u> Matthew Krikken
Role: Right-hand bat, wicket-keeper
Born: 9 April 1969, Bolton
Height: 5ft 10in **Weight:** 13st 3lbs
Nickname: Krikk, Krude
County debut: 1987 (one-day),
1989 (first-class)
County cap: 1992
50 dismissals in a season: 5
1st-Class 50s: 25
1st-Class 100s: 1
1st-Class catches: 500
1st-Class stumpings: 31
Place in batting averages: 179th av. 21.75
(2000 213th av. 17.00)
Strike rate: (career 134.00)
Parents: Brian and Irene
Wife and date of marriage: Leesha,
3 October 1998

Children: Harry Evan, 20 December 1996; Chester, 19 December 1998
Family links with cricket: Father played for Lancashire and Worcestershire
Education: Horwich Parish Church School; Rivington and Blackrod High School and
Sixth Form College
Qualifications: 6 O-levels, 3 A-levels, Level 3 coaching award
Off-season: 'Beneficiary 2002, and trying to fathom the Level 4 coaching award out'
Overseas tours: Derbyshire to Bermuda 1993, to Spain 1997, to Portugal 2000
Overseas teams played for: CBC Old Boys, Kimberley, South Africa 1988-89;
Green Island, Dunedin, New Zealand 1990-91; United CC, Cape Town 1992-93;
Rivertonians, Cape Town 1993-94; Longford CC, Victoria, Australia
Career highlights to date: 'Winning B&H in 1993. Winning Sunday League in 1990.
Runners-up in Nat West 1998 and Championship 1996'
Cricket moments to forget: 'Enjoyed all of it – even last season'
Cricketers particularly admired: Kim Barnett, Bob Taylor, Derek Randall,
Jack Russell, Alan Hill
Young players to look out for: 'Derbyshire will come of age in a few years'
Other sports played: 'Keg ball', volleyball, football
Other sports followed: Football (Wigan Athletic FC, Bolton Wanderers FC)
Injuries: Out for four weeks with left hamstring strain
Relaxations: Family
Extras: Derbyshire Supporters' Player of the Year 1991 and 1996; Derbyshire
Clubman of the Year 1993. Derbyshire vice-captain 1998-2000. Made 500th first-class

dismissal when he caught Will Kendall off Nathan Dumelow v Hampshire at Derby 2001. Granted a benefit for 2002

Best batting: 104 Derbyshire v Lancashire, Old Trafford 1996
Best bowling: 1-54 Derbyshire v Hampshire, Derby 1999

2001 Season

	M	Inns	NO	Runs	HS	Avge	100s	50s	Ct	St	O	M	Runs	Wkts	Avge	Best	5wI	10wM
Test																		
All First	14	25	5	435	93 *	21.75	-	3	34	1	7	0	27	0	-		-	-	-
1-day Int																		
C & G																		
B & H	5	4	1	26	23 *	8.66	-	-	2	4								
1-day Lge	14	12	4	203	42 *	25.37	-	-	14	8								

Career Performances

	M	Inns	NO	Runs	HS	Avge	100s	50s	Ct	St	Balls	Runs	Wkts	Avge	Best	5wI	10wM
Test																	
All First	204	305	59	5541	104	22.52	1	25	500	31	134	121	1	121.00	1-54	-	-
1-day Int																	
C & G	20	12	5	201	55	28.71	-	1	15	1							
B & H	37	24	9	314	42 *	20.93	-	-	33	8							
1-day Lge	136	99	33	1137	44 *	17.22	-	-	143	33							

---

52. Whose record of 66 competition dismissals did Jack Russell overtake v Derbyshire in the 1999 NatWest?

LAMPITT, S. R.
Worcestershire

Name: <u>Stuart</u> Richard Lampitt
Role: Right-hand bat, right-arm medium-fast bowler
Born: 29 July 1966, Wolverhampton
Height: 5ft 11in **Weight:** 14st
Nickname: Jed
County debut: 1985
County cap: 1989
Benefit: 2000
50 wickets in a season: 7
1st-Class 50s: 20
1st-Class 100s: 1
1st-Class 5 w. in innings: 20
1st-Class catches: 148
One-Day 5 w. in innings: 3
Place in batting averages: 150th av. 25.62 (2000 206th av. 17.42)
Place in bowling averages: 51st av. 27.87 (2000 28th av. 20.94)
Strike rate: 50.83 (career 53.32)
Parents: Joseph and Muriel
Wife and date of marriage: Clare, 31 March 2001
Children: Joseph Stuart, 4 September 2001
Family links with cricket: 'Used to play Subbuteo table cricket with Dad'
Education: Kingswinford Secondary School; Dudley College of Technology
Qualifications: 7 O-levels, Diploma in Business Studies, NCA advanced coach
Career outside cricket: Youth development coach
Off-season: Coaching
Overseas tours: NCA U19 to Bermuda; Worcestershire to Bahamas 1990, to Zimbabwe 1990-91, to South Africa 1991-92, to Barbados 1996, to Portugal 2000
Overseas teams played for: Mangere, Auckland 1986-88; University CC, Perth 1991-93
Career highlights to date: 'Winning Championship with Worcestershire in 1989 and receiving county cap after'
Cricket moments to forget: 'Every time I'm dismissed!!'
Cricketers particularly admired: Ian Botham, Malcolm Marshall
Young players to look out for: 'The good ones'
Other sports played: Golf, fishing
Other sports followed: Football (Wolves FC)
Injuries: Out for a month with a knee injury; 'GOA (general old age)'
Relaxations: Golf, fishing
Extras: Took five wickets and made 42 for Stourbridge in final of the William

Younger Cup at Lord's in 1986. One of the Whittingdale Young Players of the Year 1990. 'Must be the only bowler to be hit for six first ball by Adrian Jones and Phil Tufnell (two master batsmen)'

Opinions on cricket: 'Give youth a chance!!'

Best batting: 122 Worcestershire v Middlesex, Lord's 1994

Best bowling: 7-45 Worcestershire v Warwickshire, Worcester 2000

2001 Season

	M	Inns	NO	Runs	HS	Avge	100s	50s	Ct	St	O	M	Runs	Wkts	Avge	Best	5wI	10wM
Test																		
All First	10	13	5	205	42 *	25.62	-	-	4	-	203.2	49	669	24	27.87	5-22	1	-
1-day Int																		
C & G	3	2	1	19	17	19.00	-	-	1	-	18.5	2	108	5	21.60	3-36	-	
B & H	5	4	4	53	31 *	-	-	-	2	-	45	6	191	7	27.28	3-25	-	
1-day Lge	15	8	6	45	27 *	22.50	-	-	5	-	116	11	448	23	19.47	4-37	-	

Career Performances

	M	Inns	NO	Runs	HS	Avge	100s	50s	Ct	St	Balls	Runs	Wkts	Avge	Best	5wI	10wM
Test																	
All First	236	311	74	5649	122	23.83	1	20	148	-	32049	17224	601	28.65	7-45	20	-
1-day Int																	
C & G	30	22	5	242	54	14.23	-	1	8	-	1570	1116	46	24.26	5-22	1	
B & H	47	26	11	330	41	22.00	-	-	14	-	2404	1586	73	21.72	6-26	1	
1-day Lge	195	118	42	1394	41 *	18.34	-	-	59	-	7125	5432	221	24.57	5-67	1	

---

53. Which future England captain scored an unbeaten 107 out of a total of 188 for Surrey v Middlesex in the semi-finals of the 1988 NatWest?

LANEY, J. S.   Hampshire

Name: <u>Jason</u> Scott Laney
Role: Right-hand bat, occasional
off-spin bowler
Born: 27 April 1973, Winchester
Height: 5ft 10in **Weight:** 13st 7lbs
Nickname: Chucky, Hurler, Crickethead,
Cricket Badger
County debut: 1993 (one-day),
1995 (first-class)
County cap: 1996
1000 runs in a season: 1
1st-Class 50s: 25
1st-Class 100s: 5
1st-Class catches: 65
One-Day 100s: 2
Place in batting averages: (2000 175th
av. 20.37)

Strike rate: (career 192.00)
Parents: Geoff and Pam
Marital status: Single
Family links with cricket: Grandfather played good club cricket
Education: Pewsey Vale Comprehensive; St John's, Marlborough;
Leeds Metropolitan University
Qualifications: 8 GCSEs, 2 A-levels, BA (Hons) in Human Movement Studies
Overseas tours: England U18 to Canada 1991
Overseas teams played for: Waikato, New Zealand 1994-95; Matabeleland and Old
Miltonians, Zimbabwe 1995-96; DHS Old Boys, South Africa 1996-97
Cricketers particularly admired: Rupert Cox, Ian Botham, Robin Smith,
Malcolm Marshall
Young players to look out for: Lawrence Prittipaul, Chris Tremlett, Jimmy Adams
Other sports played: Golf, cards
Other sports followed: Football (Swindon Town FC)
Extras: Hampshire Young Cricketer of the Year 1995. Became first Hampshire
cricketer to score a century before lunch on debut in the NatWest Trophy 1996.
PCA representative for Hampshire
Best batting: 112 Hampshire v Oxford University, The Parks 1996
Best bowling: 1-24 Hampshire v Northamptonshire, Northampton 1999

2001 Season

	M	Inns	NO	Runs	HS	Avge	100s	50s	Ct	St	O	M	Runs	Wkts	Avge	Best	5wI	10wM
Test																		
All First	4	5	1	137	60	34.25	-	2	8	-								
1-day Int																		
C & G	1	1	0	23	23	23.00	-	-	-	-								
B & H	4	3	0	58	23	19.33	-	-	-	-								
1-day Lge	13	13	1	259	62 *	21.58	-	1	2	-								

Career Performances

	M	Inns	NO	Runs	HS	Avge	100s	50s	Ct	St	Balls	Runs	Wkts	Avge	Best	5wI	10wM
Test																	
All First	80	140	5	4125	112	30.55	5	25	65	-	384	224	2	112.00	1-24	-	-
1-day Int																	
C & G	15	14	1	658	153	50.61	1	3	6	-							
B & H	21	20	0	303	41	15.15	-	-	3	-							
1-day Lge	77	77	2	1719	106 *	22.92	1	7	20	-	3	9	0	-		-	-

LARAMAN, A. W.   Middlesex

Name: <u>Aaron</u> William Laraman
Role: Right-hand bat, right-arm
medium-fast bowler
Born: 10 January 1979, London
Height: 6ft 5in **Weight:** 14st 7lbs
Nickname: Az, Lazza, Shanky, Long
County debut: 1998
1st-Class catches: 2
One-Day 5 w. in innings: 2
Strike rate: 14.50 (career 25.83)
Parents: William and Lynda
Marital status: Engaged
Education: St Paul's C of E School;
Enfield Grammar School
Qualifications: 8 GCSEs
Career outside cricket: Cricket coaching
in winter
Off-season: Coaching

Overseas tours: England U17 to Holland 1995; England U19 to South Africa 1997-98
Overseas teams played for: Burnside CC, Christchurch, New Zealand 1999-2000;
Willetton CC, Perth 2000-01
Career highlights to date: 'Making my debut at Lord's in 1998'

Cricketers particularly admired: Steve Waugh, Glenn McGrath, Michael Atherton
Young players to look out for: Nick Compton
Other sports followed: Football (Arsenal)
Injuries: Out for most of season with stress fracture of shoulder blade
Relaxations: Working out at the gym, football, golf
Extras: Enfield Grammar School cap at the age of 13. Middlesex Colts cap. Seaxe 2nd XI Player of the Year 1997. Took 4-39 on NatWest debut v Nottinghamshire at Lord's 2000
Best batting: 29 Middlesex v Derbyshire, Southgate 2001
Best bowling: 4-33 Middlesex v Cambridge University, Fenner's 2000

2001 Season

	M	Inns	NO	Runs	HS	Avge	100s	50s	Ct	St	O	M	Runs	Wkts	Avge	Best	5wI	10wM
Test																		
All First	1	1	0	29	29	29.00	-	-	1	-	4.5	1	20	2	10.00	2-20	-	-
1-day Int																		
C & G	1	1	1	16	16 *	-	-	-	-	1	-							
B & H																			
1-day Lge																			

Career Performances

	M	Inns	NO	Runs	HS	Avge	100s	50s	Ct	St	Balls	Runs	Wkts	Avge	Best	5wI	10wM
Test																	
All First	3	1	0	29	29	29.00	-	-	2	-	155	75	6	12.50	4-33	-	-
1-day Int																	
C & G	4	2	1	18	16 *	18.00	-	-	2	-	141	66	8	8.25	4-39	-	
B & H																	
1-day Lge	10	8	4	33	11 *	8.25	-	-	4	-	400	299	17	17.58	6-42	2	

LATHWELL, M. N. Somerset

Name: <u>Mark</u> Nicholas Lathwell
Role: Right-hand bat, right-arm off-spin bowler
Born: 26 December 1971, Bletchley
Height: 5ft 8in **Weight:** 12st
Nickname: Trough, Lathers
County debut: 1991
County cap: 1992
Test debut: 1993
Tests: 2
1000 runs in a season: 4

1st-Class 50s: 57
1st-Class 100s: 11
1st-Class 200s: 1
1st-Class catches: 105
One-Day 100s: 5
Place in batting averages: 88th av. 35.10
(2000 181st av. 19.76)
Strike rate: (career 88.00)
Parents: Derek Peter and Valerie
Wife and date of marriage: Lisa,
October 1996
Children: Jason, 16 January 1995;
Sam, 27 October 1997
Family links with cricket: Father and
brother both club cricketers; father qualified
coach

Education: Overstone Primary, Wing, Bucks;
Southmead School, Braunton, North Devon;
Braunton School and Community College
Qualifications: 5 GCSEs, cricket coaching certificate
Career outside cricket: Coaching
Overseas tours: England A to Australia 1992-93, to South Africa 1993-94
Cricketers particularly admired: Ian Botham, Graham Gooch
Other sports played: Darts
Other sports followed: Snooker
Relaxations: Cooking, eating, sleeping
Extras: Played for Devon. Spent one season on Lord's groundstaff. Played for
England U19 v Australia U19 1991. PCA Young Player of the Year and Somerset
Player of the Year 1992. Cricket Writers' Club Young Cricketer of the Year 1993
Best batting: 206 Somerset v Surrey, Bath 1994
Best bowling: 2-21 Somerset v Sussex, Hove 1994

2001 Season

	M	Inns	NO	Runs	HS	Avge	100s	50s	Ct	St	O	M	Runs	Wkts	Avge	Best	5wI	10wM
Test																		
All First	13	21	1	702	99	35.10	-	8	9	-	7	0	37	0	-	-	-	-
1-day Int																		
C & G	1	1	0	101	101	101.00	1	-	-	-								
B & H	3	3	0	15	7	5.00	-	-	2	-								
1-day Lge	6	5	0	85	30	17.00	-	-	1	-								

Career Performances

	M	Inns	NO	Runs	HS	Avge	100s	50s	Ct	St	Balls	Runs	Wkts	Avge	Best	5wI	10wM
Test	2	4	0	78	33	19.50	-	-	-	-							
All First	156	272	11	8727	206	33.43	12	57	105	-	1144	721	13	55.46	2-21	-	-
1-day Int																	
C & G	19	18	0	566	103	31.44	2	2	7	-	66	23	1	23.00	1-23	-	
B & H	24	24	0	836	121	34.83	2	6	9	-	25	50	0	-	-	-	-
1-day Lge	119	116	5	2924	117	26.34	1	17	29	-	102	85	0	-	-	-	-

LAW, D. R. Durham

Name: <u>Danny</u> Richard Law
Role: Right-hand bat, right-arm
medium-fast bowler
Born: 13 July 1975, London
Height: 6ft 5in **Weight:** 16st
Nickname: Desperate
County debut: 1993 (Sussex), 1997 (Essex),
2001 (Durham)
County cap: 1996 (Sussex), 2001 (Durham)
1st-Class 50s: 12
1st-Class 100s: 2
1st-Class 5 w. in innings: 8
1st-Class catches: 53
Place in batting averages: 166th av. 23.44
(2000 197th av. 18.00)
Place in bowling averages: 39th av. 26.26
(2000 111th av. 34.73)
Strike rate: 50.14 (career 53.19)

Parents: Richard (deceased) and Claudette
Marital status: Separated
Children: Sade
Family links with cricket: Cousins play club cricket in Northampton
Education: St Andrews; Wolverstone Hall/Steyning Grammar School
Qualifications: Coach
Off-season: 'Training hard for the new season. Travelling to Oz to see my little girl.
Cape Town for the Durham tour'
Overseas tours: Sussex Schools U16 to Jersey 1991; England U18 to South Africa
1992-93, to Denmark 1993; England U19 to Sri Lanka 1993-94; Dulwich CC to
Kenya and Uganda 2000-01
Overseas teams played for: Ashburton CC, Melbourne 1992-94; Essendon,
Melbourne 1995-96

Career highlights to date: 'Winning two trophies with Essex. Being capped at Sussex and also at Durham'

Cricketers particularly admired: Viv Richards, Ian Botham, Michael Holding, Simon Brown, Martin Love, Stuart Law

Young players to look out for: Nicky Peng, Andy Pratt, Paul Collingwood, Steve Harmison

Other sports played: Golf ('badly')

Other sports followed: Football (Man Utd)

Relaxations: Cinema, music, PlayStation

Extras: Winner of Denis Compton Award 1996. Left Sussex during the 1996-97 off-season and joined Essex for 1997. Took Championship hat-trick v Durham at Riverside 1998. Left Essex at the end of the 2000 season and joined Durham for 2001. Scored maiden Championship century (103) v Hampshire at Riverside 2001, in the process sharing with James Brinkley in a record seventh-wicket partnership for Durham (127). Awarded Durham cap 2001

Opinions on cricket: 'Keep it interesting.'

Best batting: 115 Sussex v Young Australia, Hove 1995

Best bowling: 6-53 Durham v Hampshire, West End 2001

2001 Season

	M	Inns	NO	Runs	HS	Avge	100s	50s	Ct	St	O	M	Runs	Wkts	Avge	Best	5wI	10wM
Test																		
All First	16	26	1	586	103	23.44	1	1	11	-	351	70	1103	42	26.26	6-53	3	-
1-day Int																		
C & G	3	3	0	39	19	13.00	-	-	-	-	29.4	0	159	5	31.80	3-51	-	
B & H	4	4	2	91	57 *	45.50	-	1	2	-	21	2	104	3	34.66	2-22	-	
1-day Lge	13	13	2	233	47	21.18	-	-	1	-	77.5	6	368	13	28.30	3-28	-	

Career Performances

	M	Inns	NO	Runs	HS	Avge	100s	50s	Ct	St	Balls	Runs	Wkts	Avge	Best	5wI	10wM
Test																	
All First	96	150	6	2918	115	20.26	2	12	53	-	10319	6317	194	32.56	6-53	8	-
1-day Int																	
C & G	17	13	1	227	47	18.91	-	-	4	-	331	308	9	34.22	3-51	-	
B & H	16	15	3	248	57 *	20.66	-	1	3	-	288	241	4	60.25	2-22	-	
1-day Lge	99	86	14	1648	82	22.88	-	5	20	-	2025	1761	61	28.86	3-26	-	

LAW, S. G.   Lancashire

Name: <u>Stuart</u> Grant Law
Role: Right-hand bat, right-arm
occasional bowler
Born: 18 October 1968, Herston,
Brisbane, Australia
Height: 6ft   **Weight:** 14st
Nickname: LA, Judge
County debut: 1996 (Essex)
County cap: 1996 (Essex)
Test debut: 1995-96
Tests: 1
One-Day Internationals: 54
1000 runs in a season: 6
1st-Class 50s: 84
1st-Class 100s: 52
1st-Class 200s: 2
1st-Class 5 w. in innings: 1
1st-Class catches: 263
One-Day 100s: 12

Place in batting averages: 7th av. 65.55 (2000 10th av. 55.40)
Strike rate: (career 98.32)
Parents: Grant and Pam
Wife and date of marriage: Debbie-Lee, 31 December 1998
Children: Max, 9 January 2002
Family links with cricket: 'Father, grandfather, uncles all played at a reasonable standard'
Education: Stafford State School; Brisbane State High School; Craigslea State High School
Qualifications: Level 2 cricket coach
Off-season: Playing for the Queensland Bulls in Australia
Overseas tours: Young Australia to England 1995; Australia to India and Pakistan (World Cup) 1995-96, to Sri Lanka (Singer World Series), India and South Africa 1996-97, to New Zealand (one-day series) 1997-98
Overseas teams played for: Queensland 1988-89 –
Career highlights to date: 'Playing Test and one-day cricket for Australia. Being first captain to win Sheffield Shield for Queensland 1994-95'
Cricket moments to forget: 'Too many to name one. You play long enough, you should have a few good stories'
Cricketers particularly admired: Viv Richards, Greg Chappell
Young players to look out for: Mitchell Johnson
Other sports played: Golf ('socially')

Other sports followed: Rugby league (Brisbane Broncos)
Injuries: 'Broke my left index finger in three places'
Relaxations: Going to the beach; entertaining friends
Extras: Made his first-class debut for Queensland as a 19-year-old, scoring 179 on only his second appearance. Shared with Martin Love in record third-wicket partnership for Queensland (326), v Tasmania at Brisbane 1994-95. Is the most successful domestic captain in Australian cricket history, having captained Queensland to their first Sheffield Shield title in 1994-95, to their second in 1996-97, to the title in the first two Pura Cup competitions in 1999-2000 and 2000-01, and to three one-day titles. Made his Test debut for Australia against Sri Lanka at Perth in 1995-96 and scored an unbeaten 54. Played in all 17 One-Day Internationals for Australia in 1995-96. Man of the Match in the 1997 NatWest final at Lord's. One of *Wisden*'s Five Cricketers of the Year 1998. Set record for the fastest century in Australian domestic one-day cricket – 74 balls for Queensland v Tasmania at Brisbane 1998-99. Scored centuries (159 and 113*) in each innings v Yorkshire at Chelmsford 1999; Michael Vaughan scored two 100s for Yorks in the same match. Topped the first-class batting averages for 1999 (1833 runs at 73.32). Professional Cricketers' Association Player of the Year 1999. Man of the Match in inaugural Pura Milk Cup Final 1999-2000. Scored 116* and 123* v Lancashire at Old Trafford 2001, becoming the first player since Glamorgan's Hugh Morris in 1995 to score unbeaten centuries in each innings of a match; followed up with a 90-ball century (ending up with 108) v Lancashire in the ensuing Norwich Union League match at the same ground. Left Essex at the end of the 2001 season and has joined Lancashire as overseas player for 2002
Opinions on cricket: 'No consistency in policing the laws of the game.'
Best batting: 263 Essex v Somerset, Chelmsford 1999
Best bowling: 5-39 Queensland v Tasmania, Brisbane 1995-96
Stop press: Became Queensland's most-capped player when he passed Sam Trimble's record of 133 first-class appearances for the state, v Tasmania at the Gabba 2001-02

2001 Season

	M	Inns	NO	Runs	HS	Avge	100s	50s	Ct	St	O	M	Runs	Wkts	Avge	Best	5wI	10wM
Test																		
All First	13	23	3	1311	153	65.55	4	8	18	-								
1-day Int																		
C & G	2	2	0	24	20	12.00	-	-	-	-								
B & H	3	3	0	110	55	36.66	-	1	2	-								
1-day Lge	11	10	0	300	108	30.00	1	1	5	-								

Career Performances

	M	Inns	NO	Runs	HS	Avge	100s	50s	Ct	St	Balls	Runs	Wkts	Avge	Best	5wI	10wM
Test	1	1	1	54	54 *	-	-	1	1	-	18	9	0	-	-	-	-
All First	234	390	41	17590	263	50.40	54	84	263	-	7866	3883	80	48.53	5-39	1	-
1-day Int	54	51	5	1237	110	26.89	1	7	12	-	807	635	12	52.91	2-22	-	
C & G	16	15	1	706	107	50.42	3	3	12	-	439	366	8	45.75	2-36	-	
B & H	22	21	0	670	116	31.90	1	3	12	-	384	351	9	39.00	2-13	-	
1-day Lge	82	80	4	2671	126	35.14	7	9	34	-	904	791	22	35.95	4-37	-	

LEATHERDALE, D. A. Worcestershire

Name: <u>David</u> Anthony Leatherdale
Role: Right-hand bat, right-arm medium
bowler, cover fielder
Born: 26 November 1967, Bradford
Height: 5ft 10in **Weight:** 11st
Nickname: Lugsy, Spock
County debut: 1988
County cap: 1994
1000 runs in a season: 1
1st-Class 50s: 48
1st-Class 100s: 12
1st-Class 5 w. in innings: 2
1st-Class catches: 145
Place in batting averages: 164th av. 23.75
(2000 44th av. 39.00)
Place in bowling averages: 99th av. 36.25
(2000 67th av. 26.73)
Strike rate: 59.25 (career 53.45)
Parents: Paul and Rosalyn
Wife: Vanessa
Children: Callum Edward, 6 July 1990; Christian Ellis, 6 years old
Family links with cricket: Father played local cricket; brother plays for East Bierley
in Bradford League; brother-in-law played for England YC in 1979
Education: Bolton Royd Primary School; Pudsey Grangefield Secondary School
Qualifications: 8 O-levels, 2 A-levels; NCA coaching award (stage 1)
Overseas tours: England Indoor to Australia and New Zealand 1994-95
Overseas teams played for: Pretoria Police, South Africa 1987-88
Cricketers particularly admired: Mark Scott, George Batty, Peter Kippax
Other sports followed: Football, American football
Relaxations: Golf
Best batting: 157 Worcestershire v Somerset, Worcester 1991
Best bowling: 5-20 Worcestershire v Gloucestershire, Worcester 1998

2001 Season

	M	Inns	NO	Runs	HS	Avge	100s	50s	Ct	St	O	M	Runs	Wkts	Avge	Best	5wI	10wM
Test																		
All First	17	27	3	570	93	23.75	-	2	7	-	158	39	580	16	36.25	4-70	-	-
1-day Int																		
C & G	3	3	1	14	14 *	7.00	-	-	3	-	8	0	38	1	38.00	1-20	-	
B & H	5	5	1	225	58	56.25	-	3	2	-	36.1	3	165	6	27.50	2-26	-	
1-day Lge	15	14	2	319	55 *	26.58	-	1	9	-	62.5	2	263	10	26.30	3-11	-	

Career Performances

	M	Inns	NO	Runs	HS	Avge	100s	50s	Ct	St	Balls	Runs	Wkts	Avge	Best	5wI	10wM
Test																	
All First	196	316	37	9016	157	32.31	12	48	145	-	5934	3434	111	30.93	5-20	2	-
1-day Int																	
C & G	27	24	2	435	53	19.77	-	1	11	-	316	272	7	38.85	3-14	-	
B & H	36	29	7	540	66	24.54	-	4	9	-	669	464	19	24.42	4-13	-	
1-day Lge	172	145	23	2464	70 *	20.19	-	9	83	-	1941	1615	76	21.25	4-19	-	

LEHMANN, D. S.   Yorkshire

Name: <u>Darren</u> Scott Lehmann
Role: Left-hand bat, slow left-arm bowler, county captain
Born: 5 February 1970, Gawler, Australia
Nickname: Boof
Height: 5ft 11in **Weight:** 14st 2lbs
County debut: 1997
County cap: 1997
Test debut: 1997-98
Tests: 5
One-Day Internationals: 69
1000 runs in a season: 3
1st-Class 50s: 77
1st-Class 100s: 48
1st-Class 200s: 6
1st-Class catches: 104
One-Day 100s: 8
Place in batting averages: 2nd av. 83.29 (2000 4th av. 67.13)
Place in bowling averages: 64th av. 30.66
Strike rate: 69.58 (career 86.20)
Marital status: Married
Off-season: Playing for South Australia

Overseas tours: Australia to Sri Lanka 1996-97, to New Zealand 1997-98, to Sharjah (Coca-Cola Cup) 1997-98, to India 1997-98, to Pakistan 1998-99, to Bangladesh 1998-99, to West Indies 1998-99 (one-day series), to UK, Ireland and Holland (World Cup) 1999, to Sri Lanka 1999-2000 (one-day series), to Zimbabwe 1999-2000 (one-day series), to India 2000-01 (one-day series), to South Africa 2001-02

Overseas teams played for: Salisbury District CC (now Northern Districts), Adelaide; South Australia 1987-88 – 1989-90; Victoria 1990-91 – 1992-93; South Australia 1993-94 –

Other sports followed: Australian Football League (Adelaide Crows)

Relaxations: Golf, watching sport

Extras: Represented South Australia at all age groups. Scored 1128 runs (av. 57.50) in his first full Sheffield Shield season. Man of the Match in CUB second final v England at Melbourne 1998-99. Played in Australia's 1999 World Cup winning side, striking the winning runs in the final v Pakistan. Released by Yorkshire at the end of the 1998 season. Scored 1142 runs at 63.44 (including seven centuries) in the 1999-2000 Australian season and was voted Interstate Cricketer of the Year 1999-2000 at the inaugural Allan Border Medal awards January 2000. Has scored 1000 runs in an Australian season five times. Returned to Yorkshire as overseas player in 2000. Won the EDS Walter Lawrence Trophy for the fastest first-class century of the 2000 season – 89 balls for Yorkshire v Kent at Canterbury. Top run-scorer in English first-class cricket 2000 with 1477 runs at an average of 67.13. Scored a 44-ball 63 for South Australia v Western Australia at Adelaide 2000-01, in the process overtaking Dean Jones's total of 2122 runs to become the highest scoring batsman in Australian domestic one-day cricket. Voted State Player of the Year (for the second successive year) 2000-01. One of *Wisden*'s Five Cricketers of the Year 2001. Australian Cricket Board central contract 2001-02. B&H Gold Awards for his 114-ball 103 v Derbyshire at Headingley, 1-13 and 35 v Lancashire at Liverpool and 76-ball 88 v Durham at Headingley 2001 (three Gold Awards in eight days). C&G Man of the Match award for his 88 v Bedfordshire at Luton 2001. Became only the fourth player to score a Roses match double century with his 288-ball 252 v Lancashire at Headingley 2001; also scored a 24-ball 48 in the second innings. Scored 106* v Surrey at Headingley 2001, in the process sharing with Matthew Wood in a record third-wicket partnership for Yorkshire in matches against Surrey. His 103-ball 191, including 11 sixes, v Nottinghamshire at Scarborough in the Norwich Union League 2001 is the second highest score in the domestic one-day league, behind Alistair Brown's 203 for Surrey v Hampshire in 1997. Captain of South Australia since 1998-99. Vice-captain of Yorkshire in 2001. Yorkshire Player of the Year 2001. Named captain of Yorkshire for 2002, the first overseas player to be appointed to the office

Best batting: 255 South Australia v Queensland, Adelaide 1996-97

Best bowling: 4-42 Yorkshire v Kent, Maidstone 1998

Stop press: Became the highest scoring batsman in Sheffield Shield/Pura Cup history when he passed Jamie Siddons's career competition total of 10,643 runs v Victoria 2001-02. Named State Player of the Year (for the third successive year) 2001-02

2001 Season

	M	Inns	NO	Runs	HS	Avge	100s	50s	Ct	St	O	M	Runs	Wkts	Avge	Best	5wI	10wM
Test																		
All First	13	19	2	1416	252	83.29	5	5	6	-	139.1	33	368	12	30.66	3-13	-	-
1-day Int																		
C & G	3	3	0	90	88	30.00	-	1	-	-	16	0	67	3	22.33	2-39	-	
B & H	7	7	1	334	103	55.66	1	2	5	-	30	1	110	4	27.50	2-40	-	
1-day Lge	15	15	1	753	191	53.78	2	4	9	-	89.5	3	336	16	21.00	3-31	-	

Career Performances

	M	Inns	NO	Runs	HS	Avge	100s	50s	Ct	St	Balls	Runs	Wkts	Avge	Best	5wI	10wM
Test	5	8	0	228	98	28.50	-	2	3	-	102	45	2	22.50	1-6	-	-
All First	190	323	22	16890	255	56.11	54	77	104	-	4138	2041	48	42.52	4-42	-	-
1-day Int	69	62	11	1727	110 *	33.86	2	10	14	-	544	490	12	40.83	2-4	-	
C & G	10	9	1	278	105	34.75	1	1	2	-	180	112	7	16.00	3-26	-	
B & H	24	24	4	1018	119	50.90	3	5	10	-	294	197	8	24.62	2-17	-	
1-day Lge	58	58	7	2415	191	47.35	2	18	19	-	1015	724	29	24.96	3-31	-	

LEWIS, J.   Gloucestershire

Name: Jonathan (<u>Jon</u>) Lewis
Role: Right-hand bat,
right-arm fast-medium bowler
Born: 26 August 1975, Aylesbury
Height: 6ft 2in **Weight:** 13st
Nickname: Lewy, JJ, Nugget
County debut: 1995
County cap: 1998
50 wickets in a season: 3
1st-Class 50s: 2
1st-Class 5 w. in innings: 13
1st-Class 10 w. in match: 1
1st-Class catches: 19
Place in batting averages: (2000 286th
av. 8.04)
Place in bowling averages: 19th av. 21.61
(2000 27th av. 20.91)
Strike rate: 50.19 (career 52.18)
Parents: John and Jane
Marital status: Single
Education: Lawn Primary, Swindon; Churchfields Secondary, Swindon;
Swindon College

Qualifications: 9 GCSEs, BTEC in Leisure and Hospitality
Overseas tours: Bath Schools to New South Wales 1993; England A to West Indies 2000-01
Overseas teams played for: Marist, Christchurch, New Zealand 1994-95; Richmond City, Melbourne 1995-96; Wanderers, Johannesburg; Techs CC, Cape Town
Cricketers particularly admired: Courtney Walsh, Jack Russell
Young players to look out for: Chris Taylor, Matt Windows
Other sports played: Golf, football (Bristol North West FC)
Other sports followed: Football (Swindon Town FC)
Injuries: Out from June with a stress fracture of the back
Relaxations: 'Chilling out'
Extras: Was on Northamptonshire staff in 1994 but made no first-team appearance. Took Championship hat-trick (Gallian, Afzaal and Morris) v Nottinghamshire at Trent Bridge 2000. Leading first-class wicket-taker among English bowlers in 2000 with 72 wickets (av. 20.91). Gloucestershire Player of the Year 2000. Drafted into England A squad for tour of West Indies 2000-01 as replacement for the injured Steve Harmison. B&H Gold Award for his 4-23 in the quarter-final v Durham at Bristol 2001
Opinions on cricket: 'You must always be looking to improve your game, at whatever stage you are at. Keep learning every day. We are athletes and must treat ourselves as athletes.'
Best batting: 62 Gloucestershire v Worcestershire, Cheltenham 1999
Best bowling: 8-95 Gloucestershire v Zimbabweans, Gloucester 2000

2001 Season

	M	Inns	NO	Runs	HS	Avge	100s	50s	Ct	St	O	M	Runs	Wkts	Avge	Best	5wI	10wM
Test																		
All First	5	8	7	44	15 *	44.00	-	-	-	-	175.4	56	454	21	21.61	5-71	1	-
1-day Int																		
C & G																			
B & H	6	2	2	6	6 *	-	-	-	-	2	-	60	10	181	10	18.10	4-23	-
1-day Lge	3	2	1	14	12	14.00	-	-	-	-	26	7	74	6	12.33	3-20	-

Career Performances

	M	Inns	NO	Runs	HS	Avge	100s	50s	Ct	St	Balls	Runs	Wkts	Avge	Best	5wI	10wM
Test																	
All First	86	127	25	1206	62	11.82	-	2	19	-	15343	7625	294	25.93	8-95	13	1
1-day Int																	
C & G	7	5	3	14	6 *	7.00	-	-	5	-	380	222	9	24.66	3-27	-
B & H	20	9	5	70	33 *	17.50	-	-	3	-	1062	776	29	26.75	4-23	-
1-day Lge	56	36	14	221	26 *	10.04	-	-	9	-	2266	1826	58	31.48	3-20	-

LEWIS, J. J. B.   Durham

Name: Jonathan (Jon) James Benjamin Lewis
Role: Right-hand bat, county captain
Born: 21 May 1970, Isleworth, Middlesex
Height: 5ft 9in **Weight:** 12st
Nickname: Judge, JJ, Miny-Me
County debut: 1990 (Essex), 1997 (Durham)
County cap: 1994 (Essex), 1998 (Durham)
1000 runs in a season: 3
1st-Class 50s: 44
1st-Class 100s: 12
1st-Class 200s: 1
1st-Class catches: 90
One-Day 100s: 1
Place in batting averages: 105th av. 32.25
(2000 138th av. 24.80)
Strike rate: (career 120.00)
Parents: Ted and Nina
Wife and date of marriage: Fiona,
6 July 1999
Family links with cricket: Father played county schools. Uncle is a lifelong Somerset supporter. Sister is right-arm medium-fast bowler for Cisco
Education: King Edward VI School, Chelmsford; Roehampton Institute of Higher Education
Qualifications: 5 O-levels, 3 A-levels, BSc (Hons) Sports Science, NCA Senior Coach
Off-season: Playing and coaching in South Africa
Overseas teams played for: Old Hararians, Zimbabwe 1991-92; Taita District, New Zealand 1992-93; Eshowe and Zululand 1994-95; Richards Bay 1996-97; Empangeni, Natal 1997-98; Eshowe, South Africa 1998-2002
Cricketers particularly admired: John Childs, Greg Matthews, Alan Walker, Shane Warne
Young players to look out for: Nicky Peng
Other sports followed: Soccer (West Ham United), rugby (Newcastle Falcons), basketball, 'most sports really'
Relaxations: Sleep
Extras: Hit century on first-class debut in Essex's final Championship match of the 1990 season. Joined Durham for the 1997 season – 'I am slowly learning the local dialect'. Scored a double century on his debut for Durham (210* v Oxford University), placing him in a small club, alongside Peter Bowler and Neil Taylor, of players who have scored centuries on debut for two different counties. Captain of Durham since the latter stages of the 2000 season. Scored 112 v Nottinghamshire at Riverside 2001, in the process sharing in Durham's highest Championship partnership for any wicket (258) with Martin Love

Opinions on cricket: 'Central contracts appear to be working well.'
Best batting: 210* Durham v Oxford University, The Parks 1997
Best bowling: 1-73 Durham v Surrey, Riverside 1998

2001 Season

	M	Inns	NO	Runs	HS	Avge	100s	50s	Ct	St	O	M	Runs	Wkts	Avge	Best	5wI	10wM
Test																		
All First	17	32	1	1000	129	32.25	3	3	6	-								
1-day Int																		
C & G	3	3	2	92	65 *	92.00	-	1	-	-								
B & H	6	5	2	174	59 *	58.00	-	1	1	-								
1-day Lge	13	12	3	373	76 *	41.44	-	3	1	-								

Career Performances

	M	Inns	NO	Runs	HS	Avge	100s	50s	Ct	St	Balls	Runs	Wkts	Avge	Best	5wI	10wM
Test																	
All First	140	249	22	7624	210 *	33.58	13	44	90	-	120	121	1	121.00	1-73	-	-
1-day Int																	
C & G	15	15	3	236	65 *	19.66	-	1	1	-							
B & H	26	25	6	628	67	33.05	-	3	5	-							
1-day Lge	116	102	23	2312	102	29.26	1	14	18	-	8	35	0	-		-	-

LEWRY, J. D.   Sussex

Name: <u>Jason</u> David Lewry
Role: Left-hand bat, left-arm fast-medium bowler
Born: 2 April 1971, Worthing
Height: 6ft 3in **Weight:** 14st 7lbs ('depending on time of year!')
Nickname: Lewie, Urco
County debut: 1994
County cap: 1996
50 wickets in a season: 4
1st-Class 5 w. in innings: 20
1st-Class 10 w. in match: 3
1st-Class catches: 17
Place in batting averages: 228th av. 14.42 (2000 289th av. 7.84)
Place in bowling averages: 38th av. 26.23 (2000 91st av. 29.60)
Strike rate: 52.08 (career 48.63)
Parents: David and Veronica
Wife and date of marriage: Naomi Madeleine, 18 August 1997
Children: William Jason Joseph, 14 February 1998; Louis, 20 November 2000
Family links with cricket: Father coaches

Education: Thomas à Becket, Worthing; Durrington High School, Worthing; Worthing Sixth Form College
Qualifications: 6 O-levels, 3 GCSEs, City and Guilds, NCA Award
Career outside cricket: 'Still looking, but with more urgency with each passing year!'
Overseas tours: Goring CC to Isle of Wight 1992, 1993; England A to Zimbabwe and South Africa 1998-99
Cricketers particularly admired: David Gower, Martin Andrews
Young players to look out for: 'Swing bowlers'
Other sports played: Golf, squash; darts, pool
Other sports followed: Football (West Ham United)
Relaxations: Golf, pub games, films
Extras: Hat-trick v Gloucestershire at Cheltenham 1998, taking the final wicket of the Glos first innings and then striking with his first two balls in the second. Had match figures of 13-79 v Hampshire at Hove 2001, including a hat-trick (Kenway, Kendall, R. Smith), five first-ballers in all and a burst of seven wickets in 14 balls bridging the two innings. Granted a benefit for 2002
Best batting: 47 Sussex v Gloucestershire, Hove 2001
Best bowling: 7-38 Sussex v Derbyshire, Derby 1999

2001 Season

	M	Inns	NO	Runs	HS	Avge	100s	50s	Ct	St	O	M	Runs	Wkts	Avge	Best	5wI	10wM
Test																		
All First	17	18	4	202	47	14.42	-	-	7	-	512.1	126	1548	59	26.23	7-42	3	1
1-day Int																		
C & G	2	1	0	16	16	16.00	-	-	-	-	20	3	86	4	21.50	3-43	-	
B & H																		
1-day Lge	2	1	0	0	0	0.00	-	-	-	-	18	2	78	2	39.00	1-37	-	

Career Performances

	M	Inns	NO	Runs	HS	Avge	100s	50s	Ct	St	Balls	Runs	Wkts	Avge	Best	5wI	10wM
Test																	
All First	91	126	27	965	47	9.74	-	-	17	-	16051	8489	330	25.72	7-38	20	3
1-day Int																	
C & G	8	5	3	35	16	17.50	-	-	-	-	504	330	15	22.00	4-42	-	
B & H	12	8	2	69	14 *	11.50	-	-	-	-	624	498	10	49.80	2-32	-	
1-day Lge	32	17	6	43	10 *	3.90	-	-	5	-	1330	1072	44	24.36	4-29	-	

LIPTROT, C. G.   Worcestershire

Name: <u>Christopher</u> George Liptrot
Role: Left-hand bat, right-arm
fast-medium bowler
Born: 13 February 1980, Wigan
Height: 6ft 3in **Weight:** 13st 9lbs
Nickname: Lippy
County debut: 1999
1st-Class 50s: 1
1st-Class 5 w. in innings: 2
1st-Class catches: 9
Place in batting averages: 237th av. 12.80
Place in bowling averages: 48th av. 27.60
Strike rate: 52.91 (career 56.20)
Parents: Brian and Susan
Marital status: Single
Family links with cricket: 'My father and
brother played local league cricket in Wigan'
Education: Highfield Primary School; The
Deanery High School, Wigan
Qualifications: 9 GCSEs
Off-season: 'I will be playing grade cricket in Perth'
Overseas tours: Northwest Select XI to South Africa 1998; Forest Nomads to
Thailand 2000
Overseas teams played for: Sunshine Coast, Brisbane 1999-2000
Career highlights to date: 'Taking five wickets [5-51] on home debut against
Surrey 1999'
Cricketers particularly admired: Glenn McGrath, Graeme Hick
Young players to look out for: Kabir Ali
Other sports played: Football, rugby
Other sports followed: Football (Everton FC), rugby league (Wigan Warriors)
Relaxations: Music, spending time with friends
Extras: Represented England U19 in one-day and 'Test' series v Australia U19 1999.
NBC Denis Compton Award 1999. Worcestershire scholarship to Perth 2001.
Worcestershire Supporters' Association Uncapped Player of the Year 2001
Best batting: 61 Worcestershire v Warwickshire, Edgbaston 1999
Best bowling: 6-44 Worcestershire v Warwickshire, Worcester 2000

2001 Season

	M	Inns	NO	Runs	HS	Avge	100s	50s	Ct	St	O	M	Runs	Wkts	Avge	Best	5wl	10wM
Test																		
All First	12	14	4	128	22	12.80	-	-	4	-	308.4	80	966	35	27.60	3-12	-	-
1-day Int																		
C & G	1	1	1	2	2 *	-	-	-	-	-	5	2	12	2	6.00	2-12	-	
B & H	1	1	0	3	3	3.00	-	-	1	-	4	1	11	0	-		-	-
1-day Lge	2	0	0	0	0	-	-	-	1	-	10	0	59	1	59.00	1-41	-	

Career Performances

	M	Inns	NO	Runs	HS	Avge	100s	50s	Ct	St	Balls	Runs	Wkts	Avge	Best	5wl	10wM
Test																	
All First	27	33	11	271	61	12.31	-	1	9	-	3485	1955	62	31.53	6-44	2	-
1-day Int																	
C & G	1	1	1	2	2 *	-	-	-	-	-	30	12	2	6.00	2-12	-	
B & H	1	1	0	3	3	3.00	-	-	1	-	24	11	0	-		-	-
1-day Lge	6	3	3	18	15 *	-	-	-	1	-	163	176	6	29.33	3-44	-	

LLOYD, G. D.   Lancashire

Name: <u>Graham</u> David Lloyd
Role: Right-hand bat, right-arm medium bowler
Born: 1 July 1969, Accrington
Height: 5ft 9in **Weight:** 12st 10lbs
Nickname: Bumble
County debut: 1988
County cap: 1992
Benefit: 2001
One-Day Internationals: 5
1000 runs in a season: 5
1st-Class 50s: 59
1st-Class 100s: 21
1st-Class 200s: 3
1st-Class catches: 136
One-Day 100s: 3
Place in batting averages: (2000 102nd av. 28.95)
Strike rate: (career 169.50)
Parents: David and Susan
Wife and date of marriage: Sharon, 11 October 1997
Children: Joseph, 20 December 1998

Family links with cricket: Father played for Lancashire and England
Education: Peel Park Primary; Hollins County High School, Accrington
Qualifications: 3 O-levels, Level 2 coaching certificate
Career outside cricket: Bookmaker
Off-season: Contracted for 12 months
Overseas tours: England A to Australia 1992-93; Lancashire CCC to Guernsey 1995; England VI to Hong Kong 1997; England to Bangladesh (Wills International Cup) 1998
Overseas teams played for: Maroochydore CC, Queensland 1988-89 and 1991-95
Cricketers particularly admired: Steve Waugh
Young players to look out for: James Anderson, Kyle Hogg
Other sports played: Football, tennis
Other sports followed: Football (Manchester United)
Injuries: Bad back
Relaxations: Horse racing
Extras: Won the EDS Walter Lawrence Trophy (for the fastest century of the season) two years running: 1996 (70 balls v Essex) and 1997 (73 balls v Leicestershire). Lancashire Player of the Year 1996. Scored 109 before lunch (having been 17* overnight; eventually out for 126) v Somerset at Old Trafford 2000
Opinions on cricket: 'People are too quick to blame county cricket if England do badly. No mention of anything when England do well.'
Best batting: 241 Lancashire v Essex, Chelmsford 1996
Best bowling: 1-4 Lancashire v Warwickshire, Edgbaston 1996

2001 Season

	M	Inns	NO	Runs	HS	Avge	100s	50s	Ct	St	O	M	Runs	Wkts	Avge	Best	5wI	10wM
Test																		
All First	3	4	0	19	9	4.75	-	-	3	-								
1-day Int																		
C & G	4	2	1	11	6 *	11.00	-	-	-	-								
B & H	5	4	0	59	27	14.75	-	-	1	-								
1-day Lge	10	9	1	249	56	31.12	-	2	1	-								

Career Performances

	M	Inns	NO	Runs	HS	Avge	100s	50s	Ct	St	Balls	Runs	Wkts	Avge	Best	5wI	10wM
Test																	
All First	196	310	27	10830	241	38.26	24	59	136	-	339	440	2	220.00	1-4	-	-
1-day Int	5	4	1	39	22	13.00	-	-	2	-							
C & G	31	24	4	602	96	30.10	-	3	7	-	30	35	1	35.00	1-23	-	-
B & H	54	45	12	876	81 *	26.54	-	3	9	-	30	50	0	-	-	-	-
1-day Lge	179	163	28	4103	134	30.39	3	22	40	-	12	18	0	-	-	-	-

LOGAN, R. J.　　　　　　　　　Nottinghamshire

Name: <u>Richard</u> James Logan
Role: Right-hand bat, right-arm fast bowler
Born: 28 January 1980, Stone, Staffs
Height: 6ft 1in **Weight:** 13st 9lbs
Nickname: Gus, Logie
County debut: 1999 (Northants),
2001 (Notts)
1st-Class 5 w. in innings: 4
1st-Class catches: 6
One-Day 5 w. in innings: 1
Place in batting averages: 239th av. 12.46
(2000 294th av. 7.28)
Place in bowling averages: 69th av. 31.97
(2000 134th av. 41.18)
Strike rate: 45.93 (career 50.35)
Marital status: Single
Family links with cricket: Father played for
local club Cannock as batsman/wicket-keeper
Education: Walhouse C of E School, Cannock; Wolverhampton Grammar School
Qualifications: 11 GCSEs, 1 A-level, coaching awards (hockey and cricket)
Overseas tours: England U17 to Bermuda (International Youth Tournament) 1997;
England U19 to South Africa (including U19 World Cup) 1997-98, to New Zealand
1998-99
Overseas teams played for: St George, Sydney 1999-2000
Cricketers particularly admired: Sir Richard Hadlee, Malcolm Marshall
Young players to look out for: Mark Powell
Other sports played: Hockey (Cannock – 'also played for Staffordshire from age 9
and for Midlands U14')
Other sports followed: Football (Wolverhampton Wanderers)
Relaxations: 'Spending time with my mates. Training'
Extras: Played for Staffordshire at every level from U11 to U19, and as captain from
U13 to U17. Played for Midlands U14 and U15 (both as captain) and HMC Schools
U15. 1995 *Daily Telegraph*/Lombard U15 Midlands Bowler and Batsman of the Year.
Played for Northamptonshire U17 and U19 national champions in 1997. Has played
for England U15, U17 and U19, including one-day and 'Test' series v Australia U19
1999. Left Northamptonshire in the 2000-01 off-season and joined Nottinghamshire
for 2001. C&G Man of the Match award for his 5-24 v Suffolk at Mildenhall 2001; it
was his maiden one-day five-wicket return
Opinions on cricket: 'Two divisions have been good for the game. The season
doesn't end until there is nothing to play for, which happens very seldom when there
are two divisions. I still think there is too much cricket played, which means that the
quality of cricket isn't as high as it could be.'

Best batting: 37* Nottinghamshire v Hampshire, Trent Bridge 2001
Best bowling: 6-93 Nottinghamshire v Derbyshire, Trent Bridge 2001

2001 Season

	M	Inns	NO	Runs	HS	Avge	100s	50s	Ct	St	O	M	Runs	Wkts	Avge	Best	5wI	10wM
Test																		
All First	10	15	2	162	37 *	12.46	-	-	4	-	329.1	53	1375	43	31.97	6-93	3	-
1-day Int																		
C & G	2	1	0	0	0	0.00	-	-	1	-	20	3	53	6	8.83	5-24	1	
B & H	2	0	0	0	0	-	-	-	-	-	19	0	59	4	14.75	2-19	-	
1-day Lge	9	7	3	58	24	14.50	-	-	3	-	65.2	1	420	10	42.00	2-37	-	

Career Performances

	M	Inns	NO	Runs	HS	Avge	100s	50s	Ct	St	Balls	Runs	Wkts	Avge	Best	5wI	10wM
Test																	
All First	18	25	3	214	37 *	9.72	-	-	6	-	3122	2006	62	32.35	6-93	4	-
1-day Int																	
C & G	2	1	0	0	0	0.00	-	-	1	-	120	53	6	8.83	5-24	1	
B & H	4	1	0	1	1	1.00	-	-	-	-	216	160	7	22.85	3-52	-	
1-day Lge	15	10	3	83	24	11.85	-	-	5	-	553	603	13	46.38	2-31	-	

LOUDON, A. G. R.   Kent

Name: <u>Alexander</u> Guy Rushworth Loudon
Role: Right-hand top-order bat, right-arm
off-spin bowler
Born: 6 September 1980, London
Height: 6ft 3in **Weight:** 14st 8lbs
Nickname: Noisy, Minor
County debut: No first-team appearance
1st-Class catches: 1
Strike rate: 40.00 (career 40.00)
Parents: Jane and James
Marital status: Single
Family links with cricket: Brother and
father played for Hampshire 2nd XI
Education: Wellesley House; Eton College;
Durham University
Qualifications: 9 GCSEs, 1 AO-level,
3 A-levels, ECB Level 1 coaching
Off-season: Studying
Overseas tours: Kent U11 to Holland 1990; Eton College to South Africa 1995;

England U19 to Malaysia and (U19 World Cup) Sri Lanka 1999-2000; Kent to South Africa 2002
Career highlights to date: 'Captaining England U15 and U19 in two youth World Cups'
Cricket moments to forget: 'Stumbling onto my bum after ducking a ball bowled by Andrew Flintoff during my first first-class cricket match!'
Cricketers particularly admired: Michael Atherton, Nasser Hussain, Steve Waugh
Young players to look out for: Sam Northeast
Other sports played: Rugby (Durham University 1st XV), golf, squash, rackets
Other sports followed: Football (Man Utd), rugby (Newcastle Falcons)
Injuries: Out for first two months of season with back injury from rugby
Relaxations: 'Sky Sports, reading, eating, sleeping!'
Extras: Len Newbery Award for Best Schools Cricketer 1999. NBC Denis Compton Award for the most promising young Kent player 1999. Played for Durham University CCE 2001. Played for Kent Board XI in the second round of the C&G 2002, which was played in September 2001. Played for the Eton Ramblers *Cricketer* Cup winning side 2001, scoring 64 in the final
Opinions on cricket: '1. There should be fewer matches to enable players to practise and rest more. 2. The game needs to sell itself more to the public and media to maintain and enhance supporter bases.'
Best batting: 39 DUCCE v Lancashire, Durham 2001
Best bowling: 3-86 DUCCE v Worcestershire, Worcester 2001

2001 Season (did not make any first-class or one-day appearances)

Career Performances

	M	Inns	NO	Runs	HS	Avge	100s	50s	Ct	St	Balls	Runs	Wkts	Avge	Best	5wI	10wM
Test																	
All First	2	2	0	42	39	21.00	-	-	1	-	120	86	3	28.66	3-86	-	-
1-day Int																	
C & G	1	1	0	53	53	53.00	-	1	-	-	6	4	0	-		-	-
B & H																	
1-day Lge																	

54. Which county won the last ever Gillette Cup and in which year?

LOVE, M. L.   Durham

Name: <u>Martin</u> Lloyd Love
Role: Right-hand bat, right-arm
off-spin bowler
Born: 30 March 1974, Mundubbera,
Queensland
Height: 6ft **Weight:** 13st
Nickname: Lovey, Handles
County debut: 2001
County cap: 2001
1000 runs in a season: 1
1st-Class 50s: 38
1st-Class 100s: 16
1st-Class 200s: 2
1st-Class catches: 129
Place in batting averages: 29th av. 50.51
Strike rate: (career 6.00)
Parents: Ormond and Evelyn
Marital status: Single

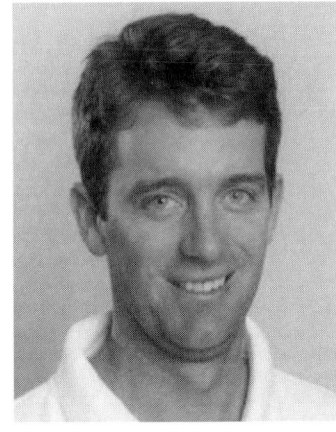

Education: Mundubbera State School; Toowoomba Grammar School;
University of Queensland
Qualifications: Bachelor of Physiotherapy
Career outside cricket: Physiotherapist
Off-season: Playing for Queensland Bulls
Overseas tours: Australia U19 to New Zealand 1992-93; Australia A to England 1995
Overseas teams played for: Queensland Bulls 1992-93 –
Career highlights to date: 'Winning Sheffield Shield with Queensland (their first
ever) in 1994-95'
Cricket moments to forget: 'Getting out twice on the same day of a match'
Cricketers particularly admired: Allan Border
Young players to look out for: Nicky Peng
Other sports played: Golf, tennis
Other sports followed: AFL (Brisbane Lions), rugby union (Queensland)
Injuries: Out for two weeks with two broken fingers; for three weeks with a
broken thumb
Relaxations: 'Going to movies; renovating home in Brisbane'
Extras: Represented Queensland U17 and U19. Made debut for Queensland in 1992-
93 Sheffield Shield final v New South Wales. Shared with Stuart Law in record third-
wicket partnership for Queensland (326), v Tasmania at Brisbane 1994-95. Scored
century (146) in 1994-95 Sheffield Shield final v South Australia at Brisbane. Shared
with Matthew Hayden in record second-wicket partnership for Queensland (368*), v
Tasmania at Hobart 1995-96. Scored century (100) in 1999-2000 Pura Milk Cup final

v Victoria at Albion. Played for Weybridge in the Surrey Championship in 1999 and for part of 2000. Scored 76 for Australia A v West Indies at Hobart 2000-01. Won the Ian Healy Trophy for Queensland Player of the Year 2000-01. Australian Cricket Board central contract 2001-02. Scored his first century for Durham (149*) v Nottinghamshire at Riverside 2001, in the process sharing in Durham's highest Championship partnership for any wicket (258) with Jon Lewis

Opinions on cricket: 'Too much cricket is played, leading to too many good cricketers being injured and so reducing the overall standard. Less matches would mean more intensity in each game and a much better quality for spectators to watch.'

Best batting: 228 Queensland v New South Wales, Brisbane 1999-2000

Best bowling: 1-5 Queensland v Western Australia, Brisbane 1997-98

2001 Season

	M	Inns	NO	Runs	HS	Avge	100s	50s	Ct	St	O	M	Runs	Wkts	Avge	Best	5wI	10wM
Test																		
All First	15	29	2	1364	149 *	50.51	1	13	20	-								
1-day Int																		
C & G	3	3	0	109	51	36.33	-	1	1	-								
B & H	4	4	0	105	59	26.25	-	1	4	-								
1-day Lge	13	13	1	431	89	35.91	-	2	8	-	2	0	7	0	-		-	-

Career Performances

	M	Inns	NO	Runs	HS	Avge	100s	50s	Ct	St	Balls	Runs	Wkts	Avge	Best	5wI	10wM
Test																	
All First	105	182	13	7647	228	45.24	18	38	129	-	6	5	1	5.00	1-5	-	-
1-day Int																	
C & G	3	3	0	109	51	36.33	-	1	1	-							
B & H	4	4	0	105	59	26.25	-	1	4	-							
1-day Lge	13	13	1	431	89	35.91	-	2	8	-	12	7	0	-		-	-

55. Whose 36-ball hundred v Devon in the 1990 NatWest remains the fastest century in the Gillette/NatWest/C&G?

LOYE, M. B.   Northamptonshire

Name: <u>Malachy</u> Bernard Loye
Role: Right-hand bat, off-spin bowler
Born: 27 September 1972, Northampton
Height: 6ft 2in **Weight:** 13st 7lbs
Nickname: Mal, Chairman
County debut: 1991
County cap: 1994
1000 runs in a season: 2
1st-Class 50s: 34
1st-Class 100s: 15
1st-Class 200s: 1
1st-Class 300s: 1
1st-Class catches: 68
One-Day 100s: 3
Place in batting averages: 21st av. 55.72
(2000 99th av. 29.64)
Parents: Patrick and Anne
Marital status: Single

Family links with cricket: Father and brother both played for Cogenhoe CC
in Northampton
Education: Brixworth Primary School; Moulton Comprehensive School
Qualifications: GCSEs and senior coaching certificate
Overseas tours: England U18 to Canada 1991; England U19 to Pakistan 1991-92;
England A to South Africa 1993-94, to Zimbabwe and South Africa 1998-99;
Northamptonshire to Cape Town 1993, to Zimbabwe 1995, 1998, to Johannesburg 1996
Overseas teams played for: Riccarton, Christchurch, New Zealand 1992-95; Onslow,
Wellington, New Zealand 1995-96; North Perth, Australia 1997-98
Cricketers particularly admired: Wayne Larkins ('talent'), Gordon Greenidge
('power'), Curtly Ambrose ('ultimate cricketer')
Young players to look out for: Monty Panesar
Other sports played: Swimming, boxing
Other sports followed: Football (Northampton Town and Liverpool FC), rugby union
(Ireland), boxing
Relaxations: 'Playing the guitar, going out to bars, swimming and sleeping'
Extras: Played for England U19 in the home series against Australia U19 in 1991 and
against Sri Lanka U19 in 1992. Voted Professional Cricketers' Association Young
Player of the Year and Whittingdale Young Player of the Year 1993. With Northants
following on v Yorkshire at Northampton in 1996, shared a county record opening
stand of 372 with Richard Montgomerie. His 322* v Glamorgan in 1998 was the
highest individual first-class score for the county until surpassed in 2001 by Mike
Hussey's 329*; during his innings, Loye put on 401 for the fifth wicket with David

Ripley, setting a new fifth wicket record for first-class cricket in England. Voted the PCA's Player of the Year in 1998. C&G Man of the Match award for his 124* v Northamptonshire Board XI at Northampton 2001

Best batting: 322* Northamptonshire v Glamorgan, Northampton 1998

2001 Season

	M	Inns	NO	Runs	HS	Avge	100s	50s	Ct	St	O	M	Runs	Wkts	Avge	Best	5wI	10wM
Test																		
All First	12	21	3	1003	197	55.72	3	4	4	-								
1-day Int																		
C & G	2	2	1	153	124 *	153.00	1	-	-	-								
B & H	5	5	0	137	77	27.40	-	1	1	-								
1-day Lge	9	9	2	284	90	40.57	-	3	2	-								

Career Performances

	M	Inns	NO	Runs	HS	Avge	100s	50s	Ct	St	Balls	Runs	Wkts	Avge	Best	5wI	10wM
Test																		
All First	138	221	22	7581	322 *	38.09	17	34	68	-	13	43	0	-	-	-	-
1-day Int																		
C & G	19	18	4	482	124 *	34.42	1	1	4	-								
B & H	28	28	5	688	77	29.91	-	4	9	-								
1-day Lge	108	104	9	2969	122	31.25	2	20	21	-								

56. Who scored 104 for Warwickshire as they reached 322-5 batting second to beat Sussex in the NatWest final 1993?

LUCAS, D. S.   Nottinghamshire

Name: <u>David</u> Scott Lucas
Role: Right-hand bat, left-arm
fast-medium bowler
Born: 19 August 1978, Nottingham
Height: 6ft 3in **Weight:** 'Too heavy, so I
hear!'
Nickname: Muke, Lukey, Luko
County debut: 1999
1st-Class 5 w. in innings: 1
1st-Class catches: 3
Place in batting averages: 209th av. 18.12
(2000 127th av. 26.28)
Place in bowling averages: (2000 106th
av. 32.88)
Strike rate: 88.50 (career 59.24)
Parents: Mary and Terry
Marital status: With partner
Education: Horsendale Primary School;
Djanogly City Technology College, Nottingham
Qualifications: 6 GCSEs, pass in Computer-Aided Design
Off-season: Playing cricket for Wanneroo in Perth, Australia
Overseas tours: England (Indoor) to Australia (Indoor Cricket World Cup) 1998
Overseas teams played for: Bankstown-Canterbury Bulldogs, Sydney 1996-97;
Wanneroo, Perth 2001-02
Career highlights to date: 'Getting Man of the Match against Derbyshire in a
close fixture'
Cricket moments to forget: 'The whole of 2001. Enough said!'
Cricketers particularly admired: Wasim Akram, Glenn McGrath, Steve Waugh,
Damien Martyn
Young players to look out for: Kevin Pietersen, Derek Kenway, 'M'goo; Colin, my
club captain'
Other sports played: Indoor cricket, football
Other sports followed: Football (Arsenal, 'keep an eye on Forest'), rugby league
(Wigan Warriors)
Relaxations: 'Food (enjoy cooking), cars, movies, music'
Extras: Won Yorkshire League with Rotherham in 1996. NBC Denis Compton Award
for the most promising young Nottinghamshire player 2000
Opinions on cricket: 'Nice to see the pitches have improved, but unfortunately
someone has decided to use tennis balls on them! It's not rocket science, chiefs! Good
pitches + good balls = good cricket!'
Best batting: 46* Nottinghamshire v Middlesex, Trent Bridge 2000
Best bowling: 5-104 Nottinghamshire v Essex, Trent Bridge 1999

2001 Season

	M	Inns	NO	Runs	HS	Avge	100s	50s	Ct	St	O	M	Runs	Wkts	Avge	Best	5wl	10wM
Test																		
All First	5	8	0	145	41	18.12	-	-	-	-	118	8	571	8	71.37	3-80	-	-
1-day Int																		
C & G																			
B & H																			
1-day Lge	1	0	0	0	0	-	-	-	-	-								

Career Performances

	M	Inns	NO	Runs	HS	Avge	100s	50s	Ct	St	Balls	Runs	Wkts	Avge	Best	5wl	10wM
Test																	
All First	21	27	8	387	46 *	20.36	-	-	3	-	2962	1853	50	37.06	5-104	1	-
1-day Int																	
C & G	1	1	1	14	14 *	-	-	-	-	-	36	40	0	-	-	-	-
B & H	2	0	0	0	0	-	-	-	-	-	54	61	1	61.00	1-33	-	
1-day Lge	16	5	1	28	19 *	7.00	-	-	2	-	657	592	19	31.15	4-27	-	

LUMB, M. J.   *Yorkshire*

Name: <u>Michael</u> John Lumb
Role: Left-hand bat, right-arm medium bowler
Born: 12 February 1980, Johannesburg, South Africa
Height: 6ft **Weight:** 13st
Nickname: Bird Doo, Lugpuss
County debut: 2000
1st-Class 50s: 2
1st-Class 100s: 1
Place in batting averages: 81st av. 36.33
Strike rate: 12.00 (career 12.00)
Parents: Richard and Susan
Marital status: Single
Family links with cricket: Father played for Yorkshire. Uncle played for Natal
Education: Montrose Primary School; St Stithians College
Qualifications: Matriculation
Overseas tours: Transvaal U19 to Barbados
Overseas teams played for: Pirates CC, Johannesburg; Wanderers CC, Johannesburg
Cricketers particularly admired: 'My father', Graham Thorpe, Darren Gough, Craig White, Jacques Kallis

Young players to look out for: Grant Elliott, Matthew Hoggard, Joe Sayers
Other sports played: Rugby ('1st team at school'), golf, football
Other sports followed: Rugby union (Super-12)
Injuries: Twisted knee
Relaxations: Surfing, reading, socialising with friends
Extras: Has Yorkshire 2nd XI cap. Scored 66* on first-class debut v Zimbabweans at Headingley 2000. Scored maiden first-class century (122) v Leicestershire at Headingley 2001; the Lumbs thus became only the fourth father and son to have scored centuries for Yorkshire
Opinions on cricket: 'Splitting the Championship has proved to be exciting and I think it's a good idea. Changes must be made to make the game more appealing to spectators, to get bigger crowds in.'
Best batting: 122 Yorkshire v Leicestershire, Headingley 2001
Best bowling: 2-10 Yorkshire v Kent, Canterbury 2001

2001 Season

	M	Inns	NO	Runs	HS	Avge	100s	50s	Ct	St	O	M	Runs	Wkts	Avge	Best	5wI	10wM
Test																		
All First	4	7	1	218	122	36.33	1	1	-	-	4	1	10	2	5.00	2-10	-	-
1-day Int																		
C & G	2	2	0	41	30	20.50	-	-	-	-								
B & H	7	5	1	52	20*	13.00	-	-	3	-								
1-day Lge	7	6	1	124	66	24.80	-	1	2	-								

Career Performances

	M	Inns	NO	Runs	HS	Avge	100s	50s	Ct	St	Balls	Runs	Wkts	Avge	Best	5wI	10wM
Test																	
All First	5	9	2	286	122	40.85	1	2	-	-	24	10	2	5.00	2-10	-	-
1-day Int																	
C & G	2	2	0	41	30	20.50	-	-	-	-							
B & H	7	5	1	52	20*	13.00	-	-	3	-							
1-day Lge	7	6	1	124	66	24.80	-	1	2	-							

LUNGLEY, T.   Derbyshire

Name: Thomas (<u>Tom</u>) Lungley
Role: Left-hand bat, right-arm medium bowler
Born: 25 July 1979, Derbyshire
Height: 6ft 2in **Weight:** 13st
Nickname: Lungo
County debut: 2000
Place in batting averages: 224th av. 15.42

Place in bowling averages: 125th av. 43.91
Strike rate: 57.83 (career 46.33)
Parents: Richard and Christina
Marital status: Single
Family links with cricket: 'Dad was captain
of Derby Road CC. Grandad was bat maker
in younger days'
Education: Risley Lower Grammar School;
Saint John Houghton School; South East
Derbyshire College
Qualifications: 9 GCSEs, Sport and
Recreation Levels 1 and 2, pool lifeguard
qualification, coaching qualifications in
cricket, tennis, basketball, football and
volleyball
Overseas teams played for: Delacombe
Park, Melbourne 1999-2000
Cricketers particularly admired:
Ian Botham, Dennis Lillee, Courtney Walsh, Curtly Ambrose, Brian Lara, Richard
Hadlee, Glenn McGrath
Other sports played: 'Enjoy playing most sports, mainly football and basketball'
Other sports followed: Football (Derby County), basketball (Derby Storm)
Relaxations: 'Shopping, watching videos, having a laugh with mates'
Extras: First homegrown cricketer to become professional from Ockbrook and
Borrowash CC. Scored 109 in Derbyshire Cup final 2000, winning Man of the Match
award
Opinions on cricket: 'Think two divisions is a good idea, and wish the wages in
cricket were the same as in football.'
Best batting: 47 Derbyshire v Warwickshire, Derby 2001
Best bowling: 3-10 Derbyshire v Cambridge University, Fenner's 2000

2001 Season

	M	Inns	NO	Runs	HS	Avge	100s	50s	Ct	St	O	M	Runs	Wkts	Avge	Best	5wI	10wM
Test																		
All First	6	11	4	108	47	15.42	-	-	-	-	115.4	14	527	12	43.91	3-58	-	-
1-day Int																		
C & G																		
B & H	1	1	0	0	0	0.00	-	-	-	-	10	0	55	3	18.33	3-55	-	
1-day Lge	8	3	1	55	45	27.50	-	-	1	-	60	6	265	16	16.56	4-28	-	

Career Performances

	M	Inns	NO	Runs	HS	Avge	100s	50s	Ct	St	Balls	Runs	Wkts	Avge	Best	5wI	10wM
Test																	
All First	7	11	4	108	47	15.42	-	-	-	-	834	568	18	31.55	3-10	-	-
1-day Int																	
C & G	1	1	0	3	3	3.00	-	-	-	-	24	24	0	-		-	-
B & H	1	1	0	0	0	0.00	-	-	-	-	60	55	3	18.33	3-55	-	
1-day Lge	11	6	1	100	45	20.00	-	-	1	-	516	369	21	17.57	4-28	-	

MADDY, D. L. Leicestershire

Name: <u>Darren</u> Lee Maddy
Role: Right-hand opening bat, right-arm medium bowler
Born: 23 May 1974, Leicester
Height: 5ft 9in **Weight:** 11st
Nickname: Roaster, Dazza, Fire Starter
County debut: 1993 (one-day), 1994 (first-class)
County cap: 1996
Test debut: 1999
Tests: 3
One-Day Internationals: 8
1000 runs in a season: 2
1st-Class 50s: 27
1st-Class 100s: 13
1st-Class 200s: 1
1st-Class 5 w. in innings: 1
1st-Class catches: 134
One-Day 100s: 5
Place in batting averages: 204th av. 18.60 (2000 128th av. 26.25)
Place in bowling averages: 56th av. 28.71
Strike rate: 50.89 (career 63.87)
Parents: William Arthur and Hilary Jean
Wife and date of marriage: Justine Marie, 7 October 2000
Family links with cricket: Father and younger brother, Greg, play club cricket
Education: Herrick Junior School, Leicester; Roundhills, Thurmaston; Wreake Valley, Syston
Qualifications: 8 GCSEs
Off-season: 'Resting until Christmas. Hopefully playing cricket in the New Year'
Overseas tours: Leicestershire to Bloemfontein 1995, to Western Transvaal 1996, to Durban 1997, to Barbados 1998, to Potchefstroom 2001; England A to Kenya and Sri

Lanka 1997-98, to Zimbabwe and South Africa 1998-99; England to South Africa and Zimbabwe 1999-2000

Overseas teams played for: Wanderers, Johannesburg 1992-93; Northern Free State, South Africa 1993-95; Rhodes University, South Africa 1995-97

Career highlights to date: 'Winning two Championship medals. Playing for England'

Cricket moments to forget: 'Too many to mention. I hate losing a cricket match and I hate getting out – losing two Lord's finals and finishing second in the Norwich Union League'

Cricketers particularly admired: Graham Gooch, Michael Atherton, Ian Botham, Viv Richards, Richard Hadlee

Young players to look out for: Steve Kirby

Other sports played: Touch rugby, golf, squash, 5-a-side football

Other sports followed: Rugby (Leicester Tigers), football (Leicester City), baseball, golf, boxing – 'most sports really except for horse racing and motor racing'

Relaxations: 'Going to the gym, playing sport, spending time with my wife, Justine; listening to music, watching TV, going on holiday, scuba diving, bungee jumping, playing the drums'

Extras: In 1994, set a new 2nd XI Championship run aggregate record (1498) beating the previous one which had stood since 1961 and winning the Rapid Cricketline 2nd XI Championship Player of the Year award. Was leading run-scorer on England A's 1997-98 tour with 687 runs at 68.7. In 1998, set a new record for the number of runs scored in the B&H competition in one season (629), previously held by Graham Gooch (591), also setting a record for the most B&H Gold Awards won in one season (five). Carried his bat (158*) for Leicestershire v Yorkshire at Leicester 1999. Recorded maiden first-class five-wicket return (5-67) v Northamptonshire at Leicester 2001

Opinions on cricket: 'Day/night cricket is a great idea to introduce cricket to the younger generation. Two divisions has proved to be a great idea in both competitions, as this has helped to make each game more competitive through the season. We must play on better pitches, which will then produce better cricketers. To stop home teams preparing wickets to suit their strengths, the opposing captain should have first choice of whether to bat or bowl, without the toss of a coin. Abolish bonus points; only give out points for first innings lead and then for a draw or win.'

Best batting: 202 England A v Kenya, Nairobi 1997-98
Best bowling: 5-67 Leicestershire v Northamptonshire, Leicester 2001

2001 Season

	M	Inns	NO	Runs	HS	Avge	100s	50s	Ct	St	O	M	Runs	Wkts	Avge	Best	5wI	10wM
Test																		
All First	17	29	1	521	111	18.60	1	2	15	-	237.3	45	804	28	28.71	5-67	1	-
1-day Int																		
C & G	5	4	2	118	49	59.00	-	-	1	-	15.5	0	82	0	-		-	-
B & H	5	5	0	133	56	26.60	-	1	2	-	29	0	136	4	34.00	2-13	-	
1-day Lge	16	14	4	279	46 *	27.90	-	-	2	-	92.3	0	464	21	22.09	3-1	-	

Career Performances

	M	Inns	NO	Runs	HS	Avge	100s	50s	Ct	St	Balls	Runs	Wkts	Avge	Best	5wI	10wM
Test	3	4	0	46	24	11.50	-	-	4	-	84	40	0	-	-	-	-
All First	138	218	11	6278	202	30.32	14	27	134	-	3513	1889	55	34.34	5-67	1	-
1-day Int	8	6	0	113	53	18.83	-	1	1	-							
C & G	18	16	2	396	89	28.28	-	2	7	-	296	248	7	35.42	2-38	-	
B & H	32	32	4	1354	151	48.35	4	7	10	-	401	342	10	34.20	3-32	-	
1-day Lge	119	107	13	2568	106 *	27.31	1	16	39	-	1796	1601	65	24.63	4-16	-	

MAHER, J. P. Glamorgan

Name: James (<u>Jimmy</u>) Patrick Maher
Role: Left-hand bat, right-arm
medium bowler
Born: 27 February 1974, Innisfail,
Queensland, Australia
Height: 6ft **Weight:** 13st 5lbs
Nickname: Rock, Mahbo
County debut: 2001
County cap: 2001
One-Day Internationals: 2
1000 runs in a season: 1
1st-Class 50s: 30
1st-Class 100s: 12
1st Class 200s: 2
1st-Class catches: 106
One-Day 100s: 1
Place in batting averages: 23rd av. 53.95
Strike rate: (career 84.00)
Parents: Marie Ann and Warren George
Wife and date of marriage: Debbie, 6 April 2001
Family links with cricket: Father and uncle played for Queensland Country
Education: St Michael's, Gordonvale; St Francis Xavier, Cairns; St Augustine's
College, Cairns; Nudgee College, Brisbane
Career outside cricket: Has part-time radio show
Off-season: Playing cricket for Queensland
Overseas tours: Queensland Academy to South Africa 1993; Australia U19 to
New Zealand
Overseas teams played for: Queensland 1993-94 –
Career highlights to date: 'Playing for Australia. Being part of Queensland's first
ever Sheffield Shield title win at The Gabba [1994-95]'
Cricket moments to forget: 'Running out Allan Border on my debut'

Cricketers particularly admired: Allan Border, Matt Hayden, Shane Warne, Glenn McGrath
Young players to look out for: Mark Wallace, Mitchell Johnson
Other sports played: Squash ('played State titles U12-U16'), tennis ('ranked in top ten in Queensland at U14')
Other sports followed: Rugby union (Queensland Reds), rugby league (Canterbury Bulldogs)
Injuries: Out for about three weeks with a broken finger
Relaxations: 'Golf, dinner with friends, couple of lagers with mates'
Extras: Represented Australia U17 and U19. Attended Australian Cricket Academy 1993. Struck a six at the Gabba that broke the glass in the press box, v Tasmania 1993-94. Scored a century (100*) aged 20 for Queensland against England on their 1994-95 tour of Australia, sharing in an unbroken fifth-wicket partnership of 205 with Andrew Symonds. Scored 102 v Western Australia in the final of the Mercantile Mutual Cup 1999-2000 at Perth. Scored 150 for Australia A v West Indies at Hobart 2000-01. Scored 1142 first-class runs at 63.44 for Queensland and Australia A 2000-01. Can throw both left and right handed. Joined Glamorgan for 2001 as overseas player. Carried his bat for 142* v Gloucestershire in the B&H at Bristol 2001. Awarded Glamorgan cap 2001; released at the end of the 2001 season
Opinions on cricket: 'Don't fiddle around with it too much. We have a great game and all cricketers owe cricket a lot.'
Best batting: 217 Glamorgan v Essex, Cardiff 2001
Best bowling: 3-11 Queensland v Western Australia, Perth 1995-96
Stop press: Selected for the Australian one-day squad for the series in South Africa 2001-02.

2001 Season

	M	Inns	NO	Runs	HS	Avge	100s	50s	Ct	St	O	M	Runs	Wkts	Avge	Best	5wI	10wM
Test																		
All First	14	23	2	1133	217	53.95	4	3	13	-	21	3	88	0	-	-	-	-
1-day Int																		
C & G	1	1	0	30	30	30.00	-	-	1	-								
B & H	5	5	1	182	142 *	45.50	1	-	4	-	9	0	52	1	52.00	1-20	-	
1-day Lge	15	15	1	453	94	32.35	-	3	7	-								

Career Performances

	M	Inns	NO	Runs	HS	Avge	100s	50s	Ct	St	Balls	Runs	Wkts	Avge	Best	5wI	10wM
Test																	
All First	106	185	24	6622	217	41.13	14	30	106	-	840	500	10	50.00	3-11	-	-
1-day Int	2	2	0	21	13	10.50	-	-	-	-							
C & G	1	1	0	30	30	30.00	-	-	1	-							
B & H	5	5	1	182	142 *	45.50	1	-	4	-	54	52	1	52.00	1-20	-	
1-day Lge	15	15	1	453	94	32.35	-	3	7	-							

Name: <u>Gregor</u> Ian Maiden
Role: Right-hand bat, right-arm
off-spin bowler
Born: 22 July 1979, Glasgow
Height: 6ft **Weight:** 10st 7lbs
Nickname: Rusty
County debut: No first-team appearance
Parents: Martin and Lynne
Marital status: Single
Education: Lochfield Primary, Paisley;
Hutchesons Grammar School, Glasgow;
Loughborough University
Qualifications: BSc PE and Sports Science
Career outside cricket: Coach
Off-season: 'Working on game abroad'
Overseas tours: Scotland to Zimbabwe
2000, to Namibia 2001, to Canada (ICC
Trophy) 2001

Overseas teams played for: South Perth 1997; Richmond, Victoria 1998; Randwick-Petersham, Sydney 2001; New Town, Tasmania 2001
Career highlights to date: 'Winning back-to-back BUSA titles with Loughborough University'
Cricket moments to forget: 'Failing to qualify for the 2003 World Cup'
Cricketers particularly admired: Curtly Ambrose, Damien Martyn
Young players to look out for: James Anderson, Steven Gilmour
Other sports played: Hockey, golf, football
Other sports followed: Football (Aberdeen FC)
Relaxations: Films
Extras: Played for Loughborough University CCE 2001. Has represented Scotland, including matches in the NatWest and C&G. Two uncles and grandfather played professional football
Opinions on cricket: 'Too much over-coaching, leading to ruining of natural talent – young players should be allowed to develop more naturally.'

---

57. Which current broadcaster is the only player to have won
three Man of the Match awards in NatWest finals?

2001 Season (did not make any first-class or one-day appearances)

Career Performances

	M	Inns	NO	Runs	HS	Avge	100s	50s	Ct	St	Balls	Runs	Wkts	Avge	Best	5wI	10wM
Test																	
All First																	
1-day Int																	
C & G	5	2	0	3	3	1.50	-	-	2	-	210	130	4	32.50	2-27	-	
B & H																	
1-day Lge																	

MALCOLM, D. E. Leicestershire

Name: <u>Devon</u> Eugene Malcolm
Role: Right-hand bat, right-arm fast bowler
Born: 22 February 1963, Kingston, Jamaica
Height: 6ft 2in **Weight:** 15st 8lbs
Nickname: Dude
County debut: 1984 (Derbyshire),
1998 (Northamptonshire), 2001
(Leicestershire)
County cap: 1989 (Derbyshire),
1999 (Northamptonshire), 2001
(Leicestershire)
Benefit: 1997 (Derbyshire)
Test debut: 1989
Tests: 40
One-Day Internationals: 10
50 wickets in a season: 8
1st-Class 50s: 2
1st-Class 5 w. in innings: 41
1st-Class 10 w. in match: 8
1st-Class catches: 41
One-Day 5 w. in innings: 2
Place in batting averages: 265th av. 9.00 (2000 306th av. 2.66)
Place in bowling averages: 54th av. 28.64 (2000 82nd av. 28.47)
Strike rate: 48.19 (career 50.87)
Parents: Albert and Brendalee (deceased)
Wife and date of marriage: Jennifer, October 1989
Children: Erica Cian, 11 June 1991; Natile Jade, 25 June 1993;
Stephany, 11 July 1995
Education: St Elizabeth Technical High School; Richmond College;
Derby College of Higher Education

Qualifications: O-levels, Diploma in Business Administration, Level II coaching certificate

Overseas tours: England to West Indies 1989-90, to Australia 1990-91, to India and Sri Lanka 1992-93, to West Indies 1993-94, to Australia 1994-95, to South Africa 1995-96; England A to Bermuda and West Indies 1991-92; Christians in Sport to South Africa 2000

Overseas teams played for: Ellerslie, Auckland 1985-87

Cricketers particularly admired: Michael Holding, Sir Richard Hadlee, Sir Viv Richards, Steve Waugh

Young players to look out for: David Sales, Ian Blackwell, Mudhsuden Panesar

Other sports played: Football, table tennis

Other sports followed: Football (Man United), boxing

Relaxations: 'Movies, music, eating, debating with Jenny (wife)'

Extras: Played league cricket for Sheffield Works and Sheffield United; he once took six wickets for no runs off 15 deliveries. Became eligible to play for England in 1987. Had match figures of 10 for 137 v West Indies in Port-of-Spain Test 1989-90. Took 9-57 v South Africa at The Oval in 1994; received the 'Century of Bottles' Award for this best performance against the touring South Africans. Was one of *Wisden*'s Five Cricketers of the Year 1995. Joined Northamptonshire for 1998. Left Northants at the end of the 2000 season and joined Leicestershire for 2001, taking 5-78 v Lancashire at Leicester in his second Championship match for the county. B&H Gold Award for his 3-13 v Lancashire at Leicester 2001. Returned Championship best innings figures of 8-63 v Surrey at Leicester 2001. First bowler to reach 50 first-class wickets in the 2001 season. Awarded Leicestershire cap 2001

Opinions on cricket: 'Two divisions have kept both Championship and one-day league closely contested to the very last games of the season. Competition like this can only develop more competitive cricketers for the national team. Central contracts have already produced much-rested and enthusiastic cricketers (bowlers) for the national team. That's the way to go.'

Best batting: 51 Derbyshire v Surrey, Derby 1989

Best bowling: 9-57 England v South Africa, The Oval 1994

2001 Season

	M	Inns	NO	Runs	HS	Avge	100s	50s	Ct	St	O	M	Runs	Wkts	Avge	Best	5wI	10wM
Test																		
All First	16	21	7	126	50	9.00	-	1	1	-	546.1	94	1948	68	28.64	8-63	4	1
1-day Int																		
C & G	1	0	0	0	0	-	-	-	1	-	6	1	17	1	17.00	1-17	-	
B & H	5	2	0	4	4	2.00	-	-	1	-	32.3	1	168	7	24.00	3-13	-	
1-day Lge	6	2	1	2	2*	2.00	-	-	-	-	33	2	177	5	35.40	3-34	-	

Career Performances

	M	Inns	NO	Runs	HS	Avge	100s	50s	Ct	St	Balls	Runs	Wkts	Avge	Best	5wI	10wM
Test	40	58	19	236	29	6.05	-	-	7	-	8480	4748	128	37.09	9-57	5	2
All First	284	340	105	1820	51	7.74	-	2	41	-	49858	29793	980	30.40	9-57	41	8
1-day Int	10	5	2	9	4	3.00	-	-	1	-	526	404	16	25.25	3-40	-	
C & G	28	13	1	31	10 *	2.58	-	-	2	-	1643	1052	39	26.97	7-35	1	
B & H	43	23	6	114	16	6.70	-	-	6	-	2354	1715	62	27.66	5-27	1	
1-day Lge	92	38	13	155	42	6.20	-	-	10	-	3895	3273	116	28.21	4-21	-	

MALIK, M. N. Nottinghamshire

Name: Muhammad Nadeem Malik
Role: Right-hand bat, right-arm
fast-medium bowler
Born: 6 October 1982, Nottingham
Height: 6ft 5in **Weight:** 14st
Nickname: Nigel, Nige, Gerz
County debut: 2001
1st-Class 5 w. in innings: 1
Place in bowling averages: 119th av. 41.40
Strike rate: 62.40 (career 62.40)
Parents: Abdul and Arshad
Marital status: Single
Education: Meadows Primary School;
Wilford Meadows Secondary School;
Bilborough College
Qualifications: 9 GCSEs
Off-season: England U19 tour to Australia
and New Zealand
Overseas tours: ZRK to Pakistan 2000; Nottinghamshire to South Africa 2001;
England U19 to India 2000-01, to Australia and (U19 World Cup) New Zealand
2001-02
Career highlights to date: '5-57 against Derbyshire 2001'
Cricket moments to forget: 'Norwich Union match v Yorkshire at Scarborough 2001
– Lehmann 191'
Cricketers particularly admired: Glenn McGrath, Wasim Akram, Curtly Ambrose
Young players to look out for: Bilal Shafayat, Gordon Muchall
Other sports played: Football
Other sports followed: Football
Relaxations: Music, games consoles
Extras: Took 15 wickets at an average of 19.40 for Nottinghamshire 2nd XI 2000.
Played for Nottinghamshire Board XI in the NatWest 2000. Represented England U19

v West Indies U19 in one-day series (1/3) 2001. Recorded maiden first-class five-wicket return (5-57) v Derbyshire at Trent Bridge 2001
Best batting: 6* Nottinghamshire v Gloucestershire, Bristol 2001
Best bowling: 5-57 Nottinghamshire v Derbyshire, Trent Bridge 2001

2001 Season

	M	Inns	NO	Runs	HS	Avge	100s	50s	Ct	St	O	M	Runs	Wkts	Avge	Best	5wI	10wM
Test																		
All First	5	6	5	12	6 *	12.00	-	-	-	-	104	21	414	10	41.40	5-57	1	-
1-day Int																		
C & G																		
B & H	2	0	0	0	0	-	-	-	-	-	13	0	62	1	62.00	1-42	-	
1-day Lge	5	2	1	4	3 *	4.00	-	-	-	-	40	3	205	5	41.00	2-34	-	

Career Performances

	M	Inns	NO	Runs	HS	Avge	100s	50s	Ct	St	Balls	Runs	Wkts	Avge	Best	5wI	10wM
Test																	
All First	5	6	5	12	6 *	12.00	-	-	-	-	624	414	10	41.40	5-57	1	-
1-day Int																	
C & G	1	1	1	1	1 *	-	-	-	-	-	36	20	0	-	-	-	-
B & H	2	0	0	0	0	-	-	-	-	-	78	62	1	62.00	1-42	-	
1-day Lge	5	2	1	4	3 *	4.00	-	-	-	-	240	205	5	41.00	2-34	-	

MANN, C.   Durham

Name: Christopher (Chris) Mann
Role: Right-hand bat, right-arm medium bowler
Born: 14 April 1981, South Shields
Height: 6ft 1in **Weight:** 10st 10lbs
Nickname: Norman
County debut: No first-team appearance
Parents: Pat and Harry
Marital status: Single
Family links with cricket: Father has played for Marsden CC for 35 years
Education: Biddick Hall Primary School; Boldon Comprehensive;
South Tyneside College
Qualifications: 6 GCSEs, Level 2 cricket coach
Off-season: Playing for Bulleen CC in Melbourne
Overseas teams played for: Bulleen CC, Melbourne 2001-02
Career highlights to date: 'Being told by Geoff Cook at the end of the 2001 season that I was going to be given a two-year professional contract with Durham'

Cricket moments to forget: 'Injuring my back in the 2000 season and being told by the specialist not to bowl again'
Cricketers particularly admired: Mike Atherton, Steve Waugh
Young players to look out for: Graham Onions, Liam Plunket
Other sports played: Football (South Tyneside; goalkeeper 1988-96)
Other sports followed: Football (Manchester United)
Injuries: Out for two months with a torn side
Relaxations: Listening to music, going to the cinema, relaxing with family and friends
Extras: Captain of Durham Cricket Academy 2001. Played for Durham Board XI in the second round of the C&G 2002, which was played in September 2001

2001 Season (did not make any first-class or one-day appearances)

Career Performances

	M	Inns	NO	Runs	HS	Avge	100s	50s	Ct	St	Balls	Runs	Wkts	Avge	Best	5wI	10wM
Test																	
All First																	
1-day Int																	
C & G	1	1	0	7	7	7.00	-	-	1	-							
B & H																	
1-day Lge																	

58. Who opened the bowling for Lancashire in the 1972 Gillette Cup final, then scored 126 as Lancashire successfully chased 235 to win?

MARSH, D. J.　　　　　Leicestershire

Name: <u>Daniel</u> James Marsh
Role: Right-hand bat, slow left-arm bowler;
all-rounder
Born: 14 June 1973, Subiaco,
Western Australia
Nickname: Marshy
County debut: 2001
1st-Class 50s: 18
1st-Class 100s: 7
1st-Class 5 w. in innings: 1
1st-Class catches: 67
Place in batting averages: 44th av. 46.15
Strike rate: 101.55 (career 86.50)
Family links with cricket: Father, Rodney,
played for Western Australia and Australia
Overseas teams played for: South Australia
1993-94 – 1995-96; Tasmania 1996-97 –
Extras: Attended Australian Cricket

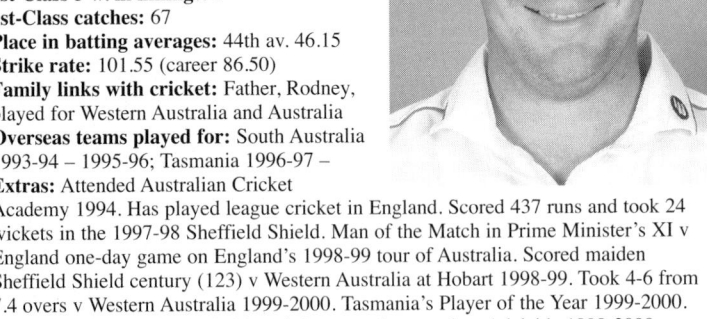

Academy 1994. Has played league cricket in England. Scored 437 runs and took 24
wickets in the 1997-98 Sheffield Shield. Man of the Match in Prime Minister's XI v
England one-day game on England's 1998-99 tour of Australia. Scored maiden
Sheffield Shield century (123) v Western Australia at Hobart 1998-99. Took 4-6 from
7.4 overs v Western Australia 1999-2000. Tasmania's Player of the Year 1999-2000.
Represented Australia A v Pakistanis in a one-day match at Adelaide 1999-2000.
Joined Leicestershire as overseas player for 2001. Took 4-44 and scored a 61-ball 67*
v Nottinghamshire at Oakham School in the Norwich Union League 2001. Season cut
short by a fractured cheekbone; replaced by Shahid Afridi
Best batting: 157 Tasmania v India, Hobart 1999-2000
Best bowling: 7-57 Tasmania v New South Wales, Sydney 1997-98

2001 Season

	M	Inns	NO	Runs	HS	Avge	100s	50s	Ct	St	O	M	Runs	Wkts	Avge	Best	5wI	10wM
Test																		
All First	9	16	3	600	138*	46.15	1	5	13	-	152.2	43	410	9	45.55	2-35	-	-
1-day Int																		
C & G	1	1	0	25	25	25.00	-	-	-	-	10	1	50	1	50.00	1-50	-	
B & H	5	5	0	140	42	28.00	-	-	2	-	23	1	115	1	115.00	1-44	-	
1-day Lge	5	5	2	206	97*	68.66	-	2	3	-	34.4	0	171	6	28.50	4-44	-	

Career Performances

	M	Inns	NO	Runs	HS	Avge	100s	50s	Ct	St	Balls	Runs	Wkts	Avge	Best	5wI	10wM
Test																	
All First	66	109	20	3464	157	38.92	7	18	67	-	10381	4974	120	41.45	7-57	1	-
1-day Int																	
C & G	1	1	0	25	25	25.00	-	-	-	-	60	50	1	50.00	1-50	-	
B & H	5	5	0	140	42	28.00	-	-	2	-	138	115	1	115.00	1-44	-	
1-day Lge	5	5	2	206	97 *	68.66	-	2	3	-	208	171	6	28.50	4-44	-	

MARTIN, P. J. Lancashire

Name: Peter James Martin
Role: Right-hand bat, right-arm
fast-medium bowler
Born: 15 November 1968, Accrington
Height: 6ft 5in **Weight:** 15st 7lbs
Nickname: Digger
County debut: 1989
County cap: 1994
Test debut: 1995
Tests: 8
One-Day Internationals: 19
50 wickets in a season: 2
1st-Class 50s: 6
1st-Class 100s: 1
1st-Class 5 w. in innings: 15
1st-Class 10 w. in match: 1
1st-Class catches: 42
One-Day 5 w. in innings: 6
Place in batting averages: 203rd av. 18.77 (2000 214th av. 16.75)
Place in bowling averages: 59th av. 29.36 (2000 7th av. 15.46)
Strike rate: 58.63 (career 61.15)
Parents: Keith and Catherine Lina
Wife and date of marriage: Bethan, 3 October 1998
Children: Oliver, 14 August 2001
Education: Danum School, Doncaster; UCLAN, Preston
Qualifications: 6 O-levels, 2 A-levels, PGCM (UCLAN), Levels 1 and 2 coaching
certificates
Off-season: Benefit year 2002
Overseas tours: England YC to Australia (U19 World Cup) 1987-88, 'and various
other tours with English Schools and NAYC'; England to South Africa 1995-96, to
India and Pakistan (World Cup) 1995-96, to Sharjah (Champions Trophy) 1997-98,
to Bangladesh (Wills International Cup) 1998-99

Overseas teams played for: Southern Districts, Queensland 1988-89; South Launceston, Tasmania 1989-90; South Canberra, ACT 1990-92
Career highlights to date: 'Playing in Lord's finals with Lancashire and representing England'
Cricketers particularly admired: 'Too many to mention'
Young players to look out for: Kyle Hogg
Other sports played: 'District soccer and basketball while at school; keen golfer'
Other sports followed: Football (Manchester United), rugby league (St Helens)
Injuries: Stress fracture of right fibula
Relaxations: Painting, wine, reading, family
Extras: Played for England A v Sri Lankans 1991. Granted a benefit for 2002
Best batting: 133 Lancashire v Durham, Gateshead Fell 1992
Best bowling: 8-32 Lancashire v Middlesex, Uxbridge 1997

2001 Season

	M	Inns	NO	Runs	HS	Avge	100s	50s	Ct	St	O	M	Runs	Wkts	Avge	Best	5wI	10wM
Test																		
All First	9	12	3	169	51 *	18.77	-	1	2	-	322.3	86	969	33	29.36	5-52	1	-
1-day Int																		
C & G	4	1	1	11	11 *	-	-	-	-	-	34	5	103	10	10.30	5-16	1	
B & H	4	2	2	3	3 *	-	-	-	-	-	38	2	135	5	27.00	2-30	-	
1-day Lge	6	3	1	14	6	7.00	-	-	-	-	48.5	4	216	7	30.85	2-24	-	

Career Performances

	M	Inns	NO	Runs	HS	Avge	100s	50s	Ct	St	Balls	Runs	Wkts	Avge	Best	5wI	10wM
Test	8	13	0	115	29	8.84	-	-	6	-	1452	580	17	34.11	4-60	-	-
All First	180	211	54	2993	133	19.06	1	6	42	-	30700	13937	502	27.76	8-32	15	1
1-day Int	20	13	7	38	6	6.33	-	-	1	-	1048	806	27	29.85	4-44	-	
C & G	27	10	7	105	31 *	35.00	-	-	1	-	1580	908	53	17.13	5-16	2	
B & H	37	12	9	46	11 *	15.33	-	-	12	-	2000	1380	51	27.05	3-31	-	
1-day Lge	119	35	18	191	35 *	11.23	-	-	22	-	4765	3407	150	22.71	5-21	4	

MARTIN-JENKINS, R. S. C. Sussex

Name: Robin Simon Christopher Martin-Jenkins
Role: Right-hand bat, right-arm medium-fast bowler
Born: 28 October 1975, Guildford
Height: 6ft 5in **Weight:** 14st
Nickname: Tucker
County debut: 1995
County cap: 2000
1st-Class 50s: 10

1st-Class 100s: 1
1st-Class 5 w. in innings: 2
1st-Class catches: 15
Place in batting averages: 38th av. 47.63
(2000 152nd av. 22.68)
Place in bowling averages: 68th av. 31.83
(2000 115th av. 36.42)
Strike rate: 62.00 (career 58.50)
Parents: Christopher and Judy
Wife and date of marriage: Flora,
19 February 2000
Family links with cricket: Father is
The Times chief cricket correspondent and
TMS commentator. Brother captains the
Radley Rangers
Education: Cranleigh Prep School, Surrey;
Radley College, Oxon; Durham University
Qualifications: 10 GCSEs, 3 A-levels,

1 AS-level, Grade 3 bassoon (with merit), BA (Hons) Social Sciences, Don Mackenzie
School of Professional Photography Certificate
Career outside cricket: Weekly columnist for *Brighton Evening Argus*
Off-season: 'Getting fitter, stronger and faster'
Overseas tours: Radley College to Barbados 1992; Sussex U19 to Sri Lanka 1995;
Durham University to Vienna 1995; MCC to Kenya 1999; Sussex to Grenada 2001
Overseas teams played for: Lima CC, Peru 1994; Bellville CC, Cape Town 2000-01
Career highlights to date: 'Maiden first-class century in same match that Sussex won
to take the division two title'
Cricket moments to forget: 'How could I choose just one moment?'
Cricketers particularly admired: Angus Fraser, Robin Smith, Jon Bond, Nick Hoyle,
Dave Lawrence
Young players to look out for: Krishna Singh
Other sports played: Golf, tennis, fives
Other sports followed: Tennis, skiing, football (Liverpool FC)
Injuries: Out for ten weeks with a torn side muscle
Relaxations: TV, film, photography
Extras: European Player of the Year, Vienna 1995. Played for ESCA from U15 to
U19. *Daily Telegraph* Bowling Award 1994. Best Performance Award for Sussex 1998.
NBC Denis Compton Award for the most promising young Sussex player 1998, 1999,
2000. Scored maiden first-class century (113) v Gloucestershire at Hove 2001,
including 109 between lunch and tea on the first day
Opinions on cricket: 'Regional cricket a must. More time for practice. England A tour
should be reinstated. Pitches improved massively this year but practice facilities still
very poor.'
Best batting: 113 Sussex v Gloucestershire, Hove 2001
Best bowling: 7-54 Sussex v Glamorgan, Hove 1998

2001 Season

	M	Inns	NO	Runs	HS	Avge	100s	50s	Ct	St	O	M	Runs	Wkts	Avge	Best	5wl	10wM
Test																		
All First	9	15	4	524	113	47.63	1	3	4	-	248	63	764	24	31.83	4-18	-	-
1-day Int																		
C & G																		
B & H	4	4	1	27	12 *	9.00	-	-	-	-	35.2	2	151	6	25.16	3-42	-	
1-day Lge	7	5	2	82	38	27.33	-	-	5	-	49	4	202	8	25.25	3-20	-	

Career Performances

	M	Inns	NO	Runs	HS	Avge	100s	50s	Ct	St	Balls	Runs	Wkts	Avge	Best	5wl	10wM
Test																	
All First	53	84	10	1936	113	26.16	1	10	15	-	7430	3830	127	30.15	7-54	2	-
1-day Int																	
C & G	2	1	0	16	16	16.00	-	-	-	-	120	52	4	13.00	2-24	-	
B & H	20	17	1	181	45	11.31	-	-	2	-	1031	751	29	25.89	4-57	-	
1-day Lge	54	36	3	332	44	10.06	-	-	18	-	2238	1534	47	32.63	3-20	-	

MASCARENHAS, A. D.   Hampshire

Name: Adrian <u>Dimitri</u> Mascarenhas
Role: Right-hand bat, right-arm
medium bowler
Born: 30 October 1977, Chiswick, London
Height: 6ft 2in **Weight:** 11st 7lbs
Nickname: Dimmie, Genii, Gibson
County debut: 1996
County cap: 1998
1st-Class 50s: 11
1st-Class 100s: 2
1st-Class 5 w. in innings: 4
1st-Class catches: 26
Place in batting averages: 156th av. 24.83
(2000 172nd av. 20.56)
Place in bowling averages: 33rd av. 25.37
(2000 81st av. 28.42)
Strike rate: 59.92 (career 65.64)
Parents: Malik and Pauline
Marital status: Single
Family links with cricket: Uncle played in Sri Lanka and brothers both play for
Melville CC in Perth, WA
Education: Our Lady's Primary, Melbourne; Trinity College, Perth

Overseas teams played for: Melville CC, Perth 1991-2000
Cricketers particularly admired: Viv Richards, Malcolm Marshall, the Waugh twins
Other sports followed: Aussie Rules (Collingwood)
Relaxations: Aussie Rules, tennis, golf, 'occasional scenario'
Extras: Played for Western Australia at U17 and U19 level as captain. Won NatWest Man of the Match awards in semi-final v Lancashire 1998 (3-28 and 73) and in quarter-final v Middlesex 2000 (4-25). Put on 90 for the tenth wicket with Simon Francis v Surrey at The Oval 2000, the pair falling just two runs short of pulling off a remarkable Championship victory. Scorer of the first Championship century recorded at the Rose Bowl (104) v Worcestershire 2001
Best batting: 104 Hampshire v Worcestershire, West End 2001
Best bowling: 6-26 Hampshire v Middlesex, West End 2001

2001 Season

	M	Inns	NO	Runs	HS	Avge	100s	50s	Ct	St	O	M	Runs	Wkts	Avge	Best	5wl	10wM
Test																		
All First	15	23	5	447	104	24.83	1	1	8	-	399.3	112	1015	40	25.37	6-26	2	-
1-day Int																		
C & G	1	1	1	35	35 *	-	-	-	-	-	8	2	41	0	-		-	-
B & H	4	3	0	34	25	11.33	-	-	-	-	30	6	134	3	44.66	2-30	-
1-day Lge	15	13	1	167	53	13.91	-	1	4	-	125	17	441	21	21.00	2-11	-

Career Performances

	M	Inns	NO	Runs	HS	Avge	100s	50s	Ct	St	Balls	Runs	Wkts	Avge	Best	5wl	10wM
Test																	
All First	70	102	11	2104	104	23.12	2	11	26	-	9125	4393	139	31.60	6-26	4	-
1-day Int																	
C & G	11	10	4	287	73	47.83	-	2	2	-	546	303	18	16.83	4-25	-
B & H	16	15	2	237	53	18.23	-	2	-	-	660	472	11	42.90	4-28	-
1-day Lge	68	58	6	921	79	17.71	-	6	21	-	2579	1901	78	24.37	3-9	-

---

59. Which England leg-spinner took a Gillette Cup hat-trick for Essex v Middlesex at Lord's in the 1968 competition?

MASON, T. J.   Essex

Name: <u>Timothy</u> James Mason
Role: Right-hand middle-order bat,
off-spin bowler
Born: 12 April 1975, Leicester
Height: 5ft 9in **Weight:** 10st 8lbs
Nickname: Biffa, Perry, Stone
County debut: 1994 (Leicestershire),
2000 (Essex)
1st-Class 50s: 1
1st-Class 5 w. in innings: 1
1st-Class catches: 8
Place in batting averages: (2000 257th
av. 11.66)
Place in bowling averages: (2000 142nd
av. 50.71)
Strike rate: 39.00 (career 90.50)
Parents: Phillip John and Anthea Jane
Marital status: Single
Family links with cricket: Father plays club cricket and is manager of Leicestershire
Schools U11
Education: Brookvale High School, Leicester; Denstone College
Qualifications: 9 GCSEs, 3 A-levels
Overseas tours: Denstone College to South Africa 1993; England U19 to Sri Lanka
1993-94; Westgold CC to Northern Transvaal 1996; Leicestershire to Sri Lanka 1999
Overseas teams played for: Eastern Freestate, South Africa 1994-95; Westgold CC,
Western Transvaal 1995-97
Cricketers particularly admired: Allan Lamb, Malcolm Marshall, Jon Dakin,
Darren 'Roasting' Maddy
Other sports followed: Rugby union (Leicester Tigers), football (Leicester City)
Relaxations: 'Going out with girlfriend and friends; listening to most types of music;
watching virtually all sports'
Extras: Captained Leicestershire Schools at all age levels. 1992 *Daily Telegraph* U19
Midlands Bowler of the Year; 1993 *Daily Telegraph* U19 National Bowler of the Year;
1993 Gray-Nicolls Outstanding Schoolboy Player of the Year. Dislocated shoulder
prevented him from going on England U18 tour to South Africa 1992-93. Played in the
Leicestershire 2nd XI team that won the Bain Hogg Trophy in 1996. Left
Leicestershire at end of the 1999 season and joined Essex for 2000. Recorded maiden
first-class five-wicket return (5-40) v Cambridge University CCE at Fenner's 2001.
Released by Essex at the end of the 2001 season
Best batting: 52* Essex v Glamorgan, Cardiff 2000
Best bowling: 5-40 Essex v CUCCE, Fenner's 2001

2001 Season

	M	Inns	NO	Runs	HS	Avge	100s	50s	Ct	St	O	M	Runs	Wkts	Avge	Best	5wI	10wM
Test																		
All First	3	5	2	85	41 *	28.33	-	-	-	-	39	13	98	6	16.33	5-40	1	-
1-day Int																		
C & G	2	2	2	25	18 *	-	-	-	-	-	13	3	31	1	31.00	1-14	-	
B & H	2	2	1	12	12	12.00	-	-	1	-	20	0	91	5	18.20	3-40	-	
1-day Lge	8	6	3	33	12	11.00	-	-	-	-	35.2	0	183	1	183.00	1-47	-	

Career Performances

	M	Inns	NO	Runs	HS	Avge	100s	50s	Ct	St	Balls	Runs	Wkts	Avge	Best	5wI	10wM
Test																	
All First	20	25	5	311	52 *	15.55	-	1	8	-	2715	1252	30	41.73	5-40	1	-
1-day Int																	
C & G	9	7	2	105	36	21.00	-	-	3	-	408	222	4	55.50	3-29	-	
B & H	10	6	3	73	30	24.33	-	-	3	-	498	362	15	24.13	3-40	-	
1-day Lge	63	42	17	221	21 *	8.84	-	-	16	-	1910	1674	34	49.23	4-12	-	

MASTERS, D. D.   Kent

Name: <u>David</u> Daniel Masters
Role: Right-hand bat, right-arm medium-fast bowler
Born: 22 April 1978, Chatham
Height: 6ft 4ins **Weight:** 12st 5lbs
Nickname: Hod, Race Horse, Hoddy
County debut: 2000
1st-Class 5 w. in innings: 3
1st-Class catches: 6
Place in batting averages: (2000 299th av. 5.46)
Place in bowling averages: (2000 51st av. 24.18)
Strike rate: 75.42 (career 57.09)
Parents: Kevin and Tracey
Marital status: Single
Family links with cricket:
'Dad was on staff at Kent 1983-86'

Education: Luton Junior School; Fort Luton High School; Mid-Kent College
Qualifications: 8 GCSEs, GNVQ in Leisure and Tourism, qualified coach in cricket, football and athletics, bricklayer and plasterer
Career outside cricket: Builder

Overseas teams played for: Double View, Perth 1998-99
Cricketers particularly admired: Ian Botham
Young players to look out for: 'My brother Daniel Masters', James Hockley
Other sports played: Football, boxing 'and most other sports'
Other sports followed: Football (Manchester United)
Relaxations: 'Going out with mates'
Extras: His 6-27 v Durham at Tunbridge Wells 2000 included a final spell of 4-9 from 10.2 overs. Joint Kent Player of the Year 2000 (with Martin Saggers). NBC Denis Compton Award for the most promising young Kent player 2000
Opinions on cricket: 'Great game.'
Best batting: 21 Kent v Hampshire, Canterbury 2000
Best bowling: 6-27 Kent v Durham, Tunbridge Wells 2000

2001 Season

	M	Inns	NO	Runs	HS	Avge	100s	50s	Ct	St	O	M	Runs	Wkts	Avge	Best	5wI	10wM
Test																		
All First	4	3	2	8	6	8.00	-	-	2	-	88	16	279	7	39.85	3-52	-	-
1-day Int																		
C & G																		
B & H	4	1	0	6	6	6.00	-	-	-	-	23.4	2	105	1	105.00	1-20	-	
1-day Lge																		

Career Performances

	M	Inns	NO	Runs	HS	Avge	100s	50s	Ct	St	Balls	Runs	Wkts	Avge	Best	5wI	10wM
Test																	
All First	20	23	9	79	21	5.64	-	-	6	-	3140	1440	55	26.18	6-27	3	-
1-day Int																	
C & G	2	1	0	1	1	1.00	-	-	-	-	109	59	1	59.00	1-23	-	
B & H	6	2	1	18	12 *	18.00	-	-	1	-	202	136	2	68.00	1-19	-	
1-day Lge	14	9	2	33	10 *	4.71	-	-	2	-	595	433	9	48.11	2-10	-	

MAUNDERS, J. K. Middlesex

Name: John Kenneth Maunders
Role: Left-hand opening bat, right-arm medium bowler
Born: 4 April 1981, Ashford, Middlesex
Height: 5ft 10in **Weight:** 13st
Nickname: Chop
County debut: 1999
1st-Class catches: 1
Parents: Kenneth and Lynn
Marital status: Single

Family links with cricket: Grandfather and two uncles play club cricket (Thames Valley Ramblers)

Education: Ashford Park Primary School; Ashford High School; Spelthorne College of Further Education

Qualifications: 10 GCSEs, coaching award

Career outside cricket: Administration clerk for Pacemaker Distribution; cricket coach

Off-season: Three months in Perth playing for University; working on game

Overseas tours: England U19 to New Zealand 1998-99, to Malaysia and (U19 World Cup) Sri Lanka 1999-2000

Overseas teams played for: University, Perth 2001-02

Career highlights to date: 'Representing England U19 and Middlesex 1st XI'

Cricket moments to forget: 'Glen "Weazel" Nash hitting me for 24 in an over and claiming my wicket twice!!'

Cricketers particularly admired: Michael Atherton, Justin Langer, Shaun Pollock

Young players to look out for: Ian Bell, Mark Wallace

Other sports followed: Football ('no particular team')

Relaxations: Spending time with girlfriend Lauren; eating out, socialising with friends; 'partial to the odd game of Boggle'

Extras: Awarded junior county cap at the age of 12. Has been Seaxe Player of Year. Represented England U17 and U19. NBC Denis Compton Award 1999. Played for Middlesex Board XI in the C&G 2001

Best batting: 9 Middlesex v Cambridge University, Fenner's 1999

2001 Season

	M	Inns	NO	Runs	HS	Avge	100s	50s	Ct	St	O	M	Runs	Wkts	Avge	Best	5wI	10wM
Test																		
All First																		
1-day Int																		
C & G	1	1	0	11	11	11.00	-	-	-	-	2.1	0	18	0	-		-	-
B & H																		
1-day Lge	2	2	0	55	49	27.50	-	-	1	-								

Career Performances

	M	Inns	NO	Runs	HS	Avge	100s	50s	Ct	St	Balls	Runs	Wkts	Avge	Best	5wI	10wM
Test																	
All First	1	2	0	13	9	6.50	-	-	1	-							
1-day Int																	
C & G	1	1	0	11	11	11.00	-	-	-	-	13	18	0	-		-	-
B & H																	
1-day Lge	2	2	0	55	49	27.50	-	-	1	-							

MAYNARD, M. P. Glamorgan

Name: <u>Matthew</u> Peter Maynard
Role: Right-hand bat, occasional wicket-keeper
Born: 21 March 1966, Oldham, Lancashire
Height: 5ft 11in **Weight:** 13st
Nickname: Ollie, Wilf
County debut: 1985
County cap: 1987
Benefit: 1996
Test debut: 1988
Tests: 4
One-Day Internationals: 14
1000 runs in a season: 10
1st-Class 50s: 117
1st-Class 100s: 45
1st-Class 200s: 3
1st-Class catches: 332
1st-Class stumpings: 7
One-Day 100s: 13

Place in batting averages: 119th av. 31.05 (2000 65th av. 34.09)
Strike rate: (career 185.16)
Parents: Ken (deceased) and Pat
Wife and date of marriage: Susan, 27 September 1986
Children: Tom, 25 March 1989; Ceri Lloyd, 5 August 1993
Family links with cricket: Father played for many years for Duckinfield. Brother Charles plays for St Fagans. Son Tom plays
Education: Ysgol David Hughes, Menai Bridge, Anglesey
Qualifications: Cricket coach
Career outside cricket: 'Ice cream taster'
Off-season: 'Captaining England VI to Hong Kong. Working for Thomas, Carroll (Group) Ltd. Fixing up my 1974 Beetle Cabriolet'

Overseas tours: North Wales XI to Barbados 1982; Glamorgan to Barbados 1982, to South Africa 1993; unofficial England XI to South Africa 1989-90; HKCC (Australia) to Bangkok and Hong Kong 1990; England VI to Hong Kong 1992, 1994, 2001 (captain); England to West Indies 1993-94; England XI to New Zealand (Cricket Max) 1997 (captain)

Overseas teams played for: St Joseph's, Whakatane, New Zealand 1986-88; Gosnells, Perth, Western Australia 1988-89; Papakura and Northern Districts, New Zealand 1990-92; Morrinsville College and Northern Districts 1991-92; Otago, New Zealand 1996-97

Career highlights to date: 'Leading Glamorgan to the County Championship in 1997. Playing for England'

Cricket moments to forget: 'Playing unsuccessfully for England'

Cricketers particularly admired: Ian Botham, Viv Richards, David Gower

Young players to look out for: Tom Maynard

Other sports played: Golf, football

Other sports followed: Rugby (Pentyrch U13), football (Pentyrch U12)

Relaxations: 'Spending time with my wife and family and relaxing'

Extras: Scored century on first-class debut v Yorkshire at Swansea in 1985, reaching his 100 with three successive straight sixes and becoming the youngest centurion for Glamorgan; he scored 1000 runs in his first full season. In 1987 set record for fastest 50 for Glamorgan (14 mins) v Yorkshire and became youngest player to be awarded Glamorgan cap. Voted Young Cricketer of the Year 1988 by the Cricket Writers' Club. Banned from Test cricket for five years for joining 1989-90 tour of South Africa; ban remitted 1992. Scored 987 runs in July 1991, including a century in each innings v Gloucestershire at Cheltenham. His 243 v Hampshire at Southampton 1991 is the highest score by a Glamorgan No. 4. Captained Glamorgan for most of 1992 in Alan Butcher's absence. Glamorgan captain 1996-2000. Voted Wombwell Cricket Lovers' Society captain of the year for 1997. Was one of *Wisden*'s Five Cricketers of the Year 1998. Appointed honorary fellow of University of Wales, Bangor. Set new Glamorgan one-day record stand for third wicket (204) with Jacques Kallis in National League match v Surrey at Pontypridd 1999. Passed 20,000 first-class runs during his 186 in Glamorgan's first innings v Yorkshire at Headingley 1999. Won Gold Award in the B&H Cup Final 2000 for his 104 from 118 balls, having also won the award in the semi-final v Surrey for his 109 from 115 balls

Opinions on cricket: 'Why are people so keen to criticise our national team? I wish they could be a lot more upbeat and get behind the team.'

Best batting: 243 Glamorgan v Hampshire, Southampton 1991

Best bowling: 3-21 Glamorgan v Oxford University, The Parks 1987

2001 Season

	M	Inns	NO	Runs	HS	Avge	100s	50s	Ct	St	O	M	Runs	Wkts	Avge	Best	5wI	10wM
Test																		
All First	13	20	0	621	145	31.05	1	3	6	-	1	1	0	0	-	-	-	-
1-day Int																		
C & G	2	2	1	110	93 *	110.00	-	1	3	1								
B & H	5	5	0	204	63	40.80	-	2	2	-								
1-day Lge	16	16	6	527	116 *	52.70	1	3	7	2								

Career Performances

	M	Inns	NO	Runs	HS	Avge	100s	50s	Ct	St	Balls	Runs	Wkts	Avge	Best	5wI	10wM
Test	4	8	0	87	35	10.87	-	-	3	-							
All First	350	569	56	21518	243	41.94	48	117	332	7	1111	861	6	143.50	3-21	-	-
1-day Int	14	12	1	156	41	14.18	-	-	3	-							
C & G	44	42	4	1669	151 *	43.92	2	13	23	1	18	8	0	-	-	-	-
B & H	59	59	6	2325	151 *	43.86	6	11	19	-	30	38	0	-	-	-	-
1-day Lge	227	219	22	6468	132	32.83	5	42	95	4	64	64	1	64.00	1-13	-	

McCAGUE, M. J.   Kent

Name: <u>Martin</u> John McCague
Role: Right-hand bat, right-arm fast bowler
Born: 24 May 1969, Larne, Northern Ireland
Height: 6ft 5in **Weight:** 17st 2lbs
Nickname: Munga, Macca
County debut: 1991
County cap: 1992
Test debut: 1993
Tests: 3
50 wickets in a season: 4
1st-Class 50s: 6
1st-Class 5 w. in innings: 25
1st-Class 10 w. in match: 2
1st-Class catches: 75
One-Day 5 w. in innings: 3
Place in batting averages: (2000 207th av. 17.36)
Place in bowling averages: (2000 90th av. 29.42)
Strike rate: 81.00 (career 50.27)
Parents: Mal and Mary
Wife and date of marriage: Leigh-Anne, 8 February 1997

Children: Monte Frederick, 15 September 1998; Clarry Richard, 21 March 2001
Education: Hedland Senior High School
Qualifications: Electrician
Off-season: 'Time with family, working and a bit of golf'
Overseas tours: England A to South Africa 1993-94; England to Australia 1994-95;
Kent Cricket Board XI to West Indies 1998-99
Overseas teams played for: Western Australia 1990-91
Career highlights to date: 'First Test cap and Kent cap'
Cricket moments to forget: 'Too many to mention'
Cricketers particularly admired: Paul Strang, Courtney Walsh
Young players to look out for: Alex Loudon, James Tredwell, Monte McCague
Other sports played: Golf
Other sports followed: Football (Crystal Palace FC), American football
Relaxations: Family time
Extras: Kent Player of the Year in 1996. Struck 20-ball 50 v Leicestershire Foxes in
National League at Canterbury 2000. Granted a benefit for 2002
Opinions on cricket: 'Players need to keep supporting the PCA in all their efforts to
make our efforts more enjoyable and secure.'
Best batting: 72 Kent v Yorkshire, Canterbury 2000
Best bowling: 9-86 Kent v Derbyshire, Derby 1994

2001 Season

	M	Inns	NO	Runs	HS	Avge	100s	50s	Ct	St	O	M	Runs	Wkts	Avge	Best	5wI	10wM
Test																		
All First	2	1	0	4	4	4.00	-	-	-	-	27	5	99	2	49.50	1-28	-	-
1-day Int																		
C & G																		
B & H	5	4	0	12	11	3.00	-	-	-	-	23	0	137	2	68.50	1-30	-	
1-day Lge	2	2	0	9	5	4.50	-	-	1	-	12.1	1	55	2	27.50	2-21	-	

Career Performances

	M	Inns	NO	Runs	HS	Avge	100s	50s	Ct	St	Balls	Runs	Wkts	Avge	Best	5wI	10wM
Test	3	5	0	21	11	4.20	-	-	1	-	593	390	6	65.00	4-121	-	-
All First	135	186	45	2324	72	16.48	-	6	75	-	22924	12392	456	27.17	9-86	25	2
1-day Int																	
C & G	16	12	7	126	31 *	25.20	-	-	4	-	882	592	22	26.90	5-26	1	
B & H	35	23	8	181	30	12.06	-	-	7	-	1670	1323	41	32.26	5-43	1	
1-day Lge	104	58	16	436	56	10.38	-	1	18	-	3946	3386	136	24.89	5-40	1	

McGARRY, A. C.   Essex

Name: <u>Andrew</u> Charles McGarry
Role: Right-hand bat, right-arm
fast-medium bowler
Born: 8 November 1981, Basildon
Height: 6ft 5in **Weight:** 12st 7lbs
Nickname: Rodders
County debut: 1999
1st-Class catches: 2
Place in bowling averages: 146th av. 63.70
Strike rate: 88.80 (career 73.50)
Parents: Christine and George
Marital status: Single
Family links with cricket: Father played,
and eldest brother plays recreational cricket
Education: Widford Lodge Preparatory
School, Chelmsford; King Edward VI GS,
Chelmsford; South East Essex College of
Arts and Technology, Southend
Qualifications: 9 GCSEs, Level 1 and 2 ECB coaching awards
Career outside cricket: Student
Overseas tours: England U19 to India 2000-01
Cricketers particularly admired: Ian Botham, Allan Donald
Young players to look out for: Justin Bishop, Monty Panesar, Mark Pettini
Other sports played: Basketball, volleyball, football
Other sports followed: Football (Aston Villa)
Relaxations: Going out, listening to music
Extras: First Brian Johnston Scholarship winner 1996. NBC Denis Compton Award
for the most promising young Essex player 2000. Represented England U19 v West
Indies U19 in one-day series (1/3) and 'Test' series (2/3) 2001
Opinions on cricket: 'Two division cricket has created a much more competitive
season.'
Best batting: 4* Essex v Kent, Tunbridge Wells 2001
Best bowling: 3-29 Essex v Worcestershire, Chelmsford 2000

---

60. In which year did the county board 'recreational' sides
join the NatWest competition?

2001 Season

	M	Inns	NO	Runs	HS	Avge	100s	50s	Ct	St	O	M	Runs	Wkts	Avge	Best	5wl	10wM
Test																		
All First	6	8	6	5	4 *	2.50	-	-	2	-	148	19	637	10	63.70	3-77	-	-
1-day Int																		
C & G																		
B & H	3	1	1	0	0 *	-	-	-	-	-	25	1	98	4	24.50	2-34	-	
1-day Lge	5	1	0	1	1	1.00	-	-	1	-	12	0	71	2	35.50	1-26	-	

Career Performances

	M	Inns	NO	Runs	HS	Avge	100s	50s	Ct	St	Balls	Runs	Wkts	Avge	Best	5wl	10wM
Test																	
All First	10	12	9	6	4 *	2.00	-	-	2	-	1470	1013	20	50.65	3-29	-	-
1-day Int																	
C & G																	
B & H	3	1	1	0	0 *	-	-	-	-	-	150	98	4	24.50	2-34	-	
1-day Lge	9	2	1	1	1	1.00	-	-	1	-	174	134	4	33.50	2-20	-	

McGRATH, A.   Yorkshire

Name: Anthony McGrath
Role: Right-hand bat, right-arm medium bowler
Born: 6 October 1975, Bradford
Height: 6ft 1in **Weight:** 14st
Nickname: Gripper, Mags
County debut: 1995
County cap: 1999
1st-Class 50s: 21
1st-Class 100s: 8
1st-Class catches: 63
One-Day 100s: 2
Place in batting averages: 106th av. 32.07 (2000 104th av. 28.84)
Strike rate: 34.00 (career 63.05)
Parents: Terry and Kathleen
Marital status: Single
Family links with cricket: Brother Dermot plays in the Bradford League. 'Sisters Anne and Catherine could have played for England Ladies. Nephews Aidan, Thomas and Niall are future stars'
Education: St Winefrides; St Blaize; Yorkshire Martyrs Collegiate School
Qualifications: 9 GCSEs, BTEC National Diploma in Leisure Studies, senior coaching award

433

Overseas tours: England U19 to West Indies 1994-95; England A to Pakistan 1995-96, to Australia 1996-97; MCC to Bangladesh 1999-2000
Overseas teams played for: Deep Dene, Melbourne 1998-99
Cricketers particularly admired: Darren Lehmann, Nasser Hussain, Ronnie Irani, Robin Smith
Other sports played: Football (Green Man FC)
Other sports followed: Football (Manchester United)
Relaxations: Watching football. Music. Socialising with friends
Extras: Captained Yorkshire Schools U13, U14, U15 and U16; captained English Schools U17. Bradford League Young Cricketer of the Year 1992 and 1993. Played for England U17, and for England U19 in home series against India U19 1994. Appeared as 12th man for England in the first Test against West Indies at Headingley in 1995
Best batting: 142* Yorkshire v Middlesex, Headingley 1999
Best bowling: 3-18 Yorkshire v Surrey, The Oval 1999

2001 Season

	M	Inns	NO	Runs	HS	Avge	100s	50s	Ct	St	O	M	Runs	Wkts	Avge	Best	5wl	10wM
Test																		
All First	9	15	2	417	116 *	32.07	1	2	6	-	17	4	53	3	17.66	2-22	-	-
1-day Int																		
C & G	1	1	0	82	82	82.00	-	1	1	-								
B & H	5	5	0	128	46	25.60	-	-	3	-								
1-day Lge	9	9	0	344	102	38.22	1	1	1	-	0.3	0	1	1	1.00	1-1	-	

Career Performances

	M	Inns	NO	Runs	HS	Avge	100s	50s	Ct	St	Balls	Runs	Wkts	Avge	Best	5wl	10wM
Test																	
All First	102	173	12	4717	142 *	29.29	8	21	63	-	1135	581	18	32.27	3-18	-	-
1-day Int																	
C & G	15	14	1	502	84	38.61	-	5	6	-	42	37	0	-	-	-	-
B & H	27	25	1	639	109 *	26.62	1	1	11	-	12	10	2	5.00	2-10	-	
1-day Lge	79	72	13	1908	102	32.33	1	12	23	-	273	188	8	23.50	2-20	-	

McLEAN, R. A. Northamptonshire

Name: <u>Ross</u> Alexander McLean
Role: Right-hand bat, right-arm medium bowler
Born: 16 March 1981, Northampton
Height: 6ft 3in **Weight:** 13st 7lbs
Nickname: Gibbon
County debut: No first-team appearance
Parents: Val and Peter

Marital status: 'Long-term relationship'
Education: Duston C of E Lower School;
Reylands Middle School; Duston Upper
School; University of Leeds
Qualifications: 3 A-levels, ECB Level 1
cricket coach, hockey and basketball awards
Career outside cricket: University student
Off-season: 'Sleeping, socialising, reading on
various topics, and, well, I suppose, studying'
Overseas tours: Northamptonshire U19 to
South Africa 2000
Career highlights to date: 'Playing under
floodlights in Boland was quite nice'
Cricket moments to forget:
'All of my ducks!'
Cricketers particularly admired:
Alec Swann, David Capel, Learie Constantine
Young players to look out for:
Dave Paynter, Rob 'Bob' White
Other sports played: Hockey, badminton
Other sports followed: Football (Northampton Town), rugby (Northampton Saints)
Injuries: Out for one week with a back injury; for one week with an ankle injury
Relaxations: 'TV, films, sleeping'
Extras: Played for Northamptonshire Board XI in NatWest 2000. Played for
Bradford/Leeds University CCE 2001
Opinions on cricket: 'A lot of TV commentators talk rubbish. Three-day cricket
should be reintroduced. There exists a dependence on the word "positive" and a
strange belief that in conjunction with the word "thinking" can produce or lead to
desired results with little regard to other aspects.'

2001 Season (did not make any first-class or one-day appearances)

Career Performances

	M	Inns	NO	Runs	HS	Avge	100s	50s	Ct	St		Balls	Runs	Wkts	Avge	Best	5wI	10wM
Test																		
All First																		
1-day Int																		
NatWest	1	1	1	10	10 *	-	-	-	-	-		60	21	1	21.00	1-21	-	
B & H																		
1-day Lge																		

MEES, T.   Warwickshire

Name: Thomas (<u>Tom</u>) Mees
Role: Right-hand bat, right-arm
fast-medium bowler
Born: 8 June 1981, Wolverhampton
Height: 6ft 3in **Weight:** 13st
Nickname: Meesy, Meesdog
County debut: No first-team appearance
1st-Class 5 w. in innings: 1
1st-Class catches: 1
Strike rate: 57.85 (career 57.85)
Parents: Mark and Christina
Marital status: Single
Family links with cricket: 'Cousin Simon
played for Worcestershire Youth. Dad played
for Cosely and umpires'

Education: Worcester Royal Grammar Prep
School; Worcester Royal Grammar School;
King Edward VI College, Stourbridge;
Oxford Brookes University
Qualifications: 9 GCSEs, 3 A-levels, ECB Level 1 coaching award
Off-season: Studying marketing and retail management at university; tour to South
Africa with British Universities cricket team
Overseas tours: British Universities to South Africa 2002
Overseas teams played for: Railways, Albany, Western Australia 1999-2000
Career highlights to date: 'Taking 6-64 v Middlesex on first-class debut for
Oxford UCCE 2001'
Cricket moments to forget: 'Playing in a Birmingham League match for Old Hill v
Walsall, mistaking the umpire for the wicket-keeper and throwing the ball over the
umpire's head for four overthrows off the last ball of the game with the opposition
needing two to win!'
Cricketers particularly admired: Ian Botham, Andrew Flintoff
Young players to look out for: James Dalrymple, Matt Stillwell, Patrick Wolff,
Ian Bell, Graham Wagg
Other sports played: Golf, football, tennis
Other sports followed: Football (Liverpool FC)
Relaxations: Playing golf, spending time with friends, shopping, going out
Extras: Played for Worcestershire Board XI in the NatWest 1999. Has played for
Warwickshire 2nd XI. Played for Oxford University CCE in 2001. Played for
Warwickshire Board XI in the C&G 2001 and in the first and second rounds of the
C&G 2002, which were played in August and September 2001. Recorded maiden
first-class five-wicket return (6-64) for OUCCE on first-class debut v Middlesex at
The Parks 2001

Opinions on cricket: 'Regional cricket should be introduced at start of season and against tourists as a trial, and then possibly used more frequently. Day/night cricket should be played more frequently. County Championship could be divided into three divisions.'

Best batting: 4 OUCCE v Warwickshire, The Parks 2001
Best bowling: 6-64 OUCCE v Middlesex, The Parks 2001

2001 Season (did not make any first-class or one-day appearances)

Career Performances

	M	Inns	NO	Runs	HS	Avge	100s	50s	Ct	St	Balls	Runs	Wkts	Avge	Best	5wl	10wM
Test																	
All First	2	2	0	8	4	4.00	-	-	1	-	405	222	7	31.71	6-64	1	-
1-day Int																	
C & G	4	2	1	4	4 *	4.00	-	-	-	-	198	144	3	48.00	3-19	-	
B & H																	
1-day Lge																	

MIDDLEBROOK, J. D.   Essex

Name: <u>James</u> Daniel Middlebrook
Role: Right-hand bat, off-spin bowler
Born: 13 May 1977, Leeds
Height: 6ft 1in   **Weight:** 13st
Nickname: Midi, Midders, Midhouse
County debut: 1998 (Yorkshire)
1st-Class 50s: 1
1st-Class 5 w. in innings: 1
1st-Class 10 w. in match: 1
1st-Class catches: 14
Place in batting averages: (2000 241st av. 13.40)
Place in bowling averages: (2000 55th av. 24.87)
Strike rate: 98.40 (career 64.57)
Parents: Ralph and Mavis
Marital status: Single
Family links with cricket: 'Dad is a senior staff coach'

Education: Greenside, Pudsey; Crawshaw, Pudsey ('at these schools with Paul Hutchison')
Qualifications: NVQ Level 2 in Coaching Sport and Recreation, ECB senior coach

Off-season: Playing in Australia
Overseas tours: Yorkshire CCC to Guernsey
Overseas teams played for: Stokes Valley CC, New Zealand; Gold Coast Dolphins, Brisbane; Surfers Paradise CC, Brisbane
Cricketers particularly admired: John Emburey, Ian Botham
Young players to look out for: Matthew Wood, Matthew Hoggard, 'Me!'
Other sports played: Golf, tennis, squash, badminton
Other sports followed: Football (Leeds United), athletics
Relaxations: 'Any music – MTV – sleeping, socialising, catching up with old friends'
Extras: Played for Pudsey Congs from age of seven. Played for Yorkshire at all age levels U11 to 1st XI. Awarded Yorkshire 2nd XI cap 1998. His maiden first-class five-wicket return (6-82) v Hampshire at Southampton 2000 included a spell of four wickets in five balls. Released by Yorkshire at the end of the 2001 season and has joined Essex for 2002
Best batting: 84 Yorkshire v Essex, Chelmsford 2001
Best bowling: 6-82 Yorkshire v Hampshire, Southampton 2000

2001 Season

	M	Inns	NO	Runs	HS	Avge	100s	50s	Ct	St	O	M	Runs	Wkts	Avge	Best	5wI	10wM
Test																		
All First	4	4	1	145	84	48.33	-	1	2	-	82	15	265	5	53.00	3-49	-	-
1-day Int																		
C & G																		
B & H	2	1	0	3	3	3.00	-	-	1	-	14	0	75	0	-		-	-
1-day Lge	3	2	1	17	10 *	17.00	-	-	1	-	19	0	78	2	39.00	2-33	-	

Career Performances

	M	Inns	NO	Runs	HS	Avge	100s	50s	Ct	St	Balls	Runs	Wkts	Avge	Best	5wI	10wM
Test																	
All First	23	31	3	485	84	17.32	-	1	14	-	3164	1458	49	29.75	6-82	1	1
1-day Int																	
C & G	2	1	1	6	6 *	-	-	-	3	-	48	38	0	-		-	-
B & H	2	1	0	3	3	3.00	-	-	1	-	84	75	0	-		-	-
1-day Lge	14	9	2	52	15 *	7.42	-	-	1	-	564	417	13	32.07	3-16	-	

61. Whose 58-ball 95 earned him the Man of the Match award
as Leicestershire beat Lancashire in the semi-finals of the 2001 C&G?

MILLNS, D. J.   Nottinghamshire

Name: <u>David</u> James Millns
Role: Left-hand bat, right-arm
fast-medium swing bowler
Born: 27 February 1965, Mansfield
Height: 6ft 3in **Weight:** 14st 7lbs
Nickname: Rocket Man
County debut: 1988 (Nottinghamshire),
1990 (Leicestershire)
County cap: 1991 (Leicestershire),
2000 (Nottinghamshire – *see* **Extras**)
Benefit: 1999 (Leicestershire)
50 wickets in a season: 4
1st-Class 50s: 8
1st-Class 100s: 3
1st-Class 5 w. in innings: 23
1st-Class 10 w. in match: 4
1st-Class catches: 76
Place in batting averages: (2000 112th
av. 27.85)
Place in bowling averages: (2000 89th av. 29.33)
Strike rate: 151.00 (career 48.04)
Parents: Bernard and Brenda
Wife and date of marriage: Wanda Marie, 25 September 1993
Children: Dylan, 17 April 1998
Family links with cricket: Andy Pick, former Notts CCC player, is brother-in-law.
Brother Paul and his son Matthew play for Clipstone MWCC
Education: Samuel Barlow Junior; Garibaldi Comprehensive; North Notts College of
Further Education; Nottingham Trent Polytechnic
Qualifications: Advanced coach
Overseas tours: England A to Australia 1992-93; Leicestershire to South Africa 1994,
1995, to Holland 1994, 1996, to Barbados 1998
Overseas teams played for: Uitenhage, Port Elizabeth, South Africa 1988-89;
Birkenhead, Auckland 1989-91; Tasmania, Australia 1994-95; Boland, South Africa
1996-97
Cricketers particularly admired: Darren Gough, Glenn McGrath
Young players to look out for: Paul Franks, Usman Afzaal, David Lucas, Chris Read
Other sports followed/played: Football (Leicester City), rugby union (Leicester
Tigers), golf ('taking money off J.J. Whitaker on the golf course gives me great
pleasure')
Relaxations: Computers and property development
Extras: Harold Larwood Bowling Award 1984. Asked to be released by

Nottinghamshire at the end of the 1989 season and joined Leicestershire in 1990. Finished third in national bowling averages in 1990. Britannic Assurance Player of the Month in August 1991 after taking 9-37 v Derbyshire, the best Leicestershire figures since George Geary's 10-18 v Glamorgan in 1929. Was players' representative on Cricketers' Association Executive for Leicestershire. Leicestershire Cricketer of the Year 1992. Leicestershire Bowling Award 1990, 1991, 1992 and 1994. Left Leicestershire at the end of the 1999 season and rejoined Nottinghamshire for 2000, taking 5-58 v Northamptonshire at Trent Bridge in his first match. Retired during the 2001 season

Opinions on cricket: 'Congratulations to the ECB for the new format.'
Best batting: 121 Leicestershire v Northamptonshire, Northampton 1997
Best bowling: 9-37 Leicestershire v Derbyshire, Derby 1991

2001 Season

	M	Inns	NO	Runs	HS	Avge	100s	50s	Ct	St	O	M	Runs	Wkts	Avge	Best	5wI	10wM
Test																		
All First	1	2	1	7	4	7.00	-	-	1	-	25.1	4	87	1	87.00	1-69	-	-
1-day Int																		
C & G																		
B & H																		
1-day Lge																		

Career Performances

	M	Inns	NO	Runs	HS	Avge	100s	50s	Ct	St	Balls	Runs	Wkts	Avge	Best	5wI	10wM
Test																	
All First	171	203	63	3082	121	22.01	3	8	76	-	26571	15129	553	27.35	9-37	23	4
1-day Int																	
C & G	11	5	3	49	29 *	24.50	-	-	2	-	648	423	12	35.25	3-22	-
B & H	30	16	9	109	39 *	15.57	-	-	6	-	1339	1013	32	31.65	4-26	-
1-day Lge	47	25	13	157	20 *	13.08	-	-	10	-	1812	1585	37	42.83	2-11	-

MONTGOMERIE, R. R.   Sussex

Name: <u>Richard</u> Robert Montgomerie
Role: Right-hand opening bat
Born: 3 July 1971, Rugby
Height: 5ft 10in **Weight:** 13st
Nickname: Monty
County debut: 1991 (Northamptonshire), 1999 (Sussex)
County cap: 1995 (Northamptonshire), 1999 (Sussex)
1000 runs in a season: 3
1st-Class 50s: 42

1st-Class 100s: 21
1st-Class catches: 137
One-Day 100s: 2
Place in batting averages: 14th av. 58.75
(2000 76th av. 32.10)
Strike rate: 36.00 (career 144.00)
Parents: Robert and Gillian
Marital status: Single
Family links with cricket: Father captained
Oxfordshire
Education: Bilton Grange; Rugby School;
Worcester College, Oxford University
Qualifications: 12 O-levels, 4 A-levels,
BA (Hons) Chemistry, Level II coaching
Off-season: Teaching/coaching at Brighton
College. Christians in Sport tour to
Bangladesh and India over New Year
Overseas tours: Oxford University to

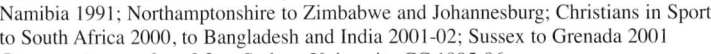

Namibia 1991; Northamptonshire to Zimbabwe and Johannesburg; Christians in Sport
to South Africa 2000, to Bangladesh and India 2001-02; Sussex to Grenada 2001
Overseas teams played for: Sydney University CC 1995-96
Career highlights to date: 'Two Lord's finals. Winning second division of National
League in 1999 and second division of County Championship in 2001. A hundred
[157] v Australians [at Hove 2001]'
Cricket moments to forget: 'Running [Northants] captain Allan Lamb out on my
Championship debut … as his runner'
Cricketers particularly admired: Steve Waugh, Mark Robinson
Young players to look out for: Matt Prior
Other sports followed: Golf, rackets, real tennis 'and many others'
Injuries: 'Very sore bruised hand/wrist. Played through it but fielding was
somewhat dodgy'
Relaxations: Any sport, good television, reading and 'occasionally testing my brain'
Extras: Oxford rackets Blue 1990. Scored unbeaten 50 in each innings of 1991
Varsity match. Faced first ball delivered by Durham in first-class cricket, for Oxford
University at The Parks 1992. Was Oxford University captain in 1994; also captained
Combined Universities 1994. Released by Northants at the end of the 1998 season and
joined Sussex for 1999. Scored his first 100 for Sussex (113*) against Northants, his
former county, at Hove 1999. Scored 160* v Nottinghamshire at Trent Bridge 2001; in
the process he shared with Murray Goodwin in a record partnership for any wicket for
Sussex in matches against Notts (372*), superseding his own record (292) set with
Michael Bevan at Hove in 2000. Scored 108 (his maiden one-day league century) v
Essex at Hove in the Norwich Union League 2001, in the process sharing with Murray
Goodwin in a Sussex record opening partnership in the one-day league (176). Man of
the Match award for his 157 in the Vodafone Challenge match against the Australians

at Hove 2001. Joint Sussex Player of the Year (with Murray Goodwin) 2001. PCA representative for Sussex

Opinions on cricket: 'The two league system is keeping players more intense and focused. County cricket is improving but too slowly. The changes in 2003 need to be effective – too long to discuss here but regional cricket and more overseas players may be good options.'

Best batting: 192 Northamptonshire v Kent, Canterbury 1995
Best bowling: 1-0 Sussex v Middlesex, Lord's 2001

2001 Season

	M	Inns	NO	Runs	HS	Avge	100s	50s	Ct	St	O	M	Runs	Wkts	Avge	Best	5wl	10wM
Test																		
All First	18	33	4	1704	160 *	58.75	8	5	17	-	6	1	17	1	17.00	1-0	-	-
1-day Int																		
C & G	2	2	0	37	33	18.50	-	-	-	-								
B & H	4	4	0	140	83	35.00	-	1	-	-								
1-day Lge	15	15	1	673	108	48.07	1	5	1	-								

Career Performances

	M	Inns	NO	Runs	HS	Avge	100s	50s	Ct	St	Balls	Runs	Wkts	Avge	Best	5wl	10wM
Test																	
All First	148	260	26	8508	192	36.35	21	42	137	-	144	89	1	89.00	1-0	-	-
1-day Int																	
C & G	12	12	3	514	109	57.11	1	5	3	-							
B & H	25	23	2	643	83	30.61	-	3	3	-	6	0	0	-		-	-
1-day Lge	80	79	5	2543	108	34.36	1	20	19	-							

MORRIS, A. C.   Hampshire

Name: <u>Alexander</u> Corfield Morris
Role: Left-hand bat, right-arm medium-fast bowler
Born: 4 October 1976, Barnsley
Height: 6ft 6in **Weight:** 'Off-season 18st; season hopefully 14st 7lbs'
County debut: 1995 (Yorkshire), 1998 (Hampshire)
County cap: 2001 (Hampshire)
50 wickets in a season: 2
1st-Class 50s: 7
1st-Class 5 w. in innings: 5
1st-Class 10 w. in match: 1
1st-Class catches: 32
Place in batting averages: 155th av. 24.88 (2000 237th av. 14.00)
Place in bowling averages: 52nd av. 28.00 (2000 98th av. 31.22)
Strike rate: 55.52 (career 49.31)

Parents: Chris and Janet
Marital status: Single
Family links with cricket: Brother Zac
played for Hampshire
Education: Wilthorpe Primary School;
Holgate School, Barnsley; Barnsley College
Qualifications: 4 GCSEs, BTEC National
Diploma in Sports Science, senior cricket
coach
Overseas tours: England U19 to West Indies
1994-95, to Zimbabwe 1995-96; England VI
to Hong Kong 1996; Michael Vaughan XI to
Tenerife 1996; Craig Dudley XI to Cyprus
1997; Anthony McGrath XI to Gran Canaria
1998; Alex Morris XI to Cyprus 1999
Cricketers particularly admired: 'Everyone
I've ever been on an overseas tour with'
Other sports followed: Football (Barnsley FC)

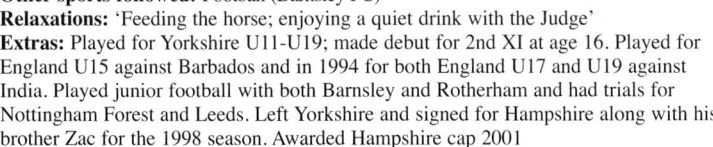

Relaxations: 'Feeding the horse; enjoying a quiet drink with the Judge'
Extras: Played for Yorkshire U11-U19; made debut for 2nd XI at age 16. Played for
England U15 against Barbados and in 1994 for both England U17 and U19 against
India. Played junior football with both Barnsley and Rotherham and had trials for
Nottingham Forest and Leeds. Left Yorkshire and signed for Hampshire along with his
brother Zac for the 1998 season. Awarded Hampshire cap 2001
Best batting: 65 Hampshire v Sussex, West End 2001
Best bowling: 5-39 Hampshire v Durham, Riverside 2001

2001 Season

	M	Inns	NO	Runs	HS	Avge	100s	50s	Ct	St	O	M	Runs	Wkts	Avge	Best	5wI	10wM
Test																		
All First	16	19	2	423	65	24.88	-	3	10	-	472	107	1428	51	28.00	5-39	2	-
1-day Int																		
C & G	1	0	0	0	0	-	-	-	1	-	6	0	37	0	-	-	-	-
B & H	4	3	1	46	25 *	23.00	-	-	1	-	30	2	131	6	21.83	3-49	-	
1-day Lge																		

Career Performances

	M	Inns	NO	Runs	HS	Avge	100s	50s	Ct	St	Balls	Runs	Wkts	Avge	Best	5wI	10wM
Test																	
All First	58	76	12	1289	65	20.14	-	7	32	-	7693	4007	156	25.68	5-39	5	1
1-day Int																	
C & G	3	2	2	4	3 *	-	-	-	1	-	132	125	2	62.50	1-43	-	
B & H	5	3	1	46	25 *	23.00	-	-	2	-	186	135	6	22.50	3-49	-	
1-day Lge	32	19	5	232	48 *	16.57	-	-	6	-	792	708	26	27.23	4-49	-	

MORRIS, J. E.   Nottinghamshire

Name: <u>John</u> Edward Morris
Role: Right-hand bat, right-arm
medium bowler
Born: 1 April 1964, Crewe
Height: 5ft 10in **Weight:** 13st 6lbs
Nickname: Animal
County debut: 1982 (Derbyshire),
1994 (Durham), 2000 (Notts)
County cap: 1986 (Derbyshire),
1998 (Durham), 2000 (Notts)
Benefit: 1999 (Durham)
Test debut: 1990
Tests: 3
One-Day Internationals: 8
1000 runs in a season: 11
1st-Class 50s: 104
1st-Class 100s: 50
1st-Class 200s: 2
1st-Class catches: 156
One-Day 100s: 10

Place in batting averages: 47th av. 45.71 (2000 95th av. 30.05)
Strike rate: (career 129.25)
Parents: George (Eddie) and Jean
Wife and date of marriage: Sally, 30 September 1990
Children: Thomas Edward, 27 June 1991
Family links with cricket: Father played for Crewe for many years as an
opening bowler
Education: Shavington Comprehensive School; Dane Bank College of Further Education
Qualifications: O-levels
Overseas tours: England to Australia 1990-91; Romany to South Africa 1993;
MCC to Bahrain 1994-95
Overseas teams played for: Umbilo, Durban, South Africa 1982-84; Alex Old Boys,
Pietermaritzburg, South Africa 1984-85; Subiaco-Floreat, Western Australia
1986-87; Griqualand West, South Africa 1988-89, 1993-94; Protea, Johannesburg,
South Africa 1993
Other sports followed: Golf, football (Derby County)
Relaxations: The golf course and home life
Extras: In 1984 became youngest player to score a Sunday League century. Was the
first batsman to pass 5000 runs for Durham. Passed 20,000 first-class runs during
Durham's first innings v Derbyshire, his former county, at Chester-le-Street 1999. Left
Durham at the end of the 1999 season and joined Nottinghamshire for 2000. Has set

up a sports management agency with Somerset's Peter Bowler. Passed 5000 Sunday/National League career runs in 2000, against his former club Durham at Trent Bridge. Scored 50th first-class century (115) v Sussex at Hove 2000. Scored two centuries (170 and 136*) in match against his old county Derbyshire at Derby 2001. Retired at the end of the 2001 season, scoring his first one-day century for Nottinghamshire (102 from 103 balls) v Surrey at Trent Bridge in the Norwich Union League in his penultimate game and a 43-ball 50 (ending up with 57) v Leicestershire at Trent Bridge in the NUL in his final match

Best batting: 229 Derbyshire v Gloucestershire, Cheltenham 1993
Best bowling: 1-6 Derbyshire v Cambridge University, Fenner's 1993

2001 Season

	M	Inns	NO	Runs	HS	Avge	100s	50s	Ct	St	O	M	Runs	Wkts	Avge	Best	5wI	10wM
Test																		
All First	8	16	2	640	170	45.71	2	4	3	-	3.2	0	19	0	-		-	-	-
1-day Int																		
C & G																		
B & H	1	1	0	6	6	6.00	-	-	1	-								
1-day Lge	5	5	0	204	102	40.80	1	1	2	-								

Career Performances

	M	Inns	NO	Runs	HS	Avge	100s	50s	Ct	St	Balls		Runs	Wkts	Avge	Best	5wI	10wM
Test	3	5	2	71	32	23.66	-	-	3	-								
All First	362	612	35	21539	229	37.32	52	104	156	-	1034		958	8	119.75	1-6	-	-
1-day Int	8	8	1	167	63 *	23.85	-	1	2	-								
C & G	31	30	3	874	109	32.37	1	5	9	-								
B & H	63	59	6	1533	145	28.92	3	7	14	-	24		14	0	-		-	-
1-day Lge	234	223	12	5492	134	26.02	6	25	53	-	9		8	0	-		-	-

---

62. When they met Yorkshire in the 1969 Gillette Cup final,
Derbyshire fielded three pace bowlers who played
in Tests for England. Name them.

Name: <u>Zachary</u> Clegg Morris
Role: Right-hand bat, left-arm
medium bowler
Born: 4 September 1978, Barnsley
Height: 6ft 2in **Weight:** 13st 7lbs
Nickname: Zaco, Z Man, Cleggy
County debut: 1998
Parents: Lance and Janet
Marital status: Single
Family links with cricket: Brother Alex
plays for Hampshire
Education: Wilthorpe Primary School;
Holgate Secondary School
Qualifications: Level 1 coaching award
Career outside cricket: 'Roundabout
caretaker'
Off-season: 'Watering plants and
flower beds'
Overseas tours: Sheffield Cricket Lovers to Holland 1990, to Magaluf 1992; England
U15 to South Africa 1993; England U19 to Pakistan 1996-97
Overseas teams played for: Strathfield CC, Sydney 1998-99; Melville CC, Perth
2000-01
Career highlights: 'Meeting so many nice and thirsty people every day I used to play'
Cricket moments to forget: 'Tended to forget them all through sheer exhaustion after
a hard day's playing'
Cricketers particularly admired: 'Everyone I had the pleasure of playing with on the
field and in various late night dancing halls around the circuit'
Young players to look out for: Derek Kenway
Other sports played: Football (Barnsley Schools age groups 11 to 16; represented
Barnsley 15 age group v London at Wembley); 'watersports are my favourite'
Other sports followed: Football (Barnsley FC, Southampton FC, England)
Relaxations: Partying
Extras: Moved to Hampshire in the 1997-98 close season along with his brother,
Alex. Represented England U19 v Pakistan U19 1998. 'Switched from bowling slow
left-arm to left-arm seam at beginning of 2000 season.' Saw Hampshire to victory by
taking seven from the last over v Worcestershire on his Norwich Union League debut
at West End 2001. Released by Hampshire at the end of the 2001 season
Opinions on cricket: 'Sky Sports commentators are one of the biggest mistakes in the
English game. The English management team aren't much better either. Great lads
play the game.'
Best batting: 10 Hampshire v Gloucestershire, Southampton 1998

2001 Season

	M	Inns	NO	Runs	HS	Avge	100s	50s	Ct	St	O	M	Runs	Wkts	Avge	Best	5wI	10wM
Test																		
All First																		
1-day Int																		
C & G																			
B & H	1	1	0	0	0	0.00	-	-	1	-	6	0	27	0	-		-	-
1-day Lge	3	3	1	7	7 *	3.50	-	-	-	-	25	2	102	3	34.00	3-31	-	

Career Performances

	M	Inns	NO	Runs	HS	Avge	100s	50s	Ct	St	Balls	Runs	Wkts	Avge	Best	5wI	10wM
Test																	
All First	2	4	0	11	10	2.75	-	-	-	-	205	99	0	-		-	-
1-day Int																	
C & G																	
B & H	1	1	0	0	0	0.00	-	-	1	-	36	27	0	-		-	-
1-day Lge	3	3	1	7	7 *	3.50	-	-	-	-	150	102	3	34.00	3-31	-	

MUCHALL, G. J.   Durham

Name: <u>Gordon</u> James Muchall
Role: Right-hand bat, right-arm
medium bowler
Born: 2 November 1982, Newcastle
upon Tyne
Height: 6ft **Weight:** 13st 3lbs
Nickname: Much, A.G.M.
County debut: No first-team appearance
Parents: Arthur and Mary
Marital status: Single
Family links with cricket: Grandfather
played for Northumberland. Younger brother
is in England U15 squad
Education: Newlands Prep School,
Newcastle; Durham School
Qualifications: 8 GCSEs, 2 A-levels
Off-season: Coaching in Perth, playing for
Fremantle; England U19 tour to Australia and
New Zealand
Overseas tours: England U19 to India 2000-01, to Australia and (U19 World Cup)
New Zealand 2001-02
Overseas teams played for: Fremantle 2001-02

Career highlights to date: 'Being picked for England U19. Getting a contract at Durham'

Cricket moments to forget: 'With the opposition needing four off the last ball to win, going into the long barrier position and the ball bouncing over my head for four'

Cricketers particularly admired: Jacques Kallis, Ian Botham, Steve Waugh, Darren Gough

Young players to look out for: Paul Muchall, Nicky Peng, Ian Bell, Kadeer Ali, Tim Bresnan

Other sports played: Rugby (at school)

Other sports followed: Football (Newcastle United), rugby (Newcastle Falcons and England)

Injuries: Out for one Durham Academy game with a sprained ankle

Relaxations: Listening to music, socialising with friends

Extras: Represented England U19 v West Indies U19 in one-day series (3/3) and 'Test' series (2/3) 2001. Played for Durham Board XI in the second round of the C&G 2002, which was played in September 2001

Opinions on cricket: 'More day/night cricket.'

2001 Season (did not make any first-class or one-day appearances)

Career Performances

	M	Inns	NO	Runs	HS	Avge	100s	50s	Ct	St	Balls	Runs	Wkts	Avge	Best	5wI	10wM
Test																	
All First																	
1-day Int																	
C & G	1	1	0	19	19	19.00	-	-	2	-	12	11	0	-	-	-	-
B & H																	
1-day Lge																	

MULLALLY, A. D.   Hampshire

Name: <u>Alan</u> David Mullally

Role: Right-hand bat, left-arm fast bowler

Born: 12 July 1969, Southend

Height: 6ft 4in **Weight:** 14st

Nickname: Spider

County debut: 1988 (Hampshire), 1990 (Leicestershire)

County cap: 1993 (Leicestershire), 2000 (Hampshire – *see Extras*)

Test debut: 1996

Tests: 19

One-Day Internationals: 50

50 wickets in a season: 5

1st-Class 50s: 2
1st-Class 5 w. in innings: 29
1st-Class 10 w. in match: 4
1st-Class catches: 40
One-Day 5 w. in innings: 2
Place in batting averages: 256th av. 10.25
(2000 297th av. 6.00)
Place in bowling averages: 5th av. 18.50
(2000 10th av. 16.97)
Strike rate: 44.78 (career 60.63)
Parents: Mick and Ann
Wife and date of marriage: Chelsey, 1997
Family links with cricket: 'Younger brother
is better'
Education: Cannington Primary and High
School, Perth, Australia; Wembley and
Carlisle Technical College
Off-season: 'Fishing with A. Hollioake'
Overseas tours: Western Australia to India; Leicestershire to Jamaica 1992-93; England
to Zimbabwe and New Zealand 1996-97, to Australia 1998-99, to Sharjah (Coca-Cola
Cup) 1998-99, to South Africa and Zimbabwe 1999-2000, to Sri Lanka 2000-01
(one-day series)
Overseas teams played for: Western Australia 1987-90; Victoria 1990-91
Career highlights to date: 'Career best 9-93 v Derbyshire. Man of the Match in
World Cup [v Zimbabwe 1999] and CUB Series v Australia [1998-99]'
Cricket moments to forget: 'Sunday League v Middlesex' (*At the Rose Bowl in 2001,
Middlesex took 35 runs off the last 13 deliveries of the game to win*)
Cricketers particularly admired: Robin Smith
Young players to look out for: Derek Kenway
Other sports followed: Australian Rules football, basketball, most sports
Relaxations: Fishing, music
Extras: English-qualified as he was born in Southend, he made his first-class debut for
Western Australia in the 1987-88 Sheffield Shield final, and played for Australian YC
1988-89. Played one match for Hampshire in 1988 before joining Leicestershire.
Represented England in the 1999 World Cup. Left Leicestershire at end of 1999 season
and rejoined Hampshire for 2000. Forced to withdraw from England one-day squads to
Kenya and Pakistan 2000-01 with recurrence of rib injury. Took 5-18 as Hampshire
bowled out the Australians for 97 at West End 2001
Opinions on cricket: 'Too much cricket. Too many teams.'
Best batting: 75 Leicestershire v Middlesex, Leicester 1996
Best bowling: 9-93 Hampshire v Derbyshire, Derby 2000

2001 Season

	M	Inns	NO	Runs	HS	Avge	100s	50s	Ct	St	O	M	Runs	Wkts	Avge	Best	5wI	10wM
Test	1	1	0	0	0	0.00	-	-	-	-	30.3	10	99	2	49.50	1-34	-	-
All First	14	13	5	82	36	10.25	-	-	4	-	477.4	151	1184	64	18.50	8-90	6	-
1-day Int	6	5	2	13	6	4.33	-	-	1	-	54	5	248	7	35.42	3-50	-	
C & G	1	0	0	0	0	-	-	-	-	-	10	1	79	2	39.50	2-79	-	
B & H	4	2	1	7	7 *	7.00	-	-	-	-	30	2	105	3	35.00	2-25	-	
1-day Lge	11	4	2	8	5 *	4.00	-	-	2	-	90.1	13	311	14	22.21	3-19	-	

Career Performances

	M	Inns	NO	Runs	HS	Avge	100s	50s	Ct	St	Balls	Runs	Wkts	Avge	Best	5wI	10wM
Test	19	27	4	127	24	5.52	-	-	6	-	4525	1812	58	31.24	5-105	1	-
All First	199	222	57	1456	75	8.82	-	2	40	-	38016	17422	627	27.78	9-93	29	4
1-day Int	50	25	10	86	20	5.73	-	-	8	-	2698	1728	63	27.42	4-18	-	
C & G	25	10	5	58	19 *	11.60	-	-	3	-	1542	866	42	20.61	5-18	1	
B & H	49	20	7	58	13	4.46	-	-	2	-	2634	1666	46	36.21	3-33	-	
1-day Lge	116	52	23	227	38	7.82	-	-	20	-	5188	3611	130	27.77	5-15	1	

MUNTON, T. A. Derbyshire

Name: <u>Timothy</u> Alan Munton
Role: Right-hand bat, right-arm
seam bowler
Born: 30 July 1965, Melton Mowbray
Height: 6ft 6in **Weight:** 17st
Nickname: Harry, Herman, Munts
County debut: 1985 (Warwicks),
2000 (Derbys)
County cap: 1990 (Warwicks),
2000 (Derbys)
Benefit: 1998 (Warwicks)
Test debut: 1991
Tests: 2
50 wickets in a season: 6
1st-Class 50s: 4
1st-Class 5 w. in innings: 35
1st-Class 10 w. in match: 6
1st-Class catches: 82
One-Day 5 w. in innings: 2
Place in batting averages: 246th av. 12.08 (2000 246th av. 12.73)
Place in bowling averages: 88th av. 34.68 (2000 99th av. 31.22)
Strike rate: 76.47 (career 59.52)

Parents: Alan and Brenda
Marital status: Engaged to Sonia
Children: Camilla Dallas, 13 August 1988; Harrison George Samuel, 17 February 1992; Thomas Edward, 13 October 2001
Family links with cricket: Father played for Buckminster CC
Education: Sarson High School; King Edward VII Upper School, Melton Mowbray
Qualifications: CSE grade 1, 9 O-levels, 1 A-level
Career outside cricket: Commercial Director of cricnet.com, the PCA's website
Off-season: 'As above, and marrying Sonia'
Overseas tours: England A to Pakistan 1990-91, to Bermuda and West Indies 1991-92, to Pakistan 1995-96
Overseas teams played for: Victoria University, Wellington, New Zealand 1985-86; Witwatersrand University, Johannesburg, South Africa 1986-87
Cricketers particularly admired: Michael Atherton, Steve Waugh, Allan Donald, Brian Lara, Steve Stubbings
Players to look out for: Nicky Peng, Keith Piper, Mark Wagh
Other sports played: Golf
Other sports followed: Football (Leicester City), rugby (Leicester Tigers)
Injuries: Out for two months with an Achilles tendon injury
Relaxations: 'Watching films; golf; spending time at home with my family'
Extras: Appeared for Leicestershire 2nd XI 1982-84. Second highest wicket-taker in 1990 with 78. Was voted Warwickshire Player of the Season 1990, 1991 and 1994. Was one of *Wisden*'s Five Cricketers of the Year 1995. Assumed the Warwickshire captaincy after the retirement of Dermot Reeve in 1996 but was replaced by Brian Lara for the 1998 season after missing the whole of the 1997 season through injury. Took Championship hat-trick v Kent at Maidstone 1999. Left Warwickshire in 1999-2000 off-season and joined Derbyshire for 2000. Vice-captain of Derbyshire 2001
Opinions on cricket: '1. Two divisional cricket should be continued but with the counties only playing each other once. This will allow time to introduce regional cricket. 2. A lot of time, energy and money needs to be spent improving the quality of club cricket to support the professional game.'
Best batting: 54* Warwickshire v Worcestershire, Worcester 1992
Best bowling: 8-89 Warwickshire v Middlesex, Edgbaston 1991

2001 Season

	M	Inns	NO	Runs	HS	Avge	100s	50s	Ct	St	O	M	Runs	Wkts	Avge	Best	5wI	10wM
Test																		
All First	9	13	1	145	50	12.08	-	1	2	-	242.1	61	659	19	34.68	5-85	1	-
1-day Int																		
C & G	1	1	0	3	3	3.00	-	-	-	-	10	1	32	1	32.00	1-32	-	
B & H	5	3	2	23	17*	23.00	-	-	-	-	49	5	175	4	43.75	3-28	-	
1-day Lge	6	2	1	4	3	4.00	-	-	-	-	51	12	166	10	16.60	4-31	-	

	M	Inns	NO	Runs	HS	Avge	100s	50s	Ct	St	Balls	Runs	Wkts	Avge	Best	5wI	10wM
Test	2	2	1	25	25 *	25.00	-	-	-	-	405	200	4	50.00	2-22	-	
All First	252	272	98	1827	54 *	10.50	-	4	82	-	43873	19065	737	25.86	8-89	35	6
1-day Int																	
C & G	38	13	6	33	17	4.71	-	-	6	-	2290	1139	40	28.47	3-36	-	
B & H	43	19	12	91	17 *	13.00	-	-	6	-	2584	1484	48	30.91	4-35	-	
1-day Lge	176	55	32	200	18	8.69	-	-	35	-	7769	4999	176	28.40	5-23	2	

MURALITHARAN, M.   Lancashire

Name: Muttiah Muralitharan
Role: Right-hand bat, off-spin bowler
Born: 17 April 1972, Kandy, Sri Lanka
Height: 5ft 5in
Nickname: Murali
County debut: 1999
County cap: 1999
Test debut: 1992-93
Tests: 66
One-Day Internationals: 174
50 wickets in a season: 2
1st-Class 50s: 1
1st-Class 5 w. in innings: 60
1st-Class 10 w. in match: 16
1st-Class catches: 71
One-Day 5 w. in innings: 5
Place in batting averages: 258th av. 10.00
Place in bowling averages: 9th av. 19.42
Strike rate: 58.18 (career 55.52)
Education: St Anthony's College, Kandy
Overseas tours: Sri Lanka to England 1991, to India 1993-94, to Zimbabwe 1994-95, to New Zealand 1994-95, 1996-97, to South Africa (Mandela Cup) 1994-95, to Sharjah (one-day tournaments) 1994-95, 1995-96, 1996-97, 1998-99, to Pakistan 1995-96, to India and Pakistan (World Cup) 1995-96, to Singapore (Singer Cup) 1995-96, to Australia 1995-96, to West Indies 1996-97, to Kenya (KCA Centenary Tournament) 1996-97, to India (Independence Cup) 1996-97, to India 1997-98, to South Africa 1997-98, to Pakistan (Independence Cup) 1997-98, to England 1998, to Bangladesh (Wills International Cup) 1998-99, to Australia (CUB series) 1998-99, to UK, Ireland and Holland (World Cup) 1999, to Zimbabwe 1999-2000, to Pakistan 1999-2000, to Kenya (ICC Knockout Trophy) 2000-01, to South Africa 2000-01
Overseas teams played for: Tamil Union Cricket and Athletic Club 1991-92 –

Extras: Took 16-220 from 113.5 overs v England at The Oval 1998, the fifth best bowling analysis in Test cricket; it included 9-65 in England's second innings, in which he took his 200th Test victim (Dominic Cork) in 42 Tests. His bowling action has attracted controversy – including calls for throwing – but was studied by the ICC in 1996 and cleared. One of *Wisden*'s Five Cricketers of the Year 1999. Was Lancashire's overseas player in 1999, taking an astonishing 66 wickets in the 12 Championship innings in which he bowled; his haul included eight returns of five or more wickets in an innings (including five returns of seven) and he had five match returns of ten or more wickets. Lancashire Player of the Year 1999. Played for an Asia XI v a World XI in Dhaka 2000. Took 13-171 at Galle in 2000, winning the Man of the Match award in Sri Lanka's first Test win over South Africa. Took 7-30 v India in the Champions Trophy in Sharjah 2000, at the time the best return in One-Day International history (superseded in 2001-02 by the 8-19 of fellow Sri Lankan Chaminda Vaas). Took 300th Test wicket (Shaun Pollock) v South Africa 2000-01 in his 58th Test; only Dennis Lillee (55 Tests) has reached this mark in fewer matches. Highest wicket-taker in Test cricket for the calendar year 2000 with 75 wickets in ten matches. Returned as Lancashire's overseas player for 2001. B&H Gold Award for his 1-4 from 10 overs v Derbyshire at Liverpool 2001. Scored 65-ball 67 in the second Test v India at Kandy 2001, in the process sharing with Ruchira Perera in a record tenth-wicket partnership for Sri Lanka in Tests (64). Took 50 Championship wickets (av. 19.42 and including five five-wicket innings) in only seven matches in 2001; in taking his 100th Championship wicket in only his 12th match overall, he became the quickest to this milestone for any county. Man of the Series v India 2001, taking 23 wickets (av. 19.30) in the three-match rubber including 8-87 (11-196 the match) in the third Test at Colombo. Released by Lancashire at the end of the 2001 season

Best batting: 67 Sri Lanka v India, Kandy 2001-02

Best bowling: 9-65 Sri Lanka v England, The Oval 1998

Stop press: Highest wicket-taker in Test cricket for the calendar year 2001 with 80 wickets in 12 matches. Took 9-51 in Zimbabwe's first innings in the second Test at Kandy January 2002, in the process passing Ian Botham's tally of 383 Test wickets in his 71st match; reached 400 Test wickets in a record 72 matches when he dismissed Henry Olonga v Zimbabwe in the third Test at Galle, January 2002 (took 30 wickets in the three-match series at an average of 9.80)

2001 Season

	M	Inns	NO	Runs	HS	Avge	100s	50s	Ct	St	O	M	Runs	Wkts	Avge	Best	5wI	10wM
Test																		
All First	7	8	1	70	21	10.00	-	-	4	-	484.5	159	971	50	19.42	6-53	5	1
1-day Int																		
C & G	2	0	0	0	0	-	-	-	-	-	20	6	45	4	11.25	3-21	-	
B & H	5	3	1	1	1 *	0.50	-	-	2	-	48	13	129	4	32.25	2-40	-	
1-day Lge	5	1	0	1	1	1.00	-	-	-	-	40	10	92	5	18.40	2-24	-	

Career Performances

	M	Inns	NO	Runs	HS	Avge	100s	50s	Ct	St	Balls	Runs	Wkts	Avge	Best	5wI	10wM
Test	66	85	34	675	67	13.23	-	1	30	-	21633	8678	350	24.79	9-65	28	7
All First	135	164	52	1258	67	11.23	-	1	71	-	37279	14562	722	20.16	9-65	60	16
1-day Int	174	80	34	250	18	5.43	-	-	78	-	9552	6335	250	25.34	7-30	5	
C & G	5	2	0	15	15	7.50	-	-	-	-	288	186	5	37.20	3-21	-	
B & H	6	3	1	1	1 *	0.50	-	-	2	-	348	143	5	28.60	2-40	-	
1-day Lge	12	2	1	14	13 *	14.00	-	-	4	-	578	280	15	18.66	3-12	-	

MURTAGH, T. J. Surrey

Name: Timothy (Tim) James Murtagh
Role: Left-hand bat, right-arm
fast-medium bowler
Born: 2 August 1981, Lambeth, London
Height: 6ft **Weight:** 12st
Nickname: Squeezer
County debut: 2000 (one-day),
2001 (first-class)
1st-Class 5 w. in innings: 1
Strike rate: 29.00 (career 26.87)
Parents: Dominic and Elizabeth
Marital status: Single
Family links with cricket: 'Chris, younger
brother, plays in Surrey age-group cricket and
is in their Development of Excellence
Programme; Uncle Andy (A. J. Murtagh)
played for Hampshire'
Education: Regina Coeli, Purley, Surrey;
John Fisher, Purley, Surrey; St Mary's University, Twickenham
Qualifications: 10 GCSEs, 2 A-levels
Career outside cricket: Student (Sports Science and Media Studies)
Overseas tours: Surrey U17 to South Africa 1997; England U19 to Malaysia and
(U19 World Cup) Sri Lanka 1999-2000
Cricketers particularly admired: Darren Gough, Glenn McGrath
Young players to look out for: Rikki Clarke, Chris Murtagh
Other sports played: Rugby (was captain of John Fisher 2nd XV), skiing ('in the past')
Other sports followed: Football (Liverpool FC), rugby
Relaxations: Playing golf, watching sport, films, reading
Extras: Represented British Universities 2000 and 2001. Represented England U19 in
one-day and 'Test' series v Sri Lanka U19 2000; named Player of the Series. Played
for Surrey Board XI and Surrey in the C&G 2001. Recorded maiden first-class
five-wicket return (6-86) for British Universities v Pakistanis at Trent Bridge 2001

Best batting: 22* British Universities v Pakistanis, Trent Bridge 2001
Best bowling: 6-86 British Universities v Pakistanis, Trent Bridge 2001

2001 Season

	M	Inns	NO	Runs	HS	Avge	100s	50s	Ct	St	O	M	Runs	Wkts	Avge	Best	5wI	10wM
Test																		
All First	2	3	1	24	22 *	12.00	-	-	-	-	33.5	8	114	7	16.28	6-86	1	-
1-day Int																		
C & G	2	2	0	13	11	6.50	-	-	1	-	18	1	86	2	43.00	1-40	-	
B & H																		
1-day Lge	7	5	4	12	4 *	12.00	-	-	1	-	52.5	5	262	10	26.20	4-31	-	

Career Performances

	M	Inns	NO	Runs	HS	Avge	100s	50s	Ct	St	Balls	Runs	Wkts	Avge	Best	5wI	10wM
Test																	
All First	3	4	2	36	22 *	18.00	-	-	-	-	215	120	8	15.00	6-86	1	-
1-day Int																	
C & G	2	2	0	13	11	6.50	-	-	1	-	108	86	2	43.00	1-40	-	
B & H																	
1-day Lge	9	6	4	12	4 *	6.00	-	-	1	-	419	364	11	33.09	4-31	-	

MUSTARD, P.   Durham

Name: Philip Mustard
Role: Left-hand bat, wicket-keeper
Born: 8 October 1982, Sunderland
Nickname: Colonel
County debut: No first-team appearance
Parents: Maureen
Marital status: Single
Education: Usworth Grange;
Usworth Comprehensive
Career outside cricket: Landscaping
Off-season: As above plus two weeks in
South Africa
Cricket moments to forget: 'The first game
I played I went out to bat and got a first-ball
duck, then went out to keep wicket and
dropped catches'
Cricketers particularly admired:
Mike Atherton ('professionalism')
Young players to look out for: Nicky Peng

Other sports followed: Football (Middlesbrough)
Relaxations: 'Socialising with friends down the pub'
Extras: Played for Durham Board XI in the NatWest 2000, in the C&G 2001 and in the second round of the C&G 2002, which was played in September 2001

2001 Season (did not make any first-class or one-day appearances)

Career Performances

	M	Inns	NO	Runs	HS	Avge	100s	50s	Ct	St	Balls	Runs	Wkts	Avge	Best	5wI	10wM
Test																	
All First																	
1-day Int																	
C & G	5	4	1	14	8	4.66	-	-	7	3							
B & H																	
1-day Lge																	

NAPIER, G. R.   Essex

Name: <u>Graham</u> Richard Napier
Role: Right-hand bat, right-arm medium bowler
Born: 6 January 1980, Colchester
Height: 5ft 10in **Weight:** 12st 7lbs
Nickname: Plank, Napes
County debut: 1997
1st-Class 50s: 2
1st-Class 100s: 1
1st-Class catches: 10
One-Day 5 w. in innings: 1
Place in batting averages: 110th av. 31.62
Place in bowling averages: 106th av. 37.75
Strike rate: 52.08 (career 53.00)
Parents: Roger and Carol
Marital status: Single
Family links with cricket: Father played for Palmers Boys School 1st XI (1965-68), Essex Police divisional teams, and Harwich Immigration CC. 'Now makes guest appearances on Walton beach'
Education: Myland School, Colchester; Gilberd School, Colchester
Qualifications: NCA coaching award
Off-season: 'Playing for North Perth and training in the sun'
Overseas tours: England U17 to Bermuda; England U19 to South Africa (including U19 World Cup) 1997-98

456

Overseas teams played for: Campbelltown CC, Sydney 2000-01; North Perth, Western Australia 2001-02
Career highlights to date: 'To test myself against the world's best and score some runs'
Cricket moments to forget: 'Being 12th man at Lord's and after a drinks break dropping the empties on a tray, towels, jumpers and anything else thrown at me in front of the MCC members'
Young players to look out for: Will Jefferson, Mark Pettini
Other sports followed: Football ('The Tractor Boys' – Ipswich Town FC)
Relaxations: 'Research on the lifecycle of the cranefly'
Extras: Represented England U19 in one-day and 'Test' series v Australia U19 1999. Scored maiden first-class century (104) v Cambridge University CCE at Fenner's 2001. Scored 73 (losing three cricket balls in the process) and recorded maiden one-day five-wicket return (6-29) v Worcestershire at Chelmsford in the Norwich Union League 2001
Opinions on cricket: 'The introduction of the cricket academy is the best move the ECB have made to help the progress of young cricketers into the first-class and hopefully the international game. Longer lunch and tea breaks.'
Best batting: 104 Essex v CUCCE, Fenner's 2001
Best bowling: 3-55 Essex v Leicestershire, Chelmsford 2001

2001 Season

	M	Inns	NO	Runs	HS	Avge	100s	50s	Ct	St	O	M	Runs	Wkts	Avge	Best	5wI	10wM
Test																		
All First	10	16	0	506	104	31.62	1	2	4	-	104.1	15	453	12	37.75	3-55	-	-
1-day Int																		
C & G	1	1	0	0	0	0.00	-	-	-	-								
B & H	3	3	1	26	22 *	13.00	-	-	-	-	6	0	45	0	-		-	-
1-day Lge	12	11	0	174	73	15.81	-	1	1	-	32.2	0	151	7	21.57	6-29	1	

Career Performances

	M	Inns	NO	Runs	HS	Avge	100s	50s	Ct	St	Balls	Runs	Wkts	Avge	Best	5wI	10wM
Test																	
All First	16	24	2	613	104	27.86	1	2	10	-	895	638	17	37.52	3-55	-	-
1-day Int																	
C & G	3	3	0	96	79	32.00	-	1	-	-	42	37	1	37.00	1-37	-	
B & H	5	3	1	26	22 *	13.00	-	-	-	-	90	107	0	-	-	-	
1-day Lge	36	29	0	474	78	16.34	-	3	7	-	404	337	14	24.07	6-29	1	

NASH, D. C.   Middlesex

Name: <u>David</u> Charles Nash
Role: Right-hand bat, wicket-keeper
Born: 19 January 1978, Chertsey
Height: 5ft 8in **Weight:** 11st 3lbs
Nickname: Nashy, Knocker
County debut: 1995 (one-day), 1997 (first-class)
County cap: 1999
50 dismissals in a season: 1
1st-Class 50s: 11
1st-Class 100s: 3
1st-Class catches: 135
1st-Class stumpings: 13
Place in batting averages: 101st av. 32.71
(2000 178th av. 20.22)
Strike rate: (career 19.00)
Parents: David and Christine
Marital status: Single
Family links with cricket: 'Father played
club cricket, and brother Glen is a very talented left-hand bat and off-spinner'
Education: Chennestone County Middle; Sunbury Manor; Malvern College, Worcs
Qualifications: 10 GCSEs, 1 A-level, NCA coaching award, qualified football referee
Career outside cricket: 'No idea – suggestions welcome!'
Off-season: 'Spending three months in Perth, Western Australia, working on game and
fitness with a few Middlesex colleagues and the Fremantle boys. Learning from B. L.
Hutton how to play so many shots at night and still not manage to get off the mark!'
Overseas tours: England U15 to South Africa 1993; British Airways Youth Team to
West Indies 1993-94; England U19 to Zimbabwe 1995-96, to Pakistan 1996-97;
England A to Kenya and Sri Lanka 1997-98
Overseas teams played for: Fremantle, Perth 2000-01
Career highlights to date: 'Being picked at 19 for England A tour to Sri Lanka.
Scoring first hundred at Lord's against Somerset whilst being "on them"!'
Cricket moments to forget: 'Getting caught on the sweep for a first ball nought
for the Bunburys against an Invitation side, the bowler being Adam Hollioake
bowling leggies!'
Cricketers particularly admired: George Simons and Gareth Rees 'for their big
hearts', 'the Sunbury CC squad', and Angus Fraser 'for always smiling and enjoying
his cricket, however unlucky he is!'
Young players to look out for: Ian Bell, John Maunders ('if he can shed a couple of
stone!'), 'and Glen Nash if he ever takes up the game again!'
Other sports played: Football ('played for Millwall U15s and my district side')
rugby, snooker ('always getting beaten by Richard Johnson')

Other sports followed: Football (Brentford), rugby union (London Irish), AFL (Fremantle Dockers)

Injuries: Out for two games with a badly dislocated finger; 'bad earache listening to Andy Strauss's dieting troubles – but managed to play'

Relaxations: 'I enjoy playing golf, listening to music, going out with my mates'

Extras: Represented Middlesex at all ages. Played for England U14, U15, U17 and U19. Once took six wickets in six balls when aged 11 – 'when I could bowl!' *Daily Telegraph* Southern England Batting Award 1993. Seaxe Young Player of the Year 1993

Opinions on cricket: 'More floodlit cricket should be played – it's the way forward to get the crowds in; and Lord's having lights would be a bonus. The technological side of the game is good with umpires getting help in run-outs, but we don't need to add to this. One-day teams should consist of at least three players under 23. Second-team cricket should mirror first-class, with pitches in particular needing to improve. The two-league system is good and has added to the competitiveness, especially at the end of the season!'

Best batting: 114 Middlesex v Somerset, Lord's 1998
Best bowling: 1-8 Middlesex v Essex, Chelmsford 1997

2001 Season

	M	Inns	NO	Runs	HS	Avge	100s	50s	Ct	St	O	M	Runs	Wkts	Avge	Best	5wI	10wM
Test																		
All First	15	19	5	458	103 *	32.71	1	4	39	4								
1-day Int																		
C & G	1	1	0	58	58	58.00	-	1	-	-								
B & H	5	4	1	55	27	18.33	-	-	6	3								
1-day Lge	13	12	3	161	57 *	17.88	-	1	7	4								

Career Performances

	M	Inns	NO	Runs	HS	Avge	100s	50s	Ct	St	Balls	Runs	Wkts	Avge	Best	5wI	10wM
Test																	
All First	71	100	17	2356	114	28.38	3	11	135	13	19	19	1	19.00	1-8	-	-
1-day Int																	
C & G	3	2	0	61	58	30.50	-	1	1	-							
B & H	10	7	3	66	27	16.50	-	-	10	4							
1-day Lge	52	40	8	613	57 *	19.15	-	1	41	11							

NEW, T. J.   Leicestershire

Name: Thomas (Tom) James New
Role: Left-hand bat, wicket-keeper
Born: 18 January 1985, Sutton-in-Ashfield
Height: 5ft 10in **Weight:** 10st 2lbs
Nickname: Newy
County debut: No first-team appearance
Parents: Martin and Louise
Marital status: Single
Education: Croft Primary School;
Quarrydale
Overseas teams played for: Geelong
Cement, Victoria 2001-02
Career highlights to date: 'Captaining
England U15 in Costcutter World Challenge
2000'
Cricket moments to forget: 'Losing
semi-final of Costcutter World Challenge
2000 to Pakistan'
Cricketers particularly admired: Ian Healy, Mark Waugh
Young players to look out for: Samit Patel
Other sports played: Rugby (County U14/U15), football
Other sports followed: Football (Mansfield Town FC)
Relaxations: Golf
Extras: Played for Leicestershire Board XI in the C&G 2001. Sir John Hobbs
Memorial Award 2001

2001 Season (did not make any first-class or one-day appearances)

Career Performances

	M	Inns	NO	Runs	HS	Avge	100s	50s	Ct	St	Balls	Runs	Wkts	Avge	Best	5wl	10wM
Test																	
All First																	
1-day Int																	
C & G	1	1	0	3	3	3.00	-	-	-	-							
B & H																	
1-day Lge																	

NEWELL, K.   Glamorgan

Name: Keith Newell
Role: Right-hand bat, right-arm
medium bowler
Born: 25 March 1972, Crawley
Height: 6ft   **Weight:** 13st
Nickname: Croc, Nightstalker, Greavsie
County debut: 1993 (one-day, Sussex),
1995 (first-class, Sussex), 1999 (Glamorgan)
1st-Class 50s: 11
1st-Class 100s: 5
1st-Class catches: 25
One-Day 100s: 1
One-Day 5 w. in innings: 1
Place in batting averages: 100th av. 32.88
(2000 201st av. 17.80)
Strike rate: (career 85.45)
Parents: Peter Charles and Julie Anne
Marital status: Single
Family links with cricket: Brother Mark played for Sussex and Derbyshire. Brother
Jonathan has played for Sussex U17 and U19
Education: Gossops Green Junior School; Ifield Community College
Qualifications: 'A few GCSEs', coaching certificate
Career outside cricket: Cricket coach
Off-season: 'Playing for the Balmain Tigers in Sydney grade'
Overseas teams played for: Zimbabwe Universals 1989-90; Bulawayo Athletic Club
1991-92, 1995-96; Riverside CC, Wellington 1992-93; Randwick CC, Sydney
1998-99; Balmain Tigers, Sydney 2001-02
Cricketers particularly admired: Ian Botham, Alan Wells
Young players to look out for: Simon Jones, Mark Wallace, 'Kirbs'
Other sports played: Table tennis
Other sports followed: Football (Spurs)
Injuries: 'None thanks to ERJ'
Relaxations: 'Watching films and going out every now and then'
Extras: Released by Sussex at end of 1998 season and joined Glamorgan. Scored a
53-ball 97 to set up victory for Glamorgan against Essex at Chelmsford in the Norwich
Union League 2001
Opinions on cricket: 'It looks like staffs are going to have to get smaller with the
amount of 2nd team cricket being reduced by so much. You have guys who aren't
playing regular 1st team cricket sitting on their backsides for too long. Is the plan for
county academies to take the place of 2nd team cricket?'
Best batting: 135 Sussex v West Indians, Hove 1995
Best bowling: 4-61 Sussex v Kent, Horsham 1997

2001 Season

	M	Inns	NO	Runs	HS	Avge	100s	50s	Ct	St	O	M	Runs	Wkts	Avge	Best	5wI	10wM
Test																		
All First	7	11	2	296	103	32.88	1	1	5	-	13	0	48	0	-	-	-	-
1-day Int																		
C & G	2	2	0	39	26	19.50	-	-	-	-	0.4	0	8	0	-	-	-	
B & H	5	5	0	91	36	18.20	-	-	-	-	15	1	63	3	21.00	3-37	-	
1-day Lge	16	16	1	476	97	31.73	-	3	1	-	4	0	23	1	23.00	1-12	-	

Career Performances

	M	Inns	NO	Runs	HS	Avge	100s	50s	Ct	St	Balls	Runs	Wkts	Avge	Best	5wI	10wM
Test																	
All First	72	123	14	2930	135	26.88	5	11	25	-	2051	1023	24	42.62	4-61	-	-
1-day Int																	
C & G	11	9	2	417	129	59.57	1	2	1	-	268	213	3	71.00	1-31	-	
B & H	21	19	1	377	62 *	20.94	-	1	3	-	339	290	7	41.42	3-37	-	
1-day Lge	86	77	5	1637	97	22.73	-	7	15	-	1139	947	29	32.65	5-33	1	

NEWELL, M.   Nottinghamshire

Name: Michael Newell
Role: Right-hand opening bat, leg-break bowler, occasional wicket-keeper
Born: 25 February 1965, Blackburn
Height: 5ft 9in **Weight:** 11st 4lbs
Nickname: Mugly, Tricky, Animal
County debut: 1984
County cap: 1987
Benefit: 1999
1000 runs in a season: 1
1st-Class 50s: 24
1st-Class 100s: 5
1st-Class 200s: 1
1st-Class catches: 93
1st-Class stumpings: 1
One-Day 100s: 1
Strike rate: (career 51.86)
Parents: Barry and Janet
Wife and date of marriage: Jayne, 23 September 1989
Children: Elizabeth Rose, 1 September 1993
Family links with cricket: Father chairman of Notts Unity CC and brother, Paul, is the captain

Education: West Bridgford Comprehensive
Qualifications: 8 O-levels, 3 A-levels, NCA advanced coach
Cricketers particularly admired: Mathew Dowman, Dominic Cork, James Hindson
Young players to look out for: Paul Franks, Mathew Dowman
Other sports followed: Rugby union, football, darts
Relaxations: Football, studying, being at home
Best batting: 203* Nottinghamshire v Derbyshire, Derby 1987
Best bowling: 2-38 Nottinghamshire v Sri Lankans, Trent Bridge 1988

2001 Season (did not make any first-class or one-day appearances)

Career Performances

	M	Inns	NO	Runs	HS	Avge	100s	50s	Ct	St	Balls	Runs	Wkts	Avge	Best	5wI	10wM
Test																	
All First	102	178	26	4636	203*	30.50	6	24	93	1	363	282	7	40.28	2-38	-	-
1-day Int																	
C & G	5	5	0	136	60	27.20	-	1	3	-	6	10	0	-		-	-
B & H	10	10	1	205	39	22.77	-	-	2	-							
1-day Lge	24	21	4	611	109*	35.94	1	3	8	-							

NEWMAN, S. A.   Surrey

Name: <u>Scott</u> Alexander Newman
Role: Left-hand bat, right-arm
medium bowler
Born: 3 November 1979, Epsom
Height: 6ft 2in **Weight:** 12st 10lbs
Nickname: Scotty, Fig Jam, Blondy
County debut: 2001 (one-day)
Parents: Sandra and Ken
Marital status: Single
Family links with cricket: Father and
brother played cricket at club level
Education: Cumnor House School, Purley;
Trinity School, Croydon; Coulsdon College;
Brighton University
Qualifications: 10 GCSEs,
GNVQ (Advanced) Business Studies
Career outside cricket: Handyman
Off-season: 'Training and then overseas
after January'
Overseas tours: SCB to Barbados

Overseas teams played for: Mount Lawley CC, Perth
Career highlights to date: 'Winning ECB 2nd XI Trophy v Somerset [2001], scoring 53'
Cricket moments to forget: 'Any time I played and won the TFC award'
Cricketers particularly admired: Carl Hooper, Brian Lara
Young players to look out for: Carl Greenidge, Christian Newman, Rupesh Amin, Rikki Clarke
Other sports played: 'Most sports'
Other sports followed: Rugby, football, American sports
Relaxations: Music, socialising, sleeping
Extras: Played for Surrey Board XI in the C&G 2001 and in the second round of the C&G 2002, which was played in September 2001
Opinions on cricket: 'Coloured kits for 2nd XI Trophy. More entertainment in Sunday League cricket.'

2001 Season

	M	Inns	NO	Runs	HS	Avge	100s	50s	Ct	St	O	M	Runs	Wkts	Avge	Best	5wI	10wM
Test																		
All First																		
1-day Int																		
C & G	3	3	0	100	49	33.33	-	-	1	-								
B & H																		
1-day Lge	2	2	0	10	10	5.00	-	-	-	-								

Career Performances

	M	Inns	NO	Runs	HS	Avge	100s	50s	Ct	St	Balls	Runs	Wkts	Avge	Best	5wI	10wM
Test																	
All First																	
1-day Int																	
C & G	3	3	0	100	49	33.33	-	-	1	-							
B & H																	
1-day Lge	2	2	0	10	10	5.00	-	-	-	-							

NIXON, P. A. Kent

Name: <u>Paul</u> Andrew Nixon
Role: Left-hand bat, wicket-keeper
Born: 21 October 1970, Carlisle
Height: 6ft **Weight:** 12st 10lbs
Nickname: Badger, Nico
County debut: 1989 (Leicestershire), 2000 (Kent)
County cap: 1994 (Leicestershire), 2000 (Kent)

1000 runs in a season: 1
50 dismissals in a season: 5
1st-Class 50s: 30
1st-Class 100s: 12
1st-Class catches: 570
1st-Class stumpings: 46
Place in batting averages: 77th av. 38.29
(2000 75th av. 32.11)
Parents: Brian and Sylvia
Wife and date of marriage: Jen,
9 October 1999
Family links with cricket: 'Grandad and
father played local league cricket. Mum made
the teas for Edenhall CC, Penrith'
Education: Langwathby Primary;
Ullswater High
Qualifications: 2 O-levels, 6 GCSEs,
coaching certificates
Career outside cricket: 'Used to be farming. Father sold up'
Off-season: 'Blade tour host to Barbados. Working on fitness and mind'
Overseas tours: Cumbria Schools U15 to Denmark 1985; Leicestershire to Barbados,
to Jamaica, to Holland, to Johannesburg, to Bloemfontein; MCC to Bangladesh 1999-
2000; England A to India and Bangladesh 1994-95; England to Pakistan and Sri Lanka
2000-01
Overseas teams played for: Melville, Western Australia; North Fremantle, Western
Australia; Mitchells Plain, Cape Town 1993; Primrose CC, Cape Town 1995-96
Career highlights to date: 'Winning the Championship in 1996 with Leicestershire.
Receiving phone call from David Graveney advising me of England [tour] selection'
Cricket moments to forget: 'Losing Lord's one-day finals'
Cricketers particularly admired: David Gower, Ian Botham, Ian Healy, Viv Richards
Young players to look out for: Rob Key
Other sports played: Golf, training with Leicester Tigers rugby team
Other sports followed: Football (Leicester City, Carlisle United, Liverpool),
rugby (Leicester Tigers)
Relaxations: Team-building; winning books and tapes; health hydros
Extras: County captain of Cumbria at football, cricket and rugby. Youngest person to
score a century against Yorkshire (at U15). Played for England U15. Played in Minor
Counties Championship for Cumberland at 16. MCC Young Pro in 1988. Took eight
catches in debut match v Warwickshire at Hinckley in 1989. Played for Carlisle
United. Leicester Young Player of the Year two years running. Only second Leicester
wicket-keeper to score 1000 runs in a season. Voted Cumbria Sports Personality of the
Year 1994-95. Was part of Leicestershire's County Championship winning side in
1996 and 1998. Left Leicestershire at end of 1999 season and joined Kent for 2000.
Captained First-Class Counties Select XI v New Zealand A at Milton Keynes 2000.
B&H Gold Award for his 65* v Surrey at Canterbury 2001

Opinions on cricket: '1. 25-over day/night league. 2. "Premier Division" rather than "Division One". 3. Regional cricket against tourists. 4. Start season four weeks later so we go on into October. 5. Bats should have any company's name on them. 6. All kids under 16 should only pay £10 per year membership. 7. Two teams go up, two teams go down in Championship divisions.'

Best batting: 134* Kent v Hampshire, Canterbury 2000

2001 Season

	M	Inns	NO	Runs	HS	Avge	100s	50s	Ct	St	O	M	Runs	Wkts	Avge	Best	5wI	10wM
Test																		
All First	18	24	7	651	87 *	38.29	-	4	44	4								
1-day Int																		
C & G	3	1	0	4	4	4.00	-	-	4	-								
B & H	5	4	1	111	65 *	37.00	-	1	4	-								
1-day Lge	14	14	1	259	55	19.92	-	1	13	6								

Career Performances

	M	Inns	NO	Runs	HS	Avge	100s	50s	Ct	St	Balls	Runs	Wkts	Avge	Best	5wI	10wM
Test																	
All First	220	309	70	7617	134 *	31.87	12	30	570	46	30	14	0	-	-	-	-
1-day Int																	
C & G	27	21	8	346	51	26.61	-	1	35	7							
B & H	34	27	7	487	65 *	24.35	-	2	40	6							
1-day Lge	168	145	25	2576	96 *	21.46	-	11	160	35							

NOON, W. M. Nottinghamshire

Name: <u>Wayne</u> Michael Noon
Role: Right-hand bat, wicket-keeper
Born: 5 February 1971, Grimsby
Height: 5ft 9in **Weight:** 11st 7lbs
Nickname: Noonie, Spain Boon
County debut: 1988 (one-day, Northants), 1989 (first-class, Northants), 1994 (Notts)
County cap: 1995 (Notts)
1st-Class 50s: 12
1st-Class catches: 187
1st-Class stumpings: 20
Parents: Trafford and Rosemary
Marital status: Engaged
Education: Caistor Grammar School
Qualifications: 5 O-levels
Career outside cricket: Manager of G. Atkins (bookmakers)

Overseas tours: Lincolnshire U15 to Pakistan 1984; Rutland tourists to South Africa 1988; England YC to Australia 1989-90; Northamptonshire to Durban 1992, to Cape Town 1993

Overseas teams played for: Burnside West, Christchurch, New Zealand 1989-90 and 1995-96; Rivertonians, Cape Town 1993-94; Canterbury, Christchurch 1994-95

Cricketers particularly admired: Ian Botham

Other sports followed: Football (Lincoln City), horse racing (flat)

Relaxations: 'Having a bet. Eating out and having a pint'

Extras: Played for England YC v New Zealand YC 1989; captain v Australian YC 1989-90 and Pakistan YC 1990. Was the

1000th player to appear in the Sunday League competition. Broke the Northants record for most 2nd XI hundreds in one season in 1993. Took seven catches for Notts in Kent's first innings at Trent Bridge 1999, breaking Bruce French's county record of six. PCA representative for Nottinghamshire

Best batting: 83 Nottinghamshire v Northamptonshire, Northampton 1997

2001 Season

	M	Inns	NO	Runs	HS	Avge	100s	50s	Ct	St	O	M	Runs	Wkts	Avge	Best	5wI	10wM
Test																		
All First																		
1-day Int																		
C & G																		
B & H																		
1-day Lge	1	1	0	17	17	17.00	-	-	2	1								

Career Performances

	M	Inns	NO	Runs	HS	Avge	100s	50s	Ct	St	Balls	Runs	Wkts	Avge	Best	5wI	10wM
Test																	
All First	89	140	22	2474	83	20.96	-	12	187	20	30	34	0	-		-	-	-
1-day Int																	
C & G	7	4	1	73	34	24.33	-	-	4	2							
B & H	18	11	3	152	46	19.00	-	-	9	4							
1-day Lge	81	52	14	477	38	12.55	-	-	62	15							

ORMOND, J.   Surrey

Name: James Ormond
Role: Right-hand bat, right-arm fast-'ish'
bowler, can also bowl off spin
Born: 20 August 1977, Walsgrave, Coventry
Height: 6ft 3in **Weight:** 15st
Nickname: Horse
County debut: 1995 (Leicestershire)
County cap: 1999 (Leicestershire)
Test debut: 2001
Tests: 1
50 wickets in a season: 1
1st-Class 50s: 1
1st-Class 5 w. in innings: 13
1st-Class catches: 12
Place in batting averages: 199th av. 19.30
(2000 254th av. 11.87)
Place in bowling averages: 57th av. 28.91
(2000 62nd av. 25.36)
Strike rate: 59.46 (career 49.98)
Parents: Richard and Margaret
Marital status: Single
Family links with cricket: 'Dad played years of cricket in Warwickshire'
Education: St Anthony's, Bedworth; St Thomas More, Nuneaton; North Warwickshire
College of Further Education
Qualifications: 6 GCSEs
Off-season: Touring with England
Overseas tours: England U19 to Zimbabwe 1995-96; England A to Kenya and Sri
Lanka 1997-98; England to India and New Zealand 2001-02 (*see **Stop press***)
Overseas teams played for: Sydney University CC 1996, 1998, 1999
Cricketers particularly admired: Curtly Ambrose, Courtney Walsh, Allan Donald,
Sachin Tendulkar, Brian Lara, Steve Griffin
Young players to look out for: Darren Stevens, Carl Crowe
Other sports played: Football, mountain biking, 'anything'
Other sports followed: Football (Coventry City)
Relaxations: Spending time with friends and family
Extras: Played for the Development of Excellence side and England U19 against
South Africa U19 in 1995. Played for England U19 against New Zealand U19 in 1996.
Won Leicestershire's 2nd XI bowling award. NBC Denis Compton Award for the most
promising young Leicestershire player 1998, 1999, 2000. B&H Gold Award for his
4-25 v Yorkshire at Leicester 2001. Made his Test debut in the fifth Test v Australia
at The Oval 2001. Left Leicestershire in the 2001-02 off-season and has joined Surrey
for 2002

Opinions on cricket: 'I think we should play less cricket; it would improve the standard – more time to prepare. It would also make games more competitive.'
Best batting: 50* Leicestershire v Warwickshire, Leicester 1999
Best bowling: 6-33 Leicestershire v Somerset, Leicester 1998
Stop press: Selected for England one-day tour to Zimbabwe 2001-02 but was forced to withdraw with tendonitis of the knee; replaced by Chris Silverwood

2001 Season

	M	Inns	NO	Runs	HS	Avge	100s	50s	Ct	St	O	M	Runs	Wkts	Avge	Best	5wI	10wM
Test	1	2	0	35	18	17.50	-	-	-	-	34	4	115	1	115.00	1-115	-	-
All First	12	18	5	251	42	19.30	-	-	2	-	485.4	113	1417	49	28.91	5-71	2	-
1-day Int																		
C & G	4	2	1	18	18 *	18.00	-	-	-	-	40	6	126	5	25.20	2-16	-	
B & H	4	4	2	25	13 *	12.50	-	-	2	-	26.4	2	96	7	13.71	4-25	-	
1-day Lge	13	7	3	42	13 *	10.50	-	-	1	-	104	13	403	15	26.86	3-16	-	

Career Performances

	M	Inns	NO	Runs	HS	Avge	100s	50s	Ct	St	Balls	Runs	Wkts	Avge	Best	5wI	10wM
Test	1	2	0	35	18	17.50	-	-	-	-	204	115	1	115.00	1-115	-	-
All First	62	71	17	737	50 *	13.64	-	1	12	-	11246	5727	225	25.45	6-33	13	-
1-day Int																	
C & G	8	5	3	29	18 *	14.50	-	-	1	-	462	292	10	29.20	2-16	-	
B & H	11	8	3	40	14 *	8.00	-	-	3	-	526	332	19	17.47	4-25	-	
1-day Lge	51	32	18	173	18	12.35	-	-	10	-	2205	1494	68	21.97	4-12	-	

63. Which current ECB executive and which current broadcaster took the new ball for Middlesex in the 1975 Gillette Cup final?

OSTLER, D. P. Warwickshire

Name: <u>Dominic</u> Piers Ostler
Role: Right-hand bat, right-arm
medium bowler
Born: 15 July 1970, Solihull
Height: 6ft 2in **Weight:** 13st 7lbs
Nickname: Ossie
County debut: 1990
County cap: 1991
Benefit: 2000
1000 runs in a season: 5
1st-Class 50s: 61
1st-Class 100s: 13
1st-Class 200s: 1
1st-Class catches: 232
One-Day 100s: 2
Place in batting averages: 40th av. 47.27

(2000 14th av. 49.81)
Strike rate: (career 233.00)
Parents: Mike and Ann
Wife: Karen
Family links with cricket: Brother used to play for Knowle and Dorridge CC
Education: Our Lady of the Wayside; Princethorpe College; Solihull College of
Technology
Qualifications: 4 O-levels, A-levels, City and Guilds Recreation Course
Career outside cricket: 'In business'
Overseas tours: Gladstone Small's Benefit Tour to Barbados 1991; England A to
Pakistan 1995-96; England to New Zealand (Cricket Max) 1997; Andy Moles' Benefit
Tour to Barbados 1997
Overseas teams played for: Avendale CC, Cape Town 1991-92
Cricketers particularly admired: Jason Ratcliffe, Simon Millington, Graeme Welch
Young players to look out for: Ian Bell, Nick Warren
Other sports played: Golf, snooker
Other sports followed: Football (Birmingham City FC)
Injuries: Out for last six Championship matches with tennis elbow
Relaxations: 'Spending time with wife, Karen; snooker and golf'
Extras: Played club cricket for Moseley in the Birmingham League. Made his
Warwickshire 2nd XI debut in 1989 and was a member of Warwickshire U19 side that
won Esso U19 County Festivals in 1988 and 1989. Has collected winner's medals for
B&H Cup, County Championship, NatWest Trophy and Sunday League. Scored 134*
off 114 balls v Gloucestershire at Edgbaston in the Norwich Union League 2001,
equalling Nick Knight's Warwickshire record for the highest individual score in the
one-day league

Best batting: 208 Warwickshire v Surrey, Edgbaston 1995
Best bowling: 1-46 Warwickshire v Middlesex, Edgbaston 2000

2001 Season

	M	Inns	NO	Runs	HS	Avge	100s	50s	Ct	St	O	M	Runs	Wkts	Avge	Best	5wI	10wM
Test																		
All First	10	12	1	520	121	47.27	2	2	22	-								
1-day Int																		
C & G	2	2	1	87	82 *	87.00	-	1	2	-								
B & H	6	6	0	175	77	29.16	-	1	1	-								
1-day Lge	6	6	2	320	134 *	80.00	1	2	6	-								

Career Performances

	M	Inns	NO	Runs	HS	Avge	100s	50s	Ct	St	Balls	Runs	Wkts	Avge	Best	5wI	10wM
Test																	
All First	186	303	24	9698	208	34.75	14	61	232	-	233	249	1	249.00	1-46	-	-
1-day Int																	
C & G	40	39	4	1126	104	32.17	1	8	19	-	15	10	1	10.00	1-4	-	
B & H	40	38	5	1257	87	38.09	-	10	18	-							
1-day Lge	159	149	22	4100	134 *	32.28	1	29	48	-	6	4	0	-		-	-

PANESAR, M. S.   Northamptonshire

Name: Mudhsuden Singh Panesar
Role: Left-hand bat, slow left-arm bowler
Born: 25 April 1982, Luton
Height: 6ft **Weight:** 12st
Nickname: Monty
County debut: 2001
Place in bowling averages: 74th av. 32.54
Strike rate: 55.36 (career 55.36)
Parents: Paramjit and Gursharan
Marital status: Single
Education: St Matthew's Junior School;
Stopsley High School; Bedford Modern
School; Loughborough University
Qualifications: 10 GCSEs, 3 A-levels
Overseas tours: Bedford Modern School to
Barbados 1999; England U19 to India
2000-01
Cricketers particularly admired:
Bishen Bedi, Sachin Tendulkar, Phil Tufnell
Other sports played: Tennis, badminton

Other sports followed: Football (Arsenal, India)
Relaxations: Sleeping, music, eating
Extras: Represented England U19 v Sri Lanka U19 in one-day and 'Test' series 2000 and v West Indies U19 in 'Test' series (1/3) 2001. Had match figures of 8-131 on first-class debut v Leicestershire at Northampton 2001, including 4-11 in the second innings
Opinions on cricket: 'Everything is good.'
Best batting: 10 Northamptonshire v Leicestershire, Northampton 2001
Best bowling: 4-11 Northamptonshire v Leicestershire, Northampton 2001

2001 Season

	M	Inns	NO	Runs	HS	Avge	100s	50s	Ct	St	O	M	Runs	Wkts	Avge	Best	5wI	10wM
Test																		
All First	2	3	2	15	10	15.00	-	-	-	-	101.3	28	358	11	32.54	4-11	-	-
1-day Int																		
C & G																			
B & H																			
1-day Lge																			

Career Performances

	M	Inns	NO	Runs	HS	Avge	100s	50s	Ct	St	Balls	Runs	Wkts	Avge	Best	5wI	10wM
Test																	
All First	2	3	2	15	10	15.00	-	-	-	-	609	358	11	32.54	4-11	-	-
1-day Int																	
C & G																		
B & H																		
1-day Lge																		

PARKIN, O. T.   Glamorgan

Name: <u>Owen</u> Thomas Parkin
Role: Right-hand bat, right-arm medium-fast swing bowler
Born: 24 September 1972, Coventry
Height: 6ft 3in **Weight:** 13st
Nickname: Parky
County debut: 1994
1st-Class 5 w. in innings: 2
1st-Class catches: 10
One-Day 5 w. in innings: 1
Place in bowling averages: (2000 11th av. 17.11)
Strike rate: 66.00 (career 55.25)
Parents: Vernon Cyrus and Sarah Patricia

Wife and date of marriage: Diane Margaret, 29 September 2001

Family links with cricket: Younger brother Morgan plays for Glamorgan at U17 and U19 level

Education: Bournemouth Grammar School; Bath University

Qualifications: 9 GCSEs, 4 A-levels, 1 S-level, BSc (Hons) Mathematics

Career outside cricket: Maths teacher

Off-season: 'Decorating new house!'

Overseas tours: Dorset Youth to Denmark

Overseas teams played for: Kew, Melbourne 1992-93; North Balwyn, Melbourne 1994-95; Balmain, Sydney 1997-99; ATW Clubites, Bundaberg, Queensland 1999-2000

Career highlights to date: 'Lord's final, and hitting winning runs against Derby in 2000' (*The latter batting at No. 11 in NUL after 10 required off 14 balls*)

Cricket moments to forget: 'Dropping Chris Adams at Hove 2000'

Cricketers particularly admired: Malcolm Marshall, Richard Hadlee

Young players to look out for: Simon Jones

Other sports played: 'Most sports socially'

Other sports followed: Rugby, football (Nottingham Forest), golf

Relaxations: '*Telegraph* crossword'

Extras: Played for Dorset in the NatWest Trophy 1992 and 1993. ASW Young Player of the Month July 1994. Took 5 for 28 on debut in Sunday League at Hove 1996 – a club record

Opinions on cricket: 'Two leagues excellent, but maybe only two up/two down.'

Best batting: 24* Glamorgan v Essex, Chelmsford 1998

Best bowling: 5-24 Glamorgan v Somerset, Cardiff, 1998

64. Which county won the first ever NatWest Trophy and which current county cricketer played on the winning side in the final?

2001 Season

	M	Inns	NO	Runs	HS	Avge	100s	50s	Ct	St	O	M	Runs	Wkts	Avge	Best	5wI	10wM
Test																		
All First	1	1	0	0	0	0.00	-	-	1	-	44	4	176	4	44.00	2-45	-	-
1-day Int																		
C & G	1	0	0	0	0	-	-	-	-	-	4	0	28	0	-		-	-
B & H																		
1-day Lge	13	3	1	2	2 *	1.00	-	-	2	-	78.5	7	418	13	32.15	3-37	-	

Career Performances

	M	Inns	NO	Runs	HS	Avge	100s	50s	Ct	St	Balls	Runs	Wkts	Avge	Best	5wI	10wM
Test																	
All First	37	44	20	203	24 *	8.45	-	-	10	-	5525	2745	100	27.45	5-24	2	-
1-day Int																	
C & G	11	5	2	3	2	1.00	-	-	5	-	520	361	10	36.10	3-23	-	
B & H	8	5	3	16	8	8.00	-	-	2	-	384	310	14	22.14	4-60	-	
1-day Lge	68	25	10	43	6	2.86	-	-	13	-	2894	2273	91	24.97	5-28	1	

PARSONS, K. A.   Somerset

Name: <u>Keith</u> Alan Parsons
Role: Right-hand bat, right-arm medium bowler
Born: 2 May 1973, Taunton
Height: 6ft 1in **Weight:** 14st
Nickname: Pilot, Pars, Orv
County debut: 1992
County cap: 1999
1st-Class 50s: 19
1st-Class 100s: 5
1st-Class 5 w. in innings: 2
1st-Class catches: 82
Place in batting averages: 82nd av. 36.28 (2000 48th av. 37.25)
Place in bowling averages: (2000 131st av. 40.27)
Strike rate: 276.00 (career 79.82)
Parents: Alan and Lynne
Wife and date of marriage: Sharon, 12 January 2002
Family links with cricket: Identical twin brother, Kevin, was on the Somerset staff 1992-94 and now captains the Somerset Board XI. Father played six seasons for Somerset 2nd XI and captained National Civil Service XI

Education: Bishop Henderson Primary School; The Castle School, Taunton; Richard Huish Sixth Form College, Taunton

Qualifications: 8 GCSEs, 3 A-levels, NCA senior coach

Off-season: 'Working for Set Square Recruitment Agency in Taunton'

Overseas tours: Castle School to Barbados 1989; Somerset CCC to Cape Town 1999, 2000, 2001

Overseas teams played for: Kapiti Old Boys, Horowhenua, New Zealand 1992-93; Taita District, Wellington, New Zealand 1993-96; Wembley Downs CC, Perth 1998

Career highlights to date: 'C&G final 2001 v Leicestershire – great to win a trophy, and Man of the Match capped a dream day'

Cricket moments to forget: 'Any bad days at Taunton'

Cricketers particularly admired: Andy Caddick, Marcus Trescothick, Glenn McGrath, Saqlain Mushtaq

Other sports followed: Rugby union (Bath RFC), football (Nottingham Forest FC), golf, horse racing

Injuries: Out for six weeks with knee trouble

Relaxations: Playing golf, watching movies, listening to music 'and the odd social pint of beer'

Extras: Captained two National Cup winning sides – Taunton St Andrews in National U15 Club Championship and Richard Huish College in National U17 School Championship. Represented English Schools at U15 and U19 level. Somerset Young Player of the Year 1993. C&G Man of the Match award for his 52-ball 60* (including sixes from the last two balls of the innings) and 2-40 in the final v Leicestershire at Lord's 2001

Opinions on cricket: 'Two division cricket has been very successful – interest in all games right up to the end of the season. Prize money in competitions should reflect the divisions teams are in, i.e. runners-up in division two shouldn't receive more than, say, third or fourth in division one.'

Best batting: 193* Somerset v West Indians, Taunton 2000

Best bowling: 5-13 Somerset v Lancashire, Taunton 2000

---

65. Which West Indies pace bowler returned the best figures in the history of the Gillette/NatWest/C&G (8-21) v Sussex at Hove in 1988?

2001 Season

	M	Inns	NO	Runs	HS	Avge	100s	50s	Ct	St	O	M	Runs	Wkts	Avge	Best	5wl	10wM
Test																		
All First	5	8	1	254	139	36.28	1	-	5	-	46	5	193	1	193.00	1-22	-	-
1-day Int																		
C & G	5	5	2	135	60 *	45.00	-	1	2	-	44	0	219	9	24.33	3-38	-	
B & H	5	4	1	92	72	30.66	-	1	4	-	28	2	104	0	-	-	-	
1-day Lge	10	9	1	201	58 *	25.12	-	1	2	-	40	1	197	5	39.40	2-32	-	

Career Performances

	M	Inns	NO	Runs	HS	Avge	100s	50s	Ct	St	Balls	Runs	Wkts	Avge	Best	5wl	10wM
Test																	
All First	92	148	15	3704	193 *	27.84	5	19	82	-	5029	2722	63	43.20	5-13	2	-
1-day Int																	
C & G	22	20	7	488	60 *	37.53	-	2	5	-	944	692	26	26.61	4-43	-	
B & H	18	15	5	232	72	23.20	-	1	10	-	408	394	4	98.50	2-60	-	
1-day Lge	102	84	15	1716	69	24.86	-	8	39	-	2352	1931	53	36.43	3-21	-	

PATEL, D. Worcestershire

Name: Depesh Patel
Role: Right-hand bat, right-arm fast-medium bowler
Born: 23 September 1981, Wolverhampton
Height: 6ft 4in **Weight:** 13st
Nickname: Dip, Dippy, Dipster
County debut: No first-team appearance
Parents: Balvant and Mena
Marital status: Single
Family links with cricket: 'Dad played for Thompson's CC for 18 years. Brother Vijay plays for Wolverhampton CC'
Education: Wilkinson Primary School; Moseley Park Grammar School; Bilston Community College
Qualifications: GCSEs, Level 1 coaching award
Cricketers particularly admired: Allan Donald, Glenn McGrath, Sachin Tendulkar
Young players to look out for: Ryan Driver, Kadeer Ali
Other sports followed: Football (Wolverhampton Wanderers)
Relaxations: 'Listening to music, playing pool, chilling with friends'

Extras: Scored 120 aged 15 against Cheshire playing for Staffordshire. Has best bowling of 7 for 1 playing against Glamorgan U11 for Staffordshire U11. Played for Worcestershire Board XI in the 1999 NatWest

2001 Season (did not make any first-class or one-day appearances)

Career Performances

	M	Inns	NO	Runs	HS	Avge	100s	50s	Ct	St	Balls	Runs	Wkts	Avge	Best	5wI	10wM
Test																	
All First																	
1-day Int																	
C & G	1	1	1	19	19 *	-	-	-	-	-	42	36	1	36.00	1-36	-	
B & H																	
1-day Lge																	

PATEL, M. M. Kent

Name: <u>Minal</u> Mahesh Patel
Role: Right-hand bat, slow left-arm orthodox bowler
Born: 7 July 1970, Bombay, India
Height: 5ft 7in **Weight:** 9st 10lbs
Nickname: Ho Chi, Diamond, Geez
County debut: 1989
County cap: 1994
Test debut: 1996
Tests: 2
50 wickets in a season: 3
1st-Class 50s: 6
1st-Class 5 w. in innings: 22
1st-Class 10 w. in match: 9
1st-Class catches: 79
Place in batting averages: 223rd av. 15.43 (2000 198th av. 17.93)
Place in bowling averages: 65th av. 30.70 (2000 58th av. 25.15)
Strike rate: 78.65 (career 72.50)
Parents: Mahesh and Aruna
Wife and date of marriage: Karuna, 8 October 1995
Family links with cricket: Father played good club cricket in India, Africa and England
Education: Maypole CP; Dartford Grammar School; Manchester Polytechnic

Qualifications: 6 O-levels, 3 A-levels, BA (Hons) Economics
Career outside cricket: Writes for *Racing Post*
Off-season: Player/coach on Club Cricket Conference tour to Australia, January 2002
Overseas tours: Dartford GS to Barbados 1988; England A to India and Bangladesh 1994-95; MCC to Malta 1997, 1999, to Fiji, Sydney and Hong Kong 1998, to East and Central Africa 1999, to Bangladesh 1999-2000 (captain), to Argentina and Chile 2001: Kent to Port Elizabeth 2001; Club Cricket Conference to Australia 2002
Overseas teams played for: St Augustine's, Cape Town 1993-94; Alberton, Johannesburg 1997-98
Career highlights to date: 'Winning 2001 Norwich Union League at Edgbaston. First Test cap. Any match-winning performance for Kent'
Cricket moments to forget: 'Being left out of the final XI for the Lord's Test v India 1996'
Cricketers particularly admired: Derek Underwood, Aravinda De Silva
Young players to look out for: Rob Key
Other sports played: Golf, snooker
Other sports followed: Football (Tottenham Hotspur), 'most sports that you can name'
Injuries: 'Mental strain caused by travelling with Rob Key for six months'
Relaxations: Spread betting, DJ-ing, golf
Extras: Played for English Schools 1988, 1989 and NCA England South 1989. Was voted Kent League Young Player of the Year 1987 while playing for Blackheath. First six overs in NatWest Trophy were all maidens. Whittingdale Young Player of the Year 1994
Opinions on cricket: 'At this early stage, the two division format has made a positive impact as far as players and their efforts for the *entire* season are concerned.'
Best batting: 67 Kent v Gloucestershire, Canterbury 1999
Best bowling: 8-96 Kent v Lancashire, Canterbury 1994

2001 Season

	M	Inns	NO	Runs	HS	Avge	100s	50s	Ct	St	O	M	Runs	Wkts	Avge	Best	5wI	10wM
Test																		
All First	17	19	3	247	38	15.43	-	-	9	-	524.2	158	1228	40	30.70	8-119	1	1
1-day Int																		
C & G	3	1	1	27	27*	-	-	-	-	-	9	0	55	0	-		-	-
B & H	3	2	0	5	3	2.50	-	-	1	-	24	3	116	2	58.00	2-34	-	
1-day Lge	13	9	2	58	15	8.28	-	-	7	-	89	6	406	15	27.06	2-27	-	

Career Performances

	M	Inns	NO	Runs	HS	Avge	100s	50s	Ct	St	Balls	Runs	Wkts	Avge	Best	5wI	10wM
Test	2	2	0	45	27	22.50	-	-	2	-	276	180	1	180.00	1-101	-	-
All First	144	194	38	2364	67	15.15	-	6	79	-	31468	13278	434	30.59	8-96	22	9
1-day Int																	
C & G	14	5	2	45	27 *	15.00	-	-	5	-	662	399	11	36.27	2-29	-	
B & H	18	10	6	59	18 *	14.75	-	-	5	-	750	580	11	52.72	2-29	-	
1-day Lge	38	22	6	109	15	6.81	-	-	12	-	1586	1203	46	26.15	3-22	-	

PATTISON, I.   Durham

Name: Ian Pattison
Role: Right-hand bat, right-arm medium bowler
Born: 5 May 1982, Sunderland
Height: 5ft 11in **Weight:** 12st 8lbs
Nickname: Patto, Patta
County debut: No first-team appearance
Parents: Stewart and Janice
Marital status: Single
Family links with cricket: Brother Stewart plays in local premier league
Education: New Seaham Primary School; Seaham Comprehensive
Qualifications: 6 GCSEs, Level 1 coaching award
Off-season: 'Rest as much as possible to make sure my injuries (knees) are fully cured'
Overseas tours: England U19 to Malaysia and (U19 World Cup) Sri Lanka 1999-2000, to India 2000-01
Career highlights to date: 'Representing England U19 in the 1999-2000 U19 World Cup'
Cricketers particularly admired: Steve Waugh, Jacques Kallis, Simon Katich, Craig White
Young players to look out for: Nicky Peng, Ian Bell
Other sports followed: Football (Sunderland AFC season-ticket holder), horse racing, 'most sports'
Injuries: Out for three weeks with injury to left foot; 'troubled throughout season' by patellar tendonitis in both knees
Relaxations: Horse racing, sleeping, golf
Extras: Played for Durham Board XI in the NatWest 2000 and in the second round of the C&G 2002, which was played in September 2001

2001 Season (did not make any first-class or one-day appearances)

Career Performances

	M	Inns	NO	Runs	HS	Avge	100s	50s	Ct	St	Balls	Runs	Wkts	Avge	Best	5wI	10wM
Test																	
All First																	
1-day Int																	
C & G	4	4	2	57	48 *	28.50	-	-	2	-	114	88	3	29.33	1-25	-	
B & H																	
1-day Lge																	

PAYNTER, D. E. Northamptonshire

Name: <u>David</u> Edward Paynter
Role: Right-hand bat, right-arm
off-spin bowler
Born: 25 January 1981, Truro
Height: 6ft 2½in **Weight:** 12st 7lbs
Nickname: Paints
County debut: No first-team appearance
One-Day 100s: 1
Parents: Mark and Carole
Marital status: Single
Family links with cricket: Great-grandfather
(Eddie Paynter) played for Lancashire
(1926-1945) and England and was on the
Bodyline tour
Education: Larchmont First School;
Clayton Middle School
Qualifications: 9 GCSEs, Level I, II and III
coaching awards
Overseas tours: Yorkshire U19 to India 1998-99
Overseas teams played for: Grafton, Auckland 1999-2001
Cricketers particularly admired: Mark Waugh, Ricky Ponting
Young players to look out for: John Sadler, Daren Drake, Craig Mowatt
Other sports played: Table tennis (Yorkshire U14), rugby (Queensbury RFC)
Other sports followed: Football (Bradford City), rugby league (Bradford Bulls)
Relaxations: Gym work, listening to music, socialising with friends
Extras: Bradford League Young Player of the Year 2000. Has attended Yorkshire and
Northamptonshire academies. Played for Worcestershire 2nd XI in 2000. Played for
Northamptonshire Board XI in the C&G 2001, scoring 104 on competition debut v
Northamptonshire at Northampton

Opinions on cricket: 'All good. Need more coverage of the county game on TV. Need to play more day/night games – they attract more families and have a great atmosphere.'

2001 Season (did not make any first-class or one-day appearances)

Career Performances

	M	Inns	NO	Runs	HS	Avge	100s	50s	Ct	St	Balls	Runs	Wkts	Avge	Best	5wI	10wM
Test																	
All First																	
1-day Int																	
C & G	1	1	0	104	104	104.00	1	-	-	-	36	46	0	-		-	-
B & H																	
1-day Lge																	

PENBERTHY, A. L.   Northamptonshire

Name: Anthony (<u>Tony</u>) Leonard Penberthy
Role: Left-hand bat, right-arm medium bowler, county vice-captain
Born: 1 September 1969, Troon, Cornwall
Height: 6ft 1in **Weight:** 12st 7lbs
Nickname: Berth, Penbers, Sir Leonard, Denzil
County debut: 1989
County cap: 1994
1st-Class 50s: 35
1st-Class 100s: 8
1st-Class 5 w. in innings: 4
1st-Class catches: 99
One-Day 5 w. in innings: 4
Place in batting averages: 66th av. 40.95 (2000 33rd av. 41.31)
Place in bowling averages: 115th av. 40.76 (2000 35th av. 22.37)
Strike rate: 81.44 (career 71.68)
Parents: Gerald (deceased) and Wendy
Wife and date of marriage: Rebecca, 9 November 1996
Children: Georgia Lily, 4 March 1998; Harry Jake, 5 October 2000
Family links with cricket: Father played in local leagues in Cornwall and became a qualified umpire instructor
Education: Troon County Primary; Camborne Comprehensive

Qualifications: 3 O-levels, 3 CSEs, Levels 1 and 2 coaching certificates
Career outside cricket: Coaching
Off-season: Planning benefit for 2002
Overseas tours: Druids to Zimbabwe 1988; Northants to Durban 1992, to Cape Town 1993, to Zimbabwe 1995, 1998, to Johannesburg 1996, to Grenada 2000, 2001
Career highlights to date: 'Wicket of Mark Taylor with first ball in first-class cricket' (*Caught behind, June 1989*)
Cricket moments to forget: 'A pair in the same game'
Cricketers particularly admired: Ian Botham, David Gower, Dennis Lillee, Viv Richards, Eldine Baptiste
Young players to look out for: Mark Powell, Monty Panesar
Other sports played: Football, golf
Other sports followed: Football (West Ham United), rugby (Northampton Saints)
Injuries: Out for two one-day games with a shoulder problem; fractured rib – no time off required; suffered from sciatica all season ('lovely')
Relaxations: Listening to music, watching films and comedy programmes, 'walking my Irish setter'
Extras: Had football trials for Plymouth Argyle but came to Northampton for cricket trials instead. Played for England YC v New Zealand YC 1989. Took only the second Sunday/National League hat-trick in Northants history v Somerset at Northampton in 1999. Vice-captain of Northamptonshire since 2001. Scored 132* v Glamorgan at Northampton 2001, in the process sharing with Russell Warren in a record sixth-wicket partnership for Northants in matches against Glamorgan (250). Took his 158th one-day league wicket (Trevor Ward) v Leicestershire at Northampton 2001 to pass Peter Willey's county record in the competition. Scored 80 v Somerset at Northampton 2001, in the process sharing with David Ripley in a record eighth-wicket partnership for Northants in matches against Somerset (161); also shared with Curtly Ambrose in the previous record stand – 145 at Taunton in 1994. Granted a benefit for 2002
Opinions on cricket: 'Two divisional system has led to more competitive cricket. Wickets must improve, and the pitch liaison officers should be more consistent with their findings. Cricket balls we have used this year were sub-standard.'
Best batting: 132* Northamptonshire v Glamorgan, Northampton 2001
Best bowling: 5-37 Northamptonshire v Glamorgan, Swansea 1993

66. Who is the only player to have won the Man of the Match award in a Gillette Cup final and in a NatWest Trophy final?

2001 Season

	M	Inns	NO	Runs	HS	Avge	100s	50s	Ct	St	O	M	Runs	Wkts	Avge	Best	5wI	10wM
Test																		
All First	15	24	1	942	132 *	40.95	3	5	11	-	339.2	70	1019	25	40.76	4-39	-	-
1-day Int																		
C & G	2	1	0	0	0	0.00	-	-	-	-	20	1	110	1	110.00	1-53	-	
B & H	5	3	0	68	58	22.66	-	1	2	-	47	4	197	3	65.66	2-21	-	
1-day Lge	12	11	1	190	52	19.00	-	2	2	-	99.3	7	453	12	37.75	3-43	-	

Career Performances

	M	Inns	NO	Runs	HS	Avge	100s	50s	Ct	St	Balls	Runs	Wkts	Avge	Best	5wI	10wM
Test																	
All First	163	242	26	6210	132 *	28.75	8	35	99	-	15340	8164	214	38.14	5-37	4	-
1-day Int																	
C & G	28	19	2	423	79	24.88	-	4	9	-	1285	945	24	39.37	5-56	1	
B & H	36	28	6	643	62	29.22	-	3	9	-	1652	1157	29	39.89	3-22	-	
1-day Lge	151	125	25	2343	81 *	23.43	-	12	37	-	5394	4432	158	28.05	5-29	3	

PENG, N.   Durham

Name: Nicky Peng
Role: Right-hand bat
Born: 18 September 1982, Newcastle upon Tyne
Height: 6ft 3in **Weight:** 12st
Nickname: Pengy, King
County debut: 2000
County cap: 2001
1st-Class 50s: 4
1st-Class 100s: 1
1st-Class catches: 9
One-Day 100s: 3
Place in batting averages: 146th av. 26.23 (2000 217th av. 16.50)
Parents: Linda and Wilf
Marital status: Single
Education: Royal Grammar School, Newcastle upon Tyne
Qualifications: 10 GCSEs

Off-season: ECB National Academy in Australia, U19 World Cup in New Zealand and Durham CCC tour to South Africa
Overseas tours: England U19 to India 2000-01, to Australia and (U19 World Cup)

New Zealand 2001-02 (captain); ECB National Academy to Australia 2001-02; Durham to South Africa 2002

Career highlights to date: 'Scoring 119 for Durham v Hampshire in June in C&G match'

Cricket moments to forget: 'Every time I get out!'

Cricketers particularly admired: Mike Atherton, Steve Waugh

Young players to look out for: Gordon Muchall, Ian Bell, Mark Wallace

Other sports followed: Football, rugby (Newcastle, especially England)

Relaxations: Socialising with friends; music and films

Extras: Full name Nicky Peng Gillender. Has represented England at U14, U15, U17 and U19 levels. Represented Minor Counties at age 15. Scored 98 on his Championship debut v Surrey at Riverside 2000. Represented England U19 v Sri Lanka U19 in one-day and 'Test' series 2000 (scoring 123 in second 'Test' at Northampton) and v West Indies U19 in 'Test' series (2/3) 2001 (captain in first 'Test'). Scored 132 in England's first innings in the second U19 'Test' at Chennai (Madras) 2000-01. NBC Denis Compton Award for the most promising young Durham player 2000. Scored maiden one-day century (112*) v Essex at Ilford in the Norwich Union League 2001. Scored maiden first-class century (101) v Middlesex at Riverside 2001. C&G Man of the Match award for his 119 v Hampshire at Riverside 2001. Durham CCC Young Player of the Year 2001. Awarded Durham cap 2001. PCA Young Player of the Year 2001

Opinions on cricket: 'Setting up of the National Academy is a major step forward for the development of young players.'

Best batting: 101 Durham v Middlesex, Riverside 2001

2001 Season

	M	Inns	NO	Runs	HS	Avge	100s	50s	Ct	St	O	M	Runs	Wkts	Avge	Best	5wI	10wM
Test																		
All First	13	23	2	551	101	26.23	1	3	8	-								
1-day Int																		
C & G	3	3	0	149	119	49.66	1	-	1	-								
B & H	2	2	0	35	32	17.50	-	-	-	-								
1-day Lge	13	13	1	495	121	41.25	2	2	4	-								

Career Performances

	M	Inns	NO	Runs	HS	Avge	100s	50s	Ct	St	Balls	Runs	Wkts	Avge	Best	5wI	10wM
Test																	
All First	21	37	2	782	101	22.34	1	4	9	-							
1-day Int																	
C & G	3	3	0	149	119	49.66	1	-	1	-							
B & H	7	6	0	65	32	10.83	-	-	-	-							
1-day Lge	17	17	1	541	121	33.81	2	2	4	-							

PENNEY, T. L.   Warwickshire

Name: <u>Trevor</u> Lionel Penney
Role: Right-hand bat, leg-break bowler,
occasional wicket-keeper
Born: 12 June 1968, Harare, Zimbabwe
Height: 6ft **Weight:** 11st 2lbs
Nickname: TP, Blondie
County debut: 1992
County cap: 1994
1000 runs in a season: 2
1st-Class 50s: 36
1st-Class 100s: 15
1st-Class catches: 91
1st-Class stumpings: 2
Place in batting averages: (2000 37th
av. 40.64)
Strike rate: (career 43.16)
Parents: George and Bets
Wife and date of marriage: Deborah-Anne,
19 December 1992
Children: Samantha Anne, 20 August 1995; Kevin, 7 June 1998
Family links with cricket: Father played club cricket. Brother Stephen captained
Zimbabwe Schools
Education: Blakiston Junior School; Prince Edward Boys High School, Zimbabwe
Qualifications: 3 O-levels
Career outside cricket: Tobacco buyer
Overseas tours: Zimbabwe U24 to England 1984; Zimbabwe to Sri Lanka 1987;
ICC Associates team to Australia (U19 World Cup) 1987-88 (captain)
Overseas teams played for: Old Hararians, Zimbabwe 1983-89 and 1992-98;
Scarborough, Perth 1989-90; Avendale, South Africa 1990-91; Boland, South Africa
1991-92; Mashonaland, Zimbabwe 1993-94 –
Cricketers particularly admired: Colin Bland, Ian Botham, Allan Donald,
Steve Waugh
Other sports played: Hockey (Zimbabwe and Africa), squash, tennis, golf and white
water rafting
Other sports followed: Basketball (Chicago Bulls), American football (San Francisco
49ers), Formula One motor racing
Relaxations: 'Playing golf and drinking cold Castles on Lake Kariba. Spending time
with my family'
Extras: Played for Zimbabwe against Sri Lanka in 1987. Played hockey for
Zimbabwe 1984-87 and also made the African team who played Asia in 1987.
Qualified to play for England in 1992. Captained Old Hararians to victory in three

Zimbabwe domestic trophies 1998-99. Coach of Zimbabwe Board XI 2000-01. C&G Man of the Match award for his 58* in the quarter-final v Yorkshire at Headingley 2001

Best batting: 151 Warwickshire v Middlesex, Lord's 1992
Best bowling: 3-18 Mashonaland v Mashonaland U24, Harare 1993-94

2001 Season

	M	Inns	NO	Runs	HS	Avge	100s	50s	Ct	St	O	M	Runs	Wkts	Avge	Best	5wI	10wM
Test																		
All First	1	1	0	1	1	1.00	-	-	3	-								
1-day Int																		
C & G	4	3	2	126	58 *	126.00	-	1	3	-								
B & H	6	6	1	124	73 *	24.80	-	1	-	-								
1-day Lge	15	10	3	171	35	24.42	-	-	5	-								

Career Performances

	M	Inns	NO	Runs	HS	Avge	100s	50s	Ct	St	Balls	Runs	Wkts	Avge	Best	5wI	10wM
Test																	
All First	157	246	45	7954	151	39.57	15	36	93	2	259	184	6	30.66	3-18	-	-
1-day Int																	
C & G	38	35	10	835	90	33.40	-	3	21	-	13	16	1	16.00	1-8	-	
B & H	39	34	7	759	73 *	28.11	-	4	14	1							
1-day Lge	146	125	41	2335	83 *	27.79	-	9	54	-	6	2	0	-	-	-

PETERS, S. D.   Worcestershire

Name: <u>Stephen</u> David Peters
Role: Right-hand bat, leg-break bowler
Born: 10 December 1978, Harold Wood
Height: 5ft 11in **Weight:** 11st
Nickname: Geezer, Pedro
County debut: 1996
1st-Class 50s: 10
1st-Class 100s: 2
1st-Class catches: 46
Place in batting averages: 175th av. 22.08 (2000 118th av. 27.36)
Strike rate: (career 23.00)
Parents: Brian and Lesley
Marital status: Single
Family links with cricket: 'All family is linked with Upminster CC'
Education: Upminster Junior School; Coopers Company and Coborn School
Qualifications: 9 GCSEs

Off-season: Cornwall CC, Auckland, New Zealand
Overseas tours: Essex U14 to Barbados; Essex U15 to Hong Kong; England U19 to Pakistan 1996-97, to South Africa (including U19 World Cup) 1997-98
Overseas teams played for: Cornwall CC, Auckland, New Zealand 2001-02
Career highlights to date: 'Winning B&H Cup in 1998 with Essex. Gaining [Championship] promotion in 2000 with Essex'
Cricketers particularly admired: 'Anyone who plays at the top level'
Other sports played: Football, golf
Other sports followed: Football (West Ham United)
Relaxations: 'My sofa; keeping in touch with my mates'
Extras: The Sir John Hobbs Jubilee Memorial Prize 1994; a *Daily Telegraph* regional batting award 1994. Represented England at U14, U15, U17 and U19. Scored century (110) on county debut v Cambridge University at Fenner's 1996, in the process becoming (at 17 years 194 days) the youngest player to score a first-class century for Essex. Essex Young Player of the Year 1996. Scored a century (107) and was Man of the Match in the U19 World Cup final in South Africa 1997-98. Left Essex during the 2001-02 off-season and has joined Worcestershire for 2002
Opinions on cricket: 'Day/night cricket is the way forward.'
Best batting: 110 Essex v Cambridge University, Fenner's 1996
Best bowling: 1-19 Essex v Oxford University, Chelmsford 1999

2001 Season

	M	Inns	NO	Runs	HS	Avge	100s	50s	Ct	St	O	M	Runs	Wkts	Avge	Best	5wI	10wM
Test																		
All First	15	26	3	508	56 *	22.08	-	1	6	-								
1-day Int																		
C & G	2	2	0	14	9	7.00	-	-	-	-								
B & H	3	3	0	73	48	24.33	-	-	1	-								
1-day Lge	13	12	1	253	66	23.00	-	1	4	-								

Career Performances

	M	Inns	NO	Runs	HS	Avge	100s	50s	Ct	St	Balls	Runs	Wkts	Avge	Best	5wI	10wM
Test																	
All First	62	102	15	2245	110	25.80	2	10	46	-	23	19	1	19.00	1-19	-	-
1-day Int																	
C & G	5	5	0	84	58	16.80	-	1	3	-							
B & H	13	11	1	265	58 *	26.50	-	1	3	-							
1-day Lge	56	49	3	807	73 *	17.54	-	4	15	-							

PETTINI, M. L. Essex

Name: <u>Mark</u> Lewis Pettini
Role: Right-hand bat, right-arm
medium bowler
Born: 7 August 1983, Brighton
Height: 5ft 11in **Weight:** 10st 12lbs
Nickname: Swampy, Michelle
County debut: 2001
1st-Class catches: 1
Parents: Pauline and Max
Marital status: Single
Family links with cricket: 'Brother Tom
plays. Mum and Dad are very keen supporters
while Grandad plays a demon game of beach
cricket'

Education: Avalon Primary School, Sydney,
Australia; Meridian Primary School;
Comberton Village College and Hills Road
Sixth Form College, Cambridge
Qualifications: 10 GCSEs, 3 A-levels, Level 1 cricket coaching award
Off-season: England U19 tour to Australia and New Zealand
Overseas tours: England U19 to Australia and (U19 World Cup) New Zealand
2001-02
Career highlights to date: 'First-class debut v Yorkshire 2001'
Cricketers particularly admired: Brian Lara, Steve Waugh, Sachin Tendulkar, 'all
the Essex 1st team'
Young players to look out for: 'Brother Tom'
Other sports played: Tennis, swimming ('keeping fit'), table tennis
Other sports followed: Tennis, basketball
Injuries: Out for three weeks with bad joint mobility in back
Relaxations: Fishing, watching sport, sleeping
Extras: Captained Cambridgeshire county sides from U11-U16. Took hat-trick against

Bedfordshire U12. Highest score of 173* v Hampshire U16 1999. Played for
Development of Excellence XI (South) v West Indies U19 at Arundel 2001
Best batting: 41 Essex v Yorkshire, Scarborough 2001

2001 Season

	M	Inns	NO	Runs	HS	Avge	100s	50s	Ct	St	O	M	Runs	Wkts	Avge	Best	5wI	10wM
Test																		
All First	1	2	0	42	41	21.00	-	-	1	-								
1-day Int																		
C & G																		
B & H																		
1-day Lge	2	1	0	14	14	14.00	-	-	1	-								

Career Performances

	M	Inns	NO	Runs	HS	Avge	100s	50s	Ct	St	Balls	Runs	Wkts	Avge	Best	5wI	10wM
Test																	
All First	1	2	0	42	41	21.00	-	-	1	-							
1-day Int																	
C & G																	
B & H																	
1-day Lge	2	1	0	14	14	14.00	-	-	1	-							

PHILLIPS, B. J.   Northamptonshire

Name: <u>Ben</u> James Phillips
Role: Right-hand bat, right-arm
fast-medium bowler
Born: 30 September 1975, Lewisham
Height: 6ft 6in **Weight:** 15st 2lbs
Nickname: Bus, Action, Barbie Doll,
Bomb, Golden Arm
County debut: 1996 (Kent)
1st-Class 50s: 2
1st-Class 100s: 1
1st-Class 5 w. in innings: 2
1st-Class catches: 8
Strike rate: (career 56.87)
Parents: Trevor and Glynis
Marital status: Single
Family links with cricket: Father and
brother keen club cricketers

Education: St Joseph's Primary, Bromley; Langley Park School for Boys, Beckenham; Langley Park Sixth Form
Qualifications: 9 GCSEs and 3 A-levels
Overseas teams played for: University of Queensland, Australia 1993-94; Cape Technikon Greenpoint, Cape Town, South Africa 1994-95, 1996-98; University of Western Australia, Perth 1998-99
Cricketers particularly admired: Carl Hooper, Courtney Walsh, Dennis Lillee
Young players to look out for: Rob Key
Other sports followed: Football (West Ham United) and basketball (Chicago Bulls)
Relaxations: 'Enjoy watching a decent film or listening to music. Slothing it on a beach somewhere sunny in the off-season'
Extras: Represented England U19 Schools in 1993-94. Set Langley Park School record for the fastest half century, off 11 balls. Released by Kent at the end of the 2001 season and has joined Northamptonshire for 2002
Best batting: 100* Kent v Lancashire, Old Trafford 1997
Best bowling: 5-47 Kent v Sussex, Horsham 1997

2001 Season (did not make any first-class or one-day appearances)

Career Performances

	M	Inns	NO	Runs	HS	Avge	100s	50s	Ct	St	Balls	Runs	Wkts	Avge	Best	5wI	10wM
Test																	
All First	27	39	4	584	100*	16.68	1	2	8	-	3697	1914	65	29.44	5-47	2	-
1-day Int																	
C & G	2	1	1	9	9*	-	-	-	1	-	90	67	3	22.33	3-14	-	
B & H	6	3	1	1	1*	0.50	-	-	1	-	242	156	10	15.60	3-13	-	
1-day Lge	18	8	2	49	29	8.16	-	-	7	-	562	443	20	22.15	4-25	-	

PHILLIPS, N. C.   Durham

Name: <u>Nicholas</u> Charles Phillips
Role: Right-hand bat, off-spin bowler
Born: 10 May 1974, Pembury, Kent
Height: 6ft **Weight:** 12st 5lbs
Nickname: Jenks, Dr W
County debut: 1994 (Sussex), 1998 (Durham)
County cap: 2001 (Durham)
1st-Class 50s: 3
1st-Class 5 w. in innings: 4
1st-Class 10 w. in match: 1
1st-Class catches: 31
Place in batting averages: 240th av. 12.42 (2000 282nd av. 8.44)

Place in bowling averages: 116th av. 40.82
Strike rate: 74.56 (career 91.11)
Parents: Robert and Joan
Marital status: Single
Family links with cricket: Father plays club cricket for Hastings. Represents Sussex Over 50s and has represented Kent 2nd XI, Kent League XI and has scored over 100 club 100s
Education: Hilden Grange School, Tonbridge; St Thomas's School, Winchelsea; William Parker School, Hastings
Qualifications: 8 GCSEs, NCA coaching award
Off-season: Spin coaching in Adelaide
Overseas tours: Sussex U18 to India 1990-91
Overseas teams played for: Marist CC, Auckland 1996-97; Taita Districts, Wellington, New Zealand 1998-99
Cricketers particularly admired: Norman Gifford
Other sports followed: Hockey, football
Relaxations: Spending time with friends and girlfriend. Listening to music. Eating out and socialising with fellow players
Extras: Represented England U19 in home series against West Indies U19 in 1993. Has played hockey for Sussex U14 and U16. Released by Sussex at the end of the 1997 season and joined Durham. Returned the best figures for a Durham spinner since the county attained first-class status with his 12-268 v Glamorgan at Cardiff 1999. Awarded Durham cap 2001
Best batting: 53 Sussex v Young Australia, Hove 1995
Best bowling: 6-97 Durham v Glamorgan, Cardiff 1999

> 67. Which non-first-class side put Worcestershire out of the 1998 NatWest?

2001 Season

	M	Inns	NO	Runs	HS	Avge	100s	50s	Ct	St	O	M	Runs	Wkts	Avge	Best	5wI	10wM
Test																		
All First	7	11	4	87	30	12.42	-	-	6	-	285.5	60	939	23	40.82	5-64	1	-
1-day Int																		
C & G	1	0	0	0	0	-	-	-	-	-	10	0	40	0	-			
B & H	5	1	0	0	0	0.00	-	-	3	-	47	1	178	6	29.66	2-35	-	
1-day Lge	8	4	2	23	13 *	11.50	-	-	3	-	67.4	3	297	13	22.84	4-21	-	

Career Performances

	M	Inns	NO	Runs	HS	Avge	100s	50s	Ct	St	Balls	Runs	Wkts	Avge	Best	5wI	10wM
Test																	
All First	54	80	16	945	53	14.76	-	3	31	-	9385	4890	103	47.47	6-97	4	1
1-day Int																	
C & G	6	4	0	42	21	10.50	-	-	-	-	269	140	4	35.00	2-16	-	
B & H	13	8	1	50	16	7.14	-	-	7	-	629	452	16	28.25	3-17	-	
1-day Lge	71	49	12	397	38 *	10.72	-	-	19	-	2807	2258	77	29.32	4-13	-	

PHILLIPS, T. J.   Essex

Name: Timothy (Tim) James Phillips
Role: Left-hand bat, slow left-arm bowler
Born: 13 March 1981, Cambridge
Height: 6ft **Weight:** 12st 4lbs
Nickname: Pips, TP
County debut: 1999
1st-Class catches: 1
Place in batting averages: 260th av. 10.00
Strike rate: 144.00 (career 94.28)
Parents: Martin (deceased) and Carolyn
Marital status: Single
Family links with cricket: Father played in Lancashire League, then local cricket for villages in Essex. Brother, Nick, played for Essex Schools, and now plays for Saffron Walden in the Essex League
Education: Felsted Preparatory School; Felsted School; Durham University
Qualifications: 10 GCSEs, 3 A-levels
Career outside cricket: Student
Off-season: Studying Sport in the Community at Durham University
Overseas tours: Felsted School to Australia 1995-96; England U19 to Malaysia and (U19 World Cup) Sri Lanka 1999-2000

Career highlights to date: 'Four wickets v Sri Lanka A on debut for Essex'
Cricket moments to forget: 'Essex Schools U11 debut – bowled for 0, first ball'
Cricketers particularly admired: Phil Tufnell
Young players to look out for: Mark Pettini, David Randall
Other sports played: Hockey (Essex Schools U14, U15; East of England U21 trials), 'squash and golf socially'
Other sports followed: 'Like watching rugby union and league, follow football a bit (Cambridge United!)'
Injuries: Out for last three games of the season with cartilage damage to left knee
Relaxations: Socialising, cinema, playing golf
Extras: Winner of *Daily Telegraph* U14 National Bowling Award 1995. Holmwoods School Cricketer of the Year runner-up 1997 and 1998. Broke Nick Knight's and Elliott Wilson's record for runs in a season for Felsted School, scoring 1200. NBC Denis Compton Award 1999. Played for Durham University CCE 2001
Opinions on cricket: 'There should be a more structured close season, keeping up fitness and working on technical problems. The new academy can only be good for the future of the game.'
Best batting: 27 Essex v Leicestershire, Chelmsford 2001
Best bowling: 4-42 Essex v Sri Lanka A, Chelmsford 1999

2001 Season

	M	Inns	NO	Runs	HS	Avge	100s	50s	Ct	St	O	M	Runs	Wkts	Avge	Best	5wI	10wM
Test																		
All First	6	8	0	80	27	10.00	-	-	-	-	144	24	582	6	97.00	2-80	-	-
1-day Int																		
C & G																		
B & H																		
1-day Lge	1	1	0	2	2	2.00	-	-	-	-	5	1	12	0	-		-	-

Career Performances

	M	Inns	NO	Runs	HS	Avge	100s	50s	Ct	St	Balls	Runs	Wkts	Avge	Best	5wI	10wM
Test																	
All First	9	12	0	107	27	8.91	-	-	1	-	1320	860	14	61.42	4-42	-	-
1-day Int																	
C & G																	
B & H																	
1-day Lge	2	2	0	2	2	1.00	-	-	1	-	78	68	2	34.00	2-56	-	

PIERSON, A. R. K.   Derbyshire

Name: <u>Adrian</u> Roger Kirshaw Pierson
Role: Right-hand bat, off-spin bowler
Born: 21 July 1963, Enfield
Height: 6ft 4in **Weight:** 12st
Nickname: Stick, Logga, Skirlog, Logarithm, Bunny
County debut: 1985 (Warwickshire), 1993 (Leicestershire), 1998 (Somerset), 2001 (Derbyshire)
County cap: 1995 (Leicestershire)
50 wickets in a season: 1
1st-Class 50s: 5
1st-Class 100s: 1
1st-Class 5 w. in innings: 14
1st-Class catches: 87
One-Day 5 w. in innings: 1
Place in batting averages: (2000 166th av. 21.00)
Strike rate: (career 75.27)
Parents: Patrick and Patricia

Wife and date of marriage: Helen Majella, 28 September 1990
Children: Eleanor, 7 February 1997; Sebastian, 28 February 2000
Education: Lochinver House Prep, Potters Bar, Herts; Kent College, Canterbury; Hatfield Polytechnic
Qualifications: 8 O-levels, 2 A-levels, NCA advanced coach, airline transport pilot's licence (frozen), flying instructor
Career outside cricket: Flying instructor
Off-season: 'Developing Derbyshire's best young players, both in age group cricket and those on the professional staff. Also teaching people to fly light aircraft (day and night flying)'
Overseas tours: Warwickshire to Barbados, St Lucia, Trinidad; Leicestershire to Jamaica, Bloemfontein, Durban
Overseas teams played for: Walmer CC, Port Elizabeth 1985-90; Manicaland, Zimbabwe 1990-91
Career highlights to date: 'Winning the County Championship with Leicestershire 1996'
Cricket moments to forget: 'Long cricket-related story cut short – making a former prime minister (prime minister on the day!) rather irate after putting him in an ignominious situation in order to help Ian Greig's benefit...'
Cricketers particularly admired: Tony Greig, Phil Edmonds, John Emburey
Young players to look out for: 'Derbyshire's diamonds!'

Other sports played: Golf – 'won the County Cricketers' Golf Society Silver Salver with my mate Colin Metson and won the *Daily Mail* Mijas trophy with Chris Balderstone in 1996'

Other sports followed: 'Any sport except horse racing, but especially Formula One motor racing'

Relaxations: Flying, driving, reading, chess

Extras: On Lord's groundstaff 1984-85 and on Warwickshire staff from 1985-91. First Championship wicket was Viv Richards. Won two Gold Awards in the Benson and Hedges. Released by Leicestershire at the end of the 1997 season and joined Somerset. Left Somerset at the end of the 2000 season and joined Derbyshire for 2001 as assistant coach. One of a select group to play first-class cricket for four counties and cricket for one minor county (Cambridgeshire 1992)

Opinions on cricket: 'We have to improve our homegrown talent – the fact that so many dual nationals are able to force a place in our county sides suggests we are not good enough at youth level. Maybe we should coach cricket at a younger age than ten?'

Best batting: 108* Somerset v Sussex, Hove 1998
Best bowling: 8-42 Leicestershire v Warwickshire, Edgbaston 1994

2001 Season

	M	Inns	NO	Runs	HS	Avge	100s	50s	Ct	St	O	M	Runs	Wkts	Avge	Best	5wI	10wM
Test																		
All First	1	2	1	10	9	10.00	-	-	1	-	10	0	28	0	-		-	-
1-day Int																		
C & G																		
B & H	3	2	0	9	7	4.50	-	-	2	-	25.3	0	110	1	110.00	1-58	-	
1-day Lge	1	0	0	0	0	-	-	-	-	-								

Career Performances

	M	Inns	NO	Runs	HS	Avge	100s	50s	Ct	St	Balls	Runs	Wkts	Avge	Best	5wI	10wM
Test																	
All First	180	224	70	2651	108*	17.21	1	5	87	-	27324	13787	363	37.98	8-42	14	-
1-day Int																	
C & G	14	7	2	42	20*	8.40	-	-	2	-	854	448	13	34.46	3-20	-	
B & H	23	16	10	66	11	11.00	-	-	8	-	1103	694	15	46.26	3-34	-	
1-day Lge	79	42	17	258	31*	10.32	-	-	35	-	2811	2306	68	33.91	5-36	1	

PIETERSEN, K. P.   Nottinghamshire

Name: <u>Kevin</u> Peter Pietersen
Role: Right-hand bat, right-arm
off-spin bowler; all-rounder
Born: 27 June 1980, Pietermaritzburg,
South Africa
Height: 6ft 4in   **Weight:** 14st 9lbs
Nickname: KP, Kapes
County debut: 2001
1000 runs in a season: 1
1st-Class 50s: 8
1st-Class 100s: 3
1st-Class 200s: 1
1st-Class catches: 24
Place in batting averages: 17th av. 57.95
Strike rate: 156.00 (career 96.59)
Parents: Jannie and Penny
Marital status: Girlfriend Kirsty
Education: Clarendon, Pietermaritzburg;
Merchiston Preparatory School; Maritzburg College; University of South Africa
Qualifications: 3 A-levels
Off-season: 'Spending time with girlfriend and family in South Africa'
Overseas tours: Natal to Zimbabwe 1999-2000, to Australia 2000-01;
Nottinghamshire to South Africa 2001
Overseas teams played for: Rovers, Durban 1997 – ; Natal Dolphins 1997-98 –
2000-01
Career highlights to date: 'First first-class century, scored at the home of
cricket – Lord's'
Cricket moments to forget: 'Losing the semi-final of the B&H to Surrey at
The Oval 2001'
Cricketers particularly admired: Errol Stewart, Shaun Pollock
Young players to look out for: Richard Logan, Matt 'Whibley' Whiley
Other sports played: Golf ('social'), swimming ('represented my state in 1992-93')
Other sports followed: Formula One (Ferrari), rugby (Natal Sharks)
Injuries: Out for a month after 'popping a joint off my spine connecting to my rib'
Relaxations: 'Going to game reserves and chilling with mates'
Extras: Played for South African Schools B 1997. Merit award for cricket from Natal
1997. Scored 61* and had figures of 4-141 from 56 overs for KwaZulu-Natal v England
on their 1999-2000 tour of South Africa. Played for Cannock in the
Birmingham League. Had trial for Warwickshire 2nd XI v Surrey 2nd XI. Scored
maiden first-class century (165*) v Middlesex at Lord's 2001, in the process sharing in
a record seventh-wicket stand for Notts in matches against Middlesex (199) with Paul

Franks. Scored 89-ball century v Worcestershire at Worcester 2001, finishing with 103* out of a total of 160. Youngest Notts player to score a 200 in a first-class match (218* v Derbyshire at Derby 2001). Scored 1275 runs in first season of county cricket 2001. Is not considered an overseas player

Opinions on cricket: 'Coming from South Africa where you play eight first-class games a season and one one-day competition, I was completely drained come the end of the season. So much cricket is played, but the only way to learn the game is to play. Brilliant!!!'

Best batting: 218* Nottinghamshire v Derbyshire, Derby 2001
Best bowling: 4-141 KwaZulu-Natal v England, Durban 1999-2000

2001 Season

	M	Inns	NO	Runs	HS	Avge	100s	50s	Ct	St	O	M	Runs	Wkts	Avge	Best	5wI	10wM
Test																		
All First	15	26	4	1275	218 *	57.95	4	6	14	-	234	52	767	9	85.22	2-46	-	-
1-day Int																		
C & G	2	1	0	15	15	15.00	-	-	2	-	1	0	13	0	-		-	-
B & H	7	5	5	171	78 *	-	-	1	4	-	55	1	224	3	74.66	1-28	-	
1-day Lge	16	16	4	386	61 *	32.16	-	3	7	-	88	1	480	11	43.63	3-39	-	

Career Performances

	M	Inns	NO	Runs	HS	Avge	100s	50s	Ct	St	Balls	Runs	Wkts	Avge	Best	5wI	10wM
Test																	
All First	25	39	6	1528	218 *	46.30	4	8	24	-	3091	1529	32	47.78	4-141	-	-
1-day Int																	
C & G	2	1	0	15	15	15.00	-	-	2	-	6	13	0	-		-	-
B & H	7	5	5	171	78 *	-	-	1	4	-	330	224	3	74.66	1-28	-	
1-day Lge	16	16	4	386	61 *	32.16	-	3	7	-	528	480	11	43.63	3-39	-	

---

68. Whose maiden one-day century helped Warwickshire to 357-3 v Somerset in the 1995 NatWest?

PIPE, D. J.   Worcestershire

Name: David <u>James</u> Pipe
Role: Right-hand bat, wicket-keeper
Born: 16 December 1977, Bradford
Height: 5ft 10in   **Weight:** 11st 7lbs
Nickname: Pipes, Pipey, Pip
County debut: 1998
1st-Class 50s: 1
1st-Class catches: 6
1st-Class stumpings: 2
Parents: David and Dorothy
Marital status: Single
Family links with cricket: 'My dad and uncle played in the local league'
Education: Stocks Lane Primary School; Hainsworth Moor Middle School; Queensbury School; BICC

Qualifications: 8 GCSEs, BTEC National in Business and Finance, HND Leisure Studies, senior coaching award
Career outside cricket: Coaching and studying
Off-season: Playing for Manly, Sydney
Overseas teams played for: Leeming Spartans CC and South Metropolitan Cricket Association, Perth 1998-99; Manly CC, Australia 1999-2002
Cricketers particularly admired: Adam Gilchrist
Young players to look out for: 'All the up-and-coming young players at Worcestershire'
Other sports followed: Rugby league (Bradford Bulls, Northern Eagles), football (Bradford City), boxing ('all British fighters'), AFL (West Coast Eagles)
Relaxations: Watching sport, watching films, playing golf, socialising with friends, listening to music
Extras: MCC School of Merit Wilf Slack Memorial Trophy winner 1995. Awarded 2nd XI cap 1999. Played for Worcestershire Board XI in NatWest 2000. Scored 54 on Championship debut v Warwickshire at Worcester 2000. Played for Worcestershire Board XI and Worcestershire in the C&G 2001; took eight catches for the latter v Hertfordshire at Hertford to set a new NatWest/C&G record for most catches in a match by a wicket-keeper, beating Alec Stewart's seven v Glamorgan in the NatWest 1994
Opinions on cricket: 'Wickets must be improved and all 2nd XI Championship games should be played over four days.'
Best batting: 54 Worcestershire v Warwickshire, Worcester 2000

2001 Season

	M	Inns	NO	Runs	HS	Avge	100s	50s	Ct	St	O	M	Runs	Wkts	Avge	Best	5wI	10wM
Test																		
All First	3	5	0	59	24	11.80	-	-	4	1								
1-day Int																		
C & G	2	1	0	4	4	4.00	-	-	10	-								
B & H																		
1-day Lge	1	1	0	26	26	26.00	-	-	-	1								

Career Performances

	M	Inns	NO	Runs	HS	Avge	100s	50s	Ct	St	Balls	Runs	Wkts	Avge	Best	5wI	10wM
Test																		
All First	8	12	0	187	54	15.58	-	1	6	2							
1-day Int																		
C & G	3	2	0	60	56	30.00	-	1	11	-							
B & H																		
1-day Lge	7	6	0	132	45	22.00	-	-	-	1							

PIPER, K. J. Warwickshire

Name: <u>Keith</u> John Piper
Role: Right-hand bat, wicket-keeper
Born: 18 December 1969, Leicester
Height: 5ft 7in **Weight:** 10st 8lbs
Nickname: Tubbsy, Garden Boy
County debut: 1989
County cap: 1992
Benefit: 2001
50 dismissals in a season: 2
1st-Class 50s: 13
1st-Class 100s: 2
1st-Class catches: 476
1st-Class stumpings: 32
Place in batting averages: 86th av. 35.50 (2000 208th av. 17.33)
Strike rate: (career 34.00)
Parents: John and Charlotte
Marital status: Single
Family links with cricket: Father plays club cricket in Leicester
Education: Seven Sisters Junior; Somerset Senior
Qualifications: Senior coaching award, basketball coaching award, volleyball coaching award

Overseas tours: Haringey Cricket College to Barbados 1986, to Trinidad 1987, to Jamaica 1988; Warwickshire to La Manga 1989, to St Lucia 1990; England A to India 1994-95, to Pakistan 1995-96

Overseas teams played for: Desmond Haynes's XI, Barbados v Haringey Cricket College

Cricketers particularly admired: Jack Russell, Alec Stewart, Dermot Reeve, Colin Metson

Other sports followed: Snooker, football, tennis

Relaxations: Music, eating

Extras: London Young Cricketer of the Year 1989 and in the last five 1992. Played for England YC 1989. Was batting partner (116*) to Brian Lara when he reached his 501*, v Durham, Edgbaston 1994

Best batting: 116* Warwickshire v Durham, Edgbaston 1994

Best bowling: 1-57 Warwickshire v Nottinghamshire, Edgbaston 1992

2001 Season

	M	Inns	NO	Runs	HS	Avge	100s	50s	Ct	St	O	M	Runs	Wkts	Avge	Best	5wl	10wM
Test																		
All First	15	17	5	426	92 *	35.50	-	2	39	1	1	0	3	0	-	-	-	-
1-day Int																		
C & G	4	2	1	24	17	24.00	-	-	4	2								
B & H	6	6	2	29	22	7.25	-	-	5	-								
1-day Lge	13	4	2	30	17	15.00	-	-	14	3								

Career Performances

	M	Inns	NO	Runs	HS	Avge	100s	50s	Ct	St	Balls	Runs	Wkts	Avge	Best	5wl	10wM
Test																	
All First	187	256	42	4318	116 *	20.17	2	13	476	32	34	60	1	60.00	1-57	-	-
1-day Int																	
C & G	38	19	10	178	19	19.77	-	-	47	7							
B & H	34	24	8	157	29	9.81	-	-	42	5							
1-day Lge	122	61	33	475	38 *	16.96	-	-	120	31							

POLLARD, P. R. Worcestershire

Name: <u>Paul</u> Raymond Pollard
Role: Left-hand opening bat, right-arm medium bowler
Born: 24 September 1968, Carlton, Nottinghamshire
Height: 5ft 11in **Weight:** 12st
Nickname: Polly, Sugar Ray
County debut: 1987 (Nottinghamshire), 1999 (Worcestershire)
County cap: 1992 (Nottinghamshire)
1000 runs in a season: 3

1st-Class 50s: 48
1st-Class 100s: 15
1st-Class catches: 158
One-Day 100s: 5
Place in batting averages: 138th av. 28.09
(2000 109th av. 28.34)
Strike rate: (career 68.75)
Parents: Eric (deceased) and Mary
Wife and date of marriage: Kate,
14 March 1992
Education: Gedling Comprehensive
Overseas teams played for: Southern
Districts, Brisbane 1988; North Perth 1990
Cricketers particularly admired:
David Gower, Derek Randall, Ian Botham,
Graham Gooch
Other sports followed: Football, golf, ice
hockey

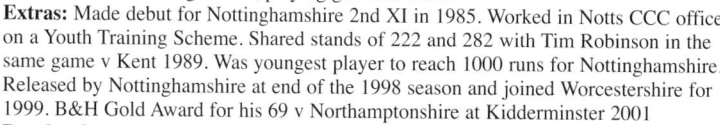

Relaxations: Watching videos, playing golf and music
Extras: Made debut for Nottinghamshire 2nd XI in 1985. Worked in Notts CCC office
on a Youth Training Scheme. Shared stands of 222 and 282 with Tim Robinson in the
same game v Kent 1989. Was youngest player to reach 1000 runs for Nottinghamshire.
Released by Nottinghamshire at end of the 1998 season and joined Worcestershire for
1999. B&H Gold Award for his 69 v Northamptonshire at Kidderminster 2001
Best batting: 180 Nottinghamshire v Derbyshire, Trent Bridge 1993
Best bowling: 2-79 Nottinghamshire v Gloucestershire, Bristol 1993

2001 Season

	M	Inns	NO	Runs	HS	Avge	100s	50s	Ct	St	O	M	Runs	Wkts	Avge	Best	5wI	10wM
Test																		
All First	10	12	1	309	131 *	28.09	1	-	5	-								
1-day Int																		
C & G																		
B & H	1	1	0	69	69	69.00	-	1	-	-								
1-day Lge	8	7	1	154	62	25.66	-	1	1	-								

Career Performances

	M	Inns	NO	Runs	HS	Avge	100s	50s	Ct	St	Balls	Runs	Wkts	Avge	Best	5wI	10wM
Test																	
All First	192	332	24	9685	180	31.44	15	48	158	-	275	272	4	68.00	2-79	-	-
1-day Int																	
C & G	17	17	2	498	96	33.20	-	3	7	-	18	9	0	-	-	-	-
B & H	36	34	3	1016	104	32.77	1	9	11	-							
1-day Lge	128	116	11	3503	132 *	33.36	4	19	43	-							

POLLOCK, S. M.   Warwickshire

Name: <u>Shaun</u> Maclean Pollock
Role: Right-hand bat, right-arm
fast-medium bowler
Born: 16 July 1973, Port Elizabeth,
South Africa
Height: 6ft 3in **Weight:** 13st 5lbs
Nickname: Polly
County debut: 1996
County cap: 1996
Test debut: 1995-96
Tests: 56
One-Day Internationals: 132
1st-Class 50s: 20
1st-Class 100s: 5
1st-Class 5 w. in innings: 18
1st-Class 10 w. in match: 1
1st-Class catches: 73
One-Day 5 w. in innings: 5
Strike rate: (career 55.46)
Parents: Peter and Inez

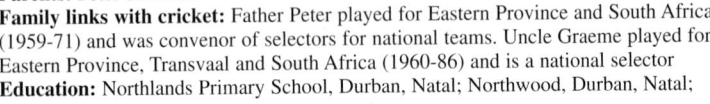

Family links with cricket: Father Peter played for Eastern Province and South Africa
(1959-71) and was convenor of selectors for national teams. Uncle Graeme played for
Eastern Province, Transvaal and South Africa (1960-86) and is a national selector
Education: Northlands Primary School, Durban, Natal; Northwood, Durban, Natal;
Natal University
Qualifications: B Comm
Off-season: Playing for South Africa
Overseas tours: South Africa Tertiary Team to Kenya and Zimbabwe 1994-95; South
Africa U24 to Sri Lanka 1995-96; South Africa to Hong Kong Sixes 1995, to India
and Pakistan (World Cup) 1995-96, to Pakistan 1997-98, to Australia 1997-98, to
England 1998, to New Zealand 1998-99, to UK, Ireland and Holland (World Cup)
1999, to Zimbabwe 1999-2000, to India 1999-2000, to Sri Lanka 2000-01, to Australia
(Super Challenge one-day series) 2000-01, to West Indies 2000-01, to Zimbabwe
2001-02, to Australia 2001-02
Overseas teams played for: Natal/KwaZulu-Natal 1991-92 –
Cricketers particularly admired: Brian Macmillan, Malcolm Marshall, Clive Rice
Other sports followed: Golf, hockey, tennis, rugby and soccer
Relaxations: Watching sport, spending time with friends and listening to music
Extras: Played for Natal Nuffield team and then selected for South Africa Schools in
1991. Made debut for Natal in all three local competitions against same team
(Northern Transvaal) at same venue (Kingsmead, Durban). Made first-class debut for

Natal B v Western Province B at Pietermaritzburg 1991-92. Was voted Player of the Series in the South Africa v England one-day series 1995-96. Won B&H Gold Award on Warwickshire debut v Leicestershire at Edgbaston 1996, during which game he became the first bowler to take four wickets (Macmillan, Whitaker, Robinson, Maddy) in four balls in the competition, ending up with 6-21. One of South Africa's five Players of the Year 1996, 1998 and 2001. Took 7-87 from 41 overs in Australia's first innings of the third Test at Adelaide 1997-98. Appointed captain of South Africa in April 2000. Was Man of the Series v Sri Lanka 2000-01, during which he became the second South African bowler to pass 200 Test wickets (at Durban) and scored a 95-ball maiden Test century (111 at Centurion, batting at No. 9). Topped batting averages (302 runs av. 75.50) and was second in bowling averages (20 wickets av. 23.20) in Test series in West Indies 2000-01, in the process scoring his second Test century batting at No. 9 (106*) in the third Test at Bridgetown and picking up Man of the Series award for Test and one-day matches. Has rejoined Warwickshire as overseas player for 2002
Best batting: 150* Warwickshire v Glamorgan, Edgbaston 1996
Best bowling: 7-33 Natal v Border, East London 1995-96
Stop press: Recorded maiden Test ten-wicket match return (10-147) in the first Test v India at Bloemfontein 2001-02, winning Man of the Match award. Scored 113* in the unofficial 'Test' v India at Centurion 2001-02, winning Man of the Match award

---

2001 Season (did not make any first-class or one-day appearances)

Career Performances

	M	Inns	NO	Runs	HS	Avge	100s	50s	Ct	St	Balls	Runs	Wkts	Avge	Best	5wl	10wM
Test	56	81	17	2015	111	31.48	2	8	36	-	12428	4695	231	20.32	7-87	12	-
All First	112	160	29	4316	150*	32.94	5	20	73	-	23296	9054	420	21.55	7-33	18	1
1-day Int	132	87	30	1411	75	24.75	-	5	47	-	6936	4380	190	23.05	6-35	3	
C & G	2	2	0	40	23	20.00	-	-	-	-	102	62	4	15.50	4-37	-	
B & H	7	4	2	98	59*	49.00	-	1	1	-	384	277	15	18.46	6-21	2	
1-day Lge	14	11	2	273	57	30.33	-	2	3	-	627	387	25	15.48	3-27	-	

---

69. Who captained Sussex to victory in the 1964 Gillette Cup final?

POPE, S. P. Gloucestershire

Name: <u>Stephen</u> Patrick Pope
Role: Right-hand bat, wicket-keeper
Born: 25 January 1983, Cheltenham
Height: 5ft 8in **Weight:** 12st
Nickame: Bod
County debut: No first-team appearance
Parents: John and Patricia
Marital status: Single
Education: Leckhampton Primary School;
Cheltenham Bournside Comprehensive
Qualifications: 11 GCSEs, 2 A-levels
Off-season: Playing in Melbourne. England
U19 tour to Australia and New Zealand
Overseas tours: ESCA South West U15 to
West Indies 1998; England U19 to Australia
and (U19 World Cup) New Zealand 2001-02
Overseas teams played for: St Kilda,
Melbourne 2001-02
Career highlights to date: 'Being selected for England U19 World Cup squad'
Cricket moments to forget: 'I've forgotten it'
Cricketers particularly admired: Jack Russell, David Partridge
Young players to look out for: Pete Baxter, Rob Hall, Tony Millard
Other sports played: Rugby union (scrum half for England U16 v Portugal and
Wales; England U18 Development Squad)
Other sports followed: Football (Arsenal FC)
Relaxations: 'Going out with my friends'
Extras: Has represented England at U14, U15, U17 and U19 levels. Played for
Gloucestershire Board XI in the NatWest 1999 and 2000 and in the C&G 2001 and the
second round of the C&G 2002, which was played in September 2001. Represented
England U19 v West Indies U19 in one-day series (3/3) and 'Test' series (1/3) 2001

2001 Season (did not make any first-class or one-day appearances)

Career Performances

	M	Inns	NO	Runs	HS	Avge	100s	50s	Ct	St	Balls	Runs	Wkts	Avge	Best	5wl	10wM
Test																	
All First																	
1-day Int																	
C & G	5	4	0	22	15	5.50	-	-	10	1							
B & H																	
1-day Lge																	

504

PORTER, J. J.   Surrey

Name: Joseph (<u>Joe</u>) James Porter
Role: Left-hand bat
Born: 5 May 1980, Hammersmith, London
Height: 5ft 11in **Weight:** 12st
Nickame: JP
County debut: 2001 (one-day)
1st-Class 50s: 4
1st-Class catches: 3
Place in batting averages: (2000 97th
av. 29.70)
Strike rate: 33.50 (career 42.50)
Parents: Bob and Judy
Marital status: Single
Education: Rokeby; St John's, Leatherhead;
Oxford Brookes University
Qualifications: 7 GCSEs, 3 A-levels
Career outside cricket: Third year at Oxford
Brookes University, reading Business Studies
and Leisure Management

Overseas tours: Surrey Cricket Board to Barbados 1999; Surrey U19 to Barbados
1999-2000; Oxford Universities to Pakistan 2000
Overseas teams played for: Havelock North, Hawkes Bay, New Zealand 1998-99
Cricketers particularly admired: Alec Stewart, Jimmy Adams, Brian Lara
Young players to look out for: Andrew Hollingsworth, Tim Murtagh
Other sports played: Rugby (Sutton and Epsom Rugby Club)
Other sports followed: Rugby (London Wasps)
Relaxations: Watching films
Extras: The Cricket Society's Wetherell Award for the leading all-rounder in schools
cricket 1998. Played for Oxford Universities in 2000 and for Oxford University CCE
in 2001 (captain). Represented British Universities in 2000 and 2001. Released by
Surrey at the end of the 2001 season
Best batting: 93 British Universities v Zimbabweans, Fenner's 2000
Best bowling: 3-50 OUCCE v Warwickshire, The Parks 2001

2001 Season

	M	Inns	NO	Runs	HS	Avge	100s	50s	Ct	St	O	M	Runs	Wkts	Avge	Best	5wI	10wM
Test																		
All First	3	6	1	102	46	20.40	-	-	3	-	22.2	1	84	4	21.00	3-50	-	-
1-day Int																		
C & G																		
B & H																		
1-day Lge	1	1	0	23	23	23.00	-	-	-	-								

Career Performances

	M	Inns	NO	Runs	HS	Avge	100s	50s	Ct	St	Balls	Runs	Wkts	Avge	Best	5wI	10wM
Test																	
All First	9	16	1	399	93	26.60	-	4	3	-	170	134	4	33.50	3-50	-	-
1-day Int																	
C & G																	
B & H																	
1-day Lge	1	1	0	23	23	23.00	-	-	-	-							

POTHAS, N.   Hampshire

Name: Nic Pothas
Role: Right-hand bat, wicket-keeper
Born: 18 November 1973, Johannesburg, South Africa
Nickname: Skeg
County debut: No first-team appearance
One-Day Internationals: 3
1st-Class 50s: 17
1st-Class 100s: 7
1st-Class catches: 238
1st-Class stumpings: 22
Marital status: Single
Education: King Edward VII School
Overseas tours: South Africa A to England 1996, to Sri Lanka 1998-99, to West Indies 2000-01; South Africa to Singapore (one-day series) 2000-01
Overseas teams played for:
Transvaal/Gauteng 1993-94 – 2001-02
Extras: Scored maiden first-class century (147) for South African Students v England tourists at Pietermaritzburg 1995-96. Selected for South Africa A tour to West Indies 2000-01 then was withdrawn temporarily onto the senior one-day tour to Singapore as

replacement for the injured Mark Boucher. Was stand-by wicket-keeper for South Africa's tour to West Indies 2000-01. Is not considered an overseas player
Best batting: 165 Gauteng v KwaZulu-Natal, Johannesburg 1998-99

2001 Season (did not make any first-class or one-day appearances)

Career Performances

	M	Inns	NO	Runs	HS	Avge	100s	50s	Ct	St	Balls	Runs	Wkts	Avge	Best	5wI	10wM
Test																	
All First	86	133	25	3890	165	36.01	7	17	238	22	6	5	0	-		-	-	-
1-day Int	3	1	0	24	24	24.00	-	-	4	1							
C & G																		
B & H																			
1-day Lge																			

POWELL, M. J.   Northamptonshire

Name: <u>Mark</u> John Powell
Role: Right-hand bat, right-arm medium bowler
Born: 4 November 1980, Northampton
Height: 5ft 11in **Weight:** 11st 12lbs
Nickname: Piggy, Perfect, Powelly
County debut: 2000
Parents: David and Philippa
Marital status: Single
Education: Flore Primary, Northants; Campion School, Bugbrooke, Northants; Loughborough University
Qualifications: 10 GCSEs, 3 A-levels, Level 1 coach
Career outside cricket: Student
Off-season: Loughborough University, final year
Overseas tours: Northants U19 to South Africa 2000
Career highlights to date: 'Making first-class debut for Northants v Worcestershire and captaining Loughborough University to BUSA Championship and to UCCE success with final at Lord's'
Cricket moments to forget: 'Bagging a pair on 2nd XI debut when 16'
Cricketers particularly admired: Steve Waugh, Adam Gilchrist, Mike Hussey

Young players to look out for: Monty Panesar, John Francis, Steve Selwood
Other sports played: Golf, touch rugby
Other sports followed: Football (Tottenham Hotspur), rugby union
(Northampton Saints)
Relaxations: 'Cinema, watching sport, going out with mates'
Extras: Played for England U15 in inaugural U15 World Cup 1996; knocked out in
semi-finals by Pakistan at Headingley. Played for Midlands U19 v Australia U19 1999.
2nd XI Player of the Month August/September 2000. Scored 50 in Loughborough
University's BUSA Championship final win at Fenner's 2000. Played for
Loughborough University CCE 2001 (captain)
Opinions on cricket: 'Too many slow, low wickets in Youth/2nd XI games, which
don't help produce good first-class/Test match players.'
Best batting: 1 Northamptonshire v Worcestershire, Worcester 2000

2001 Season (did not make any first-class or one-day appearances)

Career Performances

	M	Inns	NO	Runs	HS	Avge	100s	50s	Ct	St	Balls	Runs	Wkts	Avge	Best	5wI	10wM
Test																	
All First	1	2	0	2	1	1.00	-	-	-	-							
1-day Int																	
C & G																	
B & H																	
1-day Lge																	

POWELL, M. J. Warwickshire

Name: <u>Michael</u> James Powell
Role: Right-hand opening bat, right-arm medium bowler, county captain
Born: 5 April 1975, Bolton
Height: 5ft 10in **Weight:** 11st
Nickname: Arthur, Powelly
County debut: 1996
County cap: 1999
1000 runs in a season: 1
1st-Class 50s: 17
1st-Class 100s: 6
1st-Class 200s: 1
1st-Class catches: 53
Place in batting averages: 113th av. 31.45 (2000 26th av. 43.58)
Strike rate: 102.00 (career 91.71)
Parents: Terry and Pat

Wife and date of marriage: Sarah, 26 October 1996
Family links with cricket: 'Father played as a youngster. Brother represented Warwickshire youth teams'
Education: Horwich Parish C of E School; Rivington and Blackrod High School, Horwich; Lawrence Sheriff Boys Grammar School, Rugby
Qualifications: 6 GCSEs, 2 A-levels, Levels I-III coaching awards
Off-season: Playing for Griqualand West in South Africa
Career outside cricket: PE teacher
Overseas tours: England U18 to South Africa 1992-93 (captain), to Denmark 1993 (captain); England U19 to Sri Lanka 1993-94; England A to West Indies 2000-01

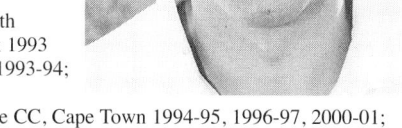

Overseas teams played for: Avendale CC, Cape Town 1994-95, 1996-97, 2000-01; Griqualand West, South Africa 2001-02
Cricketers particularly admired: Ian Botham, Dermot Reeve, Roger Twose
Young players to look out for: Graham Wagg, Ian Bell
Other sports played: Rugby (Warwickshire U16-U18), golf
Other sports followed: Football (Manchester United – 'who else?')
Relaxations: Golf, snooker, 'spending time with my wife Sarah, my dog Winston and cats Brian and Graeme'
Extras: Captained Warwickshire age-group sides U14-U19. Captained England U17 and U18. 2nd XI Player of the Month June 1996. Scored a (then) career-best 210 against Somerset 2nd XI in July 1996. Became first uncapped Warwickshire player for 49 years to carry his bat, for 70* out of 130 against Nottinghamshire at Edgbaston, May 1998. With Mark Wagh, shared in record first-wicket stand for Warwickshire in matches v Essex (230) at Chelmsford 2000. Drafted into the England A squad for the West Indies tour 2000-01 as replacement for the injured David Sales. Shared in record opening stand for England A (224) with Ian Ward v Barbados at Bridgetown 2000-01, scoring 96. Scored maiden first-class double hundred (236) v Oxford University CCE at The Parks 2001. Captain of Warwickshire since 2001
Opinions on cricket: 'Improvement of pitches around the circuit desperately needed! A new ball must be due at 80 overs, not 100! A replacement for the benefit system needed that still rewards county players for great service but prevents hangers-on and thus provides more opportunities for younger players to blossom.'
Best batting: 236 Warwickshire v OUCCE, The Parks 2001
Best bowling: 2-16 Warwickshire v Oxford University, The Parks 1998

	M	Inns	NO	Runs	HS	Avge	100s	50s	Ct	St	O	M	Runs	Wkts	Avge	Best	5wI	10wM
Test																		
All First	17	24	0	755	236	31.45	2	2	14	-	34	2	100	2	50.00	1-25	-	-
1-day Int																		
C & G	4	4	1	78	39	26.00	-	-	1	-								
B & H	6	6	1	138	55	27.60	-	1	3	-	22	0	105	2	52.50	1-33	-	
1-day Lge	15	11	1	248	78	24.80	-	1	4	-	12	0	58	0	-	-	-	-

Career Performances

	M	Inns	NO	Runs	HS	Avge	100s	50s	Ct	St	Balls	Runs	Wkts	Avge	Best	5wI	10wM
Test																	
All First	67	105	3	3348	236	32.82	7	17	53	-	642	309	7	44.14	2-16	-	-
1-day Int																	
C & G	9	9	1	149	39	18.62	-	-	7	-							
B & H	6	6	1	138	55	27.60	-	1	3	-	132	105	2	52.50	1-33	-	
1-day Lge	34	27	4	586	78	25.47	-	2	8	-	252	205	6	34.16	2-13	-	

POWELL, M. J.   Glamorgan

Name: <u>Michael</u> John Powell
Role: Right-hand bat
Born: 3 February 1977, Abergavenny
Height: 6ft 1in **Weight:** 14st 9lbs
Nickname: Powelly, Ape Man
County debut: 1997
County cap: 2000
1000 runs in a season: 1
1st-Class 50s: 18
1st-Class 100s: 7
1st-Class 200s: 1
1st-Class catches: 39
Place in batting averages: 126th av. 29.60
(2000 94th av. 30.10)
Strike rate: (career 64.00)
Parents: John and Linda
Marital status: Single
Family links with cricket: 'Dad John and
Uncle Mike both played for Abergavenny'
Education: Crickhowell Primary School; Crickhowell Secondary School;
Pontypool College
Qualifications: 5 GCSEs, BTEC National Diploma in Sports Science, Level 1
coaching award

Off-season: Training ('putting the yards in')
Overseas tours: Glamorgan to Cape Town 1999
Overseas teams played for: Wests, Brisbane 1996-97; Cornwall CC, Auckland 1998-99, 2000-01
Cricketers particularly admired: Stuart Law, Mark Waugh
Young players to look out for: Mark Wallace, Ben Powell, Mark and Andrew Coles
Other sports played: Rugby (Crickhowell RFC)
Relaxations: Eating and sleeping
Extras: Scored 200 not out on his first-class debut v Oxford University at The Parks 1997. Scored 1210 runs at 75.63 in the 1997 2nd XI Championship, the second-highest ever total behind Alan Brazier's 1212 for Surrey 2nd XI in 1948. 2nd XI Championship Player of the Year 1997. NBC Denis Compton Award for the most promising young Glamorgan player 2000. Scored the first Championship century of the 2001 season, 106 v Northamptonshire at Northampton on 20 April
Opinions on cricket: 'Great game.'
Best batting: 200* Glamorgan v Oxford University, The Parks 1997
Best bowling: 2-39 Glamorgan v Oxford University, The Parks 1999

2001 Season

	M	Inns	NO	Runs	HS	Avge	100s	50s	Ct	St	O	M	Runs	Wkts	Avge	Best	5wI	10wM
Test																		
All First	15	25	2	681	108	29.60	2	4	12	-								
1-day Int																		
C & G	2	2	1	91	52	91.00	-	1	-	-								
B & H	5	5	0	108	67	21.60	-	1	3	-								
1-day Lge	16	14	5	271	46	30.11	-	-	8	-								

Career Performances

	M	Inns	NO	Runs	HS	Avge	100s	50s	Ct	St	Balls	Runs	Wkts	Avge	Best	5wI	10wM
Test																	
All First	70	114	12	3710	200 *	36.37	8	18	39	-	128	111	2	55.50	2-39	-	-
1-day Int																	
C & G	7	7	1	111	52	18.50	-	1	2	-							
B & H	11	11	0	294	67	26.72	-	2	4	-							
1-day Lge	63	59	11	1202	86	25.04	-	3	18	-							

PRATT, A. Durham

Name: Andrew Pratt
Role: Left-hand bat, wicket-keeper
Born: 4 March 1975, Bishop Auckland
Height: 5ft 11in **Weight:** 12st
Nickname: Stumper
County debut: 1997
County cap: 2001
50 dismissals in a season: 1
1st-Class 50s: 3
1st-Class catches: 60
1st-Class stumpings: 7
Place in batting averages: 193rd av. 19.83
(2000 165th av. 21.22)
Parents: Gordon and Brenda
Marital status: Engaged to Laura
Family links with cricket: One brother was
with MCC Young Cricketers for four years.
Younger brother Gary also plays for Durham.
Father played for many years in Durham

Education: Willington Junior School; Willington Parkside Comprehensive School;
Durham New College
Qualifications: 9 GCSEs, Advanced Diploma in Information Technology, qualified
cricket coach
Off-season: 'Training, playing golf, doing martial arts and relaxing'
Overseas tours: Durham Academy to Sri Lanka
Overseas teams played for: Hallam, Melbourne 1997-98
Career highlights to date: 'Making debut for Durham'
Cricketers particularly admired: Alan Knott, Jack Russell
Other sports followed: Football (Middlesbrough FC)
Relaxations: 'Music, drinking'
Extras: Played for Durham County Schools at all levels and for the North of England
U15. Played for MCC Young Cricketers for three years. He and brother Gary became
the first brothers to play in a Championship match for Durham, against Lancashire at
Old Trafford 2000. Durham Player of the Year 2001. Awarded Durham cap 2001
Opinions on cricket: 'Less games, more practice.'
Best batting: 68* Durham v Derbyshire, Riverside 2001

2001 Season

	M	Inns	NO	Runs	HS	Avge	100s	50s	Ct	St	O	M	Runs	Wkts	Avge	Best	5wI	10wM
Test																		
All First	16	28	4	476	68 *	19.83	-	3	49	7								
1-day Int																		
C & G	3	2	1	33	26 *	33.00	-	-	3	1								
B & H	6	3	3	22	8 *	-	-	-	5	3								
1-day Lge	13	11	2	287	86	31.88	-	2	14	7								

Career Performances

	M	Inns	NO	Runs	HS	Avge	100s	50s	Ct	St	Balls	Runs	Wkts	Avge	Best	5wI	10wM
Test																	
All First	26	41	5	707	68 *	19.63	-	3	60	7							
1-day Int																	
C & G	3	2	1	33	26 *	33.00	-	-	3	1							
B & H	6	3	3	22	8 *	-	-	-	5	3							
1-day Lge	23	20	5	338	86	22.53	-	2	19	9							

PRATT, G. J.   Durham

Name: <u>Gary</u> Joseph Pratt
Role: Left-hand bat, off-spin bowler
Born: 22 December 1981, Bishop Auckland
Height: 5ft 11in **Weight:** 11st
Nickname: Gazza
County debut: 2000
1st-Class catches: 2
Parents: Gordon and Brenda
Marital status: Single
Family links with cricket: Father played for many years in Durham and one brother was on Lord's groundstaff (MCC Young Cricketers). Brother Andrew also plays for Durham
Education: Crook Junior School; Willington Parkside
Qualifications: 9 GCSEs
Off-season: In Australia
Overseas tours: England U19 to Malaysia and (U19 World Cup) Sri Lanka 1999-2000, to India 2000-01
Overseas teams played for: Melville, Perth 2001-02
Career highlights to date: 'Being the first brothers to play for Durham'

Cricketers particularly admired: Graham Thorpe, David Gower
Other sports played: Football ('ex-Sheffield Wednesday')
Relaxations: Music, cinema
Extras: Represented England U17 at the ECC Colts Festival in Northern Ireland 1999. NBC Denis Compton Award 1999. On his first-class debut, against Lancashire at Old Trafford 2000, he and brother Andrew became the first brothers to play in a Championship match for Durham. Scored century (114) for England U19 v India U19 in third 'Test' at Hyderabad 2000-01. Represented England U19 v Sri Lanka U19 in one-day and 'Test' series 2000 and v West Indies U19 in one-day series (3/3) and 'Test' series (3/3) 2001, scoring century (100) in second 'One-Day International' at Chelmsford and another (188) in the second 'Test' at Trent Bridge. Played for Durham Board XI in the second round of the C&G 2002, which was played in September 2001
Opinions on cricket: 'Tea could be a bit longer.'
Best batting: 37 Durham v Worcestershire, Riverside 2001

2001 Season

	M	Inns	NO	Runs	HS	Avge	100s	50s	Ct	St	O	M	Runs	Wkts	Avge	Best	5wI	10wM
Test																		
All First	2	4	0	53	37	13.25	-	-	1	-								
1-day Int																		
C & G	1	1	0	32	32	32.00	-	-	-	-								
B & H																		
1-day Lge																		

Career Performances

	M	Inns	NO	Runs	HS	Avge	100s	50s	Ct	St	Balls	Runs	Wkts	Avge	Best	5wI	10wM
Test																	
All First	4	7	0	92	37	13.14	-	-	2	-							
1-day Int																	
C & G	1	1	0	32	32	32.00	-	-	-	-							
B & H																	
1-day Lge																	

PRICHARD, P. J.   Essex

Name: <u>Paul</u> John Prichard
Role: Right-hand bat, cover/mid-wicket fielder
Born: 7 January 1965, Brentwood
Height: 5ft 10in **Weight:** 13st
Nickname: Pablo
County debut: 1984
County cap: 1986

Benefit: 1996
1000 runs in a season: 8
1st-Class 50s: 97
1st-Class 100s: 29
1st-Class 200s: 3
1st-Class catches: 202
One-Day 100s: 6
Place in batting averages: 207th av. 18.27
(2000 116th av. 27.67)
Strike rate: (career 144.50)
Parents: John and Margaret
Wife and date of marriage: Kate,
28 December 2000
Children: Danielle Jade, 23 April 1993;
Alexander James, 16 August 1995
Family links with cricket: Father played
club cricket in Essex
Education: Warley Primary School;
Brentwood County High School
Qualifications: Advanced cricket coaching certificate
Career outside cricket: Sales and marketing with Ridley's Brewery
Overseas tours: England A to Australia 1992-93
Overseas teams played for: VOB Cavaliers, Cape Town 1981-82; Sutherland,
Sydney 1984-87; Waverley, Sydney 1987-92
Cricketers particularly admired: Malcolm Marshall, Allan Border, David Gower,
Mark Waugh, Greg Matthews
Young players to look out for: Steve Harmison, Paul Franks
Other sports played: Golf, football (Essex cricketers' team), tennis, badminton
Other sports followed: Football (West Ham United), rugby union
Relaxations: 'Watching football and rugby live, live concerts, good food and
restaurants – all with the missus!'
Extras: Shared county record first-wicket partnership of 316 v Kent in 1994 and
county record second-wicket partnership of 403 v Leicestershire in 1990, both with
Graham Gooch at Chelmsford. Essex joint Player of the Year 1993. Essex captain 1995-1998. Won the B&H Gold Award for
his 92 from 113 balls v Leicestershire in the 1998 final at Lord's. Retired at the end of
the 2001 season
Opinions on cricket: 'Two divisions fantastic.'
Best batting: 245 Essex v Leicestershire, Chelmsford 1990
Best bowling: 1-28 Essex v Hampshire, Chelmsford 1991

2001 Season

	M	Inns	NO	Runs	HS	Avge	100s	50s	Ct	St	O	M	Runs	Wkts	Avge	Best	5wl	10wM
Test																		
All First	7	11	0	201	111	18.27	1	-	1	-								
1-day Int																		
C & G																			
B & H																			
1-day Lge	1	1	0	13	13	13.00	-	-	-	-								

Career Performances

	M	Inns	NO	Runs	HS	Avge	100s	50s	Ct	St	Balls	Runs	Wkts	Avge	Best	5wl	10wM
Test																	
All First	330	540	49	16834	245	34.28	32	97	202	-	289	497	2	248.50	1-28	-	-
1-day Int																	
C & G	36	35	5	1138	94	37.93	-	9	14	-							
B & H	59	56	8	1542	114	32.12	2	8	14	-							
1-day Lge	197	178	10	4328	107	25.76	4	19	53	-							

PRIOR, M. J. Sussex

Name: <u>Matthew</u> James Prior
Role: Right-hand bat, wicket-keeper
Born: 26 February 1982, Johannesburg, South Africa
Height: 5ft 11in **Weight:** 12st
Nickname: MP, Aldrich
County debut: 2001
1st-Class 50s: 1
1st-Class catches: 39
1st-Class stumpings: 2
Place in batting averages: 195th av. 19.68
Parents: Michael and Terri
Marital status: Single
Education: King Edward VII Prep School, Johannesburg; Brighton College, East Sussex
Qualifications: 9 GCSEs, 3 A-levels, Level 1 coaching certificate
Career outside cricket: 'Occasional coach'
Off-season: 'Training in the "Gilly" and with "Hardcore" Harley in the gym'
Overseas tours: Brighton College to India 1997-98; Sussex Academy to Cape Town 1999; Sussex to Grenada 2001
Career highlights to date: 'First-class debut. Winning second division Championship [2001]'

Cricket moments to forget: 'Falling onto my wicket at the Rose Bowl on Sky!'
Cricketers particularly admired: Steve Waugh, Murray Goodwin, Mark Boucher
Young players to look out for: Mike Yardy, Nicky Peng, Ian Bell
Other sports played: Football, golf, squash
Other sports followed: Football (Arsenal), rugby
Injuries: Out for two weeks with a strained hip flexor; 'bruised hands!!'
Relaxations: Music, gym
Extras: Has played for Sussex since U12. Represented England U14-U19, captaining England U17. Attended Sussex Academy. Played for Sussex Board XI in NatWest 2000. Reserve for England U19 tour to India 2000-01. Represented England U19 v West Indies U19 in 'Test' series (2/3) 2001, scoring 57 and 51 in the first 'Test' at Leicester
Opinions on cricket: 'Still learning too much every day to have an opinion!'
Best batting: 66 Sussex v Derbyshire, Arundel 2001

2001 Season

	M	Inns	NO	Runs	HS	Avge	100s	50s	Ct	St	O	M	Runs	Wkts	Avge	Best	5wl	10wM
Test																		
All First	16	24	2	433	66	19.68	-	1	39	2								
1-day Int																		
C & G	2	2	0	20	12	10.00	-	-	4	-								
B & H	4	3	0	12	6	4.00	-	-	2	2								
1-day Lge	11	8	1	50	25	7.14	-	-	6	1								

Career Performances

	M	Inns	NO	Runs	HS	Avge	100s	50s	Ct	St	Balls	Runs	Wkts	Avge	Best	5wl	10wM
Test																		
All First	16	24	2	433	66	19.68	-	1	39	2							
1-day Int																		
C & G	3	3	0	23	12	7.66	-	-	4	-							
B & H	4	3	0	12	6	4.00	-	-	2	2							
1-day Lge	11	8	1	50	25	7.14	-	-	6	1							

70. When Northamptonshire beat Leicestershire in the 1992 NatWest final, both overseas players were West Indies Test fast bowlers. Who were they?

PRITTIPAUL, L. R.   Hampshire

Name: <u>Lawrence</u> Roland Prittipaul
Role: Right-hand bat, right-arm medium
swing/off-spin bowler
Born: 19 October 1979, Portsmouth
Height: 6ft   **Weight:** 12st 4lbs
Nickname: Lozza, Lawrie, Lollipop
County debut: 1999 (one-day),
2000 (first-class)
1st-Class 50s: 2
1st-Class 100s: 1
1st-Class catches: 7
Place in batting averages: 206th av. 18.33
(2000 15th av. 49.66)
Parents: Roland and Christine
Marital status: 'Single?'
Family links with cricket: 'Cousin

Shivnarine Chanderpaul plays for West
Indies. Father plays for Southsea. Mum
washes his whites. Rachael (sister) played for Hampshire Girls. Kim (girlfriend)
gives support'
Education: Meon First and Middle School, Portsmouth; St John's College, Southsea;
Portsmouth College
Qualifications: GCSEs, Level 2 coaching, first aider, 'cooking and cleaning,
No. 1 romantic'
Career outside cricket: Journalism
Off-season: 'Going on holiday with girlfriend. Resting from cricket until January.
Heading off to Cape Town or Perth'
Overseas tours: Hampshire to Cape Town 2001
Overseas teams played for: Milnerton, Cape Town 1999-2001
Career highlights to date: 'Scoring 52 on debut and 152 on home debut. Any game
my father comes to watch'
Cricket moments to forget: 'Every time I was dropped from 1st XI 2001'
Cricketers particularly admired: 'My father', Jon Ayling, Carl Hooper,
Tony Middleton
Young players to look out for: Dean Wilson, Marina Stone, George Wilson,
'my future son, Luke Kendall, Archie Ayling!'
Other sports played: 'Hoovering'
Other sports followed: Football (Portsmouth)
Injuries: 'Most of winter lost after mini-operation on shoulder'
Relaxations: 'Spending time with girlfriend Kim, dog Lou Lou, Mum, Dad and
Rachael. Sleeping and watching DVDs. Being naked'

Extras: Scored first century at age 13 for St John's College. Played for Hants Colts from age 11 to 18; took 29 wickets and broke bowling record aged 11. Represented England U17. Scored 185 for Hants U19 in 1998. Won Player of the Year award in Southern League 1998. Has played for Hants 2nd XI since age 18; scored over 1000 runs for Hants 2nd XI in 1999. Scored 152 on home debut, v Derbyshire at Southampton 2000, beating Dennis Baldry's Hampshire home Championship debut record of 151 set in 1959

Opinions on cricket: 'England selectors need to come to the Rose Bowl. Foreigners need to have stricter rules for coming to play county cricket.'

Best batting: 152 Hampshire v Derbyshire, Southampton 2000

2001 Season

	M	Inns	NO	Runs	HS	Avge	100s	50s	Ct	St	O	M	Runs	Wkts	Avge	Best	5wI	10wM
Test																		
All First	7	9	0	165	84	18.33	-	1	6	-	25	1	86	0	-	-	-	-
1-day Int																		
C & G	1	1	0	9	9	9.00	-	-	-	-								
B & H																		
1-day Lge	13	12	1	201	45	18.27	-	-	6	-	3	0	18	0	-	-	-	

Career Performances

	M	Inns	NO	Runs	HS	Avge	100s	50s	Ct	St	Balls	Runs	Wkts	Avge	Best	5wI	10wM
Test																	
All First	11	15	0	463	152	30.86	1	2	7	-	150	86	0	-	-	-	-
1-day Int																	
C & G	4	4	0	75	30	18.75	-	-	3	-	156	125	4	31.25	2-53	-	
B & H																	
1-day Lge	21	16	2	288	61	20.57	-	1	8	-	24	32	0	-	-	-	

71. Who claimed the Man of the Match award for his 60 not out and 2-40 in the final of the 2001 C&G?

PYEMONT, J. P.   Derbyshire

Name: <u>James</u> Patrick Pyemont
Role: Right-hand top-order bat,
off-spin bowler
Born: 10 April 1978, Eastbourne
Height: 6ft **Weight:** 11st 7lbs
Nickname: Pumper, Pyeko, Pye, Pyemo,
Piggy, Pykethon
County debut: 1997 (Sussex),
1999 (Derbyshire)
1st-Class 50s: 5
1st-Class 100s: 1
1st-Class catches: 20
Place in batting averages: 190th av. 20.87
(2000 157th av. 22.35)
Place in bowling averages: 136th av. 51.20
Strike rate: 87.60 (career 110.27)
Parents: Christopher and Christina
Marital status: Single

Family links with cricket: Father played for Cambridge University and Sussex
2nd XI
Education: St Bede's School, Eastbourne; Tonbridge School, Kent; Trinity Hall,
Cambridge University
Qualifications: 9 GCSEs, 3 A-levels, BA (Hons) (Cantab), NCA qualified coach
Career outside cricket: Teaching, journalism, 'dabbling'
Off-season: 'Pursuing a few ideas and getting stronger'
Overseas tours: Sussex U19 to Barbados 1993; Cambridge University to Pakistan
1999; British Universities to South Africa 1999
Career highlights to date: 'Scoring maiden first-class 100 at Lord's' (*124 in the
Varsity match 2000*)
Cricket moments to forget: 'First couple of balls in Championship cricket!'
(*Recorded a king pair on Championship debut, Derbyshire v Surrey 1999*)
Cricketers particularly admired: David Gower
Young players to look out for: Stephen Stubbings
Other sports played: 'Anything'
Other sports followed: Football (Brighton & Hove Albion)
Injuries: Out for ten days with broken finger
Relaxations: Reading, films
Extras: Joined Derbyshire in 1999 from Sussex. Played in the Old Tonbridgians side
that won *The Cricketer* Cup 1998-99. Represented British Universities 2000 and 2001
(captain v Pakistanis 2001). Acted as 12th man for England v Australia at Headingley
2001. Played for Cambridge University CCE in 2001. Cambridge Blue 1998-2001
(captain 2000)

520

Opinions on cricket: 'Wickets should be prepared to ensure that the best possible cricket should be on offer both for the players and the crowd. Central contracts are an excellent idea.'

Best batting: 124 Cambridge University v Oxford University, Lord's 2000

Best bowling: 4-101 Cambridge University v Oxford University, Fenner's 2001

2001 Season

	M	Inns	NO	Runs	HS	Avge	100s	50s	Ct	St	O	M	Runs	Wkts	Avge	Best	5wI	10wM
Test																		
All First	5	9	1	167	70	20.87	-	1	4	-	146	31	512	10	51.20	4-101	-	-
1-day Int																		
C & G																		
B & H																		
1-day Lge	2	2	0	9	7	4.50	-	-	-	-								

Career Performances

	M	Inns	NO	Runs	HS	Avge	100s	50s	Ct	St	Balls	Runs	Wkts	Avge	Best	5wI	10wM
Test																	
All First	34	51	4	1005	124	21.38	1	5	20	-	1213	673	11	61.18	4-101	-	-
1-day Int																	
C & G																	
B & H	5	5	0	74	25	14.80	-	-	3	-							
1-day Lge	18	18	1	227	50	13.35	-	1	7	-							

72. Which current first-class umpire scored 112 for Surrey v Lancashire in the semi-finals of the 1986 NatWest, winning the Man of the Match award?

RAMPRAKASH, M. R.   Surrey

Name: <u>Mark</u> Ravindra Ramprakash
Role: Right-hand bat, right arm
off-spin bowler
Born: 5 September 1969, Bushey, Herts
Height: 5ft 10in   **Weight:** 12st 4lbs
Nickname: Ramps, Bloodaxe
County debut: 1987 (Middlesex),
2001 (Surrey)
County cap: 1990 (Middlesex)
Benefit: 2000 (Middlesex)
Test debut: 1991
Tests: 46

One-Day Internationals: 13
1000 runs in a season: 11
1st-Class 50s: 101
1st-Class 100s: 50
1st-Class 200s: 5
1st-Class catches: 177
One-Day 100s: 7
One-Day 5 w. in innings: 1
Place in batting averages: 30th av. 49.72 (2000 16th av. 49.29)
Strike rate: (career 120.40)
Parents: Deonarine and Jennifer
Date of marriage: 24 September 1993
Family links with cricket: Father played club cricket in Guyana
Education: Gayton High School; Harrow Weald Sixth Form College
Qualifications: 6 O-levels, 2 A-levels
Off-season: Touring with England
Overseas tours: England YC to Sri Lanka 1986-87, to Australia (U19 World Cup) 1987-88; England A to Pakistan 1990-91, to West Indies 1991-92, to India 1994-95 (vice-captain); Lion Cubs to Barbados 1993; England to New Zealand 1991-92, to West Indies 1993-94, to Australia 1994-95, to South Africa 1995-96, to West Indies 1997-98, to Australia 1998-99, to South Africa 1999-2000, to Zimbabwe (one-day series) 2001-02, to India and New Zealand 2001-02
Overseas teams played for: Nairobi Jafferys, Kenya 1988; North Melbourne 1989
Cricketers particularly admired: 'All the great all-rounders'
Other sports followed: Snooker, football
Relaxations: 'Being at home with the family, going to movies, eating out'
Extras: Did not begin to play cricket until he was nine years old; played for Bessborough CC at age 13, played for Middlesex 2nd XI aged 16 and made first-team debut for Middlesex aged 17. Scored 204* in NCA Guernsey Festival Tournament and

in 1987 made 186* on his debut for Stanmore CC. Voted Best U15 Schoolboy of 1985 by Cricket Society, Best Young Cricketer of 1986 and Most Promising Player of the Year in 1988. Man of the Match in Middlesex's NatWest Trophy final win in 1988, on his debut in the competition. Played for England YC v New Zealand YC in 1989. Won Cricket Writers' Young Cricketer of the Year award 1991. Finished top of the Whyte and Mackay batting ratings in 1995 and again in 1997. Appointed Middlesex captain during 1997 season after Mike Gatting stood down. Scored maiden Test 100 (154) v West Indies at Bridgetown 1997-98, sharing in a record sixth-wicket partnership for England in Tests v West Indies (205) with Graham Thorpe and receiving Man of the Match award. Achieved feat of scoring a century against all other first-class counties with his 128* v Glamorgan in 1998. Became the first player to score three 200s v Surrey with his 209* at Lord's 1999. Stood down as Middlesex captain at end of 1999 season. Leading run-scorer in the single-division four-day era of the County Championship with 8392 runs (av. 56.32) 1993-99. Scored two centuries in the match v Sussex at Southgate 2000 to become the first Middlesex player to record 100s in each innings of a game on four occasions; his 112 in the second innings was his 50th first-class century. Left Middlesex in the 2000-01 off-season and joined Surrey for 2001. Scored century (146) on Championship debut for Surrey v Kent at The Oval 2001. B&H Gold Award for his 97* v Essex at The Oval 2001. Scored maiden home Test century (133) in fifth Test v Australia at The Oval 2001

Best batting: 235 Middlesex v Yorkshire, Headingley 1995
Best bowling: 3-32 Middlesex v Glamorgan, Lord's 1998

2001 Season

	M	Inns	NO	Runs	HS	Avge	100s	50s	Ct	St	O	M	Runs	Wkts	Avge	Best	5wl	10wM
Test	4	8	0	318	133	39.75	1	-	3	-	8	0	31	0	-		-	-
All First	13	22	0	1094	146	49.72	4	4	7	-	59	14	115	0	-		-	-
1-day Int																		
C & G	1	1	0	51	51	51.00	-	1	-	-								
B & H	6	6	1	264	97 *	52.80	-	2	2	-	4	0	23	0	-		-	-
1-day Lge	6	6	1	214	85 *	42.80	-	2	1	-	3.3	0	23	0	-		-	-

Career Performances

	M	Inns	NO	Runs	HS	Avge	100s	50s	Ct	St	Balls	Runs	Wkts	Avge	Best	5wl	10wM
Test	46	82	6	2114	154	27.81	2	11	37	-	895	477	4	119.25	1-2	-	-
All First	300	495	62	20142	235	46.51	55	101	177	-	3853	2041	32	63.78	3-32	-	-
1-day Int	13	13	3	265	51	26.50	-	1	6	-	12	14	0	-		-	-
C & G	32	31	1	920	104	30.66	1	4	16	-	360	217	9	24.11	2-15	-	
B & H	47	46	9	1560	119 *	42.16	2	9	19	-	264	189	9	21.00	3-35	-	
1-day Lge	167	159	28	5334	147 *	40.71	4	38	53	-	502	448	15	29.86	5-38	1	

RAMSDEN, G. Yorkshire

Name: Gary Ramsden
Role: Right-hand bat, right-arm fast bowler
Born: 2 March 1983, Dewsbury
Height: 5ft 10in **Weight:** 11st 7lbs
Nickname: Rambo
County debut: 2000
Strike rate: (career 72.00)
Parents: Peter and Angela
Marital status: Single
Family links with cricket: Father plays for
local club, Moorlands CC
Education: Crowlees Junior School;
Castle Hall
Qualifications: 5 GCSEs, CSCA (leadership
award)
Overseas tours: Yorkshire CCC to Singapore
and Perth 2000

Cricketers particularly admired: Glenn
McGrath, Allan Donald
Young players to look out for: Joe Sayers, John Sadler, Steven Blackburn, 'Me'
Other sports played: Football (Huddersfield Town FC 1993-95); rugby, hockey,
tennis, rounders, basketball – all at school
Other sports followed: Football (Huddersfield Town)
Relaxations: Music, movies, socialising, keeping fit
Extras: Is a Yorkshire Academy player. Attended Dennis Lillee's MRF Pace
Foundation, Chennai (Madras) 2001
Opinions on cricket: 'More attention should be paid to the grass roots of the game to
ensure that success can be obtained more regularly in the future.'
Best bowling: 1-32 Yorkshire v Derbyshire, Derby 2000

2001 Season (did not make any first-class or one-day appearances)

Career Performances

	M	Inns	NO	Runs	HS	Avge	100s	50s	Ct	St	Balls	Runs	Wkts	Avge	Best	5wI	10wM
Test																	
All First	1	1	1	0	0 *	-	-	-	-	-	72	68	1	68.00	1-32	-	-
1-day Int																	
C & G																	
B & H																	
1-day Lge	1	0	0	0	0	-	-	-	-	-	24	26	2	13.00	2-26	-	

RANDALL, S. J.   Nottinghamshire

Name: <u>Stephen</u> John Randall
Role: Right-hand bat, right-arm
off-spin bowler
Born: 9 June 1980, Nottingham
Height: 5ft 10in **Weight:** 11st
Nickname: Rags, Rago
County debut: 1999
1st-Class catches: 4
Place in batting averages: 245th av. 12.16
Strike rate: 113.28 (career 173.37)
Parents: Robert and Glenda
Marital status: 'Living in sin with
Alexandra'
Family links with cricket: 'Dad played in
local bucket bangers league for 15 years'
Education: Heyman; West Bridgford School
Qualifications: 9 GCSEs, Level 2 coach
Career outside cricket: 'House husband'

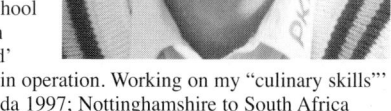

Off-season: 'Coaching and having a groin operation. Working on my "culinary skills"'
Overseas tours: England U17 to Bermuda 1997; Nottinghamshire to South Africa
1998, 1999, 2000, 2001
Career highlights to date: 'Bowling Matt Dowman'
Cricket moments to forget: 'Dropping Mr Cork on 9; he went on to make 129'
Cricketers particularly admired: Tim Robinson, Robert Croft, Eddie Hemmings,
Paul Franks
Young players to look out for: Kev Pietersen, Richard Logan, 'all backroom boys at
Notts and Ding!'
Other sports played: Golf, tennis, 'casino with Noon and Pike'
Other sports followed: Football (Mansfield Town – 'future of football')
Injuries: Groin; shoulder
Relaxations: 'Shopping with the missus'
Extras: Played for Nottinghamshire Board XI in the NatWest 1999
Opinions on cricket: 'Fantastic.'
Best batting: 28 Nottinghamshire v Gloucestershire, Bristol 2001
Best bowling: 2-64 Nottinghamshire v Derbyshire, Trent Bridge 2001

2001 Season

	M	Inns	NO	Runs	HS	Avge	100s	50s	Ct	St	O	M	Runs	Wkts	Avge	Best	5wI	10wM
Test																		
All First	4	7	1	73	28	12.16	-	-	1	-	132.1	21	465	7	66.42	2-64	-	-
1-day Int																		
C & G																		
B & H																		
1-day Lge	2	2	2	28	15 *	-	-	-	-	-	13	0	86	3	28.66	3-44	-	

Career Performances

	M	Inns	NO	Runs	HS	Avge	100s	50s	Ct	St	Balls	Runs	Wkts	Avge	Best	5wI	10wM
Test																	
All First	8	12	2	103	28	10.30	-	-	4	-	1387	811	8	101.37	2-64	-	-
1-day Int																	
C & G	1	1	0	1	1	1.00	-	-	-	-	60	43	0	-		-	-
B & H																	
1-day Lge	2	2	2	28	15 *	-	-	-	-	-	78	86	3	28.66	3-44	-	

RASHID, U. B. A.   Sussex

Name: <u>Umer</u> Bin Abdul Rashid
Role: Left-hand bat, slow left-arm bowler
Born: 6 February 1976, Southampton
Height: 6ft 2in **Weight:** 13st 5lbs
Nickname: Rash, Umie
County debut: 1995 (one-day, Middlesex),
1996 (first-class, Middlesex), 1999 (Sussex)
1st-Class 50s: 7
1st-Class 100s: 2
1st-Class 5 w. in innings: 1
1st-Class catches: 12
One-Day 5 w. in innings: 1
Place in batting averages: 205th av. 18.35
(2000 87th av. 30.78)
Place in bowling averages: 97th av. 36.18
(2000 135th av. 43.21)
Strike rate: 73.27 (career 86.04)
Parents: Mirza and Sebea
Marital status: Single
Family links with cricket: Both brothers play club and junior county level
Education: Southfield Combined First and Middle School; Ealing Green High School;
South Bank University

Qualifications: 7 GCSEs, 2 A-levels, BA (Hons) Marketing and Accounting
Career outside cricket: 'Various!'
Off-season: 'Chilling with whatever I'm doing'
Overseas tours: Sussex to Grenada 2001
Overseas teams played for: Primrose CC, South Africa; Western Province, South Africa; Kingborough CC, Tasmania
Career highlights to date: 'Being given the opportunity to play first-class cricket'
Cricketers particularly admired: 'The whole Sussex staff and everyone else!'
Young players to look out for: Matt Prior, Michael Yardy, Bas Zuiderent
Other sports played: 'Everything and anything!'
Other sports followed: Football (Southampton FC), American football
Injuries: Out for four weeks with a broken finger
Relaxations: 'Spiritualism and relaxing with family and friends'
Extras: Lord's Taverners' Cricketer of the Year 1994-95. Played for England U19 against South Africa U19 in 1995. Played for the Combined Universities side in the B&H Cup. Released by Middlesex at the end of the 1998 season and joined Sussex for 1999. Scored century (106) and had innings return of 4-9 v Durham at Riverside 2001
Opinions on cricket: 'It's getting better and better!'
Best batting: 110 Sussex v Glamorgan, Colwyn Bay 2000
Best bowling: 5-103 Sussex v Northamptonshire, Northampton 2000

2001 Season

	M	Inns	NO	Runs	HS	Avge	100s	50s	Ct	St	O	M	Runs	Wkts	Avge	Best	5wI	10wM
Test																		
All First	14	21	1	367	106	18.35	1	-	1	-	134.2	38	398	11	36.18	4-9	-	-
1-day Int																		
C & G																		
B & H	4	4	2	41	24 *	20.50	-	-	1	-	31	1	134	3	44.66	2-44	-	
1-day Lge	6	6	2	41	28	10.25	-	-	-	-	42	1	234	3	78.00	1-45	-	

Career Performances

	M	Inns	NO	Runs	HS	Avge	100s	50s	Ct	St	Balls	Runs	Wkts	Avge	Best	5wI	10wM
Test																	
All First	41	63	7	1421	110	25.37	2	7	12	-	4216	2073	49	42.30	5-103	1	-
1-day Int																	
C & G	4	2	1	29	24 *	29.00	-	-	-	-	192	144	4	36.00	3-32	-	
B & H	22	20	5	313	82	20.86	-	1	6	-	1083	849	16	53.06	2-25	-	
1-day Lge	44	28	4	241	34	10.04	-	-	17	-	1786	1402	53	26.45	5-24	1	

RATCLIFFE, J. D.   Surrey

Name: <u>Jason</u> David Ratcliffe
Role: Right-hand bat, right-arm medium/off-spin bowler, slip fielder; all-rounder
Born: 19 June 1969, Solihull
Height: 6ft 4in **Weight:** 14st 7lbs
Nickname: Ratters, Fridge
County debut: 1988 (Warwickshire), 1995 (Surrey)
County cap: 1998 (Surrey)
1st-Class 50s: 38
1st-Class 100s: 5
1st-Class 5 w. in innings: 1
1st-Class catches: 68
One-Day 100s: 1
Strike rate: (career 61.84)
Parents: David and Sheila
Wife and date of marriage: Andrea, 7 January 1995

Children: Samuel Taylor, 11 September 2001
Family links with cricket: Father (D.P. Ratcliffe) played for Warwickshire 1956-62
Education: Meadow Green Primary School; Sharmans Cross Secondary School; Solihull Sixth Form College
Qualifications: 6 O-levels, 3 A-levels, NCA staff coach
Career outside cricket: Sports PR and marketing
Off-season: Working for PCA. Training to regain full fitness after knee injury
Overseas tours: NCA (South) to Ireland 1988; Warwickshire to South Africa 1991-92
Overseas teams played for: West End, Kimberley, South Africa 1987-88; Belmont, Newcastle, NSW 1990-91; Penrith, Sydney 1992-94; Parramatta, Sydney 1999-2000
Cricketers particularly admired: Dom Ostler, Gladstone Small
Young players to look out for: Tim Murtagh, 'Martin Bicknell'
Other sports followed: Football (Birmingham City FC)
Injuries: Surgery on knee for patellar tendonitis
Relaxations: Music, reading, eating out
Extras: Has won three Championship winner's medals (Warwickshire and Surrey), a NatWest winner's medal (Warwicks), a Sunday League winner's medal (Surrey) and a B&H winner's medal (Surrey). Is treasurer of the Professional Cricketers' Association and PCA representative for Surrey
Best batting: 135 Surrey v Worcestershire, Worcester 1997
Best bowling: 6-48 Surrey v Sri Lanka A, The Oval 1999

2001 Season (did not make any first-class or one-day appearances)

Career Performances

	M	Inns	NO	Runs	HS	Avge	100s	50s	Ct	St	Balls	Runs	Wkts	Avge	Best	5wI	10wM
Test																	
All First	135	242	13	6545	135	28.58	5	38	68	-	1608	897	26	34.50	6-48	1	-
1-day Int																	
C & G	18	16	1	492	105	32.80	1	3	1	-	120	102	1	102.00	1-17	-	
B & H	16	13	3	170	41	17.00	-	-	6	-	185	121	8	15.12	3-15	-	
1-day Lge	70	60	8	1031	82	19.82	-	5	21	-	1102	842	22	38.27	3-39	-	

RAWNSLEY, M. J.   Worcestershire

Name: <u>Matthew</u> James Rawnsley
Role: Right-hand bat, slow left-arm bowler
Born: 8 June 1976, Birmingham
Height: 6ft 3in **Weight:** 12st 8lbs
Nickname: Scrawny, Dog
County debut: 1996
1st-Class 5 w. in innings: 3
1st-Class 10 w. in match: 1
1st-Class catches: 20
One-Day 5 w. in innings: 1
Place in batting averages: 236th av. 13.12
(2000 288th av. 7.84)
Place in bowling averages: 129th av. 44.85
Strike rate: 99.18 (career 91.25)
Parents: Christopher (deceased) and June
Marital status: Single
Family links with cricket: 'Brother
sometimes turns out for Old Griffinians
RFC's cricket section's 3rd XI Sunday irregulars'
Education: Northfield Manor Primary School, Birmingham; Bourneville Secondary
School, Birmingham; Brynteg Comprehensive, Bridgend
Qualifications: 9 GCSEs and 4 A-levels, NCA coaching award, qualified
canoe instructor
Career outside cricket: 'None, but have fitted windows 40 storeys up a skyscraper'
Off-season: 'Working as an estate agent until January, then going to Auckland to play
for Waitakere'
Overseas tours: Worcestershire CCC to Zimbabwe 1997; Forest Nomads to
Zimbabwe 1999
Overseas teams played for: Kumeu, Auckland 1995-96; Sunrise Sports Club, Harare,
Zimbabwe 1996-97; Old Hararians, 1999-2000; Waitakere, Auckland 2001-02

Career highlights to date: 'Playing against Australia at Worcester [2001]'
Cricket moments to forget: 'Being relegated into second division of Norwich Union League last game of the season 2000'
Cricketers particularly admired: Richard Illingworth
Young players to look out for: Kadeer Ali
Other sports played: Hockey (Wales U18), rugby (Greater Birmingham, North Midlands Colts), badminton (Glamorgan Schools)
Other sports followed: Rugby ('support my bro, who plays for Selly Oak in Birmingham')
Injuries: Out for ten days with an infected shin injury
Relaxations: 'Eating cake "me missus" makes me, with my Sky remote in the other hand'
Extras: Set record for the most wickets at the Oxford Festival (27). Warwickshire U19 Player of the Year in 1995. Took ten wickets and scored 133 not out against Gloucestershire 2nd XI in 1997. Worcestershire Denis Compton Award recipient 1997. 'Junior Lifesavers Medal; patrol leader in the Scouts'
Opinions on cricket: 'People don't realise how good things are until they are gone.'
Best batting: 39 Worcestershire v Hampshire, Worcester 2001
Best bowling: 6-44 Worcestershire v Oxford University, The Parks 1998

2001 Season

	M	Inns	NO	Runs	HS	Avge	100s	50s	Ct	St	O	M	Runs	Wkts	Avge	Best	5wI	10wM
Test																		
All First	15	21	5	210	39	13.12	-	-	6	-	446.2	122	1211	27	44.85	3-55	-	-
1-day Int																		
C & G	2	1·	0	12	12	12.00	-	-	-	-	19	1	93	2	46.50	2-49	-	
B & H	5	2	0	1	1	0.50	-	-	2	-	36.2	0	179	4	44.75	1-30	-	
1-day Lge	14	3	2	8	4 *	8.00	-	-	1	-	93	1	446	15	29.73	3-28	-	

Career Performances

	M	Inns	NO	Runs	HS	Avge	100s	50s	Ct	St	Balls	Runs	Wkts	Avge	Best	5wI	10wM
Test																	
All First	42	54	9	509	39	11.31	-	-	20	-	6570	3009	72	41.79	6-44	3	1
1-day Int																	
C & G	6	4	1	19	12	6.33	-	-	1	-	324	224	6	37.33	2-36	-	
B & H	5	2	0	1	1	0.50	-	-	2	-	218	179	4	44.75	1-30	-	
1-day Lge	38	16	5	46	7	4.18	-	-	8	-	1339	1046	37	28.27	5-26	1	

READ, C. M. W. — Nottinghamshire

Name: <u>Christopher</u> Mark Wells Read
Role: Right-hand bat, wicket-keeper
Born: 10 August 1978, Paignton
Height: 5ft 8in **Weight:** 10st 6lbs
Nickname: Readie, Little Eddie, Lambchops,
Wells Road, Bouch, Biggles
County debut: 1997 (one-day, Glos),
1998 (Notts)
County cap: 1999 (Notts)
Test debut: 1999
Tests: 3
One-Day Internationals: 9
50 dismissals in a season: 1
1st-Class 50s: 11
1st-Class 100s: 1
1st-Class catches: 217
1st-Class stumpings: 7
Place in batting averages: 122nd av. 30.27
(2000 143rd av. 23.95)

Parents: Geoffrey and Carolyn
Marital status: Single
Family links with cricket: 'Dad is now "chairman of selectors" at Paignton CC!'
Education: Roselands Primary School; Torquay Boys' Grammar School;
University of Bath; Loughborough University
Qualifications: 9 GCSEs, 4 A-levels, senior coaching award
Off-season: Studying at Loughborough University
Overseas tours: West of England U13 to Holland 1991; West of England U15 to West
Indies 1992-93; England U17 to Holland (ICC Youth tournament) 1995; England U19
to Pakistan 1996-97; England A to Kenya and Sri Lanka 1997-98, to Zimbabwe and
South Africa 1998-99, to West Indies 2000-01; England to South Africa and Zimbabwe
1999-2000
Cricketers particularly admired: Bruce French, Alan Knott, Bob Taylor,
Graham Thorpe, Jack Russell, Adam Gilchrist
Young players to look out for: Bilal Shafayat, Nadeem Malik
Other sports played: Hockey, table tennis
Other sports followed: Football (Torquay United)
Relaxations: Reading, listening to music, keeping fit and going out with friends
Extras: Represented Devon in Minor Counties Championship and NatWest in 1995,
1996 and 1997, the county winning the Minor Counties Championship three years
running. Played for England U18 against New Zealand U19 in 1996. Has also played
hockey for Devon U18 and U21 and for West of England U17. Played for England

U19 in the series against Zimbabwe U19 1997. He was selected for the England A tour to Kenya and Sri Lanka aged 18 and without having played a first-class game. Joined Nottinghamshire for 1998 season. His 160 (his maiden first-class century) v Warwickshire at Trent Bridge 1999 was the highest score by a Notts wicket-keeper for more than 30 years. Recorded eight dismissals on Test debut in the first Test v New Zealand at Edgbaston 1999

Opinions on cricket: 'We still have two one-day competitions played with a red ball where no international one-day cricket is. In day/night cricket in this country the ECB has recognised that six or eight light towers are required to illuminate the field, yet in domestic day/night games only four are used due to the large financing costs, but the players are subsequently expected to play in sub-standard conditions in often crucial games.'

Best batting: 160 Nottinghamshire v Warwickshire, Trent Bridge 1999

2001 Season

	M	Inns	NO	Runs	HS	Avge	100s	50s	Ct	St	O	M	Runs	Wkts	Avge	Best	5wI	10wM
Test																		
All First	16	27	5	666	78	30.27	-	5	43	1	3	0	25	0	-		-	-	-
1-day Int																		
C & G	2	1	0	15	15	15.00	-	-	3	-								
B & H	7	3	2	24	14 *	24.00	-	-	6	4								
1-day Lge	15	13	3	180	36	18.00	-	-	17	3								

Career Performances

	M	Inns	NO	Runs	HS	Avge	100s	50s	Ct	St	Balls	Runs	Wkts	Avge	Best	5wI	10wM
Test	3	4	0	38	37	9.50	-	-	10	1							
All First	81	122	19	2533	160	24.59	1	11	217	7	18	25	0	-		-	-	-
1-day Int	9	6	2	70	26 *	17.50	-	-	11	2							
C & G	11	9	2	131	37	18.71	-	-	11	3							
B & H	11	7	2	63	15	12.60	-	-	8	4							
1-day Lge	57	47	9	745	62	19.60	-	1	70	8							

RHODES, S. J.   Worcestershire

Name: Steven (Steve) John Rhodes
Role: Right-hand bat, wicket-keeper
Born: 17 June 1964, Bradford
Height: 5ft 8in **Weight:** 12st 8lbs
Nickname: Bumpy
County debut: 1981 (Yorkshire), 1985 (Worcestershire)
County cap: 1986 (Worcestershire)
Benefit: 1996

Test debut: 1994
Tests: 11
One-Day Internationals: 9
1000 runs in a season: 2
50 dismissals in a season: 13
1st-Class 50s: 66
1st-Class 100s: 11
1st-Class catches: 1019
1st-Class stumpings: 114
Place in batting averages: 94th av. 34.00
(2000 121st av. 26.86)
Parents: William Ernest and Norma Kathleen
Wife and date of marriage: Judy Ann,
6 March 1993
Children: Holly Jade, 20 August 1985;
George Harry, 26 October 1993;
Lily Amber, 3 March 1995
Family links with cricket: Father played for
Nottinghamshire 1959-64
Education: Bradford Moor Junior School; Lapage St Middle; Carlton-Bolling
Comprehensive, Bradford
Qualifications: 4 O-levels, Level 3 coach, 'attended Bradford Management Centre for
ECB – Coaching and Management Skills course'
Career outside cricket: Marketing department at Worcestershire CCC
Off-season: Three months coaching in Zimbabwe. Three months in marketing
department at Worcestershire CCC
Overseas tours: England A to Sri Lanka 1986, to Zimbabwe and Kenya 1989-90, to
Pakistan 1990-91, to West Indies 1991-92, to South Africa 1993-94; England to
Australia 1994-95; MCC to Kenya 1999; Blade Group to Barbados 2000-01
Overseas teams played for: Past Bros, Bundaberg, Queensland; Avis Vogeltown,
New Plymouth, New Zealand; Melville, Perth, Australia
Cricketers particularly admired: Richard Hadlee, Ian Healy, Glenn McGrath
Young players to look out for: Lawrence Prittipaul
Other sports followed: Rugby league (Bradford Bulls), horse racing
Injuries: Out for two weeks with a torn calf
Relaxations: Horse racing
Extras: Played for England YC v Australia YC in 1983 and set record for most victims
in an innings for England YC. Youngest wicket-keeper to play for Yorkshire. Released
by Yorkshire to join Worcestershire at end of 1984 season. Set one-day record of four
stumpings in an innings v Warwickshire in Sunday League at Edgbaston 1986. Was one
of four players put on stand-by as reserves for 1992 World Cup squad. One of *Wisden*'s
Five Cricketers of the Year 1995. Overtook David Bairstow (257) as the wicket-keeper
with the most dismissals in the Sunday League v Essex 1997. Made 1000th first-class
dismissal of his career when he caught Graeme Swann off Alamgir Sheriyar v
Northants at Northampton 1999. Equalled his own Worcestershire record for the most

catches in a match with nine v Gloucestershire at Worcester 2000. Made the equal highest number of first-class wicket-keeping dismissals in the 2000 season (55 with Barry Hyam). Vice captain of Worcestershire in 2001. Took 1000th first-class catch during the 2001 season. Coach of Zimbabwe U19 squad to U19 World Cup in New Zealand 2001-02. PCA representative for Worcestershire

Opinions on cricket: 'Two divisions is great. Central contracts "preserve" Test cricketers provided they are used right. The standard week should be – Mon: day off; Tue, Wed, Thu, Fri: four-day game; Sat: day off; Sun: NUL. Typically counties will say no due to costs.'

Best batting: 122* Worcestershire v Young Australia, Worcester 1995

2001 Season

	M	Inns	NO	Runs	HS	Avge	100s	50s	Ct	St	O	M	Runs	Wkts	Avge	Best	5wI	10wM
Test																		
All First	15	20	7	442	52	34.00	-	1	51	1								
1-day Int																		
C & G	2	1	1	56	56 *	-	-	1	3	1								
B & H	5	4	0	7	4	1.75	-	-	6	-								
1-day Lge	14	11	9	139	39 *	69.50	-	-	18	6								

Career Performances

	M	Inns	NO	Runs	HS	Avge	100s	50s	Ct	St	Balls	Runs	Wkts	Avge	Best	5wI	10wM
Test	11	17	5	294	65 *	24.50	-	1	46	3							
All First	397	561	149	13461	122 *	32.67	11	66	1019	114	6	30	0	-		-	-
1-day Int	9	8	2	107	56	17.83	-	1	9	2							
C & G	46	36	13	518	61	22.52	-	3	57	9	6	1	0	-		-	-
B & H	74	51	8	582	51 *	13.53	-	1	96	10							
1-day Lge	259	166	52	2240	48 *	19.64	-	-	277	83							

RICHARDSON, A.   Warwickshire

Name: Alan Richardson
Role: Right-hand bat, right-arm medium bowler
Born: 6 May 1975, Newcastle-under-Lyme, Staffs
Height: 6ft 3in **Weight:** 13st
Nickname: Richo
County debut: 1995 (Derbyshire), 1999 (Warwickshire)
1st-Class 5 w. in innings: 2
1st-Class 10 w. in match: 1
1st-Class catches: 10
Place in bowling averages: 45th av. 27.30 (2000 126th av. 38.51)
Strike rate: 65.97 (career 65.64)

Parents: Roy and Sandra

Marital status: Single

Family links with cricket: 'Dad played for and captained Little Stoke 3rd XI'

Education: Manor Hill First School; Walton Priory Middle School; Alleyne's High School, Stone; Stafford College of Further Education

Qualifications: 8 GCSEs, 2 A-levels, 2 AS-levels, senior cricket coach

Career outside cricket: 'Cutting grass'

Off-season: Playing for Northern Districts CC in Sydney grade competition

Overseas tours: Derbyshire to Malaga 1995; Warwickshire to Bloemfontein 2000, to Cape Town 2001

Overseas teams played for: Northern Natal, South Africa 1994-96; Hawkesbury CC, Sydney 1997-99; Northern Districts, Sydney 1999-2000, 2001-02

Career highlights to date: 'Getting capped by my native Staffordshire. Any attempted catch by Charlie Dagnall. Oh, and 8-51'

Cricket moments to forget: 'Grasping a tie from the open jaws of victory for Little Stoke in 1998. A true club pro at his best!'

Cricketers particularly admired: Angus Fraser, Tim Parmenter, Andrew Powers, and Jason Fellows 'for pure determination despite ability'

Young players to look out for: Jamie Spires, Jim Troughton, 'anyone from Staffordshire'

Other sports played: 'Part of sound defensive unit for the Bears football team. Hoof!!!'

Other sports followed: 'One of the many passionate and knowledgeable Stoke City fans'

Relaxations: 'Music, "Twickers", football and "Station"'

Extras: *The Cricketer*/Slazenger Cricketer of the Month June 1991. *Cricket World* award for best bowling performance in Oxford U19 Festival (8-60 v Devon). Topped Minor Counties bowling averages with Staffordshire 1998 and won Minor Counties bowling award. Most Improved 2nd XI Player 1999. Outstanding Performance of the Year 1999 for his 8-51 v Gloucestershire on home debut; besides being the season's best analysis, it was the best return by a Warwickshire player on debut at Edgbaston

Opinions on cricket: 'Tea breaks have to be longer. Will someone in authority please listen to me?!'

Best batting: 17* Warwickshire v Northamptonshire, Northampton 2000

Best bowling: 8-51 Warwickshire v Gloucestershire, Edgbaston 1999

2001 Season

	M	Inns	NO	Runs	HS	Avge	100s	50s	Ct	St	O	M	Runs	Wkts	Avge	Best	5wI	10wM
Test																		
All First	13	9	4	20	6 *	4.00	-	-	6	-	395.5	111	983	36	27.30	5-89	1	-
1-day Int																		
C & G																		
B & H																		
1-day Lge	6	2	2	8	8 *	-	-	-	1	-	39.4	3	167	7	23.85	3-17	-	

Career Performances

	M	Inns	NO	Runs	HS	Avge	100s	50s	Ct	St	Balls	Runs	Wkts	Avge	Best	5wI	10wM
Test																	
All First	33	27	14	76	17 *	5.84	-	-	10	-	5842	2622	89	29.46	8-51	2	1
1-day Int																	
C & G	3	3	0	3	3	1.00	-	-	-	-	168	116	1	116.00	1-48	-	
B & H	3	2	1	2	1 *	2.00	-	-	-	-	72	48	1	48.00	1-16	-	
1-day Lge	12	4	3	19	11 *	19.00	-	-	1	-	487	361	14	25.78	3-17	-	

RICHARDSON, S. A.   Yorkshire

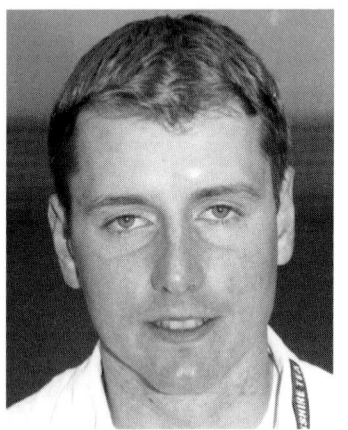

Name: <u>Scott</u> Andrew Richardson
Role: Right-hand bat, right-arm
medium bowler
Born: 5 September 1977, Oldham
Height: 6ft 2in **Weight:** 13st 6lbs
Nickname: Richo, Tickle
County debut: 2000
1st-Class 50s: 2
1st-Class catches: 6
Place in batting averages: 159th av. 23.88
Parents: Mike and Anne
Marital status: Single
Family links with cricket: 'Dad is an ex-
professional in local leagues. He owns
Romida Sports (specialist cricket shop)'
Education: Hulme Grammar School,
Oldham; Manchester Grammar School
Qualifications: 11 GCSEs, 2 A-levels
Career outside cricket: 'Work for Romida Sports'
Off-season: 'Either playing in Australia or working at Romida Sports'
Overseas tours: Manchester GS to Barbados 1993, to Cape Town 1995; MCC to
Philadelphia 2000

Overseas teams played for: Easts-Redlands, Brisbane 1996-98; Redbank Plains, Queensland 1998-99
Career highlights to date: 'Making Championship debut [2001]'
Cricket moments to forget: 'Have enjoyed every moment!'
Cricketers particularly admired: Michael Atherton, Robin Smith
Young players to look out for: Joe Sayers, David Stiff
Other sports played: Golf, football
Other sports followed: Football (Manchester United), rugby league (Oldham)
Injuries: Out for two weeks with broken left hand
Relaxations: Watching Man Utd and Oldham rugby league side; movies; playing golf
Extras: Lancashire Schools U19 Player of the Year 1995. Scored 69 v Kent at Headingley 2001, sharing in the process in the highest first-wicket partnership (152) for Yorkshire in matches against Kent for 49 years with Matthew Wood
Opinions on cricket: 'Need to keep 2nd XI because the step from board/league cricket to first-class would be too big.'
Best batting: 69 Yorkshire v Kent, Headingley 2001

2001 Season

	M	Inns	NO	Runs	HS	Avge	100s	50s	Ct	St	O	M	Runs	Wkts	Avge	Best	5wI	10wM
Test																		
All First	7	11	2	215	69	23.88	-	2	6	-								
1-day Int																		
C & G																		
B & H																		
1-day Lge																		

Career Performances

	M	Inns	NO	Runs	HS	Avge	100s	50s	Ct	St	Balls	Runs	Wkts	Avge	Best	5wI	10wM
Test																	
All First	8	13	2	229	69	20.81	-	2	6	-							
1-day Int																	
C & G																	
B & H																	
1-day Lge																	

RIPLEY, D.   Northamptonshire

Name: David Ripley
Role: Right-hand bat, wicket-keeper
Born: 13 September 1966, Leeds
Height: 5ft 11in **Weight:** 12st
Nickname: Spud, Rips, Austin
County debut: 1984
County cap: 1987
50 dismissals in a season: 4
1st-Class 50s: 34
1st-Class 100s: 8
1st-Class 200s: 1
1st-Class catches: 679
1st-Class stumpings: 84
Place in batting averages: 152nd av. 25.31
(2000 81st av. 31.66)
Strike rate: (career 30.00)
Parents: Arthur and Brenda
Wife and date of marriage: Jackie,
24 September 1988
Children: Joe David, 11 October 1989; George William, 5 March 1994;
Charlie John, 10 March 2000
Education: Woodlesford Primary; Royds High, Leeds
Qualifications: 5 O-levels, staff coach, ECB Level 3 coach
Career outside cricket: Cricket development officer for Northamptonshire
Overseas tours: England YC to West Indies 1984-85; Northants to Durban 1991-92, to
Cape Town 1992-93, to Zimbabwe 1994-95, 1998, to Johannesburg 1996, to Grenada
2000, 2001
Overseas teams played for: Marists and Poverty Bay, New Zealand 1985-87
Career highlights: 'Scoring a double hundred and avoiding a pair throughout
my career'
Cricket moments to forget: 'Two howlers at the end of last season'
Cricketers particularly admired: Alan Knott, Bob Taylor, Jack Russell 'and many
other keepers', Clive Radley, Ian Botham, Dennis Lillee
Young players to look out for: 'Sales, Swann', James Foster, Monty Panesar
Other sports played: Football (locally), golf
Other sports followed: Football (Leeds United), rugby league (Castleford), golf,
WWF wrestling ('admire The Rock'), 'local sports teams'
Injuries: Out for three weeks with thumb and finger impact injuries
Relaxations: 'Eating out, spending time with the family, improving my knowledge of
Guinness and red wine'
Extras: Finished top of wicket-keepers' dismissals list for 1988 and 1992 and was

voted Wombwell Cricket Lovers' Society Best Wicket-keeper 1992. Played for England YC v Sri Lanka YC 1986. Northamptonshire Player of the Year in 1988, 1997 and 1999. Put on 401 for the fifth wicket with Mal Loye v Glamorgan 1998, setting a new fifth-wicket partnership record for first-class cricket in England and registering a career best 209. Put on 293 for the seventh wicket with David Sales v Essex 1999, setting a new seventh-wicket partnership record for the county. Also shared in county record partnership for the eighth wicket, 164 v Lancashire in 1987 with Nick Cook. Lies second, behind K. V. Andrew, in Northants wicket-keeping dismissals list. Vice-captain of Northants 1999-2000. County captain 2001. Scored 95 v Somerset at Northampton 2001, in the process sharing with Tony Penberthy in a record eighth-wicket partnership for Northants in matches against Somerset (161). Retired at the end of the 2001 season

Best batting: 209 Northamptonshire v Glamorgan, Northampton 1998
Best bowling: 2-89 Northamptonshire v Essex, Ilford 1987

2001 Season

	M	Inns	NO	Runs	HS	Avge	100s	50s	Ct	St	O	M	Runs	Wkts	Avge	Best	5wI	10wM
Test																		
All First	15	25	6	481	95	25.31	-	2	45	3								
1-day Int																		
C & G	2	1	0	35	35	35.00	-	-	-	-								
B & H	5	2	0	28	14	14.00	-	-	3	-								
1-day Lge	11	8	2	153	40 *	25.50	-	-	9	5								

Career Performances

	M	Inns	NO	Runs	HS	Avge	100s	50s	Ct	St	Balls	Runs	Wkts	Avge	Best	5wI	10wM
Test																	
All First	307	410	104	8693	209	28.40	9	34	679	84	60	103	2	51.50	2-89	-	-
1-day Int																	
C & G	43	24	9	184	35	12.26	-	-	44	4							
B & H	54	34	13	420	36 *	20.00	-	-	58	6							
1-day Lge	178	111	45	1245	52 *	18.86	-	1	123	24							

ROBERTS, T. W.   Lancashire

Name: Timothy (<u>Tim</u>) William Roberts
Role: Right-hand bat, right-arm
off-spin bowler
Born: 4 March 1978, Kettering
Height: 5ft 7½in **Weight:** 11st
Nickname: Robbo
County debut: 2001
1st-Class catches: 1
Parents: David and Shirley
Marital status: Single
Family links with cricket: 'Brother Andy
was a leg-spinner at Northants; now captains
Bedfordshire. Dad Dave had trials for
Northants'
Education: Our Lady's Convent, Kettering;
Bishop Stopford School, Kettering;
Durham University
Qualifications: 2.1 degree in Geology,
Level 3 cricket coach
Off-season: Training
Overseas tours: England U17 to Holland 1995; Lancashire to South Africa
2000, 2001
Overseas teams played for: Eastern Suburbs, Wellington, New Zealand 1999-2000
Career highlights to date: 'Being signed by Lancashire'
Cricketers particularly admired: Andy Roberts, Ricky Ponting, Sachin Tendulkar,
Wayne Larkins
Young players to look out for: N. Coles, N. Brown, A. Daniels, S. Brett, M. Henson
Other sports played: Golf, football, badminton, squash
Other sports followed: Football (Rushden & Diamonds FC)
Relaxations: 'Having a quiet beer with the lads from FDCC – the "Dolben"!'
Extras: Played for British Universities v New Zealanders at The Parks 1999. Scored a
41-ball 50 (ending up with 55) in his second Norwich Union League match, v
Derbyshire at Derby 2001
Best batting: 49 British Universities v New Zealanders, The Parks 1999

2001 Season

	M	Inns	NO	Runs	HS	Avge	100s	50s	Ct	St	O	M	Runs	Wkts	Avge	Best	5wI	10wM
Test																		
All First	2	3	0	20	17	6.66	-	-	1	-								
1-day Int																		
C & G																		
B & H																		
1-day Lge	3	3	0	68	55	22.66	-	1	-	-	3	0	14	0	-		-	-

Career Performances

	M	Inns	NO	Runs	HS	Avge	100s	50s	Ct	St	Balls	Runs	Wkts	Avge	Best	5wI	10wM
Test																	
All First	3	5	0	108	49	21.60	-	-	1	-							
1-day Int																	
C & G																	
B & H																	
1-day Lge	3	3	0	68	55	22.66	-	1	-	-	18	14	0	-		-	-

ROBINSON, D. D. J. Essex

Name: <u>Darren</u> David John Robinson
Role: Right-hand bat, right-arm 'all sorts'
Born: 2 March 1973, Braintree, Essex
Height: 5ft 11in **Weight:** 14st
Nickname: Pie Shop
County debut: 1993
County cap: 1997
1st-Class 50s: 23
1st-Class 100s: 9
1st-Class 200s: 1
1st-Class catches: 87
One-Day 100s: 3
Place in batting averages: 99th av. 32.93
(2000 58th av. 35.06)
Parents: Dorothy (deceased) and David
Marital status: Engaged
Children: Kalli, 20 July 1998; Cameron, 20 May 2000
Family links with cricket: Father plays club cricket for Halstead
Education: Tabor High School, Braintree; Chelmsford College of Further Education
Qualifications: 5 GCSEs, BTEC National Diploma in Building and Construction
Career outside cricket: Site investigation and surveying

Off-season: 'Drinking beer with my mates'
Overseas tours: England U18 to Canada 1991; England U19 to Pakistan 1991-92
Overseas teams played for: Waverley, Sydney 1992-94; Eden Roskill CC, Auckland 1995-96
Cricketers particularly admired: Graham Gooch, Stuart Law
Young players to look out for: James Foster
Other sports followed: Golf, football, rugby, swimming
Relaxations: Reading crime novels, music, eating out, pubs
Extras: *Daily Telegraph* batting award 1988 and International Youth Tournament in Canada batting award 1991. Scored two centuries (102 and 118*) in match v Leicestershire at Chelmsford 2001
Opinions on cricket: 'Two divisions has been a revelation for the game.'
Best batting: 200 Essex v New Zealanders, Chelmsford 1999

2001 Season

	M	Inns	NO	Runs	HS	Avge	100s	50s	Ct	St	O	M	Runs	Wkts	Avge	Best	5wl	10wM
Test																		
All First	18	31	2	955	118 *	32.93	3	4	11	-	10	0	54	0	-		-	-	-
1-day Int																		
C & G	2	2	0	30	30	15.00	-	-	-	-								
B & H	3	3	0	69	69	23.00	-	1	1	-								
1-day Lge	16	15	0	304	64	20.26	-	1	2	-								

Career Performances

	M	Inns	NO	Runs	HS	Avge	100s	50s	Ct	St	Balls	Runs	Wkts	Avge	Best	5wl	10wM
Test																	
All First	107	186	9	5083	200	28.71	10	23	87	-	111	99	0	-		-	-	-
1-day Int																	
C & G	16	14	1	277	62	21.30	-	2	5	-							
B & H	20	18	3	520	137 *	34.66	2	1	3	-							
1-day Lge	88	86	8	1989	129 *	25.50	1	9	24	-	17	26	1	26.00	1-7	-	

ROBINSON, M. A. Sussex

Name: <u>Mark</u> Andrew Robinson
Role: Right-hand bat, right-arm fast-medium bowler
Born: 23 November 1966, Hull
Height: 6ft 3in **Weight:** 13st
Nickname: Coddy, Smokie, Tiger, Storm, Rodney
County debut: 1987 (Northamptonshire), 1991 (Yorkshire), 1996 (Sussex)
County cap: 1990 (Northamptonshire), 1992 (Yorkshire), 1997 (Sussex)
50 wickets in a season: 1

1st-Class 5 w. in innings: 13
1st-Class 10 w. in match: 2
1st-Class catches: 41
Place in batting averages: 281st av. 4.00
Place in bowling averages: 8th av. 19.33
(2000 110th av. 33.56)
Strike rate: 44.53 (career 64.67)
Parents: Malcolm and Joan
Wife and date of marriage: Julia,
8 October 1994
Children: Samuel Lewis, 11 January 1996;
Eleanor Grace, 20 July 2000
Family links with cricket: Grandfather a
prominent local cricketer and 'father was
hostile bowler in the back garden'

Education: Fifth Avenue Primary; Endike
Junior High; Hull Grammar School
Qualifications: 6 O-levels, 2 A-levels,
advanced cricket coach, badminton coach, rugby union coach
Career outside cricket: Self-employed cricket coach
Off-season: 'Looking for a house in Sussex'
Overseas tours: England U19 North to Bermuda; Yorkshire to Cape Town 1991-92,
1992-93, to West Indies 1993-94; Sussex to Grenada 2001
Overseas teams played for: East Shirley, Canterbury, New Zealand 1987-89;
Canterbury, New Zealand 1989-98
Career highlights to date: '9-37 v Northants'
Cricket moments to forget: 'Don't want to forget any moment of what is a
privileged existence'
Cricketers particularly admired: Peter Moores, Keith Greenfield, Tony Cottey 'and
any other player who lives for the game'
Young players to look out for: Steve Patterson, Joe Sayers, Matt Prior, Tim Ambrose,
Sam Robinson
Other sports played: Football
Other sports followed: Football (Hull City), 'all sports'
Extras: Took hat-trick with first three balls of innings in Yorkshire League playing for
Hull v Doncaster. First player to win Yorkshire U19 Bowler of the Season in two
successive years, 1984 and 1985. Northamptonshire Uncapped Player of the Year in
1989. Endured a world record 12 innings without scoring a run in 1990. Sussex
Clubman of the Year 1997 and 1998. Scored 500th first-class run on the same day as
he took 500th first-class wicket v Surrey at Hove 1999. Was not out in ten successive
innings during 1999-2000, equalling the record for county cricket. B&H Gold Award
for his 4-29 v Kent at Hastings 2001. His 5-59 v Durham at Hove 2001 included his
200th wicket for Sussex. Appointed Sussex 2nd team coach for 2002
Opinions on cricket: 'Never trust a man who likes green sweets.'

Best batting: 27 Sussex v Lancashire, Old Trafford 1997
Best bowling: 9-37 Yorkshire v Northamptonshire, Harrogate 1993

2001 Season

	M	Inns	NO	Runs	HS	Avge	100s	50s	Ct	St	O	M	Runs	Wkts	Avge	Best	5wI	10wM
Test																		
All First	14	15	7	32	10	4.00	-	-	1	-	415.4	126	1083	56	19.33	5-35	3	-
1-day Int																		
C & G	2	1	0	0	0	0.00	-	-	-	-	18	1	60	2	30.00	1-27	-	
B & H	4	1	0	1	1	1.00	-	-	1	-	40	5	145	8	18.12	4-29	-	
1-day Lge	15	7	4	8	4	2.66	-	-	1	-	131.5	16	416	19	21.89	3-17	-	

Career Performances

	M	Inns	NO	Runs	HS	Avge	100s	50s	Ct	St	Balls	Runs	Wkts	Avge	Best	5wI	10wM
Test																	
All First	228	257	111	580	27	3.97	-	-	41	-	37449	17669	579	30.51	9-37	13	2
1-day Int																	
C & G	29	11	7	19	8 *	4.75	-	-	3	-	1908	1042	38	27.42	4-32	-	
B & H	34	15	7	12	5	1.50	-	-	6	-	1906	1131	43	26.30	4-29	-	
1-day Lge	171	65	29	112	15 *	3.11	-	-	16	-	7612	5287	165	32.04	4-23	-	

ROLLINS, A. S.   Northamptonshire

Name: <u>Adrian</u> Stewart Rollins
Role: Right-hand bat, right-arm 'pie chucker
net bowler', occasional wicket-keeper
Born: 8 February 1972, Barking
Height: 6ft 5in
Nickname: Rollie, Blaaah
County debut: 1993 (Derbyshire),
2000 (Northants)
County cap: 1995 (Derbyshire)
1000 runs in a season: 3
1st-Class 50s: 38
1st-Class 100s: 10
1st-Class 200s: 2
1st-Class catches: 103
1st-Class stumpings: 1
One-Day 100s: 1
Place in batting averages: 163rd av. 23.77
(2000 123rd av. 26.50)
Strike rate: (career 90.00)

Parents: Marva
Marital status: Engaged to Debs
Children: Stepdaughter Gemma, 8 July 1993; son, Jared, 1 June 1999
Family links with cricket: 'Brother [Robert] played for Essex 1991-99. Now smacks the rubbish in Minor Counties'
Education: Avenue Primary, Manor Park, London; Little Ilford Comprehensive, Manor Park, London; Open University (2002 –)
Qualifications: 10 GCSEs, 4 A-levels, BAWLA leader's award, CCPR Community Sports Leader's award, Diploma in Sports Psychology
Career outside cricket: 'Street beggar'
Off-season: 'Back to New Zealand. Start Open Uni degree'
Overseas tours: London Federation of Boys Clubs to Barbados 1987; Northants to Grenada 2000, 2001
Overseas teams played for: Kaponga, Taranaki, New Zealand 1993-94; Taranaki, New Zealand 2000-02 (captain)
Career highlights to date: 'Hundred before lunch v Glamorgan at Chesterfield 1997'
Cricket moments to forget: 'Dropping Dave Fulton at Northampton on 13 in 2001 (he scored 197). Easiest catch in the world. Looked like an idiot – felt like an idiot – idiot'
Cricketers particularly admired: Phillip DeFreitas, Malcolm Marshall, David Gower, Viv Richards, Gordon Greenidge, Desmond Haynes, Michael Holding
Young players to look out for: Monty Panesar, Alec Swann, David Sales, 'all my little cousins; not my son, though – he'll play basketball'
Other sports played: Badminton (Essex at junior level), 'racketball master'
Other sports followed: Football (West Ham – ''nuff said')
Relaxations: 'I don't know how to relax; I have kids'
Extras: Made Championship debut on same day as brother. Became 500th first-class player for Derbyshire, for whom he was named Young Player of the Year 1993. Was the 100th Derbyshire player to score a hundred. In 1995 set record for the highest score by a Derbyshire opener to carry his bat – his 200 not out v Gloucestershire was also the longest innings by a Derbyshire player, and he became the youngest English-qualified Derbyshire double centurion. Voted Derbyshire Player of the Year for 1995. Took part in record third-wicket partnership for Derbyshire (316*) with Kim Barnett against Leicestershire 1997. Left Derbyshire at end of 1999 season and joined Northamptonshire for 2000. Scored 100 and 96 v Middlesex 2000, failing by just four runs to become the first player since Graham Gooch in 1990 to score a century in both innings at Lord's
Opinions on cricket: 'Too much negativity. Positive, aggressive cricket gets results. Look at the Aussies and the Windies of the 1970s and 1980s.'
Best batting: 210 Derbyshire v Hampshire, Chesterfield 1997
Best bowling: 1-19 Derbyshire v Essex, Chelmsford 1995

2001 Season

	M	Inns	NO	Runs	HS	Avge	100s	50s	Ct	St	O	M	Runs	Wkts	Avge	Best	5wI	10wM
Test																		
All First	6	10	1	214	65	23.77	-	1	3	-								
1-day Int																		
C & G	2	1	0	25	25	25.00	-	-	1	-								
B & H																		
1-day Lge	3	3	1	55	29	27.50	-	-	-	-								

Career Performances

	M	Inns	NO	Runs	HS	Avge	100s	50s	Ct	St	Balls	Runs	Wkts	Avge	Best	5wI	10wM
Test																	
All First	123	221	19	6871	210	34.01	12	38	103	1	90	122	1	122.00	1-19	-	-
1-day Int																	
C & G	14	13	0	323	80	24.84	-	3	9	-							
B & H	12	12	1	263	70 *	23.90	-	2	2	-							
1-day Lge	73	67	6	1139	126 *	18.67	1	1	29	-	12	15	0	-		-	-

ROSE, G. D. Somerset

Name: <u>Graham</u> David Rose
Role: Right-hand bat, right-arm fast-medium bowler, first slip
Born: 12 April 1964, Tottenham, London
Height: 6ft 4in **Weight:** 15st 7lbs
Nickname: Rosie, Hagar
County debut: 1985 (Middlesex), 1987 (Somerset)
County cap: 1988 (Somerset)
Benefit: 1997 (Somerset, £91,500)
1000 runs in a season: 1
50 wickets in a season: 5
1st-Class 50s: 41
1st-Class 100s: 11
1st-Class 5 w. in innings: 15
1st-Class 10 w. in match: 1
1st-Class catches: 116
One-Day 100s: 2
Place in batting averages: (2000 43rd av. 39.23)
Place in bowling averages: (2000 101st av. 31.31)
Strike rate: 100.00 (career 56.55)
Parents: William and Edna

Wife and date of marriage: Teresa Julie, 19 September 1987
Children: Georgina Charlotte, 6 December 1990; Felix William Michael, 11 August 1997
Family links with cricket: Father and brothers have played club cricket
Education: Northumberland Park School, Tottenham
Qualifications: 6 O-levels, 4 A-levels, NCA coaching certificate
Overseas teams played for: Carey Park, Bunbury, Western Australia 1984-85; Fremantle, Perth 1986-87; Paarl, Cape Town 1988-89
Cricketers particularly admired: Andrew Caddick, Jimmy Cook, Richard Hadlee, Malcolm Marshall, Mushtaq Ahmed
Young players to look out for: Matthew Bulbeck, Peter Trego
Other sports followed: Football, rugby, golf
Relaxations: Wine, golf, 'Georgina and Felix'
Extras: Played for England YC v Australia YC 1983. Took 6-41 on Middlesex debut in 1985 (the best innings figures by a Middlesex bowler on first-class debut), then scored 95 on debut for Somerset in 1987. Completed double of 1000 runs and 50 wickets in first-class cricket in 1990 and set records for fastest recorded centuries in NatWest Trophy (36 balls v Devon) and Sunday League (46 balls v Glamorgan; since bettered). Cricket Society's All-rounder of the Year 1997. PCA representative for Somerset
Best batting: 191 Somerset v Sussex, Taunton 1997
Best bowling: 7-47 Somerset v Nottinghamshire, Taunton 1996

2001 Season

	M	Inns	NO	Runs	HS	Avge	100s	50s	Ct	St	O	M	Runs	Wkts	Avge	Best	5wI	10wM
Test																		
All First	3	4	0	25	15	6.25	-	-	-	-	50	15	155	3	51.66	1-36	-	-
1-day Int																		
C & G																		
B & H																		
1-day Lge	1	1	0	58	58	58.00	-	1	-	-	1	0	2	0	-	-	-	-

Career Performances

	M	Inns	NO	Runs	HS	Avge	100s	50s	Ct	St	Balls	Runs	Wkts	Avge	Best	5wI	10wM
Test																		
All First	248	343	63	8653	191	30.90	11	41	116	-	34158	17868	604	29.58	7-47	15	1
1-day Int																		
C & G	25	21	3	372	110	20.66	1	1	4	-	1366	889	29	30.65	3-11	-	
B & H	56	49	5	926	79	21.04	-	4	12	-	2968	1968	68	28.94	4-21	-	
1-day Lge	205	177	34	3682	148	25.74	1	19	51	-	8060	5936	198	29.97	4-26	-	

ROSEBERRY, M. A.   Middlesex

Name: <u>Michael</u> Anthony Roseberry
Role: Right-hand opening bat, right-arm medium bowler
Born: 28 November 1966, Sunderland
Height: 6ft 2in   **Weight:** 14st 10lbs
Nickname: Micky
County debut: 1985 (Middlesex), 1995 (Durham)
County cap: 1990 (Middlesex), 1998 (Durham)
1000 runs in a season: 4
1st-Class 50s: 58
1st-Class 100s: 21
1st-Class catches: 165
One-Day 100s: 6
Place in batting averages: 139th av. 28.00 (2000 72nd av. 32.29)
Strike rate: (career 127.75)
Parents: Matthew and Jean
Wife and date of marriage: Helen Louise, 22 February 1991
Children: Jordan Louise, 29 May 1992; Lauren Ella, 19 February 1994
Family links with cricket: Brother Andrew played for Glamorgan and Leicestershire
Education: Tonstall Preparatory School, Sunderland; Durham School
Qualifications: 5 O-levels, 1 A-level, Level 3 coaching
Career outside cricket: Director in family business
Overseas tours: England YC to West Indies 1984-85; England A to Australia 1992-93; England XI and Lord's Taverners to Hong Kong 'on numerous occasions'; MCC to West Africa 1993-94; Durham CCC to South Africa 1994-95
Overseas teams played for: Fremantle, Western Australia 1986; Melville, Perth 1988; Alberton, Johannesburg 1994-96
Cricketers particularly admired: 'Desmond Haynes for the obvious and his generosity on the golf course'
Other sports played: 'Played rugby union at a good level when at school, representing Durham County at all levels except the senior side'
Other sports followed: 'Follow golf and very loyal supporter of Sunderland FC'
Relaxations: 'Eating out and spending time with my family, which is limited during the summer'
Extras: At age 16, playing for Durham School v St Bees, he hit 216 in 160 minutes. Played in Durham League as a professional while still at school. Won Lord's Taverners/MCC Cricketer of the Year 1983, Cricket Society award for Best Young

Cricketer of the Year 1984 and twice won Cricket Society award for best all-rounder in schools cricket. In 1992 scored 2044 runs – joint highest in first-class cricket with Peter Bowler – and was named Middlesex Player of the Year and Lucozade Player of the Year. Left Middlesex at end of 1994 to return to his native Durham as captain for the 1995 season but relinquished the captaincy during the 1996 season. Rejoined Middlesex for 1999. Retired at the end of the 2001 season
Best batting: 185 Middlesex v Leicestershire, Lord's 1993
Best bowling: 1-1 Middlesex v Sussex, Hove 1988

2001 Season

	M	Inns	NO	Runs	HS	Avge	100s	50s	Ct	St	O	M	Runs	Wkts	Avge	Best	5wI	10wM
Test																		
All First	11	17	2	420	87	28.00	-	2	9	-								
1-day Int																		
C & G	1	1	0	46	46	46.00	-	-	-	-								
B & H	4	3	0	0	0	0.00	-	-	1	-								
1-day Lge	6	6	0	85	35	14.16	-	-	2	-								

Career Performances

	M	Inns	NO	Runs	HS	Avge	100s	50s	Ct	St	Balls	Runs	Wkts	Avge	Best	5wI	10wM
Test																	
All First	236	401	43	11950	185	33.37	21	58	165	-	511	406	4	101.50	1-1	-	-
1-day Int																	
C & G	21	21	2	773	121	40.68	3	1	7	-	36	42	1	42.00	1-22	-	
B & H	38	35	3	710	84	22.18	-	6	9	-	6	2	0	-	-	-	
1-day Lge	151	145	17	4018	119 *	31.39	3	30	54	-	4	7	0	-	-	-	

73. Which pair of brothers played for Sussex in the
1968 and 1970 Gillette Cup finals?

RUSSELL, R. C.   Gloucestershire

Name: Robert Charles (Jack) Russell
Role: Left-hand bat, wicket-keeper
Born: 15 August 1963, Stroud
Height: 5ft 8¼in **Weight:** 9st 9lbs
County debut: 1981
County cap: 1985
Benefit: 1994
Test debut: 1988
Tests: 54
One-Day Internationals: 39
1000 runs in a season: 1
50 dismissals in a season: 15
1st-Class 50s: 81
1st-Class 100s: 8
1st-Class catches: 1120
1st-Class stumpings: 121
One-Day 100s: 2
Place in batting averages: 79th av. 37.30
(2000 98th av. 29.65)
Strike rate: (career 56.00)
Parents: John and Jennifer
Wife and date of marriage: Aileen Ann, 6 March 1985
Children: Stepson, Marcus Anthony, 1980; Elizabeth Ann, March 1988;
Victoria, 1989; Charles David, 1991; Katherine Jane, 1996
Education: Uplands County Primary School; Archway Comprehensive School; Bristol
Polytechnic ('walked out after two months of accountancy course. Couldn't
understand the sociology and economics – wanted to play cricket instead')
Qualifications: 7 O-levels, 2 A-levels
Career outside cricket: Professional artist
Off-season: Painting
Overseas tours: England A to Australia 1992-93 (vice-captain); England to Pakistan
1987-88, to India and West Indies 1989-90, to Australia 1990-91, to New Zealand
1991-92, to West Indies 1993-94, to Australia 1994-95, to South Africa 1995-96, to
Pakistan and India (World Cup) 1995-96, to Zimbabwe and New Zealand 1996-97, to
West Indies 1997-98, to Bangladesh (Wills International Cup) 1998-99
Cricketers particularly admired: Alan Knott, Bob Taylor, Ian Botham,
Rodney Marsh 'and other greats'
Young players to look out for: Chris Taylor
Other sports followed: Football (Tottenham Hotspur), rugby (England), snooker,
'anything competitive'
Relaxations: Playing cricket and painting pictures. 'I love comedians and comedies.
Life is too short, you need to laugh as much as you can'

Extras: Spotted at age nine by Gloucestershire coach, Graham Wiltshire. Became youngest Gloucestershire wicket-keeper (17 years 307 days) and set record for most dismissals in a match on first-class debut: 8 (7 caught, 1 stumped) for Gloucestershire v Sri Lankans at Bristol, 1981. Hat-trick of catches v Surrey at The Oval 1986. Represented England YC v West Indies YC in 1982. Was chosen as England's Man of the Test Series, England v Australia 1989 and was one of *Wisden's* Five Cricketers of the Year 1990. Opened Jack Russell Gallery in Chipping Sodbury, South Gloucestershire, in 1995; his paintings are sold and displayed in museums and private collections all around the world. Books of his that have been published include *A Cricketer's Art – Sketches by Jack Russell* (1988), *Sketches of a Season – illustrated by Jack Russell* (1989), *Jack Russell's Sketch Book* (1996) and *Jack Russell – Unleashed*, an autobiography which made the top ten bestsellers in 1997. He also has his own website: http://www.jackrussell.co.uk. Commissioned by Dean of Gloucester to do a drawing of Gloucester Cathedral to raise funds for 900th Anniversary. Still turns out for his original club, Stroud CC, whenever he can. Captain of Gloucestershire and Player of the Year 1995. Broke Bob Taylor's long-standing world record for the number of dismissals in a Test match with 11 (all caught) in the second Test v South Africa at Johannesburg 1995-96; his 27 Test dismissals in the series is a record for England. Awarded MBE in 1996 for services to cricket. Was the Whyte and Mackay wicket-keeper/batsman of the year 1995, 1996, 1997. Announced his retirement from international cricket in October 1998 after the Wills International Cup in Bangladesh. Became seventh wicket-keeper to take 1000 first-class catches when he caught Tim Robinson v Notts at Bristol 1999. Set a new NatWest dismissals record by claiming his 67th victim (Adrian Rollins) v Derbyshire at Bristol 1999. Man of the Match in Gloucestershire's NatWest final victory over Somerset 1999. Leading wicket-keeper in the single-division four-day County Championship era with 356 victims (335 caught/21 stumped) 1993-99. Scored 53 v Derbyshire at Derby 2001 in his 500th first-class innings for Gloucestershire

Best batting: 129* England v Boland, Paarl 1995-96
Best bowling: 1-4 Gloucestershire v West Indians, Bristol 1991

2001 Season

	M	Inns	NO	Runs	HS	Avge	100s	50s	Ct	St	O	M	Runs	Wkts	Avge	Best	5wI	10wM
Test																		
All First	10	12	2	373	91 *	37.30	-	2	42	2								
1-day Int																		
C & G	2	2	0	3	3	1.50	-	-	5	-								
B & H	2	2	0	69	62	34.50	-	1	2	-								
1-day Lge	10	9	1	65	24	8.12	-	-	7	4								

Career Performances

	M	Inns	NO	Runs	HS	Avge	100s	50s	Ct	St	Balls	Runs	Wkts	Avge	Best	5wI	10wM
Test	54	86	16	1897	128 *	27.10	2	6	153	12							
All First	435	644	134	15404	129 *	30.20	8	81	1120	121	56	68	1	68.00	1-4	-	-
1-day Int	40	31	7	423	50	17.62	-	1	41	6							
C & G	53	41	11	822	84	27.40	-	3	75	13							
B & H	78	58	21	1176	119 *	31.78	1	5	78	15							
1-day Lge	251	199	45	3581	108	23.25	1	15	206	49							

SADLER, J. L. Yorkshire

Name: <u>John</u> Leonard Sadler
Role: Left-hand bat
Born: 19 November 1981, Dewsbury
Height: 5ft 11in **Weight:** 12st 6lbs
Nickname: Sads
County debut: No first-team appearance
Parents: Mike and Sue
Marital status: Single
Family links with cricket: Father played and now coaches. Brothers Dave and Jamie play for Ossett in Central Yorkshire League; both played for Yorkshire youth teams
Education: St Ignatius Primary, Ossett; St Thomas à Becket Comprehensive, Wakefield
Qualifications: 9 GCSEs, Level 1 coaching award
Off-season: Playing club cricket for Tuart Hill, Perth. Yorkshire pre-season tour to Grenada
Overseas tours: England U19 to Malaysia and (U19 World Cup) Sri Lanka 1999-2000, to India 2000-01
Overseas teams played for: Tuart Hill, Perth 2001-02
Career highlights to date: 'Selection for England youth teams and signing for Yorkshire'
Cricket moments to forget: 'Injury to knee in Sri Lanka January 2000, leading to early return to England from U19 World Cup squad'
Cricketers particularly admired: Sachin Tendulkar, Graham Thorpe, Robin Smith
Young players to look out for: Ian Bell, Nicky Peng, Tim Bresnan
Other sports played: Football
Other sports followed: Football (Leeds United), rugby league (Leeds Rhinos)
Relaxations: 'Socialising with friends, keeping fit, sleeping'

Extras: Played for Yorkshire Schools at all levels and has been with Yorkshire Academy since 1998. Represented England at U14, U15, U16, U17 and U19 levels. Played for Yorkshire Board XI in the NatWest 1999
Opinions on cricket: 'The best game and the hardest at times.'

2001 Season (did not make any first-class or one-day appearances)

Career Performances

	M	Inns	NO	Runs	HS	Avge	100s	50s	Ct	St	Balls	Runs	Wkts	Avge	Best	5wl	10wM
Test																	
All First																	
1-day Int																	
C & G	1	1	0	9	9	9.00	-	-	-	-							
B & H																	
1-day Lge																	

SAGGERS, M. J. Kent

Name: <u>Martin</u> John Saggers
Role: Right-hand bat, right-arm fast-medium bowler
Born: 23 May 1972, King's Lynn
Height: 6ft 2in **Weight:** 14st 2lbs
Nickname: Saggs, Jurgen, Saggy Bits, Jerry, Saggsy
County debut: 1996 (Durham), 1999 (Kent)
County cap: 2001 (Kent)
50 wickets in a season: 2
1st-Class 50s: 1
1st-Class 5 w. in innings: 7
1st-Class catches: 7
One-Day 5 w. in innings: 1
Place in batting averages: 243rd av. 12.33 (2000 291st av. 7.58)
Place in bowling averages: 30th av. 24.23 (2000 22nd av. 20.14)
Strike rate: 48.04 (career 45.78)
Parents: Brian and Edna
Marital status: Single
Family links with cricket: Grandfather played in the Essex League
Education: Roseberry Avenue Primary School; Springwood High School; University of Huddersfield

Qualifications: BA (Hons) Architectural Studies International
Career outside cricket: 'This and that'
Off-season: 'Looking for a house! Also, helping run the club's website'
Overseas teams played for: Randburg CC, Johannesburg 1996-98, 2000-01; Southern Suburbs CC, Johannesburg 1998-99
Career highlights to date: 'Winning the Norwich Union League last year'
Cricket moments to forget: 'Being smashed around the ground by Shahid Afridi – twice! Also, letting a genuine long barrier stop trickle through my legs and over the boundary for four v Somerset in C&G quarter-final live on TV'
Cricketers particularly admired: Allan Donald, Neil Foster, Darren Gough, John (Jack) Russell
Young players to look out for: Rob Ferley, James Hockley, Brandon Duffield
Other sports played: Golf ('shot 74 this year in SA'), 'and anything else that includes a ball and running around like a headless chicken'
Other sports followed: Football (Tottenham Hotspur), British Touring Cars, Formula One
Injuries: Out for one week with damaged ankle ligaments
Relaxations: 'Going to the Kruger National Park in South Africa to see the wildlife, especially the big cats'
Extras: Released by Durham at end of the 1998 season and joined Kent. Took career best 7-79 against his old county, Durham, at Riverside 2000. Won Most Promising Uncapped Player Award 2000. Joint Kent Player of the Year 2000 (with David Masters). Took two hat-tricks in two weeks for Randburg CC, Johannesburg 2000-01, including one spell of five wickets in six balls. Recorded maiden one-day five-wicket return (5-22) v Gloucestershire at Canterbury in the Norwich Union League 2001. Took three wickets in four balls in last over of Norwich Union League match at Canterbury 2001, preventing Yorkshire from scoring the 13 needed to win. Kent Bowler of the Year (Underwood Trophy) 2001. Awarded Kent cap 2001
Opinions on cricket: 'Best game in the world. The new two division system creates competitive matches right through to the last game of the season.'
Best batting: 61* Kent v Lancashire, Canterbury 2001
Best bowling: 7-79 Kent v Durham, Riverside 2000

2001 Season

	M	Inns	NO	Runs	HS	Avge	100s	50s	Ct	St	O	M	Runs	Wkts	Avge	Best	5wI	10wM
Test																		
All First	17	20	5	185	61 *	12.33	-	1	1	-	512.3	118	1551	64	24.23	6-92	3	-
1-day Int																		
C & G	3	1	0	1	1	1.00	-	-	-	-	30	5	99	5	19.80	3-14	-	
B & H	1	1	1	1	1 *	-	-	-	-	-	10	0	56	1	56.00	1-56	-	
1-day Lge	13	8	4	54	21 *	13.50	-	-	1	-	94.4	10	414	25	16.56	5-22	1	

Career Performances

	M	Inns	NO	Runs	HS	Avge	100s	50s	Ct	St	Balls	Runs	Wkts	Avge	Best	5wI	10wM
Test																	
All First	43	55	15	404	61 *	10.10	-	1	7	-	7326	3660	160	22.87	7-79	7	-
1-day Int																	
C & G	5	2	0	1	1	0.50	-	-	-	-	298	197	7	28.14	3-14	-	
B & H	6	6	4	59	34 *	29.50	-	-	2	-	306	303	6	50.50	2-49	-	
1-day Lge	32	18	11	98	21 *	14.00	-	-	6	-	1370	968	55	17.60	5-22	1	

SALES, D. J. G. Northamptonshire

Name: <u>David</u> John Grimwood Sales
Role: Right-hand bat, right-arm
occasional bowler
Born: 3 December 1977, Carshalton, Surrey
Height: 6ft **Weight:** 14st 7lbs
Nickname: Jumble, Grimmers, Johnny
Hartson, Peanut
County debut: 1994 (one-day),
1996 (first-class)
County cap: 1999
1000 runs in a season: 1
1st-Class 50s: 15
1st-Class 100s: 5
1st-Class 200s: 2
1st-Class 300s: 1
1st-Class catches: 53
Place in batting averages: (2000 53rd
av. 35.65)
Strike rate: (career 33.66)
Parents: John and Daphne
Marital status: Single
Family links with cricket: Father played club cricket
Education: Cumnor House Prep School, Croydon; Caterham Boys' School
Qualifications: 7 GCSEs, cricket coach
Career outside cricket: 'Burning up golf courses!'
Overseas tours: England U15 to South Africa 1993; England U19 to West Indies
1994-95, to Zimbabwe 1995-96, to Pakistan 1996-97; England A to Kenya and Sri Lanka
1997-98, to Bangladesh and New Zealand 1999-2000, to West Indies 2000-01; Northants
to Grenada 2000
Cricketers particularly admired: Graham Gooch, Darren Cousins
Young players to look out for: Jason Brown, Mark Powell

Other sports followed: Football (Crystal Palace), golf
Injuries: Out for most of 2001 season with cruciate knee ligament damage
Relaxations: Golf and fishing
Extras: In 1994, became youngest batsman (16 years 289 days) to score a 50 in the Sunday League with his 56-ball 70* v Essex at Chelmsford. Scored 210* v Worcs 1996 to become first Englishman to score a double century on his Championship debut and the youngest ever to score a double century. Became the youngest Englishman to score a first-class 300 (303*) v Essex at Northampton 1999 aged 21 years 240 days (and became the first Englishman to 1000 runs for 1999 in the process). PCA/CGU Young Player of the Year 1999. Scored 276 off 375 balls v Nottinghamshire at Northampton 2000. Was selected for the England A tour of West Indies 2000-01 but was flown home at the start of the tour with a serious knee injury
Best batting: 303* Northamptonshire v Essex, Northampton 1999
Best bowling: 4-25 Northamptonshire v Sri Lanka A, Northampton 1999

2001 Season

	M	Inns	NO	Runs	HS	Avge	100s	50s	Ct	St	O	M	Runs	Wkts	Avge	Best	5wl	10wM
Test																		
All First																		
1-day Int																		
C & G																		
B & H																		
1-day Lge	4	4	0	52	26	13.00	-	-	-	-								

Career Performances

	M	Inns	NO	Runs	HS	Avge	100s	50s	Ct	St	Balls	Runs	Wkts	Avge	Best	5wl	10wM
Test																	
All First	74	115	10	3710	303 *	35.33	8	15	53	-	303	163	9	18.11	4-25	-	-
1-day Int																	
C & G	9	9	1	288	65	36.00	-	3	5	-	12	13	0	-		-	-
B & H	7	7	1	131	64 *	21.83	-	1	2	-							
1-day Lge	66	62	10	1402	84 *	26.96	-	7	21	-	24	17	0	-		-	-

SALISBURY, I. D. K.   Surrey

Name: <u>Ian</u> David Kenneth Salisbury
Role: Right-hand bat, leg-break bowler
Born: 21 January 1970, Moulton, Northampton
Height: 5ft 11in **Weight:** 12st 7lbs
Nickname: Solly, Dingle, Sals
County debut: 1989 (Sussex), 1997 (Surrey)
County cap: 1991 (Sussex), 1998 (Surrey)

Test debut: 1992
Tests: 15
One-Day Internationals: 4
50 wickets in a season: 6
1st-Class 50s: 17
1st-Class 100s: 1
1st-Class 5 w. in innings: 34
1st-Class 10 w. in match: 6
1st-Class catches: 160
One-Day 5 w. in innings: 1
Place in batting averages: 149th av. 25.88
(2000 142nd av. 24.07)
Place in bowling averages: 122nd av. 42.62
(2000 17th av. 18.92)
Strike rate: 88.07 (career 63.82)
Parents: Dave and Margaret
Wife and date of marriage: Emma Louise,
25 September 1993
Family links with cricket: 'Dad is vice-president of my first club, Brixworth. He also re-lays cricket squares (e.g. Lord's, Northampton, Leicester)'
Education: Moulton Primary; Moulton Comprehensive (both Northampton)
Qualifications: 7 O-levels, NCA coaching certificate, 'life'
Off-season: Six-month break
Overseas tours: England A to Pakistan 1990-91, to Bermuda and West Indies 1991-92, to India 1994-95, to Pakistan 1995-96; England to India and Sri Lanka 1992-93, to West Indies 1993-94, to Pakistan 2000-01; World Masters XI v Indian Masters XI November 1996 ('Masters aged 26?')
Overseas teams played for: University of New South Wales, Sydney 1997-2000
Cricketers particularly admired: 'Any that keep performing day in, day out, for both country and county (e.g. Saqlain, Martin Bicknell, Andrew Caddick, Steve Waugh)'
Young players to look out for: Ben Hollioake, Owais Shah, Alex Tudor, David Sales, Paul Franks, Steve Harmison, Luke Sutton
Other sports played: 'Most sports'
Other sports followed: Football (Southampton FC, Northampton Town FC), rugby union (Northampton Saints), 'any England team'
Injuries: Repetitive strain injury in wrist; Achilles injury
Relaxations: 'Spending time with wife, Emma; meeting friends and relaxing with them and eating out with good wine. Also, Sydney has its moments!!'
Extras: Picked to play two Tests for England against Pakistan in 1992, 'proudest moments of my career'. Originally selected for England A tour to Australia 1992-93 but was asked to stay on in India and played in the first two Tests of the series. In 1992 was named Young Player of the Year by both the Wombwell Cricket Lovers and the Cricket Writers. One of *Wisden's* Five Cricketers of the Year 1993. Left Sussex during the 1996-97 off-season to join Surrey. Won the Bill O'Reilly Medal for Sydney first-grade player of the year 1999-2000, taking 36 wickets at 10.31 and averaging 40

with the bat playing for University of New South Wales
Opinions on cricket: 'Improve the standard of cricket pitches (e.g. ECB-contract groundsmen, so no doctoring of pitches). Two up/two down in the Championship.'
Best batting: 100* Surrey v Somerset, The Oval 1999
Best bowling: 8-60 Surrey v Somerset, The Oval 2000

2001 Season

	M	Inns	NO	Runs	HS	Avge	100s	50s	Ct	St	O	M	Runs	Wkts	Avge	Best	5wI	10wM
Test																		
All First	15	21	4	440	54	25.88	-	1	9	-	396.2	72	1151	27	42.62	5-95	1	-
1-day Int																		
C & G																			
B & H	3	2	1	6	6 *	6.00	-	-	1	-	23	1	96	3	32.00	2-45	-	
1-day Lge	3	2	0	15	13	7.50	-	-	1	-	20	0	103	1	103.00	1-42	-	

Career Performances

	M	Inns	NO	Runs	HS	Avge	100s	50s	Ct	St	Balls	Runs	Wkts	Avge	Best	5wI	10wM
Test	15	25	3	368	50	16.72	-	1	5	-	2492	1539	20	76.95	4-163	-	-
All First	247	316	66	4861	100 *	19.44	1	17	160	-	44036	22088	690	32.01	8-60	34	6
1-day Int	4	2	1	7	5	7.00	-	-	1	-	186	177	5	35.40	3-41	-	
C & G	28	17	5	164	34 *	13.66	-	-	5	-	1685	966	33	29.27	3-28	-	
B & H	39	23	9	175	19	12.50	-	-	15	-	2055	1451	46	31.54	4-53	-	
1-day Lge	131	87	22	805	48 *	12.38	-	-	46	-	4872	4045	117	34.57	5-30	1	

SAMPSON, P. J. Surrey

Name: Philip James Sampson
Role: Right-hand bat, right-arm fast-medium bowler
Born: 6 September 1980, Manchester
Height: 6ft 1in **Weight:** 14st
Nickname: Sammo, Boss Hogg
County debut: 2000 (one-day)
Parents: Les and Kay
Marital status: Single
Family links with cricket: Father played league cricket and was chairman of the Harlequins club, Pretoria. Brother was captain of Northern Transvaal (Northerns) at Youth level
Education: Waterkloof House Preparatory School, Pretoria; Pretoria Boys High School
Qualifications: Matriculation (A-level equivalent)
Career outside cricket: 'Haven't thought about that one yet!!'
Overseas teams played for: Harlequins, Pretoria 1999, 2000, 2001

Cricketers particularly admired:
Allan Donald, Alec Stewart, Steve Waugh,
Sachin Tendulkar
Young players to look out for:
Carl Greenidge
Other sports played: Golf, social football
Other sports followed: Football (Manchester
United), Formula One motor racing
Relaxations: Going to the theatre and
movies, socialising with friends,
listening to music
Extras: Captain of school 1st XI 1998.
Trophy for best all-round cricketer at school.
Represented Northerns at U15, U18, U19.
Played for Buckinghamshire in the Minor
Counties 1999. Played for Surrey Board XI in
the NatWest 2000
Opinions on cricket: 'Changing.'

2001 Season

	M	Inns	NO	Runs	HS	Avge	100s	50s	Ct	St	O	M	Runs	Wkts	Avge	Best	5wI	10wM
Test																		
All First																		
1-day Int																		
C & G																		
B & H																		
1-day Lge	1	0	0	0	0	-	-	-	-	-	9	0	25	1	25.00	1-25	-

Career Performances

	M	Inns	NO	Runs	HS	Avge	100s	50s	Ct	St	Balls	Runs	Wkts	Avge	Best	5wI	10wM
Test																	
All First																	
1-day Int																	
C & G	1	1	1	4	4 *	-	-	-	1	-	60	26	0	-		-	-
B & H																	
1-day Lge	3	1	0	4	4	4.00	-	-	-	-	126	92	1	92.00	1-25	-

SAQLAIN MUSHTAQ   Surrey

Name: Saqlain Mushtaq
Role: Right-hand bat, off-spin bowler
Born: 29 December 1976, Lahore, Pakistan
Height: 5ft 9in **Weight:** 11st 4lbs
Nickname: Saqi, Baba
County debut: 1997
County cap: 1998
Test debut: 1995-96
Tests: 35
One-Day Internationals: 144
50 wickets in a season: 4
1st-Class 50s: 6
1st-Class 100s: 1
1st-Class 5 w. in innings: 46
1st-Class 10 w. in match: 12
1st-Class catches: 49
One-Day 5 w. in innings: 6

Place in batting averages: 235th av. 13.66
(2000 196th av. 18.08)
Place in bowling averages: 15th av. 20.74 (2000 5th av. 15.39)
Strike rate: 54.90 (career 51.08)
Parents: Nasim Akhtar and Mushtaq Ahmed
Wife and date of marriage: Sana ('Sunny') Saqlain, 11 April 2000
Education: Lahore MAO College
Career outside cricket: 'Looking after the wife'
Overseas tours: Pakistan to Australia 1995-96, to Sharjah 1995-96, 1996-97, 1997-98, to Singapore 1995-96, to England 1996, to Sri Lanka 1996-97, to Toronto and Nairobi 1996-97, to Australia 1996-97, to India 1996-97, to South Africa 1997-98, to Zimbabwe 1997-98, to Sri Lanka 1997-98, to Toronto 1997-98, 1998-99, to Bangladesh (Wills International Cup) 1998-99, to India 1998-99, to UK, Ireland and Holland (World Cup) 1999, to Australia 1999-2000, to West Indies 1999-2000, to Kenya (ICC Knockout Trophy) 2000-01, to New Zealand 2000-01, to England 2001, to Bangladesh 2001-02, to Sharjah (v West Indies) 2001-02
Overseas teams played for: PIA 1994-95 – ; Islamabad Cricket Association 1994-95
Cricketers particularly admired: Imran Khan, Wasim Akram, Waqar Younis
Young players to look out for: Younis Khan, Shoaib Malik
Other sports played: Squash
Other sports followed: Hockey (Pakistan), football (Manchester United and Arsenal)
Relaxations: 'I like listening to music when free or travelling'
Extras: Scored 79 v Zimbabwe at Sheikhupura 1996-97, in the process sharing with Wasim Akram in a world record eighth-wicket partnership in Tests (313). Won Man of

the Series award in 1998-99 Test series v India. Took only the second hat-trick in World Cup cricket, v Zimbabwe at The Oval 1999; his victims were Olonga, Huckle and Mbangwa; it was his second hat-trick in One-Day Internationals v Zimbabwe. Took the fifth hat-trick of his career, for Surrey v Sussex at Hove 1999. Topped the first-class bowling averages in 1999, taking 58 wickets at an astonishing average of 11.37 in the seven games he played for Surrey. One of *Wisden*'s Five Cricketers of the Year 2000. Took 7-11 from 9.3 overs (including a spell of 7-5 in 34 balls) v Derbyshire at The Oval 2000. Returned his best One-Day International figures (5-20) in the third One-Day International v England at Rawalpindi 2000-01, winning the Man of the Match award. Took 8-164 (all eight wickets to fall) from 74 overs in England's first innings in the first Test at Lahore 2000-01, winning the Man of the Match award. Scored maiden first-class century (101*) in second Test v New Zealand at Christchurch 2000-01. Bowled unchanged from 11 a.m. until 6 p.m. (47.2 overs) on the second day v Leicestershire at Leicester 2001, finishing with innings figures of 5-172 from a total of 52.2 overs. His 7-58 v Yorkshire at The Oval 2001 included a spell of 6-6

Opinions on cricket: 'The cricket nowadays is a lot more modernised than it was three years ago. It has become a very fast, quick and active game. It really has changed what with things such as five points being deducted if the umpire thinks there is cheating going on or if you misbehave towards the umpire. Also there are free hits (different).'

Best batting: 101* Pakistan v New Zealand, Christchurch 2000-01
Best bowling: 8-65 Surrey v Derbyshire, The Oval 1998

2001 Season

	M	Inns	NO	Runs	HS	Avge	100s	50s	Ct	St	O	M	Runs	Wkts	Avge	Best	5wI	10wM
Test	1	2	1	26	21 *	26.00	-	-	-	-	77.2	27	154	6	25.66	4-74	-	-
All First	13	18	6	164	38	13.66	-	-	2	-	567.2	157	1286	62	20.74	7-58	5	-
1-day Int	6	3	2	3	2	3.00	-	-	2	-	53	0	232	7	33.14	2-20	-	
C & G	2	1	0	24	24	24.00	-	-	-	-	16	1	77	1	77.00	1-29	-	
B & H	2	2	2	3	2 *	-	-	-	1	-	8.5	0	40	4	10.00	3-37	-	
1-day Lge	10	9	2	67	38 *	9.57	-	-	3	-	71	3	348	6	58.00	3-44	-	

Career Performances

	M	Inns	NO	Runs	HS	Avge	100s	50s	Ct	St	Balls	Runs	Wkts	Avge	Best	5wI	10wM
Test	35	56	13	710	101 *	16.51	1	2	13	-	10698	4447	151	29.45	8-164	11	2
All First	120	171	47	1922	101 *	15.50	1	6	49	-	29045	11832	566	20.90	8-65	46	12
1-day Int	144	85	31	644	37 *	11.92	-	-	35	-	7537	5371	257	20.89	5-20	6	
C & G	13	4	2	39	24	19.50	-	-	1	-	751	430	26	16.53	4-17	-	
B & H	9	5	3	21	11	10.50	-	-	3	-	435	287	14	20.50	4-46	-	
1-day Lge	37	24	8	166	38 *	10.37	-	-	9	-	1594	1130	45	25.11	3-12	-	

SAYERS, J. J.   Yorkshire

Name: Joseph (<u>Joe</u>) John Sayers
Role: Left-hand bat, right-arm
off-spin bowler
Born: 5 November 1983, Leeds
Height: 6ft **Weight:** 12st 6lbs
Nickname: Ledge, Joey
County debut: No first-team appearance
Parents: Roger and Geraldine
Marital status: Single
Family links with cricket: 'Father played at
school, but otherwise none'
Education: St Joseph's Primary School,
Otley; St Mary's RC Comprehensive School,
Menston; Worcester College, Oxford
University
Qualifications: 11 GCSEs, 4 A-levels
Career outside cricket: 'Undecided at
present, but possibly design engineering'
Off-season: Studying physics at Oxford and training with the Oxford Academy side
Overseas tours: Leeds Schools to South Africa 1998; Yorkshire U17 to South Africa
2001; England U17 to Australia 2001
Career highlights to date: 'Scoring 149* for Yorkshire 2nd XI against Durham in
2001. Fielding for Yorkshire 1st XI against Derbyshire in 2000. Captaining England
U17 against Australia in 2001'
Cricket moments to forget: 'Losing the first "Test" v Australia in Adelaide 2001'
Cricketers particularly admired: Nasser Hussain, Mike Brearley, Steve Waugh,
Jonty Rhodes, Sachin Tendulkar
Young players to look out for: Tim Bresnan, Bilal Shafayat, David Stiff
Other sports played: Football ('played as goalkeeper for Bradford City AFC for three
years'), rowing (Worcester College 2001)
Other sports followed: Football (Liverpool FC), baseball (New York Yankees)
Relaxations: Listening to music; drawing/painting; psychology
Opinions on cricket: 'World cricket is not in such a bad state as some people suggest,
and is beginning to appeal to a much wider, younger audience. One-day cricket must
take most of the credit for that, but Test cricket must remain the more prominent mode
of the game. The introduction of technology into the game to aid umpires and to
entertain crowds has been beneficial to date, but we must be careful not to overuse the
concept, for the game would lose its suspense and umpires would become redundant.'

SCHOFIELD, C. P. — Lancashire

Name: Christopher (<u>Chris</u>) Paul Schofield
Role: Left-hand bat, leg-break bowler
Born: 6 October 1978, Rochdale
Height: 6ft 1in **Weight:** 11st 5lbs
Nickname: Scoey, Junior, Scoffer
County debut: 1998
Test debut: 2000
Tests: 2
1st-Class 50s: 13
1st-Class 5 w. in innings: 4
1st-Class catches: 27
One-Day 5 w. in innings: 1
Place in batting averages: 103rd av. 32.50
(2000 124th av. 26.40)
Place in bowling averages: 141st av. 54.07
(2000 80th av. 28.25)
Strike rate: 108.07 (career 62.77)
Parents: David and Judith
Marital status: Single
Family links with cricket: Father played with local club team Whittles and brother plays with local team Littleborough
Education: St John's; Wardle High School
Qualifications: 4 GCSEs, NVQ Levels 2 and 3 in Information Technology
Off-season: In Australia with ECB National Academy
Overseas tours: England U17 to Bermuda 1997; England U19 to South Africa (including U19 World Cup) 1997-98; England A to Bangladesh and New Zealand 1999-2000, to West Indies 2000-01; ECB National Academy to Australia 2001-02
Cricketers particularly admired: Shane Warne, Stuart Law
Young players to look out for: Graeme Swann, Robert Key
Other sports played: Football (Littleborough FC, Whittles FC), snooker (Wardle Con Club – handicap of four)
Other sports followed: Football ('like watching Liverpool FC')
Relaxations: Listening to music, playing snooker, socialising
Extras: Was part of England U19 World Cup winning squad 1997-98. Won double twice in two years with Littleborough CC (Wood Cup and Lancashire Cup 1997; League and Wood Cup 1998). Awarded 2nd XI cap 1998. Won Sir Ron Brierley/Crusaders Scholarship 1998. NBC Denis Compton Award for the most promising young Lancashire player 1998, 1999, 2000. Was the only uncapped player to be contracted to England in 2000. Made Test debut in first Test v Zimbabwe at Lord's 2000 but did not get a bowl as Gough, Caddick and Giddins bowled the opposition out twice. Leading first-class wicket-taker on England A tour to West Indies

2000-01 (22 wickets av. 26.27). Recorded maiden one-day five-wicket return (5-31)
v Derbyshire at Old Trafford in the Norwich Union League 2001
Best batting: 80* Lancashire v Essex, Colchester 2001
Best bowling: 6-120 England A v Bangladesh, Chittagong 1999-2000

2001 Season

	M	Inns	NO	Runs	HS	Avge	100s	50s	Ct	St	O	M	Runs	Wkts	Avge	Best	5wI	10wM
Test																		
All First	9	14	2	390	80 *	32.50	-	4	8	-	252.1	52	757	14	54.07	3-53	-	-
1-day Int																		
C & G	4	1	0	42	42	42.00	-	-	3	-	17.5	1	91	2	45.50	1-14	-	
B & H	1	1	0	5	5	5.00	-	-	-	-	7	0	29	1	29.00	1-29	-	
1-day Lge	14	11	4	96	20	13.71	-	-	4	-	72.1	1	362	23	15.73	5-31	1	

Career Performances

	M	Inns	NO	Runs	HS	Avge	100s	50s	Ct	St	Balls	Runs	Wkts	Avge	Best	5wI	10wM
Test	2	3	0	67	57	22.33	-	1	-	-	108	73	0	-	-	-	-
All First	49	68	11	1572	80 *	27.57	-	13	27	-	8600	4295	137	31.35	6-120	4	-
1-day Int																	
C & G	8	2	0	43	42	21.50	-	-	5	-	329	257	13	19.76	4-34	-	
B & H	4	4	0	47	23	11.75	-	-	-	-	204	133	8	16.62	4-34	-	
1-day Lge	28	22	6	254	34	15.87	-	-	5	-	1026	833	36	23.13	5-31	1	

SCHOFIELD, J. E. K.   Hampshire

Name: James Edward Knowle Schofield
Role: Right-hand bat, right-arm fast-medium bowler
Born: 1 November 1978, Blackpool
Height: 6ft **Weight:** 12st 7lbs
Nickname: Schoey, Doctor, Doc, Batty, Mongrel, Mongo, Northern Monkey
County debut: 2001
1st-Class catches: 1
Place in bowling averages: 20th av. 21.92
Strike rate: 41.15 (career 41.15)
Parents: David and Victoria
Marital status: Engaged to Katy
Family links with cricket: Great grandfather played for Lancashire CCC
Education: Hagley Middle School; RGS Worcester; University of Bradford
Qualifications: 9 GCSEs, 4 A-levels, BSc Business and Management
Off-season: 'Playing for Melville in Perth and working with Paul Terry. Also sunning myself with Katy my girlfriend at Cott'
Overseas teams played for: Melville, Perth 2000-02

Career highlights to date: 'Beating the Aussies at the Rose Bowl [2001] and getting wicket with my first ball in first-class cricket'
Cricketers particularly admired: Ian Botham, Jacques Kallis, Wasim Akram, Richard Hadlee, James Tomlinson
Young players to look out for: John Francis, James Tomlinson, Nicky Peng
Other sports played: Football, rugby, tennis (played for Hereford and Worcester; won four U15 national tournaments)
Other sports followed: Football (Liverpool FC), rugby league (Bradford Bulls), 'all rugby internationals, and tennis'
Relaxations: 'Lying on the beach in Perth; spending time with Katy; listening to music; watching live sporting events; spending time with friends'

Extras: Part of Hampshire's 2nd XI Championship winning side 2001. Took a wicket (Matthew Hayden) with his first ball in first-class cricket v Australians at the Rose Bowl 2001 and also a wicket (Anurag Singh) with his first ball in the Norwich Union League on one-day debut v Worcestershire at Worcester 2001 – 'apparently a world record'
Opinions on cricket: 'Much more competitive since the introduction of two divisions. Too many so-called English players playing and taking the place of genuine English players. Need more time to practise properly and rest in between games, i.e. too much cricket.'
Best batting: 21* Hampshire v Durham, Riverside 2001
Best bowling: 4-51 Hampshire v Worcestershire, Worcester 2001

2001 Season

	M	Inns	NO	Runs	HS	Avge	100s	50s	Ct	St	O	M	Runs	Wkts	Avge	Best	5wI	10wM
Test																		
All First	3	5	2	25	21 *	8.33	-	-	1	-	89.1	17	285	13	21.92	4-51	-	-
1-day Int																		
C & G																		
B & H																		
1-day Lge	1	0	0	0	0	-	-	-	-	-	6	0	22	1	22.00	1-22	-	

	M	Inns	NO	Runs	HS	Avge	100s	50s	Ct	St	Balls	Runs	Wkts	Avge	Best	5wI	10wM
Test																	
All First	3	5	2	25	21 *	8.33	-	-	1	-	535	285	13	21.92	4-51	-	-
1-day Int																	
C & G																	
B & H																	
1-day Lge	1	0	0	0	0	-	-	-	-	-	-	36	22	1	22.00	1-22	-

SCOTT, B. J. M.   Surrey

Name: Benjamin (<u>Ben</u>) James Matthew Scott
Role: Right-hand bat, wicket-keeper
Born: 4 August 1981, Isleworth
Height: 5ft 8in **Weight:** 11st 5lbs
Nickname: Scotty, Head
County debut: No first-team appearance
Parents: Terry and Edna
Marital status: Single
Family links with cricket: Father and
brother played local club cricket
Education: Chatsworth School, Hounslow;
Whitton School, Richmond; Richmond
College
Qualifications: 9 GCSEs, 3 A-levels studied,
ECB Level 1 coach, YMCA Fitness
Instructor's Award
Career outside cricket: Fitness/gym
instructor

Off-season: 'Working as fitness/gym instructor at Richmond College and training
abroad in Australia'
Overseas tours: MCC YC to South Africa 1999-2000
Overseas teams played for: Portland CC, Victoria, Australia 1999-2000
Career highlights to date: 'ECB U19 v Australia U19. Surrey 2nd XI Trophy 2001'
Cricketers particularly admired: Alec Stewart, Alan Knott, Steve Waugh,
Jack Russell
Young players to look out for: Alan Coleman, Chad Keegan, Nick Compton
Other sports played: Squash, football
Relaxations: Music, piano, guitar
Extras: Middlesex YC cap. Represented ESCA U14 and U15. Played for
Development of Excellence XI v Australia U19 1999. Played for Middlesex Board XI
in the NatWest 1999. Finchley CC Player of the Season 2000

Opinions on cricket: 'The skill level in cricket has reached such a level that the only dividing factor between sides and cricketers is their mental toughness.'

2001 Season (did not make any first-class or one-day appearances)

Career Performances

	M	Inns	NO	Runs	HS	Avge	100s	50s	Ct	St	Balls	Runs	Wkts	Avge	Best	5wI	10wM
Test																	
All First																	
1-day Int																	
C & G	1	1	0	11	11	11.00	-	-	-	-							
B & H																	
1-day Lge																	

SCOTT, G. M.   Durham

Name: <u>Gary</u> Michael Scott
Role: Right-hand bat, right-arm off-spin bowler
Born: 21 July 1984, Sunderland
Height: 6ft 1in **Weight:** 12st 9lbs
Nickname: Scotty
County debut: 2001
1st-Class catches: 1
Parents: Mary and Michael
Marital status: Single
Education: Hetton Lyons Primary School; Hetton Comprehensive
Qualifications: 8 GCSEs
Overseas tours: England U17 to Australia 2000-01
Career highlights to date: 'Making first-class debut'
Cricket moments to forget: 'Can't remember; like to forget straightaway'

Cricketers particularly admired: Jacques Kallis, the Waugh brothers, Mike Atherton
Young players to look out for: Gordon Muchall, Bilal Shafayat
Other sports played: Football (represented Sunderland Schoolboys)
Other sports followed: Football (Newcastle Utd)
Relaxations: Football, music
Extras: Sir John Hobbs Award 1999. Played for Durham Board XI in the C&G 2001 and in the second round of the C&G 2002, which was played in September 2001.

Became youngest to play first-class cricket for Durham when he made his debut v Derbyshire at Riverside 2001 aged 17 years and 19 days. Is a Durham Academy player
Opinions on cricket: 'The standards that have been set by the England team should be set in the first-class game.'
Best batting: 25 Durham v Derbyshire, Riverside 2001

2001 Season

	M	Inns	NO	Runs	HS	Avge	100s	50s	Ct	St	O	M	Runs	Wkts	Avge	Best	5wI	10wM
Test																		
All First	1	2	0	33	25	16.50	-	-	1	-	3	1	11	0	-	-	-	-
1-day Int																		
C & G	2	2	0	30	20	15.00	-	-	-	-	20	4	54	3	18.00	2-32	-
B & H																		
1-day Lge																		

Career Performances

	M	Inns	NO	Runs	HS	Avge	100s	50s	Ct	St	Balls	Runs	Wkts	Avge	Best	5wI	10wM
Test																	
All First	1	2	0	33	25	16.50	-	-	1	-	18	11	0	-	-	-	-
1-day Int																	
C & G	2	2	0	30	20	15.00	-	-	-	-	120	54	3	18.00	2-32	-
B & H																	
1-day Lge																	

SCUDERI, J. C. Lancashire

Name: <u>Joseph</u> Charles Scuderi
Role: Right-hand bat, right-arm medium bowler
Born: 24 December 1968, Ingham, Queensland, Australia
Height: 5ft 11in **Weight:** 11st 7lbs
Nickname: Scud
County debut: 2000
1st-Class 50s: 17
1st-Class 100s: 3
1st-Class 5 w. in innings: 8
1st-Class 10 w. in match: 1
1st-Class catches: 26
Place in batting averages: 127th av. 29.60 (2000 145th av. 23.72)
Place in bowling averages: (2000 47th av. 23.78)
Strike rate: 77.11 (career 73.68)
Parents: Enrico and Nalda
Marital status: Single

Education: Macknade State Primary; Ingham State High (both Queensland)
Overseas tours: Australia U19 to New Zealand 1987
Overseas teams played for: South Australia 1988-89 – 1998-99
Cricketers particularly admired: Jeff Thomson, Ian Botham, Mike Atherton
Young players to look out for: Kyle Hogg, James Anderson
Other sports followed: Rugby league (Sydney City), football (Manchester United)
Relaxations: Listening to and playing music
Extras: South Australia Player of the Year 1991-92. Was in Australia squad of 20 for World Cup 1992. Played for Prime Minister's XI v Pakistan and England. Has played for Italy since 1998. Has played Lancashire

League cricket. Is not considered an overseas player. Released by Lancashire at the end of the 2001 season
Best batting: 125* South Australia v Western Australia, Adelaide 1991-92
Best bowling: 7-79 South Australia v New South Wales, Adelaide 1991-92

2001 Season

	M	Inns	NO	Runs	HS	Avge	100s	50s	Ct	St	O	M	Runs	Wkts	Avge	Best	5wI	10wM
Test																		
All First	12	17	2	444	89	29.60	-	3	2	-	115.4	33	318	9	35.33	3-48	-	-
1-day Int																		
C & G	1	0	0	0	0	-	-	-	1	-								
B & H	5	4	1	90	73 *	30.00	-	1	1	-	23.4	1	109	5	21.80	2-17	-	
1-day Lge	8	6	1	122	50 *	24.40	-	1	1	-	46	4	196	8	24.50	3-28	-	

Career Performances

	M	Inns	NO	Runs	HS	Avge	100s	50s	Ct	St	Balls	Runs	Wkts	Avge	Best	5wI	10wM
Test																	
All First	82	130	18	3372	125 *	30.10	3	17	26	-	13190	6073	179	33.92	7-79	8	1
1-day Int																	
C & G	3	1	0	7	7	7.00	-	-	2	-	42	31	0	-	-	-	-
B & H	7	5	1	132	73 *	33.00	-	1	1	-	160	122	5	24.40	2-17	-	
1-day Lge	14	10	2	152	50 *	19.00	-	1	2	-	456	361	12	30.08	3-28	-	

SELWOOD, S. A. Derbyshire

Name: Steven (<u>Steve</u>) Andrew Selwood
Role: Left-hand bat, left-arm spin bowler
Born: 24 November 1979, Barnet
Height: 6ft **Weight:** 12st
Nickname: Sellers, Surf Dude, Don Johnson
County debut: 2001
1st-Class catches: 1
Parents: Tim and Sarah
Marital status: 'Taken'
Family links with cricket: Father played for
Middlesex 1969-74 and Central Districts
1972-73 and is now youth coach at Finchley
Education: Belmont School, Mill Hill;
Mill Hill School; Loughborough University
Qualifications: 9 GCSEs, 2 A-levels,
Level 1 coaching
Career outside cricket: Student
Off-season: 'Doing the final year of my
Politics degree at Loughborough University. Training with the Loughborough
University CCE squad and Derbyshire'
Overseas tours: Middlesex Prep Schools to Australia 1990-91
Overseas teams played for: Manly-Warringah, Sydney 1996-97; Claremont-
Nedlands, Perth 1998-99
Career highlights to date: 'First-class debut v Gloucestershire 2001. First-team debut
v Lancashire under lights at Old Trafford'
Cricket moments to forget: 'Any time we lose and every time I fail'
Cricketers particularly admired: Don Bradman, Brian Lara, Ian Botham,
Darren Lehmann
Young players to look out for: Geoff Cullen (Western Australia), Nathan Dumelow,
Lian Wharton
Other sports played: Football, rugby ('at school')
Other sports followed: Football (Tottenham Hotspur)
Relaxations: 'Spending time with my girlfriend Melissa; travel; going out with friends
and team-mates'
Extras: Represented England U14 1994. Played for Finchley v Uxbridge in the
Evening Standard final 2000, winning Man of the Match award. Played for
Loughborough University CCE 2001
Opinions on cricket: 'In order to instil better attitudes in all cricketers, club cricket,
as a level of the game at which everyone begins, must be more relevant to the levels
above it – i.e. better wickets, two-day games and fewer clubs. In the UK the attitudes
of administrators and players alike need to be completely modernised. We need not to
be scared of progress in order to get ahead in world cricket.'

Best batting: 18 Derbyshire v Gloucestershire, Bristol 2001

2001 Season

	M	Inns	NO	Runs	HS	Avge	100s	50s	Ct	St	O	M	Runs	Wkts	Avge	Best	5wl	10wM
Test																		
All First	2	4	0	43	18	10.75	-	-	1	-								
1-day Int																		
C & G																		
B & H																		
1-day Lge	3	3	0	75	37	25.00	-	-	-	-	0.2	0	8	0	-		-	-

Career Performances

	M	Inns	NO	Runs	HS	Avge	100s	50s	Ct	St	Balls	Runs	Wkts	Avge	Best	5wl	10wM
Test																	
All First	2	4	0	43	18	10.75	-	-	1	-							
1-day Int																	
C & G																	
B & H																	
1-day Lge	3	3	0	75	37	25.00	-	-	-	-	2	8	0	-		-	-

SHAFAYAT, B. M.   Nottinghamshire

Name: <u>Bilal</u> Mustafa Shafayat
Role: Right-hand bat, right-arm medium
bowler, occasional wicket-keeper
Born: 10 July 1984, Nottingham
Height: 5ft 8in **Weight:** 10st
Nickname: Billy, Mussy
County debut: 2001
1st-Class 50s: 2
Place in batting averages: 76th av. 38.50
Parents: Mohammad Shafayat and
Mahfooza Begum
Marital status: Single
Family links with cricket: Brother played
for Notts Youth and 2nd XI. Uncle Nadeem
Khan played for PCC
Education: Greenwood Juniors; Greenwood
Dale; Nottingham Bluecoat School
Qualifications: 8 GCSEs
Career outside cricket: Student (second year of A-levels)
Off-season: 'England U19 World Cup tour to New Zealand; Notts pre-season tour to
South Africa; lots of training'

Overseas tours: ZRK to Pakistan 2000; England U17 to Australia 2000-01; England U19 to Australia and (U19 World Cup) New Zealand 2001-02

Career highlights to date: 'Notts debut at age 16 – scored 72 v Middlesex'

Cricket moments to forget: 'Dropping any catch last year in first-class cricket – e.g. Robin Smith at Trent Bridge'

Cricketers particularly admired: Sachin Tendulkar, Nasser Hussain, Andrew Jackman, Usman Afzaal

Young players to look out for: Ehsan Hussain, Akil Patel

Other sports played: Football, squash

Other sports followed: Football (Liverpool), snooker (Ronnie O'Sullivan), golf (Tiger Woods), boxing ('Naz')

Relaxations: 'Praying Namaz and spending time with loved ones'

Extras: Played for Nottinghamshire Board XI in the NatWest 2000 and for Nottinghamshire Board XI and Nottinghamshire in the C&G 2001. Represented England U19 v West Indies U19 in one-day series (3/3) and 'Test' series (2/3) 2001. Scored 72 on Championship debut v Middlesex at Trent Bridge 2001; aged 16, he also became the youngest player to represent Nottinghamshire in the competition. 'Notts have been great all last year, and my coaches have been great – e.g. Mick Newell and Andrew Jackman; I'm going to be the best and break all records, *Inshallah*'

Opinions on cricket: 'More day/night games should be introduced and better wickets in league cricket.'

Best batting: 75 Nottinghamshire v Hampshire, Trent Bridge 2001

2001 Season

	M	Inns	NO	Runs	HS	Avge	100s	50s	Ct	St	O	M	Runs	Wkts	Avge	Best	5wI	10wM
Test																		
All First	3	6	0	231	75	38.50	-	2	-	-								
1-day Int																		
C & G	2	2	0	40	36	20.00	-	-	-	-								
B & H																		
1-day Lge	5	5	0	76	31	15.20	-	-	3	-								

Career Performances

	M	Inns	NO	Runs	HS	Avge	100s	50s	Ct	St	Balls	Runs	Wkts	Avge	Best	5wI	10wM
Test																	
All First	3	6	0	231	75	38.50	-	2	-	-							
1-day Int																	
C & G	3	3	0	44	36	14.66	-	-	-	-							
B & H																	
1-day Lge	5	5	0	76	31	15.20	-	-	3	-							

SHAH, I. H. Hampshire

Name: <u>Irfan</u> Hussain Shah
Role: Right-hand bat, off-spin bowler
Born: 20 June 1979, Barking
Height: 5ft 11in **Weight:** 11st
Nickname: Irf, Shah, Saqqi
County debut: No first-team appearance
Parents: Ajaib and Nisa
Marital status: Single
Education: Cleveland Junior School, Ilford,
Essex; Loxford High School, Ilford, Essex;
London Cricket College, Haringey; City of
Westminster College
Qualifications: IT Level II, GNVQ
(Advanced) Leisure and Tourism,
NCA senior coach
Career outside cricket: 'Coaching/working
with young people at sports centres'

Cricketers particularly admired:
Saqlain Mushtaq, Steve Waugh, 'Hainault and Clayhall CC players A. Ahmed,
D. McEwan, I. Patel, Y. Patel, R. Rollins, G. Rollins'
Players to look out for: Will Kendall, Dimitri Mascarenhas, U. Shah,
M. and K. Ismail, G. Kandola, R. Bopara, Z. Sharif, R. Anderson, C. Greenidge,
K. and K. Ali, S. Khan, C. Adams
Other sports played: Badminton, snooker
Other sports followed: Snooker (Ronnie O'Sullivan), football (West Ham Utd)
Relaxations: 'Praying, worshipping; going out – club, cinema, snooker club; spending
time with family and friends; and just chilling'
Extras: Played for Northumberland in the NatWest 1999
Opinions on cricket: 'Not been involved that long to comment. I would like to say
too many good players don't get opportunities and without that opportunity you can't
see the potential.'

2001 Season (did not make any first-class or one-day appearances)

Career Performances

	M	Inns	NO	Runs	HS	Avge	100s	50s	Ct	St	Balls	Runs	Wkts	Avge	Best	5wI	10wM
Test																	
All First																	
1-day Int																	
C & G	1	0	0	0	0	-	-	-	1	-	60	64	1	64.00	1-64	-	
B & H																	
1-day Lge																	

SHAH, O. A. Middlesex

Name: <u>Owais</u> Alam Shah
Role: Right-hand bat, off-spin bowler
Born: 22 October 1978, Karachi, Pakistan
Height: 6ft 1in **Weight:** 12st
Nickname: Ace
County debut: 1995 (one-day),
1996 (first-class)
County cap: 1999
One-Day Internationals: 5
1000 runs in a season: 1
1st-Class 50s: 18
1st-Class 100s: 8
1st-Class 200s: 1
1st-Class catches: 56
One-Day 100s: 3
Place in batting averages: 61st av. 41.60
(2000 140th av. 24.45)
Strike rate: (career 57.88)
Parents: Jamshed and Mehjabeen
Marital status: Single
Family links with cricket: Father played for his college side
Education: Berkley's Junior School; Isleworth and Syon School; Lampton School;
Westminster University, Harrow
Qualifications: 7 GCSEs, 2 A-levels
Off-season: England one-day tours to Zimbabwe, India and New Zealand and ECB
National Academy to Australia
Overseas tours: England U19 to Zimbabwe 1995-96, to South Africa (including U19
World Cup) 1997-98; England A to Australia 1996-97, to Kenya and Sri Lanka
1997-98; ECB National Academy to Australia 2001-02; England to Zimbabwe
(one-day series) 2001-02, to India and New Zealand 2001-02 (one-day series)

Overseas teams played for: University of Western Australia, Perth
Career highlights to date: 'Playing for England in one-day game v Australia [2001]'
Cricket moments to forget: 'Getting a pair in first-class cricket'
Cricketers particularly admired: Viv Richards, Sachin Tendulkar, Mark Waugh
Young players to look out for: Andy Strauss, Chris Tremlett, Mark Wagh
Other sports played: Snooker
Other sports followed: Football (Manchester United)
Relaxations: TV, cinema, music
Extras: Middlesex Sports Federation Award winner. Man of the Series in U17 'Test' series against India 1994. Played for Middlesex U13, Ken Barrington Trophy (national champions) winners, and Middlesex U15, county competition winners, as captain. Scored record 232 for England U15 against England U16. Awarded 2nd XI cap in 1996. Captained the England U19 side to success in the 1997-98 U19 World Cup in South Africa, scoring 54 not out in the final. Captain of England U19 against Pakistan U19 (one-day and 'Test' matches) 1998. B&H Gold Award for his 109-ball 118* v Hampshire at Lord's 2001. Scored maiden first-class double century (203) v Derbyshire at Southgate 2001. Made One-Day International debut v Australia at Bristol in the NatWest Series 2001. Scored 62 v Pakistan at Lord's in the NatWest Series 2001, in the process sharing in a record fourth-wicket partnership for England in One-Day Internationals (170) with Marcus Trescothick. Cricket Writers' Young Player of the Year 2001
Opinions on cricket: 'There is not enough time between games to work on faults that creep into your game.'
Best batting: 203 Middlesex v Derbyshire, Southgate 2001
Best bowling: 3-33 Middlesex v Gloucestershire, Bristol 1999

2001 Season

	M	Inns	NO	Runs	HS	Avge	100s	50s	Ct	St	O	M	Runs	Wkts	Avge	Best	5wI	10wM
Test																		
All First	15	25	0	1040	203	41.60	3	4	14	-	5	1	38	0	-		-	-
1-day Int	5	5	1	104	62	26.00	-	1	2	-								
C & G	1	1	0	41	41	41.00	-	-	1	-	5	0	36	1	36.00	1-36	-	
B & H	5	4	1	168	118 *	56.00	1	-	1	-								
1-day Lge	12	11	1	244	69	24.40	-	2	5	-								

Career Performances

	M	Inns	NO	Runs	HS	Avge	100s	50s	Ct	St	Balls	Runs	Wkts	Avge	Best	5wI	10wM
Test																	
All First	78	130	8	3991	203	32.71	9	18	56	-	984	612	17	36.00	3-33	-	-
1-day Int	5	5	1	104	62	26.00	-	1	2	-							
C & G	10	10	1	227	49	25.22	-	-	3	-	30	36	1	36.00	1-36	-	
B & H	14	12	2	294	118 *	29.40	1	-	6	-	50	37	4	9.25	2-2	-	
1-day Lge	73	68	8	1659	134	27.65	2	8	18	-	151	176	3	58.66	1-4	-	

SHAHID AFRIDI Leicestershire

Name: Sahibzaha Mohammad Shahid
Khan Afridi
Role: Right-hand bat, leg-break bowler
Born: 1 March 1980, Kohat, Pakistan
County debut: 2001
Test debut: 1998-99
Tests: 11
One-Day Internationals: 131
1st-Class 50s: 12
1st-Class 100s: 6
1st-Class 5 w. in innings: 5
1st-Class catches: 42
One-Day 100s: 2
One-Day 5 w. in innings: 1
Place in batting averages: 84th av. 36.11
Place in bowling averages: 124th av. 43.76
Strike rate: 76.69 (career 53.55)
Overseas tours: Pakistan U19 to West Indies

1996-97; Pakistan to Kenya (one-day series) 1996-97, to Sharjah (one-day series)
1996-97 – 2001-02, to Australia (one-day series) 1996-97, to India (one-day series)
1996-97, to Toronto (one-day series) 1997-98, 1998-99, to Zimbabwe and South Africa
1997-98 (one-day series), to Bangladesh (Wills International Cup) 1998-99, to India
1998-99, to UK, Ireland and Holland (World Cup) 1999, to Australia 1999-2000
(one-day series), to West Indies 1999-2000 (one-day series), to New Zealand 2000-01
(one-day series), to England 2001 (one-day series), to Sharjah (v West Indies) 2001-02
Overseas teams played for: Karachi Cricket Association; Habib Bank
Extras: Set record for fastest One-Day International century – 37 balls v Sri Lanka in
Kenya 1996-97 in first ODI innings aged 16 years 217 days; innings included a
record-equalling 11 sixes. Recorded his maiden Test five-wicket innings return (5-52)
on debut v Australia at Karachi 1998-99, going on to score his maiden Test century
(141) v India at Chennai (Madras) in his second match. His quicker ball was once
timed at 86mph. Joined Leicestershire during the 2001 season as overseas player,
replacing the injured Dan Marsh. Struck 32-ball 70 on Norwich Union League debut v
Kent at Leicester 2001. C&G Man of the Match award for his 44-ball 67 in the
quarter-final v Worcestershire at Worcester 2001. C&G Man of the Match award for
his 58-ball 95 in the semi-final v Lancashire at Leicester 2001. Struck 30-ball 68 v
Somerset at Taunton in the Norwich Union League 2001. Scored 121-ball 164,
including a 74-ball century, v Northamptonshire at Northampton 2001. Scored 25-ball
58, including six sixes, v Somerset at Leicester in the Norwich Union League 2001.
Released by Leicestershire at the end of the 2001 season
Best batting: 164 Leicestershire v Northamptonshire, Northampton 2001

Best bowling: 6-101 Habib Bank v KRL, Rawalpindi 1997-98
Stop press: Won Man of the Match award for his 44-ball 83 in third One-Day
International v Bangladesh at Dhaka 2001-02

2001 Season

	M	Inns	NO	Runs	HS	Avge	100s	50s	Ct	St	O	M	Runs	Wkts	Avge	Best	5wI	10wM
Test																		
All First	6	9	0	325	164	36.11	1	1	8	-	166.1	41	569	13	43.76	5-84	1	-
1-day Int	4	4	0	68	30	17.00	-	-	2	-	26.2	3	112	5	22.40	3-15	-	
C & G	4	4	0	205	95	51.25	-	2	1	-	36	1	158	7	22.57	3-47	-	
B & H																		
1-day Lge	8	8	0	276	70	34.50	-	3	-	-	56	2	266	11	24.18	3-45	-	

Career Performances

	M	Inns	NO	Runs	HS	Avge	100s	50s	Ct	St	Balls	Runs	Wkts	Avge	Best	5wI	10wM
Test	11	20	1	594	141	31.26	1	3	7	-	1187	584	20	29.20	5-52	1	-
All First	53	88	5	2815	164	33.91	6	12	42	-	6480	3421	121	28.27	6-101	5	-
1-day Int	131	127	5	2934	109	24.04	2	16	51	-	4776	3757	90	41.74	5-40	1	
C & G	4	4	0	205	95	51.25	-	2	1	-	216	158	7	22.57	3-47	-	
B & H																	
1-day Lge	8	8	0	276	70	34.50	-	3	-	-	336	266	11	24.18	3-45	-	

74. In which year did Scotland first take part
in the Gillette/NatWest/C&G?

SHAHID, N.   Surrey

Name: Nadeem Shahid
Role: Right-hand bat, leg-spin bowler
Born: 23 April 1969, Karachi, Pakistan
Height: 6ft **Weight:** 12st
Nickname: Nad, Gonads etc
'too many to mention'
County debut: 1989 (Essex), 1995 (Surrey)
County cap: 1998 (Surrey)
1000 runs in a season: 1
1st-Class 50s: 30
1st-Class 100s: 7
1st-Class catches: 125
One-Day 100s: 2
Place in batting averages: 213th av. 17.33
(2000 52nd av. 36.16)
Strike rate: (career 70.13)
Parents: Ahmed and Salma
Marital status: Single
Family links with cricket: Brother plays cricket in Suffolk
Education: Stoke High; Northgate High; Ipswich School; Plymouth Polytechnic
Qualifications: 6 O-levels, 1 A-level, coaching certificate
Overseas tours: Ipswich School to Barbados (Sir Garfield Sobers Trophy) 1987;
England (South) to N Ireland (Youth World Tournament) 1988
Overseas teams played for: Gosnells, Perth, Western Australia 1989-91;
Fairfield, Sydney 1992-93
Cricketers particularly admired: Ian Botham, Shane Warne, Graham Thorpe and
Nasser Hussain
Young players to look out for: 'Every one'
Other sports followed: Golf, tennis, badminton, squash, 'most ball sports'
Extras: Youngest Suffolk player, aged 17. Played for HMC, MCC Schools, ESCA
U19, NCA Young Cricketers, England U25 and at every level for Suffolk. TSB Young
Player of the Year 1987, winner of the *Daily Telegraph* Bowling Award 1987 and
1988, Cricket Society's All-rounder of the Year 1988 and Laidlaw Young Player of the
Year for Essex 1993. Essex Society Player of the Year 1993. Released by Essex at end
of 1994 season and signed for Surrey. Member of the Surrey Sunday League winning
side of 1996. Member of Surrey County Championship winning squad of 1999
and 2000
Best batting: 139 Surrey v Yorkshire, The Oval 1995
Best bowling: 3-91 Essex v Surrey, The Oval 1990

2001 Season

	M	Inns	NO	Runs	HS	Avge	100s	50s	Ct	St	O	M	Runs	Wkts	Avge	Best	5wI	10wM
Test																		
All First	7	12	0	208	65	17.33	-	1	8	-								
1-day Int																		
C & G	1	0	0	0	0	-	-	-	1	-								
B & H	1	1	0	32	32	32.00	-	-	1	-								
1-day Lge	12	12	1	143	43	13.00	-	-	-	-								

Career Performances

	M	Inns	NO	Runs	HS	Avge	100s	50s	Ct	St	Balls	Runs	Wkts	Avge	Best	5wI	10wM
Test																	
All First	128	203	25	5556	139	31.21	7	30	125	-	3016	1999	43	46.48	3-91	-	-
1-day Int																	
C & G	10	7	1	163	85 *	27.16	-	1	6	-	72	30	4	7.50	3-30	-	
B & H	23	16	5	303	65 *	27.54	-	2	4	-	150	131	1	131.00	1-59	-	
1-day Lge	110	97	15	1939	109 *	23.64	2	5	34	-	66	72	0	-	-	-	

SHARIF, Z. K.   Essex

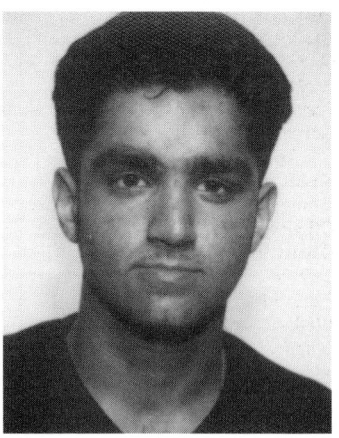

Name: Zoheb Khalid Sharif
Role: Left-hand bat, leg-spin bowler
Born: 22 February 1983, Leytonstone
Height: 5ft 10in **Weight:** 12st
Nickname: Omar, Bundles, Bomber
County debut: 2001
1st-Class catches: 1
Parents: Khalid and Robina
Marital status: Single
Education: Henry Maynard Junior School; Warwick School; Chigwell School; Coopers Company and Coburn School
Qualifications: 10 GCSEs, 3 A-levels
Career outside cricket: Student
Off-season: Playing cricket in Pakistan for Rawalpindi District
Overseas tours: Essex U13 to Holland 1995
Overseas teams played for: PNT CC, Pakistan 1997; Rawalpindi District 2001-02
Career highlights to date: 'Making my first-team debut'
Cricket moments to forget: 'No day should be worth forgetting about; it is an opportunity for a person to learn and correct things for the future'

Cricketers particularly admired: Saeed Anwar, Sachin Tendulkar, Inzamam, Wasim Akram, Imran Khan
Young players to look out for: Gurdeep Kandola, Irfan Shah, Ravi Bopara, James Foster, Carl Greenidge, Bilal Shafayat, Tony Palladino
Other sports followed: Football (Manchester United)
Relaxations: 'Music; following Islam; chillin' with my mates'
Extras: MCC Lord's Taverners' Player of the Year at U13, U15 and U19 level. Was on MCC groundstaff. Was in England U17 squad v Scotland 2000
Opinions on cricket: 'Not many people enjoy it.'
Best batting: 15 Essex v Yorkshire, Scarborough 2001

2001 Season

	M	Inns	NO	Runs	HS	Avge	100s	50s	Ct	St	O	M	Runs	Wkts	Avge	Best	5wI	10wM
Test																		
All First	1	2	0	17	15	8.50	-	-	1	-	2	0	23	0	-	-	-	-
1-day Int																		
C & G																		
B & H																		
1-day Lge																		

Career Performances

	M	Inns	NO	Runs	HS	Avge	100s	50s	Ct	St	Balls	Runs	Wkts	Avge	Best	5wI	10wM
Test																	
All First	1	2	0	17	15	8.50	-	-	1	-	12	23	0	-	-	-	-
1-day Int																	
C & G																	
B & H																	
1-day Lge																	

SHAW, A. D. Glamorgan

Name: Adrian David Shaw
Role: Right-hand bat, wicket-keeper
Born: 17 February 1972, Neath
Height: 6ft **Weight:** 13st
Nickname: Shawsy, AD, ADS, VD, Hairy Palms, C, Sea, Rick, RU
County debut: 1992 (one-day), 1994 (first-class)
County cap: 1999
50 dismissals in a season: 1
1st-Class 50s: 9
1st-Class 100s: 1

1st-Class catches: 180
1st-Class stumpings: 14
Place in batting averages: (2000 54th
av. 35.53)
Parents: David Colin and Christina
Marital status: Single
Children: 'By the time this goes to print I
will be a dad!!!'
Education: Catwg Primary; Llangatwg
Comprehensive; Neath Tertiary College
Qualifications: 9 O-levels, 3 A-levels,
various coaching badges
Career outside cricket: 'Too scary to
think about!'
Off-season: 'Due to the impending birth of my
first offspring, I am going to dedicate it to what
some would consider a mystical nirvana. I
intend to grow up and act my age (30)!'

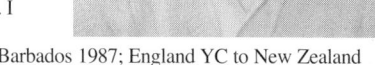

Overseas tours: Welsh Schools U17 to Barbados 1987; England YC to New Zealand
1990-91; Glamorgan pre-season tours, including to Cape Town 1999
Overseas teams played for: Welkom Police, Free State 1995-96
Career highlights to date: 'Watching people who deserve success succeed and vice
versa. Make of that what you will. Winning the Championship in 1997'
Cricket moments to forget: 'Every dropped catch and missed stumping. That's
approx 8214 moments in a 12-year career!'
Cricketers particularly admired: 'Anyone who's had to work hard – and not been
"spoonfed" – deserves admiration'
Young players to look out for: Jonathan Hughes, Tim Murtagh, Adam Harrison,
Owen Parkin ('still time, mate')
Other sports played: Rugby (formerly centre with Neath RFC; Welsh U19 and U21
squad member)
Other sports followed: Rugby ('Neath, Neath, Neath – as the song goes!!!')
Extras: One of youngest players (18 years 7 days) to play first-class rugby for Neath.
Played for Neath against Swansea six days after playing cricket against Zimbabwe for
Glamorgan, and had the 'pleasure' of marking Scott Gibbs. Neath RFC Back of the
Year 1993-94. Voted Glamorgan 2nd XI Player of the Year and Glamorgan Young
Player of the Year in 1995. 2nd XI Player of the Month, June 1996. Claimed eight
catches in the second innings and 12 for the match v Gloucestershire 2nd XI at Usk in
1998, setting two records for the 2nd XI Championship. Awarded county Young Player
of the Month for August 1999 'at the geriatric age of 27'
Opinions on cricket: 'For once I'm going to be serious. I was always brought up to
believe performance was what counted. I *now* believe it's as important to "look" the
part. For example: "He's not quick enough" – tell that to Martin Bicknell (best in
country). "His technique's not good enough" – does he score runs? "He's too big for a

keeper," etc., etc. Young cricketers: Don't get labelled! There's some bad judges out there.'

Best batting: 140 Glamorgan v Oxford University, The Parks 1999

2001 Season

	M	Inns	NO	Runs	HS	Avge	100s	50s	Ct	St	O	M	Runs	Wkts	Avge	Best	5wI	10wM
Test																		
All First	5	6	1	143	62	28.60	-	1	11	-								
1-day Int																		
C & G																		
B & H	5	5	1	90	39	22.50	-	-	1	1								
1-day Lge	4	2	1	15	9 *	15.00	-	-	-	2								

Career Performances

	M	Inns	NO	Runs	HS	Avge	100s	50s	Ct	St	Balls	Runs	Wkts	Avge	Best	5wI	10wM
Test																	
All First	76	102	16	1873	140	21.77	1	9	180	14	6	7	0	-	-	-	-
1-day Int																	
C & G	9	8	2	151	47	25.16	-	-	13	-							
B & H	19	17	3	166	39	11.85	-	-	16	7							
1-day Lge	56	38	9	436	48	15.03	-	-	29	10							

SHEIKH, M. A. Warwickshire

Name: Mohammed Avez Sheikh
Role: Left-hand bat, right-arm medium bowler
Born: 2 July 1973, Birmingham
Height: 6ft
Nickname: Sheikhy
Education: Broadway School
County debut: 1997
1st-Class 50s: 1
Strike rate: 81.87 (career 73.60)
Overseas teams played for: Western Province CC 1997-98
Extras: Has also played for Warwickshire U19 and played for both Worcestershire and Essex 2nd XIs in 1995
Best batting: 58* Warwickshire v Northamptonshire, Northampton 2000
Best bowling: 4-36 Warwickshire v Hampshire, Edgbaston 2001

2001 Season

	M	Inns	NO	Runs	HS	Avge	100s	50s	Ct	St	O	M	Runs	Wkts	Avge	Best	5wI	10wM
Test																		
All First	4	4	0	66	33	16.50	-	-	-	-	109.1	40	255	8	31.87	4-36	-	-
1-day Int																		
C & G	4	0	0	0	0	-	-	-	-	-	38	4	159	6	26.50	2-31	-	
B & H	6	3	1	27	19 *	13.50	-	-	3	-	60	9	179	7	25.57	3-27	-	
1-day Lge	15	5	3	17	12 *	8.50	-	-	3	-	120	13	383	15	25.53	4-17	-	

Career Performances

	M	Inns	NO	Runs	HS	Avge	100s	50s	Ct	St	Balls	Runs	Wkts	Avge	Best	5wI	10wM
Test																	
All First	9	11	2	223	58 *	24.77	-	1	-	-	1104	442	15	29.46	4-36	-	-
1-day Int																	
C & G	6	2	1	17	12 *	17.00	-	-	2	-	336	215	8	26.87	2-18	-	
B & H	10	4	1	34	19 *	11.33	-	-	3	-	541	277	12	23.08	3-27	-	
1-day Lge	34	16	6	103	36	10.30	-	-	8	-	1497	897	39	23.00	4-17	-	

SHERIYAR, A.   Worcestershire

Name: Alamgir Sheriyar
Role: Right-hand bat, left-arm fast bowler
Born: 15 November 1973, Birmingham
Height: 6ft 1in **Weight:** 13st
Nickname: Sheri
County debut: 1993 (one-day, Leics),
1994 (first-class, Leics), 1996 (Worcs)
County cap: 1997 (Worcs)
50 wickets in a season: 3
1st-Class 5 w. in innings: 16
1st-Class 10 w. in match: 3
1st-Class catches: 18
Place in batting averages: 273rd av. 6.45
(2000 281st av. 8.62)
Place in bowling averages: 32nd av. 25.28
(2000 121st av. 37.42)
Strike rate: 45.30 (career 48.91)
Parents: Mohammed Zaman (deceased) and
Safia Sultana
Marital status: Single
Family links with cricket: Brothers play a bit
Education: George Dixon Secondary School, Birmingham; Joseph Chamberlain Sixth
Form College, Birmingham; Oxford Brookes University

Qualifications: 6 O-levels
Overseas tours: Leicestershire to South Africa 1995; Worcestershire to Barbados 1996; England A to Bangladesh and New Zealand 1999-2000
Cricketers particularly admired: Wasim Akram
Other sports followed: Football, basketball
Relaxations: Time at home, music
Extras: Played for English Schools U17 and has also played in the Indoor National League. Became only the second player to take a hat-trick on his Championship debut, for Leics v Durham at Durham University 1994 (Vince Wells took a hat-trick for Leics in the same match); the first player to achieve the feat was H. A. Sedgwick, for Yorks v Worcs in 1906. Asked to be released by Leicestershire at the end of the 1995 season and joined Worcestershire for 1996. First bowler to reach 50 first-class wickets in 1999 and ended season as leading wicket-taker with 92. Took second first-class hat-trick of his career v Kent at Worcester 1999. His 6-88 v Durham at Kidderminster 2001 included a spell of 5-11 from 26 balls
Best batting: 21 Worcestershire v Nottinghamshire, Trent Bridge 1997
               21 Worcestershire v Pakistan A, Worcester 1997
Best bowling: 7-130 Worcestershire v Hampshire, Southampton 1999

2001 Season

	M	Inns	NO	Runs	HS	Avge	100s	50s	Ct	St	O	M	Runs	Wkts	Avge	Best	5wI	10wM
Test																		
All First	16	19	8	71	20	6.45	-	-	3	-	536.1	125	1795	71	25.28	6-88	3	-
1-day Int																		
C & G	3	1	0	4	4	4.00	-	-	1	-	22	1	97	4	24.25	2-47	-	
B & H	5	2	1	1	1 *	1.00	-	-	-	-	40.3	6	115	9	12.77	4-19	-	
1-day Lge	15	3	0	9	9	3.00	-	-	-	-	108.2	11	507	22	23.04	3-23	-	

Career Performances

	M	Inns	NO	Runs	HS	Avge	100s	50s	Ct	St	Balls	Runs	Wkts	Avge	Best	5wI	10wM
Test																	
All First	109	114	41	576	21	7.89	-	-	18	-	18393	10970	376	29.17	7-130	16	3
1-day Int																	
C & G	8	4	1	14	10	4.66	-	-	1	-	353	291	8	36.37	2-47	-	
B & H	15	6	3	29	15	9.66	-	-	1	-	682	450	20	22.50	4-19	-	
1-day Lge	69	20	11	63	19	7.00	-	-	5	-	2378	2036	79	25.77	4-18	-	

---

75. Who took 6-18 for Lancashire as Essex were bowled out
for 57 in the NatWest final 1996?

SIDEBOTTOM, R. J.   Yorkshire

Name: <u>Ryan</u> Jay Sidebottom
Role: Left-hand bat, left-arm
fast bowler
Born: 15 January 1978, Huddersfield
Height: 6ft 4in **Weight:** 14st 7lbs
Nickname: Siddy, Sexual, Jazz
County debut: 1997
County cap: 2000
Test debut: 2001
Tests: 1
1st-Class 50s: 1
1st-Class 5 w. in innings: 5
1st-Class 10 w. in match: 1
1st-Class catches: 15
One-Day 5 w. in innings: 1
Place in bowling averages: 41st av. 26.29

(2000 2nd av. 12.50)
Strike rate: 61.85 (career 54.38)
Parents: Arnie and Gillian
Marital status: Single
Family links with cricket: Father played cricket for Yorkshire and England and
football for Manchester United and Huddersfield Town
Education: Almondbury Primary, Huddersfield; Lepton Middle; King James Grammar
School, Almondbury
Qualifications: 5 GCSEs
Off-season: England one-day tour to Zimbabwe
Overseas tours: England U17 to Holland 1995; MCC to Bangladesh 1999-2000;
England A to West Indies 2000-01; England to Zimbabwe (one-day series) 2001-02
Overseas teams played for: Ringwood, Melbourne 1998
Cricketers particularly admired: Darren Gough, Chris Silverwood, Glenn McGrath
Young players to look out for: Joe Sayers, Scott Richardson
Other sports played: Football (once with Sheffield United), 'all sports'
Other sports followed: 'Love rugby league (any team)', football (Man Utd)
Relaxations: 'Music (R&B), films, clubbing, going out with my team-mates'
Extras: NBC Denis Compton Award 1999. Recorded maiden first-class five-wicket
return (5-27) v Kent at Headingley 2000, following up with 6-16 in second innings for
maiden ten-wicket match. Top English bowler in first-class averages in 2000 (second
overall) with 24 wickets at 12.50. Took 5-31 (8-65 in the match) in the Busta Cup for
England A v Jamaica at Kingston 2000-01, winning the Man of the Match award;
topped tour first-class bowling averages (16 wickets av.16.81). NBC Denis Compton
Award for the most promising young Yorkshire player 2000. Made Test debut in first

Test v Pakistan at Lord's 2001 (England's 100th Test at the ground), becoming the tenth player to follow his father into the England Test team

Opinions on cricket: 'More advertising of the game to heighten its profile. Needs better marketing for players because they work very hard.'

Best batting: 54 Yorkshire v Glamorgan, Cardiff 1998

Best bowling: 6-16 Yorkshire v Kent, Headingley 2000

Stop press: Made One-Day International debut in third ODI v Zimbabwe at Harare 2001-02. Called into the ECB National Academy squad in Australia 2001-02 as cover in the pace-bowling department

2001 Season

	M	Inns	NO	Runs	HS	Avge	100s	50s	Ct	St	O	M	Runs	Wkts	Avge	Best	5wI	10wM
Test	1	1	0	4	4	4.00	-	-	-	-	20	2	64	0	-	-	-	-
All First	9	9	4	82	40 *	16.40	-	-	3	-	278.2	75	710	27	26.29	4-49	-	-
1-day Int																		
C & G	3	1	0	6	6	6.00	-	-	1	-	30	6	103	8	12.87	4-39	-	
B & H	7	2	1	6	4	6.00	-	-	2	-	67	6	244	5	48.80	2-34	-	
1-day Lge	8	6	5	38	17 *	38.00	-	-	3	-	51.2	7	204	12	17.00	3-38	-	

Career Performances

	M	Inns	NO	Runs	HS	Avge	100s	50s	Ct	St	Balls	Runs	Wkts	Avge	Best	5wI	10wM
Test	1	1	0	4	4	4.00	-	-	-	-	120	64	0	-	-	-	-
All First	38	47	15	367	54	11.46	-	1	15	-	5602	2529	103	24.55	6-16	5	1
1-day Int																	
C & G	9	2	1	13	7 *	13.00	-	-	2	-	420	270	15	18.00	4-39	-	
B & H	17	6	2	19	8	4.75	-	-	5	-	856	570	11	51.81	2-26	-	
1-day Lge	45	23	12	117	24 *	10.63	-	-	6	-	1860	1339	49	27.32	6-40	1	

SILLENCE, R. J.   Gloucestershire

Name: <u>Roger</u> John Sillence

Role: Right-hand bat, right-arm medium-fast bowler

Born: 29 June 1977, Salisbury, Wiltshire

Height: 6ft 3in **Weight:** 13st 1lb

Nickname: Sillo, Silly

County debut: 2001

1st-Class 5 w. in innings: 1

Strike rate: 35.80 (career 35.80)

Parents: Angela May and Jacko

Marital status: 'De facto'

Education: Farley, Salisbury; Highbury, Salisbury; Salisbury Art College

Qualifications: 7 GCSEs, HND Graphic Design

Off-season: Coaching
Overseas teams played for: Napier Old
Boys, New Zealand 1997-98; St Augustine's,
Cape Town 1998-99; East Keilor, Melbourne
2000-01; Hamersley Carine, Perth 2001-02
Career highlights to date: 'Five wickets
(5-97) on debut, 2001 v Sussex at Hove'
Cricketers particularly admired: Steve
Waugh, Glenn McGrath, Sachin Tendulkar
Young players to look out for: 'Me'
Other sports followed: Football
Relaxations: Design, music, eating out, art
Extras: Played for Wiltshire in the NatWest
1999 and 2000. Wiltshire Player of the Year
2000. Recorded maiden first-class five-wicket
return (5-97) on debut v Sussex at Hove 2001
Opinions on cricket: 'To give youth a
chance in all areas of our game, from
England down to the local clubs.'

Best batting: 6 Gloucestershire v Sussex, Hove 2001
Best bowling: 5-97 Gloucestershire v Sussex, Hove 2001

2001 Season

	M	Inns	NO	Runs	HS	Avge	100s	50s	Ct	St	O	M	Runs	Wkts	Avge	Best	5wI	10wM
Test																		
All First	1	2	0	6	6	3.00	-	-	-	-	29.5	5	100	5	20.00	5-97	1	-
1-day Int																		
C & G																		
B & H																		
1-day Lge																		

Career Performances

	M	Inns	NO	Runs	HS	Avge	100s	50s	Ct	St	Balls	Runs	Wkts	Avge	Best	5wI	10wM
Test																	
All First	1	2	0	6	6	3.00	-	-	-	-	179	100	5	20.00	5-97	1	-
1-day Int																	
C & G	4	3	0	89	82	29.66	-	1	-	-	96	75	4	18.75	3-47	-	
B & H																	
1-day Lge																	

SILVERWOOD, C. E. W.   Yorkshire

Name: <u>Christopher</u> Eric Wilfred Silverwood
Role: Right-hand bat, right-arm
fast-medium bowler
Born: 5 March 1975, Pontefract
Height: 6ft 1in **Weight:** 12st 9lbs
Nickname: Spoons, Silvers, Chubby
County debut: 1993
County cap: 1996
Test debut: 1996-97
Tests: 5
One-Day Internationals: 6
50 wickets in a season: 1
1st-Class 50s: 5
1st-Class 5 w. in innings: 18
1st-Class 10 w. in match: 1
1st-Class catches: 24
One-Day 5 w. in innings: 1

Place in batting averages: 189th av. 20.87
(2000 209th av. 17.30)
Place in bowling averages: 10th av. 19.51 (2000 88th av. 29.30)
Strike rate: 38.03 (career 50.57)
Parents: Brenda
Wife and date of marriage: Emma, 3 October 1997
Family links with cricket: 'Dad played a bit'
Education: Gibson Lane School, Kippax; Garforth Comprehensive
Qualifications: 8 GCSEs, City and Guilds in Leisure and Recreation
Overseas tours: England A to Kenya and Sri Lanka 1997-98, to Bangladesh and New
Zealand 1999-2000, to West Indies 2000-01; England to Zimbabwe and New Zealand
1996-97, to West Indies 1997-98, to Bangladesh (Wills International Cup) 1998-99,
to South Africa 1999-2000 (*see **Stop press***)
Overseas teams played for: Wellington, Cape Town 1993-94, 1995-96
Cricketers particularly admired: Ian Botham, Allan Donald
Other sports played: Karate, rugby league (Kippax Welfare)
Other sports followed: Rugby league (Castleford)
Relaxations: Listening to music, watching videos, 'riding my motorbike'
Extras: Black belt in karate. Attended the Yorkshire Cricket Academy. Represented
Yorkshire at athletics. Played for England U19 in the home series against India U19 in
1994. Called up from England A tour of Bangladesh and New Zealand to England tour
of South Africa 1999-2000 as injury cover. Took his first five-wicket haul in Test
cricket (5-91) in South Africa's only innings in the fourth Test at Cape Town, January
2000. Took 4-45 from 32 overs for England A in Trinidad and Tobago's first innings in
the Busta Cup match at Port of Spain 2000-01

Best batting: 70 Yorkshire v Essex, Chelmsford 2001
Best bowling: 7-93 Yorkshire v Kent, Headingley 1997
Stop press: Called up for England one-day tour to Zimbabwe 2001-02 after the withdrawal of James Ormond through injury

2001 Season

	M	Inns	NO	Runs	HS	Avge	100s	50s	Ct	St	O	M	Runs	Wkts	Avge	Best	5wI	10wM
Test																		
All First	8	9	1	167	70	20.87	-	1	2	-	209.1	42	644	33	19.51	5-20	3	-
1-day Int																		
C & G	2	0	0	0	0	-	-	-	2	-	20	0	83	5	16.60	3-44	-	
B & H	6	4	2	24	13 *	12.00	-	-	2	-	55	5	242	8	30.25	3-30	-	
1-day Lge	4	4	3	63	27 *	63.00	-	-	1	-	29	4	102	9	11.33	4-21	-	

Career Performances

	M	Inns	NO	Runs	HS	Avge	100s	50s	Ct	St	Balls	Runs	Wkts	Avge	Best	5wI	10wM
Test	5	6	3	19	7 *	6.33	-	-	3	-	804	415	11	37.72	5-91	1	-
All First	110	142	30	1730	70	15.44	-	5	24	-	18257	9508	361	26.33	7-93	18	1
1-day Int	6	4	0	17	12	4.25	-	-	-	-	252	201	3	67.00	2-27	-	
C & G	16	5	3	25	12 *	12.50	-	-	6	-	857	529	17	31.11	3-24	-	
B & H	27	12	2	57	13 *	5.70	-	-	6	-	1372	1013	45	22.51	5-28	1	
1-day Lge	82	46	24	243	27 *	11.04	-	-	7	-	3379	2383	115	20.72	4-11	-	

---

76. Which Australian Test leg-spinner played for Devon against Yorkshire in the 1998 NatWest?

SINGH, A.   Worcestershire

Name: Anurag Singh
Role: Right-hand bat, right-arm 'all sorts'
Born: 9 September 1975, Kanpur, India
Height: 5ft 11½in **Weight:** 11st
Nickname: Ragi
County debut: 1995 (Warwickshire),
2001 (Worcestershire)
1000 runs in a season: 1
1st-Class 50s: 11
1st-Class 100s: 6
1st-Class catches: 20
One-Day 100s: 1
Place in batting averages: 80th av. 36.34
(2000 158th av. 22.28)
Parents: Vijay and Rajul
Marital status: Single
Education: Sacred Heart, Roehampton/
Bishop Gilpin, Wimbledon/Mayfield Prep,
Walsall; King Edward's School, Birmingham; Gonville and Caius College, Cambridge;
College of Law, London
Qualifications: 12 GCSEs, 1 AO-level, 4 A-levels, passed Law School exams
Career outside cricket: Solicitor at Wragge & Co in Birmingham
Overseas tours: England U19 to West Indies 1994-95; Warwickshire U21 to
South Africa; Warwickshire CCC to South Africa
Overseas teams played for: Gordon CC, Sydney; Avendale CC, Cape Town
Cricketers particularly admired: Steve Waugh, Sachin Tendulkar, Michael Atherton
Young players to look out for: Nick Warren, Kabir Ali
Other sports played: Hockey ('college and school'), football ('college and firm')
Other sports followed: Football (Aston Villa FC)
Relaxations: Reading, socialising with friends
Extras: Broke school record for number of runs in a season (1102). *Daily Telegraph*
regional award for batting (twice) and bowling (once). Tiger Smith Memorial Award
for Warwickshire Most Promising Young Cricketer 1994, Coney Edmonds Trophy for
Warwickshire Best U19 Cricketer 1994, Lord's Taverners' Trophy for Best Young
Cricketer 1994, Gray-Nicolls Len Newbery Award for ESCA U19 Best Player 1994.
Scored two centuries for England U19 against India U19 in 1994. Scored one century
against West Indies U20 and was Man of the Series 1994-95. Awarded 2nd XI cap in
1995. Cambridge Blue 1996-98; captain of Cambridge University 1997-98. With Nick
Knight, shared in record NatWest first-wicket stand for Warwickshire (185), v
Hampshire at Edgbaston 2000. Left Warwickshire at the end of the 2000 season and
joined Worcestershire for 2001. Scored maiden Championship century (168)

v Middlesex at Worcester 2001, in the process passing 1000 runs in a season for the first time and sharing with Philip Weston in a record opening partnership for Worcs in matches against Middlesex

Opinions on cricket: 'Two divisional cricket has definitely helped improve the intensity and competitiveness of every game. Should be more day/night cricket, as this makes cricket more attractive and accessible to the masses. Pitches and practice facilities must continue to improve.'

Best batting: 168 Worcestershire v Middlesex, Worcester 2001

2001 Season

	M	Inns	NO	Runs	HS	Avge	100s	50s	Ct	St	O	M	Runs	Wkts	Avge	Best	5wI	10wM
Test																		
All First	18	31	2	1054	168	36.34	2	4	5	-								
1-day Int																		
C & G	3	3	0	123	79	41.00	-	1	2	-								
B & H	5	5	0	97	83	19.40	-	1	1	-								
1-day Lge	14	14	0	299	80	21.35	-	3	4	-								

Career Performances

	M	Inns	NO	Runs	HS	Avge	100s	50s	Ct	St	Balls	Runs	Wkts	Avge	Best	5wI	10wM
Test																	
All First	61	98	5	2883	168	31.00	6	11	20	-	95	111	0	-	-	-	-
1-day Int																	
C & G	7	7	0	269	85	38.42	-	2	2	-							
B & H	22	22	1	543	123	25.85	1	4	5	-							
1-day Lge	38	38	1	823	86	22.24	-	7	11	-							

77. Which current broadcaster won the Man of the Match award in the 1983 NatWest final for his 29 and 3-30?

SMETHURST, M. P. Lancashire

Name: Michael (<u>Mike</u>) Paul Smethurst
Role: Right-hand bat, right-arm
fast bowler
Born: 11 October 1976, Oldham
Height: 6ft 5in **Weight:** 14st 6lbs
County debut: 1999
50 wickets in a season: 1
1st-Class 50s: 1
1st-Class 5 w. in innings: 3
1st-Class catches: 4
Place in batting averages: 280th av. 4.14
(2000 199th av. 17.88)
Place in bowling averages: (2000 25th
av. 20.73)
Strike rate: 85.71 (career 47.71)
Parents: Julie Martin ('Mum')
Marital status: Single
Education: Middleton Parish Primary

School; Hulme Grammar School, Oldham; University of Salford
Qualifications: 9 GCSEs, 4 A-levels, BA (Hons) Leisure Management,
Level 2 coaching award
Overseas tours: Lancashire to Cape Town 1999, 2000
Young players to look out for: Kyle Hogg, James Anderson
Other sports followed: Football (Manchester United)
Extras: Recorded maiden first-class five-wicket return (7-50) v Durham at
Riverside 2000
Best batting: 66 Lancashire v Surrey, Old Trafford 2000
Best bowling: 7-37 Lancashire v New Zealand A, Liverpool 2000

2001 Season

	M	Inns	NO	Runs	HS	Avge	100s	50s	Ct	St	O	M	Runs	Wkts	Avge	Best	5wI	10wM
Test																		
All First	5	8	1	29	7	4.14	-	-	-	-	100	17	363	7	51.85	3-32	-	-
1-day Int																		
C & G	2	0	0	0	0	-	-	-	-	-	15.1	2	64	2	32.00	2-20	-	
B & H																		
1-day Lge	5	3	2	4	2 *	4.00	-	-	1	-	25	6	106	2	53.00	1-9	-	

Career Performances

	M	Inns	NO	Runs	HS	Avge	100s	50s	Ct	St	Balls	Runs	Wkts	Avge	Best	5wI	10wM
Test																	
All First	26	31	11	195	66	9.75	-	1	4	-	3626	1901	76	25.01	7-37	3	-
1-day Int																	
C & G	5	1	1	4	4 *	-	-	-	1	-	250	173	9	19.22	4-46	-	
B & H	2	1	1	10	10 *	-	-	-	-	-	96	77	3	25.66	2-34	-	
1-day Lge	17	8	3	11	3 *	2.20	-	-	3	-	554	455	9	50.55	2-13	-	

SMITH, A. M. Gloucestershire

Name: Andrew Michael Smith
Role: Right-hand bat ('put bat to ball!'),
left-arm swing bowler
Born: 1 October 1967, Dewsbury
Height: 5ft 9in **Weight:** 12st 3lbs
Nickname: Smudge, Cyril
County debut: 1991
County cap: 1995
Benefit: 2001
Test debut: 1997
Tests: 1
50 wickets in a season: 5
1st-Class 50s: 4
1st-Class 5 w. in innings: 20
1st-Class 10 w. in match: 5
1st-Class catches: 26
One-Day 5 w. in innings: 1
Place in bowling averages: (2000 26th
av. 20.76)

Strike rate: 99.00 (career 49.43)
Parents: Hugh and Margaret
Wife and date of marriage: Sarah, 2 October 1993
Children: William James, 9 October 1994; Amelia Lucy, 14 June 1997
Family links with cricket: Father (Birstall club) and brother (East Ardsley club) local
league cricketers in Yorkshire
Education: Queen Elizabeth Grammar School, Wakefield; Exeter University;
University of the West of England, Bristol
Qualifications: 9 O-levels, 4 A-levels, BA (Hons) French and German, PGDip Law
Career outside cricket: Studying to be a lawyer
Off-season: 'Studying law; finishing my benefit year 2001; fitness'
Overseas tours: Queen Elizabeth Grammar School to Holland 1985; Bradford Junior

Cricket League to Barbados 1986; Exeter University to Barbados 1987; Gloucestershire to Kenya 1990, to Sri Lanka 1992-93, to Zimbabwe 1996, to Cape Town 2000, to South Africa 2001; England A to Pakistan 1995-96; MCC to New Zealand 1999

Overseas teams played for: Waimea, New Zealand 1990; WTTU, New Zealand 1991
Career highlights to date: 'My one Test match and the NatWest final 1999 v Somerset'
Cricket moments to forget: 'My batting in my one Test match'
Cricketers particularly admired: Wasim Akram, Malcolm Marshall, Richard Hadlee, Darren Gough, Jacques Kallis, Adam Gilchrist
Young players to look out for: Chris Taylor
Other sports played: Football, golf
Other sports followed: Football (Leeds United)
Injuries: Out for all but three games of the 2001 season with a groin injury
Relaxations: Looking after the kids ('hardly relaxing!'). Crosswords. Computers
Extras: Played for Yorkshire age groups. Played for English Schools U19, NAYC and represented Combined Universities in the B&H Cup in 1988 and 1990. Finished the 1997 season as leading first-class wicket-taker with 83 wickets. Gloucestershire Player of the Year 1997. Took 400th first-class wicket when Jack Russell caught Keith Parsons v Somerset at Bath 1999
Opinions on cricket: 'I can understand why some of our players don't want to tour every winter. However, I don't recall many Australians making the same choice. They know they will find it hard to get their place back. Time will tell whether our boys have the same problem.'
Best batting: 61 Gloucestershire v Yorkshire, Gloucester 1998
Best bowling: 8-73 Gloucestershire v Middlesex, Lord's 1996

2001 Season

	M	Inns	NO	Runs	HS	Avge	100s	50s	Ct	St	O	M	Runs	Wkts	Avge	Best	5wI	10wM
Test																		
All First	1	1	0	4	4	4.00	-	-	1	-	33	11	70	2	35.00	2-24	-	-
1-day Int																		
C & G																			
B & H																			
1-day Lge	2	2	1	3	3 *	3.00	-	-	-	-	18	6	37	4	9.25	2-18	-	

Career Performances

	M	Inns	NO	Runs	HS	Avge	100s	50s	Ct	St	Balls	Runs	Wkts	Avge	Best	5wI	10wM
Test	1	2	1	4	4 *	4.00	-	-	-	-	138	89	0	-	-	-	-
All First	134	177	48	1594	61	12.35	-	4	26	-	22544	11217	456	24.59	8-73	20	5
1-day Int																		
C & G	26	10	6	53	13	13.25	-	-	6	-	1501	800	38	21.05	4-46	-	
B & H	45	22	12	91	15 *	9.10	-	-	10	-	2472	1634	55	29.70	6-39	1	
1-day Lge	139	72	43	320	26 *	11.03	-	-	21	-	5748	4069	146	27.86	4-29	-	

SMITH, B. F. Worcestershire

Name: Benjamin (<u>Ben</u>) Francis Smith
Role: Right-hand bat, right-arm
medium bowler
Born: 3 April 1972, Corby
Height: 5ft 9in **Weight:** 11st
Nickname: Smudge
County debut: 1990 (Leicestershire)
County cap: 1995 (Leicestershire)
1000 runs in a season: 3
1st-Class 50s: 41
1st-Class 100s: 22
1st-Class 200s: 1
1st-Class catches: 97
One-Day 100s: 1
Place in batting averages: 56th av. 43.64
(2000 71st av. 32.66)
Strike rate: (career 208.50)
Parents: Keith and Janet
Wife and date of marriage: Lisa, 10 October 1998
Family links with cricket: Father, grandfather and uncles all played club and
representative cricket
Education: Tugby C of E; Kibworth High School; Robert Smyth, Market Harborough
Qualifications: 5 O-levels, 8 GCSEs, NCA coaching certificate
Off-season: Playing cricket in New Zealand
Overseas tours: England YC to New Zealand 1990-91; MCC to Bangladesh 1999-
2000; 'numerous pre-season tours to South Africa, Caribbean and Sri Lanka'
Overseas teams played for: Alexandria, Zimbabwe 1990; Bankstown-Canterbury,
Sydney 1993-96; Central Hawke's Bay CC, New Zealand 1997-98; Central Districts,
New Zealand 2000-01
Career highlights to date: 'Winning 1996 County Championship'
Cricket moments to forget: 'Lord's finals'
Cricketers particularly admired: Viv Richards, David Gower, Steve Waugh
Young players to look out for: Scott Schaw
Other sports played: Tennis, golf, touch rugby, 'Vortex'
Other sports followed: Rugby union (Leicester Tigers)
Relaxations: 'Music, DIY, good wine'
Extras: Played tennis for Leicestershire aged 12. Cricket Society Young Player of the
Year 1991. Took part in Leicestershire record fifth-wicket partnership (322) with Phil
Simmons v Notts at Worksop 1998. 'Two Championship medals so far!' Played in the
Central Districts Shell Cup winning side in New Zealand 2000-01. Vice-captain of
Leicestershire 2001. Scored 114-ball century (eventually out for 105) in one-day match

v Pakistanis at Leicester 2001. Scored 110 v Kent at Canterbury 2001, in the process sharing with Iain Sutcliffe in a Leicestershire record second-wicket partnership for matches against Kent (190). Left Leicestershire at the end of the 2001 season and has joined Worcestershire for 2002

Opinions on cricket: 'An even amount of teams in each division to play Championship games starting on the same day, to eliminate *some* weather and selection problems.'

Best batting: 204 Leicestershire v Surrey, The Oval 1998

Best bowling: 1-5 Leicestershire v Essex, Ilford 1991

Stop press: Scored 200* for Central Districts v Canterbury at New Plymouth in the New Zealand State Championship 2001-02, following up with 78 in the second innings

2001 Season

	M	Inns	NO	Runs	HS	Avge	100s	50s	Ct	St	O	M	Runs	Wkts	Avge	Best	5wI	10wM
Test																		
All First	17	30	2	1222	180 *	43.64	5	2	19	-								
1-day Int																		
C & G	5	5	2	135	64 *	45.00	-	1	4	-	3	0	15	0	-		-	-
B & H	5	5	0	170	51	34.00	-	2	1	-								
1-day Lge	16	16	4	323	65 *	26.91	-	2	4	-								

Career Performances

	M	Inns	NO	Runs	HS	Avge	100s	50s	Ct	St	Balls	Runs	Wkts	Avge	Best	5wI	10wM
Test																	
All First	187	284	35	9714	204	39.01	23	41	97	-	417	261	2	130.50	1-5	-	-
1-day Int																	
C & G	22	21	3	494	64 *	27.44	-	3	12	-	18	15	0	-		-	-
B & H	37	35	2	938	90	28.42	-	8	16	-							
1-day Lge	156	153	19	3838	115	28.64	1	20	38	-	18	15	0	-		-	-

SMITH, E. T.   Kent

Name: Edward (Ed) Thomas Smith
Role: Right-hand bat, right-arm medium bowler
Born: 19 July 1977, Pembury, Kent
Height: 6ft 2in **Weight:** 12st 8lbs
Nickname: Smudge
County debut: 1996
County cap: 2001
1000 runs in a season: 2
1st-Class 50s: 21

1st-Class 100s: 9
1st-Class catches: 23
Place in batting averages: 74th av. 39.03
(2000 150th av. 23.05)
Parents: Jonathan and Gillie
Marital status: Single
Family links with cricket: Father wrote
Good Enough? with Chris Cowdrey
Education: Tonbridge School; Peterhouse,
Cambridge University
Qualifications: 11 GCSEs, 3 A-levels,
degree in History
Career outside cricket: Journalist
Overseas teams played for: 'Several
Australian club teams'
Career highlights to date: 'Winning the
one-day league in 2001'
Cricketers particularly admired:
Martin Crowe, Mark Waugh
Young players to look out for: Ian Bell
Other sports followed: Football (Arsenal FC), baseball (New York Mets)
Relaxations: Listening to music, socialising, reading
Extras: Scored a century (101) on his first-class debut against Glamorgan in 1996 and
in doing so became the youngest player to score a century on debut for Cambridge
University. He was also the first person to score 50 or more in each of his first six
first-class games. Cambridge Blue in 1996. Played for England U19 against New
Zealand U19 in 1996. Awarded Kent cap 2001
Opinions on cricket: 'While trying to make the system better, we shouldn't constantly
run down county cricket. Is the standard of our first-class cricket really worse than most
other Test-playing countries? I doubt it.'
Best batting: 190 Cambridge University v Leicestershire, Fenner's 1997

2001 Season

	M	Inns	NO	Runs	HS	Avge	100s	50s	Ct	St	O	M	Runs	Wkts	Avge	Best	5wI	10wM
Test																		
All First	18	28	1	1054	116	39.03	3	4	5	-								
1-day Int																		
C & G																		
B & H																		
1-day Lge	4	4	0	20	10	5.00	-	-	-	-								

Career Performances

	M	Inns	NO	Runs	HS	Avge	100s	50s	Ct	St	Balls	Runs	Wkts	Avge	Best	5wI	10wM
Test																	
All First	79	131	7	4561	190	36.78	9	21	23	-		54	45	0	-	-	-	-
1-day Int																	
C & G	3	3	0	33	19	11.00	-	-	-	-							
B & H	5	5	0	79	43	15.80	-	-	3	-							
1-day Lge	22	19	2	321	72 *	18.88	-	2	2	-							

SMITH, G. J.   Nottinghamshire

Name: Gregory (Greg) James Smith
Role: Right-hand bat, left-arm fast bowler
Born: 30 October 1971, Pretoria
Height: 6ft 4in **Weight:** 15st
Nickname: Claw, Smudge, G
County debut: 2001
County cap: 2001
50 wickets in a season: 1
1st-Class 50s: 2
1st-Class 5 w. in innings: 9
1st-Class 10 w. in match: 1
1st-Class catches: 15
Place in batting averages: 212th av. 17.72
Place in bowling averages: 31st av. 25.12
Strike rate: 53.56 (career 57.39)
Parents: Fred and Nellie
Wife and date of marriage: Thea,
5 September 1999
Children: Rob, 1989; Keeghan, 1999
Education: Valhalla Primary; Pretoria BHS
Off-season: Playing for Northerns Titans in South Africa
Overseas tours: South Africa A to England 1996
Overseas teams played for: Northerns Titans 1993-94 –
Career highlights to date: 'Playing for South Africa A. Being capped by Notts'
Cricket moments to forget: 'Losing to Surrey in semi-final of B&H Cup [2001].
Losing to Natal in final of Standard Bank Cup [2000-01]'
Cricketers particularly admired: Wasim Akram, Fanie de Villiers, Kepler Wessels
Young players to look out for: Bilal Shafayat, Krier van Wyk, Jacques Rudolph
Other sports played: Golf
Other sports followed: Football (Arsenal), South African rugby
Relaxations: 'Spending time with my family and friends'

Extras: Attended national academy in South Africa. Made first-class debut for Northern Transvaal B v Transvaal B at Johannesburg 1993-94. Took hat-trick v Border in a semi-final. Recorded maiden first-class ten-wicket match return (10-101) v Sussex at Hove 2001. Took 4-18 from ten overs in the B&H quarter-final v Warwickshire at Trent Bridge 2001. Nottinghamshire Player of the Year 2001. Awarded Nottinghamshire cap 2001. Is not considered an overseas player
Opinions on cricket: 'Too much cricket in the county season.'
Best batting: 68 Northerns v Western Province, Centurion 1995-96
Best bowling: 6-35 Northerns v Western Province, Centurion 1997-98

2001 Season

	M	Inns	NO	Runs	HS	Avge	100s	50s	Ct	St	O	M	Runs	Wkts	Avge	Best	5wI	10wM
Test																		
All First	15	20	9	195	44 *	17.72	-	-	3	-	446.2	103	1256	50	25.12	5-37	3	1
1-day Int																		
C & G	2	1	0	1	1	1.00	-	-	-	-	18	0	61	7	8.71	4-25	-	
B & H	7	1	0	2	2	2.00	-	-	2	-	68.5	10	254	12	21.16	4-18	-	
1-day Lge	15	5	1	19	8	4.75	-	-	1	-	112.5	13	495	21	23.57	3-25	-	

Career Performances

	M	Inns	NO	Runs	HS	Avge	100s	50s	Ct	St	Balls	Runs	Wkts	Avge	Best	5wI	10wM
Test																	
All First	81	103	39	820	68	12.81	-	2	15	-	14407	6952	251	27.69	6-35	9	1
1-day Int																	
C & G	2	1	0	1	1	1.00	-	-	-	-	108	61	7	8.71	4-25	-	
B & H	7	1	0	2	2	2.00	-	-	2	-	413	254	12	21.16	4-18	-	
1-day Lge	15	5	1	19	8	4.75	-	-	1	-	677	495	21	23.57	3-25	-	

---

78. The fathers of three county cricketers opened the batting
for Surrey in the 1980 Gillette Cup final. Name them and their sons.

SMITH, N. M. K. Warwickshire

Name: <u>Neil</u> Michael Knight Smith
Role: Right-hand bat, off-spin bowler
Born: 27 July 1967, Solihull
Height: 6ft **Weight:** 14st 7lbs ('early season'); 15st 7lbs ('end of season')
Nickname: Gert
County debut: 1987
County cap: 1993
One-Day Internationals: 7
1000 runs in a season: 1
1st-Class 50s: 32
1st-Class 100s: 4
1st-Class 5 w. in innings: 17
1st-Class catches: 64
One-Day 100s: 2
One-Day 5 w. in innings: 3
Place in batting averages: 186th av. 21.16 (2000 132nd av. 25.77)

Place in bowling averages: 73rd av. 32.52 (2000 100th av. 31.25)
Strike rate: 75.36 (career 74.86)
Parents: Mike (M.J.K.) and Diana
Wife and date of marriage: Rachel, 4 December 1993
Family links with cricket: Father (M.J.K.) captained Warwickshire and England
Education: Warwick School
Qualifications: 3 O-levels, cricket coach Grade 1
Career outside cricket: Sports coach
Off-season: Coaching Warwick School. 'Benefit next year, so begging on the phone'
Overseas tours: England to South Africa 1995-96, to India and Pakistan (World Cup) 1995-96; England XI to New Zealand (Cricket Max) 1997-98
Overseas teams played for: Phoenix, Perth, Western Australia 1989-90
Career highlights to date: 'Playing for England'
Cricket moments to forget: 'Being known for spoiling people's breakfasts in the UK by throwing up in Pakistan during the World Cup'
Cricketers particularly admired: 'Anyone who has played for a long time'
Young players to look out for: Ian Bell, 'Mark Wagh's fielding!!', Nick Warren
Other sports played: Golf, squash, real tennis
Other sports followed: Rugby union (England, Leicester Tigers)
Relaxations: Sport, walking the dogs
Extras: Followed in his father's footsteps when he led the Warwickshire side out against Northamptonshire in the Sunday League 1997 – the first time both father and son had captained Warwicks. His 147 v Somerset at Taunton 1998 is the highest score by a Warwickshire No. 9. Warwickshire captain 1999-2000. Granted a benefit for 2002

Opinions on cricket: 'Four-day cricket is good. We must produce more spinners. And better pitches.'
Best batting: 161 Warwickshire v Yorkshire, Headingley 1989
Best bowling: 7-42 Warwickshire v Lancashire, Edgbaston 1994

2001 Season

	M	Inns	NO	Runs	HS	Avge	100s	50s	Ct	St	O	M	Runs	Wkts	Avge	Best	5wI	10wM
Test																		
All First	14	14	2	254	54	21.16	-	1	2	-	314	75	813	25	32.52	4-76	-	-
1-day Int																		
C & G	2	2	0	13	12	6.50	-	-	1	-	16	0	70	2	35.00	1-27	-	
B & H	6	6	1	129	40	25.80	-	-	-	-	36	1	162	2	81.00	1-33	-	
1-day Lge	13	8	0	97	38	12.12	-	-	2	-	71.4	2	343	14	24.50	3-19	-	

Career Performances

	M	Inns	NO	Runs	HS	Avge	100s	50s	Ct	St	Balls	Runs	Wkts	Avge	Best	5wI	10wM
Test																	
All First	191	266	34	6308	161	27.18	4	32	64	-	26801	13149	358	36.72	7-42	17	-
1-day Int	7	6	1	100	31	20.00	-	-	1	-	261	190	6	31.66	3-29	-	
C & G	43	38	8	634	72	21.13	-	4	14	-	1774	1121	47	23.85	5-17	1	
B & H	45	38	4	725	125	21.32	1	3	5	-	1559	1186	37	32.05	3-29	-	
1-day Lge	197	163	20	3182	111 *	22.25	1	18	72	-	6289	4816	186	25.89	6-33	2	

79. When Somerset met Kent in the 1967 Gillette Cup final,
the former's line-up contained four players who are now
first-class umpires. Name them.

SMITH, R. A.   Hampshire

Name: <u>Robin</u> Arnold Smith
Role: Right-hand bat, slip fielder,
county captain
Born: 13 September 1963,
Durban, South Africa
Height: 6ft **Weight:** 15st
Nickname: Judge
County debut: 1982
County cap: 1985
Benefit: 1996
Test debut: 1988
Tests: 62
One-Day Internationals: 71
1000 runs in a season: 11
1st-Class 50s: 123
1st-Class 100s: 58
1st-Class 200s: 1
1st-Class catches: 218
One-Day 100s: 27

Place in batting averages: 154th av. 24.91 (2000 173rd av. 20.51)
Strike rate: (career 78.50)
Parents: John and Joy
Wife and date of marriage: Katherine, 21 September 1988
Children: Harrison Arnold, 4 December 1991; Margaux Elizabeth, 28 July 1994
Family links with cricket: Grandfather played for Natal in Currie Cup. Brother Chris
played for Natal, Hampshire and England
Education: Northlands Boys High, Durban
Qualifications: Matriculation, '62 England caps'
Career outside cricket: 'Ducking and diving. Director of Chase Sports, which also
includes Cotton Graphics, which specialises in embroidery. Judge Tours Travel –
taking cricket lovers abroad and supporting England'
Off-season: 'Rep for Chase Sports and Masuri Helmets. Spending time expanding and
developing my business interests. Drinking the odd lager with our Hants chairman'
Overseas tours: England to India and West Indies 1989-90, to Australia 1990-91,
to Australia and New Zealand (World Cup) 1991-92, to India and Sri Lanka 1992-93,
to West Indies 1993-94, to South Africa 1995-96, to India and Pakistan (World Cup)
1995-96; England XI to New Zealand (Cricket Max) 1997-98
Overseas teams played for: Natal 1980-84; Perth, Australia 1984-85 (grade cricket)
Career highlights to date: '167* against Aussies at Edgbaston in a one-dayer [1993]
– currently still an England record. 175 at Antigua against West Indies in a Test
[1993-94]'
Cricket moments to forget: 'Too many to mention'

Cricketers particularly admired: Malcolm Marshall, Brian Lara, Graeme Hick, Graham Gooch, Allan Lamb

Young players to look out for: Chris Tremlett, Ian Bell, James Foster, 'A. Hollioake'

Other sports played: Golf – 'generally interested in all sports; trying to develop my snowboarding skills, without much luck!'

Other sports followed: 'All sports'

Injuries: Cracked rib

Relaxations: 'Reading (Leslie Thomas in particular), trout fishing, assembling a good wine cellar, keeping fit; enjoying the company of my wife and children (most of the time!)'

Extras: Played rugby for Natal Schools and for Romsey RFC as a full-back. Held 19 school athletics records and two South African schools records in shot putt and 100-metre hurdles. One of *Wisden*'s Five Cricketers of the Year 1990. Cornhill England Player of the Year 1991-92. Set record for the highest individual score for England in One-Day Internationals (167*) against Australia at Edgbaston 1993. Passed 6000 runs in Sunday/National League v Gloucestershire at Southampton 1999. Awarded an honorary MA (Honoris Causa) by Southampton Institute, November 2001. Scored a century (113) in Hampshire's victory over the Australians in the Vodafone Challenge match at West End 2001. Hampshire gained promotion to County Championship first division on his birthday 2001. Hampshire captain since 1998

Opinions on cricket: 'Not enough time spent talking about cricket in the bar after the end of the day's play. This doesn't mean you have to drink half a dozen pints, but just learn more about the game. I've enjoyed the two divisional structure – more interest throughout the whole season and certainly more competitive.'

Best batting: 209* Hampshire v Essex, Southend 1987

Best bowling: 2-11 Hampshire v Surrey, Southampton 1985

2001 Season

	M	Inns	NO	Runs	HS	Avge	100s	50s	Ct	St	O	M	Runs	Wkts	Avge	Best	5wI	10wM
Test																		
All First	16	26	2	598	118	24.91	3	1	4	-								
1-day Int																		
C & G	1	1	0	25	25	25.00	-	-	-	-	0.2	0	1	0	-		-	-
B & H	4	4	2	104	77 *	52.00	-	1	-	-								
1-day Lge	15	13	3	260	46	26.00	-	-	3	-								

Career Performances

	M	Inns	NO	Runs	HS	Avge	100s	50s	Ct	St	Balls	Runs	Wkts	Avge	Best	5wI	10wM
Test	62	112	15	4236	175	43.67	9	28	39	-	24	6	0	-	-	-	-
All First	401	677	85	24801	209 *	41.89	59	123	218	-	1099	993	14	70.92	2-11	-	-
1-day Int	71	70	8	2419	167 *	39.01	4	15	26	-							
C & G	45	44	13	2334	158	75.29	8	10	22	-	19	14	2	7.00	2-13	-	
B & H	66	63	10	2374	155 *	44.79	5	11	22	-	6	2	0	-	-	-	
1-day Lge	213	204	25	6782	131	37.88	10	40	76	-	2	0	1	0.00	1-0	-	

SMITH, T. M.   Derbyshire

Name: <u>Trevor</u> Mark Smith
Role: Left-hand bat, right-arm
fast-medium bowler
Born: 18 January 1977, Derby
Height: 6ft 3in **Weight:** 14st
Nickname: Tricky
County debut: 1997
1st-Class 50s: 1
1st-Class 5 w. in innings: 5
1st-Class 10 w. in match: 1
1st-Class catches: 11
Place in batting averages: 262nd av. 9.87
(2000 239th av. 13.81)
Place in bowling averages: 90th av. 34.81
Strike rate: 49.90 (career 48.71)
Parents: Graham and Marilyn
Marital status: Engaged to Lisa
Family links with cricket: Three brothers all
play for Sandiacre Town CC; father umpires in local league
Education: Cloudside School, Sandiacre; Friesland School, Sandiacre; Broxtowe
College of Further Education, Chilwell, Notts; Sheffield Hallam University
Qualifications: 4 GCSEs, BTEC National Diploma in Business and Finance,
ECB Level II coach, studying for BSc (Hons) PE (QTS)
Off-season: Studying
Overseas teams played for: Alma Marist CC, Cape Town 1999-2000; 'Gran Canaria
Town June 1999; Ayia Napa Select XI September 2000'
Career highlights to date: 'First 50, v Lancs [2000]. First "five-for", v South
Africans [1998]'
Cricket moments to forget: 'Being released from Derbyshire'
Cricketers particularly admired: Allan Donald, Ian Botham, Phillip DeFreitas,
Curtly Ambrose, Courtney Walsh
Other sports played: Football, golf ('very poorly')
Other sports followed: Football (Derby County; Blue Eagles – 'brother's team')
Relaxations: 'Golfing; spending time with fiancée'
Extras: Had three Championship five-wicket hauls in four innings in September 1999.
Released by Derbyshire at the end of the 2001 season
Opinions on cricket: 'The two divisions have made for more "interesting" cricket
(i.e. no meaningless end-of-season games). All we need now is good summers so we
can play!'
Best batting: 53* Derbyshire v Lancashire, Derby 2000
Best bowling: 6-32 Derbyshire v Essex, Derby 1998

2001 Season

	M	Inns	NO	Runs	HS	Avge	100s	50s	Ct	St	O	M	Runs	Wkts	Avge	Best	5wI	10wM
Test																		
All First	6	10	2	79	19	9.87	-	-	4	-	91.3	15	383	11	34.81	4-61	-	-
1-day Int																		
C & G																		
B & H	4	3	1	49	27	24.50	-	-	-	-	29.1	1	162	4	40.50	3-43	-	
1-day Lge	1	1	1	6	6 *	-	-	-	-	-	4	0	37	0	-		-	-

Career Performances

	M	Inns	NO	Runs	HS	Avge	100s	50s	Ct	St	Balls	Runs	Wkts	Avge	Best	5wI	10wM
Test																	
All First	32	42	11	377	53 *	12.16	-	1	11	-	3556	2135	73	29.24	6-32	5	1
1-day Int																	
C & G	1	0	0	0	0	-	-	-	-	-	60	25	1	25.00	1-25	-	
B & H	9	4	1	49	27	16.33	-	-	1	-	361	280	7	40.00	3-14	-	
1-day Lge	11	10	5	44	12	8.80	-	-	3	-	423	446	16	27.87	4-38	-	

SNAPE, J. N.   Gloucestershire

Name: <u>Jeremy</u> Nicholas Snape
Role: Right-hand bat, off-spin bowler; all-rounder
Born: 27 April 1973, Stoke-on-Trent
Height: 5ft 8in   **Weight:** 12st
Nickname: Snapey, Coot, Jez, Snapper
County debut: 1992 (Northamptonshire), 1999 (Gloucestershire)
County cap: 1999 (Gloucestershire)
1st-Class 50s: 19
1st-Class 100s: 3
1st-Class 5 w. in innings: 1
1st-Class catches: 60
One-Day 100s: 1
One-Day 5 w. in innings: 1
Place in batting averages: 35th av. 48.22 (2000 56th av. 35.17)
Place in bowling averages: (2000 48th av. 23.90)
Strike rate: 114.75 (career 92.21)
Parents: Keith and Barbara
Marital status: Single

Family links with cricket: 'Brother Jonathan plays league cricket for Rode Park CC in Cheshire. Dad loves cricket now, and Mum hates the sweep shot!'
Education: Denstone College, Staffordshire; Durham University
Qualifications: 8 GCSEs, 3 A-levels, BSc Natural Science
Career outside cricket: Director of Capetours – tailor-made holidays to Southern Africa (www.capetours.co.uk)
Off-season: England one-day tours to Zimbabwe, India and New Zealand
Overseas tours: England U18 to Canada 1991 (captain); England U19 to Pakistan 1991-92; Durham University to South Africa 1993, to Vienna (European Indoor Championships) 1994; Northamptonshire to Cape Town 1993; Christians in Sport to Zimbabwe 1994-95; Troubadours to South Africa 1997; Gloucestershire to Kimberley, South Africa 1999; England to Zimbabwe (one-day series) 2001-02, to India and New Zealand 2001-02 (one-day series)
Overseas teams played for: Petone, Wellington, New Zealand 1994-95; Wainuiamata, Wellington, New Zealand 1995-96; Techs CC, Cape Town 1996-99
Cricketers particularly admired: Allan Lamb, Anil Kumble, Jack Russell
Relaxations: Travelling, music, cooking, good food and wine
Extras: Sir Jack Hobbs award (U15 Schoolboy 1988). B&H Gold Award winner for Combined Universities v Worcestershire 1992 (3-34) at The Parks. Player of the Tournament at European Indoor 6-a-side Championships in 1994. Left Northants at end of 1998 season and joined Gloucestershire for 1999. Scored maiden first-class century (119) v Derbyshire at Derby 2001. Scored maiden one-day century (104*) in the Norwich Union League v Nottinghamshire at Trent Bridge 2001, in the process sharing in a record seventh-wicket partnership for domestic one-day competitions (164) with Mark Hardinges
Opinions on cricket: 'Delighted to move to Gloucestershire where the lads display a great work ethic. In general, I hope that the England side continue to do well and that our domestic game can keep pace with the world's insatiable appetite for one-day excitement!'
Best batting: 131 Gloucestershire v Sussex, Cheltenham 2001
Best bowling: 5-65 Northamptonshire v Durham, Northampton 1995
Stop press: Made One-Day International debut in first ODI v Zimbabwe at Harare 2001-02, winning Man of the Match award for his 2-39 (the Flower brothers both stumped in the same over) and brilliant catch to dismiss Guy Whittall. BBC West Country Sports Cricketer of the Year for 2001

2001 Season

	M	Inns	NO	Runs	HS	Avge	100s	50s	Ct	St	O	M	Runs	Wkts	Avge	Best	5wI	10wM
Test																		
All First	14	21	3	868	131	48.22	3	5	10	-	153	34	406	8	50.75	3-27	-	-
1-day Int																		
C & G	1	1	0	16	16	16.00	-	-	1	-								
B & H	6	6	2	152	46 *	38.00	-	-	3	-	22	0	103	4	25.75	4-32	-	
1-day Lge	12	12	4	223	104 *	27.87	1	-	4	-	38.3	3	187	10	18.70	3-30	-	

	M	Inns	NO	Runs	HS	Avge	100s	50s	Ct	St	Balls	Runs	Wkts	Avge	Best	5wI	10wM
Test																	
All First	85	126	23	3123	131	30.32	3	19	60	-	8760	4380	95	46.10	5-65	1	-
1-day Int																	
C & G	20	17	4	259	54	19.92	-	1	8	-	535	381	10	38.10	2-19	-	
B & H	36	28	6	504	52	22.90	-	2	15	-	1380	979	31	31.58	5-32	1	
1-day Lge	98	77	22	1228	104 *	22.32	1	3	33	-	2742	2173	86	25.26	4-27	-	

SOLANKI, V. S.   Worcestershire

Name: <u>Vikram</u> Singh Solanki
Role: Right-hand bat, off-spin bowler
Born: 1 April 1976, Udaipur,
Rajasthan, India
Height: 6ft **Weight:** 12st
Nickname: Vik
County debut: 1993 (one-day),
1995 (first-class)
County cap: 1998
One-Day Internationals: 8
1000 runs in a season: 2
1st-Class 50s: 37
1st-Class 100s: 12
1st-Class 5 w. in innings: 3
1st-Class 10 w. in match: 1
1st-Class catches: 157
One-Day 100s: 1
Place in batting averages: 140th av. 27.65
(2000 25th av. 43.76)
Strike rate: 251.00 (career 74.76)
Parents: Mr Vijay Singh and Mrs Florabel Solanki
Marital status: Single
Family links with cricket: Father played in India. Brother Vishal (13) is a
keen cricketer
Education: Merridale, Wolverhampton; Regis School, Wolverhampton;
Open University
Qualifications: 9 GCSEs, 3 A-levels
Off-season: Studying with the Open University
Overseas tours: England U18 to South Africa 1992-93, to Denmark (ICC Youth
Tournament) 1994; England U19 to West Indies 1994-95; Worcestershire CCC
to Barbados 1996, to Zimbabwe 1997; England A to Zimbabwe and South Africa

1998-99, to Bangladesh and New Zealand 1999-2000, to West Indies 2000-01;
England to South Africa and Zimbabwe 1999-2000 (one-day series), to Kenya
(ICC Knockout Trophy) 2000-01, to Pakistan 2000-01 (one-day series)
Overseas teams played for: Midland-Guildford, Perth, Western Australia
Career highlights to date: 'Playing for England'
Cricket moments to forget: 'Losing to Scotland' (*NatWest Trophy 1998*)
Cricketers particularly admired: Sachin Tendulkar, Graeme Hick, Tom Moody
Young players to look out for: Kabir Ali, Kadeer Ali, Chris Liptrot
Other sports played: 'Enjoy playing most sports'
Relaxations: Reading, spending time with friends and family
Extras: Scored more first-class runs (1339) in 1999 season than any other English
player. Topped batting averages with 597 first-class runs (av. 59.70) on England A tour
of Bangladesh and New Zealand 1999-2000. Drafted into England one-day squad for
Kenya and Pakistan 2000-01 as replacement for the injured Nick Knight. Took 22
catches at slip in seven first-class matches on England A tour of West Indies 2000-01
Best batting: 185 England A v Bangladesh, Chittagong 1999-2000
Best bowling: 5-69 Worcestershire v Middlesex, Lord's 1996

2001 Season

	M	Inns	NO	Runs	HS	Avge	100s	50s	Ct	St	O	M	Runs	Wkts	Avge	Best	5wI	10wM
Test																		
All First	18	29	0	802	112	27.65	3	2	16	-	83.4	17	265	2	132.50	2-41	-	-
1-day Int																		
C & G	2	2	0	64	41	32.00	-	-	2	-								
B & H	5	5	0	124	44	24.80	-	-	5	-								
1-day Lge	15	14	2	502	91 *	41.83	-	5	5	-	8	0	51	0	-		-	-

Career Performances

	M	Inns	NO	Runs	HS	Avge	100s	50s	Ct	St	Balls	Runs	Wkts	Avge	Best	5wI	10wM
Test																	
All First	126	209	14	6882	185	35.29	12	37	157	-	5389	3172	72	44.05	5-69	3	1
1-day Int	8	7	1	96	24	16.00	-	-	2	-							
C & G	12	11	0	199	50	18.09	-	1	3	-	195	149	2	74.50	1-48	-	
B & H	17	15	0	256	44	17.06	-	-	10	-	18	17	1	17.00	1-17	-	
1-day Lge	102	86	12	1975	120 *	26.68	1	11	30	-	198	206	4	51.50	1-9	-	

Name: <u>Nicholas</u> Jason Speak
Role: Right-hand bat, leg-spin bowler
Born: 21 November 1966, Manchester
Height: 6ft **Weight:** 12st 4lbs
Nickname: Speaky
County debut: 1986-87 (Lancashire), 1997 (Durham)
County cap: 1992 (Lancashire), 1998 (Durham)
1000 runs in a season: 3
1st-Class 50s: 56
1st-Class 100s: 14
1st-Class 200s: 1
1st-Class catches: 108
One-Day 100s: 1
Place in batting averages: (2000 101st av. 29.05)
Strike rate: (career 90.50)
Parents: John and Irene
Wife and date of marriage: Michele Frances, 29 March 1993
Children: Kenneth John, 24 September 1995; Ella Frances, 13 July 1997
Family links with cricket: Father and uncle were league professionals in Lancashire and Yorkshire
Education: Broad Oak, Didsbury; Parrs Wood High School, Manchester; Sixth Form College, Didsbury, Manchester
Qualifications: 5 O-levels, Levels 1 and 2 coaching
Overseas tours: Lancashire to Jamaica 1986-87, 1993, to Zimbabwe 1989, to Tasmania 1990, to Perth 1991, to Johannesburg 1992
Overseas teams played for: Maroochydore, Queensland 1988-89; South Canberra 1989-90; North Canberra 1990-91, 1992-93; Hawthorn, Melbourne 1994-96; Dandenong, Melbourne 1997-98, 2000-01
Cricketers particularly admired: Mark Waugh, Shane Warne, Sachin Tendulkar
Young players to look out for: Chris Schofield, Stephen Harmison
Other sports played: Golf, football, lacrosse
Other sports followed: Football (Manchester City FC)
Relaxations: Golf (Brancepeth Castle GC)
Extras: Scored century for Australian Capital Territories v England A at Canberra 1992-93. Released by Lancashire at the end of the 1996 season and joined Durham for 1997. Appointed Durham vice-captain for 1999. Appointed Durham captain for 2000; succeeded by Jon Lewis at the end of August. Released by Durham at the end of the 2001 season

Best batting: 232 Lancashire v Leicestershire, Leicester 1992
Best bowling: 1-0 Lancashire v Warwickshire, Edgbaston 1991

2001 Season

	M	Inns	NO	Runs	HS	Avge	100s	50s	Ct	St	O	M	Runs	Wkts	Avge	Best	5wI	10wM
Test																		
All First	3	4	1	95	45 *	31.66	-	-	-	-								
1-day Int																		
C & G																		
B & H	4	2	0	60	35	30.00	-	-	-	-								
1-day Lge																		

Career Performances

	M	Inns	NO	Runs	HS	Avge	100s	50s	Ct	St	Balls	Runs	Wkts	Avge	Best	5wI	10wM
Test																	
All First	177	307	34	9692	232	35.50	15	56	108	-	181	191	2	95.50	1-0	-	-
1-day Int																	
C & G	13	13	3	402	83	40.20	-	4	4	-	24	31	0	-		-	-
B & H	35	31	2	837	82	28.86	-	5	3	-							
1-day Lge	106	98	11	2281	102 *	26.21	1	10	21	-							

SPEARMAN, C. M.   Gloucestershire

Name: <u>Craig</u> Murray Spearman
Role: Right-hand bat
Born: 4 July 1972, Auckland, New Zealand
Height: 6ft **Weight:** 13st
Nickname: Spears
County debut: No first-team appearance
Test debut: 1995-96
Tests: 19
One-Day Internationals: 51
1st-Class 50s: 24
1st-Class 100s: 9
1st-Class catches: 81
Strike rate: (career 78.00)
Parents: Murray and Sandra
Marital status: Single
Education: Henderson Primary, Auckland;
Kelston Boys High School, Auckland;
Massey University
Qualifications: Bachelor of Business Studies (BBS; Finance major)

Overseas tours: New Zealand to India and Pakistan (World Cup) 1995-96, to West Indies 1995-96, to Sri Lanka 1997-98, to India 1999-2000, to South Africa 2000-01
Overseas teams played for: Auckland 1993-96; Central Districts 1997-2001
Career highlights to date: 'Playing international cricket; Test century; winning ICC Knockout Trophy in Kenya [2000-01]'
Cricket moments to forget: 'Misfielding on the boundary at the SCG in the fifth over and hearing about it for the next 45 overs'
Cricketers particularly admired: Desmond Haynes and Gordon Greenidge
Other sports played: Golf
Other sports followed: 'Follow most sports except motor sport'
Relaxations: 'Travelling, seeing new places and cultures'
Extras: Scored maiden Test century (112) at Auckland 1995-96, in the process sharing with Roger Twose in a record first-wicket partnership for New Zealand in Tests against Zimbabwe (214). Played in the Central Districts Shell Cup winning side in New Zealand 2000-01. 'Qualify to play for Gloucestershire because of my mother's Welsh background'
Opinions on cricket: 'Much more professional in England than in New Zealand.'
Best batting: 147 Auckland v Northern Districts, Hamilton 1994-95
Best bowling: 1-37 Central Districts v Wellington, New Plymouth 1999-2000

2001 Season (did not make any first-class or one-day appearances)

Career Performances

	M	Inns	NO	Runs	HS	Avge	100s	50s	Ct	St	Balls	Runs	Wkts	Avge	Best	5wI	10wM
Test	19	36	2	920	112	27.05	1	3	21	-							
All First	85	150	9	4888	147	34.66	9	24	83	-	78	55	1	55.00	1-37	-	-
1-day Int	51	50	0	936	86	18.72	-	5	15	-	3	6	0	-	-	-	
C & G																	
B & H																		
1-day Lge																		

80. Which West Indies pace bowler took 6-15 and the Man of the Match award as Middlesex bowled out Sussex for 115 in the semi-finals of the 1980 Gillette Cup?

SPEIGHT, M. P.

Durham

Name: <u>Martin</u> Peter Speight
Role: Right-hand bat, 'right-arm pies',
wicket-keeper
Born: 24 October 1967, Walsall
Height: 5ft 10in **Weight:** 12st 7lbs
Nickname: Sprog, Badger, Eco Warrior
County debut: 1986 (Sussex),
1997 (Durham)
County cap: 1991 (Sussex), 1998 (Durham)
1000 runs in a season: 2
50 dismissals in a season: 3
1st-Class 50s: 48
1st-Class 100s: 13
1st-Class catches: 292
1st-Class stumpings: 5
One-Day 100s: 3
Place in batting averages: 151st av. 25.33
(2000 168th av. 20.82)
Strike rate: (career 10.50)
Parents: Peter John and Val
Education: The Windmills School, Hassocks; Hurstpierpoint College Junior and
Senior Schools; Durham University (St Chad's College)
Qualifications: 13 O-levels, 3 A-levels, BA (Hons) Ancient History/Archaeology
Career outside cricket: Artist
Overseas tours: NCA U19 to Bermuda 1985; Hurstpierpoint College to India 1985-
86; England YC to Sri Lanka 1986-87
Overseas teams played for: Karori, Wellington, New Zealand 1989-90; University
CC, Wellington 1990-93; North City, Wellington 1995-96; Wellington CA 1989-90,
1992-93, 1995-96
Cricketers particularly admired: Viv Richards
Young players to look out for: Jo Wood
Other sports played: Squash
Other sports followed: 'Most sports, particularly rugby'
Relaxations: 'Art, red and white wine, good food, painting, most music'
Extras: Member of Durham University UAU winning side 1987. Played for
Combined Universities in B&H Cup 1987 and 1988. Member of Durham University's
men's hockey team to Barbados 1988. Sussex Most Promising Player 1989. Walter
Lawrence Trophy for fastest first-class 100 of 1992 – 62 balls v Lancashire at Hove.
Scored
47-ball Sunday League 100 v Somerset at Taunton 1993, the fastest 100 in the 50-over
Sunday League. Has won two Gold Awards in the Benson and Hedges competition.

Created an oil painting of the maiden first-class game at Arundel Castle between Sussex and Hampshire which was later auctioned to raise £1200 for the Sussex YC tour to India 1990-91, and of which a limited edition has also been printed and sold. Book of his paintings, *A Cricketer's View*, a collection of 54 paintings and commentary, published in 1995. Various commissions and a print of Abergavenny CC published in 1997. His paintings have also been reproduced on greetings cards and mugs, and as wooden jigsaws. Joined Durham from Sussex for the 1997 season. Oil painting of the Lord's Pavilion exhibited in the Lord's Museum 2000. Released by Durham at the end of the 2001 season

Best batting: 184 Sussex v Nottinghamshire, Eastbourne 1993
Best bowling: 1-2 Sussex v Middlesex, Hove 1988

2001 Season

	M	Inns	NO	Runs	HS	Avge	100s	50s	Ct	St	O	M	Runs	Wkts	Avge	Best	5wI	10wM
Test																		
All First	8	15	3	304	67 *	25.33	-	1	3	-								
1-day Int																		
C & G	3	2	0	18	18	9.00	-	-	1	-								
B & H	2	2	0	24	17	12.00	-	-	-	-								
1-day Lge	5	5	1	59	30	14.75	-	-	2	-								

Career Performances

	M	Inns	NO	Runs	HS	Avge	100s	50s	Ct	St	Balls	Runs	Wkts	Avge	Best	5wI	10wM
Test																	
All First	193	323	31	9225	184	31.59	13	48	292	5	21	32	2	16.00	1-2	-	-
1-day Int																	
C & G	25	22	1	480	60	22.85	-	2	12	1							
B & H	48	45	1	939	83	21.34	-	4	39	2							
1-day Lge	157	145	8	3608	126	26.33	3	17	74	14							

81. Which current ECB executive opened the batting for Middlesex v Worcestershire in the 1988 NatWest final?

SPIRES, J. A. Warwickshire

Name: James (<u>Jamie</u>) Ashley Spires
Role: Right-hand bat, slow left-arm bowler
Born: 12 November 1979, Solihull
Height: 6ft **Weight:** 12st 9lbs
Nickname: Spiro, Guff, Highlights
County debut: 2001
Strike rate: 150.00 (career 150.00)
Parents: Stuart and Carol
Marital status: Single
Family links with cricket: 'Dad used to play
with Gladstone Small and Trevor Penney at
Camp Hill CC'
Education: Eversfield School;
Solihull School
Qualifications: 11 GCSEs, 4 A-levels
Off-season: 'Six months in Cape Town on a
scholarship with Warwickshire along with
Jim Troughton'

Overseas tours: Warwickshire U19 to Cape Town 1998; Warwickshire to
Bloemfontein 2000, to Cape Town 2001
Overseas teams played for: Bloemfontein Police 1999-2000
Career highlights to date: 'Debut at Lord's for Warwickshire 2001'
Cricket moments to forget: 'Warwickshire 2nd XI v Pakistan Academy 2001 –
Younis Khan took a liking to my bowling!'
Cricketers particularly admired: Phil Tufnell, 'Gavin Franklin!'
Young players to look out for: Ian Bell, Jim Troughton, Tom Mees, Huw Jones
Other sports played: Football
Other sports followed: Football ('Nottingham Forest fan')
Relaxations: Spending time with friends
Extras: Warwickshire U19 Player of the Year 1999. Played for ECB U19 v Pakistan
U19 1999. Played for Warwickshire Board XI in the first round of the C&G 2002,
which was played in August 2001
Opinions on cricket: 'Clubs should be looking towards their youth systems before
bringing in new players.'
Best bowling: 2-73 Warwickshire v Middlesex, Lord's 2001

2001 Season

	M	Inns	NO	Runs	HS	Avge	100s	50s	Ct	St	O	M	Runs	Wkts	Avge	Best	5wI	10wM
Test																		
All First	1	0	0	0	0	-	-	-	-	-	50	8	155	2	77.50	2-73	-	-
1-day Int																		
C & G	1	0	0	0	0	-	-	-	-	-	10	0	33	1	33.00	1-33	-	
B & H																		
1-day Lge																		

Career Performances

	M	Inns	NO	Runs	HS	Avge	100s	50s	Ct	St	Balls	Runs	Wkts	Avge	Best	5wI	10wM
Test																	
All First	1	0	0	0	0	-	-	-	-	-	300	155	2	77.50	2-73	-	-
1-day Int																	
C & G	1	0	0	0	0	-	-	-	-	-	60	33	1	33.00	1-33	-	
B & H																	
1-day Lge																	

STEAD, R. A.   Yorkshire

Name: Roger <u>Alexander</u> Stead
Role: Right-hand bat, right-arm
medium bowler
Born: 18 April 1980, Dewsbury
Height: 6ft 1in **Weight:** 13st
Nickname: Zani, Steady
County debut: No first-team appearance
1st-Class catches: 1
Parents: Roger and Linda
Marital status: Single
Education: Lightcliffe Church of England
School; Hipperholme and Lightcliffe High
School; University of Durham
Qualifications: 10 GCSEs, 4 A-levels
Cricketers particularly admired:
Jacques Kallis, Steve Waugh
Young players to look out for: John Sadler
Other sports played: Football (Calderdale
district and local team), athletics (200m – Calderdale district)
Other sports followed: Football ('mad Leeds United supporter since early age')
Extras: Scored 88* on 2nd XI debut v Warwicks at Edgbaston 1998. Took 4-29 first

time he bowled for 2nd XI, v Notts at Trent Bridge 1999. Played for Durham University CCE 2001
Best batting: 28 DUCCE v Worcestershire, Worcester 2001

2001 Season (did not make any first-class or one-day appearances)

Career Performances

	M	Inns	NO	Runs	HS	Avge	100s	50s	Ct	St	Balls	Runs	Wkts	Avge	Best	5wI	10wM
Test																	
All First	2	2	0	28	28	14.00	-	-	1	-	210	107	0	-	-	-	-
1-day Int																	
C & G																	
B & H																	
1-day Lge																	

STELLING, W. F. Leicestershire

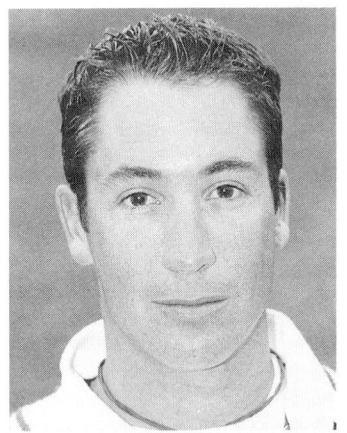

Name: <u>William</u> Frederik Stelling
Role: Right-hand bat, right-arm medium-fast bowler
Born: 30 June 1969, Johannesburg
Height: 6ft 4in **Weight:** 13st 6lbs
Nickname: Bomber, Stealth, Will
County debut: 2000
1st-Class 50s: 1
1st-Class 5 w. in innings: 1
1st-Class catches: 8
Strike rate: (career 71.30)
Parents: Kathy and William
Wife and date of marriage: Kerrie Anne, 11 March 2000
Education: St Peters Preparatory School; Michaelhouse; St Stithians College; University of Cape Town
Career outside cricket: Sports journalism
Overseas tours: Leicestershire to Anguilla 2000
Overseas teams played for: Western Province B and Western Province 1991-92, 1993-94; Boland 1994-96; Lesotho (invitational)
Cricketers particularly admired: Steve Waugh, Kepler Wessels, Hylton Ackerman (Snr)
Young players to look out for: Lawrence Prittipaul
Other sports played: Golf

Other sports followed: 'All major sports, especially rugby (Canterbury Crusaders)'
Relaxations: Internet surfing, golf, beach bats, gym, running
Extras: Made highest score of 162* in 25-over game when ten years old. Played for Transvaal Schools 1986-87. Played rugby for Transvaal U20. Made first-class cricket debut for Western Province B v Natal B at Pietermaritzburg in 1991-92. Played for Holland in 1995 NatWest Trophy. Played for East Lancs in the Lancashire League. Played for the Berkshire club Finchampstead. Won Thames Valley League Batting Award 1998. Represented Berkshire in the NatWest Trophy in 1999 and also played for them against Bangladesh in a World Cup warm-up match, taking 7-32. Scored 412 runs (av. 68.70) for Leics 2nd XI 1999 with a top score of 130 v Yorks. Joined Leicestershire for 2000 on a two-year contract; is not considered an overseas player. AON Trophy winner's medal 2000. Recorded maiden first-class five-wicket return (5-49) on Championship debut v Kent at Leicester 2000. Released by Leicestershire at the end of the 2001 season
Opinions on cricket: 'Too much cricket. Too many first-class teams. Too many contracted players. Strength versus strength is needed. Ten first-class counties, with promotion and relegation to division two and division three incorporating Minor Counties. Half as many four-day games to ensure 100 per cent effort, but no change to one-day games. A final in Championship and NCL could help.'
Best batting: 53 Western Province B v KwaZulu-Natal B, Pietermaritzburg 1991-92
Best bowling: 5-49 Leicestershire v Kent, Leicester 2000

2001 Season

	M	Inns	NO	Runs	HS	Avge	100s	50s	Ct	St	O	M	Runs	Wkts	Avge	Best	5wI	10wM
Test																		
All First																		
1-day Int																		
C & G																		
B & H	2	2	1	14	12 *	14.00	-	-	-	-	5.2	0	38	0	-		-	-
1-day Lge	1	1	0	10	10	10.00	-	-	-	-	8	1	20	2	10.00	2-20	-

Career Performances

	M	Inns	NO	Runs	HS	Avge	100s	50s	Ct	St	Balls	Runs	Wkts	Avge	Best	5wI	10wM
Test																	
All First	18	28	2	475	53	18.26	-	1	8	-	2353	1029	33	31.18	5-49	1	-
1-day Int																	
C & G	3	3	2	85	76 *	85.00	-	1	-	-	162	87	3	29.00	3-18	-
B & H	3	3	2	64	50 *	64.00	-	1	-	-	68	84	0	-	-	-
1-day Lge	2	2	1	20	10 *	20.00	-	-	-	-	102	55	5	11.00	3-35	-

STEMP, R. D.   Nottinghamshire

Name: <u>Richard</u> David Stemp
Role: Right-hand bat, slow left-arm bowler
Born: 11 December 1967, Erdington,
Birmingham
Height: 6ft **Weight:** 12st 4lbs
Nickname: Stempy, Sheriff, Badger
County debut: 1990 (Worcestershire),
1993 (Yorkshire), 1999 (Nottinghamshire)
County cap: 1996 (Yorkshire),
2000 (Nottinghamshire)
1st-Class 50s: 3
1st-Class 5 w. in innings: 14
1st-Class 10 w. in match: 1
1st-Class catches: 68
Place in batting averages: 226th av. 15.00
(2000 292nd av. 7.50)
Place in bowling averages: 126th av. 44.18
(2000 84th av. 28.66)

Strike rate: 91.75 (career 81.66)
Parents: Arnold and Rita Homer
Marital status: Single
Family links with cricket: Father played Birmingham League cricket for Old Hill
Education: Britannia High School, Rowley Regis
Qualifications: NCA coaching award
Overseas tours: England A to India 1994-95, to Pakistan 1995-96
Overseas teams played for: Pretoria Technikon 1988-89
Cricketers particularly admired: Ian Botham, Phil Tufnell
Other sports followed: Indoor cricket, American football (New England Patriots)
Relaxations: Ornithology, music, driving
Extras: Played for England indoor cricket team v Australia in ManuLife 'Test' series
1990. Moved to Yorkshire at end of 1992 season (first English non-Yorkshireman to be
signed for the county). Included in England Test squad against New Zealand in 1994.
Left Yorkshire at the end of the 1998 season and joined Notts for 1999. Released by
Notts at the end of the 2001 season
Best batting: 66 Nottinghamshire v Hampshire, West End 2001
Best bowling: 6-37 Yorkshire v Durham, Durham University 1994

2001 Season

	M	Inns	NO	Runs	HS	Avge	100s	50s	Ct	St	O	M	Runs	Wkts	Avge	Best	5wI	10wM
Test																		
All First	5	7	0	105	66	15.00	-	1	1	-	244.4	51	707	16	44.18	3-39	-	-
1-day Int																		
C & G	2	1	1	0	0 *	-	-	-	-	-	4.4	2	17	1	17.00	1-6	-	
B & H	3	1	0	29	29	29.00	-	-	-	-	29	0	129	1	129.00	1-58	-	
1-day Lge	8	2	1	1	1 *	1.00	-	-	5	-	63	3	280	11	25.45	4-25	-	

Career Performances

	M	Inns	NO	Runs	HS	Avge	100s	50s	Ct	St	Balls	Runs	Wkts	Avge	Best	5wI	10wM
Test																	
All First	165	196	63	1649	66	12.39	-	3	68	-	31361	13495	384	35.14	6-37	14	1
1-day Int																	
C & G	16	6	3	13	12	4.33	-	-	1	-	874	550	19	28.94	4-45	-	
B & H	26	6	1	34	29	6.80	-	-	-	-	1371	913	23	39.69	3-22	-	
1-day Lge	104	32	13	177	29 *	9.31	-	-	27	-	4287	3364	111	30.30	4-25	-	

STEPHENSON, J. P. Essex

Name: <u>John</u> Patrick Stephenson
Role: Right-hand bat, right-arm
medium bowler
Born: 14 March 1965, Stebbing, Essex
Height: 6ft 1in **Weight:** 12st 7lbs
Nickname: Stan
County debut: 1985 (Essex), 1995 (Hants)
County cap: 1989 (Essex), 1995 (Hants)
Benefit: 2001 (Hants)
Test debut: 1989
Tests: 1
1000 runs in a season: 5
1st-Class 50s: 72
1st-Class 100s: 23
1st-Class 200s: 1
1st-Class 5 w. in innings: 10
1st-Class catches: 174
One-Day 100s: 7
One-Day 5 w. in innings: 3
Place in batting averages: (2000 296th av. 6.40)
Place in bowling averages: (2000 136th av. 43.53)
Strike rate: 26.50 (career 61.44)

Parents: Pat and Eve
Wife and date of marriage: Fiona Maria, 24 September 1994
Children: Emma-Lydia, 19 May 1997; Camilla, 30 April 2000
Family links with cricket: Father was member of Rugby Meteors *Cricketer* Cup winning side in 1973. Three brothers played in Felsted 1st XI; Guy played for Essex 2nd XI and now plays for Teddington
Education: Felsted Prep School; Felsted Senior School; Durham University
Qualifications: 7 O-levels, 3 A-levels, BA General Arts, Level 3 coaching award, SFA registered representative
Career outside cricket: Stockbroker at Durlachers
Overseas tours: English Schools U19 to Zimbabwe 1982-83; England A to Kenya and Zimbabwe 1989-90, to Bermuda and West Indies 1991-92; MCC to Kenya 1999
Overseas teams played for: Fitzroy, Melbourne 1982-83, 1987-88; Boland, South Africa 1988-89; Gold Coast Dolphins and Bond University, Australia 1990-91; St George's, Argentina 1994-95; Belgrano, Argentina 1994-95; Victoria CC, South Africa 1995-96
Career highlights to date: 'Playing for England. Winning Championship in 1992 with Essex. Captaining Hampshire'
Cricketers particularly admired: Brian Hardie
Young players to look out for: Matthew Wood
Relaxations: Watching cricket, reading (*Sunday Telegraph*, *Wisden*, *The Cricketer*), alternative music
Extras: Awarded 2nd XI cap in 1984 when leading run-scorer with Essex 2nd XI. Essex Young Player of the Year 1985. Captained Durham University to victory in UAU Championship 1986 and was captain of Combined Universities team 1987 in the first year that it was drawn from all universities. Was leading wicket-taker on England A tour to Bermuda and West Indies 1991-92. Scored two not out centuries v Somerset at Taunton in 1992 and was on the field for the whole game (the first Essex player to achieve this). First Essex player to achieve 500 runs and 20 wickets in a Sunday League season 1993. Joined Hampshire for 1995. Took over the captaincy of Hampshire in 1996, but relinquished it at the end of the 1997 season. Founded the One Test Wonder Club in 1996. Scored 83* v Durham 2000, becoming the first opening batsman to carry his bat five times in the Sunday/National League. Released by Hampshire at the end of the 2001 season and has rejoined Essex for 2002 as 2nd XI captain/coach
Best batting: 202* Essex v Somerset, Bath 1990
Best bowling: 7-51 Hampshire v Middlesex, Lord's 1995

2001 Season

	M	Inns	NO	Runs	HS	Avge	100s	50s	Ct	St	O	M	Runs	Wkts	Avge	Best	5wl	10wM
Test																		
All First	3	6	1	128	51	25.60	-	1	1	-	17.4	3	60	4	15.00	3-48	-	-
1-day Int																		
C & G																		
B & H	4	3	0	36	31	12.00	-	-	-	-	10	0	61	1	61.00	1-40	-	
1-day Lge																		

Career Performances

	M	Inns	NO	Runs	HS	Avge	100s	50s	Ct	St	Balls	Runs	Wkts	Avge	Best	5wl	10wM
Test	1	2	0	36	25	18.00	-	-	-	-							
All First	281	474	45	13847	202 *	32.27	24	72	174	-	20401	11253	332	33.89	7-51	10	-
1-day Int																	
C & G	33	31	1	930	107	31.00	1	7	16	-	1195	920	29	31.72	5-34	1	
B & H	54	48	7	1573	142	38.36	2	11	14	-	1618	1172	43	27.25	3-22	-	
1-day Lge	184	166	23	4134	110 *	28.90	4	19	74	-	5387	4233	166	25.50	6-33	2	

STEVENS, D. I. Leicestershire

Name: <u>Darren</u> Ian Stevens
Role: Right-hand bat, right-arm
medium bowler
Born: 30 April 1976, Leicester
Height: 5ft 11in **Weight:** 12st
Nickname: Stevo
County debut: 1997
1st-Class 50s: 6
1st-Class 100s: 1
1st-Class catches: 21
One-Day 100s: 1
Place in batting averages: 183rd av. 21.58
(2000 169th av. 20.77)
Strike rate: (career 97.00)
Parents: Maddy and Bob
Marital status: Single
Family links with cricket: Father and
grandfather played league cricket in
Leicestershire
Education: Richmond Primary School; Mount Grace High School; John Cleveland
College, Hinckley; Hinckley Tech; Charles Klein College
Qualifications: 5 GCSEs, BTEC National in Sports Studies

Off-season: 'Three months at home; three months training in Cape Town'
Overseas tours: Leicestershire U19 to South Africa 1994-95; Leicestershire to Barbados 1998, to Sri Lanka 1999, to Potchefstroom 2001
Overseas teams played for: Wanderers CC, Johannesburg, South Africa 1996-97; Rhodes University, Grahamstown, South Africa 1997-98; Fairfield CC, Sydney 1998-99; Hawthorn-Waverley, Melbourne 1999-2000; Taita CC, Wellington, New Zealand 2000-01
Career highlights to date: 'The build-up to my first final at Lord's'
Cricket moments to forget: 'Losing in my first final in the C&G against Somerset 2001'
Cricketers particularly admired: Steve Waugh, Viv Richards, Ian Botham
Young players to look out for: Steve Adshead, Ian Blackwell
Other sports played: Golf, squash
Other sports followed: Football (Leicester City), rugby union (Leicester Tigers)
Relaxations: 'Music, spending time with close friends'
Extras: Received painting from Sir Colin Cowdrey on day of maiden first-class 100 (130 in fourth Championship match), v Sussex at Arundel 1999. Won Sir Ron Brierley/Crusaders Scholarship 1999
Opinions on cricket: 'A wonderful game. Possibly too many games. Not enough resting time between each game!'
Best batting: 130 Leicestershire v Sussex, Arundel 1999
Best bowling: 1-5 Leicestershire v Sussex, Eastbourne 1997

2001 Season

	M	Inns	NO	Runs	HS	Avge	100s	50s	Ct	St	O	M	Runs	Wkts	Avge	Best	5wl	10wM
Test																		
All First	8	14	2	259	63	21.58	-	1	2	-	7	1	28	0	-		-	-
1-day Int																		
C & G	4	3	0	26	23	8.66	-	-	2	-	4	0	26	2	13.00	2-26	-	
B & H	4	4	0	99	54	24.75	-	1	1	-	0.4	0	2	0	-		-	-
1-day Lge	14	12	2	343	68 *	34.30	-	3	6	-	0.3	0	1	0	-		-	-

Career Performances

	M	Inns	NO	Runs	HS	Avge	100s	50s	Ct	St	Balls	Runs	Wkts	Avge	Best	5wl	10wM
Test																	
All First	37	60	2	1316	130	22.68	1	6	21	-	97	53	1	53.00	1-5	-	-
1-day Int																	
C & G	8	7	0	251	133	35.85	1	1	2	-	24	26	2	13.00	2-26	-	
B & H	6	6	0	117	54	19.50	-	1	1	-	4	2	0	-		-	
1-day Lge	42	39	5	780	82	22.94	-	5	13	-	3	1	0	-		-	

STEWART, A. J.   Surrey

Name: <u>Alec</u> James Stewart
Role: Right-hand bat, wicket-keeper,
honorary club captain
Born: 8 April 1963, Merton, London
Height: 5ft 11in **Weight:** 13st 2lbs
Nickname: Stewie, Ming
County debut: 1981
County cap: 1985
Benefit: 1994 (£202,187)
Test debut: 1989-90
Tests: 115
One-Day Internationals: 146
1000 runs in a season: 8
50 dismissals in a season: 1
1st-Class 50s: 133
1st-Class 100s: 45
1st-Class 200s: 2
1st-Class catches: 634
1st-Class stumpings: 27
One-Day 100s: 18
Place in batting averages: 75th av. 38.73 (2000 73rd av. 32.21)
Strike rate: (career 162.33)
Parents: Michael and Sheila
Wife and date of marriage: Lynn, 28 September 1991
Children: Andrew James, 21 May 1993; Emily Elizabeth, 6 September 1996
Family links with cricket: Father (Micky) played for England (1962-64), Surrey
(1954-72) and Malden Wanderers and was team manager of England (1987-1992).
Brother Neil captains Malden Wanderers
Education: Tiffin Boys School
Qualifications: 'Streetwise'
Off-season: 'Enjoying my first winter in England for 21 years!'
Overseas tours: England to India (Nehru Cup) 1989-90, to West Indies 1989-90, to
Australia 1990-91, to Australia and New Zealand (World Cup) 1991-92, to India and
Sri Lanka 1992-93, to West Indies 1993-94, to Australia 1994-95, to South Africa
1995-96, to Pakistan and India (World Cup) 1995-96, to Zimbabwe and New Zealand
1996-97, to Sharjah (Champions Trophy) 1997-98, to West Indies 1997-98, to
Australia 1998-99 (captain), to Sharjah (Coca-Cola Cup) 1998-99, to South Africa
1999-2000, to Kenya (ICC Knockout Trophy) 2000-01, to Pakistan and Sri Lanka
2000-01
Overseas teams played for: Midland-Guildford, Perth, Western Australia 1981-89
Cricketers particularly admired: Graham Monkhouse, Graham Gooch, Alan Knott,
Geoff Arnold, K. Gartrell

Young players to look out for: Tim Murtagh
Other sports followed: Football (Chelsea)
Relaxations: 'Spending as much time with my family as possible'
Extras: Cornhill England Player of the Year (jointly with Chris Lewis) 1992-93. One of *Wisden*'s Five Cricketers of the Year 1993. Shared in a record fifth-wicket partnership for England in Tests v West Indies (150) with Graham Thorpe at Bridgetown 1993-94, becoming in that match the first Englishman to score a century in each innings against West Indies. He was the leading scorer in Test cricket in the 1996 calendar year (with 793 runs). Cornhill England Player of the Year (for the second time) 1996-97. Appointed captain of England 1998 (though had captained England in a Test match for the first time v India at Madras 1992-93). Awarded MBE in HM The Queen's birthday honours list 1998. His 164 in England's second innings v South Africa at Old Trafford in 1998 was a record by a captain/wicket-keeper in Tests. Captained England in the 1999 World Cup; stood down as captain afterwards. Leading run-scorer in world Test cricket in the 1990s with 6407 runs (av. 40.81). Captained England v West Indies in the 100th Test played at Lord's in June 2000 (his own 99th Test appearance) in place of the injured Nasser Hussain. Made 126th One-Day International appearance v Zimbabwe at The Oval 2000, breaking Graham Gooch's England record of 125 ODIs. NatWest Man of the Series v Zimbabwe and West Indies 2000; during the tournament he became the second wicket-keeper (after Adam Gilchrist) to record six dismissals in a One-Day International (v Zimbabwe at Old Trafford) and recorded scores of 74*, 101, 100 and 97 in successive ODIs. Scored century (105) on his 100th Test appearance in the third Test v West Indies 2000, in the process taking part (with Marcus Trescothick) in a record England partnership for any wicket v West Indies at Lord's (179); his century won him the Man of the Match award and, taking place as it did on The Queen Mother's 100th birthday, also won him the Slazenger 'Sheer Instinct' award for 2000. Passed 7000 runs in Test cricket in first Test v Sri Lanka at Galle 2000-01. Passed 4000 runs in One-Day Internationals v Sri Lanka at Colombo 2000-01. England central contract 2001. Took 200th Test catch for England when he caught Rashid Latif off Darren Gough at Lord's 2001 in England's 100th Test match at the ground; it was Gough's 200th Test wicket. Shared in new record seventh-wicket partnership for Surrey in matches v Essex (206) with Alex Tudor at The Oval 2001. Captained England in the second Test v Pakistan and in the NatWest Series of ODIs 2001 in the absence of the injured Nasser Hussain. Scored 65 v Australia at Edgbaston 2001, in the process sharing with Andrew Caddick in the first century stand for the last wicket (103) since 1903-04 for England in Tests v Australia. Made himself unavailable for Test tour of India 2001-02
Opinions on cricket: 'Until the standard of pitches and practice pitches improves, the quality of cricket and cricketers won't.'
Best batting: 271* Surrey v Yorkshire, The Oval 1997
Best bowling: 1-7 Surrey v Lancashire, Old Trafford 1989

2001 Season

	M	Inns	NO	Runs	HS	Avge	100s	50s	Ct	St	O	M	Runs	Wkts	Avge	Best	5wI	10wM
Test	7	12	2	385	76 *	38.50	-	2	23	-								
All First	12	18	3	581	106	38.73	1	2	36	1	1	1	0	0	-	-	-	-
1-day Int	6	6	0	79	25	13.16	-	-	6	-								
C & G	1	1	0	19	19	19.00	-	-	-	-								
B & H	5	5	0	226	92	45.20	-	3	6	-								
1-day Lge	2	2	0	19	19	9.50	-	-	3	-								

Career Performances

	M	Inns	NO	Runs	HS	Avge	100s	50s	Ct	St	Balls	Runs	Wkts	Avge	Best	5wI	10wM
Test	115	207	17	7469	190	39.31	14	38	220	11	20	13	0	-	-	-	-
All First	417	689	75	24334	271 *	39.63	47	133	634	27	487	423	3	141.00	1-7	-	-
1-day Int	146	141	11	4100	116	31.53	4	23	136	11							
C & G	47	44	7	1837	125 *	49.64	3	13	54	5							
B & H	75	75	12	3040	167 *	48.25	4	23	57	11							
1-day Lge	183	167	17	4625	125	30.83	7	26	142	13	4	8	0	-	-	-

STRAUSS, A. J.   Middlesex

Name: <u>Andrew</u> John Strauss
Role: Left-hand bat, left-arm medium bowler, county vice-captain
Born: 2 March 1977, Johannesburg, South Africa
Height: 5ft 11in **Weight:** 13st
Nickname: Straussy, Johann, Levi, Mareman, Muppet
County debut: 1997 (one-day), 1998 (first-class)
County cap: 2001
1000 runs in a season: 1
1st-Class 50s: 14
1st-Class 100s: 4
1st-Class catches: 19
Place in batting averages: 50th av. 44.81 (2000 69th av. 33.15)
Parents: David and Dawn
Marital status: Single
Education: Caldicott Prep School; Radley College; Durham University
Qualifications: 4 A-levels, BA (Hons) Economics
Off-season: ECB National Academy to Australia

Overseas tours: Durham University to Zimbabwe 1997-98; Middlesex to South Africa 2000; ECB National Academy to Australia 2001-02

Overseas teams played for: Sydney University 1998-99; Mosman, Sydney 1999-2001

Career highlights to date: 'My first first-class hundred, v Northants 2000'

Cricket moments to forget: 'Getting out second ball of the season 2001 v Oxford UCCE!'

Cricketers particularly admired: Allan Donald, Brian Lara, Saqlain Mushtaq

Young players to look out for: Ed Joyce

Other sports played: Golf (Durham University 1998), rugby (Durham University 1996-97)

Other sports followed: 'Anything with a ball'

Injuries: 'Mentally scarred by trying to run between the wickets with David Nash!'

Relaxations: 'Any new economic theory books, especially on how chaos theory can influence accepted non-linear market forecasting models'

Extras: Opened the batting for Radley with Ben Hutton, with whom he has also opened at Middlesex. Scored 112* v Hampshire at West End 2001, in the process becoming the first Middlesex batsman to carry his bat since Mark Ramprakash did so against Kent in 1997. Middlesex Player of the Year 2001. Awarded Middlesex cap 2001. Appointed Middlesex vice-captain for 2002. PCA representative for Middlesex

Opinions on cricket: 'Let's not think that English cricket is on the edge of an abyss just because we lost to the Aussies. They are a very fine side. Many improvements in structure and attitude have already taken place in domestic cricket; with a few more we may just have a system that may help rather than hinder the performance of the national side.'

Best batting: 176 Middlesex v Durham, Lord's 2001

Stop press: Scored century (113) in ECB National Academy's innings victory over Commonwealth Bank [Australian] Cricket Academy in Adelaide 2001-02

2001 Season

	M	Inns	NO	Runs	HS	Avge	100s	50s	Ct	St	O	M	Runs	Wkts	Avge	Best	5wI	10wM
Test																		
All First	17	28	1	1210	176	44.81	3	6	7	-	1	0	3	0	-	-	-	-
1-day Int																		
C & G	1	1	0	4	4	4.00	-	-	-	-								
B & H	5	4	0	112	61	28.00	-	1	2	-								
1-day Lge	13	12	0	326	59	27.16	-	3	1	-								

Career Performances

	M	Inns	NO	Runs	HS	Avge	100s	50s	Ct	St	Balls	Runs	Wkts	Avge	Best	5wI	10wM
Test																	
All First	46	79	4	2706	176	36.08	4	14	19	-	12	16	0	-	-	-	-
1-day Int																	
C & G	4	4	0	114	56	28.50	-	1	-	-							
B & H	8	7	1	160	61	26.66	-	1	2	-							
1-day Lge	36	34	2	653	90	20.40	-	4	7	-							

STRONG, M. R.   Northamptonshire

Name: <u>Michael</u> Richard Strong
Role: Left-hand bat, right-arm
fast-medium bowler
Born: 28 June 1974, Cuckfield, West Sussex
Height: 6ft 1in **Weight:** 12st 10lbs
Nickname: Strongy, Strongbow, Lager
County debut: 1997 (one-day, Sussex),
1998 (first-class, Sussex), 2000
(Northamptonshire)
1st-Class catches: 4
Place in batting averages: 244th av. 12.22
Place in bowling averages: 140th av. 52.21
(2000 37th av. 22.41)
Strike rate: 81.00 (career 74.09)
Parents: David and Gillian
Marital status: Single
Family links with cricket: Father and
brother both played club cricket in Sussex

Education: St Peter's School, Burgess Hill; Brighton College; Brunel University
College (formerly West London Institute)
Qualifications: 9 GCSEs, 3 A-levels, BA/BSc (QTS) PE and Geography,
various coaching awards
Career outside cricket: 'PE teacher and lager drinker'
Overseas tours: Brighton College to India 1991-92; Northamptonshire
to Grenada 2000
Overseas teams played for: Umbilo CC, Durban 1992-93, 1997-2000
Cricketers particularly admired: 'WG', Ranjitsinhji
Other sports played: Football (Ardingly FC)
Other sports followed: Football (Chelsea and Brighton)
Relaxations: Cooking, travelling, golf, seeing friends
Extras: 'Would like to thank the master in charge of cricket at Brighton College, John
Spencer, for all the time he spent coaching me from the age of ten.' Most Improved
Sussex Player 1998. Left Sussex in 1999-2000 off-season and joined
Northamptonshire. NatWest Man of the Match v Yorkshire 2000. Released by
Northamptonshire at the end of the 2001 season
Best batting: 35* Sussex v Leicestershire, Arundel 1999
Best bowling: 4-46 Northamptonshire v Oxford Universities, The Parks 2000

2001 Season

	M	Inns	NO	Runs	HS	Avge	100s	50s	Ct	St	O	M	Runs	Wkts	Avge	Best	5wI	10wM
Test																		
All First	9	13	4	110	34	12.22	-	-	2	-	256.3	46	992	19	52.21	3-98	-	-
1-day Int																		
C & G	1	1	0	8	8	8.00	-	-	1	-	8.5	2	29	1	29.00	1-29	-	
B & H	1	0	0	0	0	-	-	-	-	-	10	0	47	2	23.50	2-47	-	
1-day Lge	7	4	2	27	11	13.50	-	-	1	-	56.2	2	371	14	26.50	4-28	-	

Career Performances

	M	Inns	NO	Runs	HS	Avge	100s	50s	Ct	St	Balls	Runs	Wkts	Avge	Best	5wI	10wM
Test																	
All First	15	23	8	235	35 *	15.66	-	-	4	-	2297	1426	31	46.00	4-46	-	-
1-day Int																	
C & G	3	3	0	30	21	10.00	-	-	1	-	155	101	6	16.83	3-10	-	
B & H	1	0	0	0	0	-	-	-	-	-	60	47	2	23.50	2-47	-	
1-day Lge	14	10	4	33	11	5.50	-	-	2	-	596	606	18	33.66	4-28	-	

STUBBINGS, S. D.   Derbyshire

Name: Stephen David Stubbings
Role: Left-hand opening bat, 'right-arm express bowler'
Born: 31 March 1978, Huddersfield
Height: 6ft 3in **Weight:** 15st 4lbs
Nickname: Stubbo
County debut: 1997
County cap: 2001
1000 runs in a season: 2
1st-Class 50s: 10
1st-Class 100s: 4
1st-Class catches: 13
Place in batting averages: 95th av. 33.77 (2000 80th av. 31.75)
Parents: David and Marie
Marital status: Single
Family links with cricket: 'My younger brother Jonathan is also an emerging fast-bowling all-rounder with Delacombe Park CC. My father has also played for the club, and Mum has driven me to enough games and training sessions for her to know more than she probably wants to about the game'
Education: Belvedere Park Primary; Frankston High School, Victoria, Australia; Swinburne University, Australia

Qualifications: Victorian Certificate of Education (VCE)
Overseas tours: Derbyshire to Portugal 2000
Overseas teams played for: Delacombe Park CC, Melbourne 1990-94; Frankston Peninsula CC, Victoria 1994-2000; Kingborough CC, Tasmania 2000-01
Cricketers particularly admired: Mark Taylor, Michael Atherton, Steve Waugh, Matthew Mott, Ricky Ponting
Young players to look out for: James Pyemont, Will Kendall, Gary Keedy, Sam Patel
Other sports followed: Aussie Rules (Essendon Bombers)
Relaxations: 'Fishing, golf, eating out, drinking with friends, sleeping, listening to music, watching sport'
Extras: Represented Victoria at U17, U19 and Colts levels. Won two-year scholarship at the Victorian Institute of Sport. Scored maiden first-class century (135*) v Kent at Canterbury 2000, taking part in an unbroken opening partnership of 293 with Steve Titchard (141*); it was the first occasion on which Derbyshire had batted all day without losing a wicket. Derbyshire Player of the Year 2001. Awarded Derbyshire cap 2001
Opinions on cricket: 'At the moment I think the game is very healthy from an international perspective, but here in England the game is ill. Too many matches, too many teams and too little quality practice time means county cricket is struggling to produce consistent world-class performers. I also believe for the long-term good of the game England need to become a power once again, or interest in the game itself could eventually die out.'
Best batting: 135* Derbyshire v Kent, Canterbury 2000

2001 Season

	M	Inns	NO	Runs	HS	Avge	100s	50s	Ct	St	O	M	Runs	Wkts	Avge	Best	5wI	10wM
Test																		
All First	17	31	0	1047	127	33.77	3	6	6	-	4	0	36	0	-	-	-	-
1-day Int																		
C & G	1	1	0	47	47	47.00	-	-	-	-								
B & H	2	2	0	28	16	14.00	-	-	-	-								
1-day Lge	13	13	1	254	96 *	21.16	-	2	3	-								

Career Performances

	M	Inns	NO	Runs	HS	Avge	100s	50s	Ct	St	Balls	Runs	Wkts	Avge	Best	5wI	10wM
Test																	
All First	41	75	4	2176	135 *	30.64	4	10	13	-	54	77	0	-	-	-	-
1-day Int																	
C & G	3	2	0	63	47	31.50	-	-	-	-							
B & H	9	7	1	50	16	8.33	-	-	-	-							
1-day Lge	35	34	2	640	96 *	20.00	-	3	4	-							

SUCH, P. M. — Essex

Name: <u>Peter</u> Mark Such
Role: Right-hand bat, off-spin bowler
Born: 12 June 1964, Helensburgh, Scotland
Height: 6ft **Weight:** 11st 7lbs
Nickname: Sushi, Suchy
County debut: 1982 (Nottinghamshire),
1987 (Leicestershire), 1990 (Essex)
County cap: 1991 (Essex)
Benefit: 2001 (Essex)
Test debut: 1993
Tests: 11
50 wickets in a season: 6
1st-Class 50s: 2
1st-Class 5 w. in innings: 48
1st-Class 10 w. in match: 9
1st-Class catches: 119
One-Day 5 w. in innings: 3
Place in batting averages: 255th av. 10.63

(2000 298th av. 5.88)
Place in bowling averages: 142nd av. 56.58 (2000 87th av. 29.30)
Strike rate: 108.04 (career 68.82)
Parents: John and Margaret
Wife and date of marriage: Nicola Jane, 25 September 1999
Family links with cricket: Father and brother both village cricketers
Education: Lantern Lane Primary; Harry Carlton Comprehensive, East Leake, Notts
Qualifications: 9 O-levels, 3 A-levels, advanced cricket coach, three Pitman computer training courses/diplomas
Off-season: 'Finishing off my benefit year'
Overseas tours: England A to Australia 1992-93, 1996-97, to South Africa 1993-94; England to Australia 1998-99
Overseas teams played for: Kempton Park, South Africa 1982-83; Bathurst, Australia 1985-86; Matabeleland, Zimbabwe 1989-92
Career highlights to date: 'Test debut v Australia 1993. Two Championships 1991 and 1992. Three Lord's finals 1996, 1997 and 1998'
Cricketers particularly admired: Bob White, Eddie Hemmings, Graham Gooch, John Childs
Young players to look out for: James Foster, Matthew Wood
Other sports played: Golf
Other sports followed: Rugby union
Relaxations: 'Music, playing golf, socialising with mates, reading'
Extras: Played for England YC v Australian YC 1983 and for TCCB XI v New

Zealand 1985. Left Nottinghamshire at end of 1986 season; joined Leicestershire in 1987 and was released at end of 1989; signed by Essex for 1990. Played in one-day games for England A v Sri Lanka 1991. Joint winner with J.H. Childs of the Essex Player of the Year Award 1992 and shared the award again in 1993. Took 6-67 on Test debut v Australia 1993 – best figures by an England Test debutant since John Lever in India 1976-77. Set record for the most overs bowled in a County Championship innings – 86 overs against Leicestershire in August 1997; he ended up with figures of 4 for 96. Set the unenviable record of having scored the longest duck in English Test history with his 72-minute innings in the third Test v New Zealand at Old Trafford 1999. Completed the set of five-wicket returns against all the first-class counties when he took 5-51 v Middlesex at Chelmsford 2000. Was vice-chairman of the Professional Cricketers' Association. Retired at the end of the 2001 season

Opinions on cricket: 'Two divisional format has added life to what would have been dead games. Everything matters throughout the season. Pitch Liaison Officers have been a success, but clubs should have no right of appeal for poor pitches. Need to keep the pressure on clubs over pitches. Central England contracts a good idea. County cricket now needs to look after itself by playing the sort of cricket people want to see, when they want to see it. It needs a better structure/format, in which spectators' and sponsors' interests are paramount.'

Best batting: 54 Essex v Worcestershire, Chelmsford 1993
54 Essex v Nottinghamshire, Chelmsford 1996
Best bowling: 8-93 Essex v Hampshire, Colchester 1995

2001 Season

	M	Inns	NO	Runs	HS	Avge	100s	50s	Ct	St	O	M	Runs	Wkts	Avge	Best	5wI	10wM
Test																		
All First	15	20	9	117	25	10.63	-	-	7	-	432.1	98	1358	24	56.58	5-131	1	-
1-day Int																		
C & G																			
B & H																			
1-day Lge																			

Career Performances

	M	Inns	NO	Runs	HS	Avge	100s	50s	Ct	St	Balls	Runs	Wkts	Avge	Best	5wI	10wM
Test	11	16	5	67	14 *	6.09	-	-	4	-	3124	1242	37	33.56	6-67	2	-
All First	306	327	125	1645	54	8.14	-	2	119	-	58443	25932	849	30.54	8-93	48	9
1-day Int																	
C & G	25	9	5	21	8 *	5.25	-	-	4	-	1554	872	25	34.88	3-56	-	
B & H	38	14	8	46	10 *	7.66	-	-	7	-	1947	1207	32	37.71	4-43	-	
1-day Lge	139	58	34	208	19 *	8.66	-	-	37	-	5507	4240	144	29.44	5-29	3	

SUTCLIFFE, I. J.   Leicestershire

Name: <u>Iain</u> John Sutcliffe
Role: Left-hand bat, leg-spin bowler, county vice-captain
Born: 20 December 1974, Leeds
Height: 6ft 2in **Weight:** 13st
Nickname: Sutty
County debut: 1995
County cap: 1997
1000 runs in a season: 1
1st-Class 50s: 24
1st-Class 100s: 6
1st-Class 200s: 1
1st-Class catches: 54
One-Day 100s: 2
Place in batting averages: 96th av. 33.46

(2000 179th av. 19.93)
Strike rate: 36.00 (career 46.87)
Parents: John and Valerie
Marital status: Single
Education: Leeds Grammar School; Oxford University
Qualifications: 10 GCSEs, 4 A-levels, 2.1 PPE degree
Off-season: Perth, Western Australia
Overseas tours: Leeds GS to Kenya; Leicestershire to South Africa, to West Indies, to Sri Lanka
Career highlights to date: 'Championship winner's medal 1998'
Cricket moments to forget: 'Losing C&G final 2001 and B&H final 1998'
Cricketers particularly admired: Brian Lara, David Gower
Young players to look out for: S. Jones, T. Roberts
Other sports played: Boxing (Oxford Blue 1994, 1995; British Universities Light-middleweight Champion 1993)
Other sports followed: Football (Liverpool)
Relaxations: Socialising, cinema
Extras: Played NCA England U14 and NCA Development Team U18/U19. In 1995, took part (with C. Gupte) in record partnership for Oxford University against a first-class county (283 v Hampshire at The Parks), in which he scored 163*. Scored 55 out of Leicestershire's first innings total of 96 v Pakistanis at Leicester 2001. Scored maiden first-class double hundred (203) v Glamorgan at Cardiff 2001. Scored 64 v Kent at Canterbury 2001, in the process sharing with Ben Smith in a Leicestershire record second-wicket partnership for matches against Kent (190). Appointed Leicestershire vice-captain for 2002
Opinions on cricket: 'Need to play less cricket in order to improve preparation and recovery. Should be day/night competition mid-season.'

Best batting: 203 Leicestershire v Glamorgan, Cardiff 2001
Best bowling: 2-21 Oxford University v Cambridge University, Lord's 1996

2001 Season

	M	Inns	NO	Runs	HS	Avge	100s	50s	Ct	St	O	M	Runs	Wkts	Avge	Best	5wI	10wM
Test																		
All First	17	31	1	1004	203	33.46	2	5	5	-	18	3	67	3	22.33	1-7	-	-
1-day Int																		
C & G																			
B & H																			
1-day Lge	5	5	0	166	48	33.20	-	-	2	-								

Career Performances

	M	Inns	NO	Runs	HS	Avge	100s	50s	Ct	St	Balls	Runs	Wkts	Avge	Best	5wI	10wM
Test																	
All First	105	163	13	4647	203	30.98	7	24	54	-	375	279	8	34.87	2-21	-	-
1-day Int																	
C & G	8	8	2	377	103 *	62.83	1	2	2	-							
B & H	15	15	1	425	105 *	30.35	1	3	2	-							
1-day Lge	29	28	1	580	96	21.48	-	2	9	-							

SUTTON, L. D. Derbyshire

Name: <u>Luke</u> David Sutton
Role: Right-hand bat, wicket-keeper
Born: 4 October 1976, Keynsham
Height: 5ft 11in **Weight:** 12st 7lbs
Nickname: Sutts
County debut: 1997 (Somerset),
2000 (Derbyshire)
1st-Class 50s: 3
1st-Class 100s: 2
1st-Class catches: 39
1st-Class stumpings: 1
Place in batting averages: 133rd av. 28.66
(2000 120th av. 27.13)
Parents: David and Molly
Marital status: Single
Education: Edgarley Hall, Glastonbury,
Somerset; Millfield School, Street, Somerset;
Durham University
Qualifications: 9 GCSEs, 4 A-levels, 2.1 degree in Economics, various cricket
coaching awards

Off-season: Playing grade cricket in Sydney, Australia
Overseas tours: Various Somerset Schools tours to Holland; West of England U15 to West Indies 1991; Millfield School to Zimbabwe 1993, to Sri Lanka 1994; Durham University to Zimbabwe 1997
Overseas teams played for: UNSW, Sydney 1998-99; Northville, Port Elizabeth, South Africa 1999-2000; Subiaco Marist, Perth 2000-01
Career highlights to date: 'Scoring my maiden first-class 100 v Warwickshire in 2001. Carrying my bat v Sussex in 2001, scoring 140*'
Cricket moments to forget: 'Scoring 0 on my Championship debut for Somerset v Leicestershire in 1997'
Cricketers particularly admired: Ian Healy, Steve Waugh, Adrian Pierson, Alec Stewart, Paul Nixon, Ian Salisbury, Anthony Wilcox, Marcus Trescothick
Young players to look out for: Nicky Peng, Chris Tremlett, 'all the young lads at Derbyshire'
Other sports played: Golf, football
Other sports followed: Football (Newcastle United), rugby (Bath)
Injuries: Out for last three weeks of season with broken right index finger
Relaxations: 'Keeping fit; eating out with friends; going to the cinema; spending time with my girlfriend Emma'
Extras: Captain of the England U15 side that played against South Africa and also played for England U18 and U19. Won John Hobbs Award for the U16 Cricketer of the Year in 1992 and the Gray Nicolls Award for the English Schools Cricketer of the Year in 1995. Left Somerset at the end of the 1999 season and joined Derbyshire for 2000. Voted Derbyshire 2nd XI Player of the Year 2000. NBC Denis Compton Award for the most promising young Derbyshire player 2000. Scored maiden first-class century (110*) v Warwicks at Edgbaston 2001. Scored 140* v Sussex at Derby 2001, in the process becoming the first Derbyshire batsman for five years to carry his bat
Opinions on cricket: 'Some serious thinking needs to be done over the amount of foreign players, who hide behind some vague link to British nationality, who are entering county cricket. They need to be asked officially which country they want to play for. Do we want to help homegrown players or not?'
Best batting: 140* Derbyshire v Sussex, Derby 2001

2001 Season

	M	Inns	NO	Runs	HS	Avge	100s	50s	Ct	St	O	M	Runs	Wkts	Avge	Best	5wI	10wM
Test																		
All First	15	27	3	688	140 *	28.66	2	1	9	-								
1-day Int																		
C & G	1	1	0	2	2	2.00	-	-	-	-								
B & H	5	5	0	42	26	8.40	-	-	3	-								
1-day Lge	10	10	2	139	42 *	17.37	-	-	5	1								

	M	Inns	NO	Runs	HS	Avge	100s	50s	Ct	St	Balls	Runs	Wkts	Avge	Best	5wI	10wM
Test																	
All First	28	49	7	1136	140 *	27.04	2	3	39	1							
1-day Int																	
C & G	3	3	0	68	45	22.66	-	-	1	-							
B & H	10	10	1	147	60	16.33	-	1	3	-							
1-day Lge	20	19	3	272	53 *	17.00	-	1	13	3							

SWANN, A. J. Lancashire

Name: <u>Alec</u> James Swann
Role: Right-hand bat, off-spin bowler,
occasional wicket-keeper
Born: 26 October 1976, Northampton
Height: 6ft 2in **Weight:** 12st 8lbs
Nickname: Ron
County debut: 1996 (Northamptonshire)
1st-Class 50s: 7
1st-Class 100s: 5
1st-Class catches: 28
Place in batting averages: 178th av. 21.77
Strike rate: 96.00 (career 90.60)
Parents: Ray and Mavis
Marital status: Single
Family links with cricket: Dad played for
Northumberland, Bedfordshire, Northants II
and England Amateurs. Still plays local
league cricket. Brother Graeme plays for

Northants and toured South Africa and Zimbabwe with England 1999-2000
Education: Sponne School, Towcester
Qualifications: 9 GCSEs, 4 A-levels, NCA coaching award
Off-season: 'Hopefully working locally and playing plenty of golf and a bit
of football'
Overseas tours: Northants to Zimbabwe 1998, to Grenada 2000, 2001
Overseas teams played for: Wallsend, NSW, Australia 1995-96, 1997-98;
Montrose CC, Cape Town 1998-99
Career highlights to date: 'Maiden first-class century and first wicket (an unlucky
Sri Lankan)'
Cricket moments to forget: 'Missing a run-out against Sussex from about a yard
from the stumps'
Cricketers particularly admired: Mark and Steve Waugh, Robin Smith,
Russell Warren

Young players to look out for: Ian Hunter, Graeme Swann
Other sports played: Golf, snooker, occasionally football
Other sports followed: Football (Newcastle United)
Relaxations: Reading, watching films, golf
Extras: Played for England Schools U15 and U19. Opened batting for Bedfordshire (with father in Minor Counties game). *Daily Telegraph* U15 Young Cricketer of the Year 1992. Midlands Club Cricket Conference Young Cricketer of the Year 1992. Played for England U19 against New Zealand U19 in 1996. Released by Northamptonshire at the end of the 2001 season and has joined Lancashire for 2002
Opinions on cricket: 'I think county cricket is unfairly criticised a lot of the time. The only thing that could be changed is the volume. I'm glad I don't (or can't) bowl.'
Best batting: 154 Northamptonshire v Nottinghamshire, Northampton 1999
Best bowling: 2-30 Northamptonshire v Gloucestershire, Northampton 2000

2001 Season

	M	Inns	NO	Runs	HS	Avge	100s	50s	Ct	St	O	M	Runs	Wkts	Avge	Best	5wI	10wM
Test																		
All First	13	22	0	479	113	21.77	1	2	9	-	16	4	50	1	50.00	1-31	-	-
1-day Int																		
C & G	1	0	0	0	0	-	-	-	-	-								
B & H	4	2	2	137	83*	-	-	2	-	-	3	0	20	0	-		-	-
1-day Lge	12	12	4	280	54	35.00	-	1	1	-	2	0	16	0	-		-	-

Career Performances

	M	Inns	NO	Runs	HS	Avge	100s	50s	Ct	St	Balls	Runs	Wkts	Avge	Best	5wI	10wM
Test																	
All First	44	70	2	1765	154	25.95	5	7	28	-	453	246	5	49.20	2-30	-	-
1-day Int																	
C & G	4	3	0	149	74	49.66	-	1	1	-	18	16	0	-		-	-
B & H	4	2	2	137	83*	-	-	2	-	-	18	20	0	-		-	-
1-day Lge	20	20	4	460	60	28.75	-	2	3	-	12	16	0	-		-	-

SWANN, G. P.   Northamptonshire

Name: <u>Graeme</u> Peter Swann
Role: Right-hand bat, off-spin bowler, 'benefit wicket-keeper'
Born: 24 March 1979, Northampton
Height: 6ft **Weight:** 11st 7lbs
Nickname: G-spot, Swanny, Cygnet, Cyggy, Junior
County debut: 1997 (one-day), 1998 (first-class)
County cap: 1999
One-Day Internationals: 1

50 wickets in a season: 1
1st-Class 50s: 12
1st-Class 100s: 2
1st-Class 5 w. in innings: 8
1st-Class 10 w. in match: 1
1st-Class catches: 48
One-Day 5 w. in innings: 1
Place in batting averages: 181st av. 21.72
(2000 136th av. 24.87)
Place in bowling averages: 131st av. 45.50
(2000 107th av. 33.31)
Strike rate: 84.50 (career 64.70)
Parents: Ray and Mave
Marital status: Single
Family links with cricket: Dad has played
Minor Counties cricket for Bedfordshire and
Northumberland and also for England
Amateurs. Brother was contracted to
Northants, now at Lancs. 'Cat is named after Gus Logie'
Education: Abington Vale Lower School; Sponne School, Towcester
Qualifications: 10 GCSEs, 4 A-levels, NCA coaching award
Career outside cricket: 'A spot of freelance journalism'
Off-season: National Academy, Australia
Overseas tours: England U19 to South Africa (including U19 World Cup) 1997-98;
England A to Zimbabwe and South Africa 1998-99, to West Indies 2000-01; England
to South Africa 1999-2000; ECB National Academy to Australia 2001-02
Career highlights to date: 'Being picked for England's tour to South Africa 1999'
Cricket moments to forget: 'Being hit for six by Peter Such'
Cricketers particularly admired: Don Bradman, Devon Malcolm, Neil Foster,
Shane Warne, the Waugh brothers
Young players to look out for: Tim Roberts, Alec Swann, 'Gus' Logan
Other sports played: Golf, rugby (Northants county schools), football, tennis
Other sports followed: Football (Newcastle United, Northampton Town), rugby
(Northampton Saints), golf
Injuries: Out for 'a session with severe right shoulder damage'
Relaxations: 'Walking my dog; spending time with girlfriend; scuba diving'
Extras: Played for England U14, U15, U17 and U19. *Daily Telegraph* regional
bowling award winner in 1994. Gray-Nicolls Len Newbery Schools Cricketer of the
Year in 1996. Took 8-118 for England U19 in second 'Test' v Pakistan U19 1998, the
best ever figures in an U19 'Test'. Drafted into England 13 for the fourth Test
v New Zealand 1999. Completed Championship double of 500 runs and 50 wickets
1999. Drafted into England A squad in West Indies 2000-01 as replacement for Jason
Brown who was promoted to the senior tour of Sri Lanka. Had match figures of 9-62
and scored 49 runs for England A v Windward Islands in St Lucia in the Busta Cup,
winning the Man of the Match award

Opinions on cricket: 'Two divisions works. Free hit rule after a no-ball should be introduced in all cricket. The City Sixes idea from the PCA is a good one and should be well supported by all progressive minds'
Best batting: 130* Northamptonshire v Sri Lanka A, Northampton 1999
Best bowling: 6-41 Northamptonshire v Leicestershire, Northampton 1999
Stop press: Scored half-century (77) and had match figures of 3-91 in ECB National Academy's innings victory over Commonwealth Bank [Australian] Cricket Academy in Adelaide 2001-02

2001 Season

	M	Inns	NO	Runs	HS	Avge	100s	50s	Ct	St	O	M	Runs	Wkts	Avge	Best	5wI	10wM
Test																		
All First	15	25	0	543	61	21.72	-	3	9	-	422.3	87	1365	30	45.50	5-34	1	-
1-day Int																		
C & G	2	1	0	2	2	2.00	-	-	1	-	14	0	84	1	84.00	1-33	-	
B & H	4	4	1	88	51 *	29.33	-	1	1	-	20	0	92	2	46.00	1-29	-	
1-day Lge	13	12	0	348	83	29.00	-	3	3	-	68.1	2	349	6	58.16	2-35	-	

Career Performances

	M	Inns	NO	Runs	HS	Avge	100s	50s	Ct	St	Balls	Runs	Wkts	Avge	Best	5wI	10wM
Test																	
All First	74	110	7	2699	130 *	26.20	2	12	48	-	12293	6148	190	32.35	6-41	8	1
1-day Int	1	0	0	0	0	-	-	-	-	-	30	24	0	-	-	-	
C & G	8	6	0	142	42	23.66	-	-	6	-	364	300	8	37.50	2-25	-	
B & H	7	5	1	116	51 *	29.00	-	1	1	-	222	166	5	33.20	2-31	-	
1-day Lge	53	42	3	860	83	22.05	-	6	11	-	1665	1381	47	29.38	5-35	1	

SYMINGTON, M. J.   Durham

Name: <u>Marc</u> Joseph Symington
Role: Right-hand bat, right-arm medium bowler
Born: 10 January 1980, Newcastle upon Tyne
Height: 5ft 8in **Weight:** 12st 7lbs
Nickname: Simo, Skids
County debut: 1998
1st-Class catches: 1
Strike rate: (career 45.71)
Parents: Keith and Sheila
Marital status: Single
Family links with cricket: Grandfather (Ron Symington) played 24 years in Northumberland League, then umpired in same league for 21 years. Father currently plays for Norton CC in North East Premier League. Brother (Craig) plays for Norton CC and Durham U19. Mother is club committee member

Education: St Joseph's, Norton, Stockton-on-Tees; St Michael's, Billingham, Stockton-on-Tees; Stockton Sixth Form College
Qualifications: 5 GCSEs, BTEC in Sports Science, Level I coach
Off-season: 'Playing golf and then three months in Perth'
Overseas tours: Durham U21 to Sri Lanka 1996; England U19 to New Zealand 1998-99
Overseas teams played for: Claremont-Nedlands, Perth 2000-01
Career highlights to date: 'Championship debut v Derbyshire. Promotion to division one of NUL [2001]. Watching Pengy bowl'
Cricket moments to forget: 'Being hit in box against own Academy'
Cricketers particularly admired: Graham Thorpe, Darren Gough, Adam Gilchrist
Young players to look out for: Nicky Peng, Ian Bell
Other sports played: Football ('played for Middlesbrough U16'), golf, hockey, snooker
Other sports followed: Football (Middlesbrough FC)
Injuries: Out for two months with a side tear
Relaxations: Playing golf and snooker and socialising with friends
Extras: Contracted player for Norton CC in 2000, scoring 466 runs (av. 42.36) and taking 25 wickets (av. 16.20)
Opinions on cricket: 'Third umpire is beginning to be used too much. Most decisions should be left to the umpires in the middle and the players' honesty.'
Best batting: 36 Durham v Yorkshire, Riverside 2000
Best bowling: 3-55 Durham v Derbyshire, Derby 1998

2001 Season (did not make any first-class or one-day appearances)

Career Performances

	M	Inns	NO	Runs	HS	Avge	100s	50s	Ct	St	Balls	Runs	Wkts	Avge	Best	5wI	10wM
Test																	
All First	3	3	2	52	36	52.00	-	-	1	-	320	215	7	30.71	3-55	-	-
1-day Int																	
C & G																	
B & H																	
1-day Lge	10	8	0	43	16	5.37	-	-	4	-	276	282	4	70.50	1-15	-	

SYMONDS, A.   Kent

Name: Andrew Symonds
Role: Right-hand bat, right-arm
medium or off-spin bowler
Born: 9 June 1975, Birmingham
Height: 6ft 1in **Weight:** 13st 5lbs
Nickname: Roy
County debut: 1995 (Gloucestershire),
1999 (Kent)
County cap: 1999 (Kent)
One-Day Internationals: 44
1000 runs in a season: 2
1st-Class 50s: 31
1st-Class 100s: 23
1st-Class 200s: 1
1st-Class catches: 78
One-Day 5 w. in innings: 2
Place in batting averages: 41st av. 46.91
Place in bowling averages: 82nd av. 33.30
Strike rate: 63.80 (career 74.81)
Parents: Ken and Barbara
Marital status: Single
Family links with cricket: Father played Minor Counties cricket
Education: All Saints Anglican School, Gold Coast, Australia; Ballarat and Clarendon
College, Australia
Qualifications: Level 2 coaching, professional fisherman
Off-season: Playing cricket in Australia
Overseas tours: Australia A to Los Angeles 1999; Australia to Pakistan 1998-99
(one-day series), to Sri Lanka and Zimbabwe 1999-2000 (one-day series), to New
Zealand 1999-2000 (one-day series), to India 2000-01 (one-day series), to England
2001 (one-day series)
Overseas teams played for: Australian Cricket Academy 1993-94; Queensland Colts
1993-94; Queensland 1994-95 –
Cricketers particularly admired: Viv Richards, Shane Warne, Michael Holding
Other sports followed: Hockey, rugby, football
Relaxations: Fishing, camping and hunting
Extras: Nickname 'Roy' reportedly coined by his father after comic-book character
'Roy of the Rovers'. Born in England, he was brought up in Australia and attended the
Australian Cricket Academy. In his first season of first-class cricket he scored a
century (108*) for Queensland against England on their 1994-95 tour of Australia,
sharing in an unbroken fifth-wicket partnership of 205 with Jimmy Maher. Hit a world
record number of sixes (16) during his innings of 254* for Gloucestershire v
Glamorgan 1995. Professional Cricketers' Association Young Player of the Year 1995.

Turned down the invitation to tour with England A in 1995 so that he could remain eligible to play for Australia. Made One-Day International debut for Australia v Pakistan, Lahore 1998. Scored 113 off 116 balls and took 4-83 for Queensland v Western Australia in the 1998-99 Sheffield Shield final. Joined Kent for 1999 as overseas player. Awarded Kent cap 1999; released by Kent at the end of the 1999 season. Rejoined Kent as overseas player part-way through the 2001 season as replacement for the injured Daryll Cullinan. C&G Man of the Match award for his 5-21 and 40-ball 39* v Northamptonshire at Canterbury 2001. Took 5-18 in title-clinching Norwich Union League victory v Warwickshire at Edgbaston 2001. Australian Cricket Board central contract 2001-02

Best batting: 254* Gloucestershire v Glamorgan, Abergavenny 1995
Best bowling: 4-39 Queensland v Western Australia, Perth 1998-99
Stop press: Struck 43-ball 75* in Queensland's victory over Western Australia in Pura Cup match at Brisbane 2001-02

2001 Season

	M	Inns	NO	Runs	HS	Avge	100s	50s	Ct	St	O	M	Runs	Wkts	Avge	Best	5wI	10wM
Test																		
All First	8	12	0	563	131	46.91	2	2	13	-	106.2	23	333	10	33.30	3-28	-	-
1-day Int	5	3	0	69	35	23.00	-	-	1	-	23	0	129	4	32.25	2-24	-	
C & G	3	2	1	43	39 *	43.00	-	-	-	-	19.3	3	60	8	7.50	5-21	1	
B & H																		
1-day Lge	9	9	0	221	74	24.55	-	1	2	-	46	3	170	9	18.88	5-18	1	

Career Performances

	M	Inns	NO	Runs	HS	Avge	100s	50s	Ct	St	Balls	Runs	Wkts	Avge	Best	5wI	10wM
Test																	
All First	123	204	17	7878	254 *	42.12	24	31	78	-	6808	3606	91	39.62	4-39	-	-
1-day Int	44	31	6	693	68 *	27.72	-	2	16	-	1418	1173	40	29.32	4-11	-	
C & G	11	10	1	326	87	36.22	-	2	2	-	281	179	10	17.90	5-21	1	
B & H	11	11	0	291	95	26.45	-	2	4	-	24	23	0	-	-	-	-
1-day Lge	47	46	2	1225	95	27.84	-	7	23	-	775	613	24	25.54	5-18	1	

82. Which future Zimbabwean Test cricketer played for Holland in the 1997 NatWest?

TAHIR, N.   Warwickshire

Name: Naqaash Tahir
Role: Right-hand bat, right-arm fast bowler
Born: 14 November 1983, Birmingham
Height: 5ft 10in **Weight:** 10st
Nickname: Naq, Naqy
County debut: No first-team appearance
Parents: Mohammed Amin and
Ishrat Nasreen
Marital status: Single
Family links with cricket: 'Brother Sheraz
plays for Worcestershire U16 and my father
also plays cricket'
Education: Nelson Mandela; Moseley
School; Spring Hill College

Qualifications: GCSEs, Level 1 coaching
Off-season: 'Planning to tour Pakistan'
Overseas tours: Warwickshire U15 to South
Africa 1999
Career highlights to date: 'Taking six wickets for just one run in four overs when I
was 15. Taking six wickets for West Bromwich Dartmouth 2001'
Cricket moments to forget: 'When I bowled two overs for 20 runs, bowling six
wides and eight no-balls'
Cricketers particularly admired: Darren Gough, Saeed Anwar, Ricky Ponting,
Glenn McGrath, Waqar Younis, Wasim Akram
Young players to look out for: Moeen Munir, Vishaal (Warwickshire U15)
Other sports played: Football ('at school with my mates')
Injuries: Out for five months with a back injury; for six weeks with a broken finger
Relaxations: Swimming, going to the gym, listening to music
Extras: Scored 103 in a 20-over match, setting a record for Moseley Ashfield U15.
Has been Moseley Ashfield U15 Player of the Year, Warwickshire U15 Youth Player of
the Year and top wicket-taker for Warwickshire U16
Opinions on cricket: 'I think that today's game is very competitive. There are lots of
good players that are ready to play good cricket. You need to work really hard on your
fitness and on the game.'

TAYLOR, B. V.   Sussex

Name: <u>Billy</u> Victor Taylor
Role: Left-hand bat, right-arm
medium bowler
Born: 11 January 1977, Southampton
Height: 6ft 3in **Weight:** 13st 7lbs
Nickname: Crusty, Beefy, Howzat, BT
County debut: 1999
1st-Class catches: 1
Strike rate: 54.50 (career 80.87)
Parents: Victor and Jackie
Marital status: Engaged
Family links with cricket: Brother James
plays for Wiltshire CCC
Education: Townhill Park; Bitterne Park;
Southampton Tech College
Qualifications: 5 GCSEs, NVQ Level 2
Carpentry and Joinery, Level 2 coaching
Career outside cricket: Carpenter
Off-season: 'Landscape gardening; cycling in New Forest; staying away from the
running track!'
Overseas tours: Sussex/Hampshire to Cyprus 1999
Overseas teams played for: Central Hawke's Bay, New Zealand 1996-97; Manawatu
Foxton CC and Horowhenua rep team, New Zealand 1998-99, 2000-01
Cricketers particularly admired: Malcolm Marshall, Glenn McGrath,
Michael Bevan
Other sports played: Golf
Other sports followed: Cricket (Wiltshire CCC) and football (Havant &
Waterlooville) – 'brother James plays for both'
Injuries: Out for all of pre-season after operation on left ankle; for three weeks after
breaking little finger of right hand on first day back
Relaxations: 'Golf, cycling, watching Havant & Waterlooville, swimming'
Extras: Played Minor Counties cricket for Wiltshire 1996-98 and has played club
cricket for Winchester KS since 1993. Took 98 wickets in New Zealand club cricket in
1998-99. Sussex 2nd XI Player of the Year 1999, 2000
Opinions on cricket: 'Should start at 10.30. New ball at 80 overs. Should have three
less four-day matches, then there would be more rest and preparation time.'
Best batting: 24* Sussex v Gloucestershire, Cheltenham 2001
Best bowling: 3-27 Sussex v Worcestershire, Worcester 2000

2001 Season

	M	Inns	NO	Runs	HS	Avge	100s	50s	Ct	St	O	M	Runs	Wkts	Avge	Best	5wI	10wM
Test																		
All First	4	3	1	35	24 *	17.50	-	-	-	-	72.4	20	258	8	32.25	2-5	-	-
1-day Int																		
C & G	1	0	0	0	0	-	-	-	-	-	10	1	34	1	34.00	1-34	-	
B & H																		
1-day Lge	10	6	2	34	19	8.50	-	-	5	-	75	13	282	14	20.14	3-29	-	

Career Performances

	M	Inns	NO	Runs	HS	Avge	100s	50s	Ct	St	Balls	Runs	Wkts	Avge	Best	5wI	10wM
Test																	
All First	10	11	5	58	24 *	9.66	-	-	1	-	1294	771	16	48.18	3-27	-	-
1-day Int																	
C & G	4	1	0	1	1	1.00	-	-	1	-	210	126	6	21.00	4-26	-	
B & H																	
1-day Lge	30	13	6	65	21 *	9.28	-	-	7	-	1254	934	38	24.57	3-22	-	

TAYLOR, C. G.   Gloucestershire

Name: Christopher (<u>Chris</u>) Glyn Taylor
Role: Right-hand bat, right-arm off-spin bowler
Born: 27 September 1976, Bristol
Height: 5ft 8in **Weight:** 10st
Nickname: Tales, Tootsie
County debut: 2000
County cap: 2001
1st-Class 50s: 4
1st-Class 100s: 4
1st-Class catches: 14
Place in batting averages: 43rd av. 46.50 (2000 130th av. 25.89)
Strike rate: (career 55.00)
Parents: Chris and Maggie
Wife and date of marriage: Sarah, 8 December 2001
Family links with cricket: Father and grandfather both played local club cricket
Education: Brentry Primary School; Colston's Collegiate School
Qualifications: GCSEs and A-levels
Career outside cricket: Teaching

Overseas teams played for: Harbord CC, Manly, Australia 2000
Cricket moments to forget: 'This year's [2001] B&H loss to Surrey at Lord's'
Cricketers particularly admired: Jonty Rhodes, Mark Waugh
Other sports played: Rugby, hockey (both county level); squash, tennis
Other sports followed: Rugby
Injuries: Out for two Championship and three Norwich Union League matches with a broken ankle
Relaxations: Fishing
Extras: Represented England Schools U18. In 1995-96 won the Cricket Society's A. A. Thomson Fielding Prize and Wetherell Award. Set school record of 278* v Hutton Grammar School. Made his highest score of 300* for Gloucestershire 2nd XI v Somerset 1999. Scored maiden first-class century (104) in the Championship match v Middlesex 2000, becoming the first player from any county to score a century at Lord's on Championship debut; also the first player to score a century for Gloucestershire in match that was both first-class and Championship debut. NBC Denis Compton Award for the most promising young Gloucestershire player 2000. His 196 v Nottinghamshire at Trent Bridge 2001 included 100 runs scored between lunch and tea on the first day. Awarded Gloucestershire cap 2001
Opinions on cricket: 'We must try to make the game more appealing to children.'
Best batting: 196 Gloucestershire v Nottinghamshire, Trent Bridge 2001
Best bowling: 3-126 Gloucestershire v Northamptonshire, Cheltenham 2000

2001 Season

	M	Inns	NO	Runs	HS	Avge	100s	50s	Ct	St	O	M	Runs	Wkts	Avge	Best	5wI	10wM
Test																		
All First	12	20	0	930	196	46.50	3	4	6	-								
1-day Int																		
C & G	2	2	0	57	32	28.50	-	-	1	-								
B & H	8	8	1	93	23	13.28	-	-	5	-								
1-day Lge	9	9	2	111	63*	15.85	-	1	1	-								

Career Performances

	M	Inns	NO	Runs	HS	Avge	100s	50s	Ct	St	Balls	Runs	Wkts	Avge	Best	5wI	10wM
Test																	
All First	24	42	3	1422	196	36.46	4	4	14	-	165	136	3	45.33	3-126	-	-
1-day Int																	
C & G	9	8	2	114	41	19.00	-	-	6	-							
B & H	13	10	2	125	23*	15.62	-	-	5	-							
1-day Lge	22	17	3	186	63*	13.28	-	1	5	-							

TAYLOR, C. R.   Yorkshire

Name: Christopher (<u>Chris</u>) Robert Taylor
Role: Right-hand opening bat, 'right-arm
fast-medium bowler'
Born: 21 February 1981, Leeds
Height: 6ft 4in **Weight:** 14st 6lbs
Nickname: CT, Barthez, Corpse
County debut: 2001
1st-Class catches: 1
Place in batting averages: 261st av. 10.00
Parents: Phil and Elaine
Marital status: Single
Family links with cricket: Brother Matthew
plays in Bradford League for Drighlington
Education: Waterloo Infant and Junior
School, Pudsey; Benton Park High School,
Leeds

Qualifications: 9 GCSEs, 4 A-levels
Off-season: Playing for Western Suburbs CC,
Sydney ('the Magpies'). Going to Grenada with Yorkshire on pre-season tour
Overseas teams played for: Western Suburbs CC, Sydney 1999-2002
Career highlights to date: 'To have played in the team that won the 2001 County
Championship! On a personal note, my first-class debut against Surrey in August'
Cricket moments to forget: 'All the innings I didn't get any runs this season. Being
hit on the head at short leg v Essex 2001 after the ball had gone 15 feet in the air!'
Cricketers particularly admired: Geoffrey Boycott, Michael Vaughan,
Darren Lehmann, Matthew Wood
Young players to look out for: Michael Clarke (NSW), Steve Phillips (NSW)
Other sports played: Rugby, football, tennis, basketball (all for Benton Park HS
1st teams)
Other sports followed: Football (Everton – 'since I was four years old'), 'enjoy
watching all sports'
Injuries: Out for two weeks with a broken toe
Relaxations: 'Watching cricket; going to the beaches of Sydney; going out
with mates!'
Extras: Represented Yorkshire U10-U17. Represented North of England at Bunbury
Festival 1996 and was awarded Neil Lloyd Trophy for top run-scorer in festival.
Selected for England U15 team for Lombard World Cup 1996. Has also represented
England U17 and U19. Yorkshire CCC Supporters' Club Young Player of the Year
1999. Awarded Yorkshire 2nd XI cap 2001
Opinions on cricket: 'I believe the step up from 2nd XI to 1st XI is widening due to
the terrible ground conditions/practice facilities etc. in the 2nd XI. How can a 2nd XI

player improve to the standard or learn to become a first-class cricketer when playing at poor-quality club grounds with poor wickets? Also, please could we have a rule introduced for the size of changing rooms in the 2nd XI? You have to get 11 players in, not four!'

Best batting: 18 Yorkshire v Surrey, The Oval 2001

2001 Season

	M	Inns	NO	Runs	HS	Avge	100s	50s	Ct	St	O	M	Runs	Wkts	Avge	Best	5wI	10wM
Test																		
All First	3	6	0	60	18	10.00	-	-	1	-								
1-day Int																		
C & G																		
B & H																		
1-day Lge																		

Career Performances

	M	Inns	NO	Runs	HS	Avge	100s	50s	Ct	St	Balls	Runs	Wkts	Avge	Best	5wI	10wM
Test																		
All First	3	6	0	60	18	10.00	-	-	1	-								
1-day Int																		
C & G																		
B & H																		
1-day Lge																		

83. When Worcestershire skittled Lancashire for 59 in the semi-finals of the 1963 Gillette Cup, the former's bowling attack included a future FA Cup winning goalkeeper. Who was he?

TAYLOR, J. P.   Northamptonshire

Name: Jonathan <u>Paul</u> Taylor
Role: Left-hand bat, left-arm
fast-medium bowler, occasional left-arm
spin bowler
Born: 8 August 1964, Ashby-de-la-Zouch
Height: 6ft 2in **Weight:** 14st
Nickname: Roadie, PT
County debut: 1984 (Derbyshire),
1991 (Northamptonshire)
County cap: 1992 (Northamptonshire)
Benefit: 2000
Test debut: 1992-93
Tests: 2

One-Day Internationals: 1
50 wickets in a season: 6
1st-Class 50s: 9
1st-Class 5 w. in innings: 18
1st-Class 10 w. in match: 4
1st-Class catches: 61
One-Day 5 w. in innings: 1
Place in batting averages: 197th av. 19.50 (2000 267th av. 10.66)
Place in bowling averages: 133rd av. 46.37 (2000 38th av. 22.50)
Strike rate: 78.48 (career 57.31)
Parents: Derek (deceased) and Janet
Wife and date of marriage: Elaine Mary, 30 July 1993
Children: Christopher Paul, 8 July 1994; Danny Michael, 6 February 1997
Family links with cricket: Father and brother played local league cricket
Education: Pingle School, Swadlincote, Derbyshire
Qualifications: 6 O-levels, NCA senior coach
Overseas tours: Midland Club Cricket Conference to Australia 1990-91; England to
India and Sri Lanka 1992-93; England A to South Africa 1993-94; Northamptonshire
to Natal 1993, to Zimbabwe 1995, 1998, to Johannesburg 1996, to Grenada 2000
Overseas teams played for: Papakura, New Zealand 1984-85; Napier High School
Old Boys, New Zealand 1985-86; North Kalgoorlie, Western Australia 1990-91;
Great Boulder, Western Australia 1991-92; Montrose CC, Cape Town 1998-99
Cricketers particularly admired: Dennis Lillee, Courtney Walsh, Curtly Ambrose
Other sports followed: Soccer, rugby, basketball
Relaxations: 'Looking after two hyperactive little lads. Relaxing … I think not;
enjoyable … definitely!'
Extras: Spent four seasons on the staff at Derbyshire 1984-87 and played Minor
Counties cricket for Staffordshire 1989-90. Won Man of the Match in the Bain

Clarkson Final in 1987 for Derbyshire, after being released. Played first game at Lord's in NatWest Trophy final 1992. Was voted Northamptonshire's Player of the Year in 1992. Selected for England Indoor World Cup squad 1995. Scored maiden one-day 50 (57) v Kent at Canterbury in the C&G 2001. Retired at the end of the 2001 season, taking 4-100 and scoring 33 and 53 in his final Championship match v Somerset at Taunton 2001

Opinions on cricket: 'Two divisions has proved how much more competitive every game of cricket can be. Players are being asked to play under pressure all the time, which I believe will enhance the performance of the player when he makes the England team.'

Best batting: 86 Northamptonshire v Durham, Northampton 1995
Best bowling: 7-23 Northamptonshire v Hampshire, Bournemouth 1992

2001 Season

	M	Inns	NO	Runs	HS	Avge	100s	50s	Ct	St	O	M	Runs	Wkts	Avge	Best	5wI	10wM
Test																		
All First	12	17	3	273	53	19.50	-	1	3	-	379.2	49	1345	29	46.37	4-100	-	-
1-day Int																		
C & G	1	1	0	57	57	57.00	-	1	-	-	10	2	38	1	38.00	1-38	-	
B & H																		
1-day Lge	11	9	1	51	19	6.37	-	-	3	-	90	5	403	11	36.63	3-28	-	

Career Performances

	M	Inns	NO	Runs	HS	Avge	100s	50s	Ct	St	Balls	Runs	Wkts	Avge	Best	5wI	10wM
Test	2	4	2	34	17 *	17.00	-	-	-	-	288	156	3	52.00	1-18	-	-
All First	183	213	65	2253	86	15.22	-	9	61	-	32038	16618	559	29.72	7-23	18	4
1-day Int	1	1	0	1	1	1.00	-	-	-	-	18	20	0	-	-	-	-
C & G	31	13	6	97	57	13.85	-	1	6	-	1827	1220	40	30.50	4-34	-	
B & H	32	14	7	62	14	8.85	-	-	6	-	1797	1101	42	26.21	5-45	1	
1-day Lge	138	54	22	294	24	9.18	-	-	32	-	5993	4585	153	29.96	4-41	-	

84. In which year did Minor Counties first take part in the Gillette/NatWest/C&G?

THOMAS, I. J. Glamorgan

Name: <u>Ian</u> James Thomas
Role: Left-hand bat, right-arm
off-spin bowler
Born: 9 May 1979, Newport, Gwent
Height: 5ft 11in **Weight:** 14st
Nickname: Bolts, Homer, Bull
County debut: 2000
1st-Class 50s: 2
1st-Class catches: 7
Place in batting averages: 198th av. 19.40
Parents: Alun and Amanda
Marital status: Single

Family links with cricket: 'The old man is a
local legend, playing with brother for the
village team, the Machen Buzzards. Mother
brings the whites up lovely'
Education: Machen Primary School;
Bassaleg Comprehensive; University of
Wales Institute Cardiff (UWIC)
Qualifications: 9 GCSEs, 2 A-levels, BSc (Hons) Sports Development (2.2)
Career outside cricket: Management, marketing, sports development
Off-season: 'At the Paul Terry "fat camp" academy in Perth working at my fitness and
all aspects of my game'
Overseas tours: British Universities to South Africa 1999
Career highlights to date: 'Championship debut 2000'
Cricketers particularly admired: Steve James, Adrian Dale, Matthew Maynard,
Darren Thomas
Young players to look out for: Mark Wallace, Mike Powell, Simon Jones,
Matthew Wood, Richard Dawson, James Pipe
Other sports played: Rugby (Machen RFC)
Other sports followed: Rugby (Newport RFC)
Relaxations: Golf, fishing, eating out, reading, Internet
Extras: Glamorgan Young Player of the Month June, July, August and September
2000. Scored 82 on Championship debut v Essex at Southend 2000
Opinions on cricket: 'Still not enough experience to make comments.'
Best batting: 82 Glamorgan v Essex, Southend 2000

2001 Season

	M	Inns	NO	Runs	HS	Avge	100s	50s	Ct	St	O	M	Runs	Wkts	Avge	Best	5wI	10wM
Test																		
All First	6	11	1	194	59	19.40	-	1	2	-	3	1	2	0	-		-	-	-
1-day Int																		
C & G	1	1	0	11	11	11.00	-	-	1	-								
B & H																			
1-day Lge	7	6	0	179	53	29.83	-	1	1	-								

Career Performances

	M	Inns	NO	Runs	HS	Avge	100s	50s	Ct	St	Balls	Runs	Wkts	Avge	Best	5wI	10wM
Test																	
All First	10	17	3	380	82	27.14	-	2	7	-	18	2	0	-		-	-
1-day Int																	
C & G	1	1	0	11	11	11.00	-	-	1	-							
B & H																		
1-day Lge	11	10	0	279	53	27.90	-	1	3	-							

THOMAS, S. D.   Glamorgan

Name: Stuart <u>Darren</u> Thomas
Role: Left-hand bat, right-arm
fast-medium bowler
Born: 25 January 1975, Morriston
Height: 6ft **Weight:** 13st
Nickname: Teddy
County debut: 1992
County cap: 1997
50 wickets in a season: 4
1st-Class 50s: 13
1st-Class 100s: 1
1st-Class 5 w. in innings: 15
1st-Class catches: 43
One-Day 5 w. in innings: 3
Place in batting averages: 128th av. 29.57
(2000 131st av. 25.84)
Place in bowling averages: 135th av. 50.54
(2000 85th av. 28.78)
Strike rate: 76.39 (career 51.92)
Parents: Stuart and Anne
Wife and date of marriage: Claire, 30 September 2000
Family links with cricket: 'Dad used to play local club cricket for Llanelli'

Education: Old Road, Llanelli; Graig Comprehensive, Llanelli;
Neath Tertiary College
Qualifications: 5 GCSEs, BTEC National Diploma in Sports Studies,
Level 2 coaching award, 'and all the DIY knowledge in the world'
Off-season: 'Moving into my new home. A few holidays (four or five). Becoming
slim again for next year's pre-season'
Overseas tours: Glamorgan to Cape Town 1993, 1999, to Zimbabwe 1994,
to Pretoria 1995, to Portugal 1996, to Jersey 1998; England U18 to South Africa
1992-93; England U19 to Sri Lanka 1993-94; England A to Zimbabwe and South
Africa 1998-99, to Bangladesh and New Zealand 1999-2000
Overseas teams played for: Rovers CC, Welkom, Free State 1994
Career highlights to date: 'Winning the County Championship 1997'
Cricket moments to forget: 'Getting relegated this year [2001] in the four-day game'
Cricketers particularly admired: Robert Croft, Matt Maynard, Stuart Law,
Malcolm Marshall, Ian Botham
Young players to look out for: Simon Jones, Mark Wallace
Injuries: 'Ear drum injury – loss of balance due to the constant moaning of
Andrew Davies'
Relaxations: 'Enjoy seeing the globe, eating out'
Extras: Became youngest player (17 years 217 days) to take five wickets (5-80) on
debut, v Derbyshire in 1992, and finished eighth in national bowling averages. BBC
Welsh Young Sports Personality 1992. Played in third U19 'Test' against India at
Edgbaston 1994. Bettered Alan Wilkins's Glamorgan best B&H bowling figures on his
debut in the competition with 6 for 20 v Combined Universities in 1995. Took 7-16 v
Surrey in the Sunday League in 1998, the best analysis by a Glamorgan bowler in the
competition. Glamorgan Player of the Year 1998. Took 8-50 for England A v
Zimbabwe A at Harare on 1998-99 tour – the first eight-wicket haul by an England A
tourist. Scored maiden first-class century v Essex at Chelmsford 2001, his 138 being a
record Championship score by a Glamorgan No. 8
Opinions on cricket: 'Need a day's rest in between four-day cricket and one-day
cricket. Body needs time to recover. Please!'
Best batting: 138 Glamorgan v Essex, Chelmsford 2001
Best bowling: 8-50 England A v Zimbabwe A, Harare 1998-99

2001 Season

	M	Inns	NO	Runs	HS	Avge	100s	50s	Ct	St	O	M	Runs	Wkts	Avge	Best	5wI	10wM
Test																		
All First	15	21	2	562	138	29.57	1	4	5	-	420.1	56	1668	33	50.54	4-54	-	-
1-day Int																		
C & G	2	2	1	33	19 *	33.00	-	-	-	-	16	0	79	2	39.50	2-27	-	
B & H	4	4	2	67	28 *	33.50	-	-	-	-	28	3	144	2	72.00	1-45	-	
1-day Lge	16	12	5	146	25 *	20.85	-	-	3	-	87.3	5	418	18	23.22	3-27	-	

Career Performances

	M	Inns	NO	Runs	HS	Avge	100s	50s	Ct	St	Balls	Runs	Wkts	Avge	Best	5wI	10wM
Test																	
All First	127	171	35	2784	138	20.47	1	13	43	-	20564	12230	396	30.88	8-50	15	-
1-day Int																	
C & G	14	12	2	167	40	16.70	-	-	2	-	813	638	25	25.52	5-74	1	
B & H	20	15	6	180	29	20.00	-	-	5	-	848	745	26	28.65	6-20	1	
1-day Lge	73	55	11	571	38 *	12.97	-	-	11	-	2642	2206	91	24.24	7-16	1	

THORPE, A. M. Durham

Name: <u>Ashley</u> Michael Thorpe
Role: Left-hand bat, right-arm
medium bowler
Born: 2 April 1975, Kiama,
New South Wales
Height: 5ft 11in **Weight:** 14st 9lbs
Nickname: Ash, Thorpy
County debut: No first-team appearance
Parents: Michael and Helen
Wife and date of marriage: Kathleen,
18 April 1998
Children: Michael Nicholas,
11 December 1998
Family links with cricket: 'Father played for
Albion Park and now plays for Scarborough
CC veterans in Western Australia'
Education: Albion Park Primary School,
NSW; Kent St Senior High School, WA
Career outside cricket: Qualified trainer with London Electricity
Off-season: 'As above at London Electricity'
Overseas teams played for: Scarborough CC, Western Australia 1996-97
Extras: Has played for Chester-le-Street in the North East Premier League. Scored
138 and 85 on 2nd XI debut v Yorkshire 2nd XI. Is not considered an overseas player

---

85. When Sussex met Lancashire in the 1986 NatWest final,
one of the former's opening bowlers was a Pakistan Test player
and the other was a South African. Who were they?

THORPE, G. P.   Surrey

Name: <u>Graham</u> Paul Thorpe
Role: Left-hand bat, occasional
right-arm medium bowler
Born: 1 August 1969, Farnham
Height: 5ft 10in **Weight:** 12st 9lbs
Nickname: Chalky
County debut: 1988
County cap: 1991
Benefit: 2000
Test debut: 1993
Tests: 69
One-Day Internationals: 68
1000 runs in a season: 8
1st-Class 50s: 98
1st-Class 100s: 37
1st-Class 200s: 3
1st-Class catches: 240
One-Day 100s: 7
Place in batting averages: 11th av. 61.42 (2000 146th av. 23.50)
Strike rate: (career 92.84)
Parents: 'Mr and Mrs Thorpe'
Children: Henry and Amelia
Family links with cricket: Both brothers play for Farnham, father also plays cricket
and mother is 'professional scorer'
Education: Weydon Comprehensive; Farnham College
Qualifications: 7 O-levels, PE Diploma
Off-season: Touring with England
Overseas tours: England A to Zimbabwe and Kenya 1989-90, to Pakistan 1990-91,
to Bermuda and West Indies 1991-92, to Australia 1992-93; England to West Indies
1993-94, to Australia 1994-95, to South Africa 1995-96, to India and Pakistan
(World Cup) 1995-96, to Zimbabwe and New Zealand 1996-97, to Sharjah
(Champions Trophy) 1997-98, to West Indies 1997-98, to Australia 1998-99, to
Sharjah (Coca-Cola Cup) 1998-99, to Kenya (ICC Knockout Trophy) 2000-01, to
Pakistan and Sri Lanka 2000-01, to India and New Zealand 2001-02 (*see Stop press*)
Cricketers particularly admired: Grahame Clinton, Waqar Younis, Ian Botham,
Viv Richards
Young players to look out for: Ian Ward, Ben Hollioake
Other sports followed: Football (Chelsea FC), golf
Injuries: Out for much of 2001 season with a calf injury followed by a broken hand
Relaxations: Sleeping
Extras: Played for English Schools cricket U15 and U19 and England Schools

football U18. Scored a century (114*) against Australia on his Test debut at Trent Bridge 1993. Shared in a record fifth-wicket partnership for England in Tests v West Indies (150) with Alec Stewart at Bridgetown 1993-94. Shared in a record fourth-wicket partnership for England in Tests v Australia (288) with Nasser Hussain at Edgbaston 1997. England's Player of the Series and leading run-scorer in the 1997 Ashes campaign with 453 runs at an average of 50.33. Shared in a record sixth-wicket partnership for England in Tests v West Indies (205) with Mark Ramprakash at Bridgetown 1997-98. Cornhill England Player of the Year 1997-98. One of *Wisden*'s Five Cricketers of the Year 1998. Represented England in the 1999 World Cup. Reached 2000 One-Day International runs in third ODI v Pakistan at Rawalpindi 2000-01. With Craig White, shared in a new record sixth-wicket partnership for England in Tests v Pakistan (166) in the first Test at Lahore 2000-01; his century was the first in Test history to contain only one boundary (he added a second four before being out for 118). Scored match-winning 64* in third Test at Karachi 2000-01 to steer England to a series victory v Pakistan. Man of the Match in third Test v Sri Lanka at Colombo 2000-01 for his 113* followed by 32* out of 74-6 as England completed series win over Sri Lanka. Captained England in one-day series v Sri Lanka 2000-01. England central contract 2001. Shared in a record partnership for any wicket for England in Tests v Pakistan (267) with Michael Vaughan at Old Trafford 2001. England Man of the Series v Pakistan 2001

Best batting: 223* England v South Australia, Adelaide 1998-99
Best bowling: 4-40 Surrey v Australians, The Oval 1993
Stop press: Called up for England one-day tour to Zimbabwe 2001-02 after the withdrawal of Craig White through injury. Returned early from England Test tour of India 2001-02 but returned for one-day section

2001 Season

	M	Inns	NO	Runs	HS	Avge	100s	50s	Ct	St	O	M	Runs	Wkts	Avge	Best	5wI	10wM
Test	3	5	0	250	138	50.00	1	1	6	-								
All First	5	7	0	430	148	61.42	2	1	8	-	1	0	11	0	-	-	-	-
1-day Int																		
C & G																		
B & H	5	5	1	65	23 *	16.25	-	-	-	-								
1-day Lge																		

Career Performances

	M	Inns	NO	Runs	HS	Avge	100s	50s	Ct	St	Balls	Runs	Wkts	Avge	Best	5wI	10wM
Test	69	126	16	4498	138	40.89	9	28	73	-	138	37	0	-	-	-	-
All First	276	459	64	17703	223 *	44.81	40	98	240	-	2321	1305	25	52.20	4-40	-	-
1-day Int	68	64	11	2099	89	39.60	-	19	35	-	120	97	2	48.50	2-15	-	
C & G	30	29	8	1159	145 *	55.19	1	9	18	-	13	12	0	-	-	-	-
B & H	53	51	5	1718	103	37.34	1	12	20	-	168	131	4	32.75	3-35	-	
1-day Lge	129	119	17	3831	126 *	37.55	5	26	51	-	318	307	8	38.37	3-21	-	

TITCHARD, S. P. Derbyshire

Name: <u>Stephen</u> Paul Titchard
Role: Right-hand bat, right-arm
medium bowler
Born: 17 December 1967,
Warrington
Height: 6ft 3in **Weight:** 15st
Nickname: Titch, Stainy, Tyrone
County debut: 1990 (Lancs), 1999 (Derbys)
1st-Class 50s: 30
1st-Class 100s: 6
1st-Class catches: 54
Place in batting averages: (2000 85th
av. 31.17)
Strike rate: (career 97.50)
Parents: Alan and Margaret
Marital status: Single
Family links with cricket: Father, uncle and

two brothers have played for Grappenhall
1st XI in the Manchester Association League. Father also represented the Army
Education: Lymm County High School; Priestley College
Qualifications: 3 O-levels, NCA senior coaching award
Career outside cricket: Coach
Overseas tours: Lancashire to Tasmania and Western Australia 1990, to Western
Australia 1991, to Johannesburg 1992
Overseas teams played for: South Canberra, Australia 1991-92
Cricketers particularly admired: Graham Gooch, Malcolm Marshall
Other sports followed: Football (Manchester City) and rugby league (Warrington)
Relaxations: Snooker, golf, 'most sports'
Extras: Played for England U19. Made record scores for Manchester Association U18
(200*) and Cheshire Schools U19 (203*). Released by Lancashire at the end of the
1998 season and joined Derbyshire. Took part in an unbroken opening partnership of
293 with Steve Stubbings (135*) v Kent at Canterbury 2000, scoring 141*; it was the
first occasion on which Derbyshire had batted all day without losing a wicket.
Released by Derbyshire at the end of the 2001 season
Best batting: 163 Lancashire v Essex, Chelmsford 1996
Best bowling: 1-11 Lancashire v Northamptonshire, Old Trafford 1997
               1-11 Lancashire v Kent, Old Trafford 1997

	M	Inns	NO	Runs	HS	Avge	100s	50s	Ct	St	O	M	Runs	Wkts	Avge	Best	5wI	10wM
Test																		
All First	3	5	0	92	39	18.40	-	-	-	-								
1-day Int																		
C & G																		
B & H																		
1-day Lge																		

Career Performances

	M	Inns	NO	Runs	HS	Avge	100s	50s	Ct	St	Balls	Runs	Wkts	Avge	Best	5wI	10wM
Test																	
All First	107	186	14	5319	163	30.92	6	30	54	-	390	195	4	48.75	1-11	-	-
1-day Int																	
C & G	6	6	1	142	92	28.40	-	1	1	-							
B & H	8	4	0	108	82	27.00	-	1	2	-							
1-day Lge	47	46	4	1002	96	23.85	-	3	5	-	54	48	1	48.00	1-19	-	

TOLLEY, C. M.   Nottinghamshire

Name: Christopher (<u>Chris</u>) Mark Tolley
Role: Right-hand bat, left-arm medium bowler
Born: 30 December 1967, Kidderminster
Height: 5ft 9in   **Weight:** 11st 7lbs
Nickname: Red Dog, Warrior
County debut: 1989 (Worcestershire), 1996 (Nottinghamshire)
County cap: 1993 (Worcestershire), 1997 (Nottinghamshire)
1st-Class 50s: 13
1st-Class 5 w. in innings: 5
1st-Class catches: 42
One-Day 5 w. in innings: 1
Place in batting averages: (2000 111th av. 27.87)
Strike rate: (career 72.39)
Parents: Ray and Liz
Wife and date of marriage: Simone, 12 December 1998
Family links with cricket: Brother (Richard) plays for Blossomfield CC
Education: Oldswinford C of E; Redhill Comprehensive School; King Edward VI College, Stourbridge; Loughborough University

Qualifications: 9 O-levels, 3 A-levels, BSc (Hons) PE, Sports Science & Recreation Management, QTS, SMT Dip, advanced cricket coach and Level II hockey coach
Career outside cricket: PE teacher
Overseas tours: British Universities Sports Federation to Barbados, October 1989; Worcestershire to Zimbabwe and South Africa; Nottinghamshire to South Africa
Overseas teams played for: Lancaster Park, Christchurch, New Zealand 1996-97
Cricketers particularly admired: Ian Botham, Graeme Hick
Young players to look out for: Ed Joyce
Other sports played: Hockey (South Notts HC)
Relaxations: 'Food, wine and now gardening (I must be getting old)'
Extras: Played for English Schools U19 in 1986 and for the Combined Universities in B&H Cup. Asked to be released by Worcestershire at the end of the 1995 season and joined Nottinghamshire for the 1996 season. Took first-class hat-trick against Leicestershire in 1997. Appointed as a Cricket Development Officer at Nottinghamshire in autumn 2000. Played for Nottinghamshire Board XI in the C&G 2001 and in the first round of the C&G 2002, which was played in August 2001. Retired at the end of the 2001 season and is Nottinghamshire Academy director, but remains registered as a player. Granted a benefit for 2002
Opinions on cricket: 'Two divisions seems to be working – more to play for over a longer period.'
Best batting: 84 Worcestershire v Derbyshire, Derby 1994
Best bowling: 7-45 Nottinghamshire v Worcestershire, Kidderminster 1998

2001 Season

	M	Inns	NO	Runs	HS	Avge	100s	50s	Ct	St	O	M	Runs	Wkts	Avge	Best	5wI	10wM
Test																		
All First	1	0	0	0	0	-	-	-	-	-								
1-day Int																		
C & G	2	2	0	112	78	56.00	-	1	-	-	17.4	4	69	1	69.00	1-38	-	
B & H																		
1-day Lge																		

Career Performances

	M	Inns	NO	Runs	HS	Avge	100s	50s	Ct	St	Balls	Runs	Wkts	Avge	Best	5wI	10wM
Test																	
All First	107	148	31	2666	84	22.78	-	13	42	-	13682	6623	189	35.04	7-45	5	-
1-day Int																	
C & G	16	13	3	314	78	31.40	-	2	1	-	874	534	18	29.66	3-21	-	
B & H	23	20	3	414	77	24.35	-	3	3	-	1080	691	9	76.77	1-12	-	
1-day Lge	94	61	14	783	44	16.65	-	-	27	-	3257	2537	95	26.70	5-16	1	

TOMLINSON, J. A.   Hampshire

Name: <u>James</u> Andrew Tomlinson
Role: Left-hand lower-order bat,
left-arm fast bowler
Born: 12 June 1982, Winchester
Height: 6ft 1in **Weight:** 12st 4lbs
Nickname: Tommo, Dangerous Dave, Norm
County debut: No first-team appearance
Parents: Ian and Janet
Marital status: Single
Family links with cricket: Both grandfathers
played cricket and football at a high league
standard in Yorkshire
Education: Appleshaw Primary School;
Harrow Way Community School, Andover;
Cricklade College, Andover; Cardiff
University
Qualifications: 9 GCSEs, 3 A-levels
Career outside cricket: Student
(BA Education)

Off-season: 'Training with Cardiff UCCE, and my degree'
Career highlights to date: 'Making 2nd XI Championship debut v Sussex at Hove.
Winning 2nd XI Championship [2001]; doing lap of honour at West End'
Cricket moments to forget: 'Too many moments! Probably Southern League debut
v Andover – everything went wrong'
Cricketers particularly admired: Wasim Akram, Waqar Younis, Brian Lara,
Brett Lee, Shane Warne, Iain Brunnschweiler, James Hamblin
Young players to look out for: Damian Shirazi, Chris Benham, Neil Randall,
Luke Merry
Other sports played: Darts ('Walnut Tree', Appleshaw – Andover Invitation League
winners; recommended for county)
Other sports followed: Cricket (South Wilts CC), rugby league, rugby union
Relaxations: 'Walking my dog, Tinker; dancing (I enjoy dancing)'
Extras: Played for Hampshire Board XI in the NatWest 2000 and for Wiltshire in the
C&G 2001. Played for Development of Excellence XI (South) v West Indies U19 at
Arundel 2001
Opinions on cricket: 'In one-day cricket, white balls go soft too early; therefore
harder balls should be used – "the harder the ball, the farther it goes". Bouncers should
be used in one-day format and there should be no limit on bouncers in four-day or Test
match cricket. Perhaps a different ball at each end?'

2001 Season (did not make any first-class or one-day appearances)

Career Performances

	M	Inns	NO	Runs	HS	Avge	100s	50s	Ct	St	Balls	Runs	Wkts	Avge	Best	5wI	10wM
Test																	
All First																	
1-day Int																	
C & G	2	2	0	4	4	2.00	-	-	-	-	102	46	1	46.00	1-29	-	
B & H																	
1-day Lge																	

TREDWELL, J. C.   Kent

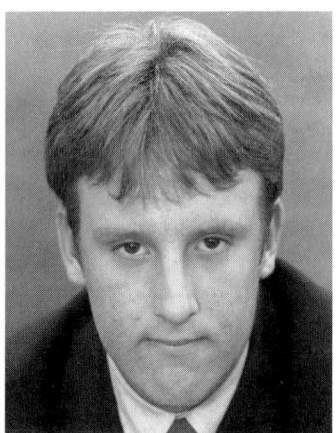

Name: James Cullum Tredwell
Role: Left-hand bat, right-arm
off-spin bowler
Born: 27 February 1982, Ashford, Kent
Height: 5ft 11in **Weight:** 14st 2lbs
Nickname: Tredders
County debut: 2001
Strike rate: 78.00 (career 78.00)
Parents: John and Rosemary
Marital status: Single
Family links with cricket: Father played
league cricket for Folkestone and previously
for Ashford
Education: Dymchurch County Primary
School; Southlands Community
Comprehensive
Qualifications: 10 GCSEs, 2 A-levels,
ECB Level 1 coach
Off-season: 'Revisiting Brisbane after 2000 winter. Training, working on fitness and
playing the odd grade match for Redlands Tigers'
Overseas tours: Kent U17 to Sri Lanka 1998-99
Overseas teams played for: Redlands Tigers, Brisbane 2000-02
Career highlights to date: 'Captaining England U19 v West Indies U19. First-class
debut v Leicestershire'
Cricket moments to forget: 'Being run out for 0 v Hampshire for Kent Board XI in
NatWest Trophy 2000'
Cricketers particularly admired: David Gower, John Emburey, Ashley Mallett
Young players to look out for: Gary Pratt, Rob Ferley, Ian Bell
Other sports followed: Football

Extras: Played for Kent Board XI in the NatWest 2000 and in the C&G 2001. Called up from England U19 for first-class debut for Kent v Leicestershire 2001, entailing a dash from Hove to Leicester on the day of the game. Represented England U19 v West Indies U19 in 'Test' series (3/3) 2001 (captain in second 'Test')
Best batting: 10 Kent v Leicestershire, Leicester 2001
Best bowling: 1-38 Kent v Leicestershire, Leicester 2001

2001 Season

	M	Inns	NO	Runs	HS	Avge	100s	50s	Ct	St	O	M	Runs	Wkts	Avge	Best	5wl	10wM
Test																		
All First	1	1	0	10	10	10.00	-	-	-	-	26	5	123	2	61.50	1-38	-	-
1-day Int																		
C & G	3	2	0	128	71	64.00	-	2	-	-	15	0	76	1	76.00	1-39	-	
B & H																		
1-day Lge																		

Career Performances

	M	Inns	NO	Runs	HS	Avge	100s	50s	Ct	St	Balls	Runs	Wkts	Avge	Best	5wl	10wM
Test																	
All First	1	1	0	10	10	10.00	-	-	-	-	156	123	2	61.50	1-38	-	-
1-day Int																	
C & G	6	5	0	166	71	33.20	-	2	1	-	234	169	3	56.33	1-31	-	
B & H																	
1-day Lge																	

---

86. Who captained Warwickshire to victory in the 1968
Gillette Cup final, winning the Man of the Match award in the process?

TREGO, P. D.　　　　　　　　　Somerset

Name: <u>Peter</u> David Trego
Role: Right-hand bat, right-arm
'quickish' bowler
Born: 12 June 1981, Weston-super-Mare
Height: 6ft **Weight:** 12st 7lbs
Nickname: Tregs 'and many more'
County debut: 2000
1st-Class 50s: 1
1st-Class catches: 3
Place in batting averages: (2000 189th
av. 19.14)
Place in bowling averages: (2000 109th
av. 33.50)
Strike rate: 87.00 (career 60.86)
Parents: Carol and Paul
Marital status: Single
Family links with cricket: 'Brother Sam
played for Somerset; Dad plays for Uphill
Castle – both strong batsmen'

Education: St Martins, Weston-super-Mare; Wyvern Comprehensive
Qualifications: Lifeguard (at Hutton Moor Leisure Centre)
Cricketers particularly admired: Ian Botham and Graham Rose – 'they have both
been huge inspirations to me'
Other sports played: Football
Other sports followed: Football (Man Utd), darts, golf
Relaxations: Golf, snooker, music, socialising with friends, shopping
Extras: Won Best Batsman award at U16 – averaged 137 in nine games. Scored
century for Somerset 2nd XI v Glos 1999. Attended Lilleshall with England U17.
Represented England U19 v Sri Lanka U19 in one-day and 'Test' series 2000, scoring
53* and taking 3-41 in the second 'One-Day International' at Cardiff. NBC Denis
Compton Award for the most promising young Somerset player 2000. Played for
Somerset Board XI in the second round of the C&G 2002, which was played in
September 2001
Best batting: 62 Somerset v Yorkshire, Taunton 2000
Best bowling: 4-84 Somerset v Yorkshire, Scarborough 2000

2001 Season

	M	Inns	NO	Runs	HS	Avge	100s	50s	Ct	St	O	M	Runs	Wkts	Avge	Best	5wI	10wM
Test																		
All First	3	5	1	117	43	29.25	-	-	-	-	58	11	243	4	60.75	3-85	-	-
1-day Int																		
C & G	1	1	0	11	11	11.00	-	-	-	-	9	1	21	2	10.50	2-21	-	
B & H																		
1-day Lge	5	4	1	44	21	14.66	-	-	-	-	15	1	81	3	27.00	1-9	-	

Career Performances

	M	Inns	NO	Runs	HS	Avge	100s	50s	Ct	St	Balls	Runs	Wkts	Avge	Best	5wI	10wM
Test																	
All First	10	13	2	251	62	22.81	-	1	3	-	1339	846	22	38.45	4-84	-	-
1-day Int																	
C & G	3	2	0	11	11	5.50	-	-	-	-	132	93	6	15.50	2-21	-	
B & H																	
1-day Lge	8	6	1	58	21	11.60	-	-	1	-	210	176	3	58.66	1-9	-	

TREMLETT, C. T. Hampshire

Name: <u>Christopher</u> Timothy Tremlett
Role: Right-hand bat, right-arm
fast-medium bowler
Born: 2 September 1981, Southampton
Height: 6ft 7in **Weight:** 15st 12lbs
Nickname: Twiggy, Goober
County debut: 2000
1st-Class catches: 2
Place in bowling averages: 12th av. 20.05
Strike rate: 39.40 (career 38.84)
Parents: Timothy and Carolyn
Marital status: Single
Family links with cricket: Grandfather
[Maurice] played county cricket for Somerset
and three Tests for England. Father played for
Hampshire and England A
Education: Otterbourne Primary, Chandlers
Ford; Thornden School, Chandlers Ford;
Taunton's College, Southampton
Qualifications: 8 GCSEs, BTEC Sports Science
Off-season: National Academy to Australia
Overseas tours: West of England U15 to West Indies; Hampshire U16 to Jersey;
England U19 to India 2000-01; ECB National Academy to Australia 2001-02

Career highlights to date: 'Taking a wicket with first ball in first-class cricket and getting promotion in 2001 to division one [of Championship]'
Cricketers particularly admired: Mark Waugh, Glenn McGrath
Young players to look out for: John Francis, Lawrence Prittipaul
Other sports played: Football, basketball, pool
Other sports followed: Football (Arsenal)
Injuries: Out for a few games at the end of the season due to sore shins
Relaxations: Watching films
Extras: Represented England U17 at the ECC Colts Festival in Northern Ireland 1999. Took wicket (Mark Richardson) with first ball in first-class cricket v New Zealand A at Portsmouth 2000; finished with debut match figures of 6-91. Hit 30 not out off 15 balls on National League debut. Represented England U19 v Sri Lanka U19 in 'Test' series 2000 and v West Indies U19 in one-day series (3/3) 2001. NBC Denis Compton Award for the most promising young Hampshire player 2000
Opinions on cricket: 'We should play less games.'
Best batting: 26 Hampshire v Nottinghamshire, West End 2001
Best bowling: 4-16 Hampshire v New Zealand A, Portsmouth 2000

2001 Season

	M	Inns	NO	Runs	HS	Avge	100s	50s	Ct	St	O	M	Runs	Wkts	Avge	Best	5wI	10wM
Test																		
All First	7	9	4	83	26	16.60	-	-	2	-	131.2	37	401	20	20.05	4-34	-	-
1-day Int																		
C & G	1	0	0	0	0	-	-	-	-	-	4	0	35	0	-		-	-
B & H																		
1-day Lge	12	9	3	59	15 *	9.83	-	-	3	-	95.3	11	364	22	16.54	3-15	-	

Career Performances

	M	Inns	NO	Runs	HS	Avge	100s	50s	Ct	St	Balls	Runs	Wkts	Avge	Best	5wI	10wM
Test																	
All First	8	11	4	116	26	16.57	-	-	2	-	1010	492	26	18.92	4-16	-	-
1-day Int																	
C & G	2	1	0	10	10	10.00	-	-	-	-	72	70	2	35.00	2-35	-	
B & H																	
1-day Lge	17	11	4	89	30 *	12.71	-	-	4	-	819	549	26	21.11	3-15	-	

TRESCOTHICK, M. E. Somerset

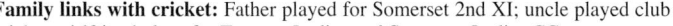

Name: <u>Marcus</u> Edward Trescothick
Role: Left-hand bat, right-arm swing bowler, reserve wicket-keeper, county vice-captain
Born: 25 December 1975, Keynsham, Bristol
Height: 6ft 3in **Weight:** 14st 7lbs
Nickname: Banger
County debut: 1993
County cap: 1999
Test debut: 2000
Tests: 16
One-Day Internationals: 21
1st-Class 50s: 36
1st-Class 100s: 10
1st-Class catches: 131
One-Day 100s: 8
Place in batting averages: 63rd av. 41.17
(2000 28th av. 43.41)
Strike rate: (career 68.94)
Parents: Martyn and Lin
Marital status: Single

Family links with cricket: Father played for Somerset 2nd XI; uncle played club cricket; girlfriend plays for Taunton Ladies and Somerset Ladies CC
Education: Sir Bernard Lovell School
Qualifications: 7 GCSEs
Off-season: Touring with England
Overseas tours: England U18 to South Africa 1992-93; England U19 to Sri Lanka 1993-94, to West Indies 1994-95 (captain); England A to Bangladesh and New Zealand 1999-2000; England to Kenya (ICC Knockout Trophy) 2000-01, to Pakistan and Sri Lanka 2000-01, to Zimbabwe (one-day series) 2001-02, to India and New Zealand 2001-02
Overseas teams played for: Melville CC, Perth 1997-99
Career highlights to date: 'Scoring my first Test hundred in Galle, Sri Lanka'
Cricket moments to forget: 'NatWest final 1999 v Gloucestershire'
Cricketers particularly admired: Adam Gilchrist, Andy Caddick
Young players to look out for: Joe Tucker, Pete Trego, Matthew Wood
Other sports followed: Golf, football (Bristol City FC)
Relaxations: 'Spending time at home (it's such a rare thing), playing golf'
Extras: Member of England U19 squad for home series against West Indies 1993. Man of the Series against India U19 in 1994, scoring most runs in the series. Whittingdale Young Player of the Month, August 1994. Captained England U19 v South Africa U19 1995. Took a hat-trick for Somerset against Young Australia in 1995.

Scored more than 1000 runs for England U19. Scored 322 in the second innings of a 2nd XI game against Warwickshire in 1997 – Somerset were chasing a target of 612 and Trescothick was the last man out with the score on 605! Made One-Day International debut v Zimbabwe in NatWest Series at The Oval 2000, scoring 79; scored 87 in same series v West Indies at Riverside, winning Man of the Match award. Made Test debut in third Test v West Indies at Old Trafford 2000; in first innings scored 66 and took part with Alec Stewart in record England partnership for any wicket in Tests v West Indies at Old Trafford (179). Scored 78 in England's first innings of the fifth Test 2000, sharing in a new record first-wicket stand for England in Tests v West Indies at The Oval (159) with Michael Atherton. PCA Player of the Year 2000. Scored maiden Test century (122) v Sri Lanka at Galle 2000-01, in the process batting throughout the third day in temperatures that topped 105 degrees Fahrenheit; also scored 57 in the second innings. England central contract 2001. Took part in Somerset record opening stand in matches v Glamorgan (240) with Piran Holloway at Cardiff 2001. B&H Gold Awards for his 113 v Glamorgan at Cardiff, 109* v Northamptonshire at Northampton and 99-ball 112 v Gloucestershire at Taunton 2001 (three B&H centuries in eight days). Man of the Match for his 142-ball 137 (his maiden ODI century) v Pakistan at Lord's in the NatWest Series 2001, in the process of scoring which he shared in a record fourth-wicket partnership for England in One-Day Internationals (170) with Owais Shah. C&G Man of the Match award for his 83-ball 121 v Glamorgan at Taunton 2001. Sports.com Cricketer of the Year 2001. Vice-captain of Somerset since 1999

Opinions on cricket: 'Two divisions are working well. Central contracts are still causing problems for the counties. If we are serious about England getting better, it's something we have to live with.'

Best batting: 190 Somerset v Middlesex, Taunton 1999

Best bowling: 4-36 Somerset v Young Australia, Taunton 1995

Stop press: Captained England v Zimbabwe in fourth One-Day International at Bulawayo 2001-02, deputising for Nasser Hussain. BBC West Country Sports Sportsman of the Year for 2001. Man of the Match award v India at Kolkata (Calcutta) 2001-02 for his 109-ball 121, which included the fastest century for England in One-Day Internationals (80 balls). Man of the Match award for his 80-ball 95 in England's series-equalling One-Day International victory over India at Mumbai (Bombay) 2001-02

2001 Season

	M	Inns	NO	Runs	HS	Avge	100s	50s	Ct	St	O	M	Runs	Wkts	Avge	Best	5wI	10wM
Test	7	13	0	484	117	37.23	1	3	6	-	5	1	16	0	-	-	-	-
All First	10	17	0	700	147	41.17	2	3	9	-	5	1	16	0	-	-	-	-
1-day Int	6	6	0	249	137	41.50	1	1	3	-								
C & G	4	4	0	186	121	46.50	1	-	2	-	2	0	13	0	-	-	-	
B & H	6	6	1	385	113	77.00	3	-	1	-	23.1	0	114	4	28.50	3-30	-	
1-day Lge	2	2	0	99	72	49.50	-	1	1	-								

Career Performances

	M	Inns	NO	Runs	HS	Avge	100s	50s	Ct	St	Balls	Runs	Wkts	Avge	Best	5wI	10wM
Test	16	30	1	1071	122	36.93	2	7	13	-	120	52	1	52.00	1-34	-	-
All First	124	207	8	6444	190	32.38	10	36	131	-	2482	1434	36	39.83	4-36	-	-
1-day Int	21	21	1	738	137	36.90	1	4	5	-	40	38	2	19.00	2-7	-	
C & G	15	14	0	555	121	39.64	2	1	4	-	174	141	4	35.25	2-23	-	
B & H	20	20	4	790	122	49.37	4	2	8	-	325	255	12	21.25	3-30	-	
1-day Lge	83	74	10	1780	110	27.81	1	9	27	-	978	823	31	26.54	4-50	-	

TROTT, B. J. Kent

Name: Benjamin (<u>Ben</u>) James Trott
Role: Right-hand bat, right-arm fast-medium bowler
Born: 14 March 1975, Wellington, Somerset
Height: 6ft 5in **Weight:** 14st
Nickname: Tony Rott, Trotsky, Trotty
County debut: 1997 (Somerset), 2000 (Kent)
1st-Class 5 w. in innings: 4
1st-Class 10 w. in match: 1
1st-Class catches: 5
One-Day 5 w. in innings: 1
Place in batting averages: 277th av. 5.70
Place in bowling averages: 40th av. 26.27
Strike rate: 47.59 (career 47.46)
Parents: Alan Robert and Jane Elizabeth
Marital status: Single
Family links with cricket: 'Younger brother Thom plays for Somerset youth sides and also plays club cricket for Wellington along with my dad'
Education: Wellesley Park Primary School, Wellington; Court Fields Community School, Taunton; The Richard Huish College, Taunton; The College of St Mark and St John, Plymouth
Qualifications: 8 GCSEs, 3 A-levels, BEd (Hons) Physical Education and Information Technology; sports coaching – cricket, rugby, football, hockey
Career outside cricket: Teacher (primary)
Off-season: 'Coaching various sports; getting fit for next season; two months in Perth, Australia'
Overseas teams played for: Claremont-Nedlands, Perth 1998-99
Career highlights to date: 'Winning the Norwich Union League 2001 with the last game of the season'
Cricketers particularly admired: Glenn McGrath, Darren Gough, Andrew Caddick

Young players to look out for: Alex Loudon, James Tredwell, Robert Ferley
Other sports played: Golf, football
Other sports followed: Football (Manchester United)
Injuries: Out for three weeks with a hamstring injury
Relaxations: 'Spending time with my girlfriend, music, golf'
Extras: Wellington Young Player of the Year in 1993. Wellington Players' Player of the Year in 1996. Played for Somerset 1997-99; has also played for Devon. Joined Kent in 2000. Recorded maiden first-class five-wicket return (5-65) v Essex at Tunbridge Wells 2001, going on to take 6-13 in the second innings for a maiden first-class ten-wicket match return. Also recorded maiden one-day five-wicket return in 2001, 5-18 v Cumberland at Barrow on C&G debut, winning Man of the Match award
Opinions on cricket: 'There should be more one-day floodlit matches as they gain the increased interest of children; they are the future of English cricket.'
Best batting: 13 Kent v Leicestershire, Leicester 2001
Best bowling: 6-13 Kent v Essex, Tunbridge Wells 2001

2001 Season

	M	Inns	NO	Runs	HS	Avge	100s	50s	Ct	St	O	M	Runs	Wkts	Avge	Best	5wI	10wM
Test																		
All First	14	13	3	57	13	5.70	-	-	3	-	372.5	68	1235	47	26.27	6-13	4	1
1-day Int																		
C & G	3	1	0	0	0	0.00	-	-	1	-	29.1	4	117	8	14.62	5-18	1	
B & H																		
1-day Lge	13	6	4	5	2 *	2.50	-	-	2	-	99	14	431	15	28.73	2-19	-	

Career Performances

	M	Inns	NO	Runs	HS	Avge	100s	50s	Ct	St	Balls	Runs	Wkts	Avge	Best	5wI	10wM
Test																	
All First	19	17	6	58	13	5.27	-	-	5	-	2753	1552	58	26.75	6-13	4	1
1-day Int																	
C & G	3	1	0	0	0	0.00	-	-	1	-	175	117	8	14.62	5-18	1	
B & H																	
1-day Lge	14	6	4	5	2 *	2.50	-	-	2	-	618	460	16	28.75	2-19	-	

---

87. In which year did the Gillette/NatWest/C&G change from
a 60-over competition to a 50-over competition?

TROUGHTON, J. O. — Warwickshire

Name: James (<u>Jim</u>) Oliver Troughton
Role: Left-hand bat, slow left-arm bowler
Born: 2 March 1979, London
Height: 5ft 11in **Weight:** 12st 12lbs
Nickname: Troughts, JT
County debut: 2001
One-Day 100s: 1
Parents: Ali and David
Marital status: Engaged to Naomi
Family links with cricket: Father was a Middlesex Colt. Great-grandfather Henry Crichton played for Warwickshire
Education: Bridgetown School, Stratford-upon-Avon; Trinity School, Leamington Spa; Birmingham University
Qualifications: 8 GCSEs, 3 A-levels, BSc Sport & Exercise Science
Career outside cricket: 'Coaching/acting'
Off-season: 'Going to Cape Town for six months, playing and coaching for Avendale CC'
Overseas tours: Warwickshire Development of Excellence squad to Cape Town 1998; MCC to Australia and Singapore 2001
Overseas teams played for: Harvinia CC, Free State, South Africa 2000; Avendale CC, Cape Town 2001-02
Career highlights to date: 'Making first-class debut v Worcestershire, August 2001'
Cricket moments to forget: 'Having to bowl at Graeme Hick on 194'
Cricketers particularly admired: Graham Thorpe, Steve Waugh, Allan Donald, Ashley Giles
Young players to look out for: Ian Bell, Andrew Gait
Other sports played: Football (Stoke City youth player)
Other sports followed: 'Hooked on Manchester United since going to their soccer school aged five'
Relaxations: 'Music, films, playing my guitar, spending time with Naomi, going abroad'
Extras: Is grandson of *Dr Who* actor Patrick Troughton; father also an actor. County colours U12-U19. Has represented England U15, U16 and U17. Represented ECB Midlands U19 v Pakistan U19 1998. Has won the Alec Hastilow Trophy and the Coney Edmonds Trophy (Warwickshire awards). Played for Warwickshire Board XI in the NatWest 1999 and 2000 and in the first and second rounds of the C&G 2002, which were played in August and September 2001; scored maiden one-day century (115*) v Cumberland at Millom in first round of C&G 2002

Opinions on cricket: 'Tight cricketing schedule sometimes overshadows the importance of improving techniques in the nets. Good to see a higher emphasis placed on fitness; you need to be an athlete in today's game. Hope summers don't get any wetter.'

Best batting: 27 Warwickshire v Worcestershire, Edgbaston 2001

2001 Season

	M	Inns	NO	Runs	HS	Avge	100s	50s	Ct	St	O	M	Runs	Wkts	Avge	Best	5wI	10wM
Test																		
All First	1	2	1	32	27	32.00	-	-	-	-	2	0	17	0	-		-	-	-
1-day Int																		
C & G	2	2	1	166	115 *	166.00	1	1	-	-	11.4	0	49	4	12.25	4-23	-	
B & H																		
1-day Lge																		

Career Performances

	M	Inns	NO	Runs	HS	Avge	100s	50s	Ct	St	Balls	Runs	Wkts	Avge	Best	5wI	10wM
Test																		
All First	1	2	1	32	27	32.00	-	-	-	-	12	17	0	-		-	-	-
1-day Int																		
C & G	4	4	1	222	115 *	74.00	1	1	2	-	130	83	7	11.85	4-23	-	
B & H																		
1-day Lge																		

TUCKER, J. P.   Somerset

Name: Joseph (Joe) Peter Tucker
Role: Right-hand bat, right-arm fast-medium bowler
Born: 14 September 1979, Bath
Height: 6ft 3in   **Weight:** 14st
Nickname: Tux, Seth, Troy, My Boy
County debut: 2000
1st-Class catches: 1
Strike rate: (career 168.00)
Parents: Geoff and Chris
Marital status: Single
Family links with cricket: 'All keen cricketers and umpire'
Education: Camely; Pensford Primary School, Bristol; Chew Valley; Colston's Collegiate School, Bristol; Richard Huish Sixth Form College, Taunton
Qualifications: 10 GCSEs, 3 A-levels, senior coaching award, 'van driver, steelworker'
Career outside cricket: Professional motocross rider (Cat Honda)

Off-season: 'My own intensive training programme (Oct-Apr); Australia (Jan) training; bustin' big on my Cat Honda 125cc'
Overseas tours: Avon to Barbados 1994; West of England U15 to West Indies 1996; England U17 to Bermuda (International Youth Tournament) 1997; England U19 to South Africa (including U19 World Cup) 1997-98, to New Zealand 1998-99
Career highlights to date: 'Getting Lara out with second ball of my career'
Cricket moments to forget: 'None. They've all been an experience'
Cricketers particularly admired: Allan Donald, Curtly Ambrose, Shoaib Akhtar, Brett Lee, Steff Jones, Geoff Tucker
Young players to look out for: Jacob Smith, Josh Tucker 'and me'
Other sports played: Motocross, football, weightlifting, golf
Other sports followed: Football (Man Utd, Bristol City), cricket (Keynsham/Purnells CC), motocross ('my cousin Martin "Airtime" Tucker for Molson's Yamaha')
Relaxations: 'Seeing my girl and my family and friends; cinema; eating out; doing my fitess programme'
Extras: Made his 2nd XI debut for Somerset at the age of 15. Took 4 for 31 against Holland for England U17 in the International Youth Tournament in Bermuda in 1997, which England U17 won. Was part of the England U19 squad that won the U19 World Cup in South Africa 1997-98. Took 7-60 for ECB South U19 v Pakistan U19 1998. Took 5-35 for England U19 in second 'Test' v New Zealand U19 1998-99. Has attended Dennis Lillee coaching school, Chennai (Madras). Missed entire 1999 season and 13 weeks at start of 2000 season due to injury and illness
Opinions on cricket: 'We are trying to make the game go forward by the divisions, academies, new fitness programmes etc. I think it's working slowly but surely. Stand by it. Don't put us down when things don't go well.'
Best batting: 14 Somerset v West Indians, Taunton 2000
Best bowling: 1-28 Somerset v West Indians, Taunton 2000

2001 Season

	M	Inns	NO	Runs	HS	Avge	100s	50s	Ct	St	O	M	Runs	Wkts	Avge	Best	5wI	10wM
Test																		
All First	1	2	2	5	5 *	-	-	-	-	-	17	2	82	0	-	-	-	-
1-day Int																		
C & G																		
B & H																		
1-day Lge																		

Career Performances

	M	Inns	NO	Runs	HS	Avge	100s	50s	Ct	St	Balls	Runs	Wkts	Avge	Best	5wI	10wM
Test																	
All First	2	3	2	19	14	19.00	-	-	1	-	168	129	1	129.00	1-28	-	-
1-day Int																	
C & G																		
B & H																		
1-day Lge																		

TUDOR, A. J.   Surrey

Name: Alexander (<u>Alex</u>) Jeremy Tudor
Role: Right-hand bat, right-arm fast bowler
Born: 23 October 1977, West Brompton, London
Height: 6ft 4in **Weight:** 13st 7lbs
Nickname: Big Al, Bambi, Tudes
County debut: 1995
County cap: 1999
Test debut: 1998-99
Tests: 5
1st-Class 50s: 4
1st-Class 100s: 1
1st-Class 5 w. in innings: 12
1st-Class catches: 20
Place in batting averages: 108th av. 31.76 (2000 110th av. 28.30)
Place in bowling averages: 92nd av. 35.65 (2000 39th av. 22.78)
Strike rate: 57.96 (career 45.47)
Parents: Daryll and Jennifer
Marital status: Single
Family links with cricket: Brother was on the staff at The Oval
Education: Wandle Primary, Earlsfield; St Mark's C of E, Fulham; City of Westminster College
Off-season: With ECB National Academy in Australia
Overseas tours: England U15 to South Africa 1992-93; England U19 to Zimbabwe 1995-96, to Pakistan 1996-97; England to Australia 1998-99, to South Africa 1999-2000, to Pakistan 2000-01; England A to West Indies 2000-01; ECB National Academy to Australia 2001-02
Cricketers particularly admired: Curtly Ambrose, Brian Lara
Other sports followed: Basketball, football (QPR)

Relaxations: Listening to music
Extras: Played for London Schools at all ages from U8. Played for England U17 against India in 1994. MCC Young Cricketer. Took 4-89 in Australia's first innings on Test debut at Perth 1998-99; his victims included both Waugh twins. Scored 99* in second innings of first Test v New Zealand at Edgbaston 1999, bettering the highest score by a nightwatchman for England (Harold Larwood's 98 v Australia at Sydney 1932-33) and winning the Man of the Match award; in total he scored 131 unbeaten runs in the match. Drafted temporarily into England Test squad for tour of Pakistan 2000-01 as replacement for the injured Andrew Flintoff. Took 5-37 for England A v West Indies B at Grenada in the Busta Cup 2000-01. Scored maiden first-class century (116) at The Oval 2001, in the process sharing in a new record seventh-wicket partnership for Surrey in matches v Essex (206) with Alec Stewart. Recorded maiden Test five-wicket return (5-44) v Australia at Trent Bridge 2001
Best batting: 116 Surrey v Essex, The Oval 2001
Best bowling: 7-48 Surrey v Lancashire, The Oval 2000

2001 Season

	M	Inns	NO	Runs	HS	Avge	100s	50s	Ct	St	O	M	Runs	Wkts	Avge	Best	5wI	10wM
Test	2	3	0	14	9	4.66	-	-	-	-	44.5	7	195	7	27.85	5-44	1	-
All First	9	14	1	413	116	31.76	1	1	2	-	251.1	53	927	26	35.65	5-44	2	-
1-day Int																		
C & G	1	0	0	0	0	-	-	-	1	-	10	2	45	1	45.00	1-45	-	
B & H	7	5	0	59	28	11.80	-	-	1	-	56.5	7	246	12	20.50	3-28	-	
1-day Lge	4	3	0	37	21	12.33	-	-	1	-	34	6	136	7	19.42	4-36	-	

Career Performances

	M	Inns	NO	Runs	HS	Avge	100s	50s	Ct	St	Balls	Runs	Wkts	Avge	Best	5wI	10wM
Test	5	9	3	180	99 *	30.00	-	1	-	-	619	434	15	28.93	5-44	1	-
All First	72	94	24	1609	116	22.98	1	4	20	-	9959	5880	217	27.09	7-48	12	-
1-day Int																	
C & G	6	2	1	11	10 *	11.00	-	-	2	-	345	229	10	22.90	4-39	-	
B & H	12	7	0	59	28	8.42	-	-	2	-	587	412	22	18.72	3-28	-	
1-day Lge	28	20	4	162	29 *	10.12	-	-	7	-	1082	848	38	22.31	4-26	-	

TUFNELL, P. C. R.   Middlesex

Name: Philip (<u>Phil</u>) Clive Roderick Tufnell
Role: Right-hand bat, slow left-arm bowler
Born: 29 April 1966, Barnet, Hertfordshire
Height: 6ft **Weight:** 12st 7lbs
Nickname: The Cat, Tuffers
County debut: 1986
County cap: 1990
Benefit: 1999
Test debut: 1990-91
Tests: 42
One-Day Internationals: 20
50 wickets in a season: 9
1st-Class 50s: 1
1st-Class 5 w. in innings: 49
1st-Class 10 w. in match: 6
1st-Class catches: 103
One-Day 5 w. in innings: 1
Place in batting averages: 279th av. 4.33
(2000 283rd av. 8.33)
Place in bowling averages: 55th av. 28.68 (2000 41st av. 23.07)
Strike rate: 69.00 (career 73.02)
Parents: Sylvia and Alan
Marital status: Single
Children: Poppy and Ellie
Education: Highgate School; Southgate School
Qualifications: O-level in Art
Career outside cricket: Media
Off-season: 'Working with Paragon Sports Management, of which I am a partner'
Overseas tours: England YC to West Indies 1984-85; England to Australia 1990-91, to New Zealand and Australia (World Cup) 1991-92, to India and Sri Lanka 1992-93, to West Indies 1993-94, to Australia 1994-95, to Zimbabwe and New Zealand 1996-97, to West Indies 1997-98, to South Africa 1999-2000
Overseas teams played for: Queensland University, Australia
Career highlights to date: 'Bowling the Aussies out at The Oval [1997]'
Cricket moments to forget: 'No moments I would like to forget'
Cricketers particularly admired: Robin Smith
Young players to look out for: 'A good crop of youngsters coming through'
Other sports followed: Football (Arsenal)
Relaxations: Sleeping and sports cars
Extras: MCC Young Cricketer of the Year 1984 and Middlesex Uncapped Bowler of the Year 1987. Had match figures of 11 for 93 in the final Test against Australia at The

Oval in 1997, winning the Man of the Match award. Played for a World XI v an Asia XI in Dhaka 2000. Took 900th first-class wicket (Guy Welton) v Nottinghamshire at Lord's 2000. Middlesex Player of the Season 2000. Took his 1000th first-class wicket (Martin Love) v Durham at Lord's 2001

Opinions on cricket: 'Cricket administration should be held more accountable.'

Best batting: 67* Middlesex v Worcestershire, Lord's 1996

Best bowling: 8-29 Middlesex v Glamorgan, Cardiff 1993

2001 Season

	M	Inns	NO	Runs	HS	Avge	100s	50s	Ct	St	O	M	Runs	Wkts	Avge	Best	5wI	10wM
Test	1	2	1	7	7*	7.00	-	-	-	-	39	2	174	1	174.00	1-174	-	-
All First	17	20	8	52	11*	4.33	-	-	-	-	690	166	1721	60	28.68	6-44	3	1
1-day Int																		
C & G	1	0	0	0	0	-	-	-	-	-	10	4	15	1	15.00	1-15	-	
B & H	2	0	0	0	0	-	-	-	-	-	17	0	71	1	71.00	1-47	-	
1-day Lge	2	1	1	0	0*	-	-	-	-	-	17.2	1	85	2	42.50	1-36	-	

Career Performances

	M	Inns	NO	Runs	HS	Avge	100s	50s	Ct	St	Balls	Runs	Wkts	Avge	Best	5wI	10wM
Test	42	59	29	153	22*	5.10	-	-	12	-	11288	4560	121	37.68	7-47	5	2
All First	302	334	128	1977	67*	9.59	-	1	103	-	73898	29636	1012	29.28	8-29	49	6
1-day Int	20	10	9	15	5*	15.00	-	-	4	-	1020	699	19	36.78	4-22	-	
C & G	9	1	0	8	8	8.00	-	-	4	-	630	338	11	30.72	3-29	-	
B & H	18	9	4	62	18	12.40	-	-	2	-	971	700	18	38.88	3-32	-	
1-day Lge	39	14	8	36	13*	6.00	-	-	5	-	1652	1277	47	27.17	5-28	1	

88. Which former Somerset and Glamorgan player took 5-26 for Holland v Kent in the 1999 NatWest, winning the Man of the Match award?

TURNER, R. J. Somerset

Name: Robert (<u>Rob</u>) Julian Turner
Role: Right-hand middle-order bat,
wicket-keeper
Born: 25 November 1967, Malvern
Height: 6ft 2in **Weight:** 14st
Nickname: Noddy, Turns
County debut: 1991
County cap: 1994
1000 runs in a season: 2
50 dismissals in a season: 6
1st-Class 50s: 38
1st-Class 100s: 9
1st-Class catches: 505
1st-Class stumpings: 39
Place in batting averages: 98th av. 33.08

(2000 174th av. 20.50)
Parents: Derek and Doris
Wife and date of marriage: Lucy,
25 September 1999
Children: Jamie Jonathan Paul, 4 April 2001
Family links with cricket: 'Father and both brothers (Richard and Simon) are closely associated with Weston-super-Mare CC. Simon played for Somerset in 1984, also as a wicket-keeper. My wife, Lucy, plays for MCC Ladies and Somerset Ladies (also as a wicket-keeper!)'
Education: Uphill Primary School, Weston-super-Mare; Broadoak Comprehensive, Weston-super-Mare; Millfield School, Street; Magdalene College, Cambridge University
Qualifications: BEng (Hons) Engineering, Diploma in Computer Science, NCA coaching award, SFA securities representative of the London Stock Exchange
Career outside cricket: Rowan Dartington stockbrokers
Off-season: 'Working for stockbrokers Rowan Dartington; preparing for my benefit year and playing with my son, Jamie'
Overseas tours: Millfield School to Barbados 1985; Combined Universities to Barbados 1989; Qantas Airlines Tournament, Kuala Lumpur, Malaysia 1992-93; English Lions to New Zealand (Cricket Max) 1997; MCC to New Zealand 1999, to Canada 2000; England A to Bangladesh and New Zealand 1999-2000 (vice-captain)
Overseas teams played for: Claremont-Nedlands, Perth, Western Australia 1991-93
Career highlights to date: 'Winning the C&G Trophy 2001 – especially catching a skyer in the Lord's final (to remove Afridi)'
Cricket moments to forget: 'None – I enjoy it all!'
Cricketers particularly admired: Jack Russell

Young players to look out for: Peter Trego, Jamie Turner
Other sports played: Golf ('badly, but holed in one at the par three fourth at Oake Manor GC!')
Other sports followed: Football ('The Villa'), hockey (Taunton Vale Ladies)
Relaxations: 'Reading, sleeping, beer and curry; the piano'
Extras: Captain of Cambridge University (Blue 1988-91) and Combined Universities 1991. Equalled Somerset records of six catches in an innings and eight dismissals in a match v West Indians at Taunton 1995; also had eight dismissals in a match v Durham at Riverside in the same season. Wombwell Cricket Lovers' Society Wicket-keeper of the Year 1999. Highest-placed Englishman in the 1999 batting averages (1217 runs at 52.91). Sheffield Cricket Lovers' Society Allrounder of the Year 1999. Was on stand-by for England tours of West Indies 1997-98 and South Africa and Zimbabwe 1999-2000. Made nine dismissals (all caught) in the match v Surrey at Taunton 2001, breaking his own (shared) Somerset record. Took seven catches in an innings v Northamptonshire at Taunton 2001, breaking his own (shared) Somerset record. Granted a benefit for 2002
Opinions on cricket: 'Two-divisional status has been a great success in terms of exciting cricket for both players and spectators. End-of-season jostling for position to gain promotion or avoid relegation adds a new dimension in both competitions.'
Best batting: 144 Somerset v Kent, Taunton 1997

2001 Season

	M	Inns	NO	Runs	HS	Avge	100s	50s	Ct	St	O	M	Runs	Wkts	Avge	Best	5wI	10wM
Test																		
All First	17	26	3	761	115 *	33.08	1	3	59	-	10	3	29	0	-	-	-	-
1-day Int																		
C & G	5	4	3	155	46	155.00	-	-	5	-								
B & H	6	4	2	17	9 *	8.50	-	-	5	-								
1-day Lge	14	13	5	209	56 *	26.12	-	1	10	3								

Career Performances

	M	Inns	NO	Runs	HS	Avge	100s	50s	Ct	St	Balls	Runs	Wkts	Avge	Best	5wI	10wM
Test																	
All First	193	296	51	7564	144	30.87	9	38	505	39	79	58	0	-	-	-	-
1-day Int																	
C & G	22	18	7	403	52	36.63	-	2	35	2							
B & H	34	29	11	574	70	31.88	-	1	31	1							
1-day Lge	121	105	31	1658	67	22.40	-	5	111	17							

UDAL, S. D.   Hampshire

Name: <u>Shaun</u> David Udal
Role: Right-hand bat, off-spin bowler
Born: 18 March 1969, Farnborough, Hants
Height: 6ft 3in **Weight:** 14st
Nickname: Shaggy
County debut: 1989
County cap: 1992
One-Day Internationals: 10
50 wickets in a season: 6
1st-Class 50s: 21
1st-Class 100s: 1
1st-Class 5 w. in innings: 25
1st-Class 10 w. in match: 4
1st-Class catches: 83
One-Day 5 w. in innings: 1
Place in batting averages: 169th av. 23.00
(2000 188th av. 19.22)
Place in bowling averages: 60th av. 29.81
(2000 71st av. 27.26)

Strike rate: 62.90 (career 70.09)
Parents: Robin Francis and Mary Elizabeth
Wife and date of marriage: Emma Jane, 5 October 1991
Children: Katherine Mary, 26 August 1992; Rebecca Jane, 17 November 1995
Family links with cricket: Father played for Camberley CC for 42 years, and also for Surrey Colts; brother is Camberley 1st XI captain. Grandfather played for Leicestershire and Middlesex
Education: Tower Hill Infants and Junior; Cove Comprehensive; 'Hampshire dressing room'
Qualifications: 8 CSEs, qualified printer, company director
Career outside cricket: Sales and marketing for the Karran Group
Off-season: 'Preparing for my benefit year and working for the Karran Group'
Overseas tours: England to Australia 1994-95; England A to Pakistan 1995-96; England XI to New Zealand (Cricket Max) 1997; Hampshire to Anguilla 1998, to Cape Town 2001
Overseas teams played for: Hamilton Wickham, Newcastle, NSW 1990-91
Career highlights to date: 'Winning NatWest and B&H with Hants and playing for England'
Cricket moments to forget: 'Getting out hooking as nightwatchman twice'
Cricketers particularly admired: Ian Botham, Shane Warne, Robin Smith
Young players to look out for: Chris Tremlett, John Francis
Other sports played: Golf (handicap of 14), football, pool, snooker, 'try anything'

Other sports followed: Football (West Ham Utd, Aldershot Town)
Injuries: Out for one week with a broken fnger
Relaxations: 'Good nights out; good food and wine; my wife and children'
Extras: Has taken two hat-tricks in club cricket. Has scored a double hundred (202) in a 40-over club game. Man of the Match on NatWest debut against Berkshire 1991. Took 8-50 v Sussex in the first game of the 1992 season, his seventh Championship match. Named Hampshire Cricket Association Player of the Year 1993. Vice-captain of Hampshire 1998-2000. Passed 500 first-class wickets during the 2001 season. Hampshire Players' Player of the Season 2001. Granted a benefit for 2002
Opinions on cricket: 'Please, everyone support the game and stop knocking it. The county game does have a future, so get behind it. England will be the best again very soon.'
Best batting: 117* Hampshire v Warwickshire, Southampton 1997
Best bowling: 8-50 Hampshire v Sussex, Southampton 1992

2001 Season

	M	Inns	NO	Runs	HS	Avge	100s	50s	Ct	St	O	M	Runs	Wkts	Avge	Best	5wI	10wM
Test																		
All First	16	20	2	414	81	23.00	-	3	5	-	566.1	143	1610	54	29.81	7-74	1	-
1-day Int																		
C & G	1	0	0	0	0	-	-	-	-	-	9	0	41	1	41.00	1-41	-	
B & H	3	2	1	25	24 *	25.00	-	-	-	-	20	0	69	3	23.00	2-33	-	
1-day Lge	15	11	3	117	28 *	14.62	-	-	8	-	123.5	12	480	15	32.00	3-23	-	

Career Performances

	M	Inns	NO	Runs	HS	Avge	100s	50s	Ct	St	Balls	Runs	Wkts	Avge	Best	5wI	10wM
Test																	
All First	183	260	46	4777	117 *	22.32	1	21	83	-	35469	17247	506	34.08	8-50	25	4
1-day Int	10	6	4	35	11 *	17.50	-	-	1	-	570	371	8	46.37	2-37	-	
C & G	28	12	5	136	39 *	19.42	-	-	12	-	1575	913	37	24.67	4-20	-	
B & H	43	26	6	264	34	13.20	-	-	13	-	2400	1561	47	33.21	4-40	-	
1-day Lge	174	116	33	1224	78	14.74	-	6	59	-	7405	5856	192	30.50	5-43	1	

89. In which year did Somerset first win the Gillette/NatWest/C&G?

VAN DER GUCHT, C. G.   Hampshire

Name: <u>Charlie</u> Graham van der Gucht
Role: Left-hand bat, left-arm orthodox
spin bowler
Born: 14 January 1980, London
Height: 6ft 1in **Weight:** 11st 5lb
Nickname: Gucht
County debut: 2000
Strike rate: 72.00 (career 51.00)
Parents: Nicky and Mike
Marital status: Single
Family links with cricket: Grandfather
played for Gloucestershire
Education: Cothill House; Radley College;
Durham University
Qualifications: 9 GCSEs, 3 A-levels,
Level 2 coaching award
Off-season: Student
Overseas tours: West of England to West
Indies 1995; British Universities to Port Elizabeth 1999; Durham University to Cape
Town 2000
Overseas teams played for: Gordon CC, Sydney 1998-99
Career highlights to date: 'First-class debut v Zimbabweans'
Cricketers particularly admired: Phil Tufnell, Muttiah Muralitharan, Gary Sobers,
Henry Fitz
Young players to look out for: Chris Tremlett
Other sports played: Rackets
Other sports followed: Football (Southampton)
Injuries: Out from July 27 with two broken legs from being run over by a taxi
Relaxations: Reading
Extras: Leading wicket-taker at Gordon club in Sydney 1998-99. Played for
Hampshire Board XI in NatWest 1999, winning Man of the Match award in fourth
round v Glamorgan at Southampton. Played for Durham University CCE in 2001.
Took 4-36 for Durham University v Loughborough University in the BUSA final at
Fenner's 2001
Opinions on cricket: 'Good game.'
Best batting: 38 DUCCE v Lancashire, Durham 2001
Best bowling: 3-75 Hampshire v Zimbabweans, Southampton 2000

2001 Season (did not make any first-class or one-day appearances)

Career Performances

	M	Inns	NO	Runs	HS	Avge	100s	50s	Ct	St	Balls	Runs	Wkts	Avge	Best	5wI	10wM
Test																	
All First	2	2	1	38	38	38.00	-	-	-	-	204	138	4	34.50	3-75	-	-
1-day Int																	
C & G	3	2	0	4	3	2.00	-	-	-	-	144	95	5	19.00	3-35	-	
B & H																	
1-day Lge																	

VAUGHAN, M. P. *Yorkshire*

Name: <u>Michael</u> Paul Vaughan
Role: Right-hand bat, off-spin bowler
Born: 29 October 1974, Eccles, Manchester
Height: 6ft 2in **Weight:** 11st 7lbs
Nickname: Frankie, Virgil
County debut: 1993
County cap: 1995
Test debut: 1999-2000
Tests: 11
One-Day Internationals: 6
1000 runs in a season: 4
1st-Class 50s: 43
1st-Class 100s: 21
1st-Class catches: 78
One-Day 100s: 1
Place in batting averages: 25th av. 52.43
(2000 29th av. 43.30)
Strike rate: 57.28 (career 77.87)
Parents: Graham John and Dee
Marital status: Single
Family links with cricket: Father played league cricket for Worsley CC. Brother plays for Sheffield Collegiate. Mother is related to the famous Tyldesley family (Lancashire and England)
Education: St Marks, Worsley, Manchester; Dore Juniors, Sheffield; Silverdale Comprehensive, Sheffield
Qualifications: 7 GCSEs
Off-season: Touring with England
Overseas tours: Yorkshire to West Indies 1994, to South Africa 1995, to Zimbabwe 1996; England U19 to India 1992-93, to Sri Lanka 1993-94 (captain); England A to India

1994-95, to Australia 1996-97, to Zimbabwe and South Africa 1998-99 (captain); England to South Africa 1999-2000, to Pakistan and Sri Lanka 2000-01, to India and New Zealand 2001-02

Career highlights to date: 'Scoring my first Test hundred. Winning the Championship with Yorkshire [2001]'

Cricket moments to forget: 'My one-day series in 2001'

Cricketers particularly admired: Darren Lehmann, 'all the Yorkshire and England squads'

Young players to look out for: Richard Dawson, Matthew Wood

Other sports played: Football (Baslow FC), golf

Other sports followed: Football (Sheffield Wednesday), all golf

Injuries: Cartilage operation

Relaxations: Most sports. 'Enjoy a good meal with friends'

Extras: Played club cricket for Sheffield Collegiate in the Yorkshire League. *Daily Telegraph* U15 Batsman of the Year 1990. Maurice Leyland Batting Award 1990. Rapid Cricketline Player of the Month, June 1993. The Cricket Society's Most Promising Young Cricketer 1993. A. A. Thompson Memorial Trophy – The Roses Cricketer of the Year 1993. Whittingdale Cricketer of the Month, July 1994. Scored 1066 runs in first full season of first-class cricket in 1994. Captained England U19 in home series against India 1994. Scored two 100s (100 and 151) v Essex at Chelmsford 1999; Stuart Law scored two 100s for Essex in the same match. Became the 600th player to represent England when he made his Test debut v South Africa at Johannesburg 1999-2000. Struck 69 in England's only innings of the rain-shortened fifth Test at Centurion, January 2000, a match-winning maiden Test 50 that earned him the Man of the Match award. Man of the Match for his 76 in England's only innings in the fourth Test v West Indies at his home ground of Headingley 2000. Took 4-46 and scored 92 v Leicestershire in the B&H at Leicester 2001. B&H Gold Award for his 128-ball 125* in the quarter-final v Somerset at Taunton 2001; it was his maiden one-day century. England central contract 2001. Scored maiden Test century (120) at Old Trafford 2001, in the process sharing in a record partnership for any wicket for England in Tests v Pakistan (267) with Graham Thorpe. Scored 89-ball 113 (century from 80 balls) v Essex at Scarborough 2001

Best batting: 183 Yorkshire v Glamorgan, Cardiff 1996

Best bowling: 4-39 Yorkshire v Oxford University, The Parks 1994

Stop press: Became the second England cricketer (after Graham Gooch) and the seventh cricketer overall in Tests to be given out handled the ball, when he was out for 64 v India in the third Test at Bangalore 2001-02

2001 Season

	M	Inns	NO	Runs	HS	Avge	100s	50s	Ct	St	O	M	Runs	Wkts	Avge	Best	5wl	10wM
Test	2	3	0	166	120	55.33	1	-	2	-	3	0	33	0	-	-	-	-
All First	9	16	0	839	133	52.43	3	4	8	-	66.5	14	198	7	28.28	4-47	-	-
1-day Int	4	4	0	7	5	1.75	-	-	1	-	2	0	17	0	-	-	-	
C & G																		
B & H	7	7	1	301	125 *	50.16	1	1	4	-	36	0	161	8	20.12	4-46	-	
1-day Lge	3	3	0	30	24	10.00	-	-	2	-								

Career Performances

	M	Inns	NO	Runs	HS	Avge	100s	50s	Ct	St	Balls	Runs	Wkts	Avge	Best	5wl	10wM
Test	11	18	0	573	120	31.83	1	2	10	-	174	131	0	-	-	-	-
All First	159	280	14	9360	183	35.18	21	43	78	-	8410	4703	108	43.54	4-39	-	-
1-day Int	6	6	0	42	26	7.00	-	-	1	-	18	20	0	-	-	-	
C & G	19	19	1	483	85	26.83	-	4	4	-	270	156	5	31.20	1-4	-	
B & H	37	35	3	1113	125 *	34.78	1	7	12	-	765	515	19	27.10	4-46	-	
1-day Lge	89	87	6	1866	72	23.03	-	8	29	-	998	813	31	26.22	4-27	-	

WADE, J.　　　　　　　Northamptonshire

Name: James Wade
Role: Right-hand top-order bat, slip fielder
Born: 7 May 1981, Bedford
Height: 5ft 11in **Weight:** 11st 8lbs
Nickname: Wadey
County debut: No first-team appearance
Parents: Nigel and Joanna
Marital status: Single
Family links with cricket: 'Dad played club cricket'
Education: Bedford Modern School; Loughborough University
Qualifications: 9 GCSEs, 3 A-levels
Career outside cricket: Student
Overseas tours: Bedford Modern School to Caribbean 1997, 1999; Northamptonshire U19 to South Africa 2000
Overseas teams played for: South Sydney 1999-2000

Cricketers particularly admired: Mark Waugh, Michael Slater, Shane Warne
Other sports played: Football (Watford School of Excellence 1994-95), golf
Relaxations: Socialising with friends, golf, snooker

Extras: Played for Northamptonshire Board XI in the C&G 2001 and in the first round of the C&G 2002, which was played in August 2001

2001 Season (did not make any first-class or one-day appearances)

Career Performances

	M	Inns	NO	Runs	HS	Avge	100s	50s	Ct	St	Balls	Runs	Wkts	Avge	Best	5wl	10wM
Test																	
All First																	
1-day Int																	
C & G	2	2	0	50	38	25.00	-	-	1	-	12	37	0	-		-	-
B & H																	
1-day Lge																	

WAGG, G. G. Warwickshire

Name: <u>Graham</u> Grant Wagg
Role: Right-hand lower-middle-order bat, left-arm fast-medium opening bowler; all-rounder
Born: 28 April 1983, Rugby
Height: 6ft **Weight:** 12st 10lbs
Nickname: Stiggy
County debut: No first-team appearance
Parents: John and Dawn
Marital status: Single
Family links with cricket: Father is qualified coach
Education: Boughton-Leigh Primary, Rugby; Ashlawn School, Rugby
Qualifications: Level 1 cricket coach
Off-season: 'Working to improve my game with the Warwickshire Academy, and coaching'

Overseas tours: Warwickshire CCC Development tour to South Africa 1998, to West Indies 2000
Overseas teams played for: Hams Tech, East London, South Africa 1999
Career highlights to date: 'Taking 5-63 v West Indies U19 touring side (and having two catches dropped), followed by 45* in 26 balls'
Cricketers particularly admired: Ian Botham, Courtney Walsh, Glenn McGrath
Young players to look out for: Ian Bell, Kyle Hogg, Alex Roberts
Other sports played: Golf, carp fishing
Other sports followed: Football (Man United)

Injuries: Out for four weeks early season with shin splints
Relaxations: Fishing, golf, football, music, clubbing
Extras: Represented England U16, U17 and U18. Played for Warwickshire Board XI in the NatWest 2000. Member of Warwickshire's ECB U19 County Championship-winning squad 2001
Opinions on cricket: 'I haven't played enough yet to have a qualified opinion.'

2001 Season (did not make any first-class or one-day appearances)

Career Performances

	M	Inns	NO	Runs	HS	Avge	100s	50s	Ct	St	Balls	Runs	Wkts	Avge	Best	5wI	10wM
Test																	
All First																		
1-day Int																		
C & G	1	1	0	0	0	0.00	-	-	-	-	30	17	0	-		-	-
B & H																		
1-day Lge																		

WAGH, M. A.　　　　　　　　　Warwickshire

Name: <u>Mark</u> Anant Wagh
Role: Right-hand bat, off-spin bowler
Born: 20 October 1976, Birmingham
Height: 6ft 2in **Weight:** 13st
Nickname: Waggy
County debut: 1997
County cap: 2000
1000 runs in a season: 1
1st-Class 50s: 18
1st-Class 100s: 10
1st-Class 200s: 1
1st-Class 300s: 1
1st-Class catches: 35
Place in batting averages: 16th av. 58.04
(2000 21st av. 45.53)
Place in bowling averages: 100th av. 36.38
Strike rate: 84.92 (career 100.83)
Parents: Mohan and Rita
Marital status: Single
Education: Harborne Infants and Junior School; King Edward's School, Birmingham; Keble College, Oxford
Qualifications: 12 GCSEs, 4 A-levels, BA degree, Level 2 coaching award

Off-season: National Academy
Overseas tours: Warwickshire U19 to South Africa 1992; ECB National Academy to Australia 2001-02
Career highlights to date: '315 at Lord's 2001'
Cricket moments to forget: 'Too many to mention'
Cricketers particularly admired: Andy Flower
Young players to look out for: Ian Bell ('obviously')
Other sports followed: Hockey, snooker, football
Relaxations: Stock market
Extras: Oxford Blue 1996-98; Oxford University captain 1997. Scored maiden first-class century (116) v Glamorgan at The Parks 1997, following up with another 100 (101) in the second innings to become the first batsman to score a century in each innings of a match for Oxford University since Imran Khan did so v Notts in 1974. Attended Zimbabwe Cricket Academy 1999. With Michael Powell, shared in record first-wicket stand for Warwickshire in matches v Essex (230) at Chelmsford 2000. His 315 v Middlesex at Lord's 2001 is the second highest score by a batsman for Warwickshire (behind Brian Lara's 501* in 1994) and the equal second highest individual Championship score made at Lord's (behind Jack Hobbs's 316 in 1926)
Best batting: 315 Warwickshire v Middlesex, Lord's 2001
Best bowling: 4-11 Warwickshire v Middlesex, Lord's 1998

2001 Season

	M	Inns	NO	Runs	HS	Avge	100s	50s	Ct	St	O	M	Runs	Wkts	Avge	Best	5wI	10wM
Test																		
All First	16	24	2	1277	315	58.04	3	6	4	-	184	37	473	13	36.38	3-3	-	-
1-day Int																		
C & G	3	3	0	68	46	22.66	-	-	-	-								
B & H	6	6	0	101	39	16.83	-	-	-	-								
1-day Lge	12	10	1	201	70 *	22.33	-	3	1	-	3	0	26	0	-		-	-

Career Performances

	M	Inns	NO	Runs	HS	Avge	100s	50s	Ct	St	Balls	Runs	Wkts	Avge	Best	5wI	10wM
Test																	
All First	82	130	13	4571	315	39.06	12	18	35	-	4336	2199	43	51.13	4-11	-	-
1-day Int																	
C & G	3	3	0	68	46	22.66	-	-	-	-							
B & H	9	9	1	137	39	17.12	-	-	-	-	174	119	3	39.66	1-39	-	
1-day Lge	18	16	1	297	70 *	19.80	-	3	1	-	42	41	0	-		-	-

WALKER, G. W.　　　　　Leicestershire

Name: <u>George</u> William Walker
Role: Left-hand bat, slow left-arm bowler
Born: 12 May 1984, Norwich
Height: 5ft 10in **Weight:** 10st 7lbs
Nickname: Walksy
County debut: No first-team appearance
Parents: John and Sarah
Marital status: Single
Education: Town Close Prep School,
Norwich; Norwich School
Qualifications: 9 GCSEs, 4 AS-levels,
ECB Level 1 coach
Career outside cricket: At school
Off-season: 'Coaching Norfolk U11
pre-season'
Career highlights to date: 'First Minor
Counties wicket – Derek Randall in his last
game for Suffolk'
Cricketers particularly admired: Ashley Giles, Brian Lara
Other sports played: Hockey, tennis, football, 'anything'
Other sports followed: Football (Norwich City); cricket, football, rugby (England national teams)
Injuries: Fractured little finger, but no games missed
Relaxations: 'Meeting up with friends; listening to a lot of music; films, videos, golf'
Extras: Played for Norfolk from U12 to 1st XI. Represented Midlands U13 and U14 and England U14, U15 and U17
Opinions on cricket: 'Introduce what they've done in New Zealand – Cricket Max – faster, more exciting game for the crowd.'

90. The Northamptonshire side that contested the 1981
NatWest final contained three players who are now
on the first-class umpires list. Who are they?

WALKER, M. J.   Kent

Name: <u>Matthew</u> Jonathan Walker
Role: Left-hand bat, right-arm medium-fast bowler
Born: 2 January 1974, Gravesend, Kent
Height: 5ft 6in **Weight:** 12st 6lbs
Nickname: Walks, Walkdog, Pumba, Sweetie Pud, Cheeky Monkey, Dicky Neurerker, Merse
County debut: 1992-93
County cap: 2000
1st-Class 50s: 14
1st-Class 100s: 6
1st-Class 200s: 1
1st-Class catches: 56
One-Day 100s: 2
Place in batting averages: 51st av. 44.77 (2000 133rd av. 25.52)
Strike rate: 60.00 (career 94.62)
Parents: Richard and June
Wife and date of marriage: Claudia, 25 September 1999
Family links with cricket: Grandfather Jack played one game for Kent as a wicket-keeper. Father played for Kent and Middlesex 2nd XIs and was on Lord's groundstaff. Mother coached ex-England Ladies captain Megan Lear
Education: Shorne C of E Primary School; King's School, Rochester
Qualifications: 9 GCSEs, 2 A-levels, advanced coaching award
Career outside cricket: Teacher
Off-season: Teaching at St Edmunds School – hockey and cricket
Overseas tours: Kent U17 to New Zealand 1990-91; England U19 to Pakistan 1991-92, to India 1992-93 (captain); Kent to Zimbabwe 1992-93, to Port Elizabeth 2001
Career highlights to date: 'Captaining England U19. Winning Norwich Union League 2001'
Cricket moments to forget: 'Losing Lord's [B&H] final against Surrey 1997'
Cricketers particularly admired: Sachin Tendulkar, Darren Lehmann, Damien Martyn
Young players to look out for: Alex Loudon, James Tredwell
Other sports played: Hockey (England U14-U21 [captain U15-U17], Kent U14-U21, South East U16-U18), rugby (Kent U18), football (trials for Chelsea and Gillingham), athletics (Kent U15 javelin champion)
Other sports followed: Football (Charlton Athletic), rugby (Gravesend RFC), hockey (Canterbury HC)
Injuries: Out for two weeks with a strained hamstring

Relaxations: Music and films ('avid collector of both'). 'Any good restaurant with a cheeky little bottle of white'

Extras: Captained England U16 cricket team and England U16 hockey team in same year. Captained England U19 v West Indies U19 in 1993 home series. Received Sir Jack Hobbs award for best young cricketer 1989, and *Daily Telegraph* U15 batting award 1989. Woolwich Kent League's Young Cricketer of the Year 1994. Scored 275 not out against Somerset in 1996 – the highest ever individual score by a Kent batsman at Canterbury – and was on the pitch for the whole game. B&H Gold Award for his 106* v Essex at Chelmsford 2001. Became an Eminent Roffensian in 1995

Opinions on cricket: 'Better wickets should be encouraged if the standard is to improve. Pitch inspectors should be stricter.'

Best batting: 275* Kent v Somerset, Canterbury 1996

Best bowling: 1-3 First-Class Counties XI v New Zealand A, Milton Keynes 2000

2001 Season

	M	Inns	NO	Runs	HS	Avge	100s	50s	Ct	St	O	M	Runs	Wkts	Avge	Best	5wI	10wM
Test																		
All First	17	25	3	985	124	44.77	4	3	9	-	20	3	69	2	34.50	1-9	-	-
1-day Int																		
C & G	3	2	0	42	36	21.00	-	-	2	-	5	0	34	1	34.00	1-34	-	
B & H	5	4	1	212	106*	70.66	1	1	1	-	4	0	16	1	16.00	1-16	-	
1-day Lge	14	14	1	205	34	15.76	-	-	3	-	19.3	0	77	9	8.55	4-24	-	

Career Performances

	M	Inns	NO	Runs	HS	Avge	100s	50s	Ct	St	Balls	Runs	Wkts	Avge	Best	5wI	10wM
Test																	
All First	87	142	15	3830	275*	30.15	7	14	56	-	757	390	8	48.75	1-3	-	-
1-day Int																	
C & G	10	9	2	254	73	36.28	-	2	2	-	102	70	2	35.00	1-33	-	
B & H	29	27	4	938	117	40.78	2	6	10	-	24	16	1	16.00	1-16	-	
1-day Lge	99	93	9	1626	80	19.35	-	7	24	-	351	281	15	18.73	4-24	-	

91. In which year did Holland first take part in the Gillette/NatWest/C&G?

WALLACE, M. A. Glamorgan

Name: <u>Mark</u> Alex Wallace
Role: Left-hand bat, wicket-keeper
Born: 19 November 1981, Abergavenny
Height: 5ft 10in **Weight:** 12st
Nickname: Wally, Marcellus, Gromit
County debut: 1999
1st-Class 50s: 4
1st-Class catches: 49
1st-Class stumpings: 1
Place in batting averages: 173rd av. 22.30
Parents: Ryland and Alvine
Marital status: Single
Family links with cricket: Father plays for
Abergavenny CC
Education: Crickhowell Primary School;
Crickhowell High School
Qualifications: 10 GCSEs, 2 A-levels
Off-season: In Adelaide with England
Academy

Overseas tours: Gwent U15 to South Africa 1996; Wales U16 to Jersey 1996, 1997;
England U19 to New Zealand 1998-99, to Malaysia and (U19 World Cup) Sri Lanka
1999-2000, to India 2000-01; ECB National Academy to Australia 2001-02
Career highlights to date: 'Beating Surrey at The Oval 2001. Being selected for
National Academy'
Cricket moments to forget: 'Leicestershire at Grace Road 2001 – nightmare'
(*Leicestershire won this crucial Championship match by ten wickets*)
Cricketers particularly admired: Ian Healy, Warren Hegg, Steve James, Keith Piper,
Adam Gilchrist
Young players to look out for: David Harrison, Simon Jones, Stephen Pope,
James Pipe, Justin Bishop, Ian Thomas, Jon Hughes
Other sports played: Football, golf, touch rugby ('badly')
Other sports followed: Football ('follow "the Martyrs" – Merthyr Tydfil FC')
Relaxations: Golf, sleep, PlayStation
Extras: Represented England U17 at the ECC Colts Festival in Northern Ireland 1999.
Represented England U19 in home series against Pakistan U19 1998, Australia U19
1999 and Sri Lanka U19 (as captain for second 'Test') 2000, although missed the one-
day series v Sri Lanka U19 due to injury. Made first-class debut v Somerset 1999 aged
17 years 287 days – youngest ever Glamorgan wicket-keeper. NBC Denis Compton
Award 1999. Took eight catches in match v Kent at Maidstone 2001, one short of
Colin Metson's Glamorgan record. Took seven catches in the match and scored 63*
and 18* in win over Surrey at The Oval 2001

Opinions on cricket: 'Tea break too short. Get rid of leg byes as part of the game.'
Best batting: 80* Glamorgan v Kent, Maidstone 2001
Stop press: Captained ECB National Academy to innings victory over Commonwealth Bank [Australian] Cricket Academy in Adelaide 2001-02

2001 Season

	M	Inns	NO	Runs	HS	Avge	100s	50s	Ct	St	O	M	Runs	Wkts	Avge	Best	5wI	10wM
Test																		
All First	10	16	3	290	80 *	22.30	-	2	27	1								
1-day Int																		
C & G																		
B & H																		
1-day Lge																		

Career Performances

	M	Inns	NO	Runs	HS	Avge	100s	50s	Ct	St	Balls	Runs	Wkts	Avge	Best	5wI	10wM
Test																	
All First	16	25	5	504	80 *	25.20	-	4	49	1							
1-day Int																	
C & G																	
B & H																	
1-day Lge	7	5	1	18	8 *	4.50	-	-	7	3							

> 92. For which county did Stewart Storey, Arnold Long and Geoff Arnold appear in the 1978 Gillette Cup final?

WARD, I. J.   Surrey

Name: <u>Ian</u> James Ward
Role: Left-hand bat
Born: 30 September 1973, Plymouth
Height: 5ft 8½in **Weight:** 12st 12lbs
Nickname: Wardy, Cocker, Son of Baboon,
Dwarf, Stumpy, Pig in a Passage
County debut: 1996
County cap: 2000
Test debut: 2001
Tests: 5
1000 runs in a season: 1
1st-Class 50s: 29
1st-Class 100s: 7
1st-Class catches: 45
Place in batting averages: 144th av. 26.53
(2000 38th av. 40.63)
Parents: Tony and Mary
Wife and date of marriage: Joanne,
15 February 1998
Children: Robert, 21 September; Lennox, 10 April
Family links with cricket: Grandfather and father played for Devon
Education: Valley End; Millfield School; 'Ben Hollioake's house'
Qualifications: 8 GCSEs, 3 A-levels, NCA coaching award
Off-season: 'Resting, training, improving and holidaying/practising in Australia'
Overseas tours: Surrey U19 to Barbados 1990; Millfield to Jamaica 1991, to
Australia; Malden Wanderers to Jersey 1994; England A to Bangladesh and New
Zealand 1999-2000, to West Indies 2000-01
Overseas teams played for: North Perth CC, Western Australia 1996-97; Perth CC,
Western Australia; Marist Newman Old Boys CC
Career highlights to date: 'Test debut'
Cricket moments to forget: 'Losing the Ashes'
Cricketers particularly admired: Graham Thorpe, Mark Wasley (North Perth CC),
Ali Brown, Justin Langer, Martin Bicknell
Young players to look out for: Gareth Batty
Other sports played: Golf and 'Foxball'
Other sports followed: Football (Liverpool), beach volleyball, Formula One
motor racing
Injuries: Out for one Norwich Union game with a thigh strain
Relaxations: 'Spending time with my wife, walking dog, running'
Extras: Released by Surrey at 18 and missed four years of cricket, returning to the
county in 1996. Surrey 2nd XI cap at the age of 23. Scored centuries in three

successive Busta Cup matches for England A in West Indies 2000-01 and was leading first-class run-scorer on tour (769 av. 64.08); during his 135 v Barbados at Bridgetown, he shared in record opening stand for England A (224) with Michael Powell. Made Test debut v Pakistan at Lord's 2001 in England's 100th Test at the ground

Opinions on cricket: 'Still play too much. More time needed to practise, train and prepare. Wickets and practice wickets *must improve* or our players will not learn how to play on good overseas pitches. Groundsmen should be contracted to ECB. ECB contracts for England players have worked well. Two divisions excellent, but points for wins in Championship cricket should be higher or points for winning on first innings awarded. Only two up/two down in present four-day format. Better still, introduce regional cricket, scrapping 2nd XI cricket and using county cricket as semi-pro feeder system.'

Best batting: 158* Surrey v Kent, Canterbury 2000

2001 Season

	M	Inns	NO	Runs	HS	Avge	100s	50s	Ct	St	O	M	Runs	Wkts	Avge	Best	5wI	10wM
Test	5	9	1	129	39	16.12	-	-	1	-								
All First	16	27	1	690	79	26.53	-	4	6	-								
1-day Int																		
C & G	2	2	1	151	81	151.00	-	2	-	-								
B & H	7	7	1	244	71 *	40.66	-	3	1	-								
1-day Lge	9	9	0	153	51	17.00	-	1	2	-								

Career Performances

	M	Inns	NO	Runs	HS	Avge	100s	50s	Ct	St	Balls	Runs	Wkts	Avge	Best	5wI	10wM
Test	5	9	1	129	39	16.12	-	-	1	-							
All First	80	134	12	4308	158 *	35.31	7	29	45	-	156	102	0	-		-	-	-
1-day Int																	
C & G	13	11	2	328	81	36.44	-	2	-	-							
B & H	12	10	1	256	71 *	28.44	-	3	2	-							
1-day Lge	63	60	8	1348	91	25.92	-	8	13	-	53	84	0	-		-	-

---

93. When Yorkshire met Surrey in the 1965 Gillette Cup final, each side fielded a player whose son is now a county cricketer. Name the fathers and the sons.

WARD, T. R.   Leicestershire

Name: <u>Trevor</u> Robert Ward
Role: Right-hand bat, occasional
off-spin bowler
Born: 18 January 1968, Farningham, Kent
Height: 5ft 11in   **Weight:** 13st
Nickname: Wardy, Chikka
County debut: 1986 (Kent),
2000 (Leicestershire)
County cap: 1989 (Kent),
2001 (Leicestershire)
Benefit: 1999 (Kent)
1000 runs in a season: 6
1st-Class 50s: 72
1st-Class 100s: 27
1st-Class 200s: 1
1st-Class catches: 212
One-Day 100s: 7
Place in batting averages: 45th av. 45.89

(2000 250th av. 12.22)
Strike rate: (career 135.37)
Parents: Robert Henry and Hazel Ann
Wife and date of marriage: Sarah Ann, 29 September 1990
Children: Holly Ann, 23 October 1995; Samuel Joseph, 25 April 1998
Family links with cricket: Father played club cricket
Education: Anthony Roper County Primary; Hextable Comprehensive
Qualifications: 7 O-levels, NCA coaching award
Overseas tours: NCA to Bermuda 1985; England YC to Sri Lanka 1986-87,
to Australia (U19 World Cup) 1987-88
Overseas teams played for: Scarborough, Perth, Western Australia 1985;
Gosnells, Perth 1993
Cricketers particularly admired: Ian Botham, Graham Gooch, Robin Smith
Other sports followed: 'Most sports'
Relaxations: Fishing, watching television, golf
Extras: Was awarded £1000 for becoming the first player to score 400 runs in the
Benson and Hedges Cup in 1995. Released by Kent at the end of the 1999 season and
joined Leicestershire for 2000. Awarded Leicestershire cap on the same day as he
scored a century (110) against his old county Kent at Leicester 2001
Best batting: 235* Kent v Middlesex, Canterbury 1991
Best bowling: 2-10 Kent v Yorkshire, Canterbury 1996

2001 Season

	M	Inns	NO	Runs	HS	Avge	100s	50s	Ct	St	O	M	Runs	Wkts	Avge	Best	5wI	10wM
Test																		
All First	12	21	2	872	160 *	45.89	4	2	7	-								
1-day Int																		
C & G	3	3	0	89	54	29.66	-	1	1	-								
B & H	2	2	0	9	9	4.50	-	-	1	-								
1-day Lge	11	11	0	180	56	16.36	-	1	4	-								

Career Performances

	M	Inns	NO	Runs	HS	Avge	100s	50s	Ct	St	Balls	Runs	Wkts	Avge	Best	5wI	10wM
Test																	
All First	225	386	22	12879	235 *	35.38	28	72	212	-	1083	647	8	80.87	2-10	-	-
1-day Int																	
C & G	27	27	1	1023	120	39.34	1	9	5	-	174	154	4	38.50	2-25	-	
B & H	56	56	3	1739	125	32.81	2	12	12	-	12	10	0	-	-	-	-
1-day Lge	196	190	6	5237	131	28.46	4	33	45	-	228	187	6	31.16	3-20	-	

WARREN, N. A.   Warwickshire

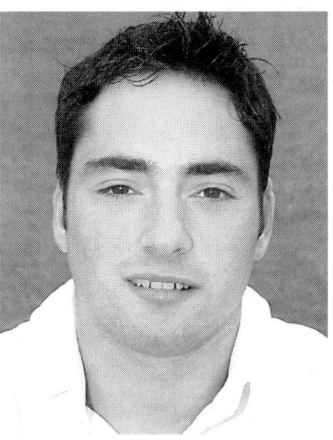

Name: Nick Alexander Warren
Role: Right-hand bat, right-arm medium-fast bowler
Born: 26 June 1982, Moseley
Height: 5ft 11in **Weight:** 12st 7lbs
Nickname: Wazza
County debut: No first-team appearance
Parents: Lesley
Marital status: Single
Education: St Martins; Wheelers Lane Boys School; Solihull Sixth Form College
Qualifications: 9 GCSEs, BTEC Sports Science
Off-season: Receiving coaching in South Africa
Overseas tours: Warwickshire U19 to Cape Town 1998-99; England U17 to Ireland 1999; England U19 to Malaysia and (U19 World Cup) Sri Lanka 1999-2000
Cricketers particularly admired: Allan Donald, Graeme Welch
Young players to look out for: Jim Troughton
Other sports played: Football
Other sports followed: Football (Birmingham City)

Relaxations: Watching films; planes, music
Extras: Played for Warwickshire Board XI in the second round of the C&G 2002, which was played in September 2001
Opinions on cricket: 'I haven't really played the game long enough.'

2001 Season (did not make any first-class or one-day appearances)

Career Performances

	M	Inns	NO	Runs	HS	Avge	100s	50s	Ct	St	Balls	Runs	Wkts	Avge	Best	5wl	10wM
Test																	
All First																	
1-day Int																	
C & G	1	1	0	0	0	0.00	-	-	2	-	36	29	0	-		-	-
B & H																	
1-day Lge																	

WARREN, R. J.   Northamptonshire

Name: <u>Russell</u> John Warren
Role: Right-hand bat, wicket-keeper
Born: 10 September 1971, Northampton
Height: 6ft 2in **Weight:** 13st 4lbs
Nickname: Rab C, Rabbit
County debut: 1992
County cap: 1995
1000 runs in a season: 1
1st-Class 50s: 30
1st-Class 100s: 8
1st-Class 200s: 1
1st-Class catches: 105
1st-Class stumpings: 3
One-Day 100s: 1
Place in batting averages: 22nd av. 54.29
(2000 61st av. 34.75)
Parents: John and Sally
Marital status: Single
Family links with cricket: 'Dad likes a bet. Mum follows scores on Teletext'
Education: Whitehills Lower School; Kingsthorpe Middle and Upper Schools
Qualifications: 8 O-levels, 2 A-levels
Overseas tours: England YC to New Zealand 1990-91; Northamptonshire to Cape Town 1993, to Zimbabwe 1995, to Johannesburg 1996, to Grenada 2000
Overseas teams played for: Lancaster Park, Christchurch, and Canterbury B, New Zealand 1991-93; Riverside CC, Lower Hutt, New Zealand 1994-95; Petone CC,

Wellington, New Zealand 1995-96; Alma Marist CC, Cape Town, South Africa
1997-98
Cricketers particularly admired: Allan Lamb, Wayne Larkins
Young players to look out for: Mark Powell
Other sports played: Golf, snooker
Other sports followed: Football (Manchester United and Northampton Town),
rugby (Northampton Saints), golf, snooker and horse racing
Relaxations: 'Music, having a bet'
Extras: Scored 175 v Glamorgan at Northampton 2001, in the process sharing with
Tony Penberthy in a record sixth-wicket partnership for Northants in matches against
Glamorgan (250). Scored 144 v Somerset at Taunton 2001, in the process sharing with
Mike Hussey in a record third-wicket partnership for Northants in matches against
Somerset (287)
Opinions on cricket: 'Smaller staffs. Scrap 2nd XI cricket.'
Best batting: 201* Northamptonshire v Glamorgan, Northampton 1996

2001 Season

	M	Inns	NO	Runs	HS	Avge	100s	50s	Ct	St	O	M	Runs	Wkts	Avge	Best	5wI	10wM
Test																		
All First	16	26	2	1303	194	54.29	4	7	8	-	1	1	0	0	-	-	-	-
1-day Int																		
C & G	2	2	1	84	70 *	84.00	-	1	1	-								
B & H	5	5	2	31	19	10.33	-	-	3	-								
1-day Lge	11	11	1	411	93	41.10	-	4	4	-								

Career Performances

	M	Inns	NO	Runs	HS	Avge	100s	50s	Ct	St	Balls	Runs	Wkts	Avge	Best	5wI	10wM
Test																	
All First	104	168	19	5398	201 *	36.22	9	30	105	3	6	0	0	-	-	-	-
1-day Int																	
C & G	19	17	3	432	100 *	30.85	1	2	21	1							
B & H	19	18	3	159	23	10.60	-	-	18	-							
1-day Lge	93	82	12	1734	93	24.77	-	8	74	9							

94. When Northamptonshire met Lancashire in the
1976 Gillette Cup final, the former's line-up included one Indian and
two Pakistani Test players. Who were they?

WATKIN, S. L. Glamorgan

Name: <u>Steven</u> Llewellyn Watkin
Role: Right-hand bat, right-arm
medium-fast bowler
Born: 15 September 1964, Dyffryn, Rhondda
Height: 6ft 3in **Weight:** 12st 8lbs
Nickname: Watty, Banger
County debut: 1986
County cap: 1989
Benefit: 1998
Test debut: 1991
Tests: 3

One-Day Internationals: 4
50 wickets in a season: 9
1st-Class 50s: 1
1st-Class 5 w. in innings: 31
1st-Class 10 w. in match: 4
1st-Class catches: 71
One-Day 5 w. in innings: 1
Place in batting averages: 202nd av. 18.80 (2000 200th av. 17.85)
Place in bowling averages: 76th av. 32.55 (2000 34th av. 22.22)
Strike rate: 65.95 (career 57.68)
Parents: John (deceased) and Sandra
Wife and date of marriage: Caryl, 8 April 2000
Family links with cricket: Brothers play for local cricket teams
Education: Cymer Afan Comprehensive; Swansea College of Further Education;
South Glamorgan Institute of Higher Education
Qualifications: 8 O-levels, 2 A-levels, BA (Hons) Human Movement Studies,
Level 3 coaching award
Career outside cricket: New Welsh Academy director
Overseas tours: British Colleges to West Indies 1987; England A to Kenya and
Zimbabwe 1989-90, to Pakistan and Sri Lanka 1990-91, to Bermuda and West Indies
1991-92; England to West Indies 1993-94
Overseas teams played for: Potchefstroom University, South Africa 1987-88;
Aurora, Durban 1991-92
Career highlights: 'Winning County Championship 1997 and Sunday League 1993.
Test caps'
Cricket moments to forget: 'Getting hit for 28 in an over against Essex in the
Norwich Union League 2001'
Cricketers particularly admired: Richard Hadlee, Dennis Lillee, Ian Botham,
Allan Donald, Alec Stewart
Young players to look out for: Mark Wallace, Dave Harrison

Other sports played: Football (Welsh Boys' Clubs cap as goalkeeper)
Other sports followed: Football ('all Welsh football clubs'), rugby (Neath and Maesteg)
Relaxations: Watching television, music, DIY, motor mechanics, 'a quiet pint'
Extras: Joint highest wicket-taker in English first-class cricket 1989 with 94 wickets and took most (92) in 1993. Sister Lynda has played for Great Britain at hockey. PCA Player of the Year and Glamorgan Player of the Year 1993. One of *Wisden*'s Five Cricketers of the Year 1994. Began Glamorgan's match v Notts at Colwyn Bay 1999 with a spell of 5-0 off 17 balls, passing 800 first-class wickets in the process. Scored maiden first-class 50 (51) v Gloucestershire at Cardiff 2000. Took 900th first-class wicket (Vince Wells lbw) v Leicestershire at Leicester 2001. Retired at the end of the 2001 season to become Welsh Academy director but his registration has been retained
Opinions on cricket: 'Let's be patient with regard to the England Test team – progress is being made! Obvious difference between first and second division in County Championship.'
Best batting: 51 Glamorgan v Gloucestershire, Cardiff 2000
Best bowling: 8-59 Glamorgan v Warwickshire, Edgbaston 1988

2001 Season

	M	Inns	NO	Runs	HS	Avge	100s	50s	Ct	St	O	M	Runs	Wkts	Avge	Best	5wI	10wM
Test																		
All First	15	17	7	188	38	18.80	-	-	5	-	472.4	113	1400	43	32.55	6-67	1	-
1-day Int																		
C & G	2	0	0	0	0	-	-	-	1	-	12	0	84	0	-		-	-
B & H	3	0	0	0	0	-	-	-	-	-	30	4	115	5	23.00	2-34	-	
1-day Lge	8	2	0	5	3	2.50	-	-	-	-	66	8	289	4	72.25	2-26	-	

Career Performances

	M	Inns	NO	Runs	HS	Avge	100s	50s	Ct	St	Balls	Runs	Wkts	Avge	Best	5wI	10wM
Test	3	5	0	25	13	5.00	-	-	1	-	534	305	11	27.72	4-65	-	-
All First	266	297	109	2037	51	10.83	-	1	71	-	52035	25191	902	27.92	8-59	31	4
1-day Int	4	2	0	4	4	2.00	-	-	-	-	221	193	7	27.57	4-49	-	
C & G	36	15	5	53	13	5.30	-	-	4	-	2237	1213	45	26.95	4-26	-	
B & H	46	24	11	100	15	7.69	-	-	9	-	2619	1671	62	26.95	4-31	-	
1-day Lge	159	66	24	270	31 *	6.42	-	-	25	-	7051	5054	187	27.02	5-23	1	

WATKINSON, M.   Lancashire

Name: Michael Watkinson
Role: Right-hand bat, right-arm medium or off-spin bowler
Born: 1 August 1961, Westhoughton
Height: 6ft 1½in   **Weight:** 13st
Nickname: Winker
County debut: 1982
County cap: 1987
Benefit: 1996 (£209,000)
Test debut: 1995
Tests: 4
One-Day Internationals: 1
1000 runs in a season: 1
50 wickets in a season: 7
1st-Class 50s: 50
1st-Class 100s: 11
1st-Class 5 w. in innings: 27
1st-Class 10 w. in match: 3
1st-Class catches: 156
One-Day 100s: 2
One-Day 5 w. in innings: 3
Strike rate: (career 64.69)
Parents: Albert and Marian
Wife and date of marriage: Susan, 12 April 1986
Children: Charlotte, 24 February 1989; Liam, 27 July 1991
Education: Rivington and Blackrod High School, Horwich
Qualifications: 8 O-levels, HTC Civil Engineering
Career outside cricket: Draughtsman
Overseas tours: England to South Africa 1995-96
Cricketers particularly admired: Clive Lloyd, Imran Khan
Other sports followed: Football
Relaxations: Watching Bolton Wanderers
Extras: Played for Cheshire in Minor Counties Championship and in NatWest Trophy (v Middlesex) 1982. Man of the Match in the first Refuge Assurance Cup final 1988 and in B&H Cup final 1990. Lancashire captain 1994-97, leading the county to one NatWest and two B&H titles. Lancashire Player of the Year 1995. 2nd XI captain and coach 2000-01. Appointed cricket manager for 2002; retired but registration retained
Best batting: 161 Lancashire v Essex, Old Trafford 1995
Best bowling: 8-30 Lancashire v Hampshire, Old Trafford 1994

Career Performances

	M	Inns	NO	Runs	HS	Avge	100s	50s	Ct	St	Balls	Runs	Wkts	Avge	Best	5wI	10wM
Test	4	6	1	167	82 *	33.40	-	1	1	-	672	348	10	34.80	3-64	-	-
All First	308	459	49	10939	161	26.68	11	50	156	-	47806	24960	739	33.77	8-30	27	3
1-day Int	1	0	0	0	0	-	-	-	-	-	54	43	0	-	-	-	-
C & G	46	40	7	1064	130	32.24	1	7	12	-	2681	1751	46	38.06	3-14	-	
B & H	73	53	12	837	76	20.41	-	4	22	-	3740	2636	88	29.95	5-44	2	
1-day Lge	236	189	38	3262	121	21.60	1	9	59	-	8730	7113	225	31.61	5-46	1	

WEEKES, L. C.   Northamptonshire

Name: Lesroy Charlesworth Weekes
Role: Right-hand bat, right-arm fast bowler
Born: 19 July 1972, Montserrat
Height: 6ft 2in   **Weight:** 16st
Nickname: Weeksey
County debut: 2000 (Yorkshire),
2001 (Northamptonshire)
1st-Class 5 w. in innings: 2
1st-Class catches: 17
Strike rate: 52.00 (career 48.49)
Parents: Winifred and Franklyn
Marital status: Single
Children: Keisha, 15 August 1998
Education: Plymouth School; Montserrat
High School; Montserrat Sports College
Qualifications: 5 GCSEs, NCA coaching
award
Career outside cricket: Football
Overseas teams played for: Leeward Islands
Cricketers particularly admired: Curtly Ambrose, Sir Viv Richards, Darren Gough
Young players to look out for: Sylvester Joseph, Liam Dickinson
Other sports played: Football, basketball
Other sports followed: Football (Manchester United)
Relaxations: 'Watching young cricketers play'
Extras: Played league cricket in Yorkshire. Played for Lincolnshire in the NatWest
1997 and for Yorkshire Board XI in the NatWest 1999. Made debut for Yorkshire 2000
v West Indians at Headingley, taking a career best 6-56. Left Yorkshire at the end of
the 2000 season and joined Northamptonshire for 2001; left Northamptonshire during
the 2001-02 off-season

Best batting: 46 Leeward Islands v Guyana, Berbice 1993-94
Best bowling: 6-56 Yorkshire v West Indians, Headingley 2000

2001 Season

	M	Inns	NO	Runs	HS	Avge	100s	50s	Ct	St	O	M	Runs	Wkts	Avge	Best	5wI	10wM
Test																		
All First	1	2	1	62	44 *	62.00	-	-	-	-	26	5	107	3	35.66	3-51	-	-
1-day Int																		
C & G	1	0	0	0	0	-	-	-	-	-	10	1	63	0	-		-	-
B & H	2	0	0	0	0	-	-	-	-	-	17	0	96	2	48.00	2-47	-	
1-day Lge	8	5	2	19	10 *	6.33	-	-	2	-	62	3	353	7	50.42	3-34	-	

Career Performances

	M	Inns	NO	Runs	HS	Avge	100s	50s	Ct	St	Balls	Runs	Wkts	Avge	Best	5wI	10wM
Test																	
All First	24	36	6	535	46	17.83	-	-	17	-	3346	1871	69	27.11	6-56	2	-
1-day Int																	
C & G	3	2	0	8	8	4.00	-	-	1	-	118	129	0	-		-	-
B & H	2	0	0	0	0	-	-	-	-	-	102	96	2	48.00	2-47	-	
1-day Lge	8	5	2	19	10 *	6.33	-	-	2	-	372	353	7	50.42	3-34	-	

WEEKES, P. N. Middlesex

Name: <u>Paul</u> Nicholas Weekes
Role: Left-hand bat, right-arm
off-spin bowler
Born: 8 July 1969, Hackney, London
Height: 5ft 10in **Weight:** 12st 6lbs
Nickname: Weekesy, Twidds
County debut: 1990
County cap: 1993
1000 runs in a season: 1
1st-Class 50s: 34
1st-Class 100s: 11
1st-Class 5 w. in innings: 4
1st-Class catches: 146
One-Day 100s: 3
Place in batting averages: 102nd av. 32.68
(2000 177th av. 20.33)
Place in bowling averages: 61st av. 29.95
Strike rate: 65.97 (career 82.71)
Parents: Robert and Carol

Marital status: Partner Christine
Children: Cherie, 4 September 1993; Shyann, 5 May 1998
Family links with cricket: Father played club cricket
Education: Manderville Primary; Homerton House, Hackney; Hackney Technical College
Qualifications: 2 O-levels, senior cricket coach
Career outside cricket: Cricket coach
Off-season: 'Working on my benefit'
Overseas tours: England A to India and Bangladesh 1994-95; BWIA to Trinidad (twice); Middlesex to Johannesburg
Overseas teams played for: Newcastle University, NSW 1988-89; Sunrise CC, Zimbabwe 1990-91
Career highlights to date: 'Scoring more than 150 (171* and 160) in each innings of a four-day match, v Somerset at Uxbridge 1996. Scoring 102* v South Africa' (*The latter innings was in a World Cup warm-up match 1999*)
Cricket moments to forget: 'Getting a pair against Essex in 1996'
Cricketers particularly admired: Viv Richards, Courtney Walsh
Young players to look out for: Owais Shah
Other sports followed: Boxing, football (Arsenal)
Relaxations: 'Music, laughing, talking rubbish'
Extras: Scored 50 in debut innings for both 2nd and 1st teams. Took two catches whilst appearing as 12th man for England in the second Test against West Indies at Lord's in 1995. Middlesex Player of the Year 1999. Only Englishman to have scored more than 150 in both innings of a first-class game. Has won six one-day Man of the Match awards (two NatWest; four B&H), including B&H Gold Award for his 4-17 v Kent at Lord's 2001. Captained Middlesex to their one-day victory over the Australians at Lord's 2001. Granted a benefit for 2002
Best batting: 171* Middlesex v Somerset, Uxbridge 1996
Best bowling: 8-39 Middlesex v Glamorgan, Lord's 1996

2001 Season

	M	Inns	NO	Runs	HS	Avge	100s	50s	Ct	St	O	M	Runs	Wkts	Avge	Best	5wI	10wM
Test																		
All First	17	27	5	719	107	32.68	1	5	15	-	439.5	100	1198	40	29.95	5-90	1	-
1-day Int																		
C & G	1	1	1	19	19 *	-	-	-	-	-	9.5	0	40	0	-	-	-	-
B & H	5	4	0	104	46	26.00	-	-	2	-	38	0	156	9	17.33	4-17	-	
1-day Lge	14	13	1	273	55	22.75	-	1	8	-	102	5	450	11	40.90	3-28	-	

Career Performances

	M	Inns	NO	Runs	HS	Avge	100s	50s	Ct	St		Balls	Runs	Wkts	Avge	Best	5wI	10wM
Test																		
All First	160	251	30	7119	171 *	32.21	11	34	146	-		16791	7937	203	39.09	8-39	4	-
1-day Int																		
C & G	20	20	4	520	143 *	32.50	2	2	6	-		987	702	19	36.94	3-35	-	
B & H	37	33	6	831	77	30.77	-	5	12	-		1658	1190	39	30.51	4-17	-	
1-day Lge	165	140	18	2979	119 *	24.41	1	12	72	-		5733	4785	173	27.65	4-26	-	

WELCH, G.   Derbyshire

Name: Graeme Welch
Role: Right-hand bat, right-arm
medium-fast bowler
Born: 21 March 1972, County Durham
Height: 6ft **Weight:** 13st
Nickname: Pop
County debut: 1992 (one-day,
Warwickshire), 1994 (first-class,
Warwickshire), 2001 (Derbyshire)
County cap: 1997 (Warwickshire),
2001 (Derbyshire)
50 wickets in a season: 1
1st-Class 50s: 9
1st-Class 5 w. in innings: 7
1st-Class 10 w. in match: 1
1st-Class catches: 33
One-Day 5 w. in innings: 1
Place in batting averages: 201st av. 18.92
(2000 216th av. 16.57)
Place in bowling averages: 103rd av. 37.06
Strike rate: 68.52 (career 62.08)
Parents: Jean and Robert
Wife and date of marriage: Emma, 4 October 1997
Children: Ethan, 4 April 2000
Family links with cricket: Brother and father play club cricket in Leeds and
Durham respectively
Education: Hetton Primary; Hetton Comprehensive
Qualifications: 9 GCSEs, City and Guilds in Sports and Leisure, senior
coaching award
Career outside cricket: Coaching
Off-season: Getting fit and coaching

Overseas tours: Warwickshire to Cape Town 1992-97; England XI to New Zealand (Cricket Max) 1997
Overseas teams played for: Avendale, Cape Town 1992-94; Wellington Collegians and Wellington 1996
Career highlights to date: 'Winning the treble with Warwickshire in 1994'
Cricket moments to forget: 'Benson and Hedges game against Lancashire in 1995' (*Became first bowler to concede 100 runs in B&H match*)
Cricketers particularly admired: Brian Lara, Allan Donald, Sachin Tendulkar
Young players to look out for: Ian Bell, Nicky Peng
Other sports played: Football
Other sports followed: Football (Newcastle United)
Relaxations: 'A beer at "The Brook"; spending time with Emma and Ethan'
Extras: Played for England YC v Australian YC 1991. Took two hat-tricks in the 2nd XI, against Durham in 1992 and against Worcestershire. Warwickshire's Most Improved Player in 1994. Won seven trophies with Warwickshire 1994-97. Left Warwickshire at the end of the 2000 season and joined Derbyshire for 2001. Recorded five-wicket innings return (5-53) and scored a 50 (64) against his old county Warwickshire at Edgbaston 2001. Awarded Derbyshire cap 2001
Opinions on cricket: 'Wickets need to improve and the balls were terrible last year and they need to improve.'
Best batting: 84* Warwickshire v Nottinghamshire, Edgbaston 1994
Best bowling: 6-30 Derbyshire v Durham, Riverside 2001

2001 Season

	M	Inns	NO	Runs	HS	Avge	100s	50s	Ct	St	O	M	Runs	Wkts	Avge	Best	5wI	10wM
Test																		
All First	16	29	2	511	64	18.92	-	1	3	-	502.3	108	1631	44	37.06	6-30	3	-
1-day Int																		
C & G	1	1	1	6	6*	-	-	-	-	-	10	1	42	0	-		-	-
B & H																		
1-day Lge	15	13	0	89	26	6.84	-	-	-	-	121.4	17	473	16	29.56	5-22	1	

Career Performances

	M	Inns	NO	Runs	HS	Avge	100s	50s	Ct	St	Balls	Runs	Wkts	Avge	Best	5wI	10wM
Test																	
All First	94	138	20	2406	84*	20.38	-	9	33	-	14155	7867	228	34.50	6-30	7	1
1-day Int																	
C & G	17	12	3	145	41	16.11	-	-	-	-	918	572	9	63.55	4-31	-	
B & H	22	16	4	241	55*	20.08	-	1	1	-	895	704	22	32.00	3-20	-	
1-day Lge	88	70	19	943	71	18.49	-	3	16	-	3389	2513	67	37.50	5-22	1	

WELLS, V. J. Leicestershire

Name: Vincent (<u>Vince</u>) John Wells
Role: Right-hand bat, right-arm medium
bowler, county captain
Born: 6 August 1965, Dartford
Height: 6ft **Weight:** 13st 4lbs
Nickname: Vinny, Wellsy, Both
County debut: 1987 (one-day, Kent),
1988 (first-class, Kent), 1992 (Leicestershire)
County cap: 1994 (Leicestershire)
Benefit: 2001 (Leicestershire)
One-Day Internationals: 9
1000 runs in a season: 2

1st-Class 50s: 41
1st-Class 100s: 13
1st-Class 200s: 3
1st-Class 5 w. in innings: 4
1st-Class catches: 114
One-Day 100s: 3
One-Day 200s: 1
One-Day 5 w. in innings: 2
Place in batting averages: 123rd av. 29.90 (2000 103rd av. 28.89)
Place in bowling averages: 50th av. 27.66 (2000 79th av. 28.17)
Strike rate: 60.33 (career 54.54)
Parents: Pat and Jack
Wife and date of marriage: Deborah Louise, 14 October 1989
Children: Harrison John, 25 January 1995; Molly Louise, 2 June 1996
Family links with cricket: Brother plays club cricket for Chestfield
Education: Downs School, Dartford; Sir William Nottidge School, Whitstable
Qualifications: 1 O-level, 8 CSEs, junior and senior coaching certificates
Off-season: 'Finishing benefit year; coaching'
Overseas tours: Leicestershire to Jamaica 1993, to Bloemfontein 1994 and 1995,
to Western Transvaal 1996, to Durban 1997, to Barbados 1998, to Anguilla 2000;
England to Australia 1998-99 (CUB Series), to Sharjah (Coca-Cola Cup) 1998-99
Overseas teams played for: Parnell, Auckland 1986; Avendale, Cape Town 1986-89,
1990-91; Potchefstroom University, North West Transvaal 1996-97; Cornwall CC,
Auckland 1998-99
Career highlights to date: 'Winning trophies for Leicestershire. Playing for England'
Cricket moments to forget: 'Losing any game, especially Lord's finals'
Cricketers particularly admired: James Whitaker, Phil Simmons, Mike Kasprowicz,
Anil Kumble – 'all play hard, practise hard and all respect the game; top people'
Young players to look out for: James Ormond

Other sports followed: Football (Chelsea and Leicester)

Injuries: Neck and back injury

Relaxations: 'Good food, pint of Guinness, spending time with my family and walking Jasper the dog'

Extras: Was a schoolboy footballer with Leyton Orient. Scored 100 not out on NatWest debut v Oxfordshire 1990. Left Kent at the end of 1991 season to join Leicestershire. Missed 1992 NatWest final owing to viral infection. Hat-trick for Leics against Durham 1994; Alamgir Sheriyar also took hat-trick for Leics in same match. Scored 201 not out against Berkshire in the 1996 NatWest Trophy. Member of England's 1999 World Cup squad and was reserve wicket-keeper. Captain of Leicestershire since retirement of James Whitaker during 1999 season. Scored century (138) and recorded five-wicket innings return (5-36) against his old county Kent at Canterbury 2001. C&G Man of the Match award for his 54* v Nottinghamshire at Trent Bridge 2001

Opinions on cricket: 'Would like to see the toss given to away side in Championship cricket to hopefully make the pitches better and take away a luck element of the game. Two up/two down promotion and relegation.'

Best batting: 224 Leicestershire v Middlesex, Lord's 1997

Best bowling: 5-18 Leicestershire v Nottinghamshire, Worksop 1998

2001 Season

	M	Inns	NO	Runs	HS	Avge	100s	50s	Ct	St	O	M	Runs	Wkts	Avge	Best	5wI	10wM
Test																		
All First	13	22	1	628	138	29.90	2	2	8	-	181	47	498	18	27.66	5-36	1	-
1-day Int																		
C & G	5	5	2	174	64 *	58.00	-	2	2	-	29.4	4	108	5	21.60	2-23	-	
B & H	5	5	0	190	76	38.00	-	2	-	-	21.3	0	114	7	16.28	2-17	-	
1-day Lge	16	16	1	191	39	12.73	-	-	7	-	86	5	394	15	26.26	4-30	-	

Career Performances

	M	Inns	NO	Runs	HS	Avge	100s	50s	Ct	St	Balls	Runs	Wkts	Avge	Best	5wI	10wM
Test																	
All First	173	268	19	8336	224	33.47	16	41	114	-	14235	6984	261	26.75	5-18	4	-
1-day Int	9	7	0	141	39	20.14	-	-	7	-	220	189	8	23.62	3-30	-	
C & G	26	25	6	832	201	43.78	2	5	3	-	1065	644	28	23.00	3-30	-	
B & H	44	38	3	929	90	26.54	-	5	13	-	1672	1242	45	27.60	6-25	1	
1-day Lge	152	145	13	3103	101	23.50	2	12	37	-	4931	3812	136	28.02	5-10	1	

WELTON, G. E.   Nottinghamshire

Name: <u>Guy</u> Edward Welton
Role: Right-hand opening bat
Born: 4 May 1978, Grimsby
Height: 6ft 1in **Weight:** 13st 7lbs
Nickname: Trigger, Giggs, Welts
County debut: 1997
1st-Class 50s: 8
1st-Class 200s: 1
1st-Class catches: 21
One-Day 100s: 1
Place in batting averages: 225th av. 15.31
(2000 77th av. 32.09)
Parents: Robert and Diana
Marital status: Single
Family links with cricket: Father is a
qualified cricket coach and keen club
cricketer

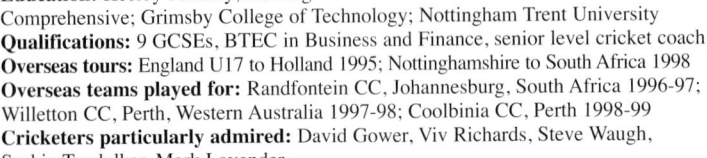

Education: Keelby Primary; Healing
Comprehensive; Grimsby College of Technology; Nottingham Trent University
Qualifications: 9 GCSEs, BTEC in Business and Finance, senior level cricket coach
Overseas tours: England U17 to Holland 1995; Nottinghamshire to South Africa 1998
Overseas teams played for: Randfontein CC, Johannesburg, South Africa 1996-97;
Willetton CC, Perth, Western Australia 1997-98; Coolbinia CC, Perth 1998-99
Cricketers particularly admired: David Gower, Viv Richards, Steve Waugh,
Sachin Tendulkar, Mark Lavender
Other sports played: Football ('youth trainee at Grimsby Town Football Club 1994-96')
Relaxations: Music and going to the gym
Extras: Completed a two-year YTS with Grimsby Town Football Club where he made
one first-team appearance as a substitute. Played cricket for England U14, U15 and
U17. Won the Lord's Taverners' Young Player Award in 1993 and was MCC Young
Cricketer 1994-95. Was 12th man for England at Lord's and The Oval against West
Indies in 1995. Scored maiden first-class century v Warwickshire at Edgbaston 2000,
going on to score 200* and become Nottinghamshire's youngest ever double
centurion; in the process he shared in a first-wicket stand of 406* with Darren Bicknell
(180*) that broke several records, including that for the highest Nottinghamshire
partnership for any wicket, formerly 398 by Arthur Shrewsbury and William Gunn v
Sussex at Trent Bridge 1890, and that for the highest unbeaten first-wicket partnership
in Championship history. B&H Gold Awards for his 71 v Leicestershire at Trent
Bridge 2001 and 75 v Durham at Riverside 2001
Best batting: 200* Nottinghamshire v Warwickshire, Edgbaston 2000

2001 Season

	M	Inns	NO	Runs	HS	Avge	100s	50s	Ct	St	O	M	Runs	Wkts	Avge	Best	5wI	10wM
Test																		
All First	12	22	0	337	61	15.31	-	2	5	-	1	0	4	0	-	-	-	-
1-day Int																		
C & G	1	1	0	13	13	13.00	-	-	1	-								
B & H	6	6	0	182	75	30.33	-	2	2	-								
1-day Lge	8	7	1	115	38	19.16	-	-	-	-								

Career Performances

	M	Inns	NO	Runs	HS	Avge	100s	50s	Ct	St	Balls	Runs	Wkts	Avge	Best	5wI	10wM
Test																	
All First	45	82	3	1773	200 *	22.44	1	8	21	-	12	5	0	-	-	-	-
1-day Int																	
C & G	2	2	0	29	16	14.50	-	-	1	-							
B & H	6	6	0	182	75	30.33	-	2	2	-							
1-day Lge	31	30	2	568	104 *	20.28	1	1	8	-							

WESTON, R. M. S.   Middlesex

Name: <u>Robin</u> Michael Swann Weston
Role: Right-hand bat, leg-break bowler
Born: 7 June 1975, Durham
Height: 6ft **Weight:** 12st 6lbs
County debut: 1995 (Durham),
1998 (Derbyshire), 2000 (Middlesex)
County cap: 2001 (Middlesex)
1st-Class 50s: 7
1st-Class 100s: 6
1st-Class catches: 33
Place in batting averages: 59th av. 42.00
(2000 192nd av. 18.88)
Strike rate: (career 93.50)
Parents: Kathleen Mary (deceased) and
Michael Philip
Marital status: Single
Family links with cricket: Father played for
Durham (and played rugby union for
England); brother Philip plays for Worcestershire
Education: Bow School; Durham School; Loughborough University
Qualifications: 10 GCSEs, 4 A-levels, degree in Economics with Accountancy, basic
cricket coaching certificate

Career outside cricket: Working in marketing
Off-season: Working in marketing for Halifax Equitable
Overseas tours: England U18 to South Africa 1992-93, to Denmark 1993; England U19 to Sri Lanka 1993-94
Overseas teams played for: Fremantle, Western Australia 1996-98; Parnell CC, Auckland 1999-2000
Cricketers particularly admired: 'Anyone at the highest level'
Young players to look out for: Andrew Strauss
Other sports played: Golf, rugby union (Loughborough Students 1994-96, England U18 1993)
Other sports followed: Football (Sunderland AFC)
Relaxations: Most sports, listening to music and socialising with friends
Extras: Became youngest to play for Durham 1st XI, in Minor Counties competition, aged 15 in 1991. Released by Durham at the end of the 1997 season and joined Derbyshire. Scored maiden first-class century v Essex at Chelmsford 1999 and followed up with centuries in the next two Championship matches. NBC Denis Compton Award 1999. Left Derbyshire at the end of 1999 season and joined Middlesex for 2000. 2nd XI Championship Player of the Year 2000. Awarded Middlesex cap 2001
Opinions on cricket: 'The two-league system seems to be creating more interest in the game, which can only be a good thing. If we are to continue to improve our standing in the world we *must* address the standard of our wickets.'
Best batting: 156 Derbyshire v Somerset, Derby 1999
Best bowling: 1-15 Derbyshire v Hampshire, Derby 1999

2001 Season

	M	Inns	NO	Runs	HS	Avge	100s	50s	Ct	St	O	M	Runs	Wkts	Avge	Best	5wI	10wM
Test																		
All First	10	17	1	672	135 *	42.00	3	1	5	-								
1-day Int																		
C & G	1	1	0	47	47	47.00	-	-	-	-								
B & H	1	1	0	10	10	10.00	-	-	-	-								
1-day Lge	8	8	1	135	80 *	19.28	-	1	3	-								

Career Performances

	M	Inns	NO	Runs	HS	Avge	100s	50s	Ct	St	Balls	Runs	Wkts	Avge	Best	5wI	10wM
Test																	
All First	51	89	4	2398	156	28.21	6	7	33	-	187	104	2	52.00	1-15	-	-
1-day Int																	
C & G	7	7	1	150	56	25.00	-	1	1	-							
B & H	2	2	0	28	18	14.00	-	-	-	-							
1-day Lge	36	35	3	599	80 *	18.71	-	3	9	-							

WESTON, W. P. C.   Worcestershire

Name: William <u>Philip</u> Christopher Weston
Role: Left-hand opening bat, left-arm
medium bowler
Born: 16 June 1973, Durham
Height: 6ft 4in   **Weight:** 13st 9lbs
Nickname: Sven, Reverend, Wesso
County debut: 1991
County cap: 1995
1000 runs in a season: 4
1st-Class 50s: 44
1st-Class 100s: 16
1st-Class 200s: 1
1st-Class catches: 83
One-Day 100s: 2
Place in batting averages: 60th av. 41.92
(2000 223rd av. 15.82)
Strike rate: (career 241.25)
Parents: Kate (deceased) and Michael
Wife and date of marriage: Sarah, 30 September 2000
Family links with cricket: Brother plays for Middlesex. Father played Minor
Counties cricket for Durham (and rugby union for England)
Education: Bow School, Durham; Durham School
Qualifications: 9 GCSEs, 4 A-levels, coaching certificates
Career outside cricket: Cricket development for Worcestershire CCC
Off-season: 'Coaching around Worcestershire for the club'
Overseas tours: England U18 to Canada 1991; England YC to New Zealand 1990-91;
England U19 to Pakistan 1991-92 (captain); Worcestershire to Zimbabwe 1996
Overseas teams played for: Melville, Perth 1992-94 and 1996-97; Swanbourne,
Perth 1995-96
Cricketers particularly admired: 'Everyone who makes the most of their talent'
Young players to look out for: Kadeer Ali, Kabir Ali
Other sports followed: Rugby union, football (Sunderland AFC)
Relaxations: 'Spending time with Sarah; travelling, cinema, property'
Extras: Played for Northants 2nd XI and Worcs 2nd XI in 1989. Scored century for
England YC v Australian YC 1991. Cricket Society's Most Promising Young Cricketer
1992. Worcestershire Uncapped Player of the Year 1992. Member of Whittingdale
Fringe Squad 1993. Scored 71 v Middlesex at Worcester 2001, in the process
sharing with Anurag Singh in a record opening partnership for Worcs in matches
against Middlesex
Opinions on cricket: 'The English domestic game and the development of its players
is being ruined by the lack of quality pitches we play on. Hard surfaces with even

bounce allowing an equal contest between bat and ball are not too much to ask for, are they? Without them, we are wasting our time.'
Best batting: 205 Worcestershire v Northamptonshire, Northampton 1997
Best bowling: 2-39 Worcestershire v Pakistanis, Worcester 1992

2001 Season

	M	Inns	NO	Runs	HS	Avge	100s	50s	Ct	St	O	M	Runs	Wkts	Avge	Best	5wI	10wM
Test																		
All First	18	31	4	1132	192	41.92	2	7	12	-	7.4	0	41	0	-		-	-	-
1-day Int																		
C & G	3	3	0	47	40	15.66	-	-	-	-								
B & H	5	5	1	91	65	22.75	-	1	2	-								
1-day Lge	11	10	0	313	134	31.30	1	1	1	-								

Career Performances

	M	Inns	NO	Runs	HS	Avge	100s	50s	Ct	St	Balls	Runs	Wkts	Avge	Best	5wI	10wM
Test																	
All First	162	284	29	8817	205	34.57	17	44	83	-	965	640	4	160.00	2-39	-	-
1-day Int																	
C & G	11	11	0	150	40	13.63	-	-	1	-							
B & H	26	25	3	325	65	14.77	-	2	11	-							
1-day Lge	90	76	8	1655	134	24.33	2	5	17	-	6	2	1	2.00	1-2	-	

WHARF, A. G. Glamorgan

Name: Alexander (<u>Alex</u>) George Wharf
Role: Right-hand bat, right-arm fast-medium bowler
Born: 4 June 1975, Bradford
Height: 6ft 4in
Nickname: Gangster
County debut: 1994 (Yorks), 1998 (Notts), 2000 (Glamorgan)
County cap: 2000 (Glamorgan)
1st-Class 50s: 3
1st-Class 100s: 2
1st-Class 5 w. in innings: 2
1st-Class catches: 22
Place in batting averages: (2000 161st av. 21.92)
Place in bowling averages: 70th av. 32.00 (2000 63rd av. 25.40)
Strike rate: 54.71 (career 54.61)
Parents: Derek and Jane
Marital status: Lives with partner
Children: Tristan Jack Busfield Wharf, 15 November 1997; Alf Alexander Busfield Wharf, 30 June 2001

Family links with cricket: Father played local cricket and brother Simon plays local cricket

Education: Marshfields First School; Preistman Middle School; Buttershaw Upper School; Thomas Danby College

Qualifications: 6 GCSEs, City and Guilds in Sports Management, NCA coaching award, junior football coaching award

Off-season: Recovering from ankle injury ready for 2002 season

Overseas tours: Various pre-season tours with Yorkshire and Notts, including Yorkshire to Cape Town 1994-95, to Guernsey 1996

Overseas teams played for: Somerset West, Cape Town 1993-95; Johnsonville CC, Wellington, New Zealand 1996-97; Universities, Wellington 1998-99

Career highlights to date: 'Playing alongside some great players!'

Cricket moments to forget: 'Too many to mention'

Cricketers particularly admired: Ian Botham

Young players to look out for: Jon Hughes

Other sports played: Football

Other sports followed: 'Follow most sports but my passion is Manchester United; also very proud of Bradford City'

Injuries: Out for three and a half months with an ankle injury

Relaxations: 'Spending time with family and friends, movies, PlayStation 2, eating (too much), TV, gym'

Extras: Attended Dennis Lillee coaching school, Chennai (Madras), during winter 1997-98. Scored 78 for Notts v Glamorgan at Colwyn Bay 1999, having arrived at the wicket with his side on 9 for 6. Left Nottinghamshire at end of the 1999 season and joined Glamorgan for 2000

Opinions on cricket: 'Maybe regional cricket should come into play to bridge the gap between first-class and Test cricket. Other than that, just get on with it.'

Best batting: 101* Glamorgan v Northamptonshire, Northampton 2000

Best bowling: 5-63 Glamorgan v Yorkshire, Swansea 2001

---

95. Which West Indies all-rounder took 5-20 and the
Man of the Match award as Kent bowled out Hampshire for 102
in the semi-finals of the 1983 NatWest?

2001 Season

	M	Inns	NO	Runs	HS	Avge	100s	50s	Ct	St	O	M	Runs	Wkts	Avge	Best	5wI	10wM
Test																		
All First	5	4	1	59	31	19.66	-	-	1	-	127.4	19	448	14	32.00	5-63	1	-
1-day Int																		
C & G	1	1	1	24	24 *	-	-	-	-	-	8	1	28	1	28.00	1-28	-	
B & H	2	1	1	4	4 *	-	-	-	-	-	17	2	71	2	35.50	2-31	-	
1-day Lge	2	0	0	0	0	-	-	-	-	-	16	1	76	5	15.20	3-23	-	

Career Performances

	M	Inns	NO	Runs	HS	Avge	100s	50s	Ct	St	Balls	Runs	Wkts	Avge	Best	5wI	10wM
Test																	
All First	43	60	8	908	101 *	17.46	2	3	22	-	5571	3391	102	33.24	5-63	2	-
1-day Int																	
C & G	5	4	1	42	24 *	14.00	-	-	-	-	276	145	7	20.71	3-18	-	
B & H	12	8	1	75	20	10.71	-	-	2	-	658	539	15	35.93	4-29	-	
1-day Lge	34	20	8	217	38 *	18.08	-	-	6	-	1342	1081	28	38.60	3-23	-	

WHARTON, L. J.   Derbyshire

Name: Lian James Wharton
Role: Left-hand bat, slow left-arm bowler
Born: 21 February 1977, Derby
Height: 5ft 9in **Weight:** 10st 9lbs
Nickname: Tetley, King, Two Thumbs
County debut: 2000
1st-Class 5 w. in innings: 1
1st-Class catches: 3
Place in batting averages: 283rd av. 3.22
Place in bowling averages: (2000 127th av. 38.66)
Strike rate: 163.12 (career 114.45)
Parents: Pete and Di
Marital status: Single
Education: Ravensdale School; Ecclesbourne; Mackworth College
Qualifications: 9 GCSEs, BTEC National Computer Studies
Career outside cricket: Salesman; indoor cricket umpire
Off-season: Coaching, working
Overseas teams played for: Merewether CC, Newcastle, NSW 2000-01
Career highlights to date: 'Taking nine wickets against the West Indians' (*Match figures of 9-179 at Derby 2000*)

Cricket moments to forget: 'Had complete nightmare fielding at Durham – running wrong way for balls, balls going through my legs etc.'

Cricketers particularly admired: Phil Tufnell, Ian Botham, Shane Warne, Stewart Edge, Ian Fraser, Daniel Vettori, Rory Williams, Andrew Williams, Ewan Craig, Alec Stubbs

Young players to look out for: James Dakin, George Moulds, Chris Windmill, Trevor Smith, Luke Sutton, Steve Stubbings, Tom Lungley, Sam Patel, Steve Selwood

Other sports played: Indoor cricket ('train with England squad'), golf, football, tennis, 'spoof'

Other sports followed: Football (Derby County), basketball (Derby Storm)

Relaxations: Reading, going to the cinema, socialising, sleeping

Extras: Had match figures of 10-58 from 37 overs on debut for Derbyshire 2nd XI

Opinions on cricket: 'Tea should be longer than 20 minutes. More day/night games – maybe a league. Two divisions has made a good improvement to the game. Relegation and promotion can go down to the last match, so there are no meaningless games. This should help improve the competitive nature of English cricketers. John the Chef should be the chef for every first-class county! Awesome!'

Best batting: 13* Derbyshire v Warwickshire, Derby 2001

Best bowling: 5-96 Derbyshire v West Indians, Derby 2000

2001 Season

	M	Inns	NO	Runs	HS	Avge	100s	50s	Ct	St	O	M	Runs	Wkts	Avge	Best	5wI	10wM
Test																		
All First	11	18	9	29	13*	3.22	-	-	1	-	217.3	58	644	8	80.50	2-74	-	-
1-day Int																		
C & G	1	1	1	0	0*	-	-	-	-	-	10	0	41	1	41.00	1-41	-	
B & H																		
1-day Lge	10	4	4	18	9*	-	-	-	-	-	85	7	337	10	33.70	3-23	-	

Career Performances

	M	Inns	NO	Runs	HS	Avge	100s	50s	Ct	St	Balls	Runs	Wkts	Avge	Best	5wI	10wM
Test																	
All First	18	27	13	44	13*	3.14	-	-	3	-	2289	1108	20	55.40	5-96	1	-
1-day Int																	
C & G	1	1	1	0	0*	-	-	-	-	-	60	41	1	41.00	1-41	-	
B & H																	
1-day Lge	17	8	8	26	9*	-	-	-	2	-	786	553	16	34.56	3-23	-	

WHILEY, M. J. A.   Leicestershire

Name: Matthew (<u>Matt</u>) Jeffrey Allen Whiley
Role: Right-hand bat, left-arm
fast bowler
Born: 6 May 1980, Nottingham
Height: 6ft 3in **Weight:** 13st 8lbs
Nickname: Whibley, Stretch
County debut: 1998 (Nottinghamshire),
2001 (Leicestershire)
1st-Class catches: 1
Strike rate: 159.50 (career 161.50)
Parents: Paul and Barbara
Marital status: Single
Family links with cricket: 'Dad played in
the local "bucket bangers" league; claims he
was quicker than Donald. Mum made the
business teas'

Education: Whitegate Primary School,
Clifton; Harry Carlton Comprehensive
School, East Leake
Qualifications: 10 GCSEs, Level 1 coaching certificate, 'University of Life'
Off-season: 'Training with Steve Long, then going on the MCC tour'
Overseas tours: England U19 to New Zealand 1998-99; Nottinghamshire to
Johannesburg 1999; Leicestershire to Potchefstroom 2001; MCC to Kenya 2002
Overseas teams played for: Manawatu-Foxton CC and Horowhenua District Cricket
Association, both New Zealand 1997-98; Melville CC, Perth 2000-01
Career highlights to date: 'Although only at U19 level, representing my country.
Making first-class debut'
Cricketers particularly admired: Devon 'the Android' Malcolm, Dennis Lillee,
Graham Dilley, Bernard Allen 'for motivation'
Young players to look out for: Paul Franks, Stephen Randall, Richard Logan,
Guy Welton
Other sports followed: Football (Man Utd)
Injuries: Out for eight weeks with a toe injury and a side strain
Relaxations: 'Training, R&B music, clothes shopping'
Extras: Visited the Dennis Lillee MRF Pace Foundation, February 2000. Awarded
Nottinghamshire 2nd XI cap September 2000. Came second in the Freeserve Speedster
Challenge; bowled the fastest delivery (86.6 mph) but was adjudged to have bowled a
no-ball. Left Nottinghamshire in the 2000-01 off-season and joined Leicestershire for
2001
Opinions on cricket: 'Happy to be given an opportunity that others aren't.'
Best batting: 1* Leicestershire v Kent, Leicester 2001
Best bowling: 1-44 Nottinghamshire v Oxford University, The Parks 1999

2001 Season

	M	Inns	NO	Runs	HS	Avge	100s	50s	Ct	St	O	M	Runs	Wkts	Avge	Best	5wI	10wM
Test																		
All First	3	5	1	2	1 *	0.50	-	-	-	-	53.1	14	188	2	94.00	1-54	-	-
1-day Int																		
C & G																		
B & H																		
1-day Lge																		

Career Performances

	M	Inns	NO	Runs	HS	Avge	100s	50s	Ct	St	Balls	Runs	Wkts	Avge	Best	5wI	10wM
Test																	
All First	6	9	2	2	1 *	0.28	-	-	1	-	646	432	4	108.00	1-44	-	-
1-day Int																	
C & G																	
B & H																	
1-day Lge																	

WHITE, C.   Yorkshire

Name: Craig White
Role: Right-hand bat, right-arm
fast-medium bowler, cover fielder
Born: 16 December 1969, Morley, Yorkshire
Height: 6ft 1in **Weight:** 11st 11lbs
Nickname: Chalky, Bassey
County debut: 1990
County cap: 1993
Test debut: 1994
Tests: 21
One-Day Internationals: 37
1st-Class 50s: 36
1st-Class 100s: 11
1st-Class 5 w. in innings: 9
1st-Class catches: 133
One-Day 100s: 2
One-Day 5 w. in innings: 2
Place in batting averages: 107th av. 31.84
(2000 247th av. 12.50)
Place in bowling averages: 91st av. 35.23 (2000 12th av. 17.20)
Strike rate: 75.58 (career 51.91)
Parents: Fred Emsley and Cynthia Anne

Wife and date of marriage: Elizabeth Anne, 19 September 1992
Family links with cricket: Father played for Pudsey St Lawrence
Education: Kennington Primary; Flora Hill High School; Bendigo Senior High School (all Victoria, Australia)
Off-season: Touring with England
Overseas tours: Australian YC to West Indies 1989-90; England A to Pakistan 1995-96, to Australia 1996-97; England to Australia 1994-95, to India and Pakistan (World Cup) 1995-96, to Zimbabwe and New Zealand 1996-97, to South Africa and Zimbabwe 1999-2000 (one-day series), to Kenya (ICC Knockout Trophy) 2000-01, to Pakistan and Sri Lanka 2000-01, to India and New Zealand 2001-02 (*see **Stop press***)
Overseas teams played for: Victoria, Australia 1990-91
Cricketers particularly admired: Graeme Hick, Mark Waugh, Brian Lara
Other sports followed: Leeds RFC, motocross, golf, tennis
Injuries: Back injury
Relaxations: Playing guitar, reading, gardening and socialising
Extras: Recommended to Yorkshire by Victorian Cricket Academy, being eligible to play for Yorkshire as he was born in the county. 'Fred Trueman and I are the only Yorkshire players to debut in the 1st XI before the 2nd XI.' Formerly bowled off-spin. Called up for one-day series v South Africa and Zimbabwe 1999-2000 after injury to Andrew Flintoff. Took 5-21 and scored 26 in second One-Day International v Zimbabwe at Bulawayo in February 2000, winning the Man of the Match award. Took National League hat-trick (Fleming, Patel, Masters) v Kent at Headingley 2000. England's leading wicket-taker in the NatWest Triangular Series v Zimbabwe and West Indies 2000 with 11 wickets. Recorded maiden Test five-wicket return (5-57) in fourth Test v West Indies on his home ground of Headingley 2000, following up with 5-32 in the fifth Test at The Oval. Scored 93 in England's first innings in the first Test at Lahore 2000-01, in the process sharing, with Graham Thorpe, in a new record sixth-wicket partnership for England in Tests v Pakistan (166); also took 4-54 in Pakistan's only innings of the match. England central contract 2001. Granted a benefit for 2002
Best batting: 186 Yorkshire v Lancashire, Old Trafford 2001
Best bowling: 8-55 Yorkshire v Gloucestershire, Gloucester 1998
Stop press: Selected for England one-day tour to Zimbabwe 2001-02 but was forced to withdraw with an injury to his right knee; replaced by Graham Thorpe. Scored maiden Test century (121) in second Test v India at Ahmedabad 2001-02, winning Man of the Match award and sharing with James Foster in a record seventh-wicket partnership for England in Tests in India (105). Ruled out of the one-day series v India 2001-02 with an injury to his left knee

---

96. Which current first-class umpire scored 113 not out
for Kent v Warwickshire in the semi-finals of the 1984 NatWest,
winning the Man of the Match award?

2001 Season

	M	Inns	NO	Runs	HS	Avge	100s	50s	Ct	St	O	M	Runs	Wkts	Avge	Best	5wI	10wM
Test	3	6	1	38	27 *	7.60	-	-	1	-	46.4	7	189	1	189.00	1-101	-	-
All First	12	21	2	605	186	31.84	2	-	6	-	214.1	52	599	17	35.23	4-57	-	-
1-day Int																		
C & G	2	2	1	84	73 *	84.00	-	1	-	-	15.1	0	80	4	20.00	3-44	-	
B & H	3	3	0	43	25	14.33	-	-	1	-	30	1	121	3	40.33	2-47	-	
1-day Lge	10	10	0	219	73	21.90	-	1	4	-	72.5	5	281	10	28.10	3-30	-	

Career Performances

	M	Inns	NO	Runs	HS	Avge	100s	50s	Ct	St	Balls	Runs	Wkts	Avge	Best	5wI	10wM
Test	21	34	4	540	93	18.00	-	2	13	-	2610	1388	38	36.52	5-32	2	-
All First	191	295	41	7886	186	31.04	11	36	133	-	17338	9129	334	27.33	8-55	9	-
1-day Int	37	29	2	337	38	12.48	-	-	8	-	1668	1207	47	25.68	5-21	1	
C & G	26	23	6	806	113	47.41	1	6	9	-	1170	754	25	30.16	3-38	-	
B & H	40	36	7	659	57 *	22.72	-	2	12	-	1800	1314	43	30.55	5-25	1	
1-day Lge	132	117	15	2461	148	24.12	1	8	40	-	4196	2996	129	23.22	4-14	-	

WHITE, G. W.   Hampshire

Name: <u>Giles</u> William White
Role: Right-hand bat, leg-break bowler
Born: 23 March 1972, Barnstaple
Height: 6ft **Weight:** 12st
Nickname: Chalky
County debut: 1991 (Somerset),
1994 (Hampshire)
County cap: 1998 (Hampshire)
1000 runs in a season: 1
1st-Class 50s: 30
1st-Class 100s: 9
1st-Class catches: 101
1st-Class stumpings: 2
Place in batting averages: 145th av. 26.39
(2000 108th av. 28.46)
Strike rate: 81.50 (career 72.54)
Parents: John and Tina
Wife and date of marriage: Samantha,
25 September 1999
Family links with cricket: Father played club cricket for Exeter CC
Education: Sandford Primary School, Devon; Exeter Cathedral School; Millfield
School; Loughborough University

Qualifications: 10 O-levels, 3 A-levels, BA (Hons) Sports Management, Computing diploma, coaching certificates
Overseas tours: Millfield School to Australia 1989; Hampshire to Anguilla, Cork and Guernsey
Overseas teams played for: Waverley, Sydney 1990-91; Tigers Parrow, Cape Town 1994-95; Techs Mutual CC, Cape Town 1995-96; Rygersdaal, Cape Town 1996-97; Wanneroo, Perth 1997-98
Cricketers particularly admired: Peter Hartley, Shane Warne, Darren Lehmann, Robin Smith, Peter Bowler
Young players to look out for: Chris Tremlett, Lawrence Prittipaul, Simon Francis
Other sports played: Golf, squash
Other sports followed: Football (Southampton FC)
Relaxations: Pubs, music, travel, friends, family
Extras: Played for Somerset before joining Hants. Hants Exiles Young Player of the Year 1997. Carried bat twice in 2000 season – for 78* v Somerset at Southampton (the first time by a Hampshire player since Paul Terry at Headingley in 1994); for 80* v Kent at Portsmouth
Opinions on cricket: 'Wickets need to improve. More time needed between games for practice. Should be two up/two down rather than three.'
Best batting: 156 Hampshire v Sri Lanka, Southampton 1998
Best bowling: 3-23 Hampshire v Nottinghamshire, Trent Bridge 1999

2001 Season

	M	Inns	NO	Runs	HS	Avge	100s	50s	Ct	St	O	M	Runs	Wkts	Avge	Best	5wI	10wM
Test																		
All First	17	32	4	739	141	26.39	2	1	17	2	27.1	0	109	2	54.50	1-29	-	-
1-day Int																		
C & G																		
B & H																		
1-day Lge	6	5	0	160	59	32.00	-	2	2	-								

Career Performances

	M	Inns	NO	Runs	HS	Avge	100s	50s	Ct	St	Balls	Runs	Wkts	Avge	Best	5wI	10wM
Test																	
All First	120	209	19	5961	156	31.37	9	30	101	2	798	565	11	51.36	3-23	-	-
1-day Int																	
C & G	11	11	0	159	69	14.45	-	1	6	-	72	45	1	45.00	1-45	-	
B & H	16	15	1	232	56	16.57	-	1	2	-							
1-day Lge	83	79	5	1710	76	23.10	-	11	26	-	22	23	0	-		-	-

WHITE, R. A. — Northamptonshire

Name: Robert (Rob) Allan White
Role: Right-hand middle-order bat, leg-spin bowler
Born: 15 October 1979, Chelmsford
Height: 5ft 11in **Weight:** 11st 7lbs
Nickname: Chalky, Toff, Zorro, Whitey, Lamb
County debut: 2000
1st-Class catches: 2
Parents: Dennis and Ann
Marital status: Single

Family links with cricket: 'Grandfather on Essex committee for many years. Dad flailed the willow and brother travels the local leagues high and low'
Education: Spratton Hall; Stowe School; St John's College, Durham University; Loughborough University
Qualifications: 9 GCSEs, 3 A-levels
Off-season: 'Continuing my Politics degree at Loughborough'
Career highlights to date: 'The success Loughborough Uni achieved last year was a big highlight and launchpad for a good season at Northants'
Cricket moments to forget: 'Franklyn Rose telling me my mates had bet £10 that he couldn't injure me, as I walked out to play Lashings last year'
Cricketers particularly admired: Ian Botham, Viv Richards, Steve Waugh
Young players to look out for: Monty Panesar ('the Asian world's answer to Jonty Rhodes'), Mark Powell ('genuine all-rounder England are desperate for')
Other sports played: Badminton, squash, golf, kabaddi
Other sports followed: Football (West Ham), rugby (Northampton Saints)
Injuries: 'A recurring hamstring injury which seems to play up during fitness tests'
Extras: Northamptonshire League Young Player of the Year and Youth Cricketer of the Year 1999. Northamptonshire Young Player of the Year 2001. Played for Loughborough University CCE in 2001, scoring 99 v Nottinghamshire at Trent Bridge and receiving the Man of the Match for his 58 in the first UCCE final at Lord's
Opinions on cricket: 'Mediocrity is standard. Dedication is questioned. Our professional standards are unprofessional. Oh, and tea is too short.'
Best batting: 20 Northamptonshire v Oxford Universities, The Parks 2000

2001 Season

	M	Inns	NO	Runs	HS	Avge	100s	50s	Ct	St	O	M	Runs	Wkts	Avge	Best	5wI	10wM
Test																		
All First	1	2	0	6	4	3.00	-	-	-	-	3	0	7	0	-	-	-	-
1-day Int																		
C & G																		
B & H																		
1-day Lge																		

Career Performances

	M	Inns	NO	Runs	HS	Avge	100s	50s	Ct	St	Balls	Runs	Wkts	Avge	Best	5wI	10wM
Test																	
All First	2	4	0	37	20	9.25	-	-	2	-	18	7	0	-	-	-	-
1-day Int																	
C & G																	
B & H																	
1-day Lge																	

WHITTICASE, P.   Leicestershire

Name: Philip (Phil) Whitticase
Role: Right-hand bat, wicket-keeper
Born: 15 March 1965, Wythall, Birmingham
Height: 5ft 8in **Weight:** 12st
Nickname: Boggy, Rat
County debut: 1984
County cap: 1987
Benefit: 1997
50 dismissals in a season: 2
1st-Class 50s: 17
1st-Class 100s: 1
1st-Class catches: 309
1st-Class stumpings: 14
Parents: Larry Gordon and Ann
Wife and date of marriage: Karen, 12 October 1996
Children: Amy, 25 September 1997; Jade, 18 November 2000
Family links with cricket: Grandfather and father were both wicket-keepers in local cricket
Education: Belle Vue Middle School; Crestwood Comprehensive
Qualifications: 6 O-levels, Diploma in Sports Psychology; Advanced, Level III and Staff Level II coaching qualifications

Overseas tours: Rutland Tourists to South Africa 1989; Leicestershire CCC to Montego Bay, to Bloemfontein
Overseas teams played for: South Bunbury, Western Australia 1982, 1984
Cricketers particularly admired: Dennis Amiss, Alan Knott, Bob Taylor
Other sports played: Football, golf
Other sports followed: Football (Birmingham City)
Relaxations: Reading (criminal psychology), all sports, keeping fit
Extras: Played schoolboy football for Birmingham City. Was Derek Underwood's last first-class victim. Lost seven teeth after being struck in the mouth by a bouncer from Neil Williams in Leicestershire's game against Essex in April 1995. Is head coach at Leicestershire
Opinions on cricket: 'The introduction of the two division system has produced more competitive cricket throughout the year, which is beneficial to the players but also the public. The involvement of agents is a little worrying, as some clubs are feeling the pinch and are therefore being priced out of the market. I hope this does not lead to an elite section of clubs, with the others going by the wayside.'
Best batting: 114* Leicestershire v Hampshire, Bournemouth 1991

2001 Season (did not make any first-class or one-day appearances)

Career Performances

	M	Inns	NO	Runs	HS	Avge	100s	50s	Ct	St	Balls	Runs	Wkts	Avge	Best	5wI	10wM
Test																	
All First	132	174	40	3113	114 *	23.23	1	17	309	14	5	7	0	-	-	-	-
1-day Int																	
C & G	13	6	1	67	32	13.40	-	-	14	-							
B & H	29	19	7	313	45	26.08	-	-	29	4							
1-day Lge	69	45	9	413	38	11.47	-	-	56	4							

97. Who captained Warwickshire to victory in
the 1989 NatWest final?

WIDDUP, S. Yorkshire

Name: Simon Widdup
Role: Right-hand bat, right-arm bowler, occasional wicket-keeper
Born: 10 November 1977, Doncaster
Height: 6ft **Weight:** 11st 11lbs
Nickname: Widds, Posh Spice, Reardo
County debut: 2000
1st-Class catches: 11
Place in batting averages: (2000 226th av. 15.46)
Strike rate: (career 15.00)
Parents: Eric and Maggie
Marital status: Single
Family links with cricket: Great uncle Richard Knowles Tyldesley played for Lancashire in 1920s and was *Wisden* Cricketer of the Year 1925
Education: Saltersgate Infants/Middle

School, Doncaster; Ridgewood Comprehensive School, Doncaster; Danum Sixth Form School, Doncaster
Qualifications: 11 GCSEs, 1 A-level, Levels 1 and 2 coaching awards
Overseas tours: England Schools U15 to South Africa 1993; England U17 to Holland (ICC Youth Tournament) 1995
Overseas teams played for: Curtin University CC, Perth 1997-98
Cricketers particularly admired: Graeme Hick, Steve Waugh, Gary Fellows
Young players to look out for: John Sadler
Other sports played: Golf (16 handicap)
Other sports followed: Football (Doncaster Rovers FC, Arsenal FC)
Relaxations: 'Music, eating out, spending time with my girlfriend'
Extras: *Daily Telegraph* Young Cricketer of the Year 1992. Set Yorkshire League opening partnership record 1994. Set Yorkshire 2nd XI opening partnership record (279 with Colin Chapman) v Northants 2nd XI 1998. Abbot Ale Cup winner with Doncaster Town CC 1998. Awarded Yorkshire 2nd XI cap. Released by Yorkshire at the end of the 2001 season
Best batting: 44 Yorkshire v Somerset, Scarborough 2000
Best bowling: 1-22 Yorkshire v Somerset, Scarborough 2000

2001 Season

	M	Inns	NO	Runs	HS	Avge	100s	50s	Ct	St	O	M	Runs	Wkts	Avge	Best	5wI	10wM
Test																		
All First	2	4	0	44	27	11.00	-	-	5	-								
1-day Int																		
C & G																		
B & H																		
1-day Lge																		

Career Performances

	M	Inns	NO	Runs	HS	Avge	100s	50s	Ct	St	Balls	Runs	Wkts	Avge	Best	5wI	10wM
Test																	
All First	11	18	1	245	44	14.41	-	-	11	-	15	22	1	22.00	1-22	-	-
1-day Int																	
C & G																	
B & H																	
1-day Lge	4	4	0	49	38	12.25	-	-	2	-							

WIGLEY, D. H. — Yorkshire

Name: David Harry Wigley
Role: Right-hand bat, right-arm fast-medium bowler
Born: 26 October 1981, Bradford
Height: 6ft 4in **Weight:** 14st 12lbs
Nickname: Wiggers, Reverend
County debut: No first-team appearance
Parents: Max and Judith
Marital status: Single
Family links with cricket: 'Dad played league cricket in Liverpool Competition, Bradford League and Durham Senior League'
Education: Pudsey Waterloo Infants and Junior Schools; St Mary's Roman Catholic Comprehensive, Menston; Loughborough University
Qualifications: 9 GCSEs, 3 A-levels, ECB Level I coaching
Off-season: Studying at Loughborough; training at ECB Centre of Excellence
Career highlights to date: 'Playing for ECB Schools v Sri Lanka U19 2000'
Cricketers particularly admired: Darren Gough, Allan Donald, Jason Gillespie
Young players to look out for: Joe Sayers, Monty Panesar, Tim Bresnan

Other sports played: Rugby union ('played until 17 for district; had county trials, during which packed it in')
Other sports followed: Football (Leeds United), rugby (Wales)
Injuries: Out from mid-July with torn hip/pelvic muscle
Relaxations: 'Watching films, listening to any good music'
Extras: Yorkshire U19 Bowling Award 2000. Played country cricket in Victoria, Australia 2001
Opinions on cricket: 'Compared to Australians, who have dominated the last decade, first-class cricketers in England play a significantly larger number of games. Australian game is more competitive as a result of players having more training and rest time.'

WILLIAMS, R. C. J. Gloucestershire

Name: <u>Richard</u> Charles James Williams
Role: Left-hand bat, wicket-keeper
Born: 8 August 1969, Bristol
Height: 5ft 10in **Weight:** 11st
Nickname: Reg
County debut: 1990
County cap: 1996
1st-Class 50s: 5
1st-Class catches: 125
1st-Class stumpings: 17
Place in batting averages: 234th av. 13.66
Parents: Michael (deceased) and Angela
Marital status: Single
Family links with cricket: Father played local club cricket
Education: Clifton College Preparatory School; Millfield School
Qualifications: PE Diploma, NCA junior coaching award

Overseas tours: Gloucestershire to Namibia 1990, to Kenya 1991, to Sri Lanka 1992-93; Romany CC to Durban & Cape Town 1993; Gloucestershire Gypsies to Zimbabwe 1994-95, to South Africa 1995-96; Christians in Sport to South Africa 2000
Overseas teams played for: Manicaland, Zimbabwe 1990-91
Cricketers particularly admired: Andy Brassington, Jack Russell, David Gower
Other sports followed: Football, hockey, squash, snooker
Relaxations: 'Eating out, pubs and clubs, strutting my funky stuff'
Extras: Rapid Cricketline 2nd XI Championship Player of the Year 1992
Best batting: 90 Gloucestershire v Oxford University, Bristol 1995
Extras: Left Gloucestershire during the off-season.

2001 Season

	M	Inns	NO	Runs	HS	Avge	100s	50s	Ct	St	O	M	Runs	Wkts	Avge	Best	5wI	10wM
Test																		
All First	5	9	0	123	33	13.66	-	-	17	1								
1-day Int																		
C & G																		
B & H	6	5	1	68	28	17.00	-	-	9	1								
1-day Lge	4	2	0	33	28	16.50	-	-	5	2								

Career Performances

	M	Inns	NO	Runs	HS	Avge	100s	50s	Ct	St	Balls	Runs	Wkts	Avge	Best	5wI	10wM
Test																	
All First	44	59	9	911	90	18.22	-	5	125	17							
1-day Int																	
C & G																	
B & H	7	5	1	68	28	17.00	-	-	10	1							
1-day Lge	25	11	2	111	28	12.33	-	-	26	6							

WILSON, E. J.   Warwickshire

Name: Elliot James Wilson
Role: Right-hand bat, right-arm medium bowler
Born: 10 November 1979, Hertford
Height: 5ft 9in **Weight:** 11st 4lbs
Nickname: Elmo, Wils
County debut: No first-team appearance
Parents: Tom and Pam
Marital status: Single
Education: The Alleyn Court School, Westcliff; The Deanes School, Thundersley, Essex; South East Essex College, Southend; Stamford College, Lincs
Qualifications: 9 GCSEs, BTEC National Diploma in Sports Science, HND Sports Injuries, Level 2 cricket coach
Off-season: 'Working in England on my game'
Overseas teams played for: Bishen Bedi Cricket Coaching Trust, New Delhi 1998-99
Career highlights to date: 'Yet to come'
Cricket moments to forget: 'A day in the field for the 2nd XI v Surrey 2nd XI, Leamington 2000 – two drops, a few through my legs; you name it, it happened'

Cricketers particularly admired: Darren Gough, Glenn McGrath, Steve Waugh
Young players to look out for: James Foster, Jim Troughton, Elliot Wilson, Graham Napier
Other sports played: Golf, football (West Ham schoolboy)
Other sports followed: Rugby union
Injuries: Out for last three weeks of season with a stress fracture of left foot
Relaxations: 'Pub lunches; time spent on my own reading the paper in a local'
Extras: Represented ECB XI v Sri Lanka U19 2000. Took 7-61 on debut for Lincolnshire v Cambridgeshire 2000
Opinions on cricket: 'Amount of cricket played is all right if only it was in a structured fixture list – i.e. a four-day game followed by a rest day, followed by a one-day game, followed by a rest day, a training day followed by a travel day.'

WILTON, N. J.   Sussex

Name: Nicholas James Wilton
Role: Right-hand bat, wicket-keeper
Born: 23 September 1978, Pembury
Height: 5ft 11in **Weight:** 12st
Nickname: Pops
County debut: 1998
1st-Class 50s: 1
1st-Class catches: 37
1st-Class stumpings: 3
Place in batting averages: (2000 215th av. 16.66)
Parents: Graham and Susan
Marital status: Single
Family links with cricket: 'Dad played local club cricket. Brother plays club cricket'
Education: St Johns C of E Primary School, Crowborough; Beacon Community College, Crowborough; City of Westminster College

Qualifications: 5 GCSEs, CFS in Sports Studies, GNVQ (Advanced) Leisure and Tourism, ECB Level 1 coaching award
Career outside cricket: 'Coach or something involved in sport'
Overseas tours: England U19 to South Africa (including U19 World Cup) 1997-98
Cricketers particularly admired: Alan Knott, Jack Russell, Ian Healy
Young players to look out for: Mike Yardy
Other sports played: Football (Sussex U10 and U11); 'I'll have a go at most things'
Other sports followed: Football (Arsenal FC)
Relaxations: 'Cinema, music; spending time with girlfriend'
Extras: Played for Sussex U10 to U19. Retained and registered by Sussex in 1997

while spending a season with the MCC Young Cricketers. Has represented England at U14, U17 and U19 levels. Part of the England U19 squad which won the U19 World Cup in South Africa 1998. Had shoulder operation in 1999 to cure recurring dislocation problem. Released by Sussex at the end of the 2001 season

Opinions on cricket: 'Two divisional cricket has led to competitive cricket all year round and a high standard, as every game has something riding on it. Day/night cricket is a massive crowd-puller and great to play in. More needed to increase the level of interest in the game.'

Best batting: 55 Sussex v Leicestershire, Arundel 1999

2001 Season

	M	Inns	NO	Runs	HS	Avge	100s	50s	Ct	St	O	M	Runs	Wkts	Avge	Best	5wl	10wM
Test																		
All First	1	1	0	1	1	1.00	-	-	-	1								
1-day Int																		
C & G																		
B & H																		
1-day Lge																		

Career Performances

	M	Inns	NO	Runs	HS	Avge	100s	50s	Ct	St	Balls	Runs	Wkts	Avge	Best	5wl	10wM
Test																		
All First	17	26	4	353	55	16.04	-	1	37	3							
1-day Int																		
C & G																		
B & H	3	2	1	10	7 *	10.00	-	-	2	-							
1-day Lge	13	9	1	18	7	2.25	-	-	9	3							

---

98. Which current county director of cricket captained
Northamptonshire in the 1981 NatWest final,
winning the Man of the Match award?

WINDOWS, M. G. N.   Gloucestershire

Name: <u>Matthew</u> Guy Newman Windows
Role: Right-hand bat, left-arm
medium bowler
Born: 5 April 1973, Bristol
Height: 5ft 7in   **Weight:** 11st 7lbs
Nickname: Steamy, Nik Nak, Bedos
County debut: 1992
County cap: 1998
1000 runs in a season: 2
1st-Class 50s: 32
1st-Class 100s: 13
1st-Class catches: 67
One-Day 100s: 2
Place in batting averages: 89th av. 35.00
(2000 49th av. 37.21)
Strike rate: (career 58.50)
Parents: Tony and Carolyn
Marital status: 'Shacked up'

Family links with cricket: Father (A.R.) played for Gloucestershire (1960-69) and
Cambridge University
Education: Clifton College Prep; Clifton College; Durham University
Qualifications: 9 GCSEs, 3 A-levels, BA (Hons) Sociology (Dunelm)
Career outside cricket: Stockbroker
Overseas tours: Clifton College to Barbados 1991; England U19 to Pakistan 1991-92;
Durham University to South Africa 1992-93; England A to Zimbabwe and South
Africa 1998-99; Gloucestershire's annual pre-season tour to South Africa
Overseas teams played for: Gold Coast Dolphins, Queensland 1996-97
Cricketers particularly admired: David Boon, Courtney Walsh, David Milne
Other sports played: Rackets (British Open runner-up 1997)
Relaxations: Reading and travelling
Extras: Played for Lincolnshire and in England U19 home series v Sri Lanka 1992.
Scored 71 on county debut v Essex in 1992. Gloucestershire Young Player of the Year
1994. Set record for highest individual score for Durham University (218*).
Gloucestershire Player of the Year 1998. B&H Gold Award for his 54 in the semi-final
v Yorkshire at Headingley 2001. C&G Man of the Match award for his 82 v Sussex
Board XI at Horsham 2001. Scored 94-ball 117 v Northamptonshire at Cheltenham in
the Norwich Union League 2001
Best batting: 184 Gloucestershire v Warwickshire, Cheltenham 1996
Best bowling: 1-6 Combined Universities v West Indians, The Parks 1995

2001 Season

	M	Inns	NO	Runs	HS	Avge	100s	50s	Ct	St	O	M	Runs	Wkts	Avge	Best	5wI	10wM
Test																		
All First	16	27	3	840	174	35.00	3	3	6	-								
1-day Int																		
C & G	2	2	0	138	82	69.00	-	2	2	-								
B & H	8	8	1	277	108 *	39.57	1	1	3	-								
1-day Lge	15	15	0	458	117	30.53	1	2	5	-								

Career Performances

	M	Inns	NO	Runs	HS	Avge	100s	50s	Ct	St	Balls	Runs	Wkts	Avge	Best	5wI	10wM
Test																	
All First	112	198	15	6296	184	34.40	13	32	67	-	117	111	2	55.50	1-6	-	-
1-day Int																	
C & G	17	16	3	371	82	28.53	-	2	5	-							
B & H	22	22	6	594	108 *	37.12	1	2	6	-							
1-day Lge	96	89	6	1773	117	21.36	1	6	31	-	48	49	0	-		-	-

WOOD, J.   Lancashire

Name: John Wood
Role: Right-hand bat, right-arm
fast-medium bowler
Born: 22 July 1970, Crofton, Wakefield
Height: 6ft 3in **Weight:** 16st 7lbs
Nickname: Woody
County debut: 1992 (Durham),
2001 (Lancashire)
County cap: 1998 (Durham)
50 wickets in a season: 1
1st-Class 50s: 2
1st-Class 5 w. in innings: 11
1st-Class catches: 23
Place in batting averages: 231st av. 14.11
(2000 252nd av. 12.06)
Place in bowling averages: (2000 74th
av. 27.81)
Strike rate: 93.22 (career 54.69)
Parents: Brian and Anne
Wife and date of marriage: Emma Louise, 30 October 1994
Children: Alexandra Mae, 7 April 1996; Joseph Samuel, 3 July 1998
Family links with cricket: 'Brother Ian plays for Spen Victoria in Bradford League;
Dad played local league cricket for Crofton'

Education: Crofton Junior School; Crofton High School; Wakefield District College; Leeds Polytechnic

Qualifications: 6 O-levels, BTEC Diploma Electronic Engineering, HND Electrical and Electronic Engineering, Level III cricket coach

Career outside cricket: '12-month contracts at Lancs'

Off-season: Pre-season tour to Cape Town

Overseas tours: Durham CCC to South Africa 1994-95

Overseas teams played for: Griqualand West Cricket Union, South Africa 1990-91; TAWA, Wellington and Wellington B, New Zealand 1993-95

Career highlights to date: 'Reaching C&G semi-final'

Cricket moments to forget: 'C&G semi-final' (*Lancashire lost to Leicestershire as Shahid Afridi struck a 58-ball 95*)

Cricketers particularly admired: Wasim Akram, David Boon, Wayne Larkins

Young players to look out for: Andrew Pratt, Steve Harmison, Paul Collingwood, Jimmy Anderson

Other sports played: Golf

Other sports followed: Football (Leeds United), rugby (England)

Injuries: Out for six weeks with ligament damage to right ankle

Relaxations: 'Spending time with my family; playing golf'

Extras: Played in the Bradford League. Made his debut for Durham (Minor Counties) in 1991. Durham Players' Player of the Year 1998. Left Durham at the end of the 2000 season and joined Lancashire for 2001

Opinions on cricket: 'Umpires should treat batsmen 1-11 the same.'

Best batting: 63* Durham v Nottinghamshire, Chester-le-Street 1993

Best bowling: 7-58 Durham v Yorkshire, Headingley 1999

2001 Season

	M	Inns	NO	Runs	HS	Avge	100s	50s	Ct	St	O	M	Runs	Wkts	Avge	Best	5wI	10wM
Test																		
All First	8	10	1	127	35	14.11	-	-	-	-	139.5	16	540	9	60.00	3-97	-	-
1-day Int																		
C & G	3	2	1	29	25	29.00	-	-	-	-	19	0	94	4	23.50	3-43	-	
B & H	3	2	1	17	15 *	17.00	-	-	-	-	27.4	3	109	4	27.25	2-39	-	
1-day Lge	10	5	2	33	19 *	11.00	-	-	2	-	66	8	319	8	39.87	2-20	-	

Career Performances

	M	Inns	NO	Runs	HS	Avge	100s	50s	Ct	St	Balls	Runs	Wkts	Avge	Best	5wI	10wM
Test																	
All First	96	142	21	1462	63 *	12.08	-	2	23	-	14719	9059	269	33.67	7-58	11	-
1-day Int																	
C & G	12	6	2	49	25	12.25	-	-	-	-	543	373	12	31.08	3-43	-	
B & H	20	13	4	103	28 *	11.44	-	-	1	-	1034	650	26	25.00	4-26	-	
1-day Lge	81	55	20	366	28 *	10.45	-	-	15	-	3477	2836	74	38.32	4-17	-	

WOOD, M. J. Somerset

Name: <u>Matthew</u> James Wood
Role: Right-hand bat, right-arm
off-spin bowler
Born: 30 September 1980, Exeter
Height: 5ft 11in **Weight:** 12st 5lbs
Nickname: Woody, Grandma
County debut: 2001
1st-Class 50s: 4
1st-Class 100s: 1
1st-Class catches: 2
Place in batting averages: 55th av. 44.08
Parents: James and Trina
Marital status: Single
Family links with cricket: Father is
chairman of Exmouth CC
Education: St Joseph's Primary, Exmouth;
Exmouth College; Exeter University
(first year)
Qualifications: 8 GCSEs, 2 A-levels, ECB Level II coach
Overseas tours: West of England U15 to West Indies 1995
Overseas teams played for: Doubleview CC, Perth 2000
Career highlights to date: '51 v Australians 2001. Maiden first-class 100
v Northants'
Cricketers particularly admired: Marcus Trescothick
Young players to look out for: Arul Suppiah
Other sports played: Football, golf
Other sports followed: Football (Liverpool FC)
Relaxations: Music, golf
Extras: Scored 71 on debut v Yorkshire at Bath 2001. Scored maiden first-class
century (122) v Northamptonshire at Taunton 2001; also scored 65 in the second
innings. Has played for Devon
Best batting: 122 Somerset v Northamptonshire, Taunton 2001

2001 Season

	M	Inns	NO	Runs	HS	Avge	100s	50s	Ct	St	O	M	Runs	Wkts	Avge	Best	5wI	10wM
Test																		
All First	7	12	0	529	122	44.08	1	4	2	-	7	1	30	0	-	-	-	-
1-day Int																		
C & G																		
B & H																		
1-day Lge	6	5	0	86	29	17.20	-	-	1	-								

Career Performances

	M	Inns	NO	Runs	HS	Avge	100s	50s	Ct	St	Balls	Runs	Wkts	Avge	Best	5wI	10wM
Test																	
All First	7	12	0	529	122	44.08	1	4	2	-	42	30	0	-	-	-	-
1-day Int																	
C & G																	
B & H																	
1-day Lge	6	5	0	86	29	17.20	-	-	1	-							

WOOD, M. J.   Yorkshire

Name: <u>Matthew</u> James Wood
Role: Right-hand bat, off-spin bowler
Born: 6 April 1977, Huddersfield
Height: 5ft 9in **Weight:** 12st
Nickname: Ronnie, Chuddy
County debut: 1997
County cap: 2001
1000 runs in a season: 2
1st-Class 50s: 13
1st-Class 100s: 8
1st-Class 200s: 1
1st-Class catches: 42
Place in batting averages: 36th av. 48.18
(2000 195th av. 18.28)
Parents: Roger and Kathryn
Marital status: Single
Family links with cricket: 'Father played for local team Emley. Mum made the teas and sister Caroline scored'
Education: Emley First School; Kirkburton Middle School; Shelley High School and Sixth Form Centre
Qualifications: 9 GCSEs, 2 A-levels, NCA coaching award
Off-season: Spending the winter in Australia with the England National Academy
Overseas tours: England U19 to Zimbabwe 1995-96; Yorkshire CCC to West Indies 1996-97, to Cape Town 1997, 1998; MCC to Kenya 1999, to Bangladesh 1999-2000; ECB National Academy to Australia 2001-02
Overseas teams played for: Somerset West CC, Cape Town 1994-95; Upper Hutt United CC, Wellington, New Zealand 1997-98; Mosman Park, Western Australia 2000-01
Career highlights to date: 'Being on the pitch as fielding 12th man for England series win v South Africa at Headingley [1998]. Winning the Championship in 2001'

Cricket moments to forget: 'Losing B&H quarter-final v Surrey 2000'
Cricketers particularly admired: Darren Lehmann, Michael Slater, Martyn Moxon, Matthew Maynard
Young players to look out for: Ben Heritage, Richard Dawson
Other sports played: Football (Kirkburton FC)
Other sports followed: Football (Liverpool FC)
Injuries: Out for seven weeks with a broken hand
Relaxations: Music, dining out, socialising, watching sport
Extras: Played for England U17 against India 1994. Spent two years at the Yorkshire Academy before graduating to the full staff in 1996. Has Yorkshire 2nd XI cap. Scored 81 on first-class debut v Lancashire at Headingley in 1997. Scored 1000 runs in first full season 1998. Shared in the highest first-wicket partnership (152) for Yorkshire in matches against Kent for 49 years with Scott Richardson at Headingley 2001. Scored 85* v Surrey at Headingley 2001, in the process sharing with Darren Lehmann in a record third-wicket partnership for Yorkshire in matches against Surrey. Awarded Yorkshire cap 2001
Opinions on cricket: 'Two divisions has been a real boost to the intensity of both forms of cricket. Under-16s should be allowed free entry to Championship fixtures.'
Best batting: 200* Yorkshire v Warwickshire, Headingley 1998

2001 Season

	M	Inns	NO	Runs	HS	Avge	100s	50s	Ct	St	O	M	Runs	Wkts	Avge	Best	5wI	10wM
Test																		
All First	14	23	1	1060	124	48.18	4	6	9	-								
1-day Int																		
C & G	3	3	0	29	24	9.66	-	-	1	-								
B & H	1	1	0	7	7	7.00	-	-	1	-								
1-day Lge	13	13	0	256	68	19.69	-	1	5	-								

Career Performances

	M	Inns	NO	Runs	HS	Avge	100s	50s	Ct	St	Balls	Runs	Wkts	Avge	Best	5wI	10wM
Test																	
All First	63	106	10	3027	200 *	31.53	9	13	42	-	18	16	0	-	-	-	-
1-day Int																	
C & G	5	5	1	97	43	24.25	-	-	1	-							
B & H	7	5	1	89	59	22.25	-	1	2	-							
1-day Lge	35	28	2	563	68	21.65	-	3	12	-							

WRIGHT, A. S.   Leicestershire

Name: <u>Ashley</u> Spencer Wright
Role: Right-hand opening bat, right-arm
medium bowler
Born: 21 October 1980, Grantham
Height: 5ft 11in **Weight:** 11st 7lbs
Nickname: Ash
County debut: 2001
One-Day 100s: 1
Parents: Keith and Anna
Marital status: Single
Family links with cricket: Father very keen
cricketer and senior coach; brother Luke also
on Leicestershire staff
Education: Redmile Primary School;
Belvoir High School; King Edward VII,
Melton Mowbray
Qualifications: 10 GCSEs, coaching award
Cricketers particularly admired: 'All the
Leicestershire players'

Young players to look out for: Darren Stevens
Other sports played: Squash
Other sports followed: Football (Leicester City, Notts County, Notts Forest)
Relaxations: Music, cinema, going to gym, going out
Extras: Hit a highest score of 158 against Staffordshire U15. Won the Livingstone
Cup for outstanding batting performance in the 2nd XI 1999. Played for Leicestershire
Board XI in the NatWest 1999 and 2000, scoring maiden one-day century (112) v
Durham Board XI at Gateshead Fell 2000. Also played for Leics Board XI in the
second round of the C&G 2002, which was played in September 2001
Best batting: 30 Leicestershire v Pakistanis, Leicester 2001

2001 Season

	M	Inns	NO	Runs	HS	Avge	100s	50s	Ct	St	O	M	Runs	Wkts	Avge	Best	5wl	10wM
Test																		
All First	1	2	0	30	30	15.00	-	-	-	-								
1-day Int																		
C & G	1	1	0	6	6	6.00	-	-	-	-	6	0	32	0	-		-	-
B & H																		
1-day Lge																		

Career Performances

	M	Inns	NO	Runs	HS	Avge	100s	50s	Ct	St	Balls	Runs	Wkts	Avge	Best	5wI	10wM
Test																	
All First	1	2	0	30	30	15.00	-	-	-	-							
1-day Int																	
C & G	3	3	0	181	112	60.33	1	1	-	-	36	32	0	-		-	-
B & H																	
1-day Lge																	

WRIGHT, L. J. — Leicestershire

Name: <u>Luke</u> James Wright
Role: Right-hand bat, right-arm medium-fast bowler
Born: 7 March 1985, Grantham
Height: 5ft 11in **Weight:** 11st 6lbs
County debut: No first-team appearance
Parents: Keith and Anna
Marital status: Single
Family links with cricket: 'Father very keen cricketer (Level 2 coach); brother Ashley also has a contract with Leicestershire'
Education: Redmile Primary School; Belvoir High School, Bottesford; Ratcliffe College
Qualifications: 8 GCSEs, 'currently studying sports science and sports massage'
Off-season: 'Keeping fit, practising hard and studying'
Overseas tours: Leicestershire U13 to South Africa; Leicestershire U15 to South Africa
Career highlights to date: 'Getting a contract with Leicestershire'
Cricketers particularly admired: Jacques Kallis
Young players to look out for: Ashley Wright, Stephen Adshead, Damian Brandy, Tom New
Other sports played: Football, hockey, squash, tennis
Other sports followed: Football (Newcastle United)
Relaxations: Music, cinema, going out
Extras: Set record for best debut for Ratcliffe College with 130. Scored 86 v MCC, the highest score by a Ratcliffe player against the club. Played for Leicestershire Board XI in the second round of the C&G 2002, which was played in September 2001

Career Performances

	M	Inns	NO	Runs	HS	Avge	100s	50s	Ct	St	Balls	Runs	Wkts	Avge	Best	5wI	10wM
Test																	
All First																	
1-day Int																	
C & G	1	1	0	16	16	16.00	-	-	-	-							
B & H																	
1-day Lge																	

YARDY, M. H. Sussex

Name: <u>Michael</u> Howard Yardy
Role: Left-hand bat, left-arm
medium-fast bowler
Born: 27 November 1980, Pembury, Kent
Height: 6ft 1in **Weight:** 14st
Nickname: Yards, Skuttler
County debut: 1999 (one-day),
2000 (first-class)
1st-Class 50s: 5
1st-Class catches: 9
Place in batting averages: 91st av. 34.60
(2000 277th av. 9.14)
Strike rate: 138.00 (career 312.00)
Parents: Beverly D'Inverno and
Howard Yardy
Marital status: Single
Family links with cricket: Brother plays
Education: St Pauls School, Hastings;
William Parker School, Hastings
Qualifications: 5 GCSEs, 2 A-levels

Off-season: 'International Academy, Port Elizabeth, South Africa (January 2002);
watching West Ham'
Overseas tours: Sussex U19 to Barbados 1997, to Cape Town 2000; Sussex to
Grenada 2001
Overseas teams played for: Cape Town CC 1999
Career highlights to date: 'Winning [second division] Championship with
Sussex 2001'
Cricket moments to forget: 'Getting out on TV debut for nought'
Cricketers particularly admired: James Kirtley, Mark Robinson, Tony Cottey,
'all Sussex players'

Young players to look out for: Greg Hobbs, Russ Jones, John McSweeney, Martin Smith, Bas Zuiderent, Dom Clapp, Matt Prior
Other sports played: American football
Other sports followed: Football (West Ham)
Injuries: Unable to bowl July-September 2001 because of sore Achilles
Relaxations: 'Drinking with mates; enjoying life'
Extras: Played in the Sussex U15 side that won the U15 County Championship 1996, the U16 side that won the U16 County Championship in 1997 and the U19 side that were runners-up in the NAYC Two-Day Cup 1997. Represented England U17 1998. Attended Sussex Academy. Played for Sussex Board XI in 1999 NatWest. Sussex Most Improved Player 2001
Opinions on cricket: 'Great game. Enjoy it – we are only here once.'
Best batting: 87* Sussex v Hampshire, Hove 2001
Best bowling: 1-13 Sussex v Derbyshire, Arundel 2001

2001 Season

	M	Inns	NO	Runs	HS	Avge	100s	50s	Ct	St	O	M	Runs	Wkts	Avge	Best	5wI	10wM
Test																		
All First	17	29	6	796	87 *	34.60	-	5	9	-	23	6	61	1	61.00	1-13	-	-
1-day Int																		
C & G	2	2	0	0	0	0.00	-	-	-	-	6.2	0	38	1	38.00	1-30	-	
B & H	3	3	0	67	59	22.33	-	1	-	-	5	1	17	1	17.00	1-10	-	
1-day Lge	5	5	0	56	24	11.20	-	-	-	-	19	0	78	2	39.00	2-34	-	

Career Performances

	M	Inns	NO	Runs	HS	Avge	100s	50s	Ct	St	Balls	Runs	Wkts	Avge	Best	5wI	10wM
Test																	
All First	21	37	7	860	87 *	28.66	-	5	9	-	312	145	1	145.00	1-13	-	-
1-day Int																	
C & G	5	5	0	28	15	5.60	-	-	4	-	146	128	2	64.00	1-30	-	
B & H	3	3	0	67	59	22.33	-	1	-	-	30	17	1	17.00	1-10	-	
1-day Lge	6	5	0	56	24	11.20	-	-	-	-	132	93	2	46.50	2-34	-	

99. In which year did Ireland first take part in the Gillette/NatWest/C&G?

YATES, G.

Lancashire

Name: Gary Yates
Role: Right-hand bat, right-arm
off-spin bowler
Born: 20 September 1967,
Ashton-under-Lyne
Height: 6ft 1in **Weight:** 13st 1lb
Nickname: Sweaty, Yugo, Pearly,
Backyard, Zippy
County debut: 1990
County cap: 1994
1st-Class 50s: 5
1st-Class 100s: 3
1st-Class 5 w. in innings: 5
1st-Class catches: 38
Strike rate: 58.25 (career 73.78)
Parents: Alan and Patricia
Marital status: Single
Children: Francis Leonard George,
1 May 1999
Family links with cricket: Father played in Lancashire Leagues
Education: Corrie County Primary School, Denton; Corrie County Junior School,
Denton; Manchester Grammar School
Qualifications: 6 O-levels, Level 2 coach, Australian Cricket Coaching Council coach
Career outside cricket: 'Sales rep with family business (Digical Ltd), selling diaries,
calendars and business gifts'
Off-season: Training with Lancashire
Overseas tours: Lancashire to Tasmania and Western Australia 1990, to Western
Australia 1991, to Johannesburg 1992, to Barbados and St Lucia 1992, to Calcutta
1997, to Cape Town 1997-98; MCC to Bangladesh 1999-2000
Overseas teams played for: South Barwon, Geelong, Australia 1987-88; Johnsonville,
Wellington, New Zealand 1989-90; Western Suburbs, Brisbane 1991-92; Old
Selbornian, East London, South Africa 1992-93; Hermanus CC, South Africa 1995-96
Cricketers particularly admired: Michael Atherton, Ian Botham, John Emburey
Other sports played: Golf ('represented Lancashire CCC at National *Times* Corporate
Golf Challenge, La Manga, Spain, December 2001')
Other sports followed: All sports, especially football (Manchester City season-ticket
holder), golf, motor rallying
Relaxations: 'Playing golf, watching football and good films, eating; spending time
with my son'
Extras: Played for Worcestershire 2nd XI in 1987. Made debut for Lancashire 2nd XI
in 1988 and taken on to county staff in 1990. Scored century (106) on Championship

debut v Nottinghamshire at Trent Bridge 1990. Rapid Cricketline Player of the Month April/May 1992. Appointed 2nd XI captain/coach for 2002. PCA representative for Lancashire

Opinions on cricket: 'I feel that over the next few years the game will enter a transitional period. There will be more emphasis on England and the number of English contracted players. There may well be less County Championship matches. I hope to see relegation and promotion restricted to two teams only.'

Best batting: 134* Lancashire v Northamptonshire, Old Trafford 1993
Best bowling: 6-64 Lancashire v Kent, Old Trafford 1999

2001 Season

	M	Inns	NO	Runs	HS	Avge	100s	50s	Ct	St	O	M	Runs	Wkts	Avge	Best	5wl	10wM
Test																		
All First	2	2	1	65	57	65.00	-	1	2	-	38.5	10	88	4	22.00	2-23	-	-
1-day Int																		
C & G	2	1	0	9	9	9.00	-	-	-	-	10	0	23	2	11.50	2-23	-	
B & H																		
1-day Lge	8	4	2	28	16	14.00	-	-	2	-	53	3	201	4	50.25	2-21	-	

Career Performances

	M	Inns	NO	Runs	HS	Avge	100s	50s	Ct	St	Balls	Runs	Wkts	Avge	Best	5wl	10wM
Test																	
All First	81	105	36	1772	134 *	25.68	3	5	38	-	13577	6949	184	37.76	6-64	5	-
1-day Int																	
C & G	21	10	5	91	34 *	18.20	-	-	5	-	1206	692	18	38.44	2-15	-	
B & H	34	15	3	135	26	11.25	-	-	6	-	1566	1093	35	31.22	3-42	-	
1-day Lge	109	48	24	374	38	15.58	-	-	27	-	3864	3131	102	30.69	4-34	-	

---

100. Which future Australian Test cricketer played
for Holland in the 1998 NatWest?

ZUIDERENT, B.   Sussex

Name: Bastiaan (<u>Bas</u>) Zuiderent
Role: Right-hand top-order bat, right-arm
off-spin bowler
Born: 3 March 1977, Utrecht, Holland
Height: 6ft 3in **Weight:** 14st 2lbs
Nickname: Bazy, Bastil
County debut: 1999 (one-day),
2001 (first-class)
One-Day Internationals: 5
1st-Class 50s: 3
1st-Class 100s: 1
1st-Class catches: 18
One-Day 100s: 1

Place in batting averages: 162nd av. 23.80
Parents: Eduard and Jacqueline
Marital status: Girlfriend Kelly
Family links with cricket: Cousins
J. J. Esmeijer and Ben Goedegebuur have
represented Holland
Education: Van Oldebarnevelt School, Rotterdam; Erasmiaans Gymnasium,
Rotterdam; University of Amsterdam ('two years; Economics')
Qualifications: Level 2 coaching
Career outside cricket: 'Still studying part-time'
Off-season: 'World Cup with Holland coming up! Spending time with family and
friends. Travelling with my girlfriend'
Overseas tours: Various Holland sides to Denmark, Kenya, South Africa and Scotland;
Holland to India and Pakistan (World Cup) 1995-96, to Malaysia (ICC Trophy) 1998
Overseas teams played for: VOC Rotterdam 1989-97; Wits Technicon, Johannesburg
1997; VRA Amsterdam 1998
Career highlights to date: 'Winning [Championship] division two with Sussex 2001.
Participating in 1995-96 World Cup'
Cricket moments to forget: 'My first-class debut'
Cricketers particularly admired: Steven Lubbers, Martin Crowe, Tim de Leede
Young players to look out for: Carl Hopkinson
Other sports played: Football (VOC Rotterdam), golf (Broekpolder), skiing,
squash, tennis
Other sports followed: Football (PSV Eindhoven 'and Man United especially for
Wayne and Sam Tucknott')
Relaxations: Music, reading, films
Extras: Has represented Holland at various levels since the age of 12. Player of the
Tournament, International Youth Tournament, Denmark 1993. Scored 54 v England in
1995-96 World Cup, becoming the second youngest player (after Sachin Tendulkar) to

score 50 in a World Cup. Scored 99 (run out) for Holland v Worcestershire in NatWest Trophy 1997, winning the Man of the Match award. Played for Brighton & Hove in their Sussex League and Challenge Cup winning season 2000, scoring an unbeaten century in the cup final. B&H Gold Award for his 102* v Hampshire at West End 2001 (his maiden one-day century). Scored maiden first-class century (122) v Nottinghamshire at Hove 2001 in only his second first-class match

Opinions on cricket: 'Still too many games played! We need more exposure and promotion of the game in the country (also Holland) to get more kids interested.'

Best batting: 122 Sussex v Nottinghamshire, Hove 2001

2001 Season

	M	Inns	NO	Runs	HS	Avge	100s	50s	Ct	St	O	M	Runs	Wkts	Avge	Best	5wl	10wM
Test																		
All First	17	27	1	619	122	23.80	1	3	18	-								
1-day Int																		
C & G	2	2	0	16	16	8.00	-	-	2	-								
B & H	4	4	1	167	102 *	55.66	1	-	2	-								
1-day Lge	10	9	0	202	65	22.44	-	2	1	-								

Career Performances

	M	Inns	NO	Runs	HS	Avge	100s	50s	Ct	St	Balls	Runs	Wkts	Avge	Best	5wl	10wM
Test																	
All First	17	27	1	619	122	23.80	1	3	18	-							
1-day Int	5	5	1	91	54	22.75	-	1	4	-							
C & G	6	6	0	149	99	24.83	-	1	3	-	12	15	0	-		-	-
B & H	6	6	1	170	102 *	34.00	1	-	3	-							
1-day Lge	19	17	0	353	68	20.76	-	3	6	-							

GUEST PLAYERS

AAMER SOHAIL   Somerset

Name: Aamer Sohail

Role: Left-hand bat, slow left-arm bowler

Born: 14 September 1966, Lahore

Extras: Played 47 Tests for Pakistan 1992 – 1999-2000 and 156 One-Day Internationals 1990-91 – 1999-2000. Scored 205 v England in the third Test at Old Trafford 1992. Played one match for Somerset against the Australian tourists at Taunton 2001

BANKS, O. A. C. Leicestershire

Name: <u>Omari</u> Ahmed Clemente Banks
Role: Right-hand bat, right-arm off-spin bowler
Born: 17 July 1982, Anguilla
Extras: Made first-class debut for Leeward Islands 2000-01. Took 7-70 (10-148 in match) v Jamaica at Molyneux 2000-01. Toured England with West Indies U19 2001, also playing in one match for Leicestershire against the Pakistani tourists at Leicester

SHOAIB AKHTAR Somerset

Name: Shoaib Akhtar
Role: Right-hand bat, right-arm fast bowler
Born: 13 August 1975, Rawalpindi
Extras: Has played 16 Tests and 45 One-Day Internationals for Pakistan 1997-98 –. Nicknamed the Rawalpindi Express. Played one match for Somerset against the Australian tourists at Taunton 2001

STOP PRESS

MASON, M. S. Worcestershire

Name: Matthew (<u>Matt</u>) Sean Mason
Role: Right-hand bat, right-arm fast-medium bowler
Born: 20 March 1974, Claremont, Western Australia
Extras: Has played for Western Australia, making his Sheffield Shield debut in 1997-98. Is not considered an overseas player

McMAHON, P. J. Nottinghamshire

Name: <u>Paul</u> Joseph McMahon
Role: Right-hand bat, right-arm off-spin bowler
Born: 12 March 1983, Wigan
Extras: Represented England U19 in the U19 World Cup in New Zealand 2001-02

NOTE: <u>Stuart</u> Rupert Clark, 26-year-old right-arm fast-medium bowler from New South Wales, has been signed by Worcestershire as temporary overseas player until Andy Bichel becomes available. Nottinghamshire have also signed South African Lance Klusener as similar cover for Chris Cairns.

THE UMPIRES

BENSON, M. R.

Name: <u>Mark</u> Richard Benson
Born: 6 July 1958, Shoreham, Sussex
Height: 5ft 10in
Nickname: Benny
Wife and date of marriage: Sarah Patricia,
20 September 1986
Children: Laurence, 16 October 1987;
Edward, 23 June 1990
Education: Sutton Valence School
Off-season: 'Looking after my properties'
Other sports played: Bridge, golf,
swimming, cycling
Relaxations: Bridge ('relaxing?')
Appointed to 1st-Class list: 2000
One-Day Internationals umpired: 1 as
TV umpire
County as player: Kent
Role: Left-hand bat
County debut: 1980
County cap: 1981
Benefit: 1991 (£174,619)
Test debut: 1986
Tests: 1
One-Day Internationals: 1
1000 runs in a season: 11
1st-Class 50s: 99
1st-Class 100s: 47
1st-Class 200s: 1
1st-Class catches: 140
One-Day 100s: 5
Overseas tours: None

Highlights of playing career: '257 v Hampshire. Winning Sunday League as captain of Kent. Two 90s to win a game against Hampshire with Malcolm Marshall bowling'
Extras: Scored 1000 runs in first full season. Kent captain 1991-95. Captained England in two one-day matches against Holland in 1993. Retired from county cricket in 1995, finishing first-class career with a batting average in excess of 40
Opinions on cricket: 'Wish the game was played in an honest fashion (à la golf). Why fellow pros cheat fellow pros is beyond me. If it happened in golf, the guilty player would probably be ostracised for the rest of his career.'
Best batting: 257 Kent v Hampshire, Southampton 1991
Best bowling: 2-55 Kent v Surrey, Dartford 1986

First-Class Career Performances

	M	Inns	NO	Runs	HS	Avge	100s	Ct	St	Runs	Wkts	Avge	Best	5wI	10wM
Test	1	2	0	51	30	25.50	-	-	-						
All First	292	491	34	18387	257	40.23	48	140	-	493	5	98.60	2-55	-	-

BURGESS, G. I.

Name: <u>Graham</u> Iefvion Burgess
Born: 5 May 1943, Glastonbury, Somerset
Education: Millfield School
Appointed to 1st-Class list: 1991
One-Day Internationals umpired: 2 as
TV umpire
County as player: Somerset
Role: Right-hand bat, right-arm
medium bowler
County debut: 1966
County cap: 1968
Testimonial: 1977
1st-Class 100s: 2
1st-Class 5 w. in innings: 18
1st-Class 10 w. in match: 2
1st-Class catches: 120
One-Day 5 w. in innings: 2
Extras: Played Minor Counties cricket for
Wilts 1981-82 and for Cambs 1983-84
Best batting: 129 Somerset v Gloucestershire, Taunton 1973
Best bowling: 7-43 Somerset v Oxford University, The Parks 1975

First-Class Career Performances

	M	Inns	NO	Runs	HS	Avge	100s	Ct	St	Runs	Wkts	Avge	Best	5wI	10wM
Test															
All First	252	414	37	7129	129	18.90	2	120	-	13543	474	28.57	7-43	18	2

CLARKSON, A.

Name: Anthony (Tony) Clarkson
Born: 5 September 1939, Killinghall,
North Yorkshire
Height: 6ft
Wife's name: Cheryl
Children: André, 5 September 1964;
Chantal, 27 May 1967; Pierre, 1 May 1969
Family links with cricket: Father was a
league professional
Education: Killinghall C of E; Harrogate
Grammar School; Leeds College of Building;
Bradford Polytechnic; Brunel College, Bristol
Career outside cricket: Architectural, civil
engineering and surveying consultant
Other sports followed: Golf and rugby
Relaxations: Golf, DIY, and gardening
Appointed to 1st-Class list: 1996
Counties as player: Yorkshire, Somerset
Role: Right-hand bat, right-arm off-spin bowler
County debut: 1963 (Yorkshire), 1965 (Somerset)
County cap: 1969 (Somerset)
1000 runs in a season: 2
1st-Class 50s: 23
1st-Class 100s: 2
1st-Class catches: 52
One-Day 100s: 1
Extras: First English player to score a century in the Sunday League. Was league
professional 1973-89
Best batting: 131 Somerset v Northamptonshire, Northampton 1969
Best bowling: 3-51 Somerset v Essex, Yeovil 1967

First-Class Career Performances

	M	Inns	NO	Runs	HS	Avge	100s	Ct	St	Runs	Wkts	Avge	Best	5wl	10wM
Test															
All First	110	189	12	4458	131	25.18	2	52	-	367	13	28.23	3-51	-	-

CONSTANT, D. J.

Name: <u>David</u> John Constant
Born: 9 November 1941,
Bradford-on-Avon, Wiltshire
Height: 5ft 7in
Nickname: Connie
Wife's name: Rosalyn
Children: Lisa, 6 July 1966;
Julie, 21 February 1969
Family links with cricket: Father-in-law,
G.E.E. Lambert, played for Gloucestershire
Education: Grove Park Secondary Modern
Off-season: Bowls
Other sports followed: Football (Millwall)
Interests/relaxations: 'Six grandchildren
and bowls'
Appointed to 1st-Class list: 1969
First appointed to Test panel: 1971
Tests umpired: 36 (plus 5 as TV umpire)
One-Day Internationals umpired: 33 (plus 5 as TV umpire)
Other umpiring honours: Stood in 1975, 1979 and 1983 World Cups
Counties as player: Kent, Leicestershire
Role: Left-hand bat, slow left-arm bowler
County debut: 1961 (Kent), 1965 (Leicestershire)
1st-Class 50s: 6
1st-Class catches: 33
Extras: County bowls player for Gloucestershire 1984-86 (outdoors). Also represented
Somerset at indoor version of the game in the Liberty Trophy
Best batting: 80 Leicestershire v Gloucestershire, Bristol 1966
Best bowling: 1-28 Leicestershire v Surrey, The Oval 1968

First-Class Career Performances

	M	Inns	NO	Runs	HS	Avge	100s	Ct	St	Runs	Wkts	Avge	Best	5wI	10wM
Test															
All First	61	93	14	1517	80	19.20	-	33	-	36	1	36.00	1-28	-	-

COWLEY, N. G.

Name: <u>Nigel</u> Geoffrey Cowley
Born: 1 March 1953, Shaftesbury, Dorset
Height: 5ft 6½in
Marital status: Divorced
Children: Mark Antony, 14 June 1973;
Darren James, 30 October 1976
Family links with cricket: Darren played
Hampshire Schools U11, U12, U13; Natal
Schools 1993, 1994, 1995; and toured India
with South Africa U19 1996
Education: Duchy Manor, Mere, Wilts
Off-season: Cricket coach at Durban
High School
Other sports played: Golf (8 handicap)
Other sports followed: Football
(Liverpool FC)

Appointed to 1st-Class list: 2000
Counties as player: Hampshire, Glamorgan
Role: Right-hand bat, off-spin bowler
County debut: 1974 (Hampshire), 1990 (Glamorgan)
County cap: 1978 (Hampshire)
Benefit: 1988 (Hampshire; £88,274)
1000 runs in a season: 1
50 wickets in a season: 2
1st-Class 50s: 36
1st-Class 100s: 2
1st-Class 5 w. in innings: 5
1st-Class catches: 105
One-Day 5 w. in innings: 1
Overseas tours: Hampshire to Barbados 1985, 1986, 1987, to Dubai 1989
Overseas teams played for: Paarl CC, 1982-83; Amanzimtoti, 1984-96
(both South Africa)
Extras: Played for Dorset 1972. NatWest Man of the Match award
Best batting: 109* Hampshire v Somerset, Taunton 1977
Best bowling: 6-48 Hampshire v Leicestershire, Southampton 1982

First-Class Career Performances

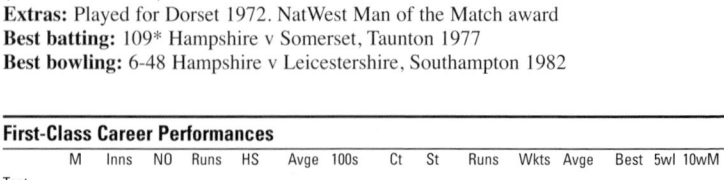

	M	Inns	NO	Runs	HS	Avge	100s	Ct	St	Runs	Wkts	Avge	Best	5wI	10wM
Test															
All First	271	375	62	7309	109*	23.35	2	105	-	14879	437	34.04	6-48	5	-

DUDLESTON, B.

Name: Barry Dudleston
Born: 16 July 1945, Bebington, Cheshire
Height: 5ft 9in
Nickname: Danny
Wife and date of marriage: Louise Wendy, 19 October 1994
Children: Sharon Louise, 29 October 1968; Matthew Barry, 12 September 1988; Jack Nicholas, 29 April 1998
Family links with cricket: 'Dad was a league cricketer'
Education: Stockport School
Career outside cricket: Managing director of Sunsport Tours & Travel
Other sports played: Golf
Other sports followed: All sports
Relaxations: Bridge, red wine
Appointed to 1st-Class list: 1984
First appointed to Test panel: 1991

Tests umpired: 2 (plus 4 as TV umpire)
One-Day Internationals umpired: 4 (plus 6 as TV umpire)
Other umpiring honours: Stood in C&G final 2001
Players to watch for the future: James Foster
Counties as player: Leicestershire, Gloucestershire
Role: Right-hand opening bat, slow left-arm bowler, occasional wicket-keeper
County debut: 1966 (Leicestershire), 1981 (Gloucestershire)
County cap: 1969 (Leicestershire)
Benefit: 1980 (Leicestershire; £25,000)
1000 runs in a season: 8
1st-Class 50s: 64
1st-Class 100s: 31
1st-Class 200s: 1
1st-Class catches: 234
One-Day 100s: 4
Overseas tours: Kent (as guest player) to West Indies 1972; D.H. Robins' XI to West Indies 1973; Wisden XI to West Indies 1984; MCC to Kenya 1993
Overseas teams played for: Rhodesia 1975-80
Highlights of playing career: 'Winning County Championship [with Leicestershire]'
Extras: Played for England U25. Holder with John Steele of the highest first-wicket partnership for Leics, 390 v Derbys at Leicester in 1979. Fastest player in Rhodesian cricket history to 1000 first-class runs in Currie Cup; second fastest ever in Currie Cup
Opinions on cricket: 'My team-mate Duncan Fletcher is doing a great job.'

Best batting: 202 Leicestershire v Derbyshire, Leicester 1979
Best bowling: 4-6 Leicestershire v Surrey, Leicester 1972

First-Class Career Performances

	M	Inns	NO	Runs	HS	Avge	100s	Ct	St	Runs	Wkts	Avge	Best	5wl	10wM
Test															
All First	295	501	47	14747	202	32.48	32	234	7	1365	47	29.04	4-6	-	-

EVANS, J. H.

Name: Jeffrey (<u>Jeff</u>) Howard Evans
Born: 7 August 1954, Llanelli
Height: 5ft 8in
Wife and date of marriage: Christine, 29 December 1983
Children: Rhian, 9 February 1986; Siân, 3 September 1987; Seren (golden retriever)
Education: Llanelli Boys Grammar School; Dudley College of Education
Career outside cricket: Supply teacher
Off-season: Teaching; coaching cricket
Other sports played: 'Used to play team squash and coach rugby in local league'
Other sports followed: 'Most sports, rugby in particular'
Relaxations: Keeping fit, walking, cycling, skiing

Appointed to 1st-Class list: 2001
Umpiring honours: Kent v New Zealanders 1999; Essex v Zimbabweans 2000; Worcestershire v West Indians 2000; England U19 v Sri Lanka U19 2000
Highlights of umpiring career: 'First Championship match – Yorkshire v Somerset, Headingley 2001'
Cricket moments to forget: 'Any error of judgment!'
Players to watch for the future: Ian Bell, Nicky Peng, Gareth Batty
County as player: Did not play first-class cricket. Played league cricket in South Wales as a right-hand bat
Extras: Coach to Welsh Schools Cricket Association team on tour to Australia 1993. Taught in the Gwendraeth Grammar School – 'the old "outside half factory"'
Opinions on cricket: 'Would like to see more honesty throughout the game.'

Did not play first-class cricket

GOULD, I. J.

Name: <u>Ian</u> James Gould
Born: 19 August 1957, Taplow, Bucks
Height: 5ft 7in
Nickname: Gunner
Wife and date of marriage: Joanne,
27 September 1986
Children: Gemma; Michael; George
Education: Westgate Secondary Modern,
Slough
Off-season: 'Driving a lorry!'
Other sports played: Golf
Other sports followed: Football (Arsenal),
racing
Relaxations: 'Going racing'
Appointed to 1st-Class list: 2002
Players to watch for the future:
Owais Shah, John Maunders,
Aaron Laraman ('when fit')

Counties as player: Middlesex, Sussex
Role: Left-hand bat, wicket-keeper
County debut: 1975 (Middlesex), 1981 (Sussex)
County cap: 1977 (Middlesex), 1981 (Sussex)
Benefit: 1990 (Sussex; £87,097)
One-Day Internationals: 18
1st-Class 50s: 47
1st-Class 100s: 4
1st-Class catches: 536
1st-Class stumpings: 67
Overseas tours: England YC to West Indies 1976; Derrick Robins' XI to Canada
1978-79; International XI to Pakistan 1980-81; England to Australia and New Zealand
1982-83; MCC to Namibia
Overseas teams played for: Auckland 1979-80
Highlights of playing career: 'Playing in the World Cup'
Extras: Represented England in the 1983 World Cup
Opinions on cricket: 'Too many long faces. Things that are funny should be
laughed at!
Best batting: 128 Middlesex v Worcestershire, Worcester 1978
Best bowling: 3-10 Sussex v Surrey, The Oval 1989

First-Class Career Performances

	M	Inns	NO	Runs	HS	Avge	100s	Ct	St	Runs	Wkts	Avge	Best	5wI	10wM
Test															
All First	297	399	63	8756	128	26.06	4	536	67	365	7	52.14	3-10	-	-

HAMPSHIRE, J. H.

Name: John Harry Hampshire
Born: 10 February 1941, Thurnscoe, Yorks
Height: 6ft
Nickname: Hamps
Wife and date of marriage: Judith Ann,
5 September 1964
Children: Ian Christopher, 6 January 1969;
Paul Wesley, 12 February 1972
Family links with cricket: Father (J.) and
brother (A.W.) both played for Yorkshire
Education: Oakwood Technical High School,
Rotherham
Other sports followed: Most sports
Relaxations: Gardening and cooking
Appointed to 1st-Class list: 1985
First appointed to Test panel: 1989
International panel: 1999 –
Tests umpired: 21 (plus 4 as TV umpire)

One-Day Internationals umpired: 20 (plus 8 as TV umpire)
Other umpiring honours: Umpired four Tests in Pakistan 1989-90. Toured
Bangladesh 1999-2000 with MCC (as umpire). Stood in Coca-Cola Cup, Sharjah
2000. Umpired NatWest final 2000 and B&H final 2001
Counties as player: Yorkshire, Derbyshire
Role: Right-hand bat, leg-spin bowler
County debut: 1961 (Yorkshire), 1982 (Derbyshire)
County cap: 1963 (Yorkshire), 1982 (Derbyshire)
Benefit: 1976 (Yorkshire)
Test debut: 1969
Tests: 11
1000 runs in a season: 15
1st-Class 50s: 142
1st-Class 100s: 43
1st-Class 5 w. in innings: 2
1st-Class catches: 445
One-Day 100s: 7

Overseas tours: MCC (England) to Australia and New Zealand 1970-71
Overseas teams played for: Tasmania, 1966-69, 1977-79
Extras: Captained Yorkshire 1979-80. Scored a century (107) at Lord's on Test debut (v West Indies 1969); the only England player to have done so. Manager/coach of the Zimbabwe squad for their first Test matches against India and New Zealand 1992-93
Best batting: 183* Yorkshire v Surrey, Hove 1971
Best bowling: 7-52 Yorkshire v Glamorgan, Cardiff 1963

First-Class Career Performances

	M	Inns	NO	Runs	HS	Avge	100s	Ct	St	Runs	Wkts	Avge	Best	5wI	10wM
Test	8	16	1	405	107	26.86	1	9	-						
All First	577	924	112	28059	183*	34.55	43	445	-	1637	30	54.56	7-52	2	-

HARRIS, M. J.

Name: <u>Michael</u> John Harris
Born: 25 May 1944, St Just-in-Roseland, Cornwall
Height: 6ft 1in
Nickname: Pasty
Wife and date of marriage: Danielle Ruth, 10 September 1969
Children: Jodie, Richard
Education: Gerrans Comprehensive
Career outside cricket: Sports teacher
Other sports followed: Squash, golf
Appointed to 1st-Class list: 1998
Counties as player: Middlesex, Notts
Role: Right-hand bat, leg-break bowler, wicket-keeper
County debut: 1964 (Middlesex), 1969 (Notts)
County cap: 1967 (Middlesex), 1970 (Notts)
1000 runs in a season: 11
1st-Class 50s: 98
1st-Class 100s: 40
1st-Class 200s: 1
1st-Class catches: 288
1st-Class stumpings: 14
One-Day 100s: 3
Overseas teams played for: Eastern Province 1971-72; Wellington 1975-76
Extras: Shared Middlesex then-record first-wicket partnership of 312 with Eric

Russell v Pakistanis at Lord's 1967. Scored nine centuries in 1971 to equal Nottinghamshire county record, scoring two centuries in a match twice and totalling 2238 runs for the season at an average of 50.86
Best batting: 201* Nottinghamshire v Glamorgan, Trent Bridge 1973
Best bowling: 4-16 Nottinghamshire v Warwickshire, Trent Bridge 1969

First-Class Career Performances

	M	Inns	NO	Runs	HS	Avge	100s	Ct	St	Runs	Wkts	Avge	Best	5wI	10wM
Test															
All First	344	581	58	19196	201*	36.70	41	288	14	3459	79	43.78	4-16	-	-

HOLDER, J. W.

Name: <u>John</u> Wakefield Holder
Born: 19 March 1945, St George, Barbados
Height: 6ft
Nickname: Benson, Hod
Wife's name: Glenda
Children: Christopher, 1968; Nigel, 1970
Education: St Giles Boys School; Combermere High School, Barbados; Rochdale College
Off-season: Keeping fit
Other sports followed: Football (Manchester United)
Relaxations: Keeping fit and watching wildlife documentaries
Appointed to 1st-Class list: 1983
First appointed to Test panel: 1988
Tests umpired: 11 (plus 5 as TV umpire)
One-Day Internationals umpired: 19 (plus 3 as TV umpire)
Other umpiring honours: Umpired in Nehru Cup in India and four Tests in Pakistan 1989-90. Has stood in Refuge Assurance Cup, B&H Cup and NatWest Trophy finals
Players to watch for the future: Alex Tudor
County as player: Hampshire
Role: Right-hand bat, right-arm fast bowler
County debut: 1968
50 wickets in a season: 1
1st-Class 5 w. in innings: 5
1st-Class 10 w. in match: 1
1st-Class catches: 12

Extras: Championship hat-trick v Kent at Southampton 1972

Opinions on cricket: 'I can see the day coming when umpires in international cricket as they are now will become redundant. TV technology is so advanced and commentators are so critical of mistakes that I think TV technology will be used more and more widely and eventually the TV umpire will make all the decisions. When that happens, for me the game will become far more impersonal.'

Best batting: 33 Hampshire v Sussex, Hove 1971

Best bowling: 7-79 Hampshire v Gloucestershire, Gloucester 1972

First-Class Career Performances

	M	Inns	NO	Runs	HS	Avge	100s	Ct	St	Runs	Wkts	Avge	Best	5wI	10wM
Test															
All First	47	49	14	374	33	10.68	-	12	-	3415	139	24.56	7-79	5	1

HOLDER, V. A.

Name: <u>Vanburn</u> Alonza Holder
Born: 8 October 1945, St Michael, Barbados
Height: 6ft 3in
Nickname: Van
Wife's name: Christine
Children: James Vanburn, 2 September 1981
Education: St Leonard's Secondary Modern; Community High
Off-season: 'Working'
Other sports followed: Football (Liverpool)
Relaxations: Music, doing crosswords
Appointed to 1st-Class list: 1992
One-Day Internationals umpired: 2 as TV umpire
County as player: Worcestershire
Role: Right-hand bat, right-arm fast-medium bowler
County debut: 1968
County cap: 1970
Benefit: 1979
Test debut: 1969
Tests: 40
One-Day Internationals: 12
1st-Class 50s: 4
1st-Class 100s: 1
1st-Class 5 w. in innings: 38

1st-Class 10 w. in match: 3
1st-Class catches: 98
One-Day 5 w. in innings: 3
Overseas tours: West Indies to England 1969, 1973, 1975 (World Cup), 1976, to India, Sri Lanka and Pakistan 1974-75, to Australia 1975-76, to India and Sri Lanka 1978-79 (vice-captain); Rest of the World to Pakistan 1973-74
Overseas teams played for: Barbados 1966-78
Extras: Made his debut for Barbados in the Shell Shield competition in 1966-67. Won John Player League 1973 and County Championship 1974 with Worcestershire. Played in West Indies 1975 World Cup winning side
Best batting: 122 Barbados v Trinidad, Bridgetown 1973-74
Best bowling: 7-40 Worcestershire v Glamorgan, Cardiff 1974

First-Class Career Performances

	M	Inns	NO	Runs	HS	Avge	100s	Ct	St	Runs	Wkts	Avge	Best	5wI	10wM
Test	40	59	11	682	42	14.20	-	16	-	3627	109	33.27	6-28	3	-
All First	311	354	81	3559	122	13.03	1	98	-	23183	948	24.45	7-40	38	3

JESTY, T. E.

Name: <u>Trevor</u> Edward Jesty
Born: 2 June 1948, Gosport, Hampshire
Height: 5ft 9in
Nickname: Jets
Wife and date of marriage: Jacqueline, 12 September 1970
Children: Graeme Barry, 27 September 1972; Lorna Samantha, 7 November 1976
Family links with cricket: Daughter played for England XI 2000
Education: Privett County Secondary Modern, Gosport
Off-season: Cricket coaching
Other sports followed: Football (Arsenal)
Relaxations: Gardening, reading
Appointed to 1st-Class list: 1994
One-Day Internationals umpired: 3 as TV umpire

Counties as player: Hampshire, Surrey, Lancashire
Role: Right-hand bat, right-arm medium bowler
County debut: 1966 (Hampshire), 1985 (Surrey), 1988 (Lancashire)
County cap: 1971 (Hampshire), 1985 (Surrey), 1990 (Lancashire)

Benefit: 1982 (Hampshire)
One-Day Internationals: 10
1000 runs in a season: 10
50 wickets in a season: 2
1st-Class 50s: 110
1st-Class 100s: 33
1st-Class 200s: 2
1st-Class 5 w. in innings: 19
1st-Class catches: 265
1st-Class stumpings: 1
One-Day 100s: 7
Overseas tours: International XI to West Indies 1982; joined England tour to Australia 1982-83; Lancashire to Zimbabwe 1989
Overseas teams played for: Border, South Africa 1973-74; Griqualand West 1974-76, 1980-81; Canterbury, New Zealand 1979-80
Highlights of playing career: 'Winning Championship with Hampshire in 1973. Playing against Australia for England in one-day match on 1982-83 tour'
Extras: One of *Wisden*'s Five Cricketers of the Year 1983
Best batting: 248 Hampshire v Cambridge University, Fenner's 1984
Best bowling: 7-75 Hampshire v Worcestershire, Southampton 1976

First-Class Career Performances

	M	Inns	NO	Runs	HS	Avge	100s	Ct	St	Runs	Wkts	Avge	Best	5wl	10wM
Test															
All First	490	777	107	21916	248	32.71	35	265	1	16075	585	27.47	7-75	19	-

JONES, A. A.

Name: <u>Allan</u> Arthur Jones
Born: 9 December 1947, Horley, Surrey
Height: 6ft 4in
Nickname: Jonah
Marital status: Single
Education: St John's College, Horsham
Career outside cricket: Sports tours
Off-season: 'Enjoying life'
Other sports played: Golf
Other sports followed: Football (Arsenal)
Relaxations: English history, reading, cooking
Appointed to 1st-Class list: 1985
First appointed to Test panel: 1996
Tests umpired: 3 as TV umpire
One-Day Internationals umpired: 1
(plus 4 as TV umpire)
Other umpiring honours: Has umpired at Hong Kong Sixes, chairman of the First-Class Umpires' Association
Players to watch for the future: Ed Joyce
Counties as player: Sussex, Somerset, Middlesex, Glamorgan
Role: Right-hand bat, right-arm fast bowler
County debut: 1964 (Sussex), 1970 (Somerset), 1976 (Middlesex), 1980 (Glamorgan)
County cap: 1972 (Somerset), 1976 (Middlesex)
50 wickets in a season: 4
1st-Class 5 w. in innings: 23
1st-Class 10 w. in match: 3
1st-Class catches: 50
One-Day 5 w. in innings: 5
Overseas teams played for: Northern Transvaal 1971-72; Orange Free State 1976-77; Auckland (Birkenhead)
Highlights of playing career: '9-51 v Sussex 1972'
Extras: Won two Championship medals with Middlesex (1976 and 1977). Was on stand-by for England tour of India 1976-77. Represented MCC v Australians 1977. Was the first person to play for four counties
Opinions on cricket: 'Groundsmen should be appointed and retained by ECB and not their counties, to achieve higher standard of pitches and more uniformity. Second XI should be scrapped; integrate club sides into counties to bring on younger players and revive more interest in amateur game, thus creating more money for schools of excellence.'
Best batting: 33 Middlesex v Kent, Canterbury 1978
Best bowling: 9-51 Somerset v Sussex, Hove 1972

First-Class Career Performances

	M	Inns	NO	Runs	HS	Avge	100s	Ct	St	Runs	Wkts	Avge	Best	5wI	10wM
Test															
All First	214	216	68	799	33	5-39	-	50	-	15414	549	28.07	9-51	23	3

KITCHEN, M. J.

Name: Mervyn (<u>Merv</u>) John Kitchen
Born: 1 August 1940, Nailsea, Somerset
Height: 5ft 11in
Nickname: MJ
Wife and date of marriage: Anne, March 1972
Children: Faye, 30 September 1975; Jody, 5 March 1976
Family links with cricket: 'Only local cricket – father played for local village, Nailsea'
Education: Blackwell Secondary Modern, Nailsea
Career outside cricket: 'Many varied winter jobs in the past – driving lorries, labourer, decorator, printing photographer, worked for a racetrack bookmaker'
Off-season: 'Resting and playing golf (weather permitting)'
Other sports played: Golf, bowls, skittles
Other sports followed: 'Avid follower of TV football and golf; no allegiance to any special team'
Relaxations: Most sports and dog-walking
Appointed to 1st-Class list: 1982
First appointed to Test panel: 1990
International panel: 1995-99
Tests umpired: 20 (plus 3 as TV umpire)
One-Day Internationals umpired: 28 (plus 8 as TV umpire)
Other umpiring honours: Stood in 1983 World Cup. Has umpired all the domestic finals. Umpired in a one-day series in Kenya between the hosts, Bangladesh and Zimbabwe, including the final, 1997-98
Highlights of umpiring career: 'My first Test match, England v New Zealand at Lord's with D. Shepherd'
Players to watch for the future: Ian Bell
County as player: Somerset

Role: Left-hand bat, occasional right-arm medium bowler
County debut: 1960
County cap: 1966
Testimonial: 1973
1000 runs in a season: 7
1st-Class 50s: 68
1st-Class 100s: 17
1st-Class catches: 157
One-Day 100s: 1
Overseas tours: Whitbread Wanderers to Rhodesia
Highlights of playing career: 'Many happy days playing'
Cricket moments to forget: 'I don't want to forget anything about my playing days, disappointment or not (but perhaps being John Holder's first first-class wicket, as he keeps reminding me)'
Extras: 'Played under eight different captains during my time at Somerset.' Won two Gillette Cup Man of the Match awards and two B&H Gold Awards. Retired in 1979 and played local cricket for Mendip Acorns
Opinions on cricket: 'Very high profile with close-up TV replays – players and umpires alike come under microscopic examination. Projection of the game to the armchair watcher is so much better.'
Best batting: 189 Somerset v Pakistanis, Taunton 1967
Best bowling: 1-4 Somerset v Sussex, Taunton 1969

First-Class Career Performances

	M	Inns	NO	Runs	HS	Avge	100s	Ct	St	Runs	Wkts	Avge	Best	5wl	10wM
Test															
All First	354	612	32	15230	189	26.25	17	157	-	109	2	54.50	1-4	-	-

LEADBEATER, B.

Name: Barrie Leadbeater
Born: 14 August 1943, Leeds
Height: 6ft
Nickname: Leady
Marital status: Widowed
Wife and date of marriage: Jacqueline, 18 September 1971 (deceased 1997)
Children: Richard Barrie, 23 November 1972; Michael Spencer, 21 March 1976; Daniel Mark Ronnie, 19 June 1981
Education: Harehills County Secondary, Leeds
Career outside cricket: LGV Class 1 driver – Renshaw Scotts
Off-season: As above
Other sports played: Golf

Other sports followed: All sport – football (Leeds United), rugby league (Leeds Rhinos)
Relaxations: 'Reading, going to the pub, running'
Appointed to 1st-Class list: 1981
Tests umpired: 2 as TV umpire
One-Day Internationals umpired: 5 (plus 2 as TV umpire)
Other umpiring honours: Stood in 1983 World Cup. MCC tours to New Zealand 1999 and to Argentina and Chile 2001. Former chairman of the First-Class Umpires' Association

County as player: Yorkshire
Role: Right-hand opening bat, right-arm medium bowler, slip fielder
County debut: 1966
County cap: 1969
Benefit: 1980 (joint benefit with G.A. Cope)
1st-Class 50s: 27
1st-Class 100s: 1
1st-Class catches: 82
Overseas tours: Duke of Norfolk's XI to West Indies 1970
Overseas teams played for: Johannesburg Municipals 1978-79
Highlights of playing career: 'Man of the Match in Gillette Cup final 1969'
Cricket moments to forget: 'I've forgotten'
Extras: Took part in London Marathon 1997, 1998, 2000. Retired from county cricket in 1980 and played social cricket
Best batting: 140* Yorkshire v Hampshire, Portsmouth 1976
Best bowling: 1-1 Yorkshire v Middlesex, Headingley 1971

First-Class Career Performances

	M	Inns	NO	Runs	HS	Avge	100s	Ct	St	Runs	Wkts	Avge	Best	5wl	10wM
Test															
All First	147	241	29	5373	140*	25.34	1	82	-	5	1	5.00	1-1	-	-

LLONG, N. J.

Name: <u>Nigel</u> James Llong
Born: 11 February 1969, Ashford, Kent
Height: 6ft
Nickname: Nidge
Wife and date of marriage: Melissa,
20 February 1999
Family links with cricket: Father and
brother played local club cricket
Education: North School for Boys, Ashford
Career outside cricket: Roofing labourer,
Melbourne
Off-season: Coaching – Kent Cricket Board;
Duke of York School, Dover
Other sports followed: Football (Arsenal),
'generally most sports'
Relaxations: Fishing, clay-pigeon shooting
Appointed to 1st-Class list: 2002
Players to watch for the future:
Ben Phillips
County as player: Kent

Role: Left-hand bat, right-arm off-spin bowler
County debut: 1991
County cap: 1993
1st-Class 50s: 16
1st-Class 100s: 6
1st-Class 5 w. in innings: 2
1st-Class catches: 59
One-Day 100s: 2
Overseas tours: Kent to Zimbabwe 1993
Overseas teams played for: Ashburton, Melbourne 1988-90, 1996-97; Greenpoint,
Cape Town, 1990-95
Highlights of playing career: 'B&H final 1997. Sunday League winners 1995. First
Championship hundred, Lord's 1993'
Cricket moments to forget: 'Sunday League [1993], last match against Glamorgan at
Canterbury – lost the match and were runners-up. Plus not making the most of my
ability'
Extras: Kent Young Player of the Year 1992. Man of the Match in 2nd XI Trophy
semi-final and final 1999. Retired from county cricket in September 1999 and played
for Norfolk in 2000
Opinions on cricket: 'Good pitches produce good players. With central contracts, we
now need two overseas players per club (especially bowlers).'

Best batting: 130 Kent v Hampshire, Canterbury 1996
Best bowling: 5-21 Kent v Middlesex, Canterbury 1996

First-Class Career Performances

	M	Inns	NO	Runs	HS	Avge	100s	Ct	St	Runs	Wkts	Avge	Best	5wI	10wM
Test															
All First	68	108	11	3024	130	31.17	6	59	-	1259	35	35.97	5-21	2	-

LLOYDS, J. W.

Name: <u>Jeremy</u> William Lloyds
Born: 17 November 1954, Penang, Malaya
Height: 5ft 11in
Nickname: Jerry
Wife and date of marriage: Janine,
16 September 1997
Children: Kaeli, 16 November 1991
Family links with cricket: Father played
cricket in Malaya. Brother Chris played for
Somerset 2nd XI
Education: Curry Rivel Primary School;
St Dunstan's Prep School; Blundell's School,
Tiverton
Career outside cricket: Coaching and setting
up Western Province Youth Programme 1992-
95 in South Africa. Coach at St Stithian's,
Johannesburg 1995-98

Other sports played: Golf (6 handicap)
Other sports followed: Golf, football (Tottenham Hotspur), American football
(San Francisco 49ers), Formula One and saloon car racing, rugby (Bath)
Relaxations: 'Reading, music and spending time at home with my family'
Appointed to 1st-Class list: 1998
Tests umpired: 2 as TV umpire
One-Day Internationals umpired: 2 (plus 2 as TV umpire)
Counties as player: Somerset, Gloucestershire
Role: Left-hand bat, off-spin bowler
County debut: 1979 (Somerset), 1985 (Gloucestershire)
County cap: 1982 (Somerset), 1985 (Gloucestershire)
1000 runs in a season: 3
1st-Class 50s: 62
1st-Class 100s: 10
1st-Class 5 w. in innings: 13

1st-Class 10 w. in match: 1
1st-Class catches: 229
Overseas tours: Somerset to Antigua 1982; Gloucestershire to Barbados 1985, to Sri Lanka 1987
Overseas teams played for: St Stithian's Old Boys, Johannesburg 1978-79; Toombull DCC, Brisbane 1980-82; North Sydney District 1982-83; Alberton, Johannesburg 1984; Preston CC, Melbourne 1986; Orange Free State 1987; Fish Hoek CC, Cape Town 1988-92
Highlights of playing career: 'Winning 1983 NatWest final'
Extras: Highest score in Brisbane Premier League 1980-81 (165). Britannic Player of the Month July 1987. Gloucestershire Player of the Year 1987. Leading run-scorer in Western Province Cricket League 1988, 1989
Opinions on cricket: 'Too much overseas influence on how to play the game in England. We have more variations in wickets and weather conditions than in most other countries. Yes, take the best of what they have and work it into our game. Also, too much emphasis on all the various levels of coaching certificates. We have been dragged too far away from the *basics* – batting, bowling and fielding. The game hasn't really changed – but people have.'
Best batting: 132* Somerset v Northamptonshire, Northampton 1982
Best bowling: 7-88 Somerset v Essex, Chelmsford 1982

First-Class Career Performances

	M	Inns	NO	Runs	HS	Avge	100s	Ct	St	Runs	Wkts	Avge	Best	5wI	10wM
Test															
All First	267	408	64	10679	132*	31.04	10	229	-	12943	333	38.86	7-88	13	1

MALLENDER, N. A.

Name: <u>Neil</u> Alan Mallender
Born: 13 August 1961, Kirk Sandall, Doncaster
Height: 6ft
Nickname: Ghostie
Marital status: Divorced
Children: Kirstie, 13; Dominic, 10; Jacob 5
Education: Beverley Grammar School
Off-season: 'Working on fitness'
Other sports played: Golf (3 handicap)
Other sports followed: Football (Leeds United), rugby union (Otago), rugby league (Hull)
Interests/relaxations: 'Interested in most sports'
Appointed to 1st-Class list: 1999
Tests umpired: 1 as TV umpire

One-Day Internationals umpired: 2
(plus 1 as TV umpire)
Other umpiring honours: Went with MCC
to umpire in Namibia March/April 2001.
PCA Umpire of the Year 2001
Highlights of umpiring career: 'Walking
out to a full house at Lord's to umpire
England v Pakistan in One-Day International'
Players to watch for the future:
Ian Hunter, Michael Lumb
Counties as player: Northamptonshire,
Somerset
Role: Right-hand bat, right-arm
fast-medium bowler
County debut: 1980 (Northamptonshire),
1987 (Somerset)
County cap: 1984 (Northamptonshire),
1987 (Somerset)
Benefit: 1994 (Somerset)
Test debut: 1992
Tests: 2

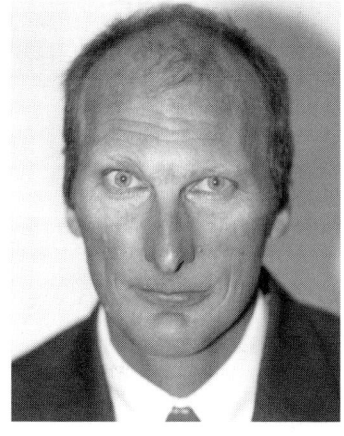

50 wickets in a season: 6
1st-Class 50s: 10
1st-Class 100s: 1
1st-Class 5 w. in innings: 36
1st-Class 10 w. in match: 5
1st-Class catches: 111
One-Day 5 w. in innings: 3
Overseas tours: England YC to West Indies 1979-80
Overseas teams played for: Kaikorai, Dunedin, New Zealand; University,
Wellington, New Zealand; Otago, New Zealand 1983-84 – 1992-93
Highlights of playing career: 'England debut at Headingley'
Extras: Represented England U19 1980-81. Took 5-50 on Test debut v Pakistan at
Headingley in 1992. Retired from county cricket in 1996
Best batting: 100* Otago v Central Districts, Palmerston North 1991-92
Best bowling: 7-27 Otago v Auckland, Auckland 1984-85

First-Class Career Performances

	M	Inns	NO	Runs	HS	Avge	100s	Ct	St	Runs	Wkts	Avge	Best	5wI	10wM
Test	2	3	0	8	4	2.66	-	-	-	215	10	21.50	5-50	1	-
All First	345	396	122	4709	100*	17.18	1	111	-	24654	937	26.31	7-27	36	5

PALMER, K. E.

Name: Kenneth (<u>Ken</u>) Ernest Palmer
Born: 22 April 1937, Winchester
Height: 5ft 10in
Nickname: Pedlar
Wife and date of marriage: Jacqueline,
24 September 1994
Children: Gary Vincent, 1 November 1965
Family links with cricket: Father played
club cricket and did the cricketer's double 13
times. Son played for Somerset, as did
brother Roy (also a Test umpire)
Education: Southbroom Secondary Modern,
Devizes
Off-season: Gardening and relaxing
Other sports played: Squash
Other sports followed: Football (Manchester
United) and rugby (Bath and England)
Relaxations: Car enthusiast. Gardening
Appointed to 1st-Class list: 1972
First appointed to Test panel: 1978
International panel: 1994
Tests umpired: 22 (plus 5 as TV umpire)
One-Day Internationals umpired: 23 (plus 3 as TV umpire)
Other umpiring honours: Has umpired six B&H finals and four NatWest finals.
Stood in 1979 and 1983 World Cups
Highlights of umpiring career: 'My first Test umpired, at Edgbaston, England
v Pakistan 1978'
Players to watch for the future: Ian Bell, Jason Brown, Mark Wagh, Andy Pratt
County as player: Somerset
Role: Right-hand bat, right-arm fast-medium bowler; all-rounder
County debut: 1955
County cap: 1958
Testimonial: 1968
Test debut: 1964-65
Tests: 1
1000 runs in a season: 1
50 wickets in a season: 2
100 wickets in a season: 4
1st-Class 50s: 27
1st-Class 100s: 2
1st-Class 5 w. in innings: 46

1st-Class 10 w. in match: 5
1st-Class catches: 156
Overseas tours: Commonwealth XI to Pakistan 1962; International Cavaliers to West Indies 1963-64
Overseas teams played for: Old Maristonian, South Africa 1964-65
Highlights of playing career: 'Playing first Test in South Africa'
Cricket moments to forget: 'My first year in county cricket, I was 17 years old, and Yorkshire's Appleyard bowled me out in both innings for nought'
Extras: Won Carling Single Wicket Competition 1961. Did the 'double' in 1961 (114 wickets, 1036 runs). With Bill Alley holds the Somerset record for sixth-wicket partnership – 265 v Northants at Northampton 1961. Had figures of 22.3-9-36-7 (all clean bowled) for Somerset v Lancashire 1963. Called into Test side while coaching in South Africa 1964-65. Won Man of the Match Award for Somerset v Lancashire 1967. 'Pleased to become an MCC member for services to cricket'
Opinions on cricket: 'I am a great believer that if dissent is shown on the field of play, the player should be banned from playing for one or two matches, not fined.'
Best batting: 125* Somerset v Northamptonshire, Northampton 1961
Best bowling: 9-57 Somerset v Nottinghamshire, Trent Bridge 1963

First-Class Career Performances

	M	Inns	NO	Runs	HS	Avge	100s	Ct	St	Runs	Wkts	Avge	Best	5wI	10wM
Test	1	1	0	10	10	10.00	-	-	-	189	1	189.00	1-113	-	-
All First	314	481	105	7771	125*	20.66	2	156	-	18485	866	21.34	9-57	46	5

PALMER, R.

Name: Roy Palmer
Born: 12 July 1942, Hampshire
Height: 6ft 3in
Nickname: Arp
Wife and date of marriage: Alyne,
5 November 1983
Children: Nick, 7 October 1968
Family links with cricket: Brother of Ken
Palmer, Test umpire and former Somerset
player; nephew Gary also played for
Somerset
Education: Southbroom Secondary Modern,
Devizes
Off-season: Golf, DIY
Relaxations: Golf
Appointed to 1st-Class list: 1980
First appointed to Test panel: 1992
Tests umpired: 2 (plus 1 as TV umpire)
One-Day Internationals umpired: 8 (plus 2 as TV umpire)
Other umpiring honours: Stood in 1983 World Cup
Players to watch for the future: Matthew Wood (Somerset)
County as player: Somerset
Role: Right-hand bat, right-arm fast-medium bowler
County debut: 1965
50 wickets in a season: 1
1st-Class 50s: 1
1st-Class 5 w. in innings: 4
1st-Class catches: 25
One-Day 5 w. in innings: 1
Extras: Won two Man of the Match Awards in the Gillette Cup
Best batting: 84 Somerset v Leicestershire, Taunton 1967
Best bowling: 6-45 Somerset v Middlesex, Lord's 1967

First-Class Career Performances

	M	Inns	NO	Runs	HS	Avge	100s	Ct	St	Runs	Wkts	Avge	Best	5wI	10wM
Test															
All First	74	110	32	1037	84	13.29	-	25	-	5439	172	31.62	6-45	4	-

SHARP, G.

Name: George Sharp
Born: 12 March 1950, West Hartlepool,
County Durham
Height: 5ft 11in
Nickname: Sharpy, Blunt, Razor, Toffee
Wife and date of marriage: Audrey,
14 September 1974
Children: Gareth James, 27 June 1984
Education: Elwick Road Secondary Modern,
Hartlepool
Career outside cricket: Watching all sports
Off-season: Working as joint director with
GSB Loams Ltd for soils and top dressing
Other sports played: Golf (8 handicap)
Other sports followed: Football (Newcastle
Utd and Middlesbrough), rugby
(Northampton Saints)
Relaxations: Golf; 'spend a lot of time in the
gym during the off-season'
Appointed to 1st-Class list: 1992
International panel: 1996 –
Tests umpired: 15 (plus 1 as TV umpire)

One-Day Internationals umpired: 31 (plus 13 as TV umpire)
Other umpiring honours: Has umpired three B&H finals and one NatWest final and
stood in the inaugural C&G final 2001. Has stood in four overseas tournaments,
including the Singer Cup (India, Sri Lanka, Pakistan) in Singapore 1995-96 and the
Singer Champions Trophy (Pakistan, Sri Lanka, New Zealand) in Sharjah 1996-97
County as player: Northamptonshire
Role: Right-hand bat, wicket-keeper
County debut: 1967
County cap: 1973
Benefit: 1982
1st-Class 50s: 21
1st-Class catches: 565
1st-Class stumpings: 90
Overseas tours: England Counties XI to Barbados and Trinidad 1975
Best batting: 98 Northamptonshire v Yorkshire, Northampton 1983
Best bowling: 1-47 Northamptonshire v Yorkshire, Northampton 1980

First-Class Career Performances

	M	Inns	NO	Runs	HS	Avge	100s	Ct	St	Runs	Wkts	Avge	Best	5wI	10wM
Test															
All First	306	396	81	6254	98	19.85	-	565	90	70	1	70.00	1-47	-	-

SHEPHERD, D. R.

Name: <u>David</u> Robert Shepherd
Born: 27 December 1940, Bideford, Devon
Height: 5ft 10in
Nickname: Shep
Marital status: Single
Family links with cricket: Father: club cricketer and local umpire. Brother Bill: MCC Young Professional, Devon CCC and North Devon CC; local umpire
Education: Barnstaple Grammar School; St Luke's College, Exeter
Career outside cricket: Schoolteacher
Off-season: 'Umpiring Tests abroad. Have written autobiography entitled *Shep*'
Other sports played: 'Used to play rugby (school, Devon Public & Grammar Schools XV, South Molton RFC)'
Other sports followed: All sports
Relaxations: Stamp collecting
Appointed to 1st-Class list: 1981
First appointed to Test panel: 1985
International panel: 1994 –
Tests umpired: 60
One-Day Internationals umpired: 97 (plus 10 as TV umpire)
Other umpiring honours: Umpired the MCC Bicentenary Test, England v Rest of the World, at Lord's in 1987. With Dickie Bird and Steve Bucknor was one of the first umpires officially sponsored by the ICC. Has stood in each World Cup since 1983, including the 1995-96 final between Australia and Sri Lanka in Lahore and the 1999 final between Australia and Pakistan at Lord's. Has umpired numerous domestic finals. Received National Grid/ICC 'bronze award' in March 1998 for long service as a Test umpire. Umpired 50th Test, India v South Africa, Mumbai (Bombay) February 2000, receiving ICC 'silver award' to acknowledge this achievement. Known for his superstition regarding 'Nelson' score 111, and multiples – 222, 333 etc
Highlights of umpiring career: 'Two World Cup finals. All Test matches'
Players to watch for the future: Andy Pratt, Rob Key

County as player: Gloucestershire
Role: Right-hand bat, right-arm ('occasional!') medium bowler
County debut: 1965
County cap: 1969
Benefit: 1978 (joint benefit with J. Davey)
1000 runs in a season: 2
1st-Class 50s: 55
1st-Class 100s: 12
1st-Class catches: 95
One-Day 100s: 2
Highlights of playing career: 'Winning the Gillette Cup in 1973 and winning the B&H in 1977'
Extras: Played Minor Counties cricket for Devon 1959-64. First player to score a century for Gloucestershire on his first-class debut, v Oxford University 1965. Retired from county cricket in 1979 and played a little club cricket for local club North Devon CC. Was awarded the MBE in 1997 for services to cricket
Opinions on cricket: 'Players at the highest level must realise that they have a tremendous responsibility to the game as a whole. Their behaviour on the field is of the utmost importance, as they set an example for the rest of the sport. Young players and schoolboys are apt to copy their peers. The game must survive!'
Best batting: 153 Gloucestershire v Middlesex, Bristol 1968
Best bowling: 1-1 Gloucestershire v Northamptonshire, Gloucester 1968

First-Class Career Performances

	M	Inns	NO	Runs	HS	Avge	100s	Ct	St	Runs	Wkts	Avge	Best	5wI	10wM
Test															
All First	282	476	40	10672	153	24.47	12	95	-	106	2	53.00	1-1	-	-

STEELE, J. F.

Name: <u>John</u> Frederick Steele
Born: 23 July 1946, Stafford
Height: 5ft 10in
Nickname: Steely
Wife and date of marriage: Susan,
17 April 1977
Children: Sarah Jane, 2 April 1982;
Robert Alfred, 10 April 1985
Family links with cricket: Uncle Stan
played for Staffordshire. Brother David
played for Northamptonshire, Derbyshire and
England. Cousin Brian Crump played for
Northamptonshire and Staffordshire
Education: Endon School, Stoke-on-Trent;
Stafford College
Career outside cricket: Work study officer.
Fireman with Staffordshire Fire Brigade
Other sports followed: Soccer (Stoke City,
Port Vale), golf

Relaxations: Music and walking
Appointed to 1st-Class list: 1997
Counties as player: Leicestershire, Glamorgan
Role: Right-hand bat, slow left-arm bowler
County debut: 1970 (Leicestershire), 1984 (Glamorgan)
County cap: 1971 (Leicestershire), 1984 (Glamorgan)
Benefit: 1983 (Leicestershire)
1000 runs in a season: 6
1st-Class 50s: 69
1st-Class 100s: 21
1st-Class 5 w. in innings: 16
1st-Class catches: 414
One-Day 100s: 1
One-Day 5 w. in innings: 4
Overseas teams played for: Springs HSOB, Northern Transvaal 1971-73;
Pine Town CC, Natal 1973-74, 1982-83; Natal 1975-76, 1978-79
Extras: Played for England U25. Was voted Natal's Best Bowler in 1975-76. First-
wicket record partnership for Leicestershire of 390 with Barry Dudleston v Derbyshire
at Leicester 1979. Won two Man of the Match Awards in the Gillette Cup and four in
the Benson and Hedges Cup. Won the award for the most catches in a season in 1984
Best batting: 195 Leicestershire v Derbyshire, Leicester 1971
Best bowling: 7-29 Natal B v Griqualand West, Umzinto 1973-74
                  7-29 Leicestershire v Gloucestershire, Leicester 1980

First-class career performances

	M	Inns	NO	Runs	HS	Avge	100s	Ct	St	Runs	Wkts	Avge	Best	5wI	10wM
Test															
All First	379	605	85	15053	195	28.94	21	414	-	15793	584	27.04	7-29	16	-

WHITEHEAD, A. G. T.

Name: <u>Alan</u> Geoffrey Thomas Whitehead
Born: 28 October 1940, Butleigh, Somerset
Appointed to 1st-Class list: 1970
First appointed to Test panel: 1982
Tests umpired: 5 (plus 5 as TV umpire)
One-Day Internationals umpired: 14
(plus 2 as TV umpire)
Other umpiring honours: Stood in the 1979
and 1983 World Cups
County as player: Somerset
Role: Left-hand bat, slow left-arm bowler
County debut: 1957
1st-Class 5 w. in innings: 3
1st-Class catches: 20
Best batting: 15 Somerset v Hampshire,
Southampton 1959
Best bowling: 6-74 Somerset v Sussex,
Eastbourne 1959

First-Class Career Performances

	M	Inns	NO	Runs	HS	Avge	100s	Ct	St	Runs	Wkts	Avge	Best	5wI	10wM
Test															
All First	38	49	25	137	15	5.70	-	20	-	2306	67	34.41	6-74	3	

WILLEY, P.

Name: Peter Willey
Born: 6 December 1949, Sedgefield, County Durham
Height: 6ft 1in
Nickname: Will, 'many unprintable'
Wife and date of marriage: Charmaine, 23 September 1971
Children: Heather Jane, 11 September 1985; David, 28 February 1990
Family links with cricket: Father played local club cricket in County Durham
Education: Seaham Secondary School, County Durham
Other sports followed: All sports
Relaxations: Gardening, dog-walking
Appointed to 1st-Class list: 1993
International panel: 1996 –
Tests umpired: 24 (plus 1 as TV umpire)
One-Day Internationals umpired: 23 (plus 7 as TV umpire)
Other umpiring honours: Stood in the 1999 World Cup and in the 1999 Benson and Hedges Super Cup final
Counties as player: Northamptonshire, Leicestershire
Role: Right-hand bat, off-break bowler
County debut: 1966 (Northamptonshire), 1984 (Leicestershire)
County cap: 1971 (Northamptonshire), 1984 (Leicestershire)
Benefit: 1981 (Northamptonshire; £31,400)
Test debut: 1976
Tests: 26
One-Day Internationals: 26
1000 runs in a season: 10
50 wickets in a season: 2
1st-Class 50s: 101
1st-Class 100s: 43
1st-Class 200s: 1
1st-Class 5 w. in innings: 26
1st-Class 10 w. in match: 3
1st-Class catches: 235
One-Day 100s: 9
Overseas tours: England to Australia and India 1979-80, to West Indies 1980-81, 1985-86; unofficial England XI to South Africa 1981-82
Overseas teams played for: Eastern Province, South Africa 1982-85

Extras: Became youngest player ever to play for Northamptonshire, at 16 years 180 days v Cambridge University in 1966. Leicestershire captain 1987. Played for Northumberland in 1992
Best batting: 227 Northamptonshire v Somerset, Northampton 1976
Best bowling: 7-37 Northamptonshire v Oxford University, The Parks 1975

First-Class Career Performances

	M	Inns	NO	Runs	HS	Avge	100s	Ct	St	Runs	Wkts	Avge	Best	5wl	10wM
Test	26	50	6	1184	102*	26.90	2	3	-	456	7	65.14	2-73	-	-
All First	559	918	121	24361	227	30.56	44	235	-	23400	756	30.95	7-37	26	3

THE PRIMARY CLUB

PO Box 12121
London NW1 9WS
Tel: 020 7267 3316
Fax: 020 7485 6808

Derek Underwood, the patron of the Primary Club, qualified for membership in some style in 1965. Playing for Kent against the South Africans he was out first ball twice in the same match.

However, members do not have to be playing Test or county cricket when the ultimate disaster strikes in order to qualify for the club. As long as you are out first ball at ANY level of cricket you are eligible to join The Primary Club.

Why join? The Primary Club is a charity (Registered Charity No. 285285) and all profits from subscriptions, donations and the range of items for sale (ties, sweaters, shirts, mugs, umbrellas, etc.) go to pay for sporting and recreational facilities for the blind and partially sighted. All the club's workers are volunteers.

For many of us sport is an important part of our every day lives; for the blind and partially sighted, sport can mean so much more. The confidence and sense of achievement they get from mastering a physical skill helps them a great deal in tackling the problems of their lives.

MEMBERSHIP APPLICATION

Name

Address

Joining subscription:	
To include City tie – £20	
To include Club tie – £20	
To include City & Club tie – £30	
To include 100% silk tie (City motif) – £27.50	
To include Bow tie – £20	
Lady, to include brooch – £15	
DONATION	
REMITTANCE TO 'THE PRIMARY CLUB' £	

Registered Charity No. 285285

The value of your remittance to The Primary Club can be increased by 28p for every £1 you give under Gift Aid tax reclaim arrangements, *at no extra cost to you.*
To enable the Club to benefit from this scheme, please sign and date the declaration below, provided that you pay income tax, or capital gains tax, of an amount equal to the tax to be reclaimed.

I wish The Primary Club to reclaim tax on all donations I make on or after the date of this declaration.

Signed   **Date**

It would be of great benefit to the Club if you pay future donations by banker's standing order. Please tick the box and a form will be sent to you.

THE BROADCASTERS

AGNEW, J. P.   BBC Test Match Special

Name: <u>Jonathan</u> Philip Agnew
Born: 4 April 1960, Macclesfield
Height: 6ft 4in
Wife's name: Emma
Children: Jennifer, 1985; Rebecca, 1988
Education: Uppingham School
Relaxations: 'Eating good food and drinking good wine amongst friends'
First broadcast for: BBC Radio Leicester 1987
Broadcasting career: Became Sports Producer at Radio Leicester in 1989. Became BBC Cricket Correspondent in 1991
Highlights of broadcasting career: 'Interviewing Nelson Mandela'
Newspapers and magazines contributed to: *Today*, *Daily Express*, *Wisden Cricket Monthly*
Books published: Include *8 Days A Week* (1988); *Over to You, Aggers* (1997); current editor of *B&H Cricket Year*

County as player: Leicestershire
Role: Right-hand bat, right-arm fast bowler
County debut: 1978
County cap: 1984
Test debut: 1984
Tests: 3
One-day Internationals: 3
50 wickets in a season: 6
100 wickets in a season: 1
1st-Class 50s: 2
1st-Class 5 w. in innings: 37
1st-Class 10 w. in match: 6
1st-Class catches: 39
One-Day 5 w. in innings: 2
Career strike rate: 53.17
Overseas tours: England to India 1984-85
Overseas teams played for: Essendon, Melbourne; Parramatta, Sydney
Highlights of playing career: 'Returning to play NatWest semi-final for Leicestershire after two years in retirement'
Extras: One of *Wisden*'s Five Cricketers of the Year 1988
Opinions on cricket: 'Need more overseas players – two per county. The sooner the two divisional Championship is scrapped – and regional cricket introduced – the better.'

Best batting: 90 Leicestershire v Yorkshire, Scarborough 1987
Best bowling: 9-70 Leicestershire v Kent, Leicester 1985

First-Class and International Career Performances

	M	Inns	NO	Runs	HS	Avge	100s	Ct	St	Runs	Wkts	Avge	Best	5wI	10wM
Test	3	4	3	10	5	10.00	-	-	-	373	4	93.25	2-51	-	-
All First	218	232	49	2118	90	11.57	-	39	-	19485	666	29.25	9-70	37	6
1-day Int	3	1	1	2	2*	-	-	1	-	120	3	40.00	3-38	-	

ALLOTT, P. J. W.   SkySports

Name: <u>Paul</u> John Walter Allott
Born: 14 September 1956, Altrincham
Height: 6ft 4in
Wife's name: Pamela
Children: Ben and Susie
Family links with cricket: Father
captain/secretary of Ashley CC for 40 years
Education: Altrincham Grammar School;
Bede College, Durham
First broadcast for: BBC Radio 5 (radio);
BBC 1 (TV)
Broadcasting career: BBC 1993-94;
BBC/Sky 1994-95; Sky Sports 1995–
Newspapers and magazines contributed to:
The Guardian, *The Cricketer*
County as player: Lancashire
Role: Right-hand bat, right-arm fast-medium
bowler
County debut: 1978
County cap: 1981
Benefit: 1990
Test debut: 1981
Tests: 13
One-Day Internationals: 13
50 wickets in a season: 5
1st-Class 50s: 10
1st-Class 5 w. in innings: 30
1st-Class catches: 134
Career strike rate: 59.61
Overseas tours: England to India and Sri Lanka 1981-82, to India 1984-85
Overseas teams played for: Wellington 1985-87

Extras: Scored 52* in his first Test innings, v Australia at Old Trafford 1981
Best batting: 88 Lancashire v Hampshire, Southampton 1987
Best bowling: 8-48 Lancashire v Northamptonshire, Northampton 1981

First-Class and International Career Performances

	M	Inns	NO	Runs	HS	Avge	100s	Ct	St	Runs	Wkts	Avge	Best	5wI	10wM
Test	13	18	3	213	52*	14.20	-	4	-	1084	26	41.69	6-61	1	-
All First	245	262	64	3363	88	16.98	-	134	-	16665	652	25.55	8-48	30	-
1-day Int	13	6	1	15	8	3.00	-	2	-	552	15	36.80	3-41	-	

ATHERTON, M. A.   Channel 4

New member of Channel 4 team for summer 2002 – see entry in Players section (p.36)

BAXTER, P. A. S.   BBC Test Match Special

Name: <u>Peter</u> Alastair St John Baxter
Born: 8 January 1947, Derby
Height: 5ft 11in
Marital status: Separated
Children: Claire, 8 November 1983;
Jamie, 5 July 1986
Education: Wellington College, Berkshire
Other sports followed: Rugby union
First broadcast for: Radio Hilversum
(Holland) 1970, reading the football results
Broadcasting career: British Forces
Broadcasting Service (Aden) 1965. BBC Radio
Outside Broadcasts, September 1965. Became
Cricket Producer, BBC Radio, March 1973
Highlights of broadcasting career: 'First
Test match commentary, Calcutta 1984-85.
Organisation of radio coverage of 1999 World
Cup'

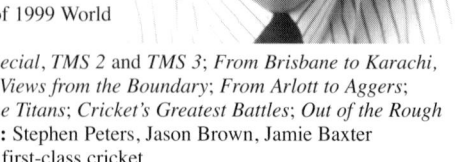

Books published: *Test Match Special, TMS 2* and *TMS 3*; *From Brisbane to Karachi,
Views from the Boundary*; *More Views from the Boundary*; *From Arlott to Aggers*;
World Cup: Cricket's Clash of the Titans; *Cricket's Greatest Battles*; *Out of the Rough*
Players to watch for the future: Stephen Peters, Jason Brown, Jamie Baxter
County as player: Did not play first-class cricket
Highlights of playing career: 'Taking eight wickets in a school game on an
impossibly wet pitch'

Opinions on cricket: 'The ECB should not lose sight of the fact that they are running the game of cricket, with all the commercial and televisual distractions around.'

Did not play first-class cricket

BENAUD, R. Channel 4

Name: Richard (<u>Richie</u>) Benaud
Born: 6 October 1930
Wife and date of marriage: Daphne, 26 July 1967
Family links with cricket: 'Lou Benaud, my father, a leg-spin bowler and all-rounder, was an outstanding country cricketer in New South Wales in the 1920s and early 1930s and then played in Sydney for Central Cumberland first and other grades from 1937-38 to 1956. Aged 43, he was in the team when I made my first-grade debut in 1946'
Education: Parramatta High School
Career outside media: 'With Daphne, as Benaud and Associates Pty Ltd, International Sports Consultants'
Other sports played: 'Tennis and soccer up to age 21; since then, golf and horse racing'

Other sports followed: Golf, soccer, rugby league, rugby union, Australian Rules. 'The first match I ever watched in England was in 1953 when Alf Ramsey was at full back for Tottenham Hotspur'
Relaxations: 'Golf, horse racing, reading and the occasional glass of Montrachet or Lynch-Bages'
Broadcasting career: BBC Radio 1960. BBC Television 1963-99; Channel 4 Television 2000 – ; Channel 9 Television 1977 –
Newspapers and magazines contributed to: Journalist with *The Sun* (Sydney newspaper) 1956-68. Freelance journalist 1968 –
Books published: *Way of Cricket* (1961); *A Tale of Two Tests* (1962); *Spin Me a Spinner* (1963); *The New Champions* (1965); *Willow Patterns* (1969); *Benaud on Reflection* (1984); *The Appeal of Cricket* (1995); *Anything but … An Autobiography* (1998)
County as player: Did not play county cricket
Role: Right-hand bat, leg-spin bowler
Test debut: 1951-52
Tests: 63
1st-Class 100s: 23

1st-Class 5 w. in innings: 56
1st-Class 10 w. in match: 9
1st-Class catches: 254
Overseas tours: Australia to England 1953, 1956, 1961 (captain), to West Indies 1954-55, to Pakistan 1956-57, 1959-60 (captain), to India 1956-57, 1959-60 (captain), to South Africa 1957-58
Overseas teams played for: Cumberland, Sydney; New South Wales 1948-49 – 1963-64
Extras: Captain of Australia 1958-59 – 1963-64 (28 Tests). Awarded OBE 1961. One of *Wisden*'s Five Cricketers of the Year 1962
Best batting: 187 Australians v Natal, Pietermaritzburg 1957-58
Best bowling: 7-18 New South Wales v MCC, Sydney 1962-63

First-Class and International Career Performances

	M	Inns	NO	Runs	HS	Avge	100s	Ct	St	Runs	Wkts	Avge	Best	5wI	10wM
Test	63	97	7	2201	122	24.45	3	65	-	6704	248	27.03	7-72	16	1
All First	259	365	44	11719	187	36.50	23	254	-	23371	945	24.73	7-18	56	9
1-day Int															

BHOGLE, H.   BBC Test Match Special

Name: <u>Harsha</u> Bhogle
Born: 19 July 1961, Hyderabad, India
Height: 5ft 10in
Wife and date of marriage: Anita, 3 November 1985
Children: Chinmay, 17 March 1988; Satchit, 11 January 1993
Family links with cricket: 'A great passion for it at home. My father had a lot of stories to tell me and was very persuasive in suggesting that I had a career in the media'
Education: Hyderabad (BTech, Chem Eng), Indian Institute of Management (Diploma in Management)
Career outside media: Early career in advertising and sports management
Other sports played: Table tennis at college level; football, hockey and volleyball 'at a decent fun-loving level'
Other sports followed: 'Virtually anything but I seem to be getting hooked on soccer. I like watching Brazil and France play and any team that Rivaldo and Roberto Carlos

play for. Fascinated by Michael Jordan, Tiger Woods and Sachin Tendulkar'

Relaxations: 'Just being at home with no deadline or shoot coming up!'

First broadcast for: All India Radio, Hyderabad v Kerala in the Ranji Trophy, 1980 (radio). Doordarshan, India v Pakistan, One-Day International, 1983 (TV)

Broadcasting career: Local radio and TV 1980-83. First One-Day in 1983, first Test in 1984. Worked with ABC in 1991-92 and followed up with work for BBC World Service. Returned to television with TWI and the newly formed Star Sports in 1993. From 1998, cricket presenter for ESPN Star Sports and involved in numerous magazine programmes. As journalist and broadcaster has covered 62 Tests and 268 One-Day Internationals. Indian Television Academy Award for Best Presenter/Commentator 2001

Highlights of broadcasting career: 'Doing live television in India virtually in the middle of the crowd with a million distractions, quite unable to hear the producer in your ear and not letting the viewers realise. But my favourite was being asked to stop throwing to studio and talking over live pictures of Pakistan doing a victory lap after a great Test match at Chennai; having to be politically correct, knowing the viewers were in a state of shock over the result and yet capturing the enormity of what was happening – an Indian crowd giving a Pakistan team a standing ovation. That was special'

Newspapers and magazines contributed to: Virtually all the Indian newspapers at some point; columnist for *The Sportstar* and for *The Week* and also writes for *Wisden Asia*. Has contributed to *The Australian*, *Daily Telegraph* and *Wisden Cricket Monthly*

Books published: *The Joy of a Lifetime* (India's Tour of England, 1990); authorised biography of Mohammed Azharuddin (1994)

Players to watch for the future: Virendar Sehwag, Tatenda Taibu, Marlon Samuels, Jacques Rudolph

County as player: Did not play first-class cricket. Played senior division cricket in Hyderabad for three years and for university in All India Inter-University event in 1981-82. Captain of the Indian Institute of Management team in 1984-85

Opinions on cricket: 'The biggest plus is that Test cricket is looking very good, better than at any time since I started covering cricket, and there seems to be a bit of a balance now with the one-day game as well. The biggest threat is that too many countries are playing "us and them", especially in the media, which has been a bit of a let-down. The issue of white versus brown/black is simmering far too close to the surface, and we need to have more dignified, statesmanlike referees.'

Did not play first-class cricket

Name: <u>Ian</u> Raphael Bishop
Born: 24 October 1967, Port of Spain, Trinidad
Height: 6ft 5in
Wife and date of marriage: Jahan, 9 October 1993
Family links with cricket: 'My uncle, Renwick Bishop, represented West Indies U19'
Education: Belmont Boys' Primary School; Belmont Secondary School
Other sports played: 'Soccer for my former school'
Other sports followed: All sports, football (Manchester United)
Relaxations: Reading, television
Broadcasting career: Cana Radio; 6.10 Radio; BBC Radio. Channel 4 Television; TWI

Highlights of broadcasting career: 'Covering the West Indies v England series in 2000 with Channel 4'
Newspapers and magazines contributed to: *Trinidad Newsday* (newspaper)
Players to watch for the future: Ravi Rampaul (Trinidad)
County as player: Derbyshire
Role: Right-hand bat, right-arm fast bowler
County debut: 1989
County cap: 1990
Test debut: 1988-89
Tests: 43
One-Day Internationals: 84
50 wickets in a season: 2
1st-Class 50s: 3
1st-Class 100s: 2
1st-Class 5 w. in innings: 23
1st-Class 10 w. in match: 1
1st-Class catches: 50
One-Day 5 w. in innings: 2
Career strike rate: 48.36
Overseas tours: West Indies to England 1988, to Australia 1988-89, to Pakistan 1990-91, to Australia 1992-93
Overseas teams played for: Trinidad and Tobago 1987-1999

Highlights of playing career: 'West Indies beating Australia by one run in Adelaide 1992-93'
Extras: Topped 1990 first-class bowling averages in England with 59 wickets at 19.05. Played for Tynedale CC in Northumberland and Reigate Priory in Surrey
Best batting: 111 Trinidad and Tobago v Barbados, Port of Spain 1996-97
Best bowling: 7-34 Derbyshire v Hampshire, Portsmouth 1992

First-Class and International Career Performances

	M	Inns	NO	Runs	HS	Avge	100s	Ct	St	Runs	Wkts	Avge	Best	5wl	10wM
Test	43	63	11	632	48	12.15	-	8	-	3909	161	24.27	6-40	6	-
All First	159	211	41	2639	111	15.52	2	50	-	12665	549	23.06	7-34	23	1
1-day Int	84	44	19	405	33*	16.20	-	12	-	3128	118	26.50	5-25	2	

BLOFELD, H. C.   BBC Test Match Special

Name: <u>Henry</u> Calthorpe Blofeld
Born: 23 September 1939, Hoveton, Norfolk
Height: 6ft
Wife's name: Bitten
Children: Suki, 1 September 1963
Education: Eton College; Cambridge University
Relaxations: Shooting, reading, bridge, collecting books
First broadcast for: Radio Jamaica, January 1971 (radio); Grenada TV, 1960s (TV)
Broadcasting career: BBC Radio's *Test Match Special* 1972 –
Newspapers and magazines contributed to: *The Times, The Guardian, The Daily Telegraph, Independent, The Observer, Daily Sketch, Daily Mirror, Independent on Sunday*
Books published: *Cricket in Three Moods; The Packer Affair; Wine, Women and Wickets;*

Caught Short of the Boundary; My Dear Old Thing; On the Edge of My Seat (1991); *One Test After Another; Cakes and Bails; "It's Just Not Cricket"* (1999); *A Thirst for Life*
County as player: Norfolk; also Cambridge University
Role: Right-hand opening bat
1st-Class 50s: 2
1st-Class 100s: 1
1st-Class catches: 11

Overseas tours: Arabs to Barbados 1966-67
Highlights of playing career: '104* for Public Schools against Combined Services at Lord's 1956'
Extras: Cambridge Blue 1959
Best batting: 138 Cambridge University v MCC, Lord's 1959

First-Class Career Performances

	M	Inns	NO	Runs	HS	Avge	100s	Ct	St	Runs	Wkts	Avge	Best	5wI	10wM
Test															
All First	17	32	1	758	138	24.45	1	11	-	15	0	-	-	-	-
1-day Int															

BOTHAM, I. T. SkySports

Name: Ian Terence Botham
Born: 24 November 1955, Heswall, Cheshire
Height: 6ft 2in
Wife and date of marriage: Kathryn, 31 January 1976
Children: Liam James, 26 August 1977; Sarah Lianne, 3 February 1979; Rebecca Kate, 13 November 1985
Education: Buckler's Mead Secondary School, Yeovil
Other sports played: Football (Scunthorpe, England Amateurs), golf
Other sports followed: Football (Chelsea FC), rugby union (Newcastle)
Relaxations: Shooting, fishing
First broadcast for: '606'
Broadcasting career: Sky 1995 –
Highlights of broadcasting career: 'Seeing Bob Willis and Paul Allott commentating on

a One-Day International at Brisbane in their underwear as the air-conditioning had broken down!'
Newspapers and magazines contributed to: Numerous, currently *The Mirror*
Books published: Include *High, Wide and Handsome*, written with Frank Keating; *It Sort of Clicks*, in collaboration with Peter Roebuck; *Cricket My Way*, with Jack Bannister; *Botham: Don't Tell Kath*; *The Botham Report* (1997)
Players to watch for the future: Michael Vaughan, Matthew Hoggard
Counties as player: Somerset, Worcestershire, Durham
Role: Right-hand bat, right-arm fast-medium bowler

County debut: 1974 (Somerset), 1987 (Worcs), 1992 (Durham)
County cap: 1976 (Somerset), 1987 (Worcs), 1992 (Durham)
Benefit: 1984 (Somerset)
Test debut: 1977
Tests: 102
One-Day Internationals: 116
1000 runs in a season: 4
50 wickets in a season: 7
100 wickets in a season: 1
1st-Class 50s: 97
1st-Class 100s: 36
1st-Class 200s: 2
1st-Class 5 w. in innings: 59
1st-Class 10 w. in match: 8
1st-Class catches: 352
One-Day 100s: 7
One-Day 5 w. in innings: 3
Career strike rate: 54.31
Overseas tours: England to Pakistan and New Zealand 1977-78, to Australia 1978-79, to Australia and India 1979-80, to West Indies 1980-81 (captain), to India 1981-82, to Australia 1982-83, to West Indies 1985-86, to Australia 1986-87, to New Zealand 1991-92, to Australia and New Zealand (World Cup) 1991-92
Overseas teams played for: Queensland
Highlights of playing career: 'Any time England beat the Aussies'
Extras: Captain of England in 12 Test matches. One of *Wisden*'s Five Cricketers of the Year 1978. BBC Sports Personality of the Year 1981. Awarded the OBE in 1992
Opinions on cricket: 'Getting better.'
Best batting: 228 Somerset v Gloucestershire, Taunton 1980
Best bowling: 8-34 England v Pakistan, Lord's 1978

First-Class and International Career Performances

	M	Inns	NO	Runs	HS	Avge	100s	Ct	St	Runs	Wkts	Avge	Best	5wI	10wM
Test	102	161	6	5200	208	33.54	14	120	-	10878	383	28.40	8-34	27	4
All First	402	617	46	19399	228	33.97	38	352	-	31942	1172	27.25	8-34	59	8
1-day Int	116	106	15	2113	79	23.21	-	36	-	4139	145	28.54	4-31	-	

COLVILE, C. E. N.

Name: <u>Charles</u> Edward Neate Colvile
Born: 29 March 1955, Rochester, Kent
Height: 6ft 4in
Wife and date of marriage: Alison Jane, 11 April 1981
Children: Raoul, 1986; Robyn, 1988; Zara, 1990; Sasha, 1993
Education: Westminster School, London
First broadcast for: BBC Radio 4 *PM* 1976 (radio); BBC *Breakfast Time* (TV)
Broadcasting career: Began broadcasting career doing a Saturday afternoon sports report on *PM* in 1976. Radio Oxford 1977. Radio 4 continuity announcer 1978. BBC Radio Sport/*Today* Sports Correspondent 1982. BBC *Breakfast Time* 1985. LWT 1988. BSB/BSkyB 1990 –
Highlights of broadcasting career: 'Some would think commentating on Warne's 1994-95 MCG hat-trick, but being a good Surrey boy, Stewart's two hundreds v West Indies in Barbados in 1993-94'
County as player: Did not play first-class cricket
Extras: Supports Surrey CCC

Did not play first-class cricket

FOWLER, G.   SkySports/BBC Test Match Special

Name: Graeme Fowler
Born: 20 April 1957, Accrington, Lancashire
Height: 5ft 9½in
Wife and date of marriage: Sarah,
14 February 1995
Children: Katherine Elizabeth, 4 August
1994; Georgina Ruby, 29 September 1995
Education: Accrington Grammar School for
Boys; College of St Hilda and St Bede,
Durham University
Career outside media: Senior cricket coach,
Durham University Cricket Centre of
Excellence since October 1996
Relaxations: Gardening, music, playing
drums (1999 and 2000 for the Mark Butcher
Band at the Royal Albert Hall; 1991 for Roy
Harper Band on a live CD called *Unhinged*)
First broadcast for: BBC Radio 4 1987
(radio); SkySports 1995 (TV)

Broadcasting career: Part of Radio 4 *Test Match Special* team since 1996. Part of
SkySports cricket commentary team since 1997
Highlights of broadcasting career: 'Any with Henry Blofeld'
Newspapers and magazines contributed to: *The Sunday Telegraph*, *Wisden Cricket
Monthly*
Books published: *Fox on the Run* (1986; Channel 4 Sports Book of the Year)
Players to watch for the future: James Foster
Counties as player: Lancashire, Durham
Role: Left-hand opening bat, right-arm medium bowler
County debut: 1979 (Lancashire), 1993 (Durham)
County cap: 1981 (Lancashire)
Benefit: 1991 (Lancashire; £152,000)
Test debut: 1982
Tests: 21
One-Day Internationals: 26
1000 runs in a season: 8
1st-Class 50s: 85
1st-Class 100s: 34
1st-Class 200s: 2
1st-Class catches: 154
1st-Class stumpings: 5
One-Day 100s: 9

Overseas tours: England to Australia 1982-83, to New Zealand and Pakistan 1983-84, to India 1984-85

Overseas teams played for: Scarborough, Perth 1979-1980, 1986-1988; Kingsborough, Hobart 1981

Highlights of playing career: '201 v India, Madras 1984-85; 106 v West Indies, Lord's 1984'

Extras: First Englishman to score a Test double century in India

Opinions on cricket: 'Technology should be fully embraced. Full tours should be abolished and replaced by a world league. Needs to be semi-professional to allow all cricketers the chance – not just a few professionals – with half the current first-class fixtures. County clubs should be limited companies not private members' clubs. The game is run indirectly and directly by people who know very little about it.'

Best batting: 226 Lancashire v Kent, Maidstone 1984

Best bowling: 2-34 Lancashire v Warwickshire, Old Trafford 1986

First-Class and International Career Performances

	M	Inns	NO	Runs	HS	Avge	100s	Ct	St	Runs	Wkts	Avge	Best	5wI	10wM
Test	21	37	0	1307	201	35.32	3	10	-	11	0	-	-	-	-
All First	292	495	27	16663	226	35.60	36	154	5	366	10	36.60	2-34	-	-
1-day Int	26	26	2	744	81*	31.00	-	4	2						

FRINDALL, W. H.   BBC Test Match Special

Name: William (Bill) Howard Frindall

Born: 3 March 1939, Epsom, Surrey

Height: 5ft 10½in

Wife and date of marriage: Deborah Margaret, 29 February 1992

Children: Alice Katharine, 24 January 1996

Family links with cricket: Father played village cricket in Surrey – took 9-45 for Walton Heath c1946

Education: Reigate Grammar School; Kingston upon Thames School of Art (Architecture Department)

Other sports played: Hockey in the RAF ('badly')

Other sports followed: None – 'don't have the time!'

Relaxations: Blind cricket (President of British Blind Sport since 1984); drawing and painting (oil and watercolour); gardening ('under my wife's supervision'); cats; philately

First broadcast for: BBC Radio – Worcestershire v West Indians 1966: first Test match was England v West Indies, Old Trafford 1966 (radio); BBC2 Rothmans Cavaliers v Surrey, Cheam 1968 (TV)

Broadcasting career: Set all questions for *Sporting Chance* (BBC Radio) 1965-67. Has scored all home Tests (and some overseas series) for *Test Match Special* since

June 1966. Involved with BBC2's coverage of John Player League 1969-75 (captions and scorer). Interviews and reports for BBC Forces Radio (*c*1970-*c*1985) and BBC Wiltshire Sound (since 1996)

Highlights of broadcasting career: 'Wait for my memoirs! Possibly when John Arlott left early and I imitated him on *TMS*'

Newspapers and magazines contributed to: *The Times*, *The Daily Telegraph*, *The Guardian*, *Daily Mail*, *Daily Express*, *Daily Mirror*, *The Sun*, *The Observer*, *Sunday Telegraph*; Cricket Correspondent of *Mail on Sunday* 1987-89; currently cricket statistician to *The Times*

Books published: *The Wisden Book of Test Cricket* (1979; 5th edition 2000); *The Wisden Book of Cricket Records* (1981; 4th edition 1998); *The Guinness Book of Cricket Facts and Feats* (1983; 4th edition 1996); *England Test Cricketers* (1989); *Ten Tests for England* (1989); *Gooch's Golden Summer* (1991); *A Tale of Two Captains* (1992); *Playfair Cricket World Cup Guide* (1996); *Limited-Overs International Cricket: the complete record* (1997); *NatWest Playfair Cricket World Cup 1999* (1999); *Playfair Cricket Annual* (1986–; ed)

Players to watch for the future: Alice Frindall (aged 6)

County as player: Did not play first-class cricket but has played for Hampshire 2nd XI (1972) and for a host of sides, including (in benefits) Yorkshire, Essex, Kent and Warwickshire

Role: Right-hand bat, right-arm medium-fast bowler ('was fast-medium')

Overseas tours: Many, including MCC to USA 1992, to Canada 1994; Lord's Taverners to Portugal 1988, to Gibraltar 1992

Overseas teams played for: Several, including Crusaders, Australia 1982-83

Highlights of playing career: 'Taking 9-21 (all bowled) for Oxford Clergy. Clean bowling Ian Botham in a benefit match'

Extras: Awarded honorary Doctor of Technology by Staffordshire University in 1998 for services to cricket statistics. President BBC Cricket Club. Cricket archivist to Sir Paul Getty

Opinions on cricket: 'Wait for the memoirs.'

Did not play first-class cricket

Name: <u>Sunil</u> Manchar Gavaskar
Born: 10 July 1949, Bombay, India
Height: 5ft 5in
Wife and date of marriage: Marshniel,
23 September 1974
Children: Rohan, 20 February 1976
Family links with cricket: Maternal uncle
M.K. Mantri played four Tests for India.
Brother-in-law is former Indian Test player
G.R. Viswanath
Education: St Xavier's College, Bombay;
Bombay University
Broadcasting career: Frequent contributor to
BBC Radio's *Test Match Special*.
County as player: Somerset
Role: Right-hand opening bat
County debut: 1980
County cap: 1980
Test debut: 1970-71
Tests: 125
One-Day Internationals: 108
1st-Class 50s: 105
1st-Class 100s: 81
1st-Class catches: 293

Extras: Scored his first century at Lord's in his final game, playing for Rest of the World v MCC in the MCC Bicentennial Match in 1987. Was the highest Test run-scorer until overtaken by Allan Border. Was one of the first players to use head protection, wearing a skull cap inside his wide-brimmed sun hat. Scored over 1000 Test runs in a calendar year on three occasions.
Best batting: 340 Bombay v Bengal, Bombay 1981-82

First-Class and International Career Performances

	M	Inns	NO	Runs	HS	Avge	100s	Ct	St	Runs	Wkts	Avge	Best	5wI	10wM
Test	125	214	16	10122	236*	51.12	34	108	-	206	1	206.00	1-34	-	-
All First	348	563	61	25834	340	51.46	81	293	-	1240	22	56.36	3-43	-	-
1-day Int	108	102	14	3092	103*	35.13	1	22	-	25	1	25.00	1-25	-	

Name: <u>Graham</u> Alan Gooch
Born: 23 July 1953, Leytonstone
Height: 6ft
Wife and date of marriage: Brenda,
23 October 1976
Children: Hannah; Megan and Sally (twins)
Family links with cricket: Father played
club cricket for East Ham Corinthians.
Second cousin Graham Saville played for
Essex and managed England U19
Education: Cannhall School and Norlington
Junior High School, Leytonstone; Redbridge
Technical College
Other sports followed: Football (West Ham)
Relaxations: Relaxing at home
First broadcast for: *TMS* at Sabina Park,
Jamaica 1995 (radio); Sky (TV)
Broadcasting career: Has made appearances
on Sky and Channel 4 and contributed to

TMS but only became a *TMS* regular in 2000. Took part in Australia's Channel 9
coverage of Australia v West Indies at Adelaide 2000-01
Highlights of broadcasting career: 'Appearing in a muck sweat on TV for pre-match
comments after a rapid shower and change having played squash with David Craven –
lesson learned!'
Books published: Include *Out of the Wilderness* (1988); *Test of Fire* (1990);
Captaincy (1992); *Gooch: My Autobiography*, with Frank Keating (1995)
Players to watch for the future: Matthew Hoggard, Alex Tudor
County as player: Essex
Role: Right-hand bat, right-arm medium bowler
County debut: 1973
County cap: 1975
Benefit: 1985 (£153,906)
Testimonial: 1995
Test debut: 1975
Tests: 118
One-Day Internationals: 125
1000 runs in a season: 20
1st-Class 50s: 217
1st-Class 100s: 115
1st-Class 200s: 12
1st-Class 300s: 1

1st-Class 5 w. in innings: 3
1st-Class catches: 555
One-Day 100s: 41
One-Day 5 w. in innings: 1
Career strike rate: 76.36
Overseas tours: England to Australia 1978-79, 1990-91 (captain), 1994-95, to Australia and India 1979-80, to West Indies 1980-81, 1989-90 (captain), to India and Sri Lanka 1981-82, to India and Pakistan (World Cup) 1987-88, to New Zealand 1991-92 (captain), to Australia and New Zealand (World Cup) 1991-92 (captain), to India 1992-93 (captain)
Overseas teams played for: Western Province, South Africa 1982-84
Highlights of playing career: 'Captaining England for the first time. Captaining England to victory over West Indies at Sabina Park 1990. Captaining Essex to first ever trophy (and scoring a century), B&H 1979'
Extras: Captained England in 34 Test matches. One of *Wisden*'s Five Cricketers of the Year 1980. Awarded OBE 1991
Best batting: 333 England v India, Lord's 1990
Best bowling: 7-14 Essex v Worcestershire, Ilford 1982

First-Class and International Career Performances

	M	Inns	NO	Runs	HS	Avge	100s	Ct	St	Runs	Wkts	Avge	Best	5wI	10wM
Test	118	215	6	8900	333	42.58	20	103	-	1069	23	46.47	3-39	-	-
All First	581	990	75	44846	333	49.01	128	555	-	8457	246	34.37	7-14	3	-
1-day Int	125	122	6	4290	142	36.98	8	45	-	1516	36	42.11	3-19	-	

GOWER, D. I.   SkySports

Name: <u>David</u> Ivon Gower
Born: 1 April 1957, Tunbridge Wells, Kent
Height: 6ft
Wife and date of marriage: Thorunn, 1992
Children: Alexandra, 25 September 1993; Samantha, 28 May 1996
Education: King's School, Canterbury; University College London
Career outside media: Director – David Gower Media, David Gower Promotions, uvine.com – the Internet Wine Exchange
Other sports played: Tennis, skiing
Relaxations: Wildlife, safaris, photography, music
First broadcast for: *Test Match Special* on England's 1989-90 tour of West Indies (radio); Channel 9 (Australia) during 1991-92 World Cup (TV)
Broadcasting career: 1994-99: commentator for BBC TV; presenter *Gower's Cricket Monthly* (BBC TV) and *David Gower's Cricket Weekly* (Radio 5). 1995 – : Team captain on *They Think It's All Over* (BBC TV). 1999 – : Presenter *SkySports Cricket*

Highlights of broadcasting career: 'Brian Lara's 375 in Antigua'

Newspapers and magazines contributed to: *Sunday Telegraph*, *Sunday Express*, *The Daily Telegraph*, *The Times*, *Daily Express*, *The Sun*, *Wisden Cricket Monthly*; currently writes for *Skylines* (BA magazine)

Books published: Include *Anyone for Cricket* (1979); *With Time to Spare* (1980); *Heroes and Contemporaries* (1983); *A Right Ambition* (1986); *Gower: The Autobiography* (1992)

Counties as player: Leicestershire, Hampshire

Role: Left-hand bat

County debut: 1975 (Leicestershire), 1990 (Hampshire)

County cap: 1977 (Leicestershire), 1990 (Hampshire)

Benefit: 1987 (Leicestershire; £121,546)

Test debut: 1978

Tests: 117

One-Day Internationals: 114

1000 runs in a season: 13

1st-Class 50s: 136

1st-Class 100s: 51

1st-Class 200s: 2

1st-Class catches: 282

1st-Class stumpings: 1

One-Day 100s: 19

Overseas tours: England to Australia 1978-79, 1982-83, 1986-87, 1990-91, to Australia and India 1979-80, to West Indies 1980-81, 1985-86, to India and Sri Lanka 1981-82, to New Zealand and Pakistan 1983-84, to India 1984-85

Overseas teams played for: Claremont-Cottesloe, Western Australia 1977-78

Highlights of playing career: 'Ashes 1985'

Extras: Captain of England in 32 Test matches. One of *Wisden*'s Five Cricketers of the Year 1979. Awarded OBE in 1992

Opinions on cricket: 'Two main things to aim for: a world Test championship and a streamlined first-class set-up in England.'

Best batting: 228 Leicestershire v Glamorgan, Leicester 1989

Best bowling: 3-47 Leicestershire v Essex, Leicester 1977

First-Class and International Career Performances

	M	Inns	NO	Runs	HS	Avge	100s	Ct	St	Runs	Wkts	Avge	Best	5wI	10wM
Test	117	204	18	8231	215	44.25	18	74	-	20	1	20.00	1-1	-	-
All First	448	727	70	26339	228	40.08	53	282	1	227	4	56.75	3-47	-	-
1-day Int	114	111	8	3170	158	30.77	7	44	-	14	0	-	-	-	-

HOLDING, M. A. SkySports

Name: <u>Michael</u> Anthony Holding
Born: 16 February 1954, Kingston, Jamaica
Height: 6ft 3in
Education: Kingston College HS
Counties as player: Lancashire, Derbyshire
Role: Right-hand bat, right-arm fast bowler
County debut: 1981 (Lancashire),
1983 (Derbyshire)
County cap: 1983 (Derbyshire)
Test debut: 1975-76
Tests: 60
One-Day Internationals: 102
50 wickets in a season: 3
1st-Class 50s: 14
1st-Class 5 w. in innings: 39
1st-Class 10 w. in match: 5
1st-Class catches: 124
One-Day 5 w. in innings: 3
Career strike rate: 49.97

Overseas tours: West Indies to Australia 1975-76, 1979-80, 1981-82, 1984-85, to England 1976, 1980, 1984, to New Zealand 1979-80, 1986-87, to India 1983-84
Overseas teams played for: Jamaica 1972-89; Tasmania 1982-83; Canterbury, New Zealand 1987-88
Extras: One of *Wisden*'s Five Cricketers of the Year 1977
Best batting: 80 Derbyshire v Yorkshire, Chesterfield 1985
Best bowling: 8-92 West Indies v England, The Oval 1976

First-Class and International Career Performances

	M	Inns	NO	Runs	HS	Avge	100s	Ct	St	Runs	Wkts	Avge	Best	5wI	10wM
Test	60	76	10	910	73	13.78	-	22	-	5898	249	23.68	8-92	13	2
All First	222	283	43	3600	80	15.00	-	124	-	18233	778	23.43	8-92	39	5
1-day Int	102	42	11	282	64	9.09	-	30	-	3034	142	21.36	5-26	1	

HUGHES, S. P.   Channel 4

Name: <u>Simon</u> Peter Hughes
Born: 20 December 1959, Kingston, Surrey
Height: 5ft 10in
Wife and date of marriage: Tanya,
June 1994
Children: Callum, March 1998;
Nancy, September 2000
Family links with cricket: Father keen club
player and coach. Uncle once hit ball over
school pavilion
Education: Latymer Upper School,
Hammersmith; Durham University
Other sports played: Football, golf, tennis
Other sports followed: Formula One
Relaxations: Modern novels, Hammond
organ
First broadcast for: LBC 1983 (radio); BBC
1991 – NatWest semi-final (TV)
Broadcasting career: 1988: Two winters

writing and reading sports news on GLR. 1992-98: Commentary and interviews for
BBC TV. 1999: Began with Channel 4 as 'the Analyst'
Newspapers and magazines contributed to: *Independent* (1986-93), *The Daily
Telegraph* (1994 –)
Books published: *From Minor to Major* (1992); *A Lot of Hard Yakka* (1997; Sports
Book of the Year); *Yakking Around the World* (2000); *Jargonbusting: the Analyst's
Guide to Test Cricket* (2001)
Players to watch for the future: Callum Hughes (aged 4)
Counties as player: Middlesex, Durham
Role: Right-hand bat, right-arm fast-medium bowler
County debut: 1980 (Middlesex), 1992 (Durham)
County cap: 1981 (Middlesex)
Benefit: 1991 (Middlesex; £110,000)
50 wickets in a season: 2
1st-Class 50s: 1
1st-Class 5 w. in innings: 10
1st-Class catches: 50
One-Day 5 w. in innings: 1
Career strike rate: 62.18
Highlights of playing career: 'Bowling the last over in pouring rain to win the 1986
B&H Cup'
Extras: Played in Championship and Gillette Cup winning sides in first season 1980

Opinions on cricket: 'Writing and talking about cricket is much easier than playing it.'
Best batting: 53 Middlesex v Cambridge University, Fenner's 1988
Best bowling: 7-35 Middlesex v Surrey, The Oval 1986

First-Class Career Performances

	M	Inns	NO	Runs	HS	Avge	100s	Ct	St	Runs	Wkts	Avge	Best	5wI	10wM
Test															
All First	205	226	70	1776	53	11.38	-	50	-	15139	466	32.48	7-35	10	-
1-day Int															

LLOYD, D. *SkySports*

Name: David Lloyd
Born: 18 March 1947, Accrington, Lancashire
Height: 6ft
Wife's name: Diana ('second marriage')
Children: Graham, Sarah, Steven, Ben
Family links with cricket: Son Graham plays for Lancashire CCC
Education: Accrington Secondary Technical School, Oswaldtwistle
Other sports played: 'Played soccer in teenage years for Burnley B, Rossendale Utd, Accrington Stanley'
Other sports followed: Football, golf
Relaxations: Golf, flyfishing, wine and draught beer
First broadcast for: *Test Match Special* (radio); BSB, 'which soon merged with BSkyB' (TV)

Highlights of broadcasting career: 'Every day in the box – what could be better?! Best seat in the house, chatting with your pals and having fun'
Newspapers and magazines contributed to: *Daily Telegraph*
Books published: *Anything But Murder*, autobiography with Alan Lee; *G'day, Ya Pommie B...*; *Out of the Rough*, with Jonathan Agnew and Peter Baxter
Players to watch for the future: Stephen Harmison, Usman Afzaal, Chris Schofield, Andrew Flintoff, Alex Tudor, Gary Keedy, Matthew Hoggard
County as player: Lancashire
Role: Left-hand bat, slow left-arm bowler
County debut: 1965

County cap: 1968
Testimonial: 1978
Test debut: 1974
Tests: 9
One-Day Internationals: 8
1000 runs in a season: 11
1st-Class 50s: 93
1st-Class 100s: 37
1st-Class 200s: 1
1st-Class 5 w. in innings: 5
1st-Class 10 w. in match: 1
1st-Class catches: 334
One-Day 100s: 7
Career strike rate: 65.81
Overseas tours: England to Australia 1974-75
Highlights of playing/coaching career: '214* England v India 1974. Coaching England and putting a structure in place – identified need for central contracts. Winning in Sharjah and playing small part in helping team in beating India, Pakistan, South Africa, Australia and New Zealand in international competition'
Opinions on cricket: 'Central contracts for England players will be a very significant development in the re-emergence of the England team. Match fixing and everything that goes with it has, on the face of it to the general public, been treated far too lightly. Pitches in England need to improve dramatically and a "standard" cricket ball (Kookaburra) should be used in cricket at first-class level. Indoor stadiums should be high on the agenda for people entrusted with the development of the game in England. ECB to provide less money to county clubs and much more to premier league development.'
Best batting: 214* England v India, Edgbaston 1974
Best bowling: 7-38 Lancashire v Gloucestershire, Lydney 1966

First-Class and International Career Performances

	M	Inns	NO	Runs	HS	Avge	100s	Ct	St	Runs	Wkts	Avge	Best	5wl	10wM
Test	9	15	2	552	214*	42.46	1	11	-	17	0	-	-	-	-
All First	407	652	74	19269	214*	33.33	38	334	-	7172	237	30.26	7-38	5	1
1-day Int	8	8	1	285	116*	40.71	1	3	-	3	1	3.00	1-3	-	

Name: <u>Simon</u> John Mann
Born: 1 November 1963, Bristol
Height: 5ft 11in
Marital status: Single
Education: Queen Elizabeth's Hospital, Bristol; Birmingham University; London College of Printing
Other sports played: Rugby (Bristol Schools XV – 'on one occasion I played opposite Stuart Barnes; by the time he had finished, I knew it was time to give up')
Other sports followed: Football ('there is only one football team in Bristol')
First broadcast for: Capital Radio, London, reading the sports news (radio); BBC TV, reporting for *Cricket Focus* (TV)
Broadcasting career: 1988-90: News and sports reporter with Capital Radio. 1990-

2000: BBC Sport; 'Summer 2000 was my first as an official member of the *Test Match Special* commentary team although I'd commentated for *TMS* during the 1995-96 World Cup and England's tour of Zimbabwe'. 2000 – : Freelance ('offers welcome')
Highlights of broadcasting career: 'Commentating on the closing overs of the South Africa v Australia World Cup semi-final for BBC TV. It was an exciting, unpredictable one-day game with a dramatic and bizarre finish. It's a shame they are not all like that'
Newspapers and magazines contributed to: *The Guardian*
Players to watch for the future: Adam Gilchrist
County as player: Did not play first-class cricket; North London CC since 1986
Role: Right-hand bat, 'bowler of very occasional slow left-arm filth'
Overseas tours: David Hopps' XI to Sri Lanka 1997
Opinions on cricket: 'The rules for one-day cricket need to be updated constantly to provide players with new challenges and make the game less formulaic. The third umpire will become as important as, if not more important than, the two in the middle in decision-making. The role television plays will inevitably increase. At the moment, it is absurd that three million people at home know a batsman is out/not out but the umpire in the middle, using the fallible naked eye, has made the incorrect decision. What's wrong with a qualified umpire, sitting in the stand, actually making the right decision? I love Test cricket, but matches must restart when the rain stops. Covers must cover the whole ground and be flexible enough to be removed within 15 minutes.'

Did not play first-class cricket

Name: <u>Victor</u> James Marks
Born: 25 June 1955, Middle Chinnock, Somerset
Height: 5ft 9in
Wife and date of marriage: Anna, 9 September 1978
Children: Amy, 27 November 1979; Rosie, 8 November 1987
Family links with cricket: 'Father was a dangerous village cricketer'
Education: Blundell's School, Tiverton; Oxford University
Career outside media: Teaching ('but not since 1981')
Other sports played: Golf, Rugby fives, social tennis
Other sports followed: Rugby, golf, Somerset CCC
Relaxations: Golf ('but it's not very relaxing'), writing for *The Observer*

First broadcast for: BBC *TMS* in India 1984, 'filling in for indisposed Mike Selvey' (radio)
Broadcasting career: *TMS* 'for last decade or so'; TV 'very rarely'
Newspapers and magazines contributed to: *The Observer*, *The Cricketer* magazine
Books published: *Somerset County Cricket Scrapbook* (1984); *Marks Out of XI* (1985); *TCCB Guide to Better Cricket* (1987); *The Ultimate One-Day Cricket Match*, with Robin Drake (1988); *The Wisden Illustrated History of Cricket* (1989); *My Greatest Match*, with Bob Holmes (1994)
County as player: Somerset; also Oxford University
Role: Right-hand bat, off-spin bowler
County debut: 1975
County cap: 1979
Benefit: 1988
Test debut: 1982
Tests: 6
One-Day Internationals: 34
1000 runs in a season: 2
50 wickets in a season: 8
1st-Class 50s: 73
1st-Class 100s: 5
1st-Class 5 w. in innings: 40
1st-Class 10 w. in match: 5

1st-Class catches: 145
One-Day 5 w. in innings: 2
Career strike rate: 73.33
Overseas tours: England to Australia 1982-83, to New Zealand and Pakistan 1983-84, to India 1984-85
Overseas teams played for: Western Australia 1986-87; Bayswater Morley, Perth 1981-82, 1986-87
Extras: Oxford Blue 1975, 1976, 1977, 1978; captain of Oxford University 1976-77
Best batting: 134 Somerset v Worcestershire, Weston-super-Mare 1984
Best bowling: 8-17 Somerset v Lancashire, Bath 1985

First-Class and International Career Performances

	M	Inns	NO	Runs	HS	Avge	100s	Ct	St	Runs	Wkts	Avge	Best	5wI	10wM
Test	6	10	1	249	83	27.66	-	-	-	484	11	44.00	3-78	-	-
All First	342	500	90	12419	134	30.29	5	145	-	28591	859	33.28	8-17	40	5
1-day Int	34	24	3	285	44	13.57	-	8	-	1135	44	25.79	5-20	2	

MARTIN-JENKINS, C. D. A.   BBC Test Match Special

Name: <u>Christopher</u> Dennis Alexander Martin-Jenkins
Born: 20 January 1945, Peterborough
Height: 6ft 3in
Wife and date of marriage: Judy, 17 April 1971
Children: James, Robin and Lucy
Family links with cricket: James captains Radley in *The Cricketer* Cup; Robin plays for Sussex
Education: Marlborough College; Cambridge University
Other sports played: Rugby fives (Cambridge 1966, 1967), golf ('gross underachiever')
Other sports followed: 'All ball games, and I have played most of them with amateur relish'
Relaxations: Music, the family, the open air

Broadcasting career: First broadcast as a freelance sports reporter in the late 1960s. BBC 1970-81 and 1984-91 (Cricket Correspondent 1973-81 and 1984-91; occasional commentator on BBC TV 1981-91). Freelance commentator 1992 –

Highlights of broadcasting career: 'Describing England winning the Ashes with monotonous regularity'
Newspapers and magazines contributed to: *Daily Telegraph* (Cricket Correspondent 1991-99), *The Times* (Cricket Correspondent 1999 –), *The Cricketer* (Assistant Editor 1966-70; Editor 1981-91)
Books published: Numerous, including *The Complete Who's Who of Test Cricketers* and *Ball by Ball: the Story of Cricket Broadcasting*
County as player: Did not play first-class cricket but played for Surrey 2nd XI and Surrey Club and Ground
Role: Right-hand bat, right-arm medium bowler ('until 21'), off-spin bowler ('since')
Highlights of playing career: 'Reached final of Surrey Single Wicket, defeating two Test players en route. Dismissed Alvin Kallicharran with unplayable long-hop, Surrey 2nd XI v Warwickshire 2nd XI, The Oval 1971'
Extras: Captain of Marlborough College 1963. Played three years for Cambridge University Crusaders
Opinions on cricket: 'Please read *The Times*!'

Did not play first-class cricket

NICHOLAS, M. C. J. Channel 4

Name: <u>Mark</u> Charles Jefford Nicholas
Born: 29 September 1957, London
Height: 6ft
Family links with cricket: Grandfather (F.W.H.) played for Essex as batsman and wicket-keeper and toured with MCC. Father played for Navy
Education: Bradfield College
Other sports followed/played: Most – football, golf, fives, squash
Newspapers and magazines contributed to: *The Daily Telegraph*
Broadcasting career: Presenter and commentator with Sky until 1999; with Channel 4 1999 –
County as player: Hampshire
Role: Right-hand bat, right-arm medium bowler
County debut: 1978
County cap: 1982
Benefit: 1991 (£174,260)

1000 runs in a season: 10
1st-Class 50s: 81
1st-Class 100s: 35
1st-Class 200s: 1
1st-Class 5 w. in innings: 2
1st-Class catches: 215
One-Day 100s: 1
Overseas tours: England B to Sri Lanka 1985-86 (captain); England A to Zimbabwe and Kenya 1989-90 (captain)
Best batting: 206* Hampshire v Oxford University, The Parks 1982
Best bowling: 6-37 Hampshire v Somerset, Southampton 1989

First-Class Career Performances

	M	Inns	NO	Runs	HS	Avge	100s	Ct	St	Runs	Wkts	Avge	Best	5wl	10wM
Test															
All First	377	620	89	18262	206*	34.39	36	215	-	3235	72	44.93	6-37	2	-
1-day Int															

REEVE, D. A.   Channel 4

Name: Dermot Alexander Reeve
Born: 2 April 1963, Kowloon, Hong Kong
Height: 6ft
Marital status: Single
Children: Emily Kaye, 14 September 1988
Family links with cricket: 'Dad and brothers Mark and Phil played at school. Mark plays for Stanmore CC'
Education: King George V School, Hong Kong
Career outside media: After-dinner speaker and company director
Other sports played: 'Still play football for North Curry FC; love my golf; swim and boxercise for fun'
Other sports followed: Football (Man Utd), 'most sports except motor racing and horse racing'
Relaxations: 'Three months in the winter in Western Australia; beach, golf, wine, guitar'
Broadcasting career: Commentated on a few games for BBC TV and Sky while still playing. Covered 1994-95 Ashes tour for Sky. Covered 1999 World Cup for BBC. Channel 4 1999 –

Highlights of broadcasting career: 'Sharing the commentary box with Richie'
Newspapers and magazines contributed to: *The Times*, *Daily Mirror*, *The Cricketer*
Books published: *Winning Ways* (1996)
Players to watch for the future: David Sales, Ian Blackwell, Matthew Hoggard, Steffan Jones, Robert Key, Matt Bulbeck
Counties as player: Sussex, Warwickshire, Somerset
Role: Right-hand bat, right-arm medium bowler
County debut: 1983 (Sussex), 1988 (Warwickshire), 1998 (one-day, Somerset)
County cap: 1986 (Sussex), 1989 (Warwickshire)
Benefit: 1996 (Warwickshire)
Test debut: 1991-92
Tests: 3
One-Day Internationals: 29
1000 runs in a season: 2
50 wickets in a season: 2
1st-Class 50s: 52
1st-Class 100s: 6
1st-Class 200s: 1
1st-Class 5 w. in innings: 8
1st-Class catches: 200
One-Day 100s: 1
One-Day 5 w. in innings: 1
Career strike rate: 64.76
Overseas tours: England to New Zealand 1991-92, to India and Pakistan (World Cup) 1995-96
Overseas teams played for: Hong Kong
Highlights of playing career: 'Being told by Graham Gooch I was in the team for my England debut'
Extras: Awarded OBE 1996. One of *Wisden*'s Five Cricketers of the Year 1996
Opinions on cricket: 'One neutral umpire for Tests has certainly helped. I would like to see more use of the third umpire – e.g. each team can have four referrals per innings if they feel a wrong decision has been given. It would slow play slightly but be great for the crowd with the big screen, great for TV audiences and reverse the odd bad decision. I would still like to see a domestic 20-over competition played in the evening. We must attract a new audience who perhaps work nine-to-five and are busy at weekends. Make this competition more dynamic by allowing a side to lose 15 wickets per innings.'
Best batting: 202* Warwickshire v Northamptonshire, Northampton 1990
Best bowling: 7-37 Sussex v Lancashire, Lytham 1987

First-Class and International Career Performances

	M	Inns	NO	Runs	HS	Avge	100s	Ct	St	Runs	Wkts	Avge	Best	5wI	10wM
Test	3	5	0	124	59	24.80	-	1	-	60	2	30.00	1-4	-	-
All First	241	322	77	8541	202*	34.86	7	200	-	12232	456	26.82	7-37	8	-
1-day Int	29	21	9	291	35	24.25	-	12	-	820	20	41.00	3-20	-	

RUSCOE, S. Channel 4

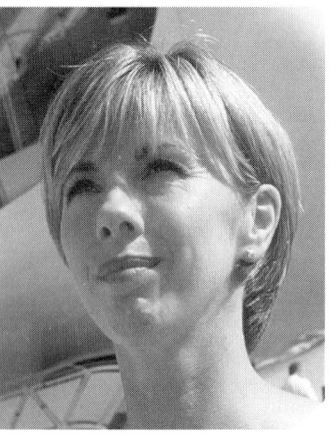

Name: Sybil Ruscoe
Born: 8 August 1960, Wem, Shropshire
Height: 5ft 3in
Marital status: Single
Family links with cricket: 'My dad played local club cricket in Shropshire. My mum knitted cricket sweaters and made fine cricket teas'
Education: Adams School, Wem
Other sports played: Skiing, golf, hockey ('had to retire from hockey at 17 after injury – blood clot on the brain')
Other sports followed: All sports, football (Stoke City)
Relaxations: Travel ('have trekked across Iceland and Chile'), poetry, the First World War, Shropshire, all music ('but especially Bob Marley, soul, Wyclef Jean, Miles Davis'), P.G. Wodehouse, *Daily Telegraph* crossword, laughing with friends
First broadcast for: Radio Wyvern, Worcester (radio); BBC TV – Top of the Pops (TV)
Broadcasting career: Local independent and BBC radio, including Radio One *Breakfast Show* with Simon Mayo and Radio 5 Live. Channel 4 cricket
Highlights of broadcasting career: 'Meeting Muhammad Ali at the Atlanta Olympics in 1996. Presenting a three-hour radio show from the Lord's Pavilion. Interviewing the anti-apartheid campaigner, the late Archbishop Trevor Huddleston'
Newspapers and magazines contributed to: *Daily Telegraph*, *Wolverhampton Express & Star*, *Newport & Market Drayton Advertiser*, *North Shropshire Journal*
Books published: 'Currently writing a semi-autobiographical cricket/media novel'
Players to watch for the future: Gary Pratt, Ian Pattison, Ben Platt (Shropshire)
County as player: Did not play first-class cricket but is an 'enthusiastic beach and garden cricketer – useful leg-spinner'
Highlights of playing career: 'Reverse-sweeping Henry Olonga on Southend beach.

Facing Allan Donald at Edgbaston. Fielding with Michael Slater at the Oswestry Disabled Cricket Club. Being complimented by Lord Cowdrey on my batting style at Arundel'

Opinions on cricket: 'The ECB, counties and MCC should all be putting even more effort into making cricket as "inclusive" as possible. Too often certain sections of people still feel excluded from the game. We should all – from broadcasters to players – be campaigning for more cricket in schools.'

Did not play first-class cricket

SELVEY, M. W. W.   BBC Test Match Special

Name: <u>Michael</u> Walter William Selvey
Born: 25 April 1948, London
Height: 6ft 2in
Wife and date of marriage: Sarah, 23 October 1992
Children: Nichola, 12 May 1975 ('by first marriage'); Joshua, Adam and Hannah, 9 January 1997 (triplets)
Education: Battersea Grammar School; University of Manchester; Cambridge University
Other sports played: Golf (6 handicap)
Other sports followed: 'Most that do not involve horses, cars, footballers, wrestlers, attempts to beat people senseless, or pastimes masquerading as sport'
Relaxations: Golf, gym, kids, pub, guitar, harmonica, reading, cooking, music
First broadcast for: *Test Match Special*, India 1985 (radio); BBC – John Player League (TV)
Broadcasting career: Regular summariser for *TMS* since 1985
Highlights of broadcasting career: 'Any England win. Any great player in top form'
Newspapers and magazines contributed to: *The Guardian* (Cricket Correspondent 1987 –), *Wisden Cricket Monthly*
Books published: *The Ashes Surrendered* (1989)
Players to watch for the future: Joshua, Adam and Hannah Selvey
Counties as player: Surrey, Middlesex, Glamorgan; also Cambridge University
Role: Right-hand bat, right-arm fast-medium bowler
County debut: 1968 (Surrey), 1972 (Middlesex), 1983 (Glamorgan)
County cap: 1973 (Middlesex), 1983 (Glamorgan)

Test debut: 1976
Tests: 3
50 wickets in a season: 6
100 wickets in a season: 1
1st-Class 50s: 4
1st-Class 5 w. in innings: 38
1st-Class 10 w. in match: 4
1st-Class catches: 80
One-Day 5 w. in innings: 2
Career strike rate: 58.90
Overseas tours: England to Australia and India 1976-77
Overseas teams played for: University-St Helier, Auckland 1978-80
Highlights of playing career: 'Taking 3-6 in first 20 balls in Tests'
Extras: Cambridge Blue 1971
Opinions on cricket: 'Not what it was, blah, blah … young players of today, blah, blah … pitches, blah, blah … spinners, blah, blah … money, blah, blah … in my day, blah blah … zzzzzz. All rubbish of course. Greatest improvements are in fielding, which is phenomenal, and the capacity to chase targets, which is equally so. Pleased that England pace bowlers have finally understood the standards required.'
Best batting: 67 Middlesex v Zimbabwe, Bulawayo 1980-81
Best bowling: 7-20 Middlesex v Gloucestershire, Gloucester 1976

First-Class and International Career Performances

	M	Inns	NO	Runs	HS	Avge	100s	Ct	St	Runs	Wkts	Avge	Best	5wI	10wM
Test	3	5	3	15	5*	7.50	-	1	-	343	6	57.16	4-41	-	-
All First	278	278	88	2399	67	12.62	-	80	-	20582	772	26.66	7-20	38	4
1-day Int															

SLATER, M. J.   Channel 4

Name: <u>Michael</u> Jonathon Slater
Role: Right-hand bat, leg-spin bowler
Born: 21 February 1970,
Wagga Wagga, New South Wales
Height: 5ft 9in
Nickname: Slats
Broadcasting career: Joined Channel 4 for the 2001 Ashes series
Books published: *Slats Opens Up* (autobiography)
County as player: Derbyshire
County debut: 1998
County cap: 1998
Test debut: 1993

Tests: 74
One-Day Internationals: 42
1st-Class 50s: 66
1st-Class 100s: 33
1st-Class catches: 108
Education: Wagga Wagga High School, NSW
Overseas tours: Australia to England 1993, to Sharjah 1993-94, to South Africa 1993-94, to Sri Lanka 1994-95, to Pakistan 1994-95, to West Indies 1994-95, to Sri Lanka 1996-97, to India 1996-97, to England 1997, to India 1997-98, to Pakistan 1998-99, to West Indies 1998-99, to Sri Lanka 1999, to Zimbabwe 1999, to New Zealand 1999-2000, to England 2001
Overseas teams played for: University of New South Wales; New South Wales

Extras: Scored three Test 100s against the 1998-99 England tourists, his 123 at Sydney (the third) accounting for 66 per cent of Australia's second innings total of 184; only Australia's Charles Bannerman had made a higher percentage of a side's innings total in a Test match. Second in list of leading Test run-scorers of 1999 with 1051 (av. 45.70).
Best batting: 221 Australia v Karachi, Karachi 1998-99
Best bowling: 1-4 Australia v Pakistan, Rawalpindi 1994-95

First-Class and International Career Performances

	M	Inns	NO	Runs	HS	Avge	100s	Ct	St	Runs	Wkts	Avge	Best	5wl	10wM
Test	74	131	7	5312	219	42.83	14	33	-	10	1	10.00	1-4	-	-
All First	196	347	18	13722	221	41.70	33	108	-	97	3	32.33	1-4	-	-
1-day Int	42	42	1	987	73	24.07	-	9	-	11	0	-	-	-	-

SMITH, I. D. S. Channel 4

Name: <u>Ian</u> David Stockley Smith
Born: 28 February 1957, Nelson, New Zealand
Height: 5ft 9in
Wife and date of marriage: Louise, 29 May 1982
Children: Jarrod (17), Jacob (10), Angus (6)
Family links with cricket: Two eldest sons play school and representative cricket
Education: Palmerston North Boys High School; Rongotai College
Career outside media: Banking
Other sports played: Played representative football at youth level, club golfer
Other sports followed: Football (Tottenham Hotspur), rugby (All Blacks, The Hurricanes, Hawkes Bay)
First broadcast for: Classic Hits 97FM (radio): TVNZ (TV)

Broadcasting career: TVNZ (6 years), SkySport, NZ (4 years), Channel 9 (Australia), Channel 4 (UK), TWI (India and West Indies), Supersport (South Africa), World Tel (India and Pakistan)
Books published: *Smithy – Just the Drummer in the Band* (1989)
Players to watch for the future: Brett Lee, Andrew Flintoff, Andre Adams, Makhaya Ntini
County as player: Did not play county cricket
Role: Right-hand bat, wicket-keeper
Test debut: 1980-81
Tests: 63
1st-Class 50s: 24
1st-Class 100s: 1
1st-Class catches: 419
1st-Class stumpings: 36
Overseas tours: 17 overseas tours to Australia, England, India, Pakistan, Sri Lanka and West Indies
Overseas teams played for: Central Districts, 1975-86; Auckland, 1986-92
Highlights of playing career: '1992 World Cup and series wins against Australia 1985 and England 1986'
Best batting: 173 New Zealand v India, Auckland 1989-90

	M	Inns	NO	Runs	HS	Avge	100s	Ct	St	Runs	Wkts	Avge	Best	5wI	10wM
Test	63	88	17	1815	173	25.56	2	168	8	5	0	-		-	-	-
All First	178	250	42	5570	173	26.77	6	419	36	37	0	-		-	-	-
1-day Int	98	77	16	1055	62*	17.29	-	81	5	-	-	-		-	-

WILLIS, R. G. D.　　　　　　　　*SkySports*

Name: Robert (<u>Bob</u>) George Dylan Willis
Born: 30 May 1949, Sunderland
Height: 6ft 6in
Family links with cricket: Brother, David, kept wicket for Blackheath CC
Education: Royal Grammar School, Guildford
Other sports played: Football (kept goal for Guildford City)
Newspapers and magazines contributed to: Include *Wisden Cricket Monthly*
Books published: Include *Diary of a Cricket Season* (1979); *Cricket Revolution* (1981)
Counties as player: Surrey, Warwickshire
Role: Right-hand bat, right-arm fast bowler
County debut: 1969 (Surrey), 1972 (Warwickshire)
County cap: 1972 (Warwickshire)
Benefit: 1981 (Warwickshire; £44,951)
Test debut: 1970-71
Tests: 90
One-Day Internationals: 64
50 wickets in a season: 5
1st-Class 50s: 2
1st-Class 5 w. in innings: 34
1st-Class 10 w. in match: 2
1st-Class catches: 134
One-Day 5 w. in innings: 4
Career strike rate: 53.37
Overseas tours: England to Australia and New Zealand 1970-71, 1974-75, to West Indies 1973-74, 1980-81 (vice-captain; returned early, injured), to Australia and India 1976-77, 1979-80 (vice-captain), to Pakistan and New Zealand 1977-78, 1983-84 (captain), to Australia 1978-79 (vice-captain), 1982-83 (captain), to India and Sri Lanka 1981-82 (vice-captain)

Extras: Captained England in 18 Test matches. One of *Wisden*'s Five Cricketers of the Year 1978. Awarded MBE 1982

Best batting: 72 Warwickshire v Indians, Edgbaston 1982

Best bowling: 8-32 Warwickshire v Gloucestershire, Bristol 1977

First-Class and International Career Performances

	M	Inns	NO	Runs	HS	Avge	100s	Ct	St	Runs	Wkts	Avge	Best	5wI	10wM
Test	90	128	55	840	28*	11.50	-	39	-	8190	325	25.20	8-43	16	-
All First	308	333	145	2690	72	14.30	-	134	-	22468	899	24.99	8-32	34	2
1-day Int	64	22	14	83	24	10.37	-	22	-	1968	80	24.60	4-11	-	

QUIZ ANSWERS

1. Alvin Kallicharran (206, Warwicks v Oxon 1984); Vince Wells (201, Leics v Berks 1996)
2. The match was abandoned and the result decided by the first 'bowl-out' tie-break, which Herts won
3. Bas Zuiderent (now of Sussex, then of Holland)
4. John Mortimore
5. Worcestershire and Gloucestershire (the player in question was Kabir Ali of Worcs)
6. Ian Gould
7. 65 (60 overs per side from 1964)
8. Chris Tavaré
9. David Smith (Sussex); Neil and Paul Smith (Warwicks)
10. Jason Laney (ended up with 153)
11. Mark Ramprakash
12. Robin Smith (8 centuries) and Chris Smith (7)
13. 2000 (Gloucestershire v Warwickshire)
14. Richard Hadlee
15. Andrew Flintoff
16. Geoffrey Boycott (146, Yorkshire v Surrey 1965)
17. Alan Knott (Kent and England); Farokh Engineer (Lancashire and India)
18. Mike Brearley
19. Peter Such
20. Rob Bailey
21. Lancashire (a total of four times)
22. Charlie van der Gucht
23. Tom Moody (180*) and Tim Curtis (136*)
24. Jack Simmons (for Lancashire)
25. Rachael Heyhoe-Flint (Sussex v Shropshire 1997; she chose James Kirtley)
26. Holland
27. James Pipe (Worcestershire; 8, all caught, v Herts 2001)
28. Sussex (although strictly speaking the competition was known as the Knockout Cup for the first year)
29. David Gower
30. Khalid 'Billy' Ibadulla
31. Colin and Alan Wells
32. Keith Fletcher
33. Jack Bond's
34. Keith Dutch
35. Waqar Younis (Surrey) and Aqib Javed (Hampshire)
36. Because there were no grass wickets in Holland
37. Andy Pick
38. David Thomas
39. Ed Joyce (Middlesex)
40. Graham Dilley
41. Lancashire and Warwickshire
42. Barrie Leadbeater (Yorkshire)
43. Rajesh Rao
44. John Lever (5-8) and Keith Boyce (5-22)
45. David Hughes
46. John Emburey
47. Kevin Parsons, brother of Somerset's Keith
48. The scores were tied, but Derbyshire won by virtue of having lost fewer wickets
49. Geoff (Greenidge) and Roger (Marshall)
50. David Graveney, Roger Knight, David Shepherd

51. Brian Hardie
52. Bob Taylor's
53. Alec Stewart
54. Middlesex in 1980
55. Graham Rose's (for Somerset)
56. Asif Din
57. Dermot Reeve (for Sussex 1986; for Warwickshire 1989, 1995)
58. Clive Lloyd
59. Robin Hobbs
60. 1999
61. Shahid Afridi's
62. Alan Ward, Harold Rhodes, Fred Rumsey
63. Tim Lamb (ECB chief executive) and Mike Selvey
64. Derbyshire; Kim Barnett
65. Michael Holding (for Derbyshire)
66. Clive Radley (for Middlesex 1977, 1984)
67. Scotland
68. Nick Knight's (151)
69. Ted Dexter
70. Curtly Ambrose (Northants) and Winston Benjamin (Leics)
71. Keith Parsons
72. Trevor Jesty
73. Tony and Mike Buss
74. 1983
75. Glen Chapple
76. Stuart MacGill
77. Vic Marks (Somerset)
78. Alan Butcher, father of Mark and Gary Butcher; Grahame Clinton, father of Richard Clinton
79. Mervyn Kitchen, Graham Burgess, Ken Palmer, Roy Palmer
80. Wayne Daniel
81. John Carr (ECB director of cricket operations)
82. Murray Goodwin
83. Jim Standen (West Ham United in 1964)
84. 1964 (the top five Minor Counties were included that year)
85. Imran Khan and Garth Le Roux
86. Alan (A.C.) Smith
87. 1999
88. Roland Lefebvre
89. 1979
90. Peter Willey, George Sharp, Neil Mallender
91. 1995
92. Sussex
93. Micky and Alec Stewart; Richard and Ben Hutton
94. Bishen Bedi (India); Mushtaq Mohammad and Sarfraz Nawaz (Pakistan)
95. Eldine Baptiste
96. Mark Benson
97. Andy Lloyd
98. Geoff Cook (director of cricket at Durham)
99. 1980
100. Colin Miller

THE 2001 SEASON

ROLL OF HONOUR 2001

CRICINFO COUNTY CHAMPIONSHIP

Division One

		P	W	L	D	T	Bt	Bl	Pts
1	Yorkshire (I/3)	16	9	3	4	0	50	45	219
2	Somerset (I/5)	16	6	2	8	0	55	44	203
3	Kent (I/6)	16	4	3	9	0	48	44	175
4	Surrey (I/1)	16	3	1	12	0	43	43	169.50
5	Leicestershire (I/4)	16	5	6	5	0	38	47	165
6	Lancashire (I/2)	16	4	5	7	0	38	39	153
7	Northamptonshire (II/1)	16	2	5	9	0	52	36	148
8	Glamorgan (II/3)	16	2	5	9	0	36	37	133
9	Essex (II/2)	16	2	7	7	0	28	36	116

The bottom three counties were relegated to Division Two for the 2002 season

Division Two

		P	W	L	D	T	Bt	Bl	Pts
1	Sussex (II/9)	16	9	3	4	0	42	42	208
2	Hampshire (I/7)	16	7	2	7	0	34	44	192
3	Warwickshire (II/6)	16	5	1	10	0	46	40	185.75
4	Gloucestershire (II/4)	16	5	5	6	0	46	43	173
5	Middlesex (II/8)	16	4	3	9	0	46	42	172
6	Worcestershire (II/5)	16	4	5	7	0	35	41	151.75
7	Nottinghamshire (II/7)	16	3	7	6	0	44	38	141.25
8	Durham (I/8)	16	3	6	7	0	32	44	140
9	Derbyshire (I/9)	16	1	9	6	0	20	37	92.25

The top three counties were promoted to Division One for the 2002 season

Teams are docked 0.25 points for each over they fail to bowl of the target figure of 16 per hour

NORWICH UNION LEAGUE

Division One

		P	W	L	T	NR	Pts
1	Kent (I/5)	16	11	2	1	2	50
2	Leicestershire (I/4)	16	11	4	0	1	46
3	Warwickshire (II/3)	16	8	5	0	3	38
4	Somerset (I/6)	16	7	7	1	1	32
5	Nottinghamshire (II/2)	16	7	8	0	1	30
6	Yorkshire (I/2)	16	7	9	0	0	28
7	Gloucestershire (I/1)	16	6	9	0	1	26
8	Surrey (II/1)	16	6	10	0	0	24
9	Northamptonshire (I/3)	16	3	12	0	1	14

The bottom three counties were relegated to Division Two for the 2002 season

Division Two

		P	W	L	T	NR	Pts
1	Glamorgan (II/6)	16	11	3	0	2	48
2	Durham (II/7)	16	9	4	0	3	42
3	Worcestershire (I/7)	16	9	5	0	2	40
4	Hampshire (II/8)	16	9	6	0	1	38
5	Sussex (I/9)	16	8	7	0	1	34
6	Lancashire (I/8)	16	5	8	0	3	26
7	Essex (II/5)	16	5	9	1	1	24
8	Middlesex (II/4)	16	3	9	1	3	20
9	Derbyshire (II/9)	16	4	12	0	0	16

The top three counties were promoted to Division One for the 2002 season

CHELTENHAM & GLOUCESTER TROPHY

Winners: Somerset
Runners-up: Leicestershire

BENSON AND HEDGES CUP

Winners: Surrey
Runners-up: Gloucestershire

2001 AVERAGES (all first-class matches)

BATTING AVERAGES – including fielding
Qualifying requirements: 6 completed innings

Name	Matches	Inns	NO	Runs	HS	Avge	100s	50s	Ct	St
D R Martyn	9	14	5	942	176*	104.66	5	3	3	-
D S Lehmann	13	19	2	1416	252	83.29	5	5	6	-
A C Gilchrist	8	10	2	663	152	82.87	3	2	27	4
M E Hussey	16	30	4	2055	329*	79.03	5	9	19	-
D P Fulton	18	27	2	1892	208*	75.68	9	3	27	-
M E Waugh	9	15	6	644	120	71.55	2	2	12	-
S G Law	13	23	3	1311	153	65.55	4	8	18	-
S R Waugh	7	11	2	583	157*	64.77	3	-	5	-
I R Bell	11	16	3	836	135	64.30	3	4	11	-
N H Fairbrother	12	19	4	939	179*	62.60	4	1	16	-
G P Thorpe	5	7	0	430	148	61.42	2	1	8	-
M W Goodwin	17	32	5	1654	203*	61.25	7	5	8	-
R T Ponting	9	15	1	844	147*	60.28	3	5	11	-
R R Montgomerie	18	33	4	1704	160*	58.75	8	5	17	-
Saeed Anwar	4	6	0	351	201	58.50	1	1	1	-
M A Wagh	16	24	2	1277	315	58.04	3	6	4	-
K P Pietersen	15	26	4	1275	218*	57.95	4	6	14	-
J Cox	15	25	3	1264	186	57.45	1	9	6	-
M A Butcher	15	25	2	1300	230	56.52	3	6	15	-
G A Hick	17	28	3	1409	201	56.36	6	3	20	-
M B Loye	12	21	3	1003	197	55.72	3	4	4	-
R J Warren	16	26	2	1303	194	54.29	4	7	8	-
J P Maher	14	23	2	1133	217	53.95	4	3	13	-
P D Collingwood	13	24	3	1108	153	52.76	3	6	10	-
M P Vaughan	9	16	0	839	133	52.43	3	4	8	-
S P Fleming	14	23	2	1091	151	51.95	4	6	22	-
C J Adams	15	23	2	1086	192	51.71	3	7	28	-
A Dale	15	23	3	1026	204	51.30	3	4	9	-
M L Love	15	29	2	1364	149*	50.51	1	13	20	-
M R Ramprakash	13	22	0	1094	146	49.72	4	4	7	-
I D Blackwell	11	17	0	839	122	49.35	4	3	5	-
D L Hemp	17	25	5	987	186*	49.35	4	2	12	-
A P Grayson	16	29	3	1275	189	49.03	6	1	7	-
W K Hegg	13	20	4	782	133	48.87	2	5	35	3
J N Snape	14	21	3	868	131	48.22	3	5	10	-
M J Wood (Yorks)	14	23	1	1060	124	48.18	4	6	9	-
G S Blewett	16	30	3	1292	137*	47.85	5	5	24	-
R S C Martin-Jenkins	9	15	4	524	113	47.63	1	3	4	-
S P James	9	15	3	568	156	47.33	1	4	5	-
D P Ostler	10	12	1	520	121	47.27	2	2	22	-
A Symonds	8	12	0	563	131	46.91	2	2	13	-
M P Bicknell	15	22	6	748	110*	46.75	1	4	5	-

Name	Matches	Inns	NO	Runs	HS	Avge	100s	50s	Ct	St
C G Taylor	12	20	0	930	196	46.50	3	4	6	-
D J Marsh	9	16	3	600	138*	46.15	1	5	13	-
T R Ward	12	21	2	872	160*	45.89	4	2	7	-
R W T Key	18	28	0	1281	132	45.75	4	7	7	-
J E Morris	8	16	2	640	170	45.71	2	4	3	-
M J DiVenuto	14	25	1	1082	165	45.08	4	5	15	-
D Byas	16	24	5	853	110*	44.89	4	2	38	-
A J Strauss	17	28	1	1210	176	44.81	3	6	7	-
M J Walker	17	25	3	985	124	44.77	4	3	9	-
K J Barnett	14	25	2	1029	114	44.73	1	7	10	-
N C Johnson	17	27	3	1073	105*	44.70	2	8	28	-
N V Knight	13	19	2	759	140	44.64	2	3	18	-
M J Wood (So)	7	12	0	529	122	44.08	1	4	2	-
B F Smith	17	30	2	1222	180*	43.64	5	2	19	-
C W G Bassano	8	14	2	523	186*	43.58	2	2	5	-
Inzamam-ul-Haq	6	7	0	299	114	42.71	1	1	4	-
R M S Weston	10	17	1	672	135*	42.00	3	1	5	-
W P C Weston	18	31	4	1132	192	41.92	2	7	12	-
O A Shah	15	25	0	1040	203	41.60	3	4	14	-
P D Bowler	14	22	2	827	164	41.35	2	4	14	-
M E Trescothick	10	17	0	700	147	41.17	2	3	9	-
N D Burns	17	28	7	862	111	41.04	1	6	65	3
A Habib	13	21	2	779	153	41.00	3	3	8	-
A L Penberthy	15	24	1	942	132*	40.95	3	5	11	-
A N Aymes	16	19	5	572	112*	40.85	1	4	43	2
I J Harvey	10	15	2	531	130*	40.84	2	1	8	-
J P Crawley	14	24	2	898	280	40.81	2	5	4	-
A J Hollioake	13	20	1	758	97	39.89	-	7	15	-
M L Hayden	10	17	1	636	142	39.75	1	3	6	-
B L Hutton	14	22	2	786	139	39.30	3	2	20	-
D R Brown	16	20	3	666	104	39.17	1	6	16	-
E T Smith	18	28	1	1054	116	39.03	3	4	5	-
A J Stewart	12	18	3	581	106	38.73	1	2	36	1
B M Shafayat	3	6	0	231	75	38.50	-	2	-	-
P A Nixon	18	24	7	651	87*	38.29	-	4	44	4
U Afzaal	15	28	1	1011	138	37.44	1	8	9	-
R C Russell	10	12	2	373	91*	37.30	-	2	42	2
A Singh	18	31	2	1054	168	36.34	2	4	5	-
M J Lumb	4	7	1	218	122	36.33	1	1	-	-
K A Parsons	5	8	1	254	139	36.28	1	-	5	-
D J Bicknell	16	29	0	1050	167	36.20	3	3	8	-
Shahid Afridi	6	9	0	325	164	36.11	1	1	8	-
M Burns	17	28	1	961	221	35.59	1	7	13	-
K J Piper	15	17	5	426	92*	35.50	-	2	39	1
D R Hewson	14	25	2	816	168	35.47	2	4	6	-
M N Lathwell	13	21	1	702	99	35.10	-	8	9	-
M G N Windows	16	27	3	840	174	35.00	3	3	6	-
Azhar Mahmood	4	7	1	209	80*	34.83	-	1	1	-
M H Yardy	17	29	6	796	87*	34.60	-	5	9	-

Name	Matches	Inns	NO	Runs	HS	Avge	100s	50s	Ct	St
D A Kenway	16	30	3	932	166	34.51	2	4	16	-
N Hussain	6	10	1	306	64	34.00	-	3	-	-
S J Rhodes	15	20	7	442	52	34.00	-	1	51	1
S D Stubbings	17	31	0	1047	127	33.77	3	6	6	-
I J Sutcliffe	17	31	1	1004	203	33.46	2	5	5	-
V H Kumar	4	7	1	199	86*	33.16	-	1	2	-
R J Turner	17	26	3	761	115*	33.08	1	3	59	-
D D J Robinson	18	31	2	955	118*	32.93	3	4	11	-
K Newell	7	11	2	296	103	32.88	1	1	5	-
D C Nash	15	19	5	458	103*	32.71	1	4	39	4
P N Weekes	17	27	5	719	107	32.68	1	5	15	-
C P Schofield	9	14	2	390	80*	32.50	-	4	8	-
M A Atherton	11	21	1	649	160	32.45	1	3	17	-
J J B Lewis	17	32	1	1000	129	32.25	3	3	6	-
A McGrath	9	15	2	417	116*	32.07	1	2	6	-
C White	12	21	2	605	186	31.84	2	-	6	-
A J Tudor	9	14	1	413	116	31.76	1	1	2	-
J L Langer	6	11	2	285	104*	31.66	2	-	5	-
G R Napier	10	16	0	506	104	31.62	1	2	4	-
R L Johnson	13	15	3	379	68	31.58	-	2	3	-
A D Brown	13	20	0	630	122	31.50	3	2	3	-
M J Powell (Warks)	17	24	0	755	236	31.45	2	2	14	-
M W Alleyne	16	26	3	718	136	31.21	2	2	12	1
A Flintoff	14	23	1	686	120	31.18	1	2	17	-
M A Carberry	6	10	0	311	84	31.10	-	1	6	-
P Johnson	13	24	2	684	149	31.09	2	2	7	-
G Chapple	13	19	3	497	155	31.06	1	2	3	-
M P Maynard	13	20	0	621	145	31.05	1	3	6	-
B C Hollioake	12	19	0	586	118	30.84	1	4	18	-
Younis Khan	4	6	0	185	65	30.83	-	2	1	-
C M W Read	16	27	5	666	78	30.27	-	5	43	1
V J Wells	13	22	1	628	138	29.90	2	2	8	-
M J Chilton	14	24	1	684	104	29.73	1	4	10	-
S K Warne	8	10	2	237	69	29.62	-	2	13	-
M J Powell (Glam)	15	25	2	681	108	29.60	2	4	12	-
J C Scuderi	12	17	2	444	89	29.60	-	3	2	-
S D Thomas	15	21	2	562	138	29.57	1	4	5	-
S J Cook	10	11	3	236	93*	29.50	-	1	3	-
K P Dutch	16	22	4	530	118	29.44	1	3	19	-
M C J Ball	12	16	3	379	68	29.15	-	3	19	-
R C Irani	17	29	2	779	119	28.85	1	6	4	-
L D Sutton	15	27	3	688	140*	28.66	2	1	9	-
J A Daley	9	16	1	428	128*	28.53	1	1	1	-
G M Fellows	12	17	1	455	63	28.43	-	3	4	-
M J Slater	8	13	1	341	77	28.41	-	2	1	-
P C L Holloway	12	21	1	567	85	28.35	-	4	3	-
P R Pollard	10	12	1	309	131*	28.09	1	-	5	-
M A Roseberry	11	17	2	420	87	28.00	-	2	9	-
V S Solanki	18	29	0	802	112	27.65	3	2	16	-

Name	Matches	Inns	NO	Runs	HS	Avge	100s	50s	Ct	St
R D B Croft	10	15	2	353	93	27.15	-	3	6	-
R J Blakey	15	21	6	405	78*	27.00	-	3	49	5
J S Foster	16	25	0	664	103	26.56	1	4	31	8
I J Ward	16	27	1	690	79	26.53	-	4	6	-
G W White	17	32	4	739	141	26.39	2	1	17	2
N Peng	13	23	2	551	101	26.23	1	3	8	-
A J Bichel	16	24	0	627	78	26.12	-	3	5	-
J W Cook	9	16	1	391	88	26.06	-	4	5	-
I D K Salisbury	15	21	4	440	54	25.88	-	1	9	-
S R Lampitt	10	13	5	205	42*	25.62	-	-	4	-
M P Speight	8	15	3	304	67*	25.33	-	1	3	-
D Ripley	15	25	6	481	95	25.31	-	2	45	3
G P Butcher	4	8	1	175	56	25.00	-	1	1	-
R A Smith	16	26	2	598	118	24.91	3	1	4	-
A C Morris	16	19	2	423	65	24.88	-	3	10	-
A D Mascarenhas	15	23	5	447	104	24.83	1	1	8	-
M J Brown	5	9	1	197	60*	24.62	-	2	2	-
M J G Davis	15	22	4	439	52	24.38	-	1	5	-
S A Richardson	7	11	2	215	69	23.88	-	2	6	-
J I D Kerr	8	12	5	167	36	23.85	-	-	1	-
D G Cork	7	11	0	262	128	23.81	1	-	6	-
B Zuiderent	17	27	1	619	122	23.80	1	3	18	-
A S Rollins	6	10	1	214	65	23.77	-	1	3	-
D A Leatherdale	17	27	3	570	93	23.75	-	2	7	-
W S Kendall	17	30	3	638	94	23.62	-	3	11	-
D R Law	16	26	1	586	103	23.44	1	1	11	-
S A A Block	4	7	1	139	56*	23.16	-	1	1	-
M A Ealham	12	15	2	299	153*	23.00	1	-	8	-
S D Udal	16	20	2	414	81	23.00	-	3	5	-
Rashid Latif	5	6	0	137	71	22.83	-	1	15	1
M P Dowman	14	26	1	567	145*	22.68	1	1	4	-
J W M Dalrymple	5	10	1	203	70	22.55	-	1	8	-
M A Wallace	10	16	3	290	80*	22.30	-	2	27	1
Abdur Razzaq	5	7	1	133	53	22.16	-	1	2	-
S D Peters	15	26	3	508	56*	22.08	-	1	6	-
D Gough	9	15	5	219	96	21.90	-	1	-	-
M V Fleming	17	23	5	393	59	21.83	-	1	6	-
A J Swann	13	22	0	479	113	21.77	1	2	9	-
K M Krikken	14	25	5	435	93*	21.75	-	3	34	1
Yousuf Youhana	6	8	0	174	80	21.75	-	1	-	-
G P Swann	15	25	0	543	61	21.72	-	3	9	-
N R C Dumelow	9	15	1	304	61	21.71	-	2	2	-
D I Stevens	8	14	2	259	63	21.58	-	1	2	-
R J Bailey	14	25	1	515	136*	21.45	1	2	8	-
B J Hyam	6	9	2	150	63	21.42	-	1	20	1
N M K Smith	14	14	2	254	54	21.16	-	1	2	-
T H C Hancock	6	11	0	230	55	20.90	-	1	7	-
V C Drakes	14	13	3	209	50	20.90	-	1	1	-
C E W Silverwood	8	9	1	167	70	20.87	-	1	2	-

Name	Matches	Inns	NO	Runs	HS	Avge	100s	50s	Ct	St
J P Pyemont	5	9	1	167	70	20.87	-	1	4	-
R S Clinton	8	15	1	283	58*	20.21	-	1	2	-
R J Cunliffe	5	8	1	141	48	20.14	-	-	5	-
A Pratt	16	28	4	476	68*	19.83	-	3	49	7
P A J DeFreitas	9	14	1	256	97	19.69	-	2	-	-
M J Prior	16	24	2	433	66	19.68	-	1	39	2
M A Gough	13	23	0	450	79	19.56	-	1	8	-
J P Taylor	12	17	3	273	53	19.50	-	1	3	-
I J Thomas	6	11	1	194	59	19.40	-	1	2	-
J Ormond	12	18	5	251	42	19.30	-	-	2	-
J M Dakin	7	11	0	211	69	19.18	-	1	1	-
G Welch	16	29	2	511	64	18.92	-	1	3	-
S L Watkin	15	17	7	188	38	18.80	-	-	5	-
P J Martin	9	12	3	169	51*	18.77	-	1	2	-
D L Maddy	17	29	1	521	111	18.60	1	2	15	-
U B A Rashid	14	21	1	367	106	18.35	1	-	1	-
L R Prittipaul	7	9	0	165	84	18.33	-	1	6	-
P J Prichard	7	11	0	201	111	18.27	1	-	1	-
B Lee	8	7	0	127	79	18.14	-	1	-	-
D S Lucas	5	8	0	145	41	18.12	-	-	-	-
I D Hunter	8	14	3	199	37	18.09	-	-	4	-
R K Illingworth	5	8	1	125	61*	17.85	-	1	-	-
G J Smith	15	20	9	195	44*	17.72	-	-	3	-
N Shahid	7	12	0	208	65	17.33	-	1	8	-
A P Cowan	15	24	3	360	68	17.14	-	2	8	-
M C Ilott	10	12	1	186	34	16.90	-	-	6	-
J J Haynes	5	8	0	133	57	16.62	-	1	7	-
P S Jones	16	16	5	180	29*	16.36	-	-	3	-
T M B Bailey	5	7	0	113	41	16.14	-	-	3	-
N G Hatch	9	16	8	129	24	16.12	-	-	1	-
J N Batty	10	16	1	239	59	15.93	-	1	26	2
D A Cosker	11	15	4	175	35	15.90	-	-	10	-
J N Gillespie	8	9	3	94	27*	15.66	-	-	3	-
M M Patel	17	19	3	247	38	15.43	-	-	9	-
T Lungley	6	11	4	108	47	15.42	-	-	-	-
G E Welton	12	22	0	337	61	15.31	-	2	5	-
R D Stemp	5	7	0	105	66	15.00	-	1	1	-
J M Golding	5	8	2	90	30	15.00	-	-	2	-
J D Lewry	17	18	4	202	47	14.42	-	-	7	-
K J Innes	4	7	1	86	40	14.33	-	-	1	-
A P Davies	4	7	1	85	40	14.16	-	-	2	-
J Wood	8	10	1	127	35	14.11	-	-	-	-
R S G Anderson	8	11	0	154	45	14.00	-	-	2	-
J B Hockley	7	13	1	166	29	13.83	-	-	6	-
R C J Williams	5	9	0	123	33	13.66	-	-	17	1
Saqlain Mushtaq	13	18	6	164	38	13.66	-	-	2	-
M J Rawnsley	15	21	5	210	39	13.12	-	-	6	-
C G Liptrot	12	14	4	128	22	12.80	-	-	4	-
G M Hamilton	8	9	0	114	34	12.66	-	-	1	-

Name	Matches	Inns	NO	Runs	HS	Avge	100s	50s	Ct	St
R J Logan	10	15	2	162	37*	12.46	-	-	4	-
N C Phillips	7	11	4	87	30	12.42	-	-	6	-
D M Cousins	8	10	3	87	27	12.42	-	-	-	-
A R C Fraser	13	12	0	149	41	12.41	-	-	4	-
M J Saggers	17	20	5	185	61*	12.33	-	1	1	-
M R Strong	9	13	4	110	34	12.22	-	-	2	-
S J Randall	4	7	1	73	28	12.16	-	-	1	-
T A Munton	9	13	1	145	50	12.08	-	1	2	-
M J Cawdron	6	9	2	82	29	11.71	-	-	1	-
K J Dean	8	12	2	117	23	11.70	-	-	2	-
R C Driver	5	8	0	93	35	11.62	-	-	5	-
G Keedy	13	15	8	81	20*	11.57	-	-	6	-
M M Betts	12	11	3	92	19	11.50	-	-	9	-
G D Bridge	7	13	2	125	39*	11.36	-	-	5	-
A R Caddick	9	15	4	122	49*	11.09	-	-	1	-
R J Kirtley	16	24	6	196	51*	10.88	-	1	8	-
P M Such	15	20	9	117	25	10.63	-	-	7	-
A D Mullally	14	13	5	82	36	10.25	-	-	4	-
J E Brinkley	10	13	2	111	65	10.09	-	1	4	-
M Muralitharan	7	8	1	70	21	10.00	-	-	4	-
P Aldred	8	13	1	120	35	10.00	-	-	5	-
T J Phillips	6	8	0	80	27	10.00	-	-	-	-
C R Taylor	3	6	0	60	18	10.00	-	-	1	-
T M Smith	6	10	2	79	19	9.87	-	-	4	-
S J Harmison	12	14	4	97	27	9.70	-	-	-	-
R K J Dawson	9	11	1	95	37	9.50	-	-	6	-
D E Malcolm	16	21	7	126	50	9.00	-	1	1	-
S P Jones	8	11	1	83	46	8.30	-	-	-	-
D W Fleming	5	6	0	49	20	8.16	-	-	-	-
Kadeer Ali	5	8	0	65	38	8.12	-	-	2	-
C D Crowe	7	10	1	73	42	8.11	-	-	4	-
J F Brown	11	12	5	56	35*	8.00	-	-	2	-
J E Bishop	8	12	2	74	18	7.40	-	-	-	-
T F Bloomfield	16	16	4	85	28	7.08	-	-	2	-
A Sheriyar	16	19	8	71	20	6.45	-	-	3	-
S P Kirby	10	10	2	49	15*	6.12	-	-	4	-
A J Harris	9	15	2	79	20*	6.07	-	-	-	-
E S H Giddins	12	14	8	36	9*	6.00	-	-	2	-
B J Trott	14	13	3	57	13	5.70	-	-	3	-
C B Keegan	7	10	2	45	30*	5.62	-	-	1	-
P C R Tufnell	17	20	8	52	11*	4.33	-	-	-	-
M P Smethurst	5	8	1	29	7	4.14	-	-	-	-
M A Robinson	14	15	7	32	10	4.00	-	-	1	-
G D Clough	4	6	0	22	8	3.66	-	-	1	-
L J Wharton	11	18	9	29	13*	3.22	-	-	1	-
J M M Averis	15	19	3	35	7*	2.18	-	-	3	-
M J Hoggard	8	8	2	11	4	1.83	-	-	-	-

BOWLING AVERAGES
Qualifying requirements: 10 wickets taken

Name	Overs	Mdns	Runs	Wkts	Avge	Best	5wI	10wM
C J Adams	40.2	6	111	10	11.10	4-28	-	-
Mushtaq Ahmed	69.2	18	176	14	12.57	8-49	1	1
G D McGrath	234.5	74	624	40	15.60	7-76	4	-
Kabir Ali	84.2	18	253	14	18.07	5-22	1	-
A D Mullally	477.4	151	1184	64	18.50	8-90	6	-
S K Warne	263	56	784	42	18.66	7-165	3	1
I J Harvey	288.4	92	773	41	18.85	5-33	2	-
M A Robinson	415.4	126	1083	56	19.33	5-35	3	-
M Muralitharan	484.5	159	971	50	19.42	6-53	5	1
C E W Silverwood	209.1	42	644	33	19.51	5-20	3	-
R S G Anderson	231.1	54	699	35	19.97	5-21	3	-
C T Tremlett	131.2	37	401	20	20.05	4-34	-	-
N Killeen	89	29	222	11	20.18	3-14	-	-
D W Fleming	138	32	390	19	20.52	6-59	1	-
Saqlain Mushtaq	567.2	157	1286	62	20.74	7-58	5	-
S P Kirby	280.3	60	980	47	20.85	7-50	3	1
M P Bicknell	541.5	132	1538	72	21.36	7-60	3	1
J E Brinkley	222.1	61	663	31	21.38	6-14	2	-
J Lewis	175.4	56	454	21	21.61	5-71	1	-
J E K Schofield	89.1	17	285	13	21.92	4-51	-	-
G Chapple	379.2	87	1174	53	22.15	6-46	4	-
Waqar Younis	119.1	23	399	18	22.16	5-23	1	-
M J Hoggard	240	58	733	32	22.90	6-51	2	-
G D Bridge	172	48	413	18	22.94	6-84	1	-
M A Ealham	226.5	68	574	25	22.96	6-64	2	-
C E Dagnall	83	16	279	12	23.25	6-50	1	-
R J Kirtley	566.3	135	1749	75	23.32	6-34	5	2
R L Johnson	463.2	89	1474	62	23.77	5-40	5	-
S J E Brown	115	29	333	14	23.78	6-70	1	-
M J Saggers	512.3	118	1551	64	24.23	6-92	3	-
G J Smith	446.2	103	1256	50	25.12	5-37	3	1
A Sheriyar	536.1	125	1795	71	25.28	6-88	3	-
A D Mascarenhas	399.3	112	1015	40	25.37	6-26	2	-
Wasim Akram	153	44	385	15	25.66	4-18	-	-
M C J Ball	348.4	94	876	34	25.76	6-23	2	-
G M Hamilton	211.2	43	672	26	25.84	5-27	1	-
K J Dean	250.5	58	888	34	26.11	6-73	2	1
J D Lewry	512.1	126	1548	59	26.23	7-42	3	1
D R Law	351	70	1103	42	26.26	6-53	3	-
B J Trott	372.5	68	1235	47	26.27	6-13	4	1
R J Sidebottom	278.2	75	710	27	26.29	4-49	-	-
M W Alleyne	374.4	87	1079	41	26.31	5-50	1	-
M M Betts	308.2	72	979	37	26.45	5-22	2	-
J M Dakin	122.3	23	427	16	26.68	4-53	-	-
A Richardson	395.5	111	983	36	27.30	5-89	1	-
A J Bichel	555.5	137	1804	66	27.33	6-44	4	1
P A J DeFreitas	303	66	934	34	27.47	6-65	1	-

Name	Overs	Mdns	Runs	Wkts	Avge	Best	5wI	10wM
C G Liptrot	308.4	80	966	35	27.60	3-12	-	-
J N Gillespie	228	54	801	29	27.62	5-37	2	-
V J Wells	181	47	498	18	27.66	5-36	1	-
S R Lampitt	203.2	49	669	24	27.87	5-22	1	-
A C Morris	472	107	1428	51	28.00	5-39	2	-
A K D Gray	92	23	281	10	28.10	4-128	-	-
D E Malcolm	546.1	94	1948	68	28.64	8-63	4	1
P C R Tufnell	690	166	1721	60	28.68	6-44	3	1
D L Maddy	237.3	45	804	28	28.71	5-67	1	-
J Ormond	485.4	113	1417	49	28.91	5-71	2	-
A R Caddick	351.2	53	1376	47	29.27	5-81	4	1
P J Martin	322.3	86	969	33	29.36	5-52	1	-
S D Udal	566.1	143	1610	54	29.81	7-74	1	-
P N Weekes	439.5	100	1198	40	29.95	5-90	1	-
T C Hicks	143	30	394	13	30.30	5-77	1	-
D R Brown	472.1	123	1284	42	30.57	6-60	1	1
D S Lehmann	139.1	33	368	12	30.66	3-13	-	-
M M Patel	524.2	158	1228	40	30.70	8-119	1	1
D Gough	321.4	55	1212	39	31.07	5-61	2	-
R K Illingworth	126.4	39	316	10	31.60	4-37	-	-
R S C Martin-Jenkins	248	63	764	24	31.83	4-18	-	-
R J Logan	329.1	53	1375	43	31.97	6-93	3	-
A G Wharf	127.4	19	448	14	32.00	5-63	1	-
M A Gough	157.3	34	449	14	32.07	5-66	1	-
R C Irani	354.5	96	1040	32	32.50	6-79	3	-
N M K Smith	314	75	813	25	32.52	4-76	-	-
M S Panesar	101.3	28	358	11	32.54	4-11	-	-
C R Miller	157.2	37	586	18	32.55	4-41	-	-
S L Watkin	472.4	113	1400	43	32.55	6-67	1	-
N M Carter	120	12	456	14	32.57	5-78	1	-
D M Cousins	333.4	54	1176	36	32.66	8-102	2	-
C B Keegan	170	38	588	18	32.66	4-54	-	-
P J Franks	149.1	33	429	13	33.00	4-65	-	-
G M Fellows	156	43	398	12	33.16	3-23	-	-
A Symonds	106.2	23	333	10	33.30	3-28	-	-
N G Hatch	248.4	43	867	26	33.34	3-42	-	-
R K J Dawson	315.5	69	1014	30	33.80	6-82	2	-
M C Ilott	287	65	921	27	34.11	5-85	1	-
P S Jones	560	100	2015	59	34.15	5-115	1	-
T F Bloomfield	479.4	79	1709	50	34.18	5-58	2	-
T A Munton	242.1	61	659	19	34.68	5-85	1	-
S J Cook	218.1	47	696	20	34.80	3-10	-	-
T M Smith	91.3	15	383	11	34.81	4-61	-	-
C White	214.1	52	599	17	35.23	4-57	-	-
A J Tudor	251.1	53	927	26	35.65	5-44	2	-
A F Giles	154.5	41	429	12	35.75	5-46	1	-
Abdur Razzaq	105.3	19	359	10	35.90	3-61	-	-
S J Harmison	419.5	86	1262	35	36.05	6-111	2	-
A N Bressington	120.4	31	397	11	36.09	3-42	-	-

Name	Overs	Mdns	Runs	Wkts	Avge	Best	5wI	10wM
U B A Rashid	134.2	38	398	11	36.18	4-9	-	-
K P Dutch	367	64	1268	35	36.22	4-32	-	-
D A Leatherdale	158	39	580	16	36.25	4-70	-	-
M A Wagh	184	37	473	13	36.38	3-3	-	-
V C Drakes	505.2	107	1537	42	36.59	5-37	1	-
E S H Giddins	352.5	83	1102	30	36.73	5-48	1	-
G Welch	502.3	108	1631	44	37.06	6-30	3	-
A R C Fraser	469.4	140	1204	32	37.62	3-46	-	-
J M M Averis	462.1	102	1621	43	37.69	5-55	1	-
G R Napier	104.1	15	453	12	37.75	3-55	-	-
J E Bishop	224	39	915	24	38.12	5-148	1	-
J P Hewitt	83	8	386	10	38.60	3-72	-	-
R D B Croft	328.3	86	927	24	38.62	5-95	2	1
A Flintoff	245.3	48	736	19	38.73	3-36	-	-
A J Harris	330.4	84	1097	28	39.17	6-98	1	-
J A R Blain	153	16	673	17	39.58	6-42	1	-
N C Johnson	252.5	42	911	23	39.60	4-20	-	-
M J G Davis	349.3	82	956	24	39.83	6-116	1	-
A L Penberthy	339.2	70	1019	25	40.76	4-39	-	-
N C Phillips	285.5	60	939	23	40.82	5-64	1	-
G Keedy	387.1	76	1150	28	41.07	5-73	2	-
M V Fleming	302.4	59	910	22	41.36	4-53	-	-
M N Malik	104	21	414	10	41.40	5-57	1	-
M J Cawdron	168	50	498	12	41.50	4-79	-	-
D A Cosker	423.5	84	1390	33	42.12	4-48	-	-
I D K Salisbury	396.2	72	1151	27	42.62	5-95	1	-
I D Hunter	181.3	27	700	16	43.75	4-55	-	-
Shahid Afridi	166.1	41	569	13	43.76	5-84	1	-
T Lungley	115.4	14	527	12	43.91	3-58	-	-
R D Stemp	244.4	51	707	16	44.18	3-39	-	-
B Lee	186.5	30	752	17	44.23	3-17	-	-
I D Blackwell	291.4	72	896	20	44.80	5-122	1	-
M J Rawnsley	446.2	122	1211	27	44.85	3-55	-	-
M Burns	138.5	23	539	12	44.91	6-54	1	-
G P Swann	422.3	87	1365	30	45.50	5-34	1	-
A P Cowan	462.4	104	1522	33	46.12	3-64	-	-
J P Taylor	379.2	49	1345	29	46.37	4-100	-	-
J F Brown	473.5	102	1407	28	50.25	5-107	1	-
S D Thomas	420.1	56	1668	33	50.54	4-54	-	-
J P Pyemont	146	31	512	10	51.20	4-101	-	-
D G Cork	206.5	44	618	12	51.50	4-122	-	-
N R C Dumelow	185.5	34	723	14	51.64	4-81	-	-
S P Jones	198.2	29	887	17	52.17	3-36	-	-
M R Strong	256.3	46	992	19	52.21	3-98	-	-
C P Schofield	252.1	52	757	14	54.07	3-53	-	-
P M Such	432.1	98	1358	24	56.58	5-131	1	-
P Aldred	189.3	30	742	13	57.07	3-102	-	-
J W M Dalrymple	203.3	47	578	10	57.80	4-86	-	-
U Afzaal	158.2	29	579	10	57.90	3-88	-	-
A C McGarry	148	19	637	10	63.70	3-77	-	

PCA AWARD WINNERS

HAYTER CUP (PCA Player of the Year)
Sponsored since 1999 by
Fleming Premier Banking

1970	Mike Procter and Jack Bond
1971	Lance Gibbs
1972	Andy Roberts
1973	Peter Lee
1974	Barry Stead
1975	Zaheer Abbas
1976	Peter Lee
1977	Mike Procter
1978	John Lever
1979	John Lever
1980	Robin Jackman
1981	Richard Hadlee
1982	Malcolm Marshall
1983	Ken McEwan
1984	Richard Hadlee
1985	Neal Radford
1986	Courtney Walsh
1987	Richard Hadlee
1988	Graeme Hick
1989	Jimmy Cook
1990	Graham Gooch
1991	Waqar Younis
1992	Courtney Walsh
1993	Steve Watkin
1994	Brian Lara
1995	Dominic Cork
1996	Phil Simmons
1997	Steve James
1998	Mal Loye
1999	Stuart Law
2000	Marcus Trescothick
2001	David Fulton

ARLOTT CUP
(PCA Young Player of the Year)
Sponsored in 2001 by Costcutter

1990	Mike Atherton
1991	Dominic Cork
1992	Mark Lathwell
1993	Malachy Loye
1994	John Crawley
1995	Andy Symonds
1996	Chris Silverwood
1997	Ben Hollioake
1998	Andrew Flintoff
1999	David Sales
2000	Matthew Hoggard
2001	Nicky Peng

HAROLD GOLDBLATT UMPIRES' CUP
Sponsored in 2001 by Accenture

1997	Peter Willey
1998	Ray Julian
1999	Ray Julian
2000	Ray Julian
2001	Neil Mallender

PCA SPECIAL MERIT AWARD *Sponsored*
since 2000 by JLT

1997	Lord Cowdrey
1998	Dickie Bird
1999	David English
2000	The Primary Club
2001	Vic Cook

SLAZENGER SHEER INSTINCT
INDIVIDUAL PERFORMANCE AWARD

1997	Alistair Brown
1998	Graeme Hick
1999	Mark Alleyne
2000	Alec Stewart
2001	Mark Butcher

INDEX OF PLAYERS BY COUNTY

*denotes not registered for the 2002 season. Where a player is known to have moved in the off-season he is listed under his new county.

INDEX OF PLAYERS BY COUNTY

INDEX OF PLAYERS BY COUNTY

LEICESTERSHIRE

ADSHEAD, S.J.
BEVAN, M.G.
BOSWELL, S.A.J.*
BRANDY, D.G.
BRIGNULL, D.S.
BURNS, N.D.
CROWE, C.D.
CUNLIFFE, R.J.
DAGNALL, C.E.
DAVIS, R.P.*
DEFREITAS, P.A.J.
GRIFFITHS, P.*
GROVE, J.O.
MADDY, D.L.
MALCOLM, D.E.
MARSH, D.J.*
NEW, T.J.
SHAHID AFRIDI*
STELLING, W.F.*
STEVENS, D.I.
SUTCLIFFE, I.J.
WALKER, G.W.
WARD, T.R.
WELLS, V.J.
WHILEY, M.J.A.
WHITTICASE, P.
WRIGHT, A.S.
WRIGHT, L.J.

MIDDLESEX

ABDUR RAZZAQ
ALLEYNE, D.
BLOOMFIELD, T.F.
BROWN, M.J.
COLEMAN, A.J.

COMPTON, N.R.D.
COOK, S.J.
CREESE, M.L.
DALRYMPLE, J.W.M.
FLEMING, S.P.*
FRASER, A.R.C.
HUNT, T.A.
HUTTON, B.L.
JOYCE, E.C.
KEEGAN, C.B.
KOENIG, S.G.
LARAMAN, A.W.
MAUNDERS, J.K.
NASH, D.C.
ROSEBERRY, M.A.*
SHAH, O.A.
STRAUSS, A.J.
TUFNELL, P.C.R.
WEEKES, P.N.
WESTON, R.M.S.

NORTHAMPTONSHIRE

ANDERSON, R.S.G.
BAILEY, T.M.B.
BAKER, T.M.
BLAIN, J.A.R.
BROPHY, G.L.
BROWN, J.F.
CASSAR, M.E.
CAWDRON, M.J.
COOK, J.W.
COUSINS, D.M.
COVERDALE, P.S.
GOODE, C.M.
GREENIDGE, C.G.
HUGGINS, T.B.
HUSSEY, M.E.K.
INNES, K.J.*

KING, R.
LOYE, M.B.
MACLEAN, R.A.
PANESAR, M.S.
PAYNTER, D.E.
PENBERTHY, A.L.
PHILLIPS, B.J.
POWELL, M.J.
RIPLEY, D.*
ROLLINS, A.S.
SALES, D.J.G.
STRONG, M.R.*
SWANN, G.P.
TAYLOR, J.P.*
WADE, J.
WARREN, R.J.
WEEKES, L.C.*
WHITE, R.A.

NOTTINGHAMSHIRE

AFZAAL, U.
BICKNELL, D.J.
BLEWETT, G.S.*
CAIRNS, C.L.
CLOUGH, G.D.
FRANKS, P.J.
GALLIAN, J.E.R.
HARRIS, A.J.
HEWISON, C.J.*
JOHNSON, P.
KLUSENER, L.
LOGAN, R.J.
LUCAS, D.S.
MALIK, M.N.
MCMAHON, P.J.
MILLNS, D.J.*
MORRIS, J.E.*
NEWELL, M.